The Academy Awards®

The Academy Awards®

The Complete Unofficial History

Gail Kinn and Jim Piazza

Black Dog
& Leventhal
Publishers
NEW YORK

Copyright © 2002 Black Dog & Leventhal Publishers, Inc.

Published by
Black Dog & Leventhal Publishers, Inc.
151 West 19th Street
New York, NY 10011

Distributed by
Workman Publishing Company
708 Broadway
New York, NY 10003

Designed by Scott Citron

Manufactured in China

Library of Congress Cataloging-in-Publication Data

Kinn, Gail.
  The Academy Awards® : the complete unofficial history / Gail Kinn and Jim Piazza.
      p. cm.
Includes bibliographical references and index.
   ISBN 1-57912-317-1
   1. Academy Awards® (Motion pictures) I. Piazza, Jim. II. Title.
   PN1993.92 .K56 2002
   791.43′079—dc21

                                            2002008684

g f e d c b a

To David Ferguson, who knows it all by heart.

—Jim

*To all the people in my life who made the movies one of my passions.
And, as always, to my niece Sarah.*

—Gail

THE AUTHORS WOULD LIKE TO BEGIN BY THANKING each other for a seamless collaboration that rarely required the threat of weapons. A project this size takes many hands, eyes, and ears. To all those at Black Dog & Leventhal without whom this book would not be possible we offer our heartfelt gratitude. To Laura Ross for pitching in with her intelligence and her professional expertise. To production director True Sims whose masterful juggling helped make this daunting concept a book. To proofreader Lesley Bruynesteyn for her attentiveness. To Reeve Chace, fashion researcher, whose vibrant insights tapped into one of our greatest Oscar obsessions—what did they wear? To copyeditor Carol Anderson, thank you, thank you for a heroic job. To book designers Scott Citron and Tony Meisel who made a complicated book easy on the eyes and inviting to read. Great thanks go to our intrepid and rock-steady editor, Will Kiester. Thanks for sharing the exhaustive days and sleepless nights. Finally to our muse and trivia genius publisher J.P. Leventhal, who stumped us at our very first lunch...Thomas Mitchell, who knew?

MANY THANKS GO TO GETTY IMAGES FOR THEIR CAVERNOUS archives and the great assist from Rosa DiSalvo, Mitch Blank, and Michael Epp. And to the generous minds and memories of the people at Photofest, particularly Howard Mandelbaum. You were always happy to help.

LIFE, LIKE THE MOVIES, IS ONLY AS GOOD as the casting. I've been fortunate with two exceptional sisters, Maryta and Terry (who will always live in Hollywood), and stellar friends who applauded this book before we'd even written a word: Richard Currier, Jim and Chris Jacques-Taylor, Robert and Rande Davis-Gedaliah and Debbie Tanklow. Hugs to starlet nieces, Amie and Shaina, and action-hero nephews Mark, Chris, Stephen, and Gil. —Jim Piazza

I AM VERY FORTUNATE TO BE SURROUNDED BY not only supportive friends and family, but by people with wonderful movie memories. To David Ferguson for knowing and sharing. To J.P. for being a friend with brilliant ideas who happens to run a publishing company. To my dear friends Ronni Stolzenberg and Debra Tanklow for being the source of true support. To my family, Mark, Hannah, Sarah, and Linda for being there, always. Finally to Alan Myers, who knew who won the Oscars without any notes. You've made my life sweeter. —Gail Kinn

THE EDITOR WOULD LIKE TO THANK Marilyn Shepard for a lifetime of movie knowledge, without which I would be a lost soul in a dark theater.

Table of Contents

OPPOSITE: Charles Farrell with Janet Gaynor in *Seventh Heaven*.

ABOVE: In a dress made for doing the Charleston, Joan Bennett is ready to dance the night away, cloche hat and all. (circa 1928)

BELOW: Clara Bow's heavily made up eyes add a touch of mischief to her otherwise feminine, flowing gown. (circa 1926)

ABOVE: Louise Brooks shows off her trademark, iconic, and oft-copied pageboy haircut. (circa 1925)

BELOW: Gloria Swanson models the bobbed hair, dark lips, and long, multiple strands of pearls that marked the style of the 1920s. (circa 1926)

THE LOOK OF THE DECADE

S THE HORRORS OF WORLD WAR I receded, the Roaring Twenties rushed in to take the place of years of worry and dread. It was time to celebrate and dance, and women literally lifted their skirts to do so. Short, drop-waisted flapper dresses, cut to reveal bare arms, exposed backs, and plunging necklines, were the new uniform for anyone who wanted to be fashionable and youthful. Transparent materials were often used to further the suggestion of nudity, and it was only the liberal use of accessories such as multiple strands of pearls, patterned silk stockings, and cloche hats that reigned the dresses in from the brink of indecency. It was a look that would make any movie star swoon, and Hollywood took to it without restraint.

OPPOSITE: Joan Crawford wears a typical flapper dress and dons all the necessary accessories: pearls, fringe, short hair, and cloche hat. (circa 1929)

1927-28

In the beginning it was mostly about the food. Sources vary as to the precise menu, but clearly losers didn't whine on empty stomachs. The 270 guests paid five bucks apiece for such festive possibilities as Lobster Eugenie, Filet of Sole au Beurre, Jumbo Squab, and, with a touch of hometown spirit, Los Angeles Salad. Dancing followed, and newcomer Janet Gaynor, just 21 and still living with her mother, was more awed by the whirl of famous faces than by the Best Actress Award she'd received.

WINGING IT

CEREMONY: May 16, 1929
Blossom Room, Hollywood
Roosevelt Hotel
HOST: Douglas Fairbanks

The orchestra was silenced when MGM chief, Louis B. Mayer, decided it was time to get down to business. The banquet, the Awards and, in fact, the very foundation of the Academy were his brainchild back in 1927. His original intention was more bottom-line than glamour. He'd hoped to unite the industry's power players in squeezing out the labor unions. When that failed, it was decided that the Academy would serve as its own censor before the government got into the act. Though the movies had become the fourth-largest industry in America, there were already rumblings about its often titillating product from concerned mothers and clergymen. The industry needed a touch of class and a public-relations coup. The idea of awarding a golden statuette to the best of the best was just the ticket.

The winners had been named three months before, which eliminated any suspense during the five-minute presentation ceremony. Douglas Fairbanks called out their names, they came forward to collect either statuettes or honorary scrolls, and sat at the head table. Producer Darryl F. Zanuck gave the only speech after picking up a Special Award for the first talkie, *The Jazz Singer*. Its star, Al Jolson, ended the evening with a song and the first big laugh in Oscar history when he said, "For the life of me I can't see what Jack Warner can do with one of these awards. It can't say yes."

BEST PICTURE
WINGS

Adolph Zukor, producer at Paramount studios in Astoria, New York, picked up the prize for the blockbuster directed by William Wellman. *Wings* provided movie audiences with an early taste of the thrill of movie magic. A spectacle about WW I aerial battles, *Wings* delivered state-of-the-art visual effects. The use of aerial photography allowed filmmakers to show "bombing machines, captive balloons, smashes and crashes of all types," noted *Variety*. Filmed in Magnascope, the movie featured a wide screen format that was a precursor to Cinemascope and other wide-screen effects that wouldn't fully emerge until the 1950s. For audiences fortunate enough to live in major cities, special offstage sound effects produced by machines mimicking the sound of airplanes could be heard. The story itself was a tearjerker in which one of two comrades in arms dies. Among the sterling cast was a 26-year-old lady killer by the name of Gary Cooper. And, departing from her famed role as a gossip columnist, was a 38-year old supporting actress named Hedda Hopper.

"Hand me now already the statuette award." —Emil Jannings

Best Production: *Wings*
Best Actor: Emil Jannings, *The Last Command,*
The Way of All Flesh
Best Actress: Janet Gaynor, *7th Heaven,*
Street Angel, Sunrise
Direction, Best Dramatic Picture: Frank Borzage,
7th Heaven
Direction, Best Comedy Picture: Lewis Milestone
Special Award: *The Jazz Singer*
Honorary Award: Charles Chaplin

OF SPECIAL NOTE

• The Academy Award statuette has remained unchanged since its original design by MGM art director Cedric Gibbons: a gold-plated naked man 14 inches tall and weighing 7 pounds, his sword plunged into a reel of film.

• The original Academy of Motion Picture Arts and Sciences consisted of 230 members, who paid a fee of $100 each.

• In the beginning, winners were selected in a three-tiered process that consisted of: (1) nominations from members; (2) a Board of Judges that narrowed each category list down to three; and (3) a final Central Board of five judges that determined the outcome. These five consisted of one member from each of the branches: writing, technical achievements, producers, directors, and performers.

SINS OF OMISSION

• There were loud complaints that Janet Gaynor's popular co-star in *7th Heaven*, Charles Farrell, had been unjustly ignored by the judges.

• The first comic superstar, Charlie Chaplin, was not well loved in Hollywood, which probably accounted for the nullification of his initial nominations for Best Actor, Best Director, and Best Writer.

UNMENTIONABLES

• Adolf Hitler was a big fan of Chaplin's—so big, in fact, that he grew his mustache like Chaplin's character the Little Tramp. Before that, Hitler's mustache was an 1880s-type handlebar.

• In her book, *Tramp: The Life of Charlie Chaplin*, Joyce Milton asserts that Nabokov's controversial classic, *Lolita*, was inspired by Chaplin's relationship with Lita Grey.

• Louis B. Mayer and Charlie Chaplin came to blows over the studio chief's snide remarks about the star's divorce from ingenue Mildred Harris. Chaplin got in the first swing, but Mayer finally decked him.

• One of Chaplin's most famous comic scenes had him eating his shoe in starved desperation (*The Gold Rush*, 1925). The shoe in question was made of black licorice.

• Mayer provided visiting East Coast VIPs with "star lookalike" escorts.

• Mayer's fierce protection of MGM stars included manslaughter coverups for Clark Gable and John Huston.

• "America's sweethearts" of the 1920s, Janet Gaynor and Charles Farrell, co-stars in twelve films, were careful to keep their homosexuality out of the public spotlight.

• Gloria Swanson and her lover and financial backer, Joseph P. Kennedy, were caught in flagrante delicto on the family yacht by his young son John Fitzgerald. The boy was so distraught that he jumped overboard and had to be rescued by the crew.

• Al Jolson paid his equally talented brother, Harry, $150 per week to stay out of show business.

BEST ACTOR
EMIL JANNINGS (1884–1950)
THE LAST COMMAND,
THE WAY OF ALL FLESH

Before coming to Hollywood, Jannings played to type, with his bearlike insistent stature, and garnered roles as rigid authoritarians, including that of Dimitri in *The Brothers Karamazov* (1920), *Othello* (1922), and *Faust* (1926, as Mephistopheles). His appearances in the F. W. Murnau classics, *The Last Laugh* (1924) and *Variety* (1925) brought Jannings to Hollywood in 1927, where he won the first Best Actor Oscar ever awarded.

With his thick German accent, there was not much for Jannings to do in the talkies. He returned to Germany, where his appearance with Marlene Dietrich in Josef von Sternberg's brilliant *The Blue Angel* (1930) was a triumph for him. Unfortunately, on his return to his native Germany he became a Nazi sympathizer and spent the next decade making Nazi propaganda films. He was named Artist of the State by Goebbels in 1941. With the fall of Hitler, Jannings found no welcomes back in the international filmmaking community. He never made another film, and died of cancer five years later.

Charles Farrell with Janet Gaynor in Seventh Heaven.

BEST ACTRESS
JANET GAYNOR (1906–1984)
7TH HEAVEN, SUNRISE (both 1927)
STREET ANGEL (1928)

Backstage, after the Awards ceremony, Gaynor was reported to have been asked what was most exciting about winning. The young actress chirped, "Meeting Douglas Fairbanks!"

The delicate, dainty Gaynor attained stardom with her ability to project sweetness without becoming cloying. She played bit parts in Hal Roach comedies and B Westerns, but her career finally took off with *The Johnstown Flood* (1926). That performance drew her into 20th Century-Fox's "Irish Mafia." She then worked with John Ford in *The Shamrock Handicap* and *The Blue Eagle* (both 1926). Gaynor garnered her Oscar-winning roles in films made by German director F. W. Murnau, who was charmed by the petite actress. Gaynor was best known for her on-screen teaming with Charles Farrell, with whom she co-starred in ten films, among them *Street Angel* (1928), the moving *Lucky Star*, and the jaunty musical *Sunny Side Up* (both 1929).

Gaynor became a big box-office star in the talkies, in such films as *Daddy Long Legs* (1931), *State Fair* (1933), and *A Star Is Born* (1937, nom.). She retired from film after appearing in *Three Loves Has Nancy* and *The Young in Heart* (both 1938), returning only once, in *Bernadine* (1957). Gaynor died following complications from a car crash that also injured actress Mary Martin.

SPECIAL AWARD
AL JOLSON (1886–1950)
THE JAZZ SINGER

Al Jolson rose from his seat saying, "I noticed they gave *The Jazz Singer* a statuette, but they, *er*, he made history by delivering the immortal line 'You ain't heard nothin' yet.'" And it was true—until then, no one had heard voices from the screen.

Jolson, the son of a cantor, ushered in the talkies—including *Mammy* (1930), *Hallelujah, I'm a Bum* (1933), *Go Into Your Dance* (1935, appearing with then-wife Ruby Keeler), and *The Singing Kid* (1936). But audiences weren't coming out in sufficient droves, and Jolson's career almost ended with the losers *Swanee River* (1939), *Hollywood Cavalcade* (1939), and *Rhapsody in Blue* (1945). Perhaps the greatest insult suffered by Jolson occurred when he was made to do a screen test for *The Jolson Story* in 1945 to determine if he could play himself!

HONORARY AWARD
CHARLES CHAPLIN (1889–1977)

Chaplin's physical and emotional genius was instrumental in shaping the film medium. In his late teens Chaplin was hired by the King of Comedy, Mack Sennett, and began appearing in films, adding bits of his Little Tramp costume with each appearance. He was a hit.

As his reputation grew, Chaplin longed for more freedom. He started United Artists with Douglas Fairbanks, Mary Pickford, and D. W. Griffith. Their first release was *A Woman of Paris* (1923), but with only a bit of Chaplin in it the movie flopped. He turned that failure into a string of classics, including *The Gold Rush* (1925) and *The Circus* (1928). In the midst of all his great professional success, Chaplin kept gossip columnists' tongues wagging with his marriages to very young women.

Chaplin moved into talkies with such landmark films as *City Lights* (1931), *Modern Times* (1936), *The Great Dictator* (1940, nom.), and *Monsieur Verdoux* (1947). The House Un-American Activities Committee went after Chaplin, pointing to two films as examples of his anti-capitalism, and he was exiled to London in 1952. Chaplin resolved never to return to America, settled in Switzerland, and made *A King in New York* (1957, released in the U.S. in 1976) and *A Countess from Hong Kong* (1967).

PICTURE
THE RACKET, The Caddo Company, Paramount Famous Lasky. Produced by Howard Hughes.
7TH HEAVEN, Fox. Produced by William Fox.
WINGS, Paramount Famous Lasky. Produced by Lucien Hubbard.

UNIQUE AND ARTISTIC PICTURE
CHANG, Paramount Famous Lasky.
THE CROWD, MGM.
SUNRISE, Fox.

ACTOR
RICHARD BARTHELMESS in *The Noose*, First National, and *The Patent Leather Kid*, First National.
EMIL JANNINGS in *The Last Command*, Paramount Famous Lasky, and *The Way of All Flesh*, Paramount Famous Lasky.

ACTRESS
LOUISE DRESSER in *A Ship Comes In*, DeMille Pictures, Pathe.
JANET GAYNOR in *7th Heaven*, Fox; *Street Angel*, Fox; and *Sunrise*, Fox.
GLORIA SWANSON in *Sadie Thompson*, Gloria Swanson Productions, UA.

DIRECTION: COMEDY PICTURE
LEWIS MILESTONE for *Two Arabian Knights*, The Caddo Company, UA.
TED WILDE for *Speedy*, Harold Lloyd Corp., Paramount Famous Lasky.
CHARLES CHAPLIN, "The Academy Board of Judges on merit awards for individual achievements in motion picture arts during the year ending August 1, 1928, unanimously decided that your name should be removed from the competitive classes, and that a special first award be conferred upon you for writing, acting, directing and producing 'The Circus.' The collective accomplishments thus displayed place you in a class by yourself." Letter from the Academy to Mr. Chaplin, dated February 19, 1929.

DIRECTION: DRAMATIC PICTURE
FRANK BORZAGE for *7th Heaven*, Fox.
HERBERT BRENON for *Sorrell and Son*, Art Cinema, UA.
KING VIDOR for *The Crowd*, MGM.

WRITING: BASED ON MATERIAL FROM ANOTHER MEDIUM
ALFRED COHN. *The Jazz Singer*, Warner Bros.
ANTHONY COLDE WAY, *Glorious Betsy*, Warner Bros.
BENJAMIN GLAZER, *7th Heaven*, Fox.

WRITING: DIRECTLY FOR THE SCREEN
LAJOS BIRO, *The Last Command*, Paramount Famous Lasky.
BEN HECHT, *Underworld*, Paramount Famous Lasky.

WRITING: TITLES
GERALD DUFFY, *The Private Life of Helen of Troy*, First National.
JOSEPH FARNHAM
GEORGE MARION, JR.

CINEMATOGRAPHY
GEORGE BARNES, *The Devil Dancer*, Samuel Goldwyn, UA; *The Magic Flame*, Samuel Goldwyn, UA; and *Sadie Thompson*, Gloria Swanson Productions, UA.
CHARLES ROSIER, *Sunrise*, Fox.
KARL STRUSS, *Sunrise*, Fox.

ART DIRECTION
ROCHUS GLIESE, *Sunrise*, Fox.
WILLIAM CAMERON MENZIES, *The Dove*, Joseph M. Schenck Productions, UA; and *Tempest*, Art Cinema, UA.
HARRY OLIVER, *7th Heaven*, Fox.

ENGINEERING EFFECTS
(NOTE: Award not given after this year)
RALPH HAMMERAS.
ROY POMEROY, *Wings*, Paramount Famous Lasky.
NUGENT SLAUGHTER.

SPECIAL AWARDS
TO WARNER BROS. for producing *The Jazz Singer*, the pioneer outstanding talking picture, which has revolutionized the industry.
TO CHARLES CHAPLIN for acting, writing, directing and producing *The Circus*.

1928-29

Hollywood managed to shut out the Depression with noise. Lots of it. For the first time ever, audiences heard slamming doors, waterfalls, dancing feet, voices in song and voices in trouble. The most overwhelming sound of all was the ringing of cash registers at every movie-house box office in the country.

The talkies were a sensation and their early critics, like MGM

MARY HAD A LITTLE SCANDAL

CEREMONY: April 30, 1930
Cocoanut Grove, Ambassador Hotel,
Los Angeles
HOST: William C. deMille,
Academy President

chief Louis B. Mayer, quickly jumped into the act. He was well aware that the brand-new Academy Awards could also bump up profits, especially if there was a little suspense involved. To that

end, winners weren't revealed until the big night. A local radio station was on hand to broadcast the announcements, the cheers, the cries of surprise. But soon enough the posh, post-banquet gathering sensed the deck was stacked. All the winning studios and stars were either on the Board of Judges or closely connected to it. The most blatantly obvious fix was the Best Actress Award. America's sweetheart, Mary Pickford, a charter member of the Academy, managed a few tears and an expression of astonishment. She wasn't the only one. She'd beat out Ruth Chatterton and the late Jeanne Eagels with her stiffly delivered starring role in the critical bomb *Coquette*.

As angry murmurs swelled to a roar of disapproval, Mayer and his Board of Judges knew the gig was up. Changes had to be made, and made fast if the Awards were to survive.

BEST PICTURE
THE BROADWAY MELODY

For MGM's first talking picture, the company opened its checkbook to make *The Broadway Melody* as loud a talkie as had ever been heard. Sporting a score by Arthur Freed, which included songs like "You Were Meant for Me" and an over-the-top dance-musical spectacle called "Wedding of the Painted Doll," *The Broadway Melody* gave the box office a record-breaking $4 million. The theater was cloaked with signs shouting, "100% Talking! 100% All Singing! 100% All Dancing!" *Variety* cheered, "The excellent bits of sound workmanship …" (in) "…the first screen musical."

"There was a time in this business when they had the eyes of the whole wide world. But that wasn't good enough for them. Oh, no! They had to have the ears of the world, too. So they opened their big mouths and out came talk, talk, talk!" —Sunset Boulevard

The envelope, please...

BEST ACTOR
WARNER BAXTER (1889–1951)
IN OLD ARIZONA

Fox lauded *In Old Arizona* as "the first 100 percent all-talking drama filmed outdoors." *Variety* described it as a Western with a climax twist. There were lots of problems to be ironed out with talking pictures. One of the first to arise was how to follow chase scenes when all the sound was recorded from a stationary position. The answer: drop the chase. And they did. But it was Warner Baxter's good looks that kept the fans coming. This generally serious leading man surprised critics and audiences alike with his flashy portrayal of the Cisco Kid. Baxter, a former salesman, learned acting in stock touring companies and got his first break in *Her Own Money* (1914). Solid, dependable, with keen eyes and a pencil mustache, the actor appeared (mostly in leading roles) in many silent films, including *The Awful Truth* (1925), *The Great Gatsby* (1926, in the title role), and *West of Zanzibar* (1928). His popularity waned, however, as his looks faded, and he ended his career with the B mystery *Crime Doctor's Diary* (1949). He may be best remembered as the stage director Julian Marsh in *42nd Street* (1933).

BEST ACTRESS
MARY PICKFORD (1893–1979)
COQUETTE

"I am sick of Cinderella parts, of wearing rags and tatters. I want to wear smart clothes and play the lover," Pickford ranted. To that end, she bought the rights to *Coquette*, launching what would become the first Academy Award campaign. The campaign worked, and the ringlet-haired Pickford soon became America's sweetheart.

Pickford worked with director D. W. Griffith and was an instant box-office success with *The New York Hat* and *The Informer* (both 1912). She later joined Famous Players, appearing in, among other films, *Rebecca of Sunnybrook Farm* (1917) and *Stella Maris* (1918).

During her prodigious career, Pickford made more than 235 films. Though reclusive, she published her autobiography, *Sunshine and Shadow*, in 1955. She had intended to have all her films destroyed after her death, fearing that no one would care about them. Fortunately, she was talked out of it.

BEST OF 1928–1929
Best Picture: *The Broadway Melody*
Best Actor: Warner Baxter, *Thunderbolt*
Best Actress: Mary Pickford, *Coquette*
Best Director: Frank Lloyd, *The Divine Lady*, *Weary River*, and *Drag*

FIRSTS
• Shortly after the ceremonies, the Academy eliminated the easily corruptible means of selection. The judging committees were replaced with a "one member, one vote policy." A technician would now have the same power as a studio chief.

• The ceremonies were publicly broadcast over the radio. Winners weren't announced until the Awards. Runners-up would not receive scrolls.

• The director of *Madame X*, Lionel Barrymore, conceived the first boom-mike, an overhang that allowed "talking" actors to move about freely on the set.

ROLE REVERSALS
Warner Baxter stepped into his winning role only after Raoul Walsh suffered a freak accident that cost him an eye.

UNMENTIONABLES
• Best Actress nominee Jeanne Eagels died shortly before the Awards of a heroin overdose.

• Best Director Frank Lloyd was most famous as a physical comedian. While posing for a publicity still, the bomb he held exploded. He briefly lost his sight, along with two fingers.

• Mary Pickford was a brilliant businesswoman who learned early on to produce her own films. By 1916 she was pulling in $10,000 per week. In 1919, along with her husband, Douglas Fairbanks, and Charlie Chaplin, she founded United Artists. Despite advice from Chaplin, she sold her shares in 1953 and missed out on far more lucrative offers down the road. The famous Pickford-Fairbanks estate in Beverly Hills, Pickfair, was the center of 1920s Hollywood society. It was purchased in the 1980s by Pia Zadora and her husband, who promptly tore the mansion down.

The Divine Lady, with Corrine Griffith and Marie Dressler

BEST DIRECTOR
FRANK LLOYD (1886–1960)
THE DIVINE LADY, WEARY RIVER, AND DRAG

One of the thirty-six founders of the Academy of Motion Picture Arts and Sciences, Lloyd won an Oscar for his first sound film. A show-business baby from the United Kingdom, where his father was a music-hall star, Lloyd came to the United States in 1914 and made dozens of films, including *A Tale of Two Cities* (1917), *Les Miserables* (both 1918), and *Oliver Twist* (1922). Continuing to make successful talkies after his first victory, Lloyd took home the Golden Boy once again for his *Mutiny on the Bounty* (1935) and followed with *Under Two Flags* (1936), *Wells Fargo* (1937), and *If I Were King* (1938).

A skillful though unnoteworthy director, whose talents were most evident in *Cavalcade* (1933, Oscar), Lloyd was also a producer who oversaw several films at Universal, including *The Spoilers*, *Invisible Agent*, and Hitchcock's *Saboteur* (all 1942). He directed James Cagney in *Japan* and *Blood on the Sun* (both 1945).

A W A R D
N O M I N A
T I O N S
1 9 2 8 – 2 9

PICTURE
ALIBI, Feature Productions, UA. Produced by Roland West.
THE BROADWAY MELODY, MGM. Produced by Harry Rapf.
THE HOLLYWOOD REVUE, MGM. Produced by Harry Rapf.
IN OLD ARIZONA, Fox. Winfield Sheehan, studio head.
THE PATRIOT, Paramount. Produced by Ernst Lubitsch.

ACTOR
GEORGE BANCROFF in *Thunderbolt*, Paramount Famous Lasky.
WARNER BAXTER in *In Old Arizona*, Fox.
CHESTER MORRIS in *Alibi*, Art Cinema, UA.

PAUL MUNI in *The Valiant*, Fox.
LEWIS STONE in *The Patriot*, Paramount Famous Lasky.

ACTRESS
RUTH CHATTERTON in *Madame X*, MGM.
BETTY COMPSON in *The Barker*, First National.
JEANNE EAGELS in *The Letter*, Paramount Famous Lasky.
CORRINE GRIFFITH in *The Divine Lady*, First National.
BESSIE LOVE in *The Broadway Melody*, MGM.
MARY PICKFORD in *Coquette*, Pickford, UA.

DIRECTION
LIONEL BARRYMORE for *Madame X*, MGM.
HARRY BEAUMONT for *The Broadway Melody*, MGM.
IRVING CUMMINGS for *In Old Arizona*, Fox.
FRANK LLOYD for *The Divine Lady*, First National.
FRANK LLOYD for *Weary River*, First National, and *Drag*, First National.
ERNST LUBITSCH for *The Patriot*, Paramount Famous Lasky.

WRITING
TOM BARRY, *The Valiant*, Fox, and *In Old Arizona*, Fox.
ELLIOT CLAWSON, *The Leatherneck*, Ralph Block, Pathe, *Sal of Singapore*, Pathe, *Skyscraper*, DeMille Pictures, Pathe, and *The Cop*, DeMille Pictures, Pathe.
HANS KRALY, *The Patriot*, Paramount Famous Lasky.
HANS KRALY, *The Last of Mrs. Cheyney*, MGM.
JOSEPHINE LOVETT, *Our Dancing Daughters*, Cosmopolitan, MGM.

BESS MEREDYTH, *Wonder of Women*, MGM, and *A Woman of Affairs*, MGM.

CINEMATOGRAPHY
GEORGE BARNES, *Our Dancing Daughters*, Cosmopolitan, MGM.
CLYDE DE VINNA, *White Shadows in the South Seas*, Cosmopolitan, MGM.
ARTHUR EDESON, *In Old Arizona*, Fox.
ERNEST PALMER, *Four Devils*, Fox, and *Street Angel*, Fox.
JOHN SEITZ, *The Divine Lady*, First National.

ART DIRECTION
HANS DREIER, *The Patriot*, Paramount Famous Lasky.
CEDRIC GIBBONS, *The Bridge of San Luis Rey* and other pictures, MGM.
MITCHELL LEISEN, *Dynamite*, Pathe, MGM.
WILLIAM CAMERON MENZIES, *Alibi*, Art Cinema, UA, and *The Awakening*, Samuel Goldwyn, UA. HARRY OLIVER, *Street Angel*, Fox.

The "annual" presentation banquet came just seven months after the last one. The industry was playing catch-up, given the sudden and complete transfer to talking pictures. Following the feasting and fox-trotting, the floor was given over to former postmaster general Will Hays, now the industry's in-house censor. Hays lectured for almost an hour about how "nothing unclean can maintain growth and vitality."

Finally, the statuettes were doled out and, as expected, *All Quiet on the Western Front* earned its due as Best Picture. It looked as if the new democratic voting process was working—until Norma Shearer was announced as Best Actress. It just so happened that she was married to MGM's second in command, Irving Thalberg. It also just so happened that she was nominated for two performances, doubling her odds. There was also the matter of those persistent rumors that Academy members who worked for MGM had been strongly advised to vote for her.

Shearer was beside herself with shock and amazement as she swept up to the podium to accept. It was by far her best performance of the year. Three days before, she'd posed for publicity pictures, award in hand, with "surprise" Best Actor winner George Arliss. Clearly, the kinks were yet to be ironed out before the Academy Awards could be taken seriously.

By evening's end, another snippet from Hays's speech had come back to haunt: "When a tree begins to collect blights, it begins to wither. So does reputation." Nonetheless, there was much to be said for a fledgling organization that could boast Thomas Edison as its special honored guest.

SHEARER COINCIDENCE

CEREMONY: November 5, 1930
Fiesta Room, Ambassador
Hotel, Los Angeles
HOST: Conrad Nagel

BEST PICTURE/BEST DIRECTOR
LEWIS MILESTONE (1895–1980)
ALL QUIET ON THE WESTERN FRONT

Louis B. Mayer announced the winner of the Best Picture Award saying, "I hear there's talk that the motion picture we honor tonight may win a Nobel Peace Prize." Both the film and its director were pacifists, but *The New Yorker*'s Pauline Kael wrote, "Milestone didn't make pacifist films with the exception of *All Quiet*, nor did anybody else working in Hollywood." *Variety* called it "a harrowing, gruesome, morbid tale of war, compelling in its realism, bigness and repulsiveness."

After Milestone was discharged from the army, he headed for Hollywood, where he was later discovered by the sometime film producer Howard Hughes. Hughes signed him up for his debut as director of *Two Arabian Knights*, for which he won an Oscar in the very first Academy Awards ceremony. Following his win for *All Quiet*, Milestone kept the films coming—though there were a few losers in the pack—with *The Front Page* (1931, nom.), *Rain* (1932), and *Hallelujah, I'm a Bum* (1933). He returned several years later with a quality film, *The General Died at Dawn* (1936). Although Milestone was a skilled craftsman, the inconsistent quality of his films attested to a lackadaisical attitude toward much of his work. During the 1950s Milestone did television work.

Lew Ayres (left)

"Novelty is always welcome, but talking pictures are just a fad."
—Irving Thalberg, MGM production chief

BEST ACTOR
GEORGE ARLISS (1868–1946)
DISRAELI

Arliss was a standout performer. With his bemused expression, the upper-class British actor took total command of audience attention. He became a big international star, frequently appearing in portraits of famous men in the 1920s and '30s. Among his films of the 1930s were *Alexander Hamilton* (1931), *The Man Who Played God* (1932), and *Voltaire* (1933). Arliss was also a gifted light comedian who played roles in such comedies as *The Working Man* and *The King's Vacation* (both 1933).

At Warners with Daryl Zanuck, Arliss made *The House of Rothschild*, *The Last Gentleman* (both 1934), and *Cardinal Richelieu* (1935). He then returned to England and made a few more films, notably *Transatlantic Tunnel* (1935), *East Meets West* (1936), and *Dr. Syn* (1937), after which he retired to care for Florence Arliss, his actress wife, who had become blind. Their son, Leslie Arliss, became a writer-director whose credits include *The Night Has Eyes* (1942) and *See How They Run* (1952).

BEST ACTRESS
NORMA SHEARER (1902–1983),
THE DIVORCEE

Her "specialty was sexy suffering in satin gowns by Adrian," wrote *The New Yorker*'s Pauline Kael. *The Divorcee* was no exception. The Hays office ordered the title—originally *Ex-Wife*—changed. The public couldn't get enough of this very risqué film.

Many suggested that Shearer achieved her fame by marrying her boss, MGM production head Irving Thalberg. Shearer was, nevertheless, a star in her own right. Thalberg groomed her for stardom. Her unconventional beauty and her awkwardly focused eyes made it necessary to work the cameras just right. Shearer appeared in silents, including Ernst Lubitsch's *The Student Prince in Old Heidelberg* (1927) and *The Latest from Paris* (1928). She made her talkie debut in *The Last of Mrs. Cheyney* (1929), which was followed by her best films, including *Their Own Desire* (1930, nom.), *Private Lives* (1931), and *The Barretts of Wimpole Street* (1934, nom.).

When Thalberg died of pneumonia at the age of 36, Shearer was devastated but continued to make films, such as *Marie Antoinette* (1938, nom.), *Idiot's Delight* (1939), and *The Women* (1939). After two of her films flopped, she retired from the screen. During her last years, Shearer showed a knack for finding star material and discovered Janet Leigh (from a picture at a ski resort) and the handsome garment-center executive Robert Evans. Though she remarried and lived well, the aging star suffered from psychiatric problems.

The Big House, with Wallace Beery (left, with machine gun), won for Best Writing and Best Sound Recording.

FIRSTS

• George Arliss was the first actor to win the Award for a role he'd played in film and on the stage.

• Norma Shearer and her brother, Douglas, MGM's sound engineer, were the first to make Oscar–winning a family affair. He got his statuette for *The Big House.*

UNMENTIONABLES

• The talkies took its toll of victims, stars who didn't have the vocal or acting chops to match their physical beauty. Among those who hopefully stashed away some of their hefty silent-era paychecks were Clara Bow, Pola Negri, Gilbert Roland, Nita Naldi, Renee Adoree, Blanche Sweet, Agnes Ayres, Vilma Banky, Rod La Rocque, Colleen Moore, and Ramon Navarro.

• Lew Ayres shot to stardom with *All Quiet on the Western Front,* but his pacifist stance during World War II effectively ended his career.

A W A R D N O M I N A T I O N S 1929-30

PICTURE

ALL QUIET ON THE WESTERN FRONT, Universal. Produced by Carl Laemmle Jr.
THE BIG HOUSE, Cosmopolitan, MGM. Produced by Irving G. Thalberg.
DISRAELI, Warner Bros. Produced by Jack L. Warner, with Darryl F. Zanuck.
THE DIVORCEE, MGM. Produced by Robert Z. Leonard.
THE LOVE PARADE, Paramount Famous Lasky. Produced by Ernst Lubitsch.

ACTOR

GEORGE ARLISS in *Disraeli,* Warner Bros., and *The Green Goddess,* Warner Bros.
WALLACE BEERY in *The Big House,* Cosmopolitan, MGM.
MAURICE CHEVALIER in *The Big Pond,* Paramount Publix, and *The Love Parade,* Paramount Famous Lasky.
RONALD COLMAN in *Bulldog Drummond,* Samuel Goldwyn, UA, and *Condemned,* Samuel Goldwyn, UA.
LAWRENCE TIBBETT in *The Rogue Song,* MGM.

ACTRESS

NANCY CARROLL in *The Devil's Holiday,* Paramount Publix.
RUTH CHATTERSON in *Sarah and Son,* Paramount Famous Lasky.
GRETA GARBO in *Anna Christie,* MGM, and *Romance,* MGM.

NORMA SHEARER in *The Divorcee,* MGM, and *Their Own Desire,* MGM.
GLORIA SWANSON in *The Trespasser,* Joseph P. Kennedy Productions UA.

DIRECTION

CLARENCE BROWN for *Anna Christie,* MG-M, and *Romance,* MGM.
ROBERT LEONARD for *The Divorcee,* MGM.
ERNST LUBITSCH for *The Love Parade,* Paramount Famous Lasky.
LEWIS MILESTONE for *All Quiet on the Western Front,* Universal.
KING VIDOR for *Hallelujah,* MGM.

WRITING

ALL QUIET ON THE WESTERN FRONT, Universal. (George Abbott, Maxwell Anderson and Del Andrews)
THE BIG HOUSE, Cosmopolitan, MGM. Frances Marion.
DISRAELI, Warner Bros. (Julian Josephson)
THE DIVORCEE, MGM. (John Meehan)
STREET OF CHANCE, Paramount Famous Lasky. (Howard Estabrook.)

CINEMATOGRAPHY

ALL QUIET ON THE WESTERN FRONT, Universal. (Arthur Edeson)
ANNA CHRISTIE, MGM. (William Daniels)
HELL'S ANGELS, The Caddo Company, UA. (Gaetano Gaudio and Harry Perry)
THE LOVE PARADE, Paramount Famous Lasky. (Victor Milner.)
WITH BYRD AT THE SOUTH POLE, Paramount Publix. Joseph T. Rucker and Willard Van Der Veer.

ART DIRECTION

BULLDOG DRUMMOND, Samuel Goldwyn, UA. (William Cameron Menzies)
KING OF JAZZ, Universal. Herman Rosse.
THE LOVE PARADE, Paramount Famous Lasky. (Hans Dreier)
SALLY, First National. (Jack Okey)
THE VAGABOND KING, Paramount Publix. (Hans Dreier)

SOUND RECORDING

THE BIG HOUSE, Cosmopolitan, MGM. Douglas Shearer for the MGM Studio Sound Dept.
THE CASE OF SERGEANT GRISCHA, RKO Radio. (John Tribby for the RKO Radio Studio Sound Dept.)

THE LOVE PARADE, Paramount Famous Lasky. (Franklin Hansen for the Paramount Famous Lasky Studio Sound Dept.)
RAFFLES, Samuel Goldwyn, UA. (Oscar Lagerstrom for the United Artists Studio Sound Dept.)
SONG OF THE FLAME, First National. (George Groves for the First National Studio Sound Dept.)

1930S

ABOVE: In a two-tone gown with a bejeweled sash, Evelyn Venable's style brings a touch of whimsy to an elegant occasion.

BELOW: Norma Shearer's floor length dress with sable-trimmed sleeves is both romantic and glamorous. (1932)

BELOW: Bette Davis looks every bit the movie star in this resplendent dress with feather details. (1939)

ABOVE: In her tastefully modest gown, Luise Rainer looks thoroughly modern in this well-cut dress that could easily be worn today. (1938)

THE LOOK OF THE DECADE

THE STOCK MARKET CRASH OF 1929 brought a somber end to the carefree parties of the Roaring Twenties. The short, flirty dresses favored by flappers and other good-time girls were put in the back of the closet, and a quieter, more subdued look took over. Minimalism was in, perhaps for the first time, and the most fashionable women of the day favored long silk or satin gowns cut on the bias. This distinctive style allowed the soft, supple fabrics to swirl around a woman's figure in the most flattering way, and helped usher in a new era of seductive elegance.

OPPOSITE: Mary Pickford looks luminous in this gorgeous dress with exquisite detailing.

1930-31

KID NAP

CEREMONY: November 10, 1931
Sala D'Oro, Biltmore Hotel,
Los Angeles
HOST: Lawrence Grant

The invitation list swelled, confusion reigned, and dinner at eight became dinner at nine-something. Awards presentations didn't kick in until well after midnight. Before then, the guest of honor, U.S. Vice-President Charles Curtis, took to the lectern with a speech that rivaled the length of the front-runner Best Picture nominee, *Cimarron*. "I have come to you tonight from the capital of our country to pay my respects to the creative minds of the world's greatest and most influential enterprise, the motion picture," he began. And with that, many of those "creative minds" slipped out into the lobby for healthy swigs from their silver flasks. It was no small irony that President Hoover's Prohibition necessitated the mass exit.

Child-star nominee Jackie Cooper was far too young for brandy and was forced to remain in his seat, but before the droning Curtis finished his first sentence, the boy had drifted into a deep sleep, nestled in the generous lap of Marie Dressler. He snoozed through Curtis, his Best Actor loss to Lionel Barrymore, and never stirred as Dressler rose to accept her award after gently shifting him to his mother's lap.

Barrymore was in the unusual position of not only beating out the youngest (and perhaps the drowsiest) nominee ever but of also besting Fredric March. March was up for his role as Lionel's brother, John, in a satire of the Barrymore clan, *The Royal Family of Broadway* (1930). The next day's *Variety* agreed with young Cooper's assessment of the ceremony by calling it "a dull evening of a nature which will repel many a Hollywoodian next year unless memories dim and time makes 'em forget." In true Academy Awards fashion, memories dimmed and people forgot.

BEST PICTURE
CIMARRON

In *Cimarron*, Richard Dix stars as an early Oklahoma settler. With his wife (Irene Dunne), he participates in the famous 1889 land grab, and helps civilize the lawless frontier town of Osage. When he leaves Dunne behind to run the newspaper that he started, her character grows from a timid housewife to become Osage's leading citizen.

At a production price of $1.5 million, *Cimarron* was one of the most expensive films of the period. Though it received good press, alas the studio lost money on the film. Pauline Kael of *The New Yorker* later called it "one of Edna Ferber's heartfelt, numbskull treks through the hardships and glories of the American heritage."

Richard Dix (left), Irene Dunne (right)

"You're only as good as your last picture." —Marie Dressler

The envelope, please...

Lionel Barrymore with Norma Shearer, Clark Gable

BEST ACTOR
LIONEL BARRYMORE (1878–1954)
A FREE SOUL

An old ham, Barrymore used the requisite skills to win an Oscar for *A Free Soul*, which was not considered the actor's finest hour. Nevertheless, he took the prize away from Fredric March and Edward G. Robinson.

The brother of thespians John and Ethel Barrymore, Lionel had the most enduring film career. From 1909 nearly up to his death, he could be seen on the screen continually, beginning with D. W. Griffith's *The Informer* and *The Musketeers of Pig Alley* (both 1912). A favorite of MGM head Louis B. Mayer, he played leading men for twenty-seven years. Frank Capra worked with Barrymore in *You Can't Take It with You* (1938) and *It's a Wonderful Life* (1946).

He appeared with his brother, John, in *Grand Hotel* (1932) and *Dinner at Eight* (1933); they were joined by sister Ethel for the only all-Barrymore endeavor, *Rasputin and the Empress* (1932).

In the 1930s Barrymore played the cantankerous Dr. Gillespie in the popular film series *Dr. Kildare*. Though wheelchair-bound with severe arthritis, he continued in parts written to accommodate his infirmity, including *Key Largo* (1948) and *Lone Star* (1952).

Marie Dressler with Wallace Beery

BEST ACTRESS
MARIE DRESSLER (1838–1934)
MIN AND BILL

The studios called Dressler "the Grand Lady of Hollywood." She was one of MGM's biggest stars by 1931, and *Min and Bill* proved to be one of its top grossers.

The large, ungainly star seemed least likely to succeed on the silver screen. But succeed she did, and audiences loved her. A has-been in the 1920s, Dressler had become a No. 1 box-office star by the 1930s. She appeared opposite Charlie Chaplin in her debut in *Tillie's Punctured Romance* (1914). Dressler rarely appeared in the silents, but among her many films were *Bringing Up Father* (1928), *Anna Christie* (1930), *Caught Short* (1930), *Emma* (1932, nom.), *Tugboat Annie*, *Dinner at Eight*, and *Christopher Bean* (all 1933), her last film. Her autobiography, *My Story*, was published in 1933.

Norman Taurog

BEST DIRECTOR
NORMAN TAUROG (1899–1981)
SKIPPY

Taurog began his prolific film career in 1919, making shorts at Vitagraph. Specializing in comedy—and some drama—he proved adept and versatile at his trade over many decades. Among his features were *If I Had a Million* (1931, with W. C. Fields), *We're Not Dressing* (1934), *The Big Broadcast of 1936* (1935), *Girl Crazy* (1943), *Blue Hawaii* (1961), *Girls! Girls! Girls!* (1962), and *Double Trouble* (1967).

Dawn Patrol (1930) took home the gold for Best Original Story.

AWARD NOMINATIONS 1930-31

PICTURE
CIMARRON, RKO Radio. Produced by William LaBaron.

EAST LYNNE, Fox. Winfield Sheehan, studio head.

THE FRONT PAGE, Cado, UA. Produced by Howard Hughes.

SKIPPY, Paramount Publix. Adolph Zukor, studio head.

TRADER HORN, MGM. Produced by Irving G. Thalberg.

ACTOR
LIONEL BARRYMORE in *A Free Soul*, MGM.

JACKIE COOPER in *Skippy*, Paramount Publix.

RICHARD DIX in *Cimarron*, RKO Radio.

FREDRIC MARCH in *The Royal Family of Broadway*, Paramount Publix.

ADOLPHE MENJOU in *The Front Page*, Caddo, UA.

ACTRESS
MARLENE DIETRICH in *Morocco*, Paramount Publix.

MARIE DRESSLER in *Min and Bill*, MGM.

IRENE DUNNE in *Cimarron*, RKO Radio.

ANN HARDING in *Holiday*, Pathe.

NORMA SHEARER in *A Free Soul*, MGM.

DIRECTION
CLARENCE BROWN for *A Free Soul*, MGM.

LEWIS MILESTONE for *The Front Page*, Caddo, UA.

WESLEY RUGGLES for *Cimarron*, RKO Radio.

NORMAN TAUROG for *Skippy*, Paramount Publix.

JOSEF VON STERNBERG for *Morocco*, Paramount Publix.

WRITING: BASED ON MATERIAL FROM ANOTHER MEDIUM
CIMARRON, RKO Radio. Howard Estabrook.

THE CRIMINAL CODE, Columbia. Seton I. Miller and Fred Niblo, Jr.

HOLIDAY, Pathe. Horace Jackson.

LITTLE CAESAR, Warner Bros.-First National. Francis Faragoh and Robert N. Lee.

SKIPPY, Paramount Publix. Joseph Mankiewicz and Sam Mintz.

WRITING: ORIGINAL STORY
THE DAWN PATROL, Warner Bros.-First National. John Monk Saunders.

THE DOORWAY TO HELL, Warner Bros. Rowland Brown.

LAUGHTER, Paramount Publix. Harry d'Abbadie d'Arrast, Douglas Doty and Donald Ogden Stewart.

THE PUBLIC ENEMY, Warner Bros. John Bright and Kubec Glasmon.

SMART MONEY, Warner Bros. Lucien Hubbard and Joseph Jackson.

CINEMATOGRAPHY
CIMARRON, RKO Radio. Edward Cronjager.

MOROCCO, Paramount Publix. Lee Garmes.

THE RIGHT TO LOVE, Paramount Publix. Charles Lang.

SVENGALI, Warner Bros. Barney "Chick" McGill.

TABU, Paramount Publix. Floyd Crosby.

ART DIRECTION
CIMARRON, RKO Radio. Max Ree.

JUST IMAGINE, Fox. Stephen Goosson and Ralph Hammeras.

MOROCCO, Paramount Publix. Hans Dreier.

SVENGALI, Warner Bros. Anton Grot.

WHOOPEE, Goldwyn, UA. Richard Day.

SOUND RECORDING
SAMUEL GOLDWYN-UA STUDIO SOUND DEPT.

MGM STUDIO SOUND DEPT.

PARAMOUNT PUBLIX STUDIO SOUND DEPT.

RKO RADIO STUDIO SOUND DEPT.

SCIENTIFIC OR TECHNICAL

CLASS I
ELECTRICAL RESEARCH PRODUCTS, INC., RCA-PHOTOPHONE, INC., and RKO RADIO PICTURES, INC., for noise reduction recording equipment.

DuPONT FILM MANUFACTURING CORP. and EASTMAN KODAK CO. for super-sensitive panchromatic film..

CLASS II
FOX FILM CORP. for effective use of synchro-projection composite photography.

CLASS III
ELECTRICAL RESEARCH PRODUCTS, INC., for moving coil microphone transmitters.

RKO RADIO PICTURES, INC., for reflex type microphone concentrators.

RCA-PHOTOPHONE, INC., for ribbon microphone transmitters.

1931-32

Franklin Delano Roosevelt had just won by a landslide, hardly the margin that carried Fredric March to his Best Actor victory for *Dr. Jekyll and Mr. Hyde.* Even as March gave grateful thanks to his makeup man, Wally Westmore, harried judges at the front table were still tabulating ballots.

Up until that moment the brightest spot of the evening was a special Disney cartoon featuring caricatures of all the biggest stars in their most famous roles. An animated Greta Garbo hugged Mickey Mouse and crooned in an exaggerated Swedish accent, "Ah tahnk ah kees you now." Given the national radio audience and limited broadcast time, there were strict orders from on high that there should be "no" speeches.

Lionel Barrymore was the first of several performers to ignore the edict. Before presenting the Best Actress statuette to Helen Hayes, he made a stentorian pitch about the integrity of the Acad-

FIT TO BE TIED

CEREMONY: November 18, 1932
Fiesta Room, Ambassador
Hotel, Los Angeles
HOST: Conrad Nagel,
Academy president

emy's voting procedure. "There is no power, however great, in any branch of the motion pictures that can exert an atom of influence beyond the marking of that secret ballot," he declared.

The stunning irony of his remarks reverberated just moments later, when a frenzied judge called host Conrad Nagel over to the table and whispered in his ear: Wallace Beery had lost to Fredric March by a single vote. According to last year's rules, that counted as a tie. Without bothering to confer with other Academy officials, Nagel sent for another statuette on the double and called Beery to the stage. To some, it looked like a last-minute salve to bruised egos—until that night, Beery had been the front-runner for his performance in *The Champ.* The next day, Academy officials felt that Nagel had exceeded his authority and considered asking Beery to give back his award. No one acted on the idea, however, sparing a great deal of embarrassment and possibly a few punched noses. Beery's tough-guy image wasn't confined to the screen.

With Prohibition about to be repealed, next year's acrimony would at least be tempered by a well-stocked bar.

BEST PICTURE
GRAND HOTEL

"I vant to be alone," insisted Garbo in what became one of Hollywood's most immortal lines; but she would hardly get her wish. In *Grand Hotel* she was accompanied by an all-star cast, the first of its kind for Hollywood. The melodrama about a penniless baron (John Barrymore) who in desperation becomes a hotel thief featured most of the stars of the day, including John Barrymore, Joan Crawford, Wallace Beery, and Lionel Barrymore. The *New York Times*'s Mordant Hall celebrated the film as a "production worthy of all the talk it has created and several motion-picture luminaries deserve to feel proud of their performances, particularly Lionel Barrymore and Greta Garbo." In the end, the melodramatic words of the film live on: "People come and go, and nothing ever happens in the Grand Hotel."

Greta Garbo, John Barrymore

"Mr. Beery and I recently adopted children. Under the circumstances, it seems a little odd that we were both given awards for the best male performance of the year." —Fredric March

The envelope, please...

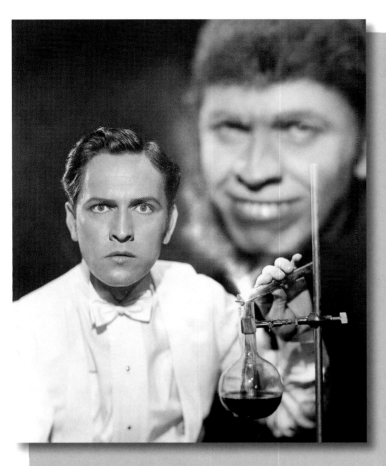

BEST ACTOR
FREDRIC MARCH (1897–1975)
DR. JEKYLL AND MR. HYDE

The controversial and tight Oscar race between March (who was reputed to be one point in the lead) and Wallace Beery resulted in a tie, which many spoke out against.

March won three Academy Award nominations for his performances in *The Royal Family of Broadway* (1930), *A Star Is Born* (1937), and *Death of a Salesman* (1951). He won an Oscar for both *Dr. Jekyll and Mr. Hyde* (1932) and *The Best Years of Our Lives* (1946).

With his leading-man good looks, March became one of Hollywood's brightest stars, with such films as *Design for Living* (1933), *The Barretts of Wimpole Street* (1934), *Anna Karenina* (1935), and *Nothing Sacred* (1937). His career continued to flourish in the 1950s and '60s, with such films as *Man on a Tightrope* (1953), *Executive Suite* (1954), *The Desperate Hours* (1955), and *The Man in the Gray Flannel Suit* (1956). In the 1960s he appeared in *Inherit the Wind* (1960), *Seven Days in May* (1964), and *The Iceman Cometh* (1973), his last film.

BEST ACTOR
WALLACE BEERY (1885–1949)
THE CHAMP

"Mr. Beery, it is my pleasure to announce that you have tied with Mr. March for the best male performance of the year for your splendid portrayal in *The Champ*," said Conrad Nagel. According to *Variety*, "some Academy members complained that Conrad overstepped his authority making such a presentation."

The bulky Beery got his start in 1915 working with a young ingenue named Gloria Swanson in the comedy *Sweedie Goes to College*. Their short-lived marriage was dissolved when Beery could not control his drinking and Gloria got tired of being black and blue.

In the 1920s Beery frequently starred in adventure films, including *The Four Horsemen of the Apocalypse* (1921) and *Robin Hood* (1922), returning to comedy in *Behind the Front* (1926).

Although Beery did not fit the image of the handsome hero, Irving Thalberg cast him in his hit *The Big House* (1930, nom.). But he was even more popular in *Min and Bill* (1930), one of the year's top moneymakers. Beery pulled in a Best Actor Oscar for *The Champ* (1931), will forever be remembered as Long John Silver in *Treasure Island* (1934), and played in *Flesh* (1932) and *Dinner at Eight* (1933). He soon became one of the top ten stars in Hollywood.

BEST OF 1931–1932
Best Picture: *Grand Hotel*
Best Director: Frank Borzage, *Bad Girl*
Best Actor: Fredric March, *Dr. Jekyll and Mr. Hyde*; Wallace Beery, *The Champ*
Best Actress: Helen Hayes, *The Sin of Madelon Claudet*
Honorary Award: Walt Disney for the creation of Mickey Mouse

FIRSTS
- *Grand Hotel* was the first and only film to take top honors without a single other nomination.

- This was the first and last time a tie would be determined by a 1–3 vote differential. From here on, a tie would be precisely what it means.

- Short Subjects were introduced with three new Award categories. This allowed Laurel and Hardy to collect their first and only statuette (Best Comedy Short, *The Music Box*).

- The Academy Awards ceremony was broadcast nationally for the first time.

- Lynne Fontanne and Alfred Lunt were the first couple to be nominated in the same year for acting.

- Fredric March would be the first and only actor to take the prize for a horror role until Anthony Hopkins scared up a win for *The Silence of the Lambs* (1991).

ROLE REVERSALS
The dual role of Dr. Jekyll and Mr. Hyde was originally intended for popular character actor Irving Pichel.

SINS OF OMISSION
Picture: *Scarface*
Director: Howard Hawks, *Scarface*
Actor: Paul Muni, *Scarface*
Actress: Marlene Dietrich, *Shanghai Express*

UNMENTIONABLES
- Walt Disney was the original voice of Mickey Mouse.

- "Fredric March was able to do a very emotional scene with tears in his eyes and pinch my fanny at the same time," said Shelley Winters.

- Wallace Beery, who ascended from character to leading roles following *The Big House*, was briefly married to Gloria Swanson, who claimed that he drunkenly brutalized her on their wedding night.

- At the age of 60, Marlene Dietrich was summoned to the White House by President Kennedy and was received in his private quarters. Seduction was inevitable, and she helped him remove the wrapping that supported his fragile back. Afterwards the president asked Dietrich if she had ever slept with his father. She said no, and the president was delighted to have "gotten somewhere first before the old man did."

BEST ACTRESS
HELEN HAYES (1900–1993)
THE SIN OF MADELON CLAUDET

Child star Hayes would become known not as a film star but rather as the "First Lady of the American Theater." Despite the fact that she never really caught on with moviegoers, she did win an Oscar for her film debut, *The Sin of Madelon Claudet*, and though her career in film would last until shortly before her death, it took forty years for Hayes to win another Golden Boy for her small role in *Airport* (1970).

Though her screen appearances were short in quantity, they were always high in quality, and included such films as *Arrowsmith* (1931), *A Farewell to Arms* (1932), *The White Sister* (1933), *What Every Woman Knows* (1934), and *Vanessa: Her Love Story* (1935). Hayes wrote three volumes of memoirs, *A Gift of Joy* (1965), *On Reflection* (1969), and *My Life in Three Acts* (1990).

Sally Eilers, James Dunn

BEST DIRECTOR
FRANK BORZAGE (1893–1962)
BAD GIRL

This was the second win—which some felt was wrong—for director Borzage, whose film *7th Heaven* took the gold in the first Oscar ceremony for Best Dramatic Picture Direction.

Borzage was perhaps Hollywood's greatest romantic, an unabashed sentimentalist who told some of the screen's most beautiful love stories using some of the most ingenious filmmaking techniques, including soft focus.

Borzage reached his peak in the late-silent and early-sound era with *Until They Get Me* (1917), *The Ghost Flower* (1918), *Humoresque* (1920), and *Secrets* (1924). His first talkie was a Will Rogers comedy, *They Had to See Paris* (1929), which was followed by *Liliom* (1930), *A Farewell to Arms* (1932), *Secrets* (1933, Mary Pickford's last movie), *Flirtation Walk* (1934), *Desire, Hearts Divided* (1936), *History Is Made at Night* (1937), *Smilin' Through* (1941), *Stage Door Canteen* (1943), *Till We Meet Again* (1944), and the low-budget psychological thriller *Moonrise* (1949). Borzage returned to the screen after a decade-long hiatus with *China Doll* (1958) and the epic *The Big Fisherman* (1959) before retiring.

HONORARY AWARD
WALT DISNEY (1901–1966)
FOR THE CREATION OF MICKEY MOUSE

Mickey Mouse was born on November 18, 1928, and grew up to become the most famous mouse in history. And with this blessed event the father of record, Walt Disney, became perhaps the most influential producer in the history of moviemaking.

Mickey's first two cartoons, *Plane Crazy* and *Gallopin' Gaucho*, were silent. Disney, ever the inventor, was adamant about technical quality and immediately began adding sound to his animations, starting with *Steamboat Willie*.

Meanwhile, Mickey himself had proved such a hit that the Disney team created a family of cartoon brothers and sisters and a girlfriend, Minnie. By 1934, the Disney organization had grown into an animation factory and fulfilled Walt's lifelong dream of feature-length pictures, the most famous of which, *Fantasia* (1940), starred Mickey.

Products based on the Disney menagerie were marketed to unprecedented success throughout the world. Disney and Mickey were no longer just characters but politically influential goodwill ambassadors. During World War II, the Walt Disney Company was recruited by the U.S. government to help in the propaganda effort, which resulted in the animated documentary *Victory Through Air Power* (1943).

In 1954 the mouse appeared on television screens across the country in the weekly series *The Mickey Mouse Club*. The following year, Disney opened Disneyland in Anaheim, California, a 160-acre family amusement park that instantly became one of the world's greatest tourist attractions.

AWARD NOMINATIONS 1931-32

PICTURE
ARROWSMITH, Goldwyn, GA. Produced by Samuel Goldwyn.
BAD GIRL, Fox. Winfield Sheehan, studio head.
THE CHAMP, MGM. Produced by King Vidor.
FIVE STAR FINAL, First National. Produced by Hal B. Wallis.
GRAND HOTEL, MGM. Produced by Irving Thalberg.
ONE HOUR WITH YOU, Paramount Publix. Produced by Ernst Lubitsch.
SHANGHAI EXPRESS, Paramount Publix. Adolph Zukor, studio head.
THE SMILING LIEUTENANT, Paramount Publix. Produced by Ernst Lubitsch.

ACTOR
WALLACE BEERY in *The Champ*, MGM.
ALFRED LUNT in *The Guardsman*, MGM.
FREDRIC MARCH in *Dr. Jekyll and Mr. Hyde*, Paramount Publix.

ACTRESS
MARIE DRESSLER in *Emma*, MGM.
LYNN FONTANNE in *The Guardsman*, MGM.
HELEN HAYES in *The Sin of Madelon Claudet*, MGM.

DIRECTION
FRANK BORZAGE for *Bad Girl*, Fox.
KING VIDOR for *The Champ*, MGM.
JOSEF VON STERNBERG for *Shanghai Express*, Paramount Publix.

WRITING: BASED ON MATERIAL FROM ANOTHER MEDIUM
ARROWSMITH, Goldwyn, UA. Sidney Howard.
BAD GIRL, Fox. Edwin Burke.
DR. JEKYLL AND MR. HYDE, Paramount Publix. Percy Heath and Samuel Hoffenstein.

WRITING: ORIGINAL STORY
THE CHAMP, MGM. Frances Marion.
LADY AND GENT, Paramount Publix. Grover Jones and William Slavens McNutt.
THE STAR WITNESS, Warner Bros. Lucien Hubbard.
WHAT PRICE HOLLYWOOD, RKO Radio. Adela Rogers St. Johns and Jane Murfin.

CINEMATOGRAPHY
ARROWSMITH, Goldwyn, UA, Ray June.
DR. JEKYLL AND MR. HYDE, Paramount Publix. Karl Struss.
SHANGHAI EXPRESS, Paramount Publix, Lee Garmes.

ART DIRECTION
A NOUS LA LIBERTE (French). Lazare Meerson.
ARROWSMITH, Goldwyn, GA. Richard Day.
TRANSATLANTIC, Fox. Gordon Wiles.

SOUND RECORDING
MGM STUDIO SOUND DEPT.
PARAMOUNT PUBLIX STUDIO SOUND DEPT.
RKO RADIO STUDIO SOUND DEPT.
WARNER BROS.-FIRST NATIONAL STUDIO SOUND DEPT.

SHORT SUBJECT: CARTOON
FLOWERS AND TREES, Disney, UA.
IT'S GOT ME AGAIN, Schlesinger, Warner Bros.
MICKEY'S ORPHANS, Disney, Columbia.

SHORT SUBJECT: COMEDY
THE LOUD MOUTH, Mack Sennett, Paramount Publix.
THE MUSIC BOX, Hal Roach, MGM. (Laurel & Hardy)
SCRATCH-AS-CATCH-CAN, RKO Radio.

SHORT SUBJECT: NOVELTY
SCREEN SOUVENIRS, Paramount Publix.
SWING HIGH, MGM.
WRESTLING SWORDFISH, Mack Sennett, Educational.

SPECIAL AWARD
TO WALT DISNEY for the creation of Mickey Mouse.

SCIENTIFIC OR TECHNICAL

CLASS II
TECHNICOLOR MOTION PICTURE CORP. for its color cartoon process.

CLASS III
EASTMAN KODAK CO. for its Type II-B sensitometer.

Seventeen months was a long time to wait for a party, especially one serving the first legal martinis since 1920. The glamorous younger set showed up to sway alongside the establishment to the satin strains of Duke Ellington's orchestra. Will Rogers was the jocular host, poking fun at Republicans, Louis B. Mayer, and even the tainted Awards ceremonies of years past.

FRANKLY EMBARRASSING

CEREMONY: March 16, 1934
Fiesta Room, Ambassador
Hotel, Los Angeles
HOST: Will Rogers

Rogers continued to play fast and loose at the podium, giving rise to what would be one of the most famously humiliating scenes in Academy Awards history. It began innocently as Rogers was handed the Best Director envelope. He tore it open and exclaimed, "Well, well, well, what do you know. I've watched this young man for a long time. Saw him come up from the bottom, and I mean the bottom. It couldn't have happened to a nicer guy. Come up and get it, Frank!" A heart-clutching Frank Capra, his dream finally realized, sprang up from his seat and rushed toward the stage. A spotlight played over the house and Capra jubilantly waved his arms, shouting, "Over here, I'm over here!" The light finally settled on the real winner, Frank Lloyd, who strode imperiously to the stage.

Capra stood frozen in the middle of the room until someone shouted, "Down in front!" He crawled back to his seat in what he later referred to as "the longest, saddest, most shattering walk in my life."

Rogers nearly caused another sensation when he called Best Actress nominees May Robson and Diana Wynyard up to the front. Another tie? No, just his way of honoring their performances. The unpopular winner was Katharine Hepburn, who, luckily, was out of town, considering the tepid applause her name registered. Charles Laughton wasn't present for his muted response, either. Future hosts learned an invaluable lesson from Capra's nightmare: No more announcements on a first-name basis. Unless, of course, it was Oscar's.

BEST PICTURE/BEST DIRECTOR
FRANK LLOYD (1886–1960)
CAVALCADE

Cavalcade cost Fox a nice piece of change. Though the studio was rewarded by the critics for this Noel Coward high-class soap opera, audiences didn't see the point. The *New York Times*'s Mordant Hall praised *Cavalcade* as "a most affecting and impressive picture...one senses the genuine quality of the film and also the advantages that have been taken of the camera's far-seeing eye." They liked Lloyd's direction, too; Hall cited his "meticulous attention to detail, not only in the settings, but also in the selection of players."

Lloyd hit show-business running while he was still a teenager. He began his Hollywood career as an actor in 1914 and turned to directing a year later. His prodigious directing career tallied more than 100 films in four decades. Among Lloyd's best works were *The Divine Lady* (1929), his first film to utilize sound; *Mutiny on the Bounty* (1935, Oscar) and *Wells Fargo* (1937), which proved his sense of style. His other works include *A Tale of Two Cities* (1917), *Riders of the Purple Sage*, *Les Misérables* (both 1918), *Madame X* (1920), *Oliver Twist* (1922), *The Lady from Cheyenne* (1941), *Saboteur* (1942), and *Blood on the Sun* (1945, with James Cagney). Lloyd's last film was *The Last Command* (1955).

Will Rogers (center), Frank Lloyd (right)

"It looks like Uncle Oscar!" — Margaret Herrick, Academy librarian

The envelope, please…

BEST ACTOR
CHARLES LAUGHTON (1899–1962)
THE PRIVATE LIFE OF HENRY VIII

Variety exclaimed that the distinctive-looking Laughton was "unquestionably the perfect pick for the part of the corpulent ruler." Others had cast their bets for the Oscar on Paul Muni. The film earned Laughton international acclaim. The actor's obesity never got in the way of his choice of roles. Audiences loved him and would never forget the famous capon-eating scene in the film. After working on the British stage, Laughton's film career took off with *Ruggles of Red Gap*, *Mutiny on the Bounty*, *Les Miserables* (all 1935), *The Hunchback of Notre Dame* (1939), *The Canterville Ghost* (1944), *Captain Kidd* (1945), and *The Big Clock* (1948).

Laughton also had a flair for comedy, which was shown to great advantage in *Sidewalks of London* (1938). In 1955 he directed his only film, the haunting *Night of the Hunter*. His last few films are among his most noteworthy performances, including *Witness for the Prosecution* (1957, nom.) and *Spartacus* (1960). His last film was *Advise and Consent* (1962).

BEST ACTRESS
KATHARINE HEPBURN (B. 1907)
MORNING GLORY

The actress dubbed "box office poison" for her stiff New England accent went on to win four Academy Awards by the end of her career. Her output was enormous, from her debut in *A Bill of Divorcement* (1932) through *Little Women* (1933), *Alice Adams* (1935, nom.), and *Stage Door* (1937). Her screen credits do include a few clinkers, among them *Christopher Strong* (1933) and *Sylvia Scarlett* (1935).

After hitting a wall, Hepburn returned to the screen with the hit *The Philadelphia Story* (1940). She was up for the prize again in 1942, for *Woman of the Year*, which cast her opposite Spencer Tracy, and began a partnership that would continue in eight subsequent films and over the next twenty-five years.

Back on her own, Hepburn picked up another Oscar nomination for *The African Queen* (1951) and also appeared in *Summertime* (1955), *Suddenly, Last Summer* (1959), and *Long Day's Journey into Night* (1962). Following her win for *Guess Who's Coming to Dinner?* (1967), Hepburn starred in the period drama *The Lion in Winter* (1968).

Hepburn won an Emmy for *Love Among the Ruins* (1975). Her 1991 autobiography, *Me*, was a best-seller, as was her more specific 1987 memoir, *The Making of* The African Queen—*Or How I Went to Africa with Bogart, Bacall and Huston and Almost Lost My Mind*.

A Farewell to Arms won Oscars for Cinematography and Sound Recording. (Gary Cooper, Helen Hayes)

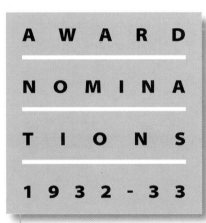

AWARD NOMINATIONS 1932-33

PICTURE
CAVALCADE, Fox. Winfield Sheehan, studio head.
A FAREWELL TO ARMS, Paramount. Adolph Zukor, studio head.
42nd STREET, Warner Bros. Produced by Darryl F. Zanuck.
I AM A FUGITIVE FROM A CHAIN GANG, Warner Bros. Produced by Hal B. Wallis.
LADY FOR A DAY, Columbia. Produced by Frank Capra.
LITTLE WOMEN, RKO Radio. Produced by Merian C. Cooper, with Kenneth MacGowan.
THE PRIVATE LIFE OF HENRY VIII, London Films, UA (British). Produced by Alexander Korda.
SHE DONE HIM WRONG, Paramount. Produced by William Le Baron.
SMILIN' THRU, MGM. Produced by Irving Thalberg
STATE FAIR, Fox. Winfield Sheehan, studio head.

ACTOR
LESLIE HOWARD in *Berkeley Square*, Fox.
CHARLES LAUGHTON in *The Private Life of Henry VIII*, London Films, UA (British).
PAUL MUNI in *I Am a Fugitive from a Chain Gang*, Warner Bros.

ACTRESS
KATHARINE HEPBURN in *Morning Glory*, RKO Radio.

MAY ROBSON in *Lady for a Day*, Columbia.
DIANA WYNYARD in *Cavalcade*, Fox.

DIRECTION
FRANK CAPRA for *Lady for a Day*, Columbia.
GEORGE CUKOR for *Little Women*, RKO Radio.
FRANK LLOYD for *Cavalcade*, Fox.

WRITING: BASED ON MATERIAL FROM ANOTHER MEDIUM
LADY FOR A DAY, Columbia. Robert Riskin.
LITTLE WOMEN, RKO Radio. Victor Heerman and Sarah Y. Mason.
STATE FAIR, Fox. Paul Green and Sonya Levien.

WRITING: DIRECTLY FOR THE SCREEN
ONE WAY PASSAGE, Warner Bros. **Robert Lord.**
THE PRIZEFIGHTER AND THE LADY, MGM. Frances Marion.
RASPUTIN AND THE EMPRESS, MGM. Charles MacArthur.

CINEMATOGRAPHY
A FAREWELL TO ARMS, Paramount. Charles Bryant Lang Jr.
REUNION IN VIENNA, MGM. George J. Folsey.
THE SIGN OF THE CROSS, Paramount Publix. Karl Struss.

ART DIRECTION
CAVALCADE, Fox. William S. Darling.
A FAREWELL TO ARMS, Paramount. Hans Dreier and Roland Anderson.
WHEN LADIES MEET, MGM. Cedric Gibbons.

SOUND RECORDING
A FAREWELL TO ARMS, Paramount, Paramount Studio Sound Dept., Franklin B. Hansen, Sound Director.
42ND STREET, Warner Bros. Warner Bros. Studio Sound Dept., Nathan Levinson, Sound Director.
GOLDDIGGERS OF 1933, Warner Bros. Warner Bros. Studio Sound Dept., Nathan Levinson, Sound Director.
I AM A FUGITIVE FROM A CHAIN GANG, Warner Bros. Warner Bros. Studio Sound Dept., Nathan Levinson, Sound Director.

ASSISTANT DIRECTOR
PERCY IKERD, Fox.
WILLIAM TUMMEL, Fox.
CHARLES DORIAN, MGM.
BUNNY DULL, MGM.
JOHN WATERS, MGM.
CHARLES BARTON, Paramount.
SIDNEY S. BROD, Paramount.
ARTHUR JACOBSON, Paramount.
EDDIE KILLEY, RKO Radio.
DEWEY STARKEY, RKO Radio.
FRED POX, UA.
BENJAMIN SILVEY, UA.
SCOTT BEAL, Universal.
JOE McDONOUGH, Universal.
W.J. REITER, Universal.
AL ALBORN, Warner Bros.
GORDON HOLLINGSHEAD, Warner Bros.
FRANK X. SHAW, Warner Bros.

SHORT SUBJECT: CARTOON
BUILDING A BUILDING, Disney, UA.
THE MERRY OLD SOUL, Lantz, Universal.
THE THREE LITTLE PIGS, Disney, UA.

SHORT SUBJECT: COMEDY
MISTER MUGG, Universal. (Comedies)
A PREFERRED LIST, Louis Brock, RKO Radio. (Headliner Series #5)
SO THIS IS HARRIS, Louis Brock, RKO Radio.

SHORT SUBJECT: NOVELTY
KRAKATOA, Joe Rock, Educational.
MENU, Pete Smith, MGM. (Oddities)
THE SEA, Educational. (Battle For Life)

SCIENTIFIC OR TECHNICAL

CLASS II
ELECTRICAL RESEARCH PRODUCTS, INC., for their wide-range recording and reproducing system.
RCA-VICTOR CO., INC., for their high-fidelity recording and reproducing system.

CLASS III
FOX FILM CORP., FRED JACKMAN and WARNER BROS. PICTURES, INC., and SIDNEY SANDERS of RKO Studios, Inc. for their development and effective use of the translucent cellulose screen in composite photography.

1934

"It's a grand and glorious feeling, but I'll be wearing the same size hat tomorrow."

—Clark Gable

 ith her gleaming mop of sausage curls, Shirley Temple, the most perfectly rehearsed child in movie history, sat at her table pretending not to know that she was about to receive a "surprise" miniature Oscar. She was the youngest of a record 1,000 attendees who had gathered for an unusually suspenseful night.

It was an edge-of-your-seat crowd, eager to watch the Academy Nominating Committee eat crow when Bette Davis won. She'd been a sensation in *Of Human Bondage*, and outrage swept through Hollywood when her performance failed to make the ballot. The sustained outcry forced the Academy's hand, and it agreed to the first sanctioned write-in. Davis was present, though none of her "official" competitors were. They'd read the writing on the wall and didn't want to suffer the embarrassment of her populist victory. Claudette Colbert was already at the train station waiting for the Super Chief to speed her off to New York for a holiday.

A GREAT NIGHT'S SWEEP

CEREMONY: February 27, 1935
Biltmore Bowl, Biltmore Hotel,
Los Angeles
HOST: Irvin S. Cobb

A funny thing happened on the way to a surefire rout. It began when Robert Riskin picked up an Oscar for his screenplay for *It Happened One Night*. He wasn't there, either. But last year's big loser, Frank Capra, was. Still smarting from the humiliation of having mistaken Frank Lloyd's name for his own, Capra wasn't quick to jump when Irvin Cobb tore open the Best Director envelope and teased, "Come on up and get it, Frank!" But this time, it was for real. *It Happened One Night* had beaten the odds.

Gable was shaken but proud of his statuette, and as for Colbert, the event mirrored a climactic scene from one of her own movies. An Academy official rushed to the depot to fetch her, and had to convince her that the Oscar was the Nobel Prize of the industry before she agreed to be rushed back to the Biltmore on the sidecar of a police motorcycle. Dazed and breathless, she accepted the Award from Shirley Temple, who stood on a chair to greet her, smile to smile. With that, Colbert was off like a shot to catch her train. Even Bette Davis joined in the sustained applause. She knew a great entrance, and an even better exit, when she saw one.

BEST PICTURE/BEST DIRECTOR
FRANK CAPRA (1897–1991)
IT HAPPENED ONE NIGHT

The film took all the awards at the Oscars, but it didn't make enough money to be held over for a second week at Radio City until word of mouth got around. Critics praised the fast-paced farce, which would usher in a whole new romantic genre: the screwball comedy. *The New Yorker*'s Pauline Kael wrote that the film had "a special American Depression-era on-the-road humor."

This was just the beginning of Sicilian-born director Frank Capra's brilliant film career, which spanned nearly half a century. Starting out as a gag writer for silent comedy kings Hal Roach and Mack Sennett, Capra later began directing films, doing everything from weepies to adventures to comedies to whodunits. In the process, he took on a host of social issues, such as Jewish assimilation in *The Younger Generation* (1929), evangelism in *The Miracle Woman* (1931), bank fraud in *American Madness* (1932), and miscegenation in *The Bitter Tea of General Yen* (1933). Capra's reputation as a director of small, sentimental films— tarred with the sobriquet "Capra-corn"—was also his strength. Among the films that cemented his reputation as a highly talented filmmaker were *Mr. Deeds Goes to Town* (1936), *You Can't Take It with You* (1938, Oscar), *Lost Horizon* (1937), *Mr. Smith Goes to Washington* (1939), *Meet John Doe* (1941), and the black comedy *Arsenic and Old Lace* (released in 1944).

Claudette Colbert, Carol Lombard, Clark Gable with Frank Capra

After the war, Capra formed Liberty Pictures, where he made the immortal *It's a Wonderful Life* (1946) and *State of the Union* (1948), both of which were box-office bombs. The 1950s was a slow period for Capra, who then tried his hand at developing educational TV programs for Bell Telephone. He did make a successful screen comeback, however, with *A Hole in the Head* (1959) and *Pocketful of Miracles* (1961). Capra's 1971 autobiography, *The Name Above the Title*, remains one of the great books on Hollywood.

The envelope, please...

BEST ACTOR
CLARK GABLE (1901–1960)
IT HAPPENED ONE NIGHT

"I feel as happy as a kid and a little foolish they picked me," said Gable, who had been loaned out to Columbia to make the film, which he considered "punishment."

Gable had instant sex appeal. The studios cast him with their finest actresses, including Garbo, Joan Crawford, and Jean Harlow. After a few weak runs following his Oscar win for *It Happened One Night*, Gable was back on top in *Mutiny on the Bounty* (1935, nom.). Success followed success with *Wife vs. Secretary* (1936), *Too Hot to Handle* (1938), *Idiot's Delight*, and, of course, *Gone with the Wind* (both 1939).

Gable's winning streak continued until, tragically, his new wife, Carole Lombard, was killed in a plane crash in 1942. He was devastated. After enlisting in the Air Corps, Gable returned to Hollywood in 1945, but without his star quality. In *The Misfits* (1961), one of Gable's last films, director John Huston was able to draw on the actor's real-life pain over the loss of Lombard. He died before the film was released, nor did he ever see the only child he fathered, John Clark Gable, who is also an actor.

BEST ACTRESS
CLAUDETTE COLBERT (1903–1996),
IT HAPPENED ONE NIGHT

With the release of the screwball comedy *Three-Cornered Moon* (1933), Parisian-born Claudette Lily Chauchoin entered America's heart. It kept beating for sixty films, among them *Bluebeard's Eighth Wife* (1938), *Midnight* (1939), and *The Palm Beach Story* (1942). Colbert proved herself a dramatic actress as well, in John Ford's *Drums Along the Mohawk* (1939), *Arise, My Love* (1940, her favorite film), and *Since You Went Away* (1944, nom.).

Time is not kind to movie stars. By the late 1940s and '50s, Colbert had lost her charm. In 1955 she filmed *Texas Lady* and returned to the stage in 1956. She wasn't seen again on film until *Parrish* (1961), her final act—with the exception of her performance in the television movie *The Two Mrs. Grenvilles*. On July 30, 1996, Colbert died, after a series of strokes, at the age of 92.

BEST OF 1934
Best Picture: *It Happened One Night*
Best Director: Frank Capra, *It Happened One Night*
Best Actor: Clark Gable, *It Happened One Night*
Best Actress: Claudette Colbert, *It Happened One Night*
Honorary Award: Shirley Temple

FIRSTS
- *It Happened One Night*'s record Oscar cleanup held until *One Flew Over the Cuckoo's Nest* in 1975.
- Editing and Music categories were introduced. The first Best Song winner was "The Continental," from *The Gay Divorcee*.
- The outcry over Bette Davis's omission gave way to the first sanctioned write-in vote.

ROLE REVERSALS
The original casting of *It Happened One Night* was to have included George Montgomery in Gable's role and Myrna Loy, Bette Davis, Miriam Hopkins, or Margaret Sullavan in Colbert's shoes.

SINS OF OMISSION
Picture: *The Scarlet Empress*
Actresses: Bette Davis, *Of Human Bondage*
Myrna Loy, *The Thin Man*

UNMENTIONABLES
- "All that French broad cares about is money," said Columbia's Harry Cohn. Claudette Colbert accepted *It Happened One Night* after an offer of $50,000 for four weeks' work.
- Colbert hated the left side of her face and once painted it green to ensure that the cameraman wouldn't shoot it.
- Colbert claimed that her longtime marriage to an Arizona physician was a success because she and her husband retained separate residences. A bisexual, she counted the ubiquitous Marlene Dietrich among her lovers.
- MGM loaned Gable out to Capra as punishment for Gable's money demands. He showed up drunk for his first meeting with the director.
- "Listen, he's no Clark Gable at home," said Carole Lombard.
- "They call me the King of Hollywood. I'm under-endowed, I've got a mouthful of false teeth and bad breath," said Clark Gable.
- When Gable peeled off his shirt in *It Happened One Night* to reveal a bare chest, men's undershirt sales plummeted.
- Bette Davis was convinced that she lost out thanks to Jack Warner's order that Warner Bros. employees not vote for her. He was irate because her great shot to stardom in *Of Human Bondage* was the result of a loan-out to RKO.
- "He was lucky and he knew it." —Clark Gable's proposed epitaph.

Shirley Temple with Irvin S. Cobb

© A.M.P.A.S®

HONORARY AWARD
SHIRLEY TEMPLE (B. 1928)

After neatly placing a hairpin in each of Shirley's fifty-two curls, Gertrude Temple's advice to her daughter was "Sparkle, Shirley, sparkle!" In the midst of the Depression, this little girl danced her way to the top of the box office. And her fans ultimately bought millions of dollars' worth of products that bore her likeness.

Temple stole the show with her number "Baby Take a Bow" in *Stand Up and Cheer* (1934). She was signed to an exclusive contract with Fox, and the studio capitalized on her fame by starring her in films backed up with hit directors and contract players from the studio ranks. She made history when she tap-danced with the great Bill "Bojangles" Robinson.

Temple's films were often remakes of famous children's stories, among them *The Littlest Rebel* (1935), *Wee Willie Winkie, Heidi* (both 1937), *Rebecca of Sunnybrook Farm*, and *Little Miss Broadway* (both 1938). Refusing to loan her to MGM to star in *The Wizard of Oz*, Darryl Zanuck tried to make his own blockbuster with *The Blue Bird* (1940) but failed.

Shirley Temple went on to do what no child star should ever do—become an adolescent. Still, she performed well in *Since You Went Away* (1944) and *The Bachelor and the Bobby-Soxer* (1947).

Shirley Temple retired from film in 1949 but returned in the late 1950s to host TV anthology programs. As the grown-up and married Shirley Temple Black, she became active in politics. Her autobiography, *Child Star*, was published in 1988.

AWARD NOMINATIONS 1933-34

PICTURE

THE BARRETTS OF WIMPOLE STREET, MGM. Produced by Irving Thalberg.

CLEOPATRA, Paramount. Produced by Cecil B. DeMille.

FLIRTATION WALK, First National. Produced by Jack L. Warner and Hal Wallis, with Robert Lord.

THE GAY DIVORCEE, RKO Radio. Produced by Pandro S. Berman.

HERE COMES THE NAVY, Warner Bros. Produced by Lou Edelman.

THE HOUSE OF ROTHSCHILD, 20th Century, UA. Produced by Darryl F. Zanuck, with William Goetz and Raymond Griffith.

IMITATION OF LIFE, Universal. Produced by John M. Stahl.

IT HAPPENED ONE NIGHT, Columbia. Produced by Harry Cohn.

ONE NIGHT OF LOVE, Columbia. Produced by Harry Cohn, with Everett Riskin.

THE THIN MAN, MGM. Produced by Hunt Stromberg.

VIVA VILLA, MGM. Produced by David O. Selznick.

THE WHITE PARADE, Fox. Produced by Jesse L. Lasky.

ACTOR

CLARK GABLE in It Happened One Night, Columbia.

FRANK MORGAN in *The Affairs of Cellini*, 20th Century, UA.

WILLIAM POWELL in *The Thin Man*, MGM.

ACTRESS

CLAUDETTE COLBERT in It Happened One Night, Columbia.

GRACE MOORE in *One Night of Love*, Columbia.

NORMA SHEARER in *The Barretts of Wimpole Street*, MGM.

DIRECTION

FRANK CAPRA for It Happened One Night, Columbia.

VICTOR SCHERTZINGER for *One Night of Love*, Columbia.

W.S. VAN DYKE for *The Thin Man*, MGM.

WRITING: BASED ON MATERIAL FROM ANOTHER MEDIUM

IT HAPPENED ONE NIGHT, Columbia. Robert Riskin.

THE THIN MAN, MGM. Frances Goodrich and Albert Hackett.

VIVA VILLA, MGM. Ben Hecht.

WRITING: DIRECTLY FOR THE SCREEN

HIDE-OUT, MGM. Mauri Grashin.

MANHATTAN MELODRAMA, Cosmopolitan, MGM. Arthur Caesar.

THE RICHEST GIRL IN THE WORLD, RKO Radio. Norman Krasna.

CINEMATOGRAPHY

THE AFFAIRS OF CELLINI, 20th Century, UA. Charles Rosher.

CLEOPATRA, Paramount. Victor Miler.

OPERATION 13, Cosmopolitan, MGM. George Folsey.

ART DIRECTION

THE AFFAIRS OF CELLINI, 20th Century, UA. Richard Day.

THE GAY DIVORCEE, RICO Radio. Van Nest Polglase and Carroll Clark.

THE MERRY WIDOW, MGM. Cedric Gibbons and Frederic Hope.

SOUND RECORDING

THE AFFAIRS OF CELLINI, 20th Century, UA. United Artists Studio Sound Dept., Thomas T. Moulton, Sound Director.

CLEOPATRA, Paramount. Paramount Studio Sound Dept., Franklin Hansen, Sound Director.

FLIRTATION WALK, First National. Warner Bros.-First National Studio Sound Dept., Nathan Levinson, Sound Director.

THE GAY DIVORCEE, RKO Radio, RKO Radio Studio Sound Dept., Carl Dreher, Sound Director.

IMITATION OF LIFE, Universal Studio Sound Dept., Theodore Soderberg, Sound Director.

ONE NIGHT OF LOVE, Columbia. Columbia Studio Sound Dept., John Livadary, Sound Director.

VIVA VILLA, MGM. MGM Studio Sound Dept., Douglas Shearer, Sound Director.

THE WHITE PARADE, Fox. Fox Studio Sound Dept., E.H. Hansen, Sound Director.

FILM EDITING

CLEOPATRA, Paramount. Anne Bauchens.

ESKIMO, MGM. Conrad Nevig.

ONE NIGHT OF LOVE, Columbia. Gene Milford.

SONG

CARIOCA *(Flying Down to Rio,* RKO Radio); Music by Vincent Youmans. Lyrics by Edward Eliscu and Gus Kahn.

THE CONTINENTAL (The Gay Divorcee, RKO Radio); Music by Con Conrad. Lyrics by Herb Magidson.

LOVE IN BLOOM *(She Loves Me Not,* Paramount); Music by Ralph Rainger. Lyrics by Leo Robin.

SCORING: ORIGINAL MUSIC

THE GAY DIVORCEE, RKO Radio. RKO Radio Studio Music Dept.; Max Steiner, head. Score by Kenneth Webb and Samuel Hoffenstein.

THE LOST PATROL, RKO Radio. RKO Radio Studio Music Dept.; Max Steiner, head. Score by Max Steiner.

ONE NIGHT OF LOVE, Columbia. Columbia Studio Music Dept.; Louis Silvers, head. Thematic music by Victor Schertzinger and Gus Kahn.

ASSISTANT DIRECTOR

SCOTT BEAL for *Imitation of Life*, Universal.

CULLEN TATE for *Cleopatra*, Paramount.

JOHN WATERS for Viva Villa, MGM.

SHORT SUBJECT: CARTOON

HOLIDAY LAND, Mintz, Columbia.

JOLLY LITTLE ELVES, Universal.

THE TORTOISE AND THE HARE, Disney, UA.

SHORT SUBJECT: COMEDY

LA CUCARACHA, RKO Radio. (Special)

MEN IN BLACK, Columbia (Broadway Comedies)

WHAT, NO MEN!, Warner Bros. (Broadway Brevities)

SHORT SUBJECTS: NOVELTY

BOSOM FRIENDS, Educational. (Treasure Chest)

CITY OF WAX, Educational. (Battle For Life)

STRIKES AND SPARES, MGM (Oddities)

SPECIAL AWARD

TO SHIRLEY TEMPLE, in grateful recognition of her outstanding contribution to screen entertainment during the year 1934.

SCIENTIFIC OR TECHNICAL

CLASS II

ELECTRICAL RESEARCH PRODUCTS, INC., for their development of the vertical cut disc method of recording sound for motion pictures (hill and dale recording).

CLASS III

COLUMBIA PICTURES CORP.; BELL AND HOWELL CO.

1935

"The casting couch? There's only one of us who ever made it to stardom without it, and that was Bette Davis."

—Claudette Colbert

Had there been a movie camera on hand, it might have panned the eighth annual banquet to find a sea of regular folk done up in their Sunday best. And there, in the small sprinkling of famous faces, would be Bette Davis, perversely attired like an executive secretary in a plain print dress. Where was everybody?

With the recent formation of the Directors Guild, its members had joined with the Actors and the Writers Guilds to boycott the

BETTE AND THE BOYCOTT

CEREMONY: March 5, 1936
Biltmore Bowl, Biltmore
Hotel, Los Angeles
HOST: Frank Capra,
Academy president

event. It was in protest of the Academy's unwillingness to intercede on behalf of union demands. Their newsletters howled, "The sooner the Academy is destroyed the better! You should not attend!" In a last-ditch effort to fill the room, the studios sent their office staff, switchboard operators, and gofers. No one took the guilds' command more seriously than Best Adapted Screenplay winner Dudley Nichols, who was not merely absent but refused his Oscar for *The Informer*.

Surprisingly, it was Columbia chief, Harry Cohn, who provided some much needed levity as he presented the Best Picture Award. "Last year we won an armful of statuettes over at Columbia, so this year we started out not to make any good pictures and we believe we succeeded," he joked. A stunning victory was handed to Hal Mohr, the cinematographer for *A Midsummer Night's Dream*. Mohr was sitting by his radio drinking a beer when he got the call. He leaped into his tux, grabbed his wife, and made it to the Biltmore in time to see Bette Davis win the Best Actress Oscar. This one was a consolation prize, and she knew it. She felt she'd been robbed last year for *Of Human Bondage* and wasn't pleased at all. She put on her happiest face, but the presenter, D. W. Griffith, a great reader of faces, seemed to sense her dissatisfaction. "You don't know how lucky you are, young lady," he said. "At your age, to be where you are, making all that money, fame and everything." Davis nodded obligingly.

Never one to trust good luck or to win a gold pin for gratitude, Davis walked out on Warner Bros. the very next day.

BEST PICTURE
MUTINY ON THE BOUNTY

Mutiny on the Bounty took the gold from powerful odds-on favorites *The Informer*, *David Copperfield*, *Ruggles of Red Gap*, *Alice Adams*, and *The Lives of a Bengal Lancer*. It had all the ingredients for becoming a winner, with its box-office power and its critical distinctions. *The New Yorker*'s Pauline Kael said of the film, "A stirring 18th-century sea adventure in the big MGM manner…The story of HMS Bounty, its brutal Captain Bligh, and the mutineers who fled… has narrative push and a popular theme—the revolt against a tyrant… But for the kind of big budget, studio controlled romantic adventure that this is, it's very well done." The *New York Times* concurred: "The weird and wonderful history…is magnificently transferred to the screen in *Mutiny on the Bounty*… Crime, brutal, sturdily romantic, made out of horror and desperate courage, it is as savagely exciting and rousingly dramatic a photoplay as has come out of Hollywood in recent years…It is superbly thrilling."

Clark Gable (left), Charles Laughton (right)

The envelope, please...

Victor McLaglen with Margot Grahame

BEST ACTOR
VICTOR MCLAGLEN (1883–1959)
THE INFORMER

According to critic Pauline Kael, "It is Hollywood legend that Ford got McLaglen boozed up so that he was bewildered and couldn't do his usual brand of acting—and it's probably true."

A great, cheerful hulk of a man whose former life as a soldier, a farmer, and a boxer was written all over his face, McLaglen appeared on the Hollywood screen after years of doing time in action roles in the British cinema. Typecast as the "two-fisted man of action," McLaglen was impressive in *The Unholy Three* (1925), *Beau Geste* (1926), and in one of his more important roles, *What Price Glory?* (1926).

McLaglen made his talkie debut in John Ford's *The Black Watch* (1929), followed by *A Devil with Women* (1930). He was reunited with Ford for his two most important roles, in *The Lost Patrol* (1934) and *The Informer* (1935). After *Fort Apache* (1948), *She Wore a Yellow Ribbon* (1949), *Rio Grande* (1950), and *The Quiet Man* (1952, nom.), his film career took a dive. An increasingly ill McLaglen retired and died of a heart attack a few years later.

Bette Davis with Franchot Tone

BEST ACTRESS
BETTE DAVIS (1908–1989)
DANGEROUS

Upon winning the Oscar, Davis was reported by *Variety* as "clasping the award in both arms and holding it tight as tears of joy ran down her cheeks," despite lingering disappointment over her no-win for *Of Human Bondage* the year before.

Although many in Hollywood doubted Davis's star potential, scoring her low on the sex-appeal chart, she proved them wrong and followed her Oscar for *Dangerous* with another for *Jezebel* (1938). She then sued the studios successfully for not giving her the big roles she felt she deserved.

After *Jezebel*, Davis tallied up an endless run of Best Actress nominations, among them *Dark Victory* (1939), *The Letter* (1940), *The Little Foxes* (1941), and *Now, Voyager* (1942). The 1940s weren't Davis's best years, though she did give Oscar-nominated performances in *All About Eve* (1950) and *The Star* (1952). She received her last Oscar nomination for *What Ever Happened to Baby Jane?* (1962); her fights with co-star Joan Crawford on that film were legendary. Davis made several not-so-laudable appearances in the 1960s, including *Hush...Hush, Sweet Charlotte* (1965) and *Connecting Rooms* (1969). She returned to the screen in *The Whales of August* (1987), along with Lillian Gish). Davis was the first female recipient of the American Film Institute's Life Achievement Award.

AWARD NOMINATIONS 1935

PICTURE
ALICE ADAMS, RKO Radio. Produced by Pandro S. Berman.
BROADWAY MELODY OF 1936, MGM. Produced by John W. Considine Jr.
CAPTAIN BLOOD, Warner Bros.-Cosmopolitan. Produced by Hal Wallis, with Harry Joe Brown and Gordon Hollingshead.
DAVID COPPERFIELD, MGM. Produced by David O. Selznick.
THE INFORMER, REQ Radio. Produced by Cliff Reid.
LES MISERABLES, 20th Century, UA. Produced by Darryl F. Zanuck.
LIVES OF A BENGAL LANCER, Paramount. Produced by Louis D. Lighton.
A MIDSUMMER NIGHT'S DREAM, Warner Bros.-First National. Produced by Henry Blanke.
MUTINY ON THE BOUNTY, MGM. Produced by Irving Thalberg, with Albert Lewin.
NAUGHTY MARIETTA, MGM. Produced by Hunt Stromberg.
RUGGLES OF RED GAP, Paramount. Produced by Arthur Hornblow Jr.
TOP HAT, RKO Radio. Produced by Pandro S. Berman.

ACTOR
CLARK GABLE in *Mutiny on the Bounty*, MGM.
CHARLES LAUGHTON in *Mutiny on the Bounty*, MGM.
VICTOR McLAGLEN in *The Informer*, RKO Radio.
FRANCHOT TONE in *Mutiny on the Bounty*, MGM.

ACTRESS
ELISABETH BERGNER in *Escape Me Never*, Wilcox, UA (British).
CLAUDETTE COLBERT in *Private Worlds*, Paramount.
BETTE DAVIS in *Dangerous*, Warner Bros.
KATHARINE HEPBURN in *Alice Adams*, RKO Radio.
MIRIAM HOPKINS in *Becky Sharp*, Pioneer, RKO Radio.
MERLE OBERON in *The Dark Angel*, Goldwyn, UA.

DIRECTION
JOHN FORD for *The Informer*, RKO Radio.
HENRY HATHAWAY for *Lives of a Bengal Lancer*, Paramount.
FRANK LLOYD for *Mutiny on the Bounty*, MGM.

WRITING: ORIGINAL STORY
BROADWAY MELODY OF 1936, MGM. Moss Hart.
THE GAY DECEPTION, Lasky, Fox. Don Hartman and Stephen Avery.
THE SCOUNDREL, Paramount. Ben Hecht and Charles MacArthur.

WRITING: SCREENPLAY
THE INFORMER, RKO Radio. Dudley Nichols.
LIVES OF A BENGAL LANCER, Paramount. Achmed Abdullah, John L. Balderston, Grover Jones, William Slavens McNutt and Waldemar Young.
MUTINY ON THE BOUNTY, MGM. Jules Furthman, Talbot Jennings and Carey Wilson.

John Ford (seated) with Victor McLaglen

BEST DIRECTOR
JOHN FORD (1894–1973)
THE INFORMER

The studio didn't think *The Informer* had "legs," so Ford was granted only a small budget. The rest is history. As film critic Leonard Maltin wrote, "Few filmmakers in the history of the medium have left their mark so indelibly on so many outstanding films."

Perhaps one of the most highly respected of American movie directors—and one of Hollywood's most colorful and irascible filmmakers—John Ford was lauded by critics for his poetic vision. The Western was his domain, and he demonstrated his mastery of the genre with such brilliant films as *Drums Along the Mohawk, Young Mr. Lincoln,* and *Stagecoach* (all 1939). In the following two years he won Oscars for *The Grapes of Wrath* (1940) and *How Green Was My Valley* (1941).

During World War II he served in the OSS and made several documentaries, including *The Battle of Midway* (1942) and *December 7th* (1943). Both were awarded Oscars. In the late 1940s Ford produced some of his most intimate films, including *Fort Apache* (1948), *She Wore a Yellow Ribbon* (1949), *Rio Grande* (1950, a trilogy), and *The Quiet Man* (1952, Oscar). *The Searchers* (1956), starring John Wayne, remains, arguably, Ford's most mythic and poetic film. Ford was the first recipient of the American Film Institute's Life Achievement Award.

CINEMATOGRAPHY
BARBARY COAST, Goldwyn, UA, Ray June.
THE CRUSADES, Paramount. Victor Miler.
LES MISERABLES, 20th Century, UA. Gregg Toland.
A MIDSUMMER NIGHT'S DREAM, Warner Bros. Hal Mohr.

ART DIRECTION
THE DARK ANGEL, Goldwyn, UA. Richard Day.
LIVES OF A BENGAL LANCER, Paramount. Hans Dreier and Roland Anderson.
TOP HAT, RKO Radio. Carroll Clark and Van Nest Polglase.

SOUND RECORDING
THE BRIDE OF FRANKENSTEIN, Universal. Universal Studio Sound Dept., Gilbert Kurland, Sound Director.
CAPTAIN BLOOD, Warner Bros. Warner Bros.-First National Studio Sound Dept., Nathan Levinson, Sound Director.
THE DARK ANGEL, Goldwyn, UA. United Artists Studio Sound Dept. Thomas T. Moulton, Sound Director.
I DREAM TOO MUCH, RKO Radio. RKO Radio Studio Sound Dept., Carl Dreher, Sound Director.
LIVES OF A BENGAL LANCER, Paramount. Paramount Studio Sound Dept., Franklin Hansen, Sound Director.
LOVE ME FOREVER, Columbia. Columbia Studio Sound Dept., John Livadary, Sound Director.
NAUGHTY MARIETTA, MGM. MGM Studio Sound Dept., Douglas Shearer, Sound Director.
1,000 DOLLARS A MINUTE, Republic. Republic Studio Sound Dept.
THANKS A MILLION, 20th Century-Fox. 20th Century-Fox Studio Sound Dept., E.H. Hansen, Sound Director.

FILM EDITING
DAVID COPPERFIELD, MGM. Robert J. Kern.
THE INFORMER, RKO Radio. George Hively.
LES MISERABLES, 20th Century, UA. Barbara McLean.
LIVES OF A BENGAL LANCER, Paramount. Ellsworth Hoagland.
A MIDSUMMER NIGHT'S DREAM, Warner Bros. Ralph Dawson.
MUTINY ON THE BOUNTY, MGM. Margaret Booth.

SONG
CHEEK TO CHEEK *(Top Hat,* RKO Radio); Music and Lyrics by Irving Berlin.

LOVELY TO LOOK AT *(Roberta,* RKO Radio); Music by Jerome Kern. Lyrics by Dorothy Fields and Jimmy McHugh.
LULLABY OF BROADWAY *(Gold Diggers of 1935,* Warner Bros.-First National); Music by Harry Warren. Lyrics by Al Dubin.

SCORING: ORIGINAL MUSIC
THE INFORMER, RKO Radio. RKO Radio Music Dept.; Max Steiner, head. Score by Max Steiner.
MUTINY ON THE BOUNTY, MGM. MGM Studio Music Dept.; Nat W. Finston, head. Score by Herbert Stothart.
PETER IBBETSON, Paramount. Paramount Studio Music Dept.; Irvin Talbot, head. Score by Ernst Toch.

ASSISTANT DIRECTOR
CLEM BEAUCRAMP for *Lives of a Bengal Lancer,* Paramount.
ERIC STACEY for *Les Miserables,* 20th Century, UA.
PAUL WING for *Lives of a Bengal Lancer,* Paramount.
JOSEPH NEWMAN for *David Copperfield,* MGM.

DANCE DIRECTION
BUSBY BERKELEY for "Lullaby of Broadway" number and "The Words are in My Heart" number from *Gold Diggers of 1935,* (Warner Bros.-First National).
BOBBY CONNOLLY for "Latin from Manhattan" number from *Go into Your Dance* (Warner Bros.-First National) and "Playboy from Paree" number from *Broadway Hostess* (Warner Bros.-First National).
DAVE GOULD for "I've Got a Feeling You're Fooling" number from *Broadway Melody of 1936* (MGM) and "Straw Hat" number from *Folies Bergere* (20th Century, UA).
SAMMY LEE for "Lovely Lady" number and "Too Good to Be True" number from *King of Burlesque* (20th Century-Fox).
HERMES PAN for "Piccolino" number and "Top Hat" number from *Top Hat* (RKO Radio).
LEROY PRINZ for "Elephant" number "It's the Animal in Me" from *Big Broadcast of 1936* (Paramount) and "Big Viennese Waltz" number from *All the King's Horses* (Paramount).
BENJAMIN ZEMACH for "Hall of Kings" number from *She* (RKO Radio).

SHORT SUBJECTS: CARTOONS
THE CALICO DRAGON, Harman-Ising, MGM.
THREE ORPHAN KITTENS, Disney, UA.
WHO KILLED COCK ROBIN?, Disney, GA.

SHORT SUBJECTS: COMEDY
HOW TO SLEEP, MGM. (Miniature)
OH, MY NERVES, Columbia. (Broadway Comedies)
TIT FOR TAT, Roach, MGM. (Laurel & Hardy)

SHORT SUBJECTS: NOVELTY
AUDIOSCOPIKS, MGM.
CAMERA THRILLS, Universal.
WINGS OVER MT. EVEREST, Educational.

SPECIAL AWARD
TO DAVID WARK GRIFFITH, for his distinguished creative achievements as director and producer and his invaluable initiative and lasting contributions to the progress of the motion-picture arts.

SCIENTIFIC OR TECHNICAL

CLASS II
AGFA ANSCO CORP. for their development of the Agfa infra-red film.
EASTMAN KODAK CO. for their development of the Eastman Pola-Screen.

CLASS III
METRO-GOLDWYN-MAYER STUDIO;
WILLIAM A. MUELLER of Warner Bros.-First National Studio Sound Dept.;
MOLE-RICHARDSON CO.;
DOUGLAS SHEARER and MGM STUDIO SOUND DEPT.;
ELECTRICAL RESEARCH PRODUCTS, INC.;
PARAMOUNT PRODUCTIONS, INC.;
NATHAN LEVINSON, director of Sound Recording for Warner Bros.-First National Studio.

BEST OF 1935
Best Picture: *Mutiny on the Bounty*
Best Director: John Ford, *The Informer*

SINS OF OMISSION
Picture: *The 39 Steps*
Director: Alfred Hitchcock, *The 39 Steps*

UNMENTIONABLES
• The studios pulled out funding for the Awards, and the Academy was forced to foot the bill for the big night.

• Thanks to union efforts, Academy membership dropped from more than 600 to 40.

• "Looking to the Academy for representation (as a screenwriter) was like trying to get laid in your mother's house," said Dorothy Parker. "Somebody was always in the parlor watching."

• Bette Davis's first screen test in 1929 sent studio boss Samuel Goldwyn into fits. "Who did this to me? She's a dog!" he ranted. Davis herself ran out of the projection room screaming.

• Bette Davis insisted that she was the one who first dubbed the Academy Award "Oscar" in honor of her first husband, Harmon Oscar Nelson. Their marriage was a disaster. She thought he might be gay and carried on affairs with Howard Hughes and the great love of her life, director William Wyler. Nelson tried to blackmail Hughes with tape recordings of his sexual liaisons with Davis.

• "Bette Davis is an egotistical little bitch," said Barbara Stanwyck.

FIRSTS
• Price Waterhouse was hired to tabulate ballots for the first time.

• *The Informer* screenwriter, Dudley Nichols, was the first winner to refuse the Oscar on political grounds.

• A flop in its initial release, *The Informer,* was the first film to financially benefit from an Oscar. It made its money back within days of its Best Actor win.

• Cinematographer Hal Mohr was the first and only write-in ballot winner.

• At $2 million, *Mutiny on the Bounty* was the most expensive motion picture made to date.

• *Mutiny on the Bounty* was the first film to garner three acting nominations (Clark Gable, Franchot Tone, Charles Laughton) and the only time the nominations were in the same category.

• MGM was the first studio to campaign with ads in the press for Oscar consideration. The movie was *Ah, Wilderness!* It didn't receive a single nomination.

1936

"Please keep your thank-you speeches brief. Remember, a fellow recently gave up the British Empire in two minutes."

Thanks to the sellout crowd of 1,150, the Academy was able to replenish its coffers by charging $25 for ringside seats. After last year's proletariat turnout, glamour was back and the champagne flowed. Lovebirds Carole Lombard and Clark Gable sipped bubbly with the recently engaged William Powell and Jean Harlow. Bette Davis even turned up in a glittery gown to present the Best Actress Award.

The last star to arrive was Norma Shearer, on the arm of Louis B. Mayer. It was Shearer's first public appearance since the death of her husband, Irving Thalberg, six months earlier. She was the presumed Best Actress winner for her extremely mature Juliet, but a quick trip downstairs to the pressroom would have eliminated the guesswork. The names of the winners had been given to reporters at 8 P.M. to meet East Coast deadlines. After an MGM publicist poked his head in to check the results, he ran to the phone to call Luise Rainer. She insisted that she couldn't make it to the ceremony, having just driven down from San Francisco. "My face is all red from the sun and wind," she said. But the young winner was quickly reminded of whom she worked for and what was required of her. Rainer arrived in plenty of time to graciously accept her Oscar from George Jessel.

Bette Davis fumed and confronted Jessel backstage. How dare he steal her role as presenter! He begged her forgiveness, claiming that he was momentarily thrown off after Victor McLaglen made a drunken shambles out of his Oscar presentation to Paul Muni.

Out front, Frank Capra ended the evening on a solemn note as he unveiled the Irving Thalberg Memorial Award. "It is to encourage the pride, the fortitude, the good taste and tolerance that Thalberg put into pictures," he said. "It is to keep permanent his message: The stars brighten the night, the laughter of children is a message to the ear." Every gaze turned to the widow's table. Her head was bowed. It had not been a good year for Norma Shearer.

GOING WITH THE FLO

CEREMONY: March 4, 1937
Biltmore Bowl, Biltmore Hotel, Los Angeles
HOST: George Jessel

BEST PICTURE
THE GREAT ZIEGFELD

"We have an arrangement in our studio where I make all the speeches," said producer Louis B. Mayer. But this time he brought the film's producer, Hunt Stromberg, to the podium. "One thing I like about working with Louis B. Mayer," Stromberg commented, "I went to him and told him that the melody numbers of *The Great Ziegfeld* would cost $250,000 and he just said, 'Shoot.'"

MGM's most expensive biopic ($2 million), *The Great Ziegfeld* made up in box-office revenue what it lacked in critical acclaim. Pauline Kael dismissed the film as a "lavish, tedious musical biography." She continued, "It goes on for a whopping three hours, but through some insane editing decision Fanny Brice is cut off in the middle of singing 'My Man.' Inexplicably this thing won the Academy Award." The *New York Times*'s slightly more forgiving Frank S. Nugent said, "If the picture overcrowds its screen, at least we must admit it is an impressive kaleidoscope; and probably nothing short of that could reflect the gaudy career of America's foremost showman…The picture has the general indifference to humor which was one of Ziegfeld's characteristics."

Luise Rainer (center)

The envelope, please…

BEST ACTOR
PAUL MUNI (1895–1967)
THE STORY OF LOUIS PASTEUR

When presenter Victor McLaglen finally got through his insufferably long introduction, Muni grabbed a moment at the microphone and said, "I have the greatest thrill of my life getting this. I will try to continue to work to make myself worthy of the Academy's high and meaningful honor." "Me too," McLaglen added, getting in the last word.

Muni (who started his career in the Yiddish theater) became a true film star with the release of *Scarface* (1932), followed by *I Am a Fugitive from a Chain Gang* (1932, nom.) and *The Good Earth* (1937). He was nominated for an Oscar for *The Life of Emile Zola* (1937), which was followed by *Juarez* (1939). In the 1940s Muni appeared in *Angel on My Shoulder* (1946). He left Hollywood and returned only once, in the Italian-made *Stranger on the Prowl* (1953). He then dabbled in television, where he appeared in *The Last Angry Man* (1959, nom.).

Luise Rainer with William Powell

BEST ACTRESS
LUISE RAINER (B. 1910)
THE GREAT ZIEGFELD

"Rainer did her heartbreak specialty smiling through tears and looking irresistibly fragile," wrote *The New Yorker*'s Pauline Kael.

MGM saw in Rainer the next Garbo—she had beauty, charm, and talent to spare—and promoted her heavily. The pretty, doll-like Austrian actress won two consecutive Oscars for *The Great Ziegfeld* (1936) and *The Good Earth* (1937) at the near-outset of her career—which was possibly too much too soon. Unable to live up to the expectations of her early successes, she was dropped by the studio.

Plagued with personal problems, and unwilling to be "molded" by Hollywood, Rainer turned on her heels, left Hollywood, and never looked back (well, almost never). She made one more film, *Hostages* (1943), before retiring from the screen. She returned to performing in the 1980s with an appearance in a 1983 episode of the TV series *The Love Boat*. She also played in a TV movie in Switzerland, *A Dancer* (1988). Rainer didn't appear in another film until 1997, when she starred in *The Gambler*. She was married to the great but troubled playwright Clifford Odets.

BEST OF 1936
Best Picture: *The Great Ziegfeld*
Best Director: Frank Capra, *Mr. Deeds Goes to Town*
Best Actor: Paul Muni, *The Story of Louis Pasteur*
Best Actress: Luise Rainer, *The Great Ziegfeld*
Best Supporting Actor: Walter Brennan, *Come and Get It*
Best Supporting Actress: Gale Sondergaard, *Anthony Adverse*

SINS OF OMISSION
Pictures: *Modern Times, My Man Godfrey*
Directors: Fritz Lang, *Fury*
Charles Chaplin, *Modern Times*
Supporting Actor: Spencer Tracy, *San Francisco*

UNMENTIONABLES
- The MGM version of *Shakespeare's Romeo and Juliet* starred Norma Shearer (36) and Leslie Howard (44) as the ill-fated teenagers.
- There was a suspiciously high number of nominees who happened to be on the Nominating Committee. Among them were Carole Lombard and Frank Capra. Following ugly accusations, the nominating duties were returned to general membership.
- There were rumors of a secret pact between Louis B. Mayer and Jack Warner: Mayer would strongly advise his employees to vote for Paul Muni if Warner would do likewise on behalf of *The Great Ziegfeld*.
- Mayer was incensed by the recent marriage of his star Luise Rainer to "that rotten Communist" playwright, Clifford Odets.
- Jean Harlow died of an inflamed gall bladder just two months after the Awards banquet. Her eccentric Christian Scientist mother refused to allow an operation, insisting that she would cure her through prayer.
- Norma Shearer retired from the screen in 1942 and married a 28-year-old ski instructor, Marti Arrouge.

FIRSTS
- Best Supporting categories were introduced. Winners received plaques rather than statuettes.
- The Irving G. Thalberg Memorial Award was dedicated. The bust was given to producers of distinction.
- Judy Garland made her feature debut in *Pigskin Parade*.
- *My Man Godfrey* was the first film to garner acting nominations in all four categories.
- Gale Sondergaard was the first performer to win Best Actress.

BEST SUPPORTING ACTOR
WALTER BRENNAN (1894–1974)
COME AND GET IT

Walter Brennan was still in his thirties when he began playing crotchety old men on screen. With his prematurely thinning hair, missing teeth, and weary expression, he had the good fortune of looking ten years older than he was, which won him plum roles.

Brennan set out to become an engineer but landed in Hollywood. In short order, he was appearing in bit parts. He became the first actor to win three Academy Awards—*Come and Get It* (1936), *Kentucky* (1938), and *The Westerner* (1940). He followed these successes with more than 100 feature films, including *My Darling Clementine* (1946), *Red River* (1948), *Bad Day at Black Rock* (1955), *Rio Bravo* (1959), and *How the West Was Won* (1962). Brennan was perhaps best known to a generation of television viewers for his role as the hobbling patriarch in the series *The Real McCoys*.

(For more on Brennan, see 1938 and 1940.)

BEST SUPPORTING ACTRESS
GALE SONDERGAARD (1895–1999)
ANTHONY ADVERSE

"Gale Sondergaard, whose leer was her fortune, plays a super-wicked villainess," wrote Pauline Kael. Sondergaard, who had started out on Broadway in the late 1920s, followed her director husband, Herbert Biberman, to Hollywood and reluctantly accepted her first film role. Her reluctance proved no "handicap," as she won a Best Supporting Actress award.

Dark, exotic-looking, and coldly attractive, Sondergaard went on to play many supporting roles as sinister, cunning women, but she still managed to land parts in such major films as *The Life of Emile Zola* (1937), *The Cat and the Canary* (1939), and *Anna and the King of Siam* (1946, nom.). Blacklisted, along with her husband, following the House Un-American Activities Committee hearings, Sondergaard made her last Hollywood film, *East Side, West Side*, in 1949.

PICTURE
ANTHONY ADVERSE, Warner Bros. Produced by Henry Blanke.
DODSWORTH, Goldwyn, UA. Produced by Samuel Goldwyn, with Merritt Hulbert.
THE GREAT ZIEGFELD, MGM. Produced by Hunt Stromberg.
LIBELED LADY, MGM. Produced by Lawrence Weingarten.
MR. DEEDS GOES TO TOWN, Columbia. Produced by Frank Capra.
ROMEO AND JULIET. MGM. Produced by Irving Thalberg.
SAN FRANCISCO, MGM. Produced by John Emerson and Bernard H. Hyman.
THE STORY OF LOUIS PASTEUR, Warner Bros. Produced by Henry Blanke.
A TALE OF TWO CITIES, MGM. Produced by David O. Selznick.
THREE SMART GIRLS, Universal. Produced by Joseph Pasternak, with Charles R. Rogers.

ACTOR
GARY COOPER in *Mr. Deeds Goes to Town*, Columbia.
WALTER HUSTON in *Dodsworth*, Goldwyn, UA.
PAUL MUNI in *The Story of Louis Pasteur*, Warner Bros.
WILLIAM POWELL in *My Man Godfrey*, Universal.
SPENCER TRACY in *San Francisco*. MGM.

ACTRESS
IRENE DUNNE in *Theodora Goes Wild*, Columbia.
GLADYS GEORGE in *Valiant Is the Word for Carrie*, Paramount.
CAROLE LOMBARD in *My Man Godfrey*, Universal.
LUISE RAINER in *The Great Ziegfeld*, MGM.
NORMA SHEARER in *Romeo and Juliet*, MGM.

SUPPORTING ACTOR
MISCHA AUER in *My Man Godfrey*, Universal.
WALTER BRENNAN in *Come and Get It*, Goldwyn, UA.
STUART ERWIN in *Pigskin Parade*, 20th Century-Fox.
BASIL RATHBONE in *Romeo and Juliet*, MGM.
AKIM TAMIROFF in *The General Died at Dawn*, Paramount.

SUPPORTING ACTRESS
BEULAH BONDI in *The Gorgeous Hussy*, MGM.
ALICE BRADY in *My Man Godfrey*, Universal.
BONITA GRANVILLE in *These Three*, Goldwyn, UA.
MARIA OUSPENSKAYA in *Dodsworth*, Goldwyn, UA.
GALE SONDERGAARD in *Anthony Adverse*, Warner Bros.

DIRECTION
FRANK CAPRA for *Mr. Deeds Goes to Town*, Columbia.
GREGORY LaCAVA for *My Man Godfrey*, Universal.
ROBERT Z. LEONARD for *The Great Ziegfeld*, MGM.
W.S. VAN DYKE for *San Francisco*, MGM.
WILLIAM WYLER for *Dodsworth*, UA.

WRITING: ORIGINAL STORY
FURY, M-G-M Norman Krasna.
THE GREAT ZIEGFELD, MGM William Anthony McGuire.
SAN FRANCISCO, MGM. Robert Hopkins.
THE STORY OF LOUIS PASTEUR. Warner Bros. Pierre Collings and Sheridan Gibney.
THREE SMART GIRLS, Universal. Adele Comandini.

WRITING: SCREENPLAY
AFTER THE THIN MAN, MGM. Frances Goodrich and Albert Hackett.
DODSWORTH, Goldwyn, UA. Sidney Howard.
MR. DEEDS GOES TO TOWN, Columbia. Robert Riskin.
MY MAN GODFREY, Universal. Eric Hatch and Morris Ryskind.
THE STORY OF LOUIS PASTEUR, Warner Bros. Pierre Collings and Sheridan Gibney.

CINEMATOGRAPHY
ANTHONY ADVERSE, Warner Bros. Gaetano Gaudio.
THE GENERAL DIED AT DAWN, Paramount. Victor Milner.
THE GORGEOUS HUSSY, MGM. George Folsey.

ART DIRECTION
ANTHONY ADVERSE, Warner Bros. Anton Grot.
DODSWORTH, Goldwyn, UA. Richard Day.
THE GREAT ZIEGFELD, MGM. Cedric Gibbons, Eddie Imazu and Edwin B. Willis.
LLOYDS OF LONDON, 20th Century-Fox. William S. Darling.
THE MAGNIFICENT BRUTE, Universal. Albert S. D'Agostino and Jack Otterson.
ROMEO AND JULIET, MGM. Cedric Gibbons, Frederic Hope and Edwin B. Willis.
WINTERSET, RKO Radio. Perry Ferguson.

SOUND RECORDING
BANJO ON MY KNEE, 20th Century-Fox. 20th Century-Fox Studio Sound Dept., E.H. Hansen, Sound Director.
THE CHARGE OF THE LIGHT BRIGADE, Warner Bros. Warner Bros. Studio Sound Dept., Nathan Levinson, Sound Director.
DODSWORTH, Goldwyn, UA. United Artists Studio Sound Dept., Thomas T. Moulton, Sound Director.
GENERAL SPANKY, Roach, MGM. Hal Roach Studio Sound Dept., Elmer A. Raguse, Sound Director.
MR. DEEDS GOES TO TOWN, Columbia. Columbia Studio Sound Dept., John Livadary, Sound Director.
SAN FRANCISCO, MGM. MGM Studio Sound Dept., Douglas Shearer, Sound Director.
THE TEXAS RANGERS, Paramount. Paramount Studio Sound Dept., Franklin Hansen, Sound Director.
THAT GIRL FROM PARIS, RKO Radio. RKO Radio Studio Sound Dept., J.O. Aalberg, Sound Director.
THREE SMART GIRLS, Universal. Universal Studio Sound Dept., Homer G. Tasker, Sound Director.

FILM EDITING
ANTHONY ADVERSE, Warner Bros. Ralph Dawson.
COME AND GET IT, Goldwyn, UA. Edward Curtiss.
THE GREAT ZIEGFELD, MGM. William S. Gray.
LLOYDS OF LONDON, 20th Century-Fox. Barbara McLean.
A TALE OF TWO CITIES, MGM. Conrad A. Nervig.
THEODORA GOES WILD, Columbia. Otto Meyer.

SONG
DID I REMEMBER *(Suzy*, M-G.M); Music by Walter Donaldson. Lyrics by Harold Adamson.
I'VE GOT YOU UNDER MY SKIN *(Born to Dance*, MGM); Music and Lyrics by Cole Porter.
A MELODY FROM THE SKY *(Trail of the Lonesome Pine*, Paramount); Music by Louis Alter. Lyrics by Sidney Mitchell.
PENNIES FROM HEAVEN *(Pennies from Heaven*, Columbia); Music by Arthur Johnston. Lyrics by Johnny Burke.
THE WAY YOU LOOK TONIGHT *(Swing Time*, RKO Radio); Music by Jerome Kern. Lyrics by Dorothy Fields.
WHEN DID YOU LEAVE HEAVEN *(Sing Baby Sing*, 20th Century-Fox); Music by Richard A. Whiting. Lyrics by Walter Bullock.

SCORING: ORIGINAL MUSIC
ANTHONY ADVERSE, Warner Bros. Warner Bros. Studio Music Dept.; Leo Forbatein, head. Score by Erich Wolfgang Korngold.
THE CHARGE OF THE LIGHT BRIGADE, Warner Bros. Warner Bros. Studio Music Dept.; Leo Forbstein, head. Score by Max Steiner.
THE GARDEN OF ALLAH, Selznick, UA. Selznick International Pictures Music Dept.; Max Steiner, head. Score by Max Steiner.
THE GENERAL DIED AT DAWN, Paramount. Paramount Studio Music Dept.; Boris Morros, head. Score by Werner Janssen.
WINTERSET, RKO Radio. RHO Radio Studio Music Dept.; Nathaniel Shilkret, head. Score by Nathaniel Shilkret.

ASSISTANT DIRECTOR
CLEM BEAUCHAMP for *Last of the Mohicans*, Reliance, UA.
WILLIAM CANNON for *Anthony Adverse*, Warner Bros.
JOSEPH NEWMAN for *San Francisco*, MGM.
ERIC G. STACEY for *The Garden of Allah*, Selznick, UA.
JACK SULLIVAN for *The Charge of the Light Brigade*, Warner Bros.

DANCE DIRECTION
BUSBY BERKELEY for "Love and War" number from *Gold Diggers of 1936*, (Warner Bros.).
BOBBY CONNOLLY for "1000 Love Songs" number from *Cain and Mabel* (Warner Bros.).
SEYMOUR FELIX for "A Pretty Girl Is Like a Melody" number from *The Great Ziegfeld* (MGM).
DAVE GOULD for "Swingin' the Jinx" number from *Born to Dance* (MGM).
JACK HASKELL for "Skating Ensemble" number from *One in a Million* (20th Century-).
RUSSELL LEWIS for "The Finale" number from *Dancing Pirate* (RKO Radio).
HERMES PAN for "Bojangles of Harlem" number from *Swing Time* (RKO Radio).

SHORT SUBJECT: CARTOON
COUNTRY COUSIN, Disney, UA.
OLD MILL POND, Harman-Ising, MGM.
SINBAD THE SAILOR, Paramount.

SHORT SUBJECT: ONE-REEL
BORED OF EDUCATION, Roach, MGM. (Our Gang)
MOSCOW MOODS, Paramount. (Headliners)
WANTED, A MASTER, MGM. (Peter Smith Specialties)

SHORT SUBJECT: TWO-REEL
DOUBLE OR NOTHING, Warner Bros. (Broadway Brevities)
DUMMY ACHE, RKO Radio. (Edgar Kennedy Comedies)
THE PUBLIC PAYS, MGM. (Crime Doesn't Pay)

SHORT SUBJECT: COLOR
GIVE ME LIBERTY, Warner Bros. (Broadway Brevities)
LA FIESTA DE SANTA BARBARA, MGM. (Musical Revues)
POPULAR SCIENCE J-6-2, Paramount.

SPECIAL AWARDS
TO MARCH OF TIME for its significance to motion pictures and for having revolutionized one of the most important branches of the industry—the newsreel.

TO W. HOWARD GREENE and HAROLD ROSSON for the color cinematography of the Selznick International Production *The Garden of Allah*.

SCIENTIFIC OR TECHNICAL

CLASS I
DOUGLAS SHEARER and the MGM STUDIO SOUND DEPARTMENT for the development of a practical two-way horn system and a biased Class A push-pull recording system.

CLASS II
E.C. WENTE and the BELL TELEPHONE LABORATORIES for their multi-cellular high-frequency horn and receiver.

CLASS III
RCA MANUFACTURING CO., INC.
ELECTRICAL RESEARCH PRODUCTS, INC.
UNITED ARTISTS STUDIO CORP.

1937

Unlike the U.S. Postal Service, rain brought a halt to the delivery of the Oscars. A record deluge gave way to flooding. Academy president, Frank Capra, was stranded in Malibu, the ceremony was canceled, and $750 worth of floral arrangements wilted on the banquet tables.

A week later Los Angeles had dried up, and so had the RSVPs. Almost none of the nominated stars showed up for the rescheduled Awards ceremony. Even the host, George Jessel, pleaded illness and was replaced at the last minute by a "hillbilly comic." The undisputed front-runner, Greta Garbo, decided that she wanted to be alone on a tour of Italy. Spencer Tracy bowed out for a less glamorous appendectomy, and Luise Rainer, who felt she didn't stand a chance of winning, opted to lounge around at home in bedroom slippers.

The most instantly recognizable face on the Biltmore stage wasn't even human. Puppet Charlie McCarthy received an honorary wooden Oscar with a movable mouth. "If you've got a gold one leftover at the end of the night, I'd like to have it," he whined through Edgar Bergen. As was the case the year before, the press knew the winners before the audience did.

Louis B. Mayer ordered one of his boys to get a sneak peek and, in an astonishing case of déjà vu, Luise Rainer got an eleventh hour call. Without time even to apply makeup, she was hustled to the Biltmore to breathlessly collect her historic back-to-back Oscar. It was a stunning upset, and the audience reacted accordingly. How could Garbo have lost for *Camille*? Perhaps for the same reason the Gershwins' "They Can't Take That Away from Me," sung by Fred Astaire in *Shall We Dance*, lost the Best Song Oscar to a catchy little ditty called "Sweet Leilani": the 12,000 members of the Screen Extras Guild were given their first opportunity to vote on the final ballot.

It was a momentous turning point in Academy history. Power shifted from the creators, stars, and studio chiefs to the less political and far less sophisticated common folk. Until their rights were revoked eight years later, they would wield far more influence on the proceedings than the weather did.

RAINER DATE

CEREMONY: March 10, 1938
Biltmore Bowl, Biltmore Hotel,
Los Angeles
HOST: Bob "Bazooka" Burns

BEST PICTURE
THE LIFE OF EMILE ZOLA

"Rich, dignified, honest, and strong," raved the *New York Times*'s Frank S. Nugent. "It is at once the finest historical film ever made and the greatest screen biography, greater even than *The Story of Louis Pasteur*, with which the Warners squared their conscience last year. Like *Pasteur*, the picture has captured the spirit of a man and his times… it has followed not merely the spirit but, to a rare degree, the very letter of his life and of the historically significant lives about him." *The Life of Emile Zola* was a natural for the Oscar just by virtue of being a large-scale biopic—the Academy's favorite category.

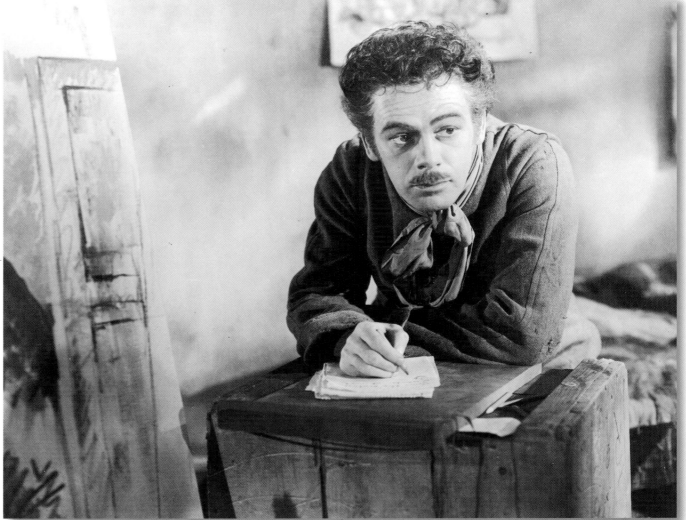

Paul Muni

The envelope, please…

Cary Grant, Irene Dunne

BEST DIRECTOR
LEO MCCAREY (1898–1969)
THE AWFUL TRUTH

"Thanks, but you gave it to me for the wrong picture," said McCarey, reminding the Academy of its disregard for *Make Way for Tomorrow*.

McCarey was one of the most inspired comedy directors in Hollywood. Among his early gigs were *Our Gang* and bits for Stan Laurel and Oliver Hardy. McCarey moved tentatively into sound before truly making it with *The Kid from Spain* (1932, with Eddie Cantor), *Duck Soup* (1933, with the Marx Brothers), *Belle of the Nineties* (1934; with Mae West), and *The Milky Way* (1936, with Harold Lloyd). But *The Awful Truth* put McCarey on the map for directing one of the best screwball comedies ever made. He was sidetracked midway through the production of another screwball, *My Favorite Wife* (1940), by a near-fatal auto accident. Garson Kanin completed the picture.

McCarey had a flair for light, romantic, and sentimental stories, including *Make Way for Tomorrow* (1937), *Going My Way* (1944, nom.), *The Bells of St. Mary's* (1945, nom.), *An Affair to Remember* (1957), and *Rally Round the Flag, Boys!* (1958). Unlike many in the film community, McCarey was fiercely anti-Communist, which got him into battles with filmmakers at the height of the House Un-American Activities Committee hearings. His film *My Son John* (1952), in fact, spoke of his outrage and earned him an Academy Award nomination for Best Screenplay. (For more on McCarey, see 1944.)

Spencer Tracy (center) with John Carradine (right)

BEST ACTOR
SPENCER TRACY (1900–1967)
CAPTAINS COURAGEOUS

Tracy was in the hospital getting so cranky by all the congratulatory calls that he disconnected the phone. Accepting the award was producer Louis B. Mayer, who said, "It is a privilege to be the stand-in for Spencer Tracy. Tracy is a fine actor, but he is most important because he understands why it is necessary to take orders from the front office." Tracy's response to the speech? "Was that a compliment or a threat?" There was a small threat, though, from the critics' corners to the Academy's judgment on this one. The *New York Times*'s F. S. Nugent wrote, "Tracy… seemed curiously unconvincing in the beginning because the accent does not become him—but made the part his in time." Danny Peary thought he was "a more appropriate candidate for Best Supporting Actor."

(For more on Tracy, see 1938.)

BEST OF 1937
Best Picture: *The Life of Emile Zola*
Best Director: Leo McCarey, *The Awful Truth*
Best Actor: Spencer Tracy, *Captains Courageous*
Best Actress: Luise Rainer, *The Good Earth*
Best Supporting Actor: Joseph Schildkraut, *The Life of Emile Zola*
Best Supporting Actress: Alice Brady, *In Old Chicago*

FIRSTS
- Luise Rainer was the first performer to win consecutive Oscars. She would be followed by only four other such winners: Spencer Tracy (*Captains Courageous*, 1937, and *Boys Town*, 1938); Katharine Hepburn (*Guess Who's Coming to Dinner*, 1967, and *The Lion in Winter*, 1968); and Tom Hanks (*Philadelphia*, 1993, and *Forrest Gump*, 1994). In the Best Supporting category, only Jason Robards Jr. pulled it off for *All the President's Men*, 1976, and *Julia*, 1977.
- The year's biggest blockbuster, *The Hurricane*, co-starred Dorothy Lamour, who introduced the sarong to popular couture.

SINS OF OMISSION
Picture: *Camille*
Director: George Cukor, *Camille*
Actress: Katharine Hepburn, *Stage Door*; Ginger Rogers, *Stage Door*; Carole Lombard, *Nothing Sacred*
Actor: Cary Grant, *The Awful Truth*

UNMENTIONABLES
- Spencer Tracy's Oscar was incorrectly engraved "Dick Tracy."
- Tracy's violent, alcoholic rages caused him to be arrested twice. His studios were careful to keep his offscreen behavior out of the press even after he destroyed a $100,000 set on the Fox lot. His extramarital affairs with Loretta Young and Joan Crawford were also hushed up. But his relationship with Katharine Hepburn was too seismic to be ignored and emerged as one of Hollywood's great romantic legends.
- A mystery man accepted the Best Supporting Actress Oscar on behalf of bedridden Alice Brady and ran off with it. The thief was never discovered and her statuette was replaced.
- Self-proclaimed "King of Comedy" Mack Sennett, creator of the Keystone Kops, was washed up and verging on bankruptcy by the time he received his Honorary Oscar in 1938.
- When Greta Garbo first arrived in Hollywood, Louis B. Mayer informed her director/mentor/lover, Mauritz Stiller, "American men don't like fat women." She lost the weight as well as Stiller, whose career dried up as hers soared. She refused to return to Sweden with him.
- Garbo was Adolf Hitler's favorite actress.
- Garbo's first talkie, *Anna Christie*, was highly publicized by MGM with the promo line "Garbo Talks!" When *Camille* opened, a Hollywood wit suggested the ad should read, "Garbo Coughs!"
- Garbo and Marlene Dietrich shared a lesbian lover, the socialite Mercedes de Acosta.
- At Mayer's insistence, Garbo reluctantly agreed to attend the Hollywood premiere of *Camille*. She wore pajamas beneath a fur coat. She waved to her fans, walked through the front door, and out the back without bothering to watch the film.
- Luise Rainer's marriage to playwright Clifford Odets ended after a shady therapist convinced Odets that sex would drain him of his creativity.

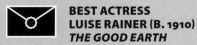

BEST ACTRESS
LUISE RAINER (B. 1910)
THE GOOD EARTH

Rainer didn't show up for the ceremony, believing what Paul Muni had told her. "Nobody wins two years in a row," he said. But he was proved wrong, and Rainer caught the dinner at the Biltmore. A nonconformist to MGM's standards of glitz and glamour, Rainer would parade around Hollywood in worn-out clothes. Tonight was no different. Studio heads had to force her to put on something presentable before dragging her to the Oscars.

Following *The Good Earth,* Rainer appeared in *The Emperor's Candlesticks* and *Big City* (both 1937), *The Toy Wife, The Great Waltz,* and *Dramatic School* (all 1938). In almost all of those films she was typecast as a trembling, dewy-eyed innocent.

After a forty-year self-banishment from Hollywood, Rainer returned for the occasional minor role and TV cameo.

(For more on Rainer, see 1936.)

Luise Rainer (right)

BEST SUPPORTING ACTOR
JOSEPH SCHILDKRAUT (1896–1964)
THE LIFE OF EMILE ZOLA

After his agent warned him that he wouldn't win, Schildkraut stayed home. Playing the suave leading man in the 1920s and '30s, he later transformed himself into a more villainous character actor.

Schildkraut appeared to great acclaim in D. W. Griffith's *Orphans of the Storm* (1922), his first film. He followed with two Cecil B. DeMille films, *Road to Yesterday* (1925) and *The King of Kings* (1927), which made him a star. Up until this time Schildkraut had performed only in silent films, but he made the transition to talkies with ease, appearing in *Cleopatra* (1934), *The Crusades* (1935), and then in his breakthrough movie *The Life of Emile Zola* (1937), *The Plainsman and The Lady* (1946), and *The Greatest Story Ever Told* (1965). Among the greatest of his late performances was *The Shop Around the Corner* (1940) and *The Diary of Anne Frank* (1959). His autobiography, *My Father and I,* was published in 1959.

BEST SUPPORTING ACTRESS
ALICE BRADY (1892–1939)
IN OLD CHICAGO

This leading lady of the silents—*La Vie de Boheme* (1916) and *Betsy Ross* (1917)—left with the talkies but made a comeback just in time to pick up some of the great comic character parts. Brady proved to have a special propensity for playing the scatterbrained socialite in such films as *The Gay Divorcee* (1934), *My Man Godfrey* (1936), and *100 Men and a Girl* (1937). Her last film was *Young Mr. Lincoln* (1939); she died of cancer before it was released.

PICTURE

THE AWFUL TRUTH, Columbia, Produced
by Leo McCarey, with Everett Riskin.
CAPTAINS COURAGEOUS, MGM.
Produced by Louis D. Lighton.
DEAD END, Goldwyn, UA. Produced by
Samuel Goldwyn, with Merritt Hulbert.
THE GOOD EARTH, MGM. Produced by
Irving Thalberg, with Albert Lewin.
IN OLD CHICAGO, 20th Century-Fox.
Produced by Darryl F. Zanuck, with
Kenneth MacGowan.
**THE LIFE OF EMILE ZOLA, Warner Bros.
Produced by Henry Blanke.**
LOST HORIZON, Columbia. Produced by
Frank Capra.
100 MEN AND A GIRL, Universal. Produced
by Charles R. Rogers, with Joe Pasternak.
STAGE DOOR, RKO Radio. Produced by
Pandro S. Berman.
A STAR IS BORN, Selznick International,
UA. Produced by David 0. Selznick.

ACTOR

CHARLES BOYER in *Conquest,* MGM.
FREDRIC MARCH in *A Star Is Born,*
Selznick, IJA.
ROBERT MONTGOMERY in *Night Must
Fall,* MGM.
PAUL MUNI in *The Life of Emile Zola,*
Warner Bros.
**SPENCER TRACY in *Captains
Courageous,* MGM.**

ACTRESS

IRENE DUNNE in *The Awful Truth,*
Columbia.
GRETA GARBO in *Camille,* MGM.
JANET GAYNOR in *A Star Is Born,* Selznick,
UA.
LUISE RAINER in *The Good Earth,* MGM.
BARBARA STANWYCK in *Stella Dallas,*
Goldwyn, UA.

SUPPORTING ACTOR

RALPH BELLAMY in *The Awful Truth,*
Columbia.
THOMAS MITCHELL in *The Hurricane,*
Goldwyn, UA.
**JOSEPH SCHILDKRAUT in *The Life of
Emile Zola,* Warner Bros.**
H.B. WARNER in *Lost Horizon,* Columbia.
ROLAND YOUNG in *Topper,* Roach, MGM.

SUPPORTING ACTRESS

**ALICE BRADY in *In Old Chicago,* 20th
Century-Fox.**
ANDREA LEEDS in *Stage Door,* RKO Radio.
ANNE SHIRLEY in *Stella Dallas,* Goldwyn,
UA.
CLAIRE TREVOR in *Dead End,* Goldwyn,
UA.
DAME MAY WHITTY in *Night Must Fall,*
MGM.

DIRECTION

WILLIAM DIETERLE for *The Life of Emile
Zola,* Warner Bros.
SIDNEY FRANKLIN for *The Good Earth,*
MGM.
GREGORY LaCAVA for *Stage Door,* RKO Radio.
**LEO McCAREY for *The Awful Truth,*
Columbia.**
WILLIAM WELLMAN for *A Star Is Born,*
Selznick, UA.

WRITING: ORIGINAL STORY

BLACK LEGION, Warner Bros. Robert Lord.

IN OLD CHICAGO, 20th Century-Fox.
Niven Busch.
THE LIFE OF EMILE ZOLA Warner Bros.
Heinz Herald and Geza Herczeg.
100 MEN AND A GIRL, Universal. Hans
Kraly.
**A STAR IS BORN, Selznick, UA. William
A. Wellman and Robert Carson.**

WRITING: SCREENPLAY

THE AWFUL TRUTH, Columbia.
Vina Delmar.
CAPTAINS COURAGEOUS, MGM Marc
Connelly, Hohn Lee Mahin and
Dale Van Every.
**THE LIFE OF EMILE ZOLA, Warner Bros.
Heinz Herald, Geza Herczeg and Norman
Reilly Raine.**
STAGE DOOR, RKO Radio. Morris Ryskind
and Anthony Veiller.
A STAR IS BORN, Selznick, UA. Alan Campbell,
Robert Carson and Dorothy Parker.

CINEMATOGRAPHY

DEAD END, Goldwyn, UA. Gregg Toland.
THE GOOD EARTH, MGM. Karl Freund.
WINGS OVER HONOLULU, Universal.
Joseph Valentine.

ART DIRECTION

CONQUEST, MGM. Cedric Gibbons and
William Horning.
A DAMSEL IN DISTRESS, RKO Radio.
Carroll Clark.
DEAD END, Goldwyn, UA. Richard Day.
EVERY DAY'S A HOLIDAY, Major Prods.,
Paramount. Wiard Ihnen.
THE LIFE OF EMILE ZOLA Warner Bros.
Anton Grot.
**LOST HORIZON, Columbia.
Stephen Goosson.**
MANHATTAN MERRY-GC-ROUND,
Republic. John Victor MacKay.
THE PRISONER OF ZENDA, Selznick, UA.
Lyle Wheeler.
SOULS AT SEA, Paramount. Hans Dreier and
Roland Anderson.
VOGUES OF 1938, Wanger, UA. Alexander
Toluboff.
WEE WILLIE WINKIE, 20th Century-Fox.
William S. Darling and David Hall.
YOU'RE A SWEETHEART, Universal. Jack
Otterson.

SONG

REMEMBER ME (*Mr. Dodd Takes the Air,*
Warner Bros.); Music by Harry Warren.
Lyrics by Al Dubin.
**SWEET LEILANI (*Waikiki Wedding,*
Paramount); Music and Lyrics by Harry
Owens.**
THAT OLD FEELING (*Vogues of 1938,*
Wanger, UA); Music by Sammy Fain. Lyrics
by Lew Brown.
THEY CAN'T TAKE THAT AWAY FROM
ME (*Shall We Dance,* RKO Radio); Music
by George Gershwin. Lyrics by Ira Gershwin.
WHISPERS IN THE DARK (*Artists and
Models,* Paramount); Music by Frederick
Hollander. Lyrics by Leo Robin.

SCORING: ORIGINAL MUSIC

THE HURRICANE, Goldwyn, CA. Samuel
Goldwyn Studio Music Dept.; Alfred
Newman, head. Score by Alfred Newman.
IN OLD CHICAGO, 20th Century-Fox. 20th
Century-Fox Studio Music Dept.; Louis
Silvers, head. (No composer credit)
THE LIFE OF EMILE ZOLA, Warner Bros.
Warner Bros. Studio Music Dept.; Leo
Forbstein, head. Score by Max Steiner.
LOST HORIZON, Columbia. Columbia
Studio Music Dept.; Morris Stoloff, head.
Score by Dimitri Tiomkin.
MAKE A WISH, Lesser, RKO Radio. Dr.
Hugo Riesenfeld, musical director. Score by
Dr. Hugo Riesenfeld.
MAYTIME, MGM, MGM Studio Music
Dept.; Nat W. Finston, head. Score by
Herbert Stothart.
**100 MEN AND A GIRL, Universal.
Universal Studio Music Dept.; Charles
Previn, head. (No composer credit)**
PORTIA ON TRIAL, Republic. Republic
Studio Music Dept.; Alberto Colombo,
head. Score by Alberto Colombo.
THE PRISONER OF ZENDA, Selznick, UA.
Selznick International Pictures Music
Dept.; Alfred Newman, musical director.
Score by Alfred Newman.

QUALITY STREET, RKO Radio. RKO Radio
Studio Music Dept.; Roy Webb, musical
director. Score by Roy Webb.
SNOW WHITE AND THE SEVEN DWARFS,
Disney, RKO Radio. Walt Disney Studio
Music Dept.; Leigh Harline, head. Score by
Frank Churchill, Leigh Harline and
Paul J. Smith.
SOMETHING TO SING ABOUT, Grand
National. Grand National Studio Music
Dept.; C. Bakaleinikoff, musical director.
Score by Victor Schertzinger.
SOULS AT SEA, Paramount. Paramount
Studio Music Dept.; Boris Morros, head.
Score by W. Franke Marling and
Milan Roder.
WAY OUT WEST, Roach, MGM. Roach
Studio Music Dept.; Marvin Hatley, head.
Score by Marvin Hatley.

SOUND RECORDING

THE GIRL SAID NO, Grand National. Grand
National Studio Sound Dept., A.E. Kaye,
Sound Director.
HITTING A NEW HIGH, RKO Radio. RKO
Radio Studio Sound Dept., John Aalberg,
Sound Director.
**THE HURRICANE, Goldwyn, UA. United
Artists Studio Sound Dept., Thomas T.
Moulton, Sound Director.**
IN OLD CHICAGO, 20th Century-Fox. 20th
Century-Fox Studio Sound Dept., E.H.
Hansen, Sound Director.
THE LIFE OF EMILE ZOLA, Warner Bros.
Warner Bros. Studio Sound Dept., Nathan
Levinson, Sound Director.
LOST HORIZON, Columbia. Columbia
Studio Sound Dept., John Livadary, Sound
Director.
MAYTIME, MGM. MGM Studio Sound
Dept., Douglas Shearer, Sound Director.
100 MEN AND A GIRL, Universal. Universal
Studio Sound Dept., Homer Tasker, Sound
Director.
TOPPER, Roach, MGM. Hal Roach Studio
Sound Dept., Elmer Raguse, Sound
Director.
WELLS FARGO, Paramount, Paramount
Studio Sound Dept., L.L. Ryder, Sound
Director.

FILM EDITING

THE AWFUL TRUTH, Columbia, Al Clark.
CAPTAINS COURAGEOUS, MGM. Elmo
Vernon.
THE GOOD EARTH, MGM Basil Wrangell.
**LOST HORIZON, Columbia. Gene Havlick
and Gene Milford.**
100 MEN AND A GIRL, Universal. Bernard
W. Burton.

ASSISTANT DIRECTOR

C.C. COLEMAN JR. for *Lost Horizon,*
Columbia.
RUSS SAUNDERS for *The Life of Emile Zola,*
Warner Bros.
ERIC STACEY for *A Star Is Born,* Selznick,
UA.
HAL WALKER for *Souls at Sea,* Paramount.
**ROBERT WEBB for *In Old Chicago,* 20th
Century-Fox.**

DANCE DIRECTION

BUSBY BERKELEY for "The Finale" number
from *Varsity Show* (Warner Bros.).
BOBBY CONNOLLY for "Too Marvelous for
Words" number from *Ready, Willing and
Able* (Warner Bros.).
DAVE GOULD for "All God's Children Got
Rhythm" number from *A Day at the Races*
(MGM).
SAMMY LEE for "Swing Is Here to Stay"
number from *Ali Baba Goes to Town* (20th
Century-Fox).
HARRY LOSEE for "Prince Igor Suite"
number from *Thin Ice* (20th Century-Fox).
**HERMES PAN for "Fun House" number
from *Damsel in Distress* (RKO Radio).**
LEROY PRINZ for "Luau" number from
Waikiki Wedding (Paramount).

SHORT SUBJECTS: CARTOONS

EDUCATED FISH, Paramount.
THE LITTLE MATCH GIRL, Mintz,
Columbia.
THE OLD MILL, Disney, RKO Radio.

SHORT SUBJECTS: ONE-REEL

A NIGHT AT THE MOVIES, MGM. (Robert
Benchley)

PRIVATE LIFE OF THE GANNETS,
Educational.
ROMANCE OF RADIUM, MGM. (Pete
Smith Specialties)

SHORT SUBJECTS: TWO-REEL

DEEP SOUTH, RKO Radio. (Radio Musical
Comedies)
SHOULD WIVES WORK, RKO Radio. (Leon
Errol Comedies)
**TORTURE MONEY, MGM. (Crime Doesn't
Pay)**

SHORT SUBJECTS: COLOR

THE MAN WITHOUT A COUNTRY,
Warner Bros. (Broadway Brevities)
**PENNY WISDOM, MGM. (Pete Smith
Specialties)**
POPULAR SCIENCE J-7-1, Paramount.

SPECIAL AWARDS

TO MACK SENNETT "for his lasting
contribution to the comedy technique of
the screen, the basic principles of which are
as important today as when they were first
put into practice, the Academy presents a
Special Award to that master of fun,
discoverer of stars, sympathetic, kindly,
understanding comedy genius, Mack
Sennett."
TO EDGAR BERGEN for his outstanding
comedy creation, Charlie McCarthy.
TO THE MUSEUM OF MODERN ART FILM
LIBRARY for its significant work in
collecting films dating from 1895 to the
present and for the first time making
available to the public the means of
studying the historical and aesthetic
development of the motion picture as one
of the major arts.
TO W. HOWARD GREENE for the color
photography of *A Star Is Born.*

IRVING G. THALBERG MEMORIAL AWARD

TO DARRYL F. ZANUCK

SCIENTIFIC OR TECHNICAL

CLASS I

AGFA ANSCO CORP. for Agfa Supreme and
Agfa Ultra Speed pan-motion-picture
negatives.

CLASS II

WALT DISNEY PRODS., LTD., for the design
and application to production of the Multi-
Plane Camera.
EASTMAN KODAK CO. for two fine-grain
duplicating film stocks.
FARCIOT EDOUART and PARAMOUNT
PICTURES, INC., for the development of
the Paramount dual-screen transparency
camera setup.
DOUGLAS SHEARER and the MGM
STUDIO SOUND DEPT. for a method of
varying the scanning width of variable
density sound tracks (squeeze tracks) for
the purpose of obtaining an increased
amount of noise reduction.

CLASS III

JOHN ARNOLD and the MGM STUDIO
CAMERA DEPT.;
JOHN LIVADARY, director of Sound
Recording for Columbia Pictures Corp.;
THOMAS T. MOULTON and the UNITED
ARTISTS STUDIO SOUND DEPT.;
RCA MANUFACTURING CO., INC.;
JOSEPH H. ROBBINS and PARAMOUNT
PICTURES, INC.;
DOUGLAS SMEARER and the MGM
STUDIO SOUND DEPARTMENT.

1938

usic Award presenter Jerome Kern cracked, "Of all the noises, I think music is the least annoying." Not as far as the Academy was concerned. After last year's embarrassment of "Sweet Leilani" winning over George Gershwin's "They Can't Take That Away from Me," the indiscriminate Screen Extras Guild was stripped of its Best Song voting privileges. It was a slap that didn't come without retaliation.

DOUBLE TAKES

**CEREMONY: February 23, 1939
Biltmore Bowl, Biltmore Hotel,
Los Angeles
HOST: Frank Capra,
Academy president**

The guild's 12,000 members pulled out the stops for one of its former members, Walter Brennan. It was his second Best Supporting Oscar in the three-year-old category. It was also the second time around the track for Spencer Tracy and the still-married Bette Davis, who swept into the Awards ceremony on the arm of her director-lover, William Wyler. Frank Capra one-upped them with his third Oscar, but the all-time champ, Walt Disney, picked up his eighth for Best Short, *Ferdinand the Bull*.

The night was far from over for the cartoon king. Shirley Temple stood on a chair to present him with a unique statuette honoring his whopping hit, *Snow White and the Seven Dwarfs*. It was a full-sized Oscar with an attached pedestal for seven mini-Oscars, one for each dwarf. Disney was overwhelmed. "I'm so proud of it I could burst," he said. Shirley brought down the house with her response: "Oh, don't do that, Mr. Disney!"

Ironically, Hollywood's own bubble had begun to burst. With war heating up in Europe and the stagnating Depression, ticket sales had slumped to record lows. With the exception of the flush Disney studio, the industry was feeling the pinch. It hardly seemed the time for risktakers and budget-be-damned visionaries. But the Hollywood dream machine was stoked for a miracle. The most astonishing year in motion-picture history was just around the corner.

BEST PICTURE/BEST DIRECTOR
FRANK CAPRA (1897–1991)
YOU CAN'T TAKE IT WITH YOU

If it wasn't clear with his second Best Director win for *Mr. Deeds Goes to Town*, this year's double win (his third Oscar-winning year, and with the Best Picture going to a comedy!) left no doubt that the 1930s belonged to Frank Capra, who later said, "The only rule in filmmaking is that there are no rules."

Capra had the ability to make stars out of actors by simplifying their personae, most famously in the case of Gary Cooper in *Mr. Deeds*. With Edward Arnold in *You Can't Take It with You*, Capra's approach to his character as a monolith of evil was thought by some to have undermined the comedic aspect of the original Broadway hit by George Kaufman and Moss Hart.

Popular with actors, writers, and directors, Capra was very politically active in Hollywood, serving as president of both the Academy and the Directors Guild. In 1938 he threatened a directors' strike and a boycott of the Oscars unless producers accepted their demands for contract negotiations.

(For more on Capra, see 1934.)

James Stewart, Jean Arthur, Edward Arnold (seated)

The envelope, please...

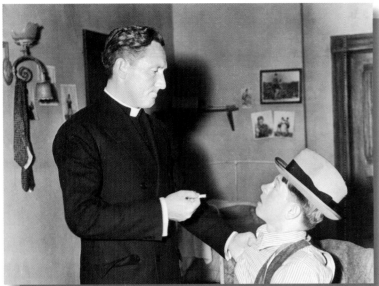

Spencer Tracy with Mickey Rooney

BEST ACTOR
SPENCER TRACY (1900–1967)
BOYS TOWN

With this new Golden Boy, Tracy became a consecutive two-time winner. In the film, Tracy plays Father Flanagan, guardian and mentor to 100 boys, with great earnestness, though the film was dubbed as sentimental by the critics.

John Ford discovered Tracy and signed him for *Up the River* (1930). After that, Tracy made sixteen films in three years. He was nominated for *San Francisco* (1936), *Father of the Bride* (1950), *Bad Day at Black Rock* (1955), *The Old Man and the Sea* (1958), *Inherit the Wind* (1960), *Judgment at Nuremberg* (1961), and *Guess Who's Coming to Dinner* (1967).

Tracy had a brief affair with Loretta Young, though as a Catholic he wouldn't divorce his first wife. No other romance, however, compared with that between Tracy and Katharine Hepburn. Somehow Tracy was best when performing with Kate, and they appeared together in many films, including *State of the Union* (1948), *Adam's Rib* (1949), and *Pat and Mike* (1952).

In the 1940s Tracy was at the top of his form, appearing in *Tortilla Flat* (1942) and *Thirty Seconds Over Tokyo* (1944). As Tracy grew white-haired and craggy-faced, his cantankerousness slipped into his roles in *Judgment at Nuremberg*, *The Devil at 4 O'Clock* (both 1961), and *It's a Mad Mad Mad Mad World* (1963). With age, and his lifelong alcohol problem, the actor became increasingly ornery, and his unique charm began to fade.

Tracy died just weeks after shooting one last film, *Guess Who's Coming to Dinner*, with his main gal. He received a posthumous Best Actor Academy Award nomination—his ninth. (For more on Tracy, see 1937.)

BEST ACTRESS
BETTE DAVIS (1908–1989)
JEZEBEL

Davis was flawless—and never ostentatious—in her role as a willful, flirtatious Southern belle of the pre–Civil War era who costs a man his life but is so brave that she risks her own life to help another woman's husband. *Jezebel* was director William Wyler's consolation prize to Davis for losing the role of Scarlett O'Hara in *Gone with the Wind* (1939), a characterization with a similar heroine. In fact, the movie has been called a black-and-white version of the famous Selznick film, which, at this point, was in the filming stage.

Jezebel was Davis's second Oscar, after *Dangerous* (1935). She soon became involved in a battle royal with Warners, accusing the studio of not giving her the roles she felt she deserved. After the lawsuit, though, her roles improved dramatically. Her career after *Jezebel* became perhaps the finest in Hollywood, as she tallied up an endless run of Best Actress nominations.

(For more on Davis, see 1935.)

BEST OF 1938
Best Picture: *You Can't Take It with You*
Best Director: Frank Capra, *You Can't Take It with You*
Best Actor: Spencer Tracy, *Boys Town*
Best Actress: Bette Davis, *Jezebel*
Best Supporting Actor: Walter Brennan, *Kentucky*
Best Supporting Actress: Fay Bainter, *Jezebel*

FIRSTS
- *Grand Illusion* was the first foreign-language film to be nominated for Best Picture.
- *Snow White and the Seven Dwarfs* was the first feature-length animated film.
- Fay Bainter was the first performer to be simultaneously nominated in two categories.
- *You Can't Take It with You* launched the collaboration of Frank Capra and James Stewart. The dynamic duo went on to make *Mr. Smith Goes to Washington* (1939) and the Christmas holiday classic *It's a Wonderful Life* (1946).

ROLE REVERSALS
Bette Davis turned down the role of Scarlett in *Gone with the Wind*, fearing that she would have to work with her least favorite leading man, Errol Flynn, as Rhett Butler.

SINS OF OMISSION
Best Picture: *Bringing Up Baby*
Best Director: Alfred Hitchcock, *The Lady Vanishes*
Best Actor: Cary Grant, *Bringing Up Baby*
Best Actress: Katharine Hepburn, *Bringing Up Baby*

UNMENTIONABLES
- Spencer Tracy refused to give his Oscar to *Boys Town*. The Academy sent the organization a commemorative duplicate.
- Studios wooed the majority bloc of screen "extra" voters with 6,000 jobs just as Awards ballots were sent out.
- The Academy refused to nominate the year's biggest hit, *Snow White and the Seven Dwarfs*, fearing that in doing so it would establish a precedent for cartoons.
- Dancer Marge Champion was the human model for Snow White.
- Shirley Temple claimed that she stopped believing in Santa Claus when she was 6 years old. Her mother took her to see him at a department store and he asked for her autograph.
- Joseph McBride's biography of Frank Capra asserted that the director was a rabid anti-Semite and an avid supporter of Mussolini.
- Despite cryogenic rumors, Walt Disney was not frozen after his death.
- Director William Wyler was a tyrannical perfectionist. He threatened to tie a weight around Bette Davis's neck if she didn't stop bobbing her head.

Loretta Young and Richard Greene with Walter Brennan

BEST SUPPORTING ACTOR
WALTER BRENNAN (1894–1974)
KENTUCKY

Brennan summed his own career up best: "I never wanted anything out of this business except a good living. Never wanted to be a star, just wanted to be good at what I was doing."

With this win, Brennan scored his second Oscar after *Come and Get It* (1936), though the victory was diluted for Brennan by claims that he won courtesy of the strong support of the thousands of extras who were permitted to vote. "They carry the balance of power," *Variety* noted the day before the Oscars.

After a failed movie stunt cost him his teeth, the 30-year-old Brennan looked much older than his years. It transformed his career; he was cast as the endearing old codger in over 200 films. His versatile range also earned him roles as corporate executives, flim-flam artists, local yokels, and military officers.

(For more on Brennan, see 1936 and 1940.)

BEST SUPPORTING ACTRESS
FAY BAINTER (1891–1968)
JEZEBEL

Bainter became the first actress to be up for two Oscars, as Best Actress in *White Banners* and for Best Supporting Actress in *Jezebel*.

Bainter was already middle-aged by the time she made her first movie, *This Side of Heaven* (1934), but her career actually began at age 5, when she made her Broadway debut. As she got older, she was frequently cast as an understanding mother or a faithful spouse, befitting her gentle manner and appearance. Her career was relatively brief, with parts in, among other films, *Daughters Courageous* (1939), *A Bill of Divorcement* (1940), *Woman of the Year* (1942), *The Secret Life of Walter Mitty* (1947), *June Bride* (1948), and her last film, *The Children's Hour* (1962). She was the mother of actor Richard Venable (1926–1974).

PICTURE
THE ADVENTURES OF ROBIN HOOD, Warner Bros. Produced by Hal B. Wallis, with Henry Blanke.
ALEXANDER'S RAGTIME BAND, 20th Century-Fox. Produced by Darryl F. Zanuck, with Harry Joe Brown.
BOYS TOWN, MGM. Produced by John W. Considine Jr.
THE CITADEL, MGM (British). Produced by Victor Saville.
FOUR DAUGHTERS, Warner Bros.-First National. Produced by Hal B. Wallis, with Henry Blanke.
GRAND ILLUSION, R.A.O. World Pictures (French). Produced by Frank Rollmer and Albert Pinkovitch.
JEZEBEL, Warner Bros. Produced by Hal B. Wallis, with Henry Blanke.
PYGMALION, MGM (British). Produced by Gabriel Pascal.
TEST PILOT, MGM. Produced by Louis D. Lighton.
YOU CAN'T TAKE IT WITH YOU, Columbia. Produced by Frank Capra.

ACTOR
CHARLES BOYER in *Algiers*, Wanger, UA.
JAMES CAGNEY in *Angels with Dirty Faces*, Warner Bros.
ROBERT DONAT in *The Citadel*, MGM (British).
LESLIE HOWARD in *Pygmalion*, MGM (British).
SPENCER TRACY in *Boys Town*, MGM.

ACTRESS
FAY BAINTER in *White Banners*, Warner Bros.
BETTE DAVIS in *Jezebel*, Warner Bros.
WENDY HILLER in *Pygmalion*, MGM (British).
NORMA SHEARER in *Marie Antoinette*, MGM.
MARGARET SULLAVAN in *Three Comrades*, MGM.

SUPPORTING ACTOR
WALTER BRENNAN in *Kentucky*, 20th Century-Fox.
JOHN GARFIELD in *Four Daughters*, Warner Bros.
GENE LOCKHART in *Algiers*, Wanger, UA.
ROBERT MORLEY in *Marie Antoinette*, MGM.
BASIL RATHBONE in *If I Were King*, Paramount.

SUPPORTING ACTRESS
FAY BAINTER in *Jezebel*, Warner Bros.
BEULAH BONDI in *Of Human Hearts*, MGM.
BILLIE BURKE in *Merrily We Live*, Roach, MGM.
SPRING BYINGTON in *You Can't Take It with You*, Columbia.
MILIZA KORJUS in *The Great Waltz*, MGM.

DIRECTION
FRANK CAPRA for *You Can't Take It with You*, Columbia.
MICHAEL CURTIZ for *Angels with Dirty Faces*, Warner Bros.
MICHAEL CURTIZ for *Four Daughters*, Warner Bros.
NORMAN TAUROG for *Boys Town*, MGM.
KING VIDOR for *The Citadel*, MGM (British).

WRITING: ORIGINAL STORY
ALEXANDER'S RAGTIME BAND, 20th Century-Fox. Irving Berlin.
ANGELS WITH DIRTY FACES, Warner Bros. Rowland Brown.
BLOCKADE, Wanger, UA. John Howard Lawson.
BOYS TOWN, MGM. Eleanore Griffin and Dore Schary.
MAD ABOUT MUSIC, Universal. Marcella Burke and Frederick Kohner.
TEST PILOT, MGM. Frank Wead.

WRITING: SCREENPLAY
BOYS TOWN, MGM. John Meehan and Dore Schary.
THE CITADEL, MGM (British). Ian Dalrymple, Elizabeth Hill and Frank Wead.
FOUR DAUGHTERS, Warner Bros. Lenore Coffee and Julius J. Epstein.
PYGMALION, MGM (British). George Bernard Shaw; adaptation by Ian Dalrymple, Cecil Lewis and W.P. Lipscomb.
YOU CAN'T TAKE IT WITH YOU, Columbia. Robert Riskin.

CINEMATOGRAPHY
ALGIERS, Wanger, UA. James Wong Howe.
ARMY GIRL, Republic. Ernest Miller and Harry Wild.
THE BUCCANEER, Paramount. Victor Milner.
THE GREAT WALTZ, MGM. Joseph Ruttenberg.
JEZEBEL, Warner Bros. Ernest Haller.
MAD ABOUT MUSIC, Universal. Joseph Valentine.
MERRILY WE LIVE, Roach, MGM. Norbert Brodine.
SUEZ, 20th Century-Fox. Peverell Marley.
VIVACIOUS LADY, RKO Radio. Robert de Grasse.
YOU CAN'T TAKE IT WITH YOU, Columbia, Joseph Walker.
THE YOUNG IN HEART, Selznick, UA. Leon Shamroy.

ART DIRECTION
THE ADVENTURES OF ROBIN HOOD, Warner Bros. Carl J. Weyl.
THE ADVENTURES OF TOM SAWYER, Selznick, UA. Lyle Wheeler.
ALEXANDER'S RAGTIME BAND, 20th Century-Fox. Bernard Herzbrun and Boris Leven.
ALGIERS, Wanger, UA. Alexander Toluboff.
CAREFREE, RKO Radio. Van Nest Polglase.
GOLDWYN FOLLIES, Goldwyn, UA. Richard Day.
HOLIDAY, Columbia. Stephen Goosson and Lionel Banks.
IF I WERE KING, Paramount. Hans Dreier and John Goodman.
MAD ABOUT MUSIC, Universal. Jack Otterson.
MARIE ANTOINETTE, MGM. Cedric Gibbons.
MERRILY WE LIVE, Roach, MGM. Charles D. Hall.

SOUND RECORDING
ARMY GIRL, Republic. Republic Studio Sound Dept., Charles Lootens, Sound Director.
THE COWBOY AND THE LADY, Goldwyn, UA. United Artists Studio Sound Dept., Thomas Moulton, Sound Director.
FOUR DAUGHTERS, Warner Bros. Warner Bros. Studio Sound Dept., Nathan Levinson, Sound Director.
IF I WERE KING, Paramount. Paramount Studio Sound Dept., L.L. Ryder, Sound Director.
MERRILY WE LIVE, Roach, MGM. Hal Roach Studio Sound Dept., Elmer Raguse, Sound Director.
SWEETHEARTS, MGM. MGM Studio Sound Dept., Douglas Shearer, Sound Director.
SUEZ, 20th Century-Fox. 20th Century-Fox Studio Sound Dept., Edmund Hansen, Sound Director.
THAT CERTAIN AGE, Universal. Universal Studio Sound Dept., Bernard B. Brown, Sound Director.
VIVACIOUS LADY, RKO Radio. RKO Radio Studio Sound Dept., James Wilkinson, Sound Director.
YOU CAN'T TAKE IT WITH YOU, Columbia. Columbia Studio Sound Dept., John Livadary, Sound Director.

FILM EDITING
THE ADVENTURES OF ROBIN ROOD, Warner Bros. Ralph Dawson.
ALEXANDER'S RAGTIME BAND, 20th Century-Fox. Barbara McLean.
THE GREAT WALTZ, MGM. Tom Held.
TEST PILOT, MGM. Tom Held.
YOU CAN'T TAKE IT WITH YOU, Columbia. Gene Havlick.

SONG
ALWAYS AND ALWAYS (*Mannequin*, MGM); Music by Edward Ward. Lyrics by Chet Forrest and Bob Wright.
CHANGE PARTNERS AND DANCE WITH ME (*Carefree*, RKO Radio); Music and Lyrics by Irving Berlin.
THE COWBOY AND THE LADY (*The Cowboy and the Lady*, Goldwyn, UA); Music by Lionel Newman. Lyrics by Arthur Quenzer.
DUST (*Under Western Stars*, Republic); Music and Lyrics by Johnny Marvin.
JEEPERS CREEPERS (*Going Places*, Warner Bros.); Music by Harry Warren. Lyrics by Johnny Mercer.
MERRILY WE LIVE (*Merrily We Live*, Roach, MGM); Music by Phil Craig. Lyrics by Arthur Quenzer.
A MIST OVER THE MOON (*The Lady Objects*, Columbia); Music by Ben Oakland. Lyrics by Oscar Hammerstein II.
MY OWN (*That Certain Age*, Universal); Music by Jimmy McHugh. Lyrics by Harold Adamson.
NOW IT CAN BE TOLD (*Alexander's Ragtime Band*, 20th Century-Fox); Music and Lyrics by Irving Berlin.
THANKS FOR THE MEMORY (*Big Broadcast of 1938*, Paramount); Music by Ralph Rainger. Lyrics by Leo Robin.

SCORING: ORIGINAL SONG SCORE AND/OR ADAPTATION
ALEXANDER'S RAGTIME BAND, 20th Century-Fox. Alfred Newman.
CAREFREE, RKO Radio. Victor Baravalle.
GIRLS SCHOOL, Columbia. Morris Stoloff and Gregory Stone.
GOLDWYN FOLLIES, Goldwyn, UA. Alfred Newman.
JEZEBEL, Warner Bros. Max Steiner.
MAD ABOUT MUSIC, Universal. Charles Previn and Frank Skinner.
STORM OVER BENGAL, Republic. Cy Feuer.
SWEETHEARTS, MGM. Herbert Stothart.
THERE GOES MY HEART, Hal Roach, UA. Marvin Hatley.
TROPIC HOLIDAY, Paramount. Boris Morros.
THE YOUNG IN HEART, Selznick, UA. Franz Waxman.

SCORING: ORIGINAL MUSIC
THE ADVENTURES OF ROBIN HOOD, Warner Bros. Erich Wolfgang Korngold.
ARMY GIRL, Republic. Victor Young.
BLOCKADE, Wringer. UA. Werner Janssen.
BLOCKHEADS, Roach, UA. Marvin Hatley.
BREAKING THE ICE, RKO Radio. Victor Young.
THE COWBOY AND THE LADY, Goldwyn, UA. Alfred Newman.
IF I WERE KING, Paramount. Richard Hageman.
MARIE ANTOINETTE, MGM. Herbert Stothart.
PACIFIC LINER, RKO Radio. Russell Bennett.
SUEZ, 20th Century-Fox. Louis Silvers.
THE YOUNG IN HEART, Selznick, UA. Franz Waxman.

SPECIAL AWARDS
TO DEANNA DURBIN and MICKEY ROONEY for their significant contribution in bringing to the screen the spirit and personification of youth, and as juvenile players setting a high standard of ability and achievement.
TO HARRY M. WARNER in recognition of patriotic service in the production of historical short subjects presenting significant episodes in the early struggle of the American people for liberty.
TO WALT DISNEY for *Snow White and the Seven Dwarfs*, recognized as a significant screen innovation which has charmed millions and pioneered a great new entertainment field for the motion-picture cartoon.
TO OLIVER MARSH and ALLEN DAVEY for the color cinematography of the MGM production *Sweethearts*.
For outstanding achievements in creating special photographic and sound effects in the Paramount production *Spawn of the North*: special effects by GORDON JENNINGS, assisted by JAN DOMELA, DEV JENNINGS, IRMIN ROBERTS and ART SMITH; transparencies by FARCIOT EDOUART, assisted by LOYAL GRIGGS; sound effects by LOREN RYDER, assisted by HARRY MILLS, LOUIS H. MESENKOP and WALTER OBERST.
TO J. ARTHUR BALL for his outstanding contributions to the advancement of color in motion picture photography.

SHORT SUBJECT: CARTOON
BRAVE LITTLE TAILOR, Disney, RKO Radio.
MOTHER GOOSE GOES HOLLYWOOD, Disney, RKO Radio.
FERDINAND THE BULL, Disney, RKO Radio.
GOOD SCOUTS, Disney, RKO Radio.
BUNNY AND SPUNKY, Paramount.

SHORT SUBJECT: ONE-REEL
THE GREAT HEART, MGM.
THAT MOTHERS MIGHT LIVE, MGM. (Miniature)
TIMBER TOPPERS, 20th Century-Fox. (Ed Thorgensen-Sports)

SHORT SUBJECT: TWO-REEL
DECLARATION OF INDEPENDENCE, Warner Bros. (Historical Featurette)
SWINGTIME IN THE MOVIES, Warner Bros. (Broadway Brevities)
THEY'RE ALWAYS CAUGHT, MGM. (Crime Doesn't Pay)

IRVING G. THALBERG MEMORIAL AWARD
TO HAL B. WALLIS

SCIENTIFIC OR TECHNICAL
CLASS III
JOHN AALBERG and the RKO RADIO STUDIO SOUND DEPT.;
BYRON HASKIN and the SPECIAL EFFECTS DEPT. of WARNER BROS. STUDIO.

1939

"Gone with the Wind is going to be the biggest flop in history. I'm just glad it'll be Clark Gable falling on his face and not me."

—Gary Cooper

I n any other year, such extraordinary contenders as *Wuthering Heights*, *Stagecoach*, *Mr. Smith Goes to Washington*, and *The Wizard of Oz* might easily have walked away with the big prize. But this was the year of the drawling monolith, *Gone with the Wind*. Its company of players, led by Pied Piper David O. Selznick, strode into the Cocoanut Grove with the luxuriant gleam of born winners.

WINDSWEPT

CEREMONY: February 29, 1940, The Cocoanut Grove, Ambassador Hotel, Los Angeles
HOST: Bob Hope

For all that, at least one of its stars, Clark Gable, was giving the performance of his career. Like Bette Davis, Gable had glimpsed the bean-spilling early edition of the *Los Angeles Times* and he knew he'd lost. He was heartbroken, but didn't let it show. That wasn't quite the case with Olivia de Havilland.

As soon as Best Supporting Actress presenter Fay Bainter began with "It is a tribute to a country where people are free to honor noteworthy achievements regardless of creed, race or color," the room knew it was all over. With a whooping "Hallelujah!" Hattie McDaniel rose majestically from her seat at the back and, under the weight of a cascade of gardenias pinned to her gown, made

her way to the stage. De Havilland leaped up simultaneously and made a beeline for the kitchen to sob. Selznick's formidable wife, Irene, followed her, told her to grow up, and ordered her back inside to congratulate McDaniel. With her prettiest Melanie smile, de Havilland did just that. After all, newsreel cameras were rolling. Best behavior wasn't merely a good idea. It was a career move.

Judy Garland didn't have to pretend anything. She was a bundle of exuberance as Mickey Rooney presented her with a Munchkin-size Juvenile Oscar. Before *Oz*, Garland's Hollywood career had been in limbo. Overnight, those ruby slippers had whisked her into the royal firmament of screen legends. Little Frances Gumm was now in the heady company of Garbo, Dietrich, and the biggest box-office draw of them all, Bette Davis.

Davis, who understood the whimsical nature of Oscar too well, didn't hesitate to give Vivien Leigh hearty congratulations. This, despite the final tabulations revealing that her loss for *Dark Victory* was a matter of just a few votes. It was a memorable night of bigger-than-life personalities, ermine capes, diamonds, drama, and vindication for David O. Selznick. He'd bet the store and won immortality.

BEST PICTURE/BEST DIRECTOR
VICTOR FLEMING (1883–1949)
GONE WITH THE WIND

Fleming was at home sick, but the monolithic producer David O. Selznick was feeling quite well when he collected his production's prize—for the most aggressively promoted, anticipated, and financially successful film of the time.

G.W.T.W. broke almost all records in Hollywood. Alleged to have suffered a nervous breakdown during production, Fleming was replaced by Sam Wood, who completed the film; George Cukor was the first of the final tally of three directors on the film.

Clocking in at 222 minutes with intermissions, the film tells Margaret Mitchell's best-selling saga of the tumultuous decade when secession, civil war, and reconstruction rent the graceful garments of the plantation era and Atlanta was burned to the ground.

The critics had mixed opinions of *G.W.T.W.*'s merits as a film, but none could deny the magnetism of its spectacle or the mesmerizing performances of the cast. And no one could say anything that would affect its massive popularity. The *New York Times*'s Frank S. Nugent tried to set the film in proper perspective when he wrote, "Is it the greatest motion picture ever made? Probably not, although it is the greatest motion mural we have seen and the most ambitious film-making venture in Hollywood's spectacular history."

A former race-car driver, Fleming never made it onto the critics' list of important Hollywood directors, but he was categorized as an action director and as the director of two of history's most beloved films: *Gone with the Wind* and *The Wizard of Oz*. In truth, Fleming often proved to be a charismatic director who could draw strong performances from his actors. Starting out as a cinematographer, he moved on to co-direct *When the Clouds Roll By* (1920). As a full-fledged director he made, among other films, *Mantrap* (1926), *The Way of All Flesh* (1927), such Westerns as *The Rough Riders* (1927) and *The Virginian* (1929), and such classics as *Red Dust* (1932), *Bombshell* (1933), and *Captains Courageous* (1937).

The envelope, please…

Robert Donat (right)

BEST ACTOR
ROBERT DONAT (1905–1958)
GOODBYE, MR. CHIPS

Writing about the actor's performance as the lovable schoolmaster, Vincent Canby said in the *New York Times*, "Donat's portrait of him is an incredibly fine characterization for its subtle underlining of the dramatic moments in an essentially undramatic life."

Robert Donat was one of those fine British leading men who could do no wrong. Audiences loved him, and deservedly so. After a distinguished career on the British stage, Donat was discovered by Hollywood and appeared in *The Count of Monte Cristo* (1934). Donat didn't feel at home in Hollywood, however, and he returned to England only to step back on America's Western shore to star in some of the best works of the 1930s, including *The 39 Steps* (1935), *Knight Without Armour* (1937), and *The Citadel* (1938, nom.). Though shadowed by constant self-doubt (and struggling with acute asthma), he continued to make his mark in such films as *Perfect Strangers* (1945), *The Winslow Boy* (1948), and *The Inn of the Sixth Happiness*. He directed and produced *The Cure for Love* in 1949.

Vivien Leigh with Clark Gable

BEST ACTRESS
VIVIEN LEIGH (1913–1967)
GONE WITH THE WIND

In what was perhaps her greatest role, Leigh continues to be celebrated for this legendary performance. Producer Selznick saw Leigh's performance in the British-filmed *A Yank at Oxford* (1938) and immediately signed her up.

The convent-educated British actress fell in love and married her co-thespian, Laurence Olivier, in 1940. Their romance became a cause célèbre. So great was her performance in *G.W.T.W.* that it overshadowed her work in later films, including *That Hamilton Woman* (1941) and *Anna Karenina* (1948). Leigh gave a riveting performance as Blanche du Bois in Tennessee Williams's *A Streetcar Named Desire* (1951, Oscar), but she didn't appear on screen for a number of years afterward. Among her last great roles were *The Roman Spring of Mrs. Stone* (1961) and *Ship of Fools* (1965). Throughout her life, she was plagued with emotional vulnerability and chronic tuberculosis (which was the cause of her death).

BEST OF 1939
Best Picture: *Gone with the Wind*
Best Director: Victor Fleming, *Gone with the Wind*
Best Actor: Robert Donat, *Goodbye, Mr. Chips*
Best Actress: Vivien Leigh, *Gone with the Wind*
Best Supporting Actor: Thomas Mitchell, *Stagecoach*
Best Supporting Actress: Hattie McDaniel, *Gone with the Wind*
Honorary Award for Outstanding Juvenile Performance: Judy Garland, *The Wizard of Oz*

FIRSTS
- *Gone with the Wind*'s ten-Award sweep (eight competitive, two honorary) was a landmark.
- With a running time of almost four hours, *G.W.T.W.* was the longest feature ever to be released.
- Hattie McDaniel broke the color barrier not only by winning an Oscar but by being the first black guest at the Academy Awards.
- Color cinematography was placed in a separate Award category.
- Directors could be nominated for only one motion picture in a single year.
- Bob Hope made his debut as Oscar host, the first of seventeen future appearances.
- Following the leak of winners' names by the *Los Angeles Times*, from this point forward only Price Waterhouse would have the names prior to the ceremony.
- *G.W.T.W.* screenwriter Sidney Howard, killed in a freak tractor mishap, was the first posthumous Oscar winner.

ROLE REVERSALS
- The seriously considered Scarletts: Jean Arthur, Claudette Colbert, Bette Davis, Jean Harlow, Tallulah Bankhead, Miriam Hopkins, Katharine Hepburn, Joan Bennett, Norma Shearer, and Carole Lombard. Among the Rhetts: Errol Flynn and Margaret Mitchell's own choice, Basil Rathbone.
- *The Wizard of Oz* was launched as a starring vehicle for Shirley Temple.

SINS OF OMISSION
Best Actors: Henry Fonda, *Young Mr. Lincoln*
Charles Laughton, *The Hunchback of Notre Dame*
Best Actress: Merle Oberon, *Wuthering Heights*

UNMENTIONABLES
- Hattie McDaniel and her escort were placed at a table in the back of the room, near the kitchen.
- McDaniel's appearance in *G.W.T.W.* was harshly criticized by the NAACP, which thought her role as the long-suffering, loyal slave Mammy was a giant step backward for the "Negro" image.
- George Cukor was fired as director of *G.W.T.W.* after Gable's ugly blowup on the set, in which the actor loudly insisted that he didn't want a "fag" telling him what to do. The official line was that Gable felt Cukor was a woman's director who wasn't paying him enough attention. But rumors persisted that Cukor had known Gable in the early years, when the struggling actor sidelined as a boy-for-hire. Quite simply, Cukor's presence was a constant embarrassment.
- Judy Garland's giggling fits were costing a small fortune in retakes. Director Victor Fleming solved the problem with a hard slap to the girl's face.
- MGM execs thought *Oz* was running too long and seriously considered cutting "Somewhere Over the Rainbow."

Claire Trevor with Thomas Mitchell

 BEST SUPPORTING ACTOR
THOMAS MITCHELL (1892–1962)
STAGECOACH

"I didn't think I was that good," Mitchell revealed as he nervously accepted his Oscar. "I don't have a speech, I'm too incoherent." When he played Scarlett O'Hara's father in *G.W.T.W.*, Mitchell had already performed in a series of memorable roles in a highly distinguished career that included some of Hollywood's most famous films, among them *Lost Horizon* (1937), *Only Angels Have Wings*, *Mr. Smith Goes to Washington*, *The Hunchback of Notre Dame*, and *Stagecoach* (all 1939). His face rings bells when he's seen playing James Stewart's inept Uncle Billy in *It's a Wonderful Life* (1946). According to Leonard Maltin, "He was playing Daniel Webster in *The Devil and Daniel Webster* (1941) when a runaway horse cart sidelined him and forced the producers to reshoot all his footage with Edward Arnold."

Vivien Leigh with Hattie McDaniel

 BEST SUPPORTING ACTRESS
HATTIE MCDANIEL (1895–1952)
GONE WITH THE WIND

The gardenia-bedecked McDaniel received a standing ovation when she rose to accept her award. "This is the happiest moment of my life," she said in a speech that had been written for her by studio publicists.

McDaniel was the first black actress to win an Academy Award. A preacher's daughter, she became a movie legend who appeared in dozens of films, generally cast as a servant. Her commanding presence, however, always stole the show. Among her films were *Alice Adams* (1935), *Show Boat* (1936), *Libeled Lady* (1936), *Saratoga*, *Nothing Sacred* (both 1937), *Carefree* (1938), *Since You Went Away* (1944), and *Song of the South* (1946). She also played Buckwheat's mother in a number of the *Our Gang* comedies. And she was one of several actresses to star as "Beulah" on radio and TV.

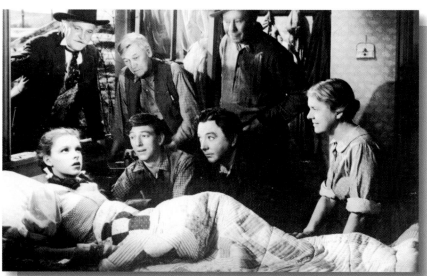
Judy Garland with Jack Haley, Ray Bolger, Clara Blandick.
(Top) Frank Morgan, Charles Grapewin, Bert Lahr

HONORARY AWARD FOR OUTSTANDING JUVENILE PERFORMANCE
JUDY GARLAND (1922–1969)
THE WIZARD OF OZ

Child star Mickey Rooney handed 17-year-old Garland her only Oscar win. She rewarded the audience by singing her heart-tugging, fairy-tale rendition of "Somewhere Over the Rainbow."

Unfortunately, the real-life story of the legendary actress was the stuff of tragedy rather than fairy tales. Garland first stole movie audiences' hearts at the age of 16, when she sang "You Made Me Love You" to a photo of Clark Gable in *Broadway Melody of 1938*. From her early films—*Babes in Arms* (1939) and *Strike Up the Band* (1940, both with Mickey Rooney)—she graduated to a starring role with Gene Kelly in *For Me and My Gal* (1942). Behind the scenes, however, Garland was hounded by a driven stage mother, and her grueling film schedule at the studio led to a lifelong dependency on pep and sleeping pills.

But in her films, including such period musicals as *Meet Me in St. Louis* (1944), *The Pirate*, and *Easter Parade* (both 1948), she was sunlight itself. She hit bottom after appearing in *Summer Stock* (1950), bounced back for the remake of *A Star Is Born* (1954, nom.), and held on until *Judgment at Nuremberg* (1961, nom.). Her emotional turmoil, however, could always be heard in her songs.

PICTURE

DARK VICTORY, Warner Bros. Produced by David Lewis.

GONE WITH THE WIND, Selznick, MGM. Produced by David O. Selznick.

GOODBYE, MR. CHIPS, MGM (British). Produced by Victor Saville.

LOVE AFFAIR, RKO Radio. Produced by Leo McCarey.

MR. SMITH GOES TO WASHINGTON, Columbia. Produced by Frank Capra.

NINOTCHKA, MGM. Produced by Sidney Franklin.

OF MICE AND MEN, Hal Roach, UA. Produced by Lewis Milestone.

STAGECOACH, Wanger, UA. Produced by Walter Wanger.

THE WIZARD OF OZ, MGM. Produced by Mervyn LeRoy.

WUTHERING HEIGHTS, Goldwyn, UA. Produced by Samuel Goldwyn.

ACTOR

ROBERT DONAT in *Goodbye, Mr. Chips*, MGM (British).

CLARK GABLE in *Gone with the Wind*, Selznick, MGM.

LAURENCE OLIVIER in *Wuthering Heights*, Goldwyn, UA.

MICKEY ROONEY in *Babes in Arms*, MGM.

JAMES STEWART in *Mr. Smith Goes to Washington*, Columbia.

ACTRESS

BETTE DAVIS in *Dark Victory*, Warner Bros.

IRENE DUNNE in *Love Affair*, RKO Radio.

GRETA GARBO in *Ninotchka*, MGM.

GREER GARSON in *Goodbye, Mr. Chips*, MGM (British).

VIVIEN LEIGH in *Gone with the Wind*, Selznick, MGM.

SUPPORTING ACTOR

BRIAN AHERNE in *Juarez*, Warner Bros.

HARRY CAREY in *Mr. Smith Goes to Washington*, Columbia.

BRIAN DONLEVY in *Beau Geste*, Paramount.

THOMAS MITCHELL in *Stagecoach*, Wanger, UA.

CLAUDE RAINS in *Mr. Smith Goes to Washington*, Columbia.

SUPPORTING ACTRESS

OLIVIA DE HAVILLAND in *Gone with the Wind*, Selznick, MGM.

GERALDINE FITZGERALD in *Wuthering Heights*, Goldwyn, UA.

HATTIE McDANIEL in *Gone with the Wind*, Selznick, MGM.

EDNA MAY OLIVER in *Drums Along the Mohawk*, 20th Century-Fox.

MARIA OUSPENSKAYA in *Love Affair*, RKO Radio.

DIRECTION

FRANK CAPRA for *Mr. Smith Goes to Washington*, Columbia.

VICTOR FLEMING for *Gone with the Wind*, Selznick MGM.

JOHN FORD for *Stagecoach*, Wanger, UA.

SAM WOOD for *Goodbye, Mr. Chips*, MGM (British).

WILLIAM WYLER for *Wuthering Heights*, Goldwyn, UA.

SHORT SUBJECT: CARTOON

DETOURING AMERICA, Warner Bros.

PEACE ON EARTH, MGM.

THE POINTER, Disney, RKO Radio.

THE UGLY DUCKLING, Disney, RKO Radio.

SHORT SUBJECT: ONE-REEL

BUSY LITTLE BEARS, Paramount. (Paragraphics)

INFORMATION PLEASE, RKO Radio.

PROPHET WITHOUT HONOR, MGM. (Miniature)

SWORD FISHING, Warner Bros. (Vitaphone Varieties)

SHORT SUBJECT: TWO-REEL

DRUNK DRIVING, MGM. (Crime Doesn't Pay)

FIVE TIMES FIVE, RKO Radio. (Special)

SONS OF LIBERTY, Warner Bros. (Historical Featurette)

FILM EDITING

GONE WITH THE WIND, Selznick, MGM. Hal C. Kern and James E. Newcom.

GOODBYE, MR. CHIPS, MGM (British). Charles Frend.

MR. SMITH GOES TO WASHINGTON, Columbia. Gene Havlick and Al Clark.

THE RAINS CAME, 20th Century-Fox. Barbara McLean.

STAGECOACH, Wanger, UA. Otho Lovering and Dorothy Spencer.

ART DIRECTION

BEAU GESTE, Paramount. Hans Dreier and Robert Odell.

CAPTAIN FURY, Roach, UA. Charles D. Hall.

FIRST LOVE, Universal. Jack Otterson and Martin Obzina.

GONE WITH THE WIND, Selznick, MGM. Lyle Wheeler.

LOVE AFFAIR, RKO Radio. Van Nest Polglase and Al Herman.

MAN OF CONQUEST, Republic. John Victor Mackay.

MR. SMITH GOES TO WASHINGTON, Columbia. Lionel Banks.

THE PRIVATE LIVES OF ELIZABETH AND ESSEX, Warner Bros. Anton Grot.

THE RAINS CAME, 20th Century-Fox. William Darling and George Dudley.

STAGECOACH, Wanger, UA. Alexander Toluboff.

THE WIZARD OF OZ, MGM. Cedric Gibbons and William A. Horning.

WUTHERING HEIGHTS, Goldwyn, UA. James Basevi.

SONG

FAITHFUL FOREVER (*Gulliver's Travels*, Paramount); Music by Ralph Rainger. Lyrics by Leo Robin.

I POURED MY HEART INTO A SONG (*Second Fiddle*, 20th Century-Fox); Music and Lyrics by Irving Berlin.

OVER THE RAINBOW (*The Wizard of Oz*, MGM); Music by Harold Arlen. Lyrics by E.Y. Harburg.

WISHING (*Love Affair*, RKO Radio); Music and Lyrics by Buddy de Sylva.

SCORING: ORIGINAL SONG SCORE AND/OR ADAPTATION

BABES IN ARMS, MGM. Roger Edens and George E. Stoll.

FIRST LOVE, Universal. Charles Previn.

THE GREAT VICTOR HERBERT, Paramount. Phil Boutelje and Arthur Lange.

THE HUNCHBACK OF NOTRE DAME, RKO Radio. Alfred Newman.

INTERMEZZO, Selznick, UA. Lou Forbes.

MR. SMITH GOES TO WASHINGTON, Columbia. Dimitri Tiomkin

OF MICE AND MEN, Roach, GA. Aaron Copland.

THE PRIVATE LIVES OF ELIZABETH AND ESSEX, Warner Bros. Erich Wolfgang Korngold.

SHE MARRIED A COP, Republic. Cy Feuer.

STAGECOACH, Wanger, UA. Richard Hageman, Frank Harling, John Leipold and Leo Shuken.

SWANEE RIVER, 20th Century-Fox. Louis Silvers.

THEY SHALL HAVE MUSIC, Goldwyn, UA. Alfred Newman.

WAY DOWN SOUTH, Lesser, RKO Radio. Victor Young.

SCORING: ORIGINAL MUSIC

DARK VICTORY, Warner Bros. Max Steiner.

ETERNALLY YOURS, Wanger, UA. Werner Janssen.

GOLDEN BOY, Columbia. Victor Young.

GONE WITH THE WIND, Selznick, MGM. Max Steiner.

GULLIVER'S TRAVELS, Paramount. Victor Young.

THE MAN IN THE IRON MASK, Small, UA. Lud Gluskin and Lucien Moraweck.

MAN OF CONQUEST, Republic. Victor Young.

NURSE EDITH CAVELL, RKO Radio. Anthony Collins.

OF MICE AND MEN, Roach, UA. Aaron Copland.

THE RAINS CAME, 20th Century-Fox. Alfred Newman.

THE WIZARD OF OZ, MGM. Herbert Stothart.

WUTHERING HEIGHTS, Goldwyn, UA. Alfred Newman.

SOUND RECORDING

BALALAIKA, MGM. MGM Studio Sound Dept., Douglas Shearer, Sound Director.

GONE WITH THE WIND, Selznick, MGM. Samuel Goldwyn Studio Sound Dept., Thomas T. Moulton, Sound Director.

GOODBYE, MR. CHIPS, MGM (British). Denham Studio Sound Dept., A.W. Watkins, Sound Director.

THE GREAT VICTOR HERBERT, Paramount. Paramount Studio Sound Dept., Loren Ryder, Sound Director.

THE HUNCHBACK OF NOTRE DAME, RKO Radio. RKO Radio Studio Sound Dept., John Aalberg, Sound Director.

MAN OF CONQUEST, Republic. Republic Studio Sound Dept., C.L. Lootens, Sound Director.

MR. SMITH GOES TO WASHINGTON, Columbia. Columbia Studio Sound Dept., John Livadary, Sound Director.

OF MICE AND MEN, Roach, MGM. Hal Roach Studio Sound Dept., Elmer Raguse, Sound Director.

THE PRIVATE LIVES OF ELIZABETH AND ESSEX, Warner Bros. Warner Bros. Studio Sound Dept., Nathan Levinson, Sound Director.

THE RAINS CAME, 20th Century-Fox. 20th Century Fox Studio Sound Dept., E.H. Hansen, Sound Director.

WHEN TOMORROW COMES, Universal. Universal Studio Sound Dept., Bernard B. Brown, Sound Director.

WRITING: ORIGINAL STORY

BACHELOR MOTHER, RKO Radio. Felix Jackson.

LOVE AFFAIR, RKO Radio. Mildred Cram and Leo McCarey.

MR. SMITH GOES TO WASHINGTON, Columbia. Lewis R. Foster.

NINOTCHKA, MGM. Melchior Lengyel.

YOUNG MR. LINCOLN, 20th Century-Fox. Lamar Trotti.

WRITING: SCREENPLAY

GONE WITH THE WIND, Selznick, MGM. Sidney Howard.

GOODBYE, MR. CHIPS, MGM (British). Eric Maschwitz, R.C. Sherriff and Claudine West.

MR. SMITH GOES TO WASHINGTON, Columbia. Sidney Buchman.

NINOTCHKA, MGM. Charles Brackett, Walter Reisch and Billy Wilder.

WUTHERING HEIGHTS, Goldwyn, UA. Ben Hecht and Charles MacArthur.

CINEMATOGRAPHY: BLACK-AND-WHITE

STAGECOACH, Wanger, UA. Bert Glennon.

WUTHERING HEIGHTS, Goldwyn, UA. Gregg Toland.

CINEMATOGRAPHY: COLOR

GONE WITH THE WIND, Selznick, MGM. Ernest Haller and Ray Rennahan.

THE PRIVATE LIVES OF ELIZABETH AND ESSEX, Warner Bros. Sol Polito and W. Howard Greene.

SPECIAL EFFECTS

GONE WITH THE WIND, Selznick, MGM. John R. Cosgrove, Fred Albin and Arthur Johns.

ONLY ANGELS HAVE WINGS, Columbia. Roy Davidson and Edwin C. Hahn.

THE PRIVATE LIVES OF ELIZABETH AND ESSEX, Warner Bros. Byron Haskin and Nathan Levinson.

THE RAINS CAME, 20th Century-Fox. E.H. Hansen and Fred Sersen.

TOPPER TAKES A TRIP, Roach, UA. Roy Seawright.

UNION PACIFIC, Paramount. Farciot Edouart, Gordon Jennings and Loren Ryder.

THE WIZARD OF OZ, MGM. A. Arnold Gillespie and Douglas Shearer.

SPECIAL AWARDS

TO DOUGLAS FAIRBANKS (Commemorative Award)—recognizing the unique and outstanding contribution of Douglas Fairbanks, first president of the Academy, to the international development of the motion picture.

TO THE MOTION PICTURE RELIEF FUND—acknowledging the outstanding services to the industry during the past year of the Motion Picture Relief Fund and its progressive leadership. Presented to JEAN HERSHOLT, President; RALPH MORGAN, Chairman of the Executive Committee; RALPH BLOCK, First Vice-President; CONRAD NAGEL.

TO JUDY GARLAND for her outstanding performance as a screen juvenile during the past year.

TO WILLIAM CAMERON MENZIES for outstanding achievement in the use of color for the enhancement of dramatic mood in the production of *Gone with the Wind*.

TO TECHNICOLOR COMPANY for its contributions in successfully bringing three-color feature production to the screen.

IRVING G. THALBERG MEMORIAL AWARD

TO DAVID O. SELZNICK

SCIENTIFIC OR TECHNICAL

CLASS III

GEORGE ANDERSON of Warner Bros. Studio

JOHN ARNOLD of Metro-Goldwyn-Mayer Studio;

THOMAS T. MOULTON, FRED ALBIN and the SOUND DEPARTMENT of the SAMUEL GOLDWYN STUDIO;

FARCIOT EDOUART, JOSEPH E. ROBBINS, WILLIAM RUDOLPH and PARAMOUNT PICTURES, INC.;

EMERY HUSE and RALPH B. ATKINSON of Eastman Kodak Co.;

HAROLD NYE of Warner Bros. Studio;

A.J. TONDREAU of Warner Bros. Studio;

F.R. ABBOTT, HALLER BELT, ALAN COOK and BAUSCH & LOMB OPTICAL CO.;

MITCHELL CAMERA CO.;

MOLE-RICHARDSON CO.;

CHARLES HANDLEY, DAVID JOY and NATIONAL CARBON CO.;

WINTON HOCH and TECHNICOLOR MOTION PICTURE CORP.;

DON MUSGRAVE and SELZNICK INTERNATIONAL PICTURES, INC.

ABOVE: Gene Tierney (with Oleg Cassini) bares her graceful shoulders in this elegant gown with a perfectly coordinated pearl choker. (1946)

BELOW: In her delicate, lace-trimmed dress, Jane Wyman (left) is positively enchanting as she accepts her best actress award from Loretta Young. (1949)

ABOVE: Cloaked in fur, Ginger Rogers is ravishing as she arrives at the 1941 Oscars (with James Stewart).

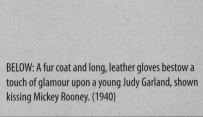

BELOW: A fur coat and long, leather gloves bestow a touch of glamour upon a young Judy Garland, shown kissing Mickey Rooney. (1940)

THE LOOK OF THE DECADE

THE EFFECTS OF WORLD WAR II on fashion could be felt even in Hollywood. Extravagance of all sorts was muted, and a softer, more lady-like way of dressing came into style. War-time rationing meant there was less fabric (among other supplies) to go around, and clothing leaned toward slim-fitting, modest garments with a more traditionally feminine look. Hats were used to express personal style because they could be made cheaply and used little material. The styles at the Awards ceremonies in the 40s reflected the times, with stars generally tempering their attire without forsaking any of their usual glamour.

OPPOSITE: Ingrid Bergman and Jennifer Jones arrive at the 1945 Oscars dressed in the bell-shaped coats of the day. Jones wears one of the elaborate hats that were *de rigueur* for well-dressed women.

1940

President Roosevelt briefly turned his attention from the war to address the banquet on a live radio hookup. He thanked the industry for its charitable fund-raising and its promotion of "the American way of life." Had he been in the room that night, he might have noticed more anxiety than charity. Despite Bette Davis's stunning performance in *The Letter*, there was no hint of a shutout. In fact, there were no hints of any kind. The Academy had finally stopped up all the press leaks, and none but Price Waterhouse knew the results of the race. The words "May I have the envelope, please" were tinged with real suspense.

NO SURE BETTE

CEREMONY: February 27, 1941
Biltmore Bowl, Biltmore Hotel,
Los Angeles
HOST: Walter Wanger,
Academy president

There was heavy betting at every table except, perhaps, in the Best Supporting Actor category. Once again, the Screen Extras Guild carried its favorite son and former $5-per-day bit player, Walter Brennan, to victory. He appeared mildly embarrassed by the tepid response to his unprecedented third Oscar.

Every other race was a tight one. Although she was a heavy favorite, Davis might be toppled by Katharine Hepburn's golden comeback role in *The Philadelphia Story*. And there was newcomer Joan Fontaine, who could be a spoiler, given the box-office success of *Rebecca*. Until the big moment, the guests settled back for some expected laughs from Bob Hope and a surprising one from Best Screenplay winner, Donald Ogden Stewart. "There has been so much niceness here tonight that I'm happy to say that I am entirely and solely responsible for the success of *The Philadelphia Story*," Stewart joked.

Walter Wanger stopped the "niceness" with his announcement "There will be no presentation of the Thalberg Award tonight, as the Academy did not think any individual deserved it," he said. Ouch! It was time to bring on the ladies for some glamorous relief. Theater legend Lynn Fontanne opened the envelope and unleashed a gleeful roar as dark horse Ginger Rogers triumphed. She rushed teary-eyed to the stage, firmly attached to her mother. Her filial devotion was contagious. Jimmy Stewart promised to send his Oscar back home to his dad in Pennsylvania.

BEST PICTURE
REBECCA

Pauline Kael dismissed the film as "romantic-gothic corn, full of Hitchcock's humor and inventiveness." The *New York Times* raved, "*Rebecca* is an altogether brilliant film, haunting…a menacing mood, fraught with…hidden meaning."

Having endured producer Selznick's notoriously controlling, authoritarian bent through the production of the film, twenty years later Hitchcock said, "When I came to America to direct *Rebecca*, David Selznick sent me a memo…I've just finished reading it. I think I may turn it into a motion picture…I plan to call it *"The Longest Story Ever Told."* Hitchcock turned this debut film into gold, making it clear that he was headed for the pantheon of great directors.

Laurence Olivier, Joan Fontaine

The envelope, please…

Katharine Hepburn with James Stewart

BEST ACTOR
JAMES STEWART (1908–1997)
THE PHILADELPHIA STORY

The shy Stewart gulped into the microphone and slowly said, "I want to assure you that this is a very, very important moment in my life."

The incomparable Jimmy Stewart remains one of America's most beloved Hollywood icons. A kindly man, Stewart was one of the few stars about whom not a bad word was ever said. Five-time Oscar nominee for *Mr. Smith Goes to Washington* (1939), *It's a Wonderful Life!* (1946), *Harvey* (1950), and *Anatomy of a Murder* (1959), he ultimately received only one Golden Boy and one Honorary Award.

Swayed from a career as an architect, Stewart performed at the Princeton Triangle Club and, upon graduation, went to Hollywood and became a leading man almost overnight. He appeared in such features as *After the Thin Man* (1936) and *You Can't Take It with You* (1938, the start of a great artistic partnership with director Frank Capra).

World War II intervened, but Stewart returned home from the army a bemedaled hero. His next film, Frank Capra's *It's a Wonderful Life* (1946), became one of America's most beloved. Among the films in his varied career are *Rope* (1948), *Broken Arrow* (1950), *The Greatest Show on Earth* (1952), *Rear Window* (1954), and *Vertigo* (1958). Stewart starred in two John Ford Westerns, *Two Rode Together* (1961), *The Man Who Shot Liberty Valance* (1962), and, finally, *The Shootist* (1976). The end of his career found him working in television and doing voice-overs.

Dennis Morgan with Ginger Rogers

BEST ACTRESS
GINGER ROGERS (1911–1995)
KITTY FOYLE

When Rogers spoke her eyes were full as she faced a cheering audience (mother at her side). "This is the greatest moment of my life," she said. "I want to thank the one who has stood by me faithfully—my mother."

Rogers caught the attention of filmgoers with her first hit, *Flying Down to Rio* (1933). Although she will forever be remembered as Fred Astaire's dynamic dance partner in their unforgettable 1930s musicals, they made only ten films together—among them *Top Hat* (1935), *Swing Time* (1936), *Shall We Dance* (1937), and *The Barkleys of Broadway* (1949).

Rogers was an actress in her own right. A delightful comedienne, she followed this year's Oscar with *Tom, Dick and Harry* (1941), *The Major and the Minor* (1942), and *Monkey Business* (1952).

Eventually, she had to admit that she couldn't compete with a newer, younger group of stars, including Marilyn Monroe. Rogers found her way back to stardom via the stage, appearing in Broadway's smash *Hello, Dolly!* (1965) and *Mame* (1969, London). Confined to a wheelchair in her later years, Rogers was active enough to promote her 1991 autobiography, *Ginger: My Story*.

BEST OF 1940
Best Picture: *Rebecca*
Best Director: John Ford, *The Grapes of Wrath*
Best Actor: James Stewart, *The Philadelphia Story*
Best Actress: Ginger Rogers, *Kitty Foyle*
Best Supporting Actor: Walter Brennan, *The Westerner*
Best Supporting Actress: Jane Darwell, *The Grapes of Wrath*

FIRSTS
- FDR was the first U.S. president to formally address the Awards ceremony.
- The Academy finally agreed to sealed envelopes. No more peeking before Awards night.
- *Rebecca* was Alfred Hitchcock's first American-made film and his first Best Director nomination.
- *The Great Dictator*'s Charlie Chaplin was the first performer to be simultaneously nominated for Best Picture, Best Director, and Best Screenplay.
- American audiences were introduced to carrot-chomping dandy Bugs Bunny.
- Walter Brennan won the first Oscar trifecta. It wasn't matched until Katharine Hepburn won her third for *Guess Who's Coming To Dinner* (1967).

ROLE REVERSALS
- Laurence Olivier won the role of Max de Winter in *Rebecca* only after William Powell and Ronald Colman took a pass.
- Ginger Rogers always bristled at the mention of Katharine Hepburn, feeling she should have been offered more of Hepburn's roles. She got her revenge when Hepburn turned down Roger's Oscar-winning part in *Kitty Foyle*.

SINS OF OMISSION
Actor: Cary Grant, *His Girl Friday*
Cary Grant, *The Philadelphia Story*
Actress: Rosalind Russell, *His Girl Friday*, Margaret Sullavan, *The Shop Around the Corner*

ALWAYS A BRIDESMAID, NEVER A BRIDE
Hitchcock didn't win Best Director this year—or any other, despite five nominations.

UNMENTIONABLES
- Jimmy Stewart's Oscar was considered a gold-plated apology for his being robbed of the award for last year's *Mr. Smith Goes to Washington*.
- The filming of *The Letter* was laced with irony. The previous year, director William Wyler had sent his lover, Bette Davis, an ultimatum letter: either dump her husband and marry him or it was over. She didn't write back.
- Ginger Rogers's tied-at-the-hip relationship with her domineering mom, Lela, proved eternal. They're buried side by side at Oakwood Memorial Park. The grave of Ginger's longtime screen partner, Fred Astaire, is just yards away.

BEST SUPPORTING ACTOR
WALTER BRENNAN, (1894–1974)
THE WESTERNER

The air was vibrating with shock when Alfred Lunt announced Brennan as the Oscar winner. Jack Oakie and James Stephenson were thought to be the undisputed contenders. Mrs. Oakie actually burst into tears while Brennan quietly accepted his third Oscar and disappeared. His performance in the role of true-life Judge Roy Bean was singled out by critic Leonard Maltin as "particularly vivid." The character of Judge Roy Bean was interpreted in several films, most famously—aside from Brennan—by Paul Newman in *The Life and Times of Judge Roy Bean* (1972).

The star of *The Westerner*, Gary Cooper, had been among Brennan's closest friends since their early Hollywood beginnings, when they both began working as extras (and Cooper's name was still Frank).

Brennan was married for fifty-four years to Ruth Welles, a childhood sweetheart. He died a wealthy businessman. (For more on Brennan, see 1936, 1938.)

Gary Cooper with Walter Brennan

BEST SUPPORTING ACTRESS
JANE DARWELL (1879–1967)
THE GRAPES OF WRATH

"Needless to say, this is my favorite role," Darwell said upon winning an Oscar for her performance as Ma Joad in *The Grapes of Wrath*. *Variety* later reported that what the then out-of-work actress said was "Awards are nice, but I'd much rather have a job."

The Grapes of Wrath was the crowning achievement of Darwell's fifty-year screen career, during which she appeared in more than 200 movies. The plump, dowdy, and kindly Darwell was usually cast in motherly roles, though she also played prison matrons and midwives. She appeared in several silent films before making her Hollywood sound debut in *Huckleberry Finn* (1931), and went on to play feature roles in *The Scarlet Empress* (1934), *All That Money Can Buy* (1941), *My Darling Clementine* (1946), and *There's Always Tomorrow* (1956). While infirm and living in retirement at the Motion Picture Country Home and Hospital, she was lured by Walt Disney personally to appear in *Mary Poppins* (1964).

Henry Fonda with Jane Darwell

BEST DIRECTOR
JOHN FORD (1894–1973)
THE GRAPES OF WRATH

"I love making pictures, but I don't like talking about them," said Ford, who snubbed the Academy and told reporters that he would be fishing—"for as long as the fish are biting"—with his star, Henry Fonda.

"The power of Ford was rooted in strong stories, classical technique and direct expression," wrote critic Roger Ebert. "Years of apprenticeship in low-budget silent films, many of them quickies shot on location, had steeled him against unnecessary set-ups and fancy camera work. There is a rigorous purity in his visual style that serves the subject well. *The Grapes of Wrath* contains not a single shot that seems careless or routine."

In some of *Wrath*'s most affecting scenes, Ford's maxim that "the main thing about directing is photograph the people's eyes" was vividly realized. Ironically, he had only one eye as the result of a freak accident during a hunting trip.

(For more on Ford, see 1935, 1941, and 1952.)

PICTURE

ALL THIS, AND HEAVEN TOO, Warner Bros, Jack L. Warner and Hall Wallis, with David Lewis.
FOREIGN CORRESPONDENT, Wanger, UA, Walter Wanger.
THE GRAPES OF WRATH, 20th Century-Fox, Darryl F. Zanuck with Nunnally Johnson.
THE GREAT DICTATOR, Chaplin, UA, Charles Chaplin.
KITTY FOYLE, RKO Radio, David Hempstead.
THE LETTER, Warner Bros, Hal B. Wallis.
THE LONG VOYAGE HOME, Wanger, UA, John Ford.
OUR TOWN, Lesser, UA, Sol Lesser.
THE PHILADELPHIA STORY, MGM. Joseph L. Mankiewicz.
REBECCA, Selznick, UA, David O. Selznick,

ACTOR

CHARLES CHAPLIN in *The Great Dictator*, Chaplin, UA.
HENRY FONDA in *The Grapes of Wrath*, 20th Century-Fox.
RAYMOND MASSEY in *Abe Lincoln in Illinois*, RKO Radio.
LAURENCE OLIVIER in *Rebecca*, Selznick, UA.
JAMES STEWART in *The Philadelphia Story*, MGM.

ACTRESS

BETTE DAVIS in *The Letter*, Warner Bros.
JOAN FONTAINE in *Rebecca*, Selznick, UA.
KATHARINE HEPBURN in *The Philadelphia Story*, MGM.
GINGER ROGERS in *Kitty Foyle*, RKO Radio.
MARTHA SCOTT in *Our Town*, Lesser, UA.

SUPPORTING ACTOR

ALBERT BASSERMANN in *Foreign Correspondent*, Wanger, UA.
WALTER BRENNAN in *The Westerner*, Goldwyn, UA.
WILLIAM GARGAN in *They Knew What They Wanted*, RKO Radio.
JACK OAKIE in *The Great Dictator*, Chaplin, UA.
JAMES STEPHENSON in *The Letter*, Warner Bros.

SUPPORTING ACTRESS

JUDITH ANDERSON in *Rebecca*, Selznick, UA.
JANE DARWELL in *The Grapes of Wrath*, 20th Century-Fox.
RUTH HUSSEY in *The Philadelphia Story*, MGM.
BARBARA O'NEIL in *All This, and Heaven Too*, Warner Bros.
MARJORIE RAMBEAU in *Primrose Path*, RKO Radio.

DIRECTION

GEORGE CUKOR for *The Philadelphia Story*, MGM.
JOHN FORD for *The Grapes of Wrath*, 20th Century-Fox.
ALFRED HITCHCOCK for *Rebecca*, Selznick, UA.
SAM WOOD for *Kitty Foyle*, RKO Radio.
WILLIAM WYLER for *The Letter*, Warner Bros.

SPECIAL EFFECTS

THE BLUE BIRD, 20th Century-Fox. Fred Sersen and E.H. Hansen.
BOOM TOWN, M.G-M. A. Arnold Gillespie and Douglas Shearer.
THE BOYS FROM SYRACUSE, Universal. John P. Fulton, Bernard B. Brown and Joseph Lapis.
DR. CYCLOPS, Paramount. Farciot Edouart and Gordon Jennings.
FOREIGN CORRESPONDENT, Wanger, UA. Paul Eagler and Thomas T. Moulton.
THE INVISIBLE MAN RETURNS, Universal. John P. Fulton, Bernard B. Brown and William Hedgecock.
THE LONG VOYAGE HOME, Argosy-Wanger, UA. R.T. Layton, R.O. Binger and Thomas T. Moulton.

ONE MILLION B.C., Roach, UA. Roy Seawright and Elmer Raguse.
REBECCA, Selznick, UA. Jack Cosgrove and Arthur Johns.
THE SEA HAWK, Warner Bros. Byron Haskin and Nathan Levinson.
SWISS FAMILY ROBINSON, RKO Radio. Vernon L. Walker and John O. Aalberg.
THE THIEF OF BAGDAD, Korda, UA. Lawrence Butler and Jack Whitney.
TYPHOON, Paramount. Farciot Edouart, Gordon Jennings and Loren Ryder.
WOMEN IN WAR, Republic. Howard J. Lydecker, William Bradford, Ellis J. Thackery and Herbert Norsch.

WRITING: ORIGINAL STORY

ARISE, MY LOVE, Paramount. Benjamin Glazer and John S. Toldy.
COMRADE X, MGM. Walter Reisch.
EDISON THE MAN, MGM. Hugo Butler and Dore Schary.
MY FAVORITE WIFE, RKO Radio. Leo McCarey, Bella Spewack and Samuel Spewack.
THE WESTERNER, Goldwyn, UA. Stuart N. Lake.

WRITING: ORIGINAL SCREENPLAY

ANGELS OVER BROADWAY, Columbia. Ben Hecht.
DR. EHRLICH'S MAGIC BULLET, Warner Bros. Norman Burnside, Heinz Herald and John Huston.
FOREIGN CORRESPONDENT, Wanger, UA. Charles Bennett and Joan Harrison.
THE GREAT DICTATOR, Chaplin, UA. Charles Chaplin.
THE GREAT McGINTY, Paramount. Preston Sturges.

WRITING: SCREENPLAY

THE GRAPES OF WRATH, 20th Century-Fox. Nunnally Johnson.
KITTY FOYLE, RKO Radio. Dalton Trumbo.
THE LONG VOYAGE HOME, Argosy-Wanger, UA. Dudley Nichols.
THE PHILADELPHIA STORY, MGM. Donald Ogden Stewart.
REBECCA, Selznick, UA. Robert E. Sherwood and Joan Harrison.

FILM EDITING

THE GRAPES OF WRATH, 20th Century-Fox. Robert E. Simpson.
THE LETTER, Warner Bros. Warren Low.
THE LONG VOYAGE HOME, Argosy-Wanger, UA. Sherman Todd.
NORTH WEST MOUNTED POLICE, DeMille, Paramount. Anne Bauchens.
REBECCA, Selznick, UA. Hal C. Kern.

CINEMATOGRAPHY

B/W

ABE LINCOLN IN ILLINOIS, RKO Radio. James Wong Howe.
ALL THIS, AND HEAVEN TOO, Warner Bros. Ernest Haller.
ARISE, MY LOVE, Paramount. Charles B. Lang Jr.
BOOM TOWN, MGM. Harold Rosson.
FOREIGN CORRESPONDENT, Wanger, UA. Rudolph Mate.
THE LETTER, Warner Bros. Gaetano Gaudio.
THE LONG VOYAGE HOME, Argosy-Wanger, UA. Gregg Toland.
REBECCA, Selznick, UA. George Barnes.
SPRING PARADE, Universal. Joseph Valentine.
WATERLOO BRIDGE, MGM. Joseph Ruttenberg.

Color

BITTER SWEET, MGM. Oliver T. Marsh and Allen Davey.
THE BLUE BIRD, 20th Century-Fox. Arthur Miller and Ray Rennahan.
DOWN ARGENTINE WAY, 20th Century-Fox. Leon Shamroy and Ray Rennahan.
NORTH WEST MOUNTED POLICE, DeMille, Paramount. Victor Milner and W. Howard Greene.
NORTHWEST PASSAGE, MGM. Sidney Wagner and William V. Skall.
THE THIEF OF BAGDAD, Korda, UA (British). George Perinal.

SOUND RECORDING

BEHIND THE NEWS, Republic. Republic Studio Sound Dept., Charles Lootens. Sound Director.
CAPTAIN CAUTION, Roach, UA. Hal Roach Studio Sound Dept., Elmer Raguse, Sound Director.
THE GRAPES OF WRATH, 20th Century-Fox. 20th Century-Fox Studio Sound Dept., E.H. Hansen, Sound Director.
THE HOWARDS OF VIRGINIA, Columbia. General Service Studio Sound Dept., Jack Whitney, Sound Director.

KITTY FOYLE, RKO Radio. RKO Radio Studio Sound Dept., John Aalberg, Sound Director.
NORTH WEST MOUNTED POLICE, Paramount. Paramount Studio Sound Dept., Loren Ryder, Sound Director.
OUR TOWN, Lesser, UA. Samuel Goldwyn Studio Sound Dept., Thomas Moulton, Sound Director.
THE SEA HAWK, Warner Bros. Warner Bros. Studio Sound Dept., Nathan Levinson, Sound Director.
SPRING PARADE, Universal. Universal Studio Sound Dept., Bernard B. Brown, Sound Director.
STRIKE UP THE BAND, MGM. MGM. Studio Sound Dept., Douglas Shearer, Sound Director.
TOO MANY HUSBANDS, Columbia. Columbia Studio Sound Dept., John Livadary, Sound Director.

ART DIRECTION

B/W

ARISE, MY LOVE, Paramount. Hans Dreier and Robert Usher.
ARIZONA, Columbia. Lionel Banks and Robert Peterson.
THE BOYS FROM SYRACUSE, Universal. John Otterson.
DARK COMMAND, Republic. John Victor Mackay.
FOREIGN CORRESPONDENT, Wanger, UA. Alexander Golitzen.
LILLIAN RUSSELL, 20th Century-Fox. Richard Day and Joseph C. Wright.
MY FAVORITE WIFE, RKO Radio. Van Nest Polglase and Mark-Lee Kirk.
MY SON, MY SON, Small, UA. John DuCasse Schulze.
OUR TOWN, Lesser, UA. Lewis J. Rachmil.
PRIDE AND PREJUDICE, MGM. Cedric Gibbons and Paul Groesse.
REBECCA, Selznick, UA. Lyle Wheeler.
THE SEA HAWK, Warner Bros. Anton Grot.
THE WESTERNER, Goldwyn, UA. James Basevi.

Color

BITTER SWEET, MGM. Cedric Gibbons and John S. Detlie.
DOWN ARGENTINE WAY, 20th Century-Fox. Richard Day and Joseph C. Wright.
NORTH WEST MOUNTED POLICE, DeMille, Paramount. Hans Dreier and Roland Anderson.
THE THIEF OF BAGDAD, Korda, UA. Vincent Korda.

SONG

DOWN ARGENTINE WAY *(Down Argentine Way*, 20th Century-Fox); Music by Harry Warren. Lyrics by Mack Gordon.
I'D KNOW YOU ANYWHERE *(You'll Find Out*, RKO Radio); Music by Jimmy McHugh. Lyrics by Johnny Mercer.
IT'S A BLUE WORLD *(Music in My Heart*, Columbia); Music and Lyrics by Chet Forrest and Bob Wright.
LOVE OF MY LIFE *(Second Chorus*, Paramount); Music by Artie Shaw, Lyrics by Johnny Mercer.
ONLY FOREVER *(Rhythm on the River*, Paramount); Music by James Monaco. Lyrics by John Burke.
OUR LOVE AFFAIR *(Strike Up the Band*, MGM); Music and Lyrics by Roger Edens and Arthur Freed.
WALTZING IN THE CLOUDS *(Spring Parade*, Universal); Music by Robert Stolz. Lyrics by Gus Kahn.
WHO AM I? *(Hit Parade of 1941*, Republic); Music by Jule Styne. Lyrics by Walter Bullock.
WHEN YOU WISH UPON A STAR *(Pinocchio*, Disney, RKO Radio); Music by Leigh Harline. Lyrics by Ned Washington.

SCORE

ARISE, MY LOVE, Paramount. Victor Young.
HIT PARADE OF 1941, Republic. Cy Feuer.
IRENE, Imperadio, RKO Radio. Anthony Collins.
OUR TOWN, Lesser, UA. Aaron Copland.
THE SEA HAWK, Warner Bros. Erich Wolfgang Korngold.
SECOND CHORUS, Paramount. Artie Shaw.
SPRING PARADE, Universal. Charles Previn.
STRIKE UP THE BAND, MGM. Georgie Stoll and Roger Edens.
TIN PAN ALLEY, 20th Century-Fox. Alfred Newman.

ORIGINAL SCORE

ARIZONA, Columbia. Victor Young.
THE DARK COMMAND, Republic. Victor Young.
THE FIGHT FOR LIFE, U.S. Government-Columbia. Louis Gruenberg.
THE GREAT DICTATOR, Chaplin, UA. Meredith Wilson.
THE HOUSE OF SEVEN GABLES, Universal. Frank Skinner

THE HOWARDS OF VIRGINIA, Columbia. Richard Hageman.
THE LETTER, Warner Bros. Max Steiner.
THE LONG VOYAGE HOME, Argosy-Wanger, UA. Richard Hageman.
THE MARK OF ZORRO, 20th Century-Fox. Alfred Newman.
MY FAVORITE WIFE, RKO Radio. Roy Webb.
NORTH WEST MOUNTED POLICE, DeMille, Paramount. Victor Young.
ONE MILLION B.C., Roach, UA. Werner Heymann.
OUR TOWN, Lesser, UA. Aaron Copland.
PINOCCHIO, Disney, RKO Radio. Leigh Harline, Paul J. Smith and Ned Washington.
REBECCA, Selznick, VA. Franz Waxman.
THE THIEF OF BAGDAD, Korda, UA. Miklos Rozsa.
WATERLOO BRIDGE, MGM. Herbert Stothart.

SHORT SUBJECT: CARTOON

MILKY WAY, MGM. (Rudolph Ising Series)
PUSS GETS THE BOOT, MGM. (Cat and Mouse Series)
A WILD HARE, Schlesinger, Warner Bros.

SHORT SUBJECT: ONE-REEL

LONDON CAN TAKE IT, Warner Bros. (Vitaphone Varieties)
MORE ABOUT NOSTRADAMUS, MGM.
QUICKER 'N A WINK, Pete Smith, MGM.
SIEGE, IIKO Radio. (Reelism)

SHORT SUBJECT: TWO-REEL

EYES OF THE NAVY, MGM. (Crime Doesn't Pay)
SERVICE WITH THE COLORS, Warner Bros. (National Defense Series)
TEDDY, THE ROUGH RIDER, Warner Bros. (Historical Featurette)

SPECIAL AWARDS

TO BOB HOPE in recognition of his unselfish services to the motion-picture industry.
TO COLONEL NATHAN LEVINSON for his outstanding service to the industry and the Army during the past nine years, which has made possible the present efficient mobilization of the motion-picture industry facilities for the production of Army training films.

SCIENTIFIC OR TECHNICAL

CLASS I

20TH CENTURY-FOX FILM CORP. for the design and construction of the 20th Century Silenced Camera, developed by DANIEL CLARK, GROVER LAUBE, CHARLES MILLER and ROBERT W. STEVENS.

CLASS III

WARNER BROS. STUDIO ART DEPARTMENT and ANTON GROT.

1941

"Of course we fight. What sisters don't battle?"

—Olivia de Havilland

a s a jittery Los Angeles scanned the horizon for enemy planes, new Academy president Bette Davis leveled her sights on the Board of Governors. She issued an ultimatum that the ceremonies be moved to a theater and tickets be sold to the public as a Red Cross fund-raiser. The Board balked, and Bette walked—all the way back to her New Hampshire farm.

THE WAR AT HOME

CEREMONY: February 26, 1942
Biltmore Bowl, Biltmore Hotel,
Los Angeles
HOST: Bob Hope

The Board did make a few "patriotic" concessions. The banquet would be referred to as a dinner and there would be no dancing or formal attire. Some stars listened and some showed up as spectacularly turned out as ever. The war on mink and ermine wasn't over by a long shot. Neither was the offensive launched on iconoclastic "boy genius" Orson Welles. After he referred to studio execs as a bunch of "overpaid office boys," they retaliated by booing his *Citizen Kane* win for Best Original Screenplay.

Pearl Harbor aside, the headlines howled over the ultimate battle in the center ring of the jam-packed Biltmore Bowl. The opponents were a feuding sister act, Olivia de Havilland and Joan Fontaine, in the race for Best Actress. De Havilland was all but a

shoo-in for *Hold Back the Dawn* until her sister's starring vehicle, *Suspicion*, opened at the very last eligible moment. The 1,600 guests eyed the two all night, as if they hoped to catch sight of concealed weapons. They barely glanced at the stage as Bob Hope and Jack Benny yucked it up over a joke Oscar done up as Benny in drag with a cigar in his mouth.

There was a pause in the sibling stare-down as crowd favorite Gary Cooper strode laconically up to the podium to accept his award. Finally, the big moment came as Ginger Rogers tore open the envelope to announce the winning sister Fontaine. She remained frozen in her seat until de Havilland leaned over and whispered, "Get up there!" Fontaine rushed to the stage, dissolved in tears, and stole the show. Her older sibling stood to await her return to the adjoining table. The room was spellbound as de Havilland proffered a thin smile and a brief handshake. The Board of Governors may have been right with their insistence that elitist glamour be maintained despite the war. It was a star's job to take the world's mind off more pressing matters for a moment or two. That being the case, Fontaine and de Havilland should have been paid overtime.

BEST PICTURE/BEST DIRECTOR
JOHN FORD (1894–1973)
HOW GREEN WAS MY VALLEY

Cecil B. DeMille committed a few verbal atrocities as he presented the Best Director award to the absent John Ford. "Some of the people who spoke before me have stolen the thunder, like Mr. Wilkie and the Jap—I mean Chinese—ambassador," he said.

"Out of the homely virtues of a group of Welsh mining folk—and a few sturdy leaders in their midst," wrote the *New York Times*'s Bosley Crowther, "Darryl Zanuck, John Ford, and their associates at Twentieth Century-Fox have fashioned a motion picture of great poetic charm and dignity, a picture rich in visual fabrication and in the vigor of its imagery, and one which may truly be regarded as an outstanding film of the year…a stunning masterpiece."

Rival nominee for Best Picture and Best Director, Orson Welles, was quoted, when asked which directors he most admired, as saying, "I like the old masters, by which I mean John Ford, John Ford, and John Ford."

(For more on Ford, see 1935, 1940, and 1952.)

The envelope, please…

Gary Cooper (right)

BEST ACTOR
GARY COOPER (1901–1961)
SERGEANT YORK

"Shucks, I've been in the business sixteen years and sometimes dreamed I might get one of these things. That's all I can say," said the awkward Cooper. "Funny, when I was dreaming I always made a good speech."

Bosley Crowther's depiction in the *New York Times* of Gary Cooper as York could stand as a description of the star himself: "the gaunt, clumsy yokel, the American hayseed—the proud, industrious, honest, simple citizen who marches in the forefront of his nation's ranks." Cooper's range ran from cowboy to light comedy and populist hero. He made his mark in Frank Capra's *Mr. Deeds Goes to Town* (1936) and *Meet John Doe* (1941). Ernest Hemingway was so impressed with Cooper's performance in *A Farewell to Arms* (1932) that he insisted that Cooper play the hero in *For Whom the Bell Tolls* (1943, nom.).

Cooper's personal profile vied with his public persona. Though married, he had many affairs with such stars as Clara Bow, Ingrid Bergman, Marlene Dietrich, Patricia Neal, Tallulah Bankhead, and Cecil Beaton (so he claimed).

BEST ACTRESS
JOAN FONTAINE (B. 1917)
SUSPICION

This was the second year in a row that Joan Fontaine was nominated for playing a victimized young bride who doesn't trust her husband. The purposeful, elegant actress became a star depicting vulnerable ingenues and made her name in Hitchcock's *Rebecca* (1940, nom.) and *Suspicion*, and in *Jane Eyre* (1944).

Prior to these films Fontaine had made some headway appearing opposite Fred Astaire in *A Damsel in Distress* and with Katharine Hepburn in *Quality Street* (both 1937), and had also starred in *Gunga Din* (1939). She took on a more challenging role in *The Constant Nymph* (1943, nom.).

As she aged, however, the delicate ingenue became the hardened schemer in *The Devil's Own* (1966), which proved to be her last leading performance.

By the 1970s, Fontaine could be seen in several made-for-TV movies. She published her autobiography, *No Bed of Roses*, in 1978.

BEST OF 1941
Best Picture: *How Green Was My Valley*
Best Director: John Ford, *How Green Was My Valley*
Best Actor: Gary Cooper, *Sergeant York*
Best Actress: Joan Fontaine, *Suspicion*
Best Supporting Actor: Donald Crisp, *How Green Was My Valley*
Best Supporting Actress: Mary Astor, *The Great Lie*

FIRSTS
• Documentaries were added to the Oscar race.
• At the ripe old age of 25, Orson Welles was the first performer to be simultaneously nominated for Best Film, Best Director, Best Actor, and Best Screenplay.
• Joan Fontaine was the first and only star of a Hitchcock film to win an Oscar.
• Walt Disney's unparalleled success streak finally hit a bump with *Fantasia*, his first commercial flop.

ROLE REVERSALS
Barbara Stanwyck picked up the starring role in *Ball of Fire* after Ginger Rogers dropped out.

SINS OF OMISSION
ACTOR: Humphrey Bogart, *The Maltese Falcon*
SUPPORTING ACTOR: Peter Lorre, *The Maltese Falcon*

ALWAYS A BRIDESMAID, NEVER A BRIDE
Despite her popularity with audiences and the Hollywood community, Barbara Stanwyck's four nominations never resulted in an Oscar.

UNMENTIONABLES
• *Citizen Kane* tops the most respected Best Film lists, but 1941 audiences stayed away in droves. It was one of the biggest box-office busts of the year.
• Barbara Stanwyck's stormy first marriage to Frank Fay finally ended after a drunken brawl during which he tossed their adopted son, Dion, into the swimming pool. Despite rumors of affairs with Marlene Dietrich and Joan Crawford, Stanwyck wed Robert Taylor, who had his own gay rumors to dispel. Their marriage started off on a sour note when his possessive mother demanded that he spend his wedding night with her rather than with Stanwyck.
• Carole Lombard was killed in a plane crash less than a month before the Oscars. Despite her mother's premonition of disaster, Lombard refused to take a train home to Los Angeles after a War Bond Rally tour. Reputedly, she was in a rush after getting wind of an alleged affair between her husband, Clark Gable, and Lana Turner.

BEST SUPPORTING ACTOR
DONALD CRISP (1880–1974)
HOW GREEN WAS MY VALLEY

"Other old-timers should be given a chance and they, too, could win awards," said Crisp, dressed in his real-life uniform as an evacuator of civilians during air raids.

New York Times critic Bosley Crowther said of Crisp's performance, "No one… could bring more strength and character to the difficult role of Gwilym Morgan than Donald Crisp."

The Oxford-educated Crisp was in pictures from film's earliest beginnings, performing on both sides of the camera. As an actor working with D. W. Griffith, he appeared in *The Birth of a Nation* (1915) and *Broken Blossoms* (1919). He directed and co-directed such silent films as *The Navigator* (1924, with Buster Keaton) and *Don Q, Son of Zorro* (1925). He had a fine acting career, often playing the tough, demanding authority figure in such films as *Red Dust* (1932), *Mutiny on the Bounty* (1935), *The Charge of the Light Brigade* (1936), *The Life of Emile Zola* (1937), *Jezebel* (1938), *Wuthering Heights* (1939), and *The Long Gray Line* (1955).

Among his last films were *The Last Hurrah* (1958), *Pollyanna* (1960), and *Spencer's Mountain* (1963).

Donald Crisp (center) with Walter Pidgeon (left) and Roddy McDowall (right)

PICTURE
BLOSSOMS IN THE DUST, MGM, Irving Asher.
CITIZEN KANE, Mercury, RKO Radio, Orson Welles.
HERE COMES MR. JORDAN, Columbia, Everett Riskin.
HOLD BACK THE DAWN, Paramount, Arthur Hornblow Jr.
HOW GREEN WAS MY VALLEY, 20th Century-Fox, Darryl F. Zanuck.
THE LITTLE FOXES, Goldwyn, RKO Radio, Samuel Goldwyn.
THE MALTESE FALCON, Warner Bros, Hal B. Wallis.
ONE FOOT IN HEAVEN, Warner Bros, Hal B. Wallis.
SERGEANT YORK, Warner Bros, Jesse L. Lasky and Hal B. Wallis.
SUSPICION, RKO Radio, RKO Radio.

ACTOR
GARY COOPER in *Sergeant York*, Warner Bros.
CARY GRANT in *Penny Serenade*, Columbia.
WALTER HUSTON in *All That Money Can Buy* (aka *The Devil and Daniel Webster*), RKO Radio.
ROBERT MONTGOMERY in *Here Comes Mr. Jordan*, Columbia.
ORSON WELLES in *Citizen Kane*, Mercury, RKO Radio.

ACTRESS
BETTE DAVIS in *The Little Foxes*, Goldwyn, RKO Radio.
OLIVIA DE HAVILLAND in *Hold Back the Dawn*, Paramount.
JOAN FONTAINE in *Suspicion*, RKO Radio.
GREER GARSON in *Blossoms in the Dust*, MGM.
BARBARA STANWYCK in *Ball of Fire*, Goldwyn, RKO Radio.

SUPPORTING ACTOR
WALTER BRENNAN in *Sergeant York*, Warner Bros.
CHARLES COBURN in *The Devil and Miss Jones*, RKO Radio.
DONALD CRISP in *How Green Was My Valley*, 20th Century-Fox.
JAMES GLEASON in *Here Comes Mr. Jordan*, Columbia.
SYDNEY GREENSTREET in *The Maltese Falcon*, Warner Bros.

SUPPORTING ACTRESS
SARA ALLGOOD in *How Green Was My Valley*, 20th Century-Fox.
MARY ASTOR in *The Great Lie*, Warner Bros.
PATRICIA COLLINGE in *The Little Foxes*, Goldwyn, RKO Radio.
TERESA WRIGHT in *The Little Foxes*, Goldwyn, RKO Radio.
MARGARET WYCHERLY in *Sergeant York*, Warner Bros.

DIRECTION
JOHN FORD for *How Green Was My Valley*, 20th Century-Fox.
ALEXANDER HALL for *Here Comes Mr. Jordan*, Columbia.
HOWARD HAWKS for *Sergeant York*, Warner Bros.
ORSON WELLES for *Citizen Kane*, Mercury, RKO Radio.
WILLIAM WYLER for *The Little Foxes*, Goldwyn, RKO Radio.

SONG
BABY MINE (*Dumbo*, Disney, RKO Radio); Music by Frank Churchill. Lyrics by Ned Washington.

BEST SUPPORTING ACTRESS
MARY ASTOR (1906–1987)
THE GREAT LIE

It had been twenty-two years since Astor appeared in a film, and she thanked co-star Bette Davis and composer Pyotr Ilich Tchaikovsky as the two people who helped her most.

Possibly better known for her inflammatory private life than for her films, Astor was nevertheless a strong actress and among the screen's greatest femme fatales. Humphrey Bogart's character in *The Maltese Falcon* (1941) said it all: "You're good…you're very good."

When her star faded, Astor tended to play "mother" roles; this was quite a switch from her beginnings as an elegant 18-year-old beauty courted by John Barrymore. She appeared with Barrymore in *Beau Brummel* (1924).

Astor's career was almost destroyed by the frank revelations of her many affairs that appeared in her diary (used as evidence in court during her divorce and custody battle). She reappeared in *Dodsworth* (1936), and her success continued with *The Prisoner of Zenda* (1937), *Midnight* (1939), and her Academy Award–winning performance in *The Great Lie*. One of her last performances was in *Hush…Hush, Sweet Charlotte* (1965). Her autobiography, *My Story*, was published in 1959.

BE HONEST WITH ME (*Ridin' on a Rainbow*, Republic); Music and Lyrics by Gene Autry and Fred Rose.

BLUES IN THE NIGHT (*Blues in the Night*, Warner Bros.); Music by Harold Arlen. Lyrics by Johnny Mercer.

BOOGIE WOOGIE BUGLE BOY OF COMPANY B (*Buck Privates*, Universal); Music by Hugh Prince. Lyrics by Don Raye.

CHATTANOOGA CHOO CHOO (*Sun Valley Serenade*, 20th Century-Fox); Music by Harry Warren. Lyrics by Mack Gordon.

DOLORES (*Las Vegas Nights*, Paramount); Music by Lou Alter. Lyrics by Frank Loesser.

THE LAST TIME I SAW PARIS (*Lady Be Good*, MGM); Music by Jerome Kern. Lyrics by Oscar Hammerstein II.

OUT OF THE SILENCE (*All American Co-Ed*, Roach, UA); Music and Lyrics by Lloyd B. Norlind.

SINCE I KISSED MY BABY GOODBYE (*You'll Never Get Rich*, Columbia); Music and Lyrics by Cole Porter.

SCORING: DRAMA

ALL THAT MONEY CAN BUY, RKO Radio. Bernard Herrmann.

BACK STREET, Universal. Frank Skinner.

BALL OF FIRE, Goldwyn, RKO Radio. Alfred Newman.

CHEERS FOR MISS BISHOP, Rowland, UA. Edward Ward.

CITIZEN KANE, Mercury, RKO Radio. Bernard Herrmann.

DR. JEKYLL AND MR. HYDE, MGM. Franz Waxman.

HOLD BACK THE DAWN, Paramount. Victor Young.

HOW GREEN WAS MY VALLEY, 20th Century-Fox. Alfred Newman.

KING OF THE ZOMBIES, Monogram. Edward Kay.

LADIES IN RETIREMENT, Columbia. Morris Stoloff and Ernst Toch.

THE LITTLE FOXES, Goldwyn, RKO Radio. Meredith Willson.

LYDIA, Korda, UA. Miklos Rozsa.

MERCY ISLAND. Republic. Cy Feuer and Walter Scharf.

SERGEANT YORK, Warner Bros. Max Steiner.

SO ENDS OUR NIGHT, Loew-Lewin, UA. Louis Greenberg.

SUNDOWN, Wanger, UA. Miklos Rozsa.

SUSPICION, RKO Radio. Franz Waxman.

TANKS A MILLION, Roach, UA. Edward Ward.

THAT UNCERTAIN FEELING, Lubitsch, UA. Werner Heymann.

THIS WOMAN IS MINE, Universal. Richard Hageman.

SCORING: MUSICAL

ALL AMERICAN CO-ED, Roach, UA. Edward Ward.

BIRTH OF THE BLUES, Paramount. Robert Emmett Dolan.

BUCK PRIVATES, Universal. Charles Previn.

THE CHOCOLATE SOLDIER, MGM. Herbert Stothart and Bronislau Kaper.

DUMBO, Disney, RKO Radio. Frank Churchill and Oliver Wallace.

ICE CAPADES, Republic. Cy Feuer.

THE STRAWBERRY BLONDE, Warner Bros. Heinz Roemheld.

SUN VALLEY SERENADE, 20th Century-Fox. Emil Newman.

SUNNY, RKO Radio. Anthony Collins.

YOU'LL NEVER GET RICH, Columbia. Morris Stoloff.

WRITING: ORIGINAL STORY

BALL OF FIRE, Goldwyn, RKO Radio. Thomas Monroe and Billy Wilder.

HERE COMES MR. JORDAN, Columbia. Harry Segall.

THE LADY EVE, Paramount. Monckton Hoffe.

MEET JOHN DOE, Warner Bros. Richard Connell and Robert Presnell.

NIGHT TRAIN, 20th Century-Fox (British). Gordon Wellesley.

WRITING: ORIGINAL SCREENPLAY

CITIZEN KANE, Mercury, RKO Radio. Herman J. Mankiewicz and Orson Welles.

THE DEVIL AND MISS JONES, RKO Radio. Norman Krasna.

SERGEANT YORK, Warner Bros. Harry Chandlee, Abem Finkel, John Huston and Howard Koch.

TALL, DARK AND HANDSOME, 20th Century-Fox. Karl Tunberg and Darrell Ware.

TOM, DICK AND HARRY, RKO Radio. Paul Jarrico.

WRITING: SCREENPLAY

HERE COMES MR. JORDAN, Columbia. Sidney Buchman and Seton I. Miller.

HOLD BACK THE DAWN, Paramount. Charles Brackett and Billy Wilder.

HOW GREEN WAS MY VALLEY, 20th Century-Fox. Philip Dunne.

THE LITTLE FOXES, Goldwyn, RKO Radio. Lillian Hellman.

THE MALTESE FALCON, Warner Bros. John Huston.

SPECIAL EFFECTS

ALOMA OF THE SOUTH SEAS, Paramount. Farciot Edouart, Gordon Jennings and Louis Mesenkop.

FLIGHT COMMAND, MGM. A. Arnold Gillespie and Douglas Shearer.

I WANTED WINGS, Paramount. Farciot Edouart, Gordon Jennings and Louis Mesenkop.

THE INVISIBLE WOMAN, Universal. John Fulton and John Hall.

THE SEA WOLF, Warner Bros. Byron Haskin and Nathan Levinson.

THAT HAMILTON WOMAN, Korda, UA. Lawrence Butler and William H. Wilmarth.

TOPPER RETURNS, Roach, UA. Roy Seawright and Elmer Raguse.

A YANK IN THE R.A.F., 20th Century-Fox. Fred Sersen and E.H. Hansen.

CINEMATOGRAPHY

B/W

THE CHOCOLATE SOLDIER, MGM. Karl Freund.

CITIZEN KANE, Mercury, RKO Radio. Gregg Toland.

DR. JEKYLL AND MR. HYDE, MGM. Joseph Ruttenberg.

HERE COMES MR. JORDAN, Columbia. Joseph Walker.

HOLD BACK THE DAWN, Paramount. Leo Tover.

HOW GREEN WAS MY VALLEY, 20th Century-Fox. Arthur Miller.

SERGEANT YORK, Warner Bros. Sol Polito.

SUN VALLEY SERENADE, 20th Century-Fox. Edward Cronjager.

SUNDOWN, Wanger, UA. Charles Lang.

THAT HAMILTON WOMAN, Korda, UA. Rudolph Mate.

Color

ALOMA OF THE SOUTH SEAS, Paramount. Wilfred M. Cline, Karl Struss and William Snyder.

BILLY THE KID, MGM. William V. Skall and Leonard Smith.

BLOOD AND SAND, 20th Century-Fox. Ernest Palmer and Ray Rennahan.

BLOSSOMS IN THE DUST, MGM. Karl Freund and W. Howard Greene.

DIVE BOMBER, Warner Bros. Bert Glennon.

LOUISIANA PURCHASE, Paramount. Harry Hallenberger and Ray Rennahan.

SHORT SUBJECT: CARTOON

BOOGIE WOOGIE BUGLE BOY OF COMPANY B, Lantz, Universal.

HIAWATHA'S RABBIT HUNT, Schlesinger, Warner Bros.

HOW WAR CAME, Columbia. (Raymond Gram Swing Series)

LEND A PAW, Disney, RKO Radio.

THE NIGHT BEFORE CHRISTMAS, MGM. (Tom and Jerry Series)

RHAPSODY IN RIVETS, Schlesinger, Warner Bros.

THE ROOKIE BEAR, MGM. (Bear Series)

RHYTHM IN THE RANKS, Paramount. (George Pal Puppetoon Series)

SUPERMAN NO. 1, Paramount.

TRUANT OFFICER DONALD, Disney, RKO Radio. (Donald Duck)

SHORT SUBJECT: ONE-REEL

ARMY CHAMPIONS, Pete Smith, MGM. (Pete Smith Specialties)

BEAUTY AND THE BEACH, Paramount. (Headliner Series)

DOWN ON THE FARM, Paramount. (Speaking of Animals)

FORTY BOYS AND A SONG, Warner Bros. (Melody Master Series)

KINGS OF THE TURF, Warner Bros. (Color Parade Series)

OF PUPS AND PUZZLES, MGM. (Passing Parade Series)

SAGEBRUSH AND SILVER, 20th Century-Fox. (Magic Carpet Series)

SHORT SUBJECT: TWO-REEL

ALIVE IN THE DEEP, Woodard Productions, Inc.

FORBIDDEN PASSAGE, MGM. (Crime Doesn't Pay)

THE GAY PARISIAN, Warner Bros. (Miniature Featurette Series)

MAIN STREET ON THE MARCH, MGM.

THE TANKS ARE COMING, Warner Bros. (National Defense Series)

ART DIRECTION—INTERIOR DECORATION

B/W

CITIZEN KANE, Mercury, RKO Radio. Perry Ferguson and Van Nest Polglase; Al Fields and Darrell Silvera.

THE FLAME OF NEW ORLEANS, Universal. Martin Obzina and Jack Otterson; Russell A. Gausman.

HOLD BACK THE DAWN, Paramount. Hans Dreier and Robert Usher; Sam Comer.

HOW GREEN WAS MY VALLEY, 20th Century-Fox. Richard Day and Nathan Juran; Thomas Little.

LADIES IN RETIREMENT, Columbia. Lionel Banks; George Montgomery.

THE LITTLE FOXES, Goldwyn, RKO Radio. Stephen Goosson; Howard Bristol.

SERGEANT YORK, Warner Bros. John Hughes; Fred MacLean.

SON OF MONTE CRISTO, Small, UA. John DuCasse Schulze; Edward G. Boyle.

SUNDOWN, Wanger, UA. Alexander Golitzen; Richard Irvine.

THAT HAMILTON WOMAN, Korda, UA. Vincent Korda; Julia Heron.

WHEN LADIES MEET, MGM. Cedric Gibbons and Randall Duell; Edwin B. Willis.

Color

BLOOD AND SAND, 20th Century-Fox. Richard Day and Joseph C. Wright; Thomas Little.

BLOSSOMS IN THE DUST, MGM. Cedric Gibbons and Urie McCleary; Edwin B. Willis.

LOUISIANA PURCHASE, Paramount. Raoul Pene du Bois; Stephen A. Seymour.

SOUND RECORDING

APPOINTMENT FOR LOVE, Universal. Universal Studio Sound Dept., Bernard B. Brown, Sound Director.

BALL OF FIRE, Goldwyn, RKO Radio. Samuel Goldwyn Studio Sound Dept., Thomas Moulton, Sound Director.

THE CHOCOLATE SOLDIER, MGM. MGM Studio Sound Dept., Douglas Shearer, Sound Director.

CITIZEN KANE, Mercury, RKO Radio. RKO Radio Studio Sound Dept., John Aalberg, Sound Director.

THE DEVIL PAYS OFF, Republic. Republic Studio Sound Dept., Charles Lootens, Sound Director.

HOW GREEN WAS MY VALLEY, 20th Century-Fox. 20th Century-Fox Studio Sound Dept., E.H. Hansen, Sound Director.

THE MEN IN HER LIFE, Columbia. Columbia Studio Sound Dept., John Livadary, Sound Director.

SERGEANT YORK, Warner Bros. Warner Bros. Studio Sound Dept., Nathan Levinson, Sound Director.

SKYLARK, Paramount. Paramount Studio Sound Dept., Loren Ryder, Sound Director.

THAT HAMILTON WOMAN, Korda, UA. General Service Studio Sound Dept., Jack Whitney, Sound Director.

TOPPER RETURNS, Roach, UA. Hal Roach Studio Sound Dept., Elmer Raguse, Sound Director.

FILM EDITING

CITIZEN KANE, Mercury, RKO Radio. Robert Wise.

DR. JEKYLL AND MR. HYDE, MGM. Harold F. Kress.

HOW GREEN WAS MY VALLEY, 20th Century-Fox. James B. Clark.

THE LITTLE FOXES, Goldwyn, RKO Radio. Daniel Mandell.

SERGEANT YORK, Warner Bros. William Holmes.

DOCUMENTARY

ADVENTURES IN THE BRONX, Film Assocs.

BOMBER, U.S. Office for Emergency Management Film Unit.

CHRISTMAS UNDER FIRE, British Ministry of Information, Warner Bros.

CHURCHILL'S ISLAND, Canadian Film Board, UA.

LETTER FROM HOME, British Ministry of Information.

LIFE OF A THOROUGHBRED, 20th Century-Fox.

NORWAY IN REVOLT, March of Time, RKO Radio.

SOLDIERS OF THE SKY, 20th Century-Fox.

WAR CLOUDS IN THE PACIFIC, Canadian Film Board.

SPECIAL AWARDS

TO REY SCOTT for his extraordinary achievement in producing *Kukan*, the film record of China's struggle, including its photography with a 16mm camera under the most difficult and dangerous conditions.

TO THE BRITISH MINISTRY OF INFORMATION for its vivid and dramatic presentation of the heroism of the RAF in the documentary film *Target For Tonight*.

TO LEOPOLD STOKOWSKI and his associates for their unique achievement in the creation of a new form of visualized music in Walt Disney's production *Fantasia*, thereby widening the scope of the motion picture as entertainment and as an art form.

TO WALT DISNEY, WILLIAM GARITY, JOHN N.A. HAWKINS and the RCA MANUFACTURING COMPANY for their outstanding contribution to the advancement of the use of sound in motion pictures through the production of *Fantasia*.

IRVING G. THALBERG MEMORIAL AWARD

TO WALT DISNEY

SCIENTIFIC OR TECHNICAL

CLASS II

ELECTRICAL RESEARCH PRODUCTS DIVISION OF WESTERN ELECTRIC CO., INC. for the development of the precision integrating sphere densitometer.

RCA MANUFACTURING CO. for the design and development of the MI-3043 Uni-directional microphone.

CLASS III

RAY WILKINSON and the PARAMOUNT STUDIO LABORATORY;

CHARLES LOOTENS and the REPUBLIC STUDIO SOUND DEPT.;

WILBUR SILVERTOOTH and the PARAMOUNT STUDIO ENGINEERING DEPT.;

PARAMOUNT PICTURES, INC., and 20TH CENTURY-FOX FILM CORP.;

DOUGLAS SHEARER and the METRO-GOLDWYN-MAYER STUDIO SOUND DEPT. and LOREN RYDER and the PARAMOUNT STUDIO SOUND DEPT.

1942

The sardine-packed crowd of stars, studio execs, and dignitaries sweated it out as Jeanette MacDonald sang every possible verse to the national anthem. Patriotic fervor peaked as two impeccably tailored buck privates, Tyrone Power and Alan Ladd, unfurled the flag with the announcement that more than 25,000 employees of the motion-picture industry had enlisted. It was an ideal setup line for Bob Hope. "The leading man shortage is so great, pretty soon we'll see Hedy Lamarr waiting to be kissed while they put a heating pad on Lewis Stone," Hope quipped.

MRS. FILIBUSTER

CEREMONY: March 4, 1943
Cocoanut Grove, Ambassador Hotel,
Los Angeles
HOST: Bob Hope

The country's most prolific songwriter, Irving Berlin, presented the music award to "someone I've known for a good many years. He's a nice kid, and I think he deserves it." With a laugh, he accepted the Oscar on his own behalf for "White Christmas."

A flurry of political speeches was occasionally interrupted by yet another Award for *Mrs. Miniver*, the night's runaway sweep. It seemed inevitable that its star, Greer Garson, would be honored as Best Actress. Even so, her jaw dropped at the mention of her name, and once on the podium she began, "I am practically unprepared." She went on to say that she felt "just like Alice in Wonderland." With that she was off on an oratorical odyssey that showed no signs of conclusion. A minute passed, then two, then three. She barely paused to take a breath. Members of the audience stifled yawns, rolled their eyes, and checked their watches. But Garson was oblivious as she unraveled her theory of competition—that there were no winners and no losers and how gracious Hollywood was to foreign-born actors. Her thoughts were heartfelt, her timing less so. Four minutes. Then five. She passed the point at which the very first Academy Awards ceremony, in 1928, had entirely completed its business. And she continued. Just shy of six minutes, her extemporaneous filibuster wound to a close and she returned to the MGM table. Astonishingly, Hope had no comment. The next day, almost everyone in Hollywood did.

Exaggeration gave birth to myth, and the Oscars of 1942 were remembered as the night Greer Garson went on for hours. Like Sally Field's "you really like me!" many years later, the unfortunate acceptance speech became the insignia of Garson's career.

BEST PICTURE/BEST DIRECTOR
WILLIAM WYLER (1902–1981)
MRS. MINIVER

Accepting the award for her husband, Mrs. Wyler said, pridefully, that he was off filming a bombing raid over Germany.

"William Wyler has directed with a sensitivity that rarely shows in films," wrote the *New York Times*'s Bosley Crowther. "Perhaps it is too soon to call this one of the greatest motion pictures ever made…One cannot speak too highly of the superb understatement and restraint exercised throughout this picture." Seeing things quite differently, Pauline Kael wrote in *The New Yorker*, "William Wyler directed this generally offensive picture… shamelessly…One of the most scandalously smug of all Academy Award winners." Though critics may have quarreled, audiences loved it. The film was a hit.

One of Hollywood's great directors, Wyler won three Academy Awards. In addition to his Best Picture and Best Director Oscars for *Mrs. Miniver*, he won the gold for *The Best Years of Our Lives* (1946) and *Ben-Hur* (1959). He was also nominated ten times for Best Picture and nine times for Best Director; thirty-six of his actors won Oscars or nominations.

During World War II, Wyler joined the service and directed two documentaries, *The Memphis Belle* and the Academy Award–winning *The Fighting Lady* (both 1944). His two most important war films bracketed the war, with *Mrs. Miniver* exploring the beginnings and *The Best Years of Our Lives* (1946) chronicling the soldiers' return home.

Among his best pictures were *Dodsworth* (1936), *Jezebel* (1938), *Wuthering Heights* (1939), *The Letter*, *The Westerner* (both 1940), and *The Little Foxes* (1941). His postwar work was equally important, and included *The Heiress* (1949), *Roman Holiday* (1953), *The Desperate Hours* (1955), his Oscar-winning epic drama *Ben-Hur* (1959), *The Children's Hour* (1962), *The Collector* (1965), and *Funny Girl* (1968). Wyler was notorious for working his actors hard.

Greer Garson, Walter Pidgeon

The envelope, please...

BEST ACTOR
JAMES CAGNEY (1899–1986)
YANKEE DOODLE DANDY

"An actor is only as good or as bad as people think he is. I am glad so many people think I was good," said Cagney, completing his speech with Cohan's famous send-off: "My mother thanks you, my father thanks you, my sisters thank you and I thank you."

Cagney learned how to be Cagney on the tough streets of New York's Lower East Side, which helped him make his mark in film with *The Public Enemy* (1931). He continued playing tough guys—*The Crowd Roars* and *Winner Take All* (both 1932)—until Prohibition turned the tables.

James Cagney (center)

Considered a troublemaker for his political activism on the part of actors, Cagney lobbied for a greater range of roles. He was able to show what a hoofer he was in *Footlight Parade* (1933). Still seeking more independence, Cagney created a production company, which got off to a bad start but came to life with *Angels with Dirty Faces* (1938, nom.), *The Roaring Twenties*, and *Each Dawn I Die* (both 1939).

The 1950s were up and down for Cagney with such quality films as *Love Me or Leave Me* (1955, nom.), *Mister Roberts*, and *Man of a Thousand Faces* (both 1957), and such losers as *Shake Hands with the Devil* (1959) and *The Gallant Hours* (1960). In 1981 Cagney came out of retirement (during which he devoted himself to painting) to appear in *Ragtime* (1981). He wrote his autobiography, *Cagney by Cagney*, in 1975.

BEST ACTRESS
GREER GARSON (1904–1996)
MRS. MINIVER

The elegant, dignified redhead made her debut in Hollywood at the ripe old age of 36 and took it by storm. Garson won six Oscar nominations for *Goodbye, Mr. Chips*, her first film (1939, nom.), *Blossoms in the Dust* (1941), *Madame Curie* (1943), *Mrs. Parkington* (1944), and *Sunrise at Campobello* (1960). But she won the gold only once, for *Mrs. Miniver*. After her success, Garson was often cast in similar "mother courage" roles but later broke out into comedy and a range of dramas. She appeared in eight films with Walter Pidgeon. In the 1950s she married an oil magnate and retired from the screen. She came out of happy retirement, however, to win an Oscar nomination for *Sunrise at Campobello* and to make a few TV and documentary appearances, including a television remake of *Little Women* in 1978.

Greer Garson with Walter Pidgeon

BEST OF 1942
Best Picture: *Mrs. Miniver*
Best Director: William Wyler, *Mrs. Miniver*
Best Actor: James Cagney, *Yankee Doodle Dandy*
Best Actress: Greer Garson, *Mrs. Miniver*
Best Supporting Actor: Van Heflin, *Johnny Eager*
Best Supporting Actress: Teresa Wright, *Mrs. Miniver*
Honorary Award: Noel Coward for *In Which We Serve*

FIRSTS
• Greer Garson's acceptance speech was the longest on record, nearly six minutes.

• *Mrs. Miniver* was the first film to earn five acting nominations.

• *The Invaders* was the first Best Picture nomination for a British-made film.

• James Cagney was the first actor to win an Oscar for a musical role.

• *Mrs. Miniver* marked Greer Garson's second in a record-breaking five consecutive nominations. From 1941 to 1945, she got the nod for *Blossoms in the Dust*, *Mrs. Miniver*, *Madame Curie*, *Mrs. Parkington*, and *The Valley of Decision*.

• The statuettes were delegated to plaster as a symbolic gesture to the war effort. Wartime winners had them replaced with the standard bronze-filled model in 1946.

SINS OF OMISSION
Picture: *Sullivan's Travels*
Actors: Joseph Cotten, *The Magnificent Ambersons*; Joel McCrea, *Sullivan's Travels*
Actress: Carole Lombard (posthumous), *To Be or Not to Be*

ALWAYS A BRIDESMAID, NEVER A BRIDE
Agnes Moorehead lost for what was considered her finest performance in *The Magnificent Ambersons*. She would strike out three more times: *Mrs. Parkington* (1944), *Johnny Belinda* (1948), and *Hush...Hush, Sweet Charlotte* (1964).

UNMENTIONABLES
• RKO exacted its revenge on resident *enfant terrible* Orson Welles. While Welles was out of the country, his *Citizen Kane* follow-up, *The Magnificent Ambersons*, was slashed by forty minutes after it received less than a favorable response from preview audiences. The edited portions were tossed onto the scrap heap. The final humiliation was its release on a double bill with the B cheapie *Mexican Spitfire Sees a Ghost*.

• Greer Garson married Richard Ney, nine years her junior, who played her son in *Mrs. Miniver*.

• Agnes Moorehead's greatest fame came with her role as Endora in the TV series *Bewitched*. Off-camera the rumor mills had her romantically linked with her devoted, early protégée, Debbie Reynolds. Moorehead was a cast member of the ill-fated *The Conqueror* (1956), which was unwittingly filmed in the Nevada desert, too close to a nuclear testing site. She died of possibly connected cancer, as did co-stars John Wayne, Susan Hayward, and Lee Van Cleef.

• Orson Welles's extraordinary Hollywood rise and fall began with *Citizen Kane* and ended with Paul Masson wine commercials and one of his final screen appearances, in *The Muppet Movie* (1979).

• As a struggling young actor, James Cagney auditioned for George M. Cohan, the stage legend he would eventually play in *Yankee Doodle Dandy*. Cohan didn't hire him.

Van Heflin with Robert Taylor

BEST SUPPORTING ACTOR
VAN HEFLIN (1910–1971)
JOHNNY EAGER

Van Heflin, an Air Force lieutenant, was one of the many men in uniform who were present at the Awards.

Van Heflin hit pay dirt early in his career with this Oscar, and though he did formidable work, it would be his first and last tango with Oscar. After a brief stage career, Heflin found his way to films playing the rugged second lead, rather than the dashing male idol. But after his Oscar win he scored leading roles as complex, intelligent, and determined heroes, the most impressive of which were in the Westerns *Shane* (1953) and *Patterns* (1956). Among his other solid efforts were *The Strange Love of Martha Ivers* (1946) and *Madame Bovary* (1949). Heflin appeared in *Airport* (1970), which was his last film. He suffered a massive heart attack while swimming at his home in Los Angeles several months later.

Teresa Wright with Richard Ney

BEST SUPPORTING ACTRESS
TERESA WRIGHT (B. 1918)
MRS. MINIVER

Upon accepting her Oscar the actress burst into tears and had to be led off the stage. Her response was consistent with her screen temperament, where she played the sweet, sensitive girl next door, and Hollywood took her straight to its heart. She earned three Academy Award nominations for her first three films—*The Little Foxes, The Pride of the Yankees* (both 1942), and *Mrs. Miniver,* for which she won the gold. Wright continued to perform in important films, including *Shadow of a Doubt* (1943), *The Best Years of Our Lives* (1946), *Miracle on 34th Street* (1955, television), *The Miracle Worker* (1957, television), and *The Rainmaker* (1999). Wright continues to work on stage and in TV movies.

AWARD NOMINATIONS 1942

PICTURE
THE INVADERS, Ortus, Columbia (British), Michael, Powell.
KINGS ROW, Warner, Bros., Hal B. Wallis.
THE MAGNIFICENT AMBERSONS, Mercury, RKO Radio, Orson Welles.
MRS. MINIVER, MGM. Sidney Franklin.
THE PIED PIPER, 20th Century-Fox, Nunnally Johnson.
THE PRIDE OF THE YANKEES, Goldwyn, RKO Radio, Samuel Goldwyn.
RANDOM HARVEST, MGM. Sidney Franklin.
THE TALK OF THE TOWN. Columbia, George Stevens.
WAKE ISLAND, Paramount, Joseph Sistrom.
YANKEE DOODLE DANDY, Warner Bros, Jack Warner and Hal. B. Wallis, with William Cagney.

ACTOR
JAMES CAGNEY in *Yankee Doodle Dandy,* Warner Bros.
RONALD COLMAN in *Random Harvest,* MGM.
GARY COOPER in *The Pride of the Yankees,* Goldwyn, RKO Radio.
WALTER PIDGEON in *Mrs. Miniver,* MGM.
MONTY WOOLLEY in *The Pied Piper,* 20th Century-Fox.

ACTRESS
BETTE DAVIS in *Now, Voyager,* Warner Bros.
GREER GARSON in *Mrs. Miniver,* MGM.
KATHARINE HEPBURN in *Woman of the Year,* MGM.
ROSALIND RUSSELL in *My Sister Eileen,* Columbia.
TERESA WRIGHT in *The Pride of the Yankees,* Goldwyn, RKO Radio.

SUPPORTING ACTOR
WILLIAM BENDIX in *Wake Island,* Paramount.
VAN HEFLIN in *Johnny Eager,* MGM.
WALTER HUSTON in *Yankee Doodle Dandy,* Warner Bros.
FRANK MORGAN in *Tortilla Flat,* MGM.
HENRY TRAVERS in *Mrs. Miniver,* MGM.

SUPPORTING ACTRESS
GLADYS COOPER in *Now, Voyager,* Warner Bros.
AGNES MOOREHEAD in *The Magnificent Ambersons,* Mercury, RKO Radio.
SUSAN PETERS in *Random Harvest,* MGM.
DAME MAY WHITTY in *Mrs. Miniver,* MGM.
TERESA WRIGHT in *Mrs. Miniver,* MGM.

DIRECTION
MICHAEL CURTIZ for *Yankee Doodle Dandy.* Warner Bros.
JOHN FARROW for *Wake Island,* Paramount.
MERVYN LeROY for *Random Harvest,* MGM.
SAM WOOD for *Kings Row,* Warner Bros.
WILLIAM WYLER for *Mrs. Miniver,* MGM.

WRITING: ORIGINAL STORY
HOLIDAY INN, Paramount. Irving Berlin.
THE INVADERS, Ortus, Columbia (British). Emeric Pressburger.
THE PRIDE OF THE YANKEES, Goldwyn, RKO Radio. Paul Gallico.
THE TALK OF THE TOWN, Columbia. Sidney Harmon.
YANKEE DOODLE DANDY, Warner Bros. Robert Buckner.

WRITING: ORIGINAL SCREENPLAY
ONE OF OUR AIRCRAFT IS MISSING, Powell, UA (British). Michael Powell and Emeric Pressburger.
THE ROAD TO MOROCCO, Paramount. Frank Butler and Don Hartman.

WAKE ISLAND, Paramount. W.R. Burnett and Frank Butler.
THE WAR AGAINST MRS. HADLEY, MGM. George Oppenheimer.
WOMAN OF THE YEAR, MGM. Michael Kanin and Ring Lardner Jr.

WRITING: SCREENPLAY
THE INVADERS, Ortus, Columbia (British). Rodney Ackland and Emeric Pressburger.
MRS. MINIVER, MGM. George Froeschel, James Hilton, Claudine West and Arthur Wimperis.
THE PRIDE OF THE YANKEES, Goldwyn, RKO Radio. Herman J. Mankiewicz and Jo Swerling.
RANDOM HARVEST, MGM. George Froeschel, Claudine West and Arthur Wimperis.
THE TALK OF THE TOWN, Columbia. Sidney Buchman and Irwin Shaw.

CINEMATOGRAPHY
B/W
KINGS ROW, Warner Bros. James Wong Howe.
THE MAGNIFICENT AMBERSONS, Mercury, RKO Radio. Stanley Cortez.
MRS. MINIVER, MGM. Joseph Ruttenberg.
MOONTIDE, 20th Century-Fox. Charles Clarke.
THE PIED PIPER, 20th Century-Fox. Edward Cronjager.
THE PRIDE OF THE YANKEES, Goldwyn, RKO Radio. Rudolph Mate.
TAKE A LETTER, DARLING, Paramount. John Mescall.
THE TALK OF THE TOWN. Columbia. Ted Tetzlaff.
TEN GENTLEMEN FROM WEST POINT, 20th Century-Fox. Leon Shamroy.
THIS ABOVE ALL, 20th Century-Fox. Arthur Miller.

Color
ARABIAN NIGHTS, Wanger, Universal. Milton Krasner, William V. Skall and W. Howard Greene.
THE BLACK SWAN, 20th Century-Fox. Leon Shamroy.
CAPTAINS OF THE CLOUDS, Warner Bros. Sol Polito.
JUNGLE BOOK, Korda, UA. W. Howard Greene.
REAP THE WILD WIND, DeMille, Paramount. Victor Milner and William V. Skall.
TO THE SHORES OF TRIPOLI, 20th Century-Fox. Edward Cronjager and William V. Skall.

ART DIRECTION—INTERIOR DECORATION
B/W
GEORGE WASHINGTON SLEPT HERE, Warner Bros. Max Parker and Mark-Lee Kirk; Casey Roberts.
THE MAGNIFICENT AMBERSONS, Mercury, RKO Radio. Albert S. D'Agostino; Al Fields and Darrell Silvera.
THE PRIDE OF THE YANKEES, Goldwyn, RKO Radio. Perry Ferguson; Howard Bristol.
RANDOM HARVEST, MGM. Cedric Gibbons and Randall Duell; Edwin B. Willis and Jack Moore.
THE SHANGHAI GESTURE, Pressburger, UA. Boris Leven.
SILVER QUEEN, Sherman, UA. Ralph Berger; Emile Kuri.
THE SPOILERS, Universal. John B. Goodman and Jack Otterson; Russell A. Gausman and Edward R. Robinson.
TAKE A LETTER, DARLING, Paramount. Hans Dreier and Roland Anderson; Sam Comer.
THE TALK OF THE TOWN, Columbia. Lionel Banks and Rudolph Sternad; Flay Babcock.
THIS ABOVE ALL, 20th Century-Fox. Richard Day and Joseph Wright; Thomas Little.

Color
ARABIAN NIGHTS, Wanger, Universal. Alexander Golitzen and Jack Otterson; Russell A. Gausman and Ira S. Webb.
CAPTAINS OF THE CLOUDS, Warner Bros. Ted Smith; Casey Roberts.
JUNGLE BOOK, Korda, UA. Vincent Korda; Julia Heron.
MY GAL SAL, 20th Century-Fox. Richard Day and Joseph Wright; Thomas Little.
REAP THE WILD WIND, DeMille, Paramount. Hans Dreier and Roland Anderson; George Sawley.

SOUND RECORDING
ARABIAN NIGHTS, Universal. Universal Studio Sound Dept., Bernard B. Brown, Sound Director.
BAMBI, Disney, RKO Radio. Walt Disney Studio Sound Dept., Sam Slyfield, Sound Director.
FLYING TIGERS, Republic. Republic Studio Sound Dept., Daniel Bloomberg, Sound Director.

FRIENDLY ENEMIES, Small, UA. Sound Service, Inc., Jack Whitney, Sound Director.
THE GOLD RUSH, Chaplin, UA. RCA Sound, James Fields, Sound Director.
MRS. MINIVER, MGM. MGM Studio Sound Dept., Douglas Shearer, Sound Director.
ONCE UPON A HONEYMOON, RKO Radio. RKO Radio Studio Sound Dept., Steve Dunn, Sound Director.
THE PRIDE OF THE YANKEES, Goldwyn, RKO Radio. Samuel Goldwyn Studio Sound Dept., Thomas Moulton, Sound Director.
ROAD TO MOROCCO, Paramount. Paramount Studio Sound Dept., Loren Ryder, Sound Director.
THIS ABOVE ALL, 20th Century-Fox. 20th Century-Fox Studio Sound Dept., E.H. Hansen, Sound Director.
YANKEE DOODLE DANDY, Warner Bros. Warner Bros. Studio Sound Dept., Nathan Levinson, Sound Director.
YOU WERE NEVER LOVELIER, Columbia. Columbia Studio Sound Dept., John Livadary, Sound Director.

FILM EDITING
MRS. MINIVER, MGM. Harold F. Kress.
THE PRIDE OF THE YANKEES, Goldwyn, RKO Radio. Daniel Mandell.
THE TALK OF THE TOWN, Columbia. Otto Meyer.
THIS ABOVE ALL, 20th Century-Fox. Walter Thompson.
YANKEE DOODLE DANDY, Warner Bros. George Amy.

SPECIAL EFFECTS
THE BLACK SWAN, 20th Century-Fox. Fred Sersen, Roger Herman and George Leverett.
DESPERATE JOURNEY, Warner Bros. Byron Haskin and Nathan Levinson.
FLYING TIGERS, Republic. Howard Lydecker and Daniel J. Bloomberg.
INVISIBLE AGENT, Universal. John Fulton and Bernard B. Brown.
JUNGLE BOOK, Korda, UA. Lawrence Butler and William H. Wilmarth.
MRS. MINIVER, MGM. A. Arnold Gillespie, Warren Newcombe and Douglas Shearer.
THE NAVY COMES THROUGH, RKO Radio. Vernon L. Walker and James G. Stewart.
ONE OF OUR AIRCRAFT IS MISSING, Powell, UA (British). Ronald Neame and C.C. Stevens.
THE PRIDE OF THE YANKEES, Goldwyn, RKO Radio. Jack Cosgrove, Ray Binger and Thomas T. Moulton.
REAP THE WILD WIND, DeMille, Paramount. Farciot Edouart, Gordon Jennings, William L. Pereira and Louis Mesenkop.

SHORT SUBJECT: CARTOON
ALL OUT FOR V, 20th Century-Fox.
THE BLITZ WOLF, MGM.
DER FUEHRER'S FACE, Disney, RKO Radio.
JUICE BOX JAMBOREE, Lantz, Universal.
PIGS IN A POLKA, Schlesinger, Warner Bros.
TULIPS SHALL GROW, Paramount. (George Pal Puppetoon)

SHORT SUBJECT: ONE-REEL
DESERT WONDERLAND, 20th Century-Fox. (Magic Carpet Series)
MARINES IN THE MAKING, MGM. (Pete Smith Specialties)
SPEAKING OF ANIMALS AND THEIR FAMILIES, Paramount. (Speaking of Animals)
UNITED STATES MARINE BAND, Warner Bros. (Melody Master Bands)

SHORT SUBJECT: TWO-REEL
BEYOND THE LINE OF DUTY, Warner Bros. (Broadway Brevities)
DON'T TALK, MGM. (Two-reel Special)
PRIVATE SMITH OF THE U.S.A., RKO Radio. (This is America Series)

SONG
ALWAYS IN MY HEART (*Always in My Heart*, Warner Bros.); Music by Ernesto Lecuona. Lyrics by Kim Gannon.
DEARLY BELOVED (*You Were Never Lovelier*, Columbia); Music by Jerome Kern. Lyrics by Johnny Mercer.
HOW ABOUT YOU? (*Babes on Broadway*, MGM); Music by Burton Lane. Lyrics by Ralph Freed.
IT SEEMS I HEARD THAT SONG BEFORE (*Youth on Parade*, Republic); Music by Jule Styne. Lyrics by Sammy Cahn.

I'VE GOT A GAL IN KALAMAZOO (*Orchestra Wives*, 20th Century-Fox); Music by Harry Warren. Lyrics by Mack Gordon.
LOVE IS A SONG (*Bambi*, Disney, RKO Radio); Music by Frank Churchill. Lyrics by Larry Morey.
PENNIES FOR PEPPINO (*Flying with Music*, Roach, UA); Music by Edward Ward. Lyrics by Chet Forrest and Bob Wright.
PIG FOOT PETE (*Keep 'Em Flying*, Universal); Music by Gene de Paul. Lyrics by Don Raye.
THERE'S A BREEZE ON LAKE LOUISE (*The Mayor of 44th Street*, RKO Radio); Music by Harry Revel. Lyrics by Mort Greene.
WHITE CHRISTMAS (Holiday Inn, Paramount); Music and Lyrics by Irving Berlin.

SCORING: DRAMA/COMEDY
ARABIAN NIGHTS, Universal. Frank Skinner.
BAMBI, Disney, RKO Radio. Frank Churchill and Edward Plumb.
THE BLACK SWAN, 20th Century-Fox. Alfred Newman.
THE CORSICAN BROTHER, Small, UA. Dimitri Tiomkin.
FLYING TIGERS, Republic. Victor Young.
THE GOLD RUSH, Chaplin, UA. Max Terr.
I MARRIED A WITCH, Cinema Guild, UA. Roy Webb.
JOAN OF PARIS, RKO Radio. Roy Webb.
JUNGLE BOOK, Korda, UA. Miklos Rozsa.
KLONDIKE FURY, Monogram. Edward Kay.
NOW, VOYAGER, Warner Bros. Max Steiner.
THE PRIDE OF THE YANKEES, Goldwyn, RKO Radio. Leigh Harline.
RANDOM HARVEST, MGM. Herbert Stothart.
THE SHANGHAI GESTURE, Pressburger, UA. Richard Hageman.
SILVER QUEEN, Sherman, UA. Victor Young.
TAKE A LETTER, DARLING, Paramount. Victor Young.
THE TALK OF THE TOWN, Columbia. Frederick Hollander and Morris Stoloff.
TO BE OR NOT TO BE, Lubitsch, UA. Werner Heymann.

SCORING: MUSICAL
FLYING WITH MUSIC, Roach, UA. Edward Ward.
FOR ME AND MY GAL, MGM. Roger Edens and Georgie Stoll.
HOLIDAY INN, Paramount. Robert Emmett Dolan.
IT STARTED WITH EVE, Universal. Charles Previn and Hans Salter.
JOHNNY DOUGHBOY, Republic. Walter Scharf.
MY GAL SAL, 20th Century-Fox. Alfred Newman.
YANKEE DOODLE DANDY, Warner Bros. Ray Heindorf and Heinz Roemheld.
YOU WERE NEVER LOVELIER, Columbia. Leigh Harline.

DOCUMENTARY
AFRICA, PRELUDE TO VICTORY, March of Time, 20th Century-Fox.
BATTLE OF MIDWAY, U.S. Navy, 20th Century-Fox.
COMBAT REPORT, U.S. Army Signal Corps.
CONQUER BY THE CLOCK, Office of War Information, RKO Pathe. Frederic Ullman, Jr.
THE GRAIN THAT BUILT A HEMISPHERE, Coordinator's Office, Motion Picture Society for the Americas. Walt Disney.
HENRY BROWNE, FARMER, U.S. Department of Agriculture, Republic.
HIGH OVER THE BORDERS, Canadian National Film Board.
HIGH STAKES IN THE EAST, Netherlands Information Bureau.
INSIDE FIGHTING CHINA, Canadian National Film Board.
IT'S EVERYBODY'S WAR, Office of War Information, 20th Century-Fox.
KOKODA FRONT LINE, Australian News Information Bureau.
LISTEN TO BRITAIN, British Ministry of Information.
LITTLE BELGIUM, Belgian Ministry of Information.
LITTLE ISLES OF FREEDOM, Warner Bros. Victor Stoloff and Edgar Loew.
MR. BLABBERMOUTH, Office of War Information, MGM.
MR. GARDENIA JONES, Office of War Information, MGM.
MOSCOW STRIKES BACK, Artkino (Russian).

NEW SPIRIT, U.S. Treasury Department, Walt Disney.
PRELUDE TO WAR, U.S. Army Special Services.
THE PRICE OF VICTORY, Office of War Information, Paramount. Pine-Thomas.
A SHIP IS BORN, U.S. Merchant Marine, Warner Bros.
TWENTY-ONE MILES, British Ministry of Information.
WE REFUSE TO DIE, Office of War Information, Paramount. William C. Thomas.
WHITE EAGLE, Cocanen Films.
WINNING YOUR WINGS, U.S. Army Air Force, Warner Bros.

SPECIAL AWARDS
TO CHARLES BOYER for his progressive cultural achievement in establishing the French Research Foundation in Los Angeles as a source of reference for the Hollywood motion-picture industry.
TO NOEL COWARD for his outstanding production achievement in *In Which We Serve*.
TO METRO-GOLDWYN-MAYER STUDIO for its achievement in representing the American way of life in the production of the *Andy Hardy* series of films.

IRVING G. THALBERG MEMORIAL AWARD
TO SIDNEY FRANKLIN

SCIENTIFIC OR TECHNICAL
CLASS II
CARROLL CLARK, F. THOMAS THOMPSON and the RKO RADIO STUDIO ART and MINIATURE DEPARTMENTS for the design and construction of a moving cloud and horizon machine.
DANIEL B. CLARK and the 20TH CENTURY-FOX CORP. for the development of a lens calibration system and the application of this system to exposure control in cinematography.

CLASS III
ROBERT HENDERSON and the PARAMOUNT STUDIO ENGINEERING and TRANSPARENCY DEPARTMENTS;
DANIEL J. BLOOMBERG and the REPUBLIC STUDIO SOUND DEPARTMENT.

1943

"Awards are meaningless for actors, unless they all play the same part."
—Bogart upon learning of his nomination for Casablanca

Three months before D-Day, Roosevelt and Churchill convened in Casablanca to map out a final strategy to crush the Axis powers. It proved perfect timing for the release of *Casablanca,* the film. A box-office smash—but a dark horse for the Oscar—it won Best Picture. Why a dark horse? It was a big year for far more sentimen-

ON THE HOLLYWOOD FRONT

**CEREMONY: March 2, 1944
Grauman's Chinese Theatre,
Hollywood
HOST: Jack Benny**

tal, patriotic war films, such as *Watch on the Rhine* and *For Whom the Bell Tolls,* than for Bogie's cynical and disaffected bar owner turned patriot. Hollywood thought of itself as the fourth wing of the armed services, galvanizing Americans for the final chapters of World War II. In many instances, Academy members followed suit by voting with a flag-waving high-mindedness rather than

with their best judgment: the award for Best Actor went to Paul Lukas for the flawlessly virtuous role of a German anti-Nazi agent in *Watch on the Rhine,* and to newcomer Jennifer Jones for her role as a canonized farm girl in the religious drama and commercial hit of the year, *The Song of Bernadette. Casablanca*'s nominee, Ingrid Bergman, playing her breakthrough role as a passion-rocked woman with a past, was sinfully under-acknowledged.

In yet another act of patriotism, Bette "If Hollywood is royalty, then I'm its queen" Davis won her campaign to open Academy doors to the public for the first time, and free passes were given to hundreds of men and women in uniform. Today's all-singing, all-dancing Academy Award extravaganza owes its existence to that night when the Academy put on its first "show" to demonstrate how Hollywood entertained its troops abroad. But neither a tuxedo nor a bejeweled gown—not even a cocktail—could be found that evening in further deference to the raging war.

**BEST PICTURE/BEST DIRECTOR
MICHAEL CURTIZ
*CASABLANCA***

Casablanca was that rare concurrence of popular appeal and subtle artistry. It's hard to imagine that a film that has become a classic began with both stars making desperate attempts to ditch their parts. "This is the worst film we've ever come across," said Bogie. "It's just a fright," Bergman complained. It all worked out in the end. *Casablanca* put Bergman on the map and defined Bogart's dissolute but idealistic character from here on.

Best Director Hungarian-born Michael Curtiz (1888-1962) had a long and stunning career that included *Angels with Dirty Faces* (1938), starring Jimmy Cagney, and *Life with Father* (1947). Accepting his Oscar for *Casablanca,* he mistakenly told the bemused audience in his tortured English, "So many times I have a speech ready but no dice. Always a bridesmaid, never a mother." A master of the film arts but obviously not of the English language, he also once directed Gary Cooper, in *Bright Leaf* (1980), to "ride off in all directions."

Paul Henreid, Ingrid Bergman, Humphrey Bogart

The envelope, please...

Bette Davis with Paul Lukas

BEST ACTOR
PAUL LUKAS (1887–1971)
WATCH ON THE RHINE

Reporters noted that Lukas was so flummoxed when he received the statuette that he nearly dropped it.

A Hungarian-born ex-wrestler, Paul Lukas "was finally back on the Hollywood heap," according to Hedda Hopper, with this role as a virtuous anti-Nazi agent. Compared with Lukas's higher-calling role, Bogart's complex part as the cynical, alcoholic bar owner wasn't quite inspirational enough for Oscar.

After fifteen years in the typecasting doldrums (always the Continental playboy or the suave villain), Lukas emerged in Hitchcock's *The Lady Vanishes* (1938) and later in *Tender Is the Night* (1962). His thick accent held him back, however, and his follow-up supporting roles were simply repeat performances.

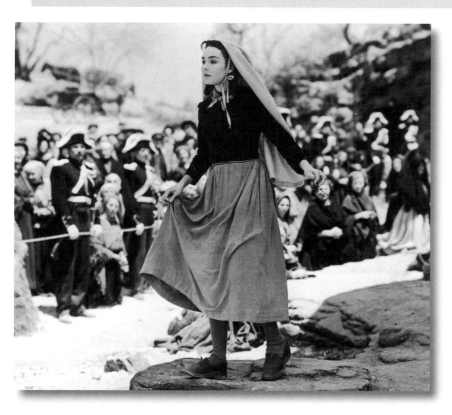

BEST ACTRESS
JENNIFER JONES (B. 1919)
THE SONG OF BERNADETTE

Jones burst into tears upon accepting the Award.

The ultimate Hollywood Cinderella story, Jones was rescued from obscurity by producer-director David O. Selznick and given Oscar-anointed sainthood as Bernadette, a young French girl who claims to have seen the Virgin Mary in a vision.

Selznick constructed her stardom and squelched her secret teen marriage to deeply troubled Robert Walker. Jones went on to play many successful, Oscar-nominated roles, including *Since You Went Away* (1944, nom.) and *Love Letters* (1945, nom.). She was wildly miscast—though nominated for an Oscar—in *Duel in the Sun* (1947), but triumphed in *Sister Carrie* (1952). Jones appeared in consistently fine performances in such films as *Madame Bovary* (1949), *Love Is a Many Splendored Thing* (1955, nom.), *The Man in the Gray Flannel Suit* (1956), *A Farewell to Arms* (1957), and *Tender Is the Night* (1961).

Selznick, who became Jones's husband in 1949, died in 1965, and she lost interest in her career. Her son, Robert Walker Jr., is also an actor (and a double of his father).

BEST OF 1943
Best Picture: *Casablanca*
Best Director: Michael Curtiz, *Casablanca*
Best Actor: Paul Lukas, *Watch on the Rhine*
Best Actress: Jennifer Jones, *Song of Bernadette*
Best Supporting Actor: Charles Coburn, *The More the Merrier*
Best Supporting Actress: Katina Patoux, *For Whom the Bell Tolls*

SINS OF OMISSION
Picture: *Shadow of a Doubt, Old Acquaintance, Hangmen Also Die, Cabin in the Sky, The Cat People, I Walked with a Zombie*
Actress: Ida Lupino for *The Hard Way*

UNMENTIONABLES
• Height-challenged Bogart had to wear platform shoes to play alongside statuesque Bergman.

• Darryl Zanuck cast his mistress, Linda Darnell, as the Virgin Mary in *The Song of Bernadette*.

• Another loser that year, Jean Arthur, was a veteran actress, who had appeared in such films as *Mr. Deeds Goes to Town, You Can't Take it with You*, and *Mr. Smith Goes to Washington*. She was Frank Capra's favorite actress despite his misgivings: "You can't get her in front of the camera without her crying, whining, vomiting, all that [expletive] she does. But when she does get in front of the camera, and you turn on the lights — wow!" Despite Arthur's sensational career, 1943 was her first nomination for the feisty, lovable underdog trapped in a dull life in *The More the Merrier*. She lost.

FIRSTS
• Oscars are made of plaster because metals were too precious during wartime.

• The Awards ceremony moved from an intimate, insiders-only banquet at Cocoanut Grove in Los Angeles to a massive public venue at Grauman's Chinese Theatre, with a seating capacity of 2,258.

• Best supporting actors and actresses finally received full-bodied Oscars rather than the miniature Oscar-on-a-plaque.

• For the first time in six years running, Bette Davis failed to win a nomination.

ROLE REVERSALS
Instead of Bogie and Bergman, the leading roles in *Casablanca* were originally slated for—are you ready?—Ronald Reagan and Hedy Lamarr.

BEST SUPPORTING ACTOR
CHARLES COBURN (1877–1961)
THE MORE THE MERRIER

"Yes, I'll accept the prize. You don't have to urge me." Everyone laughed when Coburn said, "I hope that at the end of another fifty years of service in the theater, your children and your children's children will have enough courage to vote for me again."

Playing Benjamin Dingle in the charming, funny *The More the Merrier*, Coburn slipped easily into the role of a sly matchmaker for Jean Arthur and Joel McCrea when the three wind up sharing an apartment in an overcrowded, wartime D.C. boardinghouse. A former theater manager who at one time ran his own acting troupe, Coburn entered film in 1938, at the age of 58. The combination of aristocratic Southern gentleman and slightly shady, affable cantankerousness that characterized his persona lent itself to dozens of hits, such as *The Lady Eve*

(1941), *Kings Row* (1942), and *Gentlemen Prefer Blondes* (1953). At the age of 80, Coburn starred in *How to Murder a Rich Uncle* (1957), and two years later he was cast as Benjamin Franklin in *John Paul Jones* (1959).

BEST SUPPORTING ACTRESS
KATINA PAXINOU (1900–1973)
FOR WHOM THE BELL TOLLS

In her stunning, somber acceptance speech, Paxinou—a Greek political radical—suggested that her fellow actors in the underground back home were probably all dead.

Paxinou was born to play Pilar, the Spanish Civil War revolutionary in *For Whom the Bell Tolls*. Earth mother of the Greek theater and a trench fighter in the underground, Paxinou claimed that her "grandmother learned her ABC's from a guerrilla chieftain in a cave." After only a few films in Hollywood (most prominently *Mourning Becomes Electra*, in 1947), she returned to Athens with her husband to found the Royal Theatre of Athens.

AWARD NOMINATIONS 1943

PICTURE
CASABLANCA, Warner Bros, Hal B. Wallis.
FOR WHOM THE BELL TOLLS, Paramount, Sam Wood.
HEAVEN CAN WAIT, 20th Century-Fox, Ernst Lubitsch.
THE HUMAN COMEDY, MGM, Clarence Brown.
IN WHICH WE SERVE, Two Cities, UA (British), Noel Coward.
MADAME CURIE, MGM, Sidney Franklin.
THE MORE THE MERRIER, Columbia, George Stevens.
THE OX-BOW INCIDENT, 20th Century-Fox, Lamar Trotti.
THE SONG OF BERNADETTE, 20th Century-Fox, William Perlberg.
WATCH ON THE RHINE, Warner Bros, Hal B. Wallis.

ACTOR
HUMPHREY BOGART in *Casablanca*, Warner Bros.
GARY COOPER in *For Whom the Bell Tolls*, Paramount.
PAUL LUKAS in *Watch on the Rhine*, Warner Bros.
WALTER PIDGEON in *Madame Curie*, MGM.
MICKEY ROONEY in *The Human Comedy*, MGM.

ACTRESS
JEAN ARTHUR in *The More the Merrier*, Columbia.
INGRID BERGMAN in *For Whom the Bell Tolls*, Paramount.
JOAN FONTAINE in *The Constant Nymph*, Warner Bros.
GREER GARSON in *Madame Curie*, MGM.
JENNIFER JONES in *The Song of Bernadette*, 20th Century-Fox.

SUPPORTING ACTOR
CHARLES BICKFORD in *The Song of Bernadette*, 20th Century-Fox.
CHARLES COBURN in *The More the Merrier*, Columbia.
J. CARROL NAISH in *Sahara*, Columbia.
CLAUDE RAINS in *Casablanca*, Warner Bros.
AKIM TAMIROFF in *For Whom the Bell Tolls*, Paramount.

SUPPORTING ACTRESS
GLADYS COOPER in *The Song of Bernadette*, 20th Century-Fox.
PAULETTE GODDARD in *So Proudly We Hail*, Paramount.
KATINA PAXINOU in *For Whom the Bell Tolls*, Paramount.
ANNE REVERE in *The Song of Bernadette*, 20th Century-Fox.
LUCILE WATSON in *Watch on the Rhine*, Warner Bros.

DIRECTION
CLARENCE BROWN for *The Human Comedy*, MGM.
MICHAEL CURTIZ for *Casablanca*, Warner Bros.
HENRY KING for *The Song of Bernadette*, 20th Century-Fox.
ERNST LUBITSCH for *Heaven Can Wait*, 20th Century-Fox.
GEORGE STEVENS for *The More the Merrier*, Columbia.

WRITING: ORIGINAL STORY
ACTION IN THE NORTH ATLANTIC, Warner Bros. Guy Gilpatric.

DESTINATION TOKYO, Warner Bros. Steve Fisher.
THE HUMAN COMEDY, MGM. William Saroyan.
THE MORE THE MERRIER, Columbia, Frank Ross and Robert Russell.
SHADOW OF A DOUBT, Universal, Gordon McDonnell.

WRITING: ORIGINAL SCREENPLAY
AIR FORCE, Warner Bros. Dudley Nichols.
IN WHICH WE SERVE, Two-Cities-UA (British). Noel Coward.
THE NORTH STAR, Goldwyn, RKO Radio. Lillian Hellman.
PRINCESS O'ROURKE, Warner Bros. Norman Krasna.
SO PROUDLY WE HAIL, Paramount. Allan Scott.

WRITING: SCREENPLAY
CASABLANCA, Warner Bros. Julius J. Epstein, Philip G. Epstein and Howard Koch.
HOLY MATRIMONY, 20th Century-Fox. Nunnally Johnson.
THE MORE THE MERRIER, Columbia. Richard Flournoy, Lewis R. Roster, Frank Ross and Robert Russell.
THE SONG OF BERNADETTE, 20th Century-Fox. George Seaton.
WATCH ON THE RHINE, Warner Bros. Dashiell Hammett.

CINEMATOGRAPHY
B/W
AIR FORCE, Warner Bros. James Wong Howe, Elmer Dyer and Charles Marshall.
CASABLANCA, Warner Bros. Arthur Edeson.
CORVETTE K-225, Universal. Tony Gaudio.
FIVE GRAVES TO CAIRO, Paramount. John Seitz.
THE HUMAN COMEDY, MGM. Harry Stradling.
MADAME CURIE, MGM. Joseph Ruttenberg.
THE NORTH STAR, Goldwyn, RKO Radio. James Wong Howe.
SAHARA, Columbia. Rudolph Mate.
SO PROUDLY WE HAIL, Paramount. Charles Lang.
THE SONG OF BERNADETTE, 20th Century-Fox. Arthur Miller.

Color
FOR WHOM THE BELL TOLLS, Paramount, Ray Rennahan.
HEAVEN CAN WAIT, 20th Century-Fox. Edward Cronjager.
HELLO, FRISCO, HELLO, 20th Century-Fox. Charles G. Clarke and Allen Davey.
LASSIE COME HOME, MGM. Leonard Smith.
THE PHANTOM OF THE OPERA, Universal. Hal Mohr and W. Howard Greene.
THOUSANDS CHEER, MGM. George Folsey.

ART DIRECTION-INTERIOR DECORATION
B/W
FIVE GRAVES TO CAIRO, Paramount. Hans Dreier and Ernst Fegte; Bertram Granger.
FLIGHT FOR FREEDOM, RKO Radio. Albert S. D'Agostino and Carroll Clark; Darrell Silvera and Harley Miller.
MADAME CURIE, MGM. Cedric Gibbons and Paul Groesse; Edwin B. Willis and Hugh Hunt.
MISSION TO MOSCOW, Warner Bros. Carl Weyl; George J. Hopkins.
THE NORTH STAR, Goldwyn, RKO Radio. Parry Ferguson; Howard Bristol.
THE SONG OF BERNADETTE, 20th Century-Fox. James Basevi and William Darling; Thomas Little.

Color
FOR WHOM THE BELL TOLLS, Paramount. Hans Dreir and Haldane Douglas; Bertram Granger.
THE GANG'S ALL HERE, 20th Century-Fox. James Basevi and Joseph C. Wright; Thomas Little.
THE PHANTOM OF THE OPERA, Universal. Alexander Golitzen and John B. Goodman; Russell A. Gausman and Ira S. Webb.
THIS IS THE ARMY, Warner Bros. John Hughes and Lt. John Koenig; George J. Hopkins.
THOUSANDS CHEER, MGM. Cedric Gibbons and Daniel Cathcart; Edwin B. Willis and Jacques Mersereau.

SOUND RECORDING
HANGMEN ALSO DIE, Pressburger, UA. Sound Service, Inc., Jack Whitney, Sound Director.
IN OLD OKLAHOMA, Republic. Republic Studio Sound Dept., Daniel J. Bloomberg, Sound Director.
MADAME CURIE. MGM. MGM. Studio Sound Dept., Douglas Shearer, Sound Director.
THE NORTH STAR, Goldwyn, RKO Radio. Samuel Goldwyn Studio Sound Dept., Thomas Moulton, Sound Director.

THE PHANTOM OF THE OPERA, Universal. Universal Studio Sound Dept., Bernard B. Brown, Sound Director.
RIDING HIGH, Paramount. Paramount Studio Sound Dept., Loren L. Ryder, Sound Director.
SAHARA, Columbia. Columbia Studio Sound Dept., John Livadary, Sound Director.
SALUDOS. AMIGOS, Disney, RKO Radio. Walt Disney Studio Sound Dept., C.O. Slyfield, Sound Director.
SO THIS IS WASHINGTON, Votion, RKO Radio. RCA Sound, J.L. Fields, Sound Director.
THE SONG OF BERNADETTE, 20th Century-Fox. 20th Century-Fox Studio Sound Dept., E.H. Hansen, Sound Director.
THIS IS THE ARMY, Warner Bros. Warner Bros. Studio Sound Dept., Nathan Levinson, Sound Director.
THIS LAND IS MINE, RKO Radio. RKO Radio Studio Sound Dept., Stephen Dunn, Sound Director.

FILM EDITING
AIR FORCE, Warner Bros. George Amy.
CASABLANCA, Warner Bros. Owen Marks.
FIVE GRAVES TO CAIRO, Paramount. Doane Harrison.
FOR WHOM THE BELL TOLLS, Paramount. Sherman Todd and John Link.
THE SONG OF BERNADETTE, 20th Century-Fox. Barbara McLean.

SPECIAL EFFECTS
AIR FORCE, Warner Bros. Hans Koenekamp, Rex Wimpy and Nathan Levinson.
BOMBARDIER, RKO Radio. Vernon L. Walker, James G. Stewart and Roy Granville.
CRASH DIVE, 20th Century-Fox. Fred Semen and Roger Heman.
THE NORTH STAR, Goldwyn, RKO Radio. Clarence Slifer, R.O. Binger and Thomas T. Moulton.
SO PROUDLY WE HAIL, Paramount. Farciot Edouart, Gordon Jennings and George Dutton.
STAND BY FOR ACTION, MGM. A. Arnold Gillespie, Donald Jahraus and Michael Steinore.

SONG
CHANGE OF HEART (*Hit Parade of 1943*, Republic); Music by Jule Styne. Lyrics by Harold Adamson.
HAPPINESS IS A THING CALLED JOE (*Cabin in the Sky*, MGM); Music by Harold Arlen. Lyrics by E.Y. Harburg.
MY SHINING HOUR (*The Sky's the Limit*, RKO Radio); Music by Harold Arlen. Lyrics by Johnny Mercer.
SALUDOS AMIGOS (*Saludos Amigos*, Disney, RKO Radio); Music by Charles Wolcott. Lyrics by Ned Washington.
SAY A PRAYER FOR THE BOYS OVER THERE (*Hers to Hold*, Universal); Music by Jimmy McHugh. Lyrics by Herb Magidson.
THAT OLD BLACK MAGIC (*Star Spangled Rhythm*, Paramount); Music by Harold Arlen. Lyrics by Johnny Mercer.
THEY'RE EITHER TOO YOUNG OR TOO OLD (*Thank Your Lucky Stars*, Warner Bros.); Music by Arthur Schwartz. Lyrics by Frank Loesser.
WE MUSTN'T SAY GOOD BYE (*Stage Door Canteen*, Lesser, UA); Music by James Monaco. Lyrics by Al Dubin.
YOU'D BE SO NICE TO COME HOME TO (*Something to Shout About*, Columbia); Music and Lyrics by Cole Porter.
YOU'LL NEVER KNOW (*Hello, Frisco, Hello*, 20th Century-Fox); Music by Harry Warren. Lyrics by Mack Gordon.

SCORING: DRAMA/COMEDY
THE AMAZING MRS. HOLLIDAY, Universal. Hans J. Salter and Frank Skinner.
CASABLANCA, Warner Bros. Max Steiner.
THE COMMANDOS STRIKE AT DAWN, Columbia. Louis Gruenberg and Morris Stoloff.
THE FALLEN SPARROW, RKO Radio. C. Bakaleinikoff and Roy Webb.
FOR WHOM THE BELL TOLLS, Paramount. Victor Young
HANGMEN ALSO DIE, Pressburger, UA. Hanns Eisler.
HI DIDDLE DIDDLE, Stone, UA. Phil Boutelje.
IN OLD OKLAHOMA, Republic. Walter Scharf.
JOHNNY COME LATELY, Cagney, UA. Leigh Harline.
THE KANSAN. Sherman, UA. Gerard Carbonara.
LADY OF BURLESQUE, Stromberg, UA. Arthur Lange.
MADAME CURIE, MGM. Herbert Stothart.
THE MOON AND SIXPENCE, Loew-Lewin, UA. Dimitn Tiomkin.

THE NORTH STAR, Goldwyn, RKO Radio. Aaron Copland.
THE SONG OF BERNADETTE. 20th Century-Fox. Alfred Newman.
VICTORY THROUGH AIR POWER. Disney, UA. Edward H. Plumb, Paul J. Smith and Oliver G. Wallace.

SCORING: MUSICAL
CONEY ISLAND, 20th Century-Fox. Alfred Newman.
HIT PARADE OF 1943, Republic. Walter Schart.
THE PHANTOM OF THE OPERA, Universal. Edward Ward.
SALUDOS AMIGOS, Disney, RKO Radio. Edward H. Plumb, Paul J. Smith and Charles Wolcott.
THE SKY'S THE LIMIT. RKO Radio. Leigh Harline.
SOMETHING TO SHOUT ABOUT, Columbia. Morris Stoloff.
STAGE DOOR CANTEEN, Lesser, UA. Frederic E. Rich.
STAR SPANGLED RHYTHM. Paramount. Robert Emmett Dolan.
THIS IS THE ARMY, Warner Bros. Ray Heindorf.
THOUSANDS CHEER, MGM. Herbert Stothart.

SHORT SUBJECT: CARTOON
THE DIZZY ACROBAT, Lantz, Universal. Walter Lantz, producer.
THE FIVE HUNDRED HATS OF BARTHOLOMEW CUBBINS, Paramount (Puppetoon). George Pal, producer.
GREETINGS, BAIT, Warner Bros. Leon Schlesinger, producer.
IMAGINATION, Columbia. Dave Fleischer, producer.
REASON AND EMOTION, Disney, RKO Radio. Walt Disney, producer.
YANKEE DOODLE MOUSE. MGM. Frederick Quimby, producer.

SHORT SUBJECT: ONE-REEL
AMPHIBIOUS FIGHTERS, Paramount. Grantland Rice, producer.
CAVALCADE OF THE DANCE WITH VELOZ AND YOLANDA, Warner Bros. (Melody Master Bands). Gordon Hollingshead, producer.
CHAMPIONS CARRY ON, 20th Century-Fox. (Sports Reviews). Edmund Reek, producer.
HOLLYWOOD IN UNIFORM, Columbia. (Screen Snapshots). Ralph Staub, producer.
SEEING HANDS, MG-M. (Pete Smith Specialty). Pete Smith, producer.

SHORT SUBJECT: TWO-REEL
HEAVENLY MUSIC, MGM. Jerry Bresler and Sam Coslow, producers.
LETTER TO A HERO, RKO Radio. (This Is America). Fred Ullman, producer.
MARDI GRAS, Paramount. (Musical Parade). Walter MacEwen, producer.
WOMEN AT WAR, Warner Bros. (Technicolor Special). Gordon Hollingshead, producer.

DOCUMENTARY: SHORT SUBJECT
CHILDREN OF MARS, This Is America Series, RKO Radio.
DECEMBER 7TH, U.S. Navy, Field Photographic Branch, Office of Strategic Services.
PLAN FOR DESTRUCTION, MGM.
SWEDES IN AMERICA, Office of War Information, Overseas Motion Picture Bureau.
TO THE PEOPLE OF THE UNITED STATES, U.S. Public Health Service, Walter Wanger Prods.
TOMORROW WE FLY, U.S. Navy, Bureau of Aeronautics.
YOUTH IN CRISIS, March of Time, 20th Century-Fox.

DOCUMENTARY: FEATURES
BAPTISM OF FIRE, U.S. Army, Fighting Men Series.
BATTLE OF RUSSIA, Special Service Division of the War Department.
DESERT VICTORY, British Ministry of Information.
REPORT FROM THE ALEUTIANS, U.S. Army Pictorial Service, Combat Film Series.
WAR DEPARTMENT REPORT, Field Photographic Branch, Office of Strategic Services.

SPECIAL AWARDS
TO GEORGE PAL for the development of novel methods and techniques in the production of short subjects known as Puppetoons.

IRVING G. THALBERG MEMORIAL AWARD
TO HAL B. WALLIS

SCIENTIFIC OR TECHNICAL
CLASS II
FARCIOT EDOUART, EARLE MORGAN, BARTON THOMPSON and the PARAMOUNT STUDIO ENGINEERING and TRANSPARENCY DEPARTMENTS for the development and practical application to motion-picture production of a method of duplicating and enlarging natural color photographs, transferring the image emulsions to glass plates and projecting these slides by especially designed stereopticon equipment.
PHOTO PRODUCTS DEPARTMENT, E.I. duPONT de NEMOURS AND CO., INC. for the development of fine-grain motion-picture films.

CLASS III
DANIEL J. BLOOMBERG and the REPUBLIC STUDIO SOUND DEPARTMENT;
CHARLES GALLOWAY CLARKE and the 20TH CENTURY-FOX STUDIO CAMERA DEPARTMENT;
FARCIOT EDOUART and the PARAMOUNT STUDIO TRANSPARENCY DEPARTMENT;
WILLARD H. TURNER and the RKO RADIO STUDIO SOUND DEPARTMENT.

1944

"Once or twice I've been described as a light comedian. I consider this the most accurate description of my abilities I've ever seen."

—Bing Crosby

GOING THAT WAY

CEREMONY: March 15, 1945
Grauman's Chinese Theatre,
Hollywood
HOSTS: John Cromwell, Bob Hope

The affable young priest of *Going My Way*, Bing Crosby had no faith in his chances at an Oscar. He was sure it would go to Alexander Knox for his portrayal of President Wilson. Furthermore, Crosby felt, his loss would only fuel embarrassing punch lines from his longtime cohort/rival Bob Hope. All in all, he'd rather be golfing. On the twelfth hole, he got a call from his mother. "If you don't go you'll never hear the end of it from me," she said. Her threat was enough to force Crosby into his suit, tie, and hairpiece. He arrived too late to witness Ingrid Bergman's triumphal entry into Grauman's Chinese Theatre on the arm of Jennifer Jones. The bleacher fans screamed for the star of *Gaslight*, whom they all felt should have won for *Casablanca*. Perhaps as a message to the Academy, Bergman had on the same dress she wore last year.

While Bergman's chances at an Academy Award were good, Barry Fitzgerald's were even better. He was nominated in two categories for the same role in *Going My Way*. It was the last time the Academy would allow double-dipping. Luckily for Fitzgerald, he nabbed the award for Best Supporting Actor before the rule change.

Crosby's highest hopes and worst fears were realized as he was swept in on the *Going My Way* tidal wave. He got his statuette—and endless ribbing from Hope. "Crosby winning an Oscar is like hearing that Sam Goldwyn is lecturing at Oxford," Hope quipped. The night ended on a sentimental note as the newly blond Norma Shearer, radiant after her recent marriage to a young ski instructor, presented Darryl Zanuck with his second Thalberg Memorial Award.

While it's not recorded whether Crosby finished his golf game after the ceremony, Fitzgerald certainly got into the swing of things. In the midst of raucous celebrating at home, he unleashed his four iron and his wartime plaster Oscar got in the way. The Academy quickly replaced it. Technically, Fitzgerald was the first actor to receive two statuettes for the same role.

BEST PICTURE/BEST DIRECTOR LEO MCCAREY (1898–1969) *GOING MY WAY*

The story of a progressive young Catholic priest who matches his ideas with those of the elderly pastor of a poor parish, *Going My Way* won the hearts of even the most resistant critics. "Mr. Crosby has been beautifully presented by Mr. McCarey… [The film] is a tonic delight," wrote Bosley Crowther of the *New York Times*. "[In a year] full of creepy melodramas, noir mysteries, and straight dramas…only *Going My Way* could be classified as schmaltz, in the best sense of the word… a charming film," wrote critic Danny Peary.

McCarey was lauded—and criticized—for his brilliant marriage of humor and open sentimentality. French filmmaker Jean Renoir said of the director, "Leo McCarey is one of the few directors in Hollywood who understand human beings."

(For more on McCarey, see 1937.)

The envelope, please...

Bing Crosby (center)

BEST ACTOR
BING CROSBY (1904–1977)
GOING MY WAY

"I couldn't be more surprised if I won the Kentucky Derby. Can you imagine the jokes Hope's going to write about this in his radio show? This will give him twelve straight weeks of material."

Hollywood's legendary song, dance, and straight man crooned and wooed audiences. Despite his great popularity, which included *Holiday Inn* (1942), *White Christmas* (1954), and *High Society* (1956), Crosby was nominated for Oscars for only two other films—*The Bells of St. Mary's* (1945) and *The Country Girl* (1954), his most dramatic work up to that time. For the next twenty years, he teamed up with comedian and off-camera buddy Bob Hope in the burlesque musical "Road" comedies *Road to Singapore,...Zanzibar* (1941),...*Morocco* (1942),...*Hong Kong* (1962), and others.

Crosby continued to work through the 1960s, appearing in *Robin and the Seven Hoods* (1964) and his final dramatic role, a remake of *Stagecoach* (1966). He switched over to television and starred in a half-hour sitcom, *The Bing Crosby Show*, from 1964 to 1965. Crosby published his autobiography, *Call Me Lucky*, in 1953.

BEST ACTRESS
INGRID BERGMAN (1915–1982)
GASLIGHT

"Your artistry has won our vote and your graciousness has won our hearts," said Oscar winner Jennifer Jones, handing Bergman her Golden Boy. Bergman replied, "Tomorrow I go to work in a picture with Bing and Mr. McCarey [*The Bells of St. Mary's*]. And I'm afraid if I didn't have an Oscar, too, they wouldn't speak to me."

Bergman's career was launched by a small role in the Italian film *Intermezzo* (1936). When David O. Selznick saw it he sent someone from MGM to buy the rights and remade it with Bergman as the star in 1939. The rest is history.

Uncommonly beautiful, even for Hollywood, and a great actress, Bergman was beloved. She had a brilliant career in America, appearing in *Casablanca* (1942), *For Whom the Bell Tolls* (1943, nom.), *Spellbound* (1945), and *The Bells of St. Mary's* (1945, nom.). Bergman went to Italy in 1949 to film *Stromboli* (1949) and did not return to Hollywood until 1956. Bergman retired from show business, but not before appearing in her Emmy Award–winning TV movie, *A Woman Called Golda* (1982). She died on her birthday, August 29, 1982, in London. (For more on Bergman, see 1956 and 1974.)

BEST OF 1944
Best Picture: Leo McCarey, *Going My Way*
Best Actor: Bing Crosby, *Going My Way*
Best Actress: Ingrid Bergman, *Gaslight*
Best Supporting Actor: Barry Fitzgerald, *Going My Way*
Best Supporting Actress: Ethel Barrymore, *None but the Lonely Heart*

FIRSTS
- This was the first year in which the number of Best Picture nominees would be limited to five.
- Producer/director/screenwriter Leo McCarey was the first to win three Academy Awards for the same picture.
- As the result of a change in the rules, this was the first and last time an actor (Barry Fitzgerald) would be nominated in two categories for the same film.
- The Screen Extras Guild lost its voting privileges.
- For the first time, the entire Awards ceremony would be broadcast nationally by the ABC network.

SINS OF OMISSION
Picture: *Meet Me in St. Louis*
Director: Vincente Minnelli, *Meet Me in St. Louis*
Actor: Fred McMurray, *Double Indemnity*
Actress: Judy Garland, *Meet Me in St. Louis*
Supporting Actor: Edward G. Robinson, *Double Indemnity*

UNMENTIONABLES
- Just months before the Awards ceremony, Barry Fitzgerald beat a vehicular homicide rap. He had fatally mowed down an elderly woman on Hollywood Boulevard.
- Darryl F. Zanuck wasn't in the least thrilled with his compensatory Thalberg Memorial Award. He felt that his production, *Wilson*, had been robbed of the Best Picture Oscar and he let everyone around town know it. A mercurial and eccentric cigar-chomping mogul, Zanuck decreed that none of his 20th Century-Fox male stars could appear on screen with hairy chests. William Holden was one of many who had to submit to the razor.
- Bing Crosby's uncooperatively large ears were usually taped back for his screen roles.
- During his career, Crosby amassed a fortune of more than $200 million. He left trust funds to his sons that wouldn't kick in until they reached the age of 65. Two of them, Dennis and Lindsay, committed suicide well before that. The eldest, Gary, wrote a "Daddy Dearest," claiming Bing tortured him as a child.
- Bob Hope dismissed Gary Crosby's tell-all with a quip: "Bing tortured me all the time with his singing, but I never wrote a book about it."

BEST SUPPORTING ACTOR
BARRY FITZGERALD
(1888–1966)
GOING MY WAY

When Fitzgerald shyly took the stage to make his speech, just as he had played his role as the bashful priest in the film, the audience roared. His performance in the film had been that powerful.

The Irish-born actor made his screen debut in England, in Alfred Hitchcock's *Juno and the Paycock* (1930), and was lured to Hollywood by John Ford for his film *The Plough and the Stars* (1936). With his thick brogue and his scene-stealing grin, Fitzgerald sealed his screen identity in this latter film, which established him as the archetypal Irishman.

After his Oscar win, Fitzgerald was featured in such films as *Duffy's Tavern* (1945), *Welcome Stranger* (1947), and *The Quiet Man* (1952). His last film was the British-made *Broth of a Boy* (1959).

Bing Crosby with Barry Fitzgerald

PICTURE

DOUBLE INDEMNITY, Paramount, Joseph Sistrom.
GASLIGHT, MGM. Arthur Hornblow Jr.
GOING MY WAY, Paramount, Leo McCarey.
SINCE YOU WENT AWAY, Selznick, UA, David O. Selznick.
WILSON, 20th Century-Fox, Darryl F. Zanuck.

ACTOR

CHARLES BOYER in *Gaslight*, MGM.
BING CROSBY in *Going My Way*, Paramount.
BARRY FITZGERALD in *Going My Way*, Paramount.
CARY GRANT in *None but the Lonely Heart*, RKO Radio.
ALEXANDER KNOX in *Wilson*, 20th Century-Fox.

ACTRESS

INGRID BERGMAN in *Gaslight*, MGM.
CLAUDETTE COLBERT in *Since You Went Away*, Selznick, UA.
BETTE DAVIS in *Mr. Skeffington*, Warner Bros.
GREER GARSON in *Mrs. Parkington*, MGM.
BARBARA STANWYCK in *Double Indemnity*, Paramount.

SUPPORTING ACTOR

HUME CRONYN in *The Seventh Cross*, MGM.
BARRY FITZGERALD in *Going My Way*, Paramount.
CLAUDE RAINS in *Mr. Skeffington*, Warner Bros.
CLIFTON WEBB in *Laura*, 20th Century-Fox.
MONTY WOOLLEY in *Since You Went Away*, Selznick, UA.

SUPPORTING ACTRESS

ANGELA LANSBURY in *Gaslight*, MGM.
ALINE MacMAHON in *Dragon Seed*, MGM.
AGNES MOOREHEAD in *Mrs. Parkington*, MGM.

DIRECTION

ALFRED HITCHCOCK for *Lifeboat*, 20th Century-Fox.
HENRY KING for *Wilson*, 20th Century-Fox.
LEO McCAREY for *Going My Way*, Paramount.
OTTO PREMINGER for *Laura*, 20th Century-Fox.
BILLY WILDER for *Double Indemnity*, Paramount.

WRITING: ORIGINAL STORY

GOING MY WAY, Paramount. Leo McCarey.
A GUY NAMED JOE, MGM. David Boehm and Chandler Sprague.
LIFEBOAT, 20th Century-Fox. John Steinbeck.
NONE SHALL ESCAPE, Columbia. Alfred Neumann and Joseph Than.
THE SULLIVANS, 20th Century-Fox. Edward Doherty and Jules Schermer.

WRITING: ORIGINAL SCREENPLAY

HAIL THE CONQUERING HERO, Paramount. Preston Sturges.
THE MIRACLE OF MORGAN'S CREEK, Paramount, Preston Sturges.
TWO GIRLS AND A SAILOR, MGM. Richard Connell and Gladys Lehman.
WILSON, 20th Century-Fox. Lamar Iotti.
WING AND A PRAYER, 20th Century-Fox. Jerome Cady.

WRITING: SCREENPLAY

DOUBLE INDEMNITY, Paramount. Raymond Chandler and Billy Wilder.
GASLIGHT, MGM. John L. Balderston, Walter Reisch and John Van Druten.

BEST SUPPORTING ACTRESS
ETHEL BARRYMORE (1879-1959)
NONE BUT THE LONELY HEART

Not in attendance, the proud female representative of the prestigious acting family was not particularly interested in her prize.

Having made her stage debut at the age of 15 with her uncle, John Drew—the foremost actor of his era—Ethel went on to play her first starring role on Broadway in 1900, in *Captain Jinks of the Horse Marines*. Fourteen years later, the self-proclaimed "first lady of the American theater" made her film debut in *The Nightingale* but continued to alternate between stage and film. The next time she showed up in a film it was in a talkie, *Rasputin and the Empress* (1932), in which she joined brothers John and Lionel. After landing the Oscar, she received nominations for her roles in *The Spiral Staircase* (1946), *The Paradine Case* (1947), and *Pinky* (1949). Her last film was *Johnny Trouble* (1957).

GOING MY WAY, Paramount. Frank Butler and Frank Cavett.
LAURA, 20th Century-Fox. Jay Dratler, Samuel Hoffenstein and Betty Reinhardt.
MEET ME IN ST. LOUIS, MGM. Irving Brecher and Fred F. Finkelhoffe.

CINEMATOGRAPHY
B/W
DOUBLE INDEMNITY, Paramount. John Seitz.
DRAGON SEED, MGM. Sidney Wagner.
GASLIGHT, MGM. Joseph Ruttenberg.
GOING MY WAY, Paramount. Lionel Lindon.
LAURA, 20th Century-Fox. Joseph LaShelle.
LIFEBOAT, 20th Century-Fox. Glen MacWilliams.
SINCE YOU WENT AWAY, Selznick, UA. Stanley Cortez and Lee Garmes.
THIRTY SECONDS OVER TOKYO. MGM. Robert Surtees and Harold Rosson.
THE UNINVITED, Paramount. Charles Lang.
THE WHITE CLIFFS OF DOVER, MGM. George Folsey.

Color
COVER GIRL, Columbia. Rudy Mate and Allen M. Davey.
HOME IN INDIANA, 20th Century-Fox. Edward Cronjager.
KISMET, MGM. Charles Rosher.
LADY IN THE DARK, Paramount. Ray Rennahan.
MEET ME IN ST. LOUIS, MGM. George Folsey.
WILSON, 20th Century-Fox. Leon Shamroy.

ART DIRECTION—INTERIOR DECORATION
B/W
ADDRESS UNKNOWN, Columbia. Lionel Banks and Walter Holscher; Joseph Kish.
THE ADVENTURES OF MARK TWAIN, Warner Bros. John J. Hughes; Fred MacLean.
CASANOVA BROWN, International, RKO Radio. Perry Ferguson; Julia Heron.
GASLIGHT, MGM. Cedric Gibbons and William Ferrari; Edwin Willis and Paul Huldschinsky.
LAURA, 20th Century-Fox. Lyle Wheeler and Leland Fuller; Thomas Little.
NO TIME FOR LOVE, Paramount. Hans Dreier and Robert Usher; Sam Comer.
SINCE YOU WENT AWAY, Selznick, UA. Mark-Lee Kirk; Victor A. Gangelin.
STEP LIVELY, RKO Radio, Albert S. D'Agostino and Carroll Clark; Darrell Silvera and Claude Carpenter.

Color
THE CLIMAX, Universal, John B. Goodman and Alexander Golitzen; Russell A. Gausman and Ira S. Webb.
COVER GIRL, Columbia. Lionel Banks and Cary Odell; Fay Babcock.
THE DESERT SONG, Warner Bros. Charles Novi; Jack McConaghy.
KISMET, MGM. Cedric Gibbons and Daniel B. Cathcart; Edwin B. Willis and Richard Pefferle.
LADY IN THE DARK, Paramount. Hans Dreier and Raoul Pene du Bois; Ray Moyer.
THE PRINCESS AND THE PIRATE, Goldwyn, RKO Radio. Ernst Fegte; Howard Bristol.
WILSON, 20th Century-Fox. Wiard Ihnen; Thomas Little.

FILM EDITING
GOING MY WAY, Paramount. Leroy Stone.
JANIE, Warner Bros. Owen Marks.
NONE BUT THE LONELY HEART, RKO Radio. Roland Gross.
SINCE YOU WENT AWAY, Selznick, UA. Hal C. Kern and James E. Newcom.
WILSON, 20th Century-Fox. Barbara McLean.

SPECIAL EFFECTS
THE ADVENTURES OF MARK TWAIN, Warner Bros. Paul Detlefsen, John Crouse and Nathan Levinson.
DAYS OF GLORY, Robinson, RKO Radio. Vernon L. Walker, James G. Stewart and Roy Granville.
SECRET COMMAND, Columbia. David Allen, Ray Cory, Robert Wright, Russell Malmgren and Harry Kusnick.
SINCE YOU WENT AWAY, Selznick, UA. John R. Cosgrove and Arthur Johns.
THE STORY OF DR. WASSELL, DeMille, Paramount. Farciot Edouart, Gordon Jennings and George Dutton.
THIRTY SECONDS OVER TOKYO, MGM. A. Arnold Gillespie, Donald Jahraus, Warren Newcombe and Douglas Shearer.
WILSON, 20th Century-Fox. Fred Sersen and Roger Heman.

SOUND RECORDING
BRAZIL, Republic. Republic Studio Sound Dept., Daniel J. Bloomberg, Sound Director.
CASANOVA BROWN, International, RKO Radio. Samuel Goldwyn Studio Sound Dept., Thomas T. Moulton, Sound Director.
COVER GIRL, Columbia. Columbia Studio Sound Dept., John Livadaray, Sound Director.
DOUBLE INDEMNITY, Paramount. Paramount Studio Sound Dept., Loren Ryder, Sound Director.
HIS BUTLER'S SISTER, Universal. Universal Studio Sound Dept., Bernard B. Brown, Sound Director.
HOLLYWOOD CANTEEN, Warner Bros. Studio Sound Dept., Nathan Levinson, Sound Director.
IT HAPPENED TOMORROW, Arnold, UA. Sound Services, Inc., Jack Whitney, Sound Director.
KISMET, MGM. MGM Studio Sound Dept., Douglas Shearer, Sound Director.
MUSIC IN MANHATTAN, RKO Radio. RKO Radio Studio Sound Dept., Stephen Dunn, Sound Director.
VOICE IN THE WIND, Ripley-Monter, UA. RCA Sound, W. M. Dalgleish, Sound Director.
WILSON, 20th Century-Fox. 20th Century-Fox Studio Sound Dept., E. H. Hansen, Sound Director.

SONG
I COULDN'T SLEEP A WINK LAST NIGHT *(Higher and Higher, RKO Radio)*; Music by Jimmy McHugh. Lyrics by Harold Adamson.
I'LL WALK ALONE *(Follow the Boys, Feldman, Universal)*; Music by Jule Styne. Lyrics by Sammy Cahn.
I'M MAKING BELIEVE *(Sweet and Lowdown, 20th Century-Fox)*; Music by James V. Monaco. Lyrics by Mack Gordon.
LONG AGO AND FAR AWAY *(Cover Girl, Columbia)*; Music by Jerome Kern. Lyrics by Ira Gershwin.
NOW I KNOW *(Up in Arms, Avalon, RKO Radio)*; Music by Harold Arlen. Lyrics by Ted Koehler.
REMEMBER ME TO CAROLINA *(Minstrel Man, PRC)*; Music by Harry Revel. Lyrics by Paul Webster.
RIO DE JANEIRO *(Brazil, Republic)*; Music by Ary Barroso. Lyrics by Ned Washington.
SILVER SHADOWS AND GOLDEN DREAMS *(Lady Let's Dance, Monogram)*; Music by Lew Pollack. Lyrics by Charles Newman.
SWEET DREAMS SWEETHEART *(Hollywood Canteen, Warner Bros.)*; Music by M.K. Jerome. Lyrics by Ted Koehler
SWINGING ON A STAR *(Going My Way, Paramount)*; Music by James Van Heusen. Lyrics by Johnny Burke.
TOO MUCH IN LOVE *(Song of the Open Road, Rogers, UA)*; Music by Walter Kent. Lyrics by Kim Gannon.
THE TROLLEY SONG *(Meet Me in St. Louis, MGM)*; Music and Lyrics by Ralph Blane and Hugh Martin.

SCORING: DRAMA/COMEDY
ADDRESS UNKNOWN, Columbia. Morris Stoloff and Ernst Toch.
THE ADVENTURES OF MARK TWAIN, Warner Bros. Max Steiner.
THE BRIDGE OF SAN LUIS REY, Bogeaus, UA. Dimitri Tiomkin.
CASANOVA BROWN, International, RKO Radio. Arthur Lange.
CHRISTMAS HOLIDAY, Universal. H.J. Salter.
DOUBLE INDEMNITY, Paramount. Miklos Rozsa.
THE FIGHTING SEABEES, Republic. Walter Scharf and Roy Webb.
THE HAIRY APE, Levey, UA. Michel Michelet and Edward Paul.
IT HAPPENED TOMORROW. Arnold, UA. Robert Stolz.
JACK LONDON, Bronston, UA. Frederic E. Rich.
KISMET, MGM. Herbert Stothart.
NONE BUT THE LONELY HEART, RKO Radio. C. Bakaleinikoff and Banns Eisler.
THE PRINCESS AND THE PIRATE, Goldwyn, RKO Radio. David Rose.
SINCE YOU WENT AWAY, Selznick, UA. Max Steiner.
SUMMER STORM, Angelus, UA. Karl Hajos.
THREE RUSSIAN GIRLS, R & F Prods., UA. Franke Harling.
UP IN MABEL'S ROOM, Small, UA. Edward Paul.
VOICE IN THE WIND, Ripley-Monter, UA. Michel Michelet.
WILSON, 20th Century-Fox. Alfred Newman.

WOMAN OF THE TOWN, Sherman, UA. Miklos Rozsa.

SCORING: MUSICAL
BRAZIL, Republic. Walter Scharf.
COVER GIRL, Columbia. Carmen Dragon and Morris Stoloff.
HIGHER AND HIGHER, RKO Radio. C. Bakaleinikoff.
HOLLYWOOD CANTEEN, Warner Bros. Ray Heindorf.
IRISH EYES ARE SMILING, 20th Century-Fox. Alfred Newman.
KNICKERBOCKER HOLIDAY, RCA, UA. Werner R. Heymann and Kurt Weill.
LADY IN THE DARK, Paramount. Robert Emmett Dolan.
LADY LET'S DANCE, Monogram. Edward Kay.
MEET ME IN ST. LOUIS, MGM. Georgie Stoll.
THE MERRY MONAHANS, Universal. H.J. Salter.
MINSTREL MAN, PRC. Leo Erdody and Ferdie Grofe.
SENSATIONS OF 1945, Stone, UA. Mahlon Merrick.
SONG OF THE OPEN ROAD. Rogers, UA. Charles Previn.
UP IN ARMS, Avalon, RKO Radio. Louis Forbes and Ray Heindorf.

SHORT SUBJECT: CARTOON
AND TO THINK I SAW IT ON MULBERRY STREET, Paramount. (Puppetoon). George Pal, producer.
THE DOG, CAT AND CANARY, Columbia. (Screen Gems).
FISH FRY. Universal. Walter Lantz, producer.
HOW TO PLAY FOOTBALL, Disney, RKO Radio. Walt Disney, producer.
MOUSE TROUBLE, MGM. Frederick C. Quimby, producer.
MY BOY, JOHNNY, 20th Century-Fox. Paul Terry, producer.
SWOONER CROONER, Warner Bros.

SHORT SUBJECT: ONE-REEL
BLUE GRASS GENTLEMEN, 20th Century-Fox. (Sports Review). Edmund Reed, producer.
JAMMIN' THE BLUES, Warner Bros. (Melody Master Bands). Gordon Hollingshead, producer.
MOVIE PESTS, MGM. (Pete Smith Specialty). Pete Smith, producer.
50TH ANNIVERSARY OF MOTION PICTURES, Columbia. (Screen Snapshots). Ralph Staub, producer.
WHO'S WHO IN ANIMAL LAND. Paramount. (Speaking of Animals). Jerry Fairbanks, producer.

SHORT SUBJECT: TWO-REEL
BOMBALERA, Paramount. (Musical Parade). Louis Harris, producer.
I WON'T PLAY, Warner Bros. (Featurette). Gordon Hollingshead, producer.
MAIN STREET TODAY, MGM. (Two-reel Special). Jerry Bresler, producer.

DOCUMENTARY: SHORT SUBJECTS
ARTURO TOSCANINI, Motion Picture Bureau, Overseas Branch, Office of War Information.
NEW AMERICANS, This Is America Series, RKO Radio.
WITH THE MARINES AT TARAWA, U.S. Marine Corps.

DOCUMENTARY: FEATURES
THE FIGHTING LADY, 20th Century-Fox and U.S. Navy.
RESISTING ENEMY INTERROGATION, U.S. Army Air Force.

SPECIAL AWARDS
TO MARGARET O'BRIEN, outstanding child actress of 1944.
TO BOB HOPE for his many services to the Academy, a Life Membership in the Academy of Motion Picture Arts and Sciences.

IRVING G. THALBERG MEMORIAL AWARD
TO DARRYL F. ZANUCK

SCIENTIFIC OR TECHNICAL
CLASS II
STEPHEN DUNN and the RKO RADIO STUDIO SOUND DEPARTMENT and RADIO CORPORATION OF AMERICA for the design and development of the electronic compressor-limiter.
CLASS III
LIN WOOD DUNN, CECIL LOVE and ACME TOOL MANUFACTURING CO.;
GROVER LAUBE and the 20TH CENTURY-FOX STUDIO CAMERA DEPARTMENT;
WESTERN ELECTRIC CO.;

RUSSELL BROWN, RAY HINSDALE and JOSEPH E. ROBBINS;
GORDON JENNINGS;
RADIO CORPORATION OF AMERICA and the RKO RADIO STUDIO SOUND DEPARTMENT;
DANIEL J. BLOOMBERG and the REPUBLIC STUDIO SOUND DEPARTMENT;
BERNARD B. BROWN and JOHN P. LIVADARY;
PAUL ZELL, S.J. TWINING and GEORGE SKID;
PAUL LERPAE.

1945

The war was over and the boys were back in tuxedos. It was gowns, diamonds, furs, and searchlights over Grauman's. The Awards' return to glamour would have seemed an ideal venue for the ultimate screen queen, Joan Crawford, but nerves got the best of her. Never having won anything but a pink slip from MGM, Crawford took one look at her fierce competition and suddenly decided that she had the flu.

SHAKEN AND STIRRED

CEREMONY: March 7, 1946
Grauman's Chinese Theatre,
Hollywood
HOSTS: James Stewart,
Bob Hope

Bing Crosby didn't even bother with a doctor's note. Well aware that his nominated character, Father O'Malley, wouldn't provide him with a miracle two years in a row, he took a last-minute pass. His "Road" movies sidekick, Bob Hope, was clearly miffed by his absence but was placated with a mini-Oscar for his exceptional service to the Academy. He joked about its size, suggesting that it was the *Reader's Digest* version.

It was a night of vindication for Billy Wilder, whose *Double Indemnity* had scored a humiliating six nominations, but not a single win the year before. His *Lost Weekend* hardly lost a single nomination this time around. Ray Milland's especially sweet victory after fifteen years of unnominated romantic comedy roles, left him speechless.

Joan Crawford had no intention of playing down her big moment. The star who was once quoted as saying, "If you're looking for the girl next door, go next door," Crawford was pleased to see the hordes of reporters arrive at the right address. She kept them waiting until she settled into bed with her coffee, silk peignoir, and a surrounding tableau, including *Mildred Pierce* director, Michael Curtiz, and her fan-club president. The press was finally allowed to ascend the grand staircase to interview and photograph the overwhelmed recuperative. It was a remarkable performance by all accounts, and nearly every front page the next morning featured photos of an Oscar-wielding Crawford in sumptuous sick bay. An unsuspecting reader might have thought the Academy Awards had been held in her bedroom.

BEST PICTURE/BEST DIRECTOR BILLY WILDER (1906–2002) *THE LOST WEEKEND*

"Thank you, Mrs. Miniver," said the droll Wilder to presenter and former Best Director William Wyler. When the film also won the award for Best Picture, presenter Eric Johnston, from—of all places—the Hays (read censor's) office, sounding like a child, cooed, "Oooooooh!"

Wilder had a few flings with Oscar, though he began his work life with every intention of becoming a reporter in his native Vienna. Beginning his film career in 1933 as a writer, he collaborated on the script for Ernst Lubitsch's *Bluebeard's Eighth Wife* (1938) with the urbane Charles Brackett. The collaboration worked, and the pair went on to write *What a Life*, *Ninotchka* (both 1939), the sublime *Hold Back the Dawn* (1941), and *Ball of Fire* (1942). *Ninotchka* and *Ball of Fire* were nominated for Oscars.

Ray Milland (left)

Growing increasingly frustrated with the way his witty and sophisticated scripts were being handled by directors, Wilder persuaded Paramount to let him try directing. His debut film, *The Major and the Minor* (1942), was auspicious and was followed by the equally fine *Five Graves to Cairo* (1943). Wilder's career suffered many ups and downs, but his list of great films far outweighs the clunkers and includes *Double Indemnity* (1944, nom.), *A Foreign Affair* (1948, nom.), *Sunset Boulevard* (1950, nom.), *Ace in the Hole* (1951, retitled *The Big Carnival*, nom.), *Stalag 17* (1953), *Sabrina* (1954), *The Seven Year Itch* (1955), *Love in the Afternoon* (1957), *Witness for the Prosecution* (1958), *Some Like It Hot* (1959), *The Apartment* (1960), *Irma la Douce* (1963), and *The Fortune Cookie* (1966).

Wilder turned out a few weak films in his later years, retired, and returned to his famed art collection. He remained a witty observer of the Hollywood scene, and though he didn't manage to keep up with the times, he has never been thought of as anything less than a great filmmaker.

The envelope, please...

BEST ACTOR
RAY MILLAND (1907–1986)
THE LOST WEEKEND

"Are you nervous?" asked presenter Ingrid Bergman of the obviously overwhelmed actor, who simply smiled and nodded his head to the audience without saying a word.

The charming Welsh-born Milland had a long and prolific career playing suave, romantic leading men. Milland did a number of martini-sipping roles, including *Bachelor Father* (1931) and *The Jungle Princess* (1936), and graduated to leading roles in the mid-1930s in *Beau Geste* (1939) and *The Doctor Takes a Wife* (1940). He began to show his gifts for dramatic irony in *The Major and the Minor* (1942) and *Ministry of Fear* (1944).

After impressing audiences with the depth of his acting, he starred in a range of films, including *The Big Clock* (1948, among his best), Alfred Hitchcock's *Dial M for Murder* (1954), and *The Girl in the Red Velvet Swing* (1955). In 1955 Milland directed himself in a number of films. He returned to the screen in 1970, playing a character part in *Love Story*, then resumed playing leads in low-budget horror films.

Milland's face became a familiar one on television with *The Ray Milland Show* (1953–1955).

BEST ACTRESS
JOAN CRAWFORD (1905–1977)
MILDRED PIERCE

"This is the greatest moment of my life," said Crawford from her bed, where she had retreated in fear of losing.

One of Hollywood's most brilliant actresses, Crawford was nominated four times but took home the gold only once. With her haunting eyes and awkward lips, Crawford was given roles as the tough flapper in *Taxi Dancer* (1927) and *Four Walls* (1928). She became an instant star with *Our Dancing Daughters* (1928). She wed into Hollywood's royal family by marrying Douglas Fairbanks Jr. in 1929 and was divorced by 1933.

Crawford moved on to play independent tough-minded shop girls, most notably in *The Women* (1939), but also in *Grand Hotel* (1932) and *A Woman's Face* (1941). Labeled "box-office poison" by an industry trade paper in 1938, she was fired by Louis B. Mayer after making *Above Suspicion* (1943).

Crawford didn't appear on screen for two years after that, but she persuaded Warner Bros. to cast her in the title role in *Mildred Pierce* (1945). She returned triumphant and appeared in *Humoresque* (1946), *Possessed* (1947, nom.), *Sudden Fear* (1952, nom.), *Johnny Guitar* (1954), and *The Best of Everything* (1959).

After a brief interlude, Crawford made a comeback in *What Ever Happened to Baby Jane?* (1962). In 1969 she starred in a telefilm for a series called *Night Gallery*, directed by newcomer Steven Spielberg.

BEST OF 1945
Best Picture/Best Director: Billy Wilder, *The Lost Weekend*
Best Actor: Ray Milland, *The Lost Weekend*
Best Actress: Joan Crawford, *Mildred Pierce*
Best Supporting Actor: James Dunn, *A Tree Grows in Brooklyn*
Best Supporting Actress: Anne Revere, *National Velvet*

FIRSTS
- Bing Crosby was the first actor to be nominated twice for playing the same character. It would happen again with Peter O'Toole for his King Henry II (*Becket*, 1964; *The Lion in Winter*, 1968) and Al Pacino for Michael Corleone (*The Godfather*, 1972; *The Godfather Part II*, 1974).
- Plaster statuettes were restored to bronze and gold plate.

ROLE REVERSALS
- Paramount overruled Billy Wilder's choice for *The Lost Weekend*, Jose Ferrer.
- Bette Davis or Barbara Stanwyck as Mildred Pierce? They were director Michael Curtiz's first and second choices.

SINS OF OMISSION
Picture: *To Have and Have Not*
Actor: Humphrey Bogart, *To Have and Have Not*
Supporting Actress: Lauren Bacall, *To Have and Have Not*

ALWAYS A BRIDESMAID, NEVER A BRIDE
Aside from his unsuccessful nomination for *The Story of G. I. Joe*, Robert Mitchum never got another shot at Oscar.

UNMENTIONABLES
- Ray Milland (né Reginald Alfred John Truscott-Jones) claimed he lost his hair thanks to the hot curling irons used by the makeup department for *Reap the Wild Wind* (1942). He wore a toupee in most of his subsequent movies.
- Joan Crawford's ex-husband No. 3, Phillip Terry, played Milland's brother in *The Lost Weekend*.
- Crawford's youthful arrest for prostitution was erased from the record books years later by her close friend, J. Edgar Hoover.
- 1920s starlet Lucille Fay LeSuer was renamed Joan Crawford as the result of a fan-magazine contest. She despised the name, thinking it sounded like *crawfish*.
- While the official cause of Crawford's death in 1977 was a heart attack, persistent rumors suggested suicide. Debbie Reynolds, among others, believed she wanted to end it before she was ravaged by cancer.

BEST SUPPORTING ACTOR
JAMES DUNN (1905–1967)
A TREE GROWS IN BROOKLYN

Considered a lightweight Pat O'Brien, Irish actor James Dunn worked on the stage in vaudeville and as an extra in silent movies. Noted for his performances with Shirley Temple in her first three movies—*Baby Take a Bow, Stand Up and Cheer*, and *Bright Eyes* (all 1934)—Dunn's screen character in his later films was the boy next door.

In the late 1930s Dunn was married to beautiful starlet Frances Gifford, with whom he co-starred in two potboilers, *Mercy Plane* (1939) and *Hold That Woman* (1940). His career went into a slump and he became unemployable when he began to drink heavily. He made a remarkable comeback, however, with this Oscar performance. It didn't last, though, and by 1951 he would again be unemployed and bankrupt. He appeared on television as a regular on the series *It's a Great Life* (1966).

BEST SUPPORTING ACTRESS
ANNE REVERE (1903–1990)
NATIONAL VELVET

After making her Broadway debut in 1931, Revere made her first appearance on film in *Double Door* (1934). She moved to Hollywood for keeps in 1940 and had a decade-long career for which she received two Oscar nods—*The Song of Bernadette* (1943) and *Gentleman's Agreement* (1947)—and this year's win. Among her other, less notable films were *Rainbow Island* (1944), *Forever Amber* (1947), and *A Place in the Sun* (1951).

Blacklisted in 1951 at the peak of her career for taking the Fifth Amendment before the House Un-American Activities Committee, Revere had a difficult time picking up any film or TV work for years. She returned to the screen briefly for Otto Preminger's *Tell Me That You Love Me, Junie Moon* (both 1970), and *Birch Interval* (1976).

Elizabeth Taylor with Anne Revere

A W A R D
N O M I N A
T I O N S
1 9 4 5

PICTURE
ANCHORS AWEIGH, MGM. Joe Pasternak.
THE BELLS OF ST. MARY'S, Rainbow, RKO Radio, Leo McCarey.
THE LOST WEEKEND, Paramount, Charles Brackett.
MILDRED PIERCE, Warner Bros, Jerry Wald.
SPELLBOUND, Selznick, UA, David O. Selznick.

ACTOR
BING CROSBY in *The Bells of St. Mary's*, Rainbow, RKO Radio.
GENE KELLY in *Anchors Aweigh*, MGM.
RAY MILLAND in *The Lost Weekend*, Paramount.
GREGORY PECK in *The Keys of the Kingdom*, 20th Century-Fox.
CORNEL WILDE in *A Song to Remember*, Columbia.

ACTRESS
INGRID BERGMAN in *The Bells of St. Mary's*, Rainbow, RKO Radio.
JOAN CRAWFORD in *Mildred Pierce*, Warner Bros.
GREER GARSON in *The Valley of Decision*, MGM.
JENNIFER JONES in *Love Letters*, Wallis, Paramount.
GENE TIERNEY in *Leave Her to Heaven*, 20th Century-Fox.

SUPPORTING ACTOR
MICHAEL CHEKHOV in *Spellbound*, Selznick, UA.
JOHN DALL in *The Corn Is Green*, Warner Bros.
JAMES DUNN in *A Tree Grows in Brooklyn*, 20th Century-Fox.
ROBERT MITCHUM in *The Story of G.I. Joe*, Cowan, UA.
J. CARROL NAISH in *A Medal for Benny*, Paramount.

SUPPORTING ACTRESS
EVE ARDEN in *Mildred Pierce*, Warner Bros.
ANN BLYTH in *Mildred Pierce*, Warner Bros.
ANGELA LANSBURY in *The Picture of Dorian Gray*, MGM.
JOAN LORRING in *The Corn Is Green*, Warner Bros.
ANNE REVERE in *National Velvet*, MGM.

DIRECTION
CLARENCE BROWN for *National Velvet*, MGM.
ALFRED HITCHCOCK for *Spellbound*, Selznick, UA.
LEO McCAREY for *The Bells of St. Mary's*, RKO Radio.
JEAN RENOIR for *The Southerner*, Loew-Hakim, UA.
BILLY WILDER for *The Lost Weekend*, Paramount.

WRITING: ORIGINAL STORY
THE AFFAIRS OF SUSAN, Wallis, Paramount. Laszlo Gorog and Thomas Monroe.
THE HOUSE ON 92ND STREET, 20th Century-Fox. Charles G. Booth.
A MEDAL FOR BENNY, Paramount. John Steinbeck and Jack Wagner.
OBJECTIVE, BURMA!, Warner Bros. Alvah Bessie.
A SONG TO REMEMBER, Columbia. Ernst Marischka.

WRITING: ORIGINAL SCREENPLAY
DILLINGER, Monogram. Philip Yordan.
MARIE-LOUISE, Praesens Films (Swiss). Richard Schweizer.

MUSIC FOR MILLIONS, MGM. Myles Connolly.
SALTY O'ROURKE, Paramount. Milton Holmes.
WHAT NEXT, CORPORAL HARGROVE? MGM.
Harry Kurnitz.

WRITING: SCREENPLAY
THE STORY OF G.I. JOE, Cowan, UA. Leopold
Atlas, Guy Endore and Philip Stevenson.
**THE LOST WEEKEND, Paramount. Charles
Brackett and Billy Wilder.**
MILDRED PIERCE, Warner Bros.
Ranald MacDougall.
PRIDE OF THE MARINES, Warner Bros.
Albert Maltz.
A TREE GROWS IN BROOKLYN, 20th Century-
Fox. Frank Davis and Tess Slesinger.

CINEMATOGRAPHY
B/W
THE KEYS OF THE KINGDOM, 20th Century-
Fox. Arthur Miller.
THE LOST WEEKEND, Paramount. John F. Seitz.
MILDRED PIERCE, Warner Bros. Ernest Haller.
**THE PICTURE OF DORIAN GRAY, MGM.
Harry Stradling.**
SPELLBOUND, Selznick, UA. George Barnes.

Color
ANCHORS AWEIGH, MGM. Robert Planck and
Charles Boyle.
**LEAVE HER TO HEAVEN, 20th Century-Fox.
Leon Shamory.**
NATIONAL VELVET, MGM. Leonard Smith.
A SONG TO REMEMBER, Columbia. Tony
Gaudio and Allen M. Davey.
THE SPANISH MAIN, RKO Radio.
George Barnes.

ART DIRECTION— INTERIOR DECORATION
B/W
**BLOOD ON THE SUN, Cagney, UA. Wiard
Ihnen; A. Roland Fields.**
EXPERIMENT PERILOUS, RKO Radio. Albert S.
D'Agostino and Jack Okey; Darrell Silvera and
Claude Carpenter.
THE KEYS OF THE KINGDOM, 20th Century-
Fox. James Basevi and William Darling; Thomas
Little and Frank E. Hughes.
LOVE LETTERS, Wallis, Paramount. Hans Dreier
and Roland Anderson; Sam Comer and Ray Moyer.
THE PICTURE OF DORIAN GRAY, MGM.
Cedric Gibbons and Hans Peters; Edwin B.
Willis, John Bonar and Hugh Hunt.

Color
**FRENCHMAN'S CREEK, Paramount. Hans
Dreier and Ernst Fegte; Sam Comer.**
LEAVE HER TO HEAVEN, 20th Century-Fox. Lyle
Wheeler and Maurice Ransford; Thomas Little.
NATIONAL VELVET, MGM. Cedric Gibbons
and Urie McCleary; Edwin B. Willis and
Mildred Griffiths.
SAN ANTONIO, Warner Bros. Ted Smith;
Jack McConaghy.
A THOUSAND AND ONE NIGHTS, Columbia.
Stephen Goosson and Rudolph Sternad;
Frank Tuttle.

SOUND RECORDING
**THE BELLS OF ST. MARY'S, Rainbow, RKO
Radio. RKO Radio Studio Sound Dept.,
Stephen Dunn, Sound Director.**
FLAME OF BARBARY COAST, Republic.
Republic Studio Sound Dept., Daniel J.
Bloomberg, Sound Director.
LADY ON A TRAIN, Universal. Universal Studio
Sound Dept., Bernard B. Brown, Sound Director.
LEAVE HER TO HEAVEN, 20th Century-Fox.
20th Century-Fox Studio Sound Dept., Thomas
T. Moulton, Sound Director.
RHAPSODY IN BLUE, Warner Bros. Warner
Bros. Studio Sound Dept., Nathan Levinson,
Sound Director.
A SONG TO REMEMBER, Columbia. Columbia
Studio Sound Dept., John Livadary, Sound Director.
THE SOUTHERNER, Loew-Hakim, UA. Sound
Service Inc., Jack Whitney, Sound Director.
THEY WERE EXPENDABLE, MGM. MGM
Studio Sound Dept., Douglas Shearer,
Sound Director.
THE THREE CABALLEROS, Disney, RKO Radio.
Walt Disney Studio Sound Dept., C.O. Slyfield,
Sound Director.
THREE IS A FAMILY, Master Productions, UA.
RCA Sound, W.V. Wolfe, Sound Director.
**THE UNSEEN, Paramount. Paramount Studio
Sound Dept., Loren L. Ryder, Sound Director.**

WONDER MAN, Goldwyn, RKO Radio. Samuel
Goldwyn Studio Sound Dept., Gordon Sawyer,
Sound Director.

FILM EDITING
THE BELLS OF ST. MARY'S, Rainbow, RKO
Radio. Harry Marker.
THE LOST WEEKEND, Paramount.
Doane Harrison.
NATIONAL VELVET, MGM. Robert J. Kern.
OBJECTIVE, BURMA!, Warner Bros.
George Amy.
A SONG TO REMEMBER, Columbia.
Charles Nelson.

SPECIAL EFFECTS
CAPTAIN EDDIE, 20th Century-Fox. Fred
Sersen, Sol Halprin, Roger Heman and Harry
Leonard.
SPELLBOUND, Selznick, UA. Jack Cosgrove.
THEY WERE EXPENDABLE, MGM. A. Arnold
Gillespie, Donald Jahraus, R.A. MacDonald and
Michael Steinore.
A THOUSAND AND ONE NIGHTS, Columbia.
L.W. Butler and Ray Bomba.
**WONDER MAN, Goldwyn, RKO Radio. John
Fulton and A.W. Johns.**

SONG
ACCENTUATE THE POSITIVE (*Here Come the
Waves*, Paramount); Music by Harold Arlen.
Lyrics by Johnny Mercer.
ANYWHERE (*Tonight and Every Night*,
Columbia); Music by Jule Styne. Lyrics by
Sammy Cahn.
AREN'T YOU GLAD YOU'RE YOU (*The Bells of
St. Mary's*, Rainbow, RKO Radio); Music by
James Van Heusen. Lyrics by Johnny Burke.
THE CAT AND THE CANARY (*Why Girls Leave
Home*, PRC); Music by Jay Livingston. Lyrics by
Ray Evans.
ENDLESSLY (*Earl Carroll Vanities*, Republic);
Music by Walter Kent. Lyrics by Kim Gannon.
I FALL IN LOVE TOO EASILY (*Anchors Aweigh*,
MGM); Music by Jule Styne. Lyrics by Sammy Cahn.
I'LL BUY THAT DREAM (*Sing Your Way Home*,
RKO Radio); Music by Allie Wrubel. Lyrics by
Herb Magidson.
**IT MIGHT AS WELL BE SPRING (*State Flair*,
20th Century-Fox); Music by Richard
Rodgers. Lyrics by Oscar Hammerstein II.**
LINDA (*The Story of G.I. Joe*, Cowan, UA); Music
and Lyrics by Ann Ronell.
LOVE LETTERS (*Love Letters*, Wallis,
Paramount); Music by Victor Young. Lyrics by
Edward Heyman.
MORE AND MORE (*Can't Help Singing*, Universal);
Music by Jerome Kern. Lyrics by E.Y. Harburg.
SLEIGHRIDE IN JULY (*Belle of the Yukon*,
International, RKO Radio); Music by James Van
Heusen. Lyrics by Johnny Burke.
SO IN LOVE (*Wonder Man*, Beverly Prods., RKO
Radio); Music by David Rose. Lyrics by Leo Robin.
SOME SUNDAY MORNING (*San Antonio*,
Warner Bros.); Music by Ray Heindorf and M.K.
Jerome. Lyrics by Ted Koehler.

SCORING: DRAMA/COMEDY
THE BELLS OF ST. MARY'S, Rainbow, RKO
Radio. Robert Emmet Dolan.
BREWSTER'S MILLIONS, Small, UA. Lou Forbes.
CAPTAIN KIDD, Bogeaus, UA. Werner Janssen.
ENCHANTED COTTAGE, RKO Radio. Roy Webb.
FLAME OF BARBARY COAST, Republic. Dale
Butts and Morton Scott.
G.I. HONEYMOON, Monogram. Edward J. Kay.
GUEST IN THE HOUSE, Guest in the House,
Inc., UA. Werner Janssen.
GUEST WIFE, Green Tree, Prods., UA. Daniele
Amfitheatrof.
THE KEYS OF THE KINGDOM, 20th Century-
Fox. Alfred Newman.
THE LOST WEEKEND, Paramount. Miklos Rozsa.
LOVE LETTERS, Wallis, Paramount. Victor Young.
THE MAN WHO WALKED ALONE, PRC. Karl Hajos.
OBJECTIVE, BURMA!, Warner Bros.
Franz Waxman.
PARIS—UNDERGROUND, Bennett, UA.
Alexander Tansman.
A SONG TO REMEMBER, Columbia. Miklos
Rozsa and Morris Stoloff.
THE SOUTHERNER, Loew-Hakim, UA.
Werner Janssen.
SPELLBOUND, Selznick, UA. Miklos Rozsa.
THE STORY OF G.I. JOE, Cowan, UA. Louis
Applebaum and Ann Ronell.
THIS LOVE OF OURS, Universal. H.J. Salter.
THE VALLEY OF DECISION, MGM.
Herbert Stothart.

THE WOMAN IN THE WINDOW, International,
RKO Radio. Hugo Friedhofer and Arthur
Lange.

SCORING: MUSICAL
ANCHORS AWEIGH, MGM. Georgie Stoll.
BELLE OF THE YUKON, International, RKO
Radio. Arthur Lange.
CAN'T HELP SINGING, Universal. Jerome Kern
and H.J. Salter.
HITCHHIKE TO HAPPINESS, Republic.
Morton Scott.
INCENDIARY BLONDE, Paramount. Robert
Emmett Dolan.
RHAPSODY IN BLUE, Warner Bros. Ray
Heindorf and Max Steiner.
STATE FAIR, 20th Century-Fox. Charles
Henderson and Alfred Newman.
SUNBONNET SUE, Monogram. Edward J. Kay.
THE THREE CABALLEROS, Disney, RKO Radio.
Edward Plumb, Paul J. Smith and Charles Wolcott.
TONIGHT AND EVERY NIGHT, Columbia.
Marlin Skiles and Morris Stoloff.
WHY GIRLS LEAVE HOME, PRC. Walter Greene.
WONDER MAN, Goldwyn, RKO Radio. Lou
Forbes and Ray Heindorf.

SHORT SUBJECT: CARTOON
DONALD'S CRIME, Disney, RKO Radio. (Donald
Duck). Walt Disney, producer.
JASPER AND THE BEANSTALK, Paramount.
(Jasper Puppetoon). George Pal, producer.
LIFE WITH FEATHERS, Warner Bros. (Merrie
Melodies). Eddie Selzer, producer.
MIGHTY MOUSE IN GYPSY LIFE, 20th
Century-Fox. (Tèrrytoon). Paul Terry, producer.
POET AND PEASANT, Universal. (Lantz
Cartune). Walter Lantz, producer.
**QUIET PLEASE, MGM. (Tom & Jerry Series).
Frederick Quimby, producer.**
RIPPLING ROMANCE, Columbia. (Color
Rhapsodies).

SHORT SUBJECT: ONE-REEL
ALONG THE RAINBOW TRAIL, 20th Century-
Fox. (Movietone Adventure).
Edmund Reek, producer.
SCREEN SNAPSHOTS 25TH ANNIVERSARY,
Columbia. (Screen Snapshots).
Ralph Staub, producer.
**STAIRWAY TO LIGHT, MGM. (John Nesbitt
Passing Parade). Herbert Moulton, producer.**
STORY OF A DOG. Warner Bros. (Vitaphone
Varieties). Gordon Hollingshead, producer.
WHITE RHAPSODY, Paramount. (Sportlights).
Grantland Rice, producer.
YOUR NATIONAL GALLERY, Universal.
(Variety Views). Joseph O'Brien and Thomas
Mead, producers.

SHORT SUBJECT: TWO-REEL
A GUN IN HIS HAND, MGM. (Crime Does Not
Pay). Chester Franklin, producer.
THE JURY GOES ROUND 'N' ROUND, Columbia.
(All Star Comedies). Jules White, producer.
THE LITTLE WITCH, Paramount. (Musical
Parade). George Templeton, producer.
**STAR IN THE NIGHT, Warner Bros.
(Broadway Brevities). Gordon Hollingshead,
producer.**

DOCUMENTARY: SHORT SUBJECT
HITLER LIVES?, Warner Bros.
LIBRARY OF CONGRESS, Overseas Motion
Picture Bureau, Office of War Information.
TO THE SHORES OF IWO JIMA, U.S.
Marine Corps.

DOCUMENTARY: FEATURES
THE LAST BOMB, U.S. Army Air Force.
**THE TRUE GLORY, Governments of Great
Britain and USA.**

SPECIAL AWARDS
TO WALTER WANGER for his six years of
service as President of the Academy of Motion
Picture Arts and Sciences.
TO PEGGY ANN GARNER, outstanding child
actress of 1945.
TO *THE HOUSE I LIVE IN*, tolerance short
subject; produced by Frank Ross and Mervyn
LeRoy; directed by Mervyn LeRoy; screenplay
by Albert Maltz; song *The House I Live In*, music
by Earl Robinson, lyrics by Lewis Allen; starring
Frank Sinatra; released by RKO Radio.
TO REPUBLIC STUDIO, DANIEL J.
BLOOMBERG and the REPUBLIC SOUND
DEPARTMENT for the building of an
outstanding musical scoring auditorium which

provides optimum recording and conditions
and combines all elements of acoustic and
engineering design.

SCIENTIFIC OR TECHNICAL
CLASS III
LOREN L. RYDER, CHARLES R. DAILY and the
PARAMOUNT STUDIO SOUND
DEPARTMENT. MICHAEL S. LESHING,
BENJAMIN C. ROBINSON, ARTHUR B.
CHATELAIN and ROBERT C. STEVENS of
20th CenturyFox Studio and JOHN G.
CAPSTAFF of Eastman Kodak Co.

1946

If Grauman's Chinese Theatre had become too small for the ceremony, the Shrine Auditorium was cavernous. With 6,700 seats to fill, anyone could get in for the price of a ticket. But a record number of no-shows left plenty of freebies up for grabs. Bing Crosby ignited the avalanche of absenteeism. Claiming that he hadn't performed for a live audience in years, he bowed out of singing one of the nominated songs.

FIGHT OF "OUR LIVES"

**CEREMONY: March 13, 1947
Shrine Auditorium, Los Angeles
HOST: Jack Benny**

Frank Sinatra wasn't about to show up if Crosby didn't, and he, too, canceled. Then Judy Garland got last-minute stage fright. Joan Crawford, a past master at contracting "Oscar flu," declared that she couldn't possibly attend. Olivia de Havilland, who had read the polls and suspected this was her big night, wouldn't have missed it for the world. She worked the bleacher fans into a frenzy with her splashy entrance in a hand-painted gown. Once inside, she was a bit more subdued after learning that her sister, Joan Fontaine, would be Crawford's replacement as the Best Actor presenter. It was Fontaine who had spoiled de Havilland's shot at the Oscar in 1941, and the wound had never healed. It would be reopened before the night was over.

Another notorious rift, between Sam Goldwyn and William Wyler, resulted in the end of their long collaboration. Ironically, their last film together, *The Best Years of Our Lives*, would be the high point of their careers.

Goldwyn picked up the Thalberg Memorial Award as well as an Oscar as producer of *Best Years*, and Wyler won for Best Director. The film provided Fredric March with his Oscar comeback, but it was his non-actor co-star, Harold Russell, who had the audience reaching for handkerchiefs. Having lost both hands while serving in the U.S. Navy, Russell was honored for his courage with a special Oscar by the Board of Governors. It was to be a compensation for his almost certain loss for Best Supporting Actor. But Russell made Hollywood history moments later by winning that category as well. Two Oscars for a single performance!

If there had been any statuettes left over, they would probably have gone to the battling sisters for their fiery clash backstage. When Fontaine reached out to congratulate de Havilland for her win, she was soundly rebuffed. A lucky photographer caught them in the act, and the picture made almost every front page the next morning. The simmering siblings, like Joan Crawford the year before, took precedence over Oscar. An expressionless gold statuette couldn't hope to compete with the glamour of red-hot personalities for the public's fascination.

**BEST PICTURE/BEST DIRECTOR
WILLIAM WYLER (1902–1981)
*THE BEST YEARS OF OUR LIVES***

This year it was Wilder's turn to hand the Best Director Oscar over to Wyler, calling the movie "the best-directed film I've ever seen in my life." And once again, as he had last year, Eric Johnston of the censorship office announced the Best Picture, cooing, "Oooooooh, it's *The Best Years of Our Lives*."

Though the critics had mixed feelings about the film, there was no question that *The Best Years of Our Lives* was certain to win the Best Picture prize. Writing for the *New York Times*, Bosley Crowther said, "The [film] catches the drama of veterans returning from war as no film has managed to do. It is seldom that there comes a motion picture which can be wholly and enthusiastically endorsed not only as superlative entertainment but as food for quiet and humanizing thought."

Weighing in for the middle, critic Danny Peary admitted, "It [is] so timely, so well executed—my only complaint is that the resolutions to the individual stories are too pat, too safe—that it would have been unthinkable to have given the Award to any other film." But *The New Yorker*'s Pauline Kael had little good to say: "Despite its seven Academy Awards, it's not a great picture; it's too schematic and it drags on after you get the points…however, there's something absorbing about the banality."

(For more on Wyler, see 1942 and 1959.)

Myrna Loy, Fredric March, Teresa Wright

The envelope, please...

Myrna Loy with Fredric March

BEST ACTOR
FREDRIC MARCH (1897–1975)
THE BEST YEARS OF OUR LIVES

"Fredric March is magnificent as the sergeant who breaks the ice with his family by taking his wife and daughter on a titanic binge," wrote Bosley Crowther in the *New York Times*. "His humor is sweeping yet subtle, his irony is keen as a knife, and he is altogether genuine. This is the best acting job he has ever done."

March set out to become an economist but caught the acting bug while performing bit parts in films. He seemed to have made the right career move. According to film critic Leonard Maltin, March was "one of the finest actors who ever worked on screen. [He] resisted typecasting by the studios and, in fact, refused long-term contracts, hand-picking his roles with incredible success. The result was an exemplary film career."

Along with the critics, Shelley Winters offered her own observation of March's many talents: "He was able to do a very emotional scene with tears in his eyes and pinch my fanny at the same time."

(For more on March, see 1931–32.)

BEST ACTRESS
OLIVIA DE HAVILLAND (B. 1916)
TO EACH HIS OWN

"I feel humble, too, as well as proud. I accept this Oscar in the name of my team as well as my own," de Havilland said.

A delicate beauty, de Havilland, the older sister of actress Joan Fontaine, scored a lucky break at age 19 when she was seen in a stage production by famous impresario Max Reinhardt, who helped launch her film career by casting her in *A Midsummer Night's Dream* (1935). She appeared with Errol Flynn ten times in such lavish costume pictures as *The Charge of the Light Brigade* and *Anthony Adverse* (both 1936).

De Havilland became a true star in *Gone with the Wind* (1939, nom.), which was followed by *Santa Fe Trail* (1940), *They Died with Their Boots On* (1941), and her breakthrough role in *Hold Back the Dawn* (1941)—for which she was nominated for her first Best Actress Oscar, and ironically lost to her sister. Outspoken about her treatment at Warners, where she insisted on getting better roles, de Havilland was suspended for six months. She sued the studio and won the suit.

De Havilland soon appeared victorious in *To Each His Own*, followed by *The Snake Pit* (1948, nom.) and *The Heiress* (1949, Oscar). After a brief stint on Broadway, she returned to the screen in *Not as a Stranger* (1955), *Hush...Hush, Sweet Charlotte* (1965), and *The Fifth Musketeer* (1979). In 1962 she wrote *Every Frenchman Has One*, about her experiences with her husband in Paris.
(For more on De Havilland, see 1949.)

BEST OF 1946
Best Picture/Best Director: William Wyler, *The Best Years of Our Lives*
Best Actor: Fredric March, *The Best Years of Our Lives*
Best Actress: Olivia de Havilland, *To Each His Own*
Best Supporting Actor: Harold Russell, *The Best Years of Our Lives*
Best Supporting Actress: Anne Baxter, *The Razor's Edge*
Honorary Award: Ernst Lubitsch

FIRSTS
- Only Academy members were allowed to cast ballots. The new ruling reduced the number of voters from 10,000 to fewer than 2,000.
- *The Best Years of Our Lives* was the first and only Samuel Goldwyn production to win Best Picture.
- Burt Lancaster made his screen debut in *The Killers*.

SINS OF OMISSION
Pictures: *Notorious, The Big Sleep, Brief Encounter*
Director: Alfred Hitchcock, *Notorious*
Actors: Humphrey Bogart, *The Big Sleep;* Henry Fonda, *My Darling Clementine*
Actress: Ingrid Bergman, *Notorious*
Supporting Actress: Donna Reed, *It's a Wonderful Life*

ALWAYS A BRIDESMAID, NEVER A BRIDE
Despite a rigorous campaign for votes, Rosalind Russell went home empty-handed. *Sister Kenny* was her second of four unsuccessful Best Actress nominations.

UNMENTIONABLES
- Laurence Olivier was well aware of the anti-British mood among Academy voters and stayed clear of the ceremony despite his special award for *Henry V.*
- To create a more realistic feel, female cast members of *The Best Years of Our Lives* wore everyday makeup. The men wore none.
- Gregory Peck summed up the overheated *Duel in the Sun*, nicknamed *Lust in the Dust* by critics: "A bizarre picture. I don't think the Old West was very like that."
- Four Oscars in two years went to performers playing lushes. In 1945 it was Ray Milland (*The Lost Weekend*) and James Dunn (*A Tree Grows in Brooklyn*). For 1946, it was Fredric March with a twist (*The Best Years of Our Lives*) and Anne Baxter on the rocks (*The Razor's Edge*).
- Samuel Goldwyn, *The Best Years of Our Lives* producer and Thalberg Memorial Award recipient, could have been a character in one of his own movies. A completely self-invented Polish immigrant, he was perhaps the most frequently quoted man in Hollywood thanks to his famous non sequiturs, which were dubbed Goldwynisms. A humorless man, he often delivered his statements in a rage, which made these expressions of his inadvertent wit even more memorable:

  "Include me out!"
  "In two words—impossible!"
  "It's greater than a masterpiece—it's mediocre."
  "That's the way with these directors, they're always biting the hand that lays the golden egg."
  "You've got to take the bull by the teeth."
  "Give me a smart idiot over a stupid genius any day."
  "I've gone where the hand of man has never set foot."
  "A verbal contract isn't worth the paper it's written on."

 BEST SUPPORTING ACTOR
HAROLD RUSSELL (B. 1914)
THE BEST YEARS OF OUR LIVES

Overcome by the audience's rousing applause, Russell was reduced to tears at the podium. *The New York Times* raved, "Harold Russell is incredibly fine as the sailor who has lost his hands. Mr. Russell, who actually did lose his hands in the service and does use 'hooks,' has responded to the tactful restrained direction of Mr. Wyler in a most sensitive style."

Born in Nova Scotia, Russell was training paratroopers during World War II when some TNT exploded in his hands—he lost both of them. Chosen to make an army training film called *Diary of a Sergeant*, he was spotted by Wyler, who created a part for him in *The Best Years of Our Lives*. After working to help returning veterans, he went back to films and appeared in *Inside Moves* (1980) and *Dogtown* (1997). Russell is the author of two autobiographies, *Victory in My Hands* (1949) and *The Best Years of My Life* (1981).

Hoagy Carmichael with Harold Russell

 BEST SUPPORTING ACTRESS
ANNE BAXTER (1923–1985)
THE RAZOR'S EDGE

Baxter took up acting under the tutelage of Maria Ouspenskaya at the age of 11 and made her Broadway debut at 13. She was a competent actress who relied more on charm than on great beauty to create a career marked by some shining moments. She had a special gift for playing deceptively innocent young women. Orson Welles cast her in *The Magnificent Ambersons* (1942), which revealed aspects of her that wouldn't be seen until such later films as *Five Graves to Cairo* (1943), *Angel on My Shoulder* (1946), and her vampish queen in DeMille's *The Ten Commandments* (1956).

In 1976 Baxter wrote *Intermission: A True Story*, in which she recounted her arduous life with her second husband, Randolph Galt, when she left Hollywood to live on a cattle station in the Australian outback. She made her last feature-film appearance in *Jane Austen in Manhattan* (1980) and participated in a documentary about her grandfather, the architect Frank Lloyd Wright. Baxter was a regular on the TV series *Hotel* before succumbing to cancer in 1985.

 HONORARY AWARD
ERNST LUBITSCH (1892–1947)

So distinctive were Lubitsch's films that critics described them as having the "Lubitsch touch"—films that examined sexual and social mores with a particularly sophisticated hand.

A brilliant director, Lubitsch began his film career as an actor in 1912 and joined Max Reinhardt's Deutsches Theater in Berlin. He turned to directing in the late teens and became internationally famous for a series of spectacles, including *Carmen* (1918, released in the U.S. in 1921 as *Gypsy Blood*) and *Madame Du Barry* (a.k.a. *Passion*, 1919). Silent-film star Mary Pickford had the wisdom to recognize Lubitsch's gifts and brought him to Hollywood in 1923. Their first collaboration, *Rosita* (1923), was deemed a failure, though the critics loved it. Pickford allowed Lubitsch to sign on with other studios, where he made *Lady Windermere's Fan* (1925), *So This Is Paris* (1926), and *The Patriot* (1928).

Lubitsch entered the talkies with opulence and made, among other films, *The Love Parade* (1929, nom.), *Trouble in Paradise* (1932), *Design for Living* (1933), and *The Merry Widow* (1934). In 1935 he was made head of production for Paramount, but he gave up the job in 1936 to return to directing. Lubitsch launched this stage of his career with such films as *Angel* (1937) and *Bluebeard's Eighth Wife* (1938), which were quickly followed by his best films—*Ninotchka* (1939), *The Shop Around the Corner* (1940), and the dark anti-Nazi comedy *To Be or Not to Be* (1942).

After a heart condition slowed him down, Lubitsch directed his last film to completion, the delightful *Heaven Can Wait* (1943, nom.).

PICTURE
THE BEST YEARS OF OUR LIVES, Goldwyn, RKO Radio, Samuel Goldwyn.
HENRY V, Rank-Two Cities, UA (British), Laurence Olivier.
IT'S A WONDERFUL LIFE, Liberty, RKO Radio, Frank Capra.
THE RAZOR'S EDGE, 20th Century-Fox, Darryl F. Zanuck.
THE YEARLING, MGM. Sidney Franklin.

ACTOR
FREDRIC MARCH in *The Best Years of Our Lives*, Goldwyn, RKO Radio.
LAURENCE OLIVIER in *Henry V*, Rank-Two Cities, UA (British).
LARRY PARKS in *The Jolson Story*, Columbia.
GREGORY PECK in *The Yearling*, MGM.
JAMES STEWART in *It's a Wonderful Life*, Liberty Films, RKO Radio.

ACTRESS
OLIVIA DE HAVILLAND in *To Each His Own*, Paramount.
CELIA JOHNSON in *Brief Encounter*, Rank, U-I (British).
JENNIFER JONES in *Duel in the Sun*, Selznick International.
ROSALIND RUSSELL in *Sister Kenny*, RKO Radio.
JANE WYMAN in *The Yearling*, MGM.

SUPPORTING ACTOR
CHARLES COBURN in *The Green Years*, MGM.
WILLIAM DEMAREST in *The Jolson Story*, Columbia.
CLAUDE RAINS in *Notorious*, RKO Radio.
HAROLD RUSSELL in *The Best Years of Our Lives*, Goldwyn, RKO Radio.
CLIFTON WEBB in *The Razor's Edge*, 20th Century-Fox.

SUPPORTING ACTRESS
ETHEL BARRYMORE in *The Spiral Staircase*, RKO Radio.
ANNE BAXTER in *The Razor's Edge*, 20th Century-Fox.
LILLIAN GISH in *Duel in the Sun*, Selznick International.
FLORA ROBSON in *Saratoga Trunk*, Warner Bros.
GALE SONDERGAARD in *Anna and the King of Siam*, 20th Century-Fox.

DIRECTION
CLARENCE BROWN for *The Yearling*, MGM.
FRANK CAPRA for *It's a Wonderful Life*, Liberty, RKO Radio.
DAVID LEAN for *Brief Encounter*, Rank, U-I (British).
ROBERT SIODMAK for *The Killers*, Hellinger, Universal.
WILLIAM WYLER for *The Best Years of Our Lives*, Goldwyn, RKO Radio.

WRITING: ORIGINAL STORY
THE DARK MIRROR, U-I. Vladimir Pozner.
THE STRANGE LOVE OF MARTHA IVERS, Wallis, Paramount. Jack Patrick.
THE STRANGER, International, RKO Radio. Victor Trivas.
TO EACH HIS OWN, Paramount. Charles Brackett.
VACATION FROM MARRIAGE, London Films, MGM. (British). Clemence Dane.

WRITING: ORIGINAL SCREENPLAY
THE BLUE DAHLIA, Paramount. Raymond Chandler.
CHILDREN OF PARADISE (French). Jacques Prevert.
NOTORIOUS, RKO Radio. Ben Hecht.
THE ROAD TO UTOPIA, Paramount. Norman Panama and Melvin Frank.

THE SEVENTH VEIL, Rank, Universal (British). Muriel Box and Sydney Box.

WRITING: SCREENPLAY
ANNA AND THE KING OF SIAM, 20th Century-Fox. Sally Benson and Talbot Jennings.
THE BEST YEARS OF OUR LIVES, Goldwyn, RKO Radio. Robert E. Sherwood.
BRIEF ENCOUNTER, Rank, U-I (British). Anthony Havelock-Allan, David Lean and Ronald Neame.
THE KILLERS, Hellinger, Universal. Anthony Veiller.
OPEN CITY (Italian). Sergio Amidei and F. Fellini.

CINEMATOGRAPHY
B/W
ANNA AND THE KING OF SIAM, 20th Century-Fox. Arthur Miller.
THE GREEN YEARS, MGM. George Folsey.

Color
THE JOLSON STORY, Columbia. Joseph Walker.
THE YEARLING, MGM. Charles Rasher, Leonard Smith and Arthur Arling.

ART DIRECTION—INTERIOR DECORATION
B/W
ANNA AND THE KING OF SIAM, 20th Century-Fox. Lyle Wheeler and William Darling; Thomas Little and Frank E. Hughes.
KITTY, Paramount. Hans Dreier and Walter Tyler; Sam Comer and Ray Moyer.
THE RAZOR'S EDGE, 20th Century-Fox. Richard Day and Nathan Juran; Thomas Little and Paul S. Fox.

Color
CAESAR AND CLEOPATRA, Pascal, UA (British). John Bryan.
HENRY V, Rank-Two Cities UA (British). Paul Sheriff and Carmen Dillon.
THE YEARLING, MGM. Cedric Gibbons and Paul Groesse; Edwin B. Willis.

SOUND RECORDING
THE BEST YEARS OF OUR LIVES, Goldwyn, RKO Radio. Samuel Goldwyn Studio Sound Dept., Gordon Sawyer, Sound Director.
IT'S A WONDERFUL LIFE, Liberty, RKO Radio. RKO Radio Studio Sound Dept., John Aalberg, Sound Director.
THE JOLSON STORY, Columbia. Columbia Studio Sound Dept., John Livadary, Sound Director.

FILM EDITING
THE BEST YEARS OF OUR LIVES, Goldwyn, RKO Radio. Daniel Mandell.
IT'S A WONDERFUL LIFE, Liberty, RKO Radio. William Hornbeck.
THE JOLSON STORY, Columbia. William Lyon.
THE KILLERS, Hellinger, Universal. Arthur Hilton.
THE YEARLING, MGM. Harold Kress.

SPECIAL EFFECTS
BLITHE SPIRIT, Rank-Two Cities, UA (British). Thomas Howard.
A STOLEN LIFE, Warner Bros. William McGann and Nathan Levinson.

SONG
ALL THROUGH THE DAY (*Centennial Summer*, 20th Century-Fox); Music by Jerome Kern. Lyrics by Oscar Hammerstein II.
I CAN'T BEGIN TO TELL YOU (*The Dolly Sisters*, 20th Century-Fox); Music by James Monaco. Lyrics by Mack Gordon.
OLE BUTTERMILK SKY (*Canyon Passage*, Wanger, Universal); Music by Hoagy Carmichael. Lyrics by Jack Brooks.
ON THE ATCHISON, TOPEKA AND THE SANTA FE (*The Harvey Girls*, MGM); Music by Harry Warren. Lyrics by Johnny Mercer.
YOU KEEP COMING BACK LIKE A SONG (*Blue Skies*, Paramount); Music and Lyrics by Irving Berlin.

SCORING: DRAMA/COMEDY
ANNA AND THE KING OF SIAM, 20th Century-Fox. Bernard Herrmann.
THE BEST YEARS OF OUR LIVES, Goldwyn, RKO Radio. Hugo Friedhofer.
HENRY V, Rank-Two Cities, VA (British). William Walton.
HUMORESQUE, Warner Bros. Franz Waxman.
THE KILLERS, Hellinger, Universal. Miklos Rozsa.

SCORING: MUSICAL
BLUE SKIES, Paramount. Robert Emmett Dolan.
CENTENNIAL SUMMER, 20th Century-Fox. Alfred Newman.
THE HARVEY GIRLS, MGM. Lennie Hayton.
THE JOLSON STORY, Columbia. Morris Stoloff.
NIGHT AND DAY Warner Bros. Ray Heindorf and Max Steiner.

SHORT SUBJECT: CARTOON
THE CAT CONCERTO, MGM. (Tom & Jerry). Frederick Quimby, producer.
CHOPIN'S MUSICAL MOMENTS, Universal. (Musical Miniatures). Walter Lantz, producer.
JOHN HENRY AND THE INKY POO, Paramount. (Puppetoon). George Pal, producer.
SQUATTER'S RIGHTS, Disney, RKO Radio. (Mickey Mouse). Walt Disney, producer.
WALKY TALKY HAWKY, Warner Bros. (Merrie Melodies). Edward Selzer, producer.

SHORT SUBJECT: ONE-REEL
DIVE-HI CHAMPS, Paramount. (Sportlights). Jack Eaton, producer.
FACING YOUR DANGER, Warner Bros. (Sports Parade). Gordon Hollingshead, producer.
GOLDEN HORSES, 20th Century-Fox. (Movietone Sports Review). Edmund Reek, producer.
SMART AS A FOX, Warner Bros. (Varieties). Gordon Hollingshead, producer.
SURE CURES, MGM. (Pete Smith Specialty). Pete Smith, producer.

SHORT SUBJECT: TWO-REEL
A BOY AND HIS DOG, Warner Bros. (Featurettes). Gordon Hollingshead, producer.
COLLEGE QUEEN, Paramount. (Musical Parade). George Templeton, producer.
HISS AND YELL, Columbia. (All Star Comedies). Jules White, producer.
THE LUCKIEST GUY IN THE WORLD, Warner Bros. (Two-reel Special). Jerry Bresler, producer.

DOCUMENTARY: SHORT SUBJECT
ATOMIC POWER, 20th Century-Fox.
LIFE AT THE ZOO, Artkino.
PARAMOUNT NEWS ISSUE #37, Paramount.
SEEDS OF DESTINY, U.S. War Department.
TRAFFIC WITH THE DEVIL, MGM.

SPECIAL AWARDS
TO LAURENCE OLIVIER for his outstanding achievement as actor, producer and director in bringing *Henry V* to the screen.
TO HAROLD RUSSELL for bringing hope and courage to his fellow veterans through his appearance in *The Best Years of Our Lives*.
TO ERNST LUBITSCH for his distinguished contributions to the art of the motion picture.
TO CLAUDE JARMAN JR., outstanding child actor of 1946.

IRVING G. THALBERG MEMORIAL AWARD
TO SAMUEL GOLDWYN

SCIENTIFIC OR TECHNICAL
CLASS III
HARLAN L. BAUMBACH and the PARAMOUNT WEST COAST LABORATORY;
HERBERT E. BRITT;
BURTON F. MILLER and the WARNER BROS. STUDIO SOUND and ELECTRICAL DEPARTMENTS;
CARL FAULKNER of the 20th Century-Fox Studio Sound Department;
MOLE-RICHARDSON CO.;
ARTHUR F. BLINN, ROBERT O. COOK, C.O. SLYFIELD and the WALT DISNEY STUDIO SOUND DEPARTMENT;
BURTON F. MILLER and the WARNER BROS. STUDIO SOUND DEPARTMENT;
MARTY MARTIN and HAL ADKINS of the RKO Radio Studio Miniature Department;
HAROLD NYE and the WARNER BROS. STUDIO ELECTRICAL DEPARTMENT.

1947

"We're going to the party afterward anyway. I won't be bitter."

—Rosalind Russell

If she had checked the Oscar-night weather forecast, compulsive knitter Celeste Holm would have stitched together an overcoat. It was a bizarre 30 degrees, and Hollywood's glamorously turned-out sisterhood was getting the cold shoulder. Chronic no-show Joan Crawford chose the most frigid year in Academy history to make an appearance—in an airy white crepe gown. Susan Hayward wore the most expensive dress she ever bought and worried that somebody would step on its long train. Her husband, Jess Barker, guarded against the possibility all night before finally putting his own foot on it.

SHOCKINGLY YOUNG

CEREMONY: March 20, 1948
Shrine Auditorium, Los Angeles
HOSTS: Agnes Moorehead,
Dick Powell

Front-runner Rosalind Russell, done up in white, shocking pink, and goosebumps, arrived on the arm of her own fiercely protective husband, agent Freddy Brisson, referred to in Hollywood's cattier circles as "the lizard of Roz." Dark horse Loretta Young swept through the entrance in a billowing emerald-green gown with tenuous shoulder straps. A fan shouted to her that green was an unlucky color.

Inside, Santa Claus did the trick for the year's favorite, Edmund Gwenn. Celeste Holm looked up from her knitting as her name was announced for Best Supporting Actress. Her ball of yarn skittered under her seat as she dashed up the aisle in her homemade bouffant dress. The heartthrob young star of *Gentleman's Agreement*, Gregory Peck, lost out to a matinee idol of the silent era, Ronald Colman. Colman was so shaken by the honor that he wept backstage.

With only the Best Actress statuette left on the dais, the audience began a noisy exit. Rosalind Russell was a foregone conclusion for *Mourning Becomes Electra*. She'd campaigned hard with the expert assistance of the PR agent who had earned victories for Olivia de Havilland and Joan Crawford. As Fredric March tore open the envelope, Russell confidently leaned forward and began to rise.

March was about to announce her name when he did a double take and paused. "The winner is Loretta Young!" The crowd that had already reached the door froze in its tracks. How was this possible? Russell led in every survey and poll from New York City to Las Vegas. Not even Young could believe it. After breathlessly floating to the stage, she checked the envelope herself just to be sure. Rarely had Oscar night packed such a walloping surprise win. Russell, already half out of her seat, led the standing ovation. It may have been a case of follow-through posture over murderous instinct, but it certainly looked classy.

BEST PICTURE/BEST DIRECTOR
ELIA KAZAN (B. 1909)
GENTLEMAN'S AGREEMENT

"This picture started as a gamble," said producer Darryl F. Zanuck. "We knew we were pioneering in an off-the-beaten-path film, but we weighed every sequence in the light of entertainment values…I would like to emphasize that *Gentleman's Agreement* was primarily planned for entertainment rather than for any social message. I believe that this is the chief reason for the success of the film." The Best Director accepted his prize saying, "I guess, being a comparative newcomer to the industry, I'm more grateful than most for the help that I needed and received."

Kazan, the director of such iconic films as *A Streetcar Named Desire* (1951) and *On the Waterfront* (1954), was also one of the first members of the Hollywood community to cooperate with the House Un-American Activities Committee.

Interestingly, Kazan was a true visionary of the late 1940s and early 1950s who broke new ground in social realism, creating some of the era's most memorable movies and influencing generations to come. He was also responsible for finding the genius in such actors as Marlon Brando and James Dean.

Gregory Peck, Anne Revere

Born Elia Kazanjoglou in Constantinople, Kazan began his film career by making documentaries in the mid-1930s. He was later signed on by Darryl F. Zanuck to direct *A Tree Grows in Brooklyn* (1945). Kazan knew how to draw great performances from his actors, as attested by James Dunn's Best Supporting Oscar. He took on race relations in *Boomerang!* (1947) and *Pinky* (1949), and went on to make *Man on a Tightrope* (1953), *East of Eden* (1955, nom.), *Baby Doll* (1956), *A Face in the Crowd* (1957), *Wild River* (1960), and *Splendor in the Grass* (1961). Kazan directed only three films in later decades, including *The Arrangement* (1969) and *The Last Tycoon* (1976). He published his autobiography, *A Life*, in 1988.

The envelope, please...

BEST ACTOR
RONALD COLMAN (1891–1958)
A DOUBLE LIFE

"I am very happy and very lucky," said Colman. Nominated for his roles in *Bulldog Drummond* (1929), *Condemned* (1929), and *Random Harvest* (1942), Colman got the gold only once.

The charming, elegant quintessence of British poise succeeded in becoming the No. 1 box-office star for three consecutive years, often playing Latin lovers. In the late 1920s, after breaking out with *Beau Geste* (1926), he followed that success with *The Magic Flame* (1927) and *Two Lovers* (1928).

With his smooth, cultivated voice, Colman moved gracefully into sound. He then starred in a string of well-received films (this time playing men of honor), including *A Tale of Two Cities* (1935), *Lost Horizon* (1937), *The Prisoner of Zenda* (1937), *The Talk of the Town* (1942), and *Kismet* (1944).

When Colman reached middle age it became increasingly difficult for him to find appropriate roles. After a brief hiatus, he returned to the screen in *The Late George Apley*, followed by his breakthrough role and first Academy win in *A Double Life* (both 1947). His last film appearance came ten years later, in *The Story of Mankind* (1957). He also made some television appearances on *The Jack Benny Show*.

Joseph Cotten with Loretta Young

BEST ACTRESS
LORETTA YOUNG (1913–2000)
THE FARMER'S DAUGHTER

"Up to now, this occasion for me has been a spectator sport. But I dressed, just in case," said the truly shocked Young.

Although she was never considered a great actress, Young appeared in countless films and was nominated once again for *Come to the Stable* (1949), after her Oscar win for *The Farmer's Daughter*. A child star, Young won her first contract at the age of 15 and was essentially blackballed by producer Zanuck after a series of arguments over scripts. They later reconciled.

Nevertheless, she went on to appear in a long list of films in which she was cast for her ineffable glamorous star quality. Perhaps she gave her most interesting performance in Orson Welles's *The Stranger* (1946). Among her other films were *Platinum Blonde* (1931), *Eternally Yours* (1939), *The Bishop's Wife* (1947), and *It Happens Every Thursday* (1953).

Young was best known to audiences as the star of TV's *The Loretta Young Show* (1953–1961). She published her memoirs, *The Things I Had to Learn*, in 1961, and successfully sued NBC for unlawfully broadcasting her TV shows abroad.

BEST OF 1947
Best Picture/Best Director: Elia Kazan, *Gentleman's Agreement*
Best Actor: Ronald Colman, *A Double Life*
Best Actress: Loretta Young, *The Farmer's Daughter*
Best Supporting Actor: Edmund Gwenn, *Miracle on 34th Street*
Best Supporting Actress: Celeste Holm, *Gentleman's Agreement*

FIRSTS
• Italy's *Shoeshine* was the first foreign film to receive a special Academy Award.
• *Crossfire* was the first second-tier (B movie) to be nominated for Best Picture.

ROLE REVERSALS
Ironically, Rosalind Russell turned down Loretta Young's role in *The Farmer's Daughter*.

SINS OF OMISSION
Picture: *Out of the Past*
Actors: Robert Mitchum, *Out of the Past*; Charles Chaplin, *Monsieur Verdoux*
Actress: Deborah Kerr, *Black Narcissus*
Supporting Actress: Martha Raye, *Monsieur Verdoux*

ALWAYS A BRIDESMAID, NEVER A BRIDE
"I'll be nominated for an Oscar again. Maybe not next year. Maybe I'll have to wait until the fifties. But I intend to win someday," said Susan Hayward. (She won an Oscar in 1958).

UNMENTIONABLES
• *Crossfire* producer, Adrian Scott, and its screenwriter, Edward Dmytryk, were two of the blacklisted "Hollywood Ten" castigated by the House Un-American Activities Committee.
• The curious Best Screenplay winner, *The Bachelor and the Bobby Soxer*, was penned by Sidney Sheldon, the pop-fiction novelist.
• James Baskett's special award for Uncle Remus in *Song of the South* allowed the Academy its sympathetic pitch for race relations without having to nominate him for Best Actor. Many black organizations were outraged by the recognition of Baskett's role as a happy-go-lucky slave.

Natalie Wood with Edmund Gwenn

BEST SUPPORTING ACTOR
EDMUND GWENN (1875–1959)
MIRACLE ON 34TH STREET

In an interview in *Variety*, Gwenn admitted that he believed in Santa Claus. Both audiences and critics enjoyed the plump, smiling-eyed Gwenn's performance in *Miracle on 34th Street*.

The elfin, Welsh-born actor, despite this heartwarming role in *Miracle* often played unsympathetic parts in British films of the 1930s. Before appearing in film, Gwenn was a protégé of George Bernard Shaw, and made his mark on the stage in *Man and Superman*. Gwenn was nominated once more for his role in *Mister 880* (1950).

Among his British films were Alfred Hitchcock's *The Skin Game* (1931), *Be Mine Tonight* (1932), and *Waltzes from Vienna* (1934). When he arrived in Hollywood in 1935, he was already 60 years old. He gave strong performances in, among other films, *Sylvia Scarlett* (1935), *Anthony Adverse* (1936), *Pride and Prejudice* (1940), *Foreign Correspondent* (1940), *Lassie Come Home* (1943), and *Them!* (1954). Hitchcock's *The Trouble with Harry* (1955) was Gwenn's final film. On his deathbed, he apparently said to visitor George Seaton, commenting on how tough it was to die, "It's tough…but not as tough as comedy!"

BEST SUPPORTING ACTRESS
CELESTE HOLM (B. 1919)
GENTLEMAN'S AGREEMENT

"Thank you for letting this happen," Holm said in her acceptance speech. "I'm so happy to be a part of an industry that can create so much understanding in a world that needs it so much."

After her win for *Gentleman's Agreement*, Holm was nominated for two more Oscars for her roles in *Come to the Stable* (1949) and *All About Eve* (1950). Holm's first love was the stage, where she made her mark in the original production of *Oklahoma!* She began her screen career a decade later, in 1946, and performed admirably in a variety of genres, including musicals, comedies, and serious drama—particularly in wisecracking roles.

After her many stage appearances, she returned to the screen for two MGM musicals, *The Tender Trap* (1955) and *High Society* (1956). Holm appeared on television in her own series, *Honestly Celeste* (1954), and continued to appear on stage and in films and miniseries.

PICTURE

THE BISHOP'S WIFE, Goldwyn, RKO Radio, Samuel Goldwyn.
CROSSFIRE, RKO Radio, Adrian Scott.
GENTLEMAN'S AGREEMENT, 20th Century-Fox, Darryl F. Zanuck.
GREAT EXPECTATIONS, Rank-Cineguild, U-I (British), Ronald Neame.
MIRACLE ON 34TH STREET, 20th Century-Fox, William Perlberg.

ACTOR

RONALD COLMAN in *A Double Life*, Kanin, U-I.
JOHN GARFIELD in *Body and Soul*, Enterprise, UA.
GREGORY PECK in *Gentleman's Agreement*, 20th Century-Fox.
WILLIAM POWELL in *Life with Father*, Warner Bros.
MICHAEL REDGRAVE in *Mourning Becomes Electra*, RKO Radio.

ACTRESS

JOAN CRAWFORD in *Possessed*, Warner Bros.
SUSAN HAYWARD in *Smash Up—The Story of a Woman*, Wanger, U-I.
DOROTHY McGUIRE in *Gentleman's Agreement*, 20th Century-Fox.
ROSALIND RUSSELL in *Mourning Becomes Electra*, RKO Radio.
LORETTA YOUNG in *The Farmer's Daughter*, RKO Radio.

SUPPORTING ACTOR

CHARLES BICKFORD in *The Farmer's Daughter*, RKO Radio.
THOMAS GOMEZ in *Ride the Pink Horse*, U-I.
EDMUND GWENN in *Miracle on 34th Street*, 20th Century-Fox.
ROBERT RYAN in *Crossfire*, RKO Radio.
RICHARD WIDMARK in *Kiss of Death*, 20th Century-Fox.

SUPPORTING ACTRESS

ETHEL BARRYMORE in *The Paradine Case*, Selznick Releasing Organization.
GLORIA GRAHAME in *Crossfire*, RKO Radio.
CELESTE HOLM in *Gentleman's Agreement*, 20th Century-Fox.
MARJORIE MAIN in *The Egg and I*, U-I.
ANNE REVERE in *Gentleman's Agreement*, 20th Century-Fox.

DIRECTION

GEORGE CUKOR for *A Double Life*, Kanin, U-I.
EDWARD DMYTRYK for *Crossfire*, RKO Radio.
ELIA KAZAN for *Gentleman's Agreement*, 20th Century-Fox.
HENRY KOSTER for *The Bishop's Wife*, Goldwyn, RKO Radio.
DAVID LEAN for *Great Expectations*, Rank-Cineguild, U-I (British).

WRITING: ORIGINAL STORY

A CAGE OF NIGHTINGALES, Lopert Films (French). Georges Chaperot and Rene Wheeler.
IT HAPPENED ON FIFTH AVENUE, Del Ruth, Allied Artists. Herbert Clyde Lewis and Frederick Stephani.
KISS OF DEATH, 20th Century-Fox. Eleazar Lipsky.
MIRACLE ON 34TH STREET, 20th Century-Fox. Valentine Davies.
SMASH-UP—THE STORY OF A WOMAN, Wanger, U-I. Dorothy Parker and Frank Cavett.

WRITING: ORIGINAL SCREENPLAY

THE BACHELOR AND THE BOBBYSOXER, RKO Radio. Sidney Sheldon.
BODY AND SOUL, Enterprise, UA. Abraham Polonsky.

A DOUBLE LIFE, Kanin, U-I. Ruth Gordon and Garson Kanin.
MONSIEUR VERDOUX, Chaplin, UA. Charles Chaplin.
SHOE-SHINE, Lopert Films (Italian). Sergio Amidei, Adolfo Franci, C.G. Viola and Cesare Zavattini.

WRITING: SCREENPLAY

BOOMERANG!, 20th Century-Fox. Richard Murphy.
CROSSFIRE, RKO Radio. John Paxton.
GENTLEMAN'S AGREEMENT, 20th Century-Fox. Moss Hart.
GREAT EXPECTATIONS, Rank-Cineguild, U-I (British). David Lean, Ronald Neame and Anthony Havelock-Allan.
MIRACLE ON 34TH STREET, 20th Century-Fox. George Seaton.

CINEMATOGRAPHY

B/W
THE GHOST AND MRS. MUIR, 20th Century-Fox. Charles Lang Jr.
GREAT EXPECTATIONS, Rank-Cineguild, U-I (British). Guy Green.
GREEN DOLPHIN STREET, MGM. George Folsey.

Color
BLACK NARCISSUS, Rank-Archer, U-I (British). Jack Cardiff.
LIFE WITH FATHER, Warner Bros. Peverell Marley and William V. Skall.
MOTHER WORE TIGHTS, 20th Century-Fox. Harry Jackson.

ART DIRECTION—SET DECORATION

B/W
THE FOXES OF HARROW, 20th Century-Fox. Lyle Wheeler and Maurice Ransford; Thomas Little and Paul S. Fox.
GREAT EXPECTATIONS, Rank-Cineguild, U-I (British). John Bryan; Wilfred Shingleton.

Color
BLACK NARCISSUS, Rank-Archers, U-I (British). Alfred Junge.
LIFE WITH FATHER, Warner Bros. Robert M. Haas; George James Hopkins.

SOUND RECORDING

THE BISHOP'S WIFE, Goldwyn, RKO Radio. Samuel Goldwyn Studio Sound Dept., Gordon Sawyer, Sound Director.
GREEN DOLPHIN STREET, MGM. MGM Studio Sound Dept., Douglas Shearer, Sound Director.
T-MEN, Reliance Pictures, Eagle-Lion. Sound Services, Inc., Jack Whitney, Sound Director.

FILM EDITING

THE BISHOP'S WIFE, Goldwyn, RKO Radio. Monica Collingwood.
BODY AND SOUL, Enterprise, UA. Francis Lyon and Robert Parrish.
GENTLEMAN'S AGREEMENT, 20th Century-Fox. Harmon Jones.
GREEN DOLPHIN STREET, MGM. George White.
ODD MAN OUT. Rank-Two Cities, U-I (British). Fergus McDonnell.

SPECIAL EFFECTS

GREEN DOLPHIN STREET, MGM. A. Arnold Gillespie, Warren Newcombe, Douglas Shearer and Michael Steinore.
UNCONQUERED, DeMille, Paramount. Farciot Edouart, Devereux Jennings, Gordon Jennings, Wallace Kelley, Paul Lerpae and George Dutton.

SONG

A GAL IN CALICO (*The Time, Place and the Girl*, Warner Bros.); Music by Arthur Schwartz. Lyrics by Leo Robin.
I WISH I DIDN'T LOVE YOU SO (*The Perils of Pauline*, Paramount); Music and Lyrics by Frank Loesser.
PASS THAT PEACE PIPE (*Good News*, MGM); Music and Lyrics by Ralph Blane, Hugh Martin and Roger Edens.
YOU DO (*Mother Wore Tights*, 20th Century-Fox); Music by Josef Myrow. Lyrics by Mack Gordon.
ZIP-A-DEE-DOO-DAH (Song of the South, Disney, RKO Radio); Music by Allie Wrubel. Lyrics by Ray Gilbert.

SCORING: DRAMA/COMEDY

THE BISHOP'S WIFE, Goldwyn, RKO Radio. Hugo Freidhofer.
CAPTAIN FROM CASTILE, 20th Century-Fox. Alfred Newman.
A DOUBLE LIFE, Kanin, U-I. Miklos Rozsa.

FOREVER AMBER, 20th Century-Fox. David Raksin.
LIFE WITH FATHER, Warner Bros. Max Steiner.

SCORING: MUSICAL

FIESTA, MGM. Johnny Green.
MOTHER WORE TIGHTS, 20th Century-Fox. Alfred Newman.
MY WILD IRISH ROSE, Warner Bros. Ray Heindorf and Max Steiner.
ROAD TO RIO, Paramount. Robert Emmett Dolan.
SONG OF THE SOUTH, Disney, RKO Radio. Daniele Amfitheatrof, Paul J. Smith and Charles Wolcott.

SHORT SUBJECT: CARTOON

CHIP AN' DALE, Disney, RKO Radio. (Donald Duck). Walt Disney, producer.
DR. JEKYLL AND MR. MOUSE, MGM. (Tom & Jerry). Frederick Quimby, producer.
PLUTO'S BLUE NOTE, Disney, RKO Radio. (Pluto). Walt Disney, producer.
TUBBY THE TUBA, Paramount. (Puppetoon). George Pal, producer.
TWEETIE PIE, Warner Bros. (Merrie Melodies). Edward Selzer, producer.

SHORT SUBJECT: ONE-REEL

BROOKLYN, U.S.A., Universal-International. (Variety Series). Thomas Mead, producer.
GOODBYE MISS TURLOCK, MGM. (John Nesbitt Passing Parade). Herbert Moulton, producer.
MOON ROCKETS, Paramount. (Popular Science). Jerry Fairbanks, producer.
NOW YOU SEE IT, MGM. (Pete Smith Specialty). Pete Smith, producer.
SO YOU WANT TO BE IN PICTURES, Warner Bros. (Joe McDoakes). Gordon Hollingshead, producer.

SHORT SUBJECT: TWO-REEL

CHAMPAGNE FOR TWO, Paramount. (Musical Parade Featurette). Harry Grey, producer.
CLIMBING THE MATTERHORN, Monogram. (Special). Irving Allen, producer.
FIGHT OF THE WILD STALLIONS, U-I. (Special). Thomas Mead, producer.
GIVE US THE EARTH, MGM. (Special). Herbert Morgan, producer.
A VOICE IS BORN, Columbia. (Musical Featurette). Ben Blake, producer.

DOCUMENTARY: SHORT SUBJECT

FIRST STEPS, United Nations Division of Films and Visual Education.
PASSPORT TO NOWHERE, RKO Radio. (This Is America Series). Frederic Ullman, Jr., producer.
SCHOOL IN THE MAILBOX, Australian News and Information Bureau.

DOCUMENTARY: FEATURES

DESIGN FOR DEATH, RKO Radio. Sid Rogell, executive producer; Theron Warth and Richard O. Fleischer, producers.
JOURNEY INTO MEDICINE, U.S. Department of State, Office of Information and Educational Exchange.
THE WORLD IS RICH, British Information Services. Paul Rotha, producer.

SPECIAL AWARDS

TO JAMES BASKETT for his able and heart-warming characterization of Uncle Remus, friend and storyteller to the children of the world, in Walt Disney's *Song of the South*.
TO *BILL AND COO*, in which artistry and patience blended in a novel and entertaining use of the medium of motion pictures.
TO *SHOE-SHINE*—the high quality of this Italian-made motion picture, brought to eloquent life in a country scarred by war, is proof to the world that the creative spirit can triumph over adversity.
TO COLONEL WILLIAM N. SELIG, ALBERT E. SMITH, THOMAS ARMAT and GEORGE K. SPOOR: the small group of pioneers whose belief in a new medium, and whose contributions to its development, blazed the trail along which the motion picture has progressed, in their lifetime, from obscurity to world-wide acclaim.

SCIENTIFIC OR TECHNICAL

CLASS II
C.C. DAVIS and ELECTRICAL RESEARCH PRODUCTS, DIVISION OF WESTERN ELECTRIC CO., for the development and application of an improved film drive-filter mechanism.

C.R. DAILY and the PARAMOUNT STUDIO FILM LABORATORY, STILL and ENGINEERING DEPARTMENTS for the development and first practical application to motion picture and still photography of a method of increasing film speed as first suggested to the industry by E.I. duPont de Nemours & Co.

Class III
NATHAN LEVINSON and the WARNER BROS. STUDIO SOUND DEPARTMENT;
FARCIOT EDOUART, C.R. DAILY, HAL CORL, H.G. CARTWRIGHT and the PARAMOUNT STUDIO TRANSPARENCY and ENGINEERING DEPARTMENTS;
FRED PONEDEL of Warner Bros. Studio;
KURT SINGER and the RCA-VICTOR DIVISION of the RADIO CORPORATION OF AMERICA;
JAMES GIBBONS of Warner Bros. Studio.

1948

"With all the heated rivalry going on, it wouldn't be a bad idea to hold the Oscar ceremonies in a boxing ring."
—*Variety*

 scar's twenty-first birthday party threatened to be its funeral as well. The studios stopped financing the ceremonies. The official basis for the decision was that it would end the suggestion that the studios were influencing voting practices. Behind closed doors, however, were darker motives. The Hollywood moguls were incensed by the numerous nominations for foreign films, primarily from Great Britain. Academy president Jean Hersholt furiously reminded the studios that they benefited most from the Academy Awards. But they weren't budging, especially after the front offices demanded belt-tightening following the Supreme Court's prohibition of theater monopolies. If the show was to go on, Hersholt would have to cut costs drastically. A change of venue was essential.

BATTLE OVER BRITAIN

CEREMONY: March 24, 1949
The Academy Theatre, Hollywood
HOST: George Montgomery

The cavernous Shrine Auditorium gave way to the 900-odd seat Academy Theatre. That caused an uproar among Academy members. There wouldn't be enough room for all of them. Egos were eventually salved, compromises made without blood drawn, and the Academy Awards took its first shaky but truly independent step forward. As if to mark that break from the studios, Academy voters swept in with the first non-Hollywood Best Picture, Laurence Olivier's production of *Hamlet*. Another hugely popular British import, *The Red Shoes*, picked up two Oscars, creating more than a harbinger of international influence in the future.

Hollywood weighed in with the extraordinary win of father and son Walter and John Huston for Best Director and Best Supporting Actor for *The Treasure of the Sierra Madre*. But the star of the film, Humphrey Bogart, whose performance might have given Olivier a run for his shillings, wasn't even nominated. It was considered the most outrageous omission since Bette Davis's 1934 snub for *Of Human Bondage*.

The Best Actress runoff provided the night's greatest suspense. A stunned Jane Wyman was the winner. She was the first actress since the silent era to earn an Oscar by not saying a word. Her victory was thought to be based as much on sympathy as on talent. Wyman miscarried just before filming *Johnny Belinda* and had recently divorced Ronald Reagan. Having missed her chance to be America's first lady, tonight at least, she was Hollywood's.

BEST PICTURE
HAMLET

According to *Variety*, "The gasp that went up was very similar to the one that greeted Loretta Young, last year's dark horse." The *New York Times*'s Bosley Crowther raved, "Now the matter is settled; the filmed *Hamlet* of Laurence Olivier gives absolute proof that these classics are magnificently suited to the screen…as clear an exposition of this doleful Dane's dilemma as modern-day playgoers have seen… the palace conceived for this *Hamlet* is a dark and haunted place. It is the grim and majestic setting for an uncommonly galvanic film." Pauline Kael concurred: "This is very likely the most exciting and alive production of *Hamlet* you will ever see on the screen. It's never dull."

Eileen Herlie, Laurence Olivier, Basil Sydney

The envelope, please...

BEST ACTOR
LAURENCE OLIVIER (1907–1989)
HAMLET

Generally acclaimed as the finest British stage actor of his generation, Olivier returned to Hollywood (after several failures) with Vivien Leigh—his wife from 1940 to 1960—who was hired to star as Scarlett O'Hara while he played Heathcliff in *Wuthering Heights* (1939). The film won him his first Oscar nomination. His moving performances in Hitchcock's *Rebecca* (nom.), *Pride and Prejudice* (both 1940), and *That Hamilton Woman* (1941) made him an international screen star.

After World War II, Olivier directed himself in a film version of Shakespeare's *Henry V* (1945, special Oscar, nom.), which was hailed as a milestone. He did one better with

Hamlet, making him the only performer to date to direct himself in an Academy Award–winning performance.

He also directed himself in two other films, *Richard III* (1955, nom.) and *The Prince and the Showgirl* (1957). He starred in *Carrie* (1952) and *The Entertainer* (1960, nom.), but slipped into supporting roles with *Spartacus* (1960) and *Oh! What a Lovely War* (1969). He returned to glory with *Othello* (1965, nom.) and *Sleuth* (1972, nom.). Olivier accepted roles in commercial films in the 1970s, including *Marathon Man* (1976, nom.) and *The Boys From Brazil* (1978, nom.), and he had fun with such confections as *A Little Romance* (1979).

Jane Wyman (center) with Lew Ayres (right)

BEST ACTRESS
JANE WYMAN (B. 1914)
JOHNNY BELINDA

"I accept this very gratefully for keeping my mouth shut for once. I think I will do it again," said Wyman, accepting the Oscar for her role as a deaf-mute.

Nominated for *The Yearling* (1946), *The Blue Veil* (1951), and *Magnificent Obsession* (1954), Wyman had paid her dues for ten years in routine thrillers and comedies before getting the lead in *The Lost Weekend* (1945). Following her Oscar–winning role in *Johnny Belinda*, she was pursued by the great directors and appeared in *Stage Fright* (1950), *The Glass Menagerie* (1950), and *The Story of Will Rogers* (1952)

The box-office returns showed that Americans enjoyed Wyman most in melodramas, including *The Blue Veil, So Big* (1953), *Magnificent Obsession, All That Heaven Allows* (1955), and *Miracle in the Rain* (1956). In her later years she turned to television, hosting *Fireside Theater*, which soon became *Jane Wyman Theater* (1955–1958). Wyman returned to the big screen in *Holiday for Lovers* (1959) and *Pollyanna* (1960). Her last feature was the Bob Hope–Jackie Gleason comedy *How to Commit Marriage* (1969). In addition to her starring role on *Falcon Crest* (1981–1990), Wyman starred in many made-for-TV movies.

BEST OF 1948
Best Picture: *Hamlet*
Best Director: John Huston, *The Treasure of the Sierra Madre*
Best Actor: Laurence Olivier, *Hamlet*
Best Actress: Jane Wyman, *Johnny Belinda*
Best Supporting Actor: Walter Huston, *The Treasure of the Sierra Madre*
Best Supporting Actress: Claire Trevor, *Key Largo*

FIRSTS
- *Hamlet* was the first foreign film to win Best Picture.
- Laurence Olivier's win made him and Vivien Leigh the first husband and wife to claim the gold.
- John Huston was Hollywood's first true family man, at least professionally. After directing his dad, Walter, with considerable success, he did likewise for his daughter, Anjelica, in *Prizzi's Honor*.

ROLE REVERSALS
The Red Shoes was originally written as a star vehicle for Merle Oberon.

SINS OF OMISSION
Actors: Humphrey Bogart, *The Treasure of the Sierra Madre*; John Wayne, *Red River*
Supporting Actor: Montgomery Clift, *Red River*

ALWAYS A BRIDESMAID, NEVER A BRIDE
Barbara Stanwyck kept her sense of humor despite her fourth loss. "If I get nominated next year, they'll have to give me the door prize, won't they?" she joked. She wasn't, and they didn't.

UNMENTIONABLES
- Presenter Ethel Barrymore announced the Best Picture winner with noticeable distaste. She felt that her brother John's version of *Hamlet* was far superior to Olivier's.
- Producer Walter Wanger's box-office bomb, *Joan of Arc*, drove him into bankruptcy and a dangerous state of mind. Convinced that his wife, Joan Bennett, was philandering with her agent, Wanger shot him in broad daylight in a Beverly Hills parking lot.
- Ronald Reagan was devastated by his divorce from Jane Wyman, but he managed to joke about it publicly. "I considered naming *Johnny Belinda* as a co-respondent," he said.
- John Huston had Louis B. Mayer to thank for avoiding prison after he fatally injured a pedestrian.

Tim Holt, Humphrey Bogart with Walter Huston

**BEST SUPPORTING ACTOR
WALTER HUSTON (1884–1950)**
THE TREASURE OF THE SIERRA MADRE

"Many years ago, I raised a son and I said to him, 'If you ever become a writer or a director, please find a good part for your old man.'" He did.

The audience was pleased that he did so as well. So, too, were the critics. "Equally, if not more important to the cohesion of the whole is the job done by Walter Huston," raved Bosley Crowther in the *New York Times*. "As a wise old sourdough… [he is] an unrelenting image of personality and strength. And Mr. Huston plays this ancient with such humor and cosmic gusto that he richly suffuses the picture with human vitality and warmth."

Huston had been nominated for the gold for his performances in *Dodsworth* (1936), *All That Money Can Buy* (1941), and *Yankee Doodle Dandy* (1942), so it was heartwarming and not a little ironic that he took the award for his son's film. Coming from Broadway, Huston later became a major character actor who appeared in such films as *The Outlaw*, *Mission to Moscow* (both 1943), *Duel in the Sun* (1946), *The Great Sinner* (1949), and *The Furies* (1950). His last film was completed shortly before his death.

**BEST SUPPORTING ACTRESS
CLAIRE TREVOR (1910–2000)**
KEY LARGO

"I have three boys, and I hope they grow up to be writers so they can give their old lady a part," said Trevor, mimicking the elder Huston's acceptance speech.

Every casting director in Hollywood must have felt the same way about this hard-boiled blonde, who played every conceivable type of "bad girl." She was good at it, too, judging from the Oscar she won for her turn as Edward G. Robinson's floozy in *Key Largo* (1948) and the nominations she earned for similar roles in *Dead End* and *The High and the Mighty*. Her first two films, *Life in the Raw* and *The Last Trail* (both 1933), were followed by, among other films, *Baby Take a Bow* (1934), *Stagecoach* (1939), *Texas* (1941), and *Murder, My Sweet* (1944). She began to accept secondary and character parts as well. In 1982 she played Sally Field's mother in *Kiss Me Goodbye*, and she appeared in a TV movie, *Breaking Home Ties*, in 1987.

© A.M.P.A.S®   Walter Huston with John Huston

**BEST DIRECTOR
JOHN HUSTON, (1906–1987)**
THE TREASURE OF THE SIERRA MADRE

Though the critics raved, the picture was a box-office failure. Known as a fine, though uneven, director, Huston took home the Best Director Oscar only once and was nominated for *Moulin Rouge* (1952), *The Man Who Would Be King* (1975), and *Prizzi's Honor* (1985); for screenwriting, *Sergeant York* (1941) and *Mr. Allison* (1957); and for acting in *The Cardinal* (1963).

Born into a family of actors, after a brief stint as a scriptwriter, Huston debuted as director with the *Maltese Falcon* (1941). It was a surprise hit, and catapulted Bogart to major stardom. Back in Hollywood after World War II, Huston's directorial efforts began with the Oscar-winning *Sierra Madre*, followed by *Key Largo* (1948), *The African Queen* (1951), and *Beat the Devil* (1954). It took him three years to get box-office bust *Moby Dick* (1956) on screen. Huston's later films were more uneven in quality and box-office success, among them *The Unforgiven* (1960), *The Night of the Iguana* (1964), and *Reflections in a Golden Eye* (1967). The one standout film of this period was *The Misfits* (1961).

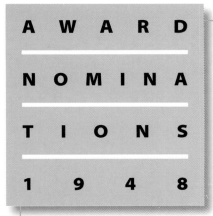

PICTURE

HAMLET, Rank-Two Cities, U-I (British), Laurence Olivier.
JOHNNY BELINDA, Warner Bros, Jerry Wald.
THE RED SHOES, Rank-Archers, Eagle-Lion (British), Michael Powell and Emeric Pressburger.
THE SNAKE PIT, 20th Century-Fox, Anatole Litvak and Robert Bassler.
THE TREASURE OF THE SIERRA MADRE, Warner Bros, Henry Blanke.

ACTOR

LEW AYRES in *Johnny Belinda*, Warner Bros.
MONTGOMERY CLIFT in *The Search*, Praesens Films (Swiss).
DAN DAILEY in *When My Baby Smiles at Me*, 20th Century-Fox.
LAURENCE OLIVIER in *Hamlet*, Rank-Two Cities, U-I (British).
CLIFTON WEBB in *Sitting Pretty*, 20th Century-Fox.

ACTRESS

INGRID BERGMAN in *Joan of Arc*, Wanger-Sierra, RKO Radio.
OLIVIA DE HAVILLAND in *The Snake Pit*, 20th Century-Fox.
IRENE DUNNE in *I Remember Mama*, RKO Radio.
BARBARA STANWYCK in *Sorry, Wrong Number*, Wallis, Paramount.
JANE WYMAN in *Johnny Belinda*, Warner Bros.

SUPPORTING ACTOR

CHARLES BICKFORD in *Johnny Belinda*, Warner Bros.
JOSE FERRER in *Joan of Arc*, Sierra, RKO Radio.
OSCAR HOMOLKA in *I Remember Mama*, RKO Radio.
WALTER HUSTON in *The Treasure of the Sierra Madre*, Warner Bros.
CECIL KELLAWAY in *The Luck of the Irish*, 20th Century-Fox.

SUPPORTING ACTRESS

BARBARA BEL GEDDES in *I Remember Mama*, RKO Radio.
ELLEN CORBY in *I Remember Mama*, RKO Radio.
AGNES MOOREHEAD in *Johnny Belinda*, Warner Bros.
JEAN SIMMONS in *Hamlet*, Rank-Two Cities, U-I (British).
CLAIRE TREVOR in *Key Largo*, Warner Bros.

DIRECTION

JOHN HUSTON for *The Treasure of the Sierra Madre*, Warner Bros.
ANATOLE LITVAK for *The Snake Pit*, 20th Century-Fox.
JEAN NEGULESCO for *Johnny Belinda*, Warner Bros.
LAURENCE OLIVIER for *Hamlet*, Rank-Two Cities, U-I (British).
FRED ZINNEMANN for *The Search* (Swiss).

CINEMATOGRAPHY

B/W
A FOREIGN AFFAIR, Paramount. Charles B. Lang Jr.
I REMEMBER MAMA, RKO Radio. Nicholas Musuraca.
JOHNNY BELINDA, Warner Bros. Ted McCord.
THE NAKED CITY Hellinger, U-I. William Daniels.
PORTRAIT OF JENNIE, Selznick Releasing Organization. Joseph August.

Color
GREEN GRASS OF WYOMING, 20th Century-Fox. Charles G. Clarke.

JOAN OF ARC, Wanger-Sierra, RKO Radio. Joseph Valentine, William V. Skall and Winton Hoch.
THE LOVES OF CARMEN, Beckworth, Columbia. William Snyder.
THE THREE MUSKETEERS, . Robert Planck.

WRITING: ORIGINAL STORY

THE LOUISIANA STORY, Robert Flaherty, Lopert. Frances Flaherty and Robert Flaherty.
THE NAKED CITY, Hellinger, U-I, Malvin Wald.
RED RIVER, Hawks-Monterey, UA. Borden Chase.
THE RED SHOES, Rank-Archers, Eagle-Lion (British), Emeric Pressburger.
THE SEARCH (Swiss). Richard Schweizer and David Wechsler.

WRITING: SCREENPLAY

A FOREIGN AFFAIR, Paramount. Charles Brackett, Billy Wilder and Richard L. Breen.
JOHNNY BELINDA, Warner Bros. Irmgard Von Cube and Allen Vincent.
THE SEARCH (Swiss). Richard Schweizer and David Wechsler.
THE SNAKE PIT, 20th Century-Fox. Frank Partos and Millen Brand.
THE TREASURE OF THE SIERRA MADRE, Warner Bros. John Huston.

ART DIRECTION—SET DECORATION

B/W
HAMLET, Rank-Two Cities, U-I (British). Roger K. Fume; Carmen Dillon.
JOHNNY BELINDA, Warner Bros. Robert Ham; William Wallace.

Color
JOAN OF ARC, Wanger-Sierra, RKO, Radio. Richard Day; Edwin Casey Roberts and Joseph Kish.
THE RED SHOES, Rank-Archers, Eagle-Lion (British). Hein Heckroth, Arthur Lawson.

COSTUME DESIGN

B/W
B.F.'S DAUGHTER, . Irene.
HAMLET, Rank-Two Cities, U-I (British). Roger K. Furse.

Color
THE EMPEROR WALTZ, Paramount. Edith Head and Gile Steele.
JOAN OF ARC, Wanger-Sierra, RKO Radio. Dorothy Jeakins and Karinska.

SOUND RECORDING

JOHNNY BELINDA, Warner Bros. Warner Bros. Sound Department.
MOONRISE, Republic. Republic Sound Department.
THE SNAKE PIT, 20th Century-Fox. 20th Century-Fox Sound Department.

FILM EDITING

JOAN OF ARC, Wanger-Sierra, RKO Radio. Frank Sullivan.
JOHNNY BELINDA, Warner Bros. David Weisbart.
THE NAKED CITY, Hellinger, U-I. Paul Weatherwax.
RED RIVER, Hawks-Monterey, UA. Christian Nyby.
THE RED SHOES, Rank-Archers, Eagle-Lion (British). Reginald Mills.

SPECIAL EFFECTS

DEEP WATERS, 20th Century-Fox. Ralph Hammeras, Fred Semen, Edward Snyder and Roger Heman.
PORTRAIT OF JENNIE, Selznick Releasing Organization. Paul Eagler, J. McMillan Johnson, Russell Shearman, Clarence Slifer, Charles Freeman and James G. Stewart.

SHORT SUBJECT: CARTOON

THE LITTLE ORPHAN, . (Tom & Jerry). Fred Quimby, producer.
MICKEY AND THE SEAL, Disney, RKO Radio. (Pluto). Walt Disney, producer.
MOUSE WRECKERS, Warner Bros. (Looney Tunes). Edward Selzer, producer.
ROBIN HOODLUM, UPA, Columbia. (Fox & Crow). United Productions of America, producer.
TEA FOR TWO HUNDRED, Disney, RKO Radio. (Donald Duck). Walt Disney, producer.

SHORT SUBJECT: ONE-REEL

ANNIE WAS A WONDER, . (John Nesbitt Passing Parade). Herbert Moulton, producer.
CINDERELLA HORSE, Warner Bros. (Sports Parade). Gordon Hollingshead, producer.
SO YOU WANT TO BE ON THE RADIO, Warner Bros. (Joe McDoakes). Gordon Hollingshead, producer.

SYMPHONY OF A CITY, 20th Century-Fox. (Movietone Specialty). Edmund H. Reek, producer.
YOU CAN'T WIN, (Pete Smith Specialty). Pete Smith, producer.

SHORT SUBJECT: TWO-REEL

CALGARY STAMPEDE, Warner Bros. (Technicolor Special). Gordon Hollingshead, producer.
GOING TO BLAZES, . (Special). Herbert Morgan, producer.
SAMBA-MANIA, Paramount. (Musical Parade). Harry Grey, producer.
SEAL ISLAND, Disney, RKO Radio. (True-Life Adventure). Walt Disney, producer.
SNOW CAPERS, U-I. (Special Series). Thomas Head, producer.

DOCUMENTARY: SHORT SUBJECT

HEART TO HEART, Fact Film Organization. Herbert Morgan, producer.
OPERATION VITTLES, U.S. Army Air Force.
TOWARD INDEPENDENCE, U.S. Army.

DOCUMENTARY: FEATURES

THE QUIET ONE, Mayer-Burstyn. Janice Loch, producer.
THE SECRET LAND, U.S. Navy, . O.O. Dull, producer.

SONG

BUTTONS AND BOWS (*The Paleface*, Paramount), Music and Lyrics by Jay Livingston and Ray Evans.
FOR EVERY MAN THERE'S A WOMAN (*Casbah*, Marston, U-I); Music by Harold Arlen. Lyrics by Leo Robin.
IT'S MAGIC (*Romance on the High Seas*, Warner Bros.); Music by Jule Styne. Lyrics by Sammy Cahn.
THIS IS THE MOMENT (*That Lady in Ermine*, 20th Century-Fox); Music by Frederick Hollander. Lyrics by Leo Robin.
THE WOODY WOODPECKER SONG (*Wee Blanket Policy*, Lantz, UA Cartoon); Music and Lyrics by Ramey Idriss and George Tibbles.

SCORING: DRAMA/COMEDY

HAMLET, Rank-Two Cities, U-I (British). William Walton.
JOAN OF ARC, Wanger-Sierra, RKO Radio. Hugo Friedhofer.
JOHNNY BELINDA, Warner Bros. Max Steiner.
THE RED SHOES, Rank-Archers, Eagle-Lion (British). Brian Easdale.
THE SNAKE PIT, 20th Century-Fox. Alfred Newman.

SCORING: MUSICAL

EASTER PARADE . Johnny Green and Roger Edens.
THE EMPEROR WALTZ, Paramount. Victor Young.
THE PIRATE. Lennie Hayton.
ROMANCE ON THE HIGH SEAS, Warner Bros. Ray Heindorf.
WHEN MY BABY SMILES AT ME, 20th Century-Fox. Alfred Newman.

SPECIAL AWARDS

TO MONSIEUR VINCENT (French)—voted by the Academy Board of Governors as the most outstanding foreign-language film released in the United States during 1948.
TO IVAN JANDL for the outstanding juvenile performance of 1948 in *The Search*.
TO SID GRAUMAN, master showman, who raised the standard of exhibition of motion pictures.
TO ADOLPH ZUKOR, a man who has been called the father of the feature film in America, for his services to the industry over a period of forty years.
TO WALTER WANGER for distinguished service to the industry in adding to its moral stature in the world community by his production of the picture *Joan of Arc*.

IRVING G. THALBERG MEMORIAL AWARD

TO JERRY WALD

SCIENTIFIC OR TECHNICAL

CLASS II
VICTOR CACCIALANZA, MAURICE AYERS and the PARAMOUNT STUDIO SET CONSTRUCTION DEPARTMENT for the development and application of "Paralite," a new lightweight plaster process for set construction.

NICK KALTEN, LOUIS J. WITT and the 20TH CENTURY FOX STUDIO MECHANICAL EFFECTS DEPARTMENT for a process of preserving and flame-proofing foliage.

CLASS III
MARTY MARTIN, JACK LANNON, RUSSELL SHEARMAN and the RKO RADIO STUDIO SPECIAL EFFECTS DEPARTMENT; A.J. MORAN and the WARNER BROS. STUDIO ELECTRICAL DEPARTMENT.

1949

O utgoing Academy president Jean Hersholt pulled off the nearly impossible—he got the studio chiefs to listen. After withdrawing their financial support in 1948, they were back in the game thanks to his insistent pressure. Flush again, the Academy could finally end its search for a permanent venue.

HOME, SWEET HOME

CEREMONY: March 23, 1950
RKO Pantages Theatre, Hollywood
HOST: Paul Douglas

The ceremonies had been moved eight times since their inception, three in the last three years. The nomadic production team had found a home at last, a sumptuous motion-picture cathedral of the Golden Age— the Pantages Theatre. Located in the mythical heart of the industry, on the corner of Hollywood and Vine, the Pantages was designed for splendor. Almost half of its space was devoted to ornate lobbies, grand staircases, and lavish restrooms. It was built in 1929 by the colorful Greek immigrant Alexander Pantages, a former boxing champ, a veteran of the Alaskan gold rush, and a theatrical impresario. He didn't live to see the 1949 Academy Awards, but he would have appreciated the showy grandeur.

Fans arrived early in the morning, and every bleacher seat had been staked out by noon. The Pantages marked a return to old-style glamour and drew almost all the nominees. This, despite one of the more predictable races in years. Newcomer Mercedes McCambridge, in her "lucky" thirteen-year-old dress, won Best Supporting Actress. She was followed up the aisle by Broderick Crawford, the veteran character actor, who was struck almost dumb by his good luck. Their movie, *All the King's Men*, earned Best Picture, though in the evening's one twist they lost Best Director and Best Screenplay to Joseph L. Mankiewicz for his *Letter to Three Wives*.

The triumph of *All the King's Men* was even less surprising than Olivia de Havilland's Oscar for *The Heiress*. For one of the screen's great beauties to play a frump was considered by voters to be as much a performance coup as chatty Jane Wyman playing a mute. Or, for that matter, high-gloss fashion queen Joan Crawford portraying a vendor of fried chicken in *Mildred Pierce*. Though it wasn't a night of stunning upsets, the ceremonies were judged a great success thanks, in part, to the snappy wit of host Paul Douglas. At one point in the show he introduced presenter George Murphy as "a man so loved, you'd think he was dead."

BEST PICTURE
ALL THE KING'S MEN

"It's been a long evening. I just can't talk," said producer/director Robert Rossen. "Robert Rossen has written and directed, as well as personally produced, a rip-roaring film," wrote the *New York Times*'s Bosley Crowther. "[He] has assembled...a piece of pictorial journalism that is remarkable for its brilliant parts. It clearly observes the beginnings of a Huey Long type of demagogue in a humble and honest lawyer fighting the 'bosses' in a sleepy dirt-road town." Pauline Kael praised the film, saying, "Broderick Crawford's Willie Stark might just make you feel better about the President you've got. Robert Penn Warren's novel about the rise of a bull-headed demagogue (modelled on Huey Long) was turned into a rousing melodrama, full of graft, double-dealing, and strong-arm excitement."

Broderick Crawford (center, light suit)

The envelope, please…

Broderick Crawford (center)

BEST ACTOR
BRODERICK CRAWFORD (1911–1986)
ALL THE KING'S MEN

The big, beefy Crawford was nominated for and got the Golden Boy only once in his prolific career. After appearing in *Beau Geste*, *The Real Story* (both 1939), and *Seven Sinners* (1940), Crawford broke out into leading roles, including *Tight Shoes* (1941) and *Butch Minds the Baby* (1942).

After several hits, Crawford went into decline; he was known for his hard drinking. He nevertheless gave some good performances in Federico Fellini's *Il Bidone* (1955), and starred in the TV series *Highway Patrol* (1955–1959) and *The Interns* (1970–1971). In the 1960s Crawford appeared mostly in poor-quality European films, but in the late 1970s he made some memorable comebacks in *The Private Files of J. Edgar Hoover* (1977) and *A Little Romance* (1979).

Olivia De Havilland with Montgomery Clift

BEST ACTRESS
OLIVIA DE HAVILLAND
THE HEIRESS

Critiquing de Havilland's performance—as the plain, vulnerable heiress who is wooed for her money by a highly eligible bachelor—on screen and on the stage, the *New York Times*'s Bosley Crowther wrote, "The story and pliant nature that Miss de Havilland gives to the shy and colorless daughter is much less shatterable by shock, and her ecstasies and her frustrations are much more open than they appeared on the stage."

"Famous people feel that they must perpetually be on the crest of the wave, not realizing that it is against all the rules of life. You can't be on top all the time, it isn't natural," said de Havilland, observing the trials of stardom. De Havilland might have earned this wisdom the hard way when she lost the Best Actress award for her role in *Hold Back the Dawn* (1941) to sister Joan Fontaine, who rode the crest for her performance in *Suspicion* that same year.

(For more on de Havilland, see 1946.)

Linda Darnell, Ann Sothern, Jeanne Crain

BEST DIRECTOR
JOSEPH L. MANKIEWICZ (1909-1993)
A LETTER TO THREE WIVES

"Thank you, brother Lupino," Mankiewicz said to presenter Ida Lupino. "She's listed in the membership list of the Directors Guild as Irving Lupino."

Sophistication and intelligence were the hallmarks of all Mankiewicz's film efforts, among them *Million Dollar Legs* (1932), *Manhattan Melodrama* (1934), *Our Daily Bread* (1934), *The Philadelphia Story* (1940), and *Woman of the Year* (1942).

Mankiewicz became a front-running director with *The Ghost and Mrs. Muir* (1947), *A Letter to Three Wives* (1949, nom.), *No Way Out* (1950, Sidney Poitier's first film), *Guys and Dolls* (1955), *Suddenly, Last Summer* (1959), *Cleopatra* (1963), and *Sleuth* (1972, nom.). His son, Tom Mankiewicz, is also a writer-director whose films include the 1987 *Dragnet*.

Dean Jagger with Gregory Peck

 **BEST SUPPORTING ACTOR**
DEAN JAGGER (1903–1991)
12 O'CLOCK HIGH

"I feel as emotional as the dickens," said Jagger.

Playing a middle-aged major, the bald, amenable Jagger became best known to a later generation for his television series *Mr. Novak* (1963–1964). The actor began his career in vaudeville and moved on to film, largely appearing in second leads and character roles, though he did land a few leading roles, among them *Wanderer of the Wasteland* (1935), *Poverty Row* (1936), *Revolt of the Zombies* (1936), and *When Strangers Marry* (1944). His character roles included *Rawhide* (1951), *Bad Day at Black Rock* (1955), *Elmer Gantry* (1960), and *Game of Death* (1978).

John Ireland with Mercedes McCambridge

 BEST SUPPORTING ACTRESS
MERCEDES MCCAMBRIDGE (B.1918)
ALL THE KING'S MEN

"I just want to say to all beginning actresses, never get discouraged. Hold on. Just look at what can happen!" Of her performance the *New York Times*'s Bosley Crowther wrote, "McCambridge is picturesque but vagrant as a hard-boiled henchman in skirts." She earned her Academy Award first time out, and Orson Welles—with whom she worked on radio's Ford Theater series—described her as "the world's greatest living radio actress." An intense and formidable presence, she followed her brilliant film debut with such powerful pictures as *Johnny Guitar* (1954) and *Giant* (1956, nom.).

A bout with alcoholism during the 1960s interrupted her career. She returned, however, as the voice of the possessed Linda Blair in *The Exorcist* (1973) and in *Thieves* (1977).

 HONORARY AWARD
FRED ASTAIRE (1899–1987)

"I'm so excited I could do handsprings down Hollywood Boulevard," Astaire said. "As for you, Ginger [who handed him the special award], you've been much too gracious. Remember, I had a partner."

On Astaire's first screen test studio casting agents wrote, "Can't sing. Can't act. Slightly balding. Can dance a little." To the contrary, not only could Astaire do everything but he left audiences speechless. After dancing for fifteen years in vaudeville with his sister Adele, Astaire made his way to Hollywood to debut in *Dancing Lady* (1933). Later that year he was teamed with Ginger Rogers in *Flying Down to Rio*. After that, no one could deny his magic.

For the next six years Astaire and Rogers danced their way through eight more films. Among their great pictures were *Top Hat* (1935), *Swing Time* (1936), *Shall We Dance* (1937), and *Carefree* (1938). Astaire went solo when Rogers decided to do straight acting jobs. He picked up singing and dancing partners, including Eleanor Powell, Gene Kelly, Judy Garland, Jane Powell, Cyd Charisse, and Audrey Hepburn.

AWARD NOMINATIONS 1949

PICTURE
ALL THE KING'S MEN, Rossen, Columbia, Robert Rossen.
BATTLEGROUND, MGM. Dore Schary.
THE HEIRESS, Paramount, Produced by William Wyler.
A LETTER TO THREE WIVES, 20th Century-Fox, Sol C. Siegel.
12 O'CLOCK HIGH, 20th Century-Fox, Darryl F. Zanuck.

ACTOR
BRODERICK CRAWFORD in *All the King's Men*, Rossen, Columbia.
KIRK DOUGLAS in *Champion*, Kramer, UA.
GREGORY PECK in *12 O'Clock High*, 20th Century-Fox.
RICHARD TODD in *The Hasty Heart*, Warner Bros.
JOHN WAYNE in *Sands of Iwo Jima*, Republic.

ACTRESS
JEANNE CRAIN in *Pinky*, 20th Century-Fox.
OLIVIA DE HAVILLAND in *The Heiress*, Paramount.
SUSAN HAYWARD in *My Foolish Heart*, Goldwyn, RKO Radio.
DEBORAH KERR in *Edward, My Son*, MGM.
LORETTA YOUNG in *Come to the Stable*, 20th Century-Fox.

SUPPORTING ACTOR
JOHN IRELAND in *All the King's Men*, Columbia.
DEAN JAGGER in *12 O'Clock High*, 20th Century-Fox.
ARTHUR KENNEDY in *Champion*, Kramer, UA.
RALPH RICHARDSON in *The Heiress*, Paramount.
JAMES WHITMORE in *Battleground*, MGM.

SUPPORTING ACTRESS
ETHEL BARRYMORE in *Pinky*, 20th Century-Fox.
CELESTE HOLM in *Come to the Stable*, 20th Century-Fox.
ELSA LANCHESTER in *Come to the Stable*, 20th Century-Fox.
MERCEDES McCAMBRIDGE in *All the King's Men*, Rosen, Columbia.
ETHEL WATERS in *Pinky*, 20th Century-Fox.

DIRECTION
JOSEPH L. MANKIEWICZ for *A Letter to Three Wives*, 20th Century-Fox.
CAROL REED for *The Fallen Idol*, London Films, SRO (British).
ROBERT ROSSEN for *All the King's Men*, Rossen, Columbia.
WILLIAM A. WELLMAN for *Battleground*, MGM.
WILLIAM WYLER for *The Heiress*, Paramount.

ART DIRECTION—SET DECORATION
B/W
COME TO THE STABLE, 20th Century-Fox. Lyle Wheeler and Joseph C. Wright; Thomas Little and Paul S. Fox.
THE HEIRESS, Paramount. John Meehan and Harry Homer; Emile Kuri.
MADAME BOVARY, MGM. Cedric Gibbons and Jack Martin Smith; Edwin B. Willis and Richard A. Pefferie.

Color
ADVENTURES OF DON JUAN, Warner Bros. Edward Carrere; Lyle Reifsnider.
LITTLE WOMEN, MGM. Cedric Gibbons and Paul Groesse; Edwin B. Willis and Jack D. Moore.
SARABAND, Rank-Ealing, Eagle-Lion (British). Jim Morahan, William KeRoer and Michael Relph.

WRITING: ORIGINAL STORY
COME TO THE STABLE, 20th Century-Fox. Clare Booth Luce.
IT HAPPENS EVERY SPRING, 20th Century-Fox. Shirley W. Smith and Valentine Davies.
SANDS OF IWO JIMA, Republic. Harry Brown.
THE STRATTON STORY, MGM. Douglas Morrow.
WHITE HEAT, Warner Bros. Virginia Kellogg.

WRITING: SCREENPLAY
ALL THE KING'S MEN, Rossen, Columbia. Robert Rossen.
THE BICYCLE THIEF, De Sica, Mayer-Burstyn (Italian). Cesare Zavattini.
CHAMPION, Kramer, UA. Carl Foreman.
THE FALLEN IDOL, London Films, SRO (British). Graham Greene.
A LETTER TO THREE WIVES, 20th Century-Fox. Joseph L. Mankiewicz.

WRITING: STORY AND SCREENPLAY
BATTLEGROUND, MGM. Robert Pirosh.
JOLSON SINGS AGAIN, Columbia. Sidney Buchman.
PAISAN, Rossellini, Mayer-Burstyn (Italian). Alfred Hayes, Federico Fellini, Sergio Amidei, Marcello Pagliero and Roberto Rossellini.
PASSPORT TO PIMLICO, Rank-Ealing, Eagle-Lion (British). T.E.B. Clarke.
THE QUIET ONE, Film Documents, Mayer-Burstyn. Helen Levitt, Janice Loeb and Sidney Meyers.

CINEMATOGRAPHY
B/W
BATTLEGROUND, MGM. Paul C. Vogel.
CHAMPION, Kramer, UA. Frank Planer.
COME TO THE STABLE, 20th Century-Fox. Joseph LaShelle.
THE HEIRESS, Paramount. Leo Tover.
PRINCE OF FOXES, 20th Century-Fox. Leon Shamroy.

Color
THE BARKLEYS OF BROADWAY, MGM. Harry Stradling.
JOLSON SINGS AGAIN, Columbia. William Snyder.
LITTLE WOMEN, MGM. Robert Planck and Charles Schoenbaum.
SAND, 20th Century-Fox. Charles G. Clarke.
SHE WORE A YELLOW RIBBON, Argosy, RKO Radio. Winton Hoch.

SOUND RECORDING
ONCE MORE, MY DARLING, U-I. Universal-International Sound Department.
SANDS OF IWO JIMA, Republic. Republic Sound Department.
12 O'CLOCK HIGH, 20th Century-Fox. 20th Century-Fox Sound Department.

FILM EDITING
ALL THE KING'S MEN, Rossen, Columbia. Robert Parrish and Al Clark.
BATTLEGROUND, MGM. John Dunning.
CHAMPION, Kramer, UA. Harry Gerstad.
SANDS OF IWO JIMA, Republic. Richard L. Van Enger.
THE WINDOW, RKO Radio. Frederic Knudtson.

SPECIAL EFFECTS
MIGHTY JOE YOUNG, Cooper, RKO Radio.
TULSA, Wanger, Eagle-Lion.

SONG
BABY, IT'S COLD OUTSIDE *(Neptune's Daughter*, MGM); Music and Lyrics by Frank Loesser.
IT'S A GREAT FEELING *(It's a Great Feeling*, Warner Bros.); Music by Jule Styne. Lyrics by Sammy Cahn.
LAVENDER BLUE *(So Dear to My Heart*, Disney, RKO Radio); Music by Eliot Daniel. Lyrics by Larry Morey.
MY FOOLISH HEART *(My Foolish Heart*, Goldwyn, RKO Radio); Music by Victor Young. Lyrics by Ned Washington.
THROUGH A LONG AND SLEEPLESS NIGHT *(Come to the Stable*, 20th Century-Fox); Music by Alfred Newman. Lyrics by Mack Gordon.

SCORING: DRAMA/COMEDY
BEYOND THE FOREST, Warner Bros. Max Steiner.
CHAMPION, Kramer, UA. Dimitri Tiomkin.
THE HEIRESS, Paramount. Aaron Copland.

SCORING: MUSICAL
JOLSON SINGS AGAIN, Columbia. Morris Stoloff and George Duning.

LOOK FOR THE SILVER LINING, Warner Bros. Ray Heindorf.
ON THE TOWN, MGM. Roger Edens and Lennie Hayton.

SHORT SUBJECT: CARTOON
FOR SCENT-IMENTAL REASONS, Warner Bros. (Looney Tunes). Edward Selzer, producer.
HATCH UP YOUR TROUBLES, MGM. (Tom & Jerry). Fred Quimby, producer.
MAGIC FLUKE, UPA, Columbia. (Fox & Crow). Stephen Bosustow, producer.
TOY TINKERS, Disney, RKO Radio. Walt Disney, producer.

SHORT SUBJECT: ONE-REEL
AQUATIC HOUSE-PARTY, Paramount. (Grantland Rice Sportlights). Jack Eaton, producer.
ROLLER DERBY GIRL, Paramount. (Pacemaker). Justin Herman, producer.
SO YOU THINK YOU'RE NOT GUILTY, Warner Bros. (Joe McDoakes). Gordon Hollingshead, producer.
SPILLS AND CHILLS, Warner Bros. (Sports Review). Walton C. Ament, producer.
WATER TRIX, MGM. (Pete Smith Specialty). Pete Smith, producer.

SHORT SUBJECT: TWO-REEL
BOY AND THE EAGLE, RKO Radio. William Lasky, producer.
CHASE OF DEATH, Irving Allen Productions, Irving Allen, producer.
THE GRASS IS ALWAYS GREENER, Warner Bros. Gordon Hollingshead, producer.
SNOW CARNIVAL, Warner Bros. Gordon Hollingshead, producer.
VAN GOGH, Canton-Weiner. Gaston Diehl and Robert Haessens, producers.

COSTUME DESIGN
B/W
THE HEIRESS, Paramount. Edith Head and Gile Steele.
PRINCE OF FOXES, 20th Century-Fox. Vittorio Nino Novarese.

Color
ADVENTURES OF DON JUAN, Warner Bros. Leah Rhodes, Travilla and Marjorie Best.
MOTHER IS A FRESHMAN, 20th Century-Fox. Kay Nelson.

DOCUMENTARY: SHORT SUBJECT
A CHANCE TO LIVE, March of Time, 20th Century-Fox. Richard de Rochemont, producer.
1848, A.F. Films, Inc. French Cinema General Cooperative, producer.
THE RISING TIDE, National Film Board of Canada. St. Francis-Xavier University (Nova Scotia), producer.
SO MUCH FOR SO LITTLE, Warner Bros. Edward Selzer, producer.

DOCUMENTARY: FEATURES
DAYBREAK IN UDI, British Information Services. Crown Film Unit, producer.
KENJI COMES HOME, A Protestant Film Commission Prod. Paul F. Heard, producer.

SPECIAL AWARDS
TO THE BICYCLE THIEF (Italian)—voted by the Academy Board of Governors as the most outstanding foreign-language film released in the United States during 1949.
TO BOBBY DRISCOLL, as the outstanding juvenile actor of 1949.
TO FRED ASTAIRE for his unique artistry and his contributions to the technique of musical pictures.
TO CECIL B. DeMILLE, distinguished motion-picture pioneer, for 37 years of brilliant showmanship.
TO JEAN HERSHOLT for distinguished service to the motion-picture industry.

SCIENTIFIC OR TECHNICAL
CLASS I
EASTMAN KODAK CO. for the development and introduction of an improved safety base motion picture film.

CLASS III
LOREN L. RYDER, BRUCE H. DENNEY, ROBERT CARR and the PARAMOUNT STUDIO SOUND DEPARTMENT;
M.B. PAUL;

HERBERT BRITT;
ANDRE COUTANT and JACQUES MATHOT;
CHARLES R. DAILY, STEVE CSILLAG and the PARAMOUNT STUDIO ENGINEERING, EDITORIAL and MUSIC DEPARTMENTS;
INTERNATIONAL PROJECTOR CORP.;
ALEXANDER VELCOFF.

1950S

BELOW: Two audience members, clad in full skirts and fur stoles, show off the new look of luxury. (1956)

ABOVE: Always impeccably dressed, Grace Kelly is stunning in a floor-length silk gown that is simple yet consummately elegant. (1954)

BELOW: This strapless dress with criss-cross detailing on the bodice lends Jean Simmons an air of refined grace. (1958)

ABOVE: Regal in a pleated gown and bejeweled tiara, Elizabeth Taylor (center) is absolutely dazzling in this 1956 ensemble.

THE LOOK OF THE DECADE

WITH THE END OF WORLD WAR II, opulence and extravagance came out of the closet—or rather, went into women's closets for the first time in almost a decade. Women who had been denying themselves luxurious clothing, whether out of necessity or tact for those less fortunate, were suddenly pining for generous cuts of sensuous fabrics to express the new sense of exuberance. Hollywood, of course, made the look even more sumptuous, and stars showed up at the Academy Awards throughout the 50s dressed in sweeping satin and silk gowns, accented by furs of all shapes and sizes.

OPPOSITE: The ever graceful Audrey Hepburn personifies the new look of the 1950s in this demure dress with a cinched waist and full skirt. (1954)

1950

"I've been resurrected from the dead."

—Bette Davis

"IT'S GOING TO BE A BUMPY NIGHT"

CEREMONY: March 29, 1951
RKO Pantages Theatre, Hollywood
HOST: Fred Astaire

*A*wards night coincided with Gloria Swanson's fifty-second birthday bash at New York's Lazambra restaurant. Her nominee-studded table included Jose Ferrer, Judy Holliday, Celeste Holm, George Cukor, and Sam Jaffe. A swarm of photographers caught them all smiling, but Swanson's nerves jangled. *Sunset Boulevard* was her huge comeback and if she were ever to win an Oscar this would be it. In any other year she might have clinched it. But 1950 was a traffic jam of extraordinary Best Actress nominees. *All About Eve*'s Margo Channing was Bette Davis's role of a lifetime. Ann Baxter's Eve was an historic performance, and Judy Holliday's Billie Dawn in *Born Yesterday* was an unparalleled screen debut.

As the audience at the Pantages Theatre in Los Angeles whooped it up with Dean Martin and Jerry Lewis's rendition of *Cinderella*'s nominated song "Bippidy-Bobbidi-Boo," Best Supporting winner George Sanders, overcome with emotion, wept backstage. But it was 50-something glamour goddess Marlene Dietrich who stole the show without bothering to be nominated for anything. Her sculpted black dress, slit above the knee to expose those famous legs, drew applause before she said a word.

At last the evening's most suspenseful moment had come, as Broderick Crawford opened the envelope in L.A. Bette Davis leaned into her radio in London, and Holliday and Swanson clutched hands at Lazambra's. "One of us is about to be very happy," whispered Swanson. Her hopes died along with the radio hookup. Holliday's acceptance speech went unheard.

Back at the Pantages, the last of the grand old studio tyrants, Louis B. Mayer, was put out to pasture with an honorary award. A shy young starlet who'd made a splash in *The Asphalt Jungle* (1950) barely looked up as she presented a Technical Achievement Oscar. It was to be Marilyn Monroe's first and only appearance at the Academy Awards.

**BEST PICTURE/BEST DIRECTOR
JOSEPH L. MANKIEWICZ (1909–1993)
*ALL ABOUT EVE***

Receiving a record-breaking fourteen nominations, *Eve*, the inside story of an ambitious actress's rise from glamour-struck girl to a flinty-eyed winner of the Siddons Prize, was a hit on every front. The *New York Times*'s Walter Goodman lauded the film for being "a witty, mature, and worldly-wise satire," adding, "dazzling and devastating mockery [are] brilliantly packed into this film." Of the director Goodman said, "Mr. Mankiewicz had been sharpening his wits and his talents a long, long time for just this go. And now, with the excellent assistance of Bette Davis and a truly sterling cast, he is wading into the theater's middle with all claws slashing and settling a lot of scores…with this cutlass-edge derision of Broadway's theatrical tribe…he let himself go and didn't know when to stop. Mr. Mankiewicz has gathered up a saga of theatrical ambition and conceit, pride and deception and hypocrisy, that just about drains the subject dry."

(For more on Mankiewicz, see 1949)

Front: Gregory Ratoff, Anne Baxter, Marilyn Monroe. Back: Gary Merrill, Celeste Holm, George Sanders

The envelope, please...

BEST ACTOR
JOSE FERRER (1909–1992)
CYRANO DE BERGERAC

"You must know that this means more to me than the honor accorded an actor," Ferrer said to a cheering crowd. "I consider it a vote of confidence and an act of faith and, believe me, I'll not let you down."

After winning the award for *Cyrano de Bergerac*, Ferrer, a commanding actor with a distinctive voice, entered a period of prolific filmmaking that included *Moulin Rouge* (1952, nom.), *The Caine Mutiny* (1954), and *Deep in My Heart* (1954). He directed himself as well in *I Accuse!* (1958).

Ferrer's poor remake of *State Fair* (1962) destroyed his career behind the camera. He continued to appear in films throughout the 1960s and the 1980s, however, among them *Lawrence of Arabia* (1962), *The Greatest Story Ever Told* (1965), *Enter Laughing* (1967), *A Midsummer Night's Sex Comedy* (1982), and *To Be or Not to Be* (1983). Ferrer appeared as a recurring character on the Bob Newhart TV sitcom in the 1980s.

Broderick Crawford with Judy Holliday

BEST ACTRESS
JUDY HOLLIDAY (1921–1965)
BORN YESTERDAY

Upon hearing Holliday's name called, her neighbor and rival for the prize, Gloria Swanson, was heard to have said, "Why couldn't you have waited till next year?" Co-star Bette Davis generously responded to the award by saying, "Good! A newcomer won. I couldn't be more pleased." "A priceless performance," wrote Bosley Crowther in the *New York Times*. "There is no doubt that Miss Holliday will leap into popularity as a leading American movie star…she illuminates so brightly the elemental wit and honesty of her blankly unlettered young lady that she puts pathos and respect into the role."

The onetime switchboard operator was rejected by the Yale Drama School, but when she replaced Jean Arthur in the Garson Kanin play *Born Yesterday*, a star was born. Her early films, *Adam's Rib* (1949) and *Born Yesterday* put her on the Hollywood map. Next came *The Marrying Kind* (1952), *It Should Happen to You* (1954), and *The Solid Gold Cadillac* (1956). Unfortunately, she would be typecast and restricted to "dumb blonde" roles for the remainder of her career.

BEST OF 1950
Best Picture: *All About Eve*
Best Director: Joseph L. Mankiewicz, *All About Eve*
Best Actor: Jose Ferrer, *Cyrano de Bergerac*
Best Actress: Judy Holliday, *Born Yesterday*
Best Supporting Actor: George Sanders, *All About Eve*
Best Supporting Actress: Josephine Hull, *Harvey*

FIRSTS
- Frank Sinatra decided to get into acting when a secretary in the advertising firm where he worked suggested it. That secretary was Greer Garson.

- Joseph L. Mankiewicz became the only person to win Best Director and Best Screenplay for two consecutive years.

ROLE REVERSALS
- Billy Wilder initially approached Mae West, Mary Pickford, and Pola Negri for Gloria Swanson's role in *Sunset Boulevard*. Montgomery Clift backed out of the film, and Fred MacMurray turned down the part that was eventually—and unforgettably—played by William Holden.

- Claudette Colbert broke her back to make *All About Eve*. Well, not exactly. Colbert broke a vertebrae while skiing and was replaced at the last minute by Bette Davis.

SINS OF OMISSION
Actor: Spencer Tracy, *Father of the Bride*
Actress: Gloria Swanson, *Sunset Boulevard*

UNMENTIONABLES
- The infamous producer Harry Cohn was heard referring to Judy Holliday as "that fat Jewish broad."

- Listed by Madonna as one of her biggest influences, Holliday co-wrote and performed songs with jazz legend Gerry Mulligan for the album *Holliday with Mulligan*.

- To help build Holliday's image, particularly in the eyes of producer Harry Cohn, Katharine Hepburn deliberately leaked stories to the gossip columns suggesting that Holliday's performance in *Adam's Rib* was so good that she had stolen the spotlight from Tracy and Hepburn. This got the attention of Cohn and won Holliday the part in *Born Yesterday*.

- Producer Darryl F. Zanuck put both stars of *All About Eve*, Anne Baxter and Bette Davis, in the running for Oscars, causing a rivalry that re-created the tension of the film.

- When Erich Von Stroheim learned of his nomination for Best Supporting Actor, he threatened to sue Paramount over the insult to his stature.

- As so many actors had been, Jose Ferrer was subpoenaed by the House Un-American Activities Committee, which he used to his advantage by taking out patriotic ads and insisting that he would swear on a stack of Bibles that he was neither a Communist nor a sympathizer.

- Discovering that her dress was torn, Marilyn Monroe burst into tears.

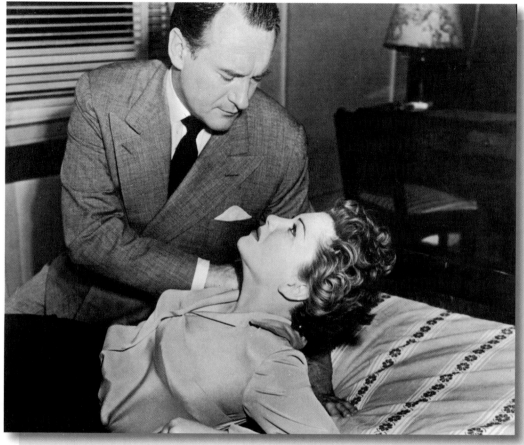

George Sanders with Anne Baxter

BEST SUPPORTING ACTOR
GEORGE SANDERS (1906–1972)
ALL ABOUT EVE

Sanders cried upon receiving his Oscar, saying, "I can't help it. This has unnerved me." Ironically, in the film Sanders plays a cynical, poker-faced theater critic, a man who was singularly incapable of being unnerved.

The suave yet sometimes sinister Sanders played everything from rakish leading man to ruthless cad. He came to Hollywood with a contract from Fox, for which he made *Allegheny Uprising* (1939), *The Son of Monte Cristo* (1940), and *Quiet Please—Murder* (1942). His star began to shine when he starred in a series of popular B thrillers, including *The Saint*. But he excelled in weightier roles, such as Hitchcock's *Foreign Correspondent* (1940) and *Rebecca* (1940), *Forever Amber* (1947), and *The Picture of Dorian Gray* (1945). After *Eve* Sanders' career flourished, and he appeared in such films as *Call Me Madam* (1953), *The Quiller Memorandum* (1966), and *The Kremlin Letter* (1970, in drag).

Saunders' autobiography, *Memoirs of a Professional Cad*, was published in 1960 and revealed a depth not seen by filmgoers. He committed suicide by taking an overdose of sleeping pills. His suicide note read, in part, "Dear World: I am leaving because I am bored."

Josephine Hull with James Stewart

BEST SUPPORTING ACTRESS
JOSEPHINE HULL (1886–1957)
HARVEY

Stumbling on the stairs to the podium, Oscar-winner Hull pretended to be accompanied by Harvey himself, saying, "I must thank you all and the wonderful six-foot Harvey. He has brought happiness to me in Hollywood." Hull also showed her appreciation to the studio, Universal International, that made the film, calling it "the gateway to the world."

Hull had had a successful fifty-year career on Broadway before bringing her roles in *Arsenic and Old Lace* (1944) and *Harvey* from the stage to the screen.

PICTURE
ALL ABOUT EVE, 20th Century-Fox, Darryl F. Zanuck.
BORN YESTERDAY, Columbia, S. Sylvan Simon.
FATHER OF THE BRIDE, MGM, Pandro S. Berman.
KING SOLOMON'S MINES, MGM, Sam Zimbalist.
SUNSET BOULEVARD, Paramount, Charles Brackett.

ACTOR
LOUIS CALHERN in *The Magnificent Yankee*, MGM.
JOSE FERRER in *Cyrano de Bergerac*, Kramer, UA.
WILLIAM HOLDEN in *Sunset Boulevard*, Paramount.
JAMES STEWART in *Harvey*, U-I.
SPENCER TRACY in *Father of the Bride*, MGM.

ACTRESS
ANNE BAXTER in *All About Eve*, 20th Century-Fox.
BETTE DAVIS in *All About Eve*, 20th Century-Fox.
JUDY HOLLIDAY in *Born Yesterday*, Columbia.
ELEANOR PARKER in *Caged*, Warner Bros.
GLORIA SWANSON in *Sunset Boulevard*, Paramount.

SUPPORTING ACTOR
JEFF CHANDLER in *Broken Arrow*, 20th Century-Fox.
EDMUND GWENN in *Mister 880*, 20th Century-Fox.
SAM JAFFE in *The Asphalt Jungle*, MGM.
GEORGE SANDERS in *All About Eve*, 20th Century-Fox.
ERICH VON STROHEIM in *Sunset Boulevard*, Paramount.

SUPPORTING ACTRESS
HOPE EMERSON in *Caged*, Warner Bros.
CELESTE HOLM in *All About Eve*, 20th Century-Fox.
JOSEPHINE HULL in *Harvey*, U-I.
NANCY OLSON in *Sunset Boulevard*, Paramount
THELMA RITTER in *All About Eve*, 20th Century-Fox.

DIRECTION
GEORGE CUKOR for *Born Yesterday*, Columbia.
JOHN HUSTON for *The Asphalt Jungle*, MGM.
JOSEPH L. MANKIEWICZ for *All About Eve*, 20th Century-Fox.
CAROL REED for *The Third Man*, Selznick-London Films, SRO (British).
BILLY WILDER for *Sunset Boulevard*, Paramount.

WRITING: ORIGINAL STORY
BITTER RICE, Lux Films (Italian). Giuseppe De Santis and Carlo Lizzani.
THE GUNFIGHTER, 20th Century-Fox. William Bowers and Andre de Toth.
MYSTERY STREET, MGM, Leonard Spigelgass.
PANIC IN THE STREETS, 20th Century-Fox. Edna Anhalt and Edward Anhalt.
WHEN WILLIE COMES MARCHING HOME, 20th Century-Fox. Sy Gomberg.

WRITING: SCREENPLAY
ALL ABOUT EVE, 20th Century-Fox. Joseph L. Mankiewicz.
THE ASPHALT JUNGLE, MGM, Ben Maddow and John Huston.
BORN YESTERDAY, Columbia. Albert Mannheimer.
BROKEN ARROW, 20th Century-Fox. Michael Blankfort.
FATHER OF THE BRIDE, MGM, Frances Goodrich and Albert Hackett.

WRITING: STORY AND SCREENPLAY
ADAM'S RIB, MGM, Ruth Gordon and Garson Kanin.

CAGED, Warner Bros. Virginia Kellogg and Bernard C. Schoenfeld.
THE MEN, Kramer, UA. Carl Foreman.
NO WAY OUT, 20th Century-Fox. Joseph L. Mankiewicz and Lesser Samuels,
SUNSET BOULEVARD, Paramount. Charles Brackett, Billy Wilder and D.M. Marshman, Jr.

CINEMATOGRAPHY
B/W
ALL ABOUT EVE, 20th Century-Fox. Milton Krasner.
THE ASPHALT JUNGLE, MGM, Harold Rossen.
THE FURIES, Walls, Paramount. Victor Milner.
SUNSET BOULEVARD, Paramount. John F. Seitz.
THE THIRD MAN, Selznick-London Films, SRO (British). Robert Krasker.

Color
ANNIE GET YOUR GUN, MGM, Charles Rosher.
BROKEN ARROW, 20th Century-Fox. Ernest Palmer.
THE FLAME AND THE ARROW, Norma-F.R., Warner Bros. Ernest Haller.
KING SOLOMON'S MINES, MGM. Robert Surtees.
SAMSON AND DELILAH, DeMille, Paramount. George Barnes.

ART DIRECTION—SET DECORATION
B/W
ALL ABOUT EVE, 20th Century-Fox. Lyle Wheeler and George Davis; Thomas Little and Walter M. Scott.
THE RED DANUBE, MGM. Cedric Gibbons and Hans Peters; Edwin B. Willis and Hugh Hunt.
SUNSET BOULEVARD, Paramount. Hans Dreier and John Meehan; Sam Comer and Ray Moyer.

Color
ANNIE GET YOUR GUN, MGM. Cedric Gibbons and Paul Groesse; Edwin B. Willis and Richard A. Pefferle.
DESTINATION MOON, Pal, Eagle-Lion. Ernst Fegte; George Sawley.
SAMSON AND DELILAH, DeMille, Paramount. Hans Dreier and Walter Tyler; Sam Comer and Ray Moyer.

COSTUME DESIGN
B/W
ALL ABOUT EVE, 20th Century-Fox. Edith Head and Charles LeMaire.
BORN YESTERDAY, Columbia. Jean Louis.
THE MAGNIFICENT YANKEE, MGM. Walter Plunkett.

Color
THE BLACK ROSE, 20th Century-Fox. Michael Whittaker.
SAMSON AND DELILAH, DeMille, Paramount. Edith Head, Dorothy Jeakins, Elois Jenssen, Gile Steele and Gwen Wakeling.
THAT FORSYTE WOMAN, MGM. Walter Plunkett and Valles.

SOUND RECORDING
ALL ABOUT EVE, 20th Century-Fox. 20th Century-Fox Sound Department.
CINDERELLA, Disney, RKO Radio. Disney Sound Department.
LOUISA, U-I. Universal-International Sound Department.
OUR VERY OWN, Goldwyn, RKO Radio. Goldwyn Sound Department.
TRIO, Rank-Sydney Box. Paramount (British).

FILM EDITING
ALL ABOUT EVE, 20th Century-Fox. Barbara McLean.
ANNIE GET YOUR GUN, MGM. James E. Newcom.
KING SOLOMON'S MINES, MGM. Ralph E. Winters and Conrad A. Nervig.
SUNSET BOULEVARD, Paramount. Arthur Schmidt and Doane Harrison.
THE THIRD MAN, Selznick-London Films, SRO (British). Oswald Hafenrichter.

SPECIAL EFFECTS
DESTINATION MOON, Pal, Eagle-Lion.
SAMSON AND DELILAH, DeMille, Paramount.

SONG
BE MY LOVE (*The Toast of New Orleans*, MGM); Music by Nicholas Brodszky. Lyrics by Sammy Cahn.
BIBBIDY-BOBBIDI-BOO (*Cinderella*, Disney, RKO Radio); Music and Lyrics by Mack David, Al Hoffman and Jerry Livingston.

MONA LISA (*Captain Carey*, *USA*, Paramount);
Music and Lyrics by Ray Evans and Jay Livingston.
MULE TRAIN (*Singing Guns*, Republic); Music and Lyrics by Fred Glickman, Hy Heath and Johnny Lange.
WILHELMINA (*Wabash Avenue*, 20th Century-Fox); Music by Josef Myrow. Lyrics by Mack Gordon.

SCORING: DRAMA/COMEDY
ALL ABOUT EVE, 20th Century-Fox. Alfred Newman.
THE FLAME AND THE ARROW, Norma, Warner Bros. Max Steiner.
NO SAD SONGS FOR ME, Columbia. George Duning.
SAMSON AND DELILAH, Paramount. Victor Young.
SUNSET BOULEVARD, Paramount. Franz Waxman.

SCORING: MUSICAL
ANNIE GET YOUR GUN, MGM. Adolph Deutsch and Roger Edens.
CINDERELLA. Disney, RKO Radio. Oliver Wallace and Paul J. Smith.
I'LL GET BY, 20th Century-Fox. Lionel Newman.
THREE LITTLE WORDS, MGM. Andre Previn.
THE WEST POINT STORY, Warner Bros. Ray Heindorf.

SHORT SUBJECTS: CARTOONS
GERALD McBOING-BOING, UPA, Columbia. (Jolly Frolics Series). Stephen Bosustow, executive producer.
JERRY'S COUSIN, MGM. (Tom & Jerry Series). Fred Quimby, producer.
TROUBLE INDEMNITY, UPA, Columbia. (Mr. Magoo Series). Stephen Bosustow, executive producer.

SHORT SUBJECT: ONE-REEL
BLAZE BUSTERS, Warner Bros. (Vitaphone Novelties). Robert Youngson, producer.
GRANDAD OF RACES Warner Bros. (Sports Parade). Gordon Hollingshead, producer.
WRONG WAY BUTCH, MGM (Pete Smith Specialty). Pete Smith, producer.

SHORT SUBJECT: TWO-REEL
GRANDMA MOSES, Falcon Films, Inc., A.F. Films. Falcon Films, Inc., producer.
IN BEAVER VALLEY, Disney, RKO Radio, (True-Life Adventure). Walt Disney, producer.
MY COUNTRY 'TIS OF THEE, Warner Bros. (Featurette Series). Gordon Hollingshead, producer.

DOCUMENTARY: SHORT SUBJECTS
THE FIGHT: SCIENCE AGAINST CANCER, National Film Board of Canada in cooperation with the Medical Film Institute of the Association of American Medical Colleges.
THE STAIRS, Film Documents, Inc.
WHY KOREA?, 20th Century-Fox Movietone, Edmund Reek, producer.

DOCUMENTARY: FEATURES
THE TITAN: STORY OF MICHELANGELO, Michelangelo Co., Classics Pictures, Inc. Robert Snyder, producer.
WITH THESE HANDS, Promotional Films Co., Inc. Jack Arnold and Lee Goodman, producers.

HONORARY AND OTHER AWARDS
TO GEORGE MURPHY for his services in interpreting the film industry to the country at large.
TO LOUIS B. MAYER for distinguished service to the motion picture industry
TO *THE WALLS OF MALAPAGA* (Franco-Italian—voted by the Board of Governors as the most outstanding foreign language film released in the United States in 1950.

IRVING G. THALBERG MEMORIAL AWARD
TO DARRYL F. ZANUCK

SCIENTIFIC OR TECHNICAL
CLASS I
None.

CLASS II
JAMES B. GORDON and the 20TH CENTURY-FOX STUDIO CAMERA DEPARTMENT for the design and development of a multiple image film viewer.
JOHN PAUL LIVADARY, FLOYD CAMPBELL, L.W. RUSSELL and the COLUMBIA STUDIO SOUND DEPARTMENT for the development of a multi-track magnetic re-recording system.

LOREN L. RYDER and the PARAMOUNT STUDIO SOUND DEPARTMENT for the first studio-wide application of magnetic sound recording to motion picture production.

CLASS III
None.

1951

"There is a strange sort of reasoning in Hollywood that musicals are less worthy of Academy consideration than dramas."

—Gene Kelly

SURPRISE PARTY

CEREMONY: March 20, 1952
RKO Pantages Theatre, Hollywood
HOST: Danny Kaye

With his muscular talent nearly bursting out of Stanley Kowalski's torn T-shirt, Marlon Brando dominated the race for Best Actor. He'd made a rebellious show of not giving a damn, much the way Humphrey Bogart reacted to his 1943 nomination for *Casablanca*. Eight years older and wiser, Bogie had begun to care deeply enough to launch a serious Oscar campaign. He arrived at the Pantages Theatre with his pregnant wife, Lauren Bacall, and a dim hope that the sentimental vote might swing his way. According to the same polls, Best Picture was a toss-up between *A Place in the Sun* and *A Streetcar Named Desire*. Perhaps in compensation for the almost certain loss of *An American in Paris*, Gene Kelly received an Honorary Oscar for outstanding achievements as an actor/dancer/choreographer.

Streetcar began its projected sweep with a Best Supporting win for Karl Malden, who made his way to the wrong microphone. Shelley Winters didn't get quite that far. When Vivien Leigh's name was announced for Best Actress, Winters swore she heard her own and leaped out of her seat. Her fiancé, Vittorio Gassman, grabbed the back of her mauve gown in time to save her from public humiliation.

Another glamorously engaged couple, Ronald Reagan and starlet Nancy Davis, applauded his ex-wife, Jane Wyman, who sang "In the Cool, Cool, Cool of the Evening" with funnyman host Danny Kaye. Moments later, two knockout punches left the audience stunned. Bogie pulled off his Best Actor bid, leaving Brando the only central character in *Streetcar* Oscar-less. Then George Stevens plucked the Best Director statuette, almost assuring a Best Picture win for *A Place in the Sun*.

The ladies began collecting their purses as early film pioneer Jesse Lasky opened the final envelope. He announced the winner, and people in the audience stopped in their tracks near the exit. Like Shelley Winters earlier in the evening, they thought they'd heard wrong. But, no, it was *An American in Paris*. An overwhelmed Gene Kelly had good reason to begin "Singin' in the Rain."

BEST PICTURE
AN AMERICAN IN PARIS

There was an audible gasp when the announcement of the main award echoed through the theater. All the naysayers (the critics) quickly recovered and erupted into applause. But despite the genius of the Gershwin songs "I Got Rhythm," "Embraceable You," "S' Wonderful," and "I'll Build a Stairway to Paradise," along with a beautiful ballet on the banks of the Seine, some reviewers were left cold by the film as a whole. Pauline Kael of *The New Yorker* called it, "too fancy and overblown." Despite the withering reviews, *An American in Paris* remains one of Hollywood's greatest musicals, up there in the pantheon with *Singin' in the Rain* and the Astaire-Rogers films.

HONORARY AWARD
GENE KELLY (1912–1996)

One of Hollywood's most charming virtuoso performers, Kelly's presence on the dance floor or singing on bended knee was magic.

Gene Kelly came to Hollywood in 1941 straight from the Broadway stage and planned to return after making *For Me and My Gal* (1942). He never went back. His robust, balletic charm and energy, like Fred Astaire's, were all his own. His partners in dance ranged from Frank Sinatra to an animated Jerry the Mouse.

Gene Kelly

A list of his films brings forth the Golden Age itself: *For Me and My Gal* (1942), *Anchors Aweigh* (1945, nom.), *Ziegfeld Follies* (1946), *The Pirate* (1948) and *Singin' in the Rain* (1952). Teamed with Stanley Donen, Kelly moved in and out of the director's chair. He co-starred with Judy Garland in *Summer Stock* (1950) and played one of his few dramatic roles in *Black Hand* (1950).

By 1952 MGM had scaled back the lavish musicals, making only *Brigadoon* (1954), *Invitation to the Dance* (1957), and *Les Girls* (1957), Kelly's last. He did, however, perform in the bittersweet *Marjorie Morningstar* (1958), and he played a cynical reporter in *Inherit the Wind* (1960). Toward the end of his career, Kelly appeared in MGM's musical compilation film, *That's Entertainment!* (1974).

The envelope, please…

© A.M.P.A.S® *Humphrey Bogart, Danny Kaye, Arthur Freed, and George Stevens*

BEST DIRECTOR
GEORGE STEVENS (1904–1975)
A PLACE IN THE SUN

Like so many others, Stevens was not present to accept the award—which everyone expected—for his melodramatic adaptation of Dreiser's *An American Tragedy*.

Stevens was a true Golden Age director who enjoyed uncommon success with many films—*Swing Time* (1936), *Gunga Din* (1939), and *Shane* (1953)—that are now considered icons of their genre. He made his way into movies as a cameraman, shooting many great comedies—including such Laurel and Hardy classics as *Two Tars* (1928), *Liberty*, and *Big Business* (both 1929).

Stevens's turning point came when he directed Katharine Hepburn in *Alice Adams* (1935), and continued his great successes with *Annie Oakley* (1935), *Vivacious Lady* (1938), *Woman of the Year* (1942), and *The More the Merrier* (1943, nom.).

During World War II, Stevens photographed the liberation of the concentration camp at Dachau, which turned him toward more serious work in *The Diary of Anne Frank* (1959). He was a demanding director with a penchant for perfection, insisting on many reshoots and recuts.

Humphrey Bogart with Katharine Hepburn

BEST ACTOR
HUMPHREY BOGART
(1899–1957)
THE AFRICAN QUEEN

Having already told reporters, "The only honest way to find the best actor would be to let everybody play *Hamlet* and let the best man win," when it was time to receive the award he said something quite different: "I'm not going to thank anybody; I'm just going to say I damn well deserve it."

Bogart was noticed by Hollywood for his stage performances, and in 1930 he was signed on with Fox. After five films, Bogie got his break in *The Petrified Forest* (1936), and from 1936 to 1940 he appeared in twenty-eight films, among them *Angels with Dirty Faces* (1938), *The Roaring Twenties* (1939), and *Dark Victory* (1939). Bogart's star began to rise in 1941 when he made *High Sierra* and *The Maltese Falcon* (both 1941), followed by *Casablanca* (1942, nom.), *To Have and Have Not* (1944, during which he met and married Lauren Bacall), *The Big Sleep* (1946), *Key Largo* (1948), *The Treasure of the Sierra Madre* (1949), *In a Lonely Place* (1950), *The Caine Mutiny* (1954, nom.), and *The Harder They Fall* (1956).

BEST OF 1951
Best Picture: *An American in Paris*
Best Director: George Stevens, *A Place in the Sun*
Best Actor: Humphrey Bogart, *The African Queen*
Best Actress: Vivien Leigh, *A Streetcar Named Desire*
Best Supporting Actor: Karl Malden, *A Streetcar Named Desire*
Best Supporting Actress: Kim Hunter, *A Streetcar Named Desire*
Honorary Award: Gene Kelly

ROLE REVERSALS
• Scarlett O'Hara might have been played by an actress called April Morn, a stage name she briefly considered before settling on Vivien Leigh.

• Edward G. Robinson was initially cast for *The Petrified Forest*, but when Leslie Howard threatened to quit unless he was accompanied by his fellow actor from the Broadway production, the part was given to Bogart.

• Bogart owes his stardom to George Raft, who turned down the two 1941 roles that boosted him to the top in *High Sierra* and *The Maltese Falcon*.

UNMENTIONABLES
• "I wasn't nice to Debbie. It's a wonder she still speaks to me."—Gene Kelly, on his working experience with Debbie Reynolds while filming *Singin' in the Rain* (1952).

• The contract system at Hollywood studios like MGM "was a very efficient system in that because we were at the studio all the time we could rehearse a lot," said Kelly. "But it also really repressed people. There were no union regulations yet, and we were all indentured servants—you can call us slaves if you want—like ball players before free agency. We had seven-year contracts but every six months the studio could decide to fire you if your picture wasn't a hit. And if you turned down a role, they cut off your salary and simply added the time to your contract."

• According to the *New York Times*, Humphrey Bogart was born on January 23, 1899, but Warner Bros. publicity decided that a Christmas birthday would be far more advantageous because "a guy born on Christmas can't be all bad."

• "The trouble with the world is that it's always one drink behind," said Bogart.

• Bogart's attributed last words were, "I should never have switched from scotch to martinis."

• Bogart suffered from manic depression.

• Olivier's first wife, Jill Esmond, named Vivien as corespondent in her February 1940 divorce from Olivier on grounds of adultery. Vivien would name Joan Plowright—Olivier's last wife—as corespondent in her 1960 divorce from Olivier, also on grounds of adultery.

• According to legend, Myron Selznick introduced Vivien to his brother—*Gone with the Wind* producer David O. Selznick—with the words "Hey, genius! Meet your Scarlett."

Vivien Leigh with Marlon Brando

BEST ACTRESS
VIVIEN LEIGH (1913–1967)
A STREETCAR NAMED DESIRE

"Vivien Leigh gives one of those rare performances that can truly be said to evoke pity and terror," wrote Pauline Kael in *The New Yorker*. "Blanche's plea, 'I don't want realism…I want magic,' is central [to the film].'"

Leigh's reputation was sealed early by her unforgettable performance, at the age of 29, as the irrepressibly charming irritant Scarlett O'Hara, in *Gone with the Wind* (1939). The rest of her fine career fell under its shadow, but the camera loved Leigh, who fell in love with Laurence Olivier while making the film *Fire Over England* (1937).

After *G.W.T.W.* Leigh appeared in *Waterloo Bridge* (1940), *That Hamilton Woman* (1941, with Olivier), and *Anna Karenina* (1948) among others.

Vivien Leigh, Kim Hunter, Peg Hillias with Karl Malden

BEST SUPPORTING ACTOR
KARL MALDEN (B. 1912)
A STREETCAR NAMED DESIRE

When his name was announced, Malden stumbled to the stage and talked into the wrong microphone. Directed back to the correct podium by a stagehand he said, "I haven't been out here very long, but I can tell you I feel—great!"

The bulbous-nosed actor didn't have the makings of a leading man, yet he managed to make his way into some of the most important films of the 1950s, beginning with his Oscar-winning performance in *A Streetcar Named Desire*. The *New York Times*'s Bosley Crowther appreciated Malden as "a timid, boorish suitor."

Success followed with *On the Waterfront* (1954, nom.). "A commanding screen presence," wrote film critic Leonard Maltin. "[He] enriches every film in which he appears, and invariably brings his innate dignity to every role he tackles." Malden's subsequent films include *Baby Doll* (1956) and *Cheyenne Autumn* (1964). From 1972 to 1977, he starred in the TV police series *The Streets of San Francisco*.

Kim Hunter with Marlon Brando

BEST SUPPORTING ACTRESS
KIM HUNTER (B. 1922)
A STREETCAR NAMED DESIRE

Hunter was at home listening to the radio when her award was announced. Bette Davis picked up the prize and said, "I wish I were Kim Hunter tonight."

Playing Stella, the torn younger sister to Leigh and wife to Brando, Hunter put up with a lot of grief from her screen husband. *Streetcar* would prove to be the high point of her movie career, which was hampered when she was blacklisted during the McCarthy era.

Beginning her career onstage at age 17, Hunter was an Actors Studio student who made an impressive screen debut in *The Seventh Victim* (1943), followed by *When Strangers Marry* (1944). She was cast by Michael Powell and Emeric Pressburger in their brilliant fantasy *Stairway to Heaven* (1946). Hunter stopped making films in 1951 and continued to appear on stage and television.

PICTURE
AN AMERICAN IN PARIS, MGM, Arthur Freed.
DECISION BEFORE DAWN, 20th Century-Fox, Anatole Litvak and Frank McCarthy.
A PLACE IN THE SUN, Paramount, George Stevens.
QUO VADIS, MGM,, Sam Zimbalist.
A STREETCAR NAMED DESIRE, Feldman, Warner Bros, Charles K. Feldman.

ACTOR
HUMPHREY BOGART in *The African Queen*, Horizon, UA.
MARLON BRANDO in *A Streetcar Named Desire*, Charles K. Feldman, Warner Bros.
MONTGOMERY CLIFT in *A Place in the Sun*, Paramount.
ARTHUR KENNEDY in *Bright Victory*, U-I.
FREDRIC MARCH in *Death of a Salesman*, Stanley Kramer, Columbia.

ACTRESS
KATHARINE HEPBURN in *The African Queen*, Horizon, UA.
VIVIEN LEIGH in *A Streetcar Named Desire*, Charles K. Feldman, Warner Bros.
ELEANOR PARKER in *Detective Story*, Paramount.
SHELLEY WINTERS in *A Place in the Sun*, Paramount.
JANE WYMAN in *The Blue Veil*, Wald-Krasna, RKO Radio.

SUPPORTING ACTOR
LEO GENN in *Quo Vadis*, MGM.
KARL MALDEN in *A Streetcar Named Desire*, Charles K. Feldman, Warner Bros.
KEVIN McCARTHY in *Death of a Salesman*, Kramer, Columbia.
PETER USTINOV in *Quo Vadis*, MGM.
GIG YOUNG in *Come Fill the Cup*, Warner Bros.

SUPPORTING ACTRESS
JOAN BLONDELL in *The Blue Veil*, Wald-Krasna, RKO Radio.
MILDRED DUNNOCK in *Death of a Salesman*, Kramer, Columbia.
LEE GRANT in *Detective Story*, Paramount.
KIM HUNTER in *A Streetcar Named Desire*, Charles K. Feldman, Warner Bros.
THELMA RITTER in *The Mating Season*, Paramount.

DIRECTION
JOHN HUSTON for *The African Queen*, Horizon-Romulus, UA.
ELIA KAZAN for *A Streetcar Named Desire*, Feldman, Warner Bros.
VINCENTE MINNELLI for *An American in Paris*, MGM.
GEORGE STEVENS for *A Place in the Sun*, Paramount.
WILLIAM WYLER for *Detective Story*, Paramount.

WRITING: ORIGINAL STORY
THE BULLFIGHTER AND THE LADY, Republic. Budd Boetticher and Ray Nazarro.
THE FROGMEN, 20th Century-Fox. Oscar Millard.
HERE COMES THE GROOM, Paramount. Robert Riskin and Liam O'Brien.
SEVEN DAYS TO NOON, Boulting Bros., Mayer-Kingsley (British). Paul Dehn and James Bernard.
TERESA, MGM. Alfred Hayes and Stewart Stern.

WRITING: SCREENPLAY
THE AFRICAN QUEEN, Horizon-Romulus, UA. James Agee and John Huston.
DETECTIVE STORY, Paramount. Philip Yordan and Robert Wyler.
LA RONDE, Commercial Pictures (French). Jacques Natanson and Max Ophuls.
A PLACE IN THE SUN, Paramount. Michael Wilson and Harry Brown.
A STREETCAR NAMED DESIRE, Feldman, Warner Bros. Tennessee Williams.

(Story and Screenplay)
AN AMERICAN IN PARIS, MGM. Alan Jay Lerner.
THE BIG CARNIVAL, Paramount. Billy Wilder, Lesser Samuels and Walter Newman.
DAVID AND BATHSHEBA, 20th Century-Fox. Philip Dunne.
GO FOR BROKE!, MGM. Robert Pirosh.
THE WELL, Popkin, UA. Clarence Greene and Russell Rouse.

CINEMATOGRAPHY
B/W
DEATH OF A SALESMAN, Kramer, Columbia. Frank Planer.
THE FROGMEN, 20th Century-Fox. Norbert Brodine.
A PLACE IN THE SUN, Paramount. William C. Mellor.
STRANGERS ON A TRAIN, Warner Bros. Robert Burks.
A STREETCAR NAMED DESIRE, Feldman, Warner Bros. Harry Stradling.

Color
AN AMERICAN IN PARIS, MGM. Alfred Gilks and John Alton.
DAVID AND BATHSHEBA, 20th Century-Fox. Leon Shamroy.
QUO VADIS, MGM. Robert Surtees and William V. Skall.
SHOW BOAT, MGM. Charles Rosher.
WHEN WORLDS COLLIDE, Pal, Paramount. John F. Seitz and W. Howard Greene.

ART DIRECTION—SET DECORATION
B/W
FOURTEEN HOURS, 20th Century-Rex. Lyle Wheeler and Leland Fuller; Thomas Little and Fred J. Rode.
HOUSE ON TELEGRAPH HILL, 20th Century-Fox. Lyle Wheeler and John DeCuir; Thomas Little and Paul S. Fox.
LA RONDE, Commercial Pictures (French). D'Eaubonne.
A STREETCAR NAMED DESIRE, Feldman, Warner Bros. Richard Day; George James Hopkins.
TOO YOUNG TO KISS, MGM. Cedric Gibbons and Paul Groesse; Edwin B. Willis and Jack D. Moore.

Color
AN AMERICAN IN PARIS, MGM. Cedric Gibbons and Preston Ames; Edwin B. Willis and Keogh Gleason.
DAVID AND BATHSHEBA, 20th Century-Fox. Lyle Wheeler and George Davis; Thomas Little and Paul S. Fox.
ON THE RIVIERA, 20th Century-Fox. Lyle Wheeler and Leland Fuller; Joseph C. Wright, Thomas Little and Walter H. Scott.
QUO VADIS, MGM. William A. Horning, Cedric Gibbons and Edward Carfagno; Hugh Hunt.
TALES OF HOFFMANN, Powell-Pressburger. Lopert (British). Hein Heckroth.

SHORT SUBJECTS: CARTOONS
LAMBERT, THE SHEEPISH LION, Disney, RKO Radio. (Special). Walt Disney, producer.
ROOTY TOOT TOOT, UPA, Columbia (Jolly Frolics). Stephen Bosustow, executive producer.
TWO MOUSEKETEERS, MGM (Tom & Jerry). Fred Quimby, producer.

SHORT SUBJECT: ONE-REEL
RIDIN' THE RAILS, Paramount. (Sportlights). Jack Eaton, producer.
THE STORY OF TIME, A Signal Films Production by Robert G. Leffingwell, Cornell Film Company (British).
WORLD OF KIDS, Warner Bros. (Vitaphone Novelties). Robert Youngson, producer.

SHORT SUBJECT: TWO-REEL
BALZAC, Les Films Du Compass, A.F. Films, Inc. (French). Les Films Du Compass, producer.
DANGER UNDER THE SEA, U-I. ibm Mead, producer.
NATURE'S HALF ACRE, Disney, RKO Radio, (True Life Adventure). Walt Disney, producer.

DOCUMENTARY: SHORT SUBJECTS
BENJY, Made by Fred Zinnemann with the cooperation of Paramount Pictures Corp. for the Los Angeles Orthopaedic Hospital.
ONE WHO CAME BACK, Owen Crump, producer. (Film sponsored by the Disabled American Veterans, in cooperation with the United States Department of Defense and the Association of Motion Picture Producers.)
THE SEEING EYE, Warner Bros. Gordon Hollingshead, producer.

DOCUMENTARY: FEATURES
I WAS A COMMUNIST FOR THE F.B.I., Warner Bros. Bryan Foy, producer.
KON-TIKI, Artfilm Prod., RKO Radio (Norwegian). Olle Nordemar, producer.

SPECIAL EFFECTS
WHEN WORLDS COLLIDE, Pal, Paramount.

SONG
IN THE COOL, COOL, COOL OF THE EVENING (*Here Comes the Groom*, Paramount); Music by Hoagy Carmichael. Lyrics by Johnny Mercer.
A KISS TO BUILD A DREAM ON (*The Strip*, MGM); Music and Lyrics by Bert Kalmar, Harry Ruby and Oscar Hammerstein, II.
NEVER (*Golden Girl*, 20th Century-Fox); Music by Lionel Newman. Lyrics by Eliot Daniel.
TOO LATE NOW (*Royal Wedding*, MGM); Music by Burton Lane. Lyrics by Alan Jay Lerner.
WONDER WHY (*Rich, Young and Pretty*, MGM); Music by Nicholas Brodsky. Lyrics by Sammy Cahn.

SCORING: DRAMA/COMEDY
DAVID AND BATHSHEBA, 20th Century-Fox. Alfred Newman.
DEATH OF A SALESMAN, Kramer, Columbia. Alex North.
A PLACE IN THE SUN, Paramount. Franz Waxman.
QUO VADIS, MGM. Miklos Rozsa.
A STREETCAR NAMED DESIRE, Feldman, Warner Bros. Alex North.

SCORING: MUSICAL
ALICE IN WONDERLAND, Disney, RKO Radio. Oliver Wallace.
AN AMERICAN IN PARIS, MGM. Johnny Green and Saul Chaplin.
THE GREAT CARUSO, MGM. Peter Herman Adler and Johnny Green.
ON THE RIVIERA, 20th Century-Fox. Alfred Newman.
SHOW BOAT, MGM. Adolph Deutsch and Conrad Salinger.

COSTUME DESIGN
B/W
KIND LADY, MGM. Walter Plunkett and Gile Steele.
THE MODEL AND THE MARRIAGE BROKER, 20th Century-Fox. Charles LeMaire and Renie.
THE MUDLARK, 20th Century-Fox. Edward Stevenson and Margaret Furse.
A PLACE IN THE SUN, Paramount. Edith Head.
A STREETCAR NAMED DESIRE. Foldman, Warner Bros. Lucinda Ballard.

Color
AN AMERICAN IN PARIS, MGM. Orry-Kelly, Walter Plunkett and Irene Sharaff.
DAVID AND BATHSHEBA, 20th Century-Fox. Charles LeMaire and Edward Stevenson.
THE GREAT CARUSO, MGM. Helen Rose and Gile Steele.
QUO VADIS, MGM. Herschel McCoy.
TALES OF HOFFMANN, Powell-Pressburger, Lopert (British). Hein Heckroth.

SOUND RECORDING
BRIGHT VICTORY, U-I. Leslie I. Carey, sound director.
THE GREAT CARUSO, MGM. Douglas Shearer, sound director.
I WANT YOU, Goldwyn, RKO Radio. Gordon Sawyer, sound director.
A STREETCAR NAMED DESIRE, Feldman, Warner Bros. Col. Nathan Levinson, sound director.
TWO TICKETS TO BROADWAY, RKO Radio. John O. Aalberg, sound director.

FILM EDITING
AN AMERICAN IN PARIS, MGM. Adrienne Fazan.
DECISION BEFORE DAWN, 20th Century-Fox. Dorothy Spencer.
A PLACE IN THE SUN, Paramount. William Hornbeck.
QUO VADIS, MGM. Ralph K. Winters.
THE WELL, Popkin, UA. Chester Schaeffer.

HONORARY AND OTHER AWARDS
TO GENE KELLY in appreciation of his versatility as an actor, singer, director and dancer, and specifically for his brilliant achievements in the art of choreography on film.
TO *RASHOMON* (Japanese)—voted by the Board of Governors as the most outstanding foreign language film released in the United States during 1951.

IRVING G. THALBERG MEMORIAL AWARD
TO ARTHUR FREED

SCIENTIFIC OR TECHNICAL
CLASS II
GORDON JENNINGS, S.L. STANCLIFFE and the PARAMOUNT STUDIO SPECIAL PHOTOGRAPHIC and ENGINEERING DEPARTMENTS for the design, construction and application of a servo-operated recording and repeating device.
OLIN L. DUPY of MGM Studio for the design, construction and application of a motion picture reproducing system.
RADIO CORPORATION OF AMERICA, VICTOR DIVISION, for pioneering direct positive recording with anticipatory noise reduction.

CLASS III
RICHARD M. HAFF, FRANK P. HERRNFELD, GARLAND C. MISENER and the ANSCO FILM DIVISION OF GENERAL ANILINE AND FILM CORP.;
FRED PONEDEL, RALPH AYRES and GEORGE BROWN of Warner Bros. Studio;
GLEN ROBINSON and the METRO-GOLDWYN-MAYER STUDIO CONSTRUCTION DEPARTMENT;
JACK GAYLORD and the METRO-GOLDWYN-MAYER STUDIO CONSTRUCTION DEPARTMENT;
CARLOS RIVAS of METRO-GOLDWYN-MAYER STUDIO.

1952

O scar's silver anniversary almost wasn't. The studios complained that TV had drained off profits and refused to fund the show. In desperation, the Academy Awards board turned to where else... TV! NBC kicked in $100,000 for broadcast rights, and millions of Americans made their own popcorn, settled back on the couch,

STAY TUNED FOR OSCAR!

CEREMONY: March 19, 1953
Simulcast: RKO Pantages Theatre, Hollywood/Century Theatre, New York City
HOSTS: Bob Hope, Conrad Nagel

and watched their movie idols live and relatively unscripted for the first time. A new national obsession was born.

Ironically, the most talked-about star of the evening was a woman most viewers had never heard of, Shirley Booth. Though in contention with screen icons Bette Davis (*The Star*) and Joan Crawford (*Sudden Fear*), Booth's deceptively natural performance in *Come Back, Little Sheba* made her the odds-on favorite.

NBC didn't want to miss a minute of the action and installed a revolutionary bicoastal hookup. As a result, the TV audience was

able to witness Booth nearly break her neck as she dashed toward the stage of New York's Century Theatre, tripped on the stairs, and went down hard.

Back in Hollywood, John Wayne accepted awards on behalf of his absent *Quiet Man* director, John Ford, and close friend Gary Cooper. "We fell off horses together and fell into the movies," he said.

The first televised Awards suffered the inevitable glitches of confused entrances and exits and miscues. But the evening's most curious turn wasn't a technical blunder. It was the announcement, by Mary Pickford, of *The Greatest Show on Earth* as Best Picture. Almost no one would have guessed that the lumbering circus epic stood a chance against *High Noon*. Its director, Cecil B. DeMille, seemed most surprised of all. Back in New York, the camera caught the audience looking too disgruntled to applaud. TV had captured the motion-picture elite with its guard down, and viewers experienced a vicarious new thrill. The sound of radios being turned off forever was deafening.

BEST PICTURE
THE GREATEST SHOW ON EARTH

Producer-director Cecil B. DeMille accepted the prize, thanking "the thousands of stars, electricians, circus people and others" who made the film. "I am only a little link in the chain that produced the picture," he added.

According to *Variety*, although "*High Noon* was a cinch to win, a great ovation resounded throughout the theater when *The Greatest Show* was announced the winner." As the crowds roared, the critics were embattled between love and hate. On the hate side was *The New Yorker*'s Pauline Kael, who called the film "a huge, mawkish, trite circus movie." She added, "[It is] awesomely melodramatic. A cornball enterprise." Bosley Crowther of the *New York Times* raved, "The captivation of this picture is in the brilliance with which it portrays the circus and all its movement, not as a mere performing thing but, as Mr. DeMille says in the narration, as a restless, mobile giant...the imagery of arriving in a town, rolling to the lot, spreading a canvas, raising the tents, and getting ready for the show have the authority and the impact of a top documentary film."

Betty Hutton

The envelope, please...

BEST ACTOR
GARY COOPER (1901–1961)
HIGH NOON

Hollywood's golden man wasn't there to receive his Golden Boy, and once again John Wayne was on hand to pick up the prize, putting the Duke in danger of being typecast as "the actor most likely to receive awards for other people."

The quintessential "strong, silent type," Cooper started as an extra in Westerns—after a brief stint as a cartoonist. He got his big break in *The Winning of Barbara Worth* (1926). He appeared with Clara Bow in *It* and *Wings* (both 1927), and in *The Virginian* (1929) before his breakthrough role in *Morocco* (1930). Though he kept a low profile, his offscreen affairs with Bow, Lupe Velez, and others were a source of infinite gossip.

A Farewell to Arms (1931) established Cooper as a romantic leading man. Miscast in *Design for Living* (1933), Cooper finally capitalized on his comedic flair in *Mr. Deeds Goes to Town* (1936, nom.). Following a brief dip in popularity, Cooper's performance in *Beau Geste* (1939) led to a winning streak with *Meet John Doe* (1941), *Sergeant York* (1941, Oscar), *Ball of Fire* (1941), *The Pride of the Yankees* (1942, nom.), *For Whom the Bell Tolls* (1943, Oscar), *The Fountainhead* (1949), *High Noon*, and *Love in the Afternoon* (1957). (For more on Cooper, see 1941.)

BEST DIRECTOR
JOHN FORD (1894–1973)
THE QUIET MAN

John Wayne accepted the award for the absent director, of whom he had previously complained, "He kept calling me a clumsy bastard and a big oaf and kept telling me that I moved like an ox." Ford admitted to the *New York Times* critic A. H. Weiler that he had "assiduously studied the Irish for forty years...but doesn't know a thing about them."

Perhaps one of the most respected of American movie directors—and one of Hollywood's most colorful and irascible filmmakers—John Ford was lauded by critics for his poetic vision. The Western was his domain, which he mastered with such brilliant films as *Drums Along the Mohawk*, *Young Mr. Lincoln*, and *Stagecoach* (all 1939). In the following two years he won Oscars for *The Grapes of Wrath* (1940) and *How Green Was My Valley* (1941).

During World War II he served in the OSS and made several documentaries including *The Battle of Midway* (1942) and *December 7th* (1943). Both were awarded Oscars. In the late 1940s Ford produced some of his most intimate pictures, including *Fort Apache* (1948), *She Wore a Yellow Ribbon* (1949), and *Rio Grande* (1950, a trilogy), and *The Quiet Man*. *The Searchers* (1956), starring John Wayne, remains, arguably, Ford's most mythic and poetic film. Ford was the first recipient of the American Film Institute's Life Achievement Award. (For more on Ford, see 1935, 1940, and 1941.)

BEST OF 1952
Best Picture: *The Greatest Show on Earth*
Best Director: John Ford, *The Quiet Man*
Best Actor: Gary Cooper: *High Noon*
Best Actress: Shirley Booth, *Come Back, Little Sheba*
Best Supporting Actor: Anthony Quinn, *Viva Zapata!*
Best Supporting Actress: Gloria Grahame, *The Bad and the Beautiful*

FIRSTS
• Oscars are on television for the first time!

• The Oscar–winning Anthony Quinn has appeared in more movies with other Oscar–winning actors (for acting) than any other Oscar–winning actor: forty-six; twenty-eight male actors, eighteen female actors.

SINS OF OMISSION
Picture: *Singin' in the Rain, The Bad and the Beautiful, Rancho Notorious, Pat and Mike*
Actor: John Wayne, *The Quiet Man*
Actress: Judy Holliday, *The Marrying Kind*

ROLE REVERSALS
Gregory Peck turned down Cooper's role in *High Noon*.

UNMENTIONABLES
• The House Un-American Activities Committee was in full throttle and subpoenaed *High Noon* screenwriter Carl Foreman while the film was still in production.

• Vivien Leigh, who was looking forward to giving the Award to Cooper, suffered a nervous breakdown shortly before the filming of past winners and was sent to a sanitorium in England. At the same time, her home in Chelsea was robbed. Included in the bounty was her Oscar for *A Streetcar Named Desire*.

• Some words of wisdom from Gloria Grahame: "It wasn't the way I looked at a man, it was the thought behind it."

• Bette Davis—nominated for her performance in *The Star*—couldn't attend the festivities. She was in the hospital recovering from jaw surgery.

• In the 1940s Gary Cooper was used politically to oppose everything left wing. He was persuaded by Cecil B. DeMille and Hedda Hopper to oppose the election of FDR, which he did willingly, adding that he "didn't like the company he's [FDR] keeping." This was thought to be a reference to FDR's Jewish advisers.

• "From what I hear about Communism, I, er, don't like it because, er, it isn't, er, on the level," Cooper said.

• Of Arthur Miller's *Death of a Salesman*, Cooper said, "Sure, there are fellows like that, but you don't have to write plays about them."

• Carl Sandburg described Cooper as "one of the most beloved illiterates America has ever known."

• Cooper had a face-lift in 1958 after he was criticized for playing an 18-year-old's lover (and wore a wig to hide his baldness).

• Unhappy with the tilt of her upper lip, Gloria Grahame often stuffed cotton along her gum line to straighten it out. The effect was cosmetically less than flattering and made it difficult for her to speak. A leading man, after kissing her, ended up with a mouth full of cotton.

BEST ACTRESS
SHIRLEY BOOTH (1898–1992)
COME BACK, LITTLE SHEBA

Booth was so excited when she heard her name that she rushed to the stage, fell down, picked herself up, ran to the podium, and said, "I am a very lucky girl. I guess this is the peak. The view has been wonderful all along the way. And I can only say, to my new friends, thanks for their hope…And to everybody thanks for their charity."

Sheba, in which Booth played a hapless woman married to a younger man, was her debut film. "Her skillful and knowing creation of a depressingly common type—the immature, mawkish, lazy housewife—is visualization at its best," wrote Bosley Crowther in the *New York Times*.

In the end, she would make only four more films: *Main Street to Broadway* (1953), *About Mrs. Leslie* (1954), *Hot Spell*, and *The Matchmaker* (both 1958). In 1961, she appeared in the long-running sitcom *Hazel*, and won two Emmys and even greater stardom.

BEST SUPPORTING ACTOR
ANTHONY QUINN (1915–2001)
VIVA ZAPATA!

Katherine Quinn (Quinn's wife and the adopted daughter of Cecil B. DeMille) accepted the award for Quinn saying, "I know he'll be a happy man." Quinn was reported to have said he didn't stand a chance but was thrilled to win because, finally, his kids wouldn't think he was just another "bum."

Mexican-born Quinn did odd jobs as a butcher, a boxer, a street corner preacher, and a slaughterhouse worker before turning to acting. He also won a scholarship to study architecture with Frank Lloyd Wright, with whom he developed a close relationship. He gave it all up for Hollywood, and in exchange became one of its most prolific character actors—and sometime leading

Anthony Quinn (left) with Marlon Brando (seated center), Arnold Moss and Joseph Wiseman (right)

man. Among the films he made in his sixty years in the movies were *Blood and Sand*, (1941), *They Died with Their Boots On* (1941), *The Ox-Bow Incident* (1943), and *Back to Bataan* (1945). (For more on Quinn, see 1956.)

BEST SUPPORTING ACTRESS
GLORIA GRAHAME (1923–1981)
THE BAD AND THE BEAUTIFUL

Grahame looked shocked when she heard her name called out. In the film, Grahame plays the seductive Southern wife of abused author Dick Powell. It was a role made for the actress who seemed genetically disposed to play bad girls, even when they were good.

Grahame gained true recognition for her first "bad girl" performance in *It's a Wonderful Life* (1946). She had sex appeal in abundance and difficulty playing sympathetic characters; she was typecast as the shady vixen. This, 1952, proved her most glorious year, with a nomination and a victory for *The Greatest*

Dick Powell with Gloria Grahame

Show on Earth and *The Bad and the Beautiful*. She also appeared in *Macao* and *Sudden Fear* in that same year. She later made such films as *Not as a Stranger* (1955) and *Blood and Lace* (1971), *The Loners* (1972), and *Melvin and Howard* (1980).

AWARD NOMINATIONS 1952

PICTURE
THE GREATEST SHOW ON EARTH, DeMille, Paramount, Cecil B. DeMille.
HIGH NOON, Kramer, UA, Stanley Kramer.
IVANHOE, MGM, Pandro S. Berman.
MOULIN ROUGE, Romulus, UA, John Huston.
THE QUIET MAN, Argosy, Republic, John Ford and Merian C. Cooper.

ACTOR
MARLON BRANDO in *Viva Zapata!*, 20th Century-Fox.
GARY COOPER in *High Noon*, Kramer, UA.
KIRK DOUGLAS in *The Bad and the Beautiful*, MGM.
JOSE FERRER in *Moulin Rouge*, Romulus, UA.
ALEC GUINNESS in *The Lavender Hill Mob*, Rank Ealing, U-I. (British).

ACTRESS
SHIRLEY BOOTH in *Come Back, Little Sheba*, Wallis, Paramount.
JOAN CRAWFORD in *Sudden Fear*, Kaufman, RKO Radio.
BETTE DAVIS in *The Star*, Friedlob, 20th Century-Fox.
JULIE HARRIS in *The Member of the Wedding*, Kramer, Columbia.
SUSAN HAYWARD in *With a Song in My Heart*, 20th Century-Fox.

SUPPORTING ACTOR
RICHARD BURTON in *My Cousin Rachel*, 20th Century-Fox.
ARTHUR HUNNICUT in *The Big Sky*, Winchester, RKO Radio.
VICTOR McLAGLEN in *The Quiet Man*, Argosy, Republic.
JACK PALANCE in *Sudden Fear*, Kaufman, RKO Radio.
ANTHONY QUINN in *Viva Zapata!*, 20th Century-Fox.

SUPPORTING ACTRESS
GLORIA CRAHAME in *The Bad and the Beautiful*, MGM.
JEAN HAGEN in *Singin' in the Rain*, MGM.
COLETTE MARCHAND in *Moulin Rouge*, Romulus, UA.
TERRY MOORE in *Come Back, Little Sheba*, Wallis, Paramount.
THELMA RITTER in *With a Song in My Heart*, 20th Century-Fox.

DIRECTION
CECIL B. DeMILLE for *The Greatest Show on Earth*, DeMille, Paramount.
JOHN FORD for *The Quiet Man*, Argosy, Republic.
JOHN HUSTON for *Moulin Rouge*, Romulus, UA.
JOSEPH L. MANKIEWICZ for *Five Fingers*, 20th Century-Fox.
FRED ZINNEMANN for *High Noon*, Stanley Kramer, UA.

WRITING: ORIGINAL STORY
THE GREATEST SHOW ON EARTH, DeMille, Paramount. Frederick M. Frank, Theodore St. John and Frank Cavett.
MY SON JOHN, Rainbow, Paramount. Leo McCarey.

THE NARROW MARGIN, RKO Radio.
Martin Goldsmith and Jack Leonard.
THE PRIDE OF ST. LOUIS, 20th Century-
Fox. Guy Trosper.
THE SNIPER, Kramer, Columbia. Edna
Anhalt and Edward Anhalt.

WRITING: SCREENPLAY
THE BAD AND THE BEAUTIFUL, MGM.
Charles Schnee.
FIVE FINGERS, 20th Century-Fox.
Michael Wilson.
HIGH NOON, Kramer, UA. Carl Foreman.
THE MAN IN THE WHITE SUIT, Rank-
Ealing, U-I (British). Roger MacDougall,
John Dighton and Alexander Mackendrick.
THE QUIET MAN, Argosy, Republic.
Frank S. Nugent.

WRITING: STORY AND SCREENPLAY
THE ATOMIC CITY, Paramount.
Sydney Boehm.
BREAKING THE SOUND BARRIER, London
Films, UA (British). Terence Rattigan.
THE LAVENDER HILL MOB, Rank-Ealing,
U-I (British). T.E.B. Clarke.
PAT AND MIKE, MGM. Ruth Gordon and
Garson Kanin.
VIVA ZAPATA!, 20th Century-Fox.
John Steinbeck.

CINEMATOGRAPHY
B/W
THE BAD AND THE BEAUTIFUL, MGM.
Robert Surtees.
THE BIG SKY, Winchester, RKO Radio.
Russell Harlan.
MY COUSIN RACHEL, 20th Century-Fox.
Joseph LaShelle.
NAVAJO, Bartlett-Foster, Lippert.
Virgil E. Miller.
SUDDEN FEAR, Kaufman, RKO Radio.
Charles B. Lang, Jr.

Color
HANS CHRISTIAN ANDERSEN, Goldwyn,
RKO Radio. Harry Stradling.
IVANHOE, MGM. F.A. Young.
MILLION DOLLAR MERMAID, MGM.
George J. Folsey.
THE QUIET MAN, Argosy, Republic.
Winton C. Hoch and Archie Stout.
THE SNOWS OF KILIMANJARO, 20th
Century-Fox. Leon Shamroy.

ART DIRECTION—SET DECORATION
B/W
THE BAD AND THE BEAUTIFUL, MGM.
Cedric Gibbons and Edward Carfagno;
Edwin B. Willis and Keogh Gleason.
CARRIE, Paramount. Hal Pereira and Roland
Anderson; Emile Kuri.
MY COUSIN RACHEL, 20th Century-Fox.
Lyle Wheeler and John DeCuir;
Walter H. Scott.
RASHOMON, RKO Radio (Japanese).
Matsuyama; H. Motsumoto.
VIVA ZAPATA!, 20th Century-Fox. Lyle
Wheeler and Leland Fuller; Thomas Little
and Claude Carpenter.
Color
HANS CHRISTIAN ANDERSEN, Goldwyn,
RKO Radio. Richard Day and Clave;
Howard Bristol.
THE MERRY WIDOW, MGM. Cedric
Gibbons and Paul Groesse; Edwin B Willis
and Arthur Krams.
MOULIN ROUGE, Romulus, UA. Paul
Sheriff; Marcel Vertes.
THE QUIET MAN, Argosy, Republic. Frank
Hotaling; John McCarthy, Jr., and
Charles Thompson.
THE SNOWS OF KILIMANJARO, 20th
Century-Fox. Lyle Wheeler and John
DeCuir; Thomas Little and Paul S. Fox.

COSTUME DESIGN
B/W
AFFAIR IN TRINIDAD, Beckworth,
Columbia. Jean Louis.
THE BAD AND THE BEAUTIFUL, MGM.
Helen Rose.
CARRIE, Paramount. Edith Head.
MY COUSIN RACHEL, 20th Century-Fox.
Charles LeMaire and Dorothy Jeakins.
SUDDEN FEAR, Kaufman, RKO Radio. Sheila
O'Brien.

Color
THE GREATEST SHOW ON EARTH,
DeMille, Paramount. Edith Head, Dorothy
Jeakins and Miles White.
HANS CHRISTIAN ANDERSEN, Goldwyn,
RKO Radio. Clave, Mary Wills and
Madame Karinska.
THE MERRY WIDOW, MGM. Helen Rose
and Gile Steele.
MOULIN ROUGE, Romulus UA.
Marcel Vertes.
WITH A SONG IN MY HEART, 20th
Century-Fox. Charles LeMaire.

SOUND RECORDING
BREAKING THE SOUND BARRIER,
London Films, UA (British). London Film
Sound Department.
HANS CHRISTIAN ANDERSEN, Goldwyn,
RKO Radio. Goldwyn Sound Department;
Gordon Sawyer, sound director.
THE PROMOTER, Rank-Neame, U-I
(British). Pinewood Studios Sound
Department.
THE QUIET MAN, Argosy, Republic.
Republic Sound Department; Daniel J.
Bloomberg, sound director.
WITH A SONG IN MY HEART, 20th
Century-Fox. 20th Century-Fox Sound
Department; Thomas T. Moulton,
sound director.

FILM EDITING
COME BACK, LITTLE SHEBA, Wallis,
Paramount. Warren Low.
FLAT TOP, Monogram. William Austin.
THE GREATEST SHOW ON EARTH,
DeMille, Paramount. Anne Bauchens.
HIGH NOON, Kramer, UA. Elmo Williams
and Harry Gerstad.
MOULIN ROUGE, Romulus, UA.
Ralph Kemplen.

SPECIAL EFFECTS
PLYMOUTH ADVENTURE, MGM.

SONG
AM I IN LOVE (*Son of Paleface*, Paramount);
Music and Lyrics by Jack Brooks.
BECAUSE YOU'RE MINE, (*Because You're*
Mine, MGM); Music by Nicholas Brodszky.
Lyrics by Sammy Cahn.
HIGH NOON (DO NOT FORSAKE ME,
OH MY DARLIN'), (*High Noon*, Kramer,
UA); Music by Dimitri Tiomkin. Lyrics by
Ned Washington.
THUMBELINA (*Hans Christian Andersen*,
Goldwyn, RKO Radio); Music and Lyrics by
Frank Loesser.
ZING A LITTLE ZONG, (*Just for You*,
Paramount); Music by Barry Warren. Lyrics
by Leo Robin.

SCORING: DRAMA/COMEDY
HIGH NOON, Kramer, UA. Dimitri Tiomkin.
IVANHOE, MGM. Miklos Rozsa.
THE MIRACLE OF FATIMA, Foy. Warner
Bros. Max Steiner.
THE THIEF, Popkin, UA. Herschel Burke
Gilbert.
VIVA ZAPATA!, 20th Century-Fox. Alex North.

SCORING: MUSICAL
HANS CHRISTIAN ANDERSEN, Goldwyn,
RKO Radio. Walter Scharf.
THE JAZZ SINGER, Warner Bros. Ray
Heindorf and Max Steiner.
THE MEDIUM, Transfilm-Lopert (Italian).
Gian-Carlo Menotti.
SINGIN' IN THE RAIN, MGM. Lennie Hayton.
WITH A SONG IN MY HEART, 20th
Century-Fox. Alfred Newman.

SHORT SUBJECTS: CARTOONS
JOHANN MOUSE, MGM. (Tom & Jerry).
Fred Quimby, producer.
LITTLE JOHNNY JET, MGM. (MGM.
Series). Fred Quimby, producer.
MADELINE, UPA, Columbia. (Jolly Frolics).
Stephen Bosustow, executive producer.
PINK AND BLUE BLUES, UPA, Columbia.
(Mister Magoo). Stephen Bosustow,
executive producer.
ROMANCE OF TRANSPORTATION,
National Film Board of Canada.
(Canadian). Tom Daly, producer.

SHORT SUBJECT: ONE-REEL
ATHLETES OF THE SADDLE, Paramount.
(Sportlights Series). Jack Eaton, producer.
DESERT KILLER, Warner Bros. (Sports
Parade). Gordon Hollingshead, producer.
LIGHT IN THE WINDOW, Art Films
Prods., 20th Century-Fox. (Art Series).
Boris Vermont, producer.
NEIGHBOURS, National Film Board of Canada
(Canadian). Norman McLaren, producer.
ROYAL SCOTLAND, Crown Film Unit,
British Information Services (British).

SHORT SUBJECT: TWO-REEL
BRIDGE OF TIME, London Film Prod.,
British Information Services (British).
DEVIL TAKE US, Theatre of Life Prod. (Theatre
of Life Series). Herbert Morgan, producer.
THAR SHE BLOWS!, Warner Bros.
(Technicolor Special). Gordon
Hollingshead, producer.
WATER BIRDS, Disney, RKO Radio. (True-
Life Adventure). Walt Disney, producer.

DOCUMENTARY: SHORT SUBJECTS
DEVIL TAKE US, Theatre of Life Prod.
Herbert Morgan, producer.
THE GARDEN SPIDER (EPEIRA
DIADEMA), Cristallo Films, I.F.E.
Releasing Corp. (Italian). Alberto
Ancilotto, producer.
MAN ALIVE!, UPA for the American Cancer
Society. Stephen Bosustow, executive producer.
NEIGHBOURS, National Film Board of
Canada, Mayer-Kingsley, Inc.
(Canadian). Norman McLaren, producer.

DOCUMENTARY: FEATURES
THE HOAXTERS, MGM. Dore Schary,
producer.
NAVAJO, Bartlett-Foster Prod., Lippert
Pictures, Inc. Hall Bartlett, producer.
THE SEA AROUND US, RKO Radio. Irwin
Allen, producer.

HONORARY AND OTHER AWARDS
TO GEORGE ALFRED MITCHELL for the
design and development of the camera
which bears his name and for his continued
and dominant presence in the field of
cinematography.
TO JOSEPH M. SCHENCK for long and
distinguished service to the motion
picture industry.
TO MERIAN C. COOPER for his many
innovations and contributions to the art of
motion pictures.
TO HAROLD LLOYD, master comedian and
good citizen.
TO BOB HOPE for his contribution to the
laughter of the world, his service to the
motion picture industry, and his devotion
to the American premise.
TO *FORBIDDEN GAMES* (French)—Best
Foreign Language Film first released in the
United States during 1952.

IRVING G. THALBERG MEMORIAL AWARD
TO CECIL B. DeMILLE

SCIENTIFIC OR TECHNICAL
CLASS I
EASTMAN KODAK CO. for the introduction
of Eastman color negative and Eastman
color print film.
ANSCO DIVISION, GENERAL ANILINE
AND FILM CORP., for the introduction of
Ansco color negative and Ansco color print
film.

CLASS II
TECHNICOLOR MOTION PICTURE CORP.
for an improved method of color motion
picture photography under incandescent light.

CLASS III
PROJECTION, STILL PHOTOGRAPHIC and
DEVELOPMENT ENGINEERING
DEPARTMENTS of METRO-GOLDWYN-
MAYER STUDIO;
JOHN G. FRAYNE and R.R. SCOVILLE and
WESTREX CORP.;
PHOTO RESEARCH CORP.;
GUSTAV JIROUCH;
CARLOS RIVAS of Metro-Goldwyn-Mayer
Studio.

1953

"Ladies and gentlemen, tomorrow's headlines will be made here tonight. This is news. This is movietown's election night."

—Oscar broadcast announcer

Frank Sinatra's roller-coaster career finally washed up on the shore of Pearl Harbor. *From Here to Eternity* was his ticket back into the party, and he strolled the red carpet of the Pantages Theatre with the easy grin of a guy holding a royal flush. The woman responsible for his winning the Best Supporting role, wife Ava Gardner, was nowhere in sight. His dates for the evening were two of his children, Frank Jr. and Nancy, whose charm bracelet would soon boast a miniature gold Oscar. They got the biggest cheers from the skimpiest crowd of fans in years.

The usually boisterous mob in the bleachers was home watching the event on TV. Viewers were treated to a bicoastal gala interspersed with Oldsmobile commercials starring Betty White and Paul Douglas. "How are you doing, Dad?" joked Donald O'Connor to his New York co-host, Fredric March. That proved to be the humorous high point of the tightly scheduled two-hour show.

The true drama belonged to Sinatra, who lost his cool long enough to be thoroughly shaken by his win. Good girl turned movie hooker Donna Reed was similarly zombified by her good fortune. The broadcast cut away to a pre-filmed segment in Shirley Booth's Philadelphia-theater dressing room. She chatted amiably on the phone with a representative from Price Waterhouse, hung up, and faced the camera to report, "The winner is William Holden!"

Back at the Pantages, the Best Actor for 1953 barely had time for a rushed "Thank you" before being cut off. Then back to New York live, as Audrey Hepburn's name was announced. She rushed onto the stage and wandered around like a stray doe until March gently guided her to the mike. She was an easily predicted winner, as were most of the others. The upset of 1952 (*The Greatest Show on Earth*) was not to be repeated. The most critically acclaimed film of the year, *From Here to Eternity*, took the top prize. While Frank may have lost Ava in the comeback rush, he found a permanent seat at Table No. 1.

PERFECTLY FRANK

CEREMONY: March 25, 1954
RKO Pantages Theatre, Hollywood
Century Theater, New York
HOSTS: Donald O'Connor
Fredric March

BEST PICTURE/BEST DIRECTOR
FRED ZINNEMANN (1907–1997)
FROM HERE TO ETERNITY

Thanking "the entire Pacific Command of the U.S. Army," Zinnemann claimed his prize for his critical and box-office bonanza, which touched a social nerve in America. In the laudatory words of *The New Yorker* critic Pauline Kael, the Pearl Harbor drama about the decadent life in Hawaii on the eve of Pearl Harbor explores "the poignance and futility of the love lives of the professional soldiers involved, as well as the indictment of commanding officers whose selfishness can break men devoted to soldiering."

Though he would win four Oscars and claim authorship of a number of classics, somehow Zinnemann never entered the pantheon of "auteur" filmmakers. As a young man Zinnemann's enthusiasm for the movies led him to Germany, where he worked with some of the great filmmakers of all time, including Billy Wilder and Robert Siodmak. He then went to Hollywood, where he was an extra in *All Quiet on the Western Front* (1930). Zinnemann's first love, though, was making films; he apprenticed himself behind the camera with documentary producer-director Robert Flaherty, and teamed with producer-writer Paul Strand to co-direct a feature film, *The Wave* (1935). He later signed a contract with MGM and won his first Oscar for the short *That Mothers Might Live* (1938).

Zinnemann got his real break when he made *The Seventh Cross* (1944), starring Spencer Tracy, and began building a reputation with *The Search* (1948) and *Act of Violence* (1949). The former film marked Montgomery Clift's screen debut and earned Zinnemann his first Best Director Oscar nomination. His best-known films came out of his collaboration with producer Stanley Kramer: *The Men* (1950), *High Noon* (1952, nom.), *The Member of the Wedding* (1952), and *From Here to Eternity* (1953, Oscar). Among Zinnemann's other notable films were *Oklahoma!* (1955), *The Nun's Story* (1959, nom.), and *The Sundowners* (1960, nom.). After his triumph with *A Man for All Seasons*, Zinnemann made only three films: *The Day of the Jackal* (1973), *Julia* (1977, nom.), and *Five Days One Summer* (1982). He published his autobiography, *Fred Zinnemann on Cinema*, in 1992. (For more on Zinnemann, see 1966.)

Deborah Kerr, Burt Lancaster

The envelope, please...

Don Taylor with William Holden

BEST ACTOR
WILLIAM HOLDEN (1918–1981)
STALAG 17

"Thank you, thank you," said the tongue-tied Holden. Holden became an overnight sensation for his performance in *Golden Boy* (1939), which led to his being typecast as the boy next door in films beneath his talent. He broke the mold after returning from World War II military service to play a gigolo in *Sunset Boulevard* (1950), followed by important performances in *Born Yesterday* (1950), *Stalag 17*, and *Picnic* (1955).

Holden remained a star during the transitional 1950s, unlike many big names of the 1930s and '40s who disappeared from the screen. He negotiated a groundbreaking contract with Columbia to star in David Lean's blockbuster *The Bridge on the River Kwai* (1957), which made him a part owner of the film. In the 1960s he showed signs of winding down and sang his swan song in the Peckinpah classic *The Wild Bunch* (1969), in which he played an aging outlaw. It was possibly one of his best performances. Among his last films were *The Towering Inferno* (1974), *Network* (1976, nom.), *Fedora* (1978), and *S.O.B* (1981).

Bob Thomas's biography *Golden Boy* revealed that beneath Holden's confident exterior, he suffered deep insecurities and essentially drank himself to death.

Audrey Hepburn with Gregory Peck

BEST ACTRESS
AUDREY HEPBURN (1929–1993)
ROMAN HOLIDAY

"This is too much," said the delicate actress. According to Pauline Kael of *The New Yorker*, "[*Roman Holiday*] is the picture that made Audrey Hepburn a movie star."

Born in Belgium, Hepburn was descended from a long line of royals. During the Nazi occupation she suffered from depression and malnutrition, which may have led to eating problems. Following her brilliant debut in *Roman Holiday* she continued to seduce audiences in *Sabrina* (1954), *Love in the Afternoon* (1957, nom.), *Funny Face* (1957, nom.) and *The Nun's Story* (1959, nom.). Hepburn reached the peak of her career in *Breakfast at Tiffany's* (1961, nom.), *Charade* (1963), *My Fair Lady* (1964), and *Wait Until Dark* (1967, nom.).

By the end of the sixties, Hepburn had decided to retire while she was on top, though she did return for *Robin and Marian* (1976) with Sean Connery. In 1988 she became a special ambassador to the United Nations UNICEF fund, helping children. With her death in 1993, in a touching epitaph, Rex Reed said of Hepburn, "In a cruel and imperfect world, she was living proof that God could still create perfection."

BEST OF 1953
Best Picture: *From Here to Eternity*
Best Director: Fred Zinnemann, *From Here to Eternity*
Best Actor: William Holden, *Stalag 17*
Best Actress: Audrey Hepburn, *Roman Holiday*
Best Supporting Actor: Frank Sinatra, *From Here to Eternity*
Best Supporting Actress: Donna Reed, *From Here to Eternity*

ROLE REVERSALS
Early in her career Audrey Hepburn turned down the lead in *Gigi*. Later, she would also turn down plum roles in important films like *40 Carats*, *Nicholas and Alexandra*, and *The Turning Point*. She decided, instead, to remain in retirement and raise her sons.

SINS OF OMISSION
Actor: Montgomery Clift, *From Here to Eternity*.

UNMENTIONABLES
- According to Mia Farrow's biography, *What Falls Away*, Frank Sinatra offered to have Woody Allen's legs broken when he was found to be having an affair with Mia's adopted daughter, Soon Yi Previn.
- Sinatra reportedly kept a picture of Ava Gardner on his mirror long after their breakup.
- A provision in Frank Sinatra's will is that if anyone contests it, he or she is automatically disinherited.
- The epitaph on Sinatra's headstone reads, "The best is yet to come."
- At Sinatra's funeral, friends and family members placed items in his coffin that had personal significance. These are reported to include ten dimes, several Tootsie Roll candies, a pack of Black Jack chewing gum, a roll of wild-cherry Life Savers candy, a ring engraved with the word *Dream*, a mini-bottle of Jack Daniel's whiskey, a pack of Camel cigarettes, and a Zippo cigarette lighter.
- Some three decades later, the Hungarian-born actress Eva Bartok claimed that her daughter, Deana, born in 1957 during Bartok's marriage to the actor Curd Jürgens, was actually fathered by Sinatra during a brief affair that he and Bartok had had following his breakup in 1956 with the sultry Ava Gardner. Sinatra never acknowledged paternity.
- "I'm for anything that gets you through the night, be it prayer, tranquilizers, or a bottle of Jack Daniels," Sinatra said.
- William Holden was said to be a hygiene fanatic, and reportedly showered as many as four times a day.
- Holden died from a laceration to his forehead, which was caused by hitting his head during a bout of heavy drinking. He apparently remained conscious for half an hour or so after the injury but never realized that he should phone for help. Had he done so, he would probably have lived.
- Everyone remembers when Marilyn Monroe serenaded President John F. Kennedy on his birthday in 1962. What is often forgotten is that Audrey Hepburn sang "Happy Birthday, Mr. President" to JFK for his final birthday, in 1963.

Frank Sinatra (right) with Montgomery Clift

BEST SUPPORTING ACTOR
FRANK SINATRA (1915–1998)
FROM HERE TO ETERNITY

"In his first straight acting part," wrote the *New York Times*'s A. H. Weiler, "[Sinatra] surprised audiences with a softly modulated, likable performance as Maggio, who loses his life because of his high spirits…a characterization rich in comic vitality and genuine pathos."

Born on the streets of Hoboken, New Jersey, Sinatra pulled every string he had to win his role in *From Here to Eternity*. His star rose steadily throughout the 1940s, when he played in a series of musical comedies, including *Anchors Aweigh* (1945), *It Happened in Brooklyn* (1947), and *On the Town* (1949).

After a few more musical numbers—*Guys and Dolls* (1955), *High Society* (1956), and *Pal Joey* (1957)—Sinatra was still hungry for dramatic roles and found them in *Some Came Running* (1958) and the Cold War thriller *The Manchurian Candidate* (1962), which was made only after Richard Condon's controversial novel was endorsed by Sinatra's friend President John F. Kennedy.

Donna Reed with Montgomery Clift

BEST SUPPORTING ACTRESS
DONNA REED (1921–1986)
FROM HERE TO ETERNITY

"It's a long walk and I didn't think I'd make it," said the breathless Reed after running up to the stage. "I'm very proud and grateful. It was a wonderful road *From Here to Eternity*, but it was even more wonderful from *Eternity* to here."

The wholesome star had shocked moviegoers when she was cast against type as a prostitute.

In real life Reed grew up on a farm and was every bit the small-town good girl she came to embody in films, particularly in Frank Capra's classic *It's a Wonderful Life* (1946). First spotted by MGM in 1941 in a college production, she was cast in a handful of bit parts that led to bigger—but always light—roles, including *Shadow of the Thin Man* (1941), *The Courtship of Andy Hardy* (1942), and *The Human Comedy* (1943). Reed's potential as a more substantial actress was rarely tested, with the exception of her roles in *They Were Expendable* (1945) and *From Here to Eternity*.

She was sent back to home and hearth for *The Donna Reed Show*, a successful, long-running sitcom (1958–1966). In one of her last appearances, Reed could be seen in the miniseries *Dallas* during the 1984–1985 season.

PICTURE
FROM HERE TO ETERNITY, Columbia, Buddy Adler.
JULIUS CAESAR, MGM, John Houseman.
THE ROBE, 20th Century-Fox, Frank Ross
ROMAN HOLIDAY, Paramount, William Wyler.
SHANE, Paramount, George Stevens.

ACTOR
MARLON BRANDO in *Julius Caesar*, 20th Century-Fox.
RICHARD BURTON in *The Robe*, 20th Century-Fox.
MONTGOMERY CLIFT in *From Here to Eternity*, Columbia.
WILLIAM HOLDEN in *Stalag 17*, Paramount.
BURT LANCASTER in *From Here to Eternity*, Columbia.

ACTRESS
LESLIE CARON in *Lili*, MGM.
AVA GARDNER in *Mogambo*, MGM.
AUDREY HEPBURN in *Roman Holiday*, Paramount.
DEBORAH KERR in *From Here to Eternity*, Columbia.
MAGGIE MCNAMARA, in *The Moon Is Blue*, Preminger-Herbert, UA.

SUPPORTING ACTOR
EDDIE ALBERT in *Roman Holiday*, Paramount.
BRANDON DE WILDE in *Shane*, Paramount.
JACK PALANCE in *Shane*, Paramount.
FRANK SINATRA in *From Here to Eternity*, Columbia.
ROBERT STRAUSS in *Stalag 17*, Paramount.

SUPPORTING ACTRESS
GRACE KELLY in *Mogambo*, MGM.
GERALDINE PAGE in *Hondo*, Wayne-Fellows, Warner Bros.
MARJORIE RAMBEAU in *Torch Song*, MGM.
DONNA REED in *From Here to Eternity*, Columbia.
THELMA RITTER in *Pickup on South Street*, 20th Century-Fox.

DIRECTION
GEORGE STEVENS for *Shane*, Paramount.
CHARLES WALTERS for *Lili*, MGM.
BILLY WILDER for *Stalag 17*, Paramount.
WILLIAM WYLER for *Roman Holiday*, Paramount.
FRED ZINNEMANN for *From Here to Eternity*, Columbia.

WRITING: ORIGINAL STORY
ABOVE AND BEYOND, MGM. Beirne Lay, Jr.
THE CAPTAIN'S PARADISE, London Films, Lopert-UA (British). Alec Coppel.
LITTLE FUGITIVE, Burstyn Releasing. Ray Ashley, Morris Engel and Ruth Orkin.
ROMAN HOLIDAY, Paramount. Dalton Trumbo.

WRITING: SCREENPLAY
THE CRUEL SEA, Rank-Ealing, U-I (British). Eric Ambler.
FROM HERE TO ETERNITY, Columbia. Daniel Taradash.
LILI, MGM. Helen Deutsch.
ROMAN HOLIDAY, Paramount. Ian McLellan Hunter and John Dighton.
SHANE, Paramount. A. B. Guthrie, Jr.

WRITING: STORY AND SCREENPLAY
THE BAND WAGON, MGM. Betty Comden and Adolph Green.
THE DESERT RATS, 20th Century-Fox. Richard Murphy.
THE NAKED SPUR, MGM. Sam Rolfe and Harold Jack Bloom.
TAKE THE HIGH GROUND, MGM. Millard Kaufman.
TITANIC, 20th Century-Fox. Charles Brackett, Walter Reisch and Richard Breen.

CINEMATOGRAPHY
B/W
THE FOUR POSTER, Kramer, Columbia. Hal Mohr.
FROM HERE TO ETERNITY, Columbia. Burnett Guffey.
JULIUS CAESAR, MGM. Joseph Ruttenberg,
MARTIN LUTHER, de Rochemont Assocs. Joseph C. Brun.
ROMAN HOLIDAY, Paramount. Frank Planer and Henri Alekan.

Color
ALL THE BROTHERS WERE VALIANT, MGM. George Folsey.
BENEATH THE 12 MILE REEF, 20th Century-Fox. Edward Cronjager.
LILI, MGM. Robert Planck.
THE ROBE, 20th Century-Fox. Leon Shamroy.
SHANE, Paramount. Loyal Griggs.

ART DIRECTION—SET DECORATION
B/W
JULIUS CAESAR, MGM. Cedric Gibbons and Edward Carfagno; Edwin B. Willis and Hugh Hunt.
MARTIN LUTHER, de Rochemont Assocs. Fritz Maurischat and Paul Markwitz.
THE PRESIDENT'S LADY, 20th Century-Fox. Lyle Wheeler and Leland Fuller; Paul S. Fox.
ROMAN HOLIDAY, Paramount. Hal Pereira and Walter Tyler.
TITANIC, 20th Century-Fox Lyle Wheeler and Maurice Ransford; Stuart Reiss.

Color
KNIGHTS OF THE ROUND TABLE, MGM. Alfred Junge and Hans Peters; John Jarvis.
LILI, MGM. Cedric Gibbons and Paul Groesse; Edwin B. Willis and Arthur Krams.
THE ROBE, 20th Century-Fox. Lyle Wheeler and George W. Davis; Walter M. Scott and Paul S. Fox.
THE STORY OF THREE LOVES, MGM. Cedric Gibbons Preston Ames, Edward Carfagno and Gabriel Scognamillo; Edwin B. Wllis, Keogh Gleason, Arthur Krams and Jack D. Moore.
YOUNG BESS, MGM. Cedric Gibbons and Uric McCleary; Edwin B. Willis and Jack D. Moore.

COSTUME DESIGN
B/W
THE ACTRESS, MGM. Walter Plunkett.
DREAM WIFE, MGM. Helen Rose and Herschel McCoy.
FROM HERE TO ETERNITY Columbia. Jean Louis.
THE PRESIDENT'S LADY, 20th Century-Fox. Charles LeMaire and Renie.
ROMAN HOLIDAY, Paramount. Edith Head.

Color
THE BAND WAGON, MGM. Mary Ann Nyberg.
CALL ME MADAM, 20th Century-Fox. Irene Sharaff.
HOW TO MARRY A MILLIONAIRE, 20th CenturyFox. Charles LeMaire and Travilla.
THE ROBE, 20th Century-Fox. Charles LeMaire and Emile Santiago.
YOUNG BESS, MGM. Walter Plunkett.

SOUND RECORDING
CALAMITY JANE, Warner Bros. Warner Bros. Sound Department; William A. Mueller, sound director.
FROM HERE TO ETERNITY, Columbia. Columbia Sound Department; John P. Livadary, sound director,
KNIGHTS OF THE ROUND TABLE, MGM. MGM. Sound Department; AW. Watkins, sound director.
THE MISSISSIPPI GAMBLER, U-I. Universal International Sound Department; Leslie I. Carey, sound director.

THE WAR OF THE WORLDS, Pal, Paramount. Paramount Sound Department; Loren L. Ryder, sound director.

FILM EDITING
CRAZY LEGS, Bartlett, Republic. Irvine (Cotton) Warburton.
FROM HERE TO ETERNITY, Columbia. William Lyon.
THE MOON IS BLUE, Preminger-Herbert, UA. Otto Ludwig.
ROMAN HOLIDAY, Paramount. Robert Swink.
THE WAR OF THE WORLDS, Pal, Paramount. Everett Douglas.

SPECIAL EFFECTS
THE WAR OF THE WORLDS, Pal, Paramount.

SONG
THE MOON IS BLUE (*The Moon Is Blue*, Preminger Herbert, UA); Music by Herschel Burke Gilbert. Lyrics by Sylvia Fine.
MY FLAMING HEART (*Small Town Girl*, MGM.); Music by Nicholas Brodszky. Lyrics by Leo Robin.
SADIE THOMPSON'S SONG (BLUE PACIFIC BLUES) (*Miss Sadie Thompson*, Beckworth, Columbia); Music by Lester Lee. Lyrics by Ned Washington.
SECRET LOVE (*Calamity Jane*, Warner Bros.); Music by Sammy Fain. Lyrics by Paul Francis Webster.
THAT'S AMORE (*The Caddy*, Paramount); Music by Harry Warren. Lyrics by Jack Brooks.

SCORING: DRAMA/COMEDY
ABOVE AND BEYOND, MGM. Hugo Friedhofter.
FROM HERE TO ETERNITY, Columbia. Morris Stoloff and George Duning. -
JULIUS CAESAR, MGM. Miklos Rozsa.
LILI, MGM. Bronislau Kaper.
THIS IS CINERAMA, Cinerama Corp. Louis Forbes.

SCORING: MUSICAL
THE BAND WAGON, MGM. Adolph Deutsch.
CALAMITY JANE, Warner Bros. Ray Heindorf.
CALL ME MADAM, 20th Century-Fox. Alfred Newman.
5,000 FINGERS OF DR. T., Kramer, Columbia. Frederick Hollander and Morris Stoloff.
KISS ME KATE, MGM. Andre Previn and Saul Chaplin.

SHORT SUBJECTS: CARTOONS
CHRISTOPHER CRUMPET, UPA, Columbia. (Jolly Frolics). Stephen Bosustow, producer.
FROM A TO Z-Z-Z-Z, Warner Bros. (Looney Tunes). Edward Selzer, producer.
RUGGED BEAR, Disney, RKO Radio. (Donald Duck). Walt Disney, producer.
THE TELL TALE HEART, UPA, Columbia. (Cartoon Special). Stephen Bosustow, producer.
TOOT, WHISTLE, PLUNK AND BOOM. Disney, Buena Vista. (Special Music Series). Walt Disney, producer.

SHORT SUBJECT: ONE-REEL
CHRIST AMONG THE PRIMITIVES, IFE Releasing Corp. (Italian). Vincenzo Lucci-Chiarissi, producer.
HERRING HUNT, National Film Board of Canada, RKO Pathe, Inc. (Canadian). (Canada Carries On Series).
JOY OF LIVING, Art Film Prods., 20th Century-Fox. (Art Film Series). Boris Vermont, producer.
THE MERRY WIVES OF WINDSOR OVERTURE, MGM. (Overture Series). Johnny Green, producer.
WEE WATER WONDERS, Paramount. (Grantland Rice Sportlights Series). Jack Eaton, producer.

SHORT SUBJECT: TWO-REEL
BEAR COUNTRY, Disney, RKO Radio. (True-Life Adventure). Walt Disney, producer.
BEN AND ME, Disney, Buena Vista (Cartoon Special Series). Walt Disney, producer.
RETURN TO GLENNASCAUL, Dublin Gate Theatre Prod., Mayer-Kingsley Inc.
VESUVIUS EXPRESS, 20th Century-Fox. (CinemaScope Shorts Series). Otto Lang, producer.
WINTER PARADISE, Warner Bros. (Technicolor Special). Cedric Francis, producer.

DOCUMENTARY: SHORT SUBJECTS
THE ALASKAN ESKIMO, Disney, RKO Radio. Walt Disney, producer.
THE LIVING CITY, Encyclopaedia Britannica Films, Inc. John Barnes, producer.
OPERATION BLUE JAY, U.S. Army Signal Corps.
THEY PLANTED A STONE, World Wide Pictures, British Information Services (British). James Cari producer.
THE WORD, 20th Century-Fox. John Healy and John Adams, producers.

DOCUMENTARY: FEATURES
THE CONQUEST OF EVEREST, Countryman Films, Group 3 Ltd., UA (British). John Taylor, Leon Clore and Grahame Tharp, producers.
THE LIVING DESERT, Disney, Buena Vista. Walt Disney, producer.
A QUEEN IS CROWNED, J. Arthur Rank, U-I. (British). Castleton Knight, producer.

HONORARY AND OTHER AWARDS
TO PETE SMITH for his witty and pungent observations on the American scene in his series of "Pete Smith Specialties."
TO 20TH CENTURY-FOX FILM CORPORATION in recognition of their imagination, showmanship and foresight in introducing the revolutionary process known as CinemaScope.
TO JOSEPH I. BREEN for his conscientious, open-minded and dignified management of the Motion Picture Production Code.
TO BELL AND HOWELL COMPANY for their pioneering and basic achievements in the advancement of the motion picture industry.

IRVING G. THALBERG MEMORIAL AWARD
TO GEORGE STEVENS

SCIENTIFIC OR TECHNICAL
CLASS I
PROFESSOR HENRI CHRETIEN and EARL SPONABLE, SQL HALPRIN, LORIN GRIGNON, HERBERT GRAGG and CARL FAULKNER of 20th Century-Fox Studios for creating, developing and engineering the equipment, processes and techniques known as CinemaScope.
FRED WALLER for designing and developing the multiple photographic and projection systems which culminated in Cinerama.

CLASS II
REEVES SOUNDCRAFT CORP. for their development of a process of applying stripes of magnetic oxide to motion picture film for sound recording and reproduction.

CLASS III
WESTREX CORP.

1954

"This must be made of gold. It must be!"

—Marlon Brando

T he evening's defining moment came in the post-Oscars pressroom as the horde of hard-boiled photographers shouted at Grace Kelly to kiss the man of the hour, Marlon Brando. Kelly looked up with a fierce smile. "I think he should kiss me," she said. Brando gladly acceded to her wish, and one thing was instantly clear: Kelly may have been young and relatively new to the game, but beneath the delicate blond beauty was galvanized U.S. steel.

Earlier that night, Kelly was embroiled in a contest that had captured the entertainment world's full attention. Her primary rival was one of Hollywood's most beloved, if exasperating, stars, Judy Garland. *A Star Is Born* was a killer comeback for Garland after a five-year public and personal nightmare of breakdowns, bankruptcy, and excess. A Best Actress Oscar would be

her vindication, and the timing couldn't have been more dramatic. The big night found her in the hospital, recuperating after the premature birth of son Joey. A camera crew had been rushed onto a precarious platform outside her window. At the moment of her win, the blinds would be opened and the perfectly made-up and coiffed new mom would express her thanks.

That was the plan, at any rate. But when the announcement was made, it was Kelly in her majestic blue silk gown and floor-length matching cape who seemed to float down the aisle to stake her claim on the Pantages stage. Garland was left with a brave smile, a switched-off mike and an abruptly abandoned hospital room. She would later remark that being a legend was a very lonely business. But for tonight, at least, the two newest legends, Kelly and Brando, were cosseted by entourages and adoring fans who couldn't get enough of their youth, brilliance, and beauty. They would never be more ready for their close-ups.

COUP DE GRACE

CEREMONY: March 30, 1955
RKO Pantages Theatre, Hollywood
Century Theater, New York
HOSTS: Bob Hope, Thelma Ritter

BEST PICTURE/BEST DIRECTOR ELIA KAZAN (B. 1909) *ON THE WATERFRONT*

"A director doesn't make a picture. A whole lot of people do," Kazan said graciously. It's ironic that the film he was accepting the award for, the one great film to emerge from the blacklisting of the McCarthy era, was a study of the morality of informing that had been created by two men, Kazan and writer Budd Schulberg, who had "named names" to the House Un-American Activities Committee. Though the film is anti-union, Kazan and Schulberg successfully manipulate us into admiring Brando's Terry Malloy for testifying against the union before a government commission.

Filmed on location in Frank Sinatra's hometown of Hoboken, New Jersey, *On the Waterfront* was praised by A. H. Weiler of the *New York Times* as a glowing tribute to Kazan's direction: "[Kazan] has forged artistry, anger, and some horrible truths into *On The Waterfront*, a violent and indelible film record of man's inhumanity to man…It is an uncommonly powerful, exciting, and imaginative use of the screen by gifted professionals."

(For more on Kazan, see 1947 and 1999.)

Karl Malden, Marlon Brando, Eva Marie Saint

The envelope, please...

 BEST ACTOR
MARLON BRANDO (B. 1924)
ON THE WATERFRONT

In *On the Waterfront*, "Brando's Malloy is a shatteringly poignant portrait of an amoral, confused, illiterate citizen of the lower depths who is goaded into decency by love, hate and murder," wrote A. H. Weiler in the *New York Times*.

Long regarded as one of America's greatest actors—and one of its most difficult personalities—Brando made his screen debut in *The Men* (1950). In his checkered career, Brando appeared in such Oscar-nominated performances as *A Streetcar Named Desire* (1951), *Viva Zapata!* (1952), and *Last Tango in Paris* (1973). He tried his gifts out on uncharacteristic roles in *Guys and Dolls* (1955) and *The Fugitive Kind* (1959). But his reputation began to suffer with the remake of *Mutiny on the Bounty* (1962) and *A Countess from Hong Kong* (1967).

In his later years, Brando would appear in everything from the sublime to the ridiculous, including *Superman* (1978), *Apocalypse Now* (1979), and *The Freshman* (1990).

Grace Kelly with William Holden

 BEST ACTRESS
GRACE KELLY (1928–1982)
THE COUNTRY GIRL

In 1952, at the age of 23, the cool, sophisticated blond model turned actress landed her second film role in *High Noon* and was catapulted into instant stardom. Throughout her career, Kelly would struggle against her ice-queen veneer.

She performed in the leading films of the 1950s including *Mogambo* (1953, nom.), *The Bridges at Toko-Ri* (1954), and the Hitchcock productions *Dial M for Murder* (1954), *Rear Window* (1954), and *To Catch a Thief* (1955). It was during the filming of the latter on the French Riviera that she met and fell in love with Prince Rainier of Monaco. She made two other films, *High Society* and *The Swan* (both 1956), and left Hollywood to become Princess Grace. She died in an auto accident near her home, shocking fans around the world.

 BEST SUPPORTING ACTOR
EDMOND O'BRIEN (1915–1985)
THE BAREFOOT CONTESSA

"The calendar says March 30, but it can't be right—this must be March 17," said the burly actor, referring to Saint Patrick's Day.

O'Brien's career seemed to run in phases: comedy and drama until he enlisted in the armed services; thrillers from 1946 to 1950; Westerns from 1950 to 1953, and a few leading-character parts, including *The Barefoot Contessa* and *Seven Days in May* (1964, nom.). Among this prolific output were *Parachute Battalion* (1941), *Powder Town* (1942), *The Killers* (1946), and *The Web* (1947). After he put on weight, O'Brien was bypassed for starring roles, but he appeared as one of the most interesting character players in Hollywood in such films as *The Girl Can't Help It* (1956), *Birdman of Alcatraz*, *The Man Who Shot Liberty Valance* (both 1962), *Seven Days in May* (1964, nom.), and *The Wild Bunch* (1969). His last movie was *Dream No Evil* (1970).

 BEST SUPPORTING ACTRESS
EVA MARIE SAINT (B. 1924)
ON THE WATERFRONT

"I might have my baby right here!" cried the joyous and very pregnant actress upon accepting her Academy Award.

In describing the shy, tender, and understanding woman who enables Brando to love, the *New York Times*'s A. H. Weiler wrote, "In casting a newcomer to movies…Mr. Kazan has come up with a pretty and blond artisan who does not have to depend on these attributes. Her parochial school training is no bar to love with the proper stranger…she gives tenderness and sensitivity to genuine romance."

Though Saint was a luminous, gifted actress, she found few vehicles for her talents. After winning an Oscar for her screen debut, she continued to perform effectively in *A Hatful of Rain* (1957), Hitchcock's *North by Northwest* (1959), and Otto Preminger's *Exodus* (1960). Despite her great work, she faded quickly from the movie screen. She reappeared on television in the 1990s *Moonlighting* playing Cybill Shepherd's mother, and she won an Emmy in 1990 for the miniseries *People Like U*.

 HONORARY AWARD
GRETA GARBO (1905–1990)

Born into poverty in Stockholm, Garbo knew from the start that she wanted to be an actress. She played second female lead in G. W. Pabst's *The Joyless Street* (1924) and left for America, where Louis Mayer reluctantly signed her up. Though there were many doubts about her acting ability, the PR people at the studio could see that there was gold in Garbo's reticence, a kind of mystique. Garbo's femme fatale presence attracted moviegoers and made her a superstar with the release of *Flesh and the Devil* (1927). Her performances in *Grand Hotel* (1932), *Queen Christina* (1933), and *Camille* (1937) didn't let fans down.

The headlines screamed, "Garbo Talks!" when the elusive queen appeared to great success in her first talkie, *Anna Christie* (1930). Her husky voice, combined with her delicate appearance, enchanted.

She disappeared from the screen for two years, returning in 1939 to make her first comedy, *Ninotchka*, whose tag line "Garbo Laughs!" was played off the line for *Anna Christie*. Next she appeared in the disaster *Two-Faced Woman* (1941), which made her skittish about taking on new parts. Soon she would disappear from the screen entirely and spend the rest of her life vacationing in Switzerland, on the French Riviera, and in Italy but making home base New York City. Although she was nominated for *Anna Christie*, *Romance* (1930), *Camille*, and *Ninotchka*, Garbo never won an Oscar for acting. Nor did the woman, whose romances were the stuff of legend, ever marry.

 HONORARY AWARD
DANNY KAYE (1913–1987)

The red-haired jester, celebrated for his tongue-twisting songs delivered at whiplash-causing speed, became a comedian when, at the age of 13, he performed stand-up at Borscht Belt Catskill resorts.

Kaye made his debut on Broadway in *Lady in the Dark* (1941), which shot him to Hollywood's Goldwyn studios, where he appeared in such frenetic comedies as *Wonder Man* (1945), *The Secret Life of Walter Mitty* (1947), *Knock on Wood* (1954), and the unforgettable *Court Jester* (1956). In 1940, he married Sylvia Fine, who managed his career and even helped develop his routines. Though Kaye remained married, rumors that he was homosexual persisted throughout his career; he was most famously linked with Sir Lawrence Olivier. Dame Peggy Ashcroft said it first: "Of course I knew Lawrence Olivier and Danny Kaye were having a long-term affair. So did all of London."

One of Kaye's most beloved films was *Hans Christian Andersen* (1952), though he also appeared in an uneven list of pictures that included *The Five Pennies* (1959, with Louis Armstrong), *On the Double* (1961), and *The Man from the Diner's Club* (1963). From 1963 to 1967, Kaye starred in an Emmy-winning TV variety series, *The Danny Kaye Show*. Later, he was cast as a concentration camp survivor in the powerful TV movie, *Skokie* (1981).

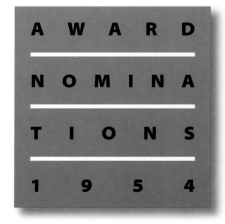

AWARD NOMINATIONS 1954

PICTURE
THE CAINE MUTINY, Kramer, Columbia, Stanley Kramer.
THE COUNTRY GIRL, Perlberg-Seaton, Paramount, William Perlberg.
ON THE WATERFRONT, Horizon-American, Columbia, Sam Spiegel.
SEVEN BRIDES FOR SEVEN BROTHERS, MGM, Jack Cummings.
THREE COINS IN THE FOUNTAIN, 20th Century-Fox, Sol C. Siegel.

ACTOR
HUMPHREY BOGART in *The Caine Mutiny*, Kramer, Columbia.
MARLON BRANDO in *On the Waterfront*, Horizon-American. Columbia.
BING CROSBY in *The Country Girl*, Perlberg-Seaton, Paramount.
JAMES MASON in *A Star Is Born*, Transcona, Warner Bros.
DAN O'HERLIHY in *Adventures of Robinson Crusoe*, Dancigers-Ehrlich, UA.

ACTRESS
DOROTHY DANDRIDGE in *Carmen Jones*, Preminger, 20th Century-Fox.
JUDY GARLAND in *A Star Is Born*, Transcona, Warner Bros.
AUDREY HEPBURN in *Sabrina*, Paramount.
GRACE KELLY in *The Country Girl*, Perlberg-Seaton, Paramount.
JANE WYMAN in *The Magnificent Obsession*, Universal-International.

SUPPORTING ACTOR
LEE J. COBB in *On the Waterfront*, Horizon-American, Columbia.
KARL MALDEN in *On the Waterfront*, Horizon-American, Columbia.
EDMOND O'BRIEN in *The Barefoot Contessa*, Figaro, UA.
ROD STEIGER in *On the Waterfront*, Horizon American, Columbia.
TOM TULLY in *The Caine Mutiny*, Kramer, Columbia.

SUPPORTING ACTRESS
NINA FOCH in *Executive Suite*, MGM.
KATY JURADO in *Broken Lance*, 20th Century-Fox.
EVA MARIE SAINT in *On the Waterfront*, Horizon-American, Columbia.
JAN STERLING in *The High and the Mighty*, Wayne-Fellows, Warner Bros.
CLAIRE TREVOR in *The High and the Mighty*, Wayne-Fellows, Warner Bros.

DIRECTION
ALFRED HITCHCOCK for *Rear Window*, Hitchcock, Paramount.
ELIA KAZAN for *On the Waterfront*, Horizon, Columbia.
GEORGE SEATON for *The Country Girl*, Perlberg-Seaton, Paramount.
WILLIAM WELLMAN for *The High and the Mighty*, Wayne-Fellows, Warner Bros.
BILLY WILDER for *Sabrina*, Paramount.

WRITING: ORIGINAL STORY
BREAD, LOVE AND DREAMS, Titanus, I.F.E. Releasing (Italian). Ettore Margadonna.
BROKEN LANCE, 20th Century-Fox. Philip Yordan.
FORBIDDEN GAMES, Times Film Corp. (French). Francois Boyer.
NIGHT PEOPLE, 20th Century-Fox. Jed Hams and Tom Reed.
THERE'S NO BUSINESS LIKE SHOW BUSINESS, 20th Century-Fox. Lamar Trotti.

WRITING: SCREENPLAY

THE CAINE MUTINY, Kramer, Columbia. Stanley Roberts.

THE COUNTRY GIRL, Perlberg-Seaton, Paramount. George Seaton.

REAR WINDOW, Hitchcock, Paramount. John Michael Hayes.

SABRINA, Paramount. Billy Wilder. Samuel Taylor and Ernest Lehman.

SEVEN BRIDES FOR SEVEN BROTHERS, MGM. Albert Hackett, Frances Goodrich and Dorothy Kingsley.

WRITING: STORY AND SCREENPLAY

THE BAREFOOT CONTESSA, Figaro, UA. Joseph Mankiewicz.

GENEVIEVE, Rank-Sirius, U-I (British). William Rose.

THE GLENN MILLER STORY, U-I. Valentine Davies and Oscar Brodney.

KNOCK ON WOOD, Dens, Paramount. Norman Panama and Melvin Frank.

ON THE WATERFRONT, Horizon, Columbia. Budd Schulberg.

CINEMATOGRAPHY

B/W

THE COUNTRY GIRL, Perlberg-Seaton, Paramount. John F. Warren.

EXECUTIVE SUITE, MGM. George Folsey.

ON THE WATERFRONT, Horizon, Columbia. Boris Kaufman.

ROGUE COP, MGM. John Seitz.

SABRINA, Paramount. Charles Lang, Jr.

Color

THE EGYPTIAN, 20th Century-Fox. Leon Shamroy.

REAR WINDOW, Hitchcock, Paramount. Robert Burks.

SEVEN BRIDES FOR SEVEN BROTHERS, MGM. George Folsey.

THE SILVER CHALICE, Saville, Warner Bros. William V. Skall.

THREE COINS IN THE FOUNTAIN, 20th CenturyFox. Milton Krasner.

ART DIRECTION—SET DECORATION

B/W

THE COUNTRY GIRL, Perlberg-Seaton, Paramount. Hal Pereira and Roland Anderson; Sam Comer and Grace Gregory.

EXECUTIVE SUITE, MGM. Cedric Gibbons and Edward Carfagno; Edwin B. Willis and Emile Kuri.

LE PLAISIR, Meyer-Kingsley (French). Max Ophuls.

ON THE WATERFRONT, Horizon, Columbia. Richard Day.

SABRINA, Paramount. Hal Pereira and Waiter Tyler; Sam Comer and Ray Moyer.

Color

BRIGADOON, MGM. Cedric Gibbons and Preston Ames; Edwin R Willis and Keogh Gleason.

DESIREE, 20th Century-Fox. Lyle Wheeler and Leland Fuller; Walter M. Scott and Paul S. Fox.

RED GARTERS, Paramount. Hal Pereira and Roland Anderson; Sam Comer and Ray Moyer.

A STAR IS BORN, Transcona, Warner Bros. Malcolm Bert, Gene Allen and Irene Sharaff; George James Hopkins.

20,000 LEAGUES UNDER THE SEA, Disney, Buena Vista. John Meehan; Emile Kuri.

COSTUME DESIGN

B/W

THE EARRINGS OF MADAME DE..., Arlan Pictures (French). Georges Annenkov and Rosine Delamare.

EXECUTIVE SUITE, MGM. Helen Rose.

INDISCRETION OF AN AMERICAN WIFE, DeSica, Columbia. Christian Dior.

IT SHOULD HAPPEN TO YOU, Columbia. Jean Louis.

SABRINA, Paramount. Edith Head.

Color

BRIGADOON, MGM. Irene Sharaff.

DESIREE, 20th Century-Fox. Charles LeMaire and Rene Hubert.

GATE OF HELL, Daiei, Edward Harrison (Japanese). Sanzo Wads.

A STAR IS BORN, Transcona, Warner Bros. Jean Louis, Mary Ann Nyberg and Irene Sharaff.

THERE'S NO BUSINESS LIKE SHOW BUSINESS, 20th Century-Fox. Charles LeMaire, Travilla and Miles White.

SOUND RECORDING

BRIGADOON, MGM. Wesley C. Miller, sound director.

THE CAINE MUTINY, Columbia. John P. Livadary, sound director.

THE GLENN MILLER STORY, U-I. Leslie I. Carey, sound director.

REAR WINDOW, Hitchcock, Paramount. Loren L. Ryder, sound director.

SUSAN SLEPT HERE, RKO Radio. John O. Aalberg, sound director.

FILM EDITING

THE CAINE MUTINY, Kramer, Columbia. William A. Lyon and Henry Batista.

THE HIGH AND THE MIGHTY, Wayne-Fellows, Warner Bros. Ralph Dawson.

ON THE WATERFRONT, Horizon, Columbia. Gene Milford.

SEVEN BRIDES FOR SEVEN BROTHERS, MGM. Ralph E. Winters.

20,000 LEAGUES UNDER THE SEA, Disney, Buena Vista. Elmo Williams.

SPECIAL EFFECTS

HELL AND HIGH WATER, 20th Century-Fox. THEM! Warner Bros.

20,000 LEAGUES UNDER THE SEA, Walt Disney Studios.

SONG

COUNT YOUR BLESSINGS INSTEAD OF SHEEP (*White Christmas, Paramount);* Music and Lyrics by Irving Berlin.

THE HIGH AND THE MIGHTY (*The High and the Mighty,* Wayne-Fellows, Warner Bros.); Music by Dimitri Tiomkin. Lyrics by Ned Washington.

HOLD MY HAND (*Susan Slept Here,* RKO Radio); Music and Lyrics by Jack Lawrence and Richard Myers.

THE MAN THAT GOT AWAY (*A Star Is Born,* Transcona, Warner Bros.); Music by Harold Arlen. Lyrics by Ira Gershwin.

THREE COINS IN THE FOUNTAIN (*Three Coins in the Fountain,* 20th Century-Fox); Music by Jule Styne. Lyrics by Sammy Cahn.

SCORING: DRAMA/COMEDY

THE CAINE MUTINY, Kramer, Columbia. Max Steiner.

GENEVIEVE, Rank-Sirius, U-I (British). Larry Adler. (NOTE: Because of the political climate of the times, *GENEVIEVE'*s arranger and orchestra conductor Muir Mathieson was credited as composer on American prints of this British-made film, and was thus credited with the nomination. Academy records have been updated to give Mr. Adler his proper credit, which Mr. Mathieson had never claimed.)

THE HIGH AND THE MIGHTY Wayne-Fellows, Warner Bros. Dimitri Tiomkin.

ON THE WATERFRONT, Horizon, Columbia. Leonard Bernstein.

THE SILVER CHALICE, Saville, Warner Bros. Franz Waxman.

SCORING: MUSICAL

CARMEN JONES, Preminger, 20th Century-Fox. Herschel Burke Gilbert.

THE GLENN MILLER STORY, U-I. Joseph Gershenson and Henry Mancini.

SEVEN BRIDES FOR SEVEN BROTHERS, MGM. Adolph Deutsch and Saul Chaplin.

A STAR IS BORN, Transcona, Warner Bros. Ray Heindorf.

THERE'S NO BUSINESS LIKE SHOW BUSINESS, 20th Century-Fox. Alfred Newman and Lionel Newman.

SHORT SUBJECTS: CARTOONS

CRAZY MIXED UP PUP, Lantz, U-I. Walter Lantz, producer.

PIGS IS PIGS, Disney, RKO Radio. Walt Disney, producer.

SANDY CLAWS, Warner Bros. Edward Selzer, producer.

TOUCHE, PUSSY CAT, MGM. Fred Quimby, producer.

WHEN MAGOO FLEW, UPA, Columbia. Stephen Hosustow, producer.

SHORT SUBJECT: ONE-REEL

THE FIRST PIANO QUARTETTE, 20th Century-Fox. Otto Lang, producer.

THE STRAUSS FANTASY, MGM. Johnny Green, producer.

THIS MECHANICAL AGE, Warner Bros. Robert Youngson, producer.

SHORT SUBJECT: TWO-REEL

BEAUTY AND THE BULL, Warner Bros. Cedric Francis, producer.

JET CARRIER, 20th Century-Fox. Otto Lang, producer.

SIAM, Disney, Buena Vista. Walt Disney, producer.

A TIME OUT OF WAR, Carnival Prods., Denis and Terry Sanders, producers.

DOCUMENTARY: SHORT SUBJECTS

JET CARRIER, 20th Century-Fox. Otto Lang producer.

REMBRANDT: A SELF-PORTRAIT, Distributors Corp. of America. Morrie Roizman, producer.

THURSDAY'S CHILDREN, British Information Services (British). World Wide Pictures and Morse Films, producers.

DOCUMENTARY: FEATURES

THE STRATFORD ADVENTURE, National Film Board of Canada, Continental (Canadian). Guy Glover, producer.

THE VANISHING PRAIRIE, Disney, Buena Vista. Walt Disney, producer.

HONORARY AND OTHER AWARDS

TO BAUSCH & LOMB OPTICAL COMPANY for their contributions to the advancement of the motion picture industry.

TO KEMP R. NIVER for the development of the Renovare Process which has made possible the restoration of the Library of Congress Paper Film Collection.

TO GRETA GARBO for her unforgettable screen performances.

TO DANNY KAYE for his unique talents, his service to the Academy, the motion picture industry, and the American people.

TO JON WHITELEY for his outstanding juvenile performance in *The Little Kidnappers.*

TO VINCENT WINTER for his outstanding performance in *The Little Kidnappers.*

TO GATE OF HELL (Japanese)—Best Foreign Language Film first released in the United States during 1954.

SCIENTIFIC OR TECHNICAL

CLASS I

PARAMOUNT PICTURES, INC., LOREN L. RYDER, JOHN R. BISHOP and all the members of the technical and engineering staff for developing a method of producing and exhibiting motion pictures known as VistaVision.

CLASS II

None.

CLASS III

DAVID S. HORSLEY and the UNIVERSAL-INTERNATIONAL STUDIO SPECIAL PHOTOGRAPHIC DEPARTMENT; KARL FREUND and FRANK CRANDELL of Photo Research Corp.;

WESLEY C. MILLER, J.W. STAFFORD, K.M. FRIERSON and the METRO-GOLDWYN-MAYER STUDIO SOUND DEPARTMENT;

JOHN P. LIVADARY, LLOYD RUSSELL and the COLUMBIA STUDIO SOUND DEPARTMENT;

ROLAND MILLER and MAX GOEPPINGER of Magnascope Corp.;

CARLOS RIVAS, G.M. SPRAGUE and the METROGOLDWYN-MAYER STUDIO SOUND DEPARTMENT;

FRED WILSON of the Samuel Goldwyn Studio Sound Department;

P.C. YOUNG of the MGM. Studio Projection Department;

FRED KNOTH and ORIEN ERNEST of the Universal International Studio Technical Department.

1955

R umored to have been made as part of a tax write-off scheme, *Marty* backfired beautifully for its producer, Burt Lancaster, and its "overnight star," Ernest Borgnine. There would be bad blood between the two down the road, thanks to a Machiavellian contract, but the night's brief glory belonged to them.

As for the glamour, Grace Kelly had it wrapped up. Her appearance as Best Actress presenter would mark her last few hours in Hollywood before jetting off for her final role as Princess Grace of Monaco. Hovering above them all was the ghost of James Dean, whose banner-headline fatal car crash just six months earlier had transformed him into an instant icon. With only three films to his credit (*East of Eden*, *Rebel Without a Cause*, and *Giant*), he'd reached the mythic status of Rudolph Valentino, whose own youthful exit had resulted in the suicides of several

adoring fans. Dean's *Rebel* co-stars, Natalie Wood and Sal Mineo, had done well by him, both earning nominations. Wood arrived on the arm of the year's second most popular teen idol, Tab Hunter, who admitted he'd done her hair.

The twenty-eighth Oscars provided the unofficial launch of Jerry Lewis's solo career. His energetic antics and one-liners made the New York half of the broadcast look like a funeral director's convention. Claudette Colbert graciously served as Lewis's straight (wo)man for much of the show. A veteran scene-stealer herself, she knew better than to compete with the new king of comedy.

Once again, Oldsmobile sponsored the broadcast. The commercials were so long that Lewis quipped, "And now a word from the Academy Awards." As the show finally culminated with *Marty*'s Best Picture win, the highly charged Lancaster nearly catapulted from his seat. Back in New York, Colbert bid good night to TV viewers and blew a congratulatory kiss westward. "Jerry, you're the cutest!" she said.

DEATH AND TAXES

CEREMONY: March 21, 1956
HOSTS: Jerry Lewis
RKO Pantages Theatre, Hollywood,
Century Theater, New York
Hosts: Claudette Colbert and Joseph
Mankiewicz, New York

BEST PICTURE/BEST DIRECTOR
DELBERT MANN (B. 1920)
MARTY

"Thank you! Thank you very much," said the winner, who was in New York at the time of the announcement and was clearly at a loss for words at his unexpected victory. Back in Los Angeles, producer Harold Hecht picked up the awards, using the opportunity to salute America and the film industry (two of Hollywood's favorite pastimes): "We are very fortunate to live in a country where any man, no matter how humble his origin, can become president—and in an industry where any picture, no matter how low the budget, can win an Oscar."

The surprise hit won the hearts of audiences, and the critics appreciated the film for what it was. "This neat little character study of a lonely fellow and a lonely girl who find each other in the prowling mob at a Bronx dance hall and get together despite their families and their friends…[is] a warm and winning film," wrote Bosley Crowther in the *New York Times*.

Ernest Borgnine, Betsy Blair

Delbert Mann won his spurs making TV films, originally directing the Paddy Chayefsky script of *Marty* for home viewers. He continued his transition to the silver screen with two more Chayefsky-penned films, *The Bachelor Party* (1957) and *Middle of the Night* (1959), as well as adaptations of *Desire Under the Elms*, *Separate Tables* (both 1958), and *The Dark at the Top of the Stairs* (1960).

Moving to less weighty material, Mann directed Doris Day in *Lover Come Back* (1961) and *That Touch of Mink* (1962), as well as the romance *Dear Heart* (1964) and the action film *The Pink Jungle* (1968). Returning to more serious fare in 1970, he shot some strong television movies, including *Jane Eyre* (1971), *A Girl Named Sooner* (1975), *All Quiet on the Western Front* (1979), and a live version of *The Member of the Wedding* (1982).

The envelope, please...

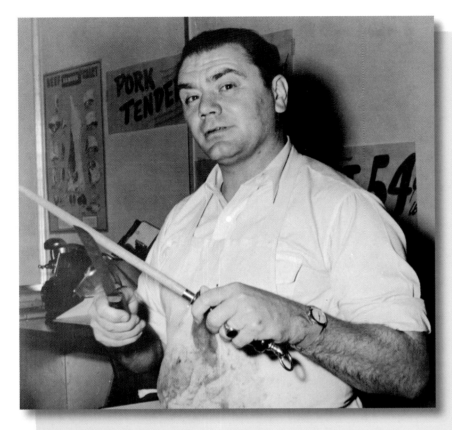

BEST ACTOR
ERNEST BORGNINE (B. 1917)
MARTY

"At the risk of sounding repetitious, I just want to thank my mother for giving me the idea of going in and doing this...my pop for being steadfast, and my lovely wife for helping me."

In *Marty*, Ernest Borgnine as the lonely man "gives a performance that burns into the mind. It is amazing to see such a performance from the actor who played the stockade sadist in *From Here to Eternity*," wrote Bosley Crowther. Borgnine's working life began with a few odd jobs after returning from the navy in 1945, but his mother, recognizing that he had a forceful personality, encouraged him to try acting. In 1949 he debuted on Broadway in *Harvey*, and quickly made the transition to film. His 1951 debut in *The Whistle at Eaton Falls* proved a great success, winning him the role of Sergeant "Fatso" in *From Here to Eternity* (1953). With that, Borgnine began a fifty-one-year career with performances in more than 100 feature films, including *Johnny Guitar* (1954), *Bad Day at Black Rock* (1955), *The Dirty Dozen* (1967), and *The Wild Bunch* (1969).

BEST ACTRESS
ANNA MAGNANI (1908–1973)
THE ROSE TATTOO

Magnani was asleep in Italy when she got the phone call announcing that she had won the Oscar for her first American production. The hot-tempered actress responded, "If you are kidding, I will get up right away and kill you—wherever you are!"

Magnani was the stuff of legend. Critic Andrew Sarris of the *Village Voice* wrote, "[Magnani] can tear a dramatic scene to tatters and in the next instant turn on a brilliant comedy style." Much like the roles she played, Magnani was born illegitimate and poor, raised by her maternal grandmother and educated in a convent. She studied drama and made her film debut in *Scampolo* (1927), followed by her triumphant critical success in Roberto Rossellini's classic *Roma Città Aperta/Open City* (1945). She became an instant international star, winning the Best Actress Award at the Venice Film Festival for her role in *L'Onorevole Angelina* (1947), and went on to star in *L'Amore* (1948), the controversial *Il Miracolo/The Miracle*, and in Renoir's *The Golden Coach* (1952).

BEST OF 1955
Best Picture: *Marty*
Best Director: Delbert Mann, *Marty*
Best Actor: Ernest Borgnine, *Marty*
Best Actress: Anna Magnani, *The Rose Tattoo*
Best Supporting Actor: Jack Lemmon, *Mister Roberts*
Best Supporting Actress: Jo Van Fleet, *East of Eden*

FIRSTS
• *Marty* was the first TV-to-motion-picture transfer to win Best Picture.
• *Marty* was the first American film to win the Palme d'Or at the Cannes Film Festival.
• *Marty* was the first American film to be shown in the Soviet Union.
• James Dean was the first actor to be nominated posthumously.

ROLE REVERSALS
The original *Marty* television leads were Rod Steiger and Nancy Marchand.

SINS OF OMISSION
Actress: Doris Day, *Love Me or Leave Me*
Director: Nicholas Ray, *Rebel Without a Cause*

UNMENTIONABLES
• "Being an actress is such a humiliating business, and as you get older it gets more humiliating because you have less to sell," said Katharine Hepburn.
• The Catholic Church was dogged in its condemnation of one of the year's biggest hits, *Lady and the Tramp*, for its portrayal of an unwed couple.
• "I don't mean to speak ill of the dead...He was selfish, petulant and believed his own press releases." —Rock Hudson
• Just months before his fatal car crash, James Dean took part in a "Safe Driving" ad campaign.
• Dean ignited the speculation about his sexual preference with the remark "I don't intend to go through life with one arm tied behind my back."
• Ethel Merman was married to Ernest Borgnine for thirty-eight days.
• The location shoot for *The Conqueror* was in the radioactive vicinity of a Nevada nuclear testing site. It may have contributed to the deaths of stars John Wayne and Susan Hayward and director Dick Powell, all of whom died of cancer.
• The four young stars of *Rebel Without a Cause* all met with tragic ends: James Dean at 24 (car crash); Natalie Wood at 43 (drowning); Nick Adams at 37 (accidental overdose); Sal Mineo at 37 (murder).

BEST SUPPORTING ACTOR
JACK LEMMON (1925–2001)
MISTER ROBERTS

The list of Lemmon's great Oscar-nominated performances represents only a fraction of his enormous output. With *Mister Roberts*, he won the supporting gold for one of his trademark performances as Ensign Pulver, the eager ne'er-do-well, but he wouldn't win the ultimate gold for quite some time, despite his amazing, nominated performances in *Some Like It Hot* (1959), *The Apartment* (1960), and *Days of Wine and Roses* (1962).

In a brilliant career that would span forty years, the Harvard-educated Lemmon showed his talent early on and continued playing the hapless victim of fate in such films as *The Fortune Cookie* (1966), *The Odd Couple* (1968), *The Front Page* (1974), and *Grumpy Old Men* (1993).

He picked up his second Oscar for *Save the Tiger* (1973) and was nominated for *The China Syndrome* (1979). He also appeared in *Tribute* (1980), *Missing* (1982), and received some of the best reviews of his career for a powerful performance in *Glengarry Glen Ross* (1992). Lemmon directed his friend Walter Matthau in *Kotch* (1971), his only take behind the camera. A lifelong pianist, he was most delighted to contribute a song to his 1957 movie *Fire Down Below*. (For more on Lemmon, see 1974)

BEST SUPPORTING ACTRESS
JO VAN FLEET (1914–1996)
EAST OF EDEN

"I could never go through this again," sighed Van Fleet backstage. Van Fleet was known for her Broadway productions and surprised moviegoers in her film debut playing James Dean's madam-mother.

Her later work was lackluster, but she always performed well when cast as abrasive, coarse women such as the drunken mistress of Kirk Douglas's Doc Holliday in *Gunfight at the O.K. Corral* (1957). Among her other films were *I'll Cry Tomorrow* (1955), *Cool Hand Luke* (1967), *I Love You, Alice B. Toklas* (1968), *The Gang That Couldn't Shoot Straight* (1971), and *The Tenant* (1976).

PICTURE

LOVE IS A MANY-SPLENDORED THING, 20th Century-Fox, Buddy Adler.
MARTY, Hecht-Lancaster, UA, Harold Hecht.
MISTER ROBERTS, Orange, Warner Bros, Leland Hayward.
PICNIC, Columbia, Fred Kohlmar.
THE ROSE TATTOO, Wallis, Paramount, Hal Wallis.

ACTOR

ERNEST BORGNINE in *Marty*, Hecht-Lancaster, UA.
JAMES CAGNEY in *Love Me or Leave Me*, MGM.
JAMES DEAN in *East of Eden*, Warner Bros.
FRANK SINATRA in *The Man with the Golden Arm*, Preminger, UA.
SPENCER TRACY in *Bad Day at Black Rock*, MGM.

ACTRESS

SUSAN HAYWARD in *I'll Cry Tomorrow*, MGM.
KATHARINE HEPBURN in *Summertime*, Lopert Lean, UA (Anglo-American).
JENNIFER JONES in *Love Is a Many-Splendored Thing*, 20th Century-Fox.
ANNA MAGNANI in *The Rose Tattoo*, Wallis, Paramount.
ELEANOR PARKER in *Interrupted Melody*, MGM.

SUPPORTING ACTOR

ARTHUR KENNEDY in *Trial*, MGM.
JACK LEMMON in *Mister Roberts*, Orange, Warner Bros.
JOE MANTELL in *Marty*, Hecht-Lancaster, UA.
SAL MINEO in *Rebel Without a Cause*, Warner Bros.
ARTHUR O'CONNELL in *Picnic*, Columbia.

SUPPORTING ACTRESS

BETSY BLAIR in *Marty*, Hecht-Lancaster, UA.
PEGGY LEE in *Pete Kelly's Blues*, Mark VII, Warner Bros.
MARISA PAVAN in *The Rose Tattoo*, Wallis, Paramount.
JO VAN FLEET in *East of Eden*, Warner Bros.
NATALIE WOOD in *Rebel Without a Cause*, Warner Bros.

DIRECTION

ELIA KAZAN for *East of Eden*, Warner Bros.
DAVID LEAN for *Summertime*, Lopert, UA (Anglo-American).
JOSHUA LOGAN for *Picnic*, Columbia.
DELBERT MANN for *Marty*, Hecht-Lancaster, UA.
JOHN STURGES for *Bad Day at Black Rock*, MGM.

WRITING: ORIGINAL STORY

LOVE ME OR LEAVE ME, MGM. Daniel Fuchs.
THE PRIVATE WAR OF MAJOR BENSON, U.-I. Joe Connelly and Bob Mosher.
REBEL WITHOUT A CAUSE, Warner Bros. Nicholas Ray.
THE SHEEP HAS 5 LEGS, U.M.P.O. (French). Jean Marsan, Henry Troyat, Jacques Perret, Henri Verneuil and Raoul Ploquin.
STRATEGIC AIR COMMAND, Paramount. Beirne Lay, Jr.

WRITING: SCREENPLAY

BAD DAY AT BLACK ROCK, MGM. Millard Kaufman.

BLACKBOARD JUNGLE, MGM. Richard Brooks.
EAST OF EDEN, Warner Bros. Paul Osborn.
LOVE ME OR LEAVE ME, MGM. Daniel Fuchs and Isobel Lennart.
MARTY, Hecht-Lancaster, UA. Paddy Chayefsky.

WRITING: STORY AND SCREENPLAY

THE COURT-MARTIAL OF BILLY MITCHELL, United States Pictures, Warner Bros. Milton Sperling and Emmet Lavery.
INTERRUPTED MELODY; MGM. William Ludwig and Sonya Levien.
IT'S ALWAYS FAIR WEATHER, MGM. Betty Comden and Adolph Green.
MR. HULOT'S HOLIDAY, GBD International Releasing (French). Jacques Tati and Henri Marquet.
THE SEVEN LITTLE FOYS, Paramount. Melville Shavelson and Jack Rose.

CINEMATOGRAPHY

B/W

BLACKBOARD JUNGLE, MGM. Russell Harlan.
I'LL CRY TOMORROW, MGM. Arthur E. Arling.
MARTY, Hecht-Lancaster, UA. Joseph LaShelle.
QUEEN BEE, Columbia. Charles Lang.
THE ROSE TATTOO, Wallis, Paramount. James Wong Howe.

Color

GUYS AND DOLLS, Goldwyn, MGM. Harry Stradling.
LOVE IS A MANY-SPLENDORED THING, 20th Century-Fox. Leon Shamroy.
A MAN CALLED PETER, 20th Century-Fox. Harold Lipstein.
OKLAHOMA!, Hornblow, Magna Corp. Robert Surtees.
TO CATCH A THIEF, Hitchcock, Paramount. Robert Burks.

ART DIRECTION—SET DECORATION

B/W

BLACKBOARD JUNGLE, MGM. Cedric Gibbons and Randall Duell; Edwin B. Willis and Henry Grace.
I'LL CRY TOMORROW, H-G-M. Cedric Gibbons and Malcolm Brown; Edwin B. Willis and Hugh B. Hunt.
THE MAN WITH THE GOLDEN ARM, Preminger, UA. Joseph C. Wright; Darrell Silvera.
MARTY, Hecht-Lancaster, UA. Edward S. Haworth and Walter Simonds; Robert Priestley.
THE ROSE TATTOO, Wallis, Paramount. Hal Pereira and Tambi Larsen; Sam Comer and Arthur Krams.

Color

DADDY LONG LEGS, 20th Century-Fox. Lyle Wheeler and John DeCuir; Walter N. Scott and Paul S. Fox.
GUYS AND DOLLS, Goldwyn, MGM. Oliver Smith and Joseph C. Wright; Howard Bristol.
LOVE IS A MANY-SPLENDORED THING, 20th Century-Fox. Lyle Wheeler and George W. Davis; Walter M. Scott and Jack Stubbs.
PICNIC, Columbia. William Flannery and Jo Mielziner; Robert Priestley.
TO CATCH A THIEF, Hitchcock, Paramount. Hal Pereira and Joseph McMillan Johnson; Sam Comer and Arthur Krams.

COSTUME DESIGN

B/W

I'LL CRY TOMORROW, MGM. Helen Rose.
THE PICKWICK PAPERS, Renown, Kingsley International (British). Beatrice Dawson.
QUEEN BEE, Columbia. Jean Louis.
THE ROSE TATTOO, Wallis, Paramount. Edith Head.
UGETSU, Daiei, Edward Harrison Releasing (Japanese). Tadaoto Kainoscho.

Color

GUYS AND DOLLS, Goldwyn, MGM. Irene Sharaff.
INTERRUPTED MELODY, MGM. Helen Rose.
LOVE IS A MANY-SPLENDORED THING, 20th Century-Fox. Charles LeMaire.
TO CATCH A THIEF, Hitchcock, Paramount. Edith Head.
THE VIRGIN QUEEN, 20th Century-Fox. Charles LeMaire and Mary Wills.

SOUND RECORDING

LOVE IS A MANY-SPLENDORED THING, 20th Century-Fox. Carl W. Faulkner, sound director.
LOVE ME OR LEAVE ME, MGM. Wesley C. Miller, sound director.
MISTER ROBERTS, Warner Bros. William A. Mueller, sound director.
NOT AS A STRANGER, Kramer, UA. RCA Sound Department; Watson Jones, sound director.
OKLAHOMA!, Hornblow, Magna. Todd-AO Sound Department; Fred Hynes, sound director.

FILM EDITING

BLACKBOARD JUNGLE, MGM. Ferris Webster.
THE BRIDGES AT TOKO-RI, Perlberg-Seaton, Paramount. Alma Macrorie.
OKLAHOMA!, Hornblow, Magna Corp. Gene Ruggiero and George Boemler.
PICNIC, Columbia. Charles Nelson and William A. Lyon.
THE ROSE TATTOO, Wallis, Paramount. Warren Low.

SPECIAL EFFECTS

THE BRIDGES AT TOKO-RI, Paramount.
THE DAM BUSTERS, Associated British, Warner Bros. (British).
THE RAINS OF RANCHIPUR, 20th Century-Fox.

SONG

I'LL NEVER STOP LOVING YOU (*Love Me or Leave Me*, MGM.); Music by Nicholas Brodszky. Lyrics by Sammy Cahn.
LOVE IS A MANY-SPLENDORED THING (*Love is a Many-Splendored Thing*, 20th Century-Fox); Music by Sammy Fain, Lyrics by Paul Francis Webster.
SOMETHING'S GOTTA GIVE (*Daddy Long Legs*, 20th Century-Fox); Music and Lyrics by Johnny Mercer.
(LOVE IS) THE TENDER TRAP (*The Tender Trap*, MGM.); Music by James Van Heusen. Lyrics by Sammy Cahn.
UNCHAINED MELODY (*Unchained*, Bartlett, Warner Bros.); Music by Alex North. Lyrics by Hy Zaret.

SCORING: DRAMA/COMEDY

BATTLE CRY, Warner Bros. Max Steiner.
LOVE IS A MANY-SPLENDORED THING, 20th Century-Fox. Alfred Newman.
THE MAN WITH THE GOLDEN ARM, Preminger, UA. Elmer Bernstein.
PICNIC, Columbia. George Duning.
THE ROSE TATTOO, Wallis Paramount. Alex North.

SCORING: MUSICAL

DADDY LONG LEGS, 20th Century-Fox. Alfred Newman.
GUYS AND DOLLS, Goldwyn, MGM. Jay Blackton and Cyril J. Mockridge.
IT'S ALWAYS FAIR WEATHER, MGM. Andre Previn.
LOVE ME OR LEAVE ME, MGM. Percy Faith and George Stoll.
OKLAHOMA!, Hornblow, Magna Corp. Robert Russell Bennett, Jay Blackton and Adolph Deutsch.

SHORT SUBJECTS: CARTOONS

GOOD WILL TO MEN, MGM. Fred Quimby, William Hanna and Joseph Barbera, producers.
THE LEGEND OF A ROCK-A-BYE POINT, Lantz, U-I. Walter Lantz, producer.
NO HUNTING, Disney, RKO Radio. Walt Disney, producer.
SPEEDY GONZALES, Warner Bros. Edward Selzer, producer.

SHORT SUBJECT: ONE-REEL

GADGETS GALORE, Warner Bros. Robert Youngson, producer.
SURVIVAL CITY, 20th Century-Fox. Edmund Reek, producer.
3RD AVE. EL, Davidson Prods., Ardee Films. Carson Davidson, producer.
THREE KISSES, Paramount. Justin Herman, producer.

SHORT SUBJECT: TWO-REEL

THE BATTLE OF GETTYSBURG, MGM. Dore Schary, producer.
THE FACE OF LINCOLN, University of Southern California, Cavalcade Pictures.

Wilbur T. Blume, producer.
ON THE TWELFTH DAY..., Go Pictures, George Brest & Assocs. George K. Arthur, producer.
SWITZERLAND, Disney, Buena Vista. Walt Disney, producer.
24 HOUR ALERT, Warner Bros. Cedric Francis, producer.

DOCUMENTARY: SHORT SUBJECTS

THE BATTLE OF GETTYSBURG, MGM. Dore Schary, producer.
THE FACE OF LINCOLN, University of Southern California, Cavalcade Pictures. Wilbur T. Blume, producer.
MEN AGAINST THE ARCTIC, Disney, Buena Vista. Walt Disney, producer.

DOCUMENTARY: FEATURES

HEARTBREAK RIDGE, Rene Risacher Prod., Tudor Pictures (French). Rene Risacher, producer.
HELEN KELLER IN HER STORY, Nancy Hamilton Presentation. Nancy Hamilton, producer.

HONORARY AND OTHER AWARDS

TO SAMURAI, *The Legend of Musashi*, (Japanese)—Best Foreign Language Film first released in the United States during 1955.

SCIENTIFIC OR TECHNICAL

CLASS I

NATIONAL CARBON CO. for the development and production of a high efficiency yellow flame carbon for motion picture color photography.

CLASS II

EASTMAN KODAK CO. for Eastman Tri-X panchromatic negative film.
FARCIOT EDOUARD, HAL CORL and the PARAMOUNT STUDIO TRANSPARENCY DEPT. for the engineering and development of a double-frame, triple-head background projector.

CLASS III

20TH CENTURY-FOX STUDIO and BAUSCH & LOMB CO.;
WALTER JOLLEY, MAURICE LARSON and R.H. SPIES of 20th Century-Fox Studio;
STEVE KRILANOVICH;
DAVE ANDERSON of 20th Century-Fox Studio;
LOREN L. RYDER, CHARLES WEST, HENRY FRACKER and PARAMOUNT STUDIO;
FARCIOT EDOUART, HAL CORL and the PARAMOUNT STUDIO TRANSPARENCY DEPARTMENT.

1956

J f the movies had suddenly grown huge thanks to CinemaScope and the trend toward spectacle to compete with tiny-screened TV, Hollywood players had also exploded into out-sized personalities. Cecil B. DeMille chose Charlton Heston for Moses because he looked precisely like Michelangelo's overwhelming sculpture.

Flash-and-cash showman Mike Todd pitched his first production, *Around the World in 80 Days*, like a latter-day Barnum, somehow managing to get legendary stars such as Marlene Dietrich to appear as "dress extras." And along the way the fast-dealing 50-year-old managed to snag the ultimate trophy wife, 25-year-old Elizabeth Taylor. She arrived at the Awards nearly stooped under the weight of all the diamonds he'd decorated her with.

Yul Brynner burst onto the scene with his glistening shaved dome and the stallion strut of a pagan king. But they all paled in the blinding halo of the reincarnated Ingrid Bergman. She'd been vindicated by the press after seven years of penance for her adulterous, very public affair with Italian filmmaker Roberto Ros-

sellini. Ed Sullivan had even asked the viewers of his popular Sunday-night show to write in their vote as to whether she should be forgiven. Two to one, they agreed she'd suffered enough.

Levity was required to counteract the hyper-grandiosity, and Jerry Lewis made hay as he buzzed around the stage puncturing the ballooning egos. But this year he had riotous competition from another larger-than-life personality, Hermione Gingold, who stood in for Best Adapted Screenplay winner S. J. Perelman. "I'm very proud to accept this objet d'art on behalf of Mr. Perelman who writes; he cannot be here for a variety of reasons, all of them spicy. He's dumbfounded, absolutely flummoxed. He never expected recognition for writing *Around the World in 80 Days* and in fact did so on the expressed understanding that the film would never be shown. He hopes he will be able to live up to it, or, rather, to live it up. And he says, 'Bless you all.'"

Sitting in the glittering Pantages audience was the man who'd started it all, despotic former MGM chief and founder of the Academy Awards, Louis B. Mayer. Shrunken, frail, his power dwindled almost to nothing, he'd been forced to scrounge for tickets to the event.

THE BIG PICTURE

CEREMONY: March 27, 1957
HOSTS: Jerry Lewis, RKO Pantages Theatre, Hollywood; Celeste Holm, NBC Century Theater, New York

BEST PICTURE
AROUND THE WORLD IN 80 DAYS

Producer Mike Todd blasted out of his seat, raced to the stage, turned back to hug Elizabeth Taylor, and raced once again to the podium. "I'd like to thank you on behalf of the sixty-odd thousand people who worked on this show," said the irrepressibly happy Todd. "I am especially thrilled. This is my first time at bat."

Clocking in at three hours, Todd's extravaganza had become the talk of the town thanks to his heavy-handed promotion campaign, which even boasted a prologue narrated by esteemed journalist Edward R. Murrow. His overzealousness attracted trouble, though, and soon he was in arbitration meetings with the Writers Guild for giving sole writing credit—when many pens went into the script—to popular humorist S.J. Perelman.

Topping the "over the top" production, Todd released the film as a "theatrical" event, complete with high prices and reserved seating. Sadly, this would prove Todd's last crack at the Golden Boy. He died in a plane crash one year before he was posthumously awarded an Oscar for his new wide-screen cinematography process, Todd-AO.

Cantinflas, David Niven

The envelope, please...

Henry Ginsberg, George Stevens, Elizabeth Taylor, Rock Hudson

BEST DIRECTOR
GEORGE STEVENS (1904–1975)
GIANT

"The director's chair is a wonderful place to see the film," Stevens said after stumbling up the stairs and onto the stage. *New York Times* film critic Bosley Crowther wrote, "Mr. Stevens and his able screenplay writers have contrived a tremendously vivid picture—drama that gushes a tawdry tragedy [with] staggering scenes of the great Texas plains and of passion-charged human relations that hold the hardness of the land and atmosphere. [Stevens] tells us the reason that Texas is as it is today. Thanks to Mr. Stevens' brilliant structure and handling of images, every scene and every moment is a pleasure. He makes 'picture' the essence of his film." The *New Yorker*'s Pauline Kael found the film "handsomely designed, big, glossy." She added, "Stevens' craftsmanship is effective at an unsubtle level, and the movie is often enter-taining." (For more on George Stevens, see 1951.)

BEST ACTOR
YUL BRYNNER (1915–1985)
THE KING AND I

"I hope this isn't a mistake," said the blushing Brynner, "because I won't give it back for anything in the world." Critic Bosley Crowther agreed that it was his alone to keep. "His perfor-mance of the volatile King of Siam...is such that there comes from [it] all sorts of dazzling little glints of a complex personality battling bravely and mightily for air. The king is the heart of this story, and Mr. Brynner makes him vigorous and big," Crowther wrote.

The commanding, kingly Brynner actu-ally came from humble gypsy origins. After a brief fling with the circus, study at the Sorbonne, acting on the Broadway stage, and directing early television, Brynner got his Hollywood wings with *The King and I* and took off. Following *King*, Brynner performed royally in such films as *Anastasia* (1956), *The Ten Commandments* (1956), *The Magnificent Seven* (1960), and *Westworld* (1973).

Brynner died of lung cancer, but not before taping a series of commercials warning of the dangers of smoking. The ads were aired—hauntingly—after his death.

BEST OF 1956
Best Picture: *Around the World in 80 Days*
Best Director: George Stevens, *Giant*
Best Actor: Yul Brynner, *The King and I*
Best Actress: Ingrid Bergman, *Anastasia*
Best Supporting Actor: Anthony Quinn, *Lust for Life*
Best Supporting Actress: Dorothy Malone, *Written on the Wind*

FIRSTS
• Every Best Picture nominee was in color.

• Screenwriters Edward Bernds and Elwood Ullman withdrew their names from the final ballot. The nominating committee had mistaken them as the authors of the big hit *High Society*. Their film of the same name was a less-than-classic Bowery Boys sequel.

• Best Original Screenplay went to *The Red Balloon*, which didn't have a single line of dialogue.

• James Dean was the only actor to be nominated posthumously twice.

SINS OF OMISSION
Pictures: *The Searchers, Invasion of the Body Snatchers, The Wrong Man*
Director: Alfred Hitchcock, *The Wrong Man, The Man Who Knew Too Much*
Actor: John Wayne, *The Searchers*
Actress: Marilyn Monroe, *Bus Stop*

ALWAYS A BRIDESMAID, NEVER A BRIDE
• Mickey Rooney muttered to fellow nominee Don Murray, "We wuz robbed!" as Anthony Quinn was announced as Best Supporting Actor.

• Cecil B. DeMille was the only director of a Best Picture nominee not to make the list.

• *Lust for Life* was Kirk Douglas's third unsuccessful Oscar bid.

• *Around the World in 80 Days* didn't receive a single acting nomination.

UNMENTIONABLES
• Honorary Awardee Eddie Cantor almost didn't make it to the podium after passing out in the lobby. He was revived with whiskey.

• Blacklisted screenwriter Dalton Trumbo won his second Oscar (*The Brave One*) under the alias Robert Rich.

• Blacklisted screenwriter for *Friendly Persuasion*, Michael Wilson, was refused a spot on the ballot.

• Deborah Kerr's singing in *The King and I* was dubbed by the ubiquitous Marni Nixon.

• An irate Charlton Heston demanded the Academy ban big stars from Best Supporting nominations, claiming, "That's not the purpose of that category." He was ignored.

BEST ACTRESS
INGRID BERGMAN (1915–1982)
ANASTASIA

Cary Grant accepted the award for the actress, who was in a self-imposed exile in Paris. Bergman was informally blacklisted from Hollywood for her adulterous relationship with Roberto Rossellini, which resulted in the out-of-wedlock birth of a son. "Dear Ingrid," said Grant, "if you can hear me or see this, I want you to know we all send you our love and admiration."

Bergman was condemned by the Vatican and even by the United States Congress, where on the floor of the Senate she was denounced as a "cheap, chiseling female…a powerful influence." *Anastasia* marked her triumphant return. Critic Bosley Crowther praised Bergman, saying, "her performance as the heroine is nothing short of superb as she traces the progress of a woman from the depths of derangement and despair through a struggle with doubt and delusion to the accomplishment of courage, pride, and love. It is a beautifully molded performance."

(For more on Bergman, see 1944 and 1974.)

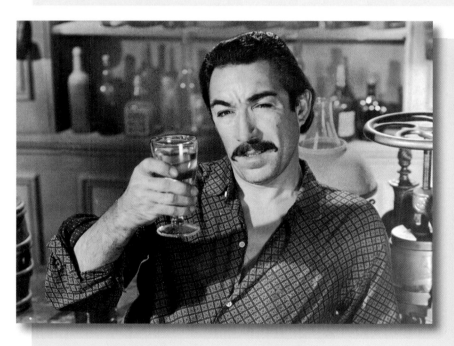

BEST SUPPORTING ACTOR
ANTHONY QUINN (1915–2001)
LUST FOR LIFE

"Acting has never been a matter of competition to me. I was only competing against myself, and I thank you for letting me win that fight with myself," said the ebullient star, who won the prize for the shortest Oscar-winning performance up to that time.

"As Gauguin, the friend but ultimate irritant to van Gogh, Anthony Quinn gives a splendid concept of a disordered, creative man," wrote Bosley Crowther.

(For more on Quinn, see 1952.)

Dorothy Malone with Rock Hudson

BEST SUPPORTING ACTRESS
DOROTHY MALONE (B. 1925)
WRITTEN ON THE WIND

Malone's lengthy "get the hook" acceptance speech, in which she thanked "all the crews I've ever worked with," was interrupted—only temporarily—by emcee Jerry Lewis, whose outstretched hand was waving a stopwatch in front of her.

Beginning her career early as a child model, Malone landed her first movie contract at 18, when she appeared in a school play and was spotted by a talent scout. For the next twelve years she played brunette nice girls without much fanfare. Then she was transformed into a promiscuous blonde and immediately won an Oscar.

But Oscar, unfortunately, didn't prove to be her knight in gold armor, and her subsequent roles were weak, with the exception of the Lon Chaney biography *Man of a Thousand Faces* (1957) and *Too Much, Too Soon* (1958). She is perhaps best known to fans for her leading role in the TV soap opera *Peyton Place* (1964–1969).

PICTURE
AROUND THE WORLD IN 80 DAYS, Todd, UA, Michael Todd.
FRIENDLY PERSUASION, Allied Artists, William Wyler.
GIANT, Warner Bros, George Stevens and Henry Ginsberg.
THE KING AND I, 20th Century-Fox, Charles Brackett.
THE TEN COMMANDMENTS, DeMille, Paramount, Cecil B. DeMille.

ACTOR
YUL BRYNNER in _The King and I_, 20th Century-Fox.
JAMES DEAN in _Giant_, Warner Bros.
KIRK DOUGLAS in _Lust for Life_, MGM.
ROCK HUDSON in _Giant_, Warner Bros.
SIR LAURENCE OLIVIER in _Richard III_, Olivier, Lopert Films (British).

ACTRESS
CARROLL BAKER in _Baby Doll_, Newtown, Warner Bros.
INGRID BERGMAN in _Anastasia_, 20th Century-Fox.
KATHARINE HEPBURN in _The Rainmaker_, Wallis, Paramount.
NANCY KELLY in _The Bad Seed_, Warner Bros.
DEBORAH KERR in _The King and I_, 20th Century-Fox.

SUPPORTING ACTOR
DON MURRAY in _Bus Stop_, 20th Century-Fox.
ANTHONY PERKINS in _Friendly Persuasion_, Allied Artists.
ANTHONY QUINN in _Lust for Life_, MGM.
MICKEY ROONEY in _The Bold and the Brave_, Filmakers Releasing, RKO Radio.
ROBERT STACK in _Written on the Wind_, U-I.

SUPPORTING ACTRESS
MILDRED DUNNOCK in _Baby Doll_, Newtown, Warner Bros.
EILEEN HECKART in _The Bad Seed_, Warner Bros.
MERCEDES McCAMBRIDGE in _Giant_, Warner Bros.
PATTY McCORMACK in _The Bad Seed_, Warner Bros.
DOROTHY MALONE in _Written on the Wind_, U-I.

DIRECTION
MICHAEL ANDERSON for _Around the World in 80 Days_, Todd, UA.
WALTER LANG for _The King and I_, 20th Century-Fox.
GEORGE STEVENS for _Giant_, Warner Bros.
KING VIDOR for _War and Peace_, Ponti-De Laurentiis, Paramount (Italo-American).
WILLIAM WYLER for _Friendly Persuasion_, Allied Artists.

WRITING: ORIGINAL STORY
THE BRAVE ONE, King Bros., RKO Radio. Dalton Trumbo (aka Robert Rich).
THE EDDY DUCHIN STORY, Columbia. Leo Katcher.
HIGH SOCIETY, Allied Artists. Edward Bernds and Elwood Ullman. (Withdrawn from final ballot.)
THE PROUD AND THE BEAUTIFUL, Kingsley International (French). Jean Paul Sartre.
UMBERTO D., Harrison & Davidson Releasing (Italian). Cesare Zavattini.

WRITING: SCREENPLAY ADAPTATION
AROUND THE WORLD IN 80 DAYS, Todd, UA. James Poe, John Farrow and S.J. Perelman.
BABY DOLL, Newtown, Warner Bros. Tennessee Williams.
GIANT, Warner Bros. Fred Guiol and Ivan Moffat.
LUST FOR LIFE, MGM. Norman Corwin
FRIENDLY PERSUASION, Allied Artists. (Writer Michael Wilson ineligible for nomination under 1956 Academy bylaws.)

WRITING: ORIGINAL SCREENPLAY
THE BOLD AND THE BRAVE, Filmakers, RKO Radio. Robert Lewin.
JULIE, Arwin, MGM. Andrew L. Stone.
LA STRADA, Ponti-De Laurentiis, Trans-Lox Dist. Corp. (Italian). Federico Fellini and Tullio Pinelli.
THE LADY KILLERS, Ealing, Continental Dist. (British). William Rose.
THE RED BALLOON, Lopert Films (French). Albert Lamorisse

CINEMATOGRAPHY
_B/W_
BABY DOLL, Newtown, Warner Bros. Boris Kaufman.
THE BAD SEED, Warner Bros. Hal Rosson.
THE HARDER THEY FALL, Columbia. Burnett Guffey.
SOMEBODY UP THERE LIKES ME, MGM. Joseph Ruttenberg.
STAGECOACH TO FURY, Regal Films, 20th Century-Fox. Walter Strenge.

Color
AROUND THE WORLD IN 80 DAYS, Todd, UA. Lionel Lindon.
THE EDDY DUCHIN STORY, Columbia. Harry Stradling.
THE KING AND I, 20th Century-Fox. Leon Shamroy.
THE TEN COMMANDMENTS, DeMille, Paramount. Loyal Griggs.
WAR AND PEACE, Ponti-De Laurentiis, Paramount (Italo-American). Jack Cardiff.

ART DIRECTION—SET DECORATION
_B/W_
THE PROUD AND THE PROFANE, Perlberg-Seaton, Paramount. Hal Pereira and A. Earl Hedrick; Samuel M. Comer and Frank B. McKelvy.
SEVEN SAMURAI, Toho, Kingsley International (Japanese). Takashi Matsuyama.
THE SOLID GOLD CADILLAC, Columbia. Ross Bellah; William R. Kiernan and Louis Diage.
SOMEBODY UP THERE LIKES ME, MGM. Cedric Gibbons and Malcolm F. Brown; Edwin B. Willis and F. Keogh Gleason.
TEENAGE REBEL, 20th Century-Fox. Lyle R. Wheeler and Jack Martin Smith; Walter M. Scott and Stuart A. Reiss.

Color
AROUND THE WORLD IN 80 DAYS, Todd, UA. James W. Sullivan and Ken Adams; Ross J. Dowd.
GIANT, Warner Bros. Boris Leven; Ralph S. Hurst.
THE KING AND I, 20th Century-Fox. Lyle B. Wheeler and John DeCuir; Walter M. Scott and Paul S. Fox.
LUST FOR LIFE, MGM. Cedric Gibbons, Hans Peters and Preston Ames; Edwin B. Willis and F. Keogh Gleason.
THE TEN COMMANDMENTS, DeMille, Paramount. Hal Pereira, Walter H. Tyler and Albert Nozaki; Sam M. Comer and Ray Moyer.

COSTUME DESIGN
_B/W_
THE POWER AND THE PRIZE, MGM. Helen Rose.
THE PROUD AND THE PROFANE, Perlberg-Seaton, Paramount. Edith Head.
SEVEN SAMURAI, Toho, Kingsley International (Japanese). Kohei Ezaki.
THE SOLID GOLD CADILLAC, Columbia. Jean Louis.
TEENAGE REBEL, 20th Century-Fox. Charles LeMaire and Mary Wills.

Color
AROUND THE WORLD IN 80 DAYS, Todd, UA. Miles White.
GIANT, Warner Bros. Moss Mabry and Marjorie Best.

THE KING AND I, 20th Century-Fox. Irene Sharaff.
THE TEN COMMANDMENTS, DeMille, Paramount. Edith Head, Ralph Jester, John Jensen, Dorothy Jeakins and Arnold Friberg.
WAR AND PEACE, Ponti-De Laurentiis, Paramount (Italo-American). Marie Be Matteis.

SOUND RECORDING
THE BRAVE ONE, King Bros., RKO Radio. John Myers, sound director.
THE EDDY DUCHIN STORY, Columbia. Columbia Studio Sound Department; John Livadary, sound director.
FRIENDLY PERSUASION, Allied Artists. Westrex Sound Services, Inc.; Gordon R. Glennan, sound director, and Samuel Goldwyn Studio Sound Department; Gordon Sawyer, sound director.
THE KING AND I, 20th Century-Fox. 20th Century-Fox Studio Sound Department; Carl Faulkner, sound director.
THE TEN COMMANDMENTS, DeMille, Paramount. Paramount Studio Sound Department; Loren L. Ryder, sound director.

FILM EDITING
AROUND THE WORLD IN 80 DAYS, Todd, UA. Gene Ruggiero and Paul Weatherwax.
THE BRAVE ONE, King Bros., RKO Radio. Merrill G. White.
GIANT, Warner Bros. William Hornbeck, Philip W. Anderson and Fred Bohanan.
SOMEBODY UP THERE LIKES ME, MGM. Albert Akst.
THE TEN COMMANDMENTS, DeMille, Paramount. Anne Bauchens.

SPECIAL EFFECTS
FORBIDDEN PLANET, MGM. A. Arnold Gillespie, Irving Ries and Wesley C. Miller.
THE TEN COMMANDMENTS, DeMille, Paramount. John Fulton.

SONG
FRIENDLY PERSUASION (THEE I LOVE) (_Friendly Persuasion_, Allied Artists); Music by Dimitri Tiomkin. Lyrics by Paul Francis Webster.
JULIE (_Julie_, Arwin, MGM.); Music by Leith Stevens. Lyrics by Tom Adair.
TRUE LOVE (_High Society_, Siegel, MGM.); Music and Lyrics by Cole Porter.
WHATEVER WILL BE, WILL BE (QUE SERA, SERA) (_The Man Who Knew Too Much_, Hitchcock, Paramount); Music and Lyrics by Jay Livingston and Ray Evans.
WRITTEN ON THE WIND (_Written on the Wind_, U-I); Music by Victor Young. Lyrics by Sammy Cahn.

SCORING: DRAMA/COMEDY
ANASTASIA, 20th Century-Fox. Alfred Newman.
AROUND THE WORLD IN 80 DAYS, Todd, UA, Victor Young.
BETWEEN HEAVEN AND HELL, 20th Century-Fox. Hugo Friedhofer.
GIANT, Warner Bros. Dimitri Tiomkin.
THE RAINMAKER, Wallis, Paramount. Alex North.

SCORING: MUSICAL
THE BEST THINGS IN LIFE ARE FREE, 20th Century-Fox. Lionel Newman.
THE EDDY DUCHIN STORY, Columbia. Morris Stoloff and George Duning.
HIGH SOCIETY, Siegel, MGM. Johnny Green and Saul Chaplin.
THE KING AND I, 20th Century-Fox. Alfred Newman and Ken Darby.
MEET ME IN LAS VEGAS, MGM. George Stoll and Johnny Green.

SHORT SUBJECTS: CARTOON
GERALD McBOING-BOING ON PLANET MOO, UPA, Columbia. Stephen Bosustow, producer.
THE JAYWALKER, UPA, Columbia. Stephen Bosustow, producer.
MISTER MAGOO'S PUDDLE JUMPER, UPA, Columbia. Stephen Bosustow, producer.

SHORT SUBJECT: ONE-REEL
CRASHING THE WATER BARRIER, Warner Bros. Konstantin Kalser, producer.
I NEVER FORGET A FACE, Warner Bros. Robert Youngson, producer.
TIME STOOD STILL, Warner Bros. Cedric Francis, producer.

SHORT SUBJECT: TWO-REEL
THE BESPOKE OVERCOAT, George K. Arthur, Go Pictures, Inc. Romulus Films, producer.
COW DOG, Disney, Buena Vista. Larry Lansburgh, producer.
THE DARK WAVE, 20th Century-Fox. John Healy, producer.
SAMOA, Disney, Buena Vista. Walt Disney, producer.

DOCUMENTARY: SHORT SUBJECTS
A CITY DECIDES, Charles Guggenheim & Assocs.
THE DARK WAVE, 20th Century-Fox. John Healy, producer.
THE HOUSE WITHOUT A NAME, U-I. Valentine Davies, producer.
MAN IN SPACE, Disney, Buena Vista. Ward Kimball, producer.
THE TRUE STORY OF THE CIVIL WAR, Camera Eye Pictures. Louis Clyde Stoumen, producer.

DOCUMENTARY: FEATURES
THE NAKED EYE, Camera Eye Pictures, Louis Clyde Stoumen, producer.
THE SILENT WORLD, Filmad-F.S.J.Y.C., Columbia (French). Jacques-Yves Cousteau, producer.
WHERE MOUNTAINS FLOAT, Brandon Films (Danish). The Government Film Committee of Denmark, producer.

FOREIGN LANGUAGE FILM
THE CAPTAIN OF KOPENICK, (West Germany), Gyula Trebitsch and Walter Koppel, producers.
GERVAISE, (France). Annie Dorfmann, producer.
HARP OF BURMA, (Japan). Masayuki Takagi, producer.
LA STRADA, (Italy). Dino De Laurentiis and Carlo Ponti, producers.
QIVITOQ, (Denmark). O. Dalsgaard-Olsen, producer.

HONORARY AND OTHER AWARDS
TO EDDIE CANTOR for distinguished service to the film industry.

IRVING G. THALBERG MEMORIAL AWARD
TO BUDDY ADLER

JEAN HERSHOLT HUMANITARIAN AWARD
TO Y. FRANK FREEMAN

SCIENTIFIC OR TECHNICAL
CLASS III
RICHARD H. RANGER of Rangertone Inc.;
TED HIRSCH, CARL HAUGE and EDWARD REICHARD of Consolidated Film Industries;
THE TECHNICAL DEPARTMENTS of PARAMOUNT PICTURES CORP;
ROY C. STEWART AND SONS of Stewart-Trans Lux Corp., DR. C.R. DAILY and the TRANSPARENCY DEPARTMENT of PARAMOUNT PICTURES CORP;
THE CONSTRUCTION DEPARTMENT of METRO GOLDWYN-MAYER STUDIO;
DANIEL J. BLOOMBERG, JOHN POND, WILLIAM WADE and the ENGINEERING and CAMERA DEPARTMENTS of REPUBLIC STUDIO.

1957

"My segment was six minutes in length. Unfortunately, that was also the length of Mr. Duck's bit of film, and they chose Donald Duck. You always have to settle for less on Best Picture: Less Laughton is great/Yeah, if you're voting for weight."
—Burt Lancaster and Kirk Douglas, singing

BRIDGE OF SIZE

CEREMONY: March 26, 1958,
RKO Pantages Theatre, Hollywood
HOSTS: Bob Hope, Rosalind Russell,
David Niven, James Stewart,
and Jack Lemmon

Despite a fashion alert that "diamonds don't photograph well on TV," Elizabeth Taylor had her considerable array of blinding stones all laid out for the big night. But four days before the Awards her husband, Mike Todd, was killed in a plane crash en route to New York City. "I was supposed to be with him but I had a cold," she wept.

Taylor and Best Actor front-runner, Alec Guinness, were the only two major nominees not present for the most glamorous, star-jammed show yet. It started off with the comeback drama of Red Buttons and the exotica of kimono-clad Miyoshi Umeki. High camp was provided by beefy heartthrob Rock Hudson and 65-year-old Mae West in a duet of "Baby, It's Cold Outside," during which he offered her a double-entendre "king-size" cigarette. But the big song of the night was the whistling "Colonel Bogey's March" from *The Bridge on the River Kwai*. It played with brain-branding repetition as David Lean's sprawling war epic picked off nearly every available statuette.

No Oscar show is complete without a Cinderella story, and newcomer Joanne Woodward earned the glass slippers. Her bumpkin-to-princess image was heightened by the strapless green dress she'd made herself for $100. The getup caused Joan Crawford no end of distress. "Miss Woodward has set Hollywood glamour back twenty years," she lamented.

The adage that Hollywood deaths come in threes proved chillingly true with the sudden exits of Todd, former Paramount chief Don Hartman, and Columbia's "prince of darkness," Harry Cohn. All passed away within a week before the Awards. Cohn's curvy protégé, Kim Novak, accepted his Oscar for Best Picture, looking appropriately forlorn. In truth, Cohn was among the most despised men in the industry. He wielded a riding crop in his office and loved firing people on Christmas Eve. At the birth of Cohn's first son, a Columbia exec expressed his hope that "he'd be just like his father." Cohn was horrified. "Don't ever say that again," he retorted. "I want him to have friends!"

BEST PICTURE/BEST DIRECTOR
DAVID LEAN (1908–1991)
THE BRIDGE ON THE RIVER KWAI

"Brilliant is the word, and no other, to describe the quality of skills that have gone into the making of this picture," wrote Bosley Crowther in the *New York Times*. "A big and engrossing [film]," wrote Pauline Kael of *The New Yorker*.

Though he didn't direct many films, Lean's epics have always been characterized by good taste, a strong sense of time and place, and superb craftsmanship. Lean's career began with a co-direction credit with Noel Coward on *In Which We Serve* (1942), but he made his first real mark and an Oscar nomination with *Brief Encounter* (1945), which he followed with adaptations of two Dickens classics, *Great Expectations* (1946) and *Oliver Twist* (1948, nom.).

His remaining films were triumphs: *Summertime* (1955, nom.), *Lawrence of Arabia* (1962), *Doctor Zhivago* (1965, nom.), and *A Passage to India* (1984, nom.). Lean's production of *The Bounty* (1980) fell through and ended up being made by others.

The envelope, please…

BEST ACTOR
ALEC GUINNESS (1914–2000)
THE BRIDGE ON THE RIVER KWAI

Guinness was in England riding in his car when he heard the news of his award from his driver: "You've won what they call an Oscar, sir."

Starting out as an ad copywriter, Guinness managed a quick change of roles to become one of Hollywood's finest actors. According to *Entertainment Tonight* film critic Leonard Maltin, "[Guinness] seems constitutionally incapable of giving a bad performance." For all the great work he had done, his myth-making role in *Star Wars* as Obi-Wan Kenobi, guardian of "the force," made him a familiar face (and voice) to a new generation.

As the star of David Lean's two Dickens adaptations, *Great Expectations* (1946) and *Oliver Twist* (1948), Guinness began his career with distinction and went on to become the heart and soul of such films as *Kind Hearts and Coronets* (1949), *The Lavender Hill Mob* (1951, nom.), *The Ladykillers* (1955), *The Horse's Mouth* (1958), and *Our Man in Havana* (1959).

BEST ACTRESS
JOANNE WOODWARD (B. 1930)
THE THREE FACES OF EVE

The plainly dressed Woodward, who had become Mrs. Paul Newman only two months earlier, raced to the podium and said, "I can only say that I've been daydreaming about this since I was nine years old." Woodward's comments before the show betrayed a different attitude: "If I had an infinite amount of respect for the people who I think gave the greatest performance, then it would matter."

Woodward landed her first film role in *Count Three and Pray* (1955) while she was still performing on the stage. She joined husband Paul Newman in *The Long Hot Summer* (1958), and the two have worked together frequently in such films as *Rally 'Round the Flag, Boys!* (1958), *A New Kind of Love* (1963), *The Drowning Pool* (1976), and *Harry and Son* (1984). They gave one of their most powerful performances in *Mr. & Mrs. Bridge* (1990, nom.).

Newman directed Woodward in some of her greatest roles, including *Rachel, Rachel* (1968, nom.), *The Effect of Gamma Rays on Man-in-the-Moon Marigolds* (1972), and the television films, *The Shadow Box* (1980) and *Summer Wishes, Winter Dreams* (1973).

Woodward, like many mature actresses, has found few worthy roles in recent years, but she has performed in exceptional TV movies, including *Sybil* (1976), *See How She Runs* (1978, Emmy), and *Do You Remember Love* (1985, Emmy).

BEST OF 1957
Best Picture: *The Bridge on the River Kwai*
Best Director: David Lean, *The Bridge on the River Kwai*
Best Actor: Alec Guinness, *The Bridge on the River Kwai*
Best Actress: Joanne Woodward, *The Three Faces of Eve*
Best Supporting Actor: Red Buttons, *Sayonara*
Best Supporting Actress: Miyoshi Umeki, *Sayonara*

FIRSTS
- The movie industry produced the TV broadcast.
- The entire show was broadcast live from the Pantages Theatre, Los Angeles.
- Academy members were made entirely responsible for nominations. Voting categories were trimmed down to twenty-three.
- Miyoshi Umeki was the first Asian actress to win an Oscar.

SINS OF OMISSION
Pictures: *Paths of Glory*, *Sweet Smell of Success*, *Funny Face*, *A Face in the Crowd*
Actor: Tony Curtis, *Sweet Smell of Success*
Actress: Marlene Dietrich, *Witness for the Prosecution*

ROLE REVERSALS
- Alec Guinness wasn't David Lean's first choice. His Oscar-winning role had been earmarked for either Noel Coward or Charles Laughton.
- Judy Garland and Jean Simmons passed on *The Three Faces of Eve* before Joanne Woodward got her first look at the script.

ALWAYS A BRIDESMAID, NEVER A BRIDE
- Deborah Kerr's nomination was her fourth unsuccessful bid.
- Paul Newman would have to wait twenty-nine years before bringing home a matching Oscar to his wife, Joanne Woodward.
- Best Supporting nominee Sessue Hayakawa was the only loser for the *Bridge on the River Kwai* team.

UNMENTIONABLES
- Ten days after the ceremonies, one of Hollywood's most notorious scandals played out at the Beverly Hills home of Best Actress nominee Lana Turner (*Peyton Place*). Her fifteen-year-old daughter, Cheryl, rushed into Lana's bedroom where the star was being savagely beaten by her live-in mobster lover, Johnny Stompanato. Cheryl fatally stabbed him with a kitchen knife. Over the years, rumors persisted that this was a cover-up and that it was Lana who wielded the weapon. What caused the handsome Stompanato to go ballistic? Lana had refused to take him to the Oscars.
- The screenplay for *The Bridge on the River Kwai* was yet another "front" job. The true authors were blacklisted Michael Wilson and Carl Foreman.
- "A film critic is a legless man who teaches running," said Frank Capra.
- Three and a half months of filming on location in Ceylon cost *Kwai* director David Lean his wife. She sued him for divorce on grounds of desertion.

Red Buttons with Marlon Brando

BEST SUPPORTING ACTOR
RED BUTTONS (B. 1919)
SAYONARA

"I'm a very happy guy," said Buttons as he accepted the award. The *Hollywood Reporter*'s W. R. Wilkerson wrote, "Red might stage such a comeback as did Frankie boy after his performance in *From Here to Eternity*."

Buttons got his start performing burlesque in the Catskill resorts and made his film debut in *Winged Victory* (1944). But it wasn't until 1952, when he hosted a TV variety series, that he became a star. After *Sayonara* he appeared in *Imitation General* (1958), *The Big Circus* (1959), *One, Two, Three* (1961), *Hatari!*, *Five Weeks in a Balloon*, *The Longest Day* (all 1962), *Stagecoach* (1966), *They Shoot Horses, Don't They?* (1969), *The Poseidon Adventure* (1972), *Gable and Lombard* (1976), and *Movie Movie* (1978).

Buttons did some TV work, spending a season on *Knots Landing* (1987). He was a regular on the Dean Martin roasts, where his "Never Got a Dinner" routine was always a crowd-pleaser.

Marlon Brando with Miyoshi Umeki

BEST SUPPORTING ACTRESS
MIYOSHI UMEKI (B. 1929)
SAYONARA

"I wish someone would help me now," said the winner at the podium. "I have nothing in my mind. Thank all American people." In the *New York Times*, Bosley Crowther wrote, "Miyoshi Umeki is droll as the Japanese girl married to (Red Buttons) an Air Force sergeant."

Born in Hokkaido, Japan, Umeki had been a radio and nightclub singer since her teens. She came to the U.S. in the 1950s and through TV exposure landed her Oscar-winning part in *Sayonara*. She also appeared on Broadway and on TV in *The Courtship of Eddie's Father*. She made only a handful of films: *Cry for Happy* (1957), *Flower Drum Song* (1961), *The Horizontal Lieutenant* (1962), and *A Girl Named Tamiko* (1963).

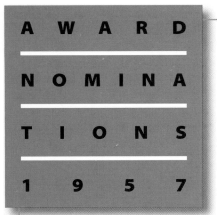

PICTURE

THE BRIDGE ON THE RIVER KWAI, Horizon, Columbia, Sam Spiegel.
PEYTON PLACE, Wald, 20th Century-Fox, Jerry Wald.
SAYONARA, Goetz, Warner Bros, William Goetz.
12 ANGRY MEN, Orion-Nova, UA, Henry Fonda and Reginald Rose.
WITNESS FOR THE PROSECUTION, Small-Hornblow, UA, Arthur Hornblow, Jr.

ACTOR

MARLON BRANDO in *Sayonara*, Goetz, Warner Bros.
ANTHONY FRANCIOSA in *A Hatful of Rain*, 20th Century-Fox.
ALEC GUINNESS in *The Bridge on the River Kwai*, Horizon, Columbia.
CHARLES LAUGHTON in *Witness for the Prosecution*, Small-Hornblow, UA.
ANTHONY QUINN in *Wild Is the Wind*, Wallis, Paramount.

ACTRESS

DEBORAH KERR in *Heaven Knows, Mr. Allison*, 20th Century-Fox.
ANNA MAGNANI in *Wild Is the Wind*, Wallis, Paramount.
ELIZABETH TAYLOR in *Raintree County*, MGM.
LANA TURNER in *Peyton Place*, Wald, 20th Century-Fox.
JOANNE WOOWARD in *The Three Faces of Eve*, 20th Century-Fox.

SUPPORTING ACTOR

RED BUTTONS in *Sayonara*, Goetz, Warner Bros.
VITTORIO DE SICA in *A Farewell to Arms*, Selznick, 20th Century-Fox.
SESSUE HAYAKAWA in *The Bridge on the River Kwai*, Horizon, Columbia.
ARTHUR KENNEDY in *Peyton Place*, Wald, 20th Century-Fox.
RUSS TAMBLYN in *Peyton Place*, Wald, 20th Century-Fox.

SUPPORTING ACTRESS

CAROLYN JONES in *The Bachelor Party*, Norma, UA.
ELSA LANCHESTER in *Witness for the Prosecution*, Small-Hornblow, UA.
HOPE LANGE in *Peyton Place*, Wald, 20th Century-Fox.
MIYOSHI UMEKI in *Sayonara*, Goetz, Warner Bros.
DIANE VARSI in *Peyton Place*, Wald, 20th Century-Fox.

DIRECTION

DAVID LEAN for *The Bridge on the River Kwai*, Horizon, Columbia.
JOSHUA LOGAN for *Sayonara*, Goetz, Warner Bros.
SIDNEY LUMET for *12 Angry Men*, Orion-Nova Prod., UA.
MARK ROBSON for *Peyton Place*, Wald, 20th Century-Fox.
BILLY WILDER for *Witness for the Prosecution*, Small-Hornblow, UA.

WRITING: BASED ON MATERIAL FROM ANOTHER MEDIUM

THE BRIDGE ON THE RIVER KWAI, Horizon, Columbia. Pierre Boulle, Carl Foreman and Michael Wilson. (NOTE: Because of the political climate of the time, only Pierre Boulle was given official on-screen credit, but actual
screenwriters Foreman and Wilson have since been acknowledged by the Academy for their contributions.)
HEAVEN KNOWS, MR. ALLISON, 20th Century-Fox. John Lee Mahin and John Huston.
PEYTON PLACE, Wald, 20th Century-Fox. John Michael Hayes.
SAYONARA, Goetz, Warner Bros. Paul Osborn.
12 ANGRY MEN, Orion-Nova Prod., UA. Reginald Rose.

WRITING: ORIGINAL STORY AND SCREENPLAY

DESIGNING WOMAN, MGM. George Wells
FUNNY FACE, Paramount. Leonard Gershe.
MAN OF A THOUSAND FACES, U-I. Ralph Wheelright, R. Wright Campbell, Ivan Goff and Ben Roberts.
THE TIN STAR, Perlberg-Seaton, Paramount. Barney Slater, Joel Kane and Dudley Nichols.
I VITELLONI, API-Janus (Italian). Federico Fellini, Ennio Flaiano, and Tullio Pinelli.

CINEMATOGRAPHY

AN AFFAIR TO REMEMBER, Wald, 20th Century-Fox. Milton Krasner.
THE BRIDGE ON THE RIVER KWAI, Horizon, Columbia. Jack Hildyard.
FUNNY FACE, Paramount. Ray June.
PEYTON PLACE, Wald, 20th Century-Fox. William Mellor.
SAYONARA, Goetz, Warner Bros. Ellsworth Fredericks.

ART DIRECTION—SET DECORATION

FUNNY FACE, Paramount. Hal Pereira and George W. Davis; Sam Comer and Ray Moyer.
LES GIRLS, Siegel, MGM. William A. Horning and Gene Allen; Edwin B. Willis and Richard Pefferle.
PAL JOEY, Essex-Sidney, Columbia. Walter Holscher; William Kiernan and Louis Diage.
RAINTREE COUNTY, MGM. William A. Horning and Urie McCleary; Edwin B. Willis and Hugh Hunt.
SAYONARA, Goetz, Warner Bros. Ted Haworth; Robert Priestly.

COSTUME DESIGN

AN AFFAIR TO REMEMBER, Wald, 20th CenturyFox. Charles LeMaire.
FUNNY FACE, Paramount. Edith Head and Hubert de Givenchy.
LES GIRLS, Siegel, MGM. Orry-Kelly.
PAL JOEY, Essex-Sidney, Columbia. Jean Louis.
RAINTREE COUNTY, MGM. Walter Plunkett.

SOUND RECORDING

GUNFIGHT AT THE O.K. CORRAL, Wallis, Paramount. Paramount Studio Sound Dept., George Dutton, Sound Director.
LES GIRLS, Siegel, MGM. MGM. Studio Sound Dept., Dr. Wesley C. Miller, Sound Director.
PAL JOEY, Essex-Sidney, Columbia. Columbia Studio Sound Dept., John P. Livadary, Sound Director.
SAYONARA, Goetz, Warner Bros. Warner Bros. Studio Sound Dept., George Groves, Sound Director.
WITNESS FOR THE PROSECUTION, Small-Hornblow, UA. Samuel Goldwyn Studio Sound Dept., Gordon Sawyer, Sound Director.

FILM EDITING

THE BRIDGE ON THE RIVER KWAI, Horizon, Columbia. Peter Taylor.
GUNFIGHT AT THE O.K. CORRAL, Wallis, Paramount. Warren Low.
PAL JOEY, Essex-Sidney, Columbia. Viola Lawrence and Jerome Thoms.
SAYONARA, Goetz, Warner Bros. Arthur Schmidt and Philip W. Anderson.
WITNESS FOR THE PROSECUTION, Small-Hornblow, UA. Daniel Mandell.

SPECIAL EFFECTS

THE ENEMY BELOW, 20th Century-Fox. Walter Rossi.
THE SPIRIT OF ST. LOUIS, Hayward-Wilder, Warner Bros. Louis Lichtenfield.

SONG

AN AFFAIR TO REMEMBER *(An Affair to Remember,* Wald, 20th Century-Fox);
Music by Harry Warren. Lyrics by Harold Adamson and Leo McCarey.
ALL THE WAY (*The Joker Is Wild*, Paramount); Music by James Van Heusen. Lyrics by Sammy Cahn.
APRIL LOVE (*April Love*, 20th Century-Fox); Music by Sammy Rain. Lyrics by Paul Francis Webster.
TAMMY (*Tammy and the Bachelor*, U-I); Music and Lyrics by Ray Evans and Jay Livingston.
WILD IS THE WIND (*Wild Is the Wind*, Wallis, Paramount); Music by Dimitri Tiomkin. Lyrics by Ned Washington.

SCORE

AN AFFAIR TO REMEMBER, Wald, 20th Century Fox. Hugo Friedhofer.
BOY ON A DOLPHIN, 20th Century-Fox. Hugo Friedhofer.
THE BRIDGE ON THE RIVER KWAI, Horizon, Columbia. Malcolm Arnold.
PERRI, Disney, Buena Vista. Paul Smith.
RAINTREE COUNTY, MGM. Johnny Green.

SHORT SUBJECTS: CARTOONS

BIRDS ANONYMOUS, Warner Bros. Edward Selzer, producer.
ONE DROOPY KNIGHT, MGM. William Hanna and Joseph Barbera, producers.
TABASCO ROAD, Warner Bros. Edward Selzer, producer.
TREES AND JAMAICA DADDY, UPA, Columbia. Stephen Bosustow, producer.
THE TRUTH ABOUT MOTHER GOOSE, Disney, Buena Vista. Walt Disney, producer.

SHORT SUBJECTS: LIVE ACTION

A CHAIRY TALE, National Film Board of Canada, Kingsley International. Norman McLaren, producer.
CITY OF GOLD, National Film Board of Canada, Kingsley International. Tom Daly, producer.
FOOTHOLD ON ANTARCTICA, World Wide Pictures, Schoenfeld Films. James Carr, producer.
PORTUGAL, Disney, Buena Vista. Ben Sharpsteen, producer.
THE WETBACK HOUND, Disney, Buena Vista. Larry Lansburgh, producer.

DOCUMENTARY: SHORT SUBJECTS

No nominations or award this year.

DOCUMENTARY: FEATURES

ALBERT SCHWEITZER, Hill and Anderson Prod., Louis de Rochemont Assocs. Jerome Hill, producer.
ON THE BOWERY, Rogosin, Film Representations, Inc. Lionel Rogosin, producer.
TORERO!, Producciones Barbachano Ponce, Columbia (Mexican). Manuel Barbachano Ponce, producer.

FOREIGN LANGUAGE FILM

THE DEVIL CAME AT NIGHT (Germany).
GATES OF PARIS (France).
MOTHER INDIA (India).
THE NIGHTS OF CABIRIA (Italy).
NINE LIVES (Norway).

HONORARY AND OTHER AWARDS

TO CHARLES BRACKETT for outstanding service to the Academy.
TO B.B. KAHANE for distinguished service to the motion picture industry.
TO GILBERT M. ("Broncho Billy") ANDERSON, motion picture pioneer, for his contributions to the development of motion pictures as entertainment.
TO THE SOCIETY OF MOTION PICTURE AND TELEVISION ENGINEERS for their contributions to the advancement of the motion picture industry.

JEAN HERSHOLT HUMANITARIAN AWARD

TO SAMUEL GOLDWYN

SCIENTIFIC OR TECHNICAL

CLASS I
TODD-AO CORP. and WESTREX CORP. for developing a method of producing and exhibiting wide-film motion pictures known as the Todd-AO System.
MOTION PICTURE RESEARCH COUNCIL for the design and development of a high efficiency projection screen for drive-in theatres.

CLASS II
SOCIETE D'OPTIQUE ET DR MECANIQUE DE HAUTE PRECISION for the development of a high speed variafocal photographic lens.
HARLAN L. BAUMBACH, LORAND WARGO, HOWARD M. LITTLE and the UNICORN ENGINEERING CORP. for the development of an automatic printer light selector.

CLASS III
CHARLES E. SUTTER, WILLIAM B. SMITH, PARAMOUNT PICTURES CORP. and GENERAL CABLE CORP.

1958

"I came here when I was 19 and I've been here twenty years. I've had it."

—Susan Hayward

 write-in campaign from shocked Midwestern viewers compelled Awards producer Jerry Wald to lay down the law: no cleavage this year! So, who else to model the costumes from *Gigi*? Jayne Mansfield, of course. Elizabeth Taylor, the target of moral outrage from every pulpit and living room across America, seemed to revel in the condemnation. It was off with the widow's weeds and into something scarlet as she pulled up at the Pantages with lover

TROUPERS AND BLOOPERS

CEREMONY: April 6, 1959
RKO Pantages Theatre, Hollywod
HOSTS: Jerry Lewis, Mort Sahl, Tony Randall, Bob Hope, David Niven, and Laurence Olivier

Eddie Fisher, husband of her ex–best friend Debbie Reynolds. Along with a record 100 million viewers, Debbie tuned in to watch Taylor lose to screen veteran Susan Hayward.

It was a night for troupers, as David Niven, after twenty-three years of stardom and no nominations, finally got his due. In his excitement to reach the stage, Niven stumbled on the stairs. It was

a minor gaffe in light of what was to come. Wald, hell-bent on running a tight ship, had cut musical numbers, monologues, and tributes as the show proceeded. The final host, Jerry Lewis, was left holding the bag: the Awards had ended twenty minutes early. Lewis was ordered to "Stretch, stretch, stretch!" He jokingly requested that all the stars come onstage to sing a hundred choruses of "There's No Business Like Show Business." When that didn't fly, he grabbed the conductor's baton and led the orchestra for a time. No laughs, no dice.

In desperation, the stars began to pair off and dance. But it was hopeless and, two by two, they waltzed into the wings and out of camera range. Half the audience had already reached the exits. Finally, NBC unceremoniously cut to a sports-show rerun. Bob Hope called it "the major goof in TV history!" The evening wasn't entirely lost to blunders. After eighteen years in the business without a single scandal to taint his image, Bugs Bunny was awarded his first cartoon Oscar.

BEST PICTURE/BEST DIRECTOR
VINCENTE MINNELLI (1903–1986)
GIGI

"*Gigi* is a charming entertainment that can stand on its own two legs," wrote Bosley Crowther in the *New York Times* (the film had been accused of copying *My Fair Lady*). "It is not only a charming confection of Colette, but it is also a lovely and lyrical enlargement upon that story's flavored mood and atmosphere. Vincente Minnelli has marshalled a cast to give a set of performances that, for quality and harmony, are superb."

The *New Yorker*'s Pauline Kael wrote of the acclaimed musical director, "Vincente Minnelli directed in a confident, confectionary style that carries all before it."

A onetime stage director, Minnelli went Hollywood and never turned back. Making his daring debut with the all-black *Cabin in the Sky* (1943), Minnelli went on to produce some of the most ingenious musicals in Hollywood, including *Meet Me in St. Louis* (1944, with Judy Garland, who became his wife), *An American in Paris* (1951, Oscar), *The Band Wagon* (1953), *Brigadoon* (1954), and *Bells Are Ringing* (1960). Minnelli also tried his hand—with the same savoir faire—at such dramas as *Madame Bovary* (1949), *Tea and Sympathy* (1956), *Some Came Running* (1959) and *Home from the Hill* (1960). Walking on the dark side, he made *The Bad and the Beautiful* (1952) and *Two Weeks in Another Town* (1962). And, according to *Entertainment Tonight* film critic Leonard Maltin, "his film *Lust for Life* (1956) remains one of the finest films ever made about the passion of a great artist, in this case Vincent van Gogh."

Minnelli's talent seemed to work its magic on every genre, including such light comedies as *Father of the Bride* (1950), *Father's Little Dividend* (1951), *Designing Woman* (1957), and *The Reluctant Debutante* (1958). He came out of retirement in 1976 to direct daughter Liza and Ingrid Bergman in *A Matter of Time*, which turned into a fiasco when Minnelli denounced the studio-edited film. His 1974 autobiography was titled *I Remember It Well*.

Louis Jourdan, Leslie Caron

The envelope, please...

David Niven with Rita Hayworth (right)

BEST ACTOR
DAVID NIVEN (1910–1983)
SEPARATE TABLES

"I'm so loaded down with good-luck charms I could hardly make it up the stairs," said the grateful winner after his stumble up to the podium.

Speaking of his role in *Separate Tables*, Niven said, "They gave me very good lines and then cut to Deborah Kerr while I was saying them." Niven's character, a proud but untrustworthy "major" who turns out to be a child molester, was thought to be his least respectable, and some thought the award was a "make-up" for his having been ignored two years before in *Around the World in 80 Days*.

The suave Brit immigrated to Hollywood, where he enjoyed a long career. Starting out in bit parts in 1935's *Mutiny on the Bounty* and *Barbary Coast*, among others, he quickly became a supporting player as the delightfully ditsy butler in the *Jeeves* films of 1936–1937. After the war, Niven applied his wit and great timing to such films as *My Man Godfrey* (1957), *Bonjour Tristesse* (1958), *Please Don't Eat the Daisies* (1960), *The Pink Panther* (1963), *Casino Royale* (1967), and *Murder by Death* (1976).

Niven also made frequent appearances on TV, starring in the series *The David Niven Show* (1959) and *The Rogues* (1964–1965).

Susan Hayward (right)

BEST ACTRESS
SUSAN HAYWARD (1917–1975)
I WANT TO LIVE!

Hayward suffered—much like the character in her winning film. She grew up in a tenement, became embattled with the press, struggled through an acrimonious custody battle for her twin sons, and attempted suicide.

In 1937 Hayward tested unsuccessfully for the role of Scarlett O'Hara in *Gone with the Wind*. Her first major role was in *Our Leading Citizen* (1939), but her star shone in *Beau Geste* (1939). Her considerable beauty and tough but vulnerable persona were apparent in *Among the Living* (1941) and *Reap the Wild Wind* (1942). She played the lead in *The Hairy Ape* (1944, one of her best roles), *Smash-Up: The Story of a Woman* (1947, nom.), and *My Foolish Heart* (1950, nom.).

Hayward was on top and chose her own roles in *I Can Get It for You Wholesale* (1951), *With a Song in My Heart* (1952, nom.), *The Lusty Men* (1952), and *Untamed* (1955). After she won for *I Want to Live!*, everything went downhill, including her role as the replacement for Judy Garland in the embarrassing *Valley of the Dolls* (1967).

BEST OF 1958
Best Picture/Best Director: Vincente Minnelli, *Gigi*
Best Actor: David Niven, *Separate Tables*
Best Actress: Susan Hayward, *I Want to Live!*
Best Supporting Actor: Burl Ives, *The Big Country*
Best Supporting Actress: Wendy Hiller, *Separate Tables*
Honorary Award: Maurice Chevalier

FIRSTS
- No Communists were allowed to receive awards.
- Sidney Poitier's nomination for *The Defiant Ones* was the first for a black actor.
- *Gigi* broke the record for the most Oscars for a single film: nine.
- Although Vincente Minnelli had nearly forty films to his credit, *Gigi* was his first and only Oscar win.
- This was Ingrid Bergman's first appearance at the Oscars since 1949.

SINS OF OMISSION
Pictures: *Vertigo, Touch of Evil, Some Came Running, Indiscreet, The Last Hurrah*
Director: Alfred Hitchcock, *Vertigo*
Actor: James Stewart, *Vertigo*
Actress: Kim Novak, *Vertigo*

UNMENTIONABLES
- Deborah Kerr's affair with writer Peter Viertel not only cost her her marriage but the custody of her two daughters.
- Weary of their vilification in the press, Elizabeth Taylor and Eddie Fisher tossed a "You Can All Go To Hell" party.
- "I've played so many hookers they don't pay me in the regular way anymore. They leave it on the dresser," said Shirley MacLaine.
- Maurice Chevalier had been branded a collaborator after performing for the Nazis in occupied Paris. He insisted that he did it in exchange for ten French prisoners. Old friend Marlene Dietrich helped restore his career and his access to all the glamorous women he claimed to have bedded over the years. At age 83, distraught by his impotency, he attempted suicide.
- Despite Debbie Reynolds's contention that her marriage was a happy one, Eddie Fisher countered that it was already dead in the water when he left her for Liz.
- The morning after the awards, studio switchboard operators were ordered to greet callers with "M-Gigi-M."

BEST SUPPORTING ACTOR
BURL IVES (1909–1995)
THE BIG COUNTRY

Known mostly as the burly, genial American folk singer, Ives began making films in 1946, playing—ironically—cantankerous old men.

In the same Oscar-winning year, Ives was unforgettable as Big Daddy in *Cat on a Hot Tin Roof*. Most producers were slow to recognize Ives's potential as an actor. He did, however, appear in a good many films, including *East of Eden* (1956), *Our Man in Havana* (1959), *Desire Under the Elms* (1960), *Let No Man Write My Epitaph* (1960), *Summer Magic* (1963), *Ensign Pulver* (1964), *The New Adventures of Heidi* (1978), *Just You and Me, Kid* (1979), and *Two-Moon Junction* (1988).

BEST SUPPORTING ACTRESS
WENDY HILLER (B. 1912)
SEPARATE TABLES

Hearing of her victory, Hiller told a London newspaper, "Never mind the honor, although I'm sure it's very nice of them. I hope this award means cash—hard cash."

For her role in *Separate Tables*, *Variety* hailed Hiller as "the efficient hotel manager who finds her romance with Burt Lancaster shattered upon the arrival of his physically attractive and fashionable ex-wife."

Though primarily a stage actress, Wendy Hiller, in her slight movie career, has contributed some of its greatest performances, including her inspired work in *Pygmalion* (1938, nom.), *Major Barbara* (1941), and *A Man for All Seasons* (1966, nom.). She has also starred in productions of *Witness for the Prosecution* (1982) and *The Importance of Being Earnest* (1985) for British TV.

Wendy Hiller with Burt Lancaster

HONORARY AWARD
MAURICE CHEVALIER (1888–1972)

For this tribute, Chevalier appeared—wearing the costume he wore in his un-nominated role in *Gigi*—onstage wandering through a chorus of dancing women singing "Thank Heaven for Little Girls."

Hollywood's most famous Frenchman, the twinkly-eyed, charming Chevalier, was an acrobat turned singer following a severe accident. Chevalier came to Hollywood in 1928 and appeared in sophisticated and often naughty films, among them *The Love Parade* (1929, nom.), *The Big Pond* (1930, nom.), and *Love Me Tonight* (1932). His later films, which were restrained by the new Production Code, were less successful as a result.

Chevalier returned to Europe in the late 1930s to make *The Beloved Vagabond* (1936), *The Man of the Hour* (1937), and *Break the News* (1938). When the war broke out he was accused—but later vindicated—of being a Nazi collaborator. He returned to the very different Hollywood of the 1950s. Among the films he made were *Love in the Afternoon* (1957), *Gigi*, in which he sang what would come to be his emblematic songs, *"I Remember It Well"* and *"Thank Heaven for Little Girls,"* *Count Your Blessings* (1959), *Can-Can* (1960), and *Fanny* (1961).

AWARD NOMINATIONS 1958

PICTURE
AUNTIE MAME, Warner Bros. Jack L. Warner, studio head.
CAT ON A HOT TIN ROOF, Avon, MGM, Lawrence Weingarten.
THE DEFIANT ONES, Kramer, UA, Stanley Kramer.
GIGI, Freed, MGM, Arthur Freed.
SEPARATE TABLES, Hecht-Hill-Lancaster, UA, Harold Hecht.

ACTOR
TONY CURTIS in *The Defiant Ones*, Kramer, UA.
PAUL NEWMAN in *Cat on a Hot Tin Roof*, Avon, MGM,
DAVID NIVEN, in *Separate Tables*, Hecht-Hill-Lancaster, UA.
SIDNEY POITIER in *The Defiant Ones*, Kramer, UA.
SPENCER TRACY in *The Old Man and the Sea*, Hayward, Warner Bros.

ACTRESS
SUSAN HAYWARD in *I Want to Live!*, Figaro, UA.
DEBORAH KERR in *Separate Tables*, Hecht-Hill-Lancaster, UA.
SHIRLEY MacLAINE in *Some Came Running*, Siegel, MGM,
ROSALIND RUSSELL in *Auntie Mame*, Warner Bros.
ELIZABETH TAYLOR in *Cat on a Hot Tin Roof*, MGM,

SUPPORTING ACTOR
THEODORE BIKEL in *The Defiant Ones*, Kramer, UA.
LEE J. COBB in *The Brothers Karamazov*, Avon, MGM,
BURL IVES in *The Big Country*, Anthony-Worldwide, UA.
ARTHUR KENNEDY in *Some Came Running*, Siegel, MGM,,
GIG YOUNG in *Teacher's Pet*, Perlberg-Seaton, Paramount.

SUPPORTING ACTRESS
PEGGY CASS in *Auntie Mame*, Warner Bros.
WENDY HILLER in *Separate Tables*, Hecht-Hill-Lancaster, UA.
MARTHA HYER in *Some Came Running*, Siegel, MGM,
MAUREEN STAPLETON in *Lonelyhearts*, Schary, UA.
CARA WILLIAMS in *The Defiant Ones*, Kramer, UA.

DIRECTION
RICHARD BROOKS for *Cat on a Hot Tin Roof*, Avon, MGM,
STANLEY KRAMER for *The Defiant Ones*, Kramer, UA.
VINCENTE MINNELLI for *Gigi*, Freed, MGM.
MARK ROBSON for *The Inn of the Sixth Happiness*, 20th Century-Fox.
ROBERT WISE for *I Want to Live!*, Wanger-Figaro, UA.

WRITING: BASED ON MATERIAL FROM ANOTHER MEDIUM
CAT ON A HOT TIN ROOF, Avon, MGM, Richard Brooks and James Poe.
GIGI, Freed, MGM, Alan Jay Lerner.
THE HORSE'S MOUTH, Lopert-UA (British). Alec Guiness.
I WANT TO LIVE!, Wanger-Figaro, UA. Nelson Gidding and Don Mankiewicz.

SEPARATE TABLES, Hecht-Hill-Lancaster, UA. Terence Rattigan and John Gay.

WRITING: ORIGINAL STORY AND SCREENPLAY
THE DEFIANT ONES, Kramer, UA. Nedrick Young and Harold Jacob Smith.
THE GODDESS, Perlman, Columbia. Paddy Chayefsky.
HOUSEBOAT, Paramount. Melville Shavelson and Jack Rose.
THE SHEEPMAN, MGM, Story by William Bowers and James Edward Grant.
TEACHER'S PET, Perlberg-Seaton, Paramount. Fay and Michael Kanin.

CINEMATOGRAPHY
B/W
THE DEFIANT ONES, Kramer, UA. Sam Leavitt.
DESIRE UNDER THE ELMS, Hartman, Paramount. Daniel L. Fapp.
I WANT TO LIVE!, Wanger-Figaro, Inc., UA. Lionel Lindon.
SEPARATE TABLES, Hecht-Hill-Lancaster, UA. Charles Lang, Jr.
THE YOUNG LIONS, 20th Century-Fox. Joe MacDonald.

Color
AUNTIE MAME, Warner Bros. Harry Stradling, Sr.
CAT ON A HOT TIN ROOF, Avon, MGM, William Daniels.
GIGI, Freed, MGM, Joseph Ruttenberg.
THE OLD MAN AND THE SEA, Hayward, Warner Bros. James Wong Howe.
SOUTH PACIFIC, Magna Corp., 20th Century-Fox. Leon Shamroy.

ART DIRECTION—SET DECORATION
(Black-and-White or Color)
AUNTIE MAME, Warner Bros. Malcolm Bert; George James Hopkins.
BELL, BOOK AND CANDLE, Phoenix, Columbia. Cary Odell; Louis Diage.
A CERTAIN SMILE, 20th Century-Fox. Lyle R. Wheeler and John DeCuir; Walter M. Scott and Paul S. Fox.
GIGI, Freed, MGM, William A. Horning and Preston Ames; Henry Grace and Keogh Gleason.
VERTIGO, Hitchcock, Paramount. Hal Pereira and Henry Bumstead; Sam Comer and Frank McKelvy.

COSTUME DESIGN
(Black-and-White or Color)
BELL, BOOK AND CANDLE, Phoenix, Columbia. Jean Louis.
THE BUCCANEER, DeMille, Paramount. Ralph Jester, Edith Head and John Jensen.
A CERTAIN SMILE, 20th Century-Fox. Charles LeMaire and Mary Wills.
GIGI, Freed, MGM, Cecil Beaton.
SOME CAME RUNNING, Siegel, MGM, Walter Plunkett.

SOUND
(No longer categorized as 'Sound Recording')
I WANT TO LIVE!, Wanger-Figaro, UA. Samuel Goldwyn Studio Sound Dept., Gordon E. Sawyer, Sound Director.
SOUTH PACIFIC, Magna Corp., 20th Century-Fox. Todd-AO Sound Department. Fred Hynes, sound director.
A TIME TO LOVE AND A TIME TO DIE, U-I. Universal-International Studio Sound Dept., Leslie I. Carey, Sound Director.
VERTIGO, Hitchcock, Paramount. Paramount Studio Sound Dept., George Dutton, Sound Director.
THE YOUNG LIONS, 20th Century-Fox. 20th Century-Fox Studio Sound Dept., Carl Faulkner, Sound Director.

FILM EDITING
AUNTIE MAME, Warner Bros. William Ziegler.
COWBOY, Phoenix, Columbia. William A. Lyon and Al Clark.
THE DEFIANT ONES, Kramer, UA. Frederic Knudtson.
GIGI, Freed, MGM, Adrienne Fazan.
I WANT TO LIVE!, Wanger-Figaro, UA. William Hornbeck.

SPECIAL EFFECTS
TOM THUMB, Pal, MG-M. Tina Howard.
TORPEDO RUN, MGM, A. Arnold Gillespie and Harold Humbrock.

SONG
ALMOST IN YOUR ARMS (Love Song from *Houseboat*) (*Houseboat*, Paramount); Music and Lyrics by Jay Livingston and Ray Evans.
A CERTAIN SMILE (*A Certain Smile*, 20th Century. Fox); Music by Sammy Fain. Lyrics by Paul Francis Webster.
GIGI (*Gigi*, Freed, MGM,); Music by Frederick Loewe. Lyrics by Alan Jay Lerner.
TO LOVE AND BE LOVED (*Some Came Running*, Siegel, MGM,); Music by James Van Heusen. Lyrics by Sammy Cahn.
A VERY PRECIOUS LOVE (*Marjorie Morningstar*, Sperling, Warner Bros.); Music by Sammy Fain. Lyrics by Paul Francis Webster.

SCORING: DRAMA/COMEDY
THE BIG COUNTRY, Anthony-Worldwide, UA. Jerome Moross.
THE OLD MAN AND THE SEA, Hayward, Warner Bros. Dimitri Tiomkin.
SEPARATE TABLES, Hecht-Hill-Lancaster, UA. David Raksin.
WHITE WILDERNESS, Disney, Buena Vista, Oliver Wallace.
THE YOUNG LIONS, 20th Century-Fox. Hugo Friedhofer.

SCORING: MUSICAL
THE BOLSHOI BALLET, Czinner-Maxwell, Rank Releasing (British). Yuri Faier and G. Rozhdestvensky.
DAMN YANKEES, Warner Bros. Ray Heindorf.
GIGI, Freed, MGM, Andre Previn.
MARDI GRAS, Wald, 20th Century-Fox. Lionel Newman.
SOUTH PACIFIC, Magna Corp., 20th Century-Fox, Alfred Newman and Ken Darby.

SHORT SUBJECTS: CARTOONS
KNIGHTY KNIGHT BUGS, Warner Bros. John W. Burton, Producer.
PAUL BUNYAN, Walt Disney Prods, Buena Vista Film Distribution. Walt Disney, producer.
SIDNEY'S FAMILY TREE, Terrytoons, 20th Century-Fox. William M. Weiss, producer.

SHORT SUBJECTS: LIVE ACTION
GRAND CANYON, Walt Disney Prods., Buena Vista. Walt Disney, producer.
JOURNEY INTO SPRING, British Transport Films, Lester A. Schoenfeld Films. Ian Ferguson, producer.
THE KISS, Cohay Prods., Continental Distributing, Inc. John Patrick Hayes, producer.
SNOWS OF AORANGI, New Zealand Screen Board. George Brest Assocs.
T IS FOR TUMBLEWEED, Continental Distributing, Inc. James A. Lebenthal, producer.

DOCUMENTARY: SHORT SUBJECTS
AMA GIRLS, Disney Prods., Buena Vista. Ben Sharpsteen, producer.
EMPLOYEES ONLY, Hughes Aircraft Co. Kenneth G. Brown, producer.
JOURNEY INTO SPRING, British Transport Films, Lester A. Schoenfeld Films. Ian Ferguson, producer.
THE LIVING STONE, National Film Board of Canada. Tom Daly, producer.
OVERTURE, United Nations Film Service. Thorold Dickinson, producer.

DOCUMENTARY: FEATURES
ANTARCTIC CROSSING, World Wide Pictures, Lester A. Schoenfeld Films. James Carr, producer.
THE HIDDEN WORLD, Small World Co. Robert Snyder, producer.
PSYCHIATRIC NURSING, Dynamic Films, Inc. Nathan Zucker, producer.
WHITE WILDERNESS, Disney Prods., Buena Vista. Ben Sharpsteen, producer.

FOREIGN LANGUAGE FILM
ARMS AND THE MAN (Germany).
LA VENGANZA (Spain).
MY UNCLE (France).
THE ROAD A YEAR LONG (Yugoslavia).

THE USUAL UNIDENTIFIED THIEVES (Italy).

HONORARY AND OTHER AWARDS
TO MAURICE CHEVALIER for his contributions to the world of entertainment for more than half a century.

IRVING G. THALBERG MEMORIAL AWARD
TO JACK L. WARNER

SCIENTIFIC OR TECHNICAL
CLASS I
None.

CLASS II
DON W. PRIDEAUX, LEROY G. LEIGHTON and the LAMP DIVISION of GENERAL ELECTRIC CO. for the development and production of an improved 10 kilowatt lamp for motion picture set lighting.
PANAVISION, INC., for the design and development of the Auto Panatar anamorphic photographic lens for 35mm CinemaScope photography.

CLASS III
WILLY BORBERG of the GENERAL PRECISION LABORATORY, INC.;
FRED PONEDEL, GEORGE BROWN and CONRAD BOYE of the WARNER BROS. SPECIAL EFFECTS DEPT.

1959

*I*n what might have sounded like a divorce proceeding, it was Hepburn vs. Hepburn in the final stretch. Audrey was up for the role of a missionary nun; Katharine for the role of the insane mother of a sexual predator eaten by cannibals. An equally disparate race shaped up on the men's side of the aisle between Charlton Heston as a hunk in a toga and sandals and wise guy Jack Lemmon in a pleated skirt and heels.

TOGAS, HABITS, AND HEELS

CEREMONY: April 4, 1960
RKO Pantages Theater, Hollywood
HOST: Bob Hope

Suspense dwindled considerably as the evening rolled along on chariot wheels. *Ben-Hur* managed to collect almost every bit of gold on the podium. Heston was swept up in its tidal wave, and he was more surprised than anyone by his good luck. "I felt as out of place among the other nominees as Zsa Zsa Gabor at a PTA meeting," he joked.

Zippy one-liners kept the show's energy above C level, with Bob Hope in especially good form. Commenting on the current Screen Actors Guild walkout, he quipped, "Welcome to Hollywood's most glamorous strike meeting. I never thought I'd live to see the day when Ronald Reagan was the only actor working."

The funniest moment came with *Pillow Talk*'s screenplay win. Only one of its co-authors, Maurice Richlin, was able to make it to the stage. He read a hastily scribbled note from his absent partner, Stanley Shapiro: "I am trapped downstairs in the gentlemen's lounge. It seems I rented a faulty tuxedo. I'd like to thank you upstairs for this great honor."

Both ladies and gentlemen voters preferred blondes this year, as Shelley Winters and Simone Signoret briefly stole the thunder from *Ben-Hur*'s onslaught. By the time the 212-minute epic took the honors as Best Picture, the show had run twenty minutes over—a flip-side no-no of last year's disastrous twenty-minute short-out.

BEST PICTURE/BEST DIRECTOR
WILLIAM WYLER (1902–1981)
BEN-HUR

After Wyler's win, Heston said backstage to the three-time Oscar-winning director, "I guess this is old hat to you." Wyler replied, "Chuck, it never gets old." Not only did *Ben-Hur* sweep the Oscars but the great epic was also lauded by the critics for its attention to dramatic detail. The *New York Times*'s Bosley Crowther wrote, "Mr. Wyler has smartly and effectively laid stress on the powerful and meaningful personal conflicts that are strong in this old heroic tale…The artistic quality and taste of Mr. Wyler have prevailed to make this a rich and glowing drama that far transcends the bounds of spectacle. His big scenes are brilliant and dramatic— that is unquestionable. There has seldom been anything in movies to compare with this picture's chariot race." *Variety* reported, "A majestic achievement, representing a superb blending of the motion picture arts by master craftsmen."

(For more on Wyler, see 1942 and 1946.)

The envelope, please...

BEST ACTOR
CHARLTON HESTON (B. 1924)
BEN-HUR

"I feel like thanking the first secretary who let me sneak into a Broadway casting call," said Heston after he stumbled en route to the stage. Backstage later, he told the press, "Somebody just asked me what scene I enjoyed doing most, and I told him that I didn't enjoy any of it. It was hard work."

Heston "was and is an actor of absolutely undeniable presence, and was never more so than during his late-1950s/early-1960s heyday, when Hollywood needed all the presence it could get to compete with television," wrote *Entertainment Tonight* film critic Leonard Maltin.

Though he had made some earlier films, Heston's performance as Moses in Cecil B. DeMille's *The Ten Commandments* (1956) landed him in the star-studded heavens. Following this he performed in a long string of historicals and other genres, including *El Cid* (1961), *The Agony and the Ecstasy* (1965), *Planet of the Apes* (1968), and *Soylent Green* (1973). In the 1970s Heston was a ubiquitous presence in disaster films, including *Earthquake* (1974). His appearance on film waned in the 1980s and '90s, but he did appear as a spokesperson for many politically conservative issues.

BEST ACTRESS
SIMONE SIGNORET (1921–1985)
ROOM AT THE TOP

"I can't say anything," said the ecstatic Signoret. "I wanted to be dignified and all that, but I can't." Writing in *The New Yorker*, Pauline Kael called Signoret "magnificent as the older woman." She added, "Her sensuality is contrasted with the virginal shallowness of [the other woman]."

The moody and seductive Signoret projected a heady sensuality and became the sex symbol of the 1950s in such films as *La Ronde* (1950) and *The Crucible* (1957). Married to French superstar—and male sex symbol—Yves Montand in 1951, she became part of the French intellectual elite and held "sophisticated" ideas about sexuality that allowed for her husband's affair with Marilyn Monroe; they remained married until Signoret's death.

Laurence Harvey with Simone Signoret

The 1960s and '70s saw Signoret in more mature roles, including *Ship of Fools* (1965, nom.) and *Madame Rosa* (1977). Her successful autobiography, *Nostalgia Isn't What It Used to Be*, was published in 1978.

BEST OF 1959
Best Picture: *Ben-Hur*
Best Director: William Wyler, *Ben-Hur*
Best Actor: Charlton Heston, *Ben-Hur*
Best Actress: Simone Signoret, *Room at the Top*
Best Supporting Actor: Hugh Griffith, *Ben-Hur*
Best Supporting Actress: Shelley Winters, *The Diary of Anne Frank*
Honorary Award: Buster Keaton

FIRSTS
- Just a year after *Gigi*'s record-breaking nine Oscars, *Ben-Hur* topped it with eleven.
- This was the first "solo host" show since 1952, when Danny Kaye did the honors.
- Simone Signoret's Oscar was the first for a Best Actress in a foreign-made film.
- Three of the year's biggest hits, *Some Like It Hot*, *Anatomy of a Murder*, and *Room at the Top* were alternately banned in Atlanta, Chicago, and all of Kansas.
- Otto Preminger was the first to break the blacklist by hiring Dalton Trumbo to write the screenplay for *Anatomy of a Murder* under his real name.

ROLE REVERSALS
- William Wyler's first choice for *Ben-Hur* was Marlon Brando. His second was Rock Hudson.
- Stephen Boyd won the role of Messala only after Kirk Douglas took a pass. Douglas was extremely disappointed not to have been offered the lead.
- When Lana Turner stormed off the set of *Anatomy of a Murder* after a long-standing row with Otto Preminger, he replaced her with an unknown, Lee Remick.

SINS OF OMISSION
Picture: *Some Like It Hot*
Actress: Marilyn Monroe, *Some Like It Hot*

ALWAYS A BRIDESMAID, NEVER A BRIDE
Thelma Ritter threw her annual "Come Over and Watch Me Lose Again" party. *Pillow Talk* was her fifth failed shot at Best Supporting Actress.

UNMENTIONABLES
- Theater owners were barred from selling snacks for the run of *Ben-Hur*. The producers considered its release an artistic event, too important to be denigratd by popcorn and candy.
- William Wyler had been an "extras director" on Cecil B. DeMille's original *Ben-Hur* production in 1926.
- Uncredited screenwriter Gore Vidal suggested an unspoken homosexual history between Boyd's Messala and Heston's Ben-Hur. Boyd liked the idea, as did Wyler, who warned him "not to tell Chuck Heston what it's all about or he'd fall apart."
- "Marilyn Monroe has breasts like granite and a brain like Swiss cheese," said Billy Wilder.
- There was open warfare on the set of *Suddenly, Last Summer* between Katharine Hepburn and Joseph L. Mankiewicz. A screaming tirade culminated in his broadside "We will resume shooting, Miss Hepburn, when the Directors Guild card I ordered for you arrives from Hollywood!"
- When the costume fitter on *Some Like It Hot* commented to Marilyn Monroe that Tony Curtis had a more shapely rear than hers, she unbuttoned her blouse and said, "He hasn't got breasts like these."

BEST SUPPORTING ACTOR
HUGH GRIFFITH (1912–1980)
BEN-HUR

"Hugh Griffith as the sheik who puts Ben-Hur into the chariot race, stands out in a very large cast," wrote Bosley Crowther in the *New York Times.*

The signature bushy-eyed character actor got a late start on the screen in 1939 after working as a bank clerk. After one feature film, Griffith was drafted into Her Majesty's Army and returned to the screen in 1947, working both in the U.S. and in England for the next thirty years. He played both big bullies and sensitive souls in such films as *Kind Hearts and Coronets* (1949), *The Beggar's Opera* (1953), *Exodus* (1960), *Tom Jones* (1963), *Oliver!* (1968), and *Start the Revolution Without Me* (1970).

BEST SUPPORTING ACTRESS
SHELLEY WINTERS (B. 1922)
THE DIARY OF ANNE FRANK

"I've waited fifteen years for this," said the jubilant Winters. She also sobbed, saying, "It takes a lot of people to put this in your hand."

Winters gained thirty pounds in order to play the whiny family friend who hides from the Nazis with the Franks. According to Bosley Crowther, "Winters is one of those actresses whose—mistaken—reputation precedes her." A favorite on the talk-show circuit, Winters began to seem like a lightweight—which she was anything but.

Her first big break came when she landed a co-starring role with Ronald Colman in *A Double Life* (1947). Following that, she was often cast as vulnerable types in such films as *The Great Gatsby* (1949) and *A Place in the Sun* (1951), but she also played the sexpot in *Frenchie* (1950) and other films. Her range is notably demonstrated in, among other films, *The Night of the Hunter* (1955), *Lolita* (1962), and *Alfie* (1966).

HONORARY AWARD
BUSTER KEATON (1895–1966)

Keaton accepted his award to a standing ovation. Making his film debut with Fatty Arbuckle in *The Butcher Boy* (1917), the two teamed up for nearly twenty two-reelers and features in which Keaton's inventive gags and surreal imagery had already become his signature.

Buster soon began making features, including *Sherlock, Jr.* (1924), *The Navigator* (1924), *The General* (1927), and *Steamboat Bill, Jr.* (1928). His career took a bad turn when his contract was sold to MGM in 1928 and his first films under this new aegis, including *The Cameraman* (1928), were compromised by the studio.

Though he continued to make his audience laugh, Keaton's private world was in turmoil. He spent a lifetime fighting a losing battle with alcoholism. With this downturn in his career, Keaton began to drink again and was reduced to playing bit parts in the 1930s and '40s.

AWARD NOMINATIONS 1959

PICTURE
ANATOMY OF A MURDER, Preminger, Columbia, Otto Preminger.
BEN-HUR, MGM, Sam Zimbalist.
THE DIARY OF ANNE FRANK, 20th Century-Fox, George Stevens.
THE NUN'S STORY, Warner Bros, Henry Blanke.
ROOM AT THE TOP, Romulus, Continental (British), John and James Woolf.

ACTOR
LAURENCE HARVEY in *Room at the Top*, Romulus, Continental (British).
CHARLTON HESTON in *Ben-Hur*, MGM.
JACK LEMMON in *Some Like It Hot*, Ashton, Mirisch, UA.
PAUL MUNI in *The Last Angry Man*, Kohlmar, Columbia.
JAMES STEWART in *Anatomy of a Murder*, Preminger, Columbia.

ACTRESS
DORIS DAY in *Pillow Talk*, Arwin, U-I.
AUDREY HEPBURN in *The Nun's Story*, Warner Bros.
KATHARINE HEPBURN in *Suddenly, Last Summer*, Horizon, Columbia.
SIMONE SIGNORET in *Room at the Top*, Romulus, Continental (British).
ELIZABETH TAYLOR in *Suddenly, Last Summer*, Horizon, Columbia.

SUPPORTING ACTOR
HUGH GRIFFITH in *Ben-Hur*, MGM.
ARTHUR O'CONNELL in *Anatomy of a Murder*, Preminger, Columbia.
GEORGE C. SCOTT in *Anatomy of a Murder*, Preminger, Columbia.
ROBERT VAUGHN in *The Young Philadelphians*, Warner Bros.
ED WYNN in *The Diary of Anne Frank*, 20th Century-Fox.

SUPPORTING ACTRESS
HERMIONE BADDELEY in *Room at the Top*, Romulus, Continental (British).
SUSAN KOHNER in *Imitation of Life*, U-I.
JUANITA MOORE in *Imitation of Life*, U-I.
THELMA RITTER in *Pillow Talk*, Arwin, U-I.
SHELLEY WINTERS in *The Diary of Anne Frank*, 20th Century-Fox.

DIRECTION
JACK CLAYTON for *Room at the Top*, Romulus, Continental (British).
GEORGE STEVENS for *The Diary of Anne Frank*, 20th Century-Fox.
BILLY WILDER for *Some Like It Hot*, Mirisch-Ashton, UA.
WILLIAM WYLER for *Ben-Hur*, MGM.
FRED ZINNEMANN for *The Nun's Story*, Warner Bros.

WRITING: BASED ON MATERIAL FROM ANOTHER MEDIUM
ANATOMY OF A MURDER, Preminger, Columbia. Wendell Mayes.
BEN-HUR, MGM. Karl Tunberg.
THE NUN'S STORY, Warner Bros. Robert Anderson.
ROOM AT THE TOP, Romulus. Continental (British). Neil Paterson.
SOME LIKE IT HOT, Mirisch-Ashton, UA. Billy Wilder and I.A.L. Diamond.

WRITING: ORIGINAL STORY AND SCREENPLAY
THE 400 BLOWS, Zenith International (French). Francois Truffaut and Marcel Moussy.

NORTH BY NORTHWEST, Hitchcock, MGM. Ernest Lehman.
OPERATION PETTICOAT, Granart, U-I. Paul King, Joseph Stone, Stanley Shapiro and Maurice Richlin.
PILLOW TALK, Arwin, U-I. Russell Rouse, Clarence Greene, Stanley Shapiro and Maurice Richlin.
WILD STRAWBERRIES, Janus Films (Swedish). Ingmar Bergman.

CINEMATOGRAPHY
B/W
ANATOMY OF A MURDER, Preminger, Columbia. Sam Leavitt.
CAREER, Wallis, Paramount. Joseph LaShelle.
THE DIARY OF ANNE FRANK, 20th Century-Fox. William C. Mellor.
SOME LIKE IT HOT, Mirisch-Ashton, UA. Charles Lang, Jr.
THE YOUNG PHILADELPHIANS, Warner Bros. Harry Stradling, Sr.

Color
BEN-HUR, MGM. Robert L. Surtees.
THE BIG FISHERMAN, Rowland V. Lee, Buena Vista. Lee Garmes.
THE FIVE PENNIES, Dena, Paramount. Daniel L. Papp.
THE NUN'S STORY, Warner Bros. Franz Planer.
PORGY AND BESS, Goldwyn, Columbia. Leon Shamroy.

ART DIRECTION—SET DECORATION
B/W
CAREER, Wallis, Paramount. Hal Pereira and Walter Tyler; Sam Comer and Arthur Krams.
THE DIARY OF ANNE FRANK, 20th Century-Fox. Lyle R. Wheeler and George W. Davis; Walter M. Scott and Stuart A. Reiss.
THE LAST ANGRY MAN, Kohlmar, Columbia. Carl Anderson; William Kiernan.
SOME LIKE IT HOT, Mirisch-Ashton, UA. Ted Haworth; Edward G. Boyle.
SUDDENLY, LAST SUMMER, Horizon, Columbia. Oliver Messel and William Kellner; Scot Slimon.

Color
BEN-HUR, MGM. William A. Horning and Edward Carfagno; Hugh Hunt.
THE BIG FISHERMAN, Rowland V. Lee, Buena Vista. John DeCuir; Julia Heron.
JOURNEY TO THE CENTER OF THE EARTH, 20th Century-Fox. Lyle R. Wheeler, Franz Bachelin and Herman A. Blumenthal; Walter M. Scott and Joseph Kish.
NORTH BY NORTHWEST, Hitchcock, MGM. William A. Horning, Robert Boyle and Merrill Pye; Henry Grace and Frank McKelvy.
PILLOW TALK, Arwin, U-I. Richard H. Riedel; Russell A. Gausman and Ruby R. Levitt.

COSTUME DESIGN
B/W
CAREER, Wallis, Paramount. Edith Head.
THE DIARY OF ANNE FRANK, 20th Century-Fox. Charles LeMaire and Mary Willis.
THE GAZEBO, Avon, MGM. Helen Rose.
SOME LIKE IT HOT, Mirisch-Ashton, UA. Orry-Kelly.
THE YOUNG PHILADELPHIANS, Warner Bros. Howard Shoup.

Color
BEN-HUR, MGM. Elizabeth Haffenden.
THE BEST OF EVERYTHING, Wald, 20th Century Fox. Adele Palmer.
THE BIG FISHERMAN, Rowland V. Lee, Buena Vista, Renie.
THE FIVE PENNIES, Dena, Paramount. Edith Head.
PORGY AND BESS, Goldwyn, Columbia. Irene Sharaff.

SOUND
BEN-HUR, MGM. Metro-Goldwyn-Mayer Studio Sound Department; Franklin E. Milton, sound director.
JOURNEY TO THE CENTER OF THE EARTH, 20th Century-Fox. 20th Century-Fox Studio Sound Department; Carl Faulkner, sound director.
LIBEL!, MGM. (British). Metro-Goldwyn-Mayer London Sound Department; A.W. Watkins, sound director.

THE NUN'S STORY, Warner Bros. Warner Bros. Studio Sound Department; George R. Groves, sound director.
PORGY AND BESS, Goldwyn, Columbia. Samuel Goldwyn Studio Sound Department; Gordon E. Sawyer, sound director; and Todd-AO Sound Dept., Fred Hunes, sound director.

FILM EDITING
ANATOMY OF A MURDER, Preminger, Columbia. Louis R. Loeffler.
BEN-HUR, MGM. Ralph E. Winters and John D. Dunning.
NORTH BY NORTHWEST, Hitchcock, MGM. George Tomasini.
THE NUN'S STORY, Warner Bros. Walter Thompson.
ON THE BEACH, Kramer, UA. Frederic Knudtson.

SPECIAL EFFECTS
BEN-HUR, MGM. A. Arnold Gillespie, Robert MacDonald and Milo Lory.
JOURNEY TO THE CENTER OF THE EARTH, 20th Century-Fox. L.B. Abbott, James B. Gordon and Carl Faulkner.

SONG
THE BEST OF EVERYTHING (*The Best of Everything*, Wald, 20th Century-Fox); Music by Alfred Newman. Lyrics by Sammy Cahn.
THE FIVE PENNIES (*The Five Pennies*, Dena, Paramount); Music and Lyrics by Sylvia Fine.
THE HANGING TREE (*The Hanging Tree*, Warner Bros.); Music by Jerry Livingston. Lyrics by Mack David.
HIGH HOPES (*A Hole in the Head*, Sincap, UA); Music by James Van Heusen. Lyrics by Sammy Cahn.
STRANGE ARE THE WAYS OF LOVE (*The Young Land*, C.V. Whitney, Columbia); Music by Dimitri Tiomkin. Lyrics by Ned Washington.

SCORING: DRAMA/COMEDY
BEN-HUR, MGM. Miklos Rozsa.
THE DIARY OF ANNE FRANK, 20th Century-Fox. Alfred Newman.
THE NUN'S STORY, Warner Bros. Franz Waxman.
ON THE BEACH, Kramer, UA. Ernest Gold.
PILLOW TALK, Arvin, U-I. Frank DeVol.

SCORING: MUSICAL
THE FIVE PENNIES, Dena, Paramount. Leith Stevens.
LI'L ABNER, Panama and Frank, Paramount. Nelson Riddle and Joseph J. Lilley.
PORGY AND BESS, Goldwyn, Columbia. Andre Previn and Ken Darby.
SAY ONE FOR ME, Crosby, 20th Century-Fox. Lionel Newman.
SLEEPING BEAUTY, Disney, Buena Vista. George Bruns.

SHORT SUBJECTS: CARTOONS
MEXICALI SHMOES, Warner Bros. John W. Burton, producer.
MOONBIRD, Storyboard-Harrison. John Hubley, producer.
NOAH'S ARK, Disney, Buena Vista. Walt Disney, producer.
THE VIOLINIST, Pintoff Prods., Kingsley International. Ernest Pintoff, producer.

SHORT SUBJECTS: LIVE ACTION
BETWEEN THE TIDES, British Transport Films, Schoenfeld Films (British). Ian Ferguson, producer.
THE GOLDEN FISH, Les Requins Associes, Columbia (French). Jacques-Yves Cousteau, producer.
MYSTERIES OF THE DEEP, Disney, Buena Vista. Walt Disney, producer.
THE RUNNING, JUMPING AND STANDING-STILL FILM, Lion International, Kingsley-Union Films (British). Peter Sellers, producer.
SKYSCRAPER, Burstyn Film Enterprises. Shirley Clarke, Willard Van Dyke and Irving Jacoby, producers.

DOCUMENTARY: SHORT SUBJECTS
DONALD IN MATHMAGIC LAND, Disney, Buena Vista. Walt Disney, producer.

FROM GENERATION TO GENERATION, Cullen Assocs., Maternity Center Assoc. Edward F. Cullen, producer.
GLASS, Netherlands Government, George K. Arthur-Go Pictures (The Netherlands). Bert Haanstra, producer.

DOCUMENTARY: FEATURES
THE RACE FOR SPACE, Wolper, Inc. David L. Wolper, producer.
SERENGETI SHALL NOT DIE, Okapia-Film Prods., Transocean Film (German). Bernhard Grzimek, producer.

FOREIGN LANGUAGE FILM
BLACK ORPHEUS (France).
THE BRIDGE (Germany).
THE GREAT WAR (Italy).
PAW (Denmark).
THE VILLAGE ON THE RIVER (The Netherlands).

HONORARY AND OTHER AWARDS
TO LEE DE FOREST for his pioneering inventions which brought sound to the motion picture.
TO BUSTER KEATON for his unique talents which brought immortal comedies to the screen.

JEAN HERSHOLT HUMANITARIAN AWARD
TO BOB HOPE

SCIENTIFIC OR TECHNICAL
CLASS I
None.

CLASS II
DOUGLAS G. SHEARER of MGM., Inc., and ROBERT E. GOTTSCHALK and JOHN R. MOORE of Panavision, Inc., for the development of a system of producing and exhibiting wide film motion pictures known as Camera 65.
WADSWORTH E. POHL, WILLIAM EVANS, WERNER HOPF, S.E. HOWSE, THOMAS P. DIXON, STANFORD RESEARCH INSTITUTE and TECHNICOLOR CORP. for the design and development of the Technicolor electronic printing timer.
WADSWORTH E. POHL, JACK ALFORD, HENRY IMUS, JOSEPH SCHMIT, PAUL FASSNACHT, AL LOFQUIST and TECHNICOLOR CORP. for the development and practical application of equipment for wet printing.
DR. HOWARD S. COLEMAN, DR. A. FRANCIS TURNER, HAROLD H. SCHROEDER, JAMES R. BENFORD and HAROLD E. ROSENBERGER of the Bausch & Lomb Optical Co. for the design and development of the Balcold projection mirror.
ROBERT P. GUTTERMAN of General Kinetics, Inc., and the LIPSNER-SMITH CORP. for the design and development of the CF-2 Ultra-sonic Film Cleaner.

CLASS III
UB IWERKS of Walt Disney Prods.
E.L. STONES, GLEN ROBINSON, WINFIELD HUBBARD and LUTHER NEWMAN of the MGM. Studio Construction Dept.

1960s

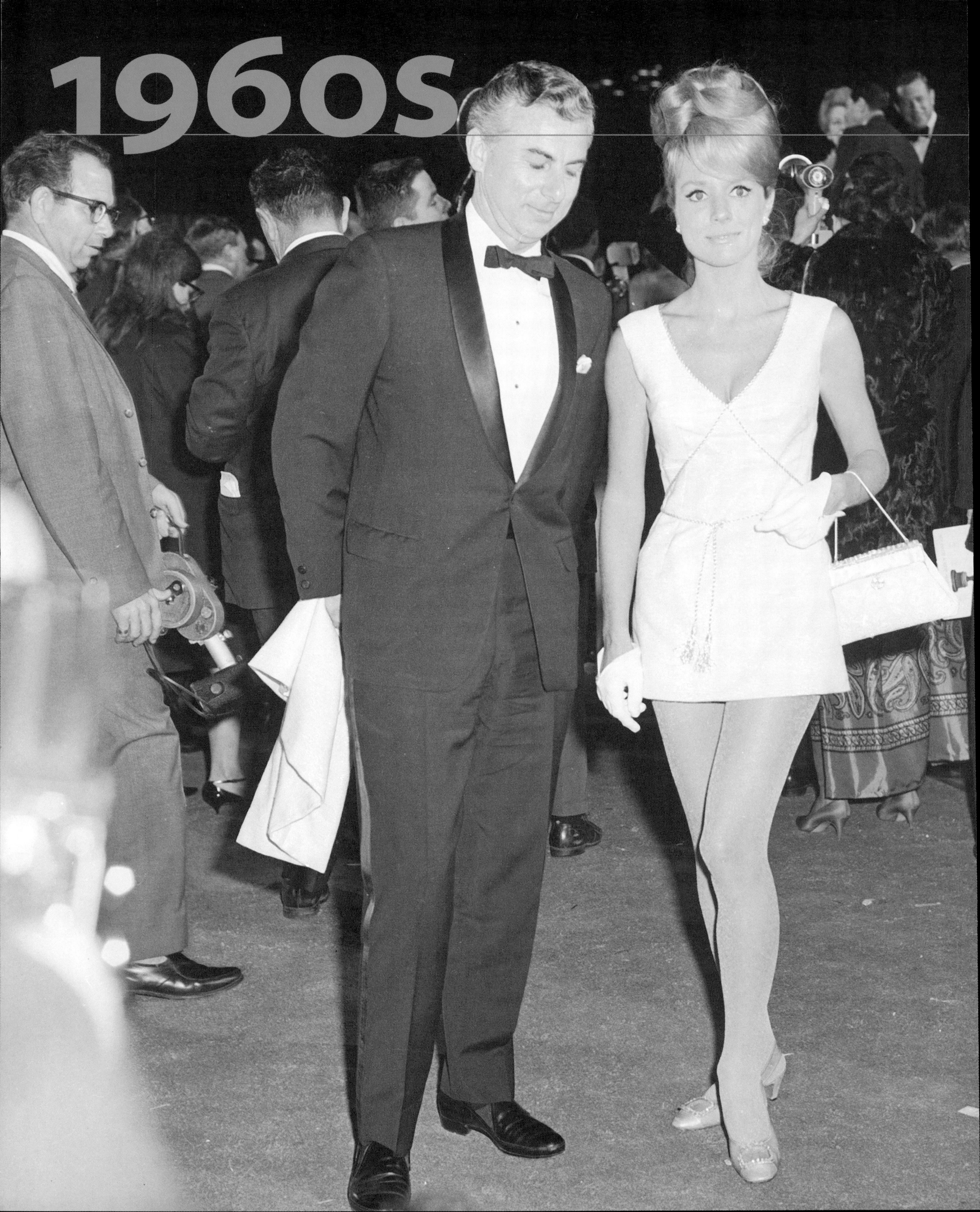

BELOW: Janet Leigh is radiant in this belted, fitted dress that brilliantly bridges the gap between 50s and 60s fashion. (1960)

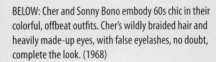

BELOW: Cher and Sonny Bono embody 60s chic in their colorful, offbeat outfits. Cher's wildly braided hair and heavily made-up eyes, with false eyelashes, no doubt, complete the look. (1968)

ABOVE: Bold, geometric patterns were a staple of 60s fashion, as modeled here by Rosemary Stack, with husband Robert. (1967)

ABOVE: In a colorful embroidered dress with matching bolero jacket, Ann-Margret draws on flower power for this playful look, here seen with her husband, Roger Smith. (1965)

THE LOOK OF THE DECADE

THE CULTURAL REVOLUTION OF THE 1960s changed everything, from the way people thought about the world to the way they dressed. Youth reigned supreme, and elegant, grown-up fashions gave way to clothes that allowed for more movement and freedom of expression. Never before had fashion taken such an extreme turn, with hemlines rising to never-before-seen heights, reflecting the sexual liberation of the decade. Hollywood, of course, presented the world with some of the most extreme takes on the new trends.

OPPOSITE: Swedish actress Inger Stevens models one of the most iconic inventions of the 60s—the miniskirt. (1967)

1960

"When Elizabeth Taylor got a hole in her throat, I canceled my plane."

—*Shirley MacLaine*

THE THROAT VOTE

CEREMONY: April 17, 1961
Santa Monica Civic Auditorium,
Santa Monica
HOST: Bob Hope

America's most famous "home wrecker" flew in directly from a London hospital, where she'd miraculously survived a near-fatal bout of pneumonia. Her swooping cleavage revealed a jagged tracheotomy scar to prove it. The million-dollar girl, the queen of the tabloid scandals, was due to collect an Oscar for a film she'd publicly despised. As she climbed out of her limo, with new husband Eddie Fisher in tow, a record mob of fans descended on the violet-eyed one for a glimpse, a touch, a memory they'd never forget. Elizabeth Taylor had come home at last. So assured of her win were the other nominees that none of them save Greer Garson bothered to attend. Taylor finally settled into her seat and the lesser show, the Awards themselves, began.

Taylor wasn't the only controversy of the evening. John Wayne's brazen Oscar campaign for his so-so epic *The Alamo* inspired one of its stars, Chill Wills, to launch a shameless hype circus of his own. He managed to get on the ballot, but in doing so made a laughingstock of himself. Bob Hope couldn't resist. "The members of the Academy will decide which actor and actress has the best press agent," he said. "I didn't know there was any campaigning until I saw my maid wearing a Chill Wills button."

There was a buzz of concern following Jimmy Stewart's tearful acceptance of an Honorary Oscar on behalf of his friend Gary Cooper. On with the show as Connie Francis warbled the naughty "Never on Sunday" and Shirley Jones picked up her Oscar for playing a hooker in *Elmer Gantry*. She was among four contenders who portrayed women of easy virtue. Conversely, Greer Garson played Eleanor Roosevelt, and the last of the mini-Oscar winners, child star Hayley Mills, was honored for *Pollyanna*. Hardly the perfect segue for the big moment, as Yul Brynner announced Taylor's win for her portrayal of a call girl in *Butterfield 8*. Startlingly gorgeous and with breathy grace, Taylor thanked everyone, floated offstage, and promptly fainted.

**BEST PICTURE/BEST DIRECTOR
BILLY WILDER (1906–2002)
*THE APARTMENT***

Upon accepting his Oscar (his third of the evening), Wilder acknowledged, "It would only be proper to cut it in half and give it to the two most valuable players—Jack Lemmon and Shirley MacLaine." The film, about a lonely insurance clerk who obliges selfish bosses by lending them the key to his apartment for their illicit assignations, was lauded by the critics. "A gleeful, tender, and even sentimental film," wrote Bosley Crowther. *Variety* exclaimed, "High in comedy and wide in warmth."

The Apartment was an all-Wilder production: he co-wrote the screenplay and produced and directed the movie. "Wilder keeps the action and the dialogue tumbling with wit," wrote Vincent Canby in the *New York Times*, "His direction is ingenious and sure, sparkled by brilliant little touches and kept to a tight sardonic line."

After Wilder had picked up his Screen Directors Guild Award, he joked, "Keep praying, cousins! We hope Oscar will say the right thing this year." Oscar heard Wilder's prayers.

(For more on Wilder, see 1945.)

Shirley MacLaine, Jack Lemmon

The envelope, please…

BEST ACTOR
BURT LANCASTER (1913–1994)
ELMER GANTRY

"I want to thank all who expressed this kind of confidence by voting for me. And right now I'm so happy I want to thank all the members who didn't vote for me." Lancaster's portrayal of Gantry, an evangelical con man, was hailed by the *New York Times* as "one of his fattest roles and one to which he gives outstanding service…a smirking, leering lecher." Pauline Kael of *The New Yorker* enthused, "You can't take your eyes off him."

With his menacing grin and muscularity, Lancaster was cast as a tough guy almost from the start. His debut in *The Killers* (1946) led to *Sorry, Wrong Number* (1948), *From Here to Eternity* (1953, nom.), *The Rose Tattoo* (1955), *Gunfight at the O.K. Corral* (1957), *Sweet Smell of Success* (1957), *Separate Tables* (1958), and *The Unforgiven* (1960). In the 1960s Lancaster landed seminal roles in important films, including *Judgment at Nuremberg* (1961), *Birdman of Alcatraz* (1962, nom.), Luchino Visconti's *The Leopard* (1963), and *Seven Days in May* (1964). One of his later films, Louis Malle's *Atlantic City*, proved to be one of his best performances (1980, nom.).

BEST ACTRESS
ELIZABETH TAYLOR (B. 1932)
BUTTERFIELD 8

Entertainment Tonight critic Leonard Maltin referred to the beautiful Taylor as "a much better actress than she has generally been given credit for." Her tempestuous personal life often overshadowed her film work. Early classics, *Lassie Come Home* (1943), *National Velvet* (1944), *Jane Eyre* (1944), and *Little Women* (1949) led to her golden age in *A Place in the Sun* (1951), *Giant* (1956), *Cat on a Hot Tin Roof* (1958, nom.), and *Suddenly, Last Summer* (1959, nom.).

Famous for her several marriages, Taylor's most scandalous was to Richard Burton, with whom she appeared, most notably, in *Cleopatra* (1963) and *Who's Afraid of Virginia Woolf?* (1966, Oscar). Her later credits include *Reflections in a Golden Eye* (1967), *The Only Game in Town* (1970), and *Night Watch* (1974). Overweight and ailing, Taylor appeared in *A Little Night Music* (1977) and *The Mirror Crack'd* (1980). Best known now for her line of fragrances and charity work for AIDS, Taylor has admitted, "My acting career is behind me." (For more on Taylor, see 1966.)

BEST OF 1960
Best Picture: *The Apartment*
Best Director: Billy Wilder, *The Apartment*
Best Actor: Burt Lancaster, *Elmer Gantry*
Best Actress: Elizabeth Taylor, *Butterfield 8*
Best Supporting Actor: Peter Ustinov, *Spartacus*
Best Supporting Actress: Shirley Jones, *Elmer Gantry*
Honorary Award: Gary Cooper, Stan Laurel, Hayley Mills (outstanding juvenile performance)

FIRSTS
• The Award ceremonies moved to the Santa Monica Civic Auditorium.
• The show moved from NBC to ABC.

ROLE REVERSALS
Billy Wilder wanted to direct *Schindler's List* (1993), but Steven Spielberg preferred to do it himself. Wilder has been quoted saying that it would have become his most personal film.

ALWAYS A BRIDESMAID, NEVER A BRIDE
Psycho gave Hitchcock his fifth Oscar nomination.

UNMENTIONABLES
• Billy Wilder once told Billy Bob Thornton that he was too ugly to be an actor and that he should write a screenplay for himself in which he could exploit his less-than-perfect features. Thornton later received an Oscar for his *Sling Blade* (1996) screenplay.

• Elizabeth Taylor has suffered more than her share of serious illnesses and near-death experiences. She was hospitalized and discharged and later rushed back after suffering a brain seizure (February 20, 1997). She underwent successful surgery to remove a benign brain tumor (February 26, 1997). While filming *Cleopatra*, the actress became seriously ill and was actually pronounced dead before being revived. It is thought that Liz's victory was the only example of an Oscar earned because of an imminent death.

• Elizabeth Taylor has also enjoyed great riches. She owns some of the world's most magnificent jewelry, including the Krupp diamond and the LaPeregina pearl.

• First-time director Richard Brooks was having a bad day: he was not nominated for *Elmer Gantry*, and the next thing he saw was a truck crashing into his sports car.

BEST SUPPORTING ACTOR
PETER USTINOV (B. 1921)
SPARTACUS

"Having been educated in English schools, we were taught for at least fifteen years of our lives how to lose gracefully, and I've been preparing myself for that all afternoon…Now I don't know quite what to say," Ustinov said in his acceptance speech.

Pauline Kael, however, didn't hesitate. Writing in *The New Yorker*, she said, "Peter Ustinov is superb as a slave dealer who, along with his groveling sycophancy and his merchant's greed, has his resentments."

The British-born character actor had been something of a boy wonder, first performing at 17, selling his first screenplay at 24, and directing his first film at 25. Nominated for his supporting role in *Quo Vadis* (1951), he won his second Oscar for *Topkapi* (1964). His film oeuvre was peopled by petulant, pompous character roles in such films as *Billy Budd* (1962), Agatha Christie's *Death on the Nile* (1978), *Evil Under the Sun* (1982), *Appointment with Death* (1988), and *Lorenzo's Oil* (1992). Ustinov published his memoir, *Dear Me*, in 1977, with more to come. (For more on Ustinov, see 1964.)

BEST SUPPORTING ACTRESS
SHIRLEY JONES (B. 1934)
ELMER GANTRY

"After I won the Oscar, my salary doubled, my friends tripled, my children became more popular at school, my butcher made a pass at me, and my maid hit me up for a raise."

In *Gantry* Shirley Jones plays a blond, brash prostitute who is violated by the menacing minister Lancaster. According to critic Leonard Maltin, "[Jones] stunned critics and moviegoers alike with her deft performance as a prostitute…it was the high point in her screen career." Jones debuted with starring roles in two classic Rodgers and Hammerstein musicals, *Oklahoma!* (1955) and *Carousel* (1956), followed by the nonmusical *April Love* (1957). She shone in *The Music Man* (1962), but tried to change her image by going brunette in *Bedtime Story* (1964), *The Secret of My Success* (1965), *Beyond the Poseidon Adventure* (1979), and *Tank* (1984), all of which were box-office bombs.

She is—much to her chagrin—remembered most for her TV mom on *The Partridge Family* (1970–1974). Jones is married to onetime actor and latter-day talent agent Marty Ingels.

HONORARY AWARD
GARY COOPER

Director William Wyler presented the honorary award, calling Cooper "the kind of American who's loved in the four corners of the earth." Cooper was gravely ill and wasn't available to accept the award; instead, Jimmy Stewart rose to the occasion. Stewart wept as he gave his speech, prompting the audience to speculate about Cooper's health. Cooper died a month after receiving the award.

"He had magic," eulogized director Fred Zinnemann. Cooper collected three Academy Awards and two nominations during his prolific career. His iconic presence was so universal that, just months before the actor died, even Pope John XXIII sent him a goodwill message.

(For more on Cooper, see 1941 and 1952.)

PICTURE

THE ALAMO, Batjac, UA, John Wayne.
THE APARTMENT, Mirisch, UA, Billy Wilder.
ELMER GANTRY, Lancaster-Brooks, U.A, Bernard Smith.
SONS AND LOVERS, Wald, 20th Century-Fox, Jerry Wald.
THE SUNDOWNERS, Warner Bros, Fred Zinnemann.

ACTOR

TREVOR HOWARD in *Sons and Lovers*, Wald, 20th Century-Fox.
BURT LANCASTER in *Elmer Gantry*, Lancaster-Brooks, UA.
JACK LEMMON in *The Apartment*, Mirisch, UA.
LAURENCE OLIVIER in *The Entertainer*, Woodfall, Continental (British).
SPENCER TRACY in *Inherit the Wind*, Kramer, UA.

ACTRESS

GREER GARSON in *Sunrise at Campobello*, Schary, Warner Bros.
DEBORAH KERR in *The Sundowners*, Warner Bros.
SHIRLEY MacLAINE in *The Apartment*, Mirisch, UA.
MELINA MERCOURI in *Never on Sunday*, Melinafilm, Lopert Pictures (Greek).
ELIZABETH TAYLOR in *Butterfield 8*, Afton-Linebrook, MGM.

SUPPORTING ACTOR

PETER FALK in *Murder, Inc.*, 20th Century-Fox.
JACK KRUSCHEN in *The Apartment*, Mirisch, UA.
SAL MINEO in *Exodus*, Preminger, UA.
PETER USTINOV in *Spartacus*, Bryna, U-I.
CHILL WILLS in *The Alamo*, Batjac, UA.

SUPPORTING ACTRESS

GLYNIS JOHNS in *The Sundowners*, Warner Bros.
SHIRLEY JONES in *Elmer Gantry*, Lancaster-Brooks, UA.
SHIRLEY KNIGHT in *The Dark at the Top of the Stairs*, Warner Bros.
JANET LEIGH in *Psycho*, Hitchcock, Paramount.
MARY URE in *Sons and Lovers*, Wald, 20th Century-Fox.

DIRECTION

JACK CARDIFF for *Sons and Lovers*, Wald, 20th Century-Fox.
JULES DASSIN for *Never on Sunday*, Melinafilm, Lopert Pictures (Greek).
ALFRED HITCHCOCK for *Psycho*, Hitchcock, Paramount.
BILLY WILDER for *The Apartment*, Mirisch, UA.
FRED ZINNEMANN for *The Sundowners*, Warner Bros.

WRITING: BASED ON MATERIAL FROM ANOTHER MEDIUM

ELMER GANTRY, Lancaster-Brooks, UA. Richard Brooks.
INHERIT THE WIND, Kramer, UA. Nedrick Young and Harold Jacob Smith.
SONS AND LOVERS, Wald, 20th Century-Fox. Gavin Lambert and T.E.B. Clarke.
THE SUNDOWNERS, Warner Bros. Isobel Lennart.
TUNES OF GLORY, Lopert Pictures (British). James Kennaway.

WRITING: ORIGINAL STORY AND SCREENPLAY

THE ANGRY SILENCE, Beaver Films, Lion International (British). Richard Gregson, Michael Craig and Bryan Forbes.
THE APARTMENT, Mirisch, UA. Billy Wilder and I.A.L. Diamond.
THE FACTS OF LIFE, Panama and Frank, UA. Norman Panama and Melvin Frank.
HIROSHIMA, MON AMOUR, Zenith International (French-Japanese). Marguerite Duras.
NEVER ON SUNDAY, Melinafilm, Lopert Pictures (Greek). Jules Dassin.

CINEMATOGRAPHY

B/W
THE APARTMENT, Mirisch, UA. Joseph LaShelle.
THE FACTS OF LIFE, Panama and Frank, UA. Charles B. Lang, Jr.
INHERIT THE WIND, Kramer, UA. Ernest Laszlo.
PSYCHO, Hitchcock, Paramount. John L. Russell.
SONS AND LOVERS, Wald, 20th Century-Fox. Freddie Francis.

Color
THE ALAMO, Batjac, UA. William H. Clothier.
BUTTERFIELD 8, Afton-Linebrook, MGM. Joseph Ruttenberg and Charles Harten.
EXODUS, Preminger, UA. Sam Leavitt.
PEPE, Sidney, Columbia. Joe MacDonald.
SPARTACUS, Bryna, U-I. Russell Metty.

ART DIRECTION—SET DECORATION

B/W
THE APARTMENT, Mirisch, UA. Alexander Trauner; Edward G. Boyle.
THE FACTS OF LIFE, Panama and Frank, UA. Joseph McMillan Johnson and Kenneth A. Reid; Ross Dowd.
PSYCHO, Hitchcock, Paramount. Joseph Hurley and Robert Clatworthy; George Milo.
SONS AND LOVERS, Wald, 20th Century-Fox. Tom Morahan; Lionel Couch.
VISIT TO A SMALL PLANET, Walls, Paramount. Hal Pereira and Walter Tyler; Sam Comer and Arthur Krams.

Color
CIMARRON, MGM. George W. Davis and Addison Hehr; Henry Grace, Hugh Hunt and Otto Siegel.
IT STARTED IN NAPLES, Paramount. Hal Pereira and Roland Anderson: Sam Comer and Arrigo Breschi.
PEPE, Sidney, Columbia. Ted Haworth; William Kiernan.
SPARTACUS, Bryna, U-I. Alexander Golitzen and Eric Orbom; Russell A. Gausman and Julia Heron.
SUNRISE AT CAMPOBELLO, Schary, Warner Bros. Edward Carrere; George James Hopkins.

COSTUME DESIGN

B/W
THE FACTS OF LIFE, Panama and Frank Prod., UA. Edith Head and Edward Stevenson.
NEVER ON SUNDAY, Melinafilm, Lopert Pictures (Greek). Denny Vachlioti.
THE RISE AND FALL OF LEGS DIAMOND, United States Prod., Warner Bros. Howard Shoup.
SEVEN THIEVES, 20th Century-Fox. Bill Thomas.
THE VIRGIN SPRING, Janus Films (Swedish). Marik Vos.

Color
CAN-CAN, Suffolk-Cummings, 20th Century-Fox. Irene Sharaff.
MIDNIGHT LACE, Hunter-Arwin, U-I. Irene.
PEPE, Sidney, Columbia. Edith Head.
SPARTACUS, Bryna, U-I. Valies and Bill Thomas.
SUNRISE AT CAMPOBELLO, Schary, Warner Bros. Marjorie Best.

SOUND

THE ALAMO. Batjac, UA. Samuel Goldwyn Studio Sound Department, Gordon K. Sawyer, sound director; and Todd-AO Sound Department, Fred Ilynes, sound director.
THE APARTMENT, Mirisch, UA. Samuel Goldwyn Studio Sound Department; Gordon K. Sawyer, sound director.
CIMARRON, MGM. Metro-Goldwyn-Mayer Studio Sound Department; Franklin K. Milton, sound director.
PEPE, Sidney, Columbia. Columbia Studio Sound Department; Charles Rice, sound director.
SUNRISE AT CAMPOBELLO, Schary, Warner Bros. Warner Bros. Studio Sound Department; George R. Groves, sound director.

FILM EDITING

THE ALAMO, Batjac, UA. Stuart Gilmore.
THE APARTMENT, Mirisch, UA. Daniel Mandell.
INHERIT THE WIND, Kramer, UA. Frederic Knudtson.
PEPE, Sidney, Columbia. Viola Lawrence and Al Clark.
SPARTACUS, Bryna, U-I. Robert Lawrence.

SPECIAL EFFECTS

THE LAST VOYAGE, Stone, MGM. AJ. Lohman.
THE TIME MACHINE, Pal, MGM. Gene Warren and Tim Baar.

SONG

THE FACTS OF LIFE (*The Facts of Life*, Panama and Frank, UA); Music and Lyrics by Johnny Mercer.
FARAWAY PART OF TOWN (*Pope*, Sidney, Columbia); Music by Andre Previn. Lyrics by Dory Langdon.
THE GREEN LEAVES OF SUMMER (*The Alamo*, Batjac, UA); Music by Dimitri Tiomkin. Lyrics by Paul Francis Webster.
NEVER ON SUNDAY (*Never on Sunday*, Melinafilm, Lopert Pictures; Greek); Music and Lyrics by Manos Hadjidakis
THE SECOND TIME AROUND (*High Time*, Crosby, 20th Century-Fox); Music by James Van Heusen. Lyrics by Sammy Cahn.

SCORING: DRAMA/COMEDY

THE ALAMO, Batjac, UA. Dimitri Tiomkin.
ELMER GANTRY, Lancaster-Brooks, UA. Andre Previn.
EXODUS, Preminger, UA. Ernest Cold.
THE MAGNIFICENT SEVEN, Mirisch-Alpha, UA. Elmer Bernstein.
SPARTACUS, Bryna, U-I. Alex North.

SCORING: MUSICAL

BELLS ARE RINGING, Freed, MGM. Andre Previn.
CAN-CAN, Suffolk-Cummings, 20th Century-Fox. Nelson Riddle.
LET'S MAKE LOVE, Wald, 20th Century-Fox. Lionel Newman and Earle H. Hagen.
PEPE, Sidney, Columbia. Johnny Green.
SONG WITHOUT END, Goetz, Columbia. Morris Stoloff and Harry Sukman.

SHORT SUBJECTS: CARTOONS

GOLIATH II, Disney, Buena Vista, Walt Disney, producer.
HIGH NOTE, Warner Bros.
MOUSE AND GARDEN, Warner Bros.
MUNRO, Rembrandt Films, Film Representations. William L. Snyder, producer.
A PLACE IN THE SUN, George K. Arthur-Go Pictures (Czechoslovakian). Frantisek Vystrecil, producer.

SHORT SUBJECTS: LIVE ACTION

THE CREATION OF WOMAN, Trident Films, Sterling World Distributors (Indian). Charles F. Schwep and Ismail Merchant, producers.
DAY OF THE PAINTER, Little Movies, Kingsley-Union Films. Ezra H. Baker, producer.
ISLANDS OF THE SEA, Disney, Buena Vista. Walt Disney, producer.
A SPORT IS BORN, Paramount. Leslie Winik, producer.

DOCUMENTARY: SHORT SUBJECTS

BEYOND SILENCE, U.S. Information Agency.
A CITY CALLED COPENHAGEN, Statens Filmcentral, Danish Film Office (Danish).
GEORGE GROSZ' INTERREGNUM, Educational Communications Corp. Charles and Altina Carey, producers.
GIUSEPPINA, Schoenfeld Films (British). James Hill, producer.
UNIVERSE, National Film Board of Canada, Schoenfeld Films (Canadian). Cohn Low, producer.

DOCUMENTARY: FEATURES

THE HORSE WITH THE FLYING TAIL, Disney, Buena Vista. Larry Lansburgh, producer.
REBEL IN PARADISE, Tiare Co. Robert D. Fraser, producer.

FOREIGN LANGUAGE FILM

KAPO (Italy).
LA VERITE (France).
MACARIO (Mexico).
THE NINTH CIRCLE (Yugoslavia).
THE VIRGIN SPRING (Sweden).

HONORARY AND OTHER AWARDS

TO GARY COOPER for his many memorable screen performances and the international recognition he, as an individual, has gained for the motion picture industry.
TO STAN LAUREL for his creative pioneering in the field of cinema comedy.
TO HAYLEY MILLS for *Pollyanna*, the most outstanding juvenile performance during 1960.

JEAN HERSHOLT HUMANITARIAN AWARD

TO SOL LESSER

SCIENTIFIC OR TECHNICAL

CLASS I
None.

CLASS II
AMPEX PROFESSIONAL PRODUCTS CO. for the production of a well-engineered multi-purpose sound system combining high standards of quality with convenience of control, dependable operation and simplified emergency provisions.

CLASS III
ARTHUR HOLCOMB, PETRO VLAHOS and COLUMBIA STUDIO CAMERA DEPT.;
ANTHONY PAGLIA and the 20TH CENTURY-FOX STUDIO MECHANICAL EFFECTS DEPT.;
CARL BADGE, ROBERT GRUBEL and EDWARD REICHARD of Consolidated Film Industries.

1961

The Sharks and the Jets came in for a landing at the Oscars to find almost nobody to greet them. Brief illness knocked out Audrey Hepburn and Judy Garland. Jackie Gleason was afraid of planes and, as Hope joked about his weight, "Vice versa." George C. Scott pulled the first of his highly publicized no-shows, claiming he would not take part in the "backstabbing parade." Sophia Loren, who made the leap from sexpot to dramatic actress, wasn't about to let millions of viewers witness her anxiety and remained in Rome.

All those empty seats left plenty of room for unknowns to steal the spotlight. Among them was curvaceous dynamo Ann-Margret, who brought down the house with her sex-kitten rendition of nominated song "Bachelor in Paradise." Her future in film was assured that night. Not so Stan Berman, a Brooklyn cabbie who marched onstage to interrupt presenters Shelley Winters and TV star Vince Edwards. "Ladies and Gentlemen, I'm the world's greatest gate crasher, and I just came here to present Bob Hope with his 1938 trophy," he announced. Winters laughingly promised the homemade Oscar would be passed on. After Berman was led off the stage, Hope deadpanned, "Who needs Price Waterhouse? All we need is a doorman."

What the show really needed that night was more show. There was a hint of drama as first time ever dual directors Jerome Robbins and Robert Wise accepted their Awards for *West Side Story*. Their bitter personal feud resulted in neither man thanking the other. Accepting for Loren was Greer Garson, who stood in the winners' circle looking almost as shell-shocked as Maximilian Schell, Rita Moreno, and George Chakiris. All three were virtually unknown before Oscar time. Despite the dark good looks of Schell and Chakiris, reigning male sex symbol Paul Newman got his first serious competition for the title from another overnight sensation. He'd escorted Natalie Wood to the Awards and had only a single movie to his credit, *Splendor in the Grass*. His name was Warren.

BROADWAY GOES HOLLYWOOD

CEREMONY: April 9, 1962
RKO Pantages Theatre, Hollywood
HOST: Bob Hope

BEST PICTURE/BEST DIRECTOR
ROBERT WISE (B. 1914) AND
JEROME ROBBINS (1918–1998)
WEST SIDE STORY

The *New York Times*'s critic Bosley Crowther called the film "nothing short of a cinema masterpiece…superbly and appropriately achieved. The strong blend of drama, dance, and music folds into a rich artistic whole."

Robert Wise had been around the block a few times by the time he made *West Side Story*, with a career dating back to 1939. He began by working as an editor and reached his crowning moment with Orson Welles's landmark *Citizen Kane* (1941, nom.). Wise's debut as director came with *The Curse of the Cat People* (1944), which he co-directed. He followed that success with *The Body Snatcher* (1945), *Blood on the Moon* (1948), and his renowned *The Set-Up* (1949).

The 1950s showed Wise to be a great filmmaker who brought intelligence and skill to his wide-ranging oeuvre, which included *The Day the Earth Stood Still* (1951), *Executive Suite* (1954), *Somebody Up There Likes Me* (1956), and *I Want to Live!* (1958, nom.), which gave Susan Hayward an Oscar. After his brilliant success on *West Side Story*, Wise got the gold again for *The Sound of Music* (1965), which cemented his reputation as a maker of "big" films. Those big films all but disappeared in the 1960s, and Wise's last two films, *Audrey Rose* (1977) and *Two People* (1986), were more intimately told stories.

Jerome Robbins, the ballet choreographer and co-ballet master at the New York City Ballet, won five Tonys for his Broadway hits *The King and I, Peter Pan, Gypsy, Fiddler on the Roof*, and *West Side Story*. In addition to winning Best Director, Robbins was awarded a special Oscar for choreography in *West Side Story*.

Robbins was subjected to the McCarthy witch hunts of the 1950s when he was called before the House Un-American Activities Committee. He admitted to having belonged to the American Communist Party's Theatrical Transient Group between 1943 and 1947, and also named eight colleagues as members. During the making of *West Side Story* tensions between the two artists led to Robbins's departure before completion of the film.

The envelope, please...

BEST ACTOR
MAXIMILIAN SCHELL (B. 1930)
JUDGMENT AT NUREMBERG

"This honors not only me but the cast and that great old man who has been nominated for the eighth time now, Spencer Tracy." Schell plays the defense lawyer for the Nazis "masterfully," wrote Bosley Crowther in the *New York Times.* "An absolutely gladiatorial job of projecting the skill, the passion and the courage of a strong, intensive man."

The darkly handsome matinee idol fought hard for more serious roles, including his American debut, *The Young Lions* (1958). Schell stepped behind the camera to produce *Topkapi* (1964), then wrote, produced, and directed *First Love* (1970) and *The Pedestrian* (1973, nom. Best Foreign Language Film).

Schell became ubiquitous in films dealing with World War II: *The Man in the Glass Booth* (1975, nom.), *A Bridge Too Far* (1977), and *Julia* (1977, nom.). In his fascinating documentary *Marlene Dietrich* (1978)—from which Dietrich dropped out at the last minute—Schell made up for the loss by using her audio interviews to create a unique portrait. Reflecting on his Oscar win, he remarked, "I had to re-start after that. I couldn't go up. I had to go down in order to scale the mountain again."

BEST ACTRESS
SOPHIA LOREN (B. 1934)
TWO WOMEN

The critics agreed that in *Two Women* Loren had broken free of the sexpot mold. Pauline Kael, as did others, viewed Loren's appearance in the film as "…deglamorized…an Anna Magnani role."

Loren, like many of her characters, was born into poverty. She dreamed of becoming an actress, and after she came in second in a beauty contest judge and future husband Carlo Ponti immediately sensed her potential. A small part in Federico Fellini's *Variety Lights* (1950) launched her career. At 19 Loren was already a leading lady. She won international stardom following her American debut in *Houseboat* (1958). She returned to Italy to make *Two Women* and followed with *El Cid*

(1961), *Boccaccio '70* (1962), *Marriage Italian Style* (1964, nom.), *Arabesque* (1966), and *A Countess from Hong Kong* (1967).

Loren's autobiography, *Sophia—Living and Loving: Her Own Story* (1980), became a TV movie in which she played herself. In 1991 she received a second, special Academy Award for lifetime achievement.

BEST OF 1961
Best Picture: *West Side Story*
Best Director: Robert Wise and Jerome Robbins, *West Side Story*
Best Actor: Maximilian Schell, *Judgment at Nuremberg*
Best Actress: Sophia Loren, *Two Women*
Best Supporting Actor: George Chakiris, *West Side Story*
Best Supporting Actress: Rita Moreno, *West Side Story*

FIRSTS
- Rita Moreno is listed in *The Guinness Book of World Records* for being the first performer to win an Oscar, a Tony, an Emmy, and a Grammy.
- Two co-directors won the Best Director Award.

SINS OF OMISSION
Pictures: *Breakfast at Tiffany's, The Misfits*
Actress: Natalie Wood, *West Side Story*

UNMENTIONABLES
- Sophia Loren had her marriage annulled to save Ponti from bigamy charges in Italy. In 1982 Loren served eighteen days in prison in Italy for tax evasion.
- Sophia Loren didn't get on with Marlon Brando during the shooting of *A Countess from Hong Kong* (1967), especially after the day they were doing a love scene and he commented, "Did you know you have hairs up your nostrils?"
- When Louella Parsons learned that Montgomery Clift and Judy Garland had been nominated for supporting roles in *Judgment at Nuremberg*, she said it was like "a bank president reducing himself to the title of bookkeeper in order to get a coffee break."
- Talking to Louella Parsons, Rita Moreno said of her co-star and off-screen boyfriend George Chakiris, "George is very soft-spoken and quiet, and his skin isn't nearly as dark in real life as it looks on the motion-picture screen."
- George C. Scott asked the Academy to remove his name for nominee as Best Supporting Actor for *The Hustler,* saying, "[It's] like a weird beauty or personality contest. I take the position that actors shouldn't be forced to out-advertise and out-stab each other." The Academy judges responded by saying they were not nominating George C. Scott but, rather, his performance.
- Carrying on the tradition of George C. Scott, Warren Beatty notified the Academy that he did not wish to be nominated for Best Supporting Actor (preferring Best Actor instead), but the Academy said it was too late. Fortunately, he didn't win.
- *Time* magazine praised *The Guns of Navarone* as "the most enjoyable consignment of baloney in months."
- Most of the singing voices in *West Side Story* were dubbed.

BEST SUPPORTING ACTOR
GEORGE CHAKIRIS (B. 1934)
WEST SIDE STORY

After being smothered with kisses by Moreno, who was sitting by his side, the visibly surprised Chakiris took the stage and whispered, "Wow, I don't believe it," to Shirley Jones. "I don't think I'll talk too much," he added. "I'll just say thank you, thank you very much."

Chakiris played the role of leader of the rival gang and the proud, heroic brother to Natalie Wood's Maria in *West Side Story*. He made his film debut at the age of 12, singing in the chorus of *Song of Love* (1947). He continued as actor/dancer, appearing in such musicals as *Gentlemen Prefer Blondes* (1953, he is one of the ballet dancers escorting Marilyn Monroe for the song "Diamonds Are a Girl's Best Friend"), *White Christmas*, *There's No Business Like Show Business*, and *Brigadoon* (all 1954). His first dramatic role came with *Under Fire* (1957).

Since making *West Side Story*, Chakiris has starred in a number of films, including *Diamond Head* (1962), *Les Demoiselles de Rochefort*, *The Big Cube* (1969), and *Jekyll and Hyde…Together Again* (1982).

Rita Moreno (center)

BEST SUPPORTING ACTRESS
RITA MORENO (B. 1931)
WEST SIDE STORY

Moreno danced up to the podium and shouted, "I can't believe it! Good Lord! I leave you with that!" Of Moreno's performance, critic Leonard Maltin would later write, "This charismatic little firecracker exploded onto movie screens as the tempestuous Anita, delivering a dynamic performance. It was the shining moment in an extensive screen career."

After *West Side Story* Moreno was almost exclusively seen in Latin roles, though she was reputedly offended by such prejudicial typecasting. She debuted on film at the age of 14 in *A Medal for Benny* (1945). After playing the fiery Latin throughout the 1950s, she did get more dimensional roles in such films as *Marlowe* (1969), *Carnal Knowledge* (1971), and *The Ritz* (1976).

Moreno was also an adjunct cast member of the 1970s landmark children's TV show *The Electric Company*. She won a Tony for *The Ritz*, and two Emmys for her appearances in *The Muppet Show* (1977) and *The Rockford Files* (1978). The versatile Moreno also released a successful exercise video. She is often seen on TV, most notably as a social worker nun in HBO's *OZ*.

A W A R D N O M I N A T I O N S 1 9 6 1

PICTURE
FANNY, Mansfield, Warner Bros, Joshua Logan.
THE GUNS OF NAVARONE, Foreman, Columbia, Carl Foreman.
THE HUSTLER, Rossen, 20th Century-Fox, Robert Rossen.
JUDGMENT AT NUREMBERG, Kramer, UA, Stanley Kramer.
WEST SIDE STORY, Mirisch-B&P Enterprises, UA, Robert Wise.

ACTOR
CHARLES BOYER in *Fanny*, Mansfield, Warner Bros.
PAUL NEWMAN in *The Hustler*, Rossen, 20th Century-Fox.
MAXIMILIAN SCHELL in *Judgment at Nuremberg*, Kramer, UA.
SPENCER TRACY in *Judgment at Nuremberg*, Kramer, UA.
STUART WHITMAN in *The Mark*, Buchman-Stross, Continental (British).

ACTRESS
AUDREY HEPBURN in *Breakfast at Tiffany's*, Jurow-Shepherd, Paramount.
PIPER LAURIE in *The Hustler*, Rossen, 20th Century-Fox.
SOPHIA LOREN in *Two Women*, Ponti, Embassy (Italian).
GERALDINE PAGE in *Summer and Smoke*, Wallis, Paramount.
NATALIE WOOD in *Splendor in the Grass*, Kazan, Warner Bros.

SUPPORTING ACTOR
GEORGE CHAKIRIS in *West Side Story*, Mirisch-B&P Enterprises, UA.
MONTGOMERY CLIFT in *Judgment at Nuremberg*, Kramer, UA.
PETER FALK in *Pocketful of Miracles*, Franton, UA.
JACKIE GLEASON in *The Hustler*, Rossen, 20th Century-Fox.
GEORGE C. SCOTT in *The Hustler*, Rossen, 20th Century-Fox.

SUPPORTING ACTRESS
FAY BAINTER in *The Children's Hour*, Mirisch-Worldwide, UA.
JUDY GARLAND in *Judgment at Nuremberg*, Kramer, UA.
LOTTE LENYA in *The Roman Spring of Mrs. Stone*, Seven Arts, Warner Bros.
UNA MERKEL in *Summer and Smoke*, Wallis, Paramount.
RITA MORENO in Mirisch-B&P Enterprises, UA.

DIRECTION
FEDERICO FELLINI for *La Dolce Vita*, Astor Pictures (Italian).
STANLEY KRAMER for *Judgment at Nuremberg*, Kramer, UA.
ROBERT ROSSEN for *The Hustler*, Rossen, 20th Century-Fox.
J. LEE THOMPSON for *The Guns of Navarone*, Foreman, Columbia.
ROBERT WISE and JEROME ROBBINS for *West Side Story*, Mirisch-Seven Arts, UA.

WRITING: BASED ON MATERIAL FROM ANOTHER MEDIUM
BREAKFAST AT TIFFANY'S, Jurow-Shepherd, Paramount, George Axelrod.
THE GUNS OF NAVARONE, Foreman, Columbia. Carl Foreman.
THE HUSTLER, Rossen, 20th Century-Fox. Sidney Carroll and Robert Rossen.

JUDGMENT AT NUREMBERG, Kramer, UA. Abby Mann.
WEST SIDE STORY, Mirisch-Seven Arts, UA. Ernest Lehman.

WRITING: ORIGINAL STORY AND SCREENPLAY
BALLAD OF A SOLDIER, Kingsley International-M.J.P. (Russian). Valentin Yoshov and Grigori Chukhrai.
GENERAL DELLA ROVERE, Continental Distributing (Italian). Sergio Amidei, Diego Febbri and Indro Montanelli.
LA DOLCE VITA, Astor Pictures (Italian). Federico Fellini, Tulio Pirelli, Ennio Flaiano and Brunello Rondi.
LOVER COME BACK, Shapiro-Arwin, U-I. Stanley Shapiro and Paul Henning.
SPLENDOR IN THE GRASS, Kazan, Warner Bros. William Inge.

CINEMATOGRAPHY
B/W
THE ABSENT MINDED PROFESSOR, Disney, Buena Vista. Edward Colman.
THE CHILDREN'S HOUR, Mirisch-Worldwide, UA. Franz F. Planer.
THE HUSTLER, Rossen, 20th Century-Fox. Eugen Shuftan.
JUDGMENT AT NUREMBERG, Kramer, UA. Ernest Laszlo.
ONE, TWO, THREE, Mirisch-Pyramid, UA. Daniel L. Fapp.

Color
FANNY, Logan, Warner Bros. Jack Cardiff.
FLOWER DRUM SONG, Hunter, U-I, Russell Metty.
A MAJORITY OF ONE, Warner Bros. Harry Stradling, Sr.
ONE-EYED JACKS, Pennebaker, Paramount. Charles Lang, Jr.
WEST SIDE STORY, Mirisch-Seven Arts, UA. Daniel L. Fapp.

ART DIRECTION—SET DECORATION
B/W
THE ABSENT-MINDED PROFESSOR, Disney, Buena Vista. Carroll Clark; Emile Kuri and Hal Gausman.
THE CHILDREN'S HOUR, Mirisch-Worldwide, UA. Fernando Carrere; Edward G. Boyle.
THE HUSTLER, Rossen, 20th Century-Fox. Harry Horner; Gene Callahan.
JUDGMENT AT NUREMBERG, Kramer, UA. Rudolph Sternad; George Milo.
LA DOLCE VITA, Astor Pictures (Italian); Piero Gherardi.

Color
BREAKFAST AT TIFFANY'S, Jurow-Shepherd, Paramount. Hal Pereira and Roland Anderson; Sam Comer and Ray Moyer.
EL CID, Bronston, Allied Artists. Veniero Colasanti and John Moore.
FLOWER DRUM SONG, Hunter, U-I. Alexander Golitzen and Joseph Wright; Howard Bristol.
SUMMER AND SMOKE, Wallis, Paramount. Hal Pereira and Walter Tyler; Sam Comer and Arthur Krams.
WEST SIDE STORY, Mirisch-Seven Arts, UA. Boris Leven; Victor A. Gangelin.

COSTUME DESIGN
B/W
THE CHILDREN'S HOUR, Mirisch-Worldwide, UA. Dorothy Jeakins.
CLAUDELLE INGLISH, Warner Bros. Howard Shoup.
JUDGMENT AT NUREMBERG, Kramer, UA. Jean Louis.
LA DOLCE VITA, Astor Pictures (Italian). Piero Gherardi.
YOJIMBO, Toho Company (Japanese). Yoshiro Muraki.

Color
BABES IN TOYLAND, Disney, Buena Vista. Bill Thomas.
BACK STREET, Hunter, U-I. Jean Louis.
FLOWER DRUM SONG, Hunter, U-I. Irene Sharaff.
POCKETFUL OF MIRACLES, Franton, UA. Edith Head and Walter Plunkett.
WEST SIDE STORY, Mirisch-Seven Arts, UA. Irene Sharaff.

SOUND
THE CHILDREN'S HOUR, Mirisch-Worldwide, UA. Samuel Goldwyn Studio Sound Dept.; Gordon E. Sawyer, sound director.
FLOWER DRUM SONG, Hunter, U-I. Revue Studio Sound Dept.; Waldon O. Watson, sound director.
THE GUNS OF NAVARONE, Foreman, Columbia. Shepperton Studio Sound Dept.; John Cox, sound director.
THE PARENT TRAP, Disney, Buena Vista. Walt Disney Studio Sound Dept.; Robert O. Cook, sound director.
WEST SIDE STORY, Mirisch-Seven Arts, UA. Todd-AO Sound Dept., Fred Hynes, sound director, and Samuel Goldwyn Studio Sound Dept.; Gordon E. Sawyer, sound director.

FILM EDITING
FANNY, Logan, Warner Bros. William H. Reynolds.
THE GUNS OF NAVARONE, Foreman, Columbia. Alan Osbiston.
JUDGMENT AT NUREMBERG, Kramer, UA. Frederic Knudtson.
THE PARENT TRAP, Disney, Buena Vista. Philip W. Anderson.
WEST SIDE STORY, Mirisch-Seven Arts, UA. Thomas Stanford.

SPECIAL EFFECTS
THE ABSENT-MINDED PROFESSOR, Disney, Buena Vista. Robert A. Mattey and Eustace Lycett.
THE GUNS OF NAVARONE, Foreman, Columbia. Bill Warrington and Vivian C. Greenham.

SONG
BACHELOR IN PARADISE (*Bachelor in Paradise*, Richmond, MGM); Music by Henry Mancini. Lyrics by Mack David.
LOVE THEME FROM EL CID (*El Cid*, Bronston, Allied Artists); Music by Miklos Rozsa. Lyrics by Paul Francis Webster.
MOON RIVER (*Breakfast at Tiffany's*, Jurow Shepherd, Paramount); Music by Henry Mancini. Lyrics by Johnny Mercer.
POCKETFUL OF MIRACLES (*Pocketful of Miracles*, Franton, UA); Music by James Van Heusen. Lyrics by Sammy Cahn.
TOWN WITHOUT PITY (*Town Without Pity*, Mirisch-Gloria, UA); Music by Dimitri Tiomkin. Lyrics by Ned Washington.

SCORING: DRAMA/COMEDY
BREAKFAST AT TIFFANY'S, Jurow-Shepherd, Paramount. Henry Mancini.
EL CID, Bronston, Allied Artists. Miklos Rozsa.
FANNY, Logan, Warner Bros. Morris Stoloff and Harry Sukman.
THE GUNS OF NAVARONE, Foreman, Columbia. Dimitri Tiomkin.
SUMMER AND SMOKE, Wallis, Paramount. Elmer Bernstein.

SCORING: MUSICAL
BABES IN TOYLAND, Disney, Buena Vista. George Bruns.
FLOWER DRUM, Hunter, U-I. Alfred Newman and Ken Darby.
KHOVANSHCHINA, Artkino (Russian), Dimitri Shostakovich.
PARIS BLUES, Pennebaker, UA. Duke Ellington.
WEST SIDE STORY, Mirisch-Seven Arts, UA. Saul Chaplin, Johnny Green, Sid Ramin and Irwin Kostal.

SHORT SUBJECTS: CARTOONS
AQUAMANIA, Disney, Buena Vista. Walt Disney, producer.
BEEP PREPARED, Warner Bros. Chuck Jones, producer.
ERSATZ (The Substitute), Zagreb Film, Hens-Lion International Corp.
NELLY'S FOLLY, Warner Bros. Chuck Jones, producer.
PIED PIPER OF GUADALUPE, Warner Bros. Friz Freleng, producer.

SHORT SUBJECTS: LIVE ACTION
BALLON VOLE (Play Ball), Cine Documents, Kingsley International.
THE FACE OF JESUS, Jennings-Stern, Inc. Dr. John D. Jennings, producer.
ROOFTOPS OF NEW YORK, McCarty-Rush-Gaffney. Columbia.

SEAWARDS THE GREAT SHIPS, Templar Film Studios, Schoenfeld Films.
VERY NICE, VERY NICE, National Film Board of Canada, Kingsley International.

DOCUMENTARY: SHORT SUBJECTS
BREAKING THE LANGUAGE BARRIER, U.S. Air Force.
CRADLE OF GENIUS, Plough Prods., Lesser Films (Irish). Jim O'Connor and Tom Hayes, producers.
KAHL, Dido-Film-GmbH., AEG-Filmdienst (German).
L'UOMO IN GRIGIO (The Man In Gray), (Italian). Benedetto Benedetti, producer.
PROJECT HOPE, Klaeger Films. Frank P. Bibas, producer.

DOCUMENTARY: FEATURES
LA GRANDE OLIMPIADE (Olympic Games 1960), Cineriz (Italian).
LE CIEL ET LA BOUE (Sky Above And Mud Beneath), Rank Films (French). Arthur Cohn and Rene Lafuite, producers.

FOREIGN LANGUAGE FILM
HARRY AND THE BUTLER, (Denmark).
IMMORTAL LOVE, (Japan).
THE IMPORTANT MAN, (Mexico).
PLACIDO, (Spain).
THROUGH A GLASS DARKLY, (Sweden).

HONORARY AND OTHER AWARDS
TO WILLIAM L. HENDRICKS for his outstanding patriotic service in the conception, writing and production of the Marine Corps film, *A Force in Readiness*, which has brought honor to the Academy and the motion picture industry.
TO FRED L. METZLER for his dedication and outstanding service to the Academy of Motion Picture Arts and Sciences.
TO JEROME ROBBINS for his brilliant achievements in the art of choreography on film.

IRVING G. THALBERG MEMORIAL AWARD
TO STANLEY KRAMER

JEAN HERSHOLT HUMANITARIAN AWARD
TO GEORGE SEATON

SCIENTIFIC OR TECHNICAL
CLASS I
None.
CLASS II
SYLVANIA ELECTRIC PRODUCTS, INC., for the development of a hand held high-power photographic lighting unit known as the Sun Gun Professional.
JAMES DALE, S. WILSON, H.E. RICE, JOHN RUDE, LAURIE ATKIN, WADSWORTH E. POHL, H. PEASGOOD and TECHNICOLOR CORP. for a process of automatic selective printing.
20TH CENTURY-FOX RESEARCH DEPT., under the direction of E.I. SPONABLE and HERBERT H. BRAGG, and DELUXE LABORATORIES, INC., with the assistance of F.D. LESLIE, R.D. WHITMORE, A.A. ALDEN, ENDEL POOL and JAMES B. GORDON for a system of decompressing and recomposing CinemaScope pictures for conventional aspect ratios.
CLASS III
HURLETRON, INC., ELECTRIC EYE DIVISION;
WADSWORTH E. POHL and TECHNICOLOR CORP.

1962

A caravan of Hollywood beauties set the fashion trend with flowing white tunic gowns inspired by *Lawrence of Arabia*. Best Actress nominee Bette Davis was having none of that. She arrived in the same dowdy black dress with the same stuck zipper she'd worn the year before. Her archrival—on-screen and off—Joan Crawford caused a sensation in a silver-beaded Edith Head original and enough diamonds to briefly blind the horde of autograph hounds who encircled her.

THE CHIC OF ARABY

CEREMONY: April 8, 1963
**Santa Monica Civic Auditorium,
Santa Monica**
HOST: Frank Sinatra

Crawford wasn't nominated for anything, but she was determined to steal the spotlight from Davis. She campaigned relentlessly to accept the Oscar for any of the nominated actresses not present. Her big moment came when dark horse Anne Bancroft, who was appearing on Broadway, was announced as the winner. Crawford made a sweeping star's entrance and, after a brief speech, clutched the statuette as if it were her own. Davis seethed backstage in a cloud of cigarette smoke, later admitting that she was so sure she'd win she "almost dropped dead" from shock.

The evening's other big upset was Ed Begley, who beat heavy favorite Omar "the next Valentino" Shariff. The unprepossessing old veteran was so astonished that all he could think to say at the podium was "I'm not Ed Begley." Sinatra introduced Sophia Loren as "the best pizza maker in the world." She thanked the Academy for last year's Oscar before opening the envelope for Best Actor.

Gregory Peck, the first California-born actor to win, was greeted with thunderous applause. The night ended with producer Sam Spiegel's Best Picture Oscar. "There's no magic formula for making a film," he told the audience. Joan Crawford might have said the same for making an entrance. Hers was months in the planning and paid off handsomely. She got more press and camera time than all the winners combined.

**BEST PICTURE/BEST DIRECTOR
DAVID LEAN (1908–1991)
*LAWRENCE OF ARABIA***

"This limey is deeply touched and gratefully honored," said Lean upon accepting his Oscar. His leading man Peter O'Toole said, "You've never seen a man more in love with the desert." Pauline Kael of *The New Yorker* raved about the film, calling it "one of the most literate and tasteful and exciting of expensive spectacles." Roger Ebert called Lean's epic "a bold, mad act of genius," adding, "Lean [had the unique] ability to imagine what it would look like to see a speck appear on the horizon of the desert and slowly grow into a human being." But the film was not all praises and huzzahs. Although he loved the scenery, Bosley Crowther of the *New York Times* complained that the film "lacks the personal magnetism, the haunting strain of mysticism and poetry that…would be dominant in a film about Lawrence the mystic and the poet…It's just a huge, thundering camel-opera."

Lean was raised by devout Quakers, who thought films were sinful. As a young boarding-school student, Lean would play truant to go to the movie theater. He continued his love for films throughout his life, and admitted with only a touch of humor, "I hope the moneymen don't find out that I'd pay them to let me do this."

(For more on Lean, see 1957.)

The envelope, please...

Gregory Peck with Mary Badham

BEST ACTOR
GREGORY PECK (B. 1916)
TO KILL A MOCKINGBIRD

Given the stiff competition, Peck was glad he had carried his lucky rabbit's foot with him to the Awards despite his favored status. *Variety* wrote "It was no surprise [Peck] was the most popular choice of Hollywood's big night."

Peck's role as the ethical Alabama lawyer who defends a black man accused of raping a white woman was perfectly suited to him. The tall, handsome former med student was Hollywood's icon for the earnest, moral, and noble man. His debut in *Days of Glory* (1944) led to his first nomination and his star-making role in *The Keys of the Kingdom* (1944). High-profile parts followed in Hitchcock's *Spellbound* (1945), *The Yearling* (1946,

nom.), *Duel in the Sun* (1946), *Gentleman's Agreement* (1947, nom.), *Twelve O'Clock High* (1949, nom.), *Roman Holiday* (1953), and *The Man in the Gray Flannel Suit* (1956).

Peck continued his long run of success with *Moby Dick* (1956), *The Guns of Navarone* (1961), and *Cape Fear* (1962). He has been chairman of the American Cancer Society and of the American Film Institute, and served as president of the Academy of Motion Picture Arts and Sciences from 1967 to 1970. In 1989 he received the American Film Institute's Life Achievement Award.

BEST ACTRESS
ANNE BANCROFT (B. 1931)
THE MIRACLE WORKER

Joan Crawford accepted on Bancroft's behalf and read Bancroft's prepared speech: "There are three reasons why I won this award—Fred Coe, Arthur Penn, and William Gibson. Thank you."

As Anne Sullivan, Bancroft played the teacher/companion of Helen Keller and was lauded by critics. "Ms. Bancroft's performance does bring to life and reveal a wondrous woman with great humor and passion...a display of physically powerful acting," Bosley Crowther wrote in the *New York Times*. Anne Bancroft created the role on Broadway and earned a Tony Award. Following her success in *The Miracle Worker*, Bancroft appeared in *The Pumpkin Eater* (1964), *7 Women* (1966), and as the iconographic Mrs. Robinson in *The Graduate* (1967, nom.).

Bancroft made several films in the 1970s for her producer/husband Mel Brooks, including *Silent Movie* (1976), *The Elephant Man* (1980), *To Be or Not to Be* (1983), and *84 Charing Cross Road* (1987). Among her other films are *The Turning Point* (1977) and *Agnes of God* (1985). Bancroft stepped behind the camera to write and direct *Fatso* (1980), which received mixed reviews.

BEST OF 1962
Best Picture: *Lawrence of Arabia*
Best Director: David Lean, *Lawrence of Arabia*
Best Actor: Gregory Peck, *To Kill a Mockingbird*
Best Actress: Anne Bancroft, *The Miracle Worker*
Best Supporting Actor: Ed Begley, *Sweet Bird of Youth*
Best Supporting Actress: Patty Duke, *The Miracle Worker*

FIRSTS
Sixteen-year-old Patty Duke became the youngest person to win an Oscar that was not a special award.

SINS OF OMISSION
Pictures: *The Manchurian Candidate, What Ever Happened to Baby Jane?, Sweet Bird of Youth, The Man Who Shot Liberty Valance*

UNMENTIONABLES
• According to *Time* magazine's Richard Schickel, Lean was so wounded by critic Pauline Kael's vicious attacks on his work, such as *Ryan's Daughter* (1970), that it kept him from directing another picture for fourteen years, until *A Passage to India* (1984).

• Gregory Peck's earliest movie memory is of being so scared by *The Phantom of the Opera* (1925) at age 9 that his grandmother allowed him to sleep in bed with her that night.

• Patty Duke has been diagnosed as being manic-depressive, and co-authored a book about the disorder, *A Brilliant Madness: Living with Manic-Depressive Illness*. She carried her good-luck charm—her pet chihuahua, named Bambi—with her to the Oscars. She hid him in a bowling bag during the ceremony.

• Ed Begley's agent almost missed the actor's unprecedented tribute to someone of his profession when his house was burglarized early on the day of the Oscars and he was left without a TV. Fortunately, the agent had tickets to the show.

• Bette Davis accused Joan Crawford of not giving up the statuette she had accepted for Anne Bancroft's Best Actress win for a whole year. The truth is that Crawford surrendered the award to its rightful owner one week later, when she went backstage after Bancroft's performance on Broadway in *Mother Courage*.

• "I wouldn't give you a dime for those two washed up b———s," said producer Jack Warner about Crawford and Davis in *What Ever Happened to Baby Jane?* Rumors abounded that the two stars were engaged in a violent feud on the set.

• Audrey Hepburn was crushed when she didn't receive an Oscar, telling *Variety*'s Army Archerd, "I have to be the first to win three! I was positive I would get it, and so was everyone in town."

BEST SUPPORTING ACTOR
ED BEGLEY (1901–1970)
SWEET BIRD OF YOUTH

Overwhelmed by his win, Begley took the podium and said, "I'm not Ed Begley." It was a surprise victory, given the competition: Omar Shariff.

In the film Begley plays a crooked political boss and the father of Shirley Knight, the innocent girlfriend of Paul Newman. Begley, the son of Irish immigrants, won his first film role in *Boomerang!* and immediately took supporting-player roles in a number of films, including *Sitting Pretty*, *Deep Waters* (both 1948), and *Lone Star* (1952). Growing into bigger roles, he starred in the TV play *Patterns* (1956) and the TV adaptation of *12 Angry Men* (1957). Following his success in *Sweet Bird*, Begley performed in *The Unsinkable Molly Brown* (1964) and the counterculture saga *Wild in the Streets* (1968). His son is actor Ed Begley Jr.

Patty Duke with Anne Bancroft

BEST SUPPORTING ACTRESS
PATTY DUKE (B. 1947)
THE MIRACLE WORKER

Choked with emotion, Duke clutched her Oscar close and whispered, "Bless you!" The youngest actress to win an Oscar at the time, she had originated the role of Helen Keller on Broadway. "Miss Duke, in those moments when she frantically pantomimes her bewilderment and desperate groping, is both gruesome and pitiable," Bosley Crowther wrote in the *New York Times*.

Ironically, Patty Duke would be best remembered for her TV comedy series *The Patty Duke Show* (1963–1966). Her screen career took a serious hit after she co-starred in the critically panned *Valley of the Dolls* (1967), and it was on TV that her real opportunities emerged. She appeared in the acclaimed telefeature *My Sweet Charlie* (1970), which won her the first of three Emmys; *Captains and the Kings* (1976); and a remake of *The Miracle Worker* (1979), in which she took the role of Anne Sullivan.

Duke's autobiography, *Call Me Anna* (1987), described her harrowing childhood; she co-produced and starred in a TV adaptation of the book in 1990. She was married to actor John Astin; their son Sean Astin is a successful actor.

A W A R D N O M I N A T I O N S 1 9 6 2

PICTURE
LAWRENCE OF ARABIA, Horizon-Spiegel-Lean, Columbia, Sam Spiegel.
THE LONGEST DAY, Zanuck, 20th Century-Fox, Darryl F. Zanuck.
THE MUSIC MAN, Warner Bros, Morton Da Costa.
MUTINY ON THE BOUNTY, Arcola, MGM, Aaron Rosenberg.
TO KILL A MOCKINGBIRD, Pakula-Mulligan-Brentwood, U-I, Alan J. Pakula.

ACTOR
BURT LANCASTER in *Bird Man of Alcatraz*, Hecht, UA.
JACK LEMMON in *Days of Wine and Roses*, Manulis-Jalem, Warner Bros.
MARCELLO MASTROIANNI in *Divorce—Italian Style*, Embassy (Italian).
PETER O'TOOLE in *Lawrence of Arabia*, Horizon-Spiegel-Lean, Columbia.
GREGORY PECK in *To Kill a Mockingbird*, Pakula-Mulligan-Brentwood, U-I.

ACTRESS
ANNE BANCROFT in *The Miracle Worker*, **Playfilms, UA.**
BETTE DAVIS in *What Ever Happened to Baby Jane?*, Seven Arts-Associates & Aldrich, Warner Bros.
KATHARINE HEPBURN in *Long Day's Journey Into Night*, Landau, Embassy.
GERALDINE PAGE in *Sweet Bird of Youth*, Roxbury, MGM.
LEE REMICK in *Days of Wine and Roses*, Manulis-Jalem, Warner Bros.

SUPPORTING ACTOR
ED BEGLEY in *Sweet Bird of Youth*, Roxbury, MGM.
VICTOR BUONO in *What Ever Happened to Baby Jane?*, Seven Arts-Associates & Aldrich, Warner Bros.
TELLY SAVALAS in *Bird Man of Alcatraz*, Hecht, UA.
OMAR SHARIFF in *Lawrence of Arabia*, Horizon-Spiegel-Lean, Columbia.
TERENCE STAMP in *Billy Budd*, Harvest, Allied Artists.

SUPPORTING ACTRESS
MARY BADHAM in *To Kill a Mockingbird*, Pakula-Mulligan-Brentwood, U-I.
PATTY DUKE in *The Miracle Worker*, Playfilms, UA.
SHIRLEY KNIGHT in *Sweet Bird of Youth*, Roxbury, MGM.
ANGELA LANSBURY in *The Manchurian Candidate*, M.C. Prod., UA.
THELMA RITTER in *Bird Man of Alcatraz*, Hecht, UA.

DIRECTION
PIETRO GERMI for *Divorce—Italian Style*, Embassy Pictures (Italian).
DAVID LEAN for *Lawrence of Arabia*, Horizon, Columbia.
ROBERT MULLIGAN for *To Kill A Mockingbird*, Pakula-Mulligan, U-I.
ARTHUR PENN for *The Miracle Worker*, Playfilms, UA.
FRANK PERRY for *David and Lisa*, Heller-Perry, Continental.

WRITING: BASED ON MATERIAL FROM ANOTHER MEDIUM
DAVID AND LISA, Heller-Perry, Continental. Eleanor Perry.
LAWRENCE OF ARABIA, Horizon, Columbia. Robert Bolt.
LOLITA, Seven Arts, MGM. Vladimir Nabokov.
THE MIRACLE WORKER, Playfilms, UA. William Gibson.
To KILL A MOCKINGBIRD, Pakula-Mulligan, U-I. Horton Foote.

WRITING: ORIGINAL STORY AND SCREENPLAY
DIVORCE—ITALIAN STYLE, Embassy Pictures (Italian). Ennio de Concini, Alfredo Giannetti and Pietro Germi.
FREUD, Huston, U-I. Charles Kaufman and Wolfgang Reinhardt.
LAST YEAR AT MARIENBAD, Astor Pictures (French). Alain Robbe-Grillet.
THAT TOUCH OF MINK, Granley-Arwin-Shapiro, U-I. Stanley Shapiro and Nate Monaster.
THROUGH A GLASS DARKLY, Janus Films (Swedish). Ingmar Bergman.

CINEMATOGRAPHY
B/W
BIRD MAN OF ALCATRAZ, Hecht, UA. Burnett Guffey.
THE LONGEST DAY, Zanuck, 20th Century-Fox. Jean Bourgoin and Walter Wottitz.
TO KILL A MOCKINGBIRD, Pakula-Mulligan, U-I. Russell Harlan.
TWO FOR THE SEESAW, Mirisch-Argyle-Talbot-Seven Arts, UA. Ted McCord.
WHAT EVER HAPPENED TO BABY JANE?, Seven Arts-Aldrich, Warner Bros. Ernest Haller.

Color
GYPSY, Warner Bros. Harry Stradling, Sr.
HATARI!, Hawks, Paramount. Russell Harlan.
LAWRENCE OF ARABIA, Horizon, Columbia. Fred A. Young.
MUTINY ON THE BOUNTY, Arcola, MGM. Robert L. Surtees.
THE WONDERFUL WORLD OF THE BROTHERS GRIMM, MGM. and Cinerama. Paul C. Vogel.

SONG
DAYS OF WINE AND ROSES (*Days of Wine and Roses*, Manulis-Jalem, Warner Bros.); Music by Henry Mancini. Lyrics by Johnny Mercer.
LOVE SONG FROM MUTINY ON THE BOUNTY (Follow Me) (*Mutiny on the Bounty*, Arcola, MGM.); Music by Bronislau Kaper. Lyrics by Paul Francis Webster.
SONG FROM TWO FOR THE SEESAW (Second Chance) (*Two for the Seesaw*, Mirisch-Argyle-Talbot-Seven Arts, UA); Music by Andre Previn. Lyrics by Dory Langdon.
TENDER IS THE NIGHT (*Tender Is the Night*, 20th Century-Fox); Music by Sammy Fain. Lyrics by Paul Francis Webster.
WALK ON THE WILD SIDE (*Walk on the Wild Side*, Feldman-Famous Artists, Columbia); Music by Elmer Bernstein. Lyrics by Mack David.

SCORING: SUBSTANTIALLY ORIGINAL
FREUD, Huston, U-I. Jerry Goldsmith.
LAWRENCE OF ARABIA, Horizon, Columbia. Maurice Jarre.
MUTINY ON THE BOUNTY, Arcola, MGM. Bronslau Kaper.
TARAS BULBA, Hecht, UA. Franz Waxman.
TO KILL A MOCKINGBIRD, Pakula-Mulligan, U-I. Elmer Bernstein.

SCORING: ADAPTATION OR TREATMENT
BILLY ROSE'S JUMBO, Euterpe-Arwin, MGM. George Stoll.
GIGOT, Seven Arts, 20th Century-Fox. Michel Magne.
GYPSY, Warner Bros. Frank Perkins.
THE MUSIC MAN, Warner Bros. Ray Heindorf.
THE WONDERFUL WORLD OF THE BROTHERS GRIMM, MGM. and Cinerama. Leigh Harline.

ART DIRECTION—SET DECORATION
B/W
DAYS OF WINE AND ROSES, Manulis-Jalem, Warner Bros. Joseph Wright; George James Hopkins.
THE LONGEST DAY, Zanuck, 20th Century-Fox. Ted Haworth, Leon Barsacq and Vincent Korda; Gabriel Bechir.
PERIOD OF ADJUSTMENT, Marten, MGM. George W. Davis and Edward Carfagno; Henry Grace and Dick Pefferle.
THE PIGEON THAT TOOK ROME, Llenroc, Paramount, Hal Pereira and Roland Anderson; Sam Comer and Frank R. McKelvy.
TO KILL A MOCKINGBIRD, Pakula-Mulligan, U-I. Alexander Golitzen and Henry Bumstead; Oliver Emert.

Color
LAWRENCE OF ARABIA, Horizon, Columbia. John Box and John Stoll; Dario Simoni.
THE MUSIC MAN, Warner Bros. Paul Groesse; George James Hopkins.
MUTINY ON THE BOUNTY, Arcola, MGM. George W. Davis and J. McMillan Johnson; Henry Grace and Hugh Hunt.
THAT TOUCH OF MINK, Granley-Arwin-Shapiro, U-I. Alexander Golitzen and Robert Clatworthy; George Milo.
THE WONDERFUL WORLD OF THE BROTHERS GRIMM, MGM. and Cinerama. George W. Davis and Edward Carfagno; Henry Grace and Dick Pefferle.

COSTUME DESIGN
B/W
DAYS OF WINE AND ROSES, Manulis-Jalem, Warner Bros. Don Feld.
THE MAN WHO SHOT LIBERTY VALANCE, Ford, Paramount. Edith Head.
THE MIRACLE WORKER, Playfilms, UA. Ruth Morley.
PHAEDRA, Dassin-Melinafilm, Lopert Pictures, Denny Vachiloti.
WHAT EVER HAPPENED TO BABY JANE?, Seven Arts-Aldrich, Warner Bros. Norma Koch.

Color
BON VOYAGE, Disney, Buena Vista. Bill Thomas.
GYPSY, Warner Bros., Orry-Kelly.
THE MUSIC MAN, Warner Bros. Dorothy Jeakins.
MY GEISHA, Sachiko, Paramount. Edith Head.
THE WONDERFUL WORLD OF THE BROTHERS GRIMM, MGM. and Cinerama. Mary Wills.

SOUND
BON VOYAGE, Disney, Buena Vista. Walt Disney Studio Sound Dept.; Robert O. Cook, sound director.
LAWRENCE OF ARABIA, Horizon, Columbia. Shepperton Studio Sound Dept.; John Cox, sound director.
THE MUSIC MAN, Warner Bros. Warner Bros. Studio Sound Dept.; George R. Groves, sound director.
THAT TOUCH OF MINK, Granley-Arwin-Shapiro, U-I. Universal City Studio Sound Dept.; Waldon O. Watson, sound director.
WHAT EVER HAPPENED TO BABY JANE?, Seven Arts-Warner Bros. Glen Glenn Sound Dept.; Joseph Kelly, sound director.

FILM EDITING
LAWRENCE OF ARABIA, Horizon, Columbia. Anne Coates.
THE LONGEST DAY, Zanuck, 20th Century-Fox. Samuel E. Beetley.
THE MANCHURIAN CANDIDATE, Axelrod-Frankenheimer, UA. Ferris Webster.
THE MUSIC MAN, Warner Bros. William Ziegler.
MUTINY ON THE BOUNTY, Arcola, MGM. John McSweeeney, Jr.

SPECIAL EFFECTS
THE LONGEST DAY, Zanuck, 20th Century-Fox. Robert MacDonald and Jacques Maumont.
MUTINY ON THE BOUNTY, Arcola, MGM., A. Arnold Gillespie and Milo Lory.

SHORT SUBJECTS: CARTOONS
THE HOLE, Storyboard Inc., Brandon Films. John and Faith Hubley, producers.
ICARUS MONTGOLFIER WRIGHT, Format Films, UA. Jules Engel, producer.
NOW HEAR THIS, Warner Bros.
SELF DEFENSE—FOR COWARDS, Rembrandt Films, Film Representations. William L. Snyder, producer.
SYMPOSIUM ON POPULAR SONGS, Disney, Buena Vista. Walt Disney, producer.

SHORT SUBJECTS: LIVE ACTION
BIG CITY BLUES, Mayfair Pictures. Martina and Charles Huguenot van der Linden, producers.
THE CADILLAC, United Producers Releasing. Robert Clouse, producer.
THE CLIFF DWELLERS, (a.k.a. *One Plus One*), Group II Film Prods., Schoenfeld Films. Hayward Anderson, producer.
HEUREUX ANNIVERSAIRE (Happy Anniversary), Atlantic Pictures (French). Pierre Etaix and J.C. Carriere, producers.
PAN, Mayfair Pictures. Herman van der Horst, producer.

DOCUMENTARY: SHORT SUBJECTS
DYLAN THOMAS, TWW Ltd., Janus Films (Welsh). Jack Howells, producer.
THE JOHN GLENN STORY, Department of the Navy, Warner Bros. William L. Hendricks, producer.
THE ROAD TO THE WALL, CBS Films, Department of Defense. Robert Saudek, producer.

DOCUMENTARY: FEATURES
ALVORADA (Brazil's Changing Pace), MW Filmproduktion (German). Hugo Niebeling, producer.
BLACK FOX, Image Prods., Heritage Films. Louis Clyde Stoumen, producer.

FOREIGN LANGUAGE FILM
ELECTRA, (Greece).
THE FOUR DAYS OF NAPLES, (Italy).
KEEPER OF PROMISES (The Given Word), (Brazil).
SUNDAYS AND CYBELE, (France).
TLAYUCAN, (Mexico).

HONORARY AND OTHER AWARDS
None given this year.

JEAN HERSHOLT HUMANITARIAN AWARD
TO STEVE BRODY

SCIENTIFIC OR TECHNICAL
CLASS I
None.

CLASS II
RALPH CHAPMAN for the design and development of an advanced motion picture camera crane.
ALBERT S. PRATT, JAMES L. WASSELL and HANS C. WOHLRAB of the Professional Division, Bell & Howell Co., for the design and development of a new and improved automatic motion picture additive color printer.
NORTH AMERICAN PHILIPS CO., INC., for the design and engineering of the Norelco Universal 70/35mm motion picture projector.
CHARLES E. SURFER, WILLIAM BRYSON SMITH and LOUIS C. KENNELL of Paramount Pictures Corp. for the engineering and application to motion picture production of a new system of electric power distribution.

CLASS III
ELECTRO-VOICE, INC.;
LOUIS G. MacKENZIE.

1963

The movie on everyone's mind that year ran less than a minute long and was shot by a horrified Dallas tourist named Zapruder. The terrifying film caught the real-life assassination of John F. Kennedy, the president most closely associated with, and beloved by, Hollywood. The grief was still palpable months later in the Santa Monica Civic Auditorium. The Awards show put on a brave front for the camera. Sammy Davis Jr. exhausted himself with songs, imitations, and one-liners for a wildly appreciative crowd of tuxedos and Jackie-inspired bouffant hairdos. The nation was in need of a laugh.

The timing of *Tom Jones*, a small British romantic comedy with a huge publicity campaign, couldn't have been better. Based on the Henry Fielding classic, *Jones* was an exuberant, wink-at-the-camera, bodice-ripping romp through the eighteenth-century English countryside. Director Tony Richardson took it to lascivious extremes with an especially erotic dinner scene that had Puritans choking on their popcorn. The film's handsome star, Albert Finney, was an overnight sensation and a heavy favorite early on in the race. He'd been pitted hunk vs. hunk with Cleveland-born Paul Newman, whose charismatic portrayal of a soulless young rancher, Hud, had fans panting with his immortal words: "The only question I ever ask a woman is, What time does your husband get home?"

Interestingly, Tom Jones was a naughty hero misconstrued as a villain, and Hud was a villain misconstrued as a hero. The latter quickly became a symbol of cool rebellion among the young. Conservative social critics worried about the wild swing of the nation's moral compass. The barrier-crashing 1960s were being born. The civil rights movement suddenly shifted into high gear, and with it Sidney Poitier's chances.

Poitier made Hollywood history that night by becoming the first black man to win Best Actor. "It's been a long journey to this moment," he said in an unprepared speech. As presenter Anne Bancroft led him off the stage, she affectionately advised him to "enjoy it, chum, it doesn't last long."

KEEPING UP WITH THE JONES BOY

CEREMONY: April 13, 1964
Santa Monica Civic Auditorium,
Santa Monica
HOST: Jack Lemmon

BEST PICTURE/BEST DIRECTOR
TONY RICHARDSON (1928–1991)
TOM JONES

Tom Jones was that rarity among Best Picture winners, an all-out comedy. But morality maven and syndicated columnist Hedda Hopper wasn't laughing. "The N.Y. critics should be slashed for choosing *Tom Jones*," she contended. Nevertheless, *Tom Jones*, which was picked up for peanuts by Universal, became the highest-grossing foreign-made film distributed in the U.S. to date.

Richardson, a stylish, influential stage and film director, was responsible for exciting the spirits of Anglophiles across America in the 1960s and '70s. He began his film career with a short feature, *Momma Don't Allow* (1955), co-directed with Karel Reisz. This was followed by film adaptations of *Look Back in Anger* (1959) and *The Entertainer* (1960). Richardson produced Karel Reisz's first feature, the seminal *Saturday Night and Sunday Morning* (1960), and directed two portraits of the working-class, *A Taste of Honey* (1961) and *The Loneliness of the Long Distance Runner* (1962). Americans were impressed by his black comedy *The Loved One* (1965), but *The Charge of the Light Brigade* (1968) was considered a disappointment.

Albert Finney, Joan Greenwood

Richardson's career was nothing if not checkered, and includes Nabokov's *Laughter in the Dark* (1969), *Hamlet* (1969), *A Delicate Balance* (1973), and *Joseph Andrews* (1977). In America, Richardson directed *The Border* (1982) and John Irving's *The Hotel New Hampshire* (1984). His last film, *Blue Sky*, was completed in 1990, before his death from complications of AIDS and released four years later, winning Jessica Lange a statuette. He was married at one time to Vanessa Redgrave; their children Natasha and Joely are also actresses. His autobiography, *The Long Distance Runner*, was published posthumously.

The envelope, please…

BEST ACTOR
SIDNEY POITIER (B. 1927)
LILIES OF THE FIELD

Poitier told the *New York Times*, "I'd like to think it will help someone, but I don't believe my Oscar will be a sort of magic wand that will wipe away the restrictions on job opportunities for Negro actors."

Poitier was raised in poverty in the Bahamas, completing only a few years of formal education. After he appeared on Broadway in *Anna Lucasta* (1948), his film debut in *No Way Out* (1950) led to *Cry, the Beloved Country* (1951). In quick succession were groundbreaking performances in *The Blackboard Jungle* (1955), *Edge of the City* (1957), *The Defiant Ones* (1958, nom.), *Porgy and Bess* (1959), *A Raisin in the Sun* (1961), and *Lilies of the Field* .

In 1967, his peak year, Poitier starred in three box-office smashes: *Guess Who's Coming to Dinner*, *To Sir, With Love*, and *In the Heat of the Night. For Love of Ivy* (1968) was Poitier's writing debut. His directorial turn was extremely successful, with such hits as *Uptown Saturday Night* (1974) and *Stir Crazy* (1980). He returned to acting in *Shoot to Kill* (1988) and played the role of Supreme Court justice Thurgood Marshall in the TV movie *Separate but Equal* (1991).

Patricia Neal with Paul Newman

BEST ACTRESS
PATRICIA NEAL (B. 1926)
HUD

"I will vote for Pat Neal to win because she has had so much personal tragedy in her life."

—Hazel Flynn, columnist for the
Hollywood Citizen News

Neal was at home on Oscar night, awaiting the birth of her fourth child. Though critics raved about her performance as the earthy housekeeper in *Hud*, her victory was marred by speculation that it was merely a sympathy vote inspired by her personal tragedies.

Following the end of a highly publicized affair with married co-star Gary Cooper in *The Fountainhead* (1949), she suffered a nervous breakdown. She then lost a daughter to measles, and a son was nearly killed when his baby carriage was struck by a car.

She continued to work, starring in *The Breaking Point* (1950), *The Day the Earth Stood Still* (1951), *A Face in the Crowd* (1957), and *In Harm's Way* (1965). Two years after filming *Hud*, she suffered a series of paralyzing strokes. After years of rehabilitation Neal made a triumphant comeback in *The Subject Was Roses* (1968, nom.), following that with *The Night Digger* (1971), *Ghost Story* (1981), and several TV movies, most notably *The Homecoming—A Christmas Story* (1971). Her autobiography, *As I Am*, was adapted as a TV movie (1981) starring Glenda Jackson.

BEST OF 1963
Best Picture: *Tom Jones*
Best Director: Tony Richardson, *Tom Jones*
Best Actor: Sidney Poitier, *Lilies of the Field*
Best Actress: Patricia Neal, *Hud*
Best Supporting Actor: Melvyn Douglas, *Hud*
Best Supporting Actress: Margaret Rutherford, *The V.I.P.s*

FIRSTS
• **"For Better or Worse"**: Rex Harrison and Rachel Roberts were the first husband and wife to be nominated in the same year since Alfred Lunt and Lynne Fontanne in 1932.

• The price tag for *Cleopatra* was $44 million, making it the most expensive picture made to date.

SINS OF OMISSION
Picture: *Bye Bye Birdie*, *The Birds*, *Hud*, *The Leopard*, *The Nutty Professor*

ROLE REVERSALS
• Queen for a Day: Marilyn Monroe was briefly considered for the role of Cleopatra.

• Federico Fellini came to the Awards to pick up his Oscar for Best Foreign Picture, *8½*, and also to try to woo Mae West and Groucho Marx to appear in his film *Juliet of the Spirits*.

UNMENTIONABLES
• "I'm never going to put myself through this [expletive] no more. Never again under no circumstances am I going to come here again and put myself through this," complained Sidney Poitier before winning Best Actor. However, he was present in 2002 to receive his Honorary Award.

• "I'm not going to be narrow enough to claim these fellows can't act. They've had plenty of practice. The weather is so foul on that tight little isle of theirs that to get in out of the rain they all gather in theaters and practice *Hamlet* on each other," said Hollywood critic and gossip columnist Hedda Hopper, responding to the British invasion.

• In the final edit of *Charade*, which opened just weeks after John F. Kennedy was killed, the word *assassinate* was over-dubbed as *eliminate*.

• Patricia Neal's struggle back from a debilitating stroke in the early 1960s was chronicled in the TV movie *The Patricia Neal Story* (1981), starring Glenda Jackson.

• When Sidney Poitier came to New York from the Caribbean to become an actor, he was so impoverished that he slept in the bus station. To get his first major role in *No Way Out* (1950), he lied to director Mankiewicz and told him he was 27 when he was actually only 22 years old.

• Stanley Kramer approached Poitier about co-starring in *The Defiant Ones* (1958), which would make him a bigger star, but informed him that if he did not take the role of Porgy in *Porgy and Bess* (1959) he might kill his chances for *The Defiant Ones*. Darryl F. Zanuck had that much clout in Hollywood.

• Cleopatra herself didn't show up for the ceremonies, and neither did most of Hollywood's star power. Newman didn't want to steal the spotlight from Poitier. Finney was doing a restful hula in Hawaii. Melvyn Douglas was shooting in Spain. And Margaret Rutherford, the beloved 72-year-old great Dame, remained at home in London, as did the very pregnant Patricia Neal. The rest of the Hollywood community, it seemed, including Judy Garland, Gregory Peck, and Charlton Heston, went to Washington for the August civil-rights march.

BEST SUPPORTING ACTOR
MELVYN DOUGLAS (1901–1981)
HUD

The debonair leading man with the signature pencil-thin mustache was the surprise winner for Best Supporting Actor, winning over John Huston's "sure thing" for *The Cardinal*. Writing in the *New York Times*, Bosley Crowther exclaimed, "Melvin Douglas is magnificent as the aging cattleman who finds his own son an abomination and disgrace to his country and home. [His] performance…fills the screen with an emotion that I've seldom felt from any film."

Douglas's great wit was at the core of many comic and dramatic classics, including *Ninotchka* (1939), *Mr. Blandings Builds His Dream House* (1948), *The Americanization of Emily* (1964), *I Never Sang for My Father* (1970, nom.), *The Candidate* (1972), *The Tenant* (1976), and *Twilight's Last Gleaming* (1977).

In the early 1950s Douglas endured the witch-hunt of his wife Helen Gahagan, who was running against Richard Nixon for Congress. During the McCarthy hearings, Nixon accused her of having ties to the Communist Party and won, despite a lack of evidence. (For more on Douglas, see 1979.)

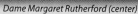
Dame Margaret Rutherford (center)

BEST SUPPORTING ACTRESS
DAME MARGARET RUTHERFORD (1892–1972)
THE V.I.P.S.

"This Oscar is the climax of my career after twenty-eight years of filmmaking. This may sound presumptuous at my age, but I like to feel that this will be the starting point of a new little phase in films. I certainly hope it will be."

Dame Margaret was the only shining light in this Elizabeth Taylor and Richard Burton vehicle. A jingoistic Hedda Hopper was forced to admit, "I'm happy Margaret Rutherford is up, even if she is English." Her kind, jowly face and British no-nonsense attitude served her image well in later years. Built like the British institution that she was, there couldn't have been a more perfect Miss Marple in Agatha Christie's *Murder Most Foul* (1964). She lent her unique presence to such classics as *Blithe Spirit* (1945), *The Importance of Being Earnest* (1952), and *Chimes at Midnight* (1966) before experiencing a fade-out in the less than choice *A Countess from Hong Kong* (1967).

Elizabeth Taylor

BEST CINEMATOGRAPHY (COLOR),
BEST ART DIRECTION (COLOR),
BEST COSTUME DESIGN (COLOR),
SPECIAL VISUAL EFFECTS
CLEOPATRA

There were those who thought *Cleopatra* was the best comedy of the year. Director Joseph L. Mankiewicz admitted, "It was conceived in a state of emergency, shot in confusion, and wound up in a blind panic."

Elizabeth Taylor was in the tub when the call came offering her the role of Cleopatra. She jokingly called out to her then-husband, Eddie Fisher, to tell them she'd do it for a million dollars. Fox agreed. Despite the film's initial box-office bonanza, it was years before its bloated budget was recouped. Taylor was embattled with the producers herself, suing Fox for failing to pay her a percentage of the gross. The studio retaliated by suing Burton and Taylor for $50 million for "depreciating the film's commercial value by their 'scandalous conduct and deportment,'" although executives admitted that the Taylor-Burton romance was what had made the movie such an eagerly awaited event. Meanwhile, Taylor was suing Eddie Fisher for divorce on grounds of abandonment.

AWARD NOMINATIONS 1963

PICTURE
AMERICA AMERICA, Athena. Warner Bros, Elia Kazan.
CLEOPATRA, 20th Century-Fox, Walter Wanger.
HOW THE WEST WAS WON, MGM. Cinerama, Bernard Smith.
LILIES OF THE FIELD, Rainbow, UA, Ralph Nelson.
TOM JONES, Woodfall, UA-Lopert (British), Tony Richardson.

ACTOR
ALBERT FINNEY in *Tom Jones*, Woodfall, UA-Lopert (British).
RICHARD HARRIS in *This Sporting Life*, Wintle-Parkyn, Reade-Sterling-Continental (British).
REX HARRISON in *Cleopatra*, 20th Century-Fox.
PAUL NEWMAN in *Hud*, Salem-Dover, Paramount.
SIDNEY POITIER in *Lilies of the Field*, Rainbow, UA.

ACTRESS
LESLIE CARON in *The L-Shaped Room*, Romulus, Columbia (British).
SHIRLEY MacLAINE in *Irma La Douce*, Mirisch-Phalanx, UA.
PATRICIA NEAL in *Hud*, Salem-Dover, Paramount.
RACHEL ROBERTS in *This Sporting Life*, Wintle-Parkwyn, Reade-Sterling-Continental (British).
NATALIE WOOD in *Love with the Proper Stranger*, Boardwalk-Rona, Paramount.

SUPPORTING ACTOR
NICK ADAMS in *Twilight of Honor*, Perlberg-Seaton, MGM.
BOBBY DARIN in *Captain Newman, MD.*, Brentwood Reynard, Universal.
MELVYN DOUGLAS in *Hud*, Salem-Dover, Paramount.
HUGH GRIFFITH in *Thin Jones*, Woodfall, UA-Lopert (British).
JOHN HUSTON in *The Cardinal*, Preminger, Columbia.

SUPPORTING ACTRESS
DIANE CILENTO in *Tom Jones*, Woodfall, UA-Lopert (British).
DAME EDITH EVANS in *Tom Jones*, Woodfall, UA Lopert (British).
JOYCE REDMAN in *Tom Jones*, Woodfall, UA-Lopert (British).
MARGARET RUTHERFORD in *The V.I.P.s*, MGM.
LILIA SKALA in *Lilies of the Field*, Rainbow, UA.

DIRECTION
FEDERICO FELLINI for *Federico Fellini's 8½*, Embassy Pictures (Italian).
ELIA KAZAN for *America America*, Kazan, Warner Bros.
OTTO PREMINGER for *The Cardinal*, Preminger, Columbia.
TONY RICHARDSON for *Tom Jones*, Woodfall, UA-Lopert (British).
MARTIN RITT for *Hud*, Salem-Dover, Paramount.

WRITING: BASED ON MATERIAL FROM ANOTHER MEDIUM
CAPTAIN NEWMAN, M.D., Brentwood-Reynard, Universal. Richard L. Breen, Phoebe and Henry Ephron.
HUD, Salem-Dover, Paramount. Irving Ravetch and Harriet Frank, Jr.
LILIES OF THE FIELD, Rainbow. UA. James Poe.
SUNDAYS AND CYBELE, Columbia (French). Serge Bourguignon and Antoine Tudal.
TOM JONES, Woodfall, UA-Lopert (British). John Osborne.

WRITING: ORIGINAL SCREENPLAY
AMERICA AMERICA, Kazan, Warner Bros. Elia Kazan.
FEDERICO FELLINI'S 8½, Embassy Pictures (Italian). Federico Fellini, Ernio Flaiano, Tulio Pinelli and Brunello Rondi.
THE FOUR DAYS OF NAPLES, Titanus, MGM. (Italian). Pasquale Festa Campanile, Massino Franciosa, Nanni Loy, Vasco Pratolini and Carlo Bernari.
HOW THE WEST WAS WON, MGM. and Cinerama. James R. Webb.
LOVE WITH THE PROPER STRANGER, Pakula-Mulligan, Paramount. Arnold Schulman.

CINEMATOGRAPHY
B/W
THE BALCONY, Allen-Hodgdon, Reade-Sterling Continental Dist. George Folsey.
THE CARETAKERS, Bartlett, UA. Lucien Ballard.
HUD, Salem-Dover, Paramount. James Wong Howe.
LILIES OF THE FIELD, Rainbow, UA. Ernest Haller.
LOVE WITH THE PROPER STRANGER, Pakula-Mulligan, Paramount. Milton Krasner.

Color
THE CARDINAL, Preminger, Columbia. Leon Shamroy.
CLEOPATRA. Wanger, 20th Century-Fox. Leon Sham roy.
HOW THE WEST WAS WON, MGM. and Cinerama. William H. Daniels, Milton Krasner, Charles Lang, Jr. and Joseph LaShelle.
IRMA LA DOUCE, Mirisch-Alperson, UA. Joseph LaShelle.
IT'S A MAD, MAD, MAD, MAD WORLD, Kramer, UA. Ernest Laszlo.

ART DIRECTION—SET DECORATION
B/W
AMERICA AMERICA, Kazan, Warner Bros. Gene Callahan.
FEDERICO FELLINI'S 8½, Embassy Pictures (Italian). Piero Gherardi.
HUD, Salem-Dover, Paramount. Hal Pereira and Tambi Larsen; Sam Comer and Robert Benton.
LOVE WITH THE PROPER STRANGER, Pakula-Mulligan, Paramount. Hal Pereira and Roland Anderson; Sam Comer and Grace Gregory.
TWILIGHT OF HONOR, Perlberg-Seaton, MGM. George W. Davis and Paul Groesse; Henry Grace and Hugh Hunt.

Color
THE CARDINAL, Preminger. Columbia. Lyle Wheeler; Gene Callahan.
CLEOPATRA, Wanger, 20th Century-Fox. John DeCuir, Jack Martin Smith, Hilyard Brown, Herman Blumenthal, Elven Webb, Maurice Pelling and Boris Juraga; Walter H. Scott, Paul S. Fox and Ray Moyer.
COME BLOW YOUR HORN, Essex-Tandem, Paramount. Hal Pereira and Roland Anderson; Sam Comer and James Payne.
HOW THE WEST WAS WON, MGM. and Cinerama. George W. Davis, William Ferrari and Addison Hehr; Henry Grace, Don Greenwood, Jr. and Jack Mills.
TOM JONES, Woodfall, UA-Lopert (British). Ralph Brinton, Ted Marshall and Jocelyn Herbert; Josie MacAvin.

COSTUME DESIGN
B/W
FEDERICO FELLINI'S 8½, Embassy Pictures (Italian). Piero Gherardi.
LOVE WITH THE PROPER STRANGER, Pakula-Mulligan, Paramount. Edith Head.
THE STRIPPER, Wald, 20th Century-Fox. Travilla.
TOYS IN THE ATTIC, Mirisch-Claude, UA. Bill Thomas.
WIVES AND LOVERS, Walls, Paramount. Edith Head.

Color
THE CARDINAL, Preminger, Columbia. Donald Brooks.
CLEOPATRA, Wanger, 20th Century-Fox. Irene Sharaff, Vittono Nino Novarese and Renie.
HOW THE WEST WAS WON, MGM. and Cinerama. Walter Plunkett.
THE LEOPARD, Titanus, 20th Century-Fox. Piero Tosi.
A NEW KIND OF LOVE, Llenroc Paramount. Edith Head.

SOUND
BYE BYE BIRDIE, Kohlmar-Sidney, Columbia. Columbia Studio Sound Dept. Charles Rice, sound director.
CAPTAIN NEWMAN, M.D., Brentwood-Reynard, Universal, Universal City Studio Sound Dept.; Waldon O. Watson, sound director.
CLEOPATRA, Wanger, 20th Century-Fox. 20th Century-Fox Studio Sound Dept.; James P. Corcoran, sound director, and Todd A-O Sound Dept., Fred Hynes, sound director.
HOW THE WEST WAS WON, MGM. and Cinerama. MGM. Studio Sound Dept.; Franklin E. Milton, sound director.
IT'S A MAD, MAD, MAD, MAD WORLD, Kramer, UA. Samuel Goldwyn Studio Sound Dept.; Gordon E. Sawyer, sound director.

FILM EDITING
THE CARDINAL, Preminger, Columbia. Louis R. Loeffler.
CLEOPATRA, Wanger, 20th Century-Fox. Dorothy Spencer.
THE GREAT ESCAPE, Mirisch-Alpha, UA. Ferris Webster.
HOW THE WEST WAS WON, MGM. and Cinerama. Harold F. Kress.
IT'S A MAD, MAD, MAD, MAD WORLD, Kramer, UA. Frederic Knudtson, Robert C. Jones and Gene Fowler, Jr.

SPECIAL VISUAL EFFECTS
THE BIRDS, Hitchcock, Universal. Ub Iwerks.
CLEOPATRA, Wanger, 20th Century-Fox. Emil Kosa, Jr.

SOUND EFFECTS
A GATHERING OF EAGLES, Universal. Robert L. Bratton.
IT'S A MAD, MAD, MAD, MAD WORLD, Kramer, UA. Walter G. Elliott.

SONG
CALL ME IRRESPONSIBLE (*Papa's Delicate Condition*, Amro, Paramount); Music by James Van Heusen. Lyrics by Sammy Cahn.
CHARADE (*Charade*, Donen, Universal); Music by Henry Mancini. Lyrics by Johnny Mercer.
IT'S A MAD, MAD, MAD, MAD WORLD, (*It's a Mad, Mad, Mad, Mad World*, Kramer, UA); Music by Ernest Gold. Lyrics by Mack David.
MORE (*Mondo Cane*, Cineriz Prods., Times Film); Music by Riz Ortolani and Nino Oliviero. Lyrics by Norman Newell.
SO LITTLE TIME (*55 Days at Peking*, Bronston, Allied Artists); Music by Dimitri Tiomkin. Lyrics by Paul Francis Webster.

SCORING: SUBSTANTIALLY ORIGINAL
CLEOPATRA, Wanger, 20th Century-Fox. Alex North.
55 DAYS AT PEKING, Bronston, Allied Artists, Dimitri Tiomkin.
HOW THE WEST WAS WON, MGM. and Cinerama. Alfred Newman and Ken Darby.
IT'S A MAD, MAD, MAD, MAD WORLD, Kramer, UA. Ernest Gold.
TOM JONES, Woodfall, UA-Lopert (British). John Addison.

SCORING: ADAPTATION OR TREATMENT
BYE BYE BIRDIE, Kohlmar-Sidney, Columbia. John Green.
IRMA LA DOUCE, Mirisch-Alperson, UA. Andre Previn.
A NEW KIND OF LOVE, Llenroc, Paramount. Leith Stevens.
SUNDAYS AND CYBELE, Columbia (French). Maurice Jarre.
THE SWORD IN THE STONE, Disney, Buena Vista. George Bruns.

SHORT SUBJECTS: CARTOONS
AUTOMANIA 2000, Pathe Contemporary Films. John Halas, producer.
THE CRITIC, Pintoff-Crossbow Prods., Columbia. Ernest Pintoff, producer.
THE GAME (Ingra), Rembrandt Films-Film Representations. Dusan Vukotic, producer.
MY FINANCIAL CAREER, National Film Board of Canada, Walter Reade-Sterling-Continental Distributing. Cohn Low and Tom Daly, producers.
PIANISSIMO, Cinema 16. Carmen D'Avino, producer.

SHORT SUBJECTS: LIVE ACTION
THE CONCERT, King Corp., George K. Arthur-Go Pictures, Ezra Baker, producer.
HOME-MADE CAR, Schoenfeld Films, James Hill, producer.
AN OCCURRENCE AT OWL CREEK BRIDGE, Janus Films, Paul de Roubaix and Marcel Ichac, producers.
SIX-SIDED TRIANGLE, Lion International, Christopher Miles, producer.
THAT'S ME, Pathe Contemporary Films, Walker Stuart, producer.

DOCUMENTARY: SHORT SUBJECTS
CHAGALL, Auerbach-Flag Films, Simon Schiffrin, producer.
THE FIVE CITIES OF JUNE, US Information Agency. George Stevens, Jr., producer.
THE SPIRIT OF AMERICA, Spotlite News, Algernon G. Walker, producer.
THIRTY MILLION LETTERS, British Transport Films. Edgar Anstey, producer.
TO LIVE AGAIN, Wilding Inc. Mel London, producer.

DOCUMENTARY: FEATURES
LE MAILLON ET LA CHAINE (The Link And The Chain), Films Du Centaure-Filmartic (French). Paul de Roubaix, producer.
ROBERT FROST: A LOVER'S QUARREL WITH THE WORLD, WGBH Educational Foundation. Robert Hughes, producer.
THE YANKS ARE COMING, David L. Wolper Prods. Marshall Flaum, producer.

FOREIGN LANGUAGE FILM
FEDERICO FELLINI'S 8½, (Italy).
KNIFE IN THE WATER, (Poland).
LOS TARANTOS, (Spain).
THE RED LANTERNS, (Greece).
TWIN SISTERS OF KYOTO, (Japan).

HONORARY AND OTHER AWARDS
None given this year.

IRVING G. THALBERG MEMORIAL AWARD
TO SAM SPIEGEL

JEAN HERSHOLT HUMANITARIAN AWARD
None given this year.

SCIENTIFIC OR TECHNICAL
CLASS I
None.

CLASS II
None.

CLASS III
DOUGLAS G. SHEARER and A. ARNOLD GILLESPIE of MGM. Studios,

1964

I t was the battle of the musical-comedy divas, Julie Andrews and Marni Nixon. Nixon, the voice behind Audrey Hepburn, had cost Hepburn a nod for Best Actress just as her singing had undermined Natalie Wood's chances for *West Side Story* in 1962. The Academy couldn't bring itself to nominate what it considered to be half a performance, and *My Fair Lady* director, George Cukor, was "just sick about it." Hepburn, always a good sport, showed up as an Awards presenter anyway, and graciously applauded when Andrews took the Oscar for her screen debut.

MY DUBBED LADY

CEREMONY: April 5, 1965
Santa Monica Civic Auditorium,
Santa Monica
HOST: Bob Hope

Andrews led the invasion of non-American acting winners across the board. Best Documentary presenters Jimmy Durante and Martha Raye hilariously mangled the slew of foreign-named nominees. Nonsensical mouthfuls continued to be the order of the evening as the New Christy Minstrels sang the Best Song, "Chim Chim Cher-ee," from *Mary Poppins*. Astonishingly, none of the more pronounceable tunes from the Beatles' *A Hard Day's Night* film were considered.

Stanley Kubrick's vehemently anti-Pentagon satire, *Dr. Strangelove or: How I Stopped Worrying and Learned to Love the Bomb*, was a strong contender but came to nothing. Hollywood's Cold War patriotism had drawn its line in the sand. America's sweetheart, Debbie Reynolds, carried the homeland banner with her career's sole nomination for *The Unsinkable Molly Brown*. The unsinkable Joan Crawford, after awarding former director George Cukor with the Oscar that had eluded him for years, hosted an informal bash in her dressing room. "It always knocks me out to be backstage with big talents at the Oscarcast," Crawford said. "I don't think I'll ever get over the sheer magic of people like Patti Page."

George Cukor with Audrey Hepburn

**BEST PICTURE/BEST DIRECTOR
GEORGE CUKOR (1899–1983)
*MY FAIR LADY***

"It is good for the soul, if not very pleasant, to sit there with your nomination and be turned down in front of a hundred million people. But when you do get it, it is a glory. Mine seemed to be an inordinately long time coming, but when I got it, it meant more to me than any other award I ever received," Cukor said backstage after receiving his prize. When he stepped onto the stage to receive the gold, he simply said, "I'm very grateful, very happy, and very lucky."

Though Cukor could boast having made films of sophistication and intelligence, he was often—to his dismay—categorized as "a woman's director." According to *Entertainment Tonight*'s Leonard Maltin, "he was a splendid director of both male and female actors, far more comfortable with pace and performance than visual technique, and his obvious skill and taste made him one of the aces of Hollywood's Golden Age."

Cukor's Hollywood career began in 1929, with the first wave of Broadway talent to be "imported" during the early years of the talkies. He was a dialogue director on *All Quiet on the Western Front* (1930), and finally made it to full-fledged director with *Tarnished Lady* (1931). Mogul David O. Selznick took to his work, establishing a partnership that resulted in such films as *A Bill of Divorcement* (1932), *Dinner at Eight* (1933), *David Copperfield* (1935), *Romeo and Juliet* (1936), *Camille* (1937), and *Holiday* (1938).

Hired by Selznick to direct *Gone with the Wind* (1939), Cukor was fired ten days after the start of production; some say his discomfort was due to Clark Gable's resentment at having to work with a director who, aside from being homosexual, lavished most of his attention on Vivien Leigh. Cukor moved on to direct some of the most memorable films to come out of Hollywood, including *The Women* (1939), *The Philadelphia Story* (1940), *Adam's Rib* (1949), *Born Yesterday* (1950), *Pat and Mike* (1952), and *A Star Is Born* (1954).

Given his record, it was astonishing that *My Fair Lady* earned Cukor his only Best Director Oscar. However, his later films, *The Chapman Report* (1962) and *Justine* (1969), were sluggish, as was his last big-screen venture, *Rich and Famous* (1981).

The envelope, please…

BEST ACTOR
REX HARRISON (1908–1990)
MY FAIR LADY

"I feel in a way I should split this [Oscar] in half between us," said Harrison of co-star Audrey Hepburn.

The quintessentially suave Englishman, Harrison followed his first appearance on Broadway with such star-making Hollywood films as *Major Barbara* (1941) and *Blithe Spirit* (1945). After serving in World War II, he scored a series of hits with *Anna and the King of Siam* (1946), *The Ghost and Mrs. Muir* (1947), and *Unfaithfully Yours* (1948).

In 1948 Harrison—then married to actress Lilli Palmer—was implicated in the suicide of his mistress, actress Carole Landis. He survived the scandal with his career intact.

Among his more popular credits were *Midnight Lace* (1960), *Cleopatra* (1963, nom.), and *The Yellow Rolls-Royce* (1965). Following his *My Fair Lady* win, the still handsome, middle-aged Harrison appeared in *The Agony and the Ecstasy* (1965), *The Honey Pot* (1967), and *Doctor Doolittle* (1967). But the leading roles became fewer, and after *Staircase* (1969) it would be nearly a decade before Harrison returned to the screen in *Crossed Swords* (1978) and his last film, *Anastasia: The Mystery of Anna* (1986).

BEST ACTRESS
JULIE ANDREWS (B. 1935)
MARY POPPINS

Time magazine was outraged when Andrews was nixed for the film version of *My Fair Lady*: "Someone, some-where, made the decision to include Andrews out of the [film]. There is an evil and rampantly lunatic force at loose in the world and it must be destroyed." Producer Jack Warner defended his actions by saying, "No one in the sticks has ever heard of her."

Ironically, Julie Andrews, not Audrey Hepburn, took home the Oscar. After scoring another nomination for *The Sound of Music* (1965), however, she was unable to sustain her meteoric success. Following *The Americanization of Emily* (1964), *Hawaii* (1966), *Torn Curtain* (1966), *Star!* (1968), and *Darling Lili* (1970), she began an exclusive collaboration with director husband Blake Edwards.

Edwards was determined to shake up her squeaky-clean image with unconventional roles in the breast-baring *S.O.B.* (1981) and gender-bending *Victor/Victoria* (1982, nom.). Following a successful stage version of *Victor/Victoria* on Broadway (1998), vocal chord surgery badly damaged Andrews's singing voice. One of the most successful musical careers in show business history came to a sudden end.

BEST OF 1964
Best Picture: *My Fair Lady*
Best Director: George Cukor, *My Fair Lady*
Best Actor: Rex Harrison, *My Fair Lady*
Best Actress: Julie Andrews, *Mary Poppins*
Best Supporting Actor: Peter Ustinov, *Topkapi*
Best Supporting Actress: Lila Kedrova, *Zorba the Greek*

FIRSTS
- The four acting Oscars were won by non-Americans.
- *My Fair Lady* was the first Best Picture Oscar for Warner Bros. since *Casablanca* (1943).

ROLE REVERSALS
- Rex Harrison without hair? *The King and I* without Yul Brynner? Harrison was offered the starring role but turned it down.
- Joan Crawford became ill during the production of *Hush…Hush, Sweet Charlotte* and was replaced by Olivia de Havilland.

SINS OF OMISSION
Picture: *Dr. Strangelove: or How I Learned to Stop Worrying and Love the Bomb*, *The Servant*, *A Hard Day's Night*, *Night of the Iguana*, *The Pink Panther*, *Zorba the Greek*
Actress: According to Hedda Hopper, Kim Stanley's performance in *Seance on a Wet Afternoon* was "by far the best acting performance of the year."

UNMENTIONABLES
- It may be one of the best-known bits of movie trivia in Hollywood-land, but it never fails to amaze that Hepburn's songs in *My Fair Lady* were all dubbed by Marni Nixon.
- Rex Harrison was named "Sexy Rexy" by movie columnists, and it annoyed him to no end that he couldn't make it go away.
- Harrison was blind in one eye as the result of a childhood illness.
- A *New York Daily News* headline screamed, "Actor Quinn Admits Love Child." It seems that Anthony Quinn had fallen for a blond wardrobe mistress while working on another film, and had two sons to show for it. The *New York Times* said, "The situation created something of an international outrage when it became public."

BEST SUPPORTING ACTOR
PETER USTINOV (B. 1921)
TOPKAPI

Accepting the award for Ustinov—who was off making another film—the wild and crazy Jonathan Winters said, "I don't know whether Peter expected this. I certainly didn't, or I would have been sure to wear black socks."

The famed actor was also a distinguished raconteur and a prized after-dinner speaker. In one of his most quotable remarks, speaking about film and stage critics, he said, "They search for ages for the wrong word, which, to give them credit, they eventually find."

(For more on Ustinov, see 1960.)

BEST SUPPORTING ACTRESS
LILA KEDROVA (1918–2000)
ZORBA THE GREEK

"Has it really happened?" asked Kedrova of her co-star Anthony Quinn, who was sitting beside her when her award was announced. "It has," he replied. And with that Kedrova raced to the stage. Thanking director Michael Cacoyannis, she said, "It is your fault, not mine. I will never, never forget it."

Kedrova learned to speak English while playing the seductive old maid who thinks attracting a man will keep her from dying. She turned out to be a quick study. She became an international star and appeared in such American films as *Flesh and the Woman* (1954), *Torn Curtain* (1966), *The Girl Who Couldn't Say No* (1969), *The Tenant* (1976), and *Tell Me a Riddle* (1980).

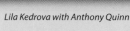

Lila Kedrova with Anthony Quinn

AWARD NOMINATIONS 1964

PICTURE
BECKET, Wallis, Paramount, Hal Wallis.
DR. STRANGELOVE OR: HOW I LEARNED TO STOP WORRYING AND LOVE THE BOMB, Hawk Films, Columbia, Stanley Kubrick.
MARY POPPINS, Disney, Buena Vista, Walt Disney and Bill Walsh.
MY FAIR LADY, Warner Bros, Jack L. Warner.
ZORBA THE GREEK, Rochley, 20th Century-Fox/ International Classics, Produced by Michael Cacoyannis.

ACTOR
RICHARD BURTON in *Becket,* Wallis, Paramount.
REX HARRISON in *My Fair Lady,* Warner Bros.
PETER O'TOOLE in *Becket,* Wallis, Paramount.
ANTHONY QUINN in *Zorba the Greek,* Rochley, 20th Century-Fox/International Classics.
PETER SELLERS in *Dr. Strangelove or: How I Learned to Stop Worrying and Love the Bomb,* Hawk Films, Columbia.

ACTRESS
JULIE ANDREWS in *Mary Poppins,* Disney, Buena Vista.
ANNE BANCROFT in *The Pumpkin Eater,* Romulus, Royal Films International/Columbia (British).
SOPHIA LOREN in *Marriage Italian Style,* Champion-Concordia, Embassy (Italian).
DEBBIE REYNOLDS in *The Unsinkable Molly Brown,* Marten, M.G.M.
KIM STANLEY in *Seance on a Wet Afternoon,* Attenborough-Forbes Artixo (British).

SUPPORTING ACTOR
JOHN GIELGUD in *Becket,* Wallis, Paramount.
STANLEY HOLLOWAY in *My Fair Lady,* Warner Bros.
EDMOND O'BRIEN in *Seven Days in May,* Joel, Paramount.
LEE TRACY in *The Best Man,* Millar-Turman, UA.
PETER USTINOV in *Topkapi,* Filmways, UA.

SUPPORTING ACTRESS
GLADYS COOPER in *My Fair Lady,* Warner Bros.
DAME EDITH EVANS in *The Chalk Garden,* Hunter, Universal.
GRAYSON HALL in *The Night of the Iguana,* Seven Arts, M.G.M.
LILA KEDROVA in *Zorba the Greek,* Rochley, 20th Century-Fox/International Classics.
AGNES MOOREHEAD in *Hush...Hush, Sweet Charlotte,* Associates & Aldrich, 20th Century-Fox.

DIRECTION
MICHAEL CACOYANNIS for *Zorba the Greek,* Rochley, International Classics/20th Century-Fox.
GEORGE CUKOR for *My Fair Lady,* Warner Bros.
PETER GLENVILLE for *Becket,* Wallis, Paramount.
STANLEY KUBRICK for *Dr. Strangelove, or: How I Learned to Stop Worrying and Love the Bomb,* Kubrick, Columbia.
ROBERT STEVENSON for *Mary Poppins,* Disney, Buena Vista.

WRITING: BASED ON MATERIAL FROM ANOTHER MEDIUM
BECKET, Wallis, Paramount. Edward Anhalt.
DR. STRANGELOVE OR: HOW I LEARNED TO STOP WORRYING AND LOVE THE BOMB, Kubrick, Columbia. Stanley Kubrick, Peter George and Terry Southern.
MARY POPPINS, Disney, Buena Vista. Bill Walsh and Don DaGradi.
MY FAIR LADY, Warner Bros. Alan Jay Lerner.

ZORBA THE GREEK, Rochley, International Classics/ 20th Century-Fox. Michael Cacoyannis.

WRITING: ORIGINAL SCREENPLAY
FATHER GOOSE, Granox, Universal. S.H. Barnett, Peter Stone and Frank Tarloff.

A HARD DAY'S NIGHT, Shenson-UA (British). Alun Owen.

ONE POTATO, TWO POTATO, Cinema V. Orville H. Hampton and Raphael Hayes.

THE ORGANIZER, Reade-Sterling-Continental (Italian). Age, Scarpelli and Mario Monicelli.

THAT MAN FROM RIO, Lopert (French). Jean-Paul Rappeneau, Ariane Mnouchkine, Daniel Boulanger and Philippe De Broca.

CINEMATOGRAPHY
B/W

THE AMERICANIZATION OF EMILY, Ransohoff, M.G.M. Philip H. Lathrop.

FATE IS THE HUNTER, Arcola, 20th Century-Fox. Milton Krasner.

HUSH...HUSH, SWEET CHARLOTTE, Aldrich, 20th Century-Fox. Joseph Biroc.

THE NIGHT OF THE IGUANA, Seven Arts, M.G.M. Gabriel Figueroa.

ZORBA THE GREEK, Rochley, International Classics/ 20th Century-Fox. Walter Lassally.

Color

BECKET, Wallis, Paramount. Geoffrey Unsworth.

CHEYENNE AUTUMN, Ford-Smith, Warner Bros. William H. Clothier.

MARY POPPINS, Disney, Buena Vista. Edward Colman.

MY FAIR LADY, Warner Bros. Harry Stradling.

THE UNSINKABLE MOLLY BROWN, Marten, M.G.M. Daniel L. Fapp.

ART DIRECTION—SET DECORATION
B/W

THE AMERICANIZATION OF EMILY, Ransohoff, M.G.M. George W. Davis, Hans Peters and Elliot Scott; Henry Grace and Robert H. Benton.

HUSH...HUSH, SWEET CHARLOTTE, Aldrich, 20th Century-Fox. William Glasgow; Raphael Bretton.

THE NIGHT OF THE IGUANA, Seven Arts, M.G.M. Stephen Grimes.

SEVEN DAYS IN MAY, Joel, Paramount. Cary Odell; Edward G. Boyle.

ZORBA THE GREEK, Rochley, International Classics/ 20th Century-Fox. Vassilis Fotopoulos.

Color

BECKET, Wallis, Paramount. John Bryan and Maurice Carter; Patrick McLoughlin and Robert Cartwright.

MARY POPPINS, Disney, Buena Vista. Carroll Clark and William H. Tuntke; Emile Kuri and Hal Gausman.

MY FAIR LADY, Warner Bros. Gene Allen and Cecil Beaton; George James Hopkins.

THE UNSINKABLE MOLLY BROWN, Marten, M.G.M. George W. Davis and Preston Ames; Henry Grace and Hugh Hunt.

WHAT A WAY TO GO, Apjac-Orchard, 20th Century-Fox. Jack Martin Smith and Ted Haworth; Walter M. Scott and Stuart A. Reiss.

COSTUME DESIGN
B/W

A HOUSE IS NOT A HOME, Greene-Rouse, Embassy Pictures. Edith Head.

HUSH...HUSH, SWEET CHARLOTTE, Aldrich, 20th Century-Fox. Norma Koch.

KISSES FOR MY PRESIDENT, Pearlayne, Warner Bros. Howard Shoup.

THE NIGHT OF THE IGUANA, Seven Arts, M.G.M. Dorothy Jeakins.

THE VISIT, DeRode, 20th Century-Fox. Rene Hubert.

Color

BECKET, Wallis, Paramount. Margaret Furse.

MARY POPPINS, Disney, Buena Vista. Tony Walton.

MY FAIR LADY, Warner Bros. Cecil Beaton.

THE UNSINKABLE MOLLY BROWN, Marten, M.G.M. Morton Haack.

WHAT A WAY TO GO, Apjac-Orchard, 20th Century-Fox. Edith Head and Moss Mabry.

SOUND
BECKET, Wallis, Paramount. Shepperton Studio Sound Dept.; John Cox, sound director.

FATHER GOOSE, Granox, Universal. Universal City Studio Sound Dept.; Waldon O. Watson, sound director.

MARY POPPINS, Disney, Buena Vista. Walt Disney Studio Sound Dept.; Robert O. Cook, sound director.

MY FAIR LADY, Warner Bros. Warner Bros. Studio Sound Dept.; George H. Groves, sound director.

THE UNSINKABLE MOLLY BROWN, Marten, M.G.M., M.G.M. Studio Sound Dept.; Franklin E. Milton, sound director.

FILM EDITING
BECKET, Wallis, Paramount. Anne Coates.

FATHER GOOSE, Granox, Universal. Ted J. Kent.

HUSH...HUSH, SWEET CHARLOTTE, Aldrich, 20th Century-Fox. Michael Luciano.

MARY POPPINS, Disney, Buena Vista. Cotton Warburton.

MY FAIR LADY, Warner Bros. William Ziegler.

SPECIAL VISUAL EFFECTS
MARY POPPINS, Disney, Buena Vista. Peter Ellenshaw, Hamilton Luske and Eustace Lycett.

7 FACES OF DR. LAO, Pal, M.G.M. Jim Danforth.

SOUND EFFECTS
GOLDFINGER, Broccoli-Saltzman-Eon, UA (British). Norman Wanstall.

THE LIVELY SET, Universal. Robert L. Bratton.

SONG
CHIM CHIM CHER-EE (*Mary Poppins*, Disney, Buena Vista); Music and Lyrics by Richard M. Sherman and Robert B. Sherman.

DEAR HEART (*Dear Heart*, Warner Bros.); Music by Henry Mancini. Lyrics by Jay Livingston and Ray Evans.

HUSH...HUSH, SWEET CHARLOTTE, (*Hush...Hush, Sweet Charlotte*, Aldrich, 20th Century-Fox); Music by Frank DeVol. Lyrics by Mack David.

MY KIND OF TOWN, (*Robin and the 7 Hoods*, Warner Bros.); Music by James Van Heusen. Lyrics by Sammy Cahn.

WHERE LOVE HAS GONE (*Where Love Has Gone*, Embassy, Paramount); Music by James Van Heusen. Lyrics by Sammy Cahn.

SCORING: SUBSTANTIALLY ORIGINAL
BECKET, Wallis, Paramount. Laurence Rosenthal.

THE FALL OF THE ROMAN EMPIRE, Bronston, Paramount. Dimitri Tiomkin.

HUSH...HUSH, SWEET CHARLOTTE, Aldrich, 20th Century-Fox. Frank DeVol.

MARY POPPINS, Disney, Buena Vista. Richard M. Sherman and Robert B. Sherman.

THE PINK PANTHER, Mirisch, UA. Henry Mancini.

SCORING: ADAPTATION OR TREATMENT
A HARD DAY'S NIGHT, Shenson, UA (British). George Martin.

MARY POPPINS, Disney, Buena Vista. Irwin Kostal.

MY FAIR LADY, Warner Bros. Andre Previn.

ROBIN AND THE 7 HOODS, Warner Bros. Nelson Riddle.

THE UNSINKABLE MOLLY BROWN, Marten, M.G.M. Robert Armbruster, Leo Arnaud, Jack Elliott, Jack Hayes, Calvin Jackson and Leo Shuken.

SHORT SUBJECTS: CARTOONS
CHRISTMAS CRACKER, National Film Board of Canada, Favorite Films of California.

HOW TO AVOID FRIENDSHIP, Rembrandt Films, Film Representations. William L. Snyder, producer.

NUDNIK #2, Rembrandt Films, Film Representations. William L. Snyder, producer.

THE PINK PHINK, Mirisch-Geoffrey, UA. David H. Depatie and Friz Freleng, producers.

SHORT SUBJECTS: LIVE ACTION
CASALS CONDUCTS: 1964, Thalia Films, Beckman Film Corp. Edward Schreiber, producer.

HELP! MY SNOWMAN'S BURNING DOWN, Pathe Contemporary Films. Carson Davidson, producer.

THE LEGEND OF JIMMY BLUE EYES, Topaz Film Corp. Robert Clouse, producer.

DOCUMENTARY: SHORT SUBJECTS
BREAKING THE HABIT, American Cancer Society, Modern Talking Picture Service. Henry Jacobs and John Korty, producers.

CHILDREN WITHOUT, National Education Association, Guggenheim Productions.

KENOJUAK, National Film Board of Canada.

NINE FROM LITTLE ROCK. US Information Agency, Guggenheim Productions.

140 DAYS UNDER THE WORLD, New Zealand National Film Unit, Rank Films. Geoffrey Scott and Oxley Hughan, producers.

DOCUMENTARY: FEATURES
THE FINEST HOURS, Le Vien Films, Columbia. Jack Le Vien, producer.

FOUR DAYS IN NOVEMBER, David L. Wolper Prods., UA. Mel Stuart, producer.

THE HUMAN DUTCH, Haanstra Filmproductie. Bert Haanstra, producer.

JACQUES-YVES COUSTEAU'S WORLD WITHOUT SUN, Columbia. Jacques-Yves Cousteau, producer.

OVER THERE, 1914-18, Zodiac Prods., Pathe Contemporary Films. Jean Aurel, producer.

FOREIGN LANGUAGE FILM
RAVEN'S END (Sweden).

SALLAH (Israel).

THE UMBRELLAS OF CHERBOURG (France).

WOMAN IN THE DUNES (Japan).

YESTERDAY, TODAY AND TOMORROW (Italy).

HONORARY AND OTHER AWARDS
TO WILLIAM TUTTLE for his outstanding make-up achievement for *7 Faces of Dr. Lao.*

JEAN HERSHOLT HUMANITARIAN AWARD
None given this year.

SCIENTIFIC OR TECHNICAL
CLASS I

PETRO VLAHOS, WADSWORTH E. POHL and UB IWERKS for the conception and perfection of techniques for Color Traveling Matte Composite Cinematography.

CLASS II

SIDNEY P. SOLOW, EDWARD H. REICHARD, CARL W. HAUGE and JOB SANDERSON of Consolidated Film Industries for the design and development of a versatile Automatic 35mm Composite Color Printer.

PIERRE ANGENIEUX for the development of a ten-to-one Zoom Lens for cinematography.

CLASS III

MILTON FORMAN, RICHARD B. GLICKMAN and DANIEL J. PEARLMAN of ColorTran Industries;

STEWART FILMSCREEN CORPORATION;

ANTHONY PAGLIA and the 20TH CENTURY-FOX STUDIO MECHANICAL EFFECTS DEPT.;

EDWARD H. REICHARD (2 citations) and CARL W. HAUGE (2 citations) and LEONARD L. SOKOLOW of Consolidated Film Industries;

NELSON TYLER.

1965

"Julie Andrews has a wonderful British strength that makes you wonder why they lost India."
—Moss Hart

Oscar made a big splash, quite literally, with an opening sequence featuring a chorus line of floodlit fountains in living color. Musically, it was an especially good year, with nominated songs including "The Shadow of Your Smile" and, sung by the young Liza Minnelli, "What's New Pussycat?" The answer to that, of course, was Julie Christie, the most charismatic British import since, well, Julie Andrews. Their press-fueled rivalry was the stuff of Oscar high drama, a contest between family-values wholesomeness and swinging sexuality in a miniskirt. Andrews could sing like an angel, but, as a *Newsweek* cover story put it, "Voom, Voom, It's Julie Christie!"

OSCAR VON TRAPP

CEREMONY: April 18, 1966
Santa Monica Civic Auditorium,
Santa Monica
HOST: Bob Hope

Best Actor Lee Marvin appeared to be having the time of his life and got a big laugh when he thanked his co-starring horse in *Cat Ballou*. Perennial host Bob Hope was honored with a gold medal for his durable service to the Academy over the years and promised to place it "in the family shrine."

After a slow start, *The Sound of Music* picked up speed and finally captured the big prize. Having lost her own Oscar bid, Julie Andrews shouted, "Oh, that's great!" But the center of the evening's glamorous gravity belonged to Christie, who gave one of the most profusely emotional acceptance speeches on record. Despite the tears, she glowed in trendy gold pajamas that perfectly matched her tightly clutched Oscar.

**BEST PICTURE/
BEST DIRECTOR
ROBERT WISE (B. 1914)**
THE SOUND OF MUSIC

Wise was in Hong Kong filming *The Sand Pebbles* when his name was called out for the big prizes, beating *Doctor Zhivago* in a close race. It all made sense, though, because full-scale Hollywood productions were one of Oscar's "favorite things."

It was no surprise, then, that the fans loved *The Sound of Music*, and saw it over and over again, breaking all known box-office records, including *Gone with the Wind*,'s and sparing 20th Century-Fox bankruptcy.

Some critics, however, abhorred the film. Pauline Kael wrote in *The New Yorker*, "A tribute to freshness that is so mechanically engineered and so shrewdly calculated that the background music rises, the already soft focus blurs and melts, and, upon the instant, you can hear all those noses blowing in the

Peggy Wood with Julie Andrews

theatre." Danny Peary, the author of *Alternate Oscars*, called it "shamelessly syrupy and manipulative." Only the lone voice of *Variety* spoke well of the film, calling it "a warmly pulsating, captivating drama…magnificently mounted." This was only one in a long line of successes for Wise, who didn't let any grass grow under his feet.

Wise was president of both the Directors Guild of America and the Academy of Motion Picture Arts and Sciences.

(For more on Wise, see 1961.)

The envelope, please...

BEST ACTOR
LEE MARVIN (1924–1987)
CAT BALLOU

Marvin's was a rare comic-performance Oscar. In the Western parody *Cat Ballou*, Marvin plays against type—the tough, rugged leading man—as a bumbling alcoholic gunslinger. Pauline Kael enjoyed his performance, particularly "his ritual preparations for a gunfight; his mistaking funeral candles for a birthday celebration."

A World War II veteran, Marvin was an unhappy plumber who dropped his wrenches to explore acting possibilities. Appearing in summer stock and Off Broadway, Marvin made his way into movies with small parts and won recognition in *The Big Heat* (1953), following up with *The Wild One* (1954) and *Bad Day at Black Rock* (1955). After a three-year stint on TV's *M Squad* (1957–1960), he won his most celebrated bad-guy role in the *The Man Who Shot Liberty Valance* (1962).

After his Oscar win for *Cat Ballou*, Marvin would appear in two all-star action blockbusters, *The Professionals* (1966) and *The Dirty Dozen* (1967). He caused a bit of a stir in the gossip columns when his longtime companion, Michelle Triola, successfully sued him for support after their breakup, bringing the word *palimony* into the American vocabulary.

BEST ACTRESS
JULIE CHRISTIE (B. 1941)
DARLING

"I don't think I can say anything except thank everyone concerned, especially my darling John Schlesinger, for this great honor."

Christie was the "It" girl of the 1960s, credited with the miniskirt craze. As the ruthless model in *Darling* who sleeps her way to the top only to regret it, critic Pauline Kael found her "extraordinary…petulant, sullen, very beautiful."

Christie's brief stage career led to *Billy Liar* (1963), which made her a star. That same year, she appeared in *Doctor Zhivago*. Her follow-ups, *Fahrenheit 451*, *Far from the Madding Crowd* (both 1967), *Petulia* (1968), and *The Go-Between* (1971), kept her star rising. An affair with Warren Beatty fueled her image and box-office power in *McCabe and Mrs. Miller* (1971, nom.), *Don't Look Now* (1973), *Shampoo* (1975), *Demon Seed* (1977), and *Heaven Can Wait* (1978).

In the 1980s and '90s Christie slowed to a crawl, appearing in only four films: *The Return of the Soldier* (1981), *Heat and Dust* (1983), *Power* (1986), and *Fools of Fortune* (1990). She earned another nomination for her acclaimed comeback role in *Afterglow* (1998).

BEST OF 1965
Best Picture: *The Sound of Music*
Best Director: Robert Wise, *The Sound of Music*
Best Actor: Lee Marvin, *Cat Ballou*
Best Actress: Julie Christie, *Darling*
Best Supporting Actor: Martin Balsam, *A Thousand Clowns*
Best Supporting Actress: Shelley Winters, *A Patch of Blue*
Honorary Award: Bob Hope

FIRSTS
- *The Sound of Music* topped *Gone with the Wind* (1939) as the biggest box-office grosser to date.
- Lee Marvin joined an extremely select group of Best Actor winners for a comic performance. His predecessors were Clark Gable for *It Happened One Night* (1934) and Rex Harrison for *My Fair Lady* (1964). James Stewart might cut it for his marginally comic performance in *The Philadelphia Story* (1940).
- Julie Christie's *Darling* launched the miniskirt as a fashion "must."
- Hiroshi Teshigahara (*Woman in the Dunes*) was the first Japanese director to be nominated.

SINS OF OMISSION
Pictures: Roman Polanski's classic chiller *Repulsion*, Tony Richardson's funereal satire *The Loved One*

ROLE REVERSALS
The Sound of Music's Mother Superior, Peggy "Climb Every Mountain" Wood, had her greatest fame playing a less celibate matriarch on the 1950s TV hit *I Remember Mama*.

ALWAYS A BRIDESMAID, NEVER A BRIDE
- *The Spy Who Came in from the Cold* marked Richard Burton's fourth of seven career nominations, none of which resulted in a win.
- *The Collector* made it a record twelve nominations for director William Wyler, who garnered three career Oscars: *Mrs. Miniver* (1942), *The Best Years of Our Lives* (1946), and *Ben-Hur* (1959).

UNMENTIONABLES
- A Cardiff widow held the bleary-eyed record for viewing *The Sound of Music* 947 times.
- Christopher Plummer referred to his most enduring film as "The Sound of Mucus."
- Critic Pauline Kael was fired by *McCall's* magazine for her scathing review of the von Trapp family saga.
- "I can't say I'm sorry Julie Andrews lost," said Julie Christie.
- Julie Christie earned $7,500 for her Oscar-winning performance in *Darling*.
- TV audiences spotted another highly publicized face in the crowd, a young woman who had never made a movie and had no intention of doing so—the president's daughter Lynda Bird Johnson, who sat beside her current beau, George Hamilton.

Jason Robards and Martin Balsam

BEST SUPPORTING ACTOR
MARTIN BALSAM (1914–1996)
A THOUSAND CLOWNS

Balsam showed up at the Awards ceremony by going AWOL from his new movie, *Hombre*. It turned out to be worth it.

A veteran of the New York stage and an alumnus of the famous Actors Studio, Balsam has appeared in dozens of movies since his debut in *On the Waterfront* (1954), followed by an excellent performance in *12 Angry Men* (1957). Balsam has presence, even when he's playing only a small role.

He played well with his co-stars in *Seven Days in May* (1964), *Tora! Tora! Tora!* (1970), *Murder on the Orient Express*, *The Taking of Pelham One Two Three* (both 1974), and *All the President's Men* (1976). Balsam did a stint on TV's *Archie Bunker's Place*, (1971–1983), and for old times' sake, he appeared in Scorcese's 1991 remake of *Cape Fear*.

Elizabeth Hartman with Shelley Winters

BEST SUPPORTING ACTRESS
SHELLEY WINTERS (B. 1922)
A PATCH OF BLUE

She cried all the way through her acceptance speech, thanking "Mr. Guy Green, who truly understood the role I played better than I did." *Variety* loved Shelley Winters' "sleazy mother" in *Blue*, but Winters was concerned that she would turn voters off with her unsympathetic role. She got that wrong.

Winters was a feisty woman—"I have bursts of being a lady, but it doesn't last long," said the actress—who spoke her mind on things both public and intimate, particularly on love and marriage. Among her many "observations" on the latter subject, Winters quipped: "In Hollywood, all the marriages are happy. It's trying to live together afterwards that causes all the problems." And, "I did a picture in England one winter, and it was so cold I almost got married." And, "The best way to find out about a man is to have lunch with his ex-wife."

(For more on Winters, see 1959.)

HONORARY AWARD
BOB HOPE (B. 1903)

"What can you say about the man who may be the most popular entertainer in the history of Western civilization?" asked critic Leonard Maltin of *Entertainment Tonight*.

From early vaudeville, Hope worked his way to Broadway, and by the early 1930s he'd made several comedy shorts. He was a regular on radio, starring on *The Pepsodent Show* (1938). That same year he made his feature-film debut in *The Big Broadcast of 1938*, in which he and Shirley Ross sang his signature song, "Thanks for the Memory." Hope was hot and appeared in a string of films, including *College Swing* (1938), *Thanks for the Memory* (1938), *Never Say Die* (1939), and *The Cat and the Canary* (1939).

Soon Hope joined forces with straight man and crooner Bing Crosby and sarong-clad Dorothy Lamour. They took to the road together in a long line of hilarious classics, including *Road to Singapore* (1940), and kept moving on to *Zanzibar* (1941), *...Morocco* (1942), *...Utopia* (1945), *...Rio* (1947), *...Bali* (1952), and *...Hong Kong* (1962). Dozens more, mostly forgettable films followed, along with a far more extraordinary TV career.

Hope remains the symbol of Hollywood patriotism, having tirelessly entertained U.S. troops all over the world. He also became synonymous with Oscar, playing host seventeen times—more than anyone else in the history of the Awards.

PICTURE
DARLING, Anglo-Amalgamated, Embassy (British), Joseph Janni.
DOCTOR ZHIVAGO, Sostar, S.A., MGM, Carlo Ponti.
SHIP OF FOOLS, Kramer, Columbia, Stanley Kramer.
THE SOUND OF MUSIC, Argyle, 20th Century-Fox, Robert Wise.
A THOUSAND CLOWNS, Harrell, UA, Fred Coe.

ACTOR
RICHARD BURTON in *The Spy Who Came In from the Cold*, Salem, Paramount.
LEE MARVIN in *Cat Ballou*, Hecht, Columbia.
LAURENCE OLIVIER in *Othello*, B.H.E. Warner Bros. (British).
ROD STEIGER in *The Pawnbroker*, Ely Landau, American International.
OSKAR WERNER in *Ship of Fools*, Kramer, Columbia.

ACTRESS
JULIE ANDREWS in *The Sound of Music*, Argyle, 20th Century-Fox.
JULIE CHRISTIE in *Darling*, Anglo-Amalgamated, Embassy (British).
SAMANTHA EGGAR in *The Collector*, Columbia.
ELIZABETH HARTMAN in *A Patch of Blue*, Berman-Green, MGM.
SIMONE SIGNORET in *Ship of Fools*, Kramer, Columbia.

SUPPORTING ACTOR
MARTIN BALSAM in *A Thousand Clowns*, Harrell, UA.
IAN BANNEN in *The Flight of the Phoenix*, Associates & Aldrich, 20th Century-Fox.
TOM COURTENAY in *Doctor Zhivago*, Sostar, S.A., MGM.
MICHAEL DUNN in *Ship of Fools*, Kramer, Columbia.
FRANK FINLAY in *Othello*, B.H.E., Warner Bros. (British).

SUPPORTING ACTRESS
RUTH GORDON in *Inside Daisy Clover*, Park Place, Warner Bros.
JOYCE REDMAN in *Othello*, B.H.E., Warner Bros. (British).
MAGGIE SMITH in *Othello*, B.H.E., Warner Bros. (British).
SHELLEY WINTERS in *A Patch of Blue*, Berman-Green, MGM.
PEGGY WOOD in *The Sound of Music*, Argyle, 20th Century-Fox.

DIRECTION
DAVID LEAN for *Doctor Zhivago*, Ponti, MGM.
JOHN SCHLESINGER for *Darling*, Embassy (British).
HIROSHI TESHIGAHARA for *Woman in the Dunes*, Pathe Contemporary Films (Japanese).
ROBERT WISE for *The Sound of Music*, 20th Century-Fox.
WILLIAM WYLER for *The Collector*, Columbia.

WRITING: BASED ON MATERIAL FROM ANOTHER MEDIUM
CAT BALLOU, Hecht, Columbia. Walter Newman and Frank H. Pierson.
THE COLLECTOR, Columbia. Stanley Mann and John Kohn.
DOCTOR ZHIVAGO, Ponti, MGM. Robert Bolt.

SHIP OF FOOLS, Kramer, Columbia. Abby Mann.
A THOUSAND CLOWNS, Harrell, UA. Herb Gardner.

WRITING: ORIGINAL SCREENPLAY
CASANOVA '70, Embassy (Italian). Age, Scarpelli, Mario Monicelli, Tonino Guerra, Giorgio Salvioni and Suso Cecchi D'Amico.
DARLING, Embassy (British). Frederic Raphael.
THOSE MAGNIFICENT MEN IN THEIR FLYING MACHINES, 20th Century-Fox. Jack Davies and Ken Annakin.
THE TRAIN, Les Prods., UA. Franklin Coen and Frank Davis.
THE UMBRELLAS OF CHERBOURG, Landau Releasing (French). Jacques Demy.

CINEMATOGRAPHY
B/W
IN HARM'S WAY, Preminger, Paramount. Loyal Griggs.
KING RAT, Coleytown, Columbia. Burnett Guffey.
MORITURI, Arcola-Colony, 20th Century-Fox. Conrad Hall.
A PATCH OF BLUE, Berman-Green, MGM. Robert Burks.
SHIP OF FOOLS, Kramer, Columbia. Ernest Laszlo.

Color
THE AGONY AND THE ECSTASY, 20th Century-Fox. Leon Shamroy.
DOCTOR ZHIVAGO, Ponti, MGM. Freddie Young.
THE GREAT RACE, Patricia-Jalem-Reynard, Warner Bros. Russell Harlan.
THE GREATEST STORY EVER TOLD, Stevens, UA. William C. Mellor and Loyal Griggs.
THE SOUND OF MUSIC, 20th Century-Fox. Ted McCord.

ART DIRECTION—SET DECORATION
B/W
KING RAT, Coleytown, Columbia. Robert Emmet Smith; Frank Tuttle.
A PATCH OF BLUE, Berman-Green, MGM. George W. Davis and Urie McCleary; Henry Grace and Charles S. Thompson.
SHIP OF FOOLS, Kramer, Columbia. Robert Clatworthy; Joseph Kish.
THE SLENDER THREAD, Paramount. Hal Pereira and Jack Poplin; Robert Benton and Joseph Kish.
THE SPY WHO CAME IN FROM THE COLD, Salem, Paramount. Hal Pereira, Tambi Larsen and Edward Marshall; Josie MacAvin.

Color
THE AGONY AND THE ECSTASY, 20th Century-Fox. John DeCuir and Jack Martin Smith; Dano Simoni.
DOCTOR ZHIVAGO, Ponti, MGM. John Box and Terry Marsh; Dario Simoni.
THE GREATEST STORY EVER TOLD, Stevens, UA. Richard Day, William Creber and David Hall; Ray Moyer, Fred MacLean and Norman Rockett.
INSIDE DAISY CLOVER, Pakula-Mulligan, Warner Bros. Robert Clatworthy; George James Hopkins.
THE SOUND OF MUSIC, 20th Century-Fox. Boris Leven; Walter H. Scott and Ruby Levitt.

COSTUME DESIGN
B/W
DARLING, Embassy (British). Julie Harris.
MORITURI, Arcola-Colony, 20th Century-Fox. Moss Mabry.
A RAGE TO LIVE, Mirisch-Araho, UA. Howard Shoup.
SHIP OF FOOLS, Kramer, Columbia. Bill Thomas and Jean Louis.
THE SLENDER THREAD, Paramount. Edith Head.

Color
THE AGONY AND THE ECSTASY, 20th Century-Fox. Vittorio Nino Novarese.
DOCTOR ZHIVAGO, Ponti, MGM. Phyllis Dalton.
THE GREATEST STORY EVER TOLD, Stevens, UA. Vittorio Nino Novarese and Marjorie Best.

INSIDE DAISY CLOVER, Pakula-Mulligan, Warner Bros. Edith Head and Bill Thomas.
THE SOUND OF MUSIC, 20th Century-Fox. Dorothy Jeakins.

SOUND
THE AGONY AND THE ECSTASY, 20th Century-Fox. 20th Century-Fox Studio Sound Dept.; James P. Corcoran, sound director.
DOCTOR ZHIVAGO, MGM. MGM. British Studio Sound Dept., A.W. Watkins, sound director; and MGM. Studio Sound Dept., Franklin E. Milton, sound director.
THE GREAT RACE, Patricia-Jalem-Reynard, Warner Bros. Warner Bros. Studio Sound Dept.; George R. Groves, sound director.
SHENANDOAH, Universal. Universal City Sound Dept.; Waldon O. Watson, sound director.
THE SOUND OF MUSIC, 20th Century-Fox. 20th Century-Fox Studio Sound Dept., James P. Corcoran, sound director; and Todd A-O Sound Dept., Fred Hynes, sound director.

FILM EDITING
CAT BALLOU, Hecht, Columbia. Charles Nelson.
DOCTOR ZHIVAGO, Ponti, MGM. Norman Savage.
THE FLIGHT OF THE PHOENIX, Aldrich, 20th Century-Fox. Michael Luciano.
THE GREAT RACE, Patricia-Jalem-Reynard, Warner Bros. Ralph E. Winters.
THE SOUND OF MUSIC, 20th Century-Fox. William Reynolds.

SPECIAL VISUAL EFFECTS
THE GREATEST STORY EVER TOLD, Stevens, UA. J. McMillan Johnson.
THUNDERBALL, Broccoli-Saltzman-McClory, UA (British). John Stears.

SOUND EFFECTS
THE GREAT RACE, Patricia-Jalem-Reynard, Warner Bros. Tregoweth Brown.
VON RYAN'S EXPRESS, 20th Century-Fox. Walter A. Rossi.

SONG
THE BALLAD OF CAT BALLOU (*Cat Ballou*, Hecht, Columbia); Music by Jerry Livingston. Lyrics by Mack David.
I WILL WAIT FOR YOU (*The Umbrellas of Cherbourg*, Landau Releasing; French); Music by Michel Legrand. Lyrics by Jacques Demy. English lyric by Norman Gimbel.
THE SHADOW OF YOUR SMILE (*The Sandpiper*, Filmways-Venice, MGM.); Music by Johnny Mandel. Lyrics by Paul Francis Webster.
THE SWEETHEART TREE (*The Great Race*, Patricia-Jalem-Reynard, Warner Bros.); Music by Henry Mancini. Lyrics by Johnny Mercer.
WHAT'S NEW PUSSYCAT? (*What's New Pussycat?*, Famous Artists-Famartists, UA); Music by Burt Bacharach. Lyrics by Hal David.

SCORING: SUBSTANTIALLY ORIGINAL
THE AGONY AND THE ECSTASY, 20th Century-Fox. Alex North.
DOCTOR ZHIVAGO, Ponti, MGM. Maurice Jarre.
THE GREATEST STORY EVER TOLD, Stevens, UA. Alfred Newman.
A PATCH OF BLUE, Berman-Green Prod., MGM. Jerry Goldsmith.
THE UMBRELLAS OF CHERBOURG, Landau Releasing (French). Michel Legrand and Jacques Demy.

SCORING: ADAPTATION OR TREATMENT
CAT BALLOU, Hecht, Columbia. DeVol.
THE PLEASURE SEEKERS, 20th Century-Fox. Lionel Newman and Alexander Courage.
THE SOUND OF MUSIC, 20th Century-Fox. Irwin Kostal.
A THOUSAND CLOWNS, Barrel, UA. Don Walker.
THE UMBRELLAS OF CHERBOURG, Landau Releasing (French). Michel Legrand.

SHORT SUBJECTS: CARTOONS
CLAY OR THE ORIGIN OF SPECIES, Harvard University, Pathe Contemporary Films, Eliot Noyes, Jr., producer.
THE DOT AND THE LINE, MGM. Chuck Jones and Les Goldman, producers.

THE THIEVING MAGPIE (La Gazza Ladra), Allied Artists. Emanuele Luzzati, producer.

SHORT SUBJECTS: LIVE ACTION
THE CHICKEN (Le Poulet). Pathe Contemporary Films (French). Claude Berri, producer.
FORTRESS OF PEACE, Farner-Looser Films, Cinerama. Lothar Wolff, producer.
SKATERDATER, Byway Prods., UA. Marshal Backlar and Noel Black, producers.
SNOW, Manson Distributing Edgar Anstey, producer.
TIME PIECE, Muppets, Inc., Pathe Contemporary Films. Jim Henson, producer.

DOCUMENTARY: SHORT SUBJECTS
MURAL ON OUR STREET, Henry Street Settlement, Pathe Contemporary Films, Kirk Smallman, producer.
OUVERTURE, Mafilm Prods., Hungarofilm-Pathe Contemporary Films.
POINT OF VIEW, Vision Associates Prod., National Tuberculosis Assoc.
TO BE ALIVE!, Johnson Wax. Francis Thompson, Inc., producer.
YEATS COUNTRY, Aengus Films for the Dept. of External Affairs of Ireland. Patrick Carey and Joe Mendoza, producers.

DOCUMENTARY: FEATURES
THE BATTLE OF THE BULGE...THE BRAVE RIFLES, Mascott Prods. Laurence E. Mascott, producer.
THE ELEANOR ROOSEVELT STORY, American International. Sidney Glazier, producer.
THE FOURTH ROAD BRIDGE, Random Film Prods., Shell-Mex and B.P Film Library. Peter Mills, producer.
LET MY PEOPLE GO, David L. Wolper Prods. Marshall Flaum, producer.
TO DIE IN MADRID, Altura Films International, Frederic Rossif, producer.

FOREIGN LANGUAGE FILM
BLOOD ON THE LAND (Greece).
DEAR JOHN (Sweden).
KWAIDAN (Japan).
MARRIAGE ITALIAN STYLE (Italy).
THE SHOP ON MAIN STREET (Czechoslovakia).

HONORARY AND OTHER AWARDS
TO BOB HOPE for unique and distinguished service to our industry and the Academy.

IRVING G. THALBERG MEMORIAL AWARD
TO WILLIAM WYLER

JEAN HERSHOLT HUMANITARIAN AWARD
TO EDMOND L. DePATIE

SCIENTIFIC OR TECHNICAL
CLASS I
None.

CLASS II
ARTHUR J. HATCH of the Strong Electric Corporation, subsidiary of General Precision Equipment Corporation, for the design and development of an Air Blown Carbon Arc Projection Lamp.
STEFAN KUDELSKI for the design and development of the Nagra portable 1/4" tape recording system for motion picture sound recording.

CLASS III
None.

1966

"How 'bout Liz and Richard?
They're a most unusual couple.
They're both expecting."
—Bob Hope

T he Redgrave family dynasty arrived en masse to cheer on nominated sisters Vanessa and Lynn. Hope singled them out in his opening monologue: "To the Redgraves, all the world's a stage and they're playing all the parts." A less weathered family dynasty of two, Mr. and Mrs. Richard Burton, were noticeably absent. Elizabeth Taylor, with her second Oscar all but clinched, was clearly miffed that her *Virginia Woolf* co-star husband would be bypassed by the Academy. Paul Scofield, the conceded front-runner, didn't bother to show, either. The only winning acting nominee in the auditorium was Walter Matthau, and he barely made it in one piece after a bone-crunching bicycle accident.

Star power, however, was in the air with the presence of four legends. The first was Patricia Neal, almost fully recuperated from three successive strokes. After receiving a standing ovation, she thanked the crowd with her emotions firmly in check. "I'm sorry I've been away so long," she said.

Following a high-voltage rendition of nominated song "Georgy Girl" by Mitzi Gaynor, the stage was cleared for the next legend up, Olivia de Havilland. The show's producers thought it would be great fun for her and sister Joan Fontaine to appear together as presenters. They'd been forerunners to Lynn and Vanessa Redgrave back in 1941, when they made the Best Actress nominations a family affair (de Havilland for *Hold Back the Dawn*, Fontaine for *Suspicion*). But the long-standing sibling rivalry was too much for Fontaine, who bowed out at the last minute.

Fred Astaire and Ginger Rogers, no strangers to reports of bad blood, were briefly reunited to announce Best Screenplay. They brought the house down with a spontaneous, perfectly executed swirl and dip. As Katharine Hepburn once said of them, "He gives her class and she gives him sex." Seventeen years after their final film together, *The Barkleys of Broadway*, the combination was still magic.

FAMILY NIGHT

CEREMONY: April 10, 1967
Santa Monica Civic Auditorium,
Santa Monica
HOST: Bob Hope

**BEST PICTURE/
BEST DIRECTOR
FRED ZINNEMANN
(1907–1997)
*A MAN FOR ALL SEASONS***

Zinnemann kissed Rosalind Russell's hand as she presented the Oscar to him. *A Man for All Seasons* swept up all the Best Film awards in the industry, with the exception of the New York Film Critics prize, though the film received mixed reviews from the critics. Writing for the *New York Times*, Bosley Crowther called it "a picture that inspires admiration, courage, and thought," adding, "Zinnemann presents us with an awesome view of a sturdy conscience and a steadfast heart." Pauline Kael, writing—less enthusiastically—for *The New Yorker*, said, "Zinnemann places himself at the service of Robert Bolt's play about the moral tug-of-war between Sir Thomas More (Paul Scofield) and Henry VIII (Robert Shaw), and the results are tasteful and moderately enjoyable." She added, "The weakness is that though Bolt's dialogue is crisp, lucid, and well-spoken, his presentation of More's martyrdom is so one-sided we don't even get to understand that side. More is the only man of honor in the movie."

Robert Shaw, Paul Scofield

As a child Zinnemann studied the violin, hoping to become a musician. As an adult he planned to become a lawyer and received a master's degree in law. When he saw the films of Erich von Stroheim and King Vidor, he dropped all previous ambitions and left for Paris and Berlin to work with some of the great filmmakers of the time.

(For more on Zinnemann, see 1953.)

The envelope, please...

BEST ACTOR
PAUL SCOFIELD (B. 1922)
A MAN FOR ALL SEASONS

Scofield remained at home in London as co-star Wendy Hiller accepted on his behalf. His performance as the sixteenth-century English chancellor Sir Thomas More was met with almost universal praise. "Scofield is brilliant," wrote Bosley Crowther in the *New York Times*. "Throughout, he gives a luminescence and power, integrity, and honor, to this man who will not 'yes' his King."

A Man for All Seasons sent Scofield into the stratosphere of great actors. Before the film version of *Man* he appeared in the Tony Award–winning Broadway production. With a preference for classical stage roles, Scofield has, however, added his dignified bearing and intelligence to many films, including *That Lady* (1955), *Carve Her Name with Pride* (1958), *The Train* (1965), *Tell Me Lies* (1968), *King Lear* (1971), *Bartleby* (1972), *A Delicate Balance* (1973), *Henry V* (1989), *Hamlet* (1990), and *Utz* (1992).

Scofield later appeared on TV and won an Emmy for *Male of the Species* (1969). He also starred in the acclaimed movie *The Attic: The Hiding of Anne Frank* (1988). Back in the film world, he played Mark Van Doren in *Quiz Show* (1994, nom.).

BEST ACTRESS
ELIZABETH TAYLOR (B. 1932)
WHO'S AFRAID OF VIRGINIA WOOLF?

All tongues were flapping on the subject of the controversial *Virginia Woolf*. Taylor put on more than 20 pounds to play the repulsive, troubled, overweight, alcoholic wife, Martha, to Burton's beaten-down George. Some critics thought Taylor's performance shrill and overdone, but most thought it one of her most interesting. Danny Peary, author of *Alternate Oscar*, suggested that Martha was a singular role for Taylor: "This time she couldn't fall back on her beauty and sex appeal...it really was a risky undertaking for Taylor."

"The role as a loudmouth unkempt woman easily was her finest personal performance to date," wrote *Entertainment Tonight* film critic Leonard Maltin." For this she would win her second Oscar and one that was more than well-deserved. Her films afterward didn't approach the intensity of that one."

(For more on Taylor, see 1960.)

BEST OF 1966
Best Picture: *A Man for All Seasons*
Best Director: Fred Zinnemann, *A Man for All Seasons*
Best Actor: Paul Scofield, *A Man for All Seasons*
Best Actress: Elizabeth Taylor, *Who's Afraid of Virginia Woolf?*
Best Supporting Actor: Walter Matthau, *The Fortune Cookie*
Best Supporting Actress: Sandy Dennis, *Who's Afraid of Virginia Woolf?*

FIRSTS
- It was a debut year for two of Hollywood's most influential directors, Mike Nichols (*Who's Afraid of Virginia Woolf?*) and Francis Ford Coppola (*You're a Big Boy Now*).
- Ronald Reagan made his first appearance at the Oscars as governor of California. On the red carpet, he was greeted with equal parts cheers and boos.
- *Who's Afraid of Virginia Woolf?* was the first of only two times that a film's entire cast was nominated. In 1972 it would be *Sleuth*'s cast of two, Laurence Olivier and Michael Caine.
- *The Fortune Cookie* was the first-time pairing of Walter Matthau and Jack Lemmon.

ROLE REVERSALS
Bette Davis fought hard to win the role of Martha in *Who's Afraid of Virginia Woolf?*, with her dream co-star Henry Fonda as George.

ALWAYS A BRIDESMAID, NEVER A BRIDE
Richard Burton's failed nomination for *Who's Afraid of Virginia Woolf?* made it 0 for 5.

UNMENTIONABLES
- Elizabeth Taylor and Lynn Redgrave each gained 20 pounds for their nominated roles.
- Taylor, irate over Burton's failed Oscar bid, chose not to send her thanks to the Academy.
- The year's biggest grosser was *The Bible*, with no Academy Award nominations. When director John Huston couldn't get Charlie Chaplin to play Noah, he took the role himself.
- In her 1990s tell-all, Lynn Redgrave confided that her father, Sir Michael, was bisexual.

BEST SUPPORTING ACTOR
WALTER MATTHAU (1920–2000)
THE FORTUNE COOKIE

Matthau, his arm in a cast, quipped, "The other day, as I was falling off my bicycle…"

The son of poor immigrants, Matthau first acted for pocket change in New York's Yiddish theater. After World War II, he honed his craft both onstage and on TV. His early films were largely dramatic or villainous roles, such as *A Face in the Crowd* (1957), *King Creole* (1958), *Gangster Story* (1960, which he also directed), *Charade* (1963), and *Failsafe* (1964). Following his comedic Oscar-winning role as an ambulance-chasing lawyer, Matthau found an avalanche of perfect vehicles in *The Odd Couple* (1968), *Hello, Dolly!* (1969), *Kotch* (1971, nom.), *The Front Page* (1974), *The Taking of Pelham One Two Three* (1974), *The Sunshine Boys* (1975, nom.), *The Bad News Bears* (1976), *House Calls* (1978), and *Hopscotch* (1980).

Matthau also appeared in such thrillers as *Charley Varrick* (1973) and *The Laughing Policeman* (1974). His later career was highlighted by *Grumpy Old Men* (1993) and *Grumpier Old Men* (1995), with longtime friend Jack Lemmon, as well as by several TV movies directed by his son Charles Matthau. Matthau's death in 2000 was particularly mourned by the industry.

BEST SUPPORTING ACTRESS
SANDY DENNIS (1937–1992)
WHO'S AFRAID OF VIRGINIA WOOLF?

Writing in the *New York Times* of Dennis's performance, Stanley Kaufman said, "Playing the bland wife, she is credibly bland." Speaking for the other side, *The New Yorker*'s Edith Oliver wrote, "When a performance is as triumphant as Miss Dennis' any description seems irrelevant."

In *Who's Afraid of Virginia Woolf?* Dennis plays George Segal's mousy wife. She was a quirky actress whose neuroses could be seen on her face, and could either captivate or repel audiences. An ardent student of method acting, Dennis won two consecutive Tony Awards for her Broadway performances in *A Thousand Clowns* and *Any Wednesday*. Among her many films are *Splendor in the Grass* (1961), *Up the Down Staircase* (1967), *A Touch of Love* (1969), *The Out-of-Towners* (1970), *Come Back to the 5 & Dime Jimmy Dean, Jimmy Dean* (1982), and *Another Woman* (1988).

AWARD NOMINATIONS 1966

PICTURE
ALFIE, Sheldrake, Paramount (British), Lewis Gilbert.
A MAN FOR ALL SEASONS, Highland Films, Columbia, Fred Zinnemann.
THE RUSSIANS ARE COMING, THE RUSSIANS ARE COMING, Mirisch, UA, Norman Jewison.
THE SAND PEBBLES, Argyle-Solar, 20th Century-Fox, Robert Wise.
WHO'S AFRAID OF VIRGINIA WOOLF?, Chenault, Warner Bros, Ernest Lehman.

ACTOR
ALAN ARKIN in *The Russians Are Coming, The Russians Are Coming,* Mirisch, UA.
RICHARD BURTON in *Who's Afraid of Virginia Woolf?* Chenault, Warner Bros.
MICHAEL CAINE in *Alfie,* Sheldrake, Paramount (British).
STEVE McQUEEN in *The Sand Pebbles,* Argyle-Solar, 20th Century-Fox.
PAUL SCOFIELD in *A Man for All Seasons,* Highland Films, Columbia.

ACTRESS
ANOUK AIMEE in *A Man and a Woman,* Allied Artists (French).
IDA KAMINSKA in *The Shop on Main Street,* Prominent Films (Czechoslovakia).
LYNNE REDGRAVE in *Georgy Girl,* Everglades, Columbia (British).
VANESSA REDGRAVE in *Morgan!,* Quintra Films, Cinema V (British).
ELIZABETH TAYLOR in *Who's Afraid of Virginia Woolf?,* Chenault, Warner Bros.

SUPPORTING ACTOR
MAKO in *The Sand Pebbles,* Argyle-Solar, 20th Century-Fox.
JAMES MASON in *Georgy Girl,* Everglades, Columbia (British).
WALTER MATTHAU in *The Fortune Cookie,* Phalanx Jalem-Mirisch, UA..
GEORGE SEGAL in *Who's Afraid of Virginia Woolf?,* Chenault, Warner Bros.
ROBERT SHAW in *A Man for All Seasons,* Highland Films, Columbia.

SUPPORTING ACTRESS
SANDY DENNIS in *Who's Afraid of Virginia Woolf?,* Chenault, Warner Bros.
WENDY HILLER in *A Man for All Seasons,* Highland Films, Columbia.
JOCELYNE LAGARDE in *Hawaii,* Mirisch, UA.
VIVIEN MERCHANT in *Alfie,* Sheldrake, Paramount (British).
GERALDINE PAGE in *You're a Big Boy Now,* Seven Arts.

DIRECTION
MICHELANGELO ANTONIONI for *Blow-Up,* Ponti, Premier Productions (British).
RICHARD BROOKS for *The Professionals,* Brooks, Columbia.
CLAUDE LELOUCH for *A Man and a Woman,* Les Films 13, Allied Artists (French).
MIKE NICHOLS for *Who's Afraid of Virginia Woolf?,* Chenault, Warner Bros.
FRED ZINNEMANN for *A Man for All Seasons,* Highland Films, Columbia.

WRITING: BASED ON MATERIAL FROM ANOTHER MEDIUM
ALFIE, Paramount (British). Bill Naughton.
A MAN FOR ALL SEASONS, Highland Films, Columbia. Robert Bolt.
THE PROFESSIONALS, Brooks, Columbia. Richard Brooks.
THE RUSSIANS ARE COMING, THE RUSSIANS ARE COMING, Mirisch, UA. William Rose.
WHO'S AFRAID OF VIRGINIA WOOLF?, Chenault, Warner Bros. Ernest Lehman.

WRITING: STORY AND SCREENPLAY WRITTEN DIRECTLY FOR THE SCREEN
BLOW-UP, Ponti Premier Procuctions (British), Michelangelo Antonioni, Tonino Guerra and Edward Bond.
THE FORTUNE COOKIE, Phalanx-Jalem-Mirisch, UA. Billy Wilder and I.A.L. Diamond.
KHARTOUM, Blaustein, UA. Robert Ardrey.
A MAN AND A WOMAN, Les Films 13, Allied Artists (French). Claude Lelouch and Pierre Uytterhoeven.
THE NAKED PREY, Theodora, Paramount. Clint Johnston and Don Peters.

CINEMATOGRAPHY
B/W
THE FORTUNE COOKIE, Phalanx-Jalem-Mirisch, UA. Joseph LaShelle.
GEORGY GIRL, Columbia (British). Ken Higgins.
IS PARIS BURNING?, Transcontinental Films-Marianne, Paramount. Marcel Grignon.
SECONDS, Paramount. James Wong Howe.
WHO'S AFRAID OF VIRGINIA WOOLF?, Chenault, Warner Bros. Haskell Wexler.

Color
FANTASTIC VOYAGE, 20th Century-Fox. Ernest Laszlo.
HAWAII, Mirisch, UA. Russell Harlan.
A MAN FOR ALL SEASONS, Highland Films, Columbia. Ted Moore.
THE PROFESSIONALS, Brooks, Columbia. Conrad Hall.
THE SAND PEBBLES, Argyle-Solar, 20th Century-Fox. Joseph MacDonald.

ART DIRECTION—SET DECORATION
B/W
THE FORTUNE COOKIE, Phalanx-Jalem-Mirisch, UA. Robert Luthardt. Edward G. Boyle.
THE GOSPEL ACCORDING TO ST. MATTHEW, Walter Reade-Continental (Italian). Luigi Scacciacnoe.
IS PARIS BURNING?, Transcontinental Films-Marianne, Paramount. Willy Holt; Marc Frederix and Pierre Guffroy.
MISTER BUDDWING, MGM. George W. Davis and Paul Groesse; Henry Grace and Hugh Hunt.
WHO'S AFRAID OF VIRGINIA WOOLF?, Chenault, Warner Bros. Richard Sylbert; George James Hopkins.

Color
FANTASTIC VOYAGE, 20th Century-Fox. Jack Martin Smith and Dale Hennessy; Walter M. Scott and Stuart A. Reiss.
GAMBIT, Universal. Alexander Golitzen and George C. Webb; John McCarthy and John Austin.
JULIET OF THE SPIRITS, Rizzoli Films (Italian). Piero Gherardi.
THE OSCAR, Greene-Rouse, Embassy. Hal Pereira and Arthur Lonergan; Robert Benton and James Payne.
THE SAND PEBBLES, Argyle-Solar, 20th Century-Fox. Boris Leven; Walter M. Scott, John Sturtevant and William Kiernan.

COSTUME DESIGN
B/W
THE GOSPEL ACCORDING TO ST. MATTHEW, Walter Reade-Continental (Italian). Danilo Donati.
MANDRAGOLA, (Italian). Danilo Donati.
MISTER BUDDWING, DDD-Cherokee, MGM. Helen Rose.
MORGAN!, (British), Cinema V. Jocelyn Rickards.
WHO'S AFRAID OF VIRGINIA WOOLF?, Chenault, Warner Bros. Irene Sharaff.

Color
GAMBIT, Universal. Jean Louis
HAWAII, Mirisch, UA. Dorothy Jeakins.
JULIET OF THE SPIRITS, Rizzoli Films (Italian). Piero Gherardi.
A MAN FOR ALL SEASONS, Highland Films, Columbia. Elizabeth Haffenden and Joan Bridge.

THE OSCAR, Greene-Rouse, Embassy. Edith Head.

SOUND
GAMBIT, Universal. Universal City Studio Sound Dept.; Waldon O. Watson, sound director.
GRAND PRIX, Lewis-Frankenheimer-Cherokee, MGM. MGM. Studio Sound Dept.; Franklin E. Milton, sound director.
HAWAII, Mirisch, UA. Samuel Goldwyn Studio Sound Dept.; Gordon E. Sawyer, sound director.
THE SAND PEBBLES, Argyle-Solar, 20th Century-Fox. 20th Century-Fox Studio Sound Dept.; James P. Corcoran, sound director.
WHO'S AFRAID OF VIRGINIA WOOLF?, Chenault, Warner Bros. Warner Bros. Studio Sound Dept.; George R. Groves, sound director.

FILM EDITING
FANTASTIC VOYAGE, 20th Century-Fox. William B Murphy.
GRAND PRIX, Lewis-Frankenheimer-Cherokee, MGM. Fredric Steinkamp, Henry Berman, Stewart Linder and Frank Santillo.
THE RUSSIANS ARE COMING, THE RUSSIANS ARE COMING, Mirisch, UA. Hal Ashby and J. Terry Williams.
THE SAND PEBBLES, Argyle-Solar, 20th Century-Fox. William Reynolds.
WHO'S AFRAID OF VIRGINIA WOOLF?, Chenault, Warner Bros. Sam O'Steen.

SPECIAL VISUAL EFFECTS
FANTASTIC VOYAGE, 20th Century-Fox. Art Cruickshank.
HAWAII, Mirisch, UA. Linwood G. Dunn.

SOUND EFFECTS
FANTASTIC VOYAGE, 20th Century-Fox. Walter Rossi.
GRAND PRIX, Lewia-Frankenheimer-Cherokee, MGM. Gordon Daniel.

SONG
ALFIE (*Alfie,* Paramount); Music by Burt Bacharach. Lyrics by Hal David.
BORN FREE (*Born Free,* Open Road-Atlas Films, Columbia; British); Music by John Barry. Lyrics by Don Black.
GEORGY GIRL (*Georgy Girl,* Columbia; British); Music by Tom Springfield. Lyrics by Jim Dale.
MY WISHING DOLL (*Hawaii,* Mirisch, UA); Music by Elmer Bernstein. Lyrics by Mack David.
A TIME FOR LOVE (*An American Dream,* Warner Bros.); Music by Johnny Mandel. Lyrics by Paul Francis Webster.

SCORING: ORIGINAL MUSIC
THE BIBLE, DeLaurentiis-Seven Arts, 20th CenturyFox. Toshiro Mayuzumi.
BORN FREE, Open Road-Atlas Films, Columbia (British). John Barry.
HAWAII, Mirisch, UA. Elmer Bernstein.
THE SAND PEBBLES, Argyle-Solar, 20th Century-Fox. Jerry Goldsmith.
WHO'S AFRAID OF VIRGINIA WOOLF?, Chenault, Warner Bros. Alex North.

SCORING: ADAPTATION OR TREATMENT
A FUNNY THING HAPPENED ON THE WAY TO THE FORUM, Frank, UA. Ken Thorne.
THE GOSPEL ACCORDING TO ST. MATTHEW, Walter-Reade-Continental (Italian). Luis Enrique Bacalov.
RETURN OF THE SEVEN, Mirisch, UA. Elmer Bernstein.
THE SINGING NUN, MGM. Harry Sukman.
STOP THE WORLD-I WANT TO GET OFF, Warner Bros. Al Ham.

SHORT SUBJECTS: CARTOONS
THE DRAG, National Film Board of Canada, Favorite Films. Wolf Koenig and Robert Verrall, producers.
HERB ALPERT AND THE TIJUANA BRASS DOUBLE FEATURE, Paramount. John and Faith Hubley, producers.
THE PINK BLUEPRINT, Mirisch-Geoffrey-DePatie-Freleng, UA. David H. DePatie and Friz Freleng, producers.

SHORT SUBJECTS: LIVE ACTION
TURKEY THE BRIDGE, Samaritan Prods., Schoenfeld Films. Derek Williams, producer.
WILD WINGS, British Transport Films, Manson Distributing. Edgar Anstey, producer.
THE WINNING STRAIN, Winik Films, Paramount. Leslie Winik, producer.

DOCUMENTARY: SHORT SUBJECTS
ADOLESCENCE, M.K. Prods. Marin Karmitz and Vladimir Forgency, producers.
COWBOY, U.S. Information Agency. Michael Ahnemann and Gary Schlosser, producers.
THE ODDS AGAINST, Vision Associates Prod. for The American Foundation Institute of Corrections. Lee R. Bobker and Helen Kristt Radin, producers.
SAINT MATTHEW PASSION, Mailm Studio, Hungarofilm.
A YEAR TOWARD TOMORROW, Sun Dial Films for Office of Economic Opportunity. Edmund A. Levy, producer.

DOCUMENTARY: FEATURES
THE FACE OF A GENIUS, WBZ-TV, Group W. Boston. Alfred R. Kelman, producer.
HELICOPTER CANADA, Centennial Commission, National Film Board of Canada. Peter Jones and Tom Daly, producers.
LE VOLCAN INTERDIT (The Forbidden Volcano), Cine Documents Tazieff, Athos Films. Haroun Tazieff, producer.
THE REALLY BIG FAMILY, David L. Wolper Prod. Alex Grasshoff, producer.
THE WAR GAME, BBC Prod. for the British Film Institute, Pathe Contemporary Films. Peter Watkins, producer.

FOREIGN LANGUAGE FILM
THE BATTLE OF ALGIERS (Italy).
LOVES OF A BLONDE (Czechoslovakia).
A MAN AND A WOMAN (France).
PHARAOH (Poland).
THREE (Yugoslavia).

HONORARY AND OTHER AWARDS
TO Y. FRANK FREEMAN for unusual and outstanding service to the Academy during his thirty years in Hollywood.
TO YAKIMA CANUTT for achievements as a stunt man and for developing safety devices to protect stunt men everywhere.

IRVING G. THALBERG MEMORIAL AWARD
TO ROBERT WISE

JEAN HERSHOLT HUMANITARIAN AWARD
TO GEORGE BAGNALL

SCIENTIFIC OR TECHNICAL
CLASS I
None.

CLASS II
MITCHELL CAMERA CORPORATION for the design and development of the Mitchell Mark II 35mm Portable Motion Picture Reflex Camera.
ARNOLD & RICHTER AG for the design and development of the Arriflex 35mm Portable Motion Picture Reflex Camera.

CLASS III
PANAVISION INCORPORATED;
CARROLL KNUDSON;
RUBY RAKSIN.

1967

The Academy's dress-code committee pleaded with invitees to attire themselves appropriately, especially the ladies, in light of last year's "unseemly" polka-dot mini worn by Julie Christie. But the tide of the 1960s cultural revolution couldn't be stemmed or, for that matter, hemmed. Short skirts, Nehru jackets, turtlenecks, love beads, and headbands signaled the sign of the times.

OSCAR TAKES THE HEAT

CEREMONY: April 10, 1968
Santa Monica Civic Auditorium, Santa Monica
HOST: Bob Hope

When Bob Hope kidded nominee Dame Edith Evans about where she'd like to go on a date, Evans, born in 1888, shot back, "How does the Pink Pussycat grab you?" In the words of Sammy Davis Jr. who crooned Best Song "Talk to the Animals," "Groovy, man!" Warren Beatty's mood that night was hardly groovy, thanks to *New York Times* critic Bosley Crowther, who led a vituperative campaign to dash the hopes of *Bonnie and Clyde* for Best Picture.

His comment that the film was "a cheap piece of bald-faced slapstick" swayed many traditional Academy voters. Its elimination left the race wide open, and the outcome was anyone's guess up until the final tense moment. Even the Best Director Oscar, almost always a barometer, didn't make *The Graduate* a sure thing. The evening's subtitle might well have been "Guess Who's Coming to the Podium?"

Finally, *In the Heat of the Night* took it, but not without grumbling from the gallery. With *Dr. Doolittle* acting as a "spoiler" in the category, *Heat*'s win was arguably by default. Fox had pulled out all the stops and hosted numerous free dinners to get its box-office dud, *Dr. Doolittle*, on the list. Truman Capote, whose *In Cold Blood* didn't get a nod, cried foul. Beatty felt he'd been robbed. Bob Hope tried to rescue the sanctity of the show's final moments with uncharacteristic humility. "The men who began our industry had at least one thing in common with the man from Atlanta. They had a dream," he said. With that, the furious 1967 Best Picture debate was muted, but not over.

BEST PICTURE
IN THE HEAT OF THE NIGHT

Jaws dropped when the winner of the Best Picture was announced. It was the ultimate surprise in an evening that had been full of surprises. Some thought political correctness with regard to race relations was the only reason for its win, considering the formidable competition. *Variety* said, "Rod Steiger's transformation from a diehard Dixie bigot to a man who learns to respect Sidney Poitier stands out in smooth comparison to the wandering solution of the murder."

Director Norman Jewison, who grew up in television and directed his first film, *Forty Pounds of Trouble*, built his reputation on his next films, *The Cincinnati Kid* (1965) and *The Russians Are Coming! The Russians Are Coming!* (1966). Jewison directed a wide range of genre films, including *The Thomas Crown Affair* (1968) *Fiddler on the Roof* (1971, nom.), *A Soldier's Story* (1984, nom.), and *Moonstruck* (1987, nom.).

Sidney Poitier (left)

The envelope, please...

BEST ACTOR
ROD STEIGER (B. 1925)
IN THE HEAT OF THE NIGHT

Steiger came to the Awards ceremony expecting to lose. When his name was called, he rose to the occasion and thanked "Mr. Sidney Poitier for the pleasure of his friendship, which gave me the knowledge and understanding of prejudice to enhance my performance. Thank you…and we shall overcome."

Known for the intensity of his work ethic, Steiger reportedly suffered a heart attack after filming *In the Heat of the Night*. A student of method acting, Steiger's bravura—sometimes over-the-top performances—became his trademark in such classics as *On the Waterfront* (1954, nom.), *Oklahoma!* (1955), *The Big Knife* (1955), *The Harder They Fall* (1956), *Al Capone* (1959),

Doctor Zhivago (1965), and *The Pawnbroker* (1965, nom.). He followed *Heat* with *No Way to Treat a Lady* (1968) and *The Illustrated Man* (1969).

In the 1970s Steiger was beset with health problems and a dearth of good roles. He made an attempted comeback in *W. C. Fields and Me* (1976), hoping it would get him back on track, but it didn't. He would later work on various minor film projects, among the more successful of which are: *F.I.S.T* (1978), *The Chosen* (1981), and *Guilty as Charged* (1992).

Katharine Hepburn with Beah Richards

BEST ACTRESS
KATHARINE HEPBURN (B. 1907)
GUESS WHO'S COMING TO DINNER

Hepburn wasn't present "in body" to receive her award, but she was there on tape, which she made on the set of her current film, *The Lion in Winter*. With this bid she tied Bette Davis for the record but was not expected to win because of the heavy competition. When her name was called, there was an audible gasp from the audience. Her director, George Cukor, accepted on her behalf, saying, "It was a very hard decision for you to make." According to the author of *Alternate Oscars*, Danny Peary, "Academy members were swayed to vote for Hepburn because she was returning to films after a five-year absence and hadn't won the Oscar since 1932–33 for *Morning Glory*. Also, her co-star and longtime lover, Spencer Tracy, had died ten days after filming—an Oscar for her would be an award for both of them. It's unfortunate that a star as incomparable as Hepburn had to appear in a bland interracial comedy."

(For more on Hepburn, see 1932–1933, 1968, 1981.)

BEST OF 1967
Best Picture: *In the Heat of the Night*
Best Director: Mike Nichols, *The Graduate*
Best Actor: Rod Steiger, *In the Heat of the Night*
Best Actress: Katharine Hepburn, *Guess Who's Coming to Dinner*
Best Supporting Actor: George Kennedy, *Cool Hand Luke*
Best Supporting Actress: Estelle Parsons, *Bonnie and Clyde*

FIRSTS
- *In the Heat of the Night* was the first detective mystery to win Best Picture.
- Movies were once again setting fashion trends, with this year's "Bonnie Look" sparked by Faye Dunaway's Depression-era gun-totin' moll.
- Alfred Hitchcock's Thalberg Memorial Oscar was the first and only one he ever received.
- Thanks to the efforts of Academy president Gregory Peck, eighteen of the twenty acting nominees were on hand, setting an attendance record.
- Separate awards for black-and-white and color films (art direction, cinematography, and costume design) were distilled into one category. The era of someone like Edith Head's being nominated for several pictures in one year were over.

SINS OF OMISSION
Song: The chart-busting theme song from the movie of the same title, "To Sir, With Love." and Paul Simon's "Mrs. Robinson" from *The Graduate*.
Actor and Actress: Audrey Hepburn and Albert Finney, as well as their portrait of a marriage, *Two for the Road*.

ROLE REVERSALS
Doris Day as Dustin Hoffman's seductress, Mrs. Robinson? Not after she read the script and found it morally reprehensible. Next up was Jeanne Moreau who, luckily for Anne Bancroft, also passed.

ALWAYS A BRIDESMAID, NEVER A BRIDE
Among Hitchcock's unsuccessful director nominations were *Rebecca* (1940), *Lifeboat* (1944), *Spellbound* (1945), *Rear Window* (1954), and *Psycho* (1960).

UNMENTIONABLES
- Spencer Tracy died less than two weeks after filming *Guess Who's Coming to Dinner*.
- Tracy's longtime lover, Katharine Hepburn, steered clear of the Oscar ceremony out of respect for his widow.
- Previous to Hepburn, the devoutly Catholic Tracy had extramarital relationships with Loretta Young and Joan Crawford.
- Warren Beatty may have felt vindicated when the *New York Times* asked Bosley Crowther to step down after his scathing review of *Bonnie and Clyde*.
- The Hersholt Humanitarian Award winner, Gregory Peck, was kept in the dark until the surprise announcement.
- Dustin Hoffman was already 30 by the time he played 23-year-old Benjamin Braddock in *The Graduate*.
- "I thought we'd win Best Picture, but then nobody likes Warren Beatty," said Estelle Parsons.

169

George Kennedy with Paul Newman

BEST SUPPORTING ACTOR
GEORGE KENNEDY (B. 1925)
COOL HAND LUKE

"I could cry. I have to thank the Academy for the greatest moment of my life."

Kennedy played the heavy, no-nonsense guy in such films as *Airport* (1970) and its three sequels. He worked steadily in the 1960s in such films as *Lonely Are the Brave* (1962), *The Man from the Diner's Club* (1963), *Charade* (1963), *Strait-Jacket* (1964), *In Harm's Way* (1965), and *The Dirty Dozen* (1967), before his award for *Cool Hand Luke*.

In the 1970s he appeared in *Earthquake* (1974), *The Eiger Sanction* (1975), and *Death on the Nile* (1978), to name a few. During the 1980s and '90s Kennedy continued to appear regularly on screen but in less memorable movies, among them *Bolero* (1984), *Radioactive Dreams* (1986), and *Nightmare at Noon* (1990). "He gently spoofed his own straightforward screen image as Leslie Nielsen's police squad colleague in the comedy hits *The Naked Gun* (1988) and its sequels," wrote *Entertainment Tonight*'s Leonard Maltin of Kennedy's performance.

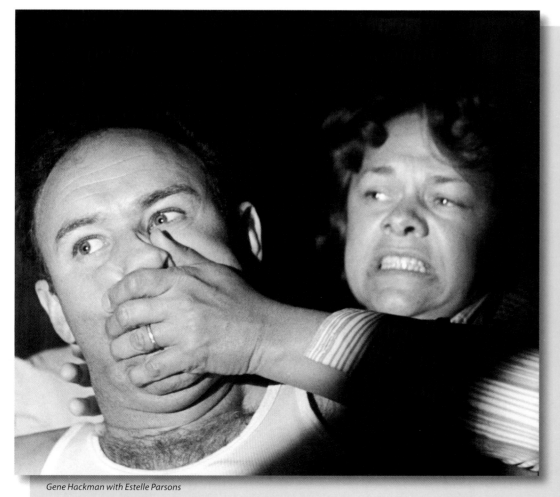

Gene Hackman with Estelle Parsons

BEST SUPPORTING ACTRESS
ESTELLE PARSONS (B. 1927)
BONNIE AND CLYDE

"Boy, it's heavy," shouted Parsons, lifting her Oscar. "I have to thank David Merrick, who let me out of my Broadway play...so I could be here this evening. Little did he know what it would mean to me, really. Thank you. It's really a great moment." Parsons did a "winning portrayal of wigged-out Blanche Barrow," wrote Leonard Maltin. The edgy Parsons was well suited to playing her part, as she had so often been in playing anxious neurotics and wild-eyed fanatics.

A former TV writer and producer who once worked on the *Today* show, Parsons took up acting in the late 1950s and, after spending several years on the stage, moved into film work. Her Oscar-winning role in *Bonnie and Clyde* was followed by another nomination for *Rachel, Rachel* (1968). In the 1980s Parsons had a major impact with her role as the annoying mother of TV's *Roseanne*.

AWARD NOMINATIONS 1967

PICTURE

BONNIE AND CLYDE, Tatira-Hiller, Warner Bros.-Seven Arts, Warren Beatty.
DOCTOR DOOLITTLE, Apjac, 20th Century-Fox, Arthur P. Jacobs.
THE GRADUATE, Nichols-Turman, Embassy, Lawrence Turman.
GUESS WHO'S COMING TO DINNER, Kramer, Columbia, Stanley Kramer.
IN THE HEAT OF THE NIGHT, Mirisch, UA, Walter Mirisch.

ACTOR

WARREN BEATTY in *Bonnie and Clyde*, Tatira-Hiller, Warner Bros.-Seven Arts.
DUSTIN HOFFMAN in *The Graduate*, Nichols Turman, Embassy.
PAUL NEWMAN in *Cool Hand Luke*, Jalem, Warner Bros.-Seven Arts,
ROD STEIGER in *In the Heat of the Night*, Mirisch, UA.
SPENCER TRACY in *Guess Who's Coming to Dinner*, Kramer, Columbia.

ACTRESS

ANNE BANCROFT in *The Graduate*, Nichols-Turman, Embassy.
FAYE DUNAWAY in *Bonnie and Clyde*, Tatira-Hiller, Warner Bros.-Seven Arts,
DAME EDITH EVANS in *The Whisperers*, Seven Pines, UA/Lopert (British).
AUDREY HEPBURN in *Wait until Dark*, Warner Bros.-Seven Arts.
KATHARINE HEPBURN in *Guess Who's Coming to Dinner*, Kramer, Columbia.

SUPPORTING ACTOR

JOHN CASSAVETES in *The Dirty Dozen*, Aldrich, MGM.
GENE HACKMAN in *Bonnie and Clyde*, Tatira-Hiller, Warner Bros.-Seven Arts,
CECIL KELLAWAY in *Guess Who's Coming to Dinner*, Kramer, Columbia,
GEORGE KENNEDY in *Cool Hand Luke*, Jalem, Warner Bros.-Seven Arts,
MICHAEL J. POLLARD in *Bonnie and Clyde*, Tatira Huller, Warner Bros,-Seven Arts.

SUPPORTING ACTRESS

CAROL CHANNING in *Thoroughly Modern Millie*, Hunter, Universal.
MILDRED NATWICK in *Barefoot in the Park*, Walls, Paramount.
ESTELLE PARSONS in *Bonnie and Clyde*, Tatira Huller, Warner Bros.-Seven Arts.
BEAH RICHARDS in *Guess Who's Coming to Dinner*, Kramer, Columbia.
KATHARINE ROSS in *The Graduate*, Nichols-Turman, Embassy.

DIRECTION

RICHARD BROOKS for *In Cold Blood*, Brooks, Columbia.
NORMAN JEWISON for *In the Heat of the Night*, Mirisch, UA.
STANLEY KRAMER for *Guess Who's Coming to Dinner*, Kramer, Columbia.
MIKE NICHOLS for *The Graduate*, Nichols-Turman, Embassy.
ARTHUR PENN for *Bonnie and Clyde*, Tatira-Hiller, Warner Bros.-Seven Arts,

WRITING: BASED ON MATERIAL FROM ANOTHER MEDIUM

COOL HAND LUKE, Jalem, Warner Bros.-Seven Arts. Donn Pearce and Frank R. Pierson.
THE GRADUATE, Nichols-Turman, Embassy. Calder Willingham and Buck Henry.

IN COLD BLOOD, Brooks, Columbia. Richard Brooks,
IN THE HEAT OF THE NIGHT, Minsch, UA. Stirling Silliphant.
ULYSSES, Walter Reade-Continental Distributing. Joseph Strick and Fred Haines.

WRITING: STORY AND SCREENPLAY WRITTEN DIRECTLY FOR THE SCREEN

BONNIE AND CLYDE, Tatira-Hiller, Warner Bros.-Seven Arts, David Newman and Robert Benton.
DIVORCE AMERICAN STYLE, Tandem-National General, Columbia Robert Kaufman and Norman Lear.
GUESS WHO'S COMING TO DINNER, Kramer, Columbia. William Rose.
LA GUERRE EST FINIE, Sofracima-Europa, Brandon Films (French). Jorge Semprun.
TWO FOR THE ROAD, Donen, 20th Century-Fox. Frederic Raphael.

CINEMATOGRAPHY

BONNIE AND CLYDE, Tatira-Hiller, Warner Bros.-Seven Arts. Burnett Guffey.
CAMELOT, Warner Bros.-Seven Arts. Richard H. Kline.
DOCTOR DOOLITTLE, Apjac, 20th Century-Fox. Robert Surtees.
THE GRADUATE, Nichols-Turman, Embassy. Robert Surtees.
IN COLD BLOOD, Brooks, Columbia. Conrad Hall.

ART DIRECTION—SET DECORATION

CAMELOT, Warner Bros.-Seven Arts. John Thiscott and Edward Carrere; John W. Brown.
DOCTOR DOOLITTLE, Apjac 20th Century-Fox. Mario Chiari, Jack Martin Smith and Ed Graves; Walter M. Scott and Stuart A. Reiss.
GUESS WHO'S COMING TO DINNER, Kramer, Columbia. Robert Clatworthy; Frank Tuttle.
THE TAMING OF THE SHREW, Royal Films International, Columbia. Renzo Hongiardino, John DeCuir, Riven Webb and Giuseppe Mariani; Dario Simoni and Luigi Gervasi.
THOROUGHLY MODERN MILLIE, Hunter, Universal. Alexander Golitzen and George C. Webb; Howard Bristol.

COSTUME DESIGN

BONNIE AND CLYDE, Tatira-Hiller, Warner Bros.-Seven Arts. Theadora Van Runkle.
CAMELOT, Warner Bros.-Seven Arts. John Truscott.
THE HAPPIEST MILLIONAIRE, Disney, Buena Vista. Bill Thomas.
THE TAMING OF THE SHREW, Royal Films International, Columbia. Irene Sharaff and Danilo Donati.
THOROUGHLY MODERN MILLIE, Hunter, Universal. Jean Louis.

SOUND

CAMELOT, Warner Bros.-Seven Arts. Warner Bros.-Seven Arts Studio Sound Dept.
THE DIRTY DOZEN, Aldrich, MGM. MGM. Studio Sound Dept.
DOCTOR DOOLITTLE, Apjac, 20th Century-Fox. 20th Century-Fox Studio Sound Dept.
IN THE HEAT OF THE NIGHT, Mirisch, UA. Samuel Goldwyn Studio Sound Dept.
THOROUGHLY MODERN MILLIE, Hunter, Universal. Universal City Studio Sound Dept.

FILM EDITING

BEACH RED, Theodora, UA. Frank P. Keller
THE DIRTY DOZEN, Aldrich, M.G-M. Michael Luciano.
DOCTOR DOOLITTLE, Apjac, 20th Century-Fox. Samuel E. Beetley and Marjorie Fowler.
GUESS WHO'S COMING TO DINNER, Kramer, Columbia. Robert C. Jones.
IN THE HEAT OF THE NIGHT, Mirisch, UA. Hal Ashby.

SPECIAL EFFECTS

DOCTOR DOOLITTLE, Apjac, 20th Century-Fox. L.B. Abbott.
TOBRUK, Gibraltar-Corman, Universal. Howard A. Anderson, Jr., and Albert Whitlock.

SOUND EFFECTS

THE DIRTY DOZEN, Aldrich, MGM. John Poyner.
IN THE HEAT OF THE NIGHT, Mirisch, UA. James A. Richard.

SONG

THE BARE NECESSITIES, (*The Jungle Book*, Disney, Buena Vista); Music and Lyrics by Terry Gilkyson.
THE EYES OF LOVE (*Banning*, Universal); Music by Quincy Jones. Lyrics by Bob Russell.
THE LOOK OF LOVE (*Casino Royale*, Famous Artists, Columbia); Music by Burt Bacharach. Lyrics by Hal David.
TALK TO THE ANIMALS (*Doctor Doolittle*, Apjac, 20th Century-Fox); Music and Lyrics by Leslie Bricusse.
THOROUGHLY MODERN MILLIE, (*Thoroughly Modern Millie*, Hunter, Universal); Music and Lyrics by James Van Heusen and Sammy Cahn.

SCORING: ORIGINAL MUSIC

COOL HAND LUKE, Jalem, Warner Bros.-Seven Arts. Lab Schifrin.
DOCTOR DOOLITTLE, Apjac, 20th Century-Fox. Leslie Bricusse.
FAR FROM THE MADDING CROWD, Appia, MGM. Richard Rodney Bennett.
IN COLD BLOOD, Brooks, Columbia. Quincy Jones.
THOROUGHLY MODERN MILLIE, Hunter, Universal. Elmer Bernstein.

SCORING: ADAPTATION OR TREATMENT

CAMELOT, Warner Bros.-Seven Arts. Alfred Newman and Ken Darby.
DOCTOR DOOLITTLE, Apjac, 20th Century-Fox. Lionel Newman and Alexander Courage.
GUESS WHO'S COMING TO DINNER, Kramer, Columbia. DeVol.
THOROUGHLY MODERN MILLIE, Hunter, Universal. Andre Previn and Joseph Gershenson.
VALLEY OF THE DOLLS, Red Lion, 20th CenturyFox. John Williams.

SHORT SUBJECTS: CARTOONS

THE BOX, Brandon Films. Fred Wolf, producer.
HYPOYHESE BETA, Films Orzeaux, Pathe Contemporary Films. Jean-Charles Meunier, producer.
WHAT ON EARTH!, National Film Board of Canada, Columbia. Robert Verrall and Wolf Koenig, producers.

SHORT SUBJECTS: LIVE ACTION

PADDLE TO THE SEA, National Film Board of Canada, Favorite Films. Julian Biggs, producer.
A PLACE TO STAND, T.D.F. Prod, for Ontario Dept. of Economics and Development, Columbia. Christopher Chapman, producer.
SKY OVER HOLLAND, Ferno Prod, for The Netherlands, Seneca International. John Ferno, producer.
STOP, LOOK AND LISTEN, MGM. Len Janson and Chuck Menville, producers.

DOCUMENTARY: SHORT SUBJECTS

MONUMENT TO THE DREAM, Guggenheim Prods. Charles E. Guggenheim, producer.
A PLACE TO STAND, T.D.F. Prod, for The Ontario Department of Economics and Development. Christopher Chapman, producer.
THE REDWOODS, King Screen Prods. Mark Harris and Trevor Greenwood, producers.
SEE YOU AT THE PILLAR, Associated British-Pathe Prod. Robert Fitchett, producer.
WHILE I RUN THIS RACE, Sun Dial Films for VISTA. Carl V. Ragsdale, producer.

DOCUMENTARY: FEATURES

THE ANDERSON PLATOON, French Broadcasting System. Pierre Schoendoerffer, producer.
FESTIVAL, Patchke Prods. Murray Lerner, producer.
HARVEST, U.S. Information Agency. Carroll Ballard, producer.
A KING'S STORY, Jack La Vien Prod. Jack La Vien, producer.

A TIME FOR BURNING, Quest Prods, for Lutheran Film Associates. William C. Jersey, producer.

FOREIGN LANGUAGE FILMS

CLOSELY WATCHED TRAINS (Czechoslovakia).
EL AMOR BRUJO (Spain).
I EVEN MET HAPPY GYPSIES (Yugoslavia).
LIVE FOR LIFE (France).
PORTRAIT OF CHIEKO (Japan).

HONORARY AND OTHER AWARDS

TO ARTHUR FREED for distinguished service to the Academy and the production of six top-rated Awards telecasts.

IRVING G. THALBERG MEMORIAL AWARD

TO ALFRED HITCHCOCK

JEAN HERSHOLT HUMANITARIAN AWARD

TO GREGORY PECK

SCIENTIFIC OR TECHNICAL

CLASS III

ELECTRO-OPTICAL DIVISION of the KOLLMORGEN CORPORATION;
PANAVISION INCORPORATED;
FRED R. WILSON of the SAMUEL GOLDWYN STUDIO SOUND DEPT.;
WALDON O. WATSON and the UNIVERSAL CITY STUDIO SOUND DEPT.

1968

"Please be sure to read everything in the envelope carefully."
—Price Waterhouse accountant, backstage, instructing Best Actress presenter Ingrid Bergman

"And the winner is. . . It's a tie!"
—Ingrid Bergman

Famed choreographer Gower Champion agreed to direct the Oscarfest only on the conditions that the show be moved to the Dorothy Chandler Pavilion, that the Dress Code regulations be loosened up, and that perennial host Bob Hope finally be dispensed with. Academy president Gregory Peck conceded and made an even more controversial decision of his own. He allowed Barbra Streisand to become an Academy voter without the usual two-year wait period following a first film release. It was a decision that would have an historic effect on the 1968 awards.

When Streisand voted for herself she caused a Best Actress tie. The result was one of the most astonishing moments ever, as she nearly tripped on her way to the podium. The camera lingered on her posterior, barely concealed in the see-through Scaasi pajamas that caused almost as much of an uproar as her win.

If Jack Albertson and Ruth Gordon got the most sentimentally inspired applause, Best Original Screenplay winner for *The Producers*, Mel Brooks, got the biggest laugh. "I'll just say what's in my heart—ba bump, ba bump, ba bump," he said. Comedienne Martha Raye was too choked up to elicit guffaws when she became the first woman to receive the Jean Hersholt Humanitarian Award for her United Service Organizations appearances in Vietnam. She couldn't even sing as scheduled, but Aretha Franklin did, giving nominated song "Funny Girl" the full, soul-stomping treatment. Frank Sinatra was appropriately blown away. "She really tore it up, didn't she?" he commented.

As the night wore on it remained a tossup between the heavy Best Picture favorites, *A Lion in Winter* and *Funny Girl*. But as is often the case, the top contenders bumped each other off, leaving room for a surprise. A wily little orphan named Oliver managed to slip through the cracks. Unlikely phenomenon Barbra Streisand, who was so disappointed that she didn't "look gorgeous on film," might well have related to his miraculous good fortune.

"HELLO, GORGEOUS!"

CEREMONY: April 14, 1969
Dorothy Chandler Pavilion,
Los Angeles Music Center,
Los Angeles
HOST: Ten Friends of Oscar

**BEST PICTURE/BEST DIRECTOR
CAROL REED (1906–1976)
OLIVER!**

There was stiff competition for this year's Best Film, with the following films in the running: *Rosemary's Baby*, *Petulia*, *Targets*, *The Conqueror Worm*, *Faces*, *The Producers*, *Pretty Poison*, *Isadora*, *The Good, the Bad, and the Ugly*, *Bullitt*, *Charly*, *Weekend*, *Belle de Jour*, and *2001: A Space Odyssey*. *Oliver!* was good enough to beat them all, and the critics agreed. Pauline Kael called *Oliver!* "not only a musical entertainment but an imaginative version of the novel as a lyrical, macabre fable," adding, "Carol Reed gives a superb demonstration of intelligent craftsmanship; he doesn't urge us to tears—he leaves us our pride."

Reed produced a long line of distinguished films, among them *The Stars Look Down* (1939), *Night Train to Munich* (1940), and the H. G. Wells story *Kipps* (1941). Like so many directors, Reed worked on propaganda features during World War II, including an Oscar-winning collaboration with American director Garson Kanin in *The True Glory* (1945).

Mark Lester

Reed's first postwar feature, *Odd Man Out* (1947), led to his five-film collaboration with producer Alexander Korda. Out of this marriage came some of Reed's best films, including *The Fallen Idol* (1948, nom.), *The Third Man* (1949, nom.), and *Our Man in Havana* (1960). In the 1950s and '60s Reed's output was equally fine, including *Trapeze* (1956), *Mutiny on the Bounty* (1962) (from which he was fired and replaced by Lewis Milestone), and *The Agony and the Ecstasy* (1965). His last film was *Follow Me* (1972, known as *The Public Eye* in the United States).

The envelope, please…

BEST ACTOR
CLIFF ROBERTSON (B. 1925)
CHARLY

Robertson, who once said he would swim across the Pacific Ocean to be present at the Oscars, was—this Oscar night—filming in the Philippines. Having originated the TV role of *Charly*, a mental retardee who briefly becomes a genius following a radical experiment, Robertson bought the film rights to assure his casting. He'd been cheated out of two other TV-turned-movie roles in *The Days of Wine and Roses* and *The Hustler*.

Robertson's other standout roles included his debut in *Picnic* (1955), *PT-109* (1963, for which he was reportedly handpicked by JFK himself), and *The Best Man* (1964). Married to actress Dina Merrill from 1966–1989, Robertson hit the scandal sheets when studio chief David Begelman forged checks in the actor's name. When Robertson blew the whistle he—not Begelman—was ostracized by Hollywood.

BEST ACTRESS
KATHARINE HEPBURN (B. 1907)
THE LION IN WINTER

BARBRA STREISAND (B. 1942)
FUNNY GIRL

"The winner is…it's a tie," shouted a stunned Ingrid Bergman.

Barbra Streisand, in a rare debut Oscar win, tore her see-through Scaasi pajamas as she raced to the stage. "I was thinking…um…the first script of *Funny Girl* was written when I was only 11 years old and, um, thank God it took so long to get it right, you know?"

Streisand, a cabaret singer and recording artist, first took Broadway by storm in *I Can Get It for You Wholesale* (1962). She soared on the big screen in *Hello, Dolly!* (1969), *On a Clear Day You Can See Forever* (1970), *The Owl and the Pussycat* (1970), *What's Up, Doc?* (1972), *Up the Sandbox* (1972), and *The Way We Were* (1973, nom.).

In association with then-lover, Jon Peters, she endured the failures of *A Star Is Born* (1976), *The Main Event* (1979), and *All Night Long* (1981). She complained that sexism was behind the Academy's pass for her direction of *Yentl* (1983). Her follow-up dramatic roles included *Nuts* (1987), *The Prince of Tides* (1991, another directorial snub), and *The Mirror Has Two Faces* (1996).

Hepburn: No-show Hepburn relayed her brief message, "When you've lived as long as I have, anything is possible" (she was only 59). It was back-to-back Oscars after the previous year's win for *Guess Who's Coming to Dinner*. Her performance in *Lion* did not receive universal raves. "Hepburn does a gallant-ravaged-great-lady number. She draws upon our feelings for her, not for the character she's playing, and the self-exploitation is hard to take," Pauline Kael groused.

(For more on Hepburn, see 1932–33, 1967, and 1981.)

(For more on Hepburn, see 1932–33, 1967, and 1981.)

BEST OF 1968
Best Picture: *Oliver!*
Best Director: Carol Reed, *Oliver!*
Best Actor: Cliff Robertson, *Charly*
Best Actress: Katharine Hepburn, *The Lion in Winter* and Barbra Streisand, *Funny Girl*
Best Supporting Actor: Jack Albertson, *The Subject Was Roses*
Best Supporting Actress: Ruth Gordon, *Rosemary's Baby*

FIRSTS
- Katharine Hepburn and Barbra Streisand were the first exact tie winners. In 1932, Wallace Beery and Fredric March shared the Best Actor honors, but Beery was unofficially one vote shy.

- This was Hepburn's record-breaking third Oscar for the top acting prize. Her first win was *Morning Glory* (1933), her second, *Guess Who's Coming to Dinner* (1967). She would win a fourth for *On Golden Pond* (1981). The only other three-time winner was Walter Brennan in the Best Supporting category for *Come and Get It* (1936), *Kentucky* (1938), and *The Westerner* (1940).

- This was the first year of Oscar at the Dorothy Chandler Pavilion.

- This marked the first worldwide telecast to thirty-seven nations.

- Best Foreign Film, *War and Peace* (U.S.S.R.), at nearly seven hours in length, was the longest film to win an Oscar.

SINS OF OMISSION
Picture: *Rosemary's Baby*
Actress: Mia Farrow, *Rosemary's Baby*

ALWAYS A BRIDESMAID, NEVER A BRIDE
- Cliff Robertson had originated the roles in two TV dramas turned feature films that went on to win Oscar nominations for his replacements, Jack Lemmon in *Days of Wine and Roses* (1962) and Paul Newman in *The Hustler* (1961).

- Before winning her Oscar, Ruth Gordon had been working in the film industry since 1915.

- *The Lion in Winter* would be the third of seven failed nominations for Peter O'Toole.

- Before finally winning for *Oliver!*, director Carol Reed had come up empty for such classics as *The Third Man* (1949) and *Our Man in Havana* (1959).

ROLE REVERSALS
With his nomination for *The Producers*, Gene Wilder was in contention with Dustin Hoffman for the lead in the upcoming *Portnoy's Complaint*. Richard Benjamin finally won the role.

UNMENTIONABLES
- Frank Sinatra filed for divorce after wife Mia Farrow ignored his demand that she turn down *Rosemary's Baby*.

- Gower Champion died just hours before the opening-night curtain rose on his biggest Broadway hit, *42nd Street* (1979). The show's producer, David Merrick, withheld the information, for full dramatic effect, until the curtain call.

- *Oliver!* co-star Oliver Reed, was director Carol Reed's nephew.

- Director Robert Aldrich made no friends when he refused to allow Cliff Robertson time off from the Philippines set of *Too Late the Hero* to attend the Oscars. Robertson pleaded, even offered to pay for the budget loss, to no avail.

- Streisand's behavior on the set of *Funny Girl* led screenwriter Isobel Lennart to admit that working with her was a "deflating, ego-crushing experience."

BEST SUPPORTING ACTOR
JACK ALBERTSON (1907–1981)
THE SUBJECT WAS ROSES

"Frank Gilroy fought for a year to make sure I got this part in the movie, and I shall never forget him for it," said the tearful actor. "I've been kicking around this business about forty years and I'm not about to be knocked over by the red-carpet treatment."

Albertson, a veteran of vaudeville, burlesque, and legitimate stage, generally played character-actor roles. He appeared in *Top Banana* (1954), re-creating his stage role. He played a wide variety of roles thereafter but seemed most comfortable in comedic parts. He also worked extensively on TV, co-starring in the sitcom *Chico and the Man* (1974–1979).

BEST SUPPORTING ACTRESS
RUTH GORDON (1896–1985)
ROSEMARY'S BABY

"I can't tell you how encouraging a thing like this is," said the 72-year-old actress. "I remember the first film I was ever in, in 1915, and here we are in 1969 and I don't know why it took me so long, though I don't think I'm backward. Thank all of you who voted for me. And to all who didn't, please excuse me."

When Gordon played the sinister neighbor in *Baby*, she already had a long list of memorable performances behind her, among them in *Abe Lincoln in Illinois* (1940), *Dr. Ehrlich's Magic Bullet* (1940), and *Two-Faced Woman* (1941). In 1942 she married playwright Garson Kanin, with whom she wrote a series of acclaimed screenplays directed by George Cukor: *A Double Life* (1947, nom.) and the Spencer Tracy–Katharine Hepburn classics *Adam's Rib* (1949, nom.) and *Pat and Mike* (1952, nom.), as well as *The Marrying Kind* (1952).

Gordon's film career picked up again with *Inside Daisy Clover* (1965, nom.), *Where's Poppa?* (1970), and *Harold and Maude* (1971). She also appeared in *Every Which Way but Loose* (1978), *Boardwalk* (1979), *My Bodyguard* (1980), and *Maxie* (1985). Before her death, Gordon penned two best-selling memoirs, *Myself Among Others* (1971) and *My Side* (1976).

PICTURE

FUNNY GIRL, Rastar, Columbia, Ray Stark.
THE LION IN WINTER, Haworth, Avco Embassy, Martin Poll.
OLIVER!, Romulus, Columbia, John Woolf.
RACHEL, RACHEL, Kayos, Warner Bros.-Seven Arts, Paul Newman.
ROMEO AND JULIET, B.H.E.-Verona-De Laurentiis, Paramount, Anthony Havelock-Allan and John Brabourne.

ACTOR

ALAN ARKIN in *The Heart is a Lonely Hunter*, Warner Bros.-Seven Arts.
ALAN BATES in *The Fixer*, Frankenheimer-Lewis, MGM.
RON MOODY in *Oliver!*, Romulus, Columbia.
PETER O'TOOLE in *The Lion in Winter*, Haworth, Avco Embassy.
CLIFF ROBERTSON in *Charly*, ABC-Selmur, Cinerama.

ACTRESS

KATHARINE HEPBURN in *The Lion in Winter*, Haworth, Avco Embassy.
PATRICIA NEAL in *The Subject Was Roses*, MGM.
VANESSA REDGRAVE in *Isadora*, Hakim, Universal.
BARBRA STREISAND in *Funny Girl*, Rastar, Columbia.
JOANNE WOODWARD in *Rachel, Rachel*, Kayos, Warner Bros.-Seven Arts.

SUPPORTING ACTOR

JACK ALBERTSON in *The Subject Was Roses*, MGM.
SEYMOUR CASSEL in *Faces*, Cassavetes, Reade-Continental.
DANIEL MASSEY in *Star!*, Wise, 20th Century-Fox.
JACK WILD in *Oliver!* Romulus, Columbia.
GENE WILDER in *The Producers*, Glazier, Avco Embassy.

SUPPORTING ACTRESS

LYNN CARLIN in *Faces*, Cassavetes, Reade-Continental.
RUTH GORDON in *Rosemary's Baby*, Castle, Paramount.
SONDRA LOCKE in *The Heart Is a Lonely Hunter*, Warner Bros.-Seven Arts.
KAY MEDFORD in *Funny Girl*, Rastar, Columbia.
ESTELLE PARSONS in *Rachel, Rachel*, Kayos, Warner Bros.-Seven Arts,

DIRECTION

ANTHONY HARVEY for *The Lion in Winter*, Haworth, Avco Embassy.
STANLEY KUBRICK for *2001: A Space Odyssey*, Polaris, MGM.
GILLO PONTECORVO for *The Battle of Algiers*, Igor-Casbash, Allied Artists (Italian).
CAROL REED for *Oliver!*, Romulus, Columbia.
FRANCO ZEFFIRELLI for *Romeo and Juliet*, B.H.E.-Verona-De Laurentiis, Paramount.

WRITING: BASED ON MATERIAL FROM ANOTHER MEDIUM

THE LION IN WINTER, Haworth, Avco Embassy. James Goldman.
THE ODD COUPLE, Koch, Paramount. Neil Simon.
OLIVER!, Romulus, Columbia. Vernon Harris.
RACHEL, RACHEL, Kayos, Warner Bros.-Seven Arts. Stewart Stern.

ROSEMARY'S BABY, Castle, Paramount. Roman Polanski.

WRITING: STORY AND SCREENPLAY WRITTEN DIRECTLY FOR THE SCREEN

THE BATTLE OF ALGIERS, Igor-Casbah, Allied Artists (Italian). Franco Solinas and Gillo Pontecorvo.
FACES, Cassavetes, Walter Reade-Continental. John Cassavetes.
HOT MILLIONS, Alberg MGM. Ira Wallach and Peter Ustinov.
THE PRODUCERS, Glazier, Avco Embassy. Mel Brooks.
2001: A SPACE ODYSSEY, Polaris, MGM. Stanley Kubrick and Arthur C. Clarke.

CINEMATOGRAPHY

FUNNY GIRL, Rastar, Columbia. Harry Stradling.
ICE STATION ZEBRA, Filmways, MGM. Daniel L. Fapp.
OLIVER! Romulus, Columbia. Oswald Morris.
ROMEO AND JULIET, B.H.E.-Verona-DeLaurentiis, Paramount. Pasqualino De Santis.
STAR!, Wise, 20th Century-Fox. Ernest Laszlo.

ART DIRECTION—SET DECORATION

OLIVER! Romulus, Columbia. John Box and Terence Marsh; Vernon Dixon and Ken Muggleston.
THE SHOES OF THE FISHERMAN, Englund, MGM. George W. Davis and Edward Carfagno.
STAR!, Wise, 20th Century-Fox. Boris Leven; Walter H. Scott and Howard Bristol.
2001: A SPACE ODYSSEY, Polaris, MGM. Tony Masters, Harry Lange and Ernie Archer.
WAR AND PEACE, Mosfilm, Walter Reade-Continental (Russian). Mikhail Bogdanov and Gennady Myasnikov; G. Koshelev and V. Uvarov.

COSTUME DESIGN

THE LION IN WINTER, Haworth, Avco Embassy. Margaret Furse.
OLIVER!, Romulus, Columbia. Phyllis Dalton.
PLANET OF THE APES, Apjac, 20th Century-Fox. Morton Haack.
ROMEO AND JULIET, B.H.E.-Verona-DeLaurentiis, Paramount. Danilo Donati.
STAR!, Wise, 20th Century-Fox. Donald Brooks.

SOUND

BULLITT, Solar, Warner Bros.-Seven Arts. Warner Bros.-Seven Arts Studio Sound Dept.
FINIAN'S RAINBOW, Warner Bros.-Seven Arts. Warner Bros.-Seven Arts Studio Sound Dept.
FUNNY GIRL, Rastar, Columbia. Columbia Studio Sound Dept.
OLIVER, Romulus, Columbia. Shepperton Studio Sound Dept.
STAR!, Wise, 20th Century-Fox. 20th Century-Fox Studio Sound Dept.

FILM EDITING

BULLITT, Solar, Warner Bros.-Seven Arts. Frank P. Keller.
FUNNY GIRL, Rastar, Columbia. Robert Swink, Maury Winetrobe and William Sands.
THE ODD COUPLE, Koch, Paramount. Frank Bracht.
OLIVER!, Romulus, Columbia. Ralph Kemplen.
WILD IN THE STREETS, American International. Fred Feitshans and Eve Newman.

SPECIAL EFFECTS

ICE STATION ZEBRA, Filmways, MGM. Hal Millar and J. McMillan Johnson.
2001: A SPACE ODYSSEY, Polaris, MGM. Stanley Kubrick.

SONG

CHITTY CHITTY BANG BANG (*Chitty Chitty Bang Bang*, Warfield, UA); Music and Lyrics by Richard M. Sherman and Robert B. Sherman.
FOR LOVE OF IVY (*For Love of Ivy*, ABC-Palomar, Cinerama); Music by Quincy Jones. Lyrics by Bob Russell.
FUNNY GIRL (*Funny Girl*, Rastar, Columbia); Music by Jule Styne. Lyrics by Bob Merrill.
STAR! (*Star!*, Wise, 20th Century-Fox); Music by Jimmy Van Heusen. Lyrics by Sammy Cahn.

THE WINDMILLS OF YOUR MIND (*The Thomas Crown Affair*, Mirisch-Simkoe-Solar, UA); Music by Michel Legrand. Lyrics by Alan and Marilyn Bergman.

ORIGINAL SCORE

THE FOX, Stross, Claridge Pictures. Lab Schifrin.
THE LION IN WINTER, Haworth, Avco Embassy. John Barry.
PLANET OF THE APES, Apjac, 20th Century-Fox. Jerry Goldsmith.
THE SHOES OF THE FISHERMAN, Englund, MGM. Alex North.
THE THOMAS CROWN AFFAIR, Mirisch-SimkoeSolar, UA. Michel Legrand.

SCORE: MUSICAL

FINIAN'S RAINBOW, Warner Bros.-Seven Arts. Ray Heindorf.
FUNNY GIRL, Rastar, Columbia. Walter Scharf.
OLIVER!, Romulus, Columbia. John Green.
STAR!, Wise, 20th Century-Fox. Lennie Hayton.
THE YOUNG GIRLS OF ROCHEFORT, Warner Bros.-Seven Arts (French). Michel Legrand and Jacques Demy.

SHORT SUBJECTS: CARTOONS

THE HOUSE THAT JACK BUILT, National Film Board of Canada, Columbia. Wolf Koenig and Jim MacKay, producers.
THE MAGIC PEAR TREE, Bing Crosby Prods, Jimmy Murakami, producer.
WINDY DAY, Hubley Studios, Paramount. John and Faith Hubley, producers.
WINNIE THE POOH AND THE BLUSTERY DAY, Disney, Buena Vista. Walt Disney, producer.

SHORT SUBJECTS: LIVE ACTION

THE DOVE, Coe-Davis, Schoenfeld Films. George Coe, Sidney Davis and Anthony Lover, producers.
DUO, National Film Board of Canada, Columbia.
PRELUDE, Prelude Company, Excelsior Dist. John Astin, producer.
ROBERT KENNEDY REMEMBERED, Guggenheim Prods., National General. Charles Guggenheim, producer.

DOCUMENTARY: SHORT SUBJECTS

THE MOUSE THAT ANANDA BUILT, Films Division, Government of India. Fali Bilimoria, producer.
THE REVOLVING DOOR, Vision Associates for American Foundation Institute of Corrections. Lee R. Broker, producer.
A SPACE TO GROW, Office of Economic Opportunity for Project Upward Bound. Thomas P. Kelly, Jr., producer.
A WAY OUT OF THE WILDERNESS, John Sutherland, Prods. Dan E. Weisburd, producer.
WHY MAN CREATES, Saul Bass & Associates. Saul Bass, producer.

DOCUMENTARY: FEATURES

A FEW NOTES ON OUR FOOD PROBLEM, U.S. Information Agency. James Blue, producer.
JOURNEY INTO SELF, Western Behavioral Sciences Institute. Bill McGaw producer.
THE LEGENDARY CHAMPIONS, Turn Of The Century Fights, William Cayton, producer.
OTHER VOICES, DHS Films. David H. Sawyer, producer.
YOUNG AMERICANS, The Young Americans Prod. Robert Cohn and Alex Grasshoff, producers.
(NOTE: YOUNG AMERICANS was originally voted the award but later [on May 7, 1969] was declared ineligible after it was learned that the picture was first shown in a theater in October 1967 and therefore not eligible for a 1968 Award. JOURNEY INTO SELF, first runner-up, was announced as the official winner on May 8, 1969.)

FOREIGN LANGUAGE

THE BOYS OF PAUL STREET (Hungary).
THE FIREMEN'S BALL (Czechoslovakia).
THE GIRL WITH THE PISTOL (Italy).
STOLEN KISSES (France).
WAR AND PEACE (Russia).

HONORARY AND OTHER AWARDS

TO JOHN CHAMBERS for his outstanding make-up achievement for *Planet Of The Apes*.
TO ONNA WHITE for her outstanding choreography achievement for *Oliver!*

JEAN HERSHOLT HUMANITARIAN AWARD

TO MARTHA RAYE

SCIENTIFIC OR TECHNICAL

CLASS I

PHILIP V. PALMQUIST of MINNESOTA MINING AND MANUFACTURING CO., to DR. HERBERT MEYER of the MOTION PICTURE AND TELEVISION RESEARCH CENTER, and to CHARLES D, STAFFELL of the RANK ORGANISATION for the development of a successful embodiment of the reflex background projection system for composite cinematography.
EASTMAN KODAK COMPANY for the development and introduction of a color reversal intermediate film for motion pictures.

CLASS II

DONALD W. NORWOOD for the design and development of the Norwood Photographic Exposure Meters.
EASTMAN KODAK COMPANY and PRODUCERS SERVICE COMPANY for the development of a new high-speed step-optical reduction printer.
EDMUND M. DIGIULIO, NIELS G. PETERSEN and NORMAN S. HUGHES of the CINEMA PRODUCT DEVELOPMENT COMPANY for the design and application of a conversion which makes available the reflex viewing system for motion picture cameras.
OPTICAL COATING LABORATORIES, INC., for the development of an improved anti-reflection coating for photographic and projection lens systems.
EASTMAN KODAK COMPANY for the introduction of a new high speed motion picture color negative film.
PANAVISION INCORPORATED for the conception, design and introduction of a 65mm hand-held motion picture camera.
TODD-AO COMPANY and the MITCHELL CAMERA COMPANY for the design and engineering of the Todd-AO hand-held motion picture camera.

CLASS III

CARL W. HAUGE and EDWARD H. REICHARD of CONSOLIDATED FILM INDUSTRIES and E. MICHAEL MEAHL and ROY J. RIDENOUR of RAMTRONICS;
EASTMAN KODAK COMPANY and CONSOLIDATED FILM INDUSTRIES.

1969

"I'm an American movie actor. I work with my clothes on. I have to. Horses are rough on your legs and your elsewheres."

—John Wayne

Jane Fonda, fresh from her controversial visit to Hanoi, flashed the peace sign, and Candice Bergen wore a mildly rebellious poncho. Elizabeth Taylor showed up with a million-dollar tan, a $1.5 million diamond on her finger, and Richard Burton on her arm.

Burton was a heavy favorite for Best Actor, and Taylor was determined to see him finally get the Oscar that had eluded him. But the crown Burton wore as Henry VIII in *Anne of the Thousand Days* was not the preferred headgear of the moment. This was the night of the cowboy hat. Nominations and awards were lassoed by *The Wild Bunch*, *Butch Cassidy and the Sundance Kid*, *Paint Your Wagon*, and, most astonishingly to many, the X-rated *Midnight Cowboy*.

King of the celluloid Wild West, John Wayne finally got his due in a surprise victory for what he considered the easiest role of his career. "I just hippity-hopped through it," he said. An indelible performance beat out bloodlines in the Best Actress category, as Maggie Smith emerged from the rear of the pack to edge out Jane Fonda and Liza Minnelli.

The old guard cheered Gig Young's win over hot newcomer Jack Nicholson (nominated for *Easy Rider*) and went wild when Frank Sinatra introduced Honorary Oscar recipient Cary Grant. The epitome of elegance—a man whose closest association to the Wild West was Mae West (*I'm No Angel*, 1933)—delivered a modest speech about the necessity for collaboration, listing the legendary directors and screenwriters who had "put up with him" all these years.

Grant's speech was the show's high-water mark until the announcement of Best Picture, *Midnight Cowboy*. The win was as scandalous as its Oscar presenter, Elizabeth Taylor, who smiled for the first time all night. Her man may have lost, but she seemed to appreciate the success of a movie about a determined young buck whose sole ambition was to satisfy the needs of beautiful women.

X-RATED COWBOY

CEREMONY: April 7, 1970
Dorothy Chandler Pavilion,
Los Angeles Music Center,
Los Angeles
HOSTS: Seventeen Friends of Oscar

BEST PICTURE/BEST DIRECTOR
JOHN SCHLESINGER (B. 1926)
MIDNIGHT COWBOY

Despite its X rating, *Midnight Cowboy's* impact was undeniable. *Entertainment Tonight's* Leonard Maltin wrote, "Like all of the director's best work, [*Cowboy*] is marked by exceptional performances and a keen sense of observation." The film also had its detractors. *The New Yorker's* Pauline Kael wrote, "Schlesinger uses fast cutting and tricky camera work to provide a satirical background as enrichment of the story, but the satire is offensively inaccurate—it cheapens the story and gives it a veneer of almost hysterical cleverness. The point of the movie must be to give us some insight into the derelicts—two of the many kinds of dreamers and failures in the city."

A lifelong movie buff, Schlesinger followed his debut feature, *A Kind of Loving* (1962), with *Billy Liar* (1963), but his Oscar nomination for *Darling* (1965) solidified his reputation. After *Darling* he went on to make accomplished and provocative films— among them *Far from the Madding Crowd* (1967, nom.), *Sunday, Bloody Sunday* (1971, nom.), *The Day of the Locust* (1975), *Marathon Man* (1976), *Yanks* (1979), *The Falcon and the Snowman* (1985), *The Believers* (1987), *Madame Sousatzka* (1988), and *The Innocent* (1993).

Jon Voight

The envelope, please…

BEST ACTOR
JOHN WAYNE (1907–1979)
TRUE GRIT

"If I'd known this was all it would take, I'd have put that eye patch on forty years ago," said Wayne in his acceptance speech. In *True Grit* Wayne played his first character role in years—a boozy, one-eyed, over-the-hill lawman. "Oscar and I have something in common," Wayne went on. "Oscar first came to the Hollywood scene in 1928. So did I. We're both a little weather-beaten, but we're still here and plan to be around for a whole lot longer."

Born Marion Morrison, Wayne supported himself as an extra while attending USC. Discovered by John Ford, he enjoyed a name change and became an overnight star with *Stagecoach* (1939). Wayne starred in countless films, including *The Spoilers* (1942), *Reap the Wild Wind* (1942), *Flying Tigers* (1942), and *They Were Expendable* (1945). The very incarnation of a war hero, Wayne was himself exempted from military service.

Following a long string of successful Westerns, Wayne collaborated with Ford again on what was perhaps his finest film, *The Searchers* (1956). His apt swan song, *The Shootist* (1976), told the story of a terminally ill, aging gunfighter. Wayne's last appearance at the 1979 Oscar ceremony was an act of courage for the cancer-ridden star, who died months later.

BEST ACTRESS
MAGGIE SMITH (B. 1934)
THE PRIME OF MISS JEAN BRODIE

One of Britain's thespian treasures, Smith has scored innumerable triumphs on the stage (both in England and on Broadway) as well as on the screen. Trained at the Oxford Playhouse School, she made her stage debut in 1952, and her first film, *Nowhere to Go*, in 1958. American moviegoers first noticed her in *The V.I.P.s* (1963) and in her brilliant performance in *Othello* (1964, nom.). Appearances in *The Pumpkin Eater* (1964), *The Honey Pot* (1967), *Hot Millions* (1968), and *Oh! What a Lovely War* (1969) didn't do much for her reputation, but her dynamic, Oscar-winning performance as an eccentric schoolmistress in *The Prime of Miss Jean Brodie* (1969) finally established her in America as a star.

She next made *Travels with My Aunt*, *Love and Pain (and the Whole Damn Thing)* (both 1972), and *California Suite* (1978, Oscar). She worked for Merchant and Ivory in *Quartet* (1981) and then snagged another Oscar nomination for *A Room with a View* (1985). A series of indelible characters culminated in yet another nomination for *Gosford Park* (2001). (For more on Smith, see 1978.)

BEST OF 1969
Best Picture: *Midnight Cowboy*
Best Director: John Schlesinger, *Midnight Cowboy*
Best Actor: John Wayne, *True Grit*
Best Actress: Maggie Smith, *The Prime of Miss Jean Brodie*
Best Supporting Actor: Gig Young, *They Shoot Horses, Don't They?*
Best Supporting Actress: Goldie Hawn, *Cactus Flower*
Honorary Award: Cary Grant

FIRSTS
- *Midnight Cowboy* was the first and only X-rated Best Picture to win an Oscar.
- Producer Hal Wallis's Best Picture nomination for *Anne of the Thousand Days* was his nineteenth, an Academy record.

ROLE REVERSALS
- Michael Sarrazin missed the chance to play the lead in *Midnight Cowboy* due to scheduling conflicts.
- Jack Nicholson replaced Rip Torn in *Easy Rider*.

SINS OF OMISSION
Picture: *They Shoot Horses, Don't They?*

ALWAYS A BRIDESMAID, NEVER A BRIDE
- *Anne of a Thousand Days* marked Richard Burton's sixth failed nomination.
- With 139 movies under his belt, John Wayne's only other Oscar nomination was *Sands of Iwo Jima* (1949).

UNMENTIONABLES
- Fending off a bogus paternity suit, Cary Grant feared that his Honorary Oscar would elicit unwanted publicity.
- In 1978 Gig Young fatally shot his wife, then himself, in their Manhattan apartment.
- Peter Fonda admitted that most of *Easy Rider's* dialogue was improvised.
- Jane Fonda famously lit up her pot pipe during a Rex Reed interview.
- Universal lured Academy voters with "champagne and filet mignon supper" screenings of its box-office flop, *Anne of the Thousand Days*.
- Henry Fonda bitterly commented on his failed track record: "How in the hell would you like to have been in this business as long as I and then have one of your kids win an Oscar before you did?"
- Liza Minnelli bore facial scars resulting from a recent motorcycle mishap with actor Tony Bill. "It was a cuckoo accident," she said. "We were only going 15 miles per hour."
- Just before Oscar night, Liza separated from her openly gay husband, singer-songwriter Peter Allen.

Gig Young (center)

BEST SUPPORTING ACTOR
GIG YOUNG (1913–1978)
THEY SHOOT HORSES, DON'T THEY?

"I'm really quite speechless," Young admitted in his acceptance speech. "In my heart, I have a special thanks—Mr. Martin Baum, who believed in me when no one else did."

Gig Young plays a dance marathon's emcee "brilliantly," said Vincent Canby in the *New York Times*. A haunting film, *They Shoot Horses* captured the desperation of the Depression by following the lives of couples at a dance marathon in which contestants drive themselves to exhaustion in order to win the cash prize.

Young's career took off in the 1950s, when he played wry bon vivants in such films as *Come Fill the Cup* (1951, nom.), *Teacher's Pet* (1958), and *Lovers and Other Strangers* (1970). Married five times, he divorced three times, was widowed, and fatally shot his last wife—only a few weeks after their marriage—and then turned the gun on himself. One of his wives wrote a book about his tragic life entitled *Final Gig*.

BEST SUPPORTING ACTRESS
GOLDIE HAWN (B. 1945)
CACTUS FLOWER

The bikini-clad go-go girl on TV's *Rowan and Martin's Laugh In* slam-dunked an Oscar in what was only her second film. The Associated Press reported, "Some observers predict, indeed, that Goldie will become as big a star as the late Marilyn." *Time* noted, "Goldie can really act."

Hawn's first venture in show business was as a can-can dancer at the 1964 World's Fair. Discovered by *Laugh-In* producer, George Schlatter, the show and Goldie were an instant smash. Her debut as a dancer in *The One and Only, Genuine, Original Family Band* (1968) led to *Cactus Flower* and one of Hollywood's most lasting careers.

Steven Spielberg freed her from the ditsy-blonde stereotype with *The Sugarland Express* (1974), and more dimensional roles followed in *Shampoo* (1975), *The Duchess and the Dirtwater Fox* (1976), *Foul Play* (1978), *Private Benjamin* (1980, nom.), *Swing Shift* (1984), *Wildcats* (1986), *Overboard* (1987), and *Bird on a Wire* (1990). A brilliant businesswoman, Hawn developed and produced many of her own films. She has a son by actor Kurt Russell, her longtime companion.

HONORARY AWARD
CARY GRANT (1904–1986)

"Everybody wants to be Cary Grant. Even I want to be Cary Grant."

Archibald Leach (a.k.a. Cary Grant) ran away from home to "join the circus." Leach began his acting career as an acrobat, juggler, and song-and-dance man, touring with small troupes and playing English music halls.

Grant hit Hollywood in 1932, and the rest is history. He was signed to a long-term contract and given his new name. His debut feature, *This Is the Night*, revealed the debonair icon to come. Grant's facility for dramas, war films, adventure epics, and comedies made him one of Hollywood's most reliable leading men. But it was his screwball comedies—*Topper* (1937), *The Awful Truth* (1937), *Holiday* (1938), *Bringing Up Baby* (1939), *His Girl Friday* (1940), *The Philadelphia Story* (1940), and *My Favorite Wife* (1940)—that secured his legend.

Hitchcock capitalized on Grant's darker side in *Suspicion* (1941) and *Notorious* (1946). They would collaborate again in *To Catch a Thief* (1955) and *North by Northwest* (1959). But one of the actor's most memorable roles was in the romantic weeper *An Affair to Remember* (1957). Grant had his share of romantic entanglements and was married—Hollywood style—several times to actresses Virginia Cherrill, Betsy Drake, heiress Barbara Hutton and Dyan Cannon, who bore his only child.

PICTURE

ANNE OF THE THOUSAND DAYS, Wallis, Universal, Hal Wallis.
BUTCH CASSIDY AND THE SUNDANCE KID, Hill Monash, 20th Century-Fox, John Foreman.
HELLO, DOLLY!, Chenault, 20th Century-Fox, Ernest Lehman.
MIDNIGHT COWBOY, Hellman-Schlesinger, UA, Jerome Hellman.
Z, Reggane Films-O.N.C.I.C., Cinema V (Algerian), Jacques Perrin and Hamed Rachedi.

ACTOR

RICHARD BURTON in *Anne of the Thousand Days*, Wallis, Universal.
DUSTIN HOFFMAN in *Midnight Cowboy*, Hellman-Schlesinger, UA.
PETER O'TOOLE in *Goodbye, Mr. Chips*, Apjac, MGM.
JON VOIGHT in *Midnight Cowboy*, Hellman-Schlesinger, UA.
JOHN WAYNE in *True Grit*, Wallis, Paramount.

ACTRESS

GENEVIEVE BUJOLD in *Anne of the Thousand Days*, Wallis, Universal.
JANE FONDA in *They Shoot Horses, Don't They?*, Chartoff-Winkler-Pollack, ABC Pictures, Cinerama.
LIZA MINNELLI in *The Sterile Cuckoo*, Boardwalk, Paramount.
JEAN SIMMONS in *The Happy Ending*, Pax Films.
MAGGIE SMITH in *The Prime of Miss Jean Brodie*, 20th Century-Fox.

SUPPORTING ACTOR

RUPERT CROSSE in *The Reivers*, Ravetch-Kramer-Solar, Cinema Center/National General.
ELLIOTT GOULD in *Bob & Carol & Ted & Alice*, Frankovich, Columbia.
JACK NICHOLSON in *Easy Rider*, Pando-Raybert, Columbia.
ANTHONY QUAYLE in *Anne of the Thousand Days*, Walls, Universal.
GIG YOUNG in *They Shoot Horses, Don't They?*, Chartoff-Winkler-Pollack, ABC Pictures, Cinerama.

SUPPORTING ACTRESS

CATHERINE BURNS in *Last Summer*, Perry-Alsid, Allied Artists.
DYAN CANNON in *Bob & Carol & Ted & Alice*, Frankovich, Columbia.
GOLDIE HAWN in *Cactus Flower*, Frankovich, Columbia.
SYLVIA MILES in *Midnight Cowboy*, Hellman-Schlesinger, UA.
SUSANNAH YORK in *They Shoot Horses, Don't They?*, Chartoff-Winkler-Pollaek, ABC Pictures, Cinerama.

DIRECTION

COSTA-GAVRAS for *Z*, Reggane Films-O.N.C.I.C., Cinema V (Algerian).
GEORGE ROY HILL for *Butch Cassidy and the Sundance Kid*, Hill-Monash, 20th Century-Fox.
ARTHUR PENN for *Alice's Restaurant*, Florin Prod., UA.
SYDNEY POLLACK for *They Shoot Horses, Don't They?*, Chartoff-Winkler-Pollack, ABC Pictures, Cinerama.
JOHN SCHLESINGER for *Midnight Cowboy*, Hellman-Schlesinger, UA.

WRITING: BASED ON MATERIAL FROM ANTOHER MEDIUM

ANNE OF THE THOUSAND DAYS, Wallis, Universal. John Hale, Bridget Boland and Richard Sokolove.
GOODBYE COLUMBUS, Willow Tree, Paramount. Arnold Schulman.
MIDNIGHT COWBOY, Hellman-Schlesinger, UA. Waldo Salt.
THEY SHOOT HORSES, DON'T THEY?, Chartoff-Winkler-Pollack, ABC Pictures, Cinerama. James Poe and Robert E. Thompson.
Z, Reggane Films-O. N.C.I.C., Cinema V (Algerian). Jorge Semprun and Costa-Gavras.

WRITING: STORY AND SCREENPLAY BASED ON MATERIAL NOT PREVIOUSLY PUBLISHED OR PRODUCED

BOB & CAROL & TED & ALICE, Frankovich, Columbia. Paul Mazursky and Larry Tucker.
BUTCH CASSIDY AND THE SUNDANCE KID, Hill-Monash, 20th Century-Fox. William Goldman.
THE DAMNED, Pegaso-Praesidens, Warner Bros. Nicola Badalucco, Enrico Medioli and Luchino Visconti.
EASY RIDER, Pando-Raybert, Columbia. Peter Fonda, Dennis Hopper and Terry Southern.
THE WILD BUNCH, Foldman, Warner Bros. Walon Green, Roy N. Sickner and Sam Peckinpah.

CINEMATOGRAPHY

ANNE OF THE THOUSAND DAYS, Wallis, Universal. Arthur Ibbetson.
BOB & CAROL & TED & ALICE, Frankovich, Columbia. Charles B. Lang
BUTCH CASSIDY AND THE SUNDANCE KID, Hill-Monash, 20th Century-Fox. Conrad Hall.
HELLO, DOLLY!, Chenault, 20th Century-Fox. Harry Stradling.
MAROONED, Frankovich-Sturges, Columbia. Daniel Fapp.

ART DIRECTION—SET DECORATION

ANNE OF THE THOUSAND DAYS, Wallis, Universal. Maurice Carter and Lionel Couch; Patrick McLoughlin.
GAILY, GAILY, Mirisch-Cartier, UA. Robert Boyle and George B. Chan; Edward Boyle and Carl Biddiscombe.
HELLO, DOLLY!, Chenault, 20th Century-Fox. John DeCuir, Jack Martin Smith and Herman Blumenthal; Walter M. Scott, George Hopkins and Raphael Bretton.
SWEET CHARITY, Universal. Alexander Golitzen and George C. Webb; Jack D. Moore.
THEY SHOOT HORSES, DON'T THEY?, Chartoff-Winkler-Pollack, ABC Pictures, Cinerama. Harry Homer; Frank McKelvey.

COSTUME DESIGN

ANNE OF THE THOUSAND DAYS, Wallis, Universal. Margaret Furse.
GAILY, GAILY, Mirisch-Cartier, UA. Ray Aghayan.
HELLO, DOLLY!, Chenault, 20th Century-Fox. Irene Sharaff.
SWEET CHARITY, Universal. Edith Head.
THEY SHOOT HORSES, DON'T THEY?, Chartoff-Winkler-Pollack, ABC Pictures, Cinerama. Donfeld.

SOUND

ANNE OF THE THOUSAND DAYS, Wallis, Universal. John Aldred.
BUTCH CASSIDY AND THE SUNDANCE KID, Hill-Monash, 20th Century-Fox. William Edmundson and David Dockendorf.
GAILY, GAILY, Mirisch-Cartier, UA. Robert Martin and Clem Portman.
HELLO, DOLLY!, Chenault, 20th Century-Fox. Jack Solomon and Murray Spivack.
MAROONED, Frankovich-Sturges, Columbia. Les Fresholtz and Arthur Piantadosi.

FILM EDITING

HELLO, DOLLY!, Chenault, 20th Century-Fox. William Reynolds.
MIDNIGHT COWBOY, Hellman-Schlesinger, UA. Hugh A. Robertson.
THE SECRET OF SANTA VITTORIA, Kramer, UA. William Lyon and Earle Herdan.
THEY SHOOT HORSES, DON'T THEY?, Chartoff-Winkler-Pollack, ABC Pictures, Cinerama. Fredric Steinkamp.

Z, Reggane Films-O.N.C.I.C., Cinema V (Algerian). Francoise Bonnot.

SPECIAL VISUAL EFFECTS

KRAKATOA, EAST OF JAVA, ABC Pictures, Cinerama. Eugene Lourie and Alex Weldon.
MAROONED, Frankovich-Sturges, Columbia. Bobbie Robertson.

SONG

COME SATURDAY MORNING (*The Sterile Cuckoo*, Boardwalk, Paramount); Music by Fred Karlin. Lyrics by Dory Previn.
JEAN (*The Prime of Miss Jean Brodie*, 20th CenturyFox); Music and Lyrics by Rod McKuen.
RAINDROPS KEEP FALLIN' ON MY HEAD (*Butch Cassidy and the Sundance Kid*, Hill-Monash, 20th Century-Fox); Music by Burt Bacharach. Lyrics by Hal David.
TRUE GRIT (*True Grit*, Wallis, Paramount); Music by Elmer Bernstein. Lyrics by Don Black.
WHAT ARE YOU DOING FOR THE REST OF YOUR LIFE? (*The Happy Ending*, Brooks, UA); Music by Michel Legrand. Lyrics by Alan and Marilyn Bergman.

ORIGINAL SCORE

ANNE OF THE THOUSAND DAYS, Wallis, Universal. Georges Delerue.
BUTCH CASSIDY AND THE SUNDANCE KID, Hill-Monash, 20th Century-Fox. Burt Bacharach.
THE REIVERS, Ravetch-Kramer-Solar, Cinema Center Films, National General. John Williams.
THE SECRET OF SANTA VITTORIA, Kramer, UA. Ernest Gold.
THE WILD BUNCH, Feldman, Warner Bros. Jerry Fielding

SCORE: MUSICAL

GOODBYE, MR. CHIPS, Apjac, MGM., Leslie Bricusse and John Williams.
HELLO, DOLLY!, Chenault, 20th Century-Fox. Lennie Hayton and Lionel Newman.
PAINT YOUR WAGON, Lemer, Paramount. Nelson Riddle.
SWEET CHARITY, Universal. Cy Coleman.
THEY SHOOT HORSES, DON'T THEY?, Chartoff-Winkler-Pollack, ABC Pictures, Cinerama. John Green and Albert Woodbury.

SHORT SUBJECTS: CARTOONS

IT'S TOUGH TO BE A BIRD, Disney, Buena Vista. Ward Kimball, producer.
OF MEN AND DEMONS, Hubley Studios, Paramount. John and Faith Hubley, producers.
WALKING, National Film Board of Canada, Columbia. Ryan Larkin, producer.

SHORT SUBJECTS: LIVE ACTION

BLAKE, National Film Board of Canada, Vaudeo Inc. Doug Jackson, producer.
THE MAGIC MACHINES, Fly-By-Night Prods., Hanson Distributing. Joan Keller Stern, producer.
PEOPLE SOUP, Pangloss Prods., Columbia. Marc Merson, producer.

DOCUMENTARY: SHORT SUBJECTS

CZECHOSLOVAKIA 1968, Sanders-Fresco Film Makers for U.S. Information Agency. Denis Sanders and Robert M. Fresco, producers.
AN IMPRESSION OF JOHN STEINBECK: WRITER, Donald Wrye Prods, for U.S. Information Agency. Donald Wrye, producer.
JENNY IS A GOOD THING, A.C.I. Prod, for Project Head Start. Joan Horvath, producer.
LEO BEUERMAN, Centron Prod. Arthur H. Wolf and Russell A. Mosser, producers.
THE MAGIC MACHINES, Fly-By-Night Prods, Manson Distributing. Joan Keller Stern, producer.

DOCUMENTARY: FEATURES

ARTHUR RUBINSTEIN—THE LOVE OF LIFE, Midem, Prod. Bernard Chevry, producer.
BEFORE THE MOUNTAIN WAS MOVED, Robert K. Sharpe Prods., for The Office of Economic Opportunity. Robert K. Sharpe, producer.
IN THE YEAR OF THE PIG, Emile de Antonio Prod. Emile de Antonio, producer.

THE OLYMPICS IN MEXICO, Film Section of the Organizing Committee for the XIX Olympic Games.
THE WOLF MEN, MGM. Irwin Rosten, producer.

FOREIGN LANGUAGE FILM

ADALEN '31, (Sweden).
THE BATTLE OF NERETVA, (Yugoslavia).
THE BROTHERS KARAMAZOV, (U.S.S.R.).
MY NIGHT WITH MAUD, (France).
Z, (Algeria).

HONORARY AND OTHER AWARDS

TO CARY GRANT for his unique mastery of the art of screen acting with the respect and affection of his colleagues.

JEAN HERSHOLT HUMANITARIAN AWARD

TO GEORGE JESSEL

SCIENTIFIC OR TECHNICAL

CLASS I
None.

CLASS II
HAZELTINE CORPORATION for the design and development of the Hazeltine Color Film Analyzer.
FOUAD SAID for the design and introduction of the Cinemobile series of equipment trucks for location motion picture production.
JUAN DE LA CIERVA and DYNA-SCIENCES CORPORATION for the design and development of the Dynalens optical image motion compensator.

CLASS III
OTTO POPELKA of Magna-Tech Electronics Co., Inc.;
FENTON HAMILTON of MGM. Studios;
PANAVISION INCORPORATED;
ROBERT M. FLYNN and RUSSELL HESSEY of Universal City Studios.

BELOW: Lauren Hutton shows off her famous toothsome grin and a prime example of 70s styling in this plunging white halter-top gown. (1975)

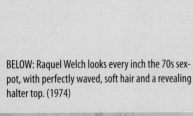

BELOW: Raquel Welch looks every inch the 70s sex-pot, with perfectly waved, soft hair and a revealing halter top. (1974)

ABOVE: Diana Ross glides down the red carpet in a loose-fitting swirl of a dress, a captivating example of the easy and eclectic glamour of the decade. (1974)

ABOVE: Ali McGraw gives a nod to the hippie movement in a crocheted cap sporting a large flower, one of the emblems of 70s style. (1974)

THE LOOK OF THE DECADE

BY THE TIME THE 1970s ROLLED AROUND, the term style could no longer be easily defined. The "Me" Decade ushered in an era of individualization, and there was no longer just one look. Bad taste was good taste, and the more eclectic the outfit, the better. From flowers and bell-bottoms to punk as high fashion, there was an ensemble to suit every person and every mood. But for the better part of a decade, Hollywood seemed to favor the sleek, form-fitting dresses inspired by disco dancing and the culture of Studio 54.

OPPOSITE: Jack Nicholson looks the part of the French dandy, while Anjelica Huston's sleek dress and straight hair evoke simple 70s sexiness. (1975)

1970

GENERAL REBELLION

CEREMONY: April 15, 1971
Dorothy Chandler Pavilion,
Los Angeles Music Center,
Los Angeles
HOST: All the nominees

Hollywood threw its biggest party of the year, and almost nobody came. Almost no winners, at any rate. Helen Hayes was doing a play in Washington, D.C.; honorary awardee Orson Welles pretended to be on location; Glenda Jackson claimed she couldn't afford the trip from London; and *Patton* screenwriter Francis Ford Coppola was back East working on a script called *The Godfather*. The recipient of the Thalberg Memorial Award, Ingmar Bergman, sent his lover, Liv Ullman, in his stead; *Patton* director, Franklin J. Schaffner, really was on location; and George C. Scott, the most recalcitrant AWOL in Academy history, was in his Manhattan apartment watching a soccer match on another channel.

In lieu of a host, thirty-two famous Friends of Oscar did the honors, and one of them, Bob Hope, fizzled badly. He got booed when he prudishly joked, "I go back to the kind of movie when a girl says 'I love you' it's a declaration, not a demonstration."

Patton had an Oscar sweep locked up early in the race and, aside from the far-distant second, *Ryan's Daughter*, there was no nail-biting competition. As is often the case, the night's big surprises were in the Best Supporting categories. Chief Dan George, the sure bet for his philosophical Sitting Bull in *Little Big Man*, was smoked out by Hayley's dad, John Mills. He was one of the few winners on hand, and his exuberance at the podium, despite the fact that his right arm was in a sling, made him the evening's anti-Scott.

Helen Hayes, as a "little old lady" stowaway in *Airport*, pulled out a win from heavyweight contenders Lee Grant and Karen Black. For some, the year's biggest surprise was Ali McGraw's nomination for the confectionery tearjerker *Love Story*. The Academy, eager for some fresh blood and higher ratings, was delighted she showed up, along with another rising young star, Jack Nicholson.

✉

BEST PICTURE/BEST DIRECTOR
FRANKLIN J. SCHAFFNER (1920–1989)
PATTON

"Since he isn't here, let me say you couldn't have given it to a better fella. I know, I was there," said *Patton*'s other star, Karl Malden. (Schaffner was in Europe working on *Nicholas and Alexandra*.)

It took two decades to bring *Patton* to the screen. Once it was released it became "most likely to succeed." *Patton* was a favorite among presidents and generals, who found in the film a warning against bowing to diplomacy in Vietnam. Fearing that the biopic about the nonconformist, visionary tank commander of World War II would lose the youth vote, the producers—in an uncharacteristic move—gave it a subtitle, *Salute to a Rebel*. As it turned out, the film was popular among a wide audience. Young co-screenwriter Francis Ford Coppola depicted Patton as an appealing military figure who recited poetry and history even as he charged ahead on the battlefield.

Schaffner, who had been best known for *Planet of the Apes* (1968), began his directing career in the 1950s on TV's *March of Time*, winning a special award for Jacqueline Kennedy's *Tour of the White House* (1962). His

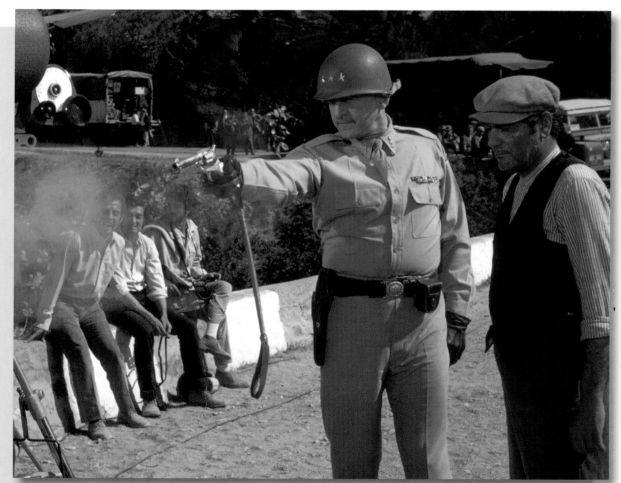

George C. Scott with Franklin J. Schaffner

first feature, *The Stripper* (1963), didn't leave much of an impression, but that all changed with *The Best Man* (1964), based on Gore Vidal's acerbic political theatrical comedy. Schaffner's career continued with the making of *Nicholas and Alexandra* (1971) and *Papillon* (1973).

The envelope, please...

BEST ACTOR
GEORGE C. SCOTT (1925–1999)
PATTON

"I respectfully request that you withdraw my name from the list of nominees for the Academy Award," wrote Scott from Spain, where he was filming.

Scott was arguably one of America's greatest performers—an actor's actor—and one of its most arrogant and temperamental. First seen in *The Hanging Tree* (1959) and *Anatomy of a Murder* (1959, nom.), in 1962 he refused the nomination for his role in *The Hustler*. He next appeared in *The List of Adrian Messenger* (1963), *Dr. Strangelove* (1964), *The Flim-Flam Man* (1967), *Petulia* (1968), *The Hospital* (1971, another nomination, another snub), and *Hardcore* (1979). He won an Emmy for a TV production of Arthur Miller's

The Price (1971), which, naturally, he refused.

Scott's first love, however, was the theater, where he remained active through the 1970s, '80s, and '90s until his death in 1999. Many of the encomiums of praise that followed his brilliant career came from fellow actors. Jack Lemmon said, "George was truly one of the greatest and most generous actors I have ever known," and Tony Randall called him "the greatest actor in American history."

BEST ACTRESS
GLENDA JACKSON (B. 1936)
WOMEN IN LOVE

The 33-year-old English actress didn't show up for the Awards ceremony reportedly because Universal wouldn't pick up the tab. An exceptionally talented actress, Jackson was often featured in intellectual, strong-willed roles, rather than for her physical attributes. In the movie version of the classic novel by D. H. Lawrence, Jackson played Gudrun, a sculptress, who together with her friend explores the complex nature of love. Said *Variety* of Jackson's talent, "The girl's no stunner...but she had punch and intelligence which give a sharp edge to all her scenes." Pauline Kael of *The New Yorker* described her performance as "bold, tense."

Jackson made her film debut in *This Sporting Life* (1963). She appeared regularly in Ken Russell's films, including *Women in Love* (1969), *The Boy Friend* (1971), *The Music Lovers* (1971), *Salome's Last Dance* (1988), and *The Rainbow* (1989). Her other classic roles include *Sunday, Bloody Sunday* (1971), *A Touch of Class* (1973), *Hedda* (1975, Jackson), and *The Romantic Englishwoman* (1975). The only member of Parliament to have received an Oscar, Jackson was an unsuccessful candidate for the new position of mayor of London. (For more on Jackson, see 1973.)

FIRSTS
• George C. Scott became the first actor to refuse an Academy Award, followed by Brando for *The Godfather*.

• Helen Hayes was the first person ever to win a Grammy, an Oscar, a Tony, and an Emmy in competitive categories.

SINS OF OMISSION
Five Easy Pieces, a landmark film for its—or any—time, is an idiosyncratic study of alienation. A young musician gives up his career to work on oil rigs and returns home for one last attempt to communicate with his dying patrician father.

ALWAYS A BRIDESMAID, NEVER A BRIDE
• (Almost) "At last, a pattern has been established in my life. See you all again in 1999." It took writer Ring Lardner Jr. twenty-nine years to win a second Oscar. He won for *Woman of the Year* in 1942, and, after a slight delay, he won again for *M*A*S*H* (1970). Helen Hayes's Best Supporting Actress win for *Airport* came thirty-nine years after her victory in *The Sin of Madelon Claudet* (1931).

• Dustin Hoffman, feeling snubbed by the Academy, told *Variety's* Army Archerd, "Sure, I'd like to win an Academy Award. I realize that intellectually it doesn't really mean very much. But it is a means to more power, which in turn enables you to be choosy about your scripts. And it makes you more money—which you can put away toward the day when you won't be in such demand." Hoffman had tallied two non-winning noms up to this point and won the gold in 1979 for *Kramer vs. Kramer.*

ROLE REVERSALS
Though the cantankerous George C. Scott gave producers more trouble than they thought he might be worth, in the end he was worth it. When the casting call for *Patton* was first announced, however, producers initially approached such stars as Burt Lancaster, Robert Mitchum, Lee Marvin, and Rod Steiger.

UNMENTIONABLES
• George C. Scott proved a tough soldier, turning the movie set into a virtual battleground. According to the *London Times,* Scott said, "Patton was misunderstood contemporaneously and he's misunderstood here—and I'm ashamed of being a part of it."

• In her review of *Love Story,* the most eagerly awaited picture of the year, *New York Herald Tribune* critic Judith Crist wrote, "Its venality and infantilism make us reach for the barf bag instead of the Kleenex."

• Speaking of the film *Airport,* Burt Lancaster said, "I don't know why it was made. It's the biggest piece of junk ever made."

• When Scott asked the Academy to rescind his nomination, some suggested that he had done so in case he lost. Rumor had it that he was a bad loser, as evidenced by his behavior when he lost Best Supporting Actor in 1959 and 1961. Not only did Scott refuse to pick up the Golden Boy, but when it was given to him by Frank McCarthy he sent it back to the Academy, where it lingers to this day.

BEST SUPPORTING ACTOR
JOHN MILLS (B. 1908)
RYAN'S DAUGHTER

In tribute to his winning role as a deaf-mute village idiot, Mills took his award silently.

Mills was one of Britain's biggest box-office stars in the 1940s and '50s, playing everything from stiff-upper-lipped officers to decent but powerful men in such films as *Goodbye, Mr. Chips* (1939), *The End of the Affair* (1955), *War and Peace* (1956), *The Human Factor* (1975), and *Hamlet* (1997). David Lean's *Great Expectations* (1946) gave Mills one of his greatest parts.

By the 1960s Mills had turned to character roles in *The Singer Not the Song* (1961), *King Rat* (1965), *The Wrong Box* (1966), and *Oh! What a Lovely War* (1969).

BEST SUPPORTING ACTRESS
HELEN HAYES (1900–1993)
AIRPORT

"I'm on the verge of tears," said Hayes to reporters, who tracked her down watching the Oscars on television. "God bless those people in Hollywood!" Pauline Kael of *The New Yorker* complained, "Helen Hayes does her loveable-old-trouper-pixie act."

Child star Hayes came to be known as the "first lady of the American theater," but the camera, unfortunately, didn't love her as much. Nevertheless, *Airport* was her second Academy Award. Her first was for *The Sin of Madelon Claudet* (1931). Among her films were *A Farewell to Arms* (1932), *My Son John* (1952), and *Anastasia* (1956). Hayes wrote three volumes of memoirs, *A Gift of Joy* (1965), *On Reflection* (1969), and *My Life in Three Acts* (1990).

(For more on Hayes, see 1931).

Helen Hayes with Van Heflin

HONORARY AWARD
ORSON WELLES (1915–1985)

"I'm not very fond of movies. I don't go to them much."

The enfant terrible didn't show up to receive the only honor he would ever get from the Academy, conveying to all that he was in Spain shooting a film.

Many of Welles's next films were commercial disasters, resulting in his exile to Europe in 1948. In 1956 he directed *Touch of Evil* (1958), which failed in the U.S. but won a prize at the 1958 Brussels World's Fair. All his films bear his signature, including *The Magnificent Ambersons* (1942), *The Lady from Shanghai* (1948), *Chimes at Midnight* (1966), and *F for Fake* (1974).

In 1975, in spite of his paltry box-office history, Welles received the American Film Institute's Lifetime Achievement Award, and in 1984 the Directors Guild of America awarded him its highest honor, the D. W. Griffith Award. His posthumous reputation as a filmmaker has climbed steadily ever since.

PICTURE

AIRPORT, Hunter, Universal. Ross Hunter.
FIVE EASY PIECES, BBS Prods., Columbia. Bob Rafelson and Richard Wechsler.
LOVE STORY, Paramount. Howard G. Minsky.
MASH, Aspen, 20th Century-Fox. Ingo Preminger.
PATTON, 20th Century-Fox. Frank McCarthy.

ACTOR

MELVYN DOUGLAS in *I Never Sang for My Father,* Jamel, Columbia.
JAMES EARL JONES in *The Great White Hope,* Turman, 20th Century-Fox.
JACK NICHOLSON in *Five Easy Pieces,* BBS Prods., Columbia.
RYAN O'NEAL in *Love Story,* Paramount.
GEORGE C. SCOTT in *Patton,* 20th Century-Fox.

ACTRESS

JANE ALEXANDER in *The Great White Hope,* Turman, 20th Century-Fox.
GLENDA JACKSON in *Women in Love,* Kramer-Rosen, UA.
ALI MacGRAW in *Love Story,* Paramount.
SARAH MILES in *Ryan's Daughter,* Faraway, MGM.
CARRIE SNODGRASS in *Diary of a Mad Housewife,* Perry, Universal.

SUPPORTING ACTOR

RICHARD CASTELLANO in *Lovers and Other Strangers,* ABC Pictures, Cinerama.
CHIEF DAN GEORGE in *Little Big Man,* Huller-Stockbridge, Cinema Center Films/National General.
GENE HACKMAN in *I Never Sang for My Father,* Jamel, Columbia.
JOHN MARLEY in *Love Story,* Paramount.
JOHN MILLS in *Ryan's Daughter,* Faraway, MGM.

SUPPORTING ACTRESS

KAREN BLACK in *Five Easy Pieces,* BBS Prods., Columbia.
LEE GRANT in *The Landlord,* Mirisch-Carter, UA.
HELEN HAYES in *Airport,* Hunter, Universal.
SALLY KELLERMAN in *M*A*S*H,* Aspen, 20th Century-Fox.
MAUREEN STAPLETON in *Airport,* Hunter, Universal.

DIRECTION

ROBERT ALTMAN for *M*A*S*H,* Aspen, 20th Century-Fox.
FEDERICO FELLINI for *Fellini Satyricon,* Frimaldi, UA (Italian).
ARTHUR HILLER for *Love Story,* Paramount.
KEN RUSSELL for *Women in Love,* Kramer-Rosen, UA.
FRANKLIN J. SCHAFFNER for *Patton,* 20th Century-Fox.

WRITING: BASED ON MATERIAL FROM ANOTHER MEDIUM

AIRPORT, Hunter, Universal. George Seaton.
I NEVER SANG FOR MY FATHER, Jamel, Columbia. Robert Anderson.
LOVERS AND OTHER STRANGERS, ABC Pictures, Cinerama. Renee Taylor, Joseph Bologna and David Zelag Goodman.
M*A*S*H, Aspen, 20th Century-Fox. Ring Lardner Jr.
WOMEN IN LOVE, Kramer-Rosen, UA. Larry Kramer.

WRITING: STORY AND SCREENPLAY BASED ON FACTUAL MATERIAL OR MATERIAL NOT PREVIOUSLY PUBLISHED OR PRODUCED

FIVE EASY PIECES, BBS Prods., Columbia. Bob Rafelson and Adrien Joyce.
JOE, Cannon Group, Cannon Releasing. Norman Wexler.
LOVE STORY, Paramount. Erich Segal.
MY NIGHT AT MAUD'S, Pathe Contemporary (French). Eric Rohmer.
PATTON, 20th Century-Fox. Francis Ford Coppola and Edmund H. North.

CINEMATOGRAPHY

AIRPORT, Hunter, Universal. Ernest Laszlo.
PATTON, 20th Century-Fox. Fred Koenekamp.
RYAN'S DAUGHTER, Faraway Prods., MGM., Freddie Young.
TORA! TORA! TORA!, 20th Century-Fox. Charles F. Wheeler, Osami Furuya, Sinsaku Himeda and Masamichi Satoh.
WOMEN IN LOVE, Kramer-Rosen, UA. Billy Williams.

ART DIRECTION—SET DECORATION

AIRPORT, Hunter, Universal. Alexander Golitzen and E. Preston Ames; Jack D. Moore and Mickey S. Michaels.
THE MOLLY MAGUIRES, Tamm Prods., Paramount. Tambi Larsen; Darrell Silvera.
PATTON, 20th Century-Fox. Urie McCleary and Gil Parrondo; Antonio Mateos and Pierre-Louis Thevenet.
SCROOGE, Waterbury Films, Cinema Center Films, National General. Terry Marsh and Bob Cartwright; Pamela Cornell.
TORA! TORA! TORA!, 20th Century-Fox. Jack Martin Smith, Yoshiro Muraki, Richard Day and Taizoh Kawashima; Walter M. Scott, Norman Rockett and Carl Biddiscombe.

COSTUME DESIGN

AIRPORT, Hunter, Universal. Edith Head.
CROMWELL, Irving Allen, Columbia. Nino Novarese.
DARLING LILI, Geoffrey Prods., Paramount. Donald Brooks and Jack Bear.
THE HAWAIIANS, Mirisch, UA. Bill Thomas.
SCROOGE, Waterbury Films, Cinema Center Films, National General. Margaret Furse.

SOUND

AIRPORT, Hunter, Universal. Ronald Pierce and David Moriarty.
PATTON, 20th Century-Fox. Douglas Williams and Don Bassman.
RYAN'S DAUGHTER, Faraway Prods., MGM., Gordon K. McCallum and John Bramall.
TORA! TORA! TORA!, 20th Century-Fox. Murray Spivack and Herman Lewis.
WOODSTOCK, Wadleigh-Maurice. Warner Bros. Dan Wallin and Larry Johnson.

FILM EDITING

AIRPORT, Hunter, Universal. Stuart Gilmore.
MASH, Aspen, 20th Century-Fox. Danford B. Greene.
PATTON, 20th Century-Fox. Hugh S. Fowler.
TORA! TORA! TORA!, 20th Century-Fox. James E. Newcom, Pembroke J. Herring and Inoue Chikaya.
WOODSTOCK, Wadleigh-Maurice, Warner Bros. Thelma Schoonmaker.

SPECIAL VISUAL EFFECTS

PATTON, 20th Century-Fox. Alex Weldon.
TORA! TORA! TORA!, 20th Century-Fox. A.D. Flowers and L.B. Abbott.

SONG

FOR ALL WE KNOW (*Lovers and Other Strangers,* ABC Pictures, Cinerama); Music by Fred Karlin. Lyrics by Robb Royer and James Griffin, aka Robb Wilson and Arthur James.
PIECES OF DREAMS (*Pieces of Dreams,* RFB Enterprises, UA); Music by Michel Legrand. Lyrics by Alan and Marilyn Bergman.
THANK YOU VERY MUCH (*Scrooge,* Waterbury Films, Cinema Center Films, National General); Music and Lyrics by Leslie Bricusse.

TILL LOVE TOUCHES YOUR LIFE (*Madron,* Four Star-Excelsior Releasing); Music by Riz Ortolani. Lyrics by Arthur Hamilton.
WHISTLING AWAY THE DARK (*Darling Lili,* Geoffrey Prods., Paramount); Music by Henry Mancini. Lyrics by Johnny Mercer.

SCORING: ORIGINAL MUSIC

AIRPORT, Hunter, Universal. Alfred Newman.
CROMWELL, Irving Allen, Columbia. Frank Cordell.
LOVE STORY, Paramount. Francis Lai.
PATTON, 20th Century-Fox. Jerry Goldsmith.
SUNFLOWER, Sostar Prod., Avco Embassy. Henry Mancini.

SCORING: ORIGINAL SONG

THE BABY MAKER, Robert Wise Prod., National General. Fred Karlin and Tylwyth Kymry.
A BOY NAMED CHARLIE BROWN, Mendelson-Melendez, Cinema Center Films, National General. Rod McKuen, John Scott Trotter, Bill Melendez, Al Shean and Vince Guaraldi.
DARLING LILI, Geoffrey Prods., Paramount. Henry Mancini and Johnny Mercer.
LET IT BE, Beatles-Apple Prods., UA. The Beatles.
SCROOGE, Waterbury Films, Cinema Center Films, National General. Leslie Bricusse, Ian Fraser and Herbert W. Spencer.

SHORT SUBJECT: CARTOON

THE FURTHER ADVENTURES OF UNCLE SAM: PART TWO, Haboush Company, Goldstone Films. Robert Mitchell and Dale Case, producers.
IS IT ALWAYS RIGHT TO BE RIGHT?, Stephen Bosustow Prods., Schoenfeld Films, Nick Bosustow, producer.
THE SHEPHERD, Cameron Guess and Associates, Brandon Films, Cameron Guess, producer.

SHORT SUBJECT: LIVE ACTION

THE RESURRECTION OF BRONCHO BILLY, University of Southern California, Dept. of Cinema, Universal. John Longenecker, producer.
SHUT UP...I'M CRYING, Robert Siegler Prods., Schoenfeld Films. Robert Siegler, producer.
STICKY MY FINGERS...FLEET MY FEET, American Film Institute, Schoenfeld Films. John Hancock, producer.

DOCUMENTARY: SHORT SUBJECT

THE GIFTS, Richter-McBride Prods., for The Water Quality Office of the Environmental Protection Agency. Robert McBride, producer.
INTERVIEWS WITH MY LAI VETERANS, Laser Film Corp. Joseph Strick, producer.
A LONG WAY FROM NOWHERE, Robert Aller Prods. Bob Aller, producer.
OISIN, An Aengue Film. Vivien and Patrick Carey, producers.
TIME IS RUNNING OUT, Gesellschaft fur bidende Filme, Horst Dallmayr and Robert Menegoz, producers.

DOCUMENTARY: FEATURE

CHARIOTS OF THE GODS, Terra-Filmkunst GmbH. Dr. Harald Reinl, producer.
JACK JOHNSON, The Big Fights. Jim Jacobs, producer.
KING: A FILMED RECORD... MONTGOMERY TO MEMPHIS, Commonwealth United Prod. Ely Landau, producer.
SAY GOODBYE, A Wolper Prod. David H. Vowell, producer.
WOODSTOCK, Wadleigh-Maurice, Warner Bros. Bob Maurice, producer.

FOREIGN LANGUAGE FILM

FIRST LOVE (Switzerland).
HOA-BINH (France).
INVESTIGATION OF A CITIZEN ABOVE SUSPICION (Italy).
PAIX SUR LES CHAMPS (Belgium).
TRISTANA (Spain).

HONORARY AND OTHER AWARDS

TO LILLIAN GISH for superlative artistry and for distinguished contribution to the progress of motion pictures.
TO ORSON WELLES for superlative artistry and versatility in the creation of motion pictures.

IRVING G. THALBERG MEMORIAL AWARD

TO INGMAR BERGMAN

JEAN HERSHOLT HUMANITARIAN AWARD

TO FRANK SINATRA

SCIENTIFIC OR TECHNICAL

CLASS II

LEONARD SOKOLOW and EDWARD H. REICHARD of Consolidated Film Industries for the concept and engineering of the Color Proofing Printer for motion pictures.

CLASS III

SYLVANIA ELECTRIC PRODUCTS, INC.;
B.J. LOSMANDY;
EASTMAN KODAK COMPANY and PHOTO ELECTRONICS CORPORATION;
ELECTRO SOUND INCORPORATED.

1971

ive minutes can be an eternity on live TV, but that's how long the standing ovation was for sole Honorary Oscar recipient Charlie Chaplin. It was an emotional homecoming for the Little Tramp, who over the years had been adored for his artistry and reviled for his left-wing politics. This was his first time in Hollywood since his self-imposed exile in 1951, and it was time to forgive and forget the

TEARS FOR THE TRAMP

CEREMONY: April 10, 1972
Dorothy Chandler Pavilion,
Los Angeles Music Center,
Los Angeles
HOSTS: Helen Hayes, Alan King,
Sammy Davis Jr., Jack Lemmon

past. When Jack Lemmon handed Chaplin his signature bowler hat and cane, the cheering nearly shook the foundation of the Chandler Pavilion.

Atonement extended to the foxy firebrand of the antiwar movement, Jane Fonda. She was Henry's kid, after all, and her performance in *Klute* could not be ignored. On the heels of her big win came Hollywood's new generation to collect their own statu-

ettes. Among them was the youngest Oscar-winning director yet, William Friedkin, and his "overnight star" of *The French Connection*, Gene Hackman.

The collision of old and new Hollywood was most startlingly realized by the pitting of *Fiddler on the Roof*, a traditional re-creation of a hit Broadway musical, against Stanley Kubrick's futuristic nightmare *A Clockwork Orange* for Best Picture. But the new Hollywood definitely had the edge, as a dangerously bejeweled Isaac Hayes roared onstage for a flashy production of his Oscar-winning score for *Shaft*. Co-host Sammy Davis Jr. whooped, "Heavy!" while Edith Head lamented "that you can lead a young actress to water and make her drink, but you can't tell her what to wear."

Underscoring Head's deep fashion concern, Jane Fonda showed up in a pantsuit. Across the aisle, Jack Nicholson skipped the jacket for a colorful shirt and a McGovern button. The iconoclastic '70s were ushering in a steady drumbeat of change. The Little Tramp could only smile with a twinkle in his eye. He'd seen it all before.

BEST PICTURE/BEST DIRECTOR
WILLIAM "HURRICANE BILLY" FRIEDKIN
(B. 1939)
THE FRENCH CONNECTION

At 32 Friedkin was the youngest director ever to win an Oscar. "I'm very much still in the learning process," he said. "Speaking personally, I think Stanley Kubrick [*A Clockwork Orange*] is the best American filmmaker of the year. In fact, not just this year but the best, period."

The French Connection, an edge-of-the-seat true-life cop story, moves at breakneck speed to tell the story of one of the biggest narcotics rings of all time, and boasts one of the most exciting chase scenes ever filmed. Friedkin's innovative semi-documentary-style film marked his commercial breakthrough. Friedkin started making documentaries right after high school, winning the Golden Gate Award at the 1962 San Francisco film festival. He became infatuated with Orson Welles after seeing *Citizen Kane*.

In 1965, he went Hollywood, where he directed television shows, including an episode of *The Alfred Hitchcock Hour*, and was introduced to the somewhat hostile practical jokes of Hitchcock, who gave the young Friedkin a hard time for not wearing a tie.

Gene Hackman with Marcel Bozzuffi

After Friedkin's Oscar win for *The French Connection*, he was nominated for *The Exorcist* (1973) and expected to become Hollywood's preeminent director. His output after *Exorcist* didn't live up to those expectations and included such films as *Sorcerer* (1977), *The Brink's Job* (1978), *Cruising* (1980), *Deal of the Century* (1983), *To Live and Die in L.A.* (1985), *Stalking Danger* (1986), and *Rampage* (1992). He also directed a pair of TV movies, *C.A.T. Squad* (1986) and *C.A.T. Squad: Python Wolf* (1988). *The Guardian* (1990) brought Friedkin back to supernatural suspense, and *Blue Chips* (1994) got him back on track. He was at one time married to actress Jeanne Moreau and is currently married to Paramount president Sherry Lansing.

The envelope, please…

Gene Hackman (right)

BEST ACTOR
GENE HACKMAN (B. 1931)
THE FRENCH CONNECTION

"When I first read the part, it seemed like a chance to do all those things I watched Jimmy Cagney do as a kid," Hackman said. He stepped up to receive his award and thanked his acting teacher and "Billy Friedkin, who brought me through this one—I wanted to quit."

Hackman is a natural in *The French Connection* as the brutal, maniacal Jimmy "Popeye" Doyle, New York City's main undercover narcotics cop—a short-tempered alcoholic bigot who is nevertheless a hardworking and dedicated police officer. The film's tag line, "Doyle is bad news—but a good cop," told the tale.

Hackman debuted in *Lilith* (1964) with Warren Beatty, which led to his Oscar-nominated role in *Bonnie and Clyde* (1967). He went on to reach great heights in *I Never Sang for My Father* (1970), *Night Moves* and *Bite the Bullet* (both 1975), and fell to the depths with *The Poseidon Adventure* (1972) and *Eureka* (1983). After a brief stalemate, Hackman regained his prestige, winning more nominations for *Mississippi Burning* (1988) and *Unforgiven* (1992, Oscar), a role he almost turned down. (For more on Hackman, see 1992.)

Donald Sutherland with Jane Fonda

BEST ACTRESS
JANE FONDA (B. 1937)
KLUTE

Fonda's appearance in *Klute*, in which she played a prostitute being stalked by a killer, stood in sharp contrast to the woman who started out doing pinup roles. This was but one of the many transformations Fonda would undergo.

Henry Fonda's daughter began her film career in 1960, in *Tall Story*, and continued to star in such romantic comedies as *Period of Adjustment* (1962), *Any Wednesday* (1966), and *Barefoot in the Park* (1967). She also played in *Cat Ballou* (1965), and made *Circle of Love* (1964) and *Barbarella* (1968) for Roger Vadim—whom she later married.

One of Fonda's greatest transformations came when she married political activist Tom Hayden and turned antiwar protester. Her appetite for a challenge led her to award-winning roles in film and theater, including *They Shoot Horses, Don't They?* (1969, nom.), *Fun with Dick and Jane* (1976), *Julia* (1977, nom.), and *The Electric Horseman* (1979). She later won a second Oscar as the wife of a Vietnam vet in *Coming Home* (1978).

(For more on Fonda, see 1978)

BEST OF 1971
Best Picture: *The French Connection*
Best Director: William Friedkin, *The French Connection*
Best Actor: Gene Hackman, *The French Connection*
Best Actress: Jane Fonda, *Klute*
Best Supporting Actor: Ben Johnson, *The Last Picture Show*
Best Supporting Actress: Cloris Leachman, *The Last Picture Show*
Honorary Award: Charles Chaplin

FIRSTS
- Jane Fonda was the only American actress in the Best Actress race.
- William Friedkin became the youngest director ever to win an Oscar.

ROLE REVERSALS
- Gene Hackman's Popeye Doyle could have been Steve McQueen's, Jackie Gleason's, or even columnist Jimmy Breslin's. Hackman, the director's seventh choice, grabbed the part without a moment's hesitation.
- Ben Johnson initially turned down the role in *The Last Picture Show,* for which he won the Academy Award, because the script contained too many expletives; with the permission of the director, Peter Bogdanovich, he rewrote his part with the offensive words removed.

UNMENTIONABLES
- Warner Bros. began to sweat when Jane Fonda's antiwar activism persuaded a number of state legislatures to pass resolutions calling for a boycott of her movies.
- In response to being compared with the great young filmmaker Orson Welles, Bogdanovich said, "I hope I'm not repeating what happened to Orson. You know, make a successful serious film like this early [*The Last Picture Show*] and then spend the rest of my life in decline."
- In making *The French Connection*, Hackman was disturbed by all the violence, saying, "I found out very quickly that I'm not a violent person, and these cops are surrounded by violence all the time. There were a couple of days when I wanted to get out of the picture."
- Vanessa Redgrave was blacklisted from attending the Awards ceremony by the Nixon administration.
- A number of stars—including Barbra Streisand—refused to present the Best Picture Award because they rejected the nomination of *A Clockwork Orange*.
- Scattered boos were heard among the cheers when Jane Fonda's name was announced for Best Actress. Before the awards, the paterfamilias said to his daughter, "I implore you not to make a political statement."
- Legend has it that when Jane Fonda attended Vassar she refused to wear the elegant white gloves and pearls that were a tradition for the daily Tea in the Rose Parlor. She was chastised and returned to the parlor wearing the gloves and the pearls, and nothing else.

Sam Bottoms with Ben Johnson

BEST SUPPORTING ACTOR
BEN JOHNSON (1918–1996)
THE LAST PICTURE SHOW

Johnson had to be talked into taking on the role of Sam the Lion by filmmaker John Ford. *Newsweek* proclaimed *The Last Picture Show* "the most impressive work by a young American director since *Citizen Kane*. A former rodeo star, Johnson broke into the movie business in 1940, first as a horse wrangler and later as a double for cowboy star Wild Bill Elliott.

He was "discovered" by director John Ford, who cast him in *She Wore a Yellow Ribbon* and *Mighty Joe Young* (both 1949), and *Rio Grande* and *Wagon Master* (both 1950). Johnson then returned to character parts, mostly in Westerns, including *Shane* (1953), *One-Eyed Jacks* (1961), and *Hang 'em High* (1968). He was also a favorite of director Sam Peckinpah, and appeared in his *Major Dundee* (1965), *The Wild Bunch* (1969), and *The Getaway* (1972). He subsequently appeared in, among other films, *Dillinger* (1973), *The Sugarland Express* (1974), and *Radio Flyer* (1992).

BEST SUPPORTING ACTRESS
CLORIS LEACHMAN (B. 1926)
THE LAST PICTURE SHOW

After thanking her piano and dancing teachers, Leachman thanked her "dad, who paid the bills."

Leachman, who played a housewife who has an affair with a younger man in *The Last Picture Show*, was a former Miss America runner-up who went on to play in such comic films as Mel Brooks's *Young Frankenstein* (1974), *High Anxiety* (1977), and *History of the World—Part 1* (1981). However, she was truly sexy in her debut film, *Kiss Me Deadly* (1955).

Leachman broke out in films in the late 1960s and early '70s, during which she made *Butch Cassidy and the Sundance Kid* (1969), *Lovers and Other Strangers* (1970), and *Crazy Mama* (1975). Leachman is best known for her television work on *Lassie*, *The Mary Tyler Moore Show* (1970–1977), and its spinoff *Phyllis* (1975–1977). She has six Emmy Awards to her credit. "I think George C. Scott was so right," she said at the Awards. "In a way, giving the award is anti-everything actors are. Still, I really want to win."

HONORARY AWARD
CHARLES CHAPLIN (1889–1977)

"Words are so futile, so feeble," said Jack Lemmon as he handed Chaplin his hat and cane. After a twenty-two-year exile, Chaplin was back.

Born into vaudeville, Chaplin drew the attention of Mack Sennett, who gave him his screen debut in *Making a Living* (1914). The Little Tramp's signature derby hat, falling trousers, and cane were first seen in *Kid Auto Races at Venice* (1914).

After thirteen films with Sennett, Chaplin made his first feature, *The Kid* (1921). He co-founded United Artists in 1919 and his first release, *A Woman of Paris* (1923), more sophisticated than his other films, failed. Chaplin returned to his Little Tramp persona in *The Gold Rush* (1925) and *The Circus* (1928).

Chaplin utilized sound to his advantage. In *City Lights* (1931) he used an orchestrated musical score; *Modern Times* (1936) remained a silent film, but with *The Great Dictator* (1940, nom.) he used dialogue for the first time.

After a hiatus of seven years, Chaplin returned to the screen with *Monsieur Verdoux* (1947, nom.). The political sentiments expressed in *Modern Times* and *Verdoux* would get Chaplin into trouble with the new House Un-American Activities Committee: he was deported despite his denial of Communist involvement. He settled in Switzerland, where he made *A King in New York* (1957) and *A Countess from Hong Kong* (1967).

PICTURE

A CLOCKWORK ORANGE, Hawk Films, Warner Bros. Stanley Kubrick.
FIDDLER ON THE ROOF, Mirisch-Cartier, UA. Norman Jewison.
THE FRENCH CONNECTION, D'Antoni-Schine-Moore, 20th Century-Fox. Philip D'Antoni.
THE LAST PICTURE SHOW, BBS Prods., Columbia. Stephen J. Friedman.
NICHOLAS AND ALEXANDRA, Horizon, Columbia. Sam Spiegel.

ACTOR

PETER FINCH in *Sunday Bloody Sunday*, Janni, UA.
GENE HACKMAN in *The French Connection*, D'Antoni-Schine-Moore, 20th Century-Fox.
WALTER MATTHAU in *Kotch*, ABC Pictures, Cinerama.
GEORGE C. SCOTT in *The Hospital*, Gottfried-Chayefsky-Hiller, UA.
TOPOL in *Fiddler on the Roof*, Mirisch-Cartier, UA.

ACTRESS

JULIE CHRISTIE in *McCabe & Mrs. Miller*, Altman Foster, Warner Bros.
JANE FONDA in *Klute*, Gus, Warner Bros.
GLENDA JACKSON in *Sunday Bloody Sunday*, Janni, UA.
VANESSA REDGRAVE in *Mary, Queen of Scots*, Wallis, Universal.
JANET SUZMAN in *Nicholas and Alexandra*, Horizon, Columbia.

SUPPORTING ACTOR

JEFF BRIDGES in *The Last Picture Show*, BBS Prods., Columbia.
LEONARD FREY in *Fiddler on the Roof*, Mirisch-Cartier, UA.
RICHARD JAECKEL in *Sometimes a Great Notion*, Newman-Foreman, Universal.
BEN JOHNSON in *The Last Picture Show*, BBS Productions, Columbia.
ROY SCHEIDER in *The French Connection*, D'Antoni-Schine-Moore, 20th Century-Fox.

SUPPORTING ACTRESS

ELLEN BURSTYN in *The Last Picture Show*, BBS Prods., Columbia.
BARBARA HARRIS in *Who Is Harry Kellerman and Why Is He Saying Those Terrible Things About Me?*, Cinema Center Films/National General.
CLORIS LEACHMAN in *The Last Picture Show*, BBS Prods., Columbia.
MARGARET LEIGHTON in *The Go-Between*, World Film Series, Columbia.
ANN MARGRET in *Carnal Knowledge*, Icarus, Avco Embassy.

DIRECTION

PETER BOGDANOVICH for *The Last Picture Show*, BBS Prods., Columbia.
WILLIAM FRIEDKIN for *The French Connection*, 20th Century-Fox.
NORMAN JEWISON for *Fiddler on the Roof*, Mirisch-Cartier, UA.
STANLEY KUBRICK for *A Clockwork Orange*, Hawk Films, Warner Bros.
JOHN SCHLESINGER for *Sunday Bloody Sunday*, Janni, UA.

WRITING: BASED ON MATERIAL FROM ANOTHER MEDIUM

A CLOCKWORK ORANGE, Hawk Films, Warner Bros. Stanley Kubrick.
THE CONFORMIST, Paramount (Italian). Bernardo Bertolucci.
THE FRENCH CONNECTION, 20th Century-Fox. Ernest Tidyman.
THE GARDEN OF THE FINZI-CONTINIS, Cinema V (Italian). Ugo Pirro and Vittorio Bonicelli.
THE LAST PICTURE SHOW, BBS Prods., Columbia. Larry McMurtry and Peter Bogdanovich.

WRITING: STORY AND SCREENPLAY BASED ON FACTUAL MATERIAL OR MATERIAL NOT PREVIOUSLY PUBLISHED OR PRODUCED

THE HOSPITAL, Gottfried-Chayefsky-Hiller, UA. Paddy Chayefsky.
INVESTIGATION OF A CITIZEN ABOVE SUSPICION, Columbia (Italian). Elio Petri and Ugo Pirro.
KLUTE, Gus Prod. Warner Bros. Andy and Dave Lewis.
SUMMER OF '42, Mulligan-Roth, Warner Bros. Herman Rancher.
SUNDAY BLOODY SUNDAY, Janni, UA. Penelope Gilliatt.

ART DIRECTION—SET DECORATION

THE ANDROMEDA STRAIN, Robert Wise Prods., Universal. Boris Leven and William Tuntke; Ruby Levitt.
BEDKNOBS AND BROOMSTICKS, Disney, Buena Vista. John B. Mansbridge and Peter Ellenshaw; Emile Kuri and Hal Gausman.
FIDDLER ON THE ROOF, Mirisch-Cartier, UA. Robert Boyle and Michael Stringer; Peter Lamont.
MARY, QUEEN OF SCOTS, Walls, Universal. Terence Marsh and Robert Cartwright; Peter Howitt.
NICHOLAS AND ALEXANDRA, Horizon, Columbia. John Box, Ernest Archer, Jack Maxsted and Gil Parrondo; Vernon Dixon.

COSTUME DESIGN

BEDKNOBS AND BROOMSTICKS, Disney, Buena Vista. Bill Thomas.
DEATH IN VENICE, Alfa Cinematografica/P.E.C.F., Warner Bros. Piero Tosi.
MARY, QUEEN OF SCOTS, Wallis, Universal. Margaret Furse.
NICHOLAS AND ALEXANDRA, Horizon, Columbia. Yvonne Blake and Antonio Castillo.
WHAT'S THE MATTER WITH HELEN? Filmways-Raymax, UA. Morton Haack.

SOUND

DIAMONDS ARE FOREVER, Broccoli-Saltzman, UA. Gordon K. McCallum, John Mitchell and Alfred J. Overton.
FIDDLER ON THE ROOF, Mirisch-Cartier, UA. Gordon K. McCallum and David Hildyard.
THE FRENCH CONNECTION, 20th Century-Fox. Theodore Soderberg and Christopher Newman.
KOTCH, ABC Pictures, Cinerama. Richard Portman and Jack Solomon.
MARY, QUEEN OF SCOTS, Wallis, Universal. Bob Jones and John Aldred.

FILM EDITING

THE ANDROMEDA STRAIN, Robert Wise Prod., Universal. Stuart Gilmore and John W. Holmes.
A CLOCKWORK ORANGE, Hawk Films, Warner Bros. Bill Butler.
THE FRENCH CONNECTION, 20th Century-Fox. Jerry Greenberg.
KOTCH, ABC Pictures, Cinerama. Ralph E. Winters.
SUMMER OF '42, Mulligan-Roth, Warner Bros. Folmar Blangsted.

CINEMATOGRAPHY

FIDDLER ON THE ROOF, Mirisch-Cartier, UA. Oswald Morris.
THE FRENCH CONNECTION, 20th Century-Fox. Owen Roizman.
THE LAST PICTURE SHOW, BBS Prods., Columbia. Robert Surtees.
NICHOLAS AND ALEXANDRA, Horizon, Columbia. Freddie Young.
SUMMER OF '42, Mulligan-Roth, Warner Bros. Robert Surtees.

SHORT SUBJECT: ANIMATED FILM

THE CRUNCH BIRD, Maxwell-Petok-Petrovich Prods., Regency Films, Ted Petok, producer.
EVOLUTION, National Film Board of Canada, Columbia. Michael Mills, producer.
THE SELFISH GIANT, Potterton Prods., Pyramid Films. Peter Sender and Murray Shostak, producers.

SHORT SUBJECT: LIVE ACTION

GOOD MORNING, E/G Films, Seymour Borde & Associates. Denny Evans and Ken Greenwald, producers.
THE REHEARSAL, Cinema Verona Prod., Schoenfeld Films. Stephen F. Verona, producer.
SENTINELS OF SILENCE, Producciones Concord, Paramount. Manuel Arango and Robert Amram, producers.

SONG

THE AGE OF NOT BELIEVING (*Bedknobs and Broomsticks*, Disney, Buena Vista); Music and Lyrics by Richard M. Sherman and Robert B. Sherman.
ALL HIS CHILDREN (*Sometimes a Great Notion*, Newman-Foreman, Universal); Music by Henry Mancini. Lyrics by Alan and Marilyn Bergman.
BLESS THE BEASTS & CHILDREN (*Bless the Beasts & Children*, Columbia); Music and Lyrics by Barry DeVorzon and Perry Botkin Jr.
LIFE IS WHAT YOU MAKE IT (Kotch, ABC Pictures, Cinerama); Music by Marvin Hamlisch. Lyrics by Johnny Mercer.
THEME FROM SHAFT (Shaft, MGM); Music and Lyrics by Isaac Hayes.

MUSIC: ORIGINAL DRAMATIC SCORE

MARY, QUEEN OF SCOTS, Walls, Universal. John Barry.
NICHOLAS AND ALEXANDRA, Horizon, Columbia. Richard Rodney Bennett.
SHAFT, MGM. Isaac Hayes.
STRAW DOGS, ABC Pictures, Cinerama. Jerry Fielding.
SUMMER OF '42, Mulligan-Roth, Warner Bros. Michel Legrand.

SCORING: ADAPTATION AND ORIGINAL SONG SCORE

BEDKNOBS AND BROOMSTICKS, Disney, Buena Vista. Richard M. Sherman, Robert B. Sherman and Irwin Kostal.
THE BOY FRIEND, Russflix, MGM. Peter Maxwell Davies and Peter Greenwell.
FIDDLER ON THE ROOF, Mirisch-Cartier, UA. John Williams.
TCHAIKOVSKY, Dimitri Tiomkin-Mosfilm Studios (U.S.S.R.). Dimitri Tiomkin.
WILLY WONKA AND THE CHOCOLATE FACTORY, Wolper, Paramount. Leslie Bricusse, Anthony Newley and Walter Scharf.

SPECIAL VISUAL EFFECTS

BEDKNOBS AND BROOMSTICKS, Disney, Buena Vista. Alan Maley, Eustace Lycett and Danny Lee.
WHEN DINOSAURS RULED THE EARTH, Hammer, Warner Bros. Jim Danforth and Roger Dicken.

DOCUMENTARY: SHORT SUBJECT

ADVENTURES IN PERCEPTION, Han van Gelder Filmproduktie for Netherlands Information Service. Han van Gelder, producer.
ART IS..., Henry Strauss Associates for Sears Roebuck Foundation. Julian Krainin and DeWitt L. Sage Jr., producers.
THE NUMBERS START WITH THE RIVER, A WH Picture for U.S. Information Agency. Donald Wrye, producer.
SENTINELS OF SILENCE, Producciones Concord, Paramount. Manuel Arango and Robert Amram, producers.
SOMEBODY WAITING, Snider Prods., for University of California Medical Film Library. Hal Riney, Dick Snider and Sherwood Omens, producers.

DOCUMENTARY: FEATURE

ALASKA WILDERNESS LAKE, Alan Landsburg Prods. Alan Landsburg, producer.
THE HELLSTROM CHRONICLE, David L. Wolper, Cinema V. Walon Green, producer.
ON ANY SUNDAY, Brown-Solar, Cinema V. Bruce Brown, producer.
THE RA EXPEDITIONS, Swedish Broadcasting Company, Interwest Film Corp. Lennart Ehrenborg and Thor Heyerdahl, producers.
THE SORROW AND THE PITY, Cinema V (French). Marcel Ophuls, producer.

FOREIGN LANGUAGE FILM

DODES'KA-DEN (Japan)
THE EMIGRANTS (Sweden)
THE GARDEN OF THE FINZI-CONTINIS (Italy)
THE POLICEMAN (Israel)
TCHAIKOVSKY (U.S.S.R.)

HONORARY AND OTHER AWARDS

TO CHARLES CHAPLIN for the incalculable effect he has had in making motion pictures the art form of this century.

SCIENTIFIC OR TECHNICAL

CLASS II

JOHN N. WILKINSON of Optical Radiation Corporation for the development and engineering of a system of xenon arc lamphouses for motion-picture projection.

CLASS III

THOMAS JEFFERSON HUTCHINSON, JAMES R. ROCHESTER and FENTON HAMILTON;
PHOTO RESEARCH, A Division of Kollmorgen Corporation;
ROBERT D. AUGUSTE and CINEMA PRODUCTS CO.;
PRODUCERS SERVICE CORPORATION and CONSOLIDATED FILM INDUSTRIES; and CINEMA RESEARCH CORPORATION and RESEARCH PRODUCTS, INC.;
CINEMA PRODUCTS CO.

1972

> "I think a man who makes $2 million playing the leader of the Mafia should at least give half of it to the Indians."
>
> —Michael Caine

INDIAN GIVER

CEREMONY: March 27, 1973
Dorothy Chandler Pavilion, Los Angeles Music Center, Los Angeles
HOSTS: Carol Burnett, Michael Caine, Charlton Heston, Rock Hudson

As Moses in *The Ten Commandments*, opening host Charlton Heston parted the Red Sea. He wasn't so lucky with L.A. traffic en route to the Oscars. A stunned Clint Eastwood was drafted at the last minute to fill in for the absent host. "This was supposed to be Charlton Heston's part of the show, but for some reason he's not here," Eastwood mumbled. "So who did they get? A guy who hasn't said three lines in twelve movies."

The night was off to a bumpy start, especially for Francis Ford Coppola, whose *Godfather* was sidelined by an early sweep for *Cabaret*. Its co-star, the diminutive Joel Grey, picked up the Oscar for Best Supporting Actor, and there was little question that Liza Minnelli would take one for the top honors. She was clearly put off by Rock Hudson's comment that "in a horse race, bloodlines count," suggesting that Minnelli's win was in compensation for mom Judy Garland's Oscar strikeout. "Thank you for giving me this award," Minnelli emphasized.

The real drama of the night came as Liv Ullman and Roger Moore opened the envelope for Best Actor. Almost everyone knew what was coming, but the effect was still stunning. With the announcement of Marlon Brando's name, a pretty young woman in full tribal regalia made her way to the microphone. "Hello, my name is Sacheen Littlefeather," she said. "I'm Apache, and I am president of the Native American Affirmative Image Committee. I'm representing Marlon Brando this evening, and he has asked me to tell you that he very regretfully cannot accept this generous award. And the reasons for this being the treatment of American Indians today by the film industry." Her appearance stopped the ceremony cold. Clint Eastwood was in the awkward position of having to follow on the heels of her moccasins to announce Best Picture. Infuriated, he finally found his voice. "I don't know if I should present this Award on behalf of all the cowboys shot in John Ford Westerns over the years," he said.

BEST PICTURE
THE GODFATHER

Robert Evans hired 32-year-old Francis Ford Coppola to direct the film of the best-selling book, even though his last three movies—*You're a Big Boy Now* (1966), the musical *Finian's Rainbow* (1968), and *The Rain People* (1969)—had been bombs. No sooner was Coppola signed than he began to argue with Paramount about raising the budget and turning *The Godfather* into an epic instead of what the studio envisioned—a low-budget gangster thriller with an exploitable title.

The *Sacramento Bee* said, "*The Godfather* was carefully structured by Coppola to resemble one of the classic gangster films that Warners studio made with James Cagney and Humphrey Bogart. It was a modern variation on the genre. You could say *The Godfather* was the greatest Warner Bros. movie that Warner Bros. never made. (It was made by Paramount.)" The *New York Times*'s Vincent Canby wrote, "Coppola has made one of the most brutal and moving chronicles of American life ever designed within the limits of popular entertainment…The Corleone family may be the mid-twentieth-century equivalent of the oil and lumber and railroad barons of nineteenth-century America."

Back row: Robert Duvall, Tere Livrano, John Cazale, Gianni Russo, Talia Shire, Morgana King, Marlon Brando, James Caan, Julie Gregg

And, indeed, Coppola put the Mafia on the map, leaving filmgoers a little bit in love with this criminal subculture. With *The Godfather*, Coppola got everything right, balancing art with commerce and turning a big-studio project into something deeply personal and resonant.

The envelope, please...

 BEST DIRECTOR
BOB FOSSE (1927–1987)
CABARET

Pauline Kael of *The New Yorker* predicted that "after *Cabaret*, it should be awhile before performers once again climb hills singing or a chorus breaks into song on a hayride."

Fosse was a dancer and stage choreographer who appeared as an actor/dancer in several Hollywood films. After *Sweet Charity*, he continued with *Lenny* and *The Little Prince* (both 1974) and *All That Jazz* (1979). His last film was *Star 80* (1983), about the doomed *Playboy* playmate Dorothy Stratten. He choreographed *My Sister Eileen* (1955) and the movie version of hit Broadway shows *The Pajama Game* (1957), *Damn Yankees* (1958), and *How to Succeed in Business Without Really Trying* (1967). "His work had bite and bravado in roughly equal doses," wrote *Entertainment Tonight* critic Leonard Maltin.

 BEST ACTOR
MARLON BRANDO (B. 1924)
THE GODFATHER

"The Brando performance is justly famous and often imitated," wrote critic Roger Ebert. "Brando embodies the character so convincingly that [at times] we are not thinking of acting at all."

In what has been a very checkered career, Brando brought life to great films in many Oscar-nominated performances, including *A Streetcar Named Desire* (1951), *Viva Zapata!* (1952), *Julius Caesar* (1953), *On the Waterfront* (1954), *Sayonara* (1957), and *Last Tango in Paris* (1973). He tried his gifts out in uncharacteristic roles in *Guys and Dolls* (1955), *The Teahouse of the August Moon* (1956), and *The Fugitive Kind* (1959). But his career was nearly destroyed with the remake of *Mutiny on the Bounty* (1962) and *A Countess from Hong Kong* (1967).

Robert Duvall with Marlon Brando

 BEST ACTRESS
LIZA MINNELLI (B. 1946)
CABARET

Cabaret was designed as a showcase for Minnelli by her friends, who wrote the Broadway musical.   al Prince thought she was too awkward for the show, which went on to become the biggest hit of the 1966–67 season.

Pauline Kael cheered Minnelli's performance in *The New Yorker* "as exuberant...Minnelli has such gaiety and electricity that she becomes a star before our eyes." By the time the play turned into a movie, Minnelli had become a star, with an Oscar nomination for *The Sterile Cuckoo* (1969). She made the cover of *Time*, *Newsweek*, and *Life*, the latter of which declared, "At 25, Liza Minnelli is still Judy's daughter, but now she is her own voice."

Liza rose above the fate of many children of famous parents and made her own career. Making her film debut at the age of 3 with her mom in In the *Good Old Summertime* (1949), she grew into a talented singer and dancer. Never quite making it as a movie star, Minnelli nevertheless drew an avid following and won three Tonys and an Oscar. Among her films are *Tell Me That You Love Me, Junie Moon* (1970), *New York, New York* (1977), and *Arthur* (1981).

BEST OF 1972
Best Picture: *The Godfather*
Best Director: Bob Fosse, *Cabaret*
Best Actor: Marlon Brando, *The Godfather*
Best Actress: Liza Minnelli, *Cabaret*
Best Supporting Actor: Joel Grey, *Cabaret*
Best Supporting Actress: Eileen Heckart, *Butterflies Are Free*

FIRSTS
Cabaret won the most Oscars—eight—without winning Best Picture.

ROLE REVERSALS
- Before signing Marlon Brando on, Paramount was torn between such possibilities as Burt Lancaster, Orson Welles, George C. Scott, and Edward G. Robinson, but Coppola knew whom he wanted: It was either Laurence Olivier or Marlon Brando. Olivier wasn't available. As for Paramount, Brando wasn't even a contender—he hadn't had a hit in a dozen years.
- The hunt for Corleone's sons was tantamount to finding four Scarlett O'Haras. It helped if you were a friend of Coppola's. Studio honchos wanted Warren Beatty, Jack Nicholson, or Dustin Hoffman as Don Corleone's No. 1 son, Michael. They scoffed at Coppola's suggestion of Al Pacino, who hadn't made much of a stir with his performance in *Panic in Needle Park* (1971).

UNMENTIONABLES
- Sacheen Littlefeather accepted the Oscar for Brando, who could not accept because, he complained, of Hollywood and American society's mistreatment of Native Americans. Littlefeather, it seems, was not an Indian activist at all but a B-movie actress who would later appear in *Playboy* magazine.
- Liza Minnelli was involved in a romance with 19-year-old Desi Arnaz Jr. Said *Modern Screen* magazine, "Liza, wrought by anxieties, may be doing everything in her power to close the [age] gap. Her makeup is kookier, her clothes more far-out. Her energy is almost frenetic."
- Liza Minnelli was romantically involved with Peter Sellers in spring 1973.
- Eileen Heckart was forced to apply for unemployment benefits after winning her Oscar.
- In 1956 Edward G. Robinson sold off his extensive art collection as part of his divorce settlement.
- Bob Fosse separated from Gwen Verdon in the 1970s but remained married to her until his death. In the interim, he was romantically involved with Ann Reinking and Jessica Lange.

BRANDO UNMENTIONABLES
- Brando balked at the prospect of Burt Reynolds playing Sonny Corleone in *The Godfather*. Brando got his way, and James Caan got the part.
- Brando's oldest son was arrested for murdering his sister's boyfriend in 1990. The boy was sentenced to ten years in March 1991 and released in January of 1996.
- In 1995, as a guest on *Larry King Live*, Brando kissed the host on the mouth.

 BEST SUPPORTING ACTOR
JOEL GREY (B. 1932)
CABARET

Cabaret brought stardom to Grey, who repeated his stage role as the master of ceremonies.

Saturday Review effused, "Nothing like Mr. Grey has happened before, not on stage and not in films. He is totally outrageous, mocking, raucous, leering, a dreadfully delightful symbol of the overall decadence." Roger Ebert wrote, "The master of sexual ambiguity and the master of motifs is Joel Grey, master of ceremonies at the Kit Kat Klub."

Grey later became a first-rate character actor, appearing in *Man on a Swing* (1974), *The Seven-Per-Cent Solution* (1976), *Remo Williams: The Adventure Begins…*(1985), *Kafka* (1991), and *The Music of Chance* (1993). His daughter is actress Jennifer Grey.

 BEST SUPPORTING ACTRESS
EILEEN HECKART (1919–2002)
BUTTERFLIES ARE FREE

"I just hope they pan the camera on me just once. I paid a lot of money for this dress…and I want my mother in Columbus, Ohio, to be able to see it."

Re-creating her Broadway role as the domineering mother in *Butterflies Are Free*, Heckart, for the benefit of the film's targeted middle-aged audience, becomes the heroine of the film. According to *Variety*, "Miss Heckart finally gets another role that enables her to display the versatility that has been evident for a long time in her stage roles."

Before her Oscar-winning performance, Heckart appeared in *Bus Stop* and *Somebody Up There Likes Me* (both 1956), *Up the Down Staircase* (1967), and *No Way to Treat a Lady* (1968). In the latter part of her career, she appeared mainly in television movies, though she did star in the films *Murder One* (1995) and *The First Wives Club* (1996).

© A.M.P.A.S®   *Eileen Heckart with Cloris Leachman*

 HONORARY AWARD
EDWARD G. ROBINSON (1893–1973)

"One of the dearest men I know," said director Mervyn LeRoy. "There is nothing that I could say about this great artist that would really praise him enough."

Robinson died two months before the award was given, but he had learned about it just before his death.

The magnetic Romanian-born star—who had considered becoming a rabbi—with the much-impersonated voice, had never been nominated for an Academy Award. He had, however, been accused and cleared of allegations of Communist affiliations in 1956, at which point he returned to Broadway in *Middle of the Night*.

Robinson became an overnight film sensation in *Little Caesar* (1930). He remained a star of many genres and appeared in *Barbary Coast* (1935), *A Slight Case of Murder* (1938), *Double Indemnity* (1944), *Key Largo* and *All My Sons* (both 1948), *The Ten Commandments* (1956), *Two Weeks in Another Town* (1962), *The Cincinnati Kid* (1965), and his last film, *Soylent Green* (1973).

PICTURE
CABARET, ABC Pictures, Allied Artists. Cy Feuer.
DELIVERANCE, Warner Bros. John Boorman.
THE EMIGRANTS, Svensk Filmindustri, Warner Bros. (Swedish) Bengt Forslund.
THE GODFATHER, Ruddy, Paramount. Albert S. Ruddy.
SOUNDER, Radnitz/Mattel, 20th Century-Fox, Robert B. Radnitz.

ACTOR
MARLON BRANDO in *The Godfather*, Ruddy, Paramount.
MICHAEL CAINE in *Sleuth*, Palomar, 20th Century-Fox.
LAURENCE OLIVIER in *Sleuth*, Palomar, 20th Century-Fox.
PETER O'TOOLE in *The Ruling Class*, Keep Films, Avco Embassy.
PAUL WINFIELD in *Sounder*, Radnitz/ Mattel, 20th Century-Fox.

ACTRESS
LIZA MINNELLI in *Cabaret*, ABC Pictures, Allied Artists.
DIANA ROSS in *Lady Sings the Blues*, Motown-Weston-Furie, Paramount.
MAGGIE SMITH in *Travels with My Aunt*, Fryer, MGM.
CICELY TYSON in *Sounder*, Radnitz/Mattel, 20th Century-Fox.
LIV ULLMANN in *The Emigrants*, Svensk Filmindustri, Warner Bros. (Swedish).

SUPPORTING ACTOR
EDDIE ALBERT in *The Heartbreak Kid*, Palomar, 20th Century-Fox.
JAMES CAAN in *The Godfather*, Ruddy, Paramount.
ROBERT DUVALL in *The Godfather*, Ruddy, Paramount.
JOEL GREY in *Cabaret*, ABC Pictures, Allied Artists.
AL PACINO in *The Godfather*, Ruddy, Paramount.

SUPPORTING ACTRESS
JEANNIE BERLIN in *The Heartbreak Kid*, Palomar, 20th Century-Fox.
EILEEN HECKART in *Butterflies Are Free*, Frankovich, Columbia.
GERALDINE PAGE in *Pete 'N' Tillie*, Ritt-Epstein, Universal.
SUSAN TYRRELL in *Fat City*, Rastar, Columbia.
SHELLEY WINTERS in *The Poseidon Adventure*, Irwin Allen, 20th Century-Fox.

DIRECTION
JOHN BOORMAN for *Deliverance*, Warner Bros.
FRANCIS FORD COPPOLA for *The Godfather*, Ruddy, Paramount.
BOB FOSSE for *Cabaret*, ABC Pictures, Allied Artists.
JOSEPH L. MANKIEWICZ for *Sleuth*, Palomar, 20th Century-Fox.
JAN TROELL for *The Emigrants*, Svensk Filmindustri, Warner Bros. (Swedish).

WRITING: BASED ON MATERIAL FROM ANOTHER MEDIUM
CABARET, ABC Pictures, Allied Artists. Jay Allen.
THE EMIGRANTS, Svensk Filmindustri, Warner Bros. (Swedish). Jan Troell and Bengt Forslund.

THE GODFATHER, Ruddy, Paramount. Mario Puzo and Francis Ford Coppola.
PETE 'N' TILLIE, Ritt-Epstein, Universal. Julius J. Epstein.
SOUNDER, Radnitz/Mattel, 20th Century-Fox. Lonne Elder III.

WRITING: STORY AND SCREENPLAY BASED ON FACTUAL MATERIAL OR MATERIAL NOT PREVIOUSLY PUBLISHED OR PRODUCED
THE CANDIDATE, Redford-Ritchie, Warner Bros. Jeremy Lamer.
THE DISCREET CHARM OF THE BOURGEOISIE, Silberman, 20th Century-Fox (French). Luis Bunuel and Jean-Claude Carriere.
LADY SINGS THE BLUES, Motown-Weston-Furie, Paramount. Terence McCloy, Chris Clark and Suzanne de Passe.
MURMUR OF THE HEART, Continental Distributing (French). Louis Malle.
YOUNG WINSTON, Open Road Films, Columbia, Carl Foreman.

CINEMATOGRAPHY
BUTTERFLIES ARE FREE, Frankovich, Columbia. Charles B. Lang.
CABARET, ABC Pictures, Allied Artists. Geoffrey Unsworth.
THE POSEIDON ADVENTURE, Irwin Allen, 20th Century-Fox. Harold E. Stine.
"1776," Jack L. Warner, Columbia. Harry Stradling Jr.
TRAVELS WITH MY AUNT, Fryer, MGM. Douglas Slocombe.

ART DIRECTION—SET DECORATION
CABARET, ABC Pictures, Allied Artists. Hoff Zehetbauer and Jurgen Kiebach. Herbert Strabel.
LADY SINGS THE BLUES, Motown-Weston-Furie, Paramount. Carl Anderson; Reg Allen.
THE POSEIDON ADVENTURE, Irwin Allen, 20th Century-Fox. William Creber; Raphael Bretton.
TRAVELS WITH MY AUNT, Fryer, MGM. John Box, Gil Parrondo and Robert W. Laing.
YOUNG WINSTON, Open Road Films, Columbia. Don Ashton, Geoffrey Drake, John Graysmark and William Hutchinson; Peter James.

COSTUME DESIGN
THE GODFATHER, Ruddy, Paramount. Anna Hill Johnstone.
LADY SINGS THE BLUES, Motown-Weston-Furie, Paramount. Bob Mackie, Ray Aghayan and Norma Koch.
THE POSEIDON ADVENTURE, Irwin Allen, 20th Century-Fox. Paul Zastupnevich.
TRAVELS WITH MY AUNT, Fryer, M.G.M., Anthony Powell.
YOUNG WINSTON, Open Road Films, Columbia. Anthony Mendleson.

SOUND
BUTTERFLIES ARE FREE, Frankovich, Columbia. Arthur Piantadosi and Charles Knight.
CABARET, ABC Pictures, Allied Artists. Robert Knudson and David Hildyard.
THE CANDIDATE, Redford-Ritchie, Warner Bros. Richard Portman and Gene Cantamessa.
THE GODFATHER, Ruddy, Paramount. Bud Grenzbach, Richard Portman and Christopher Newman.
THE POSEIDON ADVENTURE, Irwin Allen, 20th Century-Fox. Theodore Soderberg and Herman Lewis.

FILM EDITING
CABARET, ABC Pictures, Allied Artists. David Bretherton.
DELIVERANCE, Warner Bros. Tom Priestley.
THE GODFATHER, Ruddy, Paramount. William Reynolds and Peter Zinner.
THE HOT ROCK, Landers-Roberts, 20th Century-Fox. Frank P. Keller and Fred W. Berger.
THE POSEIDON ADVENTURE, Irwin Allen, 20th Century-Fox. Harold F. Kress.

SHORT SUBJECT: ANIMATED FILM
A CHRISTMAS CAROL, American

Broadcasting Company Film Services. Richard Williams, producer.
KAMA SUTRA RIDES AGAIN, Lion International Films. Bob Godfrey, producer.
TUP TUP, Zagreb Film-Corona Cinematografica, Manson Distributing. Nedejiko Dragic producer.

SHORT SUBJECT: LIVE ACTION
FROG STORY, Gidron Prods., Schoenfeld Films. Ron Satlof and Ray Gideon, producers.
NORMAN ROCKWELL'S WORLD...AN AMERICAN DREAM, Concepts Unlimited, Columbia. Richard Barclay, producer.
SOLO, Pyramid Films, UA. David Adams, producer.

DOCUMENTARY: SHORT SUBJECT
HUNDERTWASSER'S RAINY DAY, Argos Films-Schamoni Film Prod. Peter Schamoni, producer.
K-Z, Nexus Films. Giorgio Treves, producer.
SELLING OUT, Unit Productions Films. Tadeusz Jaworski, producer.
THIS TINY WORLD, A Charles Huguenot van der Linden Production. Charles and Martina Huguenot van der Linden, producers.
THE TIDE OF TRAFFIC, BP-Greenpark. Humphrey Swingler, producer.

DOCUMENTARY: FEATURES
APE AND SUPER-APE, Netherlands Ministry of Culture, Recreation and Social Welfare. Bert Haanstra, producer.
MALCOLM X., Warner Bros. Marvin Worth and Arnold Pen, producers.
MANSON, Merrick International. Robert Hendrickson and Laurence Merrick, producers.
MARJOE, Cinema X, Cinema 5, Ltd. Howard Smith and Sarah Kernochan, producers.
THE SILENT REVOLUTION, Leonaris Films. Eckehard Munck, producer.

FOREIGN LANGUAGE FILM
THE DAWNS ARE QUIET (U.S.S.R.).
THE DISCREET CHARM OF THE BOURGEOISIE (France).
I LOVE YOU ROSA (Israel).
MY DEAREST SENORITA (Spain).
THE NEW LAND (Sweden).

SONG
BEN *(Ben*, Bing Crosby Prods., Cinerama); Music by Walter Scharf. Lyrics by Don Black.
COME FOLLOW, FOLLOW ME *(The Little Ark*, Radnitz, Cinema Center Films, National General); Music by Fred Karlin. Lyrics by Marsha Karlin.
MARMALADE, MOLASSES & HONEY *(The Life and Times of Judge Roy Bean*, First Artists, National General); Music by Maurice Jarre. Lyrics by Marilyn and Alan Bergman.
THE MORNING AFTER *(The Poseidon Adventure*, Irwin Allen, 20th Century-Fox); Music and Lyrics by Al Kasha and Joel Hirschhorn.
STRANGE ARE THE WAYS OF LOVE *(The Stepmother*, Crown International); Music by Sammy Fain. Lyrics by Paul Francis Webster.

MUSIC: ORIGINAL DRAMATIC SCORE
IMAGES, Hemdale-Lion's Gate Films, Columbia. John Williams.
LIMELIGHT, Charles Chaplin, Columbia. Charles Chaplin, Raymond Rasch and Larry Russell.
NAPOLEON AND SAMANTHA, Disney, Buena Vista. Buddy Baker.
THE POSEIDON ADVENTURE, Irwin Allen, 20th Century-Fox. John Williams.
SLEUTH, Palomar Pictures, 20th Century-Fox. John Addison.

SCORING: ADAPTATION AND ORIGINAL SONG SCORE
CABARET, ABC Pictures, Allied Artists. Ralph Burns.
LADY SINGS THE BLUES, Motown-Weston-Furie, Paramount. Gil Askey.

MAN OF LA MANCHA, PEA Produzioni Europee Associate Prod., UA. Laurence Rosenthal.

SPECIAL ACHIEVEMENT AWARD
For Visual Effects: L.B. ABBOTT and A.D. FLOWERS for *The Poseidon Adventure*, Irwin Allen, 20th Century-Fox.

HONORARY AND OTHER AWARDS
TO CHARLES BOREN—Leader for 38 years of the industry's enlightened labor relations and architect of its policy of non-discrimination. With the respect and affection of all who work in films.
TO EDWARD G. ROBINSON, who achieved greatness as a player, a patron of the arts and a dedicated citizen...in sum, a Renaissance man. From his friends in the industry he loves.

JEAN HERSHOLT HUMANITARIAN AWARD
TO ROSALIND RUSSELL

SCIENTIFIC OR TECHNICAL

CLASS II
JOSEPH E. BLUTH for research and development in the field of electronic photography and transfer of video tape to motion-picture film.
EDWARD H. REICHARD and HOWARD T. LaZARE of Consolidated Film Industries, and EDWARD EFRON of IBM for the engineering of a computerized light-valve monitoring system for motion-picture printing.
PANAVISION INCORPORATED for the development and engineering of the Panaflex motion-picture camera.

CLASS III
PHOTO RESEARCH, a Division of Kollmorgen Corporation, and PCS TECHNOLOGY INC., Acme Products Division;
CARTER EQUIPMENT COMPANY, INC. and RAMTRONICS;
DAVID DEGENKOLB, HARRY LARSON, MANFRED MICHELSON and FRED SCOBEY of Deluxe General Inc.;
JIRO MURAI and RYUSHO HIROSE of Canon, Inc. and WILTON R. HOLM of the AMPTP Motion Picture and Television Research Center;
PHILIP V. PALMQUIST and LEONARD L. OLSON of the 3M Company and FRANK P. CLARK of the AMPTP Motion Picture and Television Research Center.
E.H. GEISSLER and G.M. BERGGREN of Wil-Kin Inc.

1973

"You can imagine what a trip this is for a Jewish girl from Great Neck—I get to win an Academy Award and meet Elizabeth Taylor at the same time."

—Sting producer Julia Phillips

The '70s loomed as an era of embarrassments: the George C. Scott affair; the Brando put-down; and this year a streaker, running across the stage just as Elizabeth Taylor was about to make her grand entrance. The audience howled as conductor Henry Mancini led a tongue-in-cheek rendition of "Keep Your Sunny Side Up." The uninvited naked guest, Robert Opal, proprietor of a San Francisco sex-paraphernalia shop, wasn't the night's only classless act. Burt Reynolds opened the show with a volley of insults aimed at critics of "unsophisticated Hollywood," who were really "just jealous because they weren't nominated for anything." He ended his attack with a loud Bronx cheer at the camera.

Imperial glamour was restored with the appearance of Katharine Hepburn, in pants and clogs, to present the Thalberg Memorial Award to her longtime producer, Lawrence Weingarten. She cut off the standing ovation with a warm "Thank you" and an apology for never having come to the Awards before. "I'm living proof that a person can wait forty-one years to be unselfish," she said.

William Friedkin, director of box-office sensation *The Exorcist*, wasn't quite so forgiving as his film got trampled by *The Sting*. Even his little devil of a star, Linda Blair, got checked by pint-size peer Tatum O'Neal for *Paper Moon*. Early Best Actress favorite, Barbra Streisand, chose not to perform her film's Best Song, "The Way We Were," pawning it off instead to legendary Peggy Lee.

Nostalgia continued to reign as Jack Lemmon honored a tearful Groucho Marx before collecting his own Oscar for *Save the Tiger*. Lemmon admitted that he'd had his speech all prepared—in 1959. That was the year he wrongly assumed he would win for *Some Like It Hot*. But as tonight attested, the Academy Awards could always be relied upon to end a lucky streak or provide for a naked one.

NAKED AMBITION

CEREMONY: April 2, 1974
Dorothy Chandler Pavilion,
Los Angeles Music Center,
Los Angeles
HOSTS: John Huston, David Niven,
Burt Reynolds, Diana Ross

BEST PICTURE/BEST DIRECTOR
GEORGE ROY HILL (B. 1922)
THE STING

Accepting his award, Hill suggested that to ensure the film's success the same people who worked on *The Sting* should be hired. "It helps, believe me." Many critics bemoaned the formula film, while Hill was encouraging it as the ticket to success. Ushering in the "buddy-buddy" genre, *The Sting* reunited Newman and Redford, and many wondered, "Would women ever appear in films again?"

Hill had done well in the Western with *Butch Cassidy and the Sundance Kid* (1969) and decided to make hay out of another rich period when men acted like bad boys, the Prohibition-era and its gangsters. The reviews were slim, but the BBC had good things to say: "Close attention is paid to building period detail, and one of the film's major strengths is its atmospheric re-creation of the mean streets of Chicago. The plot gets complex quickly. But don't worry. For those watching this after a large meal, intertitles with different chapter headings break the plot into easily digestible chunks."

Robert Redford, Paul Newman

Director Hill had been around the block, having launched his career in TV's Golden Age and going on to make some of the most popular American films of the last three decades. Starting out as an actor, he moved, in the early 1950s, into directing. His first films were serious adaptations of plays he had directed on Broadway: Tennessee Williams's *Period of Adjustment* (1962) and Lillian Hellman's *Toys in the Attic* (1963). With his debut film, *The World of Henry Orient* (1964), Hill showed his gift for working with actors in lively, plot-driven, and playful situations. His films run the gamut from epics to comedies to thrillers, among them *Thoroughly Modern Millie* (1967), *Slaughterhouse-Five* (1972), *The Great Waldo Pepper* (1975), *Slap Shot* (1977), *A Little Romance* (1979), *The World According to Garp* (1982), *The Little Drummer Girl* (1984), and *Funny Farm* (1989).

The envelope, please...

BEST ACTOR
JACK LEMMON (1925–2001)
SAVE THE TIGER

"There's been some criticism of this award, some of it's justified, but I think it is one hell of an honor and I'm thrilled," Lemmon said. *Save the Tiger* follows a day and a half in the life of down-on-his-luck Harry Stoner, who daydreams about his youth, tries to escape his failing business by picking up a hitchhiker/prostitute, arranges for his company's warehouse to burn down so he can collect the insurance money, and then some.

The film was a box-office disaster for which Lemmon accepted scale wages. "I did *Save the Tiger* for nothing, and I'm prouder of it than all those movies I made millions on all rolled into one," he said. But it was not only the Academy that loved the picture: *The Saturday Review* called it "the first important film of 1973 and possibly the 1970s." (For more on Lemmon, see 1955.)

BEST ACTRESS
GLENDA JACKSON (B. 1936)
A TOUCH OF CLASS

Long-shot Glenda Jackson didn't even show up to receive her Oscar because she was working. Later, she had lots to say about it, however: "I felt disgusted with myself [watching the show on television], as though I were attending a public hanging…No one should have a chance to see so much desire, so much need for a prize, and so much pain when it was not given."

The New Republic found Jackson's performance in the modern screwball comedy about adultery "a delightful surprise…absolutely first-class." Still, the reviews were mixed. *Variety* praised it, saying, "The film conjures up the warmest memories of Leo McCarey and George Stevens at their best." *Newsweek* had some doubts, suggesting that the film had "the air of a period piece in mod clothing." (For more on Jackson, see 1970.)

Glenda Jackson with George Segal

BEST OF 1973
Best Picture: *The Sting*
Best Director: George Roy Hill, *The Sting*
Best Actor: Jack Lemmon, *Save the Tiger*
Best Actress: Glenda Jackson, *A Touch of Class*
Best Supporting Actor: John Houseman, *The Paper Chase*
Best Supporting Actress: Tatum O'Neal, *Paper Moon*
Honorary Award: Groucho Marx

FIRST
Tatum O'Neal at 10 became the youngest actress ever to win an Oscar, surpassing the 16-year-old Patty Duke.

ROLE REVERSALS
• James Mason walked out on John Houseman's role in *The Paper Chase*. Director James Bridges called Houseman, who at the time was head of the Juilliard school, for ideas for a replacement. "Get Edward G. Robinson," Houseman suggested. When Bridges discovered that Robinson was too ill, the role went to Houseman. It was only his second film appearance.

• Commenting on his possible role in *The Sting*, Jack Nicholson said, "I like it. I like the period setting, the whole project, and I know it will be commercial. But I need to put my energies into a movie that really needs them. I need to take a risk."

SINS OF OMISSION
Pictures: *Last Tango in Paris, The Exorcist, American Graffiti*

ALWAYS A BRIDESMAID, NEVER A BRIDE
One outraged viewer ran an ad in *Daily Variety* that said, "Congratulations to the Academy for turning its back on talent and artistry once again by ignoring Woody Allen and his superb film *Sleeper* in the Academy Award nominations. Charlie Chaplin and the Marx Brothers never got any Oscars for their performances either. Doesn't anyone out there like to laugh?"

UNMENTIONABLES
• Ten-year-old Tatum O'Neal was escorted to the stage by her unnamed grandfather, which provoked critic Andrew Sarris to wonder, "Who was that Humbert Humbert with her?"

• The FBI created a file on Marx after he made some jokes about Communism.

• Shortly after his death, Groucho's children found a gag letter written by Dad that stated that he wanted to be buried on top of Marilyn Monroe.

• Disappointed by *The Exorcist*'s losses, William Peter Blatty complained, "*The Exorcist* is head and shoulders the finest film made this year."

John Houseman (center)

 BEST SUPPORTING ACTOR
JOHN HOUSEMAN (1902–1988)
THE PAPER CHASE

"Almost for the first time in a long and tumultuous life, I'm almost speechless," said Houseman, citing his director for "the unspeakable gall to select this aging and obscure schoolmarm for this perfectly glorious part."

James Bridges, who cast Houseman as the brilliant but sadistic Harvard law professor, had been the actor's former student. *The Paper Chase* set Houseman's film career on the fast track, where he made such movies as *Rollerball* (1975), *Three Days of the Condor* (1975), and *Another Woman* (1988).

Houseman had a diverse and extraordinary career. He was a preeminent acting coach. He co-founded the Mercury Theatre with Orson Welles; they split up, however, after a disagreement over *Citizen Kane*. Houseman was also a producer responsible for such distinguished films as *The Blue Dahlia* (1946), *They Live by Night* (1948), *The Bad and the Beautiful* (1952), *Two Weeks in Another Town* (1962), and *This Property Is Condemned* (1966).

During the 1980s he appeared on television in movies and miniseries. Houseman was working on *The Naked Gun* just weeks before his death.

Tatum O'Neal with Ryan O'Neal

 BEST SUPPORTING ACTRESS
TATUM O'NEAL (B. 1963)
PAPER MOON

Escorted by her grandfather to the stage, 9-year-old O'Neal said, "All I really want to thank is my director Peter Bogdanovich and my father." *Variety* was delighted, announcing, "Tatum O'Neal makes a sensational screen debut."

O'Neal plays the rough-talking, cigarette-smoking con artist Addie Loggins, wheeling and dealing her way through the Midwest by teaming up with a smooth-talking hustler, Moses Pray, played by her real father, Ryan O'Neal. Her gifted use of Depression-era vernacular earned Tatum what Addie was looking for throughout the film—the big score.

Tatum's film career was sadly short-lived. As an adult she married tennis star John McEnroe, from whom she is currently divorced.

HONORARY AWARD
GROUCHO MARX (1890–1977)

A tearful Groucho accepted his honors, saying, "I wish Harpo and Chico were here to share this great honor. And I wish Margaret Dumont were here, too. She was a great straight woman even though she never got any of my jokes."

The irrepressible, wisecracking Groucho was responsible for what were perhaps the funniest films in history. Groucho, in fact, could never stop joking. His son, Arthur Marx, complained about his father always being "on."

Beginning their career as a singing group, the Marx Brothers went on to make comedies—though they were unappreciated by their Depression-era audiences. Their first Broadway hit, *The Cocoanuts* (1929), eventually landed them a contract with Paramount.

Well established in Hollywood, the Marx Brothers made such original films as *Monkey Business* (1931), *Horse Feathers* (1932), *Duck Soup* (1933), *A Night at the Opera* (1935), *A Day at the Races* (1937), and *The Big Store* (1941).

The brothers later split up to pursue independent careers in and out of show business. Groucho made a few films on his own—*Copacabana* (1947), *Double Dynamite* (1951), and *Skidoo* (1968)—and did a long stint on radio.

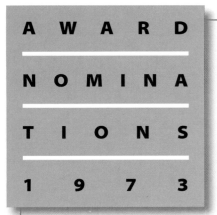

PICTURE

AMERICAN GRAFFITI, Universal-Lucasfilm, Ltd.-Coppola Co. Prod., Universal. Francis Ford Coppola, producer, Gary Kurtz, co-producer.

CRIES AND WHISPERS, Svenska Film Institutet-Cinematograph AB Prod., New World Pictures. Ingmar Bergman, producer.

THE EXORCIST, Hoya Prods., Warner Bros. William Peter Blatty, producer.

THE STING, Universal-Bill/Phillips-George Roy Hill Film Prod., Zanuck/Brown Presentation, Universal. Tony Bill, Michael and Julia Phillips, producers.

A TOUCH OF CLASS, Brut Prods., Avco Embassy, Melvin Frank, producer.

ACTOR

MARLON BRANDO in *Last Tango in Paris*, UA.

JACK LEMMON in *Save the Tiger*, Filmways-Jalem Cirandinha, Paramount.

JACK NICHOLSON in *The Last Detail*, Acrobat, Columbia.

AL PACINO in *Serpico*, De Laurentiis, Paramount.

ROBERT REDFORD in *The Sting*, Bill/Phillips-Hill, Zanuck/Brown, Universal.

ACTRESS

ELLEN BURSTYN in *The Exorcist*, Hoya, Warner Bros.

GLENDA JACKSON in *A Touch of Class*, Brut, Avco Embassy.

MARSHA MASON in *Cinderella Liberty*, Sanford, 20th Century-Fox.

BARBRA STREISAND in *The Way We Were*, Rastar, Columbia.

JOANNE WOODWARD in *Summer Wishes*, *Winter Dreams*, Rastar, Columbia.

SUPPORTING ACTOR

VINCENT GARDENIA in *Bang the Drum Slowly*, Rosenfield, Paramount.

JACK GILFORD in *Save the Tiger*, Filmways-Jalem-Cirandinha, Paramount.

JOHN HOUSEMAN in *The Paper Chase*, Thompson-Paul, 20th Century-Fox.

JASON MILLER in *The Exorcist*, Hoya, Warner Bros.

RANDY QUAID in *The Last Detail*, Acrobat, Columbia.

SUPPORTING ACTRESS

LINDA BLAIR in *The Exorcist*, Hoya, Warner Bros.

CANDY CLARK in *American Graffiti*, Lucasfilm-Coppola, Universal.

MADELINE KAHN in *Paper Moon*, Directors Company, Paramount.

TATUM O'NEAL in *Paper Moon*, Directors Company, Paramount.

SYLVIA SIDNEY in *Summer Wishes*, *Winter Dreams*, Rastar, Columbia.

DIRECTION

INGMAR BERGMAN for *Cries and Whispers*, New World Pictures (Swedish).

BERNARDO BERTOLUCCI for *Last Tango in Paris*, UA.

WILLIAM FRIEDKIN for *The Exorcist*, Hoya Prods., Warner Bros.

GEORGE ROY HILL for *The Sting*, Bill/Phillips-Hill-Zanuck/Brown, Universal.

GEORGE LUCAS for *American Graffiti*, Lucasfllm/Coppola Company, Universal.

WRITING: BEST SCREENPLAY BASED ON MATERIAL FROM ANOTHER MEDIUM

THE EXORCIST, Hoya Prods., Warner Bros. William Peter Blatty.

THE LAST DETAIL, Acrobat Films, Columbia. Robert Towne.

THE PAPER CHASE, Thompson-Paul Prods., 20th Century-Fox. James Bridges.

PAPER MOON, Directors Company, Paramount. Alvin Sargent.

SERPICO, De Laurentiis, Paramount. Waldo Salt and Norman Wexler.

WRITING: STORY AND SCREENPLAY BASED ON FACTUAL MATERIAL OR MATERIAL NOT PREVIOUSLY PUBLISHED OR PRODUCED

AMERICAN GRAFFITI, Lucasfilm/Coppola Company, Universal. George Lucas, Gloria Katz and Willard Huyck.

CRIES AND WHISPERS, New World Pictures (Swedish). Ingmar Bergman.

SAVE THE TIGER, Filmways-Jalem-Cirandinha, Paramount. Steve Shagan.

THE STING, Bill/Phillips-Hill-Zanuck/Brown, Universal. David S. Ward.

A TOUCH OF CLASS, Brut, Avco Embassy. Melvin Frank and Jack Rose.

CINEMATOGRAPHY

CRIES AND WHISPERS, New World Pictures (Swedish). Sven Nykvist.

THE EXORCIST, Hoya Prods., Warner Bros. Owen Roizman.

JONATHAN LIVINGSTON SEAGULL, Bartlett, Paramount. Jack Couffer.

THE STING, Bill/Phillips-Hill-Zanuck/Brown, Universal. Robert Surtees.

THE WAY WE WERE, Rastar, Columbia. Harry Stradling Jr.

ART DIRECTION—SET DECORATION

BROTHER SUN, SISTER MOON, Euro International-Vic Film Ltd., Paramount. Lorenzo Mongiardino and Gianni Quaranta; Carmelo Patrono.

THE EXORCIST, Hoya Prods., Warner Bros. Bill Malley; Jerry Wunderlich.

THE STING, Bill/Phillips-Hill-Zanuck/Brown, Universal. Henry Bumstead; James Payne.

TOM SAWYER, Jacobs, Reader's Digest, UA. Philip Jefferies; Robert de Vestel.

THE WAY WE WERE, Rastar, Columbia. Stephen Grimes; William Kiernan.

COSTUME DESIGN

CRIES AND WHISPERS, New World Pictures (Swedish). Marik Vos.

LUDWIG, Mega Film S.P.A. Prod., MGM. Piero Tosi.

THE STING, Bill/Phillips-Hill-Zanuck/Brown, Universal. Edith Head.

TOM SAWYER, Jacobs, Reader's Digest, UA. Donfeld.

THE WAY WE WERE, Rastar, Columbia. Dorothy Jeakins and Moss Mabry.

SOUND

THE DAY OF THE DOLPHIN, Icarus, Avco Embassy. Richard Portman and Lawrence O. Jost.

THE EXORCIST, Hoya Prods., Warner Bros. Robert Knudson and Chris Newman.

THE PAPER CHASE, Thompson-Paul Prods., 20th Century-Fox. Donald O. Mitchell and Lawrence O. Jost.

PAPER MOON, Directors Company, Paramount. Richard Portman and Les Fresholtz.

THE STING, Bill/Phillips-Hill-Zanuck/Brown, Universal. Ronald K. Pierce and Robert Bertrand.

FILM EDITING

AMERICAN GRAFFITI, Lucasfilm/Coppola Company, Universal. Verna Fields and Marcia Lucas.

THE DAY OF THE JACKAL, Warwick Films, Universal. Ralph Kemplen.

THE EXORCIST, Hoya Prods., Warner Bros. Jordan Leondopoulos, Bud Smith, Ryan Lottman and Norman Gay.

JONATHAN LIVINGSTON SEAGULL, Bartlett, Paramount. Frank P. Keller and James Galloway.

THE STING, Bill /Phillips-Hill-Zanuck/Brown, Universal. William Reynolds.

SONG

ALL THAT LOVE WENT TO WASTE *(A Touch of Class*, Brut, Avco Embassy); Music by George Barrie. Lyrics by Sammy Cahn.

LIVE AND LET DIE (*Live and Let Die*, Eon, UA); Music and Lyrics by Paul and Linda McCartney.

LOVE *(Robin Hood*, Disney, Buena Vista); Music by George Bruns. Lyrics by Floyd Huddleston.

THE WAY WE WERE *(The Way We Were*, Rastar, Columbia); Music by Marvin Hamlisch. Lyrics by Alan and Marilyn Bergman.

NICE TO BE AROUND *(Cinderella Liberty*, Sanford Prod., 20th Century-Fox); Music by John Williams. Lyrics by Paul Williams.

MUSIC: ORIGINAL DRAMATIC SCORE

CINDERELLA LIBERTY, Sanford Prod., 20th Century-Fox. John Williams.

THE DAY OF THE DOLPHIN, Learns Prods., Avco Embassy, Georges Delerue.

PAPILLON, Corona-General Prods., Allied Artists. Jerry Goldsmith.

A TOUCH OF CLASS, Brut, Avco Embassy. John Cameron.

THE WAY WE WERE, Rastar, Columbia. Marvin Hamlisch.

SCORING: ORIGINAL SONG SCORE AND/ OR ADAPTATION

JESUS CHRIST SUPERSTAR, Jewison-Stigwood, Universal. Andre Previn, Herbert Spencer and Andrew Lloyd Webber.

THE STING, Bill/Phillips-Hill-Zanuck/Brown, Universal. Marvin Hamlisch.

TOM SAWYER, Jacobs, Reader's Digest, UA.Richard M. Sherman, Robert B. Sherman and John Williams.

SHORT SUBJECT: ANIMATED FILM

FRANK FILM, Frank Mouris Prods., Frank Mouris, producer.

THE LEGEND OF JOHN HENRY, Bosustow-Pyramid Films. Nick Bosustow and David Adams, producers.

PULCINELLA, Luzzati-Gianini Prod. Emanuele Luzzati and Giulio Gianini, producers.

SHORT SUBJECT: LIVE ACTION

THE BOLERO, Allan Miller Prods. Allan Miller and William Fertik, producers.

CLOCKMAKER, James Street Prods. Richard Gayer, producer.

LIFE TIMES NINE, Insight Prods. Pen Densham and John Watson, producers.

DOCUMENTARY: SHORT SUBJECT

BACKGROUND, D'Avino and Fucci-Stone Prods. Carmen D'Avino, producer.

CHILDREN AT WORK (Paisti Ag Obair), Gael-Linn Films. Louis Marcus, producer.

CHRISTO'S VALLEY CURTAIN, Maysles Films. Albert and David Maysles, producers.

FOUR STONES FOR KANEMITSU, A Temarind Prod. Terry Sanders and June Wayne, producers.

PRINCETON: A SEARCH FOR ANSWERS, Krainin-Sage Prods. Julian Krainin and DeWitt L. Sage Jr., producers.

DOCUMENTARY: FEATURE

ALWAYS A NEW BEGINNING, Goodell Motion Pictures, John D. Goodell, producer.

BATTLE OF BERLIN, Chronos Film. Bengt von zur Muehlen, producer.

THE GREAT AMERICAN COWBOY, Merrill-Rodeo Film Prods. Kieth Merrill, producer.

JOURNEY TO TILE OUTER LIMITS, National Geographic Society and Wolper Prods. Alex Grasshoff, producer.

WALLS OF FIRE, Mentor Prods. Gertrude Ross Marks and Edmund F. Penney, producers.

FOREIGN LANGUAGE FILM

DAY FOR NIGHT (France).

THE HOUSE ON CHELOUCHE STREET (Israel).

L'INVITATION (Switzerland).

THE PEDESTRIAN (Federal Republic of West Germany).

TURKISH DELIGHT (The Netherlands).

HONORARY AND OTHER AWARDS

TO HENRI LANGLOIS for his devotion to the art of film, his massive contributions in preserving its past and his unswerving faith in its future.

TO GROUCHO MARX in recognition of his brilliant creativity and for the unequaled achievements of the Marx Brothers in the art of motion-picture comedy.

SPECIAL ACHIEVEMENT AWARD

None given this year.

IRVING G. THALBERG MEMORIAL AWARD

TO LAWRENCE WEINGARTEN

JEAN HERSHOLT HUMANITARIAN AWARD

TO LEW WASSERMAN

SCIENTIFIC OR TECHNICAL

CLASS II

JOACHIM GERB and ERICH KASTNER of The Arnold and Richter Company for the development and engineering of the Arnflex 35BL motion-picture camera.

MAGNA-TECH ELECTRONIC CO., INC. for the engineering and development of a high-speed rerecording system for motion-picture production.

WILLIAM W. VALLIANT of PSC Technology Inc., HOWARD F. OTT of Eastman Kodak Company, and GERRY DIEBOLD of The Richmark Camera Service Inc. for the development of a liquid-gate system for motion-picture printers.

HAROLD A. SCHEIB, CLIFFORD H. ELLIS and ROGER W. BANKS of Research Products Incorporated for the concept and engineering of the Model 2101 optical printer for motion-picture optical effects.

CLASS III

ROSCO LABORATORIES, INC.;

RICHARD H. VETFER of the Todd-AO Corporation.

1974

A near-biblical downpour didn't keep Jack Nicholson from arriving in sunglasses, a traditional tux, and a smile as wide as the streets of Chinatown. He entered the Chandler Pavilion a sure bet for Best Actor and left with an expression more in keeping with the weather after Art Carney's surprise win. In an odd coincidence, both Carney and Best Actress Ellen Burstyn were graduates of Jackie Gleason's TV shows.

Nominee Dustin Hoffman, in a sulky imitation of George C. Scott, was absent, but Francis Ford Coppola and entourage were on hand and ready to leap onto the stage. The first to do so was his dad, Carmine, for *Godfather Part II*'s Best Musical Score. In his excitement, the elder Coppola raced back to his seat, dropped his statuette, and broke it. The fractured Oscar was an unfortunate symbol for the vitriolic battle transpiring onstage and off. It began with the award for Best Documentary, *Hearts and Minds*, a searing indictment of the Vietnam War. Its co-producer, Bert Schneider, read a congratulatory telegram from the Vietcong delegation at the Paris peace talks. Bob Hope fumed and ignited Frank Sinatra's explosive rage. Old Blue Eyes stormed up to the podium and read his own political disclaimer "on behalf of the Academy." He was greeted with a chorus of boos and hisses.

Antiwar activist Shirley MacLaine went ballistic backstage and gave her former "ratpack" cohort a furious dressing-down. Sammy Davis Jr. tapped the ominous mood away in a tribute to Best Supporting nominee Fred Astaire, a sentimental favorite for his dramatic role in *The Towering Inferno*. Astaire didn't dance a single step in the movie. He lost to De Niro, who didn't speak a single word of English in *Godfather Part II*. Liv Ullman's blistering performance in Ingmar Bergman's *Scenes from a Marriage* was disqualified due to the film's brief showing on Swedish TV. A write-in protest by the Best Actress nominees had no effect. Ironically, Swedish-born Ingrid Bergman won Best Supporting but insisted that the Oscar should really have gone to Italy's Valentina Cortese.

COPPOLA, PART II

CEREMONY: April 8, 1975
**Dorothy Chandler Pavilion,
Los Angeles Music Center,
Los Angeles
HOSTS:** Bob Hope, Shirley MacLaine,
Sammy Davis Jr., Frank Sinatra

**BEST PICTURE/BEST DIRECTOR
FRANCIS FORD COPPOLA (B. 1939)
*THE GODFATHER PART II***

"I almost won this a few years ago for the first half of the same picture, but that's not why we did part two," said Coppola, who continued, "Thanks for giving my dad—[Carmine Coppola, Best Original Dramatic Score]—an Oscar."

Godfather II took home three gold men. "We tried to make a film that would be a really good film," said Coppola. They succeeded, yet it cost them twice as much as Part I and earned only about one-third as much.

On the heels of the first movie, Coppola was given carte blanche for *Godfather II*. "His deft directorial touches are everywhere, particularly in the earlier historical sequences," said *TV Guide*. Cinematographer Willis superbly captures the turn-of-the-century period by applying tint to flashback scenes for a softer, richer look than the sharp image of the ongoing contemporary story."

As the new don in *Godfather II*, Vito's son Michael (Al Pacino) has an "all business" attitude and seeks to consolidate his empire by making shady business deals in Cuba, only to be betrayed by those he trusts most. "Keep your friends close, but your enemies closer," says Michael. "These are words Michael comes to live by, and an ideology that climaxes in a shattering act of violence which leaves him unassailable, invincible—and utterly alone," wrote the *BBC*.

The only sequel to win an Oscar for best picture, *Godfather II* was seen by most critics as a masterpiece. "An epic vision of the corruption of America," wrote *The New Yorker*'s Pauline Kael. "It enlarges the scope and deepens the meaning of the first film…far more complexly beautiful…more shadowed, fuller."

John Cazale with Al Pacino

The envelope, please...

BEST ACTOR
ART CARNEY (B. 1918)
HARRY AND TONTO

Clearly a happy winner, Carney stood up and kicked his foot in the air, and by the time he reached the stage everyone in the audience was standing. Fifty-six-year-old Art Carney stepped into the part—originally meant for James Cagney—of a crusty 72-year-old New York widower, who, when his apartment is knocked down, takes a transcontinental journey with his cat, Tonto. Critic Danny Peary wrote, "[Carney] gave a fine performance, revealing unsuspected dramatic skills and proving that he could command our attention on the big screen as a leading man." Carney has also played other oddball roles, in such films as *W. W. and the Dixie Dancekings* (1975), *The Late Show* (1977), and *Going in Style* (1979).

BEST ACTRESS
ELLEN BURSTYN (B. 1932)
ALICE DOESN'T LIVE HERE ANYMORE

"I won't win. I never do," said Burstyn. "I just get nominated." Convinced that Gena Rowlands or Faye Dunaway were the sure bets, Burstyn asked director Martin Scorsese to accept the prize should she, on the off chance, win it. "She asked me to thank myself," said the director.

The *New York Times*'s Vincent Canby observed, "At the center of the movie and giving it visible sensibility [is] Burstyn, one of the few actresses today who is able to seem appealing, touching, intelligent, funny and bereft, all at approximately the same moment." Burstyn, having gotten so deeply into her character, improvised many of her lines.

BEST SUPPORTING ACTOR
ROBERT DE NIRO (B. 1943)
THE GODFATHER PART II

De Niro didn't say much at the podium, but later he delivered mixed messages in a *Woman's Wear Daily* interview: "It changes your life like anything that will change your life. I mean, it's not bad winning." Of De Niro, Leonard Maltin wrote, "Arguably the most impressive actor working in films today...his passion, intensity, and animal magnetism come through in every film."

De Niro, whose father was a renowned visual artist, was trained at the Stella Adler Conservatory and the American Workshop. After making *Greetings* (1968), *Bloody Mama* (1970), and *The Gang That Couldn't Shoot Straight* (1971), De Niro began to gain fame for his role in *Bang the Drum Slowly* (1973), and for *Mean Streets* (1973), his first film with director Martin Scorsese.

BEST OF 1974
Best Picture: *The Godfather, Part II*
Best Director: Francis Ford Coppola, *The Godfather Part II*
Best Actor: Art Carney, *Harry and Tonto*
Best Actress: Ellen Burstyn, *Alice Doesn't Live Here Anymore*
Best Supporting Actor: Robert De Niro, *The Godfather, Part II*
Best Supporting Actress: Ingrid Bergman, *Murder on the Orient Express*
Best Documentary Feature: *Hearts and Minds*
Best Foreign Film: *Amarcord*, Federico Fellini, Italy
Honorary Awards: Howard Hawks, Jean Renoir

FIRST
Art Carney became the oldest Best Actor since 63-year-old George Arliss won for *Disraeli* in 1929.

SINS OF OMISSION
Picture: *Chinatown*
Actor: Gene Hackman, *The Conversation*

ROLE REVERSAL
Harry of *Harry and* Tonto was written expressly for James Cagney, but the 75-year-old star refused to come out of retirement.

UNMENTIONABLES
• In an interview in *Time*, Art Carney said that he had just overcome his alcoholism.

• Ali McGraw left husband/director Robert Evans to run off with Steve McQueen.

• Robert De Niro denied any involvement when he was caught up in a Paris prostitution-ring investigation in 1998. The actor vowed never to return to France again.

 BEST SUPPORTING ACTRESS
INGRID BERGMAN (1915–1982)
MURDER ON THE ORIENT EXPRESS

"It's always nice to win an Oscar," Bergman said, "but last year when *Day for Night* opened, Valentina Cortese gave the most beautiful performance that all we actresses recognize. Here I am her rival, and I don't like it at all. Please forgive me, Valentina. I didn't mean to." Inspired by the Lindbergh kidnapping, the plot of *Murder* is secondary to the amazing cast and to Sidney Lumet's strong direction.

"*Murder on the Orient Express* is a splendidly entertaining movie of the sort that isn't made anymore. It's a classical whodunit. What I liked best about the movie is its style, both the deliberately old-fashioned visual strategies and the cheerful overacting," wrote film critic Roger Ebert in *The Movie Home Companion*.

(For more on Bergman, see 1944 and 1956.)

 HONORARY AWARD
HOWARD HAWKS (1896–1977)

"There's action only if there is danger," said Howard Hawks. John Wayne knew about danger—at least in films—and stepped up to deliver Hawks's award, saying, "Actors hate directors, and then the movie comes out, and they get great notices, and then they don't hate the director anymore."

Hawks stepped out to a standing ovation. "I remember visiting John Ford when he became sick and went out into the desert to die," said Hawks. "And he said, 'There's something I stole from you that tops the whole thing. I won the Oscar, but you made a better picture. You're going to get one.' "

After giving up his career as a pilot and race-car driver, Hawks went to Hollywood, making comedies and Westerns with such important films as *Scarface* (1932), *To Have and Have Not* (1944), and *The Big Sleep* (1946). Hawks's unforgettable screwball comedies, *Twentieth Century* (1934), *Bringing Up Baby* (1938), and *His Girl Friday* (1940), defined the genre. Some of Hollywood's brightest stars were discovered by Hawks, including Cary Grant, Carole Lombard, Lauren Bacall, Humphrey Bogart, and John Wayne. He gave Marilyn Monroe two key roles, *Monkey Business* (1952) and *Gentlemen Prefer Blondes* (1953). Of Hawks's Westerns—or any genre—*Rio Bravo* (1959) is considered his best film.

 HONORARY AWARD
JEAN RENOIR (1894–1979)

Ingrid Bergman accepted the award for the great filmmaker who had directed her in *Paris Does Strange Things* (1956). Renoir was the son of the famous Impressionist painter Pierre-Auguste Renoir—whose paintings he sold to make his first films.

In the '30s, Renoir became a political militant and French Communist Party sympathizer, and was ostracized for both. "Renoir's greatness lies in his repeated desire to take risks, to be experimental," wrote critic David Thomson. "During the 1930s there is not an adventure in natural light, camera movement, depth of focus, real location, the blending of interior and exterior that Renoir did not make."

Among his greatest films are *Grand Illusion* (1937) and *The Rules of the Game* (1939), the latter of which was severely edited and then banned for its political sentiments. Paul Mazursky, a fan of the great director, remade his film *Boudu Saved from Drowning* (1932), about a tramp who is saved from suicide only to drive his savior crazy, as *Down and Out in Beverly Hills* (1988).

Renoir had an unsatisfactory career in Hollywood, with the exception of *The Southerner* (1945 nom.), *The Golden Coach* (1953), *French Cancan* (1955), and *The Elusive Corporal* (1962).

PICTURE

CHINATOWN, Evans, Paramount. Robert Evans.

THE CONVERSATION, Directors Company, Paramount. Francis Ford Coppola.

THE GODFATHER PART II, Coppola Company, Paramount. Produced by Francis Ford Coppola; Co-produced by Gray Frederickson and Fred Roos.

LENNY, Worth, UA. Marvin Worth

THE TOWERING INFERNO, Irwin Allen, 20th Century-Fox/Warner Bros. Irwin Allen.

ACTOR

ART CARNEY in *Harry and Tonto*, 20th Century-Fox.

ALBERT FINNEY in *Murder on the Orient Express*, G.W. Films, Paramount.

DUSTIN HOFFMAN in *Lenny*, Worth, UA.

JACK NICHOLSON in *Chinatown*, Evans, Paramount.

AL PACINO in *The Godfather Part II*, Coppola Company, Paramount.

ACTRESS

ELLEN BURSTYN in *Alice Doesn't Live Here Anymore*, Warner Bros.

DIAHANN CARROLL in *Claudine*, Third World Cinema-Selznick-Pine, 20th Century-Fox.

FAYE DUNAWAY in *Chinatown*, Evans, Paramount.

VALERIE PERRINE in *Lenny*, Worth, UA.

GENA ROWLANDS in *A Woman Under the Influence*, Faces International.

SUPPORTING ACTOR

FRED ASTAIRE in *The Towering Inferno*, Irwin Allen, 20th Century-Fox/Warner Bros.

JEFF BRIDGES in *Thunderbolt and Lightfoot*, Malpaso, UA.

ROBERT DE NIRO in *The Godfather Part II*, Coppola Company, Paramount.

MICHAEL V. GAZZO in *The Godfather Part II*, Coppola Company, Paramount.

LEE STRASBERG in *The Godfather Part II*, Coppola Company, Paramount.

SUPPORTING ACTRESS

INGRID BERGMAN in *Murder on the Orient Express*, G.W. Films, Paramount.

VALENTINA CORTESE in *Day for Night* (French), Warner Bros.

MADELINE KAHN in *Blazing Saddles*, Warner Bros.

DIANE LADD in *Alice Doesn't Live Here Anymore*, Warner Bros.

TALIA SHIRE in *The Godfather Part II*, Coppola Company, Paramount.

DIRECTION

JOHN CASSAVETES for *A Woman Under the Influence*, Faces International.

FRANCIS FORD COPPOLA for *The Godfather Part II*, Coppola Company, Paramount.

BOB FOSSE for *Lenny*, Marvin Worth, UA

ROMAN POLANSKI for *Chinatown*, Robert Evans, Paramount.

FRANCOIS TRUFFAUT for *Day for Night*, Warner Bros. (French).

WRITING: ORIGINAL SCREENPLAY

ALICE DOESN'T LIVE HERE ANYMORE, Warner Bros. Robert Getchell.

CHINATOWN, Robert Evans, Paramount. Robert Towne.

THE CONVERSATION, Directors Company, Paramount. Francis Ford Coppola.

DAY FOR NIGHT, Warner Bros. (French). Francois Truffaut, Jean-Louis Richard and Suzanne Schiffman.

HARRY AND TONTO, 20th Century-Fox. Paul Mazursky and Josh Greenfeld.

WRITING: ADAPTED FROM OTHER MATERIAL

THE APPRENTICESHIP OF DUDDY KRAVITZ, International Cinemedia Centre, Paramount. Mordecai Richler and Lionel Chetwynd.

THE GODFATHER PART II, Coppola Company, Paramount. Francis Ford Coppola and Mario Puzo.

LENNY, Marvin Worth, UA. Julian Barry.

MURDER ON THE ORIENT EXPRESS, G.W. Films, Ltd., Paramount. Paul Dehn.

YOUNG FRANKENSTEIN, Gruskoff/ Venture Films-Crossbow-Jouer, 20th Century-Fox. Gene Wilder and Mel Brooks.

CINEMATOGRAPHY

CHINATOWN, Robert Evans, Paramount. John A. Alonzo.

EARTHQUAKE, Robson-Filmakers Group, Universal. Philip Lathrop.

LENNY, Marvin Worth, UA. Bruce Surtees.

MURDER ON THE ORIENT EXPRESS, G.W. Films, Ltd., Paramount. Geoffrey Unsworth.

THE TOWERING INFERNO, Irwin Allen, 20th Century-Fox/Warner Bros. Fred Koenekamp and Joseph Biroc.

ART DIRECTION—SET DECORATION

CHINATOWN, Robert Evans, Paramount. Richard Sylbert and W. Stewart Campbell; Ruby Levitt.

EARTHQUAKE, Robson-Filmakers Group, Universal. Alexander Golitzen and E. Preston Ames; Frank McKelvy.

THE GODFATHER PART II, Coppola Company, Paramount. Dean Tavoularis and Angelo Graham; George R. Nelson.

THE ISLAND AT THE TOP OF THE WORLD, Disney, Buena Vista. Peter Ellenshaw, John B. Mansbridge, Walter Tyler and Al Roelofs; Hal Gausman.

THE TOWERING INFERNO, Irwin Allen, 20th Century-Fox/Warner Bros. William Creber and Ward Preston; Raphael Bretton.

COSTUME DESIGN

CHINATOWN, Robert Evans, Paramount. Anthea Sylbert.

DAISY MILLER, Directors Company, Paramount. John Furness.

THE GODFATHER PART II, Coppola Company, Paramount. Theadora Van Runkle.

THE GREAT GATSBY, David Merrick, Paramount. Theoni V. Aldredge.

MURDER ON THE ORIENT EXPRESS, G.W. Films, Ltd., Paramount. Tony Walton.

SOUND

CHINATOWN, Robert Evans, Paramount. Bud Grenzbach and Larry Jost.

THE CONVERSATION, Directors Company, Paramount. Walter Murch and Arthur Rochester.

EARTHQUAKE, Robson-Filmakers Group, Universal. Ronald Pierce and Melvin Metcalfe Sr.

THE TOWERING INFERNO, Irwin Allen, 20th Century-Fox/Warner Bros. Theodore Soderberg and Herman Lewis.

YOUNG FRANKENSTEIN, Gruskoff/ Venture Films-Crossbow-Jouer, 20th Century-Fox. Richard Portman and Gene Cantamessa.

FILM EDITING

BLAZING SADDLES, Warner Bros. John C. Howard and Danford Greene.

CHINATOWN, Robert Evans, Paramount. Sam O'Steen.

EARTHQUAKE, Robson-Filmakers Group, Universal. Dorothy Spencer.

THE LONGEST YARD, Ruddy, Paramount. Michael Luciano.

THE TOWERING INFERNO, Irwin Allen, 20th Century-Fox/Warner Bros. Harold F. Kress and Carl Kress.

SONG

BENJI'S THEME (I FEEL LOVE) (*Benji*, Mulberry Square); Music by Euel Box. Lyrics by Betty Box.

BLAZING SADDLES (*Blazing Saddles*, Warner Bros.); Music by John Morris. Lyrics by Mel Brooks.

LITTLE PRINCE (*The Little Prince*, Stanley Donen, Paramount); Music by Frederick Loewe. Lyrics by Alan Jay Lerner.

WE MAY NEVER LOVE LIKE THIS AGAIN (*The Towering Inferno*, Irwin Allen, 20th Century-Fox/Warner Bros.); Music and Lyrics by Al Kasha and Joel Hirschhorn.

WHEREVER LOVE TAKES ME (*Gold*, Avton, Allied Artists); Music by Elmer Bernstein. Lyrics by Don Black.

MUSIC: ORIGINAL DRAMATIC SCORE

CHINATOWN, Robert Evans, Paramount. Jerry Goldsmith.

THE GODFATHER PART II, Coppola Company, Paramount. Nino Rota and Carmine Coppola.

MURDER ON THE ORIENT EXPRESS, G.W. Films, Ltd., Paramount. Richard Rodney Bennett.

SHANKS, William Castle, Paramount. Alex North.

THE TOWERING INFERNO, Irwin Allen, 20th Century-Fox/Warner Bros. John Williams.

MUSIC: SCORING — ORIGINAL SONG SCORE AND/OR ADAPTATION

THE GREAT GATSBY, David Merrick, Paramount. Nelson Riddle.

THE LITTLE PRINCE, Stanley Donen, Paramount. Alan Jay Lerner, Frederick Loewe; Angela Morley and Douglas Gamley.

PHANTOM OF THE PARADISE, Harbor Prods., 20th Century-Fox. Paul Williams and George Aliceson Tipton.

SHORT FILMS: ANIMATED FILM

CLOSED MONDAYS, Lighthouse Productions. Will Vinton and Bob Gardiner, producers.

THE FAMILY THAT DWELT APART, National Film Board of Canada. Yvon Mallette and Robert Verrall, producers.

HUNGER, National Film Board of Canada. Peter Foldes and Rene Jodoin, producers.

VOYAGE TO NEXT, Hubley Studio. Faith and John Hubley, producers.

WINNIE THE POOH AND TIGGER TOO, Disney, Buena Vista. Wolfgang Reitherman, producer.

SHORT FILMS: LIVE ACTION

CLIMB, Dewitt Jones Prods. Dewitt Jones, producer.

THE CONCERT, The Black And White Colour Film Company, Ltd. Julian and Claude Chagrin, producers.

ONE-EYED MEN ARE KINGS, C.A.P.A.C. Prods. (Paris). Paul Claudon and Edmund Sechan, producers.

PLANET OCEAN, Graphic Films. George V. Casey, producer.

THE VIOLIN, Sincinkin, Ltd. Andrew Welsh and George Pastic, producers.

DOCUMENTARY: SHORT SUBJECT

CITY OUT OF WILDERNESS, Francis Thompson Inc. Francis Thompson, producer.

DON'T, R.A. Films. Robin Lehman, producer.

EXPLORATORIUM, Jon Boorstin Prod. Jon Boorstin, producer.

JOHN MUIR'S HIGH SIERRA, Dewitt Jones Prods. Dewitt Jones and Lesley Foster, producers.

NAKED YOGA, Filmshop Prod. Ronald S. Ease and Mervyn Lloyd, producers.

DOCUMENTARY: FEATURE

ANTONIA: A PORTRAIT OF THE WOMAN, Rocky Mountain Prods. Judy Collins and Jill Godmilow, producers.

THE CHALLENGE...A TRIBUTE TO MODERN ART, World View. Herbert Kline, producer.

THE 81ST BLOW, Ghetto Fighters House. Jacquot Ehrlich, David Bergman and Haim Gouri, producers.

HEARTS AND MINDS, Touchstone-Audjeff-BBS Prod., Zuker/Jaglom-Rainbow Pictures. Peter Davis and Bert Schneider, producers.

THE WILD AND THE BRAVE, E.S.J.-

Tomorrow Entertainment-Jones/Howard Ltd. Natalie R. Jones and Eugene S. Jones, producers.

FOREIGN LANGUAGE FILM

AMARCORD (Italy).

CATSPLAY (Hungary).

THE DELUGE (Poland).

LACOMBE, LUCIEN (France).

THE TRUCE (Argentina).

HONORARY AND OTHER AWARDS

TO HOWARD HAWKS—A master American filmmaker whose creative efforts hold a distinguished place in world cinema.

TO JEAN RENOIR—A genius who, with grace, responsibility and enviable devotion through silent film, sound film, feature, documentary and television, has won the world's admiration.

SPECIAL ACHIEVEMENT AWARDS

For Visual Effects: FRANK BRENDEL, GLEN ROBINSON and ALBERT WHITLOCK for *Earthquake*, a Universal-Mark Robson-Filmakers Group Production, Universal.

JEAN HERSHOLT HUMANITARIAN AWARD

TO ARTHUR B. KRIM

SCIENTIFIC OR TECHNICAL

CLASS I

None.

CLASS II

JOSEPH D. KELLY of Glen Glenn Sound for the design of new audio-control consoles which have advanced the state of the art of sound recording and rerecording for motion-picture production.

THE BURBANK STUDIOS Sound Department for the design of new audio-control consoles engineered and constructed by the Quad-Eight Sound Corporation.

SAMUEL GOLDWYN STUDIOS Sound Department for the design of a new audio-control console engineered and constructed by the Quad-Eight Sound Corporation.

QUAD-EIGHT SOUND CORPORATION for the engineering and construction of new audio-control consoles designed by the Burbank Studios Sound Department and by the Samuel Goldwyn Studios Sound Department.

WALDON O. WATSON, RICHARD J. STUMPF, ROBERT J. LEONARD and the UNIVERSAL CITY STUDIOS Sound Department for the development and engineering of the Sensurround System for motion-picture presenstion.

CLASS III

ELEMACK COMPANY of Rome, Italy; LOUIS AMI of the Universal City Studios.

1975

ily Tomlin wore a jokey tiara, Lee Grant ran down the aisle to collect her Oscar in an old wedding dress, and presenter Rod McKuen showed up in sneakers. *Barry Lyndon*'s costume designer Ultra-Britt Soderlund accepted her Award in eighteenth-century regalia topped by a tricornered hat. In a traditional tux and shades, Jack Nicholson was handed the prize that had long eluded him. His many thanks included a smirking nod to his first agent, who told him that he "had no business being an actor."

OSCAR GOES CUCKOO

CEREMONY: March 29, 1976
Dorothy Chandler Pavilion,
Los Angeles Music Center,
Los Angeles
HOSTS: Goldie Hawn, Gene Kelly,
Walter Matthau, George Segal,
Robert Shaw

The night's dramatic high was Louise Fletcher's tearful tribute to her deaf parents in sign language. At first the audience wasn't quite sure what she was doing. Once it became clear, the Chandler Pavilion exploded in wild applause. Ironically, an Honorary Oscar was given to an actress who barely spoke a word throughout her entire career, silent-screen legend Mary Pickford. The frail Hollywood pioneer, who hadn't appeared on film since 1931, told the press that she was "eager to return to work." She might have taken her cue from Best Supporting winner George Burns, whose last outing before Neil Simon's *Sunshine Boys* was 1939's *Honolulu.*

Kirk Douglas, hardly past his prime, opted to sit out this particular ceremony, fearing that his appearance would overshadow his son, Michael. He needn't have worried. The younger Douglas spent most of the night jumping out of his seat as his first feature production, *Cuckoo's Nest*, steamrolled into Oscar history.

Thalberg Memorial Award recipient, producer/director Mervyn LeRoy (*The Wizard of Oz*, 1939), bemoaned the fact that there were no more Thalbergs left in Hollywood. But there was no shortage of originals as Gene Kelly introduced Elizabeth Taylor, who swept onstage in a flag-waving red sequin dress by Halston. With the clock running out, she was told to ditch her script and improvise. In tribute to the Bicentennial, Taylor led the audience in singing "America the Beautiful." Almost no one knew the words.

BEST PICTURE/BEST DIRECTOR
MILOS FORMAN (B. 1932)
ONE FLEW OVER THE CUCKOO'S NEST

"I spent more time in mental institutions than the others," the director said, explaining his win. Forman was one of the few foreign directors to enjoy success in Hollywood.

Cuckoo's Nest was met with mixed reviews, as was Forman's direction. The *New York Times* film critic Vincent Canby wrote, "*Cuckoo's Nest* is at its best when Mr. Forman is exercising his talents as a director of exuberant comedy that challenges preconceived notions of good taste." Pauline Kael wrote in *The New Yorker*, "Forman's tentative, literal-minded direction lacks the excitement of movie art and there's a callousness running through his work."

Orphaned by the Holocaust and raised by relatives, Forman had studied direction at the School of Cinema in Prague. Among his humorous and moving early Czech films were *Black Peter* (1963), *Loves of a Blonde* (1965, nom.), and *The Fireman's Ball* (1968). Forman was at the forefront of Czechoslovakia's film industry, but he left during the invasion of his country by the Soviet Union in 1968. He landed in Hollywood and, in only three years, made his first American film, *Taking Off* (1971).

Since *Cuckoo's* success, Forman has made many smart and well-crafted films, including *Hair*

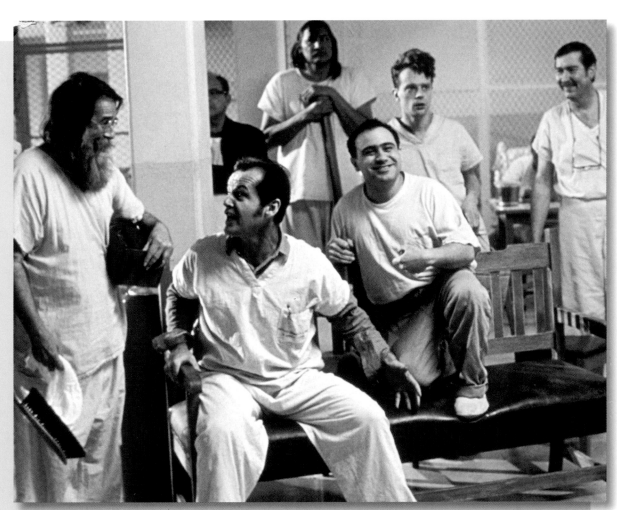

Jack Nicholson (center) with Danny DeVito (third from right)

(1979), *Ragtime* (1981), *Amadeus* (1984, eight Oscars), and *Valmont* (1989). In 1986 he appeared in the Mike Nichols film *Heartburn*. In 1978 Forman joined Columbia University as a professor of film and as co-chair of the film division of the School of the Arts. (For more on Forman, see 1984.)

The envelope, please…

BEST ACTOR
JACK NICHOLSON (B. 1937)
ONE FLEW OVER THE CUCKOO'S NEST

Having spent three months in and out of the Oregon State Asylum along with the rest of the cast, Nicholson told the *New York Daily News*, "Usually I don't have much trouble slipping out of a film role, but here I don't go home from a movie studio, I go home from a mental institution." It was appropriate training for everyone, particularly Nicholson, who played con man turned crazy man Randle McMurphy. The critics' response to Nicholson's performance changed the course of his career.

"Nicholson lets you see into him, rather than controlling what he lets you see," wrote Pauline Kael of *The New Yorker*. *The New York Times*'s Vincent Canby observed, "Nicholson slips into the role of Randle with such easy grace that it's difficult to remember him in any other film." *People* magazine predicted, correctly, "*Cuckoo's Nest* should bring Nicholson his long overdue Oscar and public acceptance as the first American actor since Marlon Brando and James Dean with the elemental energy to wildcat new wells of awareness in the national unconscious." (For more on Nicholson, see 1963, 1964, 1989.)

BEST ACTRESS
LOUISE FLETCHER (B. 1934)
ONE FLEW OVER THE CUCKOO'S NEST

Louise Fletcher, in her first film role as Nurse Ratched, played what would become an American type: the sexually repressed, overbearing, controlling, and sadistic bureaucrat. "She was nothing short of blood-curdling as the dispassionate, ruthless, and vaguely sadistic Nurse Ratched," wrote critic Leonard Maltin.

The bemused Fletcher—whose husband produced the film—couldn't help laughing as she spoke to reporters. "Suddenly, I'm having to worry about my hair," she said. "I got hot rollers for the first time in my life." Fletcher, though not a familiar face to moviegoers before *Cuckoo's Nest*, would continue to make films such as *Exorcist II: The Heretic* (1977), *Strange Invaders* and *Brainstorm* (both 1983), *Firestarter* (1984), and *Invaders from Mars* (1986). She earned an Emmy nomination for her role on *Picket Fences* but is perhaps best known to television audiences as Kai Winn from *Star Trek: Deep Space Nine* and as Nora Bloom from the cult classic *VR5*.

BEST OF 1975
Best Picture: *One Flew Over the Cuckoo's Nest*
Best Director: Milos Forman, *One Flew Over the Cuckoo's Nest*
Best Actor: Jack Nicholson, *One Flew Over the Cuckoo's Nest*
Best Actress: Louise Fletcher, *One Flew Over the Cuckoo's Nest*
Best Supporting Actor: George Burns, *The Sunshine Boys*
Best Supporting Actress: Lee Grant, *Shampoo*
Honorary Award: Mary Pickford

FIRSTS
- *Cuckoo's Nest* swept the Big Five (Best Picture, Director, Actor, Actress, Screenplay) for the first time since *It Happened One Night* in 1934. Michael Douglas was off by three years in his acceptance speech, wrongly placing Frank Capra's classic in 1937.
- George Burns, 80, was the oldest Oscar winner to date. *The Sunshine Boys* was his first film in thirty-six years.
- Louise Fletcher was the first Oscar winner to speak in sign language at the podium.
- *Nashville*'s Keith Carradine was the first Oscar-winning composer to perform his winning song in a movie.
- Record-breaking financial success *Jaws* introduced the term "blockbuster."

ROLE REVERSALS
- Louise Fletcher was at the end of a long line of contenders for the role of Nurse Ratched. Ahead of her were Angela Lansbury, Anne Bancroft, Ellen Burstyn, Geraldine Page, and Colleen Dewhurst.
- Louise Fletcher devised the role of the director of the deaf church choir in *Nashville*, which was given to Lily Tomlin. Fletcher never forgave director Robert Altman for what she considered a betrayal.

SINS OF OMISSION
Songs: Only one of *Nashville*'s dozens of original songs, "I'm Easy," was nominated.

ALWAYS A BRIDESMAID, NEVER A BRIDE
Jack Nicholson struck out twice as a front-runner for Best Actor in *The Last Detail* (1973) and *Chinatown* (1974).

UNMENTIONABLES
- Ellen Burstyn was so incensed by the lack of women's roles that she tried to organize a boycott of the Best Actress category.
- Ken Kesey, author of *One Flew Over the Cuckoo's Nest*, sued the film's producers for a bigger profit share. His name was barely mentioned in the acceptance speeches.
- Glenda Jackson neglected to pay her $50 dues as an Academy member and her ballot was deemed ineligible.
- "The market survey shows us that people care more about the clothes than about who wins," admitted Awards producer Howard Koch.
- The three mechanical sharks (named Bruce) kept sinking during early production of *Jaws*.
- According to super-agent Swifty Lazar, "You can't help but cringe over the ineptitude of some of the presenters, who mispronounce names and don't know what the hell is going on."

George Burns with Walter Matthau

BEST SUPPORTING ACTOR
GEORGE BURNS (1896–1996)
THE SUNSHINE BOYS

"It couldn't have happened to an older guy," said the cigar-chomping irrepressible elder statesman of the one-liner.

Burns started out in vaudeville with wife Gracie Allen and then broke into films, re-creating their hilarious stage routines in short subjects. They were soon signed up by Paramount to play comedy support in many of the studio's musicals and comedies, beginning with *The Big Broadcast* (1932) and continuing with *We're Not Dressing* (1934), *The Big Broadcast of 1936* (1935), and *College Swing* (1938).

After Gracie died in 1964, Burns starred in several TV series until 1985. He returned to the screen better than ever in *The Sunshine Boys*, *Oh, God!* (1977), and the less endearing sequels, *Oh God! Book II* (1980) and *Oh, God! You Devil* (1984). Burns was also a prolific memoirist, writing about his life with Gracie and his adventures in show business.

Lee Grant with Warren Beatty

BEST SUPPORTING ACTRESS
LEE GRANT (B. 1927)
SHAMPOO

"My big concern is would Brenda [Vaccaro] and Lily [Tomlin] [nominees for Best Supporting Actress] and I be talking once it's all over. We're very close friends, you know."

Grant was nominated for an Oscar three times in her career, starting off with a nomination for her debut in *Detective Story* (1951). Her great fortune, however, was stolen from her during the McCarthy era, when she was blacklisted along with her playwright husband, Arnold Manoff. She only returned to the screen in 1963, and appeared in *Divorce American Style*, *Valley of the Dolls*, *In the Heat of the Night* (all 1967), *The Landlord* (1970, nom.) *Plaza Suite* (1971), *Portnoy's Complaint* (1972), and *Voyage of the Damned* (1976, nom.).

She turned to directing in 1980 with *Tell Me a Riddle* (1980) and a documentary, *Down and Out in America* (1985), for which she won the Best Documentary Oscar. In later years, she appeared in Albert Brooks's *Defending Your Life* (1991) and the made-for-TV *Citizen*.

HONORARY AWARD
MARY PICKFORD (1892–1979)

"I could still be on the screen, you know," said the 83-year-old American sweet-heart to *Newsweek*. Her current husband said she couldn't appear because "the sheer excitement of it would be too much for her."

Pickford began her movie career working with director D. W. Griffith in 1909. The industry quickly learned that "the girl with the golden curls" was box-office gold. Among her early and most famous films were *The New York Hat* and *The Informer* (both 1912). She later joined the Famous Players Company and appeared in *The Poor Little Rich Girl* and *Rebecca of Sunnybrook Farm* (both 1917), and *Stella Maris* (1918).

Her first picture for her new company, United Artists—which she formed with Douglas Fairbanks and Charles Chaplin in 1919—*Pollyanna* (1920), was a great success and was followed by *Suds* (also 1920) and *The Love Light* (1921). Pickford moved on to more ambitious films, such as *Little Lord Fauntleroy* (1921), and worked with Ernst Lubitsch in *Rosita* (1923).

PICTURE
BARRY LYNDON, Hawk Films, Warner Bros. Stanley Kubrick.
DOG DAY AFTERNOON, Warner Bros, Martin Bregman and Martin Elfand.
JAWS, Zanuck/Brown, Universal. Richard D. Zanuck and David Brown.
NASHVILLE, ABC Entertainment-Weintraub-Altman, Paramount. Robert Altman.
ONE FLEW OVER THE CUCKOO'S NEST, Fantasy Films, UA, MGM. Saul Zaentz and Michael Douglas.

ACTOR
WALTER MATTHAU in *The Sunshine Boys*, Stark, MGM..
JACK NICHOLSON in *One Flew over the Cuckoo's Nest*, Fantasy Films, UA.
AL PACINO in *Dog Day Afternoon*, Warner Bros.
MAXIMILIAN SCHELL in *The Man in the Glass Booth*, Landau, AFT Distributing.
JAMES WHITMORE in *Give 'em Hell, Harry!*, Theatrovision, Avco Embassy.

ACTRESS
ISABELLE ADJANI in *The Story of Adele H.*, New World Pictures (French).
ANN-MARGRET in *Tommy*, Stigwood, Columbia.
LOUISE FLETCHER in *One Flew Over the Cuckoo's Nest*, Fantasy Films, UA.
GLENDA JACKSON in *Hedda*, Royal Shakespeare-Barrie/Enders, Brut Productions.
CAROL KANE in *Hester Street*, Midwest Films.

SUPPORTING ACTOR
GEORGE BURNS in *The Sunshine Boys*, M.G.M.
BRAD DOURIF in *One Flew over the Cuckoo's Nest*, Fantasy Films, UA.
BURGESS MEREDITH in *The Day of the Locust*, Bellman, Paramount.
CHRIS SARANDON in *Dog Day Afternoon*, Warner Bros.
JACK WARDEN in *Shampoo*, Rubeeker, Columbia.

SUPPORTING ACTRESS
RONEE BLAKLEY in *Nashville*, ABC Entertainment-Weintraub-Altman, Paramount.
LEE GRANT in *Shampoo*, Rubeeker, Columbia.
SYLVIA MILES in *Farewell, My Lovely*. Kastner-ITC, Avco Embassy.
LILY TOMLIN in *Nashville*, ABC Entertainment-Weintraub-Altman, Paramount.
BRENDA VACCARO in *Jacqueline Susann's Once Is Not Enough*, Koch, Paramount

DIRECTION
ROBERT ALTMAN for *Nashville*, ABC Entertainment-Weintraub-Altman, Paramount.
FEDERICO FELLINI for *Amarcord*, New World Pictures (Italian).
MILOS FORMAN for *One Flew Over the Cuckoo's Nest*, Fantasy Films, UA.
STANLEY KUBRICK for *Barry Lyndon*, Hawk Films, Warner Bros.
SIDNEY LUMET for *Dog Day Afternoon*, Warner Bros.

WRITING: ORIGINAL SCREENPLAY
AMARCORD, New World Pictures (Italian). Federico Fellini and Tonino Guerra.
AND NOW MY LOVE, Avco Embassy (French). Claude Lelouch and Pierre Uytterhoeven.
DOG DAY AFTERNOON, Warner Bros. Frank Pierson.
LIES MY FATHER TOLD ME, Pentimento-Pentacle VIII, Columbia. Ted Allan.
SHAMPOO, Rubeeker, Columbia. Robert Towne and Warren Beatty.

WRITING: ADAPTED FROM OTHER MATERIAL
BARRY LYNDON, Hawk Films, Warner Bros. Stanley Kubrick.
THE MAN WHO WOULD BE KING, Columbia/Allied Artists. John Huston and Gladys Hill.
ONE FLEW OVER THE CUCKOO'S NEST, Fantasy Films, UA. Lawrence Hauben and Bo Goldman.
SCENT OF A WOMAN, Dean Films, 20th Century-Fox (Italian). Ruggero Maccan and Dino Risi.
THE SUNSHINE BOYS, Ray Stark, MGM. Neil Simon.

CINEMATOGRAPHY
BARRY LYNDON, Hawk Films, Warner Bros. John Alcott.
THE DAY OF THE LOCUST, Jerome Hellman, Paramount. Conrad Hall.
FUNNY LADY, Rastar, Columbia. James Wong Howe.
THE HINDENBURG, Robert Wise-Filmakers Group, Universal. Robert Surtees.
ONE FLEW OVER THE CUCKOO'S NEST, Fantasy Films, UA. Haskell Wexler and Bill Butler.

ART DIRECTION—SET DECORATION
BARRY LYNDON, Hawk Films, Warner Bros. Ken Adam and Roy Walker, Vernon Dixon.
THE HINDENBURG, Robert Wise-Filmakers Group, Universal. Edward Carfagno; Frank McKelvy.
THE MAN WHO WOULD BE KING, Columbia/Allied Artists, Alexander Trauner and Tony Inglis; Peter James.
SHAMPOO, Rubeeker, Columbia. Richard Sylbert and W. Stewart Campbell; George Gaines.
THE SUNSHINE BOYS, Ray Stark, MGM. Albert Brenner, Marvin March.

COSTUME DESIGN
BARRY LYNDON, Hawk Films, Warner Bros. Ultra-Britt Soderlund and Milena Canonero.
THE FOUR MUSKETEERS, Salkind, 20th Century-Fox. Yvonne Blake, Ron Talsky.
FUNNY LADY, Rastar, Columbia. Ray Aghayan and Bob Mackie.
THE MAGIC FLUTE, Furrogate Releasing (Swedish). Henny Noremark and Karin Erskine.
THE MAN WHO WOULD BE KING, Columbia/Allied Artists, Edith Head.

SOUND
BITE THE BULLET, Brooks, Columbia. Arthur Piantodosi, Les Fresholtz, Richard Tyler and Al Overton Jr.
FUNNY LADY, Rastar, Columbia. Richard Portman, Don MacDougall, Curly Thirlwell and Jack Solomon.
THE HINDENBURG, Robert Wise-Filmakers Group, Universal. Leonard Peterson, John A. Bolger Jr., John Mack and Don K. Sharpless.
JAWS, Zanuck/Brown, Universal. Robert L. Hoyt, Roger Heman, Earl Madery and John Carter.
THE WIND AND THE LION, Herb Jaffee. MGM. Harry W. Tetrick, Aaron Rochin, William McCaughey and Roy Charman.

FILM EDITING
DOG DAY AFTERNOON, Warner Bros. Dede Allen.
JAWS, Zanuck/Brown, Universal. Verna Fields.
THE MAN WHO WOULD BE KING, Columbia/Allied Artists. Russell Lloyd.
ONE FLEW OVER THE CUCKOO'S NEST, Fantasy Films, UA. Richard Chew, Lynzee Klingman and Sheldon Kahn.
THREE DAYS OF THE CONDOR, De Laurentiis, Paramount. Fredric Steinkamp and Don Guidice.

SONG
HOW LUCKY CAN YOU GET (*Funny Lady*, Rastar, Columbia); Music and Lyrics by Fred Ebb and John Kander.
I'M EASY (*Nashville*, ABC-Weintraub-Altman, Paramount); Music and Lyrics by Keith Carradine.
NOW THAT WE'RE IN LOVE (*Whiffs*, Brut, 20th Century-Fox); Music by George Barrie. Lyrics by Sammy Cahn.
RICHARD'S WINDOW, (*The Other Side of the Mountain*, Filmways-Larry Peerce, Universal); Music by Charles Fox. Lyrics by Norman Gimbel.
THEME FROM MAHOGANY (DO YOU KNOW WHERE YOU'RE GOING TO) (*Mahogany*, Jobete, Paramount); Music by Michael Masser. Lyrics by Gerry Goffin.

SCORING: ORIGINAL MUSIC
BIRDS DO IT, BEES DO IT, Wolper, Columbia. Gerald Fried.
BITE THE BULLET, Brooks, Columbia. Alex North.
JAWS, Zanuck/Brown, Universal. John Williams.
ONE FLEW OVER THE CUCKOO'S NEST. Fantasy Films, UA. Jack Nitzsche.
THE WIND AND THE LION, Herb Jaffee. MGM. Jerry Goldsmith.

SCORING: ORIGINAL SONG SCORE AND/OR ADAPTATION
BARRY LYNDON, Hawk Films, Warner Bros. Leonard Rosenman.
FUNNY LADY, Rastar, Columbia. Peter Matz.
TOMMY, Stigwood Organization, Columbia. Peter Townshend.

SHORT FILM: ANIMATED FILM
GREAT, Grantstern, British Lion Films Ltd. Bob Godfrey, producer.
KICK ME, Swarthe Prods. Robert Swarthe, producer.
MONSIEUR POINTU, National Film Board of Canada. Rene Jodoin, Bernard Longpre and Andre Leduc, producers.
SISYPHUS, Hungarofilms. Marcell Jankovics, producer.

SHORT FILM: LIVE ACTION
ANGEL AND BIG JOE, Salzman Productions. Bert Salzman, producer.
CONQUEST OF LIGHT, Louis Marcus Films Ltd. Louis Marcus, producer.
DAWN FLIGHT, Lansburgh and Brian Lansburgh, producers.
A DAY IN THE LIFE OF BONNIE CONSOLO, Barr Films. Barry Spineilo, producer.
DOUBLETALK, Beattie Prods. Alan Beattie, producer.

DOCUMENTARY: SHORT FILM
ARTHUR AND LILLIE, Department of Communication, Stanford University. Jon Else, Steven Kovacs and Kristine Samuelson, producers.
THE END OF THE GAME, Opus Films Ltd. Claire Wilbur and Robin Lehman, producers.
MILLIONS OF YEARS AHEAD OF MAN, BASF. Manfred Baler, producer.
PROBES IN SPACE, Graphic Films. George V. Casey, producer.
WHISTLING SMITH, National Film Board of Canada. Barrie Howells and Michael Scott, producers.

DOCUMENTARY: FEATURE
THE CALIFORNIA REICH, Yasny 'Bilking Pictures. Walter F. Parkes and Keigh F. Critchiow, producers.
FIGHTING FOR OUR LIVES, A Farm Worker Film. Glen Pearcy, producer.
THE INCREDIBLE MACHINE, The National Geographic Society, Wolper Prods. Irwin Rosten, producer.
THE MAN WHO SKIED DOWN EVEREST, Crawley Films. F.R. Crawley, James Hager and Dale Hartleben, producers.
THE OTHER HALF OF THE SKY: A CHINA MEMOIR, MacLaine Prods. Shirley MacLaine, producer.

FOREIGN LANGUAGE FILM
DERSU UZALA (U.S.S.R.).
LAND OF PROMISE (Poland).
LETTERS FROM MARUSIA (Mexico).
SANDAKAN NO. 8 (Japan).
SCENT OF A WOMAN (Italy).

HONORARY AND OTHER AWARDS
TO MARY PICKFORD in recognition of her unique contributions to the film industry and the development of film as an artistic medium.

SPECIAL ACHIEVEMENT AWARDS
For Sound Effects: PETER BERKOS for The Hindenburg. Robert Wise-Filmakers Group, Universal.
For Visual Effects: ALBERT WHITLOCK and GLEN ROBINSON for The Hindenburg. Robert Wise-Filmakers Group, Universal.

IRVING G. THALBERG MEMORIAL AWARD
TO MERVYN LeROY

JEAN HERSHOLT HUMANITARIAN AWARD
TO JULES C. STEIN

SCIENTIFIC OR TECHNICAL

CLASS II
CHADWELL O'CONNOR of the O'Connor Engineering Laboratories for the concept and engineering of a fluid-damped camerahead for motion-picture photography.
WILLIAM F. MINER of Universal City Studios, Inc. and the WESTINGHOUSE ELECTRIC CORPORATION for the development and engineering of a solid-state, 500 kilowatt, direct-current static rectifier for motion-picture lighting.

CLASS III
LAWRENCE W. BUTLER and ROGER BANKS;
DAVID J. DEGENKOLB and FRED SCOBEY of Deluxe General Inc. and JOHN C. DOLAN and RICHARD DUBOIS of the Akwaklame Company; JOSEPH WESTHEIMER;
CARTER EQUIPMENT CO., INC. and RAMTRONICS;
THE HOLLYWOOD FILM COMPANY;
BELL & HOWELL;
FREDRIK SCHLYTER.

1976

"I was going to thank all the little people, but then I remembered I am the little people."

—Paul Williams, co-writer of Best Song "Evergreen"

A ROCKY ROAD

CEREMONY: March 29, 1977
Chandler Pavilion, Los Angeles Music
Center, Los Angeles
HOSTS: Jane Fonda, Ellen Burstyn,
Richard Pryor, Warren Beatty

ocky Balboa could've written the evening's script. It was a Cinderella cliff-hanger right down to the wire. The low-budget film, which director John Avildsen once predicted might "end up on a double bill at the drive-in," had become the year's biggest grosser and shot Sylvester Stallone to superstardom. It came into the Awards with the promise of a knockout in Round One. But this was also a year of superior Best Picture nominations, which included Paddy Chayefsky's media-damning *Network*, Robert Redford's Watergate mystery *All the President's Men*, and Scorsese's nightmarish masterwork *Taxi Driver*.

The ceremony's guest director, William Friedkin, wanted an evening of high-voltage entertainment and nixed Loretta Young's tribute to her recently deceased friend Rosalind Russell. Fearing a maudlin display if he won after his death, Peter Finch asked director Paddy Chayefsky if he would accept for him. He won. "I'm up here accepting an award for Peter Finch, or Finchie, as everybody knew him," Chayefsky said. "There's no rea-son for me to be here. There's only one person who should be up here, and that's the person Finch wanted to accept his award. Are you in the house, Eletha? Come on up and get your award." The composed, mink-clad Jamaican beauty did just that, and delivered an eloquent tribute to her husband. It was the highlight of the evening, and only later did Friedkin learn that Chayefsky had planned it all along. He had even written the speech for her.

Finch's widow was followed by winner Faye Dunaway, who trumped *Rocky*'s Talia Shire. Things weren't looking good for the champ, especially when *All the President's Men* began picking up a host of minor awards. Finally, Avildsen got his big moment as Best Director. Stallone knew at that point Best Picture was his for the taking. He raised his Oscar high and shouted, "To all the Rockys of the world, I love ya!" Warren Beatty closed the ceremony with prescient irony: "Thank you all for watching us congratulate ourselves." The next day's ratings were the lowest in the Awards' televised history.

BEST PICTURE
ROCKY

Sylvester Stallone, a struggling writer/actor, forfeited his salary for a screenplay about a South Philly heavyweight fighter in exchange for playing the starring role.

Many critics saw *Rocky* as a throwback to the patriotic, solid American value of pulling yourself up by your bootstraps, or, in this case, your boxing gloves. It reminded many of the films of Capra, who himself said of *Rocky*, "I think it's the best picture in the last ten years." Even the curmudgeonly John Simon liked it, saying, "*Rocky* is pugnacious, charming, grimy, a beautiful fairy tale." At *The New Yorker*, Pauline Kael admitted, "[Stallone] is amazing to watch: there's a bull-necked energy in him, smoldering, and in his deep caveman's voice he gives the most surprising, sharp, fresh shadings to his lines. The picture is poorly made, yet its naive, emotional shamelessness is funny and engaging."

One of *Rocky*'s stars, Burgess Meredith, depicted the box-office blowout as "a refreshing change after things like *Taxi Driver* and *One Flew Over the Cuckoo's Nest*—brilliant pictures, perhaps, but not rooting pictures. It's the difference between watching a sunset and a snake."

Sylvester Stallone

The envelope, please…

John G. Avildsen with Lily Tomlin

BEST DIRECTOR
JOHN G. AVILDSEN (B. 1935)
ROCKY

After giving Stallone a great big hug, Avildsen took the stage and said, "*Rocky* gave a lot of people hope. Stallone gave his guts and his heart and his best shot."

Backstage Avildsen, surprised by his win, said, "I had no idea *Rocky* would be such a hit. I thought it was going to be the second half of a double bill at a drive-in."

Avildsen shot *Rocky* with technical originality, making groundbreaking use of the Steadicam in the film's training sequences. He matched the camera movement to the momentum of Rocky's character transformation. Avildsen had worn just about every hat in filmmaking, including cinematographer, editor, assistant director, and production manager, before making his first film, *Turn On to Love* (1969). His unschooled style showed in his early films, including *Guess What We Learned in School Today?* (1970) and *Cry Uncle!* (1971). But he hit it big with the small-budget *Joe* (1970), and won the critics over with *Save the Tiger* (1973). After *Rocky*, Avildsen made some unsuccessful films before scoring with *The Karate Kid* (1984), its two sequels as well as *Lean on Me* (1989) and *The Power of One* (1992).

BEST ACTOR
PETER FINCH (1916–1977)
NETWORK

Finch was not expected to win, since the only other posthumous Oscar nominees in the past (Spencer Tracy and James Dean) had both lost. Finch's wife accepted the award, creating the emotional peak of the evening.

After being rejected by real media man Walter Cronkite and actor Henry Fonda, director Sidney Lumet finally approached Finch, who jumped at the part. Despite all this gratitude, Finch was bitter about being entered only for Best Supporting Actor. "Absolutely not!" he screamed. "Howard Beale was not a supporting role." Winning the big Oscar became an obsession with Finch.

Finch launched his screen career with a slew of minor films, among them *The Miniver Story* (1950) and Walt Disney's *The Story of Robin Hood* (1952). He won British Film Academy Awards, however, for his work in *A Town Like Alice* (1956) and *The Trials of Oscar Wilde* (1960). His real fame came with important roles in *Far from the Madding Crowd* (1967), *Sunday, Bloody Sunday* (1971, nom.), and *Lost Horizon* (1973). Finch died of a heart attack during a promotional tour for *Network*.

BEST OF 1976
Best Picture: *Rocky*
Best Director: John Avildsen, *Rocky*
Best Actor: Peter Finch, *Network*
Best Actress: Faye Dunaway, *Network*
Best Supporting Actor: Jason Robards, *All the President's Men*
Best Supporting Actress: Beatrice Straight, *Network*

FIRSTS
- *Network* was the first movie to win three acting Oscars since *A Streetcar Named Desire* (1951).
- The late Peter Finch received the first posthumous Oscar for Best Actor.
- Sylvester Stallone followed in the giant footsteps of Charlie Chaplin (1940) and Orson Welles (1944) in being nominated for Best Actor and Best Screenplay.
- Best Song composer Barbra Streisand was the first Oscar-winning actress to receive an award for music.
- *Network*'s Beatrice Straight earned her Best Supporting Oscar for the second briefest award-winning screen role (ten minutes). The shortest was Anthony Quinn's (nine minutes) in *Lust for Life* (1956).
- Lina Wertmuller vaulted the gender gap as the first woman director (*Seven Beauties*) to be nominated.

ROLE REVERSALS
- The big studios wanted *Rocky* on condition that Burt Reynolds, Ryan O'Neal, or James Caan played the lead.
- Jane Fonda declined Faye Dunaway's role in *Network*.

ALWAYS A BRIDESMAID, NEVER A BRIDE
Piper Laurie snagged a Best Supporting nomination for *Carrie* fifteen years after her last film (*The Hustler*), for which she was also nominated and lost.

UNMENTIONABLES
- *Rocky* was inspired by the World Heavyweight match between Muhammad Ali and "unknown" Chuck Wepner.
- *Rocky* was written in four days and filmed in less than a month for $960,000. Stallone defended his writing speed. "I'm astounded that it takes some people eighteen years to write something," he said. "Like that guy who wrote *Madame Bovary*. It was a lousy book, and it made a lousy movie."
- Barbra Streisand hired two limousines for the Awards. The first had a look-alike in the back seat to fool her fans.
- "If the son of a bitch hadn't died, I could've finally had my Oscar."—William Holden, referring to Peter Finch.
- Once blacklisted, Lillian Hellman was amused to be awarded by the Academy. She told the audience that "during the McCarthy era the film industry had all the force and courage of a bowl of mashed potatoes."

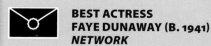

BEST ACTRESS
FAYE DUNAWAY (B. 1941)
NETWORK

"I didn't expect this to happen quite yet, but I thank you very much," Dunaway said. Lumet had trepidations while casting about for his female lead. "With all the lack of good female roles, I can name you ten actresses who would have turned it down," he remarked.

Considered one of the most important actresses of the 1970s, Dunaway broke through Hollywood's reliance on dominant leading men. She reported that her love scenes with William Holden reduced her to hysterical laughter when she was confronted with his modesty.

Dunaway made her screen debut in *The Happening* (1967) and soon appeared in Otto Preminger's *Hurry Sundown* (1967). She received her first Academy Award nomination for *Bonnie and Clyde* (1967), and followed with roles in *The Thomas Crown Affair* (1968), *Chinatown* (1974, nom.), and *Eyes of Laura Mars* (1978). Dunaway frequently clashed with director Roman Polanski during the production of *Chinatown*.

Speaking to *Woman's Wear Daily* after the *Network* win, Dunaway said, "My best work has been in the last two years. I think it's largely because I don't go home to an empty house. Marriage has filled out my life in a way that it feeds my work and my work feeds my marriage." Life in the 1990s had turned on Dunaway and, in a much-publicized incident, she was dropped as the lead in the Broadway musical *Sunset Boulevard*.

Jason Robards (center)

BEST SUPPORTING ACTOR
JASON ROBARDS (1922–2000)
ALL THE PRESIDENT'S MEN

Robards thanked Ben Bradlee, the man he portrayed in the film, "for being alive so I could come out and play with him."

Robards' first love was the theater, where he appeared in the 1956 Broadway production of Eugene O'Neill's *The Iceman Cometh*. After winning the prestigious New York Drama Critics Award for his turn in *Long Day's Journey into Night* the following year, Robards became a true stage star. Somehow his film career never measured up to the strength of his stage work. He had a busy and varied film résumé beginning with his debut in *The Journey* (1959). It took two years for Robards to reappear. It was a great return in F. Scott Fitzgerald's *Tender Is the Night* (1962) and the screen adaptation of *Long Day's Journey into Night* (1963).

Amon his many film credits are *A Thousand Clowns* (1965), *The Night They Raided Minsky's*, *Once Upon a Time in the West* (both 1968), *The Ballad of Cable Hogue* (1970), and *Melvin and Howard* (1980, nom.). He later worked in TV films, including *Haywire* (1980) and *Inherit the Wind* (1988, for which he won an Emmy). Among his last films *Parenthood* (1989) ranks as one of his best parts in years. Robards had been married to Lauren Bacall. (For more on Robards, see 1977.)

William Holden with Beatrice Straight

BEST SUPPORTING ACTRESS
BEATRICE STRAIGHT (1914–2001)
NETWORK

"I'm the dark horse, " Straight acknowledged. "It's a great, great thrill and totally unexpected."

In the upset win of the evening, Straight played the wife who struggles to keep her dignity while her husband (William Holden) confesses to having an affair with a coworker (Faye Dunaway). She was on screen for only ten minutes, the second-shortest Oscar-winning performance.

Straight was primarily a stage actress who garnered much acclaim for her appearance in the 1953 production of Arthur Miller's *The Crucible*. She proved equally skilled on the rare occasions she appeared on film. After *Network*, however, she was offered only poor roles in such films as *The Formula* (1980), *Endless Love* (1981), and *Two of a Kind* (1983). Her best role was in *Poltergeist* (1982), playing a paranormal investigator overwhelmed by malevolent spirits.

PICTURE
ALL THE PRESIDENT'S MEN, Wildwood, Warner Bros. Walter Coblenz.
BOUND FOR GLORY, UA. Robert F. Blumofe and Harold Leventhal.
NETWORK, Gottfried/Chayefsky, MGM/UA. Howard Gottfried.
ROCKY, Chartoff-Winkler, UA. Irwin Winkler and Robert Chartoff.
TAXI DRIVER, Bill/Phillips-Scorsese, Columbia. Michael Phillips and Julia Phillips.

ACTOR
ROBERT DE NIRO in *Taxi Driver*, Bill/Phillips-Scorsese, Columbia.
PETER FINCH in *Network*, Gottfried/Chayefsky, MGM/UA.
GIANCARLO GIANNINI in *Seven Beauties*, Cinema 5 (Italian).
WILLIAM HOLDEN in *Network*, Gottfried/Chayefsky, MGM/UA.
SYLVESTER STALLONE in *Rocky*, Chartoff-Winkler, UA.

ACTRESS
MARIE-CHRISTINE BARRAULT in *Cousin, Cousine*, Northal Films (French).
FAYE DUNAWAY in *Network*, Gottfried/Chayefsky, MGM/UA.
TALIA SHIRE in *Rocky*, Chartoff-Winkler, UA.
SISSY SPACEK in *Carrie*, Redbank Films, UA.
LIV ULLMANN in *Face to Face*, Paramount (Swedish).

SUPPORTING ACTOR
NED BEATTY in *Network*, Gottfried/Chayefsky, MGM/UA.
BURGESS MEREDITH in *Rocky*, Chartoff-Winkler, UA.
LAURENCE OLIVIER in *Marathon Man*, Evans-Beckerman, Paramount.
JASON ROBARDS in *All the President's Men*, Wildwood, Warner Bros.
BURT YOUNG in *Rocky*, Chartoff-Winkler, UA.

SUPPORTING ACTRESS
JANE ALEXANDER in *All the President's Men*, Wildwood, Warner Bros.
JODIE FOSTER in *Taxi Driver*, Bill/Phillips-Scorsese, Columbia.
LEE GRANT in *Voyage of the Damned*, ITC, Avco Embassy.
PIPER LAURIE in *Carrie*, Redbank Films, UA.
BEATRICE STRAIGHT in *Network*, Gottfried/Chayefsky, MGM/UA.

DIRECTION
JOHN G. AVILDSEN for *Rocky*, Chartoff-Winkler, UA.
INGMAR BERGMAN for *Face to Face*, Cinematograph, A.B., Paramount (Swedish).
SIDNEY LUMET for *Network*, Gottfried/Chayefsky, MGM/UA.
ALAN J. PAKULA for *All the President's Men*, Wildwood, Warner Bros.
LINA WERTMULLER for *Seven Beauties*, Medusa Distribuzione, Cinema 5 (Italian).

WRITING: DIRECTLY FOR THE SCREEN
COUSIN, COUSINE, Northal Film Distributors Ltd. (French). Jean-Charles Tacchella and Daniele Thompson.
THE FRONT, Columbia. Walter Bernstein.
NETWORK, Gottfried/Chayefsky, MGM/UA. Paddy Chayefsky.
ROCKY, Chartoff-Winkler, UA. Sylvester Stallone.

SEVEN BEAUTIES, Medusa Distribuzione, Cinema 5 (Italian). Lina Wertmuller.

WRITING: BASED ON MATERIAL FROM ANOTHER MEDIUM
ALL THE PRESIDENT'S MEN, Wildwood, Warner Bros. William Goldman.
BOUND FOR GLORY, UA. Robert Getchell.
FELLINI'S CASANOVA, Universal (Italian). Federico Fellini and Bernadino Zapponi.
THE SEVEN-PER-CENT SOLUTION, Herbert Ross/Winitsky-Sellers, Universal. Nicholas Meyer.
VOYAGE OF THE DAMNED, ITC Entertainment, Avco Embassy. Steve Shagan and David Butler.

CINEMATOGRAPHY
BOUND FOR GLORY, UA. Haskell Wexler.
KING KONG, De Laurentiis, Paramount, Richard H. Kline.
LOGAN'S RUN, Saul David, MGM. Ernest Laszlo.
NETWORK, Gottfried/Chayefsky, MGM/UA. Owen Roizman.
A STAR IS BORN, Barwood/Peters-First Artists, Warner Bros. Robert Surtees.

ART DECORATION—SET DECORATION
ALL THE PRESIDENT'S MEN, Wildwood, Warner Bros. George Jenkins; George Gaines.
THE INCREDIBLE SARAH, Helen M. Strauss-Reader's Digest, Seymour Borde & Associates. Elliot Scott and Norman Reynolds.
THE LAST TYCOON, Spiegel-Kazan, Paramount, Gene Callahan and Jack Collis; Jerry Wunderlich.
LOGAN'S RUN, Saul David, MGM, Dale Hennesy; Robert de Vestel.
THE SHOOTIST, Frankovich/Self-De Laurentiis, Paramount. Robert F. Boyle; Arthur Jeph Parker.

COSTUME DESIGN
BOUND FOR GLORY, UA. William Theiss.
FELLINI'S CASANOVA, Universal (Italian). Danilo Donati.
THE INCREDIBLE SARAH, Helen M. Strauss-Reader's Digest, Seymour Borde & Associates. Anthony Mendleson.
THE PASSOVER PLOT, Coast Industries-GolanGlobus, Atlas Films. Mary Wills.
THE SEVEN-PER-CENT SOLUTION, Herbert Ross/Winitsky-Sellers, Universal. Alan Barrett.

SOUND
ALL THE PRESIDENT'S MEN, Wildwood, Warner Bros. Arthur Piantadosi, Les Fresholtz, Dick Alexander and Jim Webb.
KING KONG, De Laurentiis, Paramount. Harry Warren Tetrick, William McCaughey, Aaron Rochin and Jack Solomon.
ROCKY, Chartoff-Winkler, UA. Harry Warren Tetrick, William McCaughey, Lyle Burbridge and Bud Alper.
SILVER STREAK, Frank Yablans, 20th Century-Fox. Donald Mitchell, Douglas Williams, Richard Tyler and Hal Etherington.
A STAR IS BORN, Barwood/Peters-First Artists, Warner Bros. Robert Knudson, Dan Wallin, Robert Glass and Tom Overton.

FILM EDITING
ALL THE PRESIDENT'S MEN, Wildwood, Warner Bros. Robert L. Wolfe.
BOUND FOR GLORY, UA. Robert Jones and Pembroke J. Herring.
NETWORK, Gottfried/Chayefsky, MGM/UA. Alan Heim.
ROCKY, Chartoff-Winkler, UA. Richard Halsey and Scott Conrad.
TWO-MINUTE WARNING, Filmways/Peerce-Feldman, Universal. Eve Newman and Walter Hannemann.

SONG
AVE SATANI (*The Omen*, 20th Century-Fox); Music and Lyrics by Jerry Goldsmith.
COME TO ME (*The Pink Panther Strikes Again*, Amjo, UA); Music by Henry Mancini. Lyrics by Don Black.
EVERGREEN (Love Theme from *A Star Is Born*) (*A Star Is Born*, Barwood/Peters-First Artists, Warner Bros.); Music by Barbra Streisand. Lyrics by Paul Williams.

GONNA FLY NOW (*Rocky*, Chartoff-Winkler, UA); Music by Bill Conti. Lyrics by Carol Connors and Ayn Robbins.
A WORLD THAT NEVER WAS (*Half a House*, Lenro Productions, First American Films); Music by Sammy Fain. Lyrics by Paul Francis Webster.

SCORING: ORIGINAL MUSIC
OBSESSION, Litto, Columbia. Bernard Herrmann.
THE OMEN, 20th Century-Fox, Jerry Goldsmith.
THE OUTLAW JOSEY WALES, Malpaso, Warner Bros. Jerry Fielding
TAXI DRIVER, Bill/Phillips-Scorsese, Columbia. Bernard Herrmann.
VOYAGE OF THE DAMNED, ITC Entertainment, Avco Embassy. Lalo Schifrin.

SCORING: ORIGINAL SONG SCORE AND/OR ADAPTATION
BOUND FOR GLORY, UA. Leonard Rosenman.
BUGSY MALONE, Goodtimes Enterprises, Paramount, Paul Williams.
A STAR IS BORN, Barwood/Peters-First Artists, Warner Bros. Roger Kellaway.

SHORT FILM: ANIMATED FILM
DEDALO, Cineteam Realizzazioni. Manfredo Manfredi, producer.
LEISURE, Film Australia. Suzanne Baker, producer.
THE STREET, National Film Board of Canada. Caroline Leaf and Guy Glover, producers.

SHORT FILM: LIVE ACTION
IN THE REGION OF ICE, American Film Institute. Andre Guttfreund and Peter Werner, producers.
KUDZU, A Short Production. Marjorie Anne Short, producer.
THE MORNING SPIDER, The Black and White Colour Film Company. Julian Chagrin and Claude Chagrin, producers.
NIGHTLIFE, Opus Films, Ltd. Claire Wilbur and Robin Lehman, producers.
NUMBER ONE, Number One Productions. Dyan Cannon and Vince Cannon, producers.

DOCUMENTARY: SHORT FILM
AMERICAN SHOESHINE, Titan Films, Sparky Greene, producer.
BLACKWOOD, National Film Board of Canada. Tony Ianzelo and Andy Thompson, producers.
THE END OF THE ROAD, Pelican Films. John Armstrong, producer.
NUMBER OUR DAYS, Community Television of Southern California. Lynne Littman, producer.
UNIVERSE, Graphic Films Corp. for NASA. Lester Novros, producer.

DOCUMENTARY: FEATURE
HARLAN COUNTY, U.S.A., Cabin Creek Films, Barbara Kopple, producer.
HOLLYWOOD ON TRIAL, October Films/Cinema Associates. James Gutman and David Helpern Jr., producers.
OFF THE EDGE, Pentacle Films. Michael Fifth, producer.
PEOPLE OF THE WIND, Elizabeth E. Rogers Productions. Anthony Howarth and David Koff, producers.
VOLCANO; AN INQUIRY INTO THE LIFE AND DEATH OF MALCOLM LOWRY, National Film Board of Canada. Donald Brittain and Robert Duncan, producers.

FOREIGN LANGUAGE FILM
BLACK AND WHITE IN COLOR (Ivory Coast).
COUSIN, COUSINE (France).
JACOB, THE LIAR (German Democratic Republic).
NIGHTS AND DAYS, (Poland).
SEVEN BEAUTIES (Italy).

HONORARY AND OTHER AWARDS
None given this year.

SPECIAL ACHIEVEMENT AWARDS
For Visual Effects: CARLO RAMBALDI, GLEN ROWBINSON and FRANK VAN DER VEER for *King Kong*, De Laurentiis, Paramount.

For Visual Effects: L.B. ABBOTT, GLEN ROBINSON and MATTHEW YURICICH for *Logan's Run*, Saul David, MGM.

IRVING G. THALBERG MEMORIAL AWARD
TO PANDRO S. BERMAN

SCIENTIFIC OR TECHNICAL
CLASS I
None.

CLASS II
CONSOLIDATED FILM INDUSTRIES and the BARNEBEY-CHENEY COMPANY for the development of a system for the recovery of film-cleaning solvent vapors in a motion-picture laboratory.
WILLIAM L. GRAHAM, MANFRED G. MICHELSON, GEOFFREY F. NORMAN and SIEGFRIED SEIBERT of Technicolor for the development and engineering of a continuous, high-speed, Color Motion Picture Printing System.

CLASS III
FRED BARTSCHER of the Kollmorgen Corporation and to GLENN BERGGREN of the Schneider Corporation.
PANAVISION INCORPORATED; HIROSHI SUZUKAWA of Canon and WILTON R. HOLM of AMPTP Motion Picture and Television Research Center;
CARL ZEISS COMPANY; PHOTO RESEARCH DIVISION of the KOLLMORGEN CORPORATION.

1977

O scar's Golden Anniversary show was star-packed, with a few notable absentees. "Liz Taylor's back on her farm in Virginia still trying to milk a chicken," cracked Bob Hope. Jason Robards wasn't on hand to collect his Best Supporting Oscar, and Hope insinuated that he had an ax to grind: "I think he's playing bridge with Marlon Brando and George C. Scott."

NO ORPHAN ANNIE

CEREMONY: April 3, 1978
**Dorothy Chandler Pavilion,
Los Angeles Music Center,
Los Angeles
HOST:** Bob Hope

Surprisingly, there were no zingers directed at the night's big winner, perennial no-show Woody Allen. By the time *Annie Hall* copped all the top prizes, the venom had all been used up on Vanessa Redgrave. In her early-evening acceptance speech she'd remarked on "a few Zionist hoodlums" who'd made her life a misery as the result of her campaign for a Palestinian state. The furor was immediate. Presenter Paddy

Chayefsky lambasted her for "exploiting the Academy Awards for the propagation of her propaganda." He went on to suggest to Redgrave "that her winning an Oscar is not a pivotal moment in history." He got as many boos as she did. Jack Nicholson addressed the controversy with inadvertent comic relief: "I'm not very well read. What are Zionists? Are they Reds?"

Nothing could mar the glitz and glitter of the occasion, though. "What a night—the furs, the jewels, the glamour. Looks like the opening of the Beverly Hills Taco Bell," quipped Hope. He avoided commenting on Diane Keaton's eccentric getup of ankle socks, heels, wrinkled slacks, and baggy sweater. Dubbed "the Annie Hall look," it had set off a fashion trend, like John Travolta's white disco suit in *Saturday Night Fever*. But it was *Star Wars* that truly struck gold in ancillary merchandizing, everything from Halloween masks to coffee mugs. Luckily, Princess Leia's twin-braid lump wig didn't catch on.

Woody Allen, Diane Keaton

BEST PICTURE/ BEST DIRECTOR WOODY ALLEN (B. 1935) *ANNIE HALL*

Originally titled *Anhedonia*, or "fear of pleasure," *Annie Hall* is arguably Allen's most pleasurable film. "*Annie Hall* is a comedy about urban love and incompatibility that finally establishes Woody as one of our most audacious filmmakers, as well as the only American filmmaker who is able to work seriously in the comic mode without being the least bit ponderous," Vincent Canby wrote in *The New York Times*.

Woody Allen was born Allen Konigsberg, in Brooklyn, New York. At the age of 15 he started selling one-liners to gossip columns and working as a stand-up comedian. Allen directed his first film, the crime-documentary parody *Take the Money and Run* (1969). And with that he was off to the races, making one brilliant, hilarious comedy after another, including *Bananas* (1971), *Everything You Always Wanted to Know About Sex (But Were Afraid to Ask)* (1972), *Sleeper* (1973), and *Love and Death* (1975). But *Annie Hall* was his breakthrough film. It was followed by one of his more serious films, *Interiors* (1978). Other offerings came in rapid succession, among them *Manhattan* (1979, nom.), *Stardust Memories* (1980), *A Midsummer Night's Sex Comedy* (1982), *Zelig* (1983), *Radio Days* (1987, nom.), and *Hannah and Her Sisters* (1986, Oscar).

Next came *September* (1987) and *Another Woman* (1988), both of which were weighted down by the same heavy-handedness that characterized *Interiors*. With *Crimes and Misdemeanors* (1989), however, Allen was at the top of his craft.

Allen's personal life was the subject of scandal, as he was forced to admit a romantic liaison with Mia Farrow's adopted daughter, Soon-Yi Previn. This coincided with the release of *Husbands and Wives* (1992), followed by *Manhattan Murder Mystery* (1993) and *Bullets Over Broadway* (1994).

The envelope, please...

Marsha Mason with Richard Dreyfuss

BEST ACTOR
RICHARD DREYFUSS (B. 1947)
THE GOODBYE GIRL

Acting as his own Rocky, Dreyfuss stepped onto the stage punching the air, Stallone style. "I didn't prepare anything...Wait a minute...Am I here?" he laughed. "I don't wanna leave." Dreyfuss was 29 and the youngest actor to win the big one.

Dreyfuss worked his way up playing small parts and was first noticed in *Dillinger* (1973); but his breakout film was *American Graffiti* (also 1973). Dreyfuss's performance in *The Apprenticeship of Duddy Kravitz* (1974) made him a star, and he continued to appear in leading roles in such movies

as *Jaws* (1975) and *Close Encounters of the Third Kind* (1977). Dreyfuss also produced and starred in *The Big Fix* (1978).

After a well-publicized drug problem in the 1980s, he appeared in a succession of commercial disappointments. A reformed Dreyfuss changed his fortune with *Down and Out in Beverly Hills* (1986), *Tin Men* (1987), *Postcards from the Edge* (1990), *Lost in Yonkers* (1993), and *Mr. Holland's Opus* (1995).

"Whether he's playing with his mashed potatoes [1977's *Close Encounters of the Third Kind*] or trying to murder one of his patients [1991's *What About Bob?*] this compulsively likable, extraordinarily talented actor brings to his roles a coiled-spring intensity matched by few other contemporary screen performers," wrote *Entertainment Tonight* critic Leonard Maltin.

BEST ACTRESS
DIANE KEATON (B. 1946)
ANNIE HALL

"It's simply terrific," Keaton said, giggling. "This is something...I just would like to say thanks to Woody, and thank you. Thank you very much." "As Annie Hall, Keaton emerges as Allen's Liv Ullman," wrote Vincent Canby in the *New York Times*. "His camera finds beauty and emotional resources that somehow escape the notice of other directors. [She] is a marvellous nut."

In 1970 Woody Allen cast Keaton in his Broadway run of *Play It Again, Sam*, and in 1972 she appeared in the film adaptation, and the two became intimately involved. Coppola gave her her breakout role in *The Godfather* (1972) and *The Godfather Part II* (1974). She continued to work with Allen in *Sleeper* (1973),

Love and Death (1975), *Interiors* (1978), *Manhattan* (1979), and *Murder Mystery* (1993).

In 1977 Keaton moved out of comedy and into drama with *Looking for Mr. Goodbar* (1977, Golden Globe nom.). She broke up with Allen and became involved with Warren Beatty during the production of his film *Reds* (1981, nom.). Her later, less noted films include *Mrs. Soffel* (1984) and *Crimes of the Heart* (1986). To compensate for her flagging career, Keaton began directing with the documentary *Heaven* (1987). She directed an episode of the popular TV series *Twin Peaks* (1990). Keaton made a comeback in *Unstrung Heroes* (1995), her first major feature as a director.

BEST OF 1977
Best Picture: *Annie Hall*
Best Director: Woody Allen, *Annie Hall*
Best Actor: Richard Dreyfuss, *The Goodbye Girl*
Best Actress: Diane Keaton, *Annie Hall*
Best Supporting Actor: Jason Robards, *Julia*
Best Supporting Actress: Vanessa Redgrave, *Julia*

FIRSTS
- At 29, Richard Dreyfuss became the youngest Best Actor winner.
- Woody Allen's double whammy for Best Director and Best Screenplay was an almost first. Joseph L. Mankiewicz pulled it off for *A Letter to Three Wives* in 1949.
- *Annie Hall* was the first comedy to win Best Picture since *Tom Jones* in 1963.
- *Star Wars* surpassed *Jaws* as the highest-grossing movie of all time.
- Jason Robards' two consecutive Oscar wins placed him in the elite company of Luise Rainer, Katharine Hepburn, and Spencer Tracy.

SIN OF OMISSION
The Bee Gees's chart-busting score for *Saturday Night Fever* was completely overlooked by the Academy's nominating committee. Producer Robert Stigwood protested to no avail.

ROLE REVERSAL
Director Herbert Ross almost snared Grace Kelly out of retirement for *The Turning Point*, until Prince Rainier put his royal foot down. Her co-star was to have been Audrey Hepburn.

ALWAYS A BRIDESMAID, NEVER A BRIDE
The Turning Point became the most-nominated film (eleven) that failed to score.

UNMENTIONABLES
- *Close Encounters* was originally called *Watch the Skies*.
- Vanessa Redgrave pulled up at the stage door in an ambulance to elude a mob of Jewish Defense League militants who burned her in effigy.
- Long-feuding sisters Olivia de Havilland and Joan Fontaine refused to appear anywhere near each other on the big night.
- Debbie Boone performed the Oscar winner "You Light Up My Life" with a phony sign-language chorus of children pretending to be deaf.
- Vanessa Redgrave, shunned by almost everyone at the post-Awards Governor's Ball, sat alone with two bodyguards.

 BEST SUPPORTING ACTOR
JASON ROBARDS (1922–2000)
JULIA

Robards was starring on Broadway in Eugene O'Neill's *A Touch of the Poet* and couldn't attend the Oscars. Robards' absence disturbed host Bob Hope, who angered the winner when he said, "I think he's playing bridge with Marlon Brando and George C. Scott."

Playing Dashiell Hammett to Jane Fonda's Lillian Hellman, *Julia*, Hellman's story from her memoir *Pentimento*, recounts her experience smuggling bribe money into Nazi Germany for her dear friend Julia. Given that he had been pitted against Mikhail Baryshnikov, Alec Guinness, and Peter Firth, Robards' victory one year after winning for *All the President's Men* was all the more triumphant. The reviews for the film, however, were mixed favoring the negative. *The New Yorker*'s Pauline Kael wrote, "It becomes apparant that Zimmerman and Sargeant [screenwriters] are trafficking in too many quotations and flashbacks because they can't find the core of the material."

(For more on Robards, see 1976.)

 BEST SUPPORTING ACTRESS
VANESSA REDGRAVE (B. 1937)
JULIA

Entering the pavilion through a side door because of protesters, Redgrave later took the stage to thank her colleagues and launched into her infamous political challenge: "You should feel proud that in the last few weeks you've stood firm and you have refused to be intimidated by threats of a small bunch of Zionist hoodlums whose behavior is an insult to the stature of Jews all over the world and their great and heroic record of struggle against Fascism and oppression." She was met with both boos and applause, and an uncomfortable feeling hung in the air.

Redgrave was born into a notable theatrical family. She made her screen debut in *Behind the Mask* (1958) and moved more intensively into film, winning international acclaim for her performance in *Blowup* (1966). She went on to make *A Man for All Seasons* (1966), *Morgan!* (1966, nom.), and *Camelot* (1967).

Redgrave turned away from conventional films to perform in more controversial dramas, including *Mary, Queen of Scots* (1971, nom.), *The Bostonians* (1984, nom.), and *Howards End* (1992, nom.). She met with protest when she starred as a Jewish concentration-camp survivor in the TV movie *Playing for Time* (1980). Redgrave is the mother of the actresses Natasha Richardson and Joely Richardson.

 BEST VISUAL EFFECTS
STAR WARS

The most popular film of all time also changed Hollywood. *People* magazine wrote, "Within three weeks, *Star Wars* posters were outselling Farrah Fawcett-Majors five to one." *Newsweek* said, "Not since the ominous jaws of a shark stirred the country's imagination has a film generated such a cult following."

Director/screenwriter, George Lucas, was inspired by the sci-fi comic strips of his youth for the look of the film and also lifted some of the classic formulas of the Western genre. But it was the technical wizardry that kept audiences riveted. The opening shot, in which a starship lumbers through the galaxy, awing viewers with its sheer mass and detail is, by now, part of the outer-space action/adventure canon. Other signature innovations were the use of computerized animation to suggest vast, death-defying chasms, panoramic dreamscapes, and chess-piece warriors sprung to violent life in miniature.

A W A R D

N O M I N A

T I O N S

1 9 7 7

PICTURE
ANNIE HALL, Rollins-Joffe, UA. Charles H. Joffe.
THE GOODBYE GIRL, Stark, MGM/Warner Bros. Ray Stark.
JULIA, 20th Century-Fox. Richard Roth.
STAR WARS, 20th Century-Fox. Gary Kurtz.
THE TURNING POINT, Hera Prods., 20th Century-Fox. Herbert Ross and Arthur Laurents.

ACTOR
WOODY ALLEN in *Annie Hall,* Rollins-Joffe UA.
RICHARD BURTON in *Equus,* Winkaast, UA.
RICHARD DREYFUSS in *The Goodbye Girl,* Stark, MGM/Warner Bros.
MARCELLO MASTROIANNI in *A Special Day,* Canafox Films, Cinema 5 (Italian).
JOHN TRAVOLTA in *Saturday Night Fever,* Stigwood, Paramount.

ACTRESS
ANNE BANCROFT in *The Turning Point,* Hera Prods., 20th Century-Fox.
JANE FONDA in *Julia,* 20th Century-Fox.
DIANE KEATON in *Annie Hall,* Rollins-Joffe, UA.
SHIRLEY MacLAINE in *The Turning Point,* Hera Prods., 20th Century-Fox.
MARSHA MASON in *The Goodbye Girl,* Stark, MGM/ Warner Bros.

SUPPORTING ACTOR
MIKHAIL BARYSHNIKOV in *The Turning Point,* Hera Prods., 20th Century-Fox.
PETER FIRTH in *Equus,* Winkast, UA.
ALEC GUINNESS in *Star Wars,* 20th Century-Fox.
JASON ROBARDS in *Julia,* 20th Century-Fox.
MAXIMILIAN SCHELL in *Julia,* 20th Century-Fox.

SUPPORTING ACTRESS
LESLIE BROWNE in *The Turning Point,* Hera Prods., 20th Century-Fox.
QUINN CUMMINGS in *The Goodbye Girl,* Stark, Warner Bros.
MELINDA DILLON in *Close Encounters of the Third Kind,* Columbia.
VANESSA REDGRAVE in *Julia,* 20th Century-Fox.
TUESDAY WELD in *Looking for Mr. Goodbar,* Fields, Paramount.

DIRECTION
WOODY ALLEN for *Annie Hall,* Rollins-Joffe, CA.
GEORGE LUCAS for *Star Wars,* 20th Century-Fox.
HERBERT ROSS for *The Turning Point,* Hera Prods., 20th Century-Fox.
STEVEN SPIELBERG for *Close Encounters of the Third Kind,* Columbia.
FRED ZINNEMANN for *Julia,* 20th Century-Fox.

WRITING: DIRECTLY FOR THE SCREEN
ANNIE HALL, Rollins-Joffe, Woody Allen and Marshall Brickman.
THE GOODBYE GIRL, Ray Stark, MGM/ Warner Bros. Neil Simon.
THE LATE SHOW, Lion's Gate, Warner Bros. Robert Benton.
STAR WARS, 20th Century-Fox, George Lucas.
THE TURNING POINT, Hera Prods., 20th Century-Fox. Arthur Laurents.

WRITING: BASED ON MATERIAL FROM ANOTHER MEDIUM
EQUUS, Winkast Company, UA. Peter Shaffer.
I NEVER PROMISED YOU A ROSE GARDEN, Scherick/Blatt, New World Pictures. Gavin Lambert and Lewis John Carlino.
JULIA, 20th Century-Fox. Alvin Sargent.
OH, GOD!, Warner Bros. Larry Gelbart.
THAT OBSCURE OBJECT OF DESIRE, First Artists (Spain). Luis Bunuel and Jean-Claude Carriere.

CINEMATOGRAPHY
CLOSE ENCOUNTERS OF THE THIRD KIND, Columbia. Vilmos Zsigmond.
ISLANDS IN THE STREAM, Bart/Palevsky, Paramount. Fred J. Koenekamp.
JULIA, 20th Century-Fox. Douglas Slocombe.
LOOKING FOR MR. GOODBAR, Freddie Fields, Paramount. William A. Fraker.
THE TURNING POINT, Hera Prods., 20th Century-Fox. Robert Surtees.

ART DECORATION—SET DECORATION
AIRPORT '77, Jennings Lang, Universal. George C. Webb; Mickey S. Michaels.
CLOSE ENCOUNTERS OF THE THIRD KIND, Columbia. Joe Alves and Dan Lomino; Phil Abramson.
THE SPY WHO LOVED ME, Eon, UA. Ken Adam and Peter Lamont; Hugh Scaife.
STAR WARS, 20th Century-Fox. John Barry, Norman Reynolds and Leslie Dilley; Roger Christian.
THE TURNING POINT, Hera Prods., 20th Century-Fox. Albert Brenner; Marvin March.

COSTUME DESIGN
AIRPORT '77, Jennings Lang, Universal. Edith Head and Burton Miller.
JULIA, 20th Century-Fox. Anthea Sylbert.
A LITTLE NIGHT MUSIC, Sascha-Wien/ Elliott Kastner, New World Pictures. Florence Klotz.
THE OTHER SIDE OF MIDNIGHT, Frank Yablans, 20th Century-Fox. Irene Sharaff.
STAR WARS, 20th Century-Fox. John Mollo.

SOUND
CLOSE ENCOUNTERS OF THE THIRD KIND, Columbia. Robert Knudson, Robert J. Glass, Don MacDougall and Gene S. Cantamessa.
THE DEEP, Casablanca Filmworks, Columbia. Walter Goss, Dick Alexander, Tom Beckert and Robin Gregory.
SORCERER, Friedkin, Paramount/Universal. Robert Knudson, Robert J. Glass, Richard Holley and Jean-Louis Ducarme.
STAR WARS, 20th Century-Fox. Don MacDougall, Ray West, Bob Minkler and Derek Ball.
THE TURNING POINT, Hera Prods., 20th Century-Fox. Theodore Soderberg, Paul Wells, Douglas O. Williams and Jerry Jost.

FILM EDITING
CLOSE ENCOUNTERS OF THE THIRD KIND, Columbia. Michael Kahn.
JULIA, 20th Century-Fox. Walter Murch and Marcel Durham.
SMOKEY AND THE BANDIT, Rastar, Universal. Walter Hannemann and Angelo Ross.
STAR WARS, 20th Century-Fox. Paul Hirsch, Marcia Lucas and Richard Chew.
THE TURNING POINT, Hera Productions, 20th Century-Fox. William Reynolds.

VISUAL EFFECTS
CLOSE ENCOUNTERS OF THE THIRD KIND, Columbia. Roy Arbogast, Douglas Thimbull, Matthew Yuricich, Gregory Jein and Richard Yuricich.
STAR WARS, 20th Century-Fox. John Steam, John Dykstra, Richard Edlund, Grant McCune and Robert Blalack.

SONG
CANDLE ON THE WATER (*Pete's Dragon,* Disney, Buena Vista); Music and Lyrics by Al Kasha and Joel Hirschhorn.
NOBODY DOES IT BETTER (*The Spy Who Loved Me,* Eon, UA); Music by Marvin Hamlisch. Lyrics by Carole Bayer Sager.
THE SLIPPER AND THE ROSE WALTZ (He Danced with Me/She Danced with Me) (*The Slipper and the Rose—The Story of Cinderella,* Paradine Co-Productions, Universal); Music and Lyrics by Richard M. Sherman and Robert B. Sherman.
SOMEONE'S WAITING FOR YOU (*The Rescuers,* Disney, Buena Vista); Music by Sammy Pain. Lyrics by Carol Conners and Ayn Robbins.
YOU LIGHT UP MY LIFE (*You Light Up My Life,* Session Company, Columbia); Music and Lyrics by Joseph Brooks.

SCORING: ORIGINAL MUSIC
CLOSE ENCOUNTERS OF THE THIRD KIND, Columbia. John Williams.
JULIA, 20th Century-Fox. Georges Delerue.
MOHAMMAD-MESSENGER OF GOD, Filmco International, Irwin Yablans Company. Maurice Jarre.
THE SPY WHO LOVED ME, Eon, UA. Marvin Hamlisch.
STAR WARS, 20th Century-Fox. John Williams.

SCORING: ORIGINAL SONG SCORE AND ITS ADAPTATION OR BEST ADAPTATION SCORE
A LITTLE NIGHT MUSIC, Sascha-Wien/ Elliott Kastner, New World ts, Jonathon Tunick.
PETE'S DRAGON, Disney, Buena Vista. Al Kasha, Joel Hirschhorn and Irwin Kostal.
THE SLIPPER AND THE ROSE—THE STORY OF CINDERELLA, Paradine Co-Productions, Universal. Richard M. Sherman, Robert B. Sherman and Angela Morley.

SHORT FILM: ANIMATED FILM
THE BEAD GAME, National Film Board of Canada. Ishu Patel, producer.
THE DOONESBURY SPECIAL, Hubley Studio. John and Faith Hubley and Gary Trudeau, producers.
JIMMY THE C, Motionpicker Production. James Picker, Robert Grossman and Craig Whitaker, producers.
SAND CASTLE, National Film Board of Canada. Co Hoedeman, producer.

SHORT FILM: LIVE ACTION
THE ABSENT-MINDED WAITER, Aspen Film Society. William E. McEuen, producer.
FLOATING FREE, Trans World International. Jerry Butts, producer.
I'LL FIND A WAY, National Film Board of Canada. Beverly Shaffer and Yuki Yoshida, producers.
NOTES ON THE POPULAR ARTS, Saul Bass Films. Saul Bass, producer.
SPACEBORNE, Lawrence Hall of Science Production for the Regents of the University of California with the cooperation of NASA. Philip Dauber, producer.

DOCUMENTARY: SHORT FILM
AGUEDA MARTINEZ: OUR PEOPLE, OUR COUNTRY, Esparza Production. Moctesuma Esparza, producer.
FIRST EDITION, Sage Productions. Helen Whitney and DeWitt L. Sage Jr., producers.
GRAVITY IS MY ENEMY, Joseph Production, John Joseph and Jan Stussy, producers.
OF TIME, TOMBS AND TREASURES, Charlie/Papa Production. James R. Messenger and Paul N. Raimondi, producers.
THE SHETLAND EXPERIENCE, Balfour Films. Douglas Gordon, producer.

DOCUMENTARY: FEATURE
THE CHILDREN OF THEATRE STREET, Mack-Vaganova Company. Robert Dornhelm and Earle Mack, producers.
HIGH GRASS CIRCUS, National Film Board of Canada. Hill Brind, Torben Schjoler and Tony Lanzelo, producers.
HOMAGE TO CHAGALL—THE COLOURS OF LOVE, CBC Production. Harry Rasky, producer.
UNION MAIDS, Klein, Reichert, Mogulescu Production. James Klein, Julia Reichert and Miles Mogulescu, producers.
WHO ARE THE DeBOLTS? AND WHERE DID THEY GET NINETEEN KIDS?, Korty Films/Charles M. Schulz, Sanrio Films. John Korty, Dan McCann and Warren L. Lockhart, producers.

FOREIGN LANGUAGE FILM
IPHIGENIA (Greece).
MADAME ROSA (France).
OPERATION THUNDERBOLT (Israel).
A SPECIAL DAY (Italy).
THAT OBSCURE OBJECT OF DESIRE (Spain).

HONORARY AND OTHER AWARDS
TO MARGARET BOOTH for her exceptional contribution to the art of film editing in the motion-picture industry.
TO GORDON E. SAWYER and SIDNEY P. SOLOW in appreciation for outstanding service and dedication in upholding the high standards of the Academy of Motion Picture Arts and Sciences.

SPECIAL ACHIEVEMENT AWARDS
For Sound Effects Editing: FRANK WARNER for *Close Encounters of the Third Kind,* Columbia.
For Sound Effects Creations: BENJAMIN BURTT JR. for *Star Wars,* 20th Century-Fox.

IRVING G. THALBERG MEMORIAL AWARD
TO WALTER MIRISCH

JEAN HERSHOLT HUMANITARIAN AWARD
TO CHARLTON HESTON

SCIENTIFIC OR TECHNICAL
CLASS I
GARRETT BROWN and the CINEMA PRODUCTS CORP. ENGINEERING STAFF UNDER THE SUPERVISION OF JOHN JURGENS for the invention and development of Steadicam.

CLASS II
JOSEPH D. KELLY, EMORY M. COHEN, BARRY K. HENLEY, HAMMOND H. HOLT and JOHN AGALSOFF OF GLEN GLENN SOUND for the concept and development of a post-production audio-processing system for motion-picture films.
PANAVISION INCORPORATED for the concept and engineering of the improvements incorporated in the Panaflex Motion Picture Camera.
N. PAUL KENWORTHY JR. and WILLIAM R. LATADY for the invention and development of the Kenworthy Snorkel Camera System for motion-picture photography.
JOHN C. DYKSTRA for the development of the Dykstraflex Camera, and ALVAH J. MILLER and JERRY JEFFRESS for the engineering of the Electronic Motion Control System used in concert for multiple-exposure visual-effects motion-picture photography.
THE EASTMAN KODAK COMPANY for the development and introduction of a new duplicating film for motion pictures.
STEFAN KUDELSKI of Nagra Magnetic Recorders, Inc., for the engineering of the improvements incorporated in the Nagra 4.2L, sound recorder for motion-picture production.

CLASS III
ERNST NETTMANN of the Astrovision Division of Continental Camera Systems, Inc.;
EECO (ELECTRONIC ENGINEERING COMPANY OF CALIFORNIA);
DR. BERNARD KUHL and WERNER BLOCK of OSRAM, GmbH;
PANAVISION, INCORPORATED (2 citations);
PICLEAR, INC.

1978

Future historians might suggest that it was really Jane Fonda who won the Vietnam War. Her archfoe, Richard Nixon, was forced to pull out his troops and later resigned in humiliation. Fonda went on to earn two Oscars, an incredible physique, and vindication for her militant pacifism. But in the battle for Best Picture of 1978, most brutally fought between her production *Coming Home* and Michael Cimino's *The Deer Hunter*, Fonda came up short despite a scrappy pre-Oscar campaign.

Ironically, the top award was presented by the screen's most voracious hawk, John Wayne, who hadn't seen either of the movies and mangled the pronunciation of every nominee's name. The audience didn't mind a bit. The legendary Duke, who was clearly losing his fight with cancer,

WAR OF THE ANTIWAR MOVIES

CEREMONY: April 9, 1979
Dorothy Chandler Pavilion, Los Angeles Music Center, Los Angeles
HOST: Johnny Carson

responded to the standing ovation. "That's just about the only medicine a fella'd ever really need," he said.

Special honoree Sir Laurence Olivier was just as moved by his reception, though his thanks were not quite as direct. "The prodigal, pure, human kindness of this award must be seen as a beautiful star in that firmament which shines upon me," he declared.

Presenter Shirley MacLaine minced no words as she acknowledged her sisterly pride in Warren Beatty's four nominations for *Heaven Can Wait*. "Imagine what you could accomplish if you tried celibacy," she quipped. The camera caught the flustered Beatty and date, Diane Keaton, both wearing frozen smiles. The Academy finally thawed in its selection of Best Song. Paul Jabara's thumping dance hit "Last Dance" broke through the traditional sound barrier. Its live performance by disco diva Donna Summer was one of the night's more electric moments. Johnny Carson promised the TV audience "two hours of sparkling entertainment spread out over a four-hour show." It was a promise fulfilled.

BEST PICTURE/BEST DIRECTOR
MICHAEL CIMINO (B. 1943)
THE DEER HUNTER

Before it dawned on Cimino how much outrage there was against his film, he picked up his statue and said, "I love you madly!" Cimino was taken aback by accusations that the film was racist. There were protests outside the auditorium. Jane Fonda, admitting that she hadn't even seen the film, proclaimed, "But ours—*Coming Home*—is the best picture." She also actively campaigned against the film, telling everyone that she hoped it wouldn't win.

"I am puzzled by the pickets," Cimino said backstage. But the critics were split on their assessment. Danny Peary wrote, "Cimino's film is condescending to its three white characters (we're supposed to understand better what happens to onetime POWs than they do themselves) and racist toward Vietnamese; moreover he uses a false event—the Cong guards force the three friends to play 'Russian roulette'—to give us an impression of the hellish war." From the other side, David Denby of *New York* magazine said, "Just when it seemed time to announce that the American cinema had died as an art form, *The Deer Hunter* arrives to restore a little hope."

Michael Cimino with Robert De Niro

The Deer Hunter nevertheless made Cimino's career. Originally a protégé of Clint Eastwood, Cimino co-wrote *Magnum Force* (1973) and directed *Thunderbolt and Lightfoot* (1974). A decade later he scored box-office successes with *Year of the Dragon* (1985), *The Sicilian* (1987), and *Desperate Hours* (1990). The vastly overbudget *Heaven's Gate* (1980) very nearly spelled Cimino's doom.

The envelope, please...

BEST ACTOR
JON VOIGHT (B. 1938)
COMING HOME

Overcome by Olivier's speech for his Honorary Award, Voight began his own acceptance speech by saying, "I don't think there's an actor here who doesn't acknowledge a great debt to the continuing legacy of Laurence Olivier." He further thanked the veterans in the audience, at which point he was reduced to tears.

Coming Home boasts one of the most sensual love scenes, between Voight and Fonda, in movie history. Voight's career debuted with the satire *Fearless Frank* (1967), and continued with a bang in *Midnight Cowboy* (1969, nom.), *Out of It* (1969), *Catch-22* (1970), and *Deliverance* (1972). He won a third Oscar nomination for *Runaway Train* (1985).

Voight underwent a spiritual rebirth in the late 1980s, often speaking to puzzled interviewers of the need for man's transcendence over evil. Consistent with that change, he wrote and performed in *Eternity* (1990), which had a very limited run.

BEST ACTRESS
JANE FONDA (B. 1937)
COMING HOME

When her win was announced, Fonda ran onto the stage and into the open arms of Shirley MacLaine. Fonda began her speech by signing, later explaining, "I'm signing part of what I'm saying tonight because while we were making the movie we all became more aware of the problems of the handicapped."

Fonda's second Oscar after *Klute* (1971), *Coming Home* was produced by her new film-production company from a screenplay that she commissioned. The film, about a love affair between a paraplegic Vietnam vet and the wife of an officer, was met with mixed reviews. Vincent Canby called it "soggy with sound, just as it eventually becomes soggy with good if unrealized intentions." Weakly, Pauline Kael called it "intuitive."

Fonda collected five Oscar nominations for Best Actress in *They Shoot Horses, Don't They?* (1969), *Julia* (1977), *The Morning After* (1986), and *On Golden Pond* (1981).

(For more on Fonda, see 1971.)

BEST OF 1978
Best Picture: *The Deer Hunter*
Best Director: Michael Cimino, *The Deer Hunter*
Best Actor: Jon Voight, *Coming Home*
Best Actress: Jane Fonda, *Coming Home*
Best Supporting Actor: Christopher Walken, *The Deer Hunter*
Best Supporting Actress: Maggie Smith, *California Suite*

FIRSTS
- Sir Laurence Olivier's appearance at the Oscars was his first since 1939.
- Maggie Smith won her Oscar for playing an Oscar loser.
- Warren Beatty and Buck Henry were the first nominated directorial duo since *West Side Story*'s Jerome Robbins and Robert Wise in 1961.
- Meryl Streep's nomination for *The Deer Hunter* was the first in a career total of twelve.

AND LAST
Autumn Sonata would mark the end of Ingrid Bergman's big-screen career.

SINS OF OMISSION
- John Belushi fumed over his Academy snub for *Animal House.*
- Brad Davis probably had more reason to be upset after being ignored for his starring role in *Midnight Express.*
- *An Unmarried Woman*'s Paul Mazursky was the only director of a Best Picture nominee not to be nominated.

ROLE REVERSALS
- Sir Laurence Olivier was nominated for playing a Nazi hunter in *The Boys from Brazil.* His previous nomination was for playing a Nazi on the lam in *Marathon Man.*
- The role of the paraplegic vet in *Coming Home* was offered to Jack Nicholson, Al Pacino, and Sylvester Stallone.
- Kate Jackson and Cary Grant passed on roles in *Heaven Can Wait.* She was replaced by Julie Christie, he by James Mason.

ALWAYS A BRIDESMAID, NEVER A BRIDE
- Bruce Dern's nomination for *Coming Home* was the only one he ever received.
- Maureen Stapleton struck out for a third time with her nomination for *Interiors.*

UNMENTIONABLES
- The offscreen romance of *Deer Hunter* co-stars Meryl Streep and John Cazale came to a tragic end when he died of cancer shortly before the film's release.
- Mrs. Henry Fonda admitted that she often filled out her husband's Academy ballot.
- Roger Ebert calculated that the studios' pre-Oscar campaigns cost $500 per Academy voter.

 BEST SUPPORTING ACTOR
CHRISTOPHER WALKEN (B. 1943)
THE DEER HUNTER

"I know what I'm doing onstage, but in films I have to depend on the kindness of strangers," Walken said. As recounted by Leonard Maltin, Walken described himself to a journalist as "the malevolent WASP." To director Paul Schrader, who was lighting him from below for one shot in 1991's *The Comfort of Strangers*, he said, "I don't need to be made to look evil. I can do that on my own." *The Deer Hunter* was no exception.

Walken began his acting career onstage and switched to film in 1972 with *The Anderson Tapes*. His performance in *Annie Hall* (1977) as Keaton's strange brother is engraved in filmgoers' memories. Since that time Walken has appeared in *Pennies from Heaven* (1981), in which he performed a dazzling—and unexpected—dance routine that rivaled Fred Astaire. Walken's other films include *The Dead Zone* (1983), *A View to a Kill* (1985), *At Close Range* (1986), *Batman Returns* (1992), and *Wayne's World 2* (1993).

© A.M.P.A.S® *Michael Caine with Maggie Smith*

 BEST SUPPORTING ACTRESS
MAGGIE SMITH (B. 1934)
CALIFORNIA SUITE

"I've won two Oscars and I still don't begin to understand film acting," Smith admitted backstage. Explaining why she wasn't returning to London immediately, she added, "I want to enjoy the feeling of being a winner…Oscar doesn't mean anything in England. They don't know quite what they are." Vincent Canby saluted Smith "for her best screen role since *The Prime of Miss Jean Brodie*…a part that makes use of her unique gift for comedy."

Smith has almost limitless range, and is comfortable playing everything from comedic roles in big, commercial films (*Murder by Death*, 1976) to a supercilious sci-fi character (*Clash of the Titans*, 1981), and a lonely Irish woman (*The Lonely Passion of Judith Hearne*, 1987).

(For more on Smith, see page 1969.)

 HONORARY AWARD
LAURENCE OLIVIER (1907–1989)

After an early turn on the British stage and two American film flops, Olivier went back to England only to return to Hollywood with wife Vivien Leigh. They starred together in a lavish production of *Wuthering Heights* (1939, nom.), and Olivier gained the film world's attention.

Olivier's performances in Hitchcock's *Rebecca* (1940, nom.), *Pride and Prejudice* (1940), *That Hamilton Woman* (1941), and his film version of Shakespeare's *Henry V*, (which he also directed) were hailed as among the screen's finest. *Henry V* won Olivier a special Oscar. He won four Oscars for his production of *Hamlet* (1948), making him the only performer in Oscar history to direct himself—as well as act—in an Academy Award–winning performance.

The 1950s and '60s were thin film years for Olivier, but the pictures he directed or performed in were standouts: *Richard III* (1955, nom.), *The Entertainer* (1960, nom.), *Oh! What a Lovely War* (1969, nom.), and *Sleuth* (1972, nom.).

PICTURE
COMING HOME, Hellman, UA. Jerome Hellman.
THE DEER HUNTER, EMI/Cimino, Universal, MGM. Barry Spikings, Michael Deeley, Michael Cimino and John Peverall.
HEAVEN CAN WAIT, Dogwood, Paramount. Warren Beatty.
MIDNIGHT EXPRESS, Casablanca, Columbia. Alan Marshall and David Puttnam.
AN UNMARRIED WOMAN, 20th Century-Fox. Paul Mazursky and Tony Ray.

ACTOR
WARREN BEATTY in *Heaven Can Wait*, Dogwood, Paramount.
GARY BUSEY in *The Buddy Holly Story*, Innovisions-ECA, Columbia.
ROBERT DE NIRO in *The Deer Hunter*, EMI/Cimino, Universal.
LAURENCE OLIVIER in *The Boys from Brazil*, ITC, 20th Century-Fox.
JON VOIGHT in *Coming Home*, Hellman, UA.

ACTRESS
INGRID BERGMAN in *Autumn Sonata*, Personafilm GmbH, Grade-Starger-ITC, New World Pictures.
ELLEN BURSTYN in *Same Time, Next Year*, Mirisch-Mulligan, Universal.
JILL CLAYBURGH in *An Unmarried Woman*, 20th Century-Fox.
JANE FONDA in *Coming Home*, Hellman, UA.
GERALDINE PAGE in *Interiors*, Rollins-Joffe, UA.

SUPPORTING ACTOR
BRUCE DERN in *Coming Home*, Hellman, UA.
RICHARD FARNSWORTH in *Comes a Horseman*, Chartoff-Winkler, UA.
JOHN HURT in *Midnight Express*, Casablanca, Columbia.
CHRISTOPHER WALKEN in *The Deer Hunter*, EMI/Cimino, Universal.
JACK WARDEN in *Heaven Can Wait*, Dogwood, Paramount.

SUPPORTING ACTRESS
DYAN CANNON in *Heaven Can Wait*, Dogwood, Paramount.
PENELOPE MILFORD in *Coming Home*, Hellman, UA.
MAGGIE SMITH in *California Suite*, Stark, Columbia.
MAUREEN STAPLETON in *Interiors*, Rollins-Joffe, UA.
MERYL STREEP in *The Deer Hunter*, EMI/Cimino, Universal.

DIRECTION
WOODY ALLEN for *Interiors*, Rollins-Joffe, UA
HAL ASHBY for *Coming Home*, Hellman, UA.
WARREN BEATTY and BUCK HENRY for *Heaven Can Wait*, Dogwood, Paramount
MICHAEL CIMINO for *The Deer Hunter*, EMI/Cimino, Universal
ALAN PARKER for *Midnight Express*, Casablanca, Columbia.

WRITING: DIRECTLY FOR THE SCREEN
AUTUMN SONATA, Personafilm GmbH, Grade-Starger-ITC, New World Pictures. Ingmar Bergman.

COMING HOME, Hellman, UA. Nancy Dowd, Waldo Salt and Robert C. Jones.
THE DEER HUNTER, EMI/Cimino, Universal. Michael Cimino, Deric Washburn, Louis Garfinkle, Quinn K. Redeker and Deric Washburn.
INTERIORS, Rollins-Joffe, UA. Woody Allen.
AN UNMARRIED WOMAN, 20th Century-Fox. Paul Mazursky.

WRITING: BASED ON MATERIAL FROM ANOTHER MEDIUM
BLOODBROTHERS, Warner Bros. Walter Newman.
CALIFORNIA SUITE, Stark, Columbia. Neil Simon.
HEAVEN CAN WAIT, Dogwood, Paramount. Elaine May and Warren Beatty.
MIDNIGHT EXPRESS, Casablanca, Columbia. Oliver Stone.
SAME TIME, NEXT YEAR, Mirisch-Mulligan, Universal. Bernard Slade.

CINEMATOGRAPHY
DAYS OF HEAVEN, OP, Paramount. Nestor Almendros.
THE DEER HUNTER, EMI/Cimino, Universal. Vilmos Zsigmond.
HEAVEN CAN WAIT, Dogwood, Paramount. William A. Fraker.
SAME TIME, NEXT YEAR, Mirisch-Mulligan, Universal. Robert Surtees.
THE WIZ, Motown, Universal. Oswald Morris.

ART DIRECTION—SET DECORATION
THE BRINK'S JOB, De Laurentiis, Universal. Dean Tavoularis and Angelo Graham; George R. Nelson and Bruce Kay.
CALIFORNIA SUITE, Stark, Columbia. Albert Brenner; Marvin March.
HEAVEN CAN WAIT, Dogwood, Paramount. Paul Sylbert and Edwin O'Donovan; George Games.
INTERIORS, Rollins-Joffe, UA. Mel Bourne; Daniel Robert.
THE WIZ, Motown, Universal. Tony Walton and Philip Rosenberg; Edward Stewart and Robert Drumheller.

COSTUME DESIGN
CARAVANS, Ibex-F.I.D.C.I. Universal. Renie Conley.
DAYS OF HEAVEN, OP, Paramount. Patricia Norris.
DEATH ON THE NILE, Brabourne-Goodwin, Paramount. Anthony Powell.
THE SWARM, Warner Bros. Paul Zastupnevich.
THE WIZ, Motown, Universal. Tony Walton.

SOUND
THE BUDDY HOLLY STORY, Innovisions-ECA, Columbia. Tex Rudloff, Joel Fein, Curly Thirlwell and Willie Burton.
DAYS OF HEAVEN, OP, Paramount. John K. Wilkinson, Robert W. Glass Jr., John T. Reitz and Barry Thomas.
THE DEER HUNTER, EMI/Cimino, Universal. Richard Portman, William McCaughey, Aaron Rochin and Darin Knight.
HOOPER, Warner Bros. Robert Knudson, Robert J. Glass, Don MacDougall and Jack Solomon.
SUPERMAN, Dovemead, Salkind, Warner Bros. Gordon K. McCallum, Graham Hartstone, Nicolas Le Messurier and Roy Charman.

FILM EDITING
THE BOYS FROM BRAZIL, ITC, 20th Century-Fox. Robert E. Swink.
COMING HOME, Heilman, UA. Don Zimmerman.
THE DEER HUNTER, EMI/Cimino, Universal. Peter Zinner.
MIDNIGHT EXPRESS, Casablanca, Columbia. Gerry Humbling.
SUPERMAN, Dovemead, Salkind, Warner Bros. Stuart Baird.

SONG
HOPELESSLY DEVOTED TO YOU *(Grease*, Stigwood/Carr, Paramount); Music and Lyrics by John Farrar.
LAST DANCE *(Thank God It's Friday, Casablanca-Motown, Columbia); Music and Lyrics by Paul Jabara.
THE LAST TIME I FELT LIKE THIS *(Same Time, Next Year*, Mirisch-Mulligan,

Universal); Music by Marvin Hamlisch. Lyrics by Alan and Marilyn Bergman.
READY TO TAKE A CHANCE AGAIN *(Foul Play*, Miller-Milkis/Higgins, Paramount); Music by Charles Fox. Lyrics by Norman Gimbel.
WHEN YOU'RE LOVED *(The Magic of Lassie, Lassie* Productions, The International Picture Show Company); Music and Lyrics by Richard M. Sherman and Robert B. Sherman.

SCORING: ORIGINAL MUSIC
THE BOYS FROM BRAZIL, ITC, 20th Century-Fox. Jerry Goldsmith.
DAYS OF HEAVEN, OP, Paramount. Ennio Morricone.
HEAVEN CAN WAIT, Dogwood, Paramount. Dave Grusin.
MIDNIGHT EXPRESS, Casablanca, Columbia. Giorgio Moroder.
SUPERMAN, Dovemead, Salkind, Warner Bros. John Williams.

SCORING: ORIGINAL SONG SCORE AND/ OR ADAPTATION
THE BUDDY HOLLY STORY, Innovisions-ECA, Columbia. Joe Renzetti.
PRETTY BABY, Malle, Paramount. Jerry Wexler.
THE WIZ, Motown, Universal. Quincy Jones.

SHORT FILM: ANIMATED FILM
OH MY DARLING, Nico Crama Production. Nico Crama, producer.
RIP VAN WINKLE, A Will Vinton/Billy Budd Film. Will Vinton, producer.
SPECIAL DELIVERY, National Film Board of Canada. Eunice Macaulay and John Weldon, producers.

SHORT FILM: LIVE ACTION
A DIFFERENT APPROACH, A Jim Belcher/ Brookfield Production. Jim Belcher and Fern Field, producers.
MANDY'S GRANDMOTHER, Illumination Films. Andrew Sugerman, producer.
STRANGE FRUIT, The American Film Institute. Seth Pinsker, producer.
TEENAGE FATHER, New Visions Inc. for the Children's Home Society of California. Taylor Hackford, producer.

DOCUMENTARY: SHORT FILM
THE DIVIDED TRAIL: A NATIVE AMERICAN ODYSSEY, A Jerry Aronson Production. Jerry Aronson, producer.
AN ENCOUNTER WITH FACES, Films Division, Government of India. K.K. Kapil, producer.
THE FLIGHT OF THE GOSSAMER CONDOR, A Shedd Production. Jacqueline Phillips Shedd and Ben Shedd, producers.
GOODNIGHT MISS ANN, An August Cinquegrana Films Production. August Cinquegrana, producer.
SQUIRES OF SAN QUENTIN, The J. Gary Mitchell Film Company. J. Gary Mitchell, producer.

DOCUMENTARY: FEATURE
THE LOVERS' WIND, Ministry of Culture & Arts of Iran. Albert Lamorisse, producer.
MYSTERIOUS CASTLES OF CLAY, A Survival Anglia Ltd. Production. Alan Root, producer.
RAONI, A Franco-Brazilian Production. Jean-Pierre Dutilleux, Barry Williams and Michel Gast, producers.
SCARED STRAIGHT!, A Golden West Television Production. Arnold Shapiro, producer.
WITH BABIES AND BANNERS: STORY OF THE WOMEN'S EMERGENCY BRIGADE, A Women's Labor History Film Project Production. Anne Bohlen, Lyn Goldfarb and Lorraine Gray, producers.

FOREIGN LANGUAGE FILM
GET OUT YOUR HANDKERCHIEFS (France).
THE GLASS CELL (German Federal Republic).
HUNGARIANS (Hungary).
VIVA ITALIA! (Italy).
WHITE BIM BLACK EAR (U.S.S.R.).

HONORARY AND OTHER AWARDS
TO WALTER LANTZ for bringing joy and laughter to every part of the world through

his unique animated motion pictures.
TO THE MUSEUM OF MODERN ART, DEPARTMENT OF FILM for the contribution it has made to the public's perception of movies as an art form.
TO LAURENCE OLIVIER for the full body of his work, for the unique achievements of his entire career and his lifetime of contribution to the art of film.
TO KING VIDOR for his incomparable achievements as a cinematic creator and innovator.
TO LINWOOD G. DUNN, LOREN L. RYDER and WALDON O. WATSON in appreciation for outstanding service and dedication in upholding the high standards of the Academy of Motion Picture Arts and Sciences.

SPECIAL ACHIEVEMENT AWARDS
For Visual Effects: LES BOWIE, COLIN CHILVERS. DENYS COOP, ROY FIELD, DEREK MEDDINGS and ZORAN PERISIC for "Superman," a Dovemead Ltd. Production, Alexander Salkind Presentation, Warner Bros.

IRVING G. THALERG MEMORIAL AWARD
None given this year.

JEAN HERSHOLT HUMANITARIAN AWARD
TO LEO JAFFE

SCIENTIFIC OR TECHNICAL AWARDS
EASTMAN KODAK COMPANY for the research and development of a Duplicating Color Film for Motion Pictures.
STEFAN KUDELSKI of Nagra Magnetic Recorders, Incorporated, for the continuing research, design and development of the Nagra Production Sound Recorder for Motion Pictures.
PANAVISION, INCORPORATED, and its engineering staff under the DIRECTION of Robert E. Gottschalk, for the concept, design and continuous development of the Panaflex Motion Picture Camera System.

SCIENTIFIC AND ENGINEERING AWARD
RAY M, DOLBY, IOAN R. ALLEN, DAVID P. ROBINSON, STEPHEN M, KATZ and PHILLIP S. J. BOOLE of Dolby Laboratories, Incorporated, for the development and implementation of an improved Sound Recording and Reproducing System for Motion Picture Production and Exhibition.

TECHNICAL ACHIEVEMENT AWARD
KARL MACHER and GLENN M. BERGGREN of Isco Optische Werke for the development and introduction of the Cinelux-ULTRA Lens for 35mm Motion Picture Projection.
DAVID J, DEGENKOLB, ARTHUR L. FORD and FRED J. SCOBEY of DeLuxe General, Incorporated, for the development of a Method to Recycle Motion Picture Laboratory Photographic Wash Waters by Ion Exchange.
KIICHI SEKIGUCHI of CINE-FI International for the development of the CINE-FI Auto Radio Sound System for Drive-In Theaters.
LEONARD CHAPMAN of Leonard Equipment Company, for the design and manufacture of a small, mobile, motion-picture camera platform known as the Chapman Hustler Dolly.
JAMES L. FISHER of J.L. Fisher, Incorporated, for the design and manufacture of a small, mobile, motion-picture camera platform known as the Fisher Model Ten Dolly.
ROBERT STINDT of Production Grip Equipment Company, for the design and manufacture of a small, mobile, motion-picture camera platform known as the Stindt Dolly.

1979

"I do feel like the Academy is slacking off in the class quotient. After all, I won."

—Sally Field

SORE WINNERS

CEREMONY: April 14, 1980
Dorothy Chandler Pavilion,
Los Angeles Music Center,
Los Angeles
HOST: Johnny Carson

With every major award successfully predicted long before the big night, the only suspense was just how big a fuss Dustin Hoffman was going to make on the podium. His co-star Meryl "Holy Mackerel!" Streep was genuinely thrilled with her Best Supporting Oscar. Their on screen kid, Justin Henry, fidgeted in his seat, his acceptance speech secure in his pocket. He sulked as the name of the competing, purposely absent Melvyn Douglas was announced.

Irritation seemed contagious as nominated cinematographer Haskell Wexler raged that two of the best names in his field, Caleb Deschanel (*The Black Stallion*) and Gordon Willis (*Manhattan*), had been left off the ballot. Though Sally Field gushed over her screen-debut Oscar, she appeared just as perplexed by it.

All eyes, however, were on the unpredictable Hoffman. Finally, the moment arrived. He stared at his Oscar. "He has no genitalia and he's holding a sword," he said. That got a laugh, but he wasn't nearly finished. "I'm up here with mixed feelings," he went on. "I've criticized the Academy before, with reason." An anxious hush fell. "I refuse to believe that I beat Jack Lemmon, that I beat Al Pacino, that I beat Peter Sellers. We are part of an artistic family. There are 60,000 actors in the Screen Actors Guild who don't work. You have to practice accents while you're driving a cab, 'cause when you're a broke actor you can't write and you can't paint. Most actors don't work, and a few of us are so lucky to have a chance. And to that artistic family that strives for excellence, none of you have ever lost, and I am proud to share this with you and I thank you."

Hollywood's premier bad boy had at last spoken his mind, and the ensuing cheers confirmed that he had done it beautifully. The Academy heaved a sigh of relief. The rebellious '70s had ended on a soaring note of eloquence.

BEST PICTURE/BEST DIRECTOR
ROBERT BENTON (B. 1932)
KRAMER VS. KRAMER

"This is one of the five best days of my whole life!" Benton said.

Benton had to persuade Hoffman to play the part of Ted Kramer. The actor insisted that he didn't like the script, and set an ultimatum. He wanted to be able to make changes and see the editing. "I've never let an actor in on the writing or the editing before," said Benton. "I always thought the actors were there to ruin the writer's lines." He gave in to Hoffman and ended up winning the Oscar for himself.

Producer Stanley Jaffe originally conceived that the Robert Benton script, based on the best-selling novel by Avery Corman, would be directed by François Truffaut. When Benton heard this he protested, having planned to direct his screenplay himself. It all worked out well in the end.

Kramer was the odds-on favorite for the Oscar, and led with the most bids—nine—

Dustin Hoffman, Stanley Jaffe with Robert Benton

but the early lead turned into a tie at the last minute and left *Kramer* competing with another favorite, *All That Jazz* by Bob Fosse. Vincent Canby of the *New York Times* liked *Kramer,* calling it "fine, witty, moving and intelligent…densely packed with beautifully observed detail."

Benton came to film through the word. Together with David Newman, he—both were *Esquire* editors—collaborated on the script for *Bonnie and Clyde* (1967), which brought them instant fame and an Oscar nomination. They later wrote *Superman* (1978). Benton's debut as a director came with the offbeat Western *Bad Company* (1972), and his output since has been thin but choice. His *Late Show* (1977) was an odd thriller praised for the rapport of its lead characters, played by Art Carney and Lily Tomlin. Trying to emulate Hitchcock, Benton tripped up with *Still of the Night* (1982) but bounced back with *Places in the Heart* (1984, Oscar).

The envelope, please…

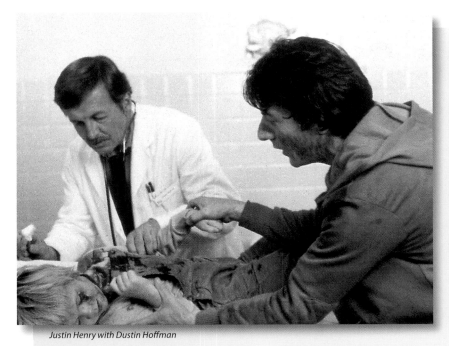

Justin Henry with Dustin Hoffman

BEST ACTOR
DUSTIN HOFFMAN (B. 1937)
KRAMER VS. KRAMER

The much-mellowed star, who, in 1974, had protested vociferously against the Oscars, decrying, "The Academy Awards are obscene, dirty, and no better than a beauty contest," accepted his prize with gratitude. "[I thank] my mother and father for not practicing birth control," he said. Continuing in a more humorous vein about his co-star Justin Henry, he joked, "If he loses again, we'll have to give him a Lifetime Achievement Award." He was applauded by the audience for his more serious words about his conflicts with Oscar.

Of Hoffmann's role in the film, Vincent Canby wrote in the *New York Times*, "Hoffman is splendid in one of the two or three best roles of his career… A delicately witty performance, funny and full of feeling that never slops over into the banal." *Time* magazine devoted a cover story to the movie and said of Hoffman, "Like Diane Keaton in *Annie Hall*, he has turned the screen into a mirror, a magical looking glass into his own head and heart."

Nominated five times, with two wins, Hoffman is perhaps the best actor in America. His extraordinary ability to inhabit completely different characters led him to star in many significant films, among them *Madigan's Million* (1966, debut), *The Graduate* (1967), *Midnight Cowboy* (1969), *Little Big Man* (1970), *Papillon* (1973), *Lenny* (1974), *All the President's Men* and *Marathon Man* (both 1976), *Straight Time* (1978), *Agatha* (1979), *Kramer vs. Kramer* (1979), and *Tootsie* (1982). He went on to make the notoriously unsuccessful *Ishtar* (1987), followed by *Family Business* (1989), *Dick Tracy* (1990, a cameo), *Billy Bathgate* (1991), *Hook* (1991), and *Outbreak* (1995). (For more on Hoffman, see 1979.)

BEST ACTRESS
SALLY FIELD (B. 1946)
NORMA RAE

"I'm going to be the one at the podium to cry tonight, I'll tell you that right now," Field said breathlessly. "They said this couldn't be done!" Field, who played a Southern textile worker who helps organize a union against all odds, is unforgettable in the famous scene in which she stands on a table to inspire the workers to unionize.

There were mixed opinions about the film, but there was high praise for its female lead. Vincent Canby wrote that this was "the plum role of her career, an opportunity to demonstrate once and for all that she is an actress of dramatic intelligence and force."

Field's career began with TV's cute and bubbly *Gidget* (1965–1966). She landed in a nun's habit in the sitcom *The Flying Nun* (1967–1970), embodied sixteen personalities in *Sybil* (1977, Emmy), and moved gracefully into her first Oscar-winning film. Said Field, "I had a terrible image because I had appeared in the TV series *Gidget* and *The Flying Nun*."

Her curriculum vitae also includes strong performances in *Steel Magnolias* (1989), *Mrs. Doubtfire* (1993), and *Forrest Gump* (1994). (For more on Fields, see 1984.)

BEST OF 1979
Best Picture: *Kramer vs. Kramer*
Best Director: Robert Benton, *Kramer vs. Kramer*
Best Actor: Dustin Hoffman, *Kramer vs. Kramer*
Best Actress: Sally Field, *Norma Rae*
Best Supporting Actor: Melvyn Douglas, *Being There*
Best Supporting Actress: Meryl Streep, *Kramer vs. Kramer*
Honorary Award: Alec Guinness

FIRST
At 8, Justin Henry became the youngest nominee.

ROLE REVERSALS
• Sally Field's screen debut almost wasn't. She was offered the part of *Norma Rae* only after Jill Clayburgh, Jane Fonda, and Faye Dunaway took a pass.

• Meryl Streep lucked out when Columbia Pictures' Sherry Lansing insisted on her over Kate Jackson.

• *China Syndrome* (originally titled *Power*) would have had a different energy with Richard Dreyfuss in Michael Douglas's role and Jack Nicholson in Jack Lemmon's shoes.

• *Apocalypse Now* was a casting nightmare. The role of the young hero sent to eliminate Marlon Brando was offered to Jack Nicholson, Robert Redford, Gene Hackman, Al Pacino, and James Caan. All said nope. Steve McQueen finally agreed, until he learned that he'd have to spend six months shooting in the jungle. Next up, Harvey Keitel, who just wasn't working out. In came Martin Sheen to save the day. Shortly afterward, he suffered a heart attack. Coppola stuck by him through his recuperation.

• Bette Midler nixed *Nashville*, *Rocky*, and *Foul Play* in favor of a part that could make her an instant screen icon: *The Pearl*, a.k.a. *The Rose*.

ALWAYS A BRIDESMAID, NEVER A BRIDE
"If I want to be up for an Academy Award, I'm either going to have to play a tour de force of some kind or have a tracheotomy just before the nominations," said Burt Reynolds (referring to Elizabeth Taylor's win in 1960).

UNMENTIONABLES
• Sally Field's stepfather, B actor Jock Mahoney, played Tarzan in three 1960s movies.

• When the Golden Globes named 9-year-old Ricky Schroeder its New Male Star of the Year, Justin Henry threw a raging tantrum.

• In the excitement of the Governor's Ball, Meryl Streep left her Oscar in the ladies' room.

• Awards producer Howard Koch fumed when unknown Documentary winner Ira Wohl gave a nearly four-minute acceptance speech. "I don't know if we should give Oscars to the people who are from nowhere," he said.

Melvyn Douglas with Peter Sellers

 BEST SUPPORTING ACTOR
MELVYN DOUGLAS (1901–1981)
BEING THERE

Offended at having to compete against an 8-year-old (Justin Henry, *Kramer vs. Kramer*), Douglas refused to appear at the ceremonies. "Douglas [plays] a poignantly ailing rich man. …His timing with [Peter Sellers] is often so perfect that the film, at its wittiest, strips conversation down to its barest maneuvers and stratagems," wrote Janet Maslin.

The debonaire leading man with the signature pencil-thin mustache, Melvyn Douglas was the surprise choice for Best Supporting Actor, winning over John Huston's perceived sure thing in *The Cardinal*. Douglas's great wit was at the core of many comic and dramatic classics, including *Ninotchka* (1939), *Mr. Blandings Builds His Dreamhouse* (1948), *The Americanization of Emily* (1964), *I Never Sang for My Father* (1970, nom.), *The Candidate* (1972), *The Tenant* (1976), and *Twilight's Last Gleaming* (1975).

In the early 1950s Douglas endured the witch-hunt of his wife, Helen Gahagan, who was running against Nixon for Congress. Nixon accused her of having ties to the Communist Party and won, despite a lack of evidence. Douglas's autobiography was published posthumously in 1986. (For more on Douglas, see 1963.)

Meryl Streep with Justin Henry

BEST SUPPORTING ACTRESS
MERYL STREEP (B. 1951)
KRAMER VS. KRAMER

"Holy mackerel!" were the first eloquent words to issue from the ladylike mouth of up-and-coming star Meryl Streep. The critics—and the audience—loved her. "One of the major performances of the year," wrote Vincent Canby. "She is fascinating."

Streep told *New York* magazine, "This hasn't changed me at all…I don't care about being a star…I feel horribly embarrassed in a limousine…I'd rather that they humanize the subways."

Streep wasn't particularly fond of working with Hoffman, who introduced himself to her at a party, burped at her, and put his hand on her breast. Their acrimonious relationship got them off to the perfect start for *Kramer*. In the end, all was well and they worked together seamlessly.

Streep's naturalistic style has enabled her to play varied, even unsympathetic roles, winning Academy Awards and ten nominations for, among other films, *The Deer Hunter* (1978), *The French Lieutenant's Woman* (1981), *Silkwood* (1983), *Out of Africa* (1985), *Ironweed* (1987), *A Cry in the Dark* (1988), *The Bridges of Madison County* (1995), *One True Thing* (1998), and *Music of the Heart* (1999).

 HONORARY AWARD
ALEC GUINNESS (1914–2000)

Guinness took his honorary award from Dustin Hoffman in front of a standing ovation and smiled. "I feel very fraudulent taking this, but…I'm grabbing this while the going's good," he said. And with that the winner disappeared with his prize.

Guinness picked himself up from highly challenged beginnings. His mother was a prostitute, and at school the headmaster told him that he would never succeed as an actor. Alec, nevertheless, rose to such a high level of achievement that in 1959 he was knighted by Queen Elizabeth.

(For more on Guinness, see 1957.)

PICTURE

ALL THAT JAZZ, 20th Century-Fox. Robert Alan Aurthur.
APOCALYPSE NOW, Omni Zoetrope, UA. Francis Coppola. Fred Roos, Gray Frederickson and Tom Sternberg.
BREAKING AWAY, 20th Century-Fox. Peter Yates.
KRAMER VS. KRAMER, Jaffe, Columbia. Stanley R. Jaffe.
NORMA RAE, 20th Century-Fox. Tamara Asseyev and Alex Rose.

ACTOR

DUSTIN HOFFMAN in *Kramer vs. Kramer*, Jaffe, Columbia.
JACK LEMMON in *The China Syndrome*, Douglas/IPC, Columbia.
AL PACINO in *...And Justice for All*, Malton, Columbia.
ROY SCHEIDER in *All That Jazz*, 20th Century-Fox.
PETER SELLERS in *Being There*, Lorimar-Fernsehproduktion GmbH, UA.

ACTRESS

JILL CLAYBURGH in *Starting Over*, Pakula/Brooks, Paramount.
SALLY FIELD in *Norma Rae*, 20th Century-Fox.
JANE FONDA in *The China Syndrome*, Douglas/IPC, Columbia.
MARSHA MASON in *Chapter Two*, Stark, Columbia.
BETTE MIDLER in *The Rose*, 20th Century-Fox.

SUPPORTING ACTOR

MELVYN DOUGLAS in *Being There*, Lorimar-Fernsehproduktion GmbH, UA.
ROBERT DUVALL in *Apocalypse Now*, Omni Zoetrope, UA.
FREDERIC FORREST in *The Rose*, 20th Century-Fox.
JUSTIN HENRY in *Kramer vs. Kramer*, Jaffe, Columbia.
MICKEY ROONEY in *The Black Stallion*, Omni Zoetrope, UA.

SUPPORTING ACTRESS

JANE ALEXANDER in *Kramer vs. Kramer*, Jaffe, Columbia.
BARBARA BARRIE in *Breaking Away*, 20th Century-Fox.
CANDICE BERGEN in *Starting Over*, Pakula/Brooks, Paramount.
MARIEL HEMINGWAY in *Manhattan*, Rollins-Joffee, UA.
MERYL STREEP in *Kramer vs. Kramer*, Jaffe, Columbia.

DIRECTION

BOB FOSSE for *All That Jazz*, 20th Century-Fox.
FRANCIS COPPOLA for *Apocalypse Now*, Omni Zoetrope, UA.
PETER YATES for *Breaking Away*, 20th Century-Fox.
ROBERT BENTON for *Kramer vs. Kramer*, Jaffe, Columbia.
EDOUARD MOLINARO for *La Cage Aux Folles*, SPA, UA.

WRITING: DIRECTLY FOR THE SCREEN

ALL THAT JAZZ, 20th Century-Fox. Robert Alan Aurthur and Bob Fosse.
...AND JUSTICE FOR ALL, Malton, Columbia. Valerie Curtin and Barry Levinson.
BREAKING AWAY, 20th Century-Fox. Steve Tesich.

THE CHINA SYNDROME, Douglas/IPC, Columbia. Mike Gray, T.S. Cook and James Bridges.
MANHATTAN, Rollins-Joffe. UA. Woody Allen and Marshall Brickman.

WRITING: BASED ON MATERIAL FROM ANOTHER MEDIUM

APOCALYPSE NOW, Omni Zoetrope, UA. John Milius and Francis Coppola.
KRAMER VS. KRAMER, Jaffe, Columbia. Robert Benton.
LA CAGE AUX FOLLES, SPA. UA. Francis Veber, Edouard Molinaro, Marcello Danon and Jean Poiret.
A LITTLE ROMANCE, Pan Arts, Orion. Allan Burns.
NORMA RAE, 20th Century-Fox. Irving Ravetch and Harriet Frank Jr.

CINEMATOGRAPHY

ALL THAT JAZZ, 20th Century-Fox. Giuseppe Rotunno.
APOCALYPSE NOW, Omni Zoetrope, UA. Vittorio Storaro.
THE BLACK HOLE, Disney. Frank Phillips.
KRAMER VS. KRAMER, Jaffe, Columbia. Nestor Almendros.
1941, Spielberg, Universal. William A. Fraker.

ART DIRECTION—SET DECORATION

ALIEN, 20th Century-Fox. Michael Seymour, Les Dilley and Roger Christian; Ian Whittaker.
ALL THAT JAZZ, 20th Century-Fox. Philip Rosenberg and Tony Walton; Edward Stewart and Gary Brink.
APOCALYPSE NOW, Omni Zoetrope, UA. Dean Tavoularis and Angelo Graham; George R. Nelson.
THE CHINA SYNDROME, Douglas/IPC, Columbia. George Jenkins; Arthur Jeph Parker.
STAR TREK–THE MOTION PICTURE, Century Associates, Paramount. Harold Michelson, Joe Jennings, Leon Harris and John Vallone; Linda DeScenna.

COSTUME DESIGN

AGATHA, Sweetwall-Casablanca-First Artists, Warner Bros. Shirley Russell.
ALL THAT JAZZ, 20th Century-Fox. Albert Wolsky.
BUTCH AND SUNDANCE: THE EARLY DAYS, 20th Century-Fox. William Ware Theiss.
THE EUROPEANS, Merchant Ivory, Levitt-Pickman. Judy Moorcroft.
LA CAGE AUX FOLLES, Les Productions Artistes Associes/Da Ma, UA. Piero Tosi, Ambra Danon.

SOUND

APOCALYPSE NOW, Omni Zoetrope, UA. Walter Murch, Mark Berger, Richard Beggs and Nat Boxer.
THE ELECTRIC HORSEMAN, Rastar/Wildwood/Pollack, Columbia. Arthur Piantadosi, Los Fresholtz, Michael Minkler and Al Overton.
METEOR, American International. William McCaughey, Aaron Rochin, Michael J. Kohut and Jack Solomon.
1941, Spielberg, Universal. Robert Knudson, Robert J. Glass, Don MacDougall and Gene S. Cantamessa.
THE ROSE, 20th Century-Fox. Theodore Soderberg, Douglas Williams, Paul Wells and Jim Webb.

FILM EDITING

ALL THAT JAZZ, 20th Century-Fox. Alan Heim.
APOCALYPSE NOW, Omni Zoetrope, UA. Richard Marks, Walter Murch, Gerald B. Greenberg and Lisa Fruchtman.
THE BLACK STALLION, Omni Zoetrope, UA. Robert Dalva.
KRAMER VS. KRAMER, Jaffe, Columbia. Jerry Greenberg.
THE ROSE, 20th Century-Fox. Robert L. Wolfe and C. Timothy O'Meara.

VISUAL EFFECTS

ALIEN, 20th Century-Fox. H.R. Giger, Carlo Rambaldi, Brian Johnson, Nick Allder and Denys Ayling.
THE BLACK HOLE, Disney. Peter Ellenshaw, Art Cruickshank, Eustace Lycett, Danny Lee, Harrison Ellenshaw and Joe Hale.

MOONRAKER, Eon, UA. Derek Meddings, Paul Wilson and John Evans.
1941, Spielberg, Universal. William A. Fraker, A.D. Flowers and Gregory Jein.
STAR TREK—THE MOTION PICTURE, Century Associates, Paramount. Douglas Trumbull, John Dykstra, Richard Yuricich, Robert Swarthe, Dave Stewart and Grant McCune.

SONG

IT GOES LIKE IT GOES *(Norma Rae*, 20th Century-Fox); Music by David Shire. Lyrics by Norman Gimbel.
THE RAINBOW CONNECTION *(The Muppet Movie*, Henson/Grade/Starger, Associated Film Distribution); Music and Lyrics by Paul Williams and Kenny Ascher.
IT'S EASY TO SAY *(10*, Geoffrey, Orion); Music by Henry Mancini. Lyrics by Robert Wells.
THROUGH THE EYES OF LOVE *(Ice Castles*, Cinemedia, Columbia); Music by Marvin Hamlisch. Lyrics by Carole Bayer Sager.
I'LL NEVER SAY "GOODBYE" *(The Promise*, Weintraub-Heller, Universal); Music by David Shire. Lyrics by Alan and Marilyn Bergman.

SCORING: ORIGINAL MUSIC

THE AMITYVILLE HORROR, American International Pictures. Lalo Schifrin.
THE CHAMP, MGM. Dave Grusin.
A LITTLE ROMANCE, Pan Arts, Orion. Georges Delerue.
STAR TREK-THE MOTION PICTURE, Century Associates, Paramount. Jerry Goldsmith.
10, Geoffrey, Orion. Henry Mancini.

SCORING: ORIGINAL SONG SCORE AND/OR ADAPTATION

ALL THAT JAZZ, 20th Century-Fox. Ralph Burns.
BREAKING AWAY, 20th Century-Fox. Patrick Williams.
THE MUPPET MOVIE, Henson/Grade/Starger, Associated Film Distribution. Paul Williams and Kenny Ascher; Paul Williams.

SHORT FILM: ANIMATED FILM

DREAM DOLL, Bob Godfrey Films/Zagreb Films/Halas and Batchelor, FilmWright. Bob Godfrey and Zlatko Grgic, producers.
EVERY CHILD, National Film Board of Canada. Derek Lamb, producer.
IT'S SO NICE TO HAVE A WOLF AROUND THE HOUSE, AR&T Productions for Learning Corporation of America. Paul Fierlinger, producer.

SHORT FILM: LIVE ACTION

BOARD AND CARE, Ron Ellis Films. Sarah Pillsbury and Ron Ellis, producers.
BRAVERY IN THE FIELD, National Film Board of Canada. Roman Kroitor and Stefan Wodoslawsky, producers.
OH BROTHER, MY BROTHER, Ross Lowell Prods., Pyramid Films, Inc. Carol and Ross Lowell, producers.
THE SOLAR FILM, Wildwood Enterprises Inc. Saul Bass and Michael Britten, producers.
SOLLY'S DINER, Mathias/Zukerman/Hankin Prods. Harry Mathias, Jay Zuckerman and Larry Hankin, producers.

DOCUMENTARY: SHORT SUBJECT

DAE, Vardar Film/Skopje. Risto Teofilovski, producer.
KORYO CELADON, Charlie/Papa Prods, Inc. Donald A. Connolly and James R. Messenger, producers.
NAILS, National Film Board of Canada. Phillip Borsos, producer.
PAUL ROBESON; TRIBUTE TO AN ARTIST, Janus Films Inc., Saul J. Turell, producer.
REMEMBER ME, Dick Young Prods, Ltd. Dick Young, producer.

DOCUMENTARY: FEATURE

BEST BOY, Only Child Motion Pictures, Inc. Ira Wohl, producer.
GENERATION ON THE WIND, More Than One Medium. David A. Vassar, producer.
GOING THE DISTANCE, National Film Board of Canada. Paul Cowan and Jacques Bobet, producers.

THE KILLING GROUND, ABC News Closeup Unit. Steve Singer and Thom Priestley, producers.
THE WAR AT HOME, Catalyst Films/Madison Film Production Co. Glenn Silber and Barry Alexander Brown, producers.

FOREIGN LANGUAGE FILM

THE MAIDS OF WILKO (Poland).
MAMA TURNS A HUNDRED (Spain).
A SIMPLE STORY (France).
THE TIN DRUM (Federal Republic of Germany).
TO FORGET VENICE (Italy).

HONORARY AND OTHER AWARDS

TO ALEC GUINNESS for advancing the art of screen acting through a host of memorable and distinguished performances.
TO HAL ELIAS for his dedication and distinguished service to the Academy of Motion Picture Arts and Sciences.
TO JOHN O. AALBERG, CHARLES G. CLARKE and JOHN G. FRAYNE in appreciation for outstanding service and dedication in upholding the high standards of the Academy of Motion Picture Arts and Sciences.

SPECIAL ACHIEVEMENT AWARDS

For SOUND Editing: ALAN SPURT for *The Black Stallion*, Omni Zoetrope, UA.

IRVING G. THALBERG MEMORIAL AWARD

TO RAY STARK

JEAN HERSHOLT HUMANITARIAN AWARD

TO ROBERT BENJAMIN

SCIENTIFIC OR TECHNICAL AWARDS: ACADEMY AWARD OF MERIT

MARK SERRURIER for the progressive development of the Moviola from the 1924 invention of his father, Iwan Serrurier, to the present Series 20 sophisticated film editing equipment.

SCIENTIFIC OR TECHNICAL AWARDS: SCIENTIFIC AND ENGINEERING AWARD

NEIMAN-TILLAR ASSOCIATES for creative development and MINI-MICRO SYSTEMS, INCORPORATED, for the design and engineering of an Automated Computer Controlled Editing Sound System (ACCESS) for motion-picture post-production.

SCIENTIFIC OR TECHNICAL AWARDS: TECHNICAL ACHIEVEMENT AWARD

MICHAEL V, CHEWEY, WALTER G. EGGERS and ALLEN HECHT of MGM Laboratories for the development of a Computer-Controlled Paper Tape Programmer System and its applications in the motion-picture laboratory.
IRWIN YOUNG, PAUL KAUFMAN and FREDRIK SCHLYTER of Du Art Film Laboratories, Incorporated, for the development of a Computer Controlled Paper Tape Programmer System and its applications in the motion-picture laboratory.
JAMES S. STANFIELD and PAUL W. TRESTER for the development and manufacture of a device for the repair or protection of sprocket holes in motion-picture film.
ZORIN PERISIC of Courier Films., Limited, for the Zoptic Special Optical Effects Device for motion-picture photography.
A.D. FLOWERS and LOGAN R. FRAZEE for the development of a device to control the flight patterns of miniature airplanes during motion picture photography.
PHOTO RESEARCH DIVISION OF KOLLMORGEN CORPORATION for the development of the Spectra Series II Cine Special Exposure Meter for motion-picture photography.
BRUCE LYON and JOHN LAMB for the development of a Video Animation System for testing motion-picture animation sequences.
ROSS LOWELL of Lowel-Light Manufacturing, Incorporated, for the development of compact lighting equipment for motion-picture photography.

ABOVE: Never one for subtlety, Cher always causes a stir with her outfits at the Academy Awards. (1988)

BELOW: With Bruce Willis at her side, 80s screen goddess Demi Moore sweeps into the Oscars in souped-up bike shorts topped with a gold brocade-trimmed bustier. (1989)

ABOVE: Goldie Hawn, escorted by Kurt Russell lives up to her name in this flaxen dress that barely clings to her torso. (1989)

BELOW: Debra Winger seems to do her best to play down her considerable charms in this ill-fitting dress. (1980)

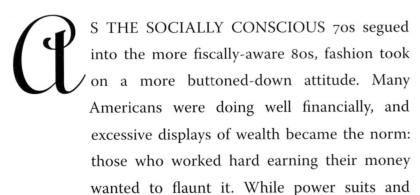

THE LOOK OF THE DECADE

*A*S THE SOCIALLY CONSCIOUS 70s segued into the more fiscally-aware 80s, fashion took on a more buttoned-down attitude. Many Americans were doing well financially, and excessive displays of wealth became the norm: those who worked hard earning their money wanted to flaunt it. While power suits and shoulder pads were all the rage among working women, movie and television stars flaunted their power through over-the-top clothes made of shiny, garish fabrics. Balloon skirts, puffed sleeves, and big hair were the order of the day, reflecting the inflated egos and bank accounts of movie stars and regular people alike.

OPPOSITE: Daryl Hannah (right) looks like a fish out of water as she attempts to recreate the glamour of the 50s screen stars in this over-the-top concoction. (1989)

1980

"I'd like to thank Jake La Motta, and my parents for having me, and my grandmothers and grandfathers for having them, and everyone else that this award means anything to, and the rest of the world... I love everyone."

—Robert De Niro

On the eve of the Awards, psychotic drifter John Hinckley, obsessed with Jodie Foster and her role in Martin Scorsese's *Taxi Driver*, shot and wounded President Reagan. While Hinckley didn't steal the show, his actions did manage to postpone it for twenty-four hours.

Quick-witted host Johnny Carson melted the tension inside the Dorothy Chandler Pavilion with his biting monologue. He introduced Motion Picture Association head Jack Valenti as "not the world's most thrilling speaker," adding, "I suggest while listening to him you do not drive or operate heavy machinery."

It brought down the house, though *Taxi Driver* star, Robert De Niro, who accepted his Best Actor Oscar for *Raging Bull* remained "deeply disturbed." He had joined a winners' circle connected by unusual coincidence. De Niro had portrayed a living person, ex-heavyweight champ Jake La Motta. Best Actress Sissy Spacek played country-and-western icon Loretta Lynn in *Coal Miner's Daughter*, and Best Supporting Actress Mary Steenburgen won for her role as the wife of real-life fortune hunter Melvin Dummar in *Melvin and Howard*. Best Actor nominee John Hurt, De Niro's closest competition, starred as Victorian England's most famous sideshow oddity, John Merrick, in *The Elephant Man*. How ironic, then, that the entirely fictional *Ordinary People* carted away the biggest prizes for Best Picture, Best Director, and Original Screenplay.

LIFE IMITATES ART IMITATES LIFE

CEREMONY: March 31, 1981
Dorothy Chandler Pavilion, Los Angeles Music Center, Los Angeles
HOST: Johnny Carson

BEST PICTURE/BEST DIRECTOR
ROBERT REDFORD (B. 1937)
ORDINARY PEOPLE

Ordinary People scored Hollywood pinup boy of the '70s his first Academy Award. "It's ironic that I won for directing," said Redford to *Variety*'s Army Archerd. Redford's only other close encounter with Oscar was in 1973 for his performance in *The Sting*. "You can only do so much as an actor," Redford explained. *Variety* declared *Ordinary People* "a remarkably intelligent and assured directorial debut in a powerfully intimate domestic drama."

"The chance to be totally responsible for my own vision was exciting," said Redford. "I have a lot of fool's courage. Despite people telling me to stop, it wouldn't work, I just plunged right in and kept going." Following his directorial debut, he continued successfully working both sides of the camera in *The Milagro Beanfield War* (1988), *A River Runs Through It* (1992), *Quiz Show* (1994), and *The Legend of Bagger Vance* (2000).

As an actor, Redford had been a big box-office draw for three decades, during which he appeared in *Inside Daisy Clover* (1966), *Butch Cassidy and the Sundance Kid* (1969), *The Candidate* (1972), *All the President's Men* (1977), and post-Oscar films, *Out of Africa* (1985), *Indecent Proposal* (1993), and *The Legend of Bagger Vance* (2000).

Mary Tyler Moore with Robert Redford

The most bankable name in film history was finally happier and more personally successful making and producing films. His groundbreaking Sundance Institute, founded in 1980, is one of the few commercial film groups to support and showcase independent cinema.

The envelope, please...

BEST ACTOR
ROBERT DE NIRO (B. 1943)
RAGING BULL

"I looked like an animal," said Robert De Niro of his portrayal of Jake La Motta. Nevertheless, this was the first time De Niro showed up to take home his prize for Best Actor.

De Niro's singular career includes—to date—sixty films, three Oscar winners, and two nominations. Though he made his film debut in Brian De Palma's *The Wedding Party* (1969), it wasn't until his emotional performance in *Bang the Drum Slowly* (1973), his ninth film, that he received real recognition. With the release of *Mean Streets* (1973), directed by Martin Scorsese, De Niro rose to become one of America's greatest and most dedicated actors.

Gaining and losing 56 pounds to play the unlikable, inarticulate, violent, and self-destructive boxer, De Niro's often improvised performance in *Raging Bull* kept audiences riveted. All the critics agreed that it was one of the most important movies of all time.

"I'm a little nervous," De Niro averred in his acceptance speech. "I'm sorry. I forgot my lines, so the director wrote them down." (For more on De Niro, see 1974.)

BEST ACTRESS
SISSY SPACEK (B. 1949)
COAL MINER'S DAUGHTER

Thanking Loretta Lynn, "the woman who gave me all that hair," Sissy Spacek, whose signature freckle face and big, pale eyes seemed made for weeping—and in films often do—took away her first Best Actress Oscar for her incarnation of country singer Lynn. "Just being nominated makes me feel like a real actress," she said. But it wasn't just her striking portrait of the rags-to-riches life of the country-music queen—for which she learned how to sing just like Lynn—that showed her to be "a real actress." Sissy Spacek was the genuine article, and would go on to boast six Oscar nominations in a career that began brilliantly with her performance in *Badlands* (1973).

Her Oscar-nominated films include *Carrie* (1976), *Missing* (1982), *The River* (1984), *Crimes of the Heart* (1986), and *In the Bedroom* (2001). Of her performance as Loretta Lynn, *Newsweek* said, "Spacek is one of the most gifted chameleons on the screen."

BEST OF 1980
Best Picture: *Ordinary People*
Best Director: Robert Redford, *Ordinary People*
Best Actor: Robert De Niro, *Raging Bull*
Best Actress: Sissy Spacek, *Coal Miner's Daughter*
Best Supporting Actor: Timothy Hutton, *Ordinary People*
Best Supporting Actress: Mary Steenburgen, *Melvin and Howard*

FIRSTS
• All the action on the set of *Raging Bull* was shut down for four months so that Robert De Niro could keep it going in his digestive system. He gained 56 pounds.

• At 20, Timothy Hutton became the youngest actor to win Best Supporting Actor.

ROLE REVERSAL
Lee Remick was considered for the role of the unyielding wife in *Ordinary People*, but Redford was interested in the dark side of Mary Tyler Moore, who herself confessed, "I tend not to be as optimistic as Mary Richards from *The Mary Tyler Moore Show*. I have anger in me that I carry from my childhood experiences. I'm not kind to myself."

ALWAYS A BRIDESMAID, NEVER A BRIDE
• Donald Sutherland, playing a straitlaced businessman in *Ordinary People*, failed to be nominated for what was perhaps the finest performance of his erratic career. Considered a Hollywood outsider for his committed antiwar protests—often standing alongside Jane Fonda—Sutherland answered questions about his status without resentment. "I know that community, and I didn't expect an Oscar," he said.

• With six Best Actor nominations, Peter O'Toole never got to take one home. "O'Toole is an acting sorcerer. An ethereal figure with strength," said the *Los Angeles Herald Examiner*. When O'Toole was asked about his plight, he responded, "I'd adore to win. Wouldn't you? The fact I've lost five times intrigues me even more."

SINS OF OMISSION
Pictures: *Melvin and Howard, Stardust Memories, My Brilliant Career, Return of the Secaucus Seven, Dressed to Kill, American Gigolo.*

UNMENTIONABLES
• Joseph La Motta, Jake La Motta's brother, portrayed by Joe Pesci, filed a $2.5 million suit against *Raging Bull* producers for the film's "unflattering" portrait of him.

• Speaking of her relationship with her son, Mary Tyler Moore said grimly, "I was kind of a perfectionist mother. I think I was responsible for a lot of alienation, although we've since become close." One month after the film's release, Moore's son committed suicide. President Carter called with his condolences.

• Ellen Burstyn, six-time Oscar nominee and five-time winner, was so outraged by the treatment of her film *Resurrection* that she vowed "to fight for the success of *Resurrection* if it kills me." One Universal executive said, "We've tried everything, but let's face it—God isn't commercial."

 BEST SUPPORTING ACTOR
TIMOTHY HUTTON (B. 1960)
ORDINARY PEOPLE

At the age of 20, Hutton was the youngest actor to score an Oscar. His character, Conrad (who was actually the star of the film and not the supporting player), wrote Kenneth Turan in *New West*, "is one of the truest portrayals of an adolescent in torment since James Dean."

Though Hutton's taste for Hollywood was next to nil, he was the subject of gossip columns when he dated Ronald Reagan's daughter Patti Davis. Hutton's intense, sensitive face and his dedication to his craft were in full display in *Ordinary People* as well as his other films, including *Taps* (1981), *The Falcon and the Snowman* (1985), and *Made in Heaven* (1987). His star dimmed in the 1990s, however, with a succession of television movies.

 BEST SUPPORTING ACTRESS
MARY STEENBURGEN (B. 1953)
MELVIN AND HOWARD

"Well, I'm gonna have to figure out something new to dream about, that's for sure," said the elated winner.

Though director Jonathan Demme's film about a Utah gas-station owner who claimed to be a beneficiary of Howard Hughes's will was charming and seductive, it had little support within the industry. In fact, it sat on the shelf for seventeen months. When it was finally released the critics loved it and it won over zealous fans. Andrew Sarris of the *Village Voice* lauded Steenburgen "as adorably giddy as the late Judy Holliday."

Steenburgen was discovered by Jack Nicholson when he was casting *Goin' South* in 1978. She met and later married its leading man in *Time After Time* (1985), Malcolm McDowell.

She continued to make such films as *Ragtime* (1981), *A Midsummers Night's Dream Sex Comedy* (1982) and *Romantic Comedy* (1983) among others.

 HONORARY AWARD
HENRY FONDA (1905–1982)

"I ain't Henry Fonda. Nobody could have that much integrity," the actor said. Fonda, born in Grand Island, Nebraska, became the founder of an acting dynasty. In his struggling early days he shared an apartment with Jimmy Stewart, whose Republican politics were off-limits to discussion. Fonda reported that Stewart's close friend Ronald Reagan made him "physically ill."

Having been to the altar five times, Fonda admitted, "I was ashamed that a guy with a solid background like mine kept screwing up his personal life." His professional life, however, was a stunning success, boasting such film classics as *You Only Live Once* (1937), *Jezebel* with Bette Davis (1938), *Young Mr. Lincoln* (1939), the John Ford Western *My Darling Clementine* (1946), *The Longest Day* (1962), and *Once Upon a Time in the West* (1968). Nominated once for his performance in *The Grapes of Wrath* (1940), he would finally take home his own golden trophy the following year for his performance in *On Golden Pond* (1981).

(For more on Fonda, see 1981.)

AWARD NOMINATIONS 1980

PICTURE
COAL MINER'S DAUGHTER, Schwartz, Universal. Produced by Bernard Schwartz.
THE ELEPHANT MAN, Brooksfilms, Paramount. Produced by Jonathan Sanger.
ORDINARY PEOPLE, Wildwood, Paramount. Produced by Ronald L. Schwary.
RAGING BULL, Chartoff-Winkler, UA. Produced by Irwin Winkler and Robert Chartoff.
TESS, Renn-Burrill, Columbia. Produced by Calude Bern. Co-produced by Timothy Burrill.

ACTOR
ROBERT DE NIRO in *Raging Bull*, Chartoff-Winkler, UA.
ROBERT DUVALL in *The Great Santini*, Orion-Crosby, Orion.
JOHN HURT in *The Elephant Man*, Brooksfilms, Paramount.
JACK LEMMON in *Tribute*, Turman-Foster, 20th Century-Fox.
PETER O'TOOLE in *The Stunt Man*, Simon, 20th Century-Fox.

ACTRESS
ELLEN BURSTYN in *Resurrection*, Universal.
GOLDIE HAWN in *Private Benjamin*, Warner Bros.
MARY TYLER MOORE in *Ordinary People*, Wildwood, Paramount.
GENA ROWLANDS in *Gloria*, Columbia.
SISSY SPACEK in *Coal Miner's Daughter*, Schwartz, Universal.

SUPPORTING ACTOR
JUDD HIRSCH in *Ordinary People*, Wildwood, Paramount.
TIMOTHY HUTTON in *Ordinary People*, Wildwood, Paramount.
MICHAEL O'KEEFE in *The Great Santini*, Orion-Crosby, Orion.
JOE PESCI in *Raging Bull*, Chartoff-Winkler, UA.
JASON ROBARDS in *Melvin and Howard*, Linson/Phillips/Demme, Universal.

SUPPORTING ACTRESS
EILEEN BRENNAN in *Private Benjamin*, Warner Bros.
EVA LE GALLIENNE in *Resurrection*, Universal.
CATHY MORIARTY in *Raging Bull*, Chartoff-Winkler, UA.
DIANA SCARWID in *Inside Moves*, Goodmark, AFD (Associated Film Distribution).
MARY STEENBURGEN in *Melvin and Howard*, Linson/Phillips/Demme, Universal.

DIRECTION
DAVID LYNCH for *The Elephant Man*, Brooksfilms, Paramount.
ROBERT REDFORD for *Ordinary People*, Wildwood, Paramount.
MARTIN SCORSESE for *Raging Bull*, Chartoff-Winkler, UA.
RICHARD RUSH for *The Stunt Man*, Simon, 20th Century-Fox.
ROMAN POLANSKI for *Tess*, Renn-Burrill, Columbia.

WRITING: DIRECTLY FOR THE SCREEN
BRUBAKER, 20th Century-Fox. W.D. Richter and Arthur Ross.
FAME, MGM. Christopher Gore.
MELVIN AND HOWARD, Linson/Phillips/Demme, Universal. Bo Goldman.
MON ONCLE D'AMERIQUE, Dussart-Andrea, New World. Jean Gruault.
PRIVATE BENJAMIN, Warner Bros. Nancy Meyers, Charles Shyer and Harvey Miller.

WRITING: BASED ON MATERIAL FROM ANOTHER MEDIUM
BREAKER MORANT, Pact Productions, New World. Jonathan Hardy, David Stevens and Bruce Beresford.
COAL MINER'S DAUGHTER, Schwartz, Universal. Tom Rickman.
THE ELEPHANT MAN, Brooksfilms, Paramount. Christopher DeVore, Eric Bergren and David Lynch.
ORDINARY PEOPLE, Wildwood, Paramount. Alvin Sargent.
THE STUNT MAN, Simon, 20th Century-Fox. Lawrence B. Marcus and Richard Rush.

CINEMATOGRAPHY
THE BLUE LAGOON, Columbia. Nestor Almendros.
COAL MINER'S DAUGHTER, Schwartz, Universal. Ralf D. Bode.
THE FORMULA, MGM. James Crabe.
RAGING BULL. Chartoff-Winkler, UA. Michael Chapman.
TESS, Renn-Burrill, Columbia. Geoffrey Unsworth and Ghislain Cloquet.

ART DIRECTION—SET DECORATION
COAL MINER'S DAUGHTER, Schwartz, Universal. John W. Corso; John M. Dwyer.
THE ELEPHANT MAN, Brooksfilms, Paramount. Stuart Craig and Bob Cartwright; Hugh Scaife.
THE EMPIRE STRIKES BACK, Lucasfilm, 20th Century-Fox. Norman Reynolds, Leslie Dilley, Harry Lange, and Alan Tomkins; Michael Ford.
KAGEMUSHA (The Shadow Warrior), Toho-Kurosawa, 20th Century-Fox. Yoshiro Muraki.
TESS, Renn-Burrill, Columbia. Pierre Guffroy and Jack Stephens.

COSTUME DESIGN
THE ELEPHANT MAN. Brooksfilms, Paramount. Patricia Norris.
MY BRILLIANT CAREER, Analysis Film Releasing Anna Senior.
SOMEWHERE IN TIME, Rastar-Deutsch, Universal. Jean-Pierre Dorleac.
TESS, Renn-Burrill, Columbia. Anthony Powell.
WHEN TIME RAN OUT, Warner Bros. Paul Zastupnevich.

SOUND
ALTERED STATES, Warner Bros. Arthur Piantadosi, Les Fresholtz, Michael Minkler and Willie D. Burton.
COAL MINER'S DAUGHTER, Schwartz, Universal. Richard Portman, Roger Heman and Jim Alexander.
THE EMPIRE STRIKES BACK, Lucasfilm, 20th Century-Fox. Bill Varney, Steve Maslow, Gregg Landaker and Peter Sutton.
FAME, MGM. Michael J. Kohut Aaron Rochin, Jay M. Harding and Chris Newman.
RAGING BULL, Chartoff-Winkler, UA. Donald O. Mitchell, Bill Nicholson, David J. Kimball and Les Lazarowitz.

FILM EDITING
COAL MINER'S DAUGHTER, Schwartz, Universal. Arthur Schmidt.
THE COMPETITION, Rastar, Columbia. David Blewitt.
THE ELEPHANT MAN, Brooksfilms, Paramount. Anne V. Coates.
FAME, MGM. Gerry Hambling.
RAGING BULL, Chartoff-Winkler, UA. Thelma Schoonmaker.

SONG
FAME (*Fame*, MGM); Music by Michael Gore. Lyrics by Dean Pitchford.
NINE TO FIVE (*Nine To Five*, 20th Century-Fox); Music and Lyrics by Dolly Parton.
ON THE ROAD AGAIN (*Honeysuckle Rose*, Warner Bros.); Music and Lyrics by Willie Nelson.
OUT HERE ON MY OWN (*Fame*, MGM); Music by Michael Gore. Lyrics by Lesley Gore.
PEOPLE ALONE (*The Competition*, Rastar, Columbia); Music by Lalo Schifrin. Lyrics by Wilbur Jennings.

SCORING: ORIGINAL MUSIC
ALTERED STATES, Warner Bros. John Corigliano.
THE ELEPHANT MAN, Brooksfilm Paramount. John Morris.
THE EMPIRE STRIKES BACK, Lucasfilm, 20th Century-Fox. John Williams.
FAME, MGM. Michael Gore.
TESS, Renn-Burrill, Columbia. Philippe Sarde.

SHORT FILMS: ANIMATED
ALL NOTHING, Radio Canada. Frederic Back, producer.
THE FLY, Pannonia Film, Budapest. Ferenc Rofusz, producer.
HISTORY OF THE WORLD IN THREE MINUTES FLAT, Michael Mills Productions Ltd. Michael Mills, producer.

SHORT FILMS: LIVE ACTION
THE DOLLAR BOTTOM, Rocking Horse Films Limited, Paramount. Lloyd Phillips, producer.
FALL LINE, Sports Imagery, Inc. Bob Carmichael and Greg Lowe, producers.
A JURY OF HER PEERS, Sally Heckel Productions. Sally Heckel, producer.

DOCUMENTARY: SHORT SUBJECTS
DON'T MESS WITH BILL, John Watson and Pen Densham's Insight Productions Inc. John Watson and Pen Densham, producers.
THE ERUPTION OF MOUNT ST. HELENS. Graphic Films Corporation. George Casey, producer.
IT'S THE SAME WORLD, Dick Young Productions, Ltd. Dick Young, producer.
KARL HESS: TOWARD LIBERTY, Halle/Ladue, Inc. Roland Halle and Peter W. Ladue, producers.
LUTHER METKE AT 94, U.C.L.A. Ethnographic Film Program. Richard Hawkins and Jorge Preloran, producers.

DOCUMENTARY: FEATURES
AGEE, James Agee Film Project. Ross Spears, producer.
THE DAY AFTER TRINITY, Jon Else Productions. Jon Else, producer.
FROM MAO TO MOZART: ISAAC STERN IN CHINA, The Hopewell Foundation. Murray Lerner, producer.
FRONT LINE, David Bradbury Productions. David Bradbury, producer.
THE YELLOW STAR—THE PERSECUTION OF THE JEWS IN EUROPE 1933-45, Chronos Films. Bengt von zur Muehlen and Arthur Cohn, producers.

FOREIGN LANGUAGE FILM
CONFIDENCE (Hungary).
KAGEMUSHA (The Shadow Warner) (Japan).
THE LAST METRO (France).
MOSCOW DOES NOT BELIEVE IN TEARS (U.S.S.R.).
THE NEST (Spain).

HONORARY AND OTHER AWARDS
TO HENRY FONDA, the consummate actor, in recognition of his brilliant accomplishments and enduring contribution to the art of motion pictures.
TO FRED HYNES, in appreciation for outstanding service and dedication in upholding the high standards of the Academy of Motion Picture Arts and Sciences. (Medal of Commendation)

SPECIAL ACHIEVEMENT AWARDS
For Visual Effects: BRIAN JOHNSON, RICHARD EDLUND, DENNIS MUREN and BRUCE NICHOLSON for *The Empire Strikes Back*, a Lucasfilm, Ltd. Production, 20th Century-Fox.

IRVING G. THALBERG MEMORIAL AWARD
None given this year.

JEAN HERSHOLT HUMANITARIAN AWARD
None given this year.

SCIENTIFIC OR TECHNICAL AWARDS: ACADEMY AWARD OF MERIT
LINWOOD G. DUNN, CECIL ID. LOVE and ACME TOOL AND MANUFACTURING COMPANY for the concept, engineering and development of the Acme-Dunn Optical Printer for motion picture special effects.

SCIENTIFIC OR TECHNICAL AWARDS: SCIENTIFIC AND ENGINEERING AWARD
JEAN-MARIE LAVALOU, ALAIN MASSERON and DAVID SAMUELSON of Samuelson Alga Cinema S.A. and Samuelson Film Service, Limited, for the engineering and development of the Louma Camera Crane and remote control system for motion picture production.
EDWARD B. KRAUSE of Filmline Corporation for the engineering and manufacture of the micro-demand drive for continuous motion picture film processors.
ROSS TAYLOR for the concept and development of a system of air guns for propelling objects used in special effects motion picture production.
DR. BERNHARD KUHL and DR. WERNER BLOCK of OSRAM GmbH, for the progressive engineering and manufacture of the OSRAM HMI light source for motion picture color photography.
DAVID A. GRAFTON for the optical design and engineering of a telecentric anamorphic lens for motion picture optical effects printers.

SCIENTIFIC OR TECHNICAL AWARDS: TECHNICAL ACHIEVEMENT AWARDS
CARTER EQUIPMENT COMPANY for the development of a continuous contact, total immersion, additive color motion picture printer.
HOLLYWOOD FILM COMPANY for the development of a continuous contact, total immersion, additive color motion picture printer.
ANDRE DeBRIE S.A. for the development of a continuous contact, total immersion, additive color, motion picture printer.
CHARLES VAUGHN and EUGENE NOTTINGHAM of Cinetron Computer Systems, Incorporated, for the development of a versatile general purpose computer system for animation and optical effects motion picture photography.
JOHN W. LANG, WALTER HRASTNIK and CHARLES J. WATSON of Bell and Howell Company for the development and manufacture of a modular continuous contact motion picture film printer.
WORTH BAIRD of LaVezzi Machine Works, Incorporated, for the advanced design and manufacture of a film sprocket for motion picture projectors.
PETER A. REGLA and DAN SLATER of Elicon for the development of a follow-focus system for motion picture optical effects printers and animation stands.

1981

"Only in America could a picture of this subject and this size be made without censorship from the people who put up the money."

—*Warren Beatty, Best Director, Reds*

THE BRITISH ARE RACING BACK

CEREMONY: March 29, 1982
Dorothy Chandler Pavilion, Los Angeles Music Center, Los Angeles
HOST: Johnny Carson

W hen Janet Maslin of the *New York Times* predicted "the most exciting Oscar night in recent years, insiders were braced for a sweep by either Warren Beatty's Communist romance, *Reds*, or the all-star family drama *On Golden Pond*. But hold your dark horses, or, in this case, your chariots! By the time the Best Costume Award was announced, a nail-biting moment for Beatty, who had bet earlier that whoever got this one would also get Best Picture, it was all but over. *Chariots of Fire*, the low-budget British period sports drama, came from behind to snatch the gold and its often combative producer, David Puttnam, gloated. His fierce rivalry with Beatty made for fun viewing as the camera panned back and forth between them.

Even more fun was Bette Midler, presenting Best Song. She chided the Academy for passing her up for her star turn in *The Rose* (1979), but then insisted "my heart is as big as the sky and I have a mind that retains absolutely nothing." She went on, "This is the Oscars. We must be dignified. We must rise to the occasion." With that she pushed up her considerable bosom and brought down the house.

On a more sentimental note, Katharine Hepburn and Henry Fonda, living symbols of "the Golden Age of Hollywood," won for their co-starring chemistry in *On Golden Pond*. A regally glamorous Jane Fonda accepted for her dad, who was too ill to appear. Another icon, Barbara Stanwyck, spectacular in red, was on hand to collect her Honorary Oscar in a tearjerker of a moment.

Loretta Young, gliding imperiously down a staircase, made it clear that not all screen legends were cause for hankies. She chided the current crop of films for their overt sex and gutter language, a direct slam at the nominated *Atlantic City*, whose presentational clips had been severely edited by network censors.

**BEST PICTURE
DAVID PUTTNAM (B. 1941),
*CHARIOTS OF FIRE***

Chariots' stunned producer, David Puttnam, picked up his Golden Boy and said to all assembled, "You are the most extraordinary, generous people on God's earth…"

His last film, *Oliver!*, made thirteen years before, was the last British film to win Best Picture. The following year would see *Gandhi* break all British film Oscar records. *Chariots*, a film about the spiritual journey of a Jew and a Scotsman running for Britain in the 1924 Olympics, had been turned down by every major American studio. After its Oscar win, *Chariots*, which was acted and directed by unknowns, became the most successful foreign film in U.S. box-office history, though not a favorite of critics.

"Chariots of Fire will get the votes of all the joggers," wrote the bemused Andrew Sarris in the *Village Voice*. A

sore winner, Puttnam went on to denigrate Beatty and *Reds*, telling columnist Marilyn Beck that Beatty's Oscar was simply "the Academy's acknowledgment that a gorgeous actor, a pretty boy, could raise $50 million to make that picture…that lumbering picture." Years later, Hollywood would take its revenge on Puttnam. He became studio head of Columbia Pictures and was fired only a year later.

The envelope, please...

Diane Keaton with Warren Beatty

BEST DIRECTOR
WARREN BEATTY (B. 1937)
REDS

Watching all but three of his twelve nominations disappear from what was initially a clear front-runner position, Warren Beatty nevertheless responded professionally to reporters. "I think we were treated very nicely," he said.

Beatty's panoramic biopic—one of the Academy's favorite categories—about American Communist and romantic figure John Reed, was described by *Time* magazine as "a big, smart movie, cast ambitiously...it combines the majestic sweep of *Lawrence of Arabia* and *Dr. Zhivago*, with the rueful comedy and historical fatalism of *Citizen Kane*."

Reds was an American film about a radical journalist theoretician whose firsthand account of Russia's October Revolution was not the sort of subject matter that producers were likely to throw their money at. Yet they did, and Beatty expressed his gratitude: "I think it reflects more particular credit on the freedom of expression we have in our American society...To get this recognition from such a mean, vitriolic, vituperative bunch is more than touching, it's paralyzing."

With *Reds*, once again Beatty—like Orson Welles—scored the most nominations ever for director, writer, actor, and producer, duplicating the milestone he had achieved in 1978 with *Heaven Can Wait*. Beatty was at the point of exhaustion when he completed *Reds*. Some believe that it was his alienation from his staff that resulted in *Reds'* failure to live up to its nomination potential. (For more on Beaty, see 1999.)

Henry Fonda with Katharine Hepburn

BEST ACTOR
HENRY FONDA (1905–1982)
ON GOLDEN POND

Though the Academy had a rule against proxies, they waived it for Henry Fonda so that daughter Jane could stand in for her bedridden dad. Watching from home when the Best Actor Oscar was announced, he called out, "Holy mackaloney." Jane, in an emotional speech, exclaimed, "Oh, Dad, I'm so happy and proud of you..."

The Fondas, not unlike the family played in the film, had a turbulent history, with the elder Fonda playing the cool and elusive father to his estranged daughter as she fought for his attention.

Determined to see that her father got the "legitimate" recognition he deserved, Jane formed her own production company and bought the rights to *On Golden Pond*. Despite the weary-making sentimentality, the moviegoing public's affection for Fonda senior gave the film a surprise box-office bonanza, and it became the highest-grossing movie of 1981 when it broke the $100 million barrier. Four months later, Fonda died at the age of 77.

(For more on Fonda, see 1980.)

BEST OF 1981
Best Picture: *Chariots of Fire*
Best Director: Warren Beatty, *Reds*
Best Actor: Henry Fonda, *On Golden Pond*
Best Actress: Katharine Hepburn, *On Golden Pond*
Best Supporting Actor: John Gielgud, *Arthur*
Best Supporting Actress: Maureen Stapleton, *Reds*
Honorary Award: Barbara Stanwyck

FIRSTS
- Katharine Hepburn's fourth win made her the current all-time Academy Award champ.
- Rick Baker received the first Oscar for makeup for his work on *An American Werewolf in London*. A fight the previous year over the Academy's refusal to create an award for John Hurt's remarkable appearance in *The Elephant Man* resulted in this first-time Oscar.
- Fonda, at 76, and Hepburn, at 74, became the oldest Best Actor and Actress winners. *On Golden Pond* was also the fifth film in Oscar history to win for both Best Actor and Best Actress—something that would not happen again until the next decade.

ROLE REVERSAL
Tom Selleck was initially slated to play Indiana Jones.

SINS OF OMISSION
Picture: *Pennies from Heaven, Cutter's Way, Body Heat, My Dinner with Andre, Rich and Famous, Mommie Dearest*

RIGHT ACTOR/WRONG FILM
Though Henry Fonda deserved the acting award for *On Golden Pond*, his was a sentimental victory and the Academy's attempt to make up for past neglects. In a virtual game of musical chairs, Fonda's victory cost Burt Lancaster an almost certain second Oscar for his ponderous figure bemoaning corruption in *Atlantic City*, Louis Malle's lamentation on a bunch of New Jersey hoods.

UNMENTIONABLES
- David Puttnam won himself the sour grapes award when, backstage, he said, "Hugh [Hudson, director, *Chariots of Fire*] is without a doubt a better director than Warren is, or ever will be. And so are Steven Spielberg and Louis Malle."
- "The return of the xenophobe." A *New York Times* headline shouted, "HOLLYWOOD FUMING OVER WIN BY 'CHARIOTS OF FIRE.'" The article quoted one unnamed Academy official as saying, "I'm afraid this could be the beginning of a trend we saw in the 1960s. Twenty years ago, we started a love affair with the English that lasted about ten years. We have extremely talented people here in America, and I don't want them to get short shrift."
- A wizened Warren Beatty told reporters, "The difference between directing yourself and being directed is the difference between masturbating and making love."

ACTRESS
It was a year of powerful female performances, yet not even a nod was given to Faye Dunaway's captivating performance in *Mommie Dearest*, Sally Field's in *Absence of Malice*, Sissy Spacek's in *Raggedy Man*, or Candice Bergen's in *Rich and Famous*. Not one of them was even nominated for an Oscar.

BEST ACTRESS
KATHARINE HEPBURN (B. 1906)
ON GOLDEN POND

With this victory, Hepburn became the most awarded actress in Academy history, winning her twelfth nomination and scoring a fourth victory. Oscar's best bets that night were for Meryl Streep in *The French Lieutenant's Woman* and Diane Keaton in *Reds*. When Jon Voight announced Hepburn's name, there was an audible gasp. Hepburn told reporters afterward, "I was so dumbfounded. I'm so touched that my fellow actors cared to vote for me, a dear old thing."

Though Fonda and Hepburn had never met, their work together made them fast friends. "Working with Henry brings tears to my eyes," Hepburn said. "He's so sensitive, so giving as an actor." Fonda said, "What a joy to be acting with Katharine. She can play all the levels of a scene, and always do something so fresh with a slight gesture or a look."

During an interview with a reporter, when Hepburn was asked if it was true that there was an aura of magic on the set, true to her "tell it like it is," style, she replied, "Who told you all that stuff?…They're all romantic."

(For more on Hepburn, see 1932–33, 1967, and 1968.)

BEST SUPPORTING ACTOR
SIR JOHN GIELGUD (1904–2000)
ARTHUR

Gielgud confessed to reporters that he was amused by the whole thing, and that he would put the Oscar on a shelf in his bathroom.

In a career that spanned more than sixty years, Gielgud regarded himself as just an "adequate character actor," despite the fact that he was considered the finest speaker of Shakespearean verse in the history of British theater. *Arthur*, in which he played Dudley Moore's butler, marked his entry into popular consciousness.

Though knighted in 1953, Gielgud was famous for his verbal blunders, known affectionately as Gielgudies. After watching a weak performance by an infirm Richard Burton in *Hamlet*, Gielgud told him, "I'll come back when you're better…in health, of course."

Gielgud was nothing if not one of the most versatile actors. His film *Becket* (1965) won him an Oscar nomination. His copious list of credits includes *Julius Caesar* (1953), *Richard III* (1955), *Around the World in Eighty Days* (1956), *The Barretts of Wimpole Street* (1957), *Chimes at Midnight* (1966), *Oh! What a Lovely War* (1969), *Murder on the Orient Express* (1974), and *The Elephant Man* (1980).

BEST SUPPORTING ACTRESS
MAUREEN STAPLETON (B. 1925)
REDS

"I expected to win because I'm old and tired and I deserved it, and I lost three times before."

Stapleton, who played the role of anarchist Emma Goldman in *Reds*, joyfully accepted the Best Supporting Actress prize, thanking "everyone I ever met in my entire life." Speaking of her film persona, Stapleton complained, "Emma Goldman had no redeeming sexual features. She beat up her lovers."

AWARD NOMINATIONS 1981

PICTURE
ATLANTIC CITY, ICC, Paramount. Produced by Denis Heroux and John Kemeny.
CHARIOTS OF FIRE, Enigma, The Ladd Company/Warner Bros. Produced by David Puttnam.
ON GOLDEN POND, ITC/IPC, Universal. Produced by Bruce Gilbert.
RAIDERS OF THE LOST ARK, Lucasfilm, Paramount. Produced by Frank Marshall.
REDS, J.R.S., Paramount. Produced by Warren Beatty.

ACTOR
WARREN BEATTY in *Reds*, J.R.S., Paramount.
HENRY FONDA in *On Golden Pond*, ITC/IPC, Universal.
BURT LANCASTER in *Atlantic City*, ICC, Paramount.
DUDLEY MOORE in *Arthur*, Rollins, Joffe, Morra and Brezner, Orion.
PAUL NEWMAN in *Absence of Malice*, Mirage, Columbia.

ACTRESS
KATHARINE HEPBURN in *On Golden Pond*, ITC/IPC, Universal.
DIANE KEATON in *Reds*, J.R.S., Paramount.
MARSHA MASON in *Only When I Laugh*, Columbia.
SUSAN SARANDON in *Atlantic City*, ICC, Paramount.
MERYL STREEP in *The French Lieutenant's Woman*, Parlon, CA.

SUPPORTING ACTOR
JAMES COCO in *Only When I Laugh*, Columbia.
JOHN GIELGUD in *Arthur*, Rollins, Joffe, Morra and Brezner, Orion.
IAN HOLM in *Chariots of Fire*, Enigma, The Ladd Company/Warner Bros.
JACK NICHOLSON in *Reds*, J.R.S., Paramount.
HOWARD E. ROLLINS, JR. in *Ragtime*, Paramount.

SUPPORTING ACTRESS
MELINDA DILLON in *Absence of Malice*, Mirage, Columbia.
JANE FONDA in *On Golden Pond*, ITC/IPC, Universal.
JOAN HACKETT in *Only When I Laugh*, Columbia.
ELIZABETH McGOVERN in *Ragtime*, Paramount.
MAUREEN STAPLETON in *Reds*, J.R.S., Paramount.

DIRECTION
LOUIS MALLE for *Atlantic City*, ICC, Paramount.
HUGH HUDSON for *Chariots of Fire*, Enigma, The Ladd Company/Warner Bros.
MARK RYDELL for *On Golden Pond*, ITC/IPC, Universal.
STEVEN SPIELBERG for *Raiders of the Lost Ark*, Lucasfilm, Paramount.
WARREN BEATTY for *Reds*, J.R.S., Paramount.

WRITING: DIRECTLY FOR THE SCREEN
ABSENCE OF MALICE, Mirage, Columbia. Kurt Luedtke.
ARTHUR, Rollins, Joffe, Morra and Brezner, Orion. Steve Gordon.
ATLANTIC CITY, ICC, Paramount. John Guare.
CHARIOT'S OF FIRE, Enigma, The Ladd Company/Warner Bros. Collin Welland.

REDS, J.R.S., Paramount. Warren Beatty and Trevor Griffiths.

WRITING: BASED ON MATERIAL FROM ANOTHER MEDIUM
THE FRENCH LIEUTENANT'S WOMAN, Parlon, CA. Harold Pinter.
ON GOLDEN POND, ITC/IPC, Universal. Ernest Thompson.
PENNIES FROM HEAVEN, Ross/Hera, MGM. Dennis Potter.
PRINCE OF THE CITY, Orion/Warner Bros. Jay Presson Allen and Sidney Lumet.
RAGTIME, Paramount. Michael Weller.

CINEMATOGRAPHY
EXCALIBUR, Orion. Alex Thomson.
ON GOLDEN POND, ITC/IPC, Universal. Billy Williams.
RAGTIME, Paramount. Miroslav Ondricek.
RAIDERS OF THE LOST ARK, Lucasfilm, Paramount. Douglas Slocombe.
REDS, J.R.S., Paramount. Vittorio Storaro.

ART DIRECTION—SET DECORATION
THE FRENCH LIEUTENANT'S WOMAN, Parlon, UA. Assheton Gorton; Ann Mollo.
HEAVEN'S GATE, Partisan, UA. Tambi Larsen; Jim Berkey.
RAGTIME, Paramount. John Graysmsrk, Patrizia Von Brandenstein and Anthony Reading; George de Titta, Sr., George de Titta, Jr. and Peter Howitt.
RAIDERS OF THE LOST ARK, Lucasfilm, Paramount. Norman Reynolds and Leslie Dilley; Michael Ford.
REDS, J.R.S., Paramount. Richard Sylbert; Michael Seirton.

COSTUME DESIGN
CHARIOTS OF FIRE, Enigma, The Ladd Company/Warner Bros. Milena Canonero.
THE FRENCH LIEUTENANT'S WOMAN, Parlon, UA. Tom Rand.
PENNIES FROM HEAVEN, Ross/Hera, MGM. Bob Mackie.
RAGTIME, Paramount. Anna Hill Johnstone.
REDS, J.R.S., Paramount. Shirley Russell.

SOUND
ON GOLDEN POND, ITC/IPC, Universal. Richard Portman and David Ronne.
OUTLAND, The Ladd Company. John K. Wilkinson, Robert W. Glass, Jr., Robert M. Thirwell and Robin Gregory.
PENNIES FROM HEAVEN, Ross/Hera, MGM. Michael.J. Kohut, Jay M. Harding, Richard Tyler and Al Overton.
RAIDERS OF THE LOST ARK, Lucasfilm, Paramount. Bill Varney, Steve Maslow, Gregg Landaker and Roy Charman.
REDS, J.R.S., Paramount. Dick Vorisek, To Fleischman and Simon Kaye.

FILM EDITING
CHARIOTS OF FIRE, Enigma, The Ladd Company/Warner Bros. Terry Rawlings.
THE FRENCH LIEUTENANT'S WOMAN, Parlon, UA. John Bloom.
ON GOLDEN POND, ITC/PC, Universal. Robert L. Wolfe.
RAIDERS OF THE LOST ARK, Lucasfilm, Paramount. Michael Kahn.
REDS, J.R.S., Paramount. Dede Allen and Craig McKay.

VISUAL EFFECTS
DRAGONSLAYER, Barwood/Robbins, Paramount. ennis Muren, Phil Tippett, Ken Ralston and Brian Johnson.
RAIDERS OF THE LOST ARK, Lucasfilm, Paramount. Richard Edlund, Kit West, Bruce Nicholson and Joe Johnston.

SONG
ARTHUR'S THEME (Best That You Can Do) (*Arthur*, Rollins, Joffe, Morra and Brezner, Orion); Music and Lyrics by Burt Bacharach, Carole Bayer Sager, Christopher Cross and Peter Allen.
ENDLESS LOVE (*Endless Love*, Barish/Lovell, Universal); Music and Lyrics by Lionel Richie.
THE FIRST TIME IT HAPPENS (*The Great Muppet Caper*, Henson/ITC, Universal); Music and Lyrics by Joe Raposo.
FOR YOUR EYES ONLY (*For Your Eyes Only*, EON, CA); Music by Bill Conti. Lyrics by Mick Leeson.

ONE MORE HOUR (*Ragtime*, Paramount); Music and Lyrics by Randy Newman.

SCORING: ORIGINAL MUSIC
CHARIOTS OF FIRE, Enigma, The Ladd Company/Warner Bros. Vangelis.
DRAGONSLAYER, Barwood/Robbins, Paramount. Alex North.
ON GOLDEN POND, ITC/IPC, Universal. Dave Grusin.
RAGTIME, Paramount. Randy Newman.
RAIDERS OF THE LOST ARK, Lucasfilm, Paramount. John Williams.

MAKEUP
AN AMERICAN WEREWOLF IN LONDON, Lycanthrope/Polygram, Universal. Rick Baker.
HEARTBEEPS, Phillips, Universal. Stan Winston.

SHORT FILMS: ANIMATED FILMS
CRAC, Societe Radio-Canada. rederic Back, producer.
THE CREATION, Will Vinton Productions. Will Vinton, producer.
THE TENDER TALE OF CINDERELLA PENGUIN, National Film Board of Canada. Janet Perlman, producer.

SHORT FILMS: LIVE ACTION
COUPLES AND ROBBERS, Flamingo Pictures Ltd. Christine Oestreicher, producer.
FIRST WINTER, National Film Board of Canada. John N. Smith, producer.
VIOLET, The American Film Institute. Paul Kemp and Shelley Levinson, producers.

DOCUMENTARY: SHORT SUBJECTS
AMERICAS IN TRANSITION, Americas in Transition, Inc. Obie Benz, producer.
CLOSE HARMONY, A Nobel Enterprise. Nigel Nobel Enterprise.
JOURNEY FOR SURVIVAL, Dick Young Productions, Inc. Dick Young producer.
SEE WHAT I SAY, Michigan Women Filmmakers Productions, Linda Chapman, Pam LeBlanc and Freddi Stevens, producers.
URGE TO BUILD, Roland Halle Productions, Inc. Roland Halle and John Hoover, producers.

DOCUMENTARY: FEATURES
AGAINST WIND AND TIDE: A CUBAN ODYSSEY, Seven League Productions, Inc. Suzanne Bauman, Paul Neshamkin and Jim Burroughs, producers.
BROOKLYN BRIDGE, Florentine Films. Ken Burns, producer.
EIGHT MINUTES TO MIDNIGHT: A PORTRAIT OF DR. HELEN CALDICOTT, The Caldicott Project. Mary Benjamin, Susanne Simpson and Boyd Estus, producers.
EL SALVADOR: ANOTHER VIETNAM, Catalyst Media Productions. Glenn Silber and Tete Vasconcellos, producers.
GENOCIDE, Arnold Schwartzman Productions, Inc. Arnold Schwartzman and Rabbi Marvin Hier, producers.

FOREIGN LANGUAGE FILM
THE BOAT IS FULL (Switzerland).
MAN OF IRON (Poland).
MEPHISTO (Hungary).
MUDDY RIVER (Japan).
THREE BROTHERS (Italy).

HONORARY
TO BARBARA STANWYCK, for superlative creativity and unique contribution to the art of screen acting

SPECIAL ACHIEVEMENT AWARDS
For Sound Effects Editing: BEN BURTT and RICHARD L. ANDERSON for *Raiders of the Lost Ark*, Lucasfilm, Paramount.

IRVING G. THALBERG MEMORIAL AWARD
TO ALBERT A. BROCCOLI

JEAN HERSHOLT HUMANITARIAN AWARD
TO DANNY KAYE

GORDON E. SAWYER AWARD
TO JOSEPH B. WALKER

SCIENTIFIC OR TECHNICAL AWARDS: ACADEMY AWARD OF MERIT
The FUJI PHOTO FILM COMPANY, LTD. for the research, development and introduction of a new Ultra-high-speed color negative film for motion pictures.

SCIENTIFIC OR TECHNICAL AWARDS: SCIENTIFIC AND ENGINEERING AWARD
NELSON TYLER for the progressive development and improvement of the Tyler Helicopter motion picture camera platform.
LEONARD SOKOLOW for the concept and design and to HOWARD T. LaZARE for the development of the Consolidated Film Industries' Stroboscan motion picture film viewer.
RICHARD EDLUND and INDUSTRIAL LIGHT AND MAGIC, INCORPORATED for the concept and engineering of a beam-splitter optical composite motion picture printer.
RICHARD EDLUND and INDUSTRIAL LIGHT AND MAGIC, INCORPORATED for the engineering of the Empire Motion Picture Camera System.
EDWARD J. BLASKO and DR. RODERICK T. RYAN of the Eastman Kodak Company for the application of the Prostar Microfilm Processor for motion picture title and special optical effects production.

SCIENTIFIC OR TECHNICAL AWARDS: TECHNICAL ACHIEVEMENT AWARD
HAL LANDAKER for the concept and to ALAN D. LANDAKER for the engineering of the Burbank Studios' Production Sound Department 24-frame color video system.
BILL HOGAN of Ruxton, Ltd. and RICHARD J. STUMPF and DANIEL R. BREWER of Universal City Studios' Production Sound Department for the engineering of a 24-frame color video system.
JOHN DeMUTH for the engineering of a 24-frame video system.
ERNST F. NETMANN of Continental Camera Systems, Inc., for the development of a pitching lens for motion picture photography.
BILL TAYLOR of Universal City Studios for the concept and specifications for a Two Format, Rotating Head, Aerial Image Optical Printer.
PETER D. PARKS of Oxford Scientific Films for the development of the OSF microcosmic zoom device for microscopic photography.
DR. LOUIS STANKIEWICZ and H.L. BLACHFORD for the development of Baryfol sound barrier materials.
DENNIS MUREN and STUART ZIFF of Industrial Light and Magic, Incorporated for the development of a Motion Picture Figure Mover for animation photography.

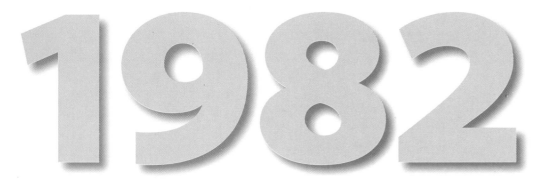

1982

"The Oscar seems to have been confused with the Nobel Peace Prize."

—Janet Maslin, The New York Times

Money talks, and this year it said, "E.T., phone home." Steven Spielberg's little charmer broke every box-office record but failed to ring up the big sale on Awards night. The image of the sweet, ugly extraterrestrial was ubiquitous, creating its own industry in cute refrigerator magnets alone. Such massive commercialism and McDonald's tie-ins may have been deemed a little too much for Academy voters. As was the gender-bending in another big hit, *Tootsie*, which led the drag parade down Main Street, America. Aside from the beautifully coiffed Dustin Hoffman, Julie Andrews wore the pants in *Victor/Victoria*, and John Lithgow high-heeled his way into a Best Supporting nomination for *The World According to Garp*. But it was a peace-loving little man in a simple white loincloth, *Gandhi*, in a debut performance by Ben Kingsley, who got the gold, thanks in large part to British director Richard Attenborough, a ferocious campaigner.

Like the real-life British invasion of the Falklands, Attenborough launched a publicity war for the film, appearing arm in arm with Coretta Scott King and Andrew Young, addressing UNICEF dignitaries, and winning the Martin Luther King Jr. Peace Prize. Politics was also at issue in *Missing*, whose story suggested that the CIA was involved in the overthrow of Chilean dictator Salvador Allende. An outraged State Department filed suit against Universal Pictures.

Movies as news and mini-industries aside, it was also the year of spectacular Oscar performances by Kingsley; Louis Gossett Jr., the first black actor to win an Academy Award since Sidney Poitier and finally, Meryl Streep, with her transcendent Sophie in *Sophie's Choice*. She had unabashedly begged on hands and knees for the role of a lifetime. Pregnant as she accepted her Oscar with a swirl of emotions that ranged from giggles to tears, she gently patted her stomach and said, "Someday I'll be able to tell him, 'You were there, darling.'"

WAGING PEACE

CEREMONY: April 11, 1983
Dorothy Chandler Pavilion, Los Angeles Music Center, Los Angeles
HOSTS: Walter Matthau, Liza Minnelli, Dudley Moore, Richard Pryor

Ben Kingsley

BEST PICTURE/BEST DIRECTOR
RICHARD ATTENBOROUGH (B. 1923)
GANDHI

"It's not me…you truly honor," Attenborough pontificated. "You honor Mahatma Gandhi and his plea to all of us to live in peace."

Not only was *Gandhi* good for the world but it proved to be a gold mine for its producers, though they were initially blind to its prospects. Attenborough had shopped the project for twenty years. Ultimately, he raised the money himself.

Arthur Knight of the *Hollywood Reporter* wrote, "*Gandhi* is more than a superb movie. It's a cinematic event…It is probably the most important film made in the last decade." Rex Reed stated, "It's the kind of massive accomplishment for which ordinary adjectives like 'brilliant' or 'sweeping' or 'magnificent' seem anemic and inadequate."

Attenborough, the stocky, buoyant British actor and director, boasted a directorial career that featured many prestigious films, among them *Oh! What a Lovely War* (1969), *Young Winston* (1972), *A Bridge Too Far* (1977), *A Chorus Line* (1985), *Cry Freedom* (1987), and *Shadowlands* (1993). This was the third year in a row that an actor turned director won the Oscar for Best Picture.

The envelope, please...

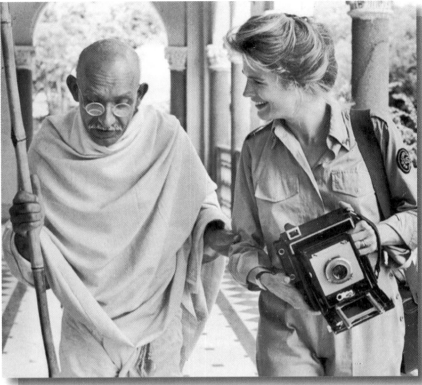

BEST ACTOR
BEN KINGSLEY (B. 1943)
GANDHI

Kingsley, born Krishna Bhanji, was an obscure, half-Indian member of the Royal Shakespeare Company when he prepared for the title role by meditating in his hotel room, surrounded by photographs of the Mahatma.

Ironically, the Best Actor competition pitted newcomer Kingsley against four Oscar-race veterans: five-time nominee (and one-time winner) Dustin Hoffman, eight-time nominee (and two-time winner) Jack Lemmon, six-time nominee Paul Newman, and seven-time nominee Peter O'Toole. "Kingsley's portrayal was so masterfully balanced and magnetic that it makes it seem as though he has stepped through black and white newsreels into the present Technicolor reincarnation," *Variety* reported.

Ben Kingsley with Candice Bergen

After *Gandhi*, Kingsley quickly became one of Britain's most perceptive and intelligent stars since Alec Guinness, providing deeply dimensional and subtle portraits in such films as *Betrayal* (1983), *Turtle Diary* (1985), *Bugsy* (1991), *Twelfth Night* (1996), and *Sexy Beast* (2000, nom.).

BEST ACTRESS
MERYL STREEP (B. 1951)
SOPHIE'S CHOICE

Streep gushed, "Oh, boy. No matter how much you try to imagine what this is like, it's just so incredibly thrilling right down to your toes."

Los Angeles Times critic Charles Champlin called Streep's portrait of a Holocaust survivor "the most moving performance by an actress, intellectually and emotionally." Streep wanted the part so badly that she approached director Alan J. Pakula, fell to her knees, and said, "I have to play this role." She did, and had to master two languages to become Sophie.

Comparisons to Garbo were made. Still, some detractors, including the *New York Daily News*, characterized her performance as "a remarkable display of acting ability, but it was also, like the movie itself, a little too studied and calculating."

BEST OF 1982
Best Picture: *Gandhi*
Best Director: Richard Attenborough, *Gandhi*
Best Actor: Ben Kingsley, *Gandhi*
Best Actress: Meryl Streep, *Sophie's Choice*
Best Supporting Actor: Louis Gossett Jr., *An Officer and a Gentleman*
Best Supporting Actress: Jessica Lange, *Tootsie*
Honorary Award: Mickey Rooney

FIRSTS
- *E.T.* became the highest-grossing film to date, grabbing $187 million.
- Louis Gossett Jr. became the first African-American actor to win Best Supporting Actor, and the first African-American actor to win an Oscar since Sidney Poitier in 1963.
- This was the first time since 1942—and the third time in Oscar history—that an actress was nominated for both Best Actress and Best Supporting Actress. This time it was Jessica Lange.
- The West German film *Das Boot* won six nominations, the highest total ever for a foreign-language film.
- It was the first year that four actors played their parts in drag: Dustin Hoffman (*Tootsie*), Julie Andrews (*Victor/Victoria*), Robert Preston (*Victor/Victoria*), and John Lithgow (*The World According to Garp*).
- Glenn Close, in *The World According to Garp*, her film debut, got the first of five nominations in a decade without winning.

ALWAYS A BRIDESMAID, NEVER A BRIDE
- Once again, as he did last year, Peter O'Toole was nominated without a win, making this his seventh time—tied with Richard Burton—to the altar without getting hitched.
- Regarding his sixth loss, Paul Newman, the quintessence of Hollywood glamour, said, "To say that I'm not interested would be hypocritical...I'm not competitive as an actor or a director, but by the same token I'm enough of a pragmatist to realize that the Academy Awards are good for the industry...you naturally want the largest number of people to see [the film]. So I would say that it's very comforting to be recognized by your peers."

SINS OF OMISSION
Pictures: *Victor/Victoria, Lola, The Road Warrior, Eating Raoul*

UNMENTIONABLES
- To prepare for his part in *Tootsie*, the film in which Dustin Hoffman wanted to explore what makes a man a man, and what makes a woman a woman, Hoffman walked around New York City dressed in women's clothing. *Newsweek* reported, "Jose Ferrer, trapped in an elevator by a strange lady in glasses [Hoffman], turned red at the woman's indecent proposal."
- "Sidney Lumet [Best Director] is the only guy I know who could double-park in front of a whorehouse. He's that fast," said Paul Newman.
- George C. Scott finally showed up for the Academy Awards and was given two tickets in the back of the auditorium.

Richard Gere with Louis Gossett Jr.

 BEST SUPPORTING ACTOR
LOUIS GOSSETT JR. (B. 1936)
AN OFFICER AND A GENTLEMAN

With this victory, Gossett became the first African-American actor to win an Oscar since Sidney Poitier. And it nearly didn't happen.

Variety raved, "Gossett does more with his eyes and facial reactions than others accomplish with pages of dialogue." *Officer*, a sexy military romance, was a box-office smash. The *Los Angeles Times* called it "tropically sexy, unabashed, uninhibited and unashamed of calling forth big emotional responses in several flavors."

'I've got a spirit that guides me, starting from my great-grandmother, who died at the age of 117," said the proud Gossett. Born to a porter and a maid, Gossett began acting at the age of 17, when he damaged his leg playing basketball, his first love. Once he tasted theater and film, Gossett was giving other black actors advice. "Don't just look for black roles," he told them. "Just look for good roles." He got them, including parts in *A Raisin in the Sun* (1961), *Iron Eagle* (1986, and its 1988 and 1992 sequels), *The Punisher* (1989), and *Toy Soldiers* (1991).

Dustin Hoffman with Jessica Lange

 BEST SUPPORTING ACTRESS
JESSICA LANGE (B. 1949)
TOOTSIE

Jessica Lange worked hard for several years to shake her reputation as the girl in King Kong's fist. "I didn't get another part for two years after *King Kong*," she said. After taking a few small roles she attracted some critical notice for her performance in *The Postman Always Rings Twice* (1981). But it wasn't until she played the challenging role of the self-destructive movie actress Frances Farmer that critics took notice. The *Los Angeles Times* called her portrayal in *Frances* a "soaring performance." The intensity of Lange's fragile Farmer provoked her co-star Kim Stanley to suggest to Lange, "Make a comedy as fast as you can." She took her advice, and several weeks later Lange landed herself a comic role in *Tootsie*—for which many said she should have won Best Actress.

Lange has continued to impress the moviegoing public with her acting ability in such films as *Country* (1984), *The Music Box* (1989), *Cape Fear* (1991), and *Blue Sky* (1994), in which she delivered another Oscar-winning performance. (For more on Lange, see 1994.)

 HONORARY AWARD
MICKEY ROONEY (B. 1920)

"When I was 19 years old," said Rooney, "I was the No. 1 star for two years. When I was 40, no one wanted me."

Rooney kissed presenter Bob Hope as he took the stage to receive an Honorary Oscar for "sixty years of work." He added, "It's really for sixty minutes of fun. of love and joy."

The dynamic, diminutive actor was perhaps one of the most famous child stars. Rooney could do anything: he could sing, dance, play piano and drums. His exuberant performances made him a household name when he joined MGM to make the Andy Hardy series and teen musicals with Judy Garland. He became the world's No. 1 box-office star for three years from 1939.

Although he was nominated for Academy Awards for *Babes in Arms* (1939), *The Human Comedy* (1943), *The Bold and the Brave* (1956), and *The Black Stallion* (1979), Rooney had won only special Oscars in 1938 and 1983. His career boasts literally hundreds of films, and he's still at it with his most recent film, *Babe: Pig in the City* (1998).

Rooney's matrimonial life was almost as prolific as his film career. He married eight times, beginning with Ava Gardner and Martha Vickers.

A W A R D N O M I N A T I O N S 1 9 8 2

PICTURE
E.T. THE EXTRA-TERRESTRIAL, Universal. Produced by Steven Spielberg and Kathleen Kennedy.
GANDHI, Columbia. Produced by Richard Attenborough.
MISSING, Lewis, Universal. Produced by Edward Lewis and Mildred Lewis.
TOOTSIE, Mirage/Punch, Columbia. Produced by Sydney Pollack and Dick Richards.
THE VERDICT, Zanuck/Brown, 20th Century-Fox. Produced by Richard D. Zanuck and David Brown.

ACTOR
DUSTIN HOFFMAN in *Tootsie*, Mirage/Punch, Columbia.
BEN KINGSLEY in *Gandhi*, Columbia.
JACK LEMMON in *Missing*, Lewis, Universal.
PAUL NEWMAN in *The Verdict*, Zanuck/Brown, 20th Century-Fox.
PETER O'TOOLE in *My Favorite Year*, Brooksfilm/Gruskoff, MGM/UA.

ACTRESS
JULIE ANDREWS in *Victor/Victoria*, MGM/UA.
JESSICA LANGE in *Frances*, Brooksfilm/EMI, Universal/A.F.D.
SISSY SPACEK in *Missing*, Lewis, Universal.
MERYL STREEP in *Sophie's Choice*, ITC/Pakula-Barish, Universal/A.FD.
DEBRA WINGER in *An Officer and a Gentleman*, Lorimar/Elfand, Paramount.

SUPPORTING ACTOR
CHARLES DURNING in *The Best Little Whorehouse in Texas*, Miller-Milkis-Boyett, Universal.
LOUIS GOSSE, JR. in *An Officer and a Gentleman*, Lorimar/Elfand, Paramount.
JOHN LITHGOW in *The World According to Garp*, Warner Bros.
JAMES MASON in *The Verdict*, Zanuck/Brown, 20th Century-Fox.
ROBERT PRESTON in *Victor/Victoria*, MGM/UA.

SUPPORTING ACTRESS
GLENN CLOSE in *The World According to Garp*, Warner Bros.
TERI GARR in *Tootsie*, Mirage/Punch, Columbia.
JESSICA LANGE in *Tootsie*, Mirage/Punch, Columbia.
KIM STANLEY in *Frances*, Brooksfilm/EMI, Universal/A.F.D.
LESLEY ANN WARREN in *Victor/Victoria*, MGM/UA.

DIRECTION
WOLFGANG PETERSON for *Das Boot*, Bavaria Atelier GmbH, Columbia/PSO.
STEVEN SPIELBERG for *E.T The Extra-Terrestrial*, Universal.
RICHARD ATTENBOROUGH for *Gandhi*, Columbia
SYDNEY POLLACK for *Tootsie*, Mirage/Punch, Columbia.
SIDNEY LUMET for *The Verdict*, Zanuck/Brown, 20 Century-Fox.

WRITING: DIRECTLY FOR THE SCREEN
DINER, Weintraub, MGM/UA. Barry Levinson.
E.T. THE EXTRA-TERRESTRIAL, Universal. Melissa Mathison.
GANDHI, Columbia. John Briley.
AN OFFICER AND A GENTLEMAN, Lorimar/Elfand Paramount. Douglas Day Stewart.
TOOTSIE, Mirage/Punch, Columbia. Larry Gelbart, Murray Schisgal and Don McGuire.

WRITING: BASED ON MATERIAL FROM ANOTHER MEDIA
DAS BOOT, Bavaria Atelier GmbH, Columbia/PSO. Wolfgang Petersen.
MISSING, Lewis, Universal. Costas-Gavras and Don Stewart.
SOPHIE'S CHOICE, ITC/Pakula-Barish, Universal/ A.F.D. Alan J. Pakula.
THE VERDICT, Zanuck/Brown, 20th Century-Fox. David Mamet.
VICTOR/VICTORIA, MGM/UA. Blake Edwards.

CINEMATOGRAPHY
DAS BOOT, Bavaria Atelier GmbH, Columbia/PSO. Jost Vacano.
E.T. THE EXTRA-TERRESTRIAL, Universal. Allen Daviau.
GANDHI, Columbia. Billy Williams and Ronnie Taylor.
SOPHIE'S CHOICE, ITC/Pakula-Barish, Universal/A.F.D. Nestor Almendros.
TOOTSIE, Mirage/Punch, Columbia. Owen Roizman.

ART DIRECTION—SET DECORATION
ANNIE, Rastar, Columbia. Dale Hennesy; Marvin March,
BLADE RUNNER, Deeley-Scott, The Ladd Company/Sir Run Run Shaw. Lawrence G. Paull and David L. Snyder; Linda DeScenna.
GANDHI, Columbia. Stuart Craig and Bob Laing; Michael Seirton.
LA TRAVIATA, Accent, Universal Classics, Franco Zeffirelli; Gianni Quaranta.
VICTOR/VICTORIA, MGM/UA. Rodger Maus, Tim Hutchinson and William Craig Smith; Harry Cordwell.

COSTUME DESIGN
GANDHI, Columbia. John Mollo and Bhanu Athaiya.
LA TRAVIATA, Accent, Universal Classics, Piero Tosi.
SOPHIE'S CHOICE, ITC/Pakula-Barish, Universal/A.F.D. Albert Wolsky.
TRON, Disney. Elois Jenssen and Rosanna Norton.
VICTOR/VICTORIA, MGM/UA, Patricia Norris.

SOUND
DAS BOOT, Bavaria Atelier GmbH, Columbia/PSO. Milan Bor, Trevor Pyke and Mike Le-Mare.
E.T. THE EXTRA-TERRESTRIAL, Universal. Robert Knudson, Robert Glass, Don Digirolamo and Gene Cantamessa.
GANDHI, Columbia. Gerry Humphreys, Robin O'Donoghue, Jonathan Bates and Simon Kaye.
TOOTSIE, Mirage/Punch, Columbia. Arthur Piantadosi, Les Fresholtz, Dick Alexander and Les Lazarowitz.
TRON, Disney. Michael Minkler, Bob Minkler, Lee Minkler and Jim La Rue.

FILM EDITING
DAS BOOT, Bavaria Atelier GmbH, Columbia/PSO. Hannes Nikel.
E.T. THE EXTRA-TERRESTRIAL, Universal. Carol Littleton.
GANDHI, Columbia. John Bloom.
AN OFFICER AND A GENTLEMAN, Lorimar/Elfand, Paramount. Peter Zinner.
TOOTSIE, Mirage/Punch, Columbia. Fredric Steinkamp and William Steinkamp.

VISUAL EFFECTS
BLADE RUNNER, Deeley-Scott, The Ladd Company/Sir Run Run Shaw. Douglas Trumbull, Richard Yuricich and David Dryer.
E.T. THE EXTRA-TERRESTRIAL, Universal. Carlo Rambaldi, Dennis Muren and Kenneth F. Smith.
POLTERGEIST, Spielberg, MGM/UA. Richard Edlund, Michael Wood and Bruce Nicholson.

SOUND EFFECTS EDITING
DAS BOOT, Bavaria Atelier GmbH, Columbia/PSO. Mike La-Mare
E.T. THE EXTRA-TERRESTRIAL, Universal. Charles L. Campbell and Ben Burtt.
POLTERGEIST, Spielberg, MGM/UA. Stephen Hunter Flick and Richard L. Anderson.

SONG
EYE OF THE TIGER (*Rocky III*, Chartoff-Winkler, MGM/UA); Music and Lyrics by Jim Peterik and Frankie Sullivan III.
HOW DO YOU KEEP THE MUSIC PLAYING? (*Best Friends*, Timberlane, Warner Bros.); Music by Michel Legrand. Lyrics by Alan and Marilyn Bergman.
IF WE WERE IN LOVE (*Yes, Giorgio*, MGM/ UA); Music by John Williams. Lyrics by Alan and Marilyn Bergman.
IT MIGHT BE YOU (*Tootsie*, Mirage/Punch, Columbia); Music by Dave Grusin. Lyrics by Alan and Marilyn Bergman.
UP WHERE WE BELONG (*An Officer and a Gentleman*, Lorimar/Elfand, Paramount); Music by Jack Nitzsche and Buffy Sainte-Marie. Lyrics by Will Jennings.

SCORING: ORIGINAL MUSIC
E.T. THE EXTRA-TERRESTRIAL, Universal. John Williams.
GANDHI, Columbia. Ravi Shankar and George Fenton.
AN OFFICER AND A GENTLEMAN, Lorimar/Elfand, Paramount. Jack Nitzsche.
POLTERGEIST, Spielberg, MGM/UA. Jerry Goldsmith.
SOPHIE'S CHOICE, ITC/Pakula-Barish, Universal/A.F.D. Marvin Hamlisch.

SCORING: ORIGINAL SONG SCORE AND/ OR ADAPTATION
ANNIE, Rastar, Columbia. Ralph Burns.
ONE FROM THE HEART, Zoetrope, Columbia. Tom Waits.
VICTOR/VICTORIA, MGM/UA. Henry Mancini and Leslie Bricusse.

MAKEUP
GANDHI, Columbia. Tom Smith.
QUEST FOR FIRE, ICC, 20th Century-Fox. Sarah Monzani and Michele Burke.

SHORT FILMS: ANIMATED
THE GREAT COGNITO, Will Vinton Productions. Will Vinton, producer.
THE SNOWMAN, Snowman Enterprises Ltd. John Coates, producer.
TANGO, Film Polski. Zbigniew Rybczynski, producer.

SHORT FILMS: LIVE ACTION
BALLET ROBOTIQUE, Bob Rogers and Company. Bob Rogers, producer.
A SHOCKING ACCIDENT, Flamingo Pictures Ltd. Christine Oestreicher, producer.
THE SILENCE, The American Film Institute. Michael ibshiyuki Uno and Joseph Benson, producers.
SPLIT CHERRY TREE, Learning Corporation of America. Jan Saunders, producer.
SREDNI VASHTAR, Laurentic Film Productions Ltd. Andrew Birkin, producer.

DOCUMENTARY: SHORT SUBJECTS
GODS OF METAL, A Richter Productions Film. Robert Richter, producer.
IF YOU LOVE THIS PLANET, National Film Board of Canada. Edward La Lorrain and Terri Nash, producers.
THE KLAN: A LEGACY OF HATE IN AMERICA, Guggenheim Productions, Inc. Charles Guggenheim and Werner Schumann, producers.
TO LIVE OR LET DIE, American Film Foundation. Freida Lee Mock, producer.
TRAVELING HOPEFULLY, Arnuthfonyus Films, Inc. John G. Avildsen, producer.

DOCUMENTARY: FEATURES
AFTER THE AXE, National Film Board of Canada. Sturla Gunnarsson and Steve Lucas, producers.
BEN'S MILL, Public Broadcasting Associates-ODYSSEY. John Karol and Michel Chalufour, producers.
IN OUR WATER, A Foresight Films Production. Meg Switzgable, producer.
JUST ANOTHER MISSING KID, Canadian Broadcasting Corporation. John Zaritsky, producer.
A PORTRAIT OF GISELLE, ABC Video Enterprises, Inc. in association with Wishupon Productions, Inc. Joseph Wishy, producer.

FOREIGN LANGUAGE FILM
ALSINO AND THE CONDOR (Nicaragua).
COUP DR TORCHON ("Clean Slate") (France).
THE FLIGHT OF THE EAGLE (Sweden).
PRIVATE LIFE (U.S.S.R.).
VOLVER A EMPEZAR (Spain).

HONORARY
TO MICKEY ROONEY, in recognition of his 60 years of versatility in a variety of memorable film performances.

JEAN HERSHOLT HUMANITARIAN AWARD
TO WALTER MIRISCH

GORDON E. SAWYER AWARD
TO JOHN O. AALBERG

SCIENTIFIC OR TECHNICAL AWARDS: ACADEMY AWARD OF MERIT
AUGUST ARNOLD and ERICH KAESTNER of Arnold & Richter, GmbH, for the concept and engineering of the first operational 35mm, handheld, spinning-mirror reflex, motion picture camera.

SCIENTIFIC OR TECHNICAL AWARDS: SCIENTIFIC AND ENGINEERING AWARD
COLIN F. MOSSMAN and THE RESEARCH AND DEVELOPMENT GROUP OF RANK FILM LABORATORIES, LONDON, for the engineering and implementation of a 4,000 meter printing system for motion picture laboratories.
SANTE ZELLI and SALVATORE ZELLI of Elemack Italia S.4.l., Rome, Italy, for the continuing engineering, design and development that has resulted in the Elemack Camera Dolly Systems for motion picture production.
LEONARD CHAPMAN for the engineering design, development and manufacture of the PeeWee Camera Dolly for motion picture production.
DR. MOHAMMAD S. NOZARI of Minnesota Mining and Manufacturing Company for the research and development of the 3M Photogard protective coating for motion picture film.
BRIANNE MURPHY and DONALD SCHISLER of Mitchell Insert Systems, Incorporated, for the concept, design and manufacture of the MISI Camera Insert Car and Process Trailer.
JACOBUS L. DIMMERS for the engineering and manufacture of the Teccon Enterprises' magnetic transducer for motion picture sound recording and playback.

SCIENTIFIC OR TECHNICAL AWARDS: TECHNICAL ACHIEVEMENT AWARD
RICHARD W. DEATS for the design and manufacture of the "Little Big Crane" for motion picture production.
CONSTANT TRESFON and ADRIAAN DE ROOY of Egripment, and to ED PHILLIPS and CARLOS DE MATTOS of Matthews Studio Equipment, Incorporated, for the design and manufacture of the "Tulip Crane" for motion picture production.
BRAN FERREN of Associates and Ferren for the design and development of a computerized lighting effect system for motion picture photography.
CHRISTIE ELECTRIC CORPORATION and LaVEZZI MACHINE WORKS, INCORPORATED, for the design and manufacture of the Ultramittent film transport for Christie motion picture projectors.

1983

"I'm gonna cry because this show has been as long as my career. I have wondered for twenty-six years what this would feel like."

—Shirley MacLaine

Things got off to a rocky start when the arriving guests were televised upside down. Host Johnny Carson deadpanned, "As you can tell if you saw our opening shot tonight, people are literally standing on their heads with excitement." But even right side up, front-runner *The Right Stuff* didn't fly despite eight nominations. Misjudged a documentary by the public, the stirring saga about the

NO UNCERTAIN TERMS

CEREMONY: April 9, 1984
Dorothy Chandler Pavilion, Los Angeles Music Center, Los Angeles
HOST: Johnny Carson

early days of the U.S. space program thudded at the box-office.

Ironically, Jack Nicholson picked up a statuette for playing a retired astronaut in *Terms of Endearment*. He got laughs and a few raised eyebrows with his mildly hallucinogenic acceptance speech, in which he encouraged "all you rock people down at the Roxy and up in the Rockies" to "rock on." The night's real drama was the snubbing of Barbra Streisand's musical opus *Yentl* and the

unmasking of Best Supporting Actress Linda Hunt's true gender. She played a man in *The Year of Living Dangerously* so convincingly that no one thought otherwise.

In keeping with her role as a competitive mother in *Terms*, Shirley MacLaine beat out her "daughter," Debra Winger, for Best Actress. Her win signaled a sweep for the human-scale family drama, halted only by Robert Duvall's win for playing a country-and-western singer in *Tender Mercies*. Presenter Dolly Parton gushed, "I think you're the greatest. I really do!"

Frank Sinatra fumbled with his cue cards, inadvertently referring to Hersholt honoree, ex-Columbia chief Mike Frankovich, as "the godfather." A faltering Frank Capra couldn't read his cards at all, and had to be interrupted by a taped announcement of Best Director nominees. A final film tribute to the recently departed Ethel Merman (it was once quipped that "Ethel may go but her voice won't") cued Liza Minnelli and Sammy Davis Jr. to lead the audience in a sing-along of "There's No Business Like Show Business." The night that began upside down ended on a high note.

BEST PICTURE/BEST DIRECTOR
JAMES L. BROOKS (B. 1940)
TERMS OF ENDEARMENT

"No!" shouted Brooks when his name was announced for Best Director. The Emmy-winning author of some of TV's best comedies, including *The Mary Tyler Moore Show* and *Taxi*, Brooks and his film took all the major awards—eleven nominations with five wins in all the top categories. And it was Brooks's first time out of the gate. Brooks's response to all the excitement? "I feel like I've been beaten up," said the prize winner as sweat poured from his brow onto the podium.

It had been only three years since a movie about a dysfunctional family, *Ordinary People*, swept the Oscars. *Terms of Endearment*, with brilliant performances by the entire cast, explores the thirty-year, alienated relationship between an exasperating and stubborn mother and her contentious daughter. Both are finally brought together by the daughter's terminal illness. By turns funny and heartbreaking, *Terms* had a great Oscar—or literary—theme: in a crisis, even the worst of us can be our better selves for the sake of those we love.

Jack Nicholson, Shirley MacLaine

The envelope, please...

BEST ACTOR
ROBERT DUVALL (B. 1931)
TENDER MERCIES

Dressed in a cowboy tux with a western tie, Duvall was given a long ovation.

In a brilliant career during which he had been nominated three times for a wide range of roles, including *The Godfather* (1972), *Apocalypse Now* (1979), and *The Great Santini* (1979), Duvall was called "one of the most resourceful, technically proficient, most remarkable actors in America today...he may well be the best we have, the American Olivier," by Vincent Canby of the *New York Times* "

Playing an ex-alcoholic country-and-western singer in *Tender Mercies*, Duvall was selected by the Academy from among five great performances. With respect to the fact that all the other nominees were British, Duvall was inspired to say, "I guess it's me against the limeys."

Shirley MacLaine with Danny DeVito

BEST ACTRESS
SHIRLEY MACLAINE (B. 1934)
TERMS OF ENDEARMENT

"I deserve this," shouted MacLaine. "With the way my mind has been, probably everybody I've ever met in my entire life, and in the other life, might have had something to do with this. God bless the potential that we all have for making anything possible if we think we deserve it."

Warren Beatty's older sister, with her pixieish face and signature red hair, was a Hollywood fixture. She had a run of successes from 1955 to 1963, during which time she was nominated Best Actress—without one win—in *The Trouble with Harry* (1955), *Some Came Running* (1959), *The Apartment* (1960), *Irma La Douce* (1963), and *What a Way to Go!* (1964). "Coming up to bat for the sixth time as Best Actress, MacLaine was a favorite to win," reported *Variety*. MacLaine agreed. "I have wondered for the last twenty-six years what this would feel like," she said. "Thank you for terminating the suspense."

BEST OF 1983
Best Picture: *Terms of Endearment*
Best Director: James L. Brooks, *Terms of Endearment*
Best Actor: Robert Duvall, *Tender Mercies*
Best Actress: Shirley MacLaine, *Terms of Endearment*
Best Supporting Actor: Jack Nicholson, *Terms of Endearment*
Best Supporting Actress: Linda Hunt, *The Year of Living Dangerously*

FIRSTS
- The Oscar show beat its own record, running a sleep-deprived three hours and forty-two minutes.
- James L. Brooks became the fourth director to win an Oscar for his first feature.
- Ingmar Bergman's *Fanny & Alexander* was named Best Foreign Film and won four awards—including cinematography, art direction, and costume design—making it the winner of the most Oscars for a foreign film to date.

ALWAYS A BRIDESMAID, NEVER A BRIDE
The most controversial omission at this year's race (perhaps a deliberate one, according to director Streisand) was *Yentl*. Written, directed, and produced by Barbra Streisand after a fifteen-year struggle to bring it to the screen, the film was the kind of passionate achievement that usually produces Oscars. "If I fail, not only would the film fail, it would set back the cause of women," Streisand told one interviewer. Outside the Chandler Pavilion, fans waved posters reading "Yentl, the Lost Cause. Best Director Nominees—1927 to the present: men 273, women 1." Many, including those who claimed not to be fans of the film, agreed that her movie represented a serious accomplishment; the Academy didn't want to admit that a woman was solely responsible for it. Seven years later, Streisand directed and starred in *The Prince of Tides* (1991). The film received rave reviews and was nominated for seven Academy Awards, including Best Picture. Once again, the Academy omitted Streisand in the Best Director category.

UNMENTIONABLES
- Mariel Hemingway took "getting into the part" to extremes by having her breasts enlarged to play Dorothy Stratton in Bob Fosse's *Star 80*. She then displayed her new ornaments across ten pages of *Playboy*.
- Fifth-time nominee Michael Caine said he lusted for the award because "it might mean I'd get more scripts without other actors' coffee stains on it."
- Taking its rightful place in history, 1983 was a banner year for a Hollywood tradition: the alcoholic on film. And what were the odds that five of the nominees for Best Actor all played men with a drinking problem? Even the *New York Daily News* noticed, commenting, "Did it strike you while watching the Oscars how many of the movies were about drunks?"

Jack Nicholson with Shirley MacLaine

BEST SUPPORTING ACTOR
JACK NICHOLSON (B. 1937)
TERMS OF ENDEARMENT

"I think you have got to have nutty goals in life," Nicholson said. "I'd like to win more Oscars than Walt Disney, and I'd like to win them in every category." Sauntering up to the podium without removing his ubiquitous sunglasses, Nicholson raised a fist and accepted his Oscar with a brief speech, which ended, "All you rock people down at the Roxy and up in the Rockies, rock on."

Nominated eight times for the Oscar, Nicholson, with his devilish smile, was frequently seen on camera as the evening's host invariably made him the subject of many of the ceremony's quips.

(For more on Nicholson, see 1975 and 1997.)

BEST SUPPORTING ACTRESS
LINDA HUNT (B. 1945)
THE YEAR OF LIVING DANGEROUSLY

"They said I would be limited as an actress. No one ever discouraged me from doing it; they only said you must prepare yourself to be limited. And how I feel is that I'm not going to be limited—the sky's the limit." With this win, Hunt became the first actress to claim an Oscar by playing a member of the opposite sex. Challenged by her 4-foot, 9-inch height, Hunt overcame some of the limitations imposed on her size, appearing in *Popeye* (1980), *Dune* and *The Bostonians* (both 1984), *Waiting for the Moon* (1987), and *Younger and Younger* (1993).

BEST FOREIGN FILM
INGMAR BERGMAN (B. 1918)
FANNY & ALEXANDER

"Thanks to the members of the Academy for having good taste," said Bergman's producer, Jorn Bonner, in his thick Swedish accent when he picked up the award for the busy director. *Fanny & Alexander* was a commercial success and introduced a new, more uplifting Bergman. He scored four Oscars, including Best Cinematography by Sven Nykvist, whose graphic boldness helped Bergman realize his own gifts as a great visual stylist. The son of a stern, disciplinary Lutheran pastor who often locked his young son in the closet for minor infractions, Bergman had a traumatic childhood that would become an important theme in his work. His dark, brooding films explored the human condition and, often, the inner lives of women. A favorite in "art" houses frequented by the baby-boom generation, Bergman broke out into more popular consciousness with his later films.

AWARD NOMINATIONS 1983

PICTURE

THE BIG CHILL, Carson, Columbia.
Produced by Michael Shamberg
THE DRESSER, Goldcrest, Columbia.
Produced by Peter Yates.
THE RIGHT STUFF, Chartoff-Winkler, The
Ladd Company through Warner Bros.
Produced by Irwin Winkler and Robert
Chartoff.
TENDER MERCIES, EMI, Universal/AFD.
Produced by Philip S. Hobel.
**TERMS OF ENDEARMENT, Brooks,
Paramount. Produced by James L. Brooks.**

ACTOR

MICHAEL CAINE in *Educating Rita*, Acorn,
Columbia.
TOM CONTI in *Reuben, Reuben*,
Saltair/Shenson, 20th Century Fox
International Classics.
TOM COURTENAY in *The Dresser*,
Goldcrest, Columbia.
**ROBERT DUVALL in *Tender Mercies*, EMI,
Universal/AFD.**
ALBERT FINNEY in *The Dresser*, Goldcrest,
Columbia.

ACTRESS

JANE ALEXANDER in *Testament*,
Entertainment Events, Paramount.
**SHIRLEY MacLAINE in *Terms of
Endearment*, Brooks, Paramount.**
MERYL STREEP in *Silkwood*, ABC, 20th
Century-Fox.
JULIE WALTERS in *Educating Rita*, Acorn,
Columbia.
DEBRA WINGER in *Terms of Endearment*,
Brooks, Paramount.

SUPPORTING ACTOR

CHARLES DURNING, in *To Be or Not To Be*,
Brooksfilms, 20th Century-Fox.
JOHN LITHGOW in *Terms of Endearment*,
Brooks, Paramount.
**JACK NICHOLSON in *Terms of
Endearment*, Brooks, Paramount.**
SAM SHEPARD in *The Right Stuff*, Chartoff-
Winkler, The Ladd Company through
Warner Bros.
RIP TORN in *Cross Creek*, Radnitz/Ritt/
Thorn EMI, Universal.

SUPPORTING ACTRESS

CHER in *Silkwood*, ABC, 20th Century Fox.
GLENN CLOSE in *The Big Chill*, Carson,
Columbia.
**LINDA HUNT in *The Year of Living
Dangerously*, Fields, M-G-M/UA.**
AMY IRVING in *Yentl*, Ladbroke/Barwood,
M-G-M/UA.
ALFRE WOODARD in *Cross Creek*, Radmtz/
Ritt/Thorn EMI, Universal.

DIRECTION

PETER YATES for *The Dresser*,
Goldcrest, Columbia.
INGMAR BERGMAN for
Fanny & Alexander, Embassy.
MIKE NICHOLS for *Silkwood*, ABC,
20th Century-Fox.
BRUCE BERESFORD for *Tender Mercies*,
EMI, Universal/AFD.
**JAMES L. BROOKS for *Terms of
Endearment*, Brooks, Paramount.**

WRITING: DIRECTLY FOR THE SCREEN

THE BIG CHILL, Carson, Columbia.
Lawrence Kasdan and Barbara Benedek.
FANNY & ALEXANDER, Embassy.
Ingmar Bergman.

SILKWOOD, ABC, 20th Century Fox. Nora
Ephron and Alice Arlen.
**TENDER MERCIES, EMI, Universal/AFD.
Horton Foote.**
WARGAMES, Goldberg, M-G-M/UA.
Lawrence Lasker and Walter F. Parkes.

WRITING: BASED ON MATERIAL FROM ANOTHER MEDIUM

BETRAYAL, Horizon, 20th Century Fox
International Classics. Harold Pinter.
THE DRESSER, Goldcrest, Columbia.
Ronald Harwood.
EDUCATING RITA, Acorn, Columbia.
Willy Russell.
REUBEN, REUBEN, Saltair/Shenson, 20th
Century Fox International Classics.
Julius J. Epstein.
**TERMS OF ENDEARMENT, Brooks,
Paramount. James L. Brooks.**

CINEMATOGRAPHY

**FANNY & ALEXANDER, Embassy.
Sven Nykvist.**
FLASHDANCE, Polygram, Paramount.
Don Peterman.
THE RIGHT STUFF, Chartoff-Winkler, The
Ladd Company through Warner Bros.
Caleb Deschanel.
WARGAMES, Goldberg, M-G-M/UA.
William A. Fraker.
ZELIG, Rollins and Joffe, Orion/Warner Bros.
Gordon Willis.

ART DIRECTION—SET DECORATION

**FANNY & ALEXANDER, Embassy.
Anna Asp.**
RETURN OF THE JEDI, Lucasfilm, 20th
Century Fox. Norman Reynolds, Fred Hole
and James Schoppe; Michael Ford.
THE RIGHT STUFF, Chartoff-Winkler, The
Ladd Company through Warner Bros.
Geoffrey Kirkland, Richard J. Lawrence, W.
Stewart Campbell and Peter Romero; Pat
Pending and George R. Nelson.
TERMS OF ENDEARMENT, Brooks,
Paramount. Polly Platt and Harold Michelson;
Tom Pedigo and Anthony Mondello.
YENTL, Ladbroke/Barwood, M-G-M/UA. Roy
Walker and Leslie Tomkins; Tessa Davies.

COSTUME DESIGN

CROSS CREEK, Radnitz/Ritt/Thorn EMI,
Universal. Joe I. Tompkins.
FANNY & ALEXANDER, Embassy. Marik Vos.
HEART LIKE A WHEEL, Aurora, 20th
Century Fox. William Ware Theiss.
THE RETURN OF MARTIN GUERRE,
Marcel Dassault-FR3, European
International Distribution. Anne-Marie
Marchand.
ZELIG, Rollins and Joffe, Orion/Warner Bros.
Santo Loquasto.

SOUND

NEVER CRY WOLF, Disney. Alan R. Splet,
Todd Boekelheide, Randy Thom and
David Parker.
RETURN OF THE JEDI, Lucasfllm, 20th
Century Fox. Ben Burtt, Gary Summers,
Randy Thom and Tony Dawe.
**THE RIGHT STUFF, Chartoff-Winkler,
The Ladd Company through Warner
Bros. Mark Berger, Tom Scott, Randy
Thom and David MacMillan.**
TERMS OF ENDEARMENT, Brooks,
Paramount. Donald O. Mitchell, Rick
Kline, Kevin O'Connell and Jim Alexander.
WARGAMES, Goldberg, M-G-M/UA.
Michael J. Kohut, Carlos de Larios, Aaron
Rochin and Willie D. Burton.

FILM EDITING

BLUE THUNDER, Rastar, Columbia. Frank
Morriss and Edward Abroms.
FLASHDANCE, Polygram, Paramount. Bud
Smith and Walt Mulconery.
**THE RIGHT STUFF, Chartoff-Winkler,
The Ladd Company through Warner
Bros. Glenn Parr, Lisa Fruchtman,
Stephen A. Rotter, Douglas Stewart and
Tom Rolf.**
SILKWOOD, ABC, 20th Century Fox.
Sam O'Steen.
TERMS OF ENDEARMENT, Brooks,
Paramount. Richard Marks.

SOUND EFFECTS EDITING

RETURN OF THE JEDI, Lucasfilm, 20th
Century Fox. Ben Burtt.

THE RIGHT STUFF, Chartoff-Winkler,
The Ladd Company through Warner
Bros. Jay Boekelheide.

SONG

FLASHDANCE ...WHAT A FEELING
(*Flashdance*, Polygram, Paramount);
Music by Giorgio Moroder. Lyrics by
Keith Forsey and Irene Cam.
MANIAC (*Flashdance*, Polygram,
Paramount); Music and Lyrics by Michael
Sembello and Dennis Matkosky.
OVER YOU (*Tender Mercies*, EMI, Universal/
AFD); Music and Lyrics by Austin Roberts
and Bobby Hart.
PAPA, CAN YOU HEAR ME? (*Yentl*,
Ladbroke/Barwood, M-G-M/UA); Music by
Michel Legrand. Lyrics by Alan and
Marilyn Bergman.
THE WAY HE MAKES ME FEEL (*Yentl*,
Ladbroke/Barwood, M-G-M/UA); Music by
Michel Legrand. Lyrics by Alan and
Marilyn Bergman.

SCORING: ORIGINAL MUSIC

CROSS CREEK, Radnitz/Ritt/Thorn EMI,
Universal. Leonard Rosenman.
RETURN OF THE JEDI, Lucasfilm, 20th
Century Fox. John Williams.
**THE RIGHT STUFF, Chartoff-Winkler,
The Ladd Company through Warner
Bros. Bill Conti.**
TERMS OF ENDEARMENT, Brooks,
Paramount. Michael Gore.
UNDER FIRE, Lions Gate, Orion. Jerry
Goldsmith.

SCORING: ORIGINAL SONG SCORE AND/ OR ITS ADAPTATION

THE STING II, Lang, Universal. Lab Schifrin.
TRADING PLACES, Russo, Paramount.
Elmer Bernstein.
**YENTL, Ladbroke/Barwood, M-G-M/UA.
Michel Legrand, Alan and Marilyn
Bergman.**

SHORT FILMS: ANIMATED

MICKEY'S CHRISTMAS CAROL, Disney,
Burny Mattinson, producer.
SOUND OF SUNSHINE—SOUND OF
RAIN, A Hallinan Plus Production. Eda
Godel Hallinan, producer.
**SUNDAE IN NEW YORK, A Motionpicker
Production, Jimmy Picker, producer.**

SHORT FILMS: LIVE ACTION

**BOYS AND GIRLS, An Atlantis Films Ltd.
Production. Janice L. Platt, producer.**
GOODIE-TWO-SHOES, A Timeless Films
Production. Ian Emes, producer.
OVERNIGHT SENSATION, A Bloom Film
Production. Jon H. Bloom, producer.

DOCUMENTARY: SHORT SUBJECTS

**FLAMENCO AT 5:15, A National Film
Board of Canada Production. Cynthia
Scott and Adam Symansky, producers.**
IN THE NUCLEAR SHADOW: WHAT CAN
THE CHILDREN TELL US?, An Impact
Production. Vivienne Verdon-Roe and Eric
Thiermann, producers.
SEWING WOMAN, A DeepFocus
Production. Arthur Doug, producer.
SPACES: THE ARCHITECTURE OF PAUL
RUDOLPH, An Eisenhardt Production.
Robert Eisenhardt, producer.
YOU ARE FREE (IHR ZENT FREI), A
Brokman/Landis Production. Des Brokman
and Ilene Landis, producers.

DOCUMENTARY: FEATURES

CHILDREN OF DARKNESS, A Children of
Darkness Production. Richard Kotuk and
Ara Chekmayan, producers.
FIRST CONTACT, An Arundel Production. Bob
Connolly and Robin Anderson, producers.
**HE MAKES ME FEEL LIKE DANCIN', An
Edgar J. Scherick Associates Production.
Emile Ardolino, producer.**
THE PROFESSION OF ARMS (WAR SERIES
FILM #3), A National Film Board of Canada
Production. Michael Bryans and Tina
Viljoen, producers.
SEEING RED, A Heartland Production. James
Klein and Julia Reichert, producers.

FOREIGN LANGUAGE FILM

CARMEN (Spain).
ENTRE NOUS (France).
FANNY & ALEXANDER (Sweden).

JOB'S REVOLT (Hungary).
LE BAL (Algeria).

HONORARY

TO HAL ROACH, in recognition of his
unparalled record of distinguished
contributions to the motion picture art form.

SPECIAL ACHIEVEMENT AWARD

For Visual Effects: RICHARD EDLUND,
DENNIS MUREN, KEN RALSTON and
PHIL TIPPETT for *Return of the Jedi*,
Lucasfilm, 20th Century Fox.

JEAN HERSHOLT HUMANITARIAN AWARD

TO M.J. FRANKOVICH

GORDON E. SAWYER AWARD

TO DR. JOHN G. FRAYNE

SCIENTIFIC OR TECHNICAL AWARDS: ACADEMY AWARD OF MERIT

DR. KURT LARCHE of OSRAM GmbH for
the research and development of xenon
short-arc discharge lamps for motion
picture projection.

SCIENTIFIC OR TECHNICAL AWARDS: SCIENTIFIC AND ENGINEERING AWARD

JONANTHAN ERLAND and ROGER
DORNEY of Apogee, Incorporated, for the
engineering and development of a reverse
bluescreen traveling matte process for
special effects photography.
GERALD L. TURPIN of Lighttlex
International Limited for the design,
engineering and development of an on-
camera device providing contrast control,
sourceless fill light and special effects for
motion picture photography.
GUNNAR P. MICHELSON for the
engineering and development of an
improved, electronic, high-speed, precision
light valve for use in motion picture
printing machines.

SCIENTIFIC OR TECHNICAL AWARDS: TECHNICAL ACHIEVEMENT AWARDS

WILLIAM G. KROKAUGGER of Mole-
Richardson Company for the design and
engineering of a portable, 12,000 watt,
lighting-control dimmer for use in motion
picture production.
CHARLES J. WATSON, LARRY L.
LANGREHR and JOHN H. STEINER for
the development of the BHP (ekctro-
mechanical) fader for use on continuous
motion picture contact printers.
ELIZABETH D. DE LA MARE of De La Mare
Engineering, Incorporated, for the
progressive development and continuous
research of special effects pyrotechnics
originally designed by Glenn W. De La
Mare for motion picture production.
DOUGLAS FRIES, JOHN LACEY and
MICHAEL SIGRIST for the design and
engineering of a 35mm reflex conversion
camera system for special effects
photography.
JACK CASHIN of Ultra-Stereo Labs,
Incorporated, for the engineering and
development of a 4-channel, stereophonic,
decoding system for optical motion picture
sound track reproduction.
DAVID J. DEGENKOLB for the design and
development of an automated device used
in the silver recovery process in motion
picture laboratories.

1984

The true star of the show, Wolfgang Amadeus Mozart, a flamboyant upstart in his day, might well have appreciated fellow nominee the artist formerly known as Prince, who pulled up in front of the Chandler Pavilion in a purple Rolls-Royce with matching cape. But showy streaks of rebellion were not confined to the young. The venerable Sir Laurence Olivier, presenting Best Picture, tossed out a prepared speech and winged it, to the horror of the show's producers. "Ladies and gentlemen," he began, "I hope I won't let the occasion down too badly." He did just that by not bothering to mention the nominees, simply announcing the winner, as the first entry on the alphabetical list, *Amadeus*. Olivier lucked out by getting it accidentally right. The film's producer, Saul Zaentz, graciously read the names of his competitors while holding his statuette high.

This was the year of Sally Field's moist, immortal "You *like* me!" speech and a gold rush for unknowns. Best Actor F. Murray Abraham pretty much admitted he'd barely heard of himself, and Best Supporting, Dr. Haing S. Ngor, the heart and soul of *The Killing Fields*, wasn't even an actor. The ceremony, which had run far too long in the past (and always would!) had been time-trimmed with the help of stopwatches and tyrannical red warning lights. It resulted in a telecast that looked rushed and too orderly. Shirley MacLaine griped, "They haven't allowed time for any real emotions." But Honorary Oscar recipient James Stewart managed to get in at least one authentic moment from the heart when he looked into the camera and thanked "all you wonderful people out there. You've given me a wonderful life."

MOSTLY MOZART

CEREMONY: March 25, 1985
Dorothy Chandler Pavilion, Los
Angeles Music Center, Los Angeles
HOST: Jack Lemmon

BEST PICTURE/BEST DIRECTOR
MILOS FORMAN (B. 1932)
AMADEUS

"I love this show! I love the Oscars!" said the ordinarily cool critic of the Academy Awards. This time he gushed onstage. As soon as he got backstage, he told a different tale. Forman let it all hang out, insisting, "It's a game, and we'll celebrate tonight and not to worry because tomorrow's another day. Another day, another game."

Amadeus and *A Passage to India* were tied 11 to 11 in the nominations war—both were "prestige" pictures. *Amadeus* had a double advantage in the realm of "most likely to win the Oscar." It fit nicely into two of Oscar's most successful genres: the biopic and the musical or the "behind-the-scenes in the entertainment world"—even classical composers fit the bill. It didn't hurt, either, that *Amadeus* was a large-scale, epic production. With this win, *Amadeus* became the seventh movie in the Award's history to garner eight Oscars. The film commanded great performances by both Abraham and Tom Hulce, and was a box-office hit.

Tom Hulce

This was Forman's second Oscar—the first went to *One Flew Over the Cuckoo's Nest* (1975)—in a dynamic career that began during the Prague Spring of the 1960s in Czechoslovakia. Ironic comedy and an eye for human foibles are hallmarks of Forman's films. Among his Czech films are the delightful *Loves of a Blonde* (1965) and *The Firemen's Ball* (1967). His critically acclaimed American films include *Taking Off* (1971), *Visions of Eight* (1973), and *Hair* (1979). The son of a Jewish professor and his Protestant wife, Forman lost both parents in Nazi concentration camps and was raised by relatives. (For more on Foreman. see 1975.)

The envelope, please…

BEST ACTOR
F. MURRAY ABRAHAM (B. 1939)
AMADEUS

"I still ride the subway and no one recognizes me," said the Hollywood newcomer, who is best known for his role as a piece of fruit in a Fruit of the Loom underwear commercial. For his performance playing Salieri, the court composer who's driven mad by his jealousy of Mozart, Abraham became a member of the small club of actors who won an Oscar the first time they were nominated. Some critics thought his acting was one of the best aspects of the film. "He gave himself heart and soul to the role of Salieri," raved *Los Angeles* magazine's Merrill Shindler. "When he was on the screen—which was through most of the film—goose bumps would flow up and down my spine."

Prior to his film debut the tall, serious-minded Abraham was best known as a New York stage actor. His film career, however, has been an interesting one and includes, among other movies, *The Ritz* (1976), *The Big Fix* (1978), *Scarface* (1983), *The Name of the Rose* (1986), *An Innocent Man* (1989), and *The Bonfire of the Vanities* (1990).

BEST ACTRESS
SALLY FIELD (B. 1946)
PLACES IN THE HEART

"I haven't had an orthodox career, and I wanted more than anything to have your respect. The first time [that I won for *Norma Rae*] I didn't feel it, but this time I feel it, and I can't deny the fact you like me. Right now, you like me!" It was undeniably the most unforgettable acceptance speech in Academy history. Critics reviewed her speech as much as they did her performance in the film. Gene Siskel praised it as "one of the most open, honest admissions of the nervousness that every performer has…a beautiful moment." *USA Today* called it a "teary, 'I'm O.K.—you're O.K.' acceptance speech."

Though the critics didn't think much of the film, Roger Ebert, writing for the *Chicago Sun-Times* said, "*Places in the Heart* is the kind of movie where people tend to dismiss the parts they don't like. I've seen some reviews where the story of Field and the farm is the only part of the movie the critics refer to."

(For more on Field, see 1979)

BEST OF 1984
Best Picture: *Amadeus*
Best Director: Milos Forman, *Amadeus*
Best Actor: F. Murray Abraham, *Amadeus*
Best Actress: Sally Field, *Places in the Heart*
Best Supporting Actor: Haing S. Ngor, *The Killing Fields*
Best Supporting Actress: Peggy Ashcroft, *A Passage to India*
Honorary Award: James Stewart

FIRST
Tri-Star, a brand-new studio formed by Columbia, CBS, and Home Box Office, released its first film, *The Natural*, to a good box-office return.

SIN OF OMISSION
Steve Martin was conspicuously absent from the Oscar list for his display of comic genius in *All of Me*. Then again, Oscar almost never saw a comedy it liked.

ALWAYS A BRIDESMAID, NEVER A BRIDE
Geraldine Page became the only woman alongside Richard Burton and Peter O'Toole to garner seven nominations and no win. The following year she would receive her eighth nomination.

FADE TO BLACK
Ralph Richardson died shortly before he would have discovered that he was one of the nominees for Best Supporting Actor.

UNMENTIONABLES
• Distressed by Hugh Hudson's rewrite of his script, Robert Towne removed his name from the writing credits of *Greystoke* and replaced them with the name of his dog, P. H. Vazak.

• Leading lady Andie MacDowell had not been able to drop her thick Southern accent for her role in *Greystoke*. The voice you really hear is that of Glenn Close, dubbed in. "Now don't bother to ask either Glenn or Warners about this," syndicated columnist Liz Smith cautioned. "Everybody had dummied up in the best whatever-are-you-talking-about fashion."

• David Lean, director of *A Passage to India*, was reported to have complained at a party, "The people at the heads of studios can't or won't read. It makes you wonder if there shouldn't be a hell of a shakeup at the studios."

• Though she had been nominated, everyone knew Vanessa Redgrave was never going to take home the Best Actress prize for *The Bostonians*. Critic Dale Pollack of the *Los Angeles Times* reminded readers that Redgrave was "one of the most controversial winners in Oscar history for her fiery anti-Zionist speech at the 1977 Awards."

• Steven Spielberg raged when the Awards producers considered barring his unwed and pregnant lover, Amy Irving, from appearing on the show.

ROLE REVERSAL
Glenn Close skipped out on James Ivory's adaptation of Henry James's *The Bostonians* to appear in Robert Redford's adaptation of Bernard Malamud's *The Natural*. Said Close, "Finally, I got to play opposite every woman's fantasy, Robert Redford, and I never got to touch him!"

BEST SUPPORTING ACTOR
HAING S. NGOR (1950–1996)
THE KILLING FIELDS

Onstage and backstage were different realities for the survivor of the Vietnam War. When he stepped to the podium to take his award, Ngor raised the Oscar high and said, "This is unbelievable, but so is my entire life." He thanked "God—Buddha—that I am even here tonight." Backstage, however, his anger came through. He said, "The film is real, but not real enough; the cruelty of the Khmer Rouge is not bad enough." Ngor had been a doctor in Cambodia, and after being tortured by the Khmer Rouge and spending four years as a slave laborer he escaped to the U.S. in 1980. Oddly, he landed a film role when he ran into a casting agent at a wedding. Critics found both the film and Ngor's performance remarkable. The *New York Times*'s Vincent Canby wrote, "Dr. Ngor reveals an extraordinary screen presence."

Perhaps the greatest of the film's effects was the reunion that it brought about between Ngor and his niece in France. She had not seen her uncle in ten years, and recognized him in an article about the film. "I found all of my family that is left. I can't speak anymore," Ngor said. After making the film, Ngor returned to his job at an employment agency in Chinatown. He did, however, make a few more films but was tragically murdered by a gang of drug dealers in 1996 while picking up his car in a parking garage.

BEST SUPPORTING ACTRESS
PEGGY ASHCROFT (1907–1991)
A PASSAGE TO INDIA

A no-show at the Awards ceremony, Ashcroft, one of Britain's most distinguished actresses, was a diminutive, humble figure. She rarely appeared in films, confining her career mainly to the stage. Her films include *The Wandering Jew* (1933), *The 39 Steps* (1935), *The Nun's Story* (1959), *Sunday, Bloody Sunday* (1971), and *Madame Sousatzka* (1988).

Said director Lean of Ashcroft's win, "I'm sure she's the most amazed person in the business. She didn't even think she was terribly good in the film."

HONORARY AWARD
JAMES STEWART (1908–1997)

"Sometimes I wonder if I'm doing a Jimmy Stewart imitation of myself."

James Stewart's golden statue was placed in the window of his father's hardware shop in 1940 when he won Best Supporting Actor for *The Philadelphia Story*, and that's where it remained. Stewart was the very incarnation of the earnest, kind, and hardworking young American male. And being this, he won America's heart.

Stewart stumbled into acting accidentally when Joshua Logan, a classmate at Princeton, urged him to join the University Players. His dream, though, was to become an architect. But the die was cast with his drama group, though Stewart never took an acting lesson in his life. America's leading man with the slow drawl emitted an honesty, thoughtfulness, and the kind of sensitivity that brought a lump to the throat.

Stewart was nominated for Oscars for *Mr. Smith Goes to Washington* (1939), *It's a Wonderful Life!* (1946), *Harvey* (1950), and *Anatomy of a Murder* (1959). Among his other films are *You Can't Take It with You* (1938), *Made for Each Other* (1939), and *The Shop Around the Corner* (1940). (For more on Stewart, see 1940.)

AWARD NOMINATIONS 1984

PICTURE
AMADEUS, Zaentz, Orion. Produced by Saul Zaentz.
THE KILLING FIELDS, Enigma, Warner Bros. Produced by David Puttnam.
A PASSAGE TO INDIA, G.W. Films, Columbia. Produced by John Brabourne and Richard Goodwin.
PLACES IN THE HEART, Tri-Star. Produced by Arlene Donovan.
A SOLDIER'S STORY, Caldix, Columbia. Produced by Norman Jewison, Ronald L. Schwary and Patrick Palmer.

ACTOR
F. MURRAY ABRAHAM in *Amadeus*, Zaentz, Orion.
JEFF BRIDGES in *Starman*, Columbia.
ALBERT FINNEY in *Under the Volcano*, Ithaca, Universal.
TOM HULCE in *Amadeus*, Zaentz, Orion.
SAM WATERSTON in *The Killing Fields*, Enigma, Warner Bros.

ACTRESS
JUDY DAVIS in *A Passage to India*, G.W. Films, Columbia.
SALLY FIELD in *Places in the Heart*, Tri-Star.
JESSICA LANGE in *Country*, Touchstone, Buena Vista.
VANESSA REDGRAVE in *The Bostonians*, Merchant Ivory, Almi.
SISSY SPACEK in *The River*, Universal.

SUPPORTING ACTOR
ADOLPH CAESAR in *A Soldier's Story*, Caldix, Columbia.
JOHN MALKOVICH in *Places in the Heart*, Tri-Star.
NORIYUKI "PAT" MORITA in *The Karate Kid*, Columbia.
HAING S. NGOR in *The Killing Fields*, Enigma, Warner Bros.
RALPH RICHARDSON in *Greystoke: The Legend of Tarzan, Lord of the Apes*, Warner Bros.

SUPPORTING ACTRESS
PEGGY ASHCROFT in *A Passage to India*, G.W. Films, Columbia.
GLENN CLOSE in *The Natural*, Tri-Star.
LINDSAY CROUSE in *Places in the Heart*, Tri-Star.
CHRISTINE LAHTI in *Swing Shift*, Warner Bros.
GERALDINE PAGE in *The Pope of Greenwich Village*, Koch/Kirkwood, MGM/UA.

DIRECTION
MILOS FORMAN for *Amadeus*, Zaentz, Orion.
WOODY ALLEN for *Broadway Danny Rose*, Rollins and Joffe, Orion.
ROLAND JOFFE for *The Killing Fields*, Enigma, Warner Bros.
DAVID LEAN for *A Passage to India*, G.W. Films, Columbia.
ROBERT BENTON for *Places in the Heart*, Tri-Star.

WRITING: DIRECTLY FOR THE SCREEN
BEVERLY HILLS COP, Simpson/Bruckheimer, Paramount. Daniel Petrie, Jr. and Danilo Bach.
BROADWAY DANNY ROSE, Rollins/Joffe, Orion. Woody Allen.
EL NORTE, Cinecom International/Island Alive. Gregory Nava and Anna Thomas.
PLACES IN THE HEART, Tri-Star. Robert Benton.
SPLASH, Touchstone, Buena Vista. Lowell Ganz, Babaloo Mandel, Bruce Jay Friedman and Brian Grazer.

WRITING: BASED ON MATERIAL FROM ANOTHER MEDIUM
AMADEUS, Zaentz, Orion. Peter Shaffer.
GREYSTOKE: THE LEGEND OF TARZAN, LORD OF THE APES, Warner Bros. P.H. Vazak and Michael Austin.
THE KILLING FIELDS, Enigma, Warner Bros. Bruce Robinson.
A PASSAGE TO INDIA, G.W. Films, Columbia. David Lean.
A SOLDIER'S STORY, Caldix, Columbia. Charles Fuller.

CINEMATOGRAPHY
AMADEUS, Zaentz, Orion. Miroslav Ondricek.
THE KILLING FIELDS, Enigma, Warner Bros. Chris Menges.
THE NATURAL, Tri-Star. Caleb Deschanel.
A PASSAGE TO INDIA, G.W. Films, Columbia. Ernest Day.
THE RIVER, Universal. Vilmos Zsigmond.

ART DIRECTION—SET DECORATION
AMADEUS, Zaentz, Orion. Patrizia Von Brandenstein; Karel Cerny.
THE COTTON CLUB, Orion. Richard Sylbert; George Gaines and Les Bloom.
THE NATURAL, Tri-Star. Angelo Graham, Mel Bourne, James J. Murakami and Speed Hopkins; Bruce Weintraub.
A PASSAGE TO INDIA, G.W. Films, Columbia. John Box and Leslie Tomkins; Hugh Scaife.
2010, Hyams, MGM/UA. Albert Brenner; Rick Simpson.

COSTUME DESIGN
AMADEUS, Zaentz, Orion. Theodor Pistek.
THE BOSTONIANS, Merchant Ivory, Almi. Jenny Beavan and John Bright.
A PASSAGE TO INDIA, G.W. Films, Columbia. Judy Moorcroft.
PLACES IN THE HEART, Tri-Star. Ann Roth.
2010, Hyams, MGM/UA. Patricia Norris.

SOUND
AMADEUS, Zaentz, Orion. Mark Berger, Tom Scott, Todd Boekelheide and Chris Newman.
DUNE, De Laurentiis, Universal. Bill Varney, Steve Maslow, Kevin O'Connell and Nelson Stoll.
A PASSAGE TO INDIA, G.W. Films, Columbia. Graham V. Hartstone, Nicolas Le Messuier, Michael A. Carter and John Mitchell.
THE RIVER, Universal. Nick Alphin, Robert Thirlwell, Richard Portman and David Boone.
2010, Hyams, MGM/UA. Michael J. Kohut, Aaron Rochin, Carlos De Larios and Gene S. Cantamessa.

FILM EDITING
AMADEUS, Zaentz, Orion. Nena Danevic and Michael Chandler.
THE COTTON CLUB, Orion. Barry Malkin and Robert Q. Lovett.
THE KILLING FIELDS, Enigma, Warner Bros. Jim Clark.
A PASSAGE TO INDIA, G.W. Films, Columbia. David Lean.
ROMANCING THE STONE, El Corazon, 20th Century Fox. Donn Cambern and Frank Morriss.

VISUAL EFFECTS
GHOSTBUSTERS, Columbia. Richard Edlund, John Bruno, Mark Vargo and Chuck Gaspar.
INDIANA JONES AND THE TEMPLE OF DOOM, Lucasfilm, Paramount. Dennis Muren, Michael McAlister, Lorne Peterson and George Gibbs.
2010, Hyams, MGM/UA. Richard Edlund, Neil Krepela, George Jenson and Mark Stetson.

SONG
AGAINST ALL ODDS (TAKE A LOOK AT ME NOW) (*Against All Odds*, New Visions, Columbia); Music and Lyrics by Phil Collins.
FOOTLOOSE (*Footloose*, Melnick, Paramount); Music and Lyrics by Kenny Loggins and Dean Pitchford.
GHOSTBUSTERS (*Ghostbusters*, Columbia); Music and Lyrics by Ray Parker, Jr.
I JUST CALLED TO SAY I LOVE YOU (*The Woman in Red*, Orion); Music and Lyrics by Stevie Wonder.
LET'S HEAR IT FOR THE BOY (*Footloose*, Melnick, Paramount); Music and Lyrics by Tom Snow and Dean Pitchford.

SCORING: ORIGINAL MUSIC
INDIANA JONES AND THE TEMPLE OF DOOM, Lucasfilm, Paramount. John Williams.
THE NATURAL, Tri-Star. Randy Newman.
A PASSAGE TO INDIA, G.W. Films, Columbia. Maurice Jarre.
THE RIVER, Universal. John Williams
UNDER THE VOLCANO, Ithaca, Universal. Alex North.

SCORING: ORIGINAL SONG SCORE AND/OR ADAPTATION
THE MUPPETS TAKE MANHATTAN, Tri-Star. Jeff Moss.
PURPLE RAIN, Warner Bros. Prince.
SONGWRITER, Tri-Star. Kris Kristofferson.

MAKEUP
AMADEUS, Zaentz, Orion. Paul LeBlanc and Dick Smith.
GREYSTOKE: THE LEGEND OF TARZAN, LORD OF THE APES, Warner Bros. Rick Baker and Paul Engelen.
2010, Hyams, MGM/UA. Michael Westmore.

SHORT FILMS: ANIMATED FILMS
CHARADE, A Sheridan College Production. Jon Minnis, Producer.
DOCTOR DE SOTO, Michael Sporn Animation, Inc. Morton Schindel and Michael Sporn, Producers.
PARADISE, National Film Board of Canada. Ishu Patel, Producer.

SHORT FILMS: LIVE ACTION
THE PAINTED DOOR, Atlantis Films Limited in association with the National Film Board of Canada. Michael MacMillan and Janice L. Platt, producer.
TALES OF MEETING AND PARTING, The American Film Institute—Directing Workshop for Women. Sharon Oreck and Lesli Linka Glatter, Producers.
UP, Pyramid Films. Mike Hoover, Producer.

DOCUMENTARY: SHORT SUBJECTS
THE CHILDREN OF SOONG CHING LING, UNICEF and The Soong Ching Ling Foundation. Gary Bush and Paul T.K. Lin, Producers.
CODE GRAY: ETHICAL DILEMMAS IN NURSING, The Nursing Ethics Project/Penlight Productions. Ben Achtenberg and Joan Sawyer, Producers.
THE GARDEN OF EDEN, Florentine Films. Lawrence R. Bott and Roger M. Sherman, Producers.
RECOLLECTIONS OF PAVLOVSK, Leningrad Documentary Film Studio. Irma Kalinina, Producer.
THE STONE CARVERS, Paul Wagner Productions. Marjorie Hunt and Paul Wagner, Producers.

DOCUMENTARY: FEATURES
HIGH SCHOOLS, Guggenheim Productions, Inc. Charles Guggenheim and Nancy Sloss, Producers.
IN THE NAME OF THE PEOPLE, Pan American Films. Alex W. Drehsler and Frank Christopher, Producers.
MARLENE, Zev Braun Pictures, Inc./OKO Film Produktion. Karel Dirka and Zev Braun, Producers.
STREETWISE, Bear Creek Productions, Inc. Cheryl McCall, Producer.
THE TIMES OF HARVEY MILK, Black Sand Educational Productions, Inc. Robert Epstein and Richard Schmiechen, Producers.

FOREIGN LANGUAGE FILM
BEYOND THE WALLS (Israel).
CAMILA (Argentina).
DANGEROUS MOVES (Switzerland).
DOUBLE FEATURE (Spain).
WARTIME ROMANCE (U.S.S.R.).

HONORARY AND OTHER AWARDS
TO JAMES STEWART for his fifty years of memorable performances. For his high ideals both on and off the screen. With the respect and affection of his colleagues.
TO THE NATIONAL ENDOWMENT FOR THE ARTS in recognition of its 20th anniversary and its dedicated commitment to fostering artistic and creative activity and excellence in every area of the arts.

SPECIAL ACHIEVEMENT AWARDS
For Sound Effects Editing: KAY ROSE for *The River*, a Universal Pictures Production.

JEAN HERSHOLT HUMANITARIAN AWARD
TO DAVID L. WOLPER

GORDON E. SAWYER AWARD
TO LINDWOOD G. DUNN

SCIENTIFIC OR TECHNICAL AWARDS: SCENTIFIC AND ENGINEERING AWARD
DONALD A. ANDERSON and DIANA REINERS of 3M Company for the development of "Cinetrak" Magnetic Film #350/351 for motion picture sound recording.
BARRY M. STULTZ, RUBEN AVILA and WES KENNEDY of Film Processing Corporation for the development of FPC 200 PB Fullcoat Magnetic Film for motion picture sound recording.
BARRY M. STULTZ, RUBEN AVILA and WES KENNEDY of Film Processing Corporation for the formulation and application of an improved sound track stripe to 70mm motion picture film, and to JOHN MOSELY for the engineering research involved therein.
KENNETH RICHTER of Richter Clue Equipment for the design and engineering of the R-2 AutoCollimator for examining image quality at the focal plane of motion picture camera lenses.
GUNTHER SCHAIDT and ROSCO LABORATORIES, INCORPORATED, for the development of an improved, non-toxic fluid for creating fog and smoke for motion picture production.
JOHN WHITNEY, JR. and GARY DEMOS of Digital Productions, Incorporated, for the practical simulation of motion picture photography by means of computer-generated images.

SCIENTIFIC OR TECHNICAL AWARDS: TECHNICAL ACHIEVEMENT AWARD
NAT TIFFEN of Tiffen Manufacturing Corporation for the production of high-quality, durable, laminated color filters for motion picture photography.
DONALD TRUMBULL, JONATHAN ERLAND, STEPHEN FOG and PAUL BURK of Apogee, Incorporated, for the design and development of the "Blue Max" highpower, blue-flux projector for traveling matte composite photography.
JONATHAN ERLAND and ROBERT BEALMEAR of Apogee, Incorporated, for an innovative design for front projection screens and an improved method for their construction.
HOWARD J. PRESTON of Preston Cinema Systems for the design and development of a variable speed control device with automatic exposure compensation for motion picture cameras.

1985

Robin Williams, a human hurricane of offbeat humor, breathed fresh, new life into the Awards ceremony, as did the inimitable Cher, who pranced onto the stage in an otherworldly porcupine headdress designed by Bob Mackie. "As you can see, I did read my Academy manual on how to dress like a serious actress," she said. Best Actress Geraldine Page even managed to upstage her own standing ovation by misplacing her shoes.

It was an impromptu, wildly entertaining party for everyone except Steven Spielberg, humiliated by the 0–11 nomination shutout for his first "grown-up" movie, *The Color Purple*. He'd even failed to make the Best Director cut. Adding insult to injury, Irene Cara sang an opening tribute number entitled "Here's to the Losers," in which three Spielberg films—*Jaws*, *Raiders of the Lost Ark*, and *E.T.*—were celebrated. Seventy-seven-year-old Don Ameche got the house to its feet with his sentimental Best Supporting win for *Cocoon*. Bob Hope cracked, "First it was George Burns, now it's Don Ameche—I hope it's a trend."

Anjelica Huston, in a startling green gown that she designed herself, dedicated her Best Supporting Oscar to her terminally ill director dad, John. Barbra Streisand, still smarting from her *Yentl* snub, sang about the trials of putting a movie together before the announcement of Best Director, Sidney Pollack, who led a surprise sweep for the blatantly old-fashioned, romantic biopic *Out of Africa*. Pollack, clearly stunned, rushed to the stage, but not before stopping to shake Spielberg's outstretched hand. Even as Williams shouted a final "Ciao!" to the camera, none of the gala crowd seemed cognizant of the fact that President Reagan had ordered the bombing of Libya simultaneous to the broadcast. In Hollywood, at least, the bombing of *The Color Purple* was the hottest topic around.

FADED PURPLE

CEREMONY: March 24, 1986
Dorothy Chandler Pavilion, Los Angeles Music Center, Los Angeles
HOSTS: Jane Fonda, Alan Alda, Robin Williams

BEST PICTURE/BEST DIRECTOR
SYDNEY POLLACK (B. 1934)
OUT OF AFRICA

"I thought Mr. Huston would get it," said Pollack. No one was more surprised than the director that his film would be the one.

It had been a difficult project to produce from the get-go. Countless directors had tried for years to produce a film out of Isak Dinesen's unforgettable memoir, among them Orson Welles, David Lean, and Nicolas Roeg; the lyrical prose made the book difficult to translate into film. "I thought it was too delicate," said Pollack. "That there was no way to do it as a movie." Somehow he managed, as he had done in the past.

An actor, a director, and a producer, Pollack made some of the most striking and memorable films of the 1960s and '70s, including *They Shoot Horses, Don't They?* (1969), *Jeremiah Johnson* (1972), *The Way We Were* (1973), and *Three Days of the Condor* (1975).

Picket lines of protesters were pitted against well-turned-out stars, claiming that the film "promoted racial stereotypes." Making matters worse, *The Color Purple*, the African-American favorite and *Out of Africa*'s rival at eleven nominations each, lost all of its votes to the Dinesen biopic. But *Africa*, with its epic scope, romance, and stirring locations, made it a safe Oscar bet.

The controversy began during production, when the Kenyans complained that they were being treated with the same disrespect as Ms. Dinesen. Worse still, it was discovered that black extras were being paid less than their white counterparts. Once the news got out, however, salaries were adjusted.

The film was met with equal measures of good and bad reviews. *The Hollywood Reporter* proclaimed, "*Out of Africa* is a splendid, beautifully composed love story in a resplendent holiday film and it should appeal to a worldwide audience." *Time*'s Richard Schickel called it "the free-spirited, full-hearted gesture that everyone has been waiting for." But according to Andrew Sarris of *The Village Voice*, the film "plods along at an elephantine pace."

Meryl Streep, Robert Redford

244

The envelope, please...

William Hurt with Raul Julia

BEST ACTOR
WILLIAM HURT (B. 1950)
KISS OF THE SPIDER WOMAN

"My honor is my work, there is none greater," said Hurt, who isn't one of Oscar's biggest fans. In fact, Hurt's friend Steven Spielberg reprimanded him when he considered sitting it out. "If people are going to honor you, how dare you not accept that?" Spielberg told Hurt.

"Hurt's mesmerizing performance was no stunt," wrote *Time* magazine. "Risking foolishness, he achieves a heartbreaking metamorphosis." Ambivalent about stardom, Hurt lives a reclusive life by Hollywood standards, although he has suffered several scandalous divorces. Perhaps the best of Hurt's career took shape in the 1980s, when he appeared in *Body Heat* (1981), *The Big Chill* (1983), *Children of a Lesser God* (1986), *Broadcast News* (1987), and *The Accidental Tourist* (1988). He went through a brief period of

performing lesser parts in *Alice* (1990) and *Smoke* (1995). But his star rose again with *Jane Eyre* and *Michael* (both 1996), and *A.I.* (2001). He has said of himself, "I'm a character actor trapped in a leading man's body."

Rebecca De Mornay with Geraldine Page

BEST ACTRESS
GERALDINE PAGE (1925–1987)
THE TRIP TO BOUNTIFUL

"Yea, for geriatrics!" shouted an excited Geraldine Page in the pressroom. Just moments before, onstage, F. Murray Abraham had opened the envelope and melted. "Oh, I consider this woman the greatest actress in the English language," he said. No doubt, all the nominees thought he might have been talking about them. But the winner was Page, who, with this win lost her place on the list of those "most likely to win the nomination and lose the award."

Page's thirty-five-year career, in which she was nominated eight times, was legendary. Though deserving, many thought the timing of this award was more a career tribute than a recognition of her touching performance.

Page, who was married to screen star Rip Torn, began her acting career on the stage, performing in the works of Tennessee Williams and often cast as a fading Southern belle. Her film career testified to her seriousness as an actress. Among her best films were *Summer and Smoke* (1961), *Sweet Bird of Youth* (1962), *You're a Big Boy Now* (1967), *Pete 'n' Tillie* (1972), *The Day of the Locust* (1975), *Interiors* (1978), and *The Pope of Greenwich Village* (1984).

BEST OF 1985
Best Picture: *Out of Africa*
Best Director: Sydney Pollack, *Out of Africa*
Best Actor: William Hurt, *Kiss of the Spider Woman*
Best Actress: Geraldine Page, *The Trip to Bountiful*
Best Supporting Actor: Don Ameche, *Cocoon*
Best Supporting Actress: Anjelica Huston, *Prizzi's Honor*
Honorary Award: Paul Newman

FIRSTS
- Two African-American actresses, Oprah Winfrey and Margaret Avery, were nominated—and for their debut performances.
- John Huston, at 79, was the oldest person to be nominated for Best Director.
- All ten nominees for Best Actor and Best Actress were Americans.
- Argentina won its first Oscar for *The Official Story*, a devastating film about the *desaparecidos*—"the disappeared"—the citizens, particularly the children, many of them infants, who were abducted during Argentina's junta in the 1970s.

ROLE REVERSALS
- "I will always thank God that Tina Turner was not able to do *The Color Purple*." Tina Turner was Spielberg's first choice to play the role for which Margaret Avery won a Best Supporting Actress nomination.
- Burt Lancaster was originally offered William Hurt's Oscar-winning role in *Kiss of the Spider Woman*. Director Hector Babenco initially feared that Hurt was too handsome and well built for the part.

SINS OF OMISSION
- *Brazil*, which won the Los Angeles Critics Best Picture, Best Director, and Best Screenplay awards, was given barely a nod by the Academy, with two nominations for Art Direction and Original Screenplay—which it lost.
- Spielberg's roster of losses was taking on conspiratorial proportions. But when *The Color Purple* was snubbed, losing all of its eleven nominations, the *New York Post* called it "Omission Impossible."

ALWAYS A BRIDESMAID, NEVER A BRIDE
For the forty-sixth year, Bob Hope was brought out as the Academy's winner of the most losses. "I think they oughta give me an Oscar just for attendance, don't you?" he quipped. "But I'm happy to be here at this annual Hollywood lottery known at my house as Passover."

UNMENTIONABLES
Many people in the African-American community took offense at *The Color Purple*, insisting that it promoted racial stereotypes by portraying black men as violent and sadistic. Protests came from all fronts, including the NAACP, the coalition against black exploitation. When Oprah Winfrey was accused of playing an Aunt Jemima role, she said, "At first I was very kind. Now I'm just ready to slap them." Quincy Jones remarked, "It's impossible to put the whole story of the black race in America into one picture." In the end the controversy served the movie, making it a hit at the box office.

 **BEST SUPPORTING ACTOR**
DON AMECHE (1908–1993)
COCOON

"Ameche is adorably impish as a dapper bon vivant and he brings the house down with his gloriously triumphant breakdancing," wrote Kathleen Carroll in the *Daily News*.

So nice they made it twice: *Cocoon* proved to be such a box-office bonanza that *Cocoon: The Return* was released in 1988. The suave leading man with the pencil mustache, Ameche sustained his stardom over an unusually long period, appearing in such films as *The Three Musketeers* and *Midnight* (both 1939), *That Night in Rio* (1941), *Heaven Can Wait* (1943), *Wing and a Prayer* (1944), *Suppose They Gave a War and Nobody Came* (1970), *Trading Places* (1983), *Coming to America* (1988), *Homeward Bound: The Incredible Journey* (1993), and *Corrina, Corrina* (1994).

Gwen Verdon with Don Ameche

 BEST SUPPORTING ACTRESS
ANJELICA HUSTON (B. 1951)
PRIZZI'S HONOR

"This means a lot to me, since it comes from a role in which I was directed by my father. And I know it means a lot to him. God, I've got to win another, because then it will be really real, really serious," said Huston in her acceptance speech.

Representing the third generation of a Hollywood royal family, beginning with her grandfather Walter Huston, Anjelica made her film debut at 18 in her father's film *A Walk with Love and Death* (1969). After arriving in Hollywood in 1973, she met Jack Nicholson and began a tempestuous seventeen-year relationship. Her film career began in earnest with *The Postman Always Rings Twice* (1981), and she continued to prove herself a versatile and three-time Oscar nominee. Her films include *This Is Spinal Tap* (1984), *The Dead* (1987), *Enemies, A Love Story* (1989), *The Grifters* (1990), *Manhattan Murder Mystery* and *Addams Family Values* (both 1993), *Agnes Brown* (1999), which she also directed, and *The Golden Bowl* (2001).

 HONORARY AWARD
PAUL NEWMAN (B. 1925)

Beamed in via satellite (no one could persuade him to appear in person), Newman accepted his award saying, "I certainly want to thank the members of the Academy, and I'm especially grateful that this does not come wrapped as a gift certificate to Forest Lawn." According to critic Gene Siskel, Newman later said, "I was relieved that I finally had evened the score with my wife," and that he found the timing of the Award, "very strange."

Newman first dazzled audiences in 1956 with the emotional power of his performance in the biopic *Somebody Up There Likes Me*. And that was the beginning of a career that earned him eight Oscar nominations, but only one win for Scorsese's *The Color of Money* (1986).

Among his other charged performances and Oscar-nominated films are *Cat on a Hot Tin Roof* (1958), *The Hustler* (1961), *Hud* (1963), *Cool Hand Luke* (1967), *Butch Cassidy and the Sundance Kid* (1969), *The Sting* (1973), *Absence of Malice* (1981), and *The Verdict* (1982).

Newman also directed films—the most notable of which starred his new wife, Joanne Woodward, in *Rachel, Rachel* (1968)—that earned him four Academy Award nominations. Newman aggressively committed himself to social causes in the 1970s. (For more on Newman, see 1966.)

PICTURE

THE COLOR PURPLE, Warner Bros. Produced by Steven Spielberg, Kathleen Kennedy, Frank Marshall and Quincy Jones

KISS OF THE SPIDER WOMAN, Island Alive. Produced by David Weisman.

OUT OF AFRICA, Universal. Produced by Sydney Pollack.

PRIZZI'S HONOR, ABC, 20th Century Fox, Produced by John Foreman.

WITNESS, Feldman, Paramount, Produced by Edward S. Feldman.

ACTOR

HARRISON FORD in *Witness*, Feldman, Paramount.

JAMES GARNER in *Murphy's Romance*, Fogwood, Columbia.

WILLIAM HURT in *Kiss of the Spider Woman*, Island Alive.

JACK NICHOLSON in *Prizzi's Honor*, ABC, 20th Century Fox.

JON VOIGHT in *Runaway Train*, Cannon.

ACTRESS

ANNE BANCROFT in *Agnes of God*, Columbia.

WHOOPI GOLDBERG in *The Color Purple*, Warner Bros.

JESSICA LANGE in *Sweet Dreams*, HBO, Tri-Star.

GERALDINE PAGE in *The Trip to Bountiful*, Island.

MERYL STREEP in *Out of Africa*, Universal.

SUPPORTING ACTOR

DON AMECHE in *Cocoon*, Zanuck-Brown, 20th Century Fox,

CLAUS MARIA BRANDAUER in *Out of Africa*, Universal.

WILLIAM HICKEY in *Prizzi's Honor*, ABC, 20th Century Fox.

ROBERT LOGGIA in *Jagged Edge*, Columbia.

ERIC ROBERTS in *Runaway Train*, Cannon.

SUPPORTING ACTRESS

MARGARET AVERY in *The Color Purple*, Warner Bros.

ANJELICA HUSTON in *Prizzi's Honor*, ABC, 20th Century Fox.

AMY MADIGAN in *Twice in a Lifetime*, Bud Yorkin Productions.

MEG TILLY in *Agnes of God*, Columbia.

OPRAH WINFREY in *The Color Purple*, Warner Bros.

DIRECTION

HECTOR BABENCO for *Kiss of the Spider Woman*, Island Alive.

SYDNEY POLLACK for *Out of Africa*, Universal.

JOHN HUSTON for *Prizzi's Honor*, ABC, 20th Century Fox.

AKIRA KUROSAWA for *Ran*, Orion Classics.

PETER WEIR for *Witness*, Feldman, Paramount.

WRITING: DIRECTLY FOR THE SCREEN

BACK TO THE FUTURE, Amblin, Universal. Robert Zemeckis and Bob Gale.

BRAZIL, Embassy International, Universal. Terry Gililam, Tom Stoppard and Charles McKeown.

THE OFFICIAL STORY, Almi. Luis Puenzo and Aida Bortnik.

THE PURPLE ROSE OF CAIRO, Rollins and Joffe, Orion. Woody Allen.

WITNESS, Feldman, Paramount. William Kelley, Pamela Wallace and Earl W. Wallace.

WRITING: BASED ON MATERIAL FROM ANOTHER MEDIUM

THE COLOR PURPLE, Warner Bros. Menno Mayjes.

KISS OF THE SPIDER WOMAN, Island Alive. Leonard Schrader.

OUT OF AFRICA, Universal. Kurt Luedtke.

PRIZZI'S HONOR, ABC, 20th Century Fox. Richard Condon and Janet Roach.

THE TRIP TO BOUNTIFUL, Island. Horton Foote.

CINEMATOGRAPHY

THE COLOR PURPLE, Warner Bros. Alien Daviau.

MURPHY'S ROMANCE, Fogwood, Columbia. William A. Fraker.

OUT OF AFRICA, Universal. David Watkin.

RAN, Orion Classics. Takao Saito, Masaharu Ueda and Asakazu Nakai.

WITNESS, Feldman, Paramount. John Scale.

ART DIRECTION—SET DECORATION

BRAZIL, Embassy International, Universal. Norman Garwood; Maggie Gray.

THE COLOR PURPLE, Warner Bros. J. Michael Riva and Robert W. Welch; Linda DeScenna.

OUT OF AFRICA, Universal. Stephen Grimes; Josie Maccm.

RAN, Orion Classics. Yoshiro Muraki and Shinobu Muraki.

WITNESS, Feldman, Paramount. Stan Jolley; John Anderson.

COSTUME DESIGN

THE COLOR PURPLE, Warner Bros. Aggie Guerard Rodgers.

THE JOURNEY OF NATTY GANN, Disney and Silver Screen Partners II, Buena Vista. Albert Wolsky.

OUT OF AFRICA, Universal. Milena Canonero.

PRIZZI'S HONOR, ABC, 20th Century Fox. Donfeld.

RAN, Orion Classics. Emi Wada.

SOUND

BACK TO THE FUTURE, Amblin, Universal. Bill Varney, B. Tennyson Sebastian II, Robert Thirlwell and William B. Kaplan.

A CHORUS LINE, Embassy/Polygram, Columbia. Donald O. Mitchell, Michael Minkler, Gerry Humphreys and Chris Newman.

LADYHAWKE, Warner Bros. Las Fresholtz, Dick Alexander, Vern Poore and Bud Alper.

OUT OF AFRICA, Universal. Chris Jenkins, Gary Alexander, Larry Stensvold and Peter Handford.

SILVERADO, Columbia. Donald O. Mitchell, Rick Kline, Kevin O'Connell and David Ronne.

FILM EDITING

A CHORUS LINE, Embassy/Polygram, Columbia. John Bloom.

OUT OF AFRICA, Universal. Fredric Steinkamp, William Steinkamp, Pembroke Herring and Sheldon Kahn.

PRIZZI'S HONOR, ABC, 20th Century Fox. Rudi Fehr and Kaja Fehr.

RUNAWAY TRAIN, Cannon. Henry Richardson.

WITNESS, Feldman, Paramount. Thom Noble.

VISUAL EFFECTS

COCOON, Zanuck-Brown, 20th Century Fox. Ken Ralston, Ralph McQuarrie, Scott Farrar and David Berry.

RETURN TO OZ, Disney and Silver Screen Partners II, Buena Vista. Will Vinton, Ian Wingrove, Zoran Perisic and Michael Lloyd.

YOUNG SHERLOCK HOLMES, Amblin/Winkler/Birnbaum, Paramount. Dennis Muren, Kit West, John Ellis and David Allen.

SOUND EFFECTS EDITING

BACK TO THE FUTURE, Amblin, Universal. Charles L. Campbell and Robert Rutledge.

LADYHAWKE, Warner Bros. Bob Henderson and Alan Murray.

RAMBO: FIRST BLOOD PART II, Tri-Star. Frederick J. Brown.

SONG

MISS CELIE'S BLUES (SISTER) (*The Color Purple*, Warner Bros.); Music by Quincy Jones and Rod Temperton. Lyrics by Quincy Jones, Rod Temperton and Lionel Richie.

THE POWER OF LOVE (*Back to the Future*, Amblin, Universal); Music by Chris Hayes and Johnny Colla. Lyrics by Huey Lewis.

SAY YOU, SAY ME (*White Nights*, Columbia); Music and Lyrics by Lionel Richie.

SEPARATE LIVES (*White Nights*, Columbia); Music and Lyrics by Stephen Bishop.

SURPRISE, SURPRISE (*A Chorus Line*, Embassy/Polygram, Columbia); Music by Marvin Hamlisch. Lyrics by Edward Kleban.

SCORING: ORIGINAL MUSIC

AGNES OF GOD, Columbia, Georges Delerue.

THE COLOR PURPLE, Warner Bros. Quincy Jones, Jeremy Lubbock, Rod Temperton, Caiphus Semenya, Andrae Crouch, Chris Boardman, Jorge Calandrelli, Joel Rosenbaum, Fred Steiner, Jack Hayes, Jerry Hey and Randy Kerber.

OUT OF AFRICA, Universal. John Barry.

SILVERADO, Columbia. Bruce Broughton.

WITNESS, Feldman, Paramount. Maurice Jarre.

MAKEUP

THE COLOR PURPLE, Warner Bros. Ken Chase.

MASK, Universal. Michael Westmore and Zoltan Elek.

REMO WILLIAMS: THE ADVENTURE BEGINS, Clark/Spiegel/Bergman, Orion. Carl Fullerton.

SHORT FILMS: ANIMATED FILM

ANNA & BELLA, The Netherlands. Cilia Van Dijk, Producer.

THE BIG SNIT, National Film Board of Canada. Richard Condie and Michael Scott, Producers.

SECOND CLASS MAIL, National Film & Television School. Alison Snowden, Producer.

SHORT FILMS: LIVE ACTION FILMS

GRAFFITI, The American Film Institute. Dianna Costello, Producer.

MOLLY'S PILGRIM, Phoenix Films Jeff Brown and Chris Peizer, Producers.

RAINBOW WAR, Bob Rogers and Company. Bob Rogers, Producers.

DOCUMENTARY: SHORT SUBJECTS

THE COURAGE TO CARE, a United Way Production. Robert Gardner, Producer.

KEATS AND HIS NIGHTINGALE: A BLIND DATE, a Production of the Rhode Island Committee for the Humanities. Michael Crowley and James Wolpaw, Producers.

MAKING OVERTURES—THE STORY OF A COMMUNITY ORCHESTRA, a Rhombus Media, Inc. Production. Barbara Willis Sweete, Producer.

WITNESS TO WAR: DR. CHARLIE CLEMENTS, a Skylight Picture Production. David Goodman, Producer.

THE WIZARD OF THE STRINGS, a Seventh Hour Production. Alan Edelstein, Producer.

DOCUMENTARY: FEATURES

BROKEN RAINBOW, an Earthworks Films Production. Maria Florlo and Victoria Mudd, Producers.

LAS MADRES—THE MOTHERS OF PLAZA DE MAYO, Sponsored by Film Arts Foundation. Susana Munoz and Lourdes Portihlo, Producers.

SOLDIERS IN HIDING, a Filinworks, Inc. Production. Japhet Asher, Producer.

THE STATUE OF LIBERTY, a Florentine Films Production. Ken Burns and Buddy Squires, Producers.

UNFINISHED BUSINESS, a Mouchette Films Production. Steven Okazaki, Producer.

FOREIGN LANGUAGE FILM

ANGRY HARVEST (Federal Republic of Germany).

COLONEL REDL (Hungary).

THE OFFICIAL STORY (Argentina).

THREE MEN AND A CRADLE (France).

WHEN FATHER WAS AWAY ON BUSINESS (Yugoslavia).

HONORARY AND OTHER AWARDS

TO PAUL NEWMAN in recognition of his many and memorable compelling screen performances and for his personal integrity and dedication to his craft.

TO ALEX NORTH in recognition of his brilliant artistry in the creation of memorable music for a host of distinguished motion pictures.

TO JOHN H. WHITNEY, SR. for Cinematic Pioneering.

JEAN HERSHOLT HUMANITARIAN AWARD

TO CHAS (BUDDY) ROGERS

SCIENTIFIC AND ENGINEERING AWARDS: SCIENTIFIC AND ENGINEERING AWARD

IMAX SYSTEMS CORPORATION for a method of filming and exhibiting high-fidelity, large-format, wide-angle motion pictures.

ERNST NETTMAN of E.F. Nettman & Associates for the invention, and to EDWARD PHILLIPS and CARLOS DeMATTOS of Matthews Studio Equipment Inc., for the development, of the Cam-Remote for motion picture photography.

MYRON GORDIN, JOE P. CROOKHAM, JIM DROST and DAVID CROOKHAM of Musco Mobile Lighting, Ltd., for the invention of a method of transporting adjustable, highintensity Luminaires and their application to the motion picture industry.

SCIENTIFIC AND ENGINEERING AWARDS: TECHNICAL ACHIEVEMENT AWARD

DAVID W. SPENCER for the development of an Animation Photo Transfer (APT) process.

HARRISON & HARRISON, OPTICAL ENGINEERS, for the invention and development of Harrison Diffusion Filters for motion picture photography.

LARRY BARTON of Cinematography Electronics, Inc., for a Precision Speed, Crystal-controlled Device for motion picture photography.

ALAN LANDAKER of the Burbank Studios for the Mark IIII Camera Drive for motion picture photography.

1986

F ew movies could have captured the romantic moment when presenter William Hurt opened the envelope and signed the name of his deaf lover, Marlee Matlin, for Best Actress. The beautiful couple hugged and kissed as the audience swooned. Loser Jane Fonda whispered appreciatively, "That's great!" Matlin's film *Children of a Lesser God* was only one among a parade of non-Hollywood nominees led by Oliver Stone's antiwar epic *Platoon*, Woody Allen's *Hannah and Her Sisters*, the eighteenth-century action/thriller *The Mission*, with Robert De Niro, and the picturesque nineteenth-century romance *A Room with a View.*

This could also be called the year of the no-shows. At key points in the ceremony, all we got were vintage photos of winners hastily put up on the screen. Among the missing were the aggressively non-present Woody Allen for Best Screenplay, Michael Caine for Best Supporting, and legendary blue-eyed boy Paul Newman, who felt that he might get lucky if he kept his distance.

The Thalberg Memorial Award went to Steven Spielberg, perhaps in compensation for last year's *Color Purple* shutout. Ironically, Spielberg, the wizard of cinematic technology, announced, "It's time to renew our romance with the word. I'm as culpable as anyone in exalting the image at the expense of the word." The announcement of Paul Newman's win for Best Actor provided the evening's high point, as presenter Bette Davis got riotously befuddled by miscues from the show's director. She then interrupted Newman's proxy, director Robert Wise, with an off-the-cuff speech of her own and refused to get off the stage. Co-host Goldie Hawn dissolved in a fit of giggles, and home viewers were treated to the sometimes magical mess of live TV. *Platoon* finally carried the day, and a somber Oliver Stone was counterbalanced by his glamorous, all-in-pink presenter, who received thunderous applause just for saying, "Hi, I'm Elizabeth Taylor."

GOING UN-HOLLYWOOD

CEREMONY: March 30, 1987
**Dorothy Chandler Pavilion,
Los Angeles Music Center,
Los Angeles**
HOSTS: Paul Hogan, Chevy Chase,
Goldie Hawn

**BEST PICTURE/BEST DIRECTOR
OLIVER STONE (B. 1946)**
PLATOON

"Shocked" was director Stone's first word when his win was announced. "I really think that through this award you're acknowledging the Vietnam veteran," he said. "And I think what you're saying is that you now understand what happened over there, and that it shouldn't happen again. This award really does belong to the Vietnam veterans, both living and dead."

A grunt's-eye view of the Vietnam War, *Platoon* was championed for its realistic evocation of the harrowing experience of the war. More specifically, Stone portrays the battle between two father figures for a young soldier's soul. Critic Joseph McBride commended the film for its "ability to demonstrate how even a good-willed person can become caught up in the process of dehumanizing the enemy and wantonly killing civilians."

Tom Berenger, Mark Moses with Willem Dafoe

After ten years of doors being slammed on the project, Stone was finally able to cobble together support by doing other films, finally winning the backing of independent Hemdale—which had lost money producing Stone's other film that year, *Salvador*—which brought *Platoon* to the screen. Vincent Canby of the *New York Times* called the film "a singular achievement...vivid, terse, exceptionally moving...the tension builds and never lets up...a major piece of work." It soon became a box-office hit, at which point *Time* magazine finally joined the raves with a cover story, "*Platoon* the picture is now *Platoon* the phenomenon." (For more on Stone, see 1989.)

The envelope, please…

BEST ACTOR
PAUL NEWMAN (B. 1925)
THE COLOR OF MONEY

"[It's] like chasing a beautiful woman for eighty years. Finally, she relents and you say, 'I am terribly sorry. I'm tired,'" said Newman to the Associated Press to justify not appearing at the Awards. "I'm superstitious," Newman went on. "I've been there six times and lost. Maybe if I stay away, I'll win." Newman was back, and as bad as ever in this remake of *The Hustler* (1961). Newman had previously been nominated without a win for *Cat on a Hot Tin Roof* (1958), *Hud* (1963), *Cool Hand Luke* (1967), *Absence of Malice* (1981), and *The Verdict* (1982). (For more on Newman, see 1985.)

William Hurt with Marlee Matlin

BEST ACTRESS
MARLEE MATLIN (B. 1965)
CHILDREN OF A LESSER GOD

"I love you," said the hearing-impaired actress who plays a spunky deaf student in the film. William Hurt, her co-star both in the film and in her love life, had the privilege of opening the envelope.

Critics thought Kathleen Turner had Oscar in the bag for her performance as a 42-year-old woman who time-travels back to age 17, when she attends her high-school prom, in *Peggy Sue Got Married*. But dark horse Matlin, in what some called the "handicap challenge," charged up from the rear. *Variety*'s Army Archerd called Matlin's victory "one of the most dramatic moments" in Oscar history.

There was a downside to Matlin's win, though. Her romance with Hurt came to a quick end. "It really shocked him when I won the Oscar," she told *Glamour* magazine, "because it took him a long time to win. Matlin's career, however, goes on. Since winning the Oscar, she has made many cameo appearances on television's *Seinfeld*, *Judging Amy*, and *West Wing*, and was the star of *Reasonable Doubt*.

BEST OF 1986
Best Picture: *Platoon*
Best Director: Oliver Stone, *Platoon*
Best Actor: Paul Newman, *The Color of Money*
Best Actress: Marlee Matlin, *Children of a Lesser God*
Best Supporting Actor: Michael Caine, *Hannah and her Sisters*
Best Supporting Actress: Dianne Wiest, *Hannah and Her Sisters*

FIRSTS
• Marlee Matlin, at 21, became the youngest actress to win the top actress Oscar for *Children of a Lesser God*—and it was her debut performance.

• Sigourney Weaver was nominated Best Actress, the first nomination ever for a woman playing an all-action role.

• *The Hustler* caused a surge in the sale of pool tables in 1961. In *The Color of Money* Paul Newman returns as "Fast Eddie" Felson's manager, and the remake sent shoppers out again. According to *Variety*, "sales of pool tables and billiards-related supplies have leaped dramatically since the October release of *The Color of Money*."

• Oscar nominations were announced on national television for the first time since 1955.

• *Hannah and Her Sisters* became the highest-grossing Allen film to date.

SECOND
Paul Newman and Joanne Woodward became the second married couple to win acting Oscars after Laurence Olivier and Vivien Leigh.

SIN OF OMISSION
"I don't think I'm the sort of material movie stars are made of—I'm 5 foot 6 inches and cubic," said Bob Hoskins, who had the bad fortune to come up against Paul Newman that year. He had won all the Best Actor awards from Cannes to the Golden Globe for his performance in *Mona Lisa*. Hoskins is terrific as an earnest, naive ex-con who gets a job driving a beautiful black prostitute to her various assignations and to search for a young drug-addicted friend. Kathleen Carroll, writing in the *New York Daily News*, said, "He makes you believe this thick-skulled Frog Prince actually possesses an inner beauty."

ROLE REVERSALS
• Debra Winger was originally cast for Kathleen Turner's part in *Peggy Sue Got Married* when a back injury took her out of the running. Turner, best known for playing seductresses, arrived and bragged to an interviewer, "I'm bankable."

• James Woods turned down the starring role in *Platoon*, explaining, "I couldn't take the mud."

UNMVENTIONABLES
• Upon winning the Best Screenplay award, Woody Allen's response was, "If you make a popular movie, you start to think, Where have I failed? I must be doing something that's unchallenging, or reinforcing the prejudices of the middle class, or being simplistic and sentimental."

• According to *Entertainment Tonight*, "Stone still held a grudge against a 1949 Best Actor nominee: 'I love John Wayne, but *Sands of Iwo Jima* sent me to Vietnam believing that it was exciting and I could make a man out of myself. I don't believe John Wayne ever went to war.'"

• In the battle for best war movie, things got a little ugly when Oliver Stone, speaking about chief rival *Top Gun* in *Premiere* magazine, said, "The message of this movie is 'I get a girlfriend if I start World War III.'"

Mia Farrow with Michael Caine

BEST SUPPORTING ACTOR
MICHAEL CAINE (B. 1933)
HANNAH AND HER SISTERS

"I was too drunk to be nervous," said Caine to his daughter, Natasha, when she called him from agent "Swifty" Lazar's annual fete. Caine was a no-show at the event. David Ansen of *Newsweek* depicted Caine's performance playing Mia Farrow's adulterous husband as "both sympathetic and exasperating, equally a torturer and the one who is tortured."

Among his many films, Caine has appeared in *Zulu* (1964), *The Ipcress File* (1965), *Alfie*, (1966, Oscar nom.), *Gambit* (1966), *Sleuth* (1972, Oscar nom.), *The Man Who Would Be King* (1975), and *Educating Rita* (1983), for which he received a third Oscar nomination. He later appeared in, among other films, *Jaws The Revenge* (1987), *Without a Clue* and *Dirty Rotten Scoundrels* (both 1988). (For more on Caine, see 1999.)

Barbara Hershey with Dianne Wiest

BEST SUPPORTING ACTRESS
DIANNE WIEST (B. 1948)
HANNAH AND HER SISTERS

"Gee, this isn't like what I imagined it would be in the bathtub!" Wiest said when she accepted her award. She also probably never imagined rushing back to the microphone after walking offstage to shout, "I left Woody Allen out of my speech!" Hard to imagine, given that Wiest had become a regular in the Allen repertoire, appearing in *Radio Days* (1987) and *Bullets Over Broadway* (1994).

Wiest is also a regular on television's *Law and Order*. "DIANNE WIEST MAKES NEUROSIS A SUCCESS STORY," read a headline in *The New York Times*. In *Hannah*, Wiest plays the most neurotic of three sisters—the least being Mia Farrow, the rock, for whom this film is a love song—whose romantic escapades are charted over a two-year period. The award couldn't have come at a better time. Wiest's three-year romance with her agent, Sam Cohn, had just come to an end, although he continued to manage her career. (For more on Wiest, see 1994.)

AWARD NOMINATIONS 1986

PICTURE
CHILDREN OF A LESSER GOD, Sugarman, Paramount. Produced by Burt Sugarman and Patrick Palmer.
HANNAH AND HER SISTERS, Rollins and Joffee, Orion. Produced by Robert Greenhut.
THE MISSION, Warner Bros. Produced by Fernando Ghia and David Puttnam.
PLATOON, Hemdale, Orion. Produced by Arnold Kopelson.
A ROOM WITH A VIEW, Merchant Ivory, Cinecom. Produced by Ismail Merchant.

ACTOR
DEXTER GORDON in 'Round Midnight, Winkler, Warner Bros.
BOB HOSKINS in Mona Lisa, Island.
WILLIAM HURT in Children of a Lesser God, Sugarman, Paramount.
PAUL NEWMAN in The Color of Money, Touchstone with Silver Screen Partners II, Buena Vista.
JAMES WOODS in Salvador, Hemdale.

ACTRESS
JANE FONDA in The Morning After, Lorimar, 20th Century Fox.
MARLEE MATLIN in Children of a Lesser God, Sugarman, Paramount.
SISSY SPACEK in Crimes of the Heart, De Laurentiis Entertainment Group.
KATHLEEN TURNER in Peggy Sue Got Married, Rastar, Tri-Star.
SIGOURNEY WEAVER in Aliens, 20th Century Fox.

SUPPORTING ACTOR
TOM BERENGER in Platoon, Hemdale, Orion.
MICHAEL CAINE in Hannah and Her Sisters, Rollins and Joffe, Orion.
WILLEM DAFOE in Platoon, Hemdale, Orion.
DENHOLM ELLIOT in A Room with a View, Merchant Ivory, Cinecom.
DENNIS HOPPER in Hoosiers, de Haven, Orion.

SUPPORTING ACTRESS
TESS HARPER in Crimes of the Heart, De Laurentiis Entertainment Group.
PIPER LAURIE in Children of a Lesser God, Sugarman, Paramount.
MARY ELIZABETH MASTRANTONIO in The Color of Money, Touchstone with Silver Screen Partners II, Buena Vista.
MAGGIE SMITH in A Room with a View, Merchant Ivory, Cinecom.
DIANNE WIEST in Hannah and Her Sisters, Rollins and Joffe, Orion.

DIRECTION
DAVID LYNCH for Blue Velvet, De Laurentiis Entertainment Group.
WOODY ALLEN for Hannah and Her Sisters, Rollins and Joffe, Orion.
ROLAND JOFFE for The Mission, Warner Bros.
OLIVER STONE for Platoon, Hemdale, Orion.
JAMES IVORY for A Room with a View, Merchant Ivory, Cinecom.

WRITING: DIRECTLY FOR THE SCREEN
"CROCODILE" DUNDEE, Rimfire, Paramount. Paul Hogan, Ken Shadie and John Cornell.
HANNAH AND HER SISTERS, Rollins and Joffe, Orion. Woody Allen.
MY BEAUTIFUL LAUNDRETTE, Orion Classics. Hanif Kureishi.
PLATOON, Hemdale, Orion. Oliver Stone.
SALVADOR, Hemdale. Oliver Stone and Richard Boyle.

WRITING: BASED ON MATERIAL FROM ANOTHER MEDIUM
CHILDREN OF A LESSER GOD, Sugarman, Paramount. Hesper Anderson and Mark Medoff.
THE COLOR OF MONEY, Touchstone with Silver Screen Partners II, Buena Vista. Richard Price.
CRIMES OF THE HEART, De Laurentiis Entertainment Group. Beth Henley.
A ROOM WITH A VIEW, Merchant Ivory, Cinecom. Ruth Prawer Jhabvala.
STAND BY ME, Act III, Columbia. Raynold Gideon and Bruce A. Evans.

CINEMATOGRAPHY
THE MISSION, Warner Bros. Chris Menges.
PEGGY SUE GOT MARRIED, Rastar, Tri-Star. Jordan Cronenweth.
PLATOON, Hemdale, Orion. Robert Richardson.
A ROOM WITH A VIEW, Merchant Ivory, Cinecom. Tony Pierce-Roberts.
STAR TREK IV: THE VOYAGE HOME, Bennett, Paramount. Don Peterman.

ART DIRECTION—SET DECORATION
ALIENS, 20th Century Fox. Peter Lamont; Crispian Sallis.
THE COLOR OF MONEY, Touchstone with Silver Screen Partners II, Buena Vista. Boris Leven; Karen A. O'Hara.
HANNAH AND HER SISTERS, Rollins and Joffe, Orion. Stuart Wurtzel; Carol Joffe.
THE MISSION, Warner Bros. Stuart Craig; Jack Stephens.
A ROOM WITH A VIEW, Merchant Ivory, Cinecom. Gianni Quaranta and Brian Ackland-Snow; Brian Savegar and Elio Altramura.

COSTUME DESIGN
THE MISSION, Warner Bros. Enrico Sabbatini.
OTELLO, Cannon. Anna Anni and Maurizio Millenotti.
PEGGY SUE GOT MARRIED, Rastar, Tri-Star. Theadora Van Runkle.
PIRATES, Cannon. Anthony Powell.
A ROOM WITH A VIEW, Merchant Ivory, Cinecom. Jenny Beavan and John Bright.

SOUND
ALIENS, 20th Century Fox. Graham V. Hartstone, Nicolas Le Messurier, Michael A. Carter and Roy Charman.
HEARTBREAK RIDGE, Warner Bros. Les Fresholtz, Dick Alexander, Vern Poore and William Nelson.
PLATOON, Hemdale, Orion. John K. Wilkinson, Richard Rogers, Charles "Bud" Grenzbach and Simon Kaye.
STAR TREK IV: THE VOYAGE HOME, Bennett, Paramount. Terry Porter, Dave Hudson, Mel Metcalfe and Gene S. Cantamessa.
TOP GUN, Simpson/Bruckheimer, Paramount. Donald O. Mitchell, Kevin O'Connell, Rick Kline and William B. Kaplan.

FILM EDITING
ALIENS, 20th Century Fox. Ray Lovejoy.
HANNAH AND HER SISTERS, Rollins and Joffe, Orion. Susan E. Morse.
THE MISSION, Warner Bros. Jim Clark.
PLATOON, Hemdale, Orion. Claire Simpson.
TOP GUN, Simpson/Bruckheimer, Paramount. Billy Weber and Chris Lebenzon.

SOUND EFFECTS EDITING
ALIENS, 20th Century Fox. Don Sharpe.
STAR TREK IV: THE VOYAGE HOME, Benett, Paramount. Mark Mangini.
TOP GUN, Simpson/Bruckheimer, Paramount. Cecelia Hall and George Watters II.

VISUAL EFFECTS
ALIENS, 20th Century Fox. Robert Skotak, Stan Winston, John Richardson and Susanne Benson.
LITTLE SHOP OF HORRORS, Geffen, through Warner Bros. Lyle Conway, Bran Ferren and Martin Gutteridge.
POLTERGEIST II: THE OTHER SIDE, Victor-Grais, MGM. Richard Edlund, John Bruno, Garry Wailer and William Neil.

SONG
GLORY OF LOVE (The Karate Kid Part II, Columbia); Music by Peter Cetera and David Foster. Lyrics by Peter Cetera and Diane Nini.
LIFE IN A LOOKING GLASS (That's Life, Columbia); Music by Henry Mancini. Lyrics by Leslie Bricusse.
MEAN GREEN MOTHER FROM OUTER SPACE (Little Shop of Horrors, The Geffen Company through Warner Bros.); Music by Alan Menken. Lyrics by Howard Ashman.
SOMEWHERE OUT THERE (An American Tail, Amblin, Universal); Music by James Horner and Barry Mann. Lyrics by Cynthia Weil.
TAKE MY BREATH AWAY (Top Gun, Simpson/Bruckheimer, Paramount); Music by Giorgio Moroder. Lyrics by Tom Whitlock.

SCORING: ORIGINAL MUSIC
ALIENS, 20th Century Fox. James Horner.
HOOSIERS, De Haven, Orion. Jerry Goldsmith.
THE MISSION, Warner Bros. Ennio Morricone.
ROUND MIDNIGHT, Winkler, Warner Bros. Herbie Hancock.
STAR TREK IV: THE VOYAGE HOME, Bennett, Paramount. Leonard Rosenman.

MAKEUP
THE CLAN OF THE CAVE BEAR, Warner Bros. Michael G. Westmore and Michele Burke.
THE FLY, Brooksfilms, 20th Century Fox. Chris Walas and Stephan Dupuis.
LEGEND, Universal. Rob Bottin and Peter Robb-King.

ANIMATED
THE FROG, THE DOG AND THE DEVIL, New Zealand National Film Unit. Bob Stenhouse, producer.
A GREEK TRAGEDY, CineTe pvba. Linda Van Tulden and Willem Thijssen, producers.
LUXO JR., Pixar Productions. John Lasseter and William Reeves, producers.

SHORT FILMS: LIVE ACTION
EXIT, Rai Radiotelevisione Italiana/RAI-UNO. Stefano Reali and Pino Quartullo, producers.
LOVE STRUCK, Rainy Day Productions. Fredda Weiss, producer.
PRECIOUS IMAGES, Calliope Films, Inc. Chuck Workman, producer.

DOCUMENTARY: SHORT SUBJECTS
DEBONAIR DANCERS, an Alison Nigh-Strelich Production. Alison Nigh-Strelich, producer.
THE MASTERS OF DISASTER, Indiana University Audio Visual Center. Sonya Friedman, producer.
RED GROOMS; SUNFLOWER IN A HOTHOUSE, a Polaris Entertainment Production, Thomas L. Neff and Madeline Bell, producers.
SAM, a Film by Aaron D. Weisblatt. Aaron D. Weisblatt, producer.
WOMEN—FOR AMERICA, FOR THE WORLD, Educational Film & Video Project. Vivienne Verdon-Roe, producer.

DOCUMENTARY: FEATURES
ARTIE SHAW: TIME IS ALL YOU'VE GOT, a Bridge Film Production. Brigitte Berman, producer.
CHILE: HASTA CUANDO?, a David Bradbury Production. David Bradbury, producer.
DOWN AND OUT IN AMERICA, a Joseph Feury Production. Joseph Feury and Milton Justice, producers,
ISAAC IN AMERICA: A Journey with Isaac Bashevis Singer, Amram Nowak Associates. Kirk Simon and Amram Nowak, producers.
WITNESS TO APARTHEID, a Production of Developing News Inc. Sharon I. Sopher, producer.

FOREIGN LANGUAGE FILM
THE ASSAULT (The Netherlands).
BETTY BLUE (France).
THE DECLINE OF THE AMERICAN EMPIRE (Canada).
MY SWEET LITTLE VILLAGE (Czechoslovakia).
"38" (Austria).

HONORARY AND OTHER AWARDS
TO RALPH BELLAMY, for his unique artistry and his distinguished service to the profession of acting.
TO E.M. (AL) LEWIS, in appreciation for outstanding service and dedication in upholding the high standards of the Academy of Motion Picture Arts and Sciences.

IRVING G. THALBERG MEMORIAL AWARD
TO STEVEN SPIELBERG

SCIENTIFIC OR TECHNICAL AWARDS: SCIENTIFIC AND ENGINEERING AWARD
BRAN FERREN, CHARLES HARRISON and KENNETH WISNER of Associates and Ferren for the concept and design of an advanced optical printer.
RICHARD BENJAMIN GRANT and RON GRANT of Auricle Control Systems for their invention of the Film Composer's Time Processor.
ANTHONY D. BRUNO and JOHN L. BAPTISTA of Metro-Goldwyn-Mayer Laboratories, Incorporated, and to MANFRED G. MICHELSON and BRUCE W. KELLER of Technical Film Systems, Incorporated, for the design and engineering of a Continuous-Feed Printer.
ROBERT GREENBERG, JOEL HYNEK and EUGENE MAMUT of R/Greenberg Associates, Incorporated, and to DR. ALFRED THUMIM, ELAN LIPSHITZ and DARRYL A. ARMOUR of the Oxberry Division of Richmark Camera Service, Incorporated, for the design and development of the RGA/Oxberry Compu-Quad Special Effects Optical Printer.
PROFESSOR FRITZ SENNHEISER of Sennheiser Electronic Corporation for the invention of an interference tube DIRECTIONal microphone.
RICHARD EDLUND, GENE WHITEMAN, DAVID GRAfTON, MARK WEST, JERRY JEFFRESS and BOB WILCOX of Boss Film Corporation for the design and development of a Zoom Aerial (ZAP) 65mm Optical Printer.
WILLIAM L. FREDRICK and HAL NEEDHAM for the design and development of the Shotmaker Elite camera car and crane.

SCIENTIFIC OR TECHNICAL AWARDS: TECHNICAL ACHIEVEMENT AWARD
LEE ELECTRIC (LIGHTING) LIMITED for the design and development of an electronic, flicker-free, discharge lamp control system.
PETER D. PARKS of Oxford Scientific Films' Image Quest Division for the development of a live aerocompositor for special effects photography.
MATT SWEENEY and LUCINDA STRUB for the development of an automatic capsule gun for simulating bullet hits for motion picture special effects.
CARL HOLMES of Carl E. Holmes Company and to ALEXANDER BRYCE of The Burbank Studios for the development of a mobile DC power supply unit for motion picture production photography.
BRAN FERREN of Associates and Ferren for the development of a laser synchro-cue system for applications in the motion picture industry.
JOHN L. BAFFISTA of Metro-Goldwyn-Mayer Laboratories, Inc. for the development and installation of a computerized silver recovery operation.
DAVID W. SAMUELSON for the development of programs incorporated into a pocket computer for motion picture cinematographers, and to WILLIAM B. POLLARD for contributing new algorithms on which the programs are based.
HAL LANDAKER and ALAN LANDAKER of The Burbank Studios for the development of the Beat System low-frequency cue track for motion picture production sound recording.

1987

ROYAL FLUSH

CEREMONY: April 11, 1988
Los Angeles Shrine Auditorium,
Los Angeles
HOST: Chevy Chase

A listless *Chorus Line* opening number tapped to a half-empty Shrine Auditorium, thanks to the biggest "limo jam" in Oscar history. Late arrival Cher, in a see-through gown, rushed down the aisle, nearly colliding with Best Supporting Actress Olympia Dukakis en route to the podium. Their film, *Moonstruck*, was off and running. But Paramount's huge-grossing sex thriller, *Fatal Attraction*, couldn't manage to pull a rabbit out of the hat, much less out of a pot of boiling water.

The evening belonged to Bernardo Bertolucci, whose visual feast, *The Last Emperor*, managed the near-impossible—nine Oscars for nine nominations, including Best Picture. The win was all the more impressive because the film had failed to score at the box office.

As the result of a writers' strike, hosts and presenters were compelled to think on their feet. Robin Williams "channeled the spirit of Georgie Jessel," and Chevy Chase resorted to picking his nose for laughs. Attendees got plenty of exercise, thanks to several standing ovations. The first was for Best Supporting Actor Sean Connery, followed by another for presenters Gregory Peck and Audrey Hepburn, and again for Thalberg Memorial recipient director Billy Wilder (*Sunset Boulevard, Some Like It Hot, The Apartment*). Wilder credited his career to a Mexican official who, during the 1940s, offered him safe harbor after he escaped Nazi Germany.

Michael Douglas, enjoying a double-whammy year with *Fatal Attraction* and *Wall Street*, dedicated his Best Actor Oscar to his dad, Kirk. Best Actress Cher, Hollywood's most adored "classless act," profusely thanked her makeup man and her hairdresser. Her chutzpah was rivaled only by fellow nominee Sally Kirkland, who launched a tireless but failed campaign for her work in a little-known Czech film, *Anna*. Kirkland, a former Warhol Factory starlet, had once posed nude while riding a pig.

BEST PICTURE/BEST DIRECTOR
BERNARDO BERTOLUCCI (B. 1940)
THE LAST EMPEROR

While accepting his Oscars Bertolucci spoke of the Academy Awards as "a distant ceremony, something fascinating, very remote—something I really didn't belong to." Once his fortunes changed, he said, "I became immediately a kind of Oscar victim. I started to learn the rules of the game and to check the odds, to start with the colitis." Bertolucci, never known to treat his subjects superficially, went all out for this production—the autobiography of the child Pu Yi, who at the age of 3 was made emperor of the Manchu dynasty only to be deposed three years later, with the onset of Communism, and winds up as a Peking gardener. The film, made in Italy and China, employed 19,000 extras and included 9,000 costumes. *Newsweek*'s David Ansen said, "Turning Bernardo Bertolucci loose in the treasure chest of Imperial China is like locking a chocoholic inside a Godiva factory for the night. He may be the last emperor of the epic." Coming from the rear, *New Republic*'s Stanley Kaufman complained that "Pu Yi is simply an eccentricity of history, worth a paragraph in the *Reader's Digest*, not a nearly three-hour film." Bertolucci, one of the international

Richard Vuu

cinema's most politically sophisticated, committed filmmakers, is responsible for such unforgettable films as *Before the Revolution* (1964), *The Conformist* (1970), *Last Tango in Paris* (1972), *Bertolucci's 1900* (1977), *La Luna* (1979), and, later, *The Sheltering Sky* (1990) and *Little Buddha* (1994).

The envelope, please...

Charlie Sheen with Michael Douglas

BEST ACTOR
MICHAEL DOUGLAS (B. 1944)
WALL STREET

"Greed is good." The real-life Douglas expressed a very different sentiment from the "pearl of wisdom" he cited in the film. Douglas dedicated his second Oscar to dad Kirk "for helping a son step out of a shadow," adding, "I'll be eternally grateful to you, Dad." Douglas had also appeared that year in the controversial, "adultery can be dangerous to men" *Fatal Attraction*. Said director Oliver Stone, "I was warned by everyone in Hollywood that Michael couldn't act." But Douglas surprised Stone and all his detractors. David Denby, writing in *New York* magazine, said, "He's never acted with this kind of gusto and power before." The *Los Angeles Times* said, "It appears he's tapped into a lifetime of personal observations of high-level power types in action—the movie looks as though it could easily have been transferred to studio executive suites in Hollywood." Douglas already had a prolific career, having appeared in such films as *The China Syndrome* (1979), *Romancing the Stone* (1984), *Jewel of the Nile* (1985), *A Chorus Line* (1985), and later *War of the Roses* (1989), *The American President* (1995), *Wonder Boys* (2000), and *Traffic* (2000).

BEST ACTRESS
CHER (B. 1946)
MOONSTRUCK

"I don't think this means I'm somebody...but I guess I'm on my way," Cher said in her acceptance speech. Demonstrating her great versatility, Cher appeared in three movies that year—*The Witches of Eastwick*, *Suspect*, and *Moonstruck*. It was all the audience could do to get Cher to remove her cloak to reveal what she wasn't wearing this year. Finally, when she walked up to the stage to claim her Oscar for her performance as an offbeat Italian widow, she dropped her wrap to reveal her transparent silk net gown. The crowd was not disappointed. Cher has rarely disappointed, either in her Oscar couture or in her film performances, which include *Good Times* (1967), *Chastity* (1969), *Come Back to the Five & Dime Jimmy Dean, Jimmy Dean* (1982), *Silkwood* (1983), *Mask* (1985), *Mermaids* (1990), and *Tea with Mussolini* (1999). She also made a directorial debut with a segment of the HBO special *If These Walls Could Talk* (1996).

FIRSTS
• Not one American director was nominated.

• For the first time since 1946, the Oscar ceremony had been moved from the Dorothy Chandler Pavilion to the "skid row" location of the Shrine Auditorium. Though maps were distributed among the drivers responsible for ferrying the stars, many got lost and the stars lost their patience, jumping out of their cars to make a mad dash to the stage. Passersby gasped at the sight of an eight months pregnant Glenn Close climbing over fenders to get to the Shrine on time. Many others were in the same boat, including Meryl Streep, Tom Bradley, the mayor of Los Angeles, septuagenarian Joan Fontaine, and Ann Sothern, walking with the help of a cane.

• Robin Williams scored his first Best Actor nomination.

FOURTHS
Nicholson's sixth Best Actor nomination, for *Ironweed*, made this his ninth nomination and placed him in a tie for fourth with Spencer Tracy in the most nominated category.

ALWAYS A BRIDESMAID, NEVER A BRIDE
• How can they do that? Make that two years that Steve Martin disappeared from the Oscar nominations, though he was recognized by the Los Angeles Critics Award for his comic portrait of the unrequited lover with a big nose, Cyrano de Bergerac, in *Roxanne*. Said Martin to the *Los Angeles Times*, "I would have turned handsprings to have gotten nominated for *All of Me* [1984]. It's not as important as it would have been several years ago."

• Maintaining his score as an Oscar wanna-be, Steven Spielberg nevertheless managed to pull Best Picture and Best Director from the National Board of Review, and Best Picture from the Golden Globes for *Empire of the Sun*, the story of a British boy stranded in Japan-occupied China during World War II. When he was asked if he thought he would be nominated for an Oscar, Spielberg replied, "I have a strong feeling I won't be nominated...just a hunch."

• It was Glenn Close's fourth Oscar nomination. Though her brave performance as the sexy, scorned, and deadly "other woman" in *Fatal Attraction* was totally convincing—frighteningly so—she couldn't even manipulate a date with Oscar that night.

ROLE REVERSALS
• Third time's the charm. *Fatal Attraction* director, Britain's Adrian Lyne (*Flashdance*, 1983), was the third director approached to make the film. It had been turned down by Brian De Palma, who thought the film was too much like Clint Eastwood's *Play Misty for Me* (1971), and by John Boorman, who preferred to make *Hope and Glory*, the memoir of his wartime childhood in England.

• John Patrick Shanley wrote Cher's Oscar-winning role in *Moonstruck* for Sally Field.

253

Sean Connery with Kevin Costner

BEST SUPPORTING ACTOR
SEAN CONNERY (B. 1930)
THE UNTOUCHABLES

"The name's Connery. Sean Connery," said the deep-voiced 007 to a standing ovation as he stepped to the podium to announce the Visual Effects Oscar. He also picked up his own Oscar for his soulful portrayal of the street-smart cop who teaches fed agent Elliot Ness (Kevin Costner) how to fight dirty. Voted *People*'s Sexiest Man Alive in 1989, and the Sexiest Man of the Century in 1999, Connery made his name playing James Bond, the suave British agent. But after six rounds he was bound to break free of Bond. His appearances in other roles include *The Longest Day* (1962), *Murder on the Orient Express* (1974), *The Man Who Would Be King*, and *The Wind and the Lion* (both 1975), *Dressed to Kill* (1980), and *The Name of the Rose* (1986). After *The Untouchables*, Connery made a variety of pictures, among them *Robin Hood: Prince of Thieves* (1991), *The Hunt for Red October* and *The Russia House* (both 1990), *Rising Sun* (1993), and *Just Cause* (1995).

BEST SUPPORTING ACTRESS
OLYMPIA DUKAKIS (B. 1931)
MOONSTRUCK

Holding Oscar high, Dukakis bellowed to her cousin Michael, who was running in the presidential race that year, "Come on, Michael, let's go!" Dukakis later said to reporters, "Winning the Oscar made me a player, a name to be considered…People think of Oscar as the culmination of your life, payment for so many sacrifices. To me, it's less about reward than evolution." Dukakis debuted in *Lilith* (1964), followed by *John and Mary* (1969), *Made for Each Other* (1971), *Death Wish* (1974), and *The Wanderers* (1979). She later appeared in *Working Girl* (1988), *Steel Magnolias* and *Dad* (both 1989), and *Look Who's Talking Now* (1993).

AWARD NOMINATIONS 1987

PICTURE

BROADCAST NEWS, 20th Century Fox. Produced by James L. Brooks.
FATAL ATTRACTION, Jaffe/Lansing, Paramount. Produced by Stanley R. Jaffe and Sherry Lansing.
HOPE AND GLORY, Davros, Columbia. Produced by John Boorman.
THE LAST EMPEROR, Hemdale, Columbia. Produced by Jeremy Thomas.
MOONSTRUCK, MGM, Produced by Patrick Palmer and Norman Jewison.

ACTOR

WILLIAM HURT in *Broadcast News*, 20th Century Fox.
MICHAEL DOUGLAS in *Wall Street*, Oaxatal, 20th Century Fox.
ROBIN WILLIAMS in *Good Morning, Vietnam*, Touchstone with Silver Screen Partners III, Buena Vista.
MARCELLO MASTROIANNI in *Dark Eyes*, Excelsior, Island Pictures.
JACK NICHOLSON in *Ironweed*, Taft/Barish, Tri-Star.

ACTRESS

CHER in *Moonstruck*, Palmer/Jewison, MGM.
MERYL STREEP in *Ironweed*, Taft/Barish, Tri-Star.
SALLY KIRKLAND in *Anna*, Magnus, Vestron.
GLENN CLOSE in *Fatal Attraction*, Jaffe/Lansing, Paramount.
HOLLY HUNTER in *Broadcast News*, 20th Century Fox.

SUPPORTING ACTOR

ALBERT BROOKS in *Broadcast News*, 20th Century Fox.
MORGAN FREEMAN in *Street Smart*, Cannon.
SEAN CONNERY in *The Untouchables*, Linson, Paramount.
DENZEL WASHINGTON in *Cry Freedom*, Marble Arch, Universal.
VINCENT GARDENIA in *Moonstruck*, Palmer/Jewison, MGM.

SUPPORTING ACTRESS

NORMA ALEANDRO in *Gaby—A True Story*, Brimmer, Tri-Star.
ANN SOTHERN in *The Whales of August*, Alive Films.
OLYMPIA DUKAKIS in *Moonstruck*, Palmer/Jewison, MGM.
ANNE ARCHER in *Fatal Attraction*, Jaffe/Lansing, Paramount.
ANNE RAMSEY in *Throw Momma from the Train*, Rollins, Morra, & Brezner, Orion.

DIRECTION

BERNARDO BERTOLUCCI for *The Last Emperor*, Hemdale, Columbia.
JOHN BOORMAN for *Hope and Glory*, Davros, Columbia.
LASSE HALLSTROM for *My Life as a Dog*, Svensk Filmindustri/Filmteknik, Skouras Pictures.
NORMAN JEWISON for *Moonstruck*, Palmer/Jewison, MGM.
ADRIAN LYNE for *Fatal Attraction*, Jaffe/Lansing, Paramount.

WRITING: DIRECTLY FOR THE SCREEN

AU REVOIR LES ENFANTS (GOODBYE, CHILDREN), NEF, Orion Classics. Louis Malle.
BROADCAST NEWS, 20th Century Fox. James L. Brooks.

HOPE AND GLORY, Davros, Columbia. John Boorman.
MOONSTRUCK, Palmer/Jewison, MGM. John Patrick Shanley.
RADIO DAYS, Rollins and Joffe, Orion. Woody Allen.

WRITING: BASED ON MATERIAL FROM ANOTHER MEDIUM

THE DEAD. Liffey, Vestron. Tony Huston.
FATAL ATTRACTION, Jaffe/Lansing, Paramount. James Dearden.
FULL METAL JACKET, Nataunt, Warner Bros. Stanley Kubrick, Michael Herr and Gustav Hasford.
THE LAST EMPEROR, Hemdale, Columbia. Mark Peploe and Bernardo Bertolucci.
MY LIFE AS A DOG, Svensk Filinindustri/Filmteknik, Skouras Pictures. Lasse Hallstrom, Reidar Jonsson, Brasse Brannstrom and Per Berglund.

CINEMATOGRAPHY

BROADCAST NEWS, 20th Century Fox. Michael Ballhaus.
THE LAST EMPEROR, Hemdale, Columbia. Vittorio Storaro.
HOPE AND GLORY, Davros, Columbia. Philippe Rousselot.
MATEWAN, Red Dog, Cinecom. Haskell Wexler.
EMPIRE OF THE SUN, Warner Bros. Allen Daviau.

ART DIRECTION—SET DECORATION

THE LAST EMPEROR, Hemdale, Columbia. Ferdinando Scarfiotti; Bruno Cesari and Osvaldo Desideri.
RADIO DAYS, Rollins and Joffe, Orion. Santo Loquasto; Carol Joffe, Les Bloom and George DeTitta, Jr.
HOPE AND GLORY, Davros, Columbia. Anthony Pratt; Joan Woolard.
THE UNTOUCHABLES, Linson, Paramount. Patrizia Von Brandenstein and William A. Elliott; Hal Gausman.
EMPIRE OF THE SUN, Warner Bros. Norman Reynolds; Harry Cordwell.

COSTUME DESIGN

MAURICE, Merchant Ivory, Cinecom. Jenny Beavan and John Bright.
EMPIRE OF THE SUN, Warner Bros. Bob Ringwood.
THE UNTOUCHABLES, Linson, Paramount. Marilyn Vance-Straker.
THE DEAD, Liffey, Vestron. Dorothy Jeakins.
THE LAST EMPEROR, Hemdale, Columbia. James Acheson.

SOUND

EMPIRE OF THE SUN. Warner Bros. Robert Knudson, Don Digirolamo, John Boyd and Tony Dawe.
THE LAST EMPEROR, Hemdale, Columbia. Bill Rowe and Ivan Sharrock.
LETHAL WEAPON, Warner Bros. Los Fresholtz, Dick Alexander, Vern Poore and Bill Nelson.
ROBOCOP, Tobor, Orion. Michael J. Kohut, Carlos de Larios, Aaron Rochin and Robert Wald.
THE WITCHES OF EASTWICK, Warner Bros. Wayne Artman, Tom Beckert, Tom Dahl and Art Rochester.

FILM EDITING

THE LAST EMPEROR, Hemdale, Columbia. Gabriella Cristiani.
FATAL ATTRACTION, Jaffe/Lansing, Paramount. Michael Kahn and Peter E. Berger.
ROBOCOP, Tobor, Orion. Frank J. Urioste.
EMPIRE OF THE SUN, Warner Bros. Michael Kahn.
BROADCAST NEWS, 20th Century Fox. Richard Marks.

VISUAL EFFECTS

PREDATOR, 20th Century Fox. Joel Hynek, Robert M. Greenberg, Richard Greenberg and Stan Winston.
INNERSPACE, Warner Bros. Dennis Muren, William George, Harley Jessup and Kenneth Smith.

SONG

CRY FREEDOM, (*Cry Freedom*, Marble Arch, Universal); Music and Lyrics by George Fenton and Jonas Gwangwa.

(I'VE HAD) THE TIME OF MY LIFE (*Dirty Dancing*, Vestron); Music by Franke Previte, John DeNicola and Donald Markowitz. Lyrics by Franke Previte.
NOTHING'S GONNA STOP US NOW (*Mannequin*, Gladden, 20th Century Fox); Music and Lyrics by Albert Hammond and Diane Warren.
SHAKEDOWN (*Beverly Hills Cop II*, Simpson/Bruckheimer, Paramount); Music by Harold Poltermeyer and Keith Forsey. Lyrics by Harold Faltermeyer, Keith Forsey and Bob Seger.
STORYBOOK LOVE (*The Princess Bride*, Act III, 20th Century Fox); Music and Lyrics by Willy DeVille.

SCORING: ORIGINAL MUSIC

CRY FREEDOM, Marble Arch, Universal. George Fenton and Jonas Gwangwa.
EMPIRE OF THE SUN. Warner Bros. John Williams.
THE LAST EMPEROR, Hemdale, Columbia. Ryuichi Sakamoto, David Byrne and Cong Su.
THE WITCHES OF EASTWICK, Warner Bros. John Williams.
THE UNTOUCHABLES, Linson, Paramount. Ennio Morricone.

MAKEUP

HARRY AND THE HENDERSONS, Amblin, Universal. Rick Baker.
HAPPY NEW YEAR, Columbia. Bob Laden.

SHORT FILMS: ANIMATED

GEORGE AND ROSEMARY, National Film Board of Canada. Eunice Macaulay, producer.
THE MAN WHO PLANTED TREES, Societe RadioCanada/Canadian Broadcasting Corporation. Frederic Back, producer.
YOUR FACE, Bill Plympton Productions. Bill Plympton, producer.

SHORT FILMS: LIVE ACTION

MAKING WAVES, The Production Pool Ltd. Ann Wingate, producer.
RAY'S MALE HETEROSEXUAL DANCE HALL, Chanticleer Films. Jonathan Sanger and Jana Sue Memel, producers.
SHOESHINE, Tom Abrams Productions. Robert A. Katz, producer.

DOCUMENTARY: SHORT SUBJECTS

FRANCES STELOFF: MEMOIRS OF A BOOKSELLER, a Winterlude Films, Inc. Production. Deborah Dickson, producer.
IN THE WEE WEE HOURS..., School of Cinema/TV, University of Southern California. Dr. Frank Daniel and Izak Ben-Meir, producers.
LANGUAGE SAYS IT ALL, a Tripod Production. Megan Williams, producer.
SILVER INTO GOLD, Department of Communications, Stanford University. Lynn Mueller, producer.
YOUNG AT HEART, a Sue Marx Films, Inc. Production. Sue Marx and Pamela Conn, producers.

DOCUMENTARY: FEATURES

EYES ON THE PRIZE: AMERICA'S CIVIL RIGHTS YEARS/Bridge to Freedom 1965, a Blackside, Inc. Production. Callie Crossley and James A. DeVinney, producers.
HELLFIRE: A JOURNEY FROM HIROSHIMA, John Junkerman and John W. Dower, producers.
RADIO BIKINI, a Production of Crossroads Film Project, Ltd. Robert Stone, producer.)
A STITCH FOR TIME, a Production of Peace Quilters Production Company, Inc. Barbara Herbich and Cyril Christo, producers.
THE TEN-YEAR LUNCH: THE WIT AND LEGEND OF THE ALGONQUIN ROUND TABLE, an Aviva Films Production. Aviva Slesin, producer.

FOREIGN LANGUAGE FILMS

AU REVOIR LES ENFANTS (GOODBYE, CHILDREN) (France).
BABETTE'S FEAST (Denmark).
COURSE COMPLETED (Spain).
THE FAMILY (Italy).
PATHFINDER (Norway).

SPECIAL ACHIEVEMENT AWARDS

For Sound Effects Editing: STEPHEN FLICK and JOHN POSPISIL for *Robocop*.

IRVING G. THALBERG MEMORIAL AWARD

TO BILLY WILDER

GORDON E. SAWYER AWARD

TO FRED HYNES

SCIENTIFIC OR TECHNICAL AWARDS: ACADEMY AWARD OF MERIT

BERNARD KUHL and WERNER BLOCK and to the OSRAM GmbH RESEARCH AND DEVELOPMENT DEPARTMENT for the invention and the continuing improvement of the OSRAM HMI light source for motion picture photography.

SCIENTIFIC OR TECHNICAL AWARDS: SCIENTIFIC AND ENGINEERING AWARD

WILLI BURTH and KINOTONE CORPORATION for the invention and development of the Non-rewind Platter System for motion picture presentations.
MONTAGE GROUP, LTD. for the development, and to RONALD C. BARKER and CHESTER L. SCHULER for the invention, of the Montage Picture Processor electronic film editing system.
COLIN F. MOSSMAN and RANK FILM LABORATORIES' DEVELOPMENT GROUP for creating a fully-automated film handling system for improving productivity of high speed film processing.
EASTMAN KODAK COMPANY for the development of Eastman Color High Speed Daylight Negative Film 5297/7297.
EASTMAN KODAK COMPANY for the development of Eastman Color High Speed SA Negative Film 5295 for blue-screen traveling matte photography.
FRITZ GABRIEL BAUER for the invention and development of the improved features of the Moviecam Camera System.
ZORAN PERISIC of Courier Films Ltd. for the Zoptic dual-zoom front projection system for VISUAL EFFECTS photography.
CARL ZEISS COMPANY for the design and development of a series of super-speed lenses for motion picture photography.

SCIENTIFIC OR TECHNICAL AWARDS: TECHNICAL ACHIEVEMENT AWARD

IOAN ALLEN of Dolby Laboratories, Inc., for the Cat. 43 playback-only noise reduction unit and its practical application to motion picture sound recordings.
JOHN EPPOLITO, WALLY GENTLEMAN, WILLIAM MESA, LES PAUL ROBLEY and GEOFFREY H. WILLIAMSON for refinements to a dual screen, front projection, image-compositing system.
JAN JACOBSEN for the application of a dual screen, front projection system to motion picture special effects photography.
THAINE MORRIS and DAVID PIER for the development of DSC Spark Devices for motion picture special effects.
TADEUZ KRZANOWSKI of Industrial Light and Magic, Inc., for the development of a Wire Rig Model Support Mechanism used to control the movements of miniatures in special effects.
DAN C. NORRIS and TIM COOK of Norris Film Products for the development of a single-frame exposure system for motion picture photography.

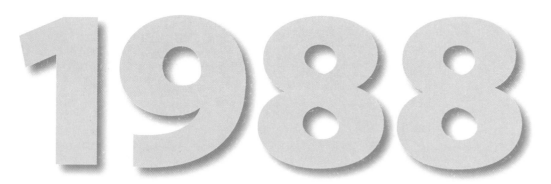

1988

"We're all a little bit autistic."
—Dustin Hoffman

First-time Awards producer Alan Carr promised an unforgettable show. And *that* it was. The opening number starred a worldly Snow White singing "Proud Mary" with off-key Prince Charming Rob Lowe. The backdrop was a re-creation of Hollywood 1940s hot spot the Cocoanut Grove, whose dancing waiters were done up in Carmen Miranda fruit-basket hats. Seated customers included former stars of the era, who leaned forward to hear "band crooner" Merv Griffin. The continued onslaught of bizarre tableaux threatened to overshadow the tight race for the top prize.

RAIN DATE

CEREMONY: April 29, 1989
Shrine Civic Auditorium,
Los Angeles
Host: Robin Williams

"The Oscar race this year is going to resemble a friendly game of bingo. The center spot—Best Picture—is free," wrote Jack Matthews in the *Los Angeles Times*. Surprise Best Supporting winner Geena Davis briefly stole the show with her storybook, ice-blue princess gown, complete with bustle and train. She was followed by another upset when Kevin Kline nudged out front-runner Martin Landau for Best Supporting Actor. Audience favorite Jodie Foster got the gold for *The Accused* and earned a thunderous cheer. It was proceeded by an anxious pause as Dustin Hoffman accepted his well-deserved Oscar for *Rain Man*, the night's big winner. Notorious for his often meandering, oblique sermonizing, Hoffman didn't let his detractors down. He even forgot to thank co-star Tom Cruise. Liz Smith, in her column the next day, chided him for "his general egotism in thinking he never has to be prepared."

Carr's deliriously overbaked show was briefly salvaged by presenters Bob Hope and Lucille Ball, who rose above the occasion. Ball, at 77, was the epitome of ageless glamour in a dress slit high enough to reveal the former chorine's still shapely gams. It was difficult to imagine that less than a month later everybody's lovable Lucy would be gone.

**BEST PICTURE/
BEST DIRECTOR
BARRY LEVINSON (B. 1942)
*RAIN MAN***

In *Rain Man* a young hustler (Tom Cruise) tries to swindle his father's inheritance from the institutionalized, autistic older brother he didn't know he had. Instead of doing his sibling bad, though, he learns to love and care for him. Around Hollywood, *Rain Man* was known as "the buddy-buddy road movie about mental illness."

Levinson began his career writing for *The Carol Burnett Show* (1967) and was hired by Mel Brooks to write *Silent Movie* (1976) and *High Anxiety* (1977). He earned a writing Oscar for *And Justice for All* (1979). Levinson's outstanding film career—which earned him five Oscar nominations and one win—began with the critically acclaimed *Diner* (1982), followed by such films as *The Natural* (1984), *Tin Men* (1987), and *Good Morning Vietnam* (1987). He later directed *Avalon* (1990), *Bugsy* (1991), *Toys* (1992), *Disclosure* (1994), *Wag the Dog* and *Donnie Brasco* (both 1997), *Liberty Heights* (1999), *The Perfect Storm* (2000), and *Bandits* (2001).

Tom Cruise, Dustin Hoffman

The envelope, please...

Tom Cruise with Dustin Hoffman

BEST ACTOR
DUSTIN HOFFMAN (B. 1937)
RAIN MAN

The only serious challenger to Hoffman's autistic heir was Gene Hackman, who plays an FBI agent caught in the cross fire of the civil-rights struggles in *Mississippi Burning*. Arguably Hollywood's best and most risk-taking actor, Hoffman delivered a captivating performance in *Rain Man* that didn't disappoint. The difficult-to-work-for-actor (Sydney Pollack called him "impossible" in *Tootsie*) was Coppola's original choice for Michael Corleone.

Nominated five times, with two winners, the films Hoffman did perform in resonate with his uncanny gift for transformation: *The Graduate* (1967), *Madigan's Million* (1968), *Midnight Cowboy* (1969), *Little Big Man* (1970), *Papillon* (1973), *Lenny* (1974), *All the President's Men* and *Marathon Man* (both 1976), *Straight Time* (1978), *Agatha* and *Kramer vs. Kramer* (both 1979), and *Tootsie* (1982). He went on to make *Ishtar* (1987), *Family Business* (1989), *Dick Tracy* (1990, a cameo), *Billy Bathgate* (1991), *Hook* (1991), and *Outbreak* (1995). (For more on Hoffman, see 1979.)

BEST ACTRESS
JODIE FOSTER (B. 1962)
THE ACCUSED

"Cruelty might be human and it might be very cultural, but it is not acceptable," said Foster. Taking on the role of a young, provocative woman who is brutally gang-raped in a bar as onlookers cheer was an act of courage for this 26-year-old, whose Hollywood star rose like lightning with this film. "It is the sort of role Jodie Foster has been training for, and she invests it with nuances of character that might have escaped a lesser actress," said the London *Evening Standard*.

Foster began her career at age 2, making commercials and a debut on the television series *Mayberry R.F.D.* (1968). Earning three Oscar nominations, with one win, she first appeared on film in *Napoleon and Samantha* (1972), continuing with performances in *Alice Doesn't Live Here Anymore* (1974), *Bugsy Malone* (1976), and *Freaky Friday* (1977).

In 1981, her role in *Taxi Driver* (1976) provoked a gunman to shoot President Ronald Reagan. After a period of recovery from that shocking incident, Foster returned to make *The Hotel New Hampshire* (1984), *Silence of the Lambs* (1991, Oscar), *Little Man Tate* (1991), *Sommersby* (1993), and *Nell* (1994). For more on Foster, see 1991.)

BEST OF 1988
Best Picture: *Rain Man*
Best Director: Barry Levinson, *Rain Man*
Best Actor: Dustin Hoffman, *Rain Man*
Best Actress: Jodie Foster, *The Accused*
Best Supporting Actor: Kevin Kline, *A Fish Called Wanda*
Best Supporting Actress: Geena Davis, *The Accidental Tourist*

FIRSTS
• In *Working Girl*, Melanie Griffith played the modern Eve Harrington—in reverse, she was the good guy—in the business world and got her first Best Actress nomination.

• Sigourney Weaver, who played Bette Davis to Griffith's Joan Bennett (only this time she was the bad guy) in *Working Girl*, received simultaneous nominations for Best Actress and Supporting Actress. She lost both.

SIN OF OMISSION
Picture: *A World Apart*

ALWAYS A BRIDESMAID, NEVER A BRIDE
Glenn Close won her sixth D.O.A. nomination for her role as a conniving pre-Revolutionary French royal in *Dangerous Liaisons*. *Newsweek*'s David Ansen said, "Here, in a performance of controlled venom and deeply hidden pathos, she's superb."

ROLE REVERSALS
• Tom Cruise was originally cast as the autistic brother in *Rain Man*, but Hoffman, preferring to play that role, switched. When the writer pointed out that Cruise was twenty years too young for the part, the producers fired him. Three writers and several directors later—the original director was Martin Brest—it was then turned down by Spielberg and Pollack. The latter refused, declaring *Tootsie* the worst experience of his life—Barry Levinson stepped in and brought back the original writer. Later, Hoffman declared that he wanted out and told the director to get Richard Dreyfuss. It all settled down in the end into a deeply felt and brilliantly performed *Rain Man*.

• Before choosing Melanie Griffith for her Oscar-nominated role in *Working Girl*, director Mike Nichols offered the job to Cher, Goldie Hawn, and Shelley Long.

• Once again a string of potential leading ladies walked through director Lawrence Kasdan's office vying for a quirky role in *The Accidental Tourist*, including Mary Steenburgen, Laura Dern, Amy Madigan, and JoBeth Williams. Kasdan chose *Body Heat*'s star Kathleen Turner as the wife and Geena Davis as the daffy eccentric.

UNMENTIONABLES
• "I feel my life's been a fairy tale," confessed *Working Girl*'s Melanie Griffith in a cover story in *Vanity Fair*, where she spoke about her redemption from alcoholism "with true love at the end and the two of us the most fortunate people around."

• The First Temptation for Scorsese. Scorsese couldn't have paid for better publicity than the vocal outrage—and sometimes violence—raised against *The Last Temptation of Christ*. Even Roy Rogers and Dale Evans spoke out against the "too human" portrait of Christ. The film provoked thousands of letters of protest, pushing the studio to the brink of pulling the plug. Blackmail was among the many attempts at censorship: a Christian group offered to give the studio $10 million to hand over all the prints. Taking advantage of all the activity, Universal moved the release date up ahead of schedule.

BEST SUPPORTING ACTOR
KEVIN KLINE (B. 1947)
A FISH CALLED WANDA

"There's a lot of Brits here tonight. Scary. But I have to thank a few of them myself," Kline said. "Charlie Crichton, who at 77 proves that, even with twenty-five years off, there's no such thing as growing old when you've got a dream."

Kevin Kline's win marked a hoped-for turning point in Oscar's notorious rejection of comedy. Though noted for his fine dramatic acting Kline was outrageously funny alongside his accomplice, Jamie Lee Curtis, in this farce about a couple of ne'er-do-well thieves.

Though best known for his Tony-winning stage performances,

Michael Palin with Kevin Kline

Kline has appeared in *The Big Chill* (1983, nom.), *Silverado* (1985), *Violets Are Blue* (1986), and *Cry Freedom* (1987). His later films include *The January Man* (1989), *I Love You to Death* (1990), *Soapdish* (1991), *Grand Canyon* (1991), *Chaplin* (1992), *French Kiss* (1995), and the Academy Award-featuring *The Anniversary Party* (2001).

BEST SUPPORTING ACTRESS
GEENA DAVIS (B. 1957)
THE ACCIDENTAL TOURIST

In preparation for the role Davis told *Entertainment Tonight*, "From now on, I'll be Muriel when somebody reads the book after seeing the movie. They'll only be able to think of me."

In an upset victory Geena, not Sigourney, took the gold first time out. Davis thanked Anne Tyler "for writing such a wonderful book. My dear friends Larry Kasdan, Bill Hurt, Ruth Meyers... my wonderful acting coach Roy London, and my other wonderful acting coach and darling husband, Jeff Goldblum," who was grinning from ear to ear. Just to spoil the party, Cynthia Heimel

Geena Davis with William Hurt

was quoted in the *Village Voice* as saying, "I predict Geena's win will put a rift in her and Jeff's relationship." Davis's warmth and quirky humor led her to several terrific performances in *Tootsie* (1982), *Beetlejuice* (1988), and, later, *Thelma & Louise* (1991)—for which she earned a Best Actress nomination—and *A League of Their Own* (1992). At this point, her career seemed to take a turn for the worse and she began appearing in such flops as *Speechless* (1994) and *Cutthroat Island* (1995). The latter film, as well as *Long Kiss Goodnight* (1996) were directed by Renny Harlin, whom Davis married, thus fulfilling Heimel's prediction.

BEST VISUAL EFFECTS, EDITING, SOUND EFFECTS, AND A SPECIAL ACHIEVEMENT AWARD FOR ANIMATOR RICHARD WILLIAMS
WHO FRAMED ROGER RABBIT

Though *Roger Rabbit* was left off the list for Best Picture, it tied *Rain Man* as the most noted film, garnering four Oscars—and the amazed adoration of audiences across the country. An act of inspired filmmaking, *Roger Rabbit* is outstanding for its technical, visual, and hilarious combination of cartoon and live action set in the Hollywood of the 1940s. In *Roger Rabbit* the cartoon characters steal the scene from some of moviedom's greatest, including Bob Hoskins.

Bob Hoskins

A FISH CALLED WANDA, Michael Shamberg-Prominent Features. M.G-M. Screenplay by John Cleese. Story by John Cleese and Charles Crichton.

RAIN MAN, Guber-Peters Company, United Artists. Screenplay by Ronald Bass and Barry Morrow. Story by Barry Morrow.

RUNNING ON EMPTY, Lorimar Production, Warner Bros. Naomi Foner.

WRITING: BASED ON MATERIAL FROM ANOTHER MEDIUM

THE ACCIDENTAL TOURIST, Warner Bros. Frank Gatali and Lawrence Kasdan.

DANGEROUS LIAISONS, Warner Bros. Christopher Hampton.

GORILLAS IN THE MIST. Warner Bros./Universal. Screenplay by Anna Hamilton Phelan. Story by Anna Hamilton Phelan and Tab Murphy.

LITTLE DORRIT, Sands Films. Cannon. Christine Edzard.

THE UNBEARABLE LIGHTNESS OF BEING, Saul Zaentz Company, Orion. Jean-Claude Carriere and Philip Kaufman.

CINEMATOGRAPHY

MISSISSIPPI BURNING, Frederick Zollo, Orion. Peter Biziou.

RAIN MAN, Guber-Peters Company. United Artists. John Seale.

TEQUILA SUNRISE, Mount Company Production, Warner Bros. Conrad L. Hall.

THE UNBEARABLE LIGHTNESS OF BEING, Saul Zaentz Company, Orion. Sveo Nykvist.

WHO FRAMED ROGER RABBIT, Amblin Entertainment and Touchstone Pictures, Buena Vista. Dean Cundey.

ART DIRECTION—SET DECORATION

BEACHES, Touchstone Pictures in Association with Silver Screen Partners III, Buena Vista. Albert Brenuer; Garrett Lewis.

DANGEROUS LIAISONS. Warner Bros. Stuart Craig; Gerard James.

RAIN MAN, Guber-Peters Company, United Artists. Ida Random; Linda DeScenna

TUCKER THE MAN AND HIS DREAM, Lucasfilm. Paramount. Dean Tavoularis; Armin Ganz.

WHO FRAMED ROGER RABBIT, Amblin Entertainment and Touchstone Pictures, Buena Vista.

COSTUME DESIGN

COMING TO AMERICA. Eddie Murphy. Paramount. Deborah Nadoolman.

DANGEROUS LIAISONS, Warner Bros. James Acheson.

A HANDFUL OF DUST, Stage Screen, New Line. Jane Robinson.

SUNSET, Hudson Hawk, Tri-Star. Patricia Norris.

TUCKER THE MAN AND HIS DREAM. Lucasfilm, Paramount. Milena Canonero.

SOUND

BIRD, Malpaso, Warner Bros. Les Fresholtz, Dick Alexander, Vera Poore and Willie D. Burton.

DIE HARD, 20th Century Fox. Don Bassman, Kevin F. Cleary, Richard Overton and Al Overton.

GORILLAS IN THE MIST, Warner Bros./Universal. Andy Nelson, Brian Saunders and Peter Handford.

MISSISSIPPI BURNING, Frederick Zollo, Orion. Robert Litt, Elliot Tyson, Rick Kline and Danny Michael.

WHO FRAMED ROGER RABBIT, Amblin Entertainment and Touchstone Pictures, Buena Vista. Robert Knudson, John Boyd, Don Digirolamo and Tony Dawe.

FILM EDITING

DIE HARD, 20th Century Fox. Frank J. Urioste and John F. Link.

GORILLAS IN THE MIST, Warner Bros./Universal. Stuart Baird.

MISSISSIPPI BURNING, Frederick Zollo, Orion. Gerry Hambling.

RAIN MAN, Guber-Peters Company, United Artists. Stu Linder.

WHO FRAMED ROGER RABBIT, Amblin Entertainment and Touchstone Pictures, Buena Vista. Arthur Schmidt.

SOUND EFFECTS EDITING

DIE HARD, 20th Century Fox. Stephen H. Flick and Richard Shorr.

WHO FRAMED ROGER RABBIT, Amblin Entertainment Touchstone, Buena Vista. Charles L. Campbell and Louis L. Edemann.

WILLOW. Lucasfilm with Imagine Entertainment. MGM. Ben Burtt and Richard Hymns.

VISUAL EFFECTS

DIE HARD. 20th Century Fox. Richard Edlund, Al DiSarro, Brent Boates and Thaine Morris.

WHO FRAMED ROGER RABBIT, Amblin Entertainment-Touchstone, Buena Vista. Ken Ralston, Richard Williams, Edward Jones and George Gibbs.

WILLOW, Lucasfilm with Imagine Entertainment, M-G-M. Dennis Muren, Michael McAlister. Phil Tippett and Chris Evans.

SONG

CALLING YOU (*Bagdad Cafe*, Pelemele Film, Island); Music and lyrics by Bob Telson.

LET THE RIVER RUN (*Working Girl*, 20th Century Fox); Music and lyrics by Carly Simon.

TWO HEARTS (*Foster*, N.F.H. Hemdale); Music by I.amont Dozier. Lyrics by Phil Collins.

SCORING: ORIGINAL MUSIC

THE ACCIDENTAL TOURIST. Warner Bros. John Williams.

DANGEROUS LIAISONS. Warner Bros. George Fenton.

GORILLAS IN THE MIST, Warner Bros./Universal. Maurice Jarre.

THE MILAGRO BEANFIELD WAR, Robert Redford/Moctesuma Esparza, Universal. Dave Grusin.

RAIN MAN, Guber/Peters. United Artists. Hans Zimmer.

MAKEUP

BEETLEJUICE. Geffen/Warner Bros. Ve Neill, Steve LaPorte and Robert Short.

COMING TO AMERICA Eddie Murphy, Paramount. Rick Baker.

SCROOGED, Art Unson, Paramount. Tom Burman and Bari Dreiband-Burman.

SHORT FILMS: ANIMATED

THE CAT CAME BACK National Film Board of Canada. Cordell Barker.

TECHNOLOGICAL THREAT, Kroyer Films, Inc. Bill Kroyer and Brian Jennings.

TIN TOY, Pixar. John Lasseter and William Reeves.

SHORT FILMS: LIVE ACTION

THE APPOINTMENTS OF DENNIS JENNINGS, Schooner Productions, Inc. Dean Parisot and Steven Wright.

CADILLAC DREAMS, Cadillac Dreams Production. Matia Karrell and Abbee Goldstein.

GULLAH TALES, Georgia State University. George deGolian and Gary Moss.

DOCUMENTARY: SHORT SUBJECTS

THE CHILDREN'S STOREFRONT, a Simon and Goodman Picture Company Production. Karen Goodman, producer.

FAMILY GATHERING, a Lese Yasui Production. Lese Yasui and Ann Tegnell, producers.

GANG COPS, Produced at the Center for Visual Anthropology and the School of Cinema/Television, University of Southern California. Thomas B. Fleming and Daniel J. Marks, producers.

PORTRAIT OF IMOGEN, A Pacific Pictures Production. Nancy Hale and Meg Partridge, producers.

YOU DON'T HAVE TO DIE, a Tiger Rose Production in Association with Filmworks, Inc. William Gutlentag and Malcolm Clarke, producers.

DOCUMENTARY: FEATURES

THE CRY OF REASON--BEYERS NAUDE: AN AFRIKANER SPEAKS OUT, a production of Worldwide Documentaries, Inc. Robert Bilheimer and Roland Mix, producers.

HOTEL TERMINUS: THE LIFE AND TIMES OF KLAUS BARBIE, a production of The Memory Pictures Company. Marcel Ophuls, producer.

LET'S GET LOST, a production of Little Bear Films, Inc. Bruce Weber and Nan Bush, producers.

PROMISES TO KEEP, a production of Durrin Productions. Inc. Ginny Dorm, producer.

WHO KILLED VINCENT CHIN?, a production of film News Now Foundation and Detroit Educational Television Foundation. Renee Tajima and Christine Choy, producers.

FOREIGN LANGUAGE FILMS

HANUSSEN (Hungary).

THE MUSIC TEACHER (Belgium).

PELLE THE CONQUEROR (Denmark).

SALAAM BOMBAY! (India).

WOMEN ON THE VERGE OF A NERVOUS BREAKDOWN (Spain).

SPECIAL ACHIEVEMENT AWARD

For Animation DIRECTION: RICHARD WILLIAMS for *Who Fronted Roger Rabbit.*

HONORARY AND OTHER AWARDS

TO NATIONAL FILM BOARD OF CANADA in recognition of its 50th anniversary and its dedicated commitment to originate artistic, creative and technological activity and excellence in every area of film making.

TO EASTMAN KODAK COMPANY in recognition of the company's fundamental contributions to the art of motion picturesduring the first century of film history.

GORDON E. SAWYER AWARD

GORDON HENRY COOK

SCIENTIFIC OR TECHNICAL AWARD: ACADEMY AWARD OF MERIT

RAY DOLBY and IOAN ALLEN of Dolby Laboratories Incorporated for their continuous contributions to motion picture sound through the research and development programs of Dolby Laboratories.

SCIENTIFIC OR TECHNICAL AWARD: SCIENTIFIC AND ENGINEERING AWARD

ROY W. EDWARDS and the Engineering Staff of PHOTO SONICS, INCORPORATED for the design and development of the Photo-Sonics 35mm-4ER High-Speed Motion Picture Camera with Reflex Viewing and Video Assist.

THE ARNOLD & RICHTER Engineering Staff, OTFO BLASCHEK and ARRIFLEX CORPORATION for the concept and engineering of the Arriflex 35-3 Motion Picture Camera.

BILL TONDREAU of Tondreau Systems/ALVAH MILLER and PAUL JOHNSON of Lynx Robotics/PETER A. REGLA of ELICON/DAN SLATER/BUD ELAM, JOE PARKER and BILL BRYAN of Interactive Motion Control/and JERRY JEFFRESS, RAY FEENEY, BILL HOLLAND and KRIS BROWN for their individual contributions and the collective advancements they have brought to the motion picture industry in the field of motion control technology.

SCIENTIFIC OR TECHNICAL AWARD: TECHNICAL ACHIEVEMENT AWARD

GRANT LOUCKS of Alan Gordon Enterprises Incorporated for the design concept, and GEOFFREY H. WILLIAMSON of Wilcam for the mechanical and electrical engineering, of the Image 300 35mm High-Speed Motion Picture Camera.

MICHAEL V. CHEWEY III for the development of the motion picture industry's first paper tape reader incorporating microprocessor technology.

BHP, Inc., successor to the Bell & Howell Professional Equipment Division, for the development of a high speed reader incorporating microprocessor technology for motion picture laboratories.

HOLLYWOOD FILM COMPANY for the development of a high-speed reader incorporating microprocessor technology for motion picture laboratories.

BRUCE W. KELLER and MANFRED C. MICHELSON of Technical Film Systems for the design and development of a high-speed light valve controller and constant current power supply for motion picture laboratories.

DR. ANFAL LISZIEWICZ and GLENN M. BERGGREN of ISCO-OPTIC GmbH for the design and development of the Ultra-Star series of motion picture lenses.

JAMES K. BRANCH of Spectra Cine, Incorporated, and WILLIAM L. BLOWERS and NASIR J. ZAIDI for the design and development of the Spectra CineSpot one-degree spotmeter for measuring the brightness of motion picture screens.

BOB BADAMI, DICK BERNSTEIN and BILL BERNSTEIN of Offbeat Systems for the design and development of the Streamline Scoring System, Mark IV, for motion picture music editing.

GARY ZELLER of Zeller International Limited for the development of Zel-Jel fire protection barrier for motion picture stunt work.

EMANUEL TRILLIING of Trilling Resources Limited for the development of Stunt-Gel fire protection barrier for motion picture stunt work.

PAUL A. ROOS for the invention of a method known as Video Assist, whereby a scene being photographed on motion picture film can be viewed on a monitor and/or recorded on video tape.

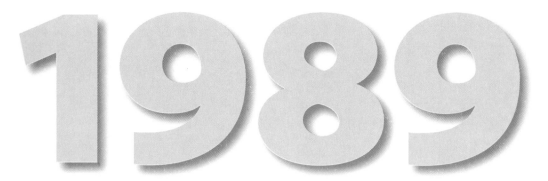

1989

"When you're lying drunk at the airport you're Irish. When you win an Oscar you're British."
—Brenda Fricker

To the tune of "Walking My Baby Back Home," Crystal sang "Gee, it's great/in a segregated state/*Driving Miss Daisy* back home." It was a tribute to the sweetly sentimental little $10 million movie that sparked the biggest controversy in years. Though it earned nine nominations, the Academy snubbed its director, Bruce Beresford. He had good company in the isolation tank with his leading man, Morgan Freeman, and inflammatory director Spike

BLACK-EYED DAISY

CEREMONY: March 26, 1990
Shrine Auditorium, Los Angeles
HOST: Billy Crystal

Lee, whose *Do the Right Thing*, Roger Ebert's pick for Best Film of the Year, had been left by the wayside. Cries of racism were briefly muted when Denzel Washington handily won Best Supporting for *Glory*, making him the fourth African-American to clutch the gold. But the pro-Lee crowd was relentless. Led by a bizarrely dressed Kim Basinger, escorted to the ceremony by current beau, rock star Prince, she hesitated as she presented clips of Best Picture nominees to remind the audience of *Do the Right Thing*'s glaring omission. She was greeted with hisses from the balcony.

Nominated director Oliver Stone bided his time in hopes that the controversy would swing Best Picture his way for *Born on the Fourth of July*. But *Daisy* took it, along with a statuette for its octogenarian star, Jessica Tandy, who raised the award high and shouted, "I am on cloud nine!" Her actor husband of fifty years, Hume Cronyn, later cracked that "if this had happened earlier in our marriage we'd be divorced by now."

A wired Diana Ross led a final number, "Somewhere Over the Rainbow," demanding that everyone join in. The camera cut to its live hookup in Sydney, Australia, where Mel Gibson continued to eat through the song. The big winner of the night was designer Giorgio Armani, who had dressed more than half of the Oscar recipients, including Washington and surprise Best Actor victor Daniel Day-Lewis.

Crystal's biggest laugh came at the expense of a highly publicized plagiarism suit launched by Art Buchwald against Paramount for Eddie Murphy's *Coming to America*. Following a montage titled "100 Years at the Movies," Crystal quipped, "There are 330 pieces of film in that montage, and what's amazing is that, according to Paramount, not one has yet to go into profits."

BEST PICTURE
DRIVING MISS DAISY

"We're up here for one very simple reason," said producers Richard and Lili Zanuck. "Bruce Beresford is a brilliant director." Ironically, Beresford had, on the eve of the Oscars, just survived a major driving accident in Nigeria, where he was filming.

Driving Miss Daisy was based on a prize-winning play that subtly chronicles the changes in Southern race relations from 1948 through 1973 as reflected in the complex relationship between a white widow and her black chauffeur. Director Beresford sensitively renders the nuances of the slowly evolving friendship between Miss Daisy and Hoke. Beresford's sensibilities, according to Roger Ebert, "seem curiously in tune with the American South." His credits include the superb *Tender Mercies* (1983) and *Crimes of the Heart* (1986). The film's emotional restraint pays powerful dividends.

Jessica Tandy, Morgan Freeman

The envelope, please...

BEST DIRECTOR
OLIVER STONE (B. 1946)
BORN ON THE FOURTH OF JULY

"How sweet it is, and how fleeting," Stone told the crowd. "I always wanted to make movies, and would give everything of myself when I had the chance."

Stone began his career as a screenwriter, winning an Oscar for his screenplay of *Midnight Express* (1978). His directorial debut came with the highly-charged *Salvador* (1986) and continued with the Academy Award–winning *Platoon* (1986) and *Wall Street* (1987), followed by *Talk Radio* (1988). He later produced *Reversal of Fortune* (1990) and directed *The Doors* (1991), the Oscar-nominated *JFK* (1991), and *Natural Born Killers* (1994), among other films.

BEST ACTOR
DANIEL DAY-LEWIS (B. 1957)
MY LEFT FOOT

Day-Lewis brilliantly portrays the true story of a petulant, spastic quadriplegic Irish artist who uses his only functional limb—his foot—to write and draw.

The word from the set was that Day-Lewis really learned how to write with his foot and never came out of his wheelchair for the six weeks of filming. A London stage actor, Day-Lewis made his auspicious film debut in *My Beautiful Laundrette* (1985), followed by *A Room with a View* (1985). He later appeared in *The Age of Innocence* (1993) and *The Boxer* (1998).

© A.M.P.A.S®

BEST ACTRESS
JESSICA TANDY (1909–1994)
DRIVING MISS DAISY

"I never expected in a million years that I would be in this position," said Tandy. "It's a miracle. I thank my lucky stars and [producers] Richard and Lili Zanuck, who had the faith to give me this wonderful chance and, also, most especially, to that forgotten man, my director, Bruce Beresford."

Tandy, a London stage actress, appeared as Blanche du Bois in the original production of *A Streetcar Named Desire* in New York (1947). Tandy married actor Hume Cronyn in 1942, and they became a Hollywood pair.

BEST OF 1989
Best Picture: *Driving Miss Daisy*
Best Director: Oliver Stone, *Born on the Fourth of July*
Best Actor: Daniel Day-Lewis, *My Left Foot*
Best Actress: Jessica Tandy, *Driving Miss Daisy*
Best Supporting Actor: Denzel Washington, *Glory*
Best Supporting Actress: Brenda Fricker, *My Left Foot*
Honorary Award: Akira Kurosawa

FIRSTS
- "Am I? Well, good for me" was Jessica Tandy's response to being told that she had just become the oldest actress to win the Oscar.
- *Driving Miss Daisy* became the first film to win Best Picture without a Best Director nomination since *Grand Hotel* (1931–32).
- Dustin Hoffman made his debut as director of the poetic *Dead Poets Society* but dropped out and turned the cameras over to Peter Weir.
- *My Left Foot* became the first Irish film ever to win a Best Picture nomination. After the nomination, its box office skyrocketed.

SECONDS
Denzel Washington became the second African-American man to win Best Supporting Actor since Louis Gossett Jr. in 1982. On the other hand, Morgan Freeman's performance in *Daisy* redefined the word dignity, and was nominated for best actor.

ROLE REVERSALS
- Robin Williams scooped up the lead in *Dead Poets Society* after Dustin Hoffman dropped out.
- Danny Aiello's role in *Do the Right Thing* was originally offered to Robert De Niro.
- Jessica Tandy beat Katharine Hepburn, Bette Davis, and Angela Lansbury to the back seat of *Driving Miss Daisy*.

SINS OF OMISSION
Pictures: *Do the Right Thing,* Spike Lee's controversial film, set during one long, hot day in a Brooklyn ghetto, in which racial tensions involving a white-owned pizzeria come to a head.
- *Roger & Me ,* Michael Moore's iconoclastic documentary.
- *Crimes and Misdemeanors,* Woody Allen's morality play in which a wealthy doctor arranges for the murder of his demanding mistress and comes to ignore his conscience.
- *Henry V,* Kenneth Branagh's inventive, gritty, emotional, and expressive rendering of Shakespeare's play, the most important film production of which had been Olivier's in 1945.
- *Enemies, A Love Story,* Based on the novel by Isaac Bashevis Singer, Paul Mazursky's directorial effort produced a resonant tragedy about a post-Holocaust Jew who cannot choose between three women: his current wife, his mistress (who hid him during the war), and his prewar, presumed dead wife.

UNMENTIONABLES
- It was a big night for Jane Fonda, who proudly displayed both her newly augmented breasts and her new boyfriend, Ted Turner. Even *Newsweek* was moved to comment on "her newly fashioned body swathed in a blue Valkyrie-in-love dress with glittery abstract breast plate. "
- Backstage, Oscar recipient Denzel Washington talked to reporters about the content of *Glory*: "I was stunned I wasn't taught this in school," he said.

BEST SUPPORTING ACTOR
DENZEL WASHINGTON (B. 1954)
GLORY

Saluting "the black soldiers who helped to make this country free," Denzel picked up his well-deserved Oscar for his eloquent, heart-tugging, daring performance as a runaway slave who joins the all-black regiment during the Civil War.

Washington's breakthrough came in 1987, with an Oscar-nominated supporting role in Cry Freedom. His career continued apace, with a starring role that earned him a Best Actor nomination in Malcolm X (1992), followed by star turns in such films as Philadelphia and The Pelican Brief (both 1993), Devil in a Blue Dress (1995), and The Bone Collector (1999).

Brenda Fricker with Daniel Day-Lewis

BEST SUPPORTING ACTRESS
BRENDA FRICKER (B. 1945)
MY LEFT FOOT

"I don't believe this," gasped the deserving star for her deeply moving performance as the warm, loving mother of the cantankerous boy prodigy—one among her brood of twenty-two. She continued, "I'd like to thank Mrs. Brown"—her real-life film character. "Anyone who gives birth twenty-two times deserves one of these."

She's best known in London for her starring role in the medical soap opera *Casualty*. After the show Fricker, joking with reporters, said, "I don't even have a mantel to put this on. I'll have to buy a new home." Several weeks after the ceremony, she told *Good Morning America*'s Joan Lunden, "It's weird. I come down and the Oscar's still sitting on the table, and I think, What's that doing in my house still?"

HONORARY AWARD
AKIRA KUROSAWA (1910–1998)

Introduced by Steven Spielberg as a "man many of us believe to be one of the few true visionaries ever to work in our medium," Kurosawa rose from his seat to a standing ovation, after a brief documentary montage prepared by Richard Schickel was shown. It ended with Kurosawa's words: "In a mad world, only the mad are sane."

Best known for his great film *Rashoman* (1950) and its innovative use of varying points of view to tell the same story, Kurosawa, a giant of the cinema, is as close as one can get to a household name in foreign filmmakers. In fact, Kurosawa is more popular in the West than he is in his native Japan. After a dry spell in the 1960s, Kurosawa attempted suicide. Fortunately, he survived to make more unforgettable films that run the gamut from action films to historical epics to humanistic dramas to works of great imagination.

Among his stirring films, which often take their inspiration from American Westerns and the classics of Shakespeare, Dostoyevsky, and Gorky, are *Ikiru* (1952), *The Seven Samurai* (1954, his most famous film), *Yojimbo* (1961), *Sanjuro* (1962), and, more recently, *Kagemusha* (1980), *Ran* (1985), and *Rhapsody in August* (1991). His memoir, *Something Like an Autobiography*, was published in 1982.

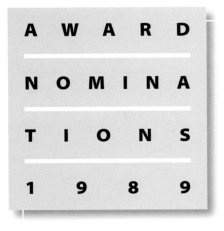

PICTURE

BORN ON THE FOURTH OF JULY, A. Kitman Ho & Ixtlan, Universal. Produced by A. Kitman Ho and Oliver Stone.
DEAD POETS SOCIETY. Touchstone Pictures with Silver Screen Partners IV, Buena Vista. Produced by Steven Haft, Paul Junger Witt and Tony Thomas.
DRIVING MISS DAISY, Zanuck Company, Warner Bros. Produced by Richard D. Zanuck and Lili Fini Zanuck.
FIELD OF DREAMS, Gordon Company, Universal. Produced by Lawrence Gordon and Charles Gordon.
MY LEFT FOOT, Ferndale/Granada, Miramax. Produced by Noel Pearson.

ACTOR

KENNETH BRANAGH in *Henry V*, Renaissance Films with BBC, Samuel Goldwyn Company.
TOM CRUISE in *Born on the Fourth of July*, A. Kitman Ho & Ixtlan, Universal.
DANIEL DAY LEWIS in *My Left Foot*, Ferndale/Granada, Miramax.
MORGAN FREEMAN in *Driving Miss Daisy*, Zanuck Company, Warner Bros.
ROBIN WILIAMS in *Dead Poets Society*, Touchstone Pictures with Silver Screen Partners IV, Buena Vista.

ACTRESS

ISABELLE ADJANI in *Camille Claudel*, Films Christian Fechner-Lilith Films-Gaumont-A2 TV France-Films A2-DD, Orion Classics.
PAULINE COLLINS in *Shirley Valentine*, Lewis Gilbert/Willy Russell, Paramount.
JESSICA LANGE in *Music Box*, Carolco, TriStar.
MICHELLE PFEIFFER in *The Fabulous Baker Boys*, Gladden Entertainment, Mirage. 20th Century Fox.
JESSICA TANDY in *Driving Miss Daisy*, Zanuck Company, Warner Bros.

SUPPORTING ACTOR

DANNY AIELLO in *Do the Right Thing*, Forty Acres and a Mule Filmworks, Universal.
DAN AYKROYD in *Driving Miss Daisy*, Zanuck Company, Warner Bros.
MARLON BRANDO in *A Dry White Season*, Paula Weinstein, MGM.
MARTIN LANDAU in *Crimes and Misdemeanors*, Jack Rollins and Charles H. Joffe, Orion.
DENZEL WASHINGTON in *Glory*, Tri-Star.

SUPPORTING ACTRESS

BRENDA FRICKER in *My Left Foot*, Ferndale/Granada, Miramax.
ANJELICA HUSTON in *Enemies, a Love Story*, Morgan Creek, 20th Century Fox.
LENA OLIN in *Enemies, a Love Story*, Morgan Creek, 20th Century Fox.
JULIA ROBERTS in *Steel Magnolias*, Rastar Production, Tri-Star.
DIANNE WEIST in *Parenthood*, Imagine Entertainment Universal.

DIRECTION

WOODY ALLEN for *Crimes and Misdemeanors*, Jack Rollins and Charles H. Joffe, Orion.
KENNETH BRANAGH for *Henry V*, Renaissance Films with BBC, Samuel Goldwyn Company.
JIM SHERIDAN for *My Left Foot*, Ferndale/Granada, Miraman.
OLIVER STONE for *Born on the Fourth of July*, A. Kitman Ho & Ixtlan, Universal.

PETER WEIR for *Dead Poets Society*, Touchstone with Silver Screen Partners IV, Buena Vista.

WRITING: DIRECTLY FOR THE SCREEN

CRIMES AND MISDEMEANORS, Jack Rollins and Charles H. Joffe, Orion. Woody Allen.
DEAD POETS SOCIETY, Touchstone with Silver Screen Partners IV, Buena Vista. Tom Schulman.
DO THE RIGHT THING, Forty Acres and a Mule Filmworks, Universal. Spike Lee.
SEX, LIES, AND VIDEOTAPE. Outlaw, Miramax. Steven Soderbergh.
WHEN HARRY MET SALLY..., Castle Rock, Columbia. Nom Ephron.

WRITING: BASED ON MATERIAL FROM ANOTHER MEDIUM

BORN ON THE FOURTH OF JULY, A. Kitman Ho & Ixtlan, Universal. Oliver Stone and Ron Kovic.
DRIVING MISS DAISY, Zanuck Company. Warner Bros. Alfred Uhry.
ENEMIES, A LOVE STORY, Morgan Creek, 20th Century Fox. Roger L. Simon and Paul Mazursky.
FIELD OF DREAMS, Gordon Company. Universal. Phil Alden Robinson.
MY LEFT FOOT, Ferndale/Granada, Miramax. Jim Sheridan and Shane Connaughton.

CINEMATOGRAPHY

THE ABYSS, 20th Century Fox. Mikael Salomon.
BLAZE, Touchtone with Silver Screen Partners IV, Buena Vista. Haskell Wexler.
BORN ON THE FOURTH OF JULY, A. Kitman Ho & Ixtlan. Universal. Robert Richardson.
THE FABULOUS BAKER BOYS, Gladden Entertainment, Mirage, 20th Century Fox. Michael Ballhaus.
GLORY, Tri-Star Pictures, Tri-Star, Freddie Francis.

ART DIRECTION—SET DECORATION

THE ABYSS, 20th Century Fox. Leslie Dilley; Anne Kuljian.
THE ADVENTURES OF BARON MUNCHAUSEN, Prominent Features & Laura Film. Columbia. Dante Feretti; Francesca Lo Schiavo.
BATMAN, Warner Bros. Anton Furst; Peter Young.
DRIVING MISS DAISY, Zanuck Company. Warner Bros. Bruno Rubeo; Crispian Sallis.
GLORY, Tri-Star Pictures, Tri-Star. Norman Garwood; Garret Lewis.

COSTUME DESIGN

THE ADVENTURES OF BARON MUNCHAUSEN, Prominent Features & Laura Film, Columbia. Gabriella Pescucci.
DRIVING MISS DAISY, Zanuck. Warner Bros. Elizabeth McBride.
HARLEM NIGHTS, Eddie Murphy, Paramount Joe I. Tompkins.
HENRY V, Renaissance Films with BBC, Samuel Goldwyn Company. Phyllis Dalton.
VALMONT, Claude Bern and Renn. Orion. Theodor Pistek.

SOUND

THE ABYSS, 20th Century Fox. Don Bassman, Kevin F. Cleary, Richard Overton and Lee Orloff.
BLACK RAIN, Jaffe/Lansing with Michael Douglas. Paramount. Donald O. Mitchell, Kevin O'Connell, Greg P. Russell and Keith A. Wester.
BORN ON THE FOURTH OF JULY. A. Kitman Ho & Ixtlan, Universal. Michael Minkler, Gregory H. Watkins. Wylie Slateman and Tod A. Maitland.
GLORY, Tri-Star. Donald O. Mitchell, Gregg C. Rudloff, Elliot Tyson and Russell Williams II.
INDIANA JONES AND THE LAST CRUSADE. Lucasfilm, Paramount Ben Burtt, Gary Summers, Shawn Murphy and Tony Dawe.

FILM EDITING

THE BEAR, Renn, Tri-Star. Noelle Boisson.
BORN ON THE FOURTH OF JULY, A. Kitman Ho & Ixtlan, Universal. David Brenner and Joe Hutshing.

DRIVING MISS DAISY, Zanuck Company Production, Warner Bros. Mark Warner.
THE FABULOUS BAKER BOYS, Gladden Entertainment, Mirage, 20th Century Fox. William Steinkamp.
GLORY, Tri-Star. Steven Rosenblum.

SOUND EFFECTS EDITING

BLACK RAIN, Jaffe/Lansing with Michael Douglas, Paramount. Milton C. Burrow and William L. Manger.
INDIANA JONES AND THE LAST CRUSADE, Lucasfilm, Paramount Ben Burtt and Richard Hymns.
LETHAL WEAPON 2, Warner Bros. Robert Henderson and Alan Robert Murray.

VISUAL EFFECTS

THE ABYSS, 20th Century Fox. John Bruno. Dennis Muren, Hoyt Yeatman and Dennis Skotak.
THE ADVENTURES OF BARON MUNCHAUSEN, Prominent Features & Laura Film, Columbia. Richard Conway and Kent Houston.
BACK TO THE FUTURE PART II, Universal Pictures/Amblin Entertainment, Universal. Ken Ralston, Michael Lantieri, John Bell and Steve Gawley.

SONG

AFTER ALL (*Chances Are*, Tri-Star); Music by Tom Snow. Lyrics by Dean Pitchford.
THE GIRL WHO USED TO BE ME (*Shirley Valentine*, Lewis Gilbert/Willy Russell, Paramount); Music by Marvin Hamlisch. Lyrics by Alan and Marilyn Bergman.
I LOVE TO SEE YOU SMILE (*Parenthood*, Imagine Entertainment, Universal); Music and lyrics by Randy Newman.
KISS THE GIRL (*The Little Mermaid*, Walt Disney Pictures with Silver Screen Partners IV, BuenaVista); Music by Alan Menken. Lyrics by Howard Ashman.
UNDER THE SEA (*The Little Mermaid*, Walt Disney Pictures with Silver Screen Partners IV, Buena Vista); Music by Alan Menken. Lyrics by Howard Ashman.

SCORING: ORIGINAL MUSIC

BORN ON THE FOURTH OF JULY, A. Kitman Ho & Ixtlan, Universal. John Williams.
THE FABULOUS BAKER BOYS, Gladden Entertainment, Mirage, 20th Century Fox. David Grusin.
FIELD OF DREAMS, Gordon Company, Universal. James Horner.
INDIANA JONES AND THE LAST CRUSADE, Lucasfilm, Paramount John Williams.
THE LITTLE MERMAID, Walt Disney Pictures with Silver Screen Partners IV, Buena Vista. Alan Menken.

MAKEUP

THE ADVENTURES OF BARON MUNCHAUSEN, Prominent Features & Laura Film, Columbia. Maggie Weston and Fabrizio Sforza.
DAD, Universal Plctures/Amblin Entertainment, Universal. Dick Smith, Ken Diaz and Greg Nelson.
DRIVING MISS DAISY, Zanuck Company, Warner Bros. Manlio Rocchetti, Lynn Barber and Kevin Haney.

SHORT FILMS: ANIMATED

BALANCE, a Lauenstein Production. Christoph Lanenslein and Wolfgang Lauenstein.
THE COW, The "Pilot" Co-op Animated Film Studio with VPTO Videofilm. Alexander Petrov.
THE HILL FARM, National Film & Television School. Mark Baker.

SHORT FILMS: LIVE ACTION

AMAZON DIARY, Determined Production, Inc. Robert Nixon.
THE CHILDEATER, Stephen-Tammuz Productions, Ltd. Jonathan Tammuz.
WORK EXPERIENCE, North Inch Production, Ltd. James Hendrie.

DOCUMENTARY: SHORT SUBJECTS

FINE FOOD, FINE PASTRIES, OPEN 6 TO 9, a production of David Petersen Productions. David Petersen, producer.

THE JOHNSTOWN FLOOD, a production of Guggenheim Production, Inc. Charles Guggenheim, producer.
YAD VASHEM: PRESERVING THE PAST TO ENSURE THE FUTURE, a Ray Errol Fox Production. Ray Errol Fox, producer.

DOCUMENTARY: FEATURES

ADAM CLAYTON POWELL, a production of RKB Productions. Richard Killberg and Yvonne Smith, producers.
COMMON THREADS: STORIES FROM THE QUILT, a Telling Pictures and The Couturie Company Production. Robert Epstein and Bill Couturie, producers.
CRACK USA: COUNTY UNDER SIEGE, a production of Half-Court Productions, Ltd. Vince DiPersio and William Guttentag, producers.
FOR ALL MANKIND, a production of Apollo Associates/FAM Productions Inc. Al Reinert and Betsy Broyles Breier, producers.
SUPER CHIEF: THE LIFE AND LEGACY OF EARL WARREN, a Quest Production. Judith Leonard and Bill Jersey, producers.

FOREIGN LANGUAGE FILMS

CAMILLE CLAUDEL (France).
CINEMA PARADISO (Italy).
JESUS OF MONTREAL (Canada).
WALTZING REGITZE (Denmark).
WHAT HAPPENED TO SANTIAGO (Puerto Rico).

HONORARY AND OTHER AWARDS

TO AKIRA KUROSAWA, for accomplishments that have inspired, delighted, enriched and entertained audiences and influenced filmmakers throughout the world.
The Academy of Motion Picture Arts and Sciences' Board of Governors commends the contributions of the members of the ENGINEERING COMMITTEES OF THE SOCIETY OF MOTION PICTURE AND TELEVISION ENGINEERS (SMPTE). By establishing industry standards, they have greatly contributed to making film a primary form of international communication.

JEAN HERSHOLT HUMANITARIAN AWARD

TO HOWARD W. KOCH

GORDON E. SAWYER AWARD

TO PIERRE ANGENIEUX

SCIENTIFIC OR TECHNICAL AWARDS: SCIENTIFIC AND ENGINEERING AWARD

JAMES KETCHUM of JSK Engineering, for the excellence in engineering and the broad adaptability of the SDA521B Advance/Retard system for magnetic film sound dubbing.
J. NOXON LEAVTIT, for the invention of, and ISTEC, INCORPORATED, for the Continuing development of the Wescam Stabilized Camera System.
GEOFFREY H, WILLIAMSON of Wilcam Photo Research, Incorporated, for the design and development, and to ROBERT D. AUGUSTE for the electronic design and development of the Wilcam W-7 200 frames-per-second VistaVision Rotating Mirror Reflex Camera.
J.L FISHER of J.L. Fisher, Incorporated, for the design and manufacture of a small, mobile motion picture camera platform known as the Fisher Model Ten Dolly.
KLAUS RESCH for the design, ERICH FITZ and FGV SCHMIDLE & FITZ for the development of the Super Panther MS-180 Camera Dolly.

SCIENTIFIC OR TECHNICAL AWARDS: TECHNICAL ACHIEVEMENT AWARD

DR. LEO CATOZZO for the design and development of the CIR-Catozzo Self-Perforating Adhesive Tape Film Splicer.
MAGNA-TECH ELECTRONIC COMPANY far the introduction of the first remotely controlled Advance/Retard function for magnetic film sound dubbing.

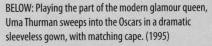

BELOW: Her hair is too tight and her dress too loose, but Gwyneth Paltrow looks lovely nonetheless in a pink gown that's fit for a princess. (1998)

BELOW: Playing the part of the modern glamour queen, Uma Thurman sweeps into the Oscars in a dramatic sleeveless gown, with matching cape. (1995)

ABOVE: Hilary Swank sports an ornate diamond necklace, most likely borrowed from Harry Winston, the jeweler to the stars who loans out his priceless pieces to many actresses on Oscar night. (1999)

ABOVE: Looking every bit the classic screen goddess, Winona Ryder was one of the first stars to appear at the Oscars in a vintage dress. This beaded gown is complemented beautifully by her perfectly coifed 20s-style hair. (1996)

©A.M.P.A.S.®

THE LOOK OF THE DECADE

$\mathcal{A}$S THE EXCESS OF THE GLITTERING 80s began to fade, the fashion flocks embraced minimalism as the new look of style and grace. Simplicity and understatement were back in style, although luxury was still a staple of any well-dressed woman's wardrobe. Though still thoroughly glamorous, the stars of the 90s tempered their extravagance by paying more attention to craftsmanship than to flashy shows of vulgarity. Simple yet striking gowns became the picks of many actresses, and the designer of the dress was, for the first time, as important as the dress itself. It was in the 90s that watching the fashion parade ceased to be a fun diversion on Oscar night and instead became the *raison d'être* for many people who watched the ceremonies.

OPPOSITE : Susan Sarandon's shimmering copper, generously-cut gown evokes the glamour of the 1950s. (1995)

1990

"I will never forget what happened here tonight. . . people I went to school with will never forget."

—Kevin Costner

Just five days after a cease-fire in the Persian Gulf, the tense political situation transformed the rain-battered entrance of the Shrine Auditorium. In lieu of front-line bleacher seats there were metal detectors, federal agents, and bomb-sniffing dogs. Inside, a battle of a different sort brewed between hearts and minds. Cerebral cinephiles, outraged that their living legend, Martin Scorsese, had been shut out in the past, were hoping to gun down the aspirations of the touchy-feely bloc behind the sentimental Western *Dances with Wolves.* But the odds were against Scorsese's *GoodFellas*, a blood-red mosaic of casual mob violence. Its only win went to Best Supporting Actor, Joe Pesci, who delivered the shortest acceptance speech on record: "Thank you, it was my privilege."

The groundswell for *Wolves* erupted in a tidal wave of Oscars for Sound, Editing, Score, Cinematography, and Best Adapted Screenplay. The *Wolves* pack was briefly sidelined by three exceptional women who brought down the house. The first was the sure-bet winner for Best Supporting Actress, Whoopi Goldberg (*Ghost*), whose emotions could barely be contained at being the first black actress to win an Oscar since Hattie McDaniel in 1939. Next up was honorary Oscar recipient Sophia Loren, whose ageless, monumental presence earned her a standing ovation. Following her "Grazie, America" and her regal exit, an unlikely new face emerged from anonymity.

Kathy Bates, with her gussied-up PTA-mom looks, grasped the Best Actress gold for her chilling portrait of a psychotic fan in *Misery*. Costner was stalled one last time, with an anxious hand to his face, as Best Actor went to gaunt British matinee idol Jeremy Irons for his eerie Claus von Bulow portrayal in *Reversal of Fortune*. Finally, the dam burst and the boyishly handsome Costner bounded to the stage twice in a row for Best Director and Best Picture. It was a triumph of perseverance and faith for the first-time director. He'd put his own money into the faltering early days of the production, which had been archly dubbed "Costner's Last Stand."

DANCES WITH OSCARS

CEREMONY: March 25, 1991
Shrine Auditorium, Los Angeles
HOST: Billy Crystal

**BEST PICTURE/
BEST DIRECTOR
KEVIN COSTNER (B. 1955)
*DANCES WITH WOLVES***

"That's how we used to make them," said former president Ronald Reagan after a special birthday viewing. But they never made them this long (183 minutes), and rarely, if ever, were white men portrayed as the enemy!

Costner's accidental Civil War hero heads west to Dakota country to see it "before it's all gone." Said the *Washington Post*, "Costner creates a vision so childlike, so willfully romantic, it's hard to put up a fight." The *Austin Chronicle* enthused, "It's an old-fashioned movie with a smart, contemporary perspective." And Roger Ebert felt it had "the epic sweep of a Western by John Ford." The reviews were generally sterling, with one notable exception: the soon-to-retire Pauline Kael of *The New Yorker* suggested

that Costner was a bland amateur whose film might be better called *Plays with Camera*. But there was high praise, especially from the Native American community, for his generous use of the Sioux-Lakota language and a detailed view of their culture and tragic history.

It took Costner a long time to get to the top, first as a studio stage manager, then in small forgotten roles. His first major exposure didn't even show his face; he was the handsomely turned-out suicide's corpse in the credits of *The Big Chill* (1983).

The envelope, please…

BEST ACTOR
JEREMY IRONS (B. 1948)
REVERSAL OF FORTUNE

"I'd love to meet [Claus von Bulow] and tell him what he's all about," said Irons. As the imperious, twice-tried husband of comatose Newport heiress Sunny, Irons gave von Bulow almost sympathetic dimension. The classic line from the film came from von Bulow's mistress during a key scene in which the two contemplated the ideal defense lawyer. "Get the Jew," she said, meaning none other than Alan Dershowitz.

The self-effacing Brit told reporters that he thought by and large Americans were better film actors. Meanwhile, American viewers thought him "the thinking girl's pinup." Irons began his career as a London street singer who made his first major leap as the conflicted hero in the British series *Brideshead Revisited* (1981). From then on life was a golden time, with a series of diverse leading roles in such films as

The French Lieutenant's Woman (1981), *Betrayal* (1983), *Dead Ringers* (1988), and a voice-over in *The Lion King* (1994).

BEST ACTRESS
KATHY BATES (B. 1948)
MISERY

Her victory announced, the grateful, overwhelmed Bates closed her eyes and turned to kiss her fiancé, Tomy Campisi. Though known to theater audiences for her mesmerizing Broadway debut in *'Night, Mother*, Bates was a virtual unknown to mass audiences until she was rescued from obscurity by director Rob Reiner to play *Misery*'s Annie, a mercurial psycho nurse who holds a romance novelist (James Caan) captive until he revives her favorite character.

Bates's career was in danger of going the route of Anthony Perkins after the actor played a psycho in the film *Psycho* (ironically, his character was called Norman Bates). But her average looks saved her. She confided to talk-show host Charlie Rose the basis of her level-headed ego. "I had just given out my first autograph on a scrap of paper," she said. "I was thrilled. Later that night, while walking my dog, I was looking for something to scoop up his business. And there it was, crumpled up on the sidewalk, my autograph."

Bates has shown her gifts time and again in such films as *Fried Green Tomatoes* (1991), *Prelude to a Kiss* (1992), *Dolores Claiborne* (1995), *Titanic* (1997), and *Primary Colors* (1998).

BEST OF 1990
Best Picture: *Dances with Wolves*
Best Director: Kevin Costner, *Dances with Wolves*
Best Actor: Jeremy Irons, *Reversal of Fortune*
Best Actress: Kathy Bates, *Misery*
Best Supporting Actor: Joe Pesci, *GoodFellas*
Best Supporting Actress: Whoopi Goldberg, *Ghost*

FIRST
Dances with Wolves was the first Western to win Best Picture since *Cimarron* in 1931.

ROLE REVERSALS
• Hard to imagine Melanie Griffith playing the con-artist Oedipal mom in *The Grifters*, but someone at the top actually did. Sanity was restored with the casting of the irreplaceable Anjelica Huston.

• Before agreeing to the role of an alcoholic Hollywood has-been in Carrie Fisher's thinly disguised autobio *Postcards from the Edge*, Shirley MacLaine asked Fisher's mom, Debbie Reynolds, for her okay.

ALWAYS A BRIDESMAID, NEVER A BRIDE
The second Honorary Oscar went to screen legend Myrna Loy—known to all for *The Thin Man* series—who was too ill to make it to the ceremony. Bed-bound in her Manhattan apartment, all the 85-year-old Loy could say in a frail voice was "You've made me very happy. Thank you very much." In a six-decade career full of signature roles, she was never once nominated. As such, she joined the ranks of the shamefully overlooked, which include Dirk Bogarde, John Barrymore, Joseph Cotten, Ida Lupino, Tyrone Power, Rita Hayworth, Peter Lorre, and Marilyn Monroe.

UNMENTIONABLES
• Novelist/screenwriter Michael Blake was so broke while penning *Dances with Wolves* that he often slept in his car.

• Bob Hope was the only entrant to the 1990 Academy Awards who wasn't required to walk through a metal detector.

• In the original script of *Pretty Woman* (then called *3000*), Julia Roberts's hooker was a drug addict who was dumped back on the streets after spending a week with a wealthy client. Disney and director Gary Marshall turned to *Cinderella* for a re-think and a smash hit.

• You couldn't have separated Julia Roberts and her fiancé, Kiefer Sutherland, with a crowbar on Oscar night. "I finally know what true love is," she told reporters. Just days after the ceremony, she unceremoniously ran off with Jason Patric, leaving Kiefer holding the garter.

• "My wife doesn't get jealous," revealed Jeremy Irons. "When she sees me in sex scenes she says to herself, 'Oh, he is only acting. I know he can't last that long.'"

• "What is this highbrow shit?" Madonna griped after hearing the songs Stephen Sondheim had written for *Dick Tracy*.

• Anticipating a huge bonanza in *Dick Tracy* paraphernalia, New York men's stores unwisely stocked up on copies of Warren Beatty's bright yellow cashmere trench coat. Sales of his two-way wristwatch radio didn't fare much better. The new generation of kids had never heard of the cartoon hero.

BEST SUPPORTING ACTOR
JOE PESCI (B. 1943)
GOODFELLAS

"I kind of hope Al [Pacino] gets it," Pesci said. Nice guy, clearly, and a key member of the Scorsese ensemble. It wasn't easy for him to get inside the character of Tommy De Vito, the comically insane killer in *GoodFellas*. The only way he could justify shooting an innocent kid in the foot was to imagine "that someday he'd grow up to be a rat."

That same year, Pesci also became the iconic villain to kids playing the stooge burglar one-upped by Macaulay Culkin in *Home Alone*. His acting break came—after careers as a child star on Broadway, a nightclub singer, and a restaurant owner—with Scorsese's masterpiece *Raging Bull* (1980). He'd get his first shot at a leading role in the hilarious *My Cousin Vinny* (1992). But then came *8 Heads in a Duffel Bag* (1997) to slow things down a bit.

BEST SUPPORTING ACTRESS
WHOOPI GOLDBERG (B. 1949)
GHOST

"Ever since I was a little kid, I've wanted this!" Goldberg said upon accepting her award. And she certainly deserved it after completely transforming her role in *Ghost* as the fake clairvoyant who accidentally gets it right for once. "I'm gonna really celebrate once I get these damn shoes off," she quipped after the Award show.

The dreadlocked comedienne had a tough climb to the top, starting out as a cabaret singer, failing in her first film, and doing a long haul of TV sitcoms and made-for-TV movies in the early '90s. Before *Ghost*, she was nominated for *The Color Purple* (1985). Goldberg went on to appear in *Sister Act* (1992), *Corrina, Corrina* (1994), *How Stella Got Her Groove Back* (1998), and *Girl, Interrupted* (1999).

AWARD NOMINATIONS 1990

PICTURE
AWAKENINGS, Columbia. Produced by Walter F. Parkes and Lawrence Lasker.
DANCES WITH WOLVES, Tig, Orion. Produced by Jim Wilson and Kevin Costner.
GHOST, Howard W. Koch. Paramount. Produced by Lisa Weinstein.
THE GODFATHER, PART III, Zoetrope Studios. Paramount. Produced by Francis Ford Coppola.
GOODFELLAS, Warner Bros. Produced by Irwin Winkler.

ACTOR
KEVIN COSTNER in *Dances With Wolves*, Tig. Orion.
ROBERT DE NIRO in *Awakenings*, Columbia.
GERARD DEPARDIEU in *Cyrano de Bergerac*, Hachette Premiere/Camera One, Orion Classics.
RICHARD HARRIS in *The Field*, Granada, Avenue Pictures.
JEREMY IRONS in *Reversal of Fortune*, Reversal Films, Warner Bros.

ACTRESS
KATHY BATES in *Misery*, Castle Rock Entertainment, Columbia.
ANJELICA HUSTON in *The Grifters*, Martin Scorsese, Miramax.
JULIA ROBERIS in *Pretty Woman*, Touchstone Pictures, Buena Vista.
MERYL STREEP in *Postcards from the Edge*, Columbia.
JOANNE WOODWARD in *Mr. & Mrs. Bridge*, Merchant Ivory, Miramax.

SUPPORTING ACTOR
BRUCE DAVISON in *Longtime Companion*, American Playhouse, Samuel Goldwyn Company.
ANDY GARCIA in *The Godfather, Part III*, Zoetrope Studios, Paramount.
GRAHAM GREENE in *Dances With Wolves*, Tig, Orion.
AL PACINO in *Dick Tracy*, Touchstone Pictures, Buena Vista.
JOE PESCI in *GoodFellas*, Warner Bros.

SUPPORTING ACTRESS
ANNETTE BENING in *The Grifters*, Martin Scorsese, Miramax.
LORRAINE BRACCO in *Good Fellas*, Warner Bros.
WHOOPI GOLDBERG in *Ghost*, Howard W. Koch, Paramount.
DIANE LADD in *Wild at Heart*, Polygram/Propaganda Films, Samuel Goldwyn Company.
MARY McDONNELL in *Dances With Wolves*, Tig, Orion.

DIRECTION
FRANCIS FORD COPPOLA for *The Godfather, Part III*, Zoetrope Studios, Paramount.
KEVIN COSTNER, for *Dances With Wolves*, Tig, Orion.
STEPHEN FREARS for *The Grifters*, Martin Scorsese, Miramax.
BARBET SCHROEDER for *Reversal of Fortune*, Reversal Films, Warner Bros.
MARTIN SCORSESE for *Good Fellas*, Warner Bros.

WRITING: DIRECTLY FOR THE SCREEN
ALICE, Jack Rollins and Charles H. Joffe, Orion. Woody Allen.
AVALON, Tri-Star. Barry Levinson.
GHOST, Howard W. Koch, Paramount. Bruce Joel Rubin.
GREEN CARD, Green Card Company, Buena Vista. Peter Weir.

METROPOLITAN, Westerly Film-Video. New Line. Whit Stillman.

WRITING: BASED ON MATERIAL FROM ANOTHER MEDIUM
AWAKENINGS, Columbia. Steven Zaillian.
DANCES WITH WOLVES. Tig. Orion. Michael Blake.
GOOD FELLAS, Warner Bros. Nicholas Pileggi and Martin Scorsese.
THE GRIFTERS, Martin Scorsese, Miramax. Donald K. Westlake.
REVERSAL OF FORTUNE, Reversal Films, Warner Bros. Nicholas Kazan.

CINEMATOGRAPHY
AVALON, Tri-Star,Tri.Star. Allen Daviau.
DANCES WITH WOLVES, Tig. Orion. Dean Semler.
DICK TRACY, Touchstone Pictures, Buena Vista. Vittorio Storaro.
THE GODFATHER, PART III, Zoetrope Studios. Paramount. Gordon Willis.
HENRY & JUNE. Walrus & Associates, Universal. Philippe Rousselot.

ART DIRECTION—SET DECORATION
CYRANO DE BERGERAC, Hachette Premiere/Camera One, Orion Classics. Ezio Frigerio; Jacques Round.
DANCES WITH WOLVES, Tig. Orion. Jeffrey Beecroft; Lisa Dean.
DICK TRACY, Touchstone Pictures, Buena Vista. Richard Sylbert, Rick Simpson.
THE GODFATHER, PART III, Zoetrope Studios, Paramount. Dean Tavoularis; Gary Fettis.
HAMLET, Icon, Warner Bros. Dante Ferretti; Francesca Lo Schiavo.

COSTUME DESIGN
AVALON, Tri-Star. Gloria Gresham.
CYRANO DE BERGERAC, Hachette Premiere/Camera One, Orion Classics. Franca Squarciapino.
DANCES WITH WOLVES. Tig, Orion. Elsa Zamparelli.
DICK TRACY, Touchstone Pictures, Buena Vista. Milena Canonero.
HAMLET, Icon, Warner Bros. Maurizio Millenotti.

SOUND
DANCES WITH WOLVES, Tig, Orion. Jeffrey Perkins. Bill W. Benton, Greg Watkins and Russell Williams II.
DAYS OF THUNDER, Don Simpson and Jerry Bruckheimer, Paramount. Donald O. Mitchell, Rick Mine, Kevin O'Connell and Charles Wilborn.
DICK TRACY, Touchstone Pictures, Buena Vista. Chris Jenkins, David E. Campbell, D.M. Hemphill and Thomas Causey.
THE HUNT FOR RED OCTOBER, Mace Neufeld/Jerry Sherlock, Paramount. Don Bassman, Richard Overton, Kevin F. Cleary and Richard Bryce Goodman.
TOTAL RECALL, Carolco Pictures, Tri-Star. Michael J. Kohut, Carlos de Larios, Aaron Rochin and Nelson Stoll.

FILM EDITING
DANCES WITH WOLVES, Tig, Orion. Neil Travis.
GHOST, Howard W. Koch, Paramount. Walter Murch.
THE GODFATHER, PART III, Zoetrope Studios, Paramount. Barry Malkin, Lisa Fruchtman and Walter Murch.
GOOD FELLAS, Warner Bros. Thelma Schoonmaker.
THE HUNT FOR RED OCTOBER, Mace Neurfeld/Jerry Sherlock, Paramount. Dennis Virkler and John Wright.

SOUND EFFECTS EDITING
FLATLINERS, Stonebridge Entertainment Production, Columbia. Charles L Campbell and Richard Franklin.
THE HUNT FOR RED OCTOBER, Mace Neufeld/Jerry Sherlock, Paramount, Cecelia Hall and George Watters II.
TOTAL RECALL, Carolco Pictures, Tri-Star. Stephen H. Flick.

SONG
BLAZE OF GLORY (*Young Guns II*, Morgan Creek, 20th Century-Fox); Music and Lyrics by Jon Bon Jovi.
I'M CHECKIN' OUT (*Postcards from the Edge*, Columbia); Music and Lyrics by Shel Silverstein.
PROMISE ME YOU'LL REMEMBER (*The Godfather, Part III*, Zoetrope Studios, Paramount); Music by Carmine Coppola. Lyrics by John Bettis.
SOMEWHERE IN MY MEMORY (*Home Alone*, 20th Century-Fox); Music by John Williams. Lyrics by Leslie Bricusse.
SOONER OR LATER (I ALWAYS GET MY MAN) (*Dick Tracy*, Touchstone Pictures, Buena Vista); Music and Lyrics by Stephen Sondheim.

SCORING: ORIGINAL MUSIC
AVALON, Tri -Star. Randy Newman.
DANCES WITH WOLVES, Tig. Orion. John Barry.
GHOST, Howard W. Koch, Paramount Maurice Jarre.
HAVANA, Universal Pictures Limited, Universal. David Grusin.
HOME ALONE, 20th Century-Fox. John Williams.

MAKEUP
CYRANO DE BERGERAC, Hachette Premiere/Camera One, Orion Classics. Michele Burke and Jean-Pierre Eychenne.
DICK TRACY, Touchstone Pictures, Buena Vista. John Caglione, Jr. and Doug Drexler.
EDWARD SCISSORHANDS, 20th Century-Fox. Ve Neill and Stan Winston.

SHORT FILMS: ANIMATED
CREATURE COMFORTS, an Aardman Animations Limited Production. Nick Park, producer.
A GRAND DAY OUT, a National Film and Television School Production. Nick Park, producer.
GRASSHOPPERS (CAVALLETTE), a Bruno Bozzetto Production. Bruno Bozzetto, producer.

SHORT FILMS: LIVE ACTION
BRONX CHEERS, an American Film Institute Production. Raymond De Felitta and Matthew Gross, producers.
DEAR ROSIE, a World's End Production. Peter Cattaneo and Barnaby Thompson, producers.
THE LUNCH DATE, an Adam Davidson Production. Adam Davidson, producer.
SENZENI NA? (WHAT HAVE WE DONE?), an American Film Institute Production. Bernard Joffa and Anthony E, Nicholas, producers.
12:01 PM, a Chanticleer Films Production. Hilary Ripps and Jonathan Heap, producers.

DOCUMENTARY: SHORT SUBJECTS
BURNING DOWN TOMORROW, an Interscope Communications, Inc. Production. Kit Thomas, producer.
CHIMPS: SO LIKE US, a Simon & Goodman Picture Company Production. Karen Goodman and Kirk Simon, producers.
DAYS OF WAITING, a Mouchette Films Production. Steven Okazaki, producer.
JOURNEY INTO LIFE: THE WORLD OF THE UNBORN, an ABC/Kane Productions International, Inc. Production. Derek Bromhall, producer.
ROSE KENNEDY: A LIFE TO REMEMBER, a production of Sanders & Mock Productions and American Film Foundation. Freida Lee Mock and Terry Sanders, producers.

DOCUMENTARY: FEATURES
AMERICAN DREAM, a Cabin Creek Films Production. Barbara Kopple and Arthur Cohn, producers.
BERKELEY IN THE SIXTIES, a production of Berkeley in the Sixties Production Partnership. Mark Kitchell, producer.
BUILDING BOMBS, a Mori/Robinson Production. Mark Mori and Susan Robinson, producers.
FOREVER ACTIVISTS: STORIES FROM THE VETERANS OF THE ABRAHAM LINCOLN BRIGADE, a Judith Montell Production. Judith Montell, producer.
WALDO SALT: A SCREENWRITER'S JOURNEY, a Waldo Productions, Inc. Production. Robert Hillmann and Eugene Corr, producers.

FOREIGN LANGUAGE FILM
CYRANO DR BERGERAC (France).
JOURNEY OF HOPE (Switzerland).
JU DOU (People's Republic of China).
THE NASTY GIRL (Germany).
OPEN DOORS (Italy).

HONORARY AND OTHER AWARDS
TO SOPHIA WREN, one of the genuine treasures of world cinema who, in a career rich with memorable performances, has added permanent luster to our art form.
TO MYRNA LOY, in recognition of her extraordinary qualities both on screen and off, with appreciation for a lifetime's worth of indelible performances.
TO RODERICK T. RYAN, DON TRUMBULL and GEOFFREY H. WILLIAMSON, in appreciation for outstanding service and dedication in upholding the high standards of the Academy of Motion Picture Arts and Sciences.

SPECIAL ACHIEVEMENT AWARDS
For Visual Effects: ERIC BREVIG, ROB BOTTIN, TIM McGOVERN and ALEX FUNKE for *Total Recall*, a Carolco Pictures Production, Tri -Star.

IRVING G. THALBERG MEMORIAL AWARD
TO RICHARD D. ZANUCK and DAVID BROWN

JEAN HERSHOLT HUMANITARIAN AWARD
None given this year.

GORDON E. SAWYER AWARD
TO STEFAN KUDELSKI

SCIENTIFIC OR TECHNICAL AWARDS: ACADEMY AWARD OF MERIT
EASTMAN KODAK COMPANY for the development of T-Grain technology and the introduction of EXR color negative films which utilize this technology.

SCIENTIFIC AND ENGINEERING AWARD
BRUCE WILTON and CARLOS ICINKOFF of Mechanical Concepts, Incorporated, for the development of the Mechanical Concepts Optical Printer Platform.
ENGINEERING DEPARTMENT of ARNOLD & RICHTER for the continued design improvements of the Arriflex BL Camera System, culminating in the 3SBL-4S model.
FUJI PHOTO FILM COMPANY, LIMITED, for the development and introduction of the F-Series of color negative films covering the range of film speeds from EI 64 to EI 500.
MANFRED G. MICHELSON of Technical Film Systems, Incorporated, for the design and development of the first sprocket-driven film transport system for color print film processors which permits transport speeds in excess of 600 feet per minute.
JOHN W. LANG, WALTER HRASTNIK and CHARLES J. WATSON of Bell and Howell Company for the development and manufacture of a modular continuous contact motion picture film printer.

SCIENTIFIC OR TECHNICAL AWARDS: TECHNICAL ACHIEVEMENT AWARD
WILLIAM L. BLOWERS of Belco Associates, Incorporated, and THOMAS F. DENOVE for the development and manufacture of the Belco/Denove Cinemeter. This digital/analog exposure meter was specifically and uniquely designed for the cinematographer.
IAIN NEIL for optical design; TAKUO MIYAGISHIMA for the mechanical design; and PANAVISION, INCORPORATED, for the concept and development of the Prima Series of spherical prime lenses for 35mm cinematography.
CHRISTOPHER S. GILMAN and HARVEY HUBERT, JR., the Diligent Dwarves Effects Lab for the development of the Actor Climate System, consisting of heat-transferring undergarments.
JIM GRAVES of J&G Enterprises for the development of the Cool Suit System, consisting of heat-transferring undergarments.
BENJT O. ORHALL, KENNETH LUND, BJORN SELIN and KJELL HOGBERG of AB Film-Teknik for the development and manufacture of the Mark IV film subtitling processor, which has increased the speed, simplified the operation and improved the quality of subtitling.
RICHARD MULA and PETE ROMANO of HydroImage, Incorporated, for the development of the SeaPar 1200 watt HMI Underwater Lamp.
DEDO WEIGERT of Dedo Weigert Film GmbH for the development of the Dedolight, a miniature low-voltage tungsten-halogen lighting fixture.
DR. FRED KOLB. JR., and PAUL PREO for the concept and development of a 35mm projection test film.
PETER BALDWIN for the design; DR. PAUL KIANKHOOY and the Lightmaker Company for the development of the Lightmaker AC/DC HMI Ballast
ALL-UNION CINEMA AND PHOTO RESEARCH INSTI'TU'TE (NIKFI) for continuously improving and providing 3-D presentations to Soviet motion picture audiences for the last 25 years.

1991

"The stage is set for the most wide-open Oscar race in years."

—*Variety*

$\mathcal{R}$arely had the oddsmakers been so wildly off the mark, but then there had never been such a diverse jumble of nominated films. From Warren Beatty's chilly, mood-driven gangster bio, *Bugsy*, to Oliver Stone's paranoid conspiracy thriller, *JFK*, to the first animated feature—a musical—to make it into the top spot, *Beauty and the Beast*. And then, of course, there was the otherwise safe bet, *The Prince of Tides*, whose sweeping emotions and melodramatic love angle were usually just the ticket. But with the snubbing of its director, Barbra Streisand, it was clouded by bad feelings all around. While *Lambs* director, Jonathan Demme, had been nominated, he wasn't popular in Hollywood after referring to it in the press as "La La Land." Another strike against *Lambs* was its horrific content of psycho killers and cannibalism, just the sort of spine-tingling entrée Hitchcock served up for decades without a nod from Oscar.

As if the Awards outcome weren't curious enough, along came Jack Palance, 72, and his showstopping one-arm push-ups after winning Best Supporting Actor. The display of septuagenarian macho fueled Crystal with enough one-liners to keep him sailing through the nearly four-hour broadcast. "Jack Palance just bungee-jumped off the Hollywood sign!" he cracked.

Among the evening's highlights was a tribute to Indian filmmaking legend Satyajit Ray, who thanked the Academy from his hospital bed.

As the shouts of thousands of gay activists protesting the treatment of gays in *Lambs* and *JFK* filled the air outside the Dorothy Chandler Pavilion, *Lambs* began its clobberfest inside to a collective gasp of surprise. It gulped down the five top Oscars, a rare feat accomplished only twice before by *One Flew Over the Cuckoo's Nest* (1975) and *It Happened One Night* (1934).

NO LOST LAMBS

CEREMONY: March 30, 1992
Dorothy Chandler Pavilion, Los Angeles Music Center, Los Angeles
HOST: Billy Crystal

Billy Crystal (wearing mask) with Anthony Hopkins

BEST PICTURE/BEST DIRECTOR
JONATHAN DEMME (B. 1944)
THE SILENCE OF THE LAMBS

"The idea of a serial killer repels me," said Demme when he was first approached to direct the film. He was, however, convinced by the book.

"Demme [is] a true maverick among the herd of Hollywood hacks," said *Rolling Stone*. "[He] can intermingle comedy and drama because he builds on a solid foundation of character. *Silence* is a powerhouse that shows Demme at his best and boldest." Demme could be perceived as an outside "insider," a director with mainstream success who kept his eccentricities intact.

He began his career under the tutelage of schlock-shock producer Roger Corman, with such drive-in movie fodder as *Caged Heat* (1974) and *Crazy Mama* (1975). His rise to more artful material such as *Melvin and Howard* (1980) earned him two Oscars but no box-office gold. *Lambs* would finally launch him into that rare orbit of directors who manage to garner accolades for both quality and—monetary—quantity. "Hair-frying, a masterwork of unbearable maximum anxiety and tension that will leave you limp as a dead butterfly's wing," quivered Rex Reed. "*Silence of the Lambs*," wrote Roger Ebert, "is not merely a thrill show. It is also about two of the most memorable characters in movie history, Clarice and Hannibal, and their strange, strained relationships." Despite the raves, there were those who didn't see the film in quite the same way. Gene Siskel complained that the conclusion "is nothing more than a grisly version of every mad-slasher picture you've ever missed." A retired Pauline Kael, still opining, told *Newsday*, "The film has no soul. It's pulp material treated as art, and I think that's a bit of a fraud." Opinions about the film may have split the critics but not the audiences, who gave it a $100-million gross and a great life on video.

The envelope, please…

© A.M.P.A.S.®

BEST ACTOR
ANTHONY HOPKINS (B. 1937)
THE SILENCE OF THE LAMBS

"My God, I can't believe it!" Hopkins, along with almost everyone else, thought Nick Nolte, the emotionally defended hero of *The Prince of Tides*, was a shoo-in. But somebody out there loved Hannibal, and it wasn't only Clarice.

Roger Ebert said, "Hopkins, in a still, sly way, brings such wit and style to the character. He may be a cannibal, but as a dinner party guest he would give value for money (if he didn't eat you)." According to Hopkins, his approach to Lecter's personality was inspired by HAL 9000 in *2001: A Space Odyssey*. "He is a dispassionate, brilliant machine, superb at logic, deficient in emotions," the actor said. A piano virtuoso who conquered alcoholism, Hopkins began his career on the London stage, and later accumulated

a brilliant film résumé with *The Lion in Winter* (1968), *The Elephant Man* (1980), *Howards End* (1992), and *Nixon* (1995), to name a few of his major accomplishments.

Anthony Hopkins with Jody Foster

BEST ACTRESS
JODIE FOSTER (B. 1962)
THE SILENCE OF THE LAMBS

"Whenever I win an award, I have this really annoying habit—I can't stop laughing," Foster said. She must have been doing a lot of laughing, having just picked up an Oscar for *Accused* three years earlier.

She shone as *Lamb*'s G-woman, Clarice, who responded to the mind-reading Lecter with a vulnerability she rarely betrayed in some of her more romantic roles. Writing in the *Washington Post*, Rita Kempley observed, "As adapted by Demme and screenwriter Ted Tally, the story manages a feminist perspective without turning Clarice into some phallic Nancy Drew. Neither boyish nor overtly sexual, she solves her crimes very much as a cerebral young woman would, with brainpower and more than the ordinary allotment of gumption."

"Foster has the less showy role," observed the *Dallas Morning News*. "But she plays it with quiet authority, sly humor, and a stalwart grace under pressure." (For more on Foster, see 1988.)

BEST OF 1991
Best Picture: *The Silence of the Lambs*
Best Director: Jonathan Demme, *The Silence of the Lambs*
Best Actor: Anthony Hopkins, *The Silence of the Lambs*
Best Actress: Jodie Foster, *The Silence of the Lambs*
Best Supporting Actor: Jack Palance, *City Slickers*
Best Supporting Actress: Mercedes Ruehl, *The Fisher King*

FIRSTS
- John Singleton, at 24, was the youngest director to be nominated for his absorbing "tell it like it is" ghetto drama *Boyz N the Hood*. "It's so cool, so cool. I'm the first person in my neighborhood to get an Oscar nomination," he exclaimed.
- *Silence*, which opened in February 1990, was the first nominated film to be released on video before winning an Oscar.
- Thanks to its technical achievements, *Terminator 2: Judgment Day*, starring Arnold Schwarzenegger, racked up an astonishing four Oscars, just behind *Lambs*'s total roundup.
- Jack Palance holds the record for the longest pause between nominations to date.

ROLE REVERSALS
Before Foster, Michelle Pfeiffer was set to play Clarice in *Lambs*, though the "material frightened me," she admitted. And an early thought for Hannibal—even before Gene Hackman—was Louis Gossett Jr.

SINS OF OMISSION
Picture: *An Angel at My Table*, *Fried Green Tomatoes*, *The Vanishing* (Best Foreign Film), *Paris Is Burning* (Best Documentary)

ALWAYS A BRIDESMAID, NEVER A BRIDE
"I'm trying hard not to take this personally. It's hard because I don't want to be bitter. I don't take it as a personal affront. I look at it as a larger problem," Barbra Streisand said to *Variety* after she failed to get a Best Director nomination for *The Prince of Tides*.

UNMENTIONABLES
- Best Screenplay nominee and Act Up founder Larry Kramer (*Women in Love*, 1970) sparked the protest against *Lambs* for its representation of gays. He held special contempt for Jodie Foster, whom the gay and lesbian community had long presumed to be one of its own.
- Best Actress nominee Susan Sarandon (*Thelma & Louise*) railed against criticism of her character's moral fiber to *Redbook* magazine: "I didn't realize everyone would be so touchy. I mean, did people think *Pretty Woman* was such a great role model? Did they think it's better to get your way by giving blow jobs?"
- "I am a screen star in the tradition of Shirley Temple, Liv Ullman, and Miss Piggy," said Best Actress nominee Bette Midler (*For the Boys*) in *Time* magazine.
- Anthony Hopkins was inspired by the voices of Katharine Hepburn and Truman Capote in his choice of the eerie cadence for Hannibal Lecter.

BEST SUPPORTING ACTOR
JACK PALANCE (B. 1919)
CITY SLICKERS

"Billy Crystal? I crap bigger than him," Palance shot back in malevolent deadpan. A long career as the Neanderthal, handsome heavy served him well this time around. Palance managed to combine his villainous image with humor in a character that executive producer/star Crystal described as "a saddlebag with eyes."

Palance had two close calls with Oscar very early in his career for his debut in *Sudden Fear* (1952) and *Shane* (1953). His method-y ferocity once resulted in his knocking out a fellow actor in an all too realistic fight scene.

PICTURE

BEAUTY AND THE BEAST, Walt Disney Pictures. Buena Vista. Produced by Don Hahn.
BUGSY, TriStar. Produced by Mark Johnson. Barry Levinson and Warren Beatty.
JFK, Camelot, Warner Bros. Produced by A. Kitman Ho and Oliver Stone.
THE PRINCE OF TIDES, Barwood/Longfellow, Columbia. Produced by Barbra Streisand and Andrew Karsch.
THE SILENCE OF THE LAMBS, Strong Heart/ Demme, Orion. Produced by Edward Saxon, Kenneth Utt and Ron Bozman.

ACTOR

WARREN BEATIY in *Bugsy*, TriStar.
ROBERT DE NIRO in *Cape Fear*, Amblin' Entertainment with Cappa Films and Tribeca Productions, Universal.
ANTHONY HOPKINS in *The Silence of the Lambs*, Strong Heart/Demme, Orion.
NICK NOLTE in *The Prince of Tides*, Barwood/ Longfellow, Columbia.
ROBIN WILLIAMS in *The Fisher King*, TriStar.

ACTRESS

GEENA DAVIS in *Thelma & Louise*, Pathe Entertainment, MGM.
LAURA DERN in *Rambling Rose*, Carolco, Seven Arts.
JODIE FOSTER in *The Silence of the Lambs*, Strong Heart/Demme, Orion.
BETTE MIDLER in *For the Boys*, 20th Century-Fox.
SUSAN SARANDON in *Thelma & Louise*, Pathe Entertainment, MGM.

SUPPORTING ACTOR

TOMMY LEE JONES in *JFK*, Camelot, Warner Bros.
HARVEY KEITEL in *Bugsy*, TriStar.
BEN KINGSLEY in *Bugsy*, TriStar.
MICHAEL LERNER in *Barton Fink*, Barton Circle, 20th Century-Fox.
JACK PALANCE in *City Slickers*, Castle Rock Entertainment, Columbia.

SUPPORTING ACTRESS

DIANE LADD in *Rambling Rose*, Carolco Pictures, Seven Arts.
JULIETTE LEWIS in *Cape Fear*, Amblin Entertainment with Cappa Films and Tribeca, Universal.
KATE NELLIGAN in *The Prince of Tides*, Barwood/Longfellow, Columbia.
MERCEDES RUEHL in *The Fisher King*, TriStar.
JESSICA TANDY in *Fried Green Tomatoes*, Act III Communications with Electric Shadow, Universal.

DIRECTION

JONATHAN DEMME for *The Silence of the Lambs*, Strong Heart/Demme, Orion.
BARRY LEVINSON for *Bugsy*, TriStar.
RIDLEY SCOTT for *Thelma & Louise*, Pathe Entertainment, MGM.
JOHN SINGLETON for *Boyz N the Hood*, Columbia.
OLIVER STONE for *JFK*, Camelot, Warner Bros.

WRITING: DIRECTLY FOR THE SCREEN

BOYZ N THE HOOD, Columbia. John Singleton.
BUGSY, TriStar. James Toback.
THE FISHER KING, TriStar. Richard LaGravenese.
GRAND CANYON, 20th Century-Fox. Lawrence Kasdan and Meg Kasdan.
THELMA & LOUISE, Pathe Entertainment MGM, Callie Khouri.

BEST SUPPORTING ACTRESS
MERCEDES RUEHL (B. 1948)
THE FISHER KING

"I shall never waitress again, and you are my witnesses," Ruehl cried after winning a Golden Globe for *The Fisher King* earlier in the year. "Ruehl, with a deep voice and décolletage is the most reasonable presence in the movie, a woman who loves even when it is not convenient, but can be pushed only so far," waxed Roger Ebert.

Ruehl had distinguished herself in the theater as well as in film, winning an Obie for her performance in Christopher Durang's *The Marriage of Bette and Boo* and in the stage production of *Other People's Money*. Often appearing as the distinctly accented, streetwise New Yorker, Ruehl debuted in *The Warriors* (1979), and made a handful of films. But it wasn't until she wowed audiences in *Married to the Mob* (1988) that she won better roles, among them *Big* (1988, as Tom Hanks's mom), *Slaves of New York* (1989), and *Crazy People* (1990).

Mercedes Ruehl with Amanda Plummer

WRITING: BASED ON MATERIAL FROM ANOTHER MEDIUM

EUROPA EUROPA, CCC-Filmkunst and Les Films du Losange, Orion Classics. Agnieszka Holland.

FRIED GREEN TOMATOES, ACT III Communications with Electric Shadow, Universal. Fannie Flagg and Carol Sobieski.

JFK, Camelot, Warner Bros. Oliver Stone and Zachary Sklar.

THE PRINCE OF TIDES, Barwood/Longfellow, Columbia Pat Conroy and Becky Johnston.

THE SILENCE OF THE LAMBS, Strong Heart/Demme, Orion. Ted Tally.

CINEMATOGRAPHY

BUGSY, TriStar. Allen Daviau.

JFK, Camelot, Warner Bros. Robert Richardson.

THE PRINCE OF TIDES, Barwood/Longfellow, Columbia, Stephen Goldblatt.

TERMINATOR 2: JUDGMENT DAY, a Carolco, TriStar. Adam Greenberg.

THELMA & LOUISE, Pathe Entertainment, MG M. Adrian Biddle.

ART DIRECTION—SET DECORATION

BARTON FINK, Barton Circle, 20th Century-Fox. Dennis Gassner; Nancy Haigh.

BUGSY, TriStar. Dennis Gassner; Nancy Haigh.

THE FISHER KING, TriStar. Mel Bourne; Cindy Carr.

HOOK, TriStar. Norman Garwood; Garrett Lewis.

THE PRINCE OF TIDES, Barwood/Longfellow, Columbia. Paul Sylbert; Caryl Heller.

COSTUME DESIGN

THE ADDAMS FAMILY, Scott Rudin, Paramount. Ruth Myers.

BARTON FINK, Barton Circle, 20th Century-Fox. Richard Hornung.

BUGSY, TriStar. Albert Wolsky.

HOOK, TriStar. Anthony Powell.

MADAME BOVARY, MK2/C.E.D./FR3 Films, Samuel Goldwyn Company. Corinne Jorry.

SOUND

BACKDRAFT, Trilogy Entertainment Group/Brian Grazer. Universal. Gary Summers, Randy Thom, Gary Rydstrom and Glenn Williams.

BEAUTY AND THE BEAST, Walt Disney Pictures. Buena Vista. Terry Porter, Mel Metcalte. David J. Hudson and Doc Kane.

JFK, Camelot, Warner Bros. Michael Minkler, Gregg Landaker and Tod A. Maitland.

THE SILENCE OF THE LAMBS, Strong Heart/Demme. Orion. Tom Fleischman and Christopher Newman.

TERMINATOR 2: JUDGMENT DAY, Carolco, TriStar. Tom Johnson. Gary Rydutrom, Gary Summers and Lee Orloff.

FILM EDITING

THE COMMITMENTS, Beacon Communications, 20th Century-Fox. Gerry Hambling.

JFK, Camelot, Warner Bros. Joe Hutshing and Pietro Scalia.

THE SILENCE OF THE LAMBS, Strong Heart/Demme. Orion. Craig McKay.

TERMINATOR 2: JUDGMENT DAY, Carolco, TriStar. Conrad Buff, Mark Goldblatt and Richard A. Harris.

THELMA & LOUISE, Pathe Entertainment, MGM. Thom Noble.

SOUND EFFECTS EDITING

BACKDRAFT, Trilogy Entertainment Group/Brian Grazer. Universal. Gary Rydstrom and Richard Hymns.

STAR TREK VI: THE UNDISCOVERED COUNTRY, Paramount Pictures. Paramount. George Watters II and F. Hudson Miller.

TERMINATOR 2: JUDGMENT DAY, Carolco. TriStar. Gary Rydstrom and Gloria S. Borders.

VISUAL EFFECTS

BACKDRAFT, Trilogy Entertainment Group/Brian Grazer. Universal. Mikael Solomon. Allen Hall. Clay Pinney and Scott Farrar,

HOOK, TriStar. Eric Brevig. Harley Jessup, Mark Sullivan and Michael Lantieri.

TERMINATOR 2: JUDGMENT DAY, Carolco, TriStar. Dennis Muren. Stan Winston, Gene Warren, Jr., and Robert Skotak.

SONG

BE OUR GUEST (*Beauty and the Beast*, Walt Disney Pictures. Buena Vista); Music by Alan Menken. Lyrics by Howard Ashman.

BEAUTY AND THE BEAST (*Beauty and the Beast*, Walt Disney Pictures. Buena Vista); Music by Alan Menken. Lyrics by Howard Ashman.

BELLE (*Beauty and the Beast*, Wall Disney Pictures, Buena Vista); Music by Alan Menken. Lyric by Howard Ashman.

(EVERYTHING I DO) I DO IT FOR YOU (*Robin Hood: Prince of Thieves*, Morgan Creek, Warner Bros); Music by Michael Kamen. Lyrics by Bryan Adams and Robert John Lange.

WHEN YOU'RE ALONE (*Hook*, TriStar Pictures. TriStar); Music by John Williams. Lyrics by Leslie Bricusse.

SCORING: ORIGINAL MUSIC

BEAUTY AND THE BEAST, Walt Disney Pictures, Buena Vista Alan Menken.

BUGSY, TriStar. Funk, Morricone.

THE FISHER KING, TriStar. George Fenton.

JFK, Camelot, Warner Bros. John Williams.

THE PRINCE OF TIDES, Barwood/Longfellow. Columbia. James Newton Howard.

MAKEUP

HOOK, TriStar. Christina Smith, Manly Westmore and Greg Cannom.

STAR TREK VI: THE UNDISCOVERED COUNTRY, Paramount. Michael Mills, Edward French and Richard Snell.

TERMINATOR 2: JUDGMENT DAY, Carolco, TriStar. Stan Winston and Jeff Dawn.

SHORT FILMS: ANIMATED

BLACKFLY, a National Film Board at Canada Production. Christopher Hinton.

MANIPULATION, a Tandem Films Production. Daniel Greaves.

STRINGS, a National Film Board at Canada Production. Wendy Tilby.

SHORT FILMS: LIVE ACTION

BIRCH STREET GYM, a Chanticleer Films Production. Stephen Kessler and Thomas K. Conroy.

LAST BREEZE OF SUMMER, an American Film Institute Production. David M. Massey.

SESSION MAN, a Chanticleer Films Production. Seth Winston and Rob Fried.

DOCUMENTARY: SHORT SUBJECTS

BIRDNESTERS OF THAILAND (aka "Shadow Hunters"), an Antenne 2/National Geographic Society/M.D.I./Wind Horse Production. Eric Valli and Alain Majani, producers.

DEADLY DECEPTION: GENERAL ELECTRIC, NUCLEAR WEAPONS AND OUR ENVIRONMENT, a Women's Educational Media. Inc. Production. Debra Chasnoff. producer.

A LITTLE VICIOUS, a Film and Video Workshop, Inc. Production. Immy Humes, producer.

THE MARK OF THE MAKER, a McGowan Film and Video, Inc. Production. David McGowan, producer.

MEMORIAL LETTERS FROM AMERICAN SOLDIERS, a Couturie Company Production. Bill Couturie and Bernard Edelman, producers.

DOCUMENTARY: FEATURES

DEATH ON THE JOB, a Half-Court Pictures, Ltd. Production. Vince DiPersio and William Guttentag, producers.

DOING TIME: LIFE INSIDE THE BIG HOUSE, a Video Verite Production. Alan Raymond and Susan Raymond, producers.

IN THE SHADOW OF THE STARS, a Light-Saraf Films Production. Allie Light and Irving Saraf, producers.

THE RESTLESS CONSCIENCE, a Hava Kohav Beller Production. Hava Kohav Beller, producer.

WILD BY LAW, a Florentine Films Production. Lawrence Hall and Diane Garey, producers.

FOREIGN LANGUAGE FILM

CHILDREN OF NATURE (Iceland).

THE ELEMENTARY SCHOOL (Czechoslovakia).

MEDITERRANEO (Italy).

THE OX (Sweden).

RAISE THE RED LANTERN (Hong Kong).

HONORARY AND OTHER AWARDS

TO SATYAJIT RAY, in recognition of his rare mastery of the art of motion pictures, and of his profound humanitarian outlook, which has had an indelible influence on filmmakers and audiences throughout the world.

TO PETE COMANDINI, RICHARD T. DAYTON, DONALD HAGANS and RICHARD T. RYAN of YCM Laboratories for the creation and development of a motion picture film restoration process using liquid gate and registration correction on a contact printer.

TO RICHARD J. STUMPF and JOSEPH WESTHEIMER for outstanding service and dedication in upholding the high standards at the Academy of Motion Picture Arts and Sciences.

IRVING G. THALBERG MEMORIAL AWARD

TO GEORGE LUCAS

JEAN HERSHOLT HUMANITARIAN AWARD

None gives this year.

GORDON E. SAWYER AWARD

TO RAY HARRYHAUSEN

SCIENTIFIC OR TECHNICAL AWARDS: SCIENTIFIC AND ENGINEERING AWARD

IAIN NEIL for the optical design; ALBERT SAIKI for the mechanical design; and PANAVISION, INCORPORATED, for the concept and development of the Prima Zoom Lens for 35mm cinematography.

GEORG THOMA for the design; HEINZ FEIERLEIN and the engineering department of Sachtler AG for the development of a range at fluid tripod heads.

HARRY J. BAKER for the design and development of the first full fluidaction tripod head with adjustable degrees at viscous drag.

GUIDO CARTONI for his pioneering work in developing the technology to achieve selectable and repeatable viscous drag modules in fluid tripod heads.

RAY FEENEY, RICHARD KEENEY and RICHARD J. LUNDELL for the software development and adaptation of the Solitaire Film Recorder that provides a flexible, cast-effective film recording system.

FAR FAZAKAS, BRIAN HENSON, DAVE HOUSMAN, PETER MILLER and JOHN STEPHENSON for the development at the Henson Performance Control System.

MARIO CELSO for his pioneering work in the design, development and manufacture of equipment for carbon arc and xenon power supplies and igniters used in motion picture projection.

RANDY CARTWRIGHT, DAVID B. COONS, LEM DAVIS, THOMAS HAHN, JAMES HOUSTON, MARK KIMBALL, PETER NYE, MICHAEL SHANTZIS, DAVID F. WOLF and the Walt Disney Feature Animation Department for the design and development of the 'CAPS' production system for feature film animation.

GEORGE WORRALL for the design, development and manufacture of the Worrall geared camera head for motion picture production.

SCIENTIFIC OR TECHNICAL AWARDS: TECHNICAL ACHIEVEMENT AWARD

ROBERT W. STOKER, JR., for the design and development at a cobweb gun, for applying non-toxic cobweb effects on motion picture sets with bath safety and ease of operation.

JAMES DOYLE for the design and development of the Dry Fogger, which uses liquid nitrogen to produce a safe, dense, low-hanging fog effect.

DICK CAVDEK, STEVE HAMERSKI and OTTO NEMENZ INTERNATIONAL, INCORPORATED, for the opto-mechanical design and development of the Canon/Nemenz Zoom Lens.

KEN ROBINGS and CLAIRMONT CAMERA for the opto-mechanical design and development of the Canon/Clairmont Camera Zoom Lens.

CENTURY PRECISION OPTICS for the opto-mechanical design and development of the Canon/Century Precision Optics Zoom Lens.

1992

ost Billy Crystal set the royal tone as he entered atop an Oscar chariot pulled by Jack Palance. The Chandler Pavilion was geared up for the coronation of Clint Eastwood, a longtime Hollywood player who had never won anything except the mayoralty of Carmel, California. The critically acclaimed, deconstructed Western *Unforgiven* was his crowning achievement—and the crown awaited. There were a couple of minor glitches to the otherwise low-key evening. The first was its theme "Oscar Salutes Women and the Movies," which was especially ironic considering the lack of solid women's roles in studio projects. The Academy's rare glance at Uruguay caused a minor tempest when that country's Best Foreign Film entry was withdrawn from nomination for being an essentially Argentinean production. It was hardly the stuff of headlines. But an upset for Best Supporting Actress was. The winner, Marisa Tomei, for her foxy automotive genius in *My Cousin Vinny*, beat out heavyweights

ALL IS UNFORGIVEN

CEREMONY: March 29, 1993
Dorothy Chandler Pavilion, Los Angeles Music Center, Los Angeles
HOST: Billy Crystal

Vanessa Redgrave and Joan Plowright for reasons, some felt, that had more to do with her being the only American in the lineup.

The gala crowd was thrilled to see Al Pacino finally get his due as Best Actor (*Scent of a Woman*). He had the additional insurance of a Best Supporting nomination (*Glengarry Glen Ross*), just in case. That category's gold went, as expected, to veteran Gene Hackman (*Unforgiven*), who beat out the most exotic nominee, Jaye Davidson, an unknown, whose gender-bending role in *The Crying Game* gave the film a big push at the box office. Emma Thompson's Best Actress win for *Howards End* established her as a star in her own right and not just as the talented wife of actor-director Kenneth Branagh.

Two women who had been legends since their first moments on film, Elizabeth Taylor and Audrey Hepburn, were honored with the Hersholt Humanitarian Award: Taylor for her efforts on behalf of AIDS research and Hepburn as a UNICEF ambassador. It was a wrenching final tribute to Hepburn, who died just weeks before the ceremony.

BEST PICTURE/BEST DIRECTOR
CLINT EASTWOOD (B. 1930)
UNFORGIVEN

"Any man don't wanna get killed better clear on out the back." For his sixteenth directorial distinction Eastwood told *Variety* that he wanted to make "a film where violence can not only be painful, it's also not without consequences for the perpetrators of violence as well as the victims."

Falling into line with a tradition of old gunslingers who hang up their hats, Eastwood, in the role of William Munny, a retired gunman who gave up his violent ways for the love of a good woman, now dead, teams up with a former partner in hell-raising to collect a bounty for the attacker of a prostitute.

Eastwood was concerned that *Unforgiven*'s antiviolence message would make it a box-office drag, which proved not to be the case. The critics, for the most part, loved it. *Time* magazine's Richard Corliss described *Unforgiven* as "a dark, passionate drama with good guys so twisted and bad guys so persuasive that virtue and villainy become

two views of the same soul." Peter Travers in *Rolling Stone* exclaimed, "In the three decades of climbing into the saddle, Eastwood has never ridden so tall."

The star of more than thirty-six films, Eastwood had come a long way from digging swimming pools to support a fledgling acting career in the 1950s. He made a name for himself as Rowdy Yates on TV's popular series *Rawhide*. Growing restless, he took the gamble to star in the low-budget spaghetti Western *A Fistful of Dollars* (1964), and his film persona was born. His first display of acumen behind the camera combined his love for jazz and suspense in *Play Misty for Me* (1971), followed by a string of commercial hits such as *The Outlaw—Josey Wales* (1976), *Tightrope* (1984), and *The Bridges of Madison County* (1995).

The envelope, please...

Al Pacino with Gabrielle Anwar

BEST ACTOR
AL PACINO (B. 1939)
SCENT OF A WOMAN

"You have broken my streak," said the delighted Pacino to the Academy. "This is a proud and hopeful moment for me. I've gotten used to not receiving awards," Pacino confessed. A poor kid from the mean streets of East Harlem, Pacino found an early mentor in star turned acting coach Charles Laughton. After only two films, *Me Natalie* (1969) and *Panic in Needle Park* (1971), Pacino could pretty much write his ticket. He chose wisely in a shortlist of what would become iconic films, among them *Serpico* (1973), *Dog Day Afternoon* (1975), and *Scarface* (1983). In *Scent of a Woman*, Pacino plays retired lieutenant colonel Frank Slade, blinded as the result of a booze-induced accident, who longs for the life he once had. While some critics questioned the overall quality of the role in comparison to his past triumphs, none could deny the impact of the film's set piece, a joyous tango with a beautiful young woman.

After a few failures, Pacino returned to the screen with *Sea of Love* (1989), *The Godfather, Part III* (1990), *Glengarry Glen Ross* (1992, nom.), and *The Insider* (1999).

Emma Thompson with Helena Bonham Carter

BEST ACTRESS
EMMA THOMPSON (B. 1959)
HOWARDS END

"I owe a lot of my performance to the corset I had to wear...the blood rushes to your face...so that explains 'radiant.'"

Playing the poor but intellectually liberated young Margaret Schlegel, duped out of the surprising inheritance of a country estate, Thompson displayed her gilded talent and supreme confidence on film. "Emma Thompson is superb in the central role, quiet, ironic, observant, with steel inside," said Roger Ebert. *Rolling Stone*'s Peter Travers said Thompson brings a "depth of feeling to Margaret. Growing less verbal and more reflective, she absorbs betrayals, initiates change and creates the balance necessary for the warring factions around her to achieve a hard-won harmony."

Thompson burst into film lovers' passions in a late start. She began her movie career at age 30 with *The Tall Guy* and *Henry V* (both 1989), and was later nominated for Oscar performances in *Remains of the Day* (1993), *In the Name of the Father* (1993), and *Sense and Sensibility* (1995).

BEST OF 1992
Best Picture: *Unforgiven*
Best Director: Clint Eastwood, *Unforgiven*
Best Actor: Al Pacino, *Scent of a Woman*
Best Actress: Emma Thompson, *Howards End*
Best Supporting Actor: Gene Hackman, *Unforgiven*
Best Supporting Actress: Marisa Tomei, *My Cousin Vinny*
Honorary Award: Federico Fellini

FIRSTS
- Al Pacino becomes the first actor to be nominated for Best Actor and for Best Supporting Actor in two different roles.
- Best Supporting Actor and real-life war hero Harold Russell (*The Best Years of Our Lives*, 1946) was forced to auction off his statuette to pay for his wife's surgery. The winning bid: $55,000.

SINS OF OMISSION
Picture: *The Player, Husbands and Wives*
Actors: Tim Robbins, Best Actor (*The Player* and *Bob Roberts*), Jack Lemmon, Best Supporting Actor (*Glengarry Glen Ross*)

UNMENTIONABLES
- Joe Pesci wore an adhesive face-lift for his youthful role in *My Cousin Vinny*.
- To maintain a sense of time and place, director Eastwood barred access to cars and trucks on his *Unforgiven* location shoot.
- Unfounded post-Oscar gossip had it that presenter Jack Palance misread the name of the Best Supporting Actress winner, thus awarding Marisa Tomei by accident.
- Clint Eastwood's date for the evening was his 85-year-old mother. He forgot to thank her after winning Best Director for *Unforgiven* but was thrilled to get a second chance when the film grabbed Best Picture.
- 8 1/2 Hankies: After Sofia Loren and Marcello Mastroianni presented filmmaker Federico Fellini with an honorary Oscar, Fellini paused in his thank-you to plead with his wife in the audience, actress Giulietta Masina: "Please, stop crying, Giulietta."
- Nominated for Best Director and Best Adapted Screenplay for his film *The Player*, Robert Altman delivered a stunning comeback movie that failed to be nominated for the top spot. A dead-on satire of contemporary Hollywood mores among the studio movers and shakers, it may have cut too close to the bone for the Academy's nominating committee.
- Neil Jordan (*The Crying Game*) almost didn't make it to the podium in time. "Sorry, I didn't know these nominations were coming up," he breathlessly informed the audience. "I was in the bathroom when I heard it."

BEST SUPPORTING ACTOR
GENE HACKMAN (B. 1931)
UNFORGIVEN

Hackman dedicated his Oscar to an uncle who, early on, worried over whether he would be able to support himself as an actor. Hackman left home at 16 for a three-year hitch with the Marines and later studied journalism and television production on the GI Bill. He was over 30 years old when he finally decided to take his chance at acting by enrolling at the Pasadena Playhouse in California.

Legend has it that Hackman and Dustin Hoffman were voted "least likely to succeed." That was rarely a problem for Hackman, whose unprepossessing looks, versatility, and subdued cauldron of emotions won him some of the best character roles around. After an Oscar nomination for *Bonnie and Clyde* (1967), he won Best Actor the next time up for *The French Connection* (1971). At 40, the versatile

Hackman was a Hollywood star whose work would rise to the heights with *Night Moves* and *Bite the Bullet* (both 1975) or fall to the depths with *The Poseidon Adventure* (1972) and *Eureka* (1983). (For more on Hackman, see 1971.)

Joe Pesci with Marisa Tomei

BEST SUPPORTING ACTRESS
MARISA TOMEI (B. 1964)
MY COUSIN VINNY

"It [Oscar] feels like a barbell," Tomei said, hefting her Golden Boy. Inspired by her screen debut, a one-line part in *Flamingo Kid* (1984), Tomei dropped out of college and landed a job on the daytime soap *As the World Turns*. After a few minor stumbles in forgettable films, she hit pay dirt as Mona Lisa Vito, Joe Pesci's gum-chomping, carburetor-know-it-all fiancée in *My Cousin Vinny*. In the film's immortal line, Tomei's killer retort to Pesci's critique of her Brooklyn bombshell outfit, "Yeah, you blend," became an instant pop catchphrase.

She was soon given her first starring role in *Untamed Heart* (1993). In *Only You* (1994) she proved that she could handle comedy, but bad luck hit with the critically thrashed *Four Rooms* (1995). She again turned in strong work in *Welcome to Sarajevo* (1997), *Slums of Beverly Hills* (1998), *The Watcher* (2001), and *In the Bedroom* (2001, nom.).

PICTURE
THE CRYING GAME, Palace Pictures, Miramax. Produced by Stephen Woolley.
A FEW GOOD MEN, Castle Rock Entertainment, Colombia. Produced by David Brown, Rob Reiner, and Andrew Scheinman.
HOWARDS END, Merchant Ivory, Sony Pictures Classics. Produced by Ismail Merchant.
SCENT OF A WOMAN, Universal Release/City Lights Films, Universal. Produced by Martin Brest.
UNFORGIVEN, Warner Bros. Produced by Clint Eastwood.

ACTOR
ROBERT DOWNEY, JR. in *Chaplin*, Carolco Pictures, TriStar.
CLINT EASTWOOD in *Unforgiven*, Warner Bros.
AL PACINO in *Scent of a Woman*, Universal Release/City Lights Films, Universal.
STEPHEN REA in *The Crying Game*, Palace Pictures. Miramax.
DENZEL WASHINGTON in *Malcolm X*, By Any Means Necessary Cinema, Universal.

ACTRESS
CATHERINE DENEUVE in *Indochine*, Paradis Films/La Generale d'Images/BAC Films/Orly Films/Cine Cinq, Sony Pictures Classics.
MARY McDONNELL in *Passion Fish*, Atchafalaya Films. Miramax.
MICHELLE PFEIFFER in *Love Field*, Sanford/Pillsbury. Orion.
SUSAN SARANDON in *Lorenzo's Oil*, Kennedy Miller Films. Universal.
EMMA THOMPSON in *Howards End*, Merchant Ivory, Sony Pictures Classics.

SUPPORTING ACTOR
JAYE DAVIDSON in *The Crying Game*, Palace Pictures. Miramax.
GENE HACKMAN in *Unforgiven*, Warner Bros.
JACK NICHOLSON in *A Few Good Men*, Castle Rock Entertainment, Columbia.
AL PACINO in *Glengarry Glen Ross*, Stephanie Lynn. New Line.
DAVID PAYMER in *Mr. Saturday Night*, Castle Rock Entertainment, Columbia.

SUPPORTING ACTRESS
JUDY DAVIS in *Husbands and Wives*, TriStar.
JOAN PLOWRIGHT in *Enchanted April*, BBC Films with Greenpoint Films, Miramax.
VANESSA REDGRAVE in *Howards End*, Merchant Ivory. Sony Pictures Classics.
MIRANDA RICHARDSON in *Damage*, SKREBA/Damage/ NEF/Le Studio Canal+, New Line.
MARISA TOMEI in *My Cousin Vinny*, 20th Century-Fox.

DIRECTION
ROBERT ALTMAN for *The Player*, Avenue Pictures, Fine Line.
MARTIN BREST for *Scent of a Woman*, Universal Release/ City Lights Films, Universal.
CLINT EASTWOOD for *Unforgiven*, Warner Bros.
JAMES IVORY for *Howards End*, Merchant Ivory, Sony Pictures Classics.
NEIL JORDAN for *The Crying Game*, Palace Pictures. Miramax.

WRITING: DIRECTLY FOR THE SCREEN
THE CRYING GAME, Palace Pictures, Miramax. Neil Jordan.
HUSBANDS AND WIVES, TriStar. Woody Allen.
LORENZO'S OIL Kennedy Miller Films, Universal. George Miller and Nick Enright.

PASSION FISH, Atchafalaya Films, Miramax. John Sayles.
UNFORGIVEN, Warner Bros. David Webb Peoples.

WRITING: BASED ON MATERIAL FROM ANOTHER MEDIUM
ENCHANTED APRIL, BBC Films with Greenpoint Films, Miramax. Peter Barnes.
HOWARDS END, Merchant Ivory. Sony Pictures Classics. Ruth Prawer Jhabvala.
THE PLAYER, Avenue Pictures. Fine Line. Michael Tolkin.
A RIVER RUNS THROUGH IT, Columbia. Richard Friedenberg.
SCENT OF A WOMAN, Universal Release/ City Lights Films, Universal. Bo Goldman.

CINEMATOGRAPHY
HOFFA, 20th Century-Fox. Stephen H. Burum.
HOWARDS END, Merchant Ivory. Sony Pictures Classics. Tony Pierce-Roberts.
THE LOVER, Renn/Burrill Productions/ Films A2, MGM/UA. Robert Fraisse.
A RIVER RUNS THROUGH IT, Columbia. Philippe Rousselot.
UNFORGIVEN, Warner Bros. Jack N. Green.

ART DIRECTION-SET DECORATION
BRAM STOKER'S DRACULA, Columbia. Thomas Sanders; Garrett Lewis.
CHAPLIN, Carolco Pictures, TriStar. Stuart Craig; Chris A. Hotter.
HOWARDS END, Merchant Ivory, Sony Pictures Classics. Luciana Arrighi, Ian Whittaker.
TOYS, 20th Century-Fox. Ferdinando Scarfiotti; Linda DeScenna.
UNFORGIVEN, Warner Bros. Henry Bumstead; Janice Blackie. Goodine.

COSTUME DESIGN
BRAM STOKER'S DRACULA, Columbia. Eiko Ishioka.
ENCHANTED APRIL, BBC Films with Greenpoint Films. Miramax. Sheena Napier.
HOWARDS END, Merchant Ivory, Sony Pictures Classics. Jenny Beavan and John Bright.
MALCOLM X, By Any Means Necessary Cinema. Warner Bros. Ruth Carter.
TOYS, 20th Century-Fox. Albert Wolsky.

SOUND
ALADDIN, Walt Disney Pictures. Buena Vista. Terry Porter, Mel Metcalfe, David J. Hudson, and Doe Kane.
A FEW GOOD MEN, Castle Rock Entertainment, Columbia. Kevin O'Connell and Rick Mine and Bob Eber.
THE LAST OF THE MOHICANS, 20th Century-Fox. Chris Jenkins, Doug Hemphill. Mark Smith, and Simon Kaye.
UNDER SIEGE, Northeast, Warner Bros. Donald O. Mitchell, Frank A. Montano, Rick Hart, and Scott Smith.
UNFORGIVEN, Warner Bros. Les Fresholtz, Vern Poore, Dick Alexander, and Rob Young.

FILM EDITING
BASIC INSTINCT, Carolco, TriStar. Frank J. Urioste.
THE CRYING GAME, Palace Pictures, Miramax. Kant Pan.
A FEW GOOD MEN, Castle Rock Entertainment. Columbia. Robert Leighton.
THE PLAYER, Avenue Pictures, Fine Line. Geraldine Peroni.
UNFORGIVEN. Warner Bros. Joel Cox.

SOUND EFFECTS EDITING
ALADDIN, Walt Disney Pictures. Buena Vista. Mark Mangini.
BRAM STOKER'S DRACULA, Columbia. Tom C. McCarthy and David E. Stone.
UNDER SIEGE. Northeast, Warner Bros. John Leveque and Bruce Stambler.

VISUAL EFFECTS
ALLEN 3, 20th Century-Fox. Richard Edlund, Alec Gillis. Tom Woodruff.Jr.. and George Gibbs.
BATMAN RETURNS, Warner Bros. Michael Fink, Craig Barron, John Bruno and Dennis Skotak.
DEATH BECOMES HER. Universal. Ken Ralston, Doug Chiang, Doug Smythe, and Tom Woodruff, Jr.

SONG
BEAUTIFUL MARIA OF MY SOUL (*The Mambo Kings*, Northwest. Warner Bros.); Music by Robert Kraft. Lyrics by Arne Glimcher.
FRIEND LIKE ME (*Aladdin*, Walt Disney Pictures. Buena Vista); Music by Alan Menken. Lyrics by Howard Ashman.
I HAVE NOTHING (*The Bodyguard*, Warner Bros.); Music by David Foster. Lyrics by Linda Thompson.
RUN TO YOU (*The Bodyguard*, Warner Bros.): Music by Jud Friedman. Lyrics by Allan Rich.
A WHOLE NEW WORLD (*Aladdin*, Walt Disney Pictures. Buena Vista): Music by Alan Menken. Lyrics by Tim Rice.

SCORING: ORIGINAL MUSIC
ALADDIN, Walt Disney Pictures. Buena Vista. Alan Menken.
BASIC INSTINCT, Carolco, TriStar. Jerry Goldsmith.
CHAPLIN, Carolco. TriStar. John Barry.
HOWARDS END, Merchant Ivory, Sony Pictures Classics. Richard Robbins.
A RIVER RUNS THROUGH IT, Columbia. Mark Isham.

MAKEUP
BATMAN RETURNS, Warner Bros. Ve Neill, Ronnie Specter and Stan Winston.
BRAM STOKER'S DRACULA, Columbia. Greg Cannom, Michele Burke and Matthew W. Mangle.
HOFFA, 20th Century-Fox. Ve Neill, Greg Cannom and John Blake.

SHORT FILMS: ANIMATED
ADAM, an Aardman Animations Ltd. Production. Peter Lord, producer.
MONA LISA DESCENDING A STAIRCASE, a Joan C. Gratz Production. Joan C. Gratz, producer.
RECI, RECI, RECI...(WORD, WORDS, WORDS), a Kratky Film Production. Michaela Pavlatova, producer.
THE SANDMAN, a Batty Berry Mackinnon Production. Paul Berry, producer.
SCREEN PLAY, a Bare Boards Film Production. Barry J.C. Purves, producer.

SHORT FILMS: LIVE ACTION
CONTACT, a Chanticleer Films, Inc. Production. Jonathan Darby and Jana Sue Memel, producers.
CRUISE CONTROL, a Palmieri Pictures Production. Matt Palmieri, producer.
THE LADY IN WAITING, a Taylor Made Films Production. Christian M. Taylor, producer.
OMNIBUS, a Lazennec tout court/Le C.R.R.A.V. Production. Sam Karmann, producer.
SWAN SONG, a Renaissance Films PLC Production. Kenneth Branagh and David Parfitt, producers.

DOCUMENTARY: SHORT SUBJECT
AT THE EDGE OF CONQUEST: THE JOURNEY OF CHIEF WAI-WAI, a Realis Pictures Inc. Production. Geoffrey O'Connor, producer.
BEYOND IMAGINING: MARGARET ANDERSON AND THE "LITTLE REVIEW," a Wendy L. Weinberg Production. Wendy L.Weinberg, producer.
THE COLOURS OF MY FATHER A PORTRAIT OF SAM BORENSTEIN, an Imageries P.B. Ltd. Production in coproduction with the National Film Board of Canada. Richard Elson and Sally Bochner, producers.
EDUCATING PETER, a State of the Art, Inc. Production. Thomas C. Goodwin and Gerardine Wurzburg, producers.
WHEN ABORTION WAS ILLEGAL: UNTOLD STORIES, a Concentric Media Production. Dorothy Fadiman, producer.

DOCUMENTARY: FEATURES
CHANGING OUR MINDS: THE STORY OF DR. EVELYN HOOKER, an Intrepid Production. David Haugland, producer.
FIRES OF KUWAIT, a Black Sun Films. Ltd./ IMAX Corporation Production. Sally Dundas, producer.
LIBERATORS: FIGHTING ON TWO FRONTS IN WORLD WAR II, a Miles

Educational Film Productions, Inc. Production. William Miles and Nina Rosenblum, producers.
MUSIC FOR THE MOVIES: BERNARD HERRMANN, an Alternate Current Inc./ Les Films d'Ici Production. Margaret Smilow and Roma Baran, producers.
THE PANAMA DECEPTION, an Empowerment Project Production. Barbara Trent and David Kasper, producers.

FOREIGN LANGUAGE FILM
CLOSE TO EDEN (Russia).
DAENS (Belgium).
INDOCHINE (France).
SCHTONK (Germany).

HONORARY AND OTHER AWARDS
TO FEDERICO FELLINI, in recognition of his place as one of the screen's master storytellers.
TO PETRO VLAHOS in appreciation for outstanding service and dedication in upholding the high standards of the Academy of Motion Picture Arts and Sciences.

JEAN HERSHOLT HUMANITARIAN AWARD
TO AUDREY HEPBURN
TO ELIZABETH TAYLOR

GORDON E. SAWYER AWARD
TO ERICH KAESTNER

SCIENTIFIC AND TECHNICAL AWARDS: ACADEMY AWARD OF MERIT
CHADWELL O'CONNOR of the O'Connor Engineering Laboratories for the concept and engineering of the fluid-damped camera-head for motion picture photography.

SCIENTIFIC AND TECHNICAL AWARDS: SCIENTIFIC AND ENGINEERING AWARD
LOREN CARPENTER, ROB COOK, ED CATMULL, TOM PORTER, PAT HANRAHAN, TONY APODACA, and DARWYN PEACHEY for the development of "RenderMan" software which produces images used in motion pictures from 3D computer descriptions of shape and appearance.
CLAUS WIEDEMANN and ROBERT ORBAN for the design and Dolby Laboratories for the development of the Dolby Labs "Container."
KEN BATES for the design and development of the Bates Decelerator System for accurately and safely arresting the descent of stunt persons in high freefalls.
AL MAYER for the camera design; IAIN NEIL and GEORGE KRAEMER for the optical design; HANS SPIRAWSKI and BILL ESUCK for the opto-mechanical design; and DON EARL for technical support in developing the Panavision System 65 Studio Sync Sound Reflex Camera for 65mm motion picture photography.
DOUGLAS TRUMBULL for the concept; GEOFFREY H. WILLIAMSON for the movement design; ROBERT D. AUGUSTE for the electronic design and EDMUND M. DIGIULIO for the camera system design of the CP-65 Showscan Camera System for 65mm motion picture photography.
ARRIFLEX CORPORATION, OTTO BLASCHEK and the ENGINEERING DEPARTMENT OF ARRI, AUSTRIA for the design and development of the Arriflex 765 Camera System for 65mm motion picture photography.

SCIENTIFIC AND TECHNICAL AWARDS: TECHNICAL ACHIEVEMENT AWARD
IRA TIFFEN of Tiffen Manufacturing Corporation for the production of the Ultra Contrast Filter Series for motion picture photography.
ROBERT R. BURTON of Audio Rents, Incorporated, for the development of the Model S.27, 4-Band Splitter/Combiner.
IAIN NEIL for the optical design and KAZ FUDANO for the mechanical design of the Panavision Slant Focus Lens for motion picture photography.
TOM BRIGHAM for the original concept and pioneering work; and DOUGLAS SMYTHE and the Computer Graphics Department of

Industrial Light & Magic for the development and the first implementation in feature motion pictures of the "MORF" system for digital metamorphosis of high resolution images.

1993

$\mathcal{H}$ollywood liberals were in a giddy mood. William Jefferson Clinton had just captured the White House, and Whoopi Goldberg had been chosen as the first woman—the first African-American, no less—to host the Academy Awards. There was some anxiety that the often X-rated comedienne might veer embarrassingly from the script. But from her first moment onstage, it was clear that she was on her best behavior.

The biggest news of the night was that producer-director Steven Spielberg had put away his boyish obsessions for sentimental aliens (*E.T.*) and things that go bump in the water (*Jaws*) to make an honest to God grown-up movie, *Schindler's List*. The *Los Angeles Times* reported that "the question is not if *Schindler's List* will win but how broad the victory would be." Its final tally of seven Oscars was nearly a record, as it turned out. Ironically, it won no acting awards.

Jane Campion's *The Piano* grabbed Best Actress for Holly Hunter, who spoke not a word of dialogue in the film, and Best Supporting Actress for Anna Paquin, just 11, whose dad hadn't allowed her to see the R-rated movie yet. Little Anna, barely able to catch her breath, nearly lost control of her senses at the podium. She held her Oscar as if it were a doll and broke tradition by skipping back to her seat in the audience. Best Supporting Actor went to Tommy Lee Jones for his intrepid cop in *The Fugitive*, a popular choice. But it was Best Actor Tom Hanks, as a gay lawyer with AIDS in *Philadelphia*, who stole the show with his "one from the heart" acceptance speech. He particularly thanked his gay high-school drama teacher and ended with "God bless America." Another highlight was a live performance by "the Boss," Bruce Springsteen, singing his haunting Oscar-winning song "Streets of Philadelphia."

Former heartthrob turned philanthropist, Paul Newman received the Hersholt Humanitarian Award. And one of the last surviving grand dames of her generation of stars, a frail but beaming Deborah Kerr, was finally given her due with an honorary Oscar. "I've never been so frightened in all my life—but I feel better now because I know I'm among friends," Kerr said. Yes, she was.

THE A LIST

CEREMONY: March 21, 1994
Dorothy Chandler Pavilion, Los Angeles Music Center, Los Angeles
HOST: Whoopi Goldberg

BEST PICTURE/BEST DIRECTOR STEVEN SPIELBERG (B. 1947) *SCHINDLER'S LIST*

"This movie has changed my life. I don't even know how, but I'm not the same person I was when I went to Poland in 1993."

Based on the best-seller by Thomas Keneally, the film tells the story of Oscar Schindler, a man who saw his chance at the beginning of World War II and moved to Nazi-occupied Poland to open a factory and employ Jews at starvation wages. His goal was to become a millionaire. By the end of the war he had, instead, risked his life and spent his fortune to save those Jews. *Schindler*, the movie, received the gamut of reviews, from raves to ridicule, but went on to become a succès d'estime and box office success.

Rolling Stone's Peter Travers wrote, "The film's near-certain victory is based less on merit than on the marketing of its ambitious intentions. The Academy doesn't judge movies, it weighs them by subject matter." Others, however, thought Spielberg's direc-

Liam Neeson (center)

tion masterful. "What is most amazing about this film is how completely Spielberg serves his story," wrote Roger Ebert. "Individual scenes are masterpieces of art direction, cinematography, special effects, crowd control…There is a single-mindedness to the enterprise that is awesome."

A lonely child of divorce and a teen prodigy, Spielberg never doubted what he wanted to do when he grew up. He signed a seven-year contract with Universal at 21 and made his first splash directing an episode of the TV series *Night Gallery* (1969). His first feature, *The Sugarland Express* (1974), paved the way for *Jaws* (1975), his first blockbuster. Since then Spielberg has directed the ten biggest moneymakers of all time, including *Close Encounters of the Third Kind* (1977) and *Raiders of the Lost Ark* (1981), many of which richly deserved nominations. But it wasn't until he made a "serious" film that the Academy took notice, and many of the critics took exception to this selection for their golden statuette.

The envelope, please…

BEST ACTOR
TOM HANKS (B. 1956)
PHILADELPHIA

At times on the verge of tears, Hanks delivered what the *Hollywood Reporter* called "one of the most dramatic acceptance speeches of any Oscar year." In his film, he plays an AIDS-stricken young lawyer who moves from shame to defiance, confronting homophobia with all the valor of a war hero. More than just a politically correct take on a nontraditional role, Hanks' immersion was complete and devastatingly honest. *Philadelphia* was not without its controversy, however. Larry Kramer complained, "*Philadelphia* doesn't have anything to do with the AIDS I know, or with the gay world I know."

Many didn't believe the film was either brave or groundbreaking, but they supported its intentions never-theless. *Philadelphia* did, however, become a box-office success, as Andrew Sarris of the *Village Voice* observed, "for many of the same reasons it has been so bitterly denounced by much of the radical gay activist community." As to Hanks, little need be said about his becoming America's most popular light comedian since Cary Grant, although, he too, has appeared in more serious roles. Hanks went on to win an Academy Award for his role in *Forrest Gump* (1994). (For more on Hanks, see 1994.)

Anna Paquin with Holly Hunter

BEST ACTRESS
HOLLY HUNTER (B. 1958)
THE PIANO

"I feel really, really, really happy. I felt happy before. But now I feel really, really happy," Hunter said backstage. "It changes the economics of my career, at least momentarily."

Hunter pulled off a deafening feat as Ada the mute nineteenth-century mail-order bride. Said Roger Ebert, "Director Campion understood the eroticism of slowness and restraint, and the power that Ada gains by pretending to care nothing for her mail-order husband. The performances are as original as the characters. Hunter's Ada is pale, grim and hatchet-faced at first, although she is capable of warming. It is one of those rare movies that is not just about a story, or some characters, but about a whole universe of feeling—of how people can be shut off from each other, lonely and afraid, about how help can come from unexpected sources, and about how you'll never know if you never ask."

Jami Bernard in the *New York Daily News* warned, "Try to see it before the inevitable backlash begins." A film showing a lusty sexual woman was more than most people—particularly men—could take. To wit: an article published by *New York* magazine was entitled "Seven Reasons Not to Like *The Piano*."

Hunter came late to film but shot to the top quickly with her nominations for *Broadcast News* (1987) and *The Firm* (1993).

BEST OF 1993
Best Picture: *Schindler's List*
Best Director: Steven Spielberg, *Schindler's List*
Best Actor: Tom Hanks, *Philadelphia*
Best Actress: Holly Hunter, *The Piano*
Best Supporting Actor: Tommy Lee Jones, *The Fugitive*
Best Supporting Actress: Anna Paquin, *The Piano*
Honorary Award: Deborah Kerr

FIRSTS
• Steven Spielberg and Tom Hanks had a double-whammy year. Alongside his Oscar win, *Schindler's List*, Spielberg's *Jurassic Park* was the big box-office grosser that also netted him three technical-achievement awards. As for Hanks, aside from his win for *Philadelphia*, he made the girls laugh and cry in the smash hit *Sleepless in Seattle*.

• Holly Hunter took home the seventh Oscar awarded for a completely nonspeaking role. Among her talented and hushed predecessors were Jane Wyman (*Johnny Belinda*, 1948); Marlee Matlin (*Children of a Lesser God*, 1986) and Patty Duke (*The Miracle Worker*, 1962), who, to be precise, did manage one word: "water."

• Ever the gentleman, Tom Hanks asked permission of his former high-school drama teacher, Rawley Farnsworth, 69, before outing him in his acceptance speech. What followed, for perhaps the first and only time, was a movie inspired by an acceptance speech, *In & Out*. The reclusive Farnsworth took it all in stride but remained curious as to how Hanks knew he was gay.

• *Schindler's List* was the first black-and-white film to win Best Picture since *The Apartment* in 1960.

ROLE REVERSALS
Holly Hunter's nominated role in *Broadcast News* (1987) was originally offered to Debra Winger. Steven Spielberg had been set to direct Harrison Ford in what would turn out to be one of Tom Hanks's early hits, *Big* (1988). Hanks then turned down the leading roles in *Jerry Maguire* (1996) and *American Beauty* (1999).

UNMENTIONABLES
• Vivien Leigh's Best Actress Oscar for *Gone with the Wind* was recently auctioned off for $500,000. Leigh made $15,000 for playing the role of Scarlett O'Hara.

• Winona Ryder told the press as she arrived at the Dorothy Chandler Pavilion, "I'm very nauseous and dizzy and totally freaked out." Her condition might have sounded familiar to adherents of her godfather, Dr. Timothy Leary, who promoted the use of LSD back in the '60s.

• It's all about whom you know: Tom Hanks is a direct descendant of Nancy Hanks, the mother of Abraham Lincoln.

• "Tom Hanks does not act in this movie. His makeup does his acting. I haven't seen so many changes hinged on shades of Max Factor since James Cagney in *Man of a Thousand Faces*," complained Larry Kramer.

SINS OF OMISSION
Actor: Denzel Washington, *Philadelphia;* Jeff Bridges, *Fearless.*

 BEST SUPPORTING ACTOR
TOMMY LEE JONES (B. 1946)
THE FUGITIVE

"The only thing a man can say at a time like this is, 'I am not really bald.'" Jones was preparing for an upcoming role (*Heaven & Earth*, 1993) even as he accepted the Oscar for his turn as the richly defined, scene-stealing U.S. marshal in *The Fugitive*. "Jones is the best thing about this all-too-often predictable chase film," wrote Marc Savlov in the *Austin Chronicle*.

Jones won a football scholarship to Harvard and roomed for four years with Al Gore. Four years on the daytime soap *One Life to Live* provided the springboard to the big screen, and he was noticed pretty quickly. Said Roger Ebert in the *Chicago Tribune*, "He has the charm of a hangman promising to make things as comfortable as possible." Jones's dangerous good looks have put him in some demanding roles, among them *Coal Miner's Daughter* (1980), *JFK* (1991), *Blue Sky* (1994), and *Men in Black* (1997).

© A.M.P.A.S.®

 BEST SUPPORTING ACTRESS
ANNA PAQUIN (B. 1982)
THE PIANO

Backstage, after nervously thanking the Academy for "permitting me to be here today…and for Beany, for taking such good care of me during the making of the film," Paquin said that when she heard Gene Hackman call her name, she thought, This can't be happening, and then, Oh, my gosh. Campion described Paquin as a completely raw and almost complete natural talent. "It was daunting," Campion said of directing Paquin. "And I did nothing really to bring that performance out except to make sure she wasn't exhausted after lunch."

Anna Paquin herself did not get to see the film in its entirety. Her father said it would stay that way for a while. Apparently, it was her distinctive voice that won her the role of a very young lifetime over 5,000 other girls. It was hardly a formulaic kid's performance, as she went from a vulnerable mother's confidante to a betrayer.

Deborah Kerr in Tea and Sympathy *(1956)*

 HONORARY AWARD
DEBORAH KERR (B. 1921)

This lovely red-haired Scottish-born leading lady once said to an interviewer, "All the most successful people seem to be neurotic—and I'm so confoundedly normal."

Kerr's graceful British reserve had her typecast in ladylike roles for too many years, until she finally broke free in *From Here to Eternity* (1953). Her inflamed, horizontal kiss with Burt Lancaster on the crashing Honolulu surf is perhaps one of the most indelibly sexy and romantic screen images of all time.

Nominated six times for Best Actress, Kerr was never united with her Golden Boy, though she delivered outstanding performances in her many films, including *The Prisoner of Zenda* (1952), *Tea and Sympathy* (1956), *Separate Tables* (1958), *The Night of the Iguana* (1964), and *The Arrangement* (1969).

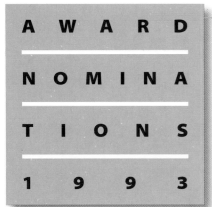

AWARD NOMINATIONS 1993

BEST PICTURE
THE FUGITIVE, Warner Bros. Arnold Kopelsan, Producer.
IN THE NAME OF THE FATHER, Hell's Kitchen/Gabriel Byrne, Universal. Jim Sheridan, Producer.
THE PIANO, Jan Chapman & CIBY 2000, Miramax. Jan Chapman, Producer.
THE REMAINS OF THE DAY, Mike Nichols/John Calley/Merchant Ivory, Columbia. Mike Nichols, John Calley and Ismail Merchant, Producers
SCHINDLER'S LIST, Universal/Amblin, Universal. Steven Spielberg, Gerald R. Molen and Branko Lustig, Producers.

ACTOR
DANIEL DAY-LEWIS in *In the Name of the Father*, Hell's Kitchen/Gabriel Byrne, Universal.
LAURENCE FISHBURNE in *What's Love Got to Do with It*, Touchstone, Bum Vista.
TOM HANKS in *Philadelphia*, TriStar.
ANTHONY HOPKINS in *The Remains of the Day*, Mike Nichols/John Calley/Merchant Ivory, Columbia.
LIAM NEESON in *Schindler's List*, Univernat/Amblin, Universal.

ACTRESS
ANGELA BASSETT in *What's Love Got to Do with It*, Touchstone, Buena Vista.
STOCKARD CHANNING in *Six Degrees of Separation*, MGM/UA.
HOLLY HUNTER in *The Piano*, Jan Chapman & CIBY 2000, Miramax.
EMMA THOMPSON in *The Remains of the Day*, Mike Nichols/John Calley/Merchant Ivory, Columbia.
DEBRA WINGER in *Shadowlands*, Shadowlands Production, Savoy.

SUPPORTING ACTOR
LEONARDO DICAPRIO in *What's Eating Gilbert Grape*, Matalon Teper Ohlsson, Paramount.
RALPH FIENNES in *Schindler's List*, Universal/Amblin, Universal
TOMMY LEE JONES in *The Fugitive*, Warner Bros.
JOHN MALKOVICH in *In the Line of Fire*, Castle Rock, Columbia.
PETE POSTLETHWAITE in *In the Name of the Father*, Hell's Kitchen/Gabriel Byrne, Universal.

SUPPORTING ACTRESS
HOLLY HUNTER in *The Firm*, John Davis/Scott Rudin/Mirage, Paramount.
ANNA PAQUIN in *The Piano*, Jan Chapman & CIBY 2000, Miramax.
ROSIE PEREZ in *Fearless*, Warner Bros.
WINONA RYDER in *The Age of Innocence*, Cappa/De Fina, Columbia.
EMMA THOMPSON in *In the Name of the Father*, Hell's Kitchen/Gabriel Byrne, Universal.

DIRECTION
JIM SHERIDAN for *In the Name of the Father*, Hell's Kitchen/Gabriel Byrne, Universal.
JANE CAMPION for *The Piano*, Jan Chapman & CIBY 2000, Miramax.
JAMES IVORY for *The Remains of the Day*, Mike Nichols/John Calley/Merchant Ivory, Columbia.
STEVEN SPIELBERG for *Schindler's List*, Universal/Amblin, Universal
ROBERT ALTMAN for *Short Cuts*, Avenue Pictures, Fine Line Features.

WRITING: BASED ON MATERIAL FROM ANOTHER MEDIUM
THE AGE OF INNOCENCE, Cappa/De Fina, Colombia. Jay Cocks, Martin Scorsese.
IN THE NAME OF THE FATHER, Hell's Kitchen/Gabriel Byrne. Universal Terry George, Jim Sheridan.
THE REMAINS OF THE DAY, Mike Nichols/John Calley/Merchant Ivory, Columbia. Ruth Prawer Jhabvala.
SCHINDLER'S LIST, Universal/Amblin, Universal. Steven Zaillian.
SHADOWLANDS, Shadowlands Production, Savoy. William Nicholson.

WRITING: DIRECTLY FOR THE SCREEN
DAVE, Warner Bros. Gary Ross.
IN THE LINE OF FIRE. Castle Rock. Columbia. Jeff Maguire.
PHILADELPHIA, TriStar. Ron Nyswaner.
THE PIANO, Jan Chapman & CIBY 2000, Miramax. Jane Campion.
SLEEPLESS IN SEATTLE, TriStar. Screenplay by Nora Ephron, David S. Ward, Jeff Arch; Story by Jeff Arch.

ART DIRECTION—SET DECORATION
ADDAMS FAMILY VALUES, Scott Rudin, Paramount. Ken Adam; Marvin March.
THE AGE OF INNOCENCE, Cappa/De Fina, Columbia. Dante Ferretti; Robert J. Franco.
ORLANDO, Adventures Pictures, Sony Pictures Classes. Ben Van Os, Jan Roelfs.
THE REMAINS OF THE DAY, Mike Nichols/John Calley/Merchant Ivory, Columbia. Luciana Arrighi; Ian Whittaker.
SCHINDLER'S LIST, Universal/Amblin, Universal. Allan Starski; Ewa Braun.

CINEMATOGRAPHY
FAREWELL MY CONCUBINE, Tomson (HK) Films, Miramart. Gu Changwei.
THE FUGITIVE, Warner Bros. Michael Chapman.
THE PIANO, Jan Chapman & CIBY 2000, Miramax. Stuart Dryburgh.
SCHINDLER'S LIST, Universal/Amblin, Universal. Janusz Kaminski.
SEARCHING FOR BOBBY FISCHER, Scott Rudin/Mirage, Paramount. Conrad L. Hall.

COSTUME DESIGN
THE AGE OF INNOCENCE, Cappa/De Fina, Columbia. Gabriella Pesuucci.
ORLANDO, Adventures Pictures, Sony Pictures Classics. Sandy Powell.
THE PIANO, Jan Chapman & CIBY 2000, Miramax. Janet Patterson.
THE REMAINS OF THE DAY. Mike Nichols/John Calley/Merchant Ivory, Columbia. Jenny Beavan, John Bright
SCHINDLER'S LIST, Universal/Amblin, Universal, Anna Biedrzycka-Sheppard.

FILM EDITING
THE FUGITIVE, Warner Bros. Dennis Virkler, David Finfer, Dean Goodhill, Don Brochu, Richard Nord, Dov Hoenig
IN THE LINE OF FIRE, Castle Rock, Columbia. Anne V. Coates.
IN THE NAME OF THE FATHER, Hell's Kitchen/Gabriel Byrne, Universal. Gerry Hambling.
THE PIANO, Jan Chapman & CIBY 2000, Miramax. Veronika Jenet.
SCHINDLER'S LIST, Universal/Amblin, Universal. Michael Kahn.

MAKEUP
MRS. DOUBTFIRE, 20th Century-Fox. Greg Cannom, Ve Neill, Yolanda Toussieng.
PHILADELPHIA, TriStar. Carl Fullerton, Alan D'Angerio.
SCHINDLER'S LIST, Universal/Amblin, Universal. Christina Smith, Matthew Mungle, Judy Alexander Cory.

SONG
AGAIN (*Poetic Justice*, Columbia). Music and Lyric by Janet Jackson, James Harris III, Terry Lewis.
THE DAY I FALL IN LOVE (*Beethoven's 2nd*, Universal). Music and Lyric by Carole Bayer Sager, James Ingram, Clif Magness.
PHILADELPHIA (*Philadelphia*, TriStar). Music and Lyric by Neil Young.
STREETS OF PHILADELPHIA (*Philadelphia*, TriStar). Music and Lyric by Bruce Springsteen.

A WINK AND A SMILE (*Sleepless in Seattle*, TriStar. Music by Marc Shaiman; Lyric by Ramsey McLean.

SCORING: ORIGINAL MUSIC
THE AGE OF INNOCENCE, Cappa/De Fina, Columbia. Elmer Bernstein.
THE FIRM, John Davis/Scott Rudin/Mirage, Paramount. Dave Grusin.
THE FUGITIVE, Warner Bros. James Newton Howard.
THE REMAINS OF THE DAY, Mike Nichols,John Calley/Merchant Ivory, Columbia. Richard Robbins.
SCHINDLER'S LIST, Universal/Amblin, Universal. John Williams.

SOUND
CLIFFHANGER, Cliffhanger B.V., TriStar. Michael Minkler, Bob Beemer, Tim Cooney.
THE FUGITIVE, Warner Bros. Donald O. Mitchell, Michael Herbick, Frank A. Montano, Scott D Smith.
GERONIMO: AN AMERICAN LEGEND, Columbia. Chris Carpenter, D.M. Hemphill, Bill W. Benton, Lee Orloff.
JURASSIC PARK, Amblin, Universal. Gary Summers, Gary Rydstrom, Shawn Murphy, Ron Judkins.
SCHINDLER'S LIST, Universal/Amblin, Universal. Andy Nelson, Steve Pederson, Scott Millan, Ron Judkins.

SOUND EFFECTS EDITING
CLIFFHANGER, Cliffhanger B.V., TriStar. Wylie Stalensan, Gregg Baxter.
THE FUGITIVE, Warner Bros. John Leveque, Bruce Stumbler.
JURASSIC PARK, Amblin, Universal. Gary Rydstrom, Richard Hymns.

VISUAL EFFECTS
CLIFFHANGER, Cliffhanger B.V. Production, TriStar. Neil Krepela, John Richardson, John Bruno, Pamela Easley.
JURASSIC PARK, Amblin Entertainment Production; Universal. Dennis Muren, Stan Winston, Phil Tippett, Michael Lantieri.
THE NIGHTMARE BEFORE CHRISTMAS, Touchstone Pictures Production; Buena Vista, Pete Kozachik, Eric Leighton, Ariel Velasco Show, Gordon Baker.

DOCUMENTARY: FEATURE
THE BROADCAST TAPES OF DR. PETER, Canadian Broadcasting Corporation/HBO Films Production. (Canada) David Paperny and Arthur Ginsberg.
CHILDREN OF FATE, Young/Friedson Production. Susan Todd and Andrew Young.
FOR BETTER OR FOR WORSE, David Collier Production. David Collier and Betsy Thompson.
I AM A PROMISE: THE CHILDREN OF STANTON ELEMENTARY SCHOOL, Verite Films Production. Susan Raymond and Alan Raymond.
THE WAR ROOM, R.J. Cutler/Wendy Ettinger/Frazer Pennebaker Production. D.A. Pennebaker and Chris Hegedus.

DOCUMENTARY: SHORT SUBJECT
BLOOD TIES: THE LIFE AND WORK OF SALLY MANN, Moving Target Production. Steven Cantor and Peter Spirer.
CHICKS IN WHITE SATIN, University of Southern California School of Cinema/Television. Elaine Holliman and Jason Schneider.
DEFENDING OUR LIVES, Cambridge Documentary Films Production. Margaret Lazarus and Renner Wunderlich.

FOREIGN LANGUAGE FILM
BELLE EPOQUE, (Spain).
FAREWELL MY CONCUBINE, (Hong Kong).
HEDD WYN, (United Kingdom/Wales)
THE SCENT OF GREEN PAPAYA, (Vietnam).
THE WEDDING BANQUET, (Taiwan).

SHORT FILMS: ANIMATED
BLINDSCAPE, National Film & Television School. Stephen Palmer.
THE MIGHTY RIVER, Canadian

Broadcasting Corporation/Societe Radio-Canada Production. Frederic Back, Hubert Tison.
SMALL TALK, Bob Godfrey Films, Ltd. Bob Godfrey, Kevin Baldwin.
THE VILLAGE, Pizazz Pictures Production. Mark Baker.
THE WRONG TROUSERS, Aardman Animations Limited Production. Nick Park.
THE WEDDING BANQUET, (Taiwan).

SHORT FILMS: LIVE ACTION
BLACK RIDER (SCHWARZFAHRER), Thins-Film GmbH Production. Pepe Daoqaart.
DOWN ON THE WATERFRONT, Stacy Title/Jonathan Penner Production. Stacy Title, Jonathan Penner.
THE DUTCH MASTER, Regina Ziegler Film Production. Susan Seidelman, Jonathan Brett.
PARTNERS, Chanticleer Films. Peter Wetter, Jana Sue Memel.
THE SCREW (LA VIS), Perla Films Production. Didier Flamand.

HONORARY AND OTHER AWARDS
TO DEBORAH KERR in appreciation for a full career's worth of elegant and beautifully crafted performances.

JEAN HERSHOLT HUMANITARIAN AWARD
TO PAUL NEWMAN

GORDON E. SAWYER AWARD
TO PETRO VLAHOS

SCIENTIFIC AND TECHNICAL AWARDS: ACADEMY AWARD OF MERIT
PANAVISION for the Auto Panatar anamorphic photographic lens.
MANFRED G. MICHELSON of Technical Film Systems, Incorporated, for the design and development of the first sprocket-driven film transport system for color print film processors which permits transport speeds in excess of 600 feet per minute.

SCIENTIFIC AND TECHNICAL AWARDS: SCIENTIFIC AND ENGINEERING AWARD
MARK LEATHER, LES DITTERT, DOUGLAS SMYTHE and GEORGE JOBLOVE for the concept and development of the Digital Motion Picture Retouching System for removing visible rigging and dirt/damage artifacts from original motion picture imagery
FRITZ GABRIEL BAUER for the design, development and manufacture of the Moviecam Compact Modular 35mm motion picture camera system.

SCIENTIFIC AND TECHNICAL AWARDS: TECHNICAL ACHIEVEMENT AWARD
WALLY MILLS for the concept; and GARY STADLER and GUSTAVE PARADA for the design of the Cinemills Lamp Protection System.
GARY NUZZI, DAVID JOHNSRUD and WILLIAM BLETHEN for the design and development of the Unilux H3000 Strobe Lighting System.
HARRY J. BAKER for the design and development of the Ronford Baker Metal Tripods for motion picture photography.
MICHAEL DORROUGH for the design and development of the compound meter known as the Dorrough Audio Level Meter.
DAVID DEGENKOLB for the development of a Silver Recovery Exchange System to eliminate hazardous waste (silver ion) in wash water and allow recycling of this water.

1994

If there had been an award for Most Talked About Dress at the Oscars, it would have gone to Lizzy Gardiner, co-costume designer of *The Adventures of Priscilla, Queen of the Desert*, whose frock was made entirely of American Express Gold Cards. Following a commercial break midway through the show, David Letterman quipped, "While we were gone, Lizzy Gardiner's dress expired."

PLAY IT AGAIN, TOM

CEREMONY: March 27, 1995
Shrine Auditorium, Los Angeles
HOST: David Letterman

It was an evening of unusual twists and turns. Jessica Lange won Best Actress for her role as a manic-depressive military wife in *Blue Sky*, a film that had been sitting on a shelf for three years. Tom Hanks plucked his second consecutive Best Actor Oscar, a double-ringer that hadn't been pulled off since Spencer Tracy in 1937 and 1938. "When in doubt, go with *Gump*," the *Los Angeles Times* had predicted. And the Academy did just that, giving the year's biggest blockbuster hit thirteen nominations and six wins.

Earlier in the race there had been some hope for Quentin Tarantino's iconoclastic *Pulp Fiction*, but when he picked up an Oscar for Best Original Screenplay, he saw the writing on *Gump*'s "box of chocolates." *Pulp*'s real winner was Best Actor nominee John Travolta, whose career catapulted into a sizzling second act thanks to his mind-blowing performance as a junkie hit man.

Dianne Wiest was served well for a second time by Woody Allen, winning a Best Supporting Actress statuette for *Bullets Over Broadway* after nabbing one for 1986's *Hannah and Her Sisters*. Martin Landau was the only first-timer in the pack for his tragicomic portrayal of Bela Lugosi in *Ed Wood*. Clint Eastwood, 1992's Oscar sweeper, made a triumphal return to claim the Irving Thalberg Memorial Award, and composer/producer/record magnate Quincy Jones picked up the Hersholt Humanitarian Award. Jack Nicholson, sans the ubiquitous shades, presented an Honorary Oscar to virtuoso Italian director Michelangelo Antonioni, 82.

By show's end, it was apparent that Letterman's less than starstruck irony hadn't caught fire with the Hollywood crowd, who felt that he'd turned their big night into a stand-up routine.

BEST PICTURE/BEST DIRECTOR
ROBERT ZEMECKIS (B. 1952)
FORREST GUMP

"Norman Rockwell painting the baby boomers," Zemeckis said of his picaresque sentimental satire of the past fifty years. *Forrest Gump*'s story is about his magical—*"Zelig"*-like—journey through four decades of American culture, taking him to the frontlines of the civil rights movement and Watergate. He even teaches Elvis to shake his hips. He is credited with coining the term "Have a nice day." Roger Ebert wrote, "He's on the Dick Cavett show with John Lennon, and he addresses a Vietnam-era peace rally on the Mall in Washington." Audiences left the theater convinced that actor Gary Sinise was actually a double amputee.

No matter which side of the argument you were on when it came to the merits of *Gump*—and the disagreements were bitter—everyone was reduced to tears. Pauline Kael, writing in *Entertainment Weekly,* summed up her own response briefly: "I hated it thoroughly." The rest of the audience, both critics and ticket payers, were crying too, but it was for Tom Hanks's moving performance. "Hanks is so charming as

Sally Field with Tom Hanks

Gump, so heroic in his guilelessness and belief in simple virtues, that you want to excuse the film's excesses and overlook Zemeckis's weakness for easy, maudlin sentiment," wrote the *San Francisco Chronicle*.

Zemeckis, a.k.a. the "whiz kid with special effects," learned it all when he made special-effects vehicles *Romancing the Stone* (1984), *Back to the Future* (1985), and *Who Framed Roger Rabbit* (1988). Specializing in entertainment films, Zemeckis's work delivers fun. His later work, though, has become more thoughtful, with *Forrest Gump* and *Contact* (1997) both critically acclaimed. These films, too, incorporate stunning effects, but Zemeckis has proved that he can combine a serious story with special effects—an unusual accomplishment for most directors. No matter what people thought of *Gump*, enough of them raced to theaters to make it the box-office blockbuster of the year.

The envelope, please...

BEST ACTOR
TOM HANKS (B. 1956)
FORREST GUMP

"Believe me, the power and the pleasure of this moment is a constant speed of light. It will never be diminished, nor will my appreciation and the meaning between two simple words that I can only offer you here: Thank you." There wasn't a dry eye in the house, including Hanks's.

It was impossible to imagine anyone but Hanks in the role of Gump, a childlike presence that Hanks did so well with in, among other films, Penny Marshall's *Big* (1988). A college dropout, Hanks had a lively, spontaneous acting style that was just the ticket . Handsome in a gawky sort of way, the thin, curly-topped Hanks made his film debut in the slasher thriller *He Knows You're Alone* (1980). He hit pay dirt when he appeared as a cross-dresser in the TV sitcom *Bosom Buddies* (1980–1982). And he was beloved by fans and critics alike for his performances in *Splash* (1984), *Turner & Hooch* (1989), and *The Bonfire of the Vanities* (1990).

In 1992 he put on pounds to play in *A League of Their Own*. His box-office success continued with *Sleepless in Seattle* and *Philadelphia* (both 1993), the latter winning him an Oscar.

(For more on Hanks, see 1993.)

BEST ACTRESS
JESSICA LANGE (B. 1949)
BLUE SKY

"Well, you know, they need some old girls sometimes," said the 45-year-old actress in answer to questions from reporters. Lange was once described by co-star Jack Nicholson (*The Postman Always Rings Twice*, 1981) as "a delicate fawn, crossed with a Buick." The actress called upon her steely inner resources to overcome her disastrous screen performance in the remake of *King Kong* (1976).

In *Blue Sky*, Lange plays the sexy, beautiful, out-of-control, adored wife of an army officer (Tommy Lee Jones) whose career is threatened by her behavior. Said Roger Ebert, "*Blue Sky* is the kind of movie that is constantly surprising us with the originality of its developments. We think we know some of this material, and where it will lead, and how it can be resolved, and we are wrong."

Lange has proved herself in some of the most demanding roles. She reached her career high-water mark with an Oscar-nominated tour de force as the tragic Frances Farmer in *Frances* (1982). Among her many films are *Tootsie* (1982 Oscar), *Country* (1984), *Sweet Dreams* (1985), *Crimes of the Heart* (1986), *Music Box* (1989), and *Cape Fear* (1991).

BEST OF 1994
Best Picture: *Forrest Gump*
Best Director: Robert Zemeckis, *Forrest Gump*
Best Actor: Tom Hanks, *Forrest Gump*
Best Actress: Jessica Lange, *Blue Sky*
Best Supporting Actor: Martin Landau, *Ed Wood*
Best Supporting Actress: Dianne Wiest, *Bullets Over Broadway*

FIRSTS
• *Entertainment Weekly* chose Tom Hanks as the only actor worthy of $20 million.

• By 1994 *Forrest Gump* was the most financially successful ($300 million) movie to win Best Picture.

• Until 1994 only three other films matched *Forrest*'s thirteen nominations: *Gone with the Wind* (1939), *Mary Poppins* (1964), and *Who's Afraid of Virginia Wolf?* (1966). The all-time champion, with fourteen, was *All About Eve*.

• *The Lion King*'s Elton John and Tim Rice outdid themselves and everybody else in Academy history, with three nominated songs in a single year.

SINS OF OMISSION
• There was a storm of protest when Linda Fiorentino's erotically charged starring performance in *The Last Seduction* failed to get Oscar consideration due to the film's brief showing on HBO.

• The Academy's Documentary nominating committee was roundly criticized when it failed to add to its list the acclaimed *Hoop Dreams*, a highly personal chronicle of two inner-city boys' attempts to dribble their way into professional basketball careers.

ALWAYS A BRIDESMAID, NEVER A BRIDE
While Tom Hanks won two consecutive Oscars, two of the most honored actors in film, Richard Burton and Peter O'Toole, hold the record for seven nominations apiece without a single win.

UNMENTIONABLES
• The House of Harry Winston lent more than $12 million in rare jewelry to presenters and nominees. Jennifer Tilly (*Bullets Over Broadway*) fairly drooped—dripped!—with $1.2 million worth of diamond bracelets, diamond and platinum ear clips, and a blinding diamond choker.

• Let's Get This Straight: Perennial heartthrob Richard Gere and his wife, superstar model Cindy Crawford, hoped to squelch rumors once and for all by taking out a full-page ad in the *London Times* insisting on their heterosexuality.

BEST SUPPORTING ACTOR
MARTIN LANDAU (B. 1931)
ED WOOD

"I feel almost like I'm having an out-of-body experience. My God, what a night, what a life, what a moment, what everything!" The audience seemed as delighted by the win as Landau, who had eerily transformed himself into tragic early-horror star Bela Lugosi in Tim Burton's *Ed Wood*.

Landau, a contemporary and friend of James Dean and Steve McQueen, spent his early career as a young actor at the Actors Studio in New York City under the mentorship of Lee Strasberg. After playing the heavy in such classics as *North by Northwest* (1959), he made his real mark on '60s TV in *Mission Impossible*, and was first offered the role of Dr. Spock on *Star Trek*. He had previously been nominated for Best Supporting Actor for *Tucker* (1988) and *Crimes and Misdemeanors* (1989).

BEST SUPPORTING ACTRESS
DIANNE WIEST (B. 1948)
BULLETS OVER BROADWAY

In response to winning two Oscars, Wiest said, "I think I'm going to make them into earrings. This is as surprising and marvelous as it was the first time, although this time I need glasses."

Playing the Norma Desmond-like fading alcoholic stage star, Wiest got belly laughs just by putting her finger to the lips of John Cusack's character, a deadly serious playwright and whispering, "Don't speak." Of Wiest's performance *Rolling Stone*'s Peter Travers exclaimed, "[She] delivers a comic tour de force. Wiest skirts caricature by finding the threatened child in this aging, boozing diva."

Wiest's career began on the stage and moved into film in the 1980s, when she appeared in many of Woody Allen's films, including *The Purple Rose of Cairo* (1985), *Hannah and Her Sisters* (1986), and *Radio Days* (1987). She also kept herself busy with performances in *Edward Scissorhands* (1990), *Little Man Tate* (1991), and *The Horse Whisperer* (1998). (For more on Wiest, see 1986.)

AWARD NOMINATIONS 1994

BEST PICTURE
FORREST GUMP, Steve Tisch/Wendy Finerman, Paramount. Wendy Finerman, Steve Tisch and Steve Starkey, Producers.
FOUR WEDDINGS AND A FUNERAL, Working Title, Gramercy. Duncan Kenworthy, Producer.
PULP FICTION, A Band Apart/Jersey Films, Miramax, Lawrence Bender, Producer.
QUIZ SHOW, Hollywood Pictures/Wildwood/Baltimore Pictures, Buena Vista. Robert Redford, Michael Jacobs, Julian Krainin and Michael Nozik, Producers.
THE SHAWSHANK REDEMPTION, Castle Rock, Columbia. Niki Marvin, Producer.

ACTOR
MORGAN FREEMAN in *The Shawshank Redemption*, Castle Rock, Columbia.
TOM HANKS in *Forrest Gump*, Steve Tisch/Wendy Finerman, Paramount.
NIGEL HAWTHORNE in *The Madness of King George*, Close Call Films, Goldwyn/Channel Four.
PAUL NEWMAN in *Nobody's Fool*, Scott Rudin/Cinehaus, Paramount/Capella International.
JOHN TRAVOLTA in *Pulp Fiction*, A Band Apart/Jersey Films, Miramax.

ACTRESS
JODIE FOSTER in *Nell*, 20th Century-Fox.
JESSICA LANGE in *Blue Sky*, Robert H. Solo, Orion.
MIRANDA RICHARDSON in *Tom & Viv*, New Era, Miramax.
WINONA RYDER in *Little Women*, Di Novi, Columbia.
SUSAN SARANDON in *The Client*, Client Production, Warner Bros.

SUPPORTING ACTOR
SAMUEL L. JACKSON in *Pulp Fiction*, A Band Apart/ Jersey Films, Miramax.
MARTIN LANDAU in *Ed Wood*, Touchstone, Buena Vista.
CHAZZ PALMINTERI in *Bullets over Broadway*, Jean Doumanian, Miramax.
PAUL SCOFIELD in *Quiz Show*, Hollywood Pictures/Wildwood/Baltimore Pictures, Buena Vista.
GARY SINISE in *Forrest Gump*, Steve Tisch/Wendy Finerman, Paramount.

SUPPORTING ACTRESS
ROSEMARY HARRIS in *Tom & Viv*, New Era, Miramax.
HELEN MIRREN in *The Madness of King George*, Close Call Films, Goldwyn/Channel Four.
UMA THURMAN in *Pulp Fiction*, A Band Apart/Jersey Films, Miramax.
JENNIFER TILLY in *Bullets over Broadway*, Jean Doumanian, Miramax.
DIANNE WIEST in *Bullets over Broadway*, Jean Doumanian, Miramax.

DIRECTION
WOODY ALLEN for *Bullets over Broadway*, Jean Doumanian, Miramax.
ROBERT ZEMECKIS for *Forrest Gump*, Steve Tisch/Wendy Finerman, Paramount.
QUENTIN TARANTINO for *Pulp Fiction*, A Band Apart/Jersey Films, Miramax.
ROBERT REDFORD for *Quiz Show*, Hollywood Pictures/Wildwood/Baltimore Pictures, Buena Vista.
KRZYSZTOF KIESLOWSKI for *Red*, CAB/MK2/TOR, Miramax.

WRITING: BASED ON MATERIAL FROM ANOTHER MEDIUM

FORREST GUMP Steve Tisch/Wendy Finerman, Paramount. Eric Roth.

THE MADNESS OF KING GEORGE, Close Call Films, Goldwyn/Channel Four. Alan Bennett.

NOBODY'S FOOL, Scott Rudin/Cinehaus, Paramount/Capella International. Robert Benton.

QUIZ SHOW, Hollywood Pictures/Wildwood/Baltimore Pictures, Buena Vista. Paul Attanasio.

THE SHAWSHANK REDEMPTION, Castle Rock, Columbia. Frank Darabont.

WRITING: DIRECTLY FOR THE SCREEN

BULLETS OVER BROADWAY, Jean Doumanian, Miramax. Woody Allen, Douglas McGrath.

FOUR WEDDINGS AND A FUNERAL, Working Title, Gramercy. Richard Curtis.

HEAVENLY CREATURES, Wingnut, Miramax. Frances Walsh, Peter Jackson.

PULP FICTION, A Band Apart/Jersey Films, Miramax. Screenplay by Quentin Tarantino. Stories by Quentin Tarantino & Roger Avary.

RED, CAB/MK2/TOR, Miramax. Krzysztof Piesiewicz, Krzysztof Kieslowski.

ART DIRECTION—SET DECORATION

BULLETS OVER BROADWAY, Jean Doumanian, Miramax. Santo Loquasto; Susan Bode.

FORREST GUMP, Steve Tisch/Wendy Finerman, Paramount. Rick Carter; Nancy Haigh.

INTERVIEW WITH THE VAMPIRE, Geffen, Warner Bros. Dante Ferretti; Francesca Lo Schiavo.

LEGENDS OF THE FALL, TriStar. Lilly Kilvert; Dorree Cooper.

THE MADNESS OF KING GEORGE, Close Call Films, Goldwyn/Channel Four. Ken Adam; Carolyn Scott.

CINEMATOGRAPHY

FORREST GUMP Steve Tisch/Wendy Finerman, Paramount. Don Burgess.

LEGENDS OF THE FALL, TriStar. John Toll.

RED, CAB/MK2/TOR, Miramax. Piotr Sobocinski.

THE SHAWSHANK REDEMPTION, Castle Rock, Columbia. Roger Deakins.

WYATT EARP, Tig, Warner Bros. Owen Roizman.

COSTUME DESIGN

THE ADVENTURES OF PRISCILLA, QUEEN OF THE DESERT, Latent Images, Gramercy. Lizzy Gardiner, Tim Chappel.

BULLETS OVER BROADWAY, Jean Doumanian, Miramax. Jeffrey Kurland.

LITTLE WOMEN, Di Novi, Columbia. Colleen Atwood.

MAVERICK, Icon, Warner Bros. April Ferry.

QUEEN MARGOT, Renn, Miramax. Moidele Bickel.

FILM EDITING

FORREST GUMP, Steve Tisch/Wendy Finerman, Paramount Arthur Schmidt.

HOOP DREAMS, Kartemquin, Fine Line Features, Frederick Marx, Steve James, Bill Haugse.

PULP FICTION, A Band Apart/Jersey Films, Miramax. Sally Menke.

THE SHAWSHANK REDEMPTION, Castle Rock, Columbia. Richard Francis-Bruce.

SPEED, 20th Century-Fox. John Wright.

MAKEUP

ED WOOD, Touchstone, Buena Vista. Rick Baker, Ve Neill, Yolanda Toussieng.

FORREST GUMP Steve Tisch/Wendy Finerman, Paramount Daniel C. Striepeke, Hallie D'Amore, Judith A. Cory.

MARY SHELLEY'S FRANKENSTEIN, TriStar. Daniel Parker, Paul Engelen, Carol Hemming.

SONG

CAN YOU FEEL THE LOVE TONIGHT (*The Lion King*, Disney, Buena Vista). Music by Elton John; Lyric by Tim Rice.

CIRCLE OF LIFE (*The Lion King*, Buena Vista). Music by Elton John; Lyric by Tim Rice.

HAKUNA MATATA (*The Lion King*, Disney, Buena Vista). Music by Elton John; Lyric by Tim Rice.

LOOK WHAT LOVE HAS DONE (*Junior*, Northern Lights, Universal). Music and Lyric by Carole Bayer Sager, James Newton Howard, James Ingram, Patty Smyth.

MAKE UP YOUR MIND (*The Paper*, Imagine, Universal). Music and Lyric by Randy Newman.

SCORING: ORIGINAL MUSIC

FORREST GUMP, Steve Tisch/Wendy Finerman, Paramount Alan Silvestri.

INTERVIEW WITH THE VAMPIRE, Geffen, Warner Bros. Elliot Goldenthal.

THE LION KING, Disney, Buena Vista. Hans Zimmer.

LITTLE WOMEN, Di Novi, Columbia. Thomas Newman.

THE SHAWSHANK REDEMPTION, Castle Rock, Columbia. Thomas Newman.

SOUND

CLEAR AND PRESENT DANGER, Mace Neufeld/Robert Rehme, Paramount. Donald O. Mitchell, Michael Herbick, Frank A. Montano, Arthur Rochester.

FORREST GUMP, Steve Tisch/Wendy Finerman, Paramount. Randy Thom, Tom Johnson, Dennis Sands, William B. Kaplan.

LEGENDS OF THE FALL, TriStar. Paul Massey, David Campbell, Christopher David, Douglas Ganton.

THE SHAWSHANK REDEMPTION, Castle Rock, Columbia. Robert J. Litt, Elliot Tyson, Michael Herbick, Willie Burton.

SPEED, 20th Century-Fox. Gregg Landaker, Steve Maslow, Bob Beemer, David R. B MacMillan.

SOUND EFFECTS EDITING

CLEAR AND PRESENT DANGER, Mace Neufeld/Robert Rehire, Paramount. Bruce Stambler, John Leveque.

FORREST GUMP, Steve Tisch/Wendy Finerman, Paramount. Gloria S. Borders, Randy Thom.

SPEED, 20th Century-Fox. Stephen Hunter Flick.

VISUAL EFFECTS

FORREST GUMP, Steve Tisch/Wendy Finerman Productions; Paramount. Ken Ralston, George Murphy, Stephen Rosenbaum, Allen Hall.

THE MASK, Katja Motion Picture Production; New Line. Scott Squires, Steve Williams, Tom Bertino, Jon Farhat.

TRUE LIES, Lightstorm Entertainment Production; 20th Century-Fox. John Bruno, Thomas L Fisher, Jacques Stroweis, Patrick McClung.

DOCUMENTARY: FEATURE

COMPLAINTS OF A DUTIFUL DAUGHTER, D/D Production, Deborah Hoffmann.

D-DAY REMEMBERED, Guggenheim Productions, Inc. Production for the National D-Day Museum. Charles Guggenheim.

FREEDOM ON MY MIND, Clarity Film Production. Connie Field, Marilyn Mulford.

A GREAT DAY IN HARLEM, Jean Bach Production; Castle Hill. Jean Bach.

MAYA LIN: A STRONG CLEAR VISION, American Film Foundation/Sanders and Mock Productions, Freida Lee Mock, Terry Sanders.

DOCUMENTARY: SHORT SUBJECT

BLUES HIGHWAY, Half-Court Pictures, Ltd./National Geographic Society Production. Vince DiPersio, Bill Guttentag.

89MM OD EUROPY (89MM FROM EUROPE), Studio Filmowe "Kalejdoskop"/Telewizja Polska Production. (Poland) Marcel Lozinski.

SCHOOL OF ASSASSINS, A Richter Productions Film. Robert Richter.

STRAIGHT FROM THE HEART, Woman Vision Production. Dee Mosbacher, Frances Reid.

A TIME FOR JUSTICE, Guggenheim Productions, Inc. Production for the Southern Poverty Law Center. Charles Guggenheim.

FOREIGN LANGUAGE FILM

BEFORE THE RAIN, (Macedonia).

BURNT BY THE SUN, (Russia).

EAT DRINK MAN WOMAN, (Taiwan).

FARINELLI: IL CASTRATO, (Belgium).

STRAWBERRY AND CHOCOLATE, (Cuba).

SHORT FILMS: ANIMATED

THE BIG STORY, Spitting Image Production. Tim Watts, David Stoten.

BOB'S BIRTHDAY, Snowden Fine Animation for Channel Four/National Film Board of Canada Production. Alison Snowden, David Fine.

THE JANITOR, Vanessa Schwartz Production. Vanessa Schwartz.

THE MONK AND THE FISH, Folimage Valence Production. Michael Dudok de Wit.

TRIANGLE, Gingco Ltd. Production for Channel Four. Erica Russell.

SHORT FILMS: LIVE ACTION

FRANZ KAFKA'S IT'S A WONDERFUL LIFE, Conundrum Films Production. Peter Capaldi, Ruth Kenley-Letts.

KANGAROO COURT, Lava Entertainment Production. Sean Astin, Christine Astin.

ON HOPE, Chanticleer Films. JoBeth Williams, Michele McGuire.

SYRUP, First Choice Production. Paul Unwin, Nick Vivian.

TREVOR, Rajski/Stone Production. Peggy Rajski, Randy Stone.

HONORARY AND OTHER AWARDS

TO MICHELANGELO ANTONIONI in recognition of his place as one of the cinema's master visual stylists.

TO JOHN A. BONNER in appreciation for outstanding service and dedication in upholding the high standards of the Academy of Motion Picture Arts and Sciences.

IRVING G. THALBERG MEMORIAL AWARD

TO CLINT EASTWOOD

JEAN HERSHOLT HUMANITARIAN AWARD

TO QUINCY JONES

GORDON E. SAWYER AWARD

None given this year.

SCIENTIFIC AND TECHNICAL AWARDS: ACADEMY AWARD OF MERIT

PETRO VLAHOS and PAUL VLAHOS for the conception and development of the Ultimatte Electronic Blue Screen Compositing Process for motion pictures.

EASTMAN KODAK COMPANY for the development of the Eastman EXR Color Intermediate Film 5244.

SCIENTIFIC AND TECHNICAL AWARDS: SCIENTIFIC AND ENGINEERING AWARD

GARY DEMOS and DAN CAMERON of Information International, DAVID DiFRANCESCO and GARY STARK WEATHER of Pixar, and SCOTT SQUIRES of Industrial Light & Magic for their pioneering work in the field of film input scanning.

RAY FEENEY, WILL McCOWN and BILL BISHOP of RFX, Inc., and LES DITTERT of Pacific Data Images for their development work with area array CCD (Charge Coupled Device) film input scanning systems.

LINCOLN HU and MICHAEL MACKENZIE of Industrial Light & Magic and GLENN KENNEL and MIKE DAVIS of Eastman Kodak for their joint development work on a linear array CCD (Charge Coupled Device) film input scanning system.

IAIN NEIL for the optical design, AL SAIKI for the mechanical design and PANAVISION INTERNATIONAL L.P. for the development of the Panavision 11:1 Primo Zoom Lens for motion picture photography.

JAMES KETCHAM of JSK Engineering for the concept and design of the MC211 microprocessor-based motion controller for synchronizing sprocketed film with timecode-based machines.

WILLIAM J. WARNER and ERIC C. PETERS for the concept, MICHAEL E. PHILLIPS and TOM A. OHANLAN for the system design and PATRICK D. O'CONNOR and JOE H. RICE for the engineering of the Avid Film Composer for motion picture editing.

PAUL BAMBOROUGH for the concept, NICK POLLACK and ARTHUR WRIGHT for the hardware development and NEIL HARRIS and DUNCAN MacLEAN for the software development of The Lightworks Editor for motion picture editing.

GEORGE SAUVE, BILL BISHOP, ARPAG DADOURIAN, RAY FEENEY and RICHARD PATTERSON for the Cinefusion software, implementation of the Ultimatte Blue Screen Compositing Technology.

SCIENTIFIC AND TECHNICAL AWARDS: TECHNICAL ACHIEVEMENT AWARDS

B. RUSSELL HESSEY of Special Effects Spectacular, Inc., and VINCENT T. KELTON for the hardware design and GEORGE JACKMAN of De La Mare Engineering, Inc. for the pyrotechnic development which together comprise the non-gun safety blank firing system.

FRIEDER HOCHHEIM, GARY SWINE, DR. JOE ZHOU and DON NORTHROP for the development of the Kino Flo Portable, Flicker-Free, High-Output Fluorescent Lighting System for motion picture set illumination.

EMANUEL PREVINAIRE of Flying-Cam for his pioneering concept and for the development of mounting a motion picture camera on a remotely controlled miniature helicopter.

JACQUES SAX of Sonosax for the design and development of the Sonosax SX-S portable audio mixer.

CLAY DAVIS and JOHN CARTER of Todd-AO for the pioneering effort of computer controlled list management style ADR (Automated Dialogue Replacement).

STEPHEN W. POTTER, JOHN B. ASMAN, CHARLES PELL and RICHARD LARSON of LarTec Systems for the advancement and refinement of the computer controlled list management style ADR (Automated Dialogue Replacement) system via the LarTec ADR System that he established itself as a standard of the industry.

AUDIO TRACKS, INC. for the design and development of the ADE (Advanced Data Encoding) System which creates an encoded timecode track and database during the initial transfer of the production sound "dailies."

COLIN BROAD of CB Electronics for the design and development of the EDL (Edit Decision List) lister which creates an encoded timecode track and database during the initial transfer of the production sound "dailies."

DIETER STURM of Sturm's Special Effects Int'l, for the creation and development of the Die-Snow 2 Flake.

DAVID A. ADDLEMAN and LLOYD A. ADDLEMAN for the development of the Cyberware 3030 3D Digitizer.

MARK R. SCHNEIDER, HERBERT R. JONES, CHRISTOPHER D. CONOVER and JOHN R.B. BROWN for the development of the Polhemus 3 Space Digitizing System.

JACK C. SMITH, MICHAEL CRICHTON and EMIL SAFIER for pioneering computerized motion picture budgeting and scheduling.

STEPHEN GREENFIELD and CHRIS HUNTLEY of Screenplay Systems for development of the "Scriptor" software.

ART FRITZEN of the California Fritzen Propeller Company as the designer and sole manufacturer of the Eight-Bladed Ritter Fan Propellers.

DR. MIKE BOUDRY of the Computer Film Company for his pioneering work in the field of film input scanning.

1995

I t was a guessing game right down to the wire, with no overwhelming favorites for Best Actor. In all the awards leading up to the Oscars, Nicolas Cage had "won everything but the New Hampshire primary" for his role in *Leaving Las Vegas*. In a strange twist, some of the best-known stars were nominated and won for work that had nothing to do with acting: Emma Thompson for Best Adapted Screenplay, *Sense and Sensibility*; Mel Gibson, for Best Director, *Braveheart*; and Christine Lahti for Best Short Live Action Film, *Lieberman in Love*.

The most outstanding actress roles were for hookers, including Elizabeth Shue in *Leaving Las Vegas*, Sharon Stone in *Casino*, and the winning "working girl," Mira Sorvino, for Woody Allen's *Mighty Aphrodite*, for which Allen's directorial insight into Sorvino's character was "Not only is she cheap—but she's stupid." After four previous nominations, Susan Sarandon was finally recognized for her most distinctively powerful and uninhibited performance since her first film, *Joe* (1970). This time she won for her role as a nun in *Dead Man Walking*. Sean Penn had come closest to nabbing the prize from Cage and had picked up a Golden Globe earlier in the year, for which he delivered his own spin on Sally Field's famous "You like me" Academy Award moment: "You tolerate me. You really, really tolerate me."

The heartbreaking story behind four-category nominee *The Postman* (*Il Postino*)—"the little Italian movie that could"—resulted in tumultuous applause at the mention of its star, Massimo Troisi, 41, who died just a few hours after filming his final scene. *Braveheart*'s five-Oscar tally, including the top two spots, provided the evening's gasping surprise finish.

NONE BUT THE BRAVEHEART

CEREMONY: March 25, 1996
Dorothy Chandler Pavilion, Los Angeles Music Center, Los Angeles
HOST: Whoopi Goldberg

BEST PICTURE/ BEST DIRECTOR MEL GIBSON (B. 1956) *BRAVEHEART*

David and Goliath in kilts, *Braveheart* was a grand-scale historical action epic nearly three hours long. With stunning cinematography and sometimes bumpy direction in the first half, *Braveheart* told the story of avenging thirteenth-century Scotsman William Wallace (Gibson), who martyred himself after a series of guerrilla strikes against a villainous King Edward I.

Gibson's death scene (drawn, quartered, and decapitated) was not for the squeamish. This was the actor's second directorial effort following *The Man Without a Face* (1993). Clearly, this was not a pretty boy willing to push his romantic image too far. The Aussie had already

Mel Gibson (left)

made his mark as an actor appearing as the futuristic hero in the box-office blockbusters *Mad Max* (1979) and *The Road Warrior* (1982). Gibson won his serious acting spurs with the Australian Film Institute's Award for Best Actor in Peter Weir's *Gallipoli* (1981). He returned to action hero—and slapstick—status with his *Lethal Weapon* series, beginning in 1987.

The envelope, please...

Elisabeth Shue with Nicolas Cage

BEST ACTOR
NICOLAS CAGE (B. 1964)
LEAVING LAS VEGAS

Nicolas Cage has a keen instinct for the right role, as he demonstrated in *Leaving Las Vegas*, in which he played a congenial drunk bent on suicide.

Having had the great good luck to be born Francis Ford Coppola's nephew, Cage rose above the taint of nepotism. He has played teen pranksters, killers, victims, thieves, and lovers, beginning with his debut in *Fast Times at Ridgemont High* (1982) and later in Scorsese's *Bringing Out the Dead* (1999). But Cage found his true aura as the strange yet charming everyman. Cher saw that aura and cast him as her love interest in *Moonstruck* (1987), and the Coen brothers revealed it in their comedy *Raising Arizona* (1987). He was warned by his agent not to do what the agent feared was a career-killing role in the low-budget indie *Leaving Las Vegas*. But challenged by the opportunity to explore the full dimensions of alcoholism, Cage said yes. In a sad irony, the author of the adapted novel, Jack O'Brien, killed himself soon after the deal was made. "*Leaving Las Vegas* was my son's suicide note," O'Brien's father said.

BEST ACTRESS
SUSAN SARANDON (B. 1946)
DEAD MAN WALKING

Sarandon's fifth time up was the charm after her nominations for *Atlantic City* (1980), *Thelma & Louise* (1991), *Lorenzo's Oil* (1992), and *The Client* (1994).

A ballet-trained "Jersey girl," Sarandon soon dumped the toe shoes and hit the sound stage running, with more than forty mostly top-notch films to her credit. But she'll be forever enshrined in film history for her role in *The Rocky Horror Picture Show* (1975).

Her performance in *Dead Man* as a death-row nun struggling with her bond to a condemned prisoner was lauded by the critics. Writing for the *Chicago Tribune*, Roger Ebert raved, "The performances in this film are beyond comparison...Sarandon finds not the right technique for a character so much as the right humanity."

BEST OF 1995
Best Picture: *Braveheart*
Best Director: Mel Gibson, *Braveheart*
Best Actor: Nicolas Cage, *Leaving Las Vegas*
Best Actress: Susan Sarandon, *Dead Man Walking*
Best Supporting Actor: Kevin Spacey, *The Usual Suspects*
Best Supporting Actress: Mira Sorvino, *Mighty Aphrodite*
Honorary Awards: Kirk Douglas, Chuck Jones

FIRST
Susan Sarandon was the first person to win Best Actress playing a nun.

FADE TO BLACK
• Of the fifty-three actors with AIDS who appeared in 1993's *Philadelphia*, forty-three died.

• Oscar-winning Ginger Rogers (*Kitty Foyle*, 1940), who claimed, "I did everything Fred Astaire did, only backwards and in heels," died at 83.

IT'S GOOD TO BE BAD
• It's not only the oldest profession but the second-best way for an actress to win over the Academy. Mira Sorvino was the eighth actress to bring home the Golden Boy by playing a prostitute; hers had a heart of gold and a sense of humor. Elizabeth Shue played a streetwalker who provided ballast to the fragile Nicolas Cage in *Leaving Las Vegas*. For a woman to win an Oscar in pre-1970s Hollywood, she had a choice of few parts: a service professional, teacher, or nurse; an "entertainer," actress, singer, dancer, or prostitute. One out of three working women in Oscar-winning roles has been either an actress or a prostitute, and sometimes both. And what do these jobs have in common? They all aim to please.

• Anne Baxter, *The Razor's Edge*, Best Supporting Actress (1946). Baxter becomes a prostitute after the deaths of her husband and child.

• Claire Trevor, *Key Largo*, Best Supporting Actress (1948). Trevor plays a onetime nightclub singer turned gangster's alcoholic mistress.

• Donna Reed, *From Here to Eternity*, Best Supporting Actress (1953). Reed plays a club "hostess." In the novel, she's a prostitute.

• Jo Van Fleet, *East of Eden*, Best Supporting Actress (1955). Van Fleet plays James Dean's estranged mother, who becomes a madam.

• Dorothy Malone, *Written on the Wind*, Best Supporting Actress (1956). Malone plays a frustrated nymphomaniac who seduces gas-station attendants.

• Elizabeth Taylor, *Butterfield 8*, Best Actress (1960). Taylor plays a seedy prostitute who wants to go straight and settle down.

• Shirley Jones, *Elmer Gantry*, Best Supporting Actress (1960). Jones turns to a life of prostitution when she becomes the ex-girlfriend of a fallen Southern preacher.

• Jane Fonda, *Klute*, Best Actress (1971). Fonda, a prostitute and would-be actress, is stalked by a killer.

Benicio Del Toro, Gabriel Byrne with Kevin Spacey

 BEST SUPPORTING ACTOR
KEVIN SPACEY (B. 1959)
THE USUAL SUSPECTS

"Nothing is usual about *The Usual Suspects*," wrote *Rolling Stone*'s Peter Travers. The story unfolds with the confession of crippled, lazy-eyed con man Verbal Kint (Spacey). "In stark contrast to his hyper roles of before [Spacey] is a credible, slow-witted, over-chatty loser, who merits the nickname Verbal," wrote Desson Howe in the *Washington Post*. Before appearing on the silver screen, Spacey had a prolific career on the stage, which all changed after his brief film debut in *Heartburn* (1986).

Spacey attracted attention for his turn as the villain in TV's *Wiseguy* (1987). Profitt was the first in a long line of dark, manipu-lative characters that would eventually make Kevin Spacey a household name in such films as *Glengarry Glen Ross* (1992) and *Swimming with Sharks* (1994). Spacey made his own directorial debut with *Albino Alligator* (1997). He reappeared in *L.A. Confidential* and *Midnight in the Garden of Good and Evil* (both 1997), and *American Beauty* (1999), for which he won a Best Actor Oscar. (For more on Spacey, see 1999.)

 BEST SUPPORTING ACTRESS
MIRA SORVINO (B. 1967)
MIGHTY APHRODITE

Mira Sorvino explained, as the camera caught her dad, Paul, in a puddle of tears over her win, "We're a very emotional family." Sorvino is Linda, a prostitute who is the birth mother of the adopted son of divorced sportswriter Lenny (Allen). "I'm always attracted to losers," says Linda. "You got no confidence. I like that in a man." A critic from the *San Francisco Examiner* wrote, "Sorvino is an inspired comedian. She has the timing and non-chalance of Judy Holliday. A gifted mimic (she played a Spaniard in *Barcelona*), she gives Linda an adenoidal voice that could strip paint."

Many have compared Sorvino's career track to that of Marisa Tomei, who also won Best Supporting early on for *My Cousin Vinny* (1992), and followed up with several lackluster films. At the post-Awards party, Dad said of her, "I always knew Mira as the dancer, the jazz singer, the athlete…but I never knew that she was funny."

 HONORARY AWARD
KIRK DOUGLAS (B. 1916)

"I've made a career of playing sons of bitches."

Douglas's "bitchy" but brilliant career spans almost sixty years, during which he appeared in some of the most dramatic films ever made. Though nominated three times, Douglas never won an Academy Award.

Douglas was born Issur Danielovitch (later changed to Isidore Demsky) in Amsterdam, New York, to Russian immigrants. He made his acting debut on Broadway in *Champion* (1949), which he re-created on film in an Oscar-nominated performance.

Down but not out after suffering a debilitating stroke several years before, Douglas received his honorary Oscar in person. With halting speech, he profusely thanked the industry he loved and respected, and for which he made more than seventy films, among them *The Strange Love of Martha Ivers* (1946), *Mourning Becomes Electra* and *Out of the Past* (both 1947), *Champion* (1949, nom.), *The Big Carnival* (originally titled *Ace in the Hole*, 1951, nom.), *The Bad and the Beautiful* (1952, nom.), *Lust for Life* (1956), *Gunfight at the O.K. Corral* (1957), *Paths of Glory* (1958), *Spartacus* (1960), *The List of Adrian Messenger* (1963), and *The Arrangement* (1969).

© A.M.P.A.S®

WRITING: BASED ON MATERIAL FROM ANOTHER MEDIUM

APOLLO 13, Imagine, Universal William Broyles, Jr., Al Reinert.
BABE, Kennedy Miller, Universal. George Miller, Chris Noonan.
LEAVING LAS VEGAS. Initial Productions, MGM/UA. Mike Figgis.
THE POSTMAN (IL POSTINO), Cecchi Gori Group Tiger Cinematografico Production/Pentafilm/Estreno Mediterraneo/Blue Dahlia, Minims. Anna Pavignano, Michael Radford, Furio Scarpelli, Giacomo Scarpelli, Massimo Troisi.
SENSE AND SENSIBILITY, Mirage, Columbia. Emma Thompson

WRITING: DIRECTLY FOR THE SCREEN

BRAVEHEART, Icon/Ladd Company, Paramount Randall Wallace.
MIGHTY APHRODITE, Sweetheart, Miramax. Woody Allen.
NIXON, Hollywood Pictures/Cinergi, Buena Vista. Stephen J. Rivele, Christopher Wilkinson, Oliver Stone.
TOY STORY, Disney/Pixar, Buena Vista. Screenplay by Joss Whedon, Andrew Stanton, Joel Cohen, Alec Sokolow; Story by John Lasseter, Peter Darter, Andrew Stanton, Joe Rant.
THE USUAL SUSPECTS, Blue Parcel, Gramercy. Christopher McQuarrie.

ART DIRECTION—SET DECORATION

APOLLO 13, Imagine, Universal. Michael Corenblith; Merideth Boswell.
BABE, Kennedy Miller, Universal. Roger Ford; Kerrie Brown.
A LITTLE PRINCESS, Warner Bros. Bo Welch, Cheryl Carasik.
RESTORATION, Segue/Avenur Pictures/Oxford Film Company, Miramax. Eugenio Zanetti.
RICHARD III, Richard III Limited Production, MGM/UA. Tony Burrough.

CINEMATOGRAPHY

BATMAN FOREVER, Warner Bros. Stephen Goldblatt.
BRAVEHEART, Icon/Ladd Company, Paramount. John Toll
A LITTLE PRINCESS, Warner Bros. Emmanuel Lubezki.
SENSE AND SENSIBILITY, Mirage, Columbia. Michael Coulter.
SHANGHAI TRIAD, Shanghai Film Studios, Sony Pictures Classics. Lu Yue.

COSTUME DESIGN

BRAVEHEART, Icon/Ladd Company, Paramount. Charles Knode.
RESTORATION, Segue/Avenue Pictures/Oxford Film Company, Miramax. James Acheson.
RICHARD III, Richard III Limited Production, MGM/UA. Shuna Harwood.
SENSE AND SENSIBILITY, Mirage, Colombia. Jenny Beacon, John Bright.
12 MONKEYS, Atlas/Classics, Universal. Julie Weiss.

FILM EDITING

APOLLO 13, Imagine, Universal. Mike Hill, Dan Hanley.
BABE, Kennedy Miller, Universal. Marcus D'Arcy, Jay Friedkin.
BRAVEHEART, Icon/Ladd Company, Paramount Steven Rosenblum.
CRIMSON TIDE, Hollywood Pictures, Buena Vista. Chris Lebenzon.
SEVEN, Juno Pix, New Line. Richard Francis-Bruce.

MAKEUP

BRAVEHEART, Icon/Ladd Company, Paramount. Peter Frampton, Paul Pattison, Lois Burwell.
MY FAMILY, MI FAMILIA, New Line. Ken Diaz, Mark Sanchez.
ROOMMATES, Hollywood Pictures/Interscope, Buena Vista. Greg Cannum, Bob Laden, Colleen Callaghan.

SONG

COLORS OF THE WIND (Pocahontas, Disney, Buena Vista).Music by Alan Menken; Lyric by Stephen Schwartz.
DEAD MAN WALKIN' (Dead Man Walking, Working Title/Havoc, Gramercy). Music and Lyric by Bruce Springsteen.

HAVE YOU EVER REALLY LOVED A WOMAN (Don Juan DeMarco, Juno Pix, New Line). Music and Lyric by Michael Kamen, Bryan Adams, Robert John Lange.
MOONLIGHT (Sabrina, Mirage/Scott Rudin/Sandollar, Paramount/Constellation Films). Music by John Williams; Lyric by Alan Bergman, Marilyn Bergman.
YOU'VE GOT A FRIEND IN ME (Toy Story, Disney/Pixar, Buena Vista). Music and Lyric by Randy Newman.

SCORING: ORIGINAL DRAMATIC MUSIC

APOLLO 13, Imagine, Universal. James Horner.
BRAVEHEART, Icon/Ladd Company, Paramount. James Horner.
NIXON, Hollywnod Pictures/Cinergi, Buena Vista. John Williams.
THE POSTMAN (IL POSTINO), Cecchi Gori Group Tiger Cinematografica Production/Pentafilm/Esterno Mediterraneo/Blue Dahlia, Miramax. Luis Enrique Bacalov.
SENSE AND SENSIBILITY, Mirage, Columbia. Patrick Doyle.

SCORING: ORIGINAL MUSICAL OR COMEDY MUSIC

THE AMERICAN PRESIDENT, Castle Rock, Columbia. Marc Shaiman.
POCAHANTAS, Disney, Buena Vista. Music by Alan Menken; Lyrics by Stephen Schwartz; Orchestral Score by Alan Menken.
SABRINA, Mirage/Scott Rudin/Sandollar, Paramount/Constellation Films. John Williams.
TOY STORY, Disney/Pixar, Buena Vista. Randy Newman.
UNSTRUNG HEROES, Hollywood Pictures, Buena Vista. Thomas Newman.

SOUND

APOLLO 13, Imagine, Universal. Rick Dior, Steve Pederson, Scott Milan, David MacMillan.
BATMAN FOREVER, Warner Bros. Donald O. Mitchell, Frank A. Montano, Michael Herbick, Petur Hliddal.
BRAVEHEART, Icon/Ladd Company, Paramount Andy Nelson, Scott Milan, Anna Behlmer, Brian Simmons.
CRIMSON TIDE, Hollywood Pictures, Buena Vista. Kevin O'Connell, Rick Kline, Gregory H. Watkins, William B. Kaplan.
WATERWORLD, Universal. Steve Maslow, Gregg Landaker, Keith A. Wester.

SOUND EFFECTS EDITING

BATMAN FOREVER, Warner Bros. John Leveque, Brace Stambler.
BRAVEHEART, Icon/Ladd Company, Paramount. Lou Bender, Per Hallberg.
CRIMSON TIDE, Hollywood Pictures, Buena Vista. George Watters II.

VISUAL EFFECTS

APOLLO 13, Imagine; Universal. Robert Legato, Michael Kanfer, Leslie Ekker, Matt Sweeney.
BABE, Kennedy Miller Pictures; Universal. Scott E. Anderson, Charles Gibson, Neal Scanlon, John Cox.

DOCUMENTARY: FEATURE

ANNE FRANK REMEMBERED, Jon Blair Film Company Limited Production; Sony Pictures Classics. Jon Blair.
THE BATTLE OVER CITIZEN KANE, Lennon Documentary Group Production for The American Experience. Thomas Lennon, Michael Epstein.
FIDDLEFEST—ROBERTA TZAVARAS AND HER EAST HARLEM VIOLIN PROGRAM, Four Oaks Foundation Production. Allan Miller, Walter Scheuer.
HANK AARON: CHASING THE DREAM, Turner Original Production. Mike Tollin, Fredric Golding.
TROUBLESOME CREEK: A MIDWESTERN, West City Films, Inc., Production. Jeanne Jordan, Steven Ascher.

DOCUMENTARY: SHORT SUBJECT

JIM DINE: A SELF-PORTRAIT ON THE WALLS, Outside in July, Inc., Production. Nancy Dine, Richard Stilwell.

THE LIVING SEA, MacGillivray Freeman Film Production. Greg MacGillivray, Alec Lorimore.
NEVER GIVE UP: THE 20TH CENTURY ODYSSEY OF HERBERT ZIPPER, American Film Foundation. Terry Sanders, Freida Lee Mock.
ONE SURVIVOR REMEMBERS, Home Box Office and The United Slates Holocaust Memorial Museum Production. Katy Antholis.
THE SHADOW OF HATE, Guggenheim Productions, Inc. Production for the Southern Poverty Law Center. Charles Guggenheim.

FOREIGN LANGUAGE FILM

ALL THINGS FAIR, (Sweden).
ANTONIA'S LINE, (The Netherlands).
DUST OF LIFE, (Algeria).
O QUATRILHO, (Brazil).
THE STAR MAKER, (Italy).

SHORT FILMS: ANIMATED

THE CHICKEN FROM OUTER SPACE, Stretch Films, Inc./Hanna-Barbera Cartoons, Inc./Cartoon Network Production, John R. Dilworth.
A CLOSE SHAVE, Aardman Animations Limited Production. Nick Park.
THE END, Alias/Wavefront Production. Chris Landreth, Robin Bargar.
GAGARIN, Second Frog Animation Group Production. Alexij Kharitidi.
RUNAWAY BRAIN, Walt Disney Pictures Production. Chris Bailey.

SHORT FILMS: LIVE ACTION

BROOMS, Yes/No Production. Luke Cresswell, Steve McNicholas.
DUKE OF GROOVE, Chanticleer Films. Griffin Dunne, Thom Colwell.
LIEBERMAN IN LOVE, Chanticleer Films. Christine Lahti, Jana Sue Memel.
LITTLE SURPRISES, Chanticleer Films. Jeff Goldblum, Tikki Goldberg.
TUESDAY MORNING RIDE, Chanticleer Films. Dianne Houston, Joy Ryan.

HONORARY AND OTHER AWARDS

TO KIRK DOUGLAS for fifty years as a creative and moral force in the motion picture community.
TO CHUCK JONES for the creation of classic cartoons which have brought worldwide joy for more than half a century.
1995 SPECIAL ACHIEVEMENT AWARD TO JOHN LASSETER for his inspired leadership of the Pixar Toy Story team, resulting in the first feature-length computer-animated film.

GORDON E. SAWYER AWARD

TO DONALD C. ROGERS

SCIENTIFIC AND TECHNICAL AWARDS: SCIENTIFIC AND ENGINEERING AWARD

HOWARD FLEMMING and RONALD UHLIG for their pioneering work leading to motion picture digital sound.
DIGITAL THEATER SYSTEMS for the design and development of the DTS Digital Sound System for motion picture exhibition.
DOLBY LABORATORIES for the design and development of the SR.D Digital Sound System for motion picture exhibition.
SONY CORPORATION for the design and development of the SDDS Digital Sound System for motion picture exhibition
COLIN MOSSMAN, JOE WARY, HANS LEISINGER, GERALD PAINTER and DELUXE LABORATORIES for the design and development of the Deluxe Quad Formal Digital Sound Printing Head.
DAVID GILMARTIN, JOHANNES BORGGREBE, JEAN-PIERRE GAGNON, FRANK RICOTTA and TECHNICOLOR, INC. for the design and development of the Technicolor Contact Printer Sound Head.
RONALD C. GOODMAN, ATTILA SZALAY, STEVEN SASS and SPACECAM SYSTEMS, INC. for the design of the SpaceCam gyroscopically stabilized camera system.
MARTIN S. MUELLER for the design and development of the MSM 9801 IMAX 65mm/15 perf production motion picture camera.

IAIN NEIL for the optical design; RICK GELBARD for the mechanical design, ERIC DUBBERKE for the engineering and PANAVISION INTERNATIONAL, I.P., for the development of the Prima 3:1 Zoom Lens.
ARNOLD AND RICHTER CINE TECHNIK for the development of the Arriflex 535 Series of Cameras far motion picture cinematography.
ALVY RAY SMITH, ED CATMULL, THOMAS PORTER and TOM DUFF for their pioneering inventions in digital image compositing.

SCIENTIFIC AND TECHNICAL AWARDS: TECHNICAL ACHIEVEMENT AWARD

DAVID PRINGLE and YAN ZHONG FANG for the design and development of "Lightning Strikes," a flexible, high-performance electronic lightning effect system.
AL JENSEN, CHUCK HEADLEY, JEAN MESSNER and HAZEM NABULSI of CEI Technology for producing a self-contained, flicker-free Color Video-Assist Camera.
PETER DENZ of Prazisions-Entwicklung Denz for developing a flicker-free Color Video-Assist Camera.
GARY DEMOS, DAVID RUHOFF, DAN CAMERON and MICHELLE FERAUD for their pioneering efforts in the creation of the Digital Productions Digital Film Compositing System.
DOUGLAS SMYTHE, LINCOLN HU, DOUGLAS S. KAY and INDUSTRIAL LIGHT AND MAGIC for their pioneering efforts in the creation of the ILM Digital Film Compositing System.
COMPUTER FILM COMPANY for their pioneering efforts in the creation of the CFC Digital Film Compositing System.
JOE FINNEGAN (a.k.a. Joe Yrigoyen) for his pioneering work in developing the Air Ram for motion picture stunt effects.
INSTITUT NATIONAL POLYTECHNIQUE DE TOULOUSE for the concept; KODAK PATHE CTP CINE for the prototype; and ECLAIR LABORATORIES and MARTINEAU INDUSTRIES for the development and further implementation of the Toulouse Electrolytic Silver Recovery Cell.
BHP, INCORPORATED for their pioneering efforts in developing digital sound printing heads for motion pictures.
JAMES DEAS of the Warner Bros. Studio Facility for the design and subsequent development of an Automated Patchbay and Metering System far motion picture sound transfer and dubbing operations.
CLAY DAVIS and JOHN CARTER of Todd AO for their pioneering efforts in creating an Automated Patchbay System for motion picture sound transfer and dubbing operations.
PASCAL CHEDEVILLE for the design of the L.C. Concept Digital Sound System for motion picture exhibition.

1996

THE INDIES ARE COMING!

CEREMONY: March 24, 1997
Shrine Auditorium, Los Angeles
HOST: Billy Crystal

There were only two things everybody knew for certain as they gathered at the Shrine Auditorium: the pint-size David of the industry, the indie (independent) film, had become an overnight Goliath, gobbling up every Best Picture nomination except TriStar's *Jerry Maguire*; the second sure thing was that Lauren Bacall would win Best Supporting Actress for her comeback role as Barbra Streisand's narcissistic mama in *The Mirror Has Two Faces*. Bacall, widow of Humphrey Bogart and Hollywood legend, had never been known for her vulnerability, but she looked fragile as the camera zeroed in for her big moment.

Then, the nearly impossible! An audible gasp of an upset as Juliette Binoche's name was pulled from the envelope. She made her way to the podium like the proverbial deer caught in headlights and apologized for winning. Not so Cuba Gooding Jr., the man from *Jerry Maguire*. He danced and shouted, thanked God and his agent, among others, and set the room afire with his explosive joy. From then on, however, *The English Patient* avalanche left the hope of long shots in the rubble.

By the time Andrew Lloyd Weber picked up his statuette for Best Song, *Evita*'s "You Must Love Me," all he could say was "Well, thank heavens there wasn't a song in *The English Patient*." Best Actor Geoffrey Rush was another survivor, for his towering performance as a mentally disabled concert pianist in *Shine*. But just when it seemed clear where things were going, *Patient*'s Grace Kelly-like star, Kristen Scott Thomas, was left in the dust by "plain as a Minnesota morning" Frances McDormand, who struck Best Actress gold for her intrepid and very pregnant police detective in *Fargo*. But by then *The English Patient*'s sack brimmed with nine Oscars, including the well-deserved Thalberg Memorial Award for its producer, Saul Zaentz. *The English Patient* was Zaentz's third Oscar-winning film—his first and second were *One Flew Over the Cuckoo's Nest* (1975) and *Amadeus* (1984).

The trifecta had been accomplished only twice before, by Darryl F. Zanuck and Sam Spiegel. By evening's end, the final tally for *The English Patient* led host Billy Crystal to quip, "Aside from wheat and auto parts, America's biggest export is now the Oscar."

BEST PICTURE/BEST DIRECTOR
ANTHONY MINGHELLA (B. 1954)
THE ENGLISH PATIENT

"Swoon," whispers the debonair Hungarian lover (Ralph Fiennes) to his married mistress (Kristen Scott Thomas). "I'll catch you."

Based on the novel by Michael Ondaatje, *The English Patient* is a conventional tragic romance set in World War II, strengthened by powerful cinematography. In one scene, the curves of a naked woman are seamlessly transfigured into the erotic contours of a desert landscape. "The film has so many facets, and combines them in such fascinating and fluid style that its cumulative effect is much stronger than the sum of its parts," said Janet Maslin in the *New York Times*. But it was the kind of prestigious tragic love story, set against an exotic background, that the Academy loved. Still, the film met with both lovers and detractors.

Minghella attended the University of Hull in England. He briefly worked as a university professor when he started writing music and plays. He won the London Theatre Critics Award in 1984 for Most Promising Playwright and in 1986 for Best Play with *Made in Bangkok*.

Ralph Fiennes

The envelope, please…

BEST ACTOR
GEOFFREY RUSH (B. 1951)
SHINE

"To all those people who were happy to bankroll the film as long as I wasn't in it!" Rush said with jubilant revenge and a contemptuous fist in the air. But their anxiety wasn't entirely unfounded. Few outside the Australian theater community had ever heard of Rush, who came to films very late in his career. "Instead of having a midlife crisis, I suddenly got into the movies," he quipped. *Shine* was essentially his star-making debut, and he made the most of it, virtually inhabiting the soul of his real-life character, the mentally unbalanced concert pianist David Helfgott. Rush was nominated for *Shakespeare in Love* (1998) and *Quills* (2000). He also appeared in *Mystery Men* and *House on Haunted Hill* (both 1999), *The Tailor of Panama* and *Lantana* (both 2001).

BEST ACTRESS
FRANCES MCDORMAND
(B. 1957)
FARGO

"I want to thank Ethan Coen [screenwriter], who made an actor of me, his brother Joel [director/husband], who made a woman of me, and my son, Pedro, who made a mother of me."

In a deceptively comic performance as a pregnant, small-town Minnesota homicide detective, McDormand gave *Fargo* its heart and soul. Based on a true 1987 crime, it was a classic film noir, wryly dubbed a "film blanc," thanks to the snow-blanketed backdrop. McDormand never considered herself a star. "I'm a character actress, plain and simple," she said. The daughter of an evangelical preacher, she caught the acting bug playing Lady Macbeth in high school. While at the Yale School of Drama, she befriended classmate Holly Hunter, who told her about "two weird guys" who were auditioning actors for a film. The "weirdos" were the Coen brothers, the film was *Blood Simple* (1984), and McDormand's love life and career were launched. She later appeared in *Raising Arizona* (1987), *Mississippi Burning* (1988, nom.), *Miller's Crossing, Hidden Agenda, Chattahoochee, Darkman* (all 1990), *The Butcher's Wife* (1991), *Passed Away* (1992), and *Short Cuts* (1993). She has also appeared on TV's *Hill Street Blues*.

BEST OF 1996
Best Picture: *The English Patient*
Best Director: Anthony Minghella, *The English Patient*
Best Actor: Geoffrey Rush, *Shine*
Best Actress: Frances McDormand, *Fargo*
Best Supporting Actor: Cuba Gooding Jr., *Jerry Maguire*
Best Supporting Actress: Juliette Binoche, *The English Patient*

FIRSTS
- With its nine Oscars *The English Patient* tied with *Gigi* (1958) and *The Last Emperor* (1987) as the third most awarded film in the Academy's history. The second was *West Side Story* (1961) with ten and that chariot on fire, *Ben-Hur* (1959), with eleven.
- Director Joel Coen and his star, Frances McDormand, were the first married couple to be nominated for the same film (*Fargo*) since John Cassavetes and Gena Rowlands in 1974 for *Woman Under the Influence*.

ROLE REVERSAL
- Debbie Reynolds's big comeback in Albert Brooks's *Mother* almost wasn't. The starring role was first offered to former first lady Nancy Reagan, then to Esther Williams.
- Early in the project, Fox pushed hard for Demi Moore as the doomed romantic heroine in *The English Patient*. Director Minghella's refusal caused the studio to pull up stakes.

SIN OF OMISSION
Best Supporting Actress: Debbie Reynolds, *Mother.*

ALWAYS A BRIDESMAID, NEVER A BRIDE
Lauren Bacall has won Broadway's Tony Award but never an Oscar. She's joined in that rarefied bicoastal category by Angela Lansbury, Julie Harris, Richard Burton, James Earl Jones, Mickey Rooney, Rosalind Russell, Ralph Fiennes, Christopher Plummer, Alan Cummings, and Natasha Richardson, among others.

UNMENTIONABLES
- Guns 'N Moses! Charlton Heston was elected vice-president of the National Rifle Association and claimed it was more rewarding than winning the position of president of the Screen Actors Guild.
- The hilariously obsessive Barbra Streisand "Hello, Gorgeous" Museum opened in San Francisco.
- A Reynolds Wrap: Box-office king for six years, Burt Reynolds filed for bankruptcy.
- Upset that it was up for auction, producer/director Steven Spielberg paid $550,000 for Clark Gable's Best Actor Oscar for *Gone with the Wind* and donated it to the Academy. "The Oscar statuette is the most personal recognition of good work our industry can ever bestow, and it strikes me as a sad sign of our times that this icon could be confused with a commercial treasure," Spielberg said.
- It was hugs and kisses when Billy Bob "Lord, have mercy!" Thornton won for Best Original Screenplay (*Sling Blade*). A week later, he and his wife, Pietra, divorced.

© A.M.P.A.S®

BEST SUPPORTING ACTOR
CUBA GOODING JR. (B. 1968)
JERRY MAGUIRE

"I've always been a sucker for attention," Gooding said. Well-deserved attention, as it turned out. The son of one-hit wonder '70s R&B singer Cuba Sr. (the song: "Everybody Plays the Fool"), Gooding was discovered by an agent who caught his high-school debut in *L'il Abner.* He made his first big splash in John Singleton's *Boyz N the Hood* (1991), which was followed by less showy, run-of-the-mill roles. Then along came *Gladiator* (1992), *Lightning Jack* (1994), *Outbreak* (1995), *Jerry Maguire* (1996), *As Good As It Gets* (1997), *What Dreams May Come* (1998), *Instinct* (1999), and *Men of Honor* (2000).

© A.M.P.A.S®

BEST SUPPORTING ACTRESS
JULIETTE BINOCHE (B. 1965)
THE ENGLISH PATIENT

"I don't know why I got this. It's not my fault." Binoche's stunned apologetic reaction to beating out Lauren Bacall was very much in keeping with her elegant modesty.

Born into a noted French theatrical family, she became a star at 21 and found an international audience with *The Unbearable Lightness of Being* (1988). The ethereal beauty and simple goodness of Binoche's nurse, Hana, in *The English Patient*, offered a warm contrast to the war-blasted backdrop. Hana's sensuality turned Binoche into a kind of "thinking man's pinup girl," and her popularity soared.

© A.M.P.A.S® *Will Smith, George Foreman, Muhammad Ali*
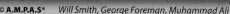

BEST DOCUMENTARY
WHEN WE WERE KINGS

Muhammad Ali and George Foreman were greeted with thunderous, tearful applause as they made their way to the stage following the win of Leon Gast and David Sonenberg's *When We Were Kings* for Best Documentary. The film chronicled the pugilists' 1974 "Rumble in the Jungle" world heavyweight bout in Zaire. The fight was eventually canceled, but not before we saw Ali in a new light as the underdog. His frail appearance at the Academy Awards, the result of a battle with Parkinson's disease, was a bittersweet reminder that even "the greatest" was only mortal, after all. This was the man who had poetically blasted his way into superstardom in the world's center ring. "Only last week," he chants in the film, "I murdered a rock, injured a stone, hospitalized a brick. I'm so mean, I make medicine sick!"

A W A R D
N O M I N A
T I O N S
1 9 9 6

BEST PICTURE
THE ENGLISH PATIENT. Tiger Moth, Miramax. Saul Zaentz, Producer.
FARGO, Working Title, Gramercy. Ethan Coen, Producer.
JERRY MAGUIRE, TriStar. James L Brooks, Laurence Mark, Richard Sakai and Cameron Crowe, Producers.
SECRETS & LIES, CIBY 2000/Thin Man Films, October Films, Simon Channing-Williams, Producer.
SHINE, Momentum Films, Fine Line Features. Jane Scott, Producer,

ACTOR
TOM CRUISE in *Jerry Maguire*, TriStar.
RALPH FIENNES in *The English Patient*, Tiger Moth, Miramax.
WOODY HARRELSON in *The People vs. Larry Flynt*, Ixtlan, Columbia.
GEOFFREY RUSH in *Shine*, Momentum Films, Fine Line Features.
BILLY BOB THORNTON in *Sling Blade*, Shooting Gallery, Miramax.

ACTRESS
BRENDA BLETHYN in *Secrets & Lies*, CIBY 2000/Thin Man Films, October Films.
DIANE KEATON in *Marvin's Room*, Marvin's Room Production, Miramax.
FRANCES McDORMAND in *Fargo*, Working Title, Gramercy.
KRISTIN SCOTT THOMAS in *The English Patient*, Tiger Moth, Miramax.
EMILY WATSON in *Breaking the Waves*, Zentropa Entertainment/Trust Film Svenska/Liberator/Argus Film/Northern Lights, October Films.

SUPPORTING ACTOR
CUBA GOODING, JR. in *Jerry Maguire*, TriStar.
WILLIAM H. MACY in *Fargo*, Working Title, Gramercy.
ARMIN MUELLER-STAHL in *Shine*, Momentum Films, Fine Line Features.
EDWARD NORTON in *Primal Fear*, Gary Lucchesi, Paramount in assoc. w/Rysher Entertainment.
JAMES WOODS in *Ghosts of Mississippi*, Castle Rock, Columbia.

SUPPORTING ACTRESS
JOAN ALLEN in *The Crucible*, 20th Century-Fox.
LAUREN BACALL in *The Mirror Has Two Faces*, TriStar.
JULIETTE BINOCHE in *The English Patient*, Tiger Moth, Miramax.
BARBARA HERSHEY in *The Portrait of a Lady*, Polygram, Gramercy.
MARIANNE JEAN-BAPTISTE in *Secrets & Lies*, CIBY 2000/Thin Man Films, October Films.

DIRECTION
ANTHONY MINGHELLA for *The English Patient*, Tiger Moth, Miramax.
JOEL COEN for *Fargo*, Working Title, Gramercy.
MILOS FORMAN for *The People vs. Larry Flynt*, Ixtlan, Columbia
MIKE LEIGH for *Secrets & Lies*, CIBY 2000/Thin Man Films, October Films.
SCOTT HICKS for *Shine*, Momentum Films, Fine Line Features.

WRITING: BASED ON MATERIAL FROM ANOTHER MEDIUM
THE CRUCIBLE, 20th Century-Fox. Arthur Miller.
THE ENGLISH PATIENT, Tiger Moth, Miramax. Anthony Minghella.
HAMLET, Castle Rock, Columbia. Kenneth Branagh.

SLING BLADE, Shorting Gallery, Miramax. Billy Bob Thornton.
TRAINSPOTTING, Channel Four Film, Miramax. John Hodge.

WRITING: DIRECTLY FOR THE SCREEN
FARGO, Working Title, Gramercy. Ethan Coen, Joel Coen.
JERRY MAGUIRE, TriStar. Cameron Crowe.
LONE STAR, Castle Rock. Sony Pictures Classics, John Sayles.
SECRETS & LIES, CIBY 2000/Thin Man Films, October Films. Mike Leigh.
SHINE, Momentum Films, Fine Line Features. Screenplay by Jan Sardi; Story by Scott Hicks.

ART DIRECTION—SET DECORATION
THE BIRDCAGE. United Artists, MGM/UA. Bo Welch; Cheryl Carasik.
THE ENGLISH PATIENT, Tiger Moth, Miramax. Stuart Craig; Stephenie McMillan.
EVITA, Hollywood Pictures/Cinergi Pictures, Buena Vista. Brian Morris; Philippe Turlure.
HAMLET, Castle Rock, Columbia. Tim Harvey.
WILLIAM SHAKESPEARE'S ROMEO & JULIET, 20th Century-Fox. Catherine Martin; Brigitte Broch.

CINEMATOGRAPHY
THE ENGLISH PATIENT, Tiger Moth, Miramax. Jobn Seale.
EVITA, Hollywood Pictures/Cinergi Pictures, Buena Vista. Darius Khondji.
FARGO, Working Title, Gramercy. Roger Deakins.
FLY AWAY HOME, Sandollar, Columbia. Caleb Deschanel.
MICHAEL COLLINS, Geffen Pictures, Warner Bros. Chris Menges.

COSTUME DESIGN
ANGELS AND INSECTS, Playhouse International, Goldwyn. Paul Brown.
EMMA, Matchmaker Films/Haft Entertainment, Miramax. Ruth Myers.
THE ENGLISH PATIENT, Tiger Moth, Miramax. Ann Roth.
HAMLET, Castle Rock, Columbia. Alex Byrne.
THE PORTRAIT OF A LADY, Polygram, Gramercy. Janet Patterson.

FILM EDITING
THE ENGLISH PATIENT, Tiger Moth, Miramax, Walter Murch.
EVITA, Hollywood Pictures/Cinergi Pictures, Buena Vista. Gerry Hambling.
FARGO, Working Title, Gramercy. Roderick Jaynes.
JERRY MAGUIRE, TriStar. Joe Hutshing.
SHINE, Momentum Films, Fine Line Features. Pip Karmel.

MAKEUP
GHOSTS OF MISSISSIPPI, Castle Rock, Columbia. Matthew W. Mangle, Deborah La Mia Denaver.
THE NUTTY PROFESSOR, Imagine, Universal. Rick Baker, David LeRoy Anderson.
STAR TREK: FIRST CONTACT, Rick Berman, Paramount. Michael Westmore, Scott Wheeler, Jake Garber.

SONG
BECAUSE YOU LOVED ME, (*Up Close and Personal*, Touchstone, Buena Vista). Music and Lyric by Diane Warren.
FOR THE FIRST TIME, (*One Fine Day*, 20th Century-Fox). Music and Lyric by James Newton Howard, Jud J. Friedman, Allan Dennis Rich.
I FINALLY FOUND SOMEONE (*The Mirror Has Two Faces*, TriStar. Music and Lyric by Barbra Streisand, Marvin Hamlisch, Bryan Adams, Robert "Mutt" Lange.
THAT THING YOU DO! (*That Thing You Do!*, 20th Century-Fox). Music and Lyric by Adam Schlesinger.
YOU MUST LOVE ME (*Evita*, Hollywood Pictures/Cinergi Pictures, Buena Vista). Music by Andrew Lloyd Webber; Lyric by Tim Rice.

SCORING: ORIGINAL DRAMATIC MUSIC
THE ENGLISH PATIENT, Tiger Moth, Miramax, Gabriel Yared.

HAMLET, Castle Rock, Columbia. Patrick Doyle.
MICHAEL COLLINS, Geffen Pictures, Warner Bros. Elliot Goldenthal.
SHINE, Momentum Films, Fine Line Features, David Hirschfelder.
SLEEPERS, Propaganda Films, Warner Bros. John Williams.

SCORING: ORIGINAL MUSICAL OR COMEDY MUSIC
EMMA, Matchmaker Films/Haft Entertarnnient, Miramax. Rachel Portman.
THE FIRST WIVES CLUB, Scott Rudin, Paramount. Marc Shannon.
THE HUNCHBACK OF NOTRE DAME, Watt Disney, Buena Vista. Music by Alan Menken; Lyrics by Stephen Schwartz; Orchestral Score by Alan Menken.
JAMES AND THE GIANT PEACH. Walt Disney, Buena Vista. Randy Newman.
THE PREACHER'S WIFE, Touchstone/Goldwyn, Buena Vista. Hans Zimmer.

SOUND
THE ENGLISH PATIENT, Tiger Moth, Miramax. Walter Murch, Mark Berger, David Parker, Chris Newman.
EVITA, Hollywood Pictures/Cinergi Pictures, Buena Vista. Andy Nelson, Anna Behlmer, Ken Weston.
INDEPENDENCE DAY, 20th Century-Fox. Chris Carpenter, Bill W. Benton, Bob Beemer, Jeff Wexler.
THE ROCK, Hollywood Pictures, Buena Vista. Kevin O'Connell, Greg P. Russell, Keith A. Wester.
TWISTER, Warner Bros/Universal. Steve Maslow, Gregg Landaker, Kevin O'Connell, Geoffrey Patterson.

SOUND EFFECTS EDITING
DAYLIGHT, Davis Entertainment/Joseph M. Singer, Universal. Richard L. Anderson, David A. Whittaker.
ERASER, Warner Bros. Alan Robert Murray, Bob Asman.
THE GHOST AND THE DARKNESS, Douglas/Reuther, Paramount. Bruce Stambler.

VISUAL EFFECTS
DRAGONHEART, Raffaella De Laurentiis, Universal. Scott Squires, Phil Tippett, James Straus, Kit West.
INDEPENDENCE DAY, 20th Century-Fox. Volker Engel, Douglas Smith, Clay Pinney, Joseph Viskocil.
TWISTER, Warner Bros./Universal. Stefen Fangmeier, John Frazier, Habib Zargarpour, Henry La Bounta.

DOCUMENTARY: FEATURE
THE LINE KING: THE AL HIRSCHFELD STORY, New York Times History Production; Castle Hill. Susan W. Dryfoos.
MANDELA, Clinica Estetico, Ltd. Production; Island Pictures Jo Menell, Angus Gibson.
SUZANNE FARRELL: ELUSIVE MUSE, Seahorse Films, Inc. Production. Anne Belle, Deborah Dickson.
TELL THE TRUTH AND RUN: GEORGE SELDES AND THE AMERICAN PRESS, Never Tire Production. Rick Goldsmith.
WHEN WE WERE KINGS, DASFilms Ltd. Production; Gramercy. Leon Gast, David Sonenberg.

DOCUMENTARY: SHORT SUBJECT
BREATHING LESSONS: THE LIFE AND WORK OF MARK O'BRIEN, Inscrutable Films/Pacific News Service Production. Jessica Yu.
COSMIC VOYAGE, Cosmic Voyage Inc. Production. Jeffrey Marvin, Bayley Silleck.
AN ESSAY ON MATISSE, Great Projects Film Company, Inc. Production. Perry Wolff.
SPECIAL EFFECTS, NOVA/WGBH Boston Production. Susanne Simpson, Ben Burtt.
THE WILD BUNCH: AN ALBUM IN MONTAGE, Tyrus Entertainment Production. Paul Seydor, Nick Redman.

FOREIGN LANGUAGE FILM
A CHEF IN LOVE, (Georgia).
KOLYA, (Czech Republic).
THE OTHER SIDE OF SUNDAY, (Norway).

PRISONER OF THE MOUNTAINS, (Russia), RIDICULE, (France).

SHORT FILMS: ANIMATED
CANHEAD, Timothy Hittle Production. Timothy Hittle, Chris Peterson.
LA SALLA, National Film Board of Canada. Richard Condie.
QUEST, Thomas Stellmach Animation Production. Tyron Montgomery, Thomas Stellmach.
WAT'S PIG, Aardman Animations Limited Production. Peter Lord.

SHORT FILMS: LIVE ACTION
DE TRIPAS, CORAZON, IMCINE/DPC/Universidad de Guadalajara Production, Antonio Urrutia
DEAR DIARY, DreamWorks SKG Production. David Frankel, Barry Jossen.
ERNST & LYSET. M & M Production. Kim Magnusson, Andes Thomas Jensen.
ESPOSADOS, Zodiac Films/Juan Carlos Fresnadillo P.C. Production. Juan Carlos Fresnadillo.
WORDLESS, Film Trust Italia Production. Bernadette Carranza, Antonello De Leo.

HONORARY AND OTHER AWARDS
TO MICHAEL KIDD in recognition of his services to the art of the dance in the art of the screen.
TO VOLKER W. BAHNEMANN and BURTON "BUD" STONE in appreciation for outstanding service and dedication in upholding the high standards of the Academy of Motion Picture Arts and Sciences.
TO JOE LOMBARDI in celebration of fifty years in the motion picture industry. His knowledge and leadership in the field of pyrotechnics and special effects along with his uncompromising promotion of safety on the set have established the standard for today's special effects technicians.

IRVING G. THALBERG MEMORIAL AWARD
TO SAUL ZAENTZ

SCIENTIFIC AND TECHNICAL AWARDS: ACADEMY AWARD OF MERIT
IMAX CORPORATION for the method of filming and exhibiting high-fidelity, large-format, wide-angle motion pictures.

SCIENTIFIC AND TECHNICAL AWARDS: SCIENTIFIC AND ENGINEERING AWARDS
JOHN SCHLAG, BRIAN KNEP, ZORAN KACIC-ALESIC and THOMAS WILLIAMS for the development of the Viewpaint 3D Paint System for film production work.
WILLIAM REEVES for the original concept and the development of particle systems used to create computer generated VISUAL EFFECTS in motion pictures.
JIM HOURIHAN for the primary design and development of the interactive language-based control of particle systems as embodied in the Dynamation software package.
JONATHAN ERLAND and KAY BEVING ERLAND for the development of the Digital Series Traveling Matte Backing System used for composite photography in motion pictures.

SCIENTIFIC AND TECHNICAL AWARDS: TECHNICAL ACHIEVEMENT AWARDS
PERRY KIVOLOWITZ, for the primary design, and DR. GARTH A. DICKIE for the development of the algorithms for the shape-driven warping and morphing subsystem of the Elastic Reality Special Effects System.
KEN PERLIN for the development of Perlin Noise, a technique used to produce natural appearing textures on computer-generated surfaces for motion picture visual effects.
NESTOR BURTNYK and MARCELI WEIN of the National Research Council of Canada for their pioneering work in the development of software techniques for Computer Assisted Key Framing for Character Animation.
GRANT LOUCKS for the concept and specifications of the Mark V Director's Viewfinder.

BRIAN KNEP, CRAIG HAYES, RICK SAYRE and THOMAS WILLIAMS for the creation and development of the Direct Input Device.
JAMES KAJIYA and TIMOTHY KAY for their pioneering work in producing computer-generated fur and hair in motion pictures.
JEFFREY YOST, CHRISTIAN ROUET, DAVID BENSON and FLORIAN KAINZ for the development of a system to create and control computer-generated fur and hair in motion pictures.
RICHARD A. PREY and WILLIAM N. MASTEN for the design and development of the Nile Sun II lighting crane and camera platform.

1997

"Titanic got 14 nominations.
One per lifeboat."
—Jim Mullen, *Entertainment Weekly*

ost Billy Crystal appeared on the big screen, inserted into a clip from *Titanic*, returned live for his frenzied, comic song medley tribute to the nominees, and wound up by plopping in Jack Nicholson's lap. "Sit back, relax, forget *Mars Attacks*," he sang to Hollywood's legendary bad boy.

The buoyant pace continued through the early Best Supporting Actress award, as a clearly stunned Kim Basinger, in a glamour-goddess white sheath, knocked out the sentimental favorite, 87-year-old Gloria Stuart. From that point on, few icebergs halted the progress of *Titanic*'s super win of eleven Oscars out of a possible fourteen nominations. Only two other films registered high on the radar, *As Good as It Gets*, with the one-two punch for Best Actor and Actress and *Good Will Hunting* for Best Supporting Actor and Best Original Screenplay. The early prediction that Matt Damon and Ben Affleck would win "because they'd look so cute up on the podium" had proved true. They were also among the youngest to appear onstage that night.

Just when the show looked like a wrap, out came all the surviving Oscar-winning stars in alphabetical order, slowly taking their places for a "class photo." Many in the audience were surprised and delighted to realize that Luise Rainer, two-time winner in 1936 and 1937, was still very much alive. But for sheer nostalgia nothing topped the honorary Award to Stanley Donen, the 73-year-old director-choreographer of *Singin' in the Rain* and *Royal Wedding*. More astonishing than his elegant song and dance to "Cheek to Cheek" with Oscar in hand was the fact that he had never received an Academy Award before. He'd never even been nominated!

The clock ticked down on the longest ceremony yet, culminating in James Cameron's big "I'm king of the world!" moment. He got more raised eyebrows than applause after requesting a moment of silence for the victims of the *Titanic*, followed by another directive to "party until dawn!"

SUNKEN TREASURE

CEREMONY: March 23, 1998
Shrine Auditorium, Los Angeles
HOST: Billy Crystal

**BEST PICTURE/
BEST DIRECTOR
JAMES CAMERON (B. 1954)
*TITANIC***

"If I'd known it would cost $200 million, I wouldn't have made it," Cameron said. Previous to its release, reports of budget overruns, delays, accidents, and directorial excesses led to wide speculation that *Titanic* would be the flop of the century. What we got instead was a rebirth of the mammoth romantic epic whose scope, as the *New York Times*'s Janet Maslin suggested, "honestly invites comparison to *Gone with the Wind*. Just as David O. Selznick had Atlanta to burn, now James Cameron has a ship to sink."

Cameron, the man behind *Aliens* (1986), *The Abyss* (1989), and *Terminator 2: Judgment Day* (1991), had everything riding on *Titanic*. No expense was spared to duplicate the original Titanic, including specially woven carpets, woodworking, and chandeliers. Updating the Romeo and Juliet scenario for Leonardo DiCaprio and Kate Winslet, Cameron's script wanted us to believe the iceberg was ignored by

Kate Winslet, Leonardo DiCaprio

the lookout crew as they spied on the young lovers kissing in the shadows. Such scenes led Kenneth Turan of the *Los Angeles Times* to comment, "What really brings on the tears is Cameron's insistence that writing this kind of movie is within his abilities." Richard Corliss of *Time* magazine felt, "The regretful verdict here: dead in the water."

The envelope, please...

BEST ACTOR
JACK NICHOLSON (B. 1937)
AS GOOD AS IT GETS

"I dropped about three quarts of water the minute I heard my name," said Nicholson. It might have been easy to detest his character, a manic-depressive author who starts out by tossing a neighbor's dog down the incinerator. But by the time he'd bonded with lonely gay Greg Kinnear and successfully romanced single-mom waitress Helen Hunt, Nicholson had the audience and the movie in his back pocket.

That notorious arched brow and smirk have served him well since his earliest days starring in Roger Corman's schlock horror flick *The Cry Baby Killer* (1958). But *Five Easy Pieces* (1970) put him on the road to one of the most successful careers in Hollywood, which included such films as *Carnal Knowledge* (1971), *The King of Marvin Gardens* (1972), *The Last Detail* (1973, nom.), *Chinatown* (1974, nom.), *The Passenger* (1975), *Goin' South* (1978), *The Shining* (1980), and *The Postman Always Rings Twice* (1981).

He later earned Oscars and nominations for *Reds* (1981, nom.), *Terms of Endearment* (1983, Oscar), *Prizzi's Honor* (1985), *Heartburn* (1986, nom.), *Ironweed* (1987), *Batman* (1989), and *A Few Good Men* (1992, nom.). In 1994 he received the American Film Institute Life Achievement Award. (For more on Nicholson, see 1965, 1975.)

BEST ACTRESS
HELEN HUNT (B. 1963)
AS GOOD AS IT GETS

Hunt was in an unusual race—she was the only American nominee. She was also a TV star (*Mad About You*), which raised the issue of "Why should I pay for what I can get for free?" with regard to her big-screen career. Diligent and perceptive, she chose projects that helped her with the crossover—particularly *Twister* (1996), a monster moneymaker ($240 million) that made her instantly viable.

Ironically, it was *As Good As It Gets* director/screenwriter James Brooks, best known for his TV work (*The Mary Tyler Moore Show*), who cast her as the beleaguered waitress who finally fell for Jack. A former child star and the daughter of director Gordon Hunt, Hunt performed one of her earliest film roles as Kathleen Turner and Nicolas Cage's daughter in *Peggy Sue Got Married* (1986).

BEST OF 1997
Best Picture: *Titanic*
Best Director: James Cameron, *Titanic*
Best Actor: Jack Nicholson, *As Good As It Gets*
Best Actress: Helen Hunt, *As Good As It Gets*
Best Supporting Actor: Robin Williams, *Good Will Hunting*
Best Supporting Actress: Kim Basinger, *L.A. Confidential*
Honorary Award: Stanley Donen

FIRSTS
• With fourteen nominations (matching the record set by *All About Eve*) and eleven Oscars, *Titanic* tied for first place with *Ben-Hur* (1958) as the most honored picture of all time.
• *Titanic* was the highest-grossing movie in history, earning more than $1 billion worldwide.
• Helen Hunt became the first Best Actress winner to simultaneously star in a TV series. Previously, Goldie Hawn and Cloris Leachman had pulled off the same trick as Best Supporting Actresses.
• Jack Nicholson, with his third Oscar, was preceded only by Katharine Hepburn (four), Walter Brennan (three), and Ingrid Bergman (three). He topped all his male counterparts with an accumulated eleven nominations.
• Woody Allen's nomination for Best Screenplay (*Deconstructing Harry*) was his thirteenth in that category, beating out Billy Wilder's long held record of twelve.

ROLE REVERSAL
Helen Hunt got her role in *As Good As It Gets* only after Holly Hunter turned it down.

SINS OF OMISSION
Best Supporting Actor: Kevin Spacey, *L.A. Confidential*; Philip Seymour Hoffman, *Boogie Nights*; Rupert Everett, *My Best Friend's Wedding*.
Best Actor: Ian Holm, *The Sweet Hereafter*.

ALWAYS A BRIDESMAID, NEVER A BRIDE
Of Best Director nominees, Peter Cattaneo (*The Full Monty*) was the least well known. Surprisingly, he was the only one who'd been nominated previously: for a short film, *Dear Rosie*, he'd made while still in college.

UNMENTIONABLES
• "I thought my chances of being nominated (*Boogie Nights*) were the same as there being a Richard Simmons Jr.," said Burt Reynolds.
• Mishaps on the *Titanic* production included assorted broken bones and the sprinkling of "angel dust" in the commissary's fish chowder.
• "We feel like impostors—the Milli Vanilli of screenwriters," said Matt Damon, following his Oscar win with co-writer Ben Affleck.
• "Kate Winslet should get the Oscar for Best Bust. Anyone with those two floaters doesn't need a lifeboat," said feminist Camille Paglia.
• Best Supporting Actress nominee Gloria Stuart (*Titanic*) gained nearly as much fame for living directly across the street from Nicole Brown Simpson at the time of her murder.

BEST SUPPORTING ACTOR
ROBIN WILLIAMS (B. 1951)
GOOD WILL HUNTING

"Thank you, Ben and Matt. I still want to see some ID. But most of all, thank you to my father, up there, who, when I said, 'I want to be an actor,' he said, 'Wonderful—just have a backup profession, like welding.'"

The fourth nomination following *Good Morning Vietnam* (1987), *Dead Poets Society* (1989), and *The Fisher King* (1991) was the charm for Williams, whose manic, stream-of-consciousness humor made him a star before 30 on the sitcom *Mork and Mindy*. As the psychotherapist with problems of his own in *Good Will Hunting*, Williams pulled off his first fully dramatic performance without a shred of shtick. "So this is acting! I don't have to act. I just have to be!" he said.

BEST SUPPORTING ACTRESS
KIM BASINGER (B. 1953)
L.A. CONFIDENTIAL

"Oh, my God, yes! I just want to thank everybody I've ever met in my entire life!" An early favorite for her performance as a Veronica Lake look-alike call girl in the noir thriller, Basinger had almost passed on the script. "The role and the reaction to it have shocked me completely," she later said.

As it did most everyone else, considering she began her career as a Breck Shampoo Girl, *Playboy* model, and a Bond girl. With new respect as an actress of depth, Basinger could finally escape the ageless sex-toy image made most famous in *9 ½ Weeks* (1984), in which she performed unmentionable acts with ice cubes and Mickey Rourke.

© A.M.P.A.S®

HONORARY AWARD
STANLEY DONEN (B. 1924)

There was Vincente Minnelli, and there was Stanley Donen: together they made the Hollywood musical the Hollywood musical. Donen started out on Broadway as a choreographer, met Gene Kelly on Broadway, and together they went Hollywood. They revolutionized the musical, co-directing the classics starting with *On the Town* (1949). Donen's own work was a masterful mix of invention and exhilaration. Among his great musicals are *Take Me Out to the Ball Game* (1949), *Royal Wedding* (1951), *Give a Girl a Break* (1953), *Seven Brides for Seven Brothers* (1954), and *Funny Face* (1957).

Later, Donen turned to romantic comedy, making such exquisite films as *Indiscreet* (1958), *The Grass Is Greener* (1960), and *Charade* (1963). Donen made a few losers, *Bedazzled* and *Two for the Road* (both 1967), and *The Little Prince* (1974). His last film to date is the sex farce *Blame It on Rio* (1984).

PICTURE
AS GOOD AS IT GETS, Gracie Films, TriStar. James L Brooks, Bridget Johnson and Kristi Zea, Producers.
THE FULL MONTY, Redwave Films, Fox Searchlight Uberto Pasolini, Producer.
GOOD WILL HUNTING, Be Gentlemen, Miramax. Lawrence Bender, Producer.
L.A. CONFIDENTIAL, Arnon Milchan/David L. Wolper, Warner Bros. Anton Mitchan, Curtis Hanson and Michael Nathanson, Pruducers.
TITANIC, Lightstorm Entertainment, 20th Century-Fox and Paramount. James Cameron and Jon Landau, Producers.

ACTOR
MATT DAMON in *Good Will Hunting*, Be Gentlemen, Miramax.
ROBERT DUVALL in *The Apostle*, Butcher's Run, October Films.
PETER FONDA in *Ulee's Gold*, Nunez-Gowart/ Clinica Estetico, Orion.
DUSTIN HOFFMAN in *Wag the Dog*, New Line.
JACK NICHOLSON in *As Good As It Gets*, Gracie Films, TriStar.

ACTRESS
HELENA BONHAM CARTER in *The Wings of the Dove*, Renaissance Films, Miramax.
JULIE CHRISTIE in *Afterglow*, Moonstone Entertainment, Sony Pictures Classics.
JUDI DENCH in *Mrs. Brown*, Ecosse Films, Miramax.
HELEN HUNT in *As Good As It Gets*, Gracie Films, TriStar.
KATE WINSLET in *Titanic*, Lightstorm Entertainment, 20th Century-Fox and Paramount.

SUPPORTING ACTOR
ROBERT FORSTER in *Jackie Brown*, Mighty, Mighty Afrodite, Miramax.
ANTHONY HOPKINS in *Amistad*, Dream Works.
GREG KINNEAR in *An Good As It Gets*, Gracie Films, TriStar.
BURT REYNOLDS in *Boogie Nights*, New Line.
ROBIN WILLIAMS in *Good Will Hunting*, Be Gentlemen, Miramax.

SUPPORTING ACTRESS
KIM BASINGER in *L.A. Confidential*, Arnon Milchan/David L. Wolper, Warner Bros.
JOAN CUSACK in *In & Out*, Scott Radio, Paramount in association with Spelling Films.
MINNIE DRIVER in *Good Will Hunting*, Be Gentlemen, Miramax.
JULIANNE MOORE in *Boogie Nights*, New Line.
GLORIA STUART in *Titanic*, Lightstorm Entertainment, 20th Century-Fox and Paramount.

DIRECTION
JAMES CAMERON for *Titanic*, Lightstorm Entertainment, 20th Century-Fox and Paramount.
PETER CATTANEO for *The Full Monty*, Redwave Films, Fox Searchlight
ATOM EGOYAN for *The Sweet Hereafter*, Ego Film Arts, Fine Line Features
CURTIS HANSON for *L.A. Confidential*, Arson Milchanl/David L. Wolper, Warner Bros.
GUS VAN SANT for *Good Will Hunting*, Be Gentlemen, Miramax.

WRITING: BASED ON MATERIAL FROM ANOTHER MEDIUM
DONNIE BRASCO, Mandalay Entertainment, TriStar. Paul Attanasio.

L.A. CONFIDENTIAL, Arnon Milchan/ David L. Wolper, Warner Bros. **Brian Helgeland and Curtis Hanson.**
THE SWEET HEREAFTER, Ego Film Arts, Fine Line Features. Atom Egoyan.
WAG THE DOG, New Line. Hilary Henkin and David Mamet.
THE WINGS OF THE DOVE, Renaissance Films, Miramax. Hossein Amini.

WRITING: DIRECTLY FOR THE SCREEN
AS GOOD AS IT GETS, Gracie Films, TriStar. Mark Andrus and James L Brooks.
BOOGIE NIGHTS, New Line. Paul Thomas Anderson.
DECONSTRUCTING HARRY, Jean Doumanian, Fine Line Features. Woody Allen.
THE FULL MONTY, Redwave Films, Fox Searchlight. Simon Beaufoy.
GOOD WILL HUNTING, Be Gentlemen, Miramax. Ben Affleck and Matt Damon.

CINEMATOGRAPHY
AMISTAD, DreamWorks. Janusz Kaminski.
KUNDUN, Touchstone Pictures, Buena Vista. Roger Deakins.
L.A. CONFIDENTIAL, Anton Milchan/ David L. Wolper, Warner Bros. Dante Spinotti.
TITANIC, Lightstorm Entertainment. 20th Century-Fox and Paramount. Russell Carpenter.
THE WINGS OF THE DOVE, Renaissance Films, Miramax. Eduardo Serra.

ART DIRECTION—SET DECORATION
GATTACA, Jersey Films, Columbia. Jan Roelfs; Nancy Nye.
KUNDUN, Touchstone Pictures, Buena Vista. Dante Ferretti; Francesca La Schiavo.
L.A. CONFIDENTIAL, Arnon Milchan/ David L. Wolper, Warner Bros. Jeannine Oppewall; Jay R. Hart.
MEN IN BLACK, Amblin Entertainment, Columbia. Bo Welch; Cheryl Carasik.
TITANIC, Lightstorm Entertainment, 20th Century-Fox and Paramount. Peter Lamont; Michael Ford.

COSTUME DESIGN
AMISTAD, DreamWorks. Ruth E. Carter.
KUNDUN, Touchstone Pictures, Buena Vista. Dante Ferretti.
OSCAR AND LUCINDA, Dalton Films, Fox Searchlight. Janet Patterson.
TITANIC, Lightstorm Entertainment. 20th Century-Fox and Paramount. Deborah L. Scott.
THE WINGS OF THE DOVE, Renaissance Films, Miramax. Sandy Powell.

SOUND
AIR FORCE ONE, Beacon Pictures/Columbia Pictures, Columbia. Paul Massey, Rick Kline, D.M. Hemphill and Keith A. Wester.
CON AIR, Touchstone Pictures, Buena Vista. Kevin O'Connell, Greg P. Russell and Arthur Rochester.
CONTACT, Warner Bros. Randy Thom, Tom Johnson, Dennis Sands and William B. Kaplan.
L.A. CONFIDENTIAL, Arnon Milchan/ David L. Wolper, Warner Bros. Andy Nelson, Anna Behlmer and Kirk Francis.
TITANIC, Lightstorm Entertainment, 20th Century-Fox and Paramount. Gary Rydstrom, Tom Johnson, Gary Summers and Mark Ulano.

FILM EDITING
AIR FORCE ONE, Beacon Pictures/Columbia Pictures, Columbia. Richard Francis-Bruce.
AS GOOD AS IT GETS, Gracie Films, TriStar. Richard Marks.
GOOD WILL HUNTING, Be Gentlemen, Miramax. Pietro Scalia.
L.A. CONFIDENTIAL, Arnon Milchan/ David L. Wolper, Warner Bros. Peter Honess.
TITANIC, Lightstorm Entertainment, 20th Century-Fox and Paramount. Conrad Buff, James Cameron and Richard A. Harris.

SOUND EFFECTS EDITING
FACE/OFF, Douglas/Reuther/WCG/David Permut, Paramount and Touchstone. Mark P. Stoeckinger and Per Hallberg.
THE FIFTH ELEMENT, Gaumont, Columbia. Mark Mangini.

TITANIC, Ligbtstorm Entertainment, 20th Century-Fox and Paramount. **Tom Bellfort and Christopher Boyes.**

SONG
GO THE DISTANCE, (*Hercules*, Walt Disney Pictures, Buena Vista); Music by Alan Menken. Lyric by David Zippel.
HOW DO I LIVE, (*Con Air*, Touchstone Pictures, Buena Vista); Music and Lyric by Diane Warren.
JOURNEY TO THE PAST (*Anastasia*, 20th Century-Fox); Music by Stephen Flaherty; Lyric by Lynn Ahrens.
MISS MISERY, (*Good Will Hunting*, Be Gentlemen, Miramax); Music and Lyric by Elliott Smith.
MY HEART WILL GO ON, (*Titanic*, Lightstorm Entertainment, 20th Century-Fox and Paramount); Music by James Horner; Lyric by Will Jennings.

ORIGINAL DRAMATIC SCORE
AMISTAD, DreamWorks. John Williams.
GOOD WILL HUNTING, Be Gentlemen, Miramax. Danny Elfman.
KUNDUN, Touchstone Pictures, Buena Vista. Philip Glass.
L.A. CONFIDENTIAL, Arnon Milchan/ David L. Wolper, Warner Bros. Jerry Goldsmith.
TITANIC, Lightstorm Entertainment. 20th Century-Fox and Paramount. James Homer.

SCORING: ORIGINAL SONG SCORE AND/ OR ADAPTATION
ANASTASIA, 20th Century-Fox. Music by Stephen Flaherty; Lyrics by Lynn Ahrens; Orchestral Score by David Newman.
AS GOOD AS IT GETS, Gracie Films, TriStar. Hans Zimmer.
THE FULL MONTY, Redwave Films, Fox Searchlight Anne Dudley.
MEN IN BLACK, Amblin Entertainment, Columbia. Danny Elfman.
MY BEST FRIEND'S WEDDING, Jerry Zucker/Predawn, TriStar. James Newton Howard.

MAKEUP
MEN IN BLACK, Amblin Entertainment, Columbia. Rick Baker and David LeRoy Anderson.
MRS. BROWN, Ecosse Films, Miramax. Lisa Westcott, Veronica Brebner and Beverley Binda.
TITANIC, Lightstorm Entertainment, 20th Century-Fox and Paramount. Tina Earnshaw, Greg Cannom and Simon Thompson.

SHORT FILMS: ANIMATED
FAMOUS FRED, TVC London Production for Channel 4 and S4C. Joanna Quinn.
GERI'S GAME, Pixar Animation Studios Production. Jan Pinkava.
LA VIEILLE DAME ET LES PIGEONS (THE OLD LADY AND THE PIGEONS), Productions Pascal Blais/Les Armateurs/ Odec Kid Cartoons Production. Sylvain Chomet.
THE MERMAID, Film Company "DAGO"/ "SHAR" School-Studio/Studio "PANORAMA," Yaroslavl Production. Alexander Petrov.
REDUX RIDING HOOD, Walt Disney Television Animation Production. Steve Moore and Dan O'Shannon.

SHORT FILMS: LIVE ACTION
DANCE LEXIE DANCE, Raw Nerve Production for Northern Lights. Pear-se Moore and Tim Loane.
IT'S GOOD TO TALK, Feasible Films Production. Roger Goldby and Barney Reins.
SWEETHEARTS?, Metronome Productions/ Victoria Film Production. Birger Larsen and Thomas Lydholm.
VISAS AND VIRTUE, Cedar Grove Production. Chris Tashima and Chris Donahue.
WOLFGANG, M&M Production for Duosk Novellefilm. Kim Magnosnon and Anders Thomas Jensen.

DOCUMENTARY: SHORT SUBJECTS
ALASKA: SPIRIT OF THE WILD, Graphic Films Corporation, George Casey and Paul Novras.

AMAZON, Ogden Entertainment Production. Kieth Merrill and Jonathan Stern.
DAUGHTER OF THE BRIDE, Term Randall Film and Video Production. Terri Randall.
STILL KICKING: THE FABULOUS PALM SPRINGS FOLLIES, Little Apple Film Production. Mel Damski and Andrea Blaugrund.
A STORY OF HEALING, Dewey-Obenchain Films Production. Donna Dewey and Carol Pasternak.

DOCUMENTARY: FEATURES
AYN RAND: A SENSE OF LIFE, AG Media Corporation Limited Production, Strand Releasing. Michael Paxton.
COLORS STRAIGHT UP, Echo Pictures Production. Michele Ohayon and Julia Schachter.
4 LITTLE GIRLS, HBO Documentary Film/ 40 Acres and a Mule Filmworks Production. Spike Lee and Sam Pollard.
THE LONG WAY HOME, Mariah Films Production at the Simon Wiesenthal Center, Seventh Art. Rabbi Marvin Hier and Richard Trank.
WACO: THE RULES OF ENGAGEMENT, SomFord Entertainment/Fifth Estate Production. Dan Gifford and William Gazecki.

FOREIGN LANGUAGE FILM
BEYOND SILENCE (Germany).
CHARACTER (The Netherlands).
FOUR DAYS IN SEPTEMBER (Brazil).
SECRETS OF THE HEART (Spain).
THE THIEF (Russia).

VISUAL EFFECTS
THE LOST WORLD: JURASSIC PARK, Universal/Amblin Entertainment, Universal. Dennis Muren, Stan Winston, Randal M. Dulva and Michael Lantieri.
STARSHIP TROOPERS, TriStar Pictures/ Touchstone Pictures, TriStar. Phil Tippett, Scott E. Anderson. Alec Gillis and John Richardson.
TITANIC, Lightstorm Entertainment, 20th Century-Fox and Paramount. Robert Legato, Mark Lasoff, Thomas L Fisher and Michael Kanfer.

HONORARY AWARDS
TO STANLEY DONEN in appreciation of a body of work marked by grace, elegance, wit and visual innovation.
TO PETE CLARK, in appreciation for outstanding service and dedication in upholding the high standards of the Academy of Motion Picture Arts and Sciences. (John A. Banner Medal of Commendation.)

GORDON E. SAWYER AWARD
TO DON IWERKS

SCIENTIFIC AND TECHNICAL AWARDS: ACADEMY AWARD OF MERIT
GUNNAR P. MICHELSON for the engineering and development of an improved, electronic, high-speed, precision light valve for use in motion picture printing machines.

SCIENTIFIC OR TECHNICAL AWARDS: SCIENTIFIC AND ENGINEERING AWARD
WILLIAM KOVACS for his creative leadership and ROY HALL for his principal engineering efforts that led to the Wavefront Advanced Visualizer computer graphics system.
JOHN GIBSON, ROB KRIEGER, MILAN NOVACEK, GLEN OZYMOK and DAVE SPRINGER for the development of the geometric modeling component of the Alias PowerAnimator System.
DOMINIQUE BOISVERT, REJEAN GAGNE, DANIEL LANGLOIS and RICHARD LAPERRIERE for the development of the "Actor" animation component of the Softimage computer animation system.
EBEN OSTBY, WILLIAM REEVES, SAMUEL J. LEFFLER and TOM DUFF for the development of the Marionette Three Dimensional Computer Animation System.
CRAIG W. REYNOLDS for his pioneering contributions to the development of three-dimensional computer animation for motion picture production.

RICHARD SHOUP, ALVY RAY SMITH and THOMAS PORTER for their pioneering efforts in the development of digital paint systems used in motion picture production.
KIRK HANDLEY, RAY MELUCH, SCOTT ROBINSON, WILSON H. ALLEN and JOHN NEARY for the design, development and implementation of the Dolby CP5OO Digital Cinema Processor.
JOEL W. JOHNSON of the O'Connor Laboratories for the unique design improvement in fluid head counter-balancing techniques as used in their Model 2575.
AL JENSEN, CHUCK HEADLEY, JEAN MESSNER and HAZEM NABULSI of CEI Technology for the production of a self-contained, flicker-free, Color Video-Assist Camera.

SCIENTIFIC OR TECHNICAL AWARDS: TECHNICAL ACHIEVEMENT AWARDS
CLARK F. CRITES for the design and development of the Christie ELF 1-C Endless Loop Film Transport and Storage System.
DAN LEIMETER and ROBERT WEITZ for the development and implementation of a Portable Adjustment Tool for T-Style Slit Lens Assemblies.
PHILIP C. CORY for the design and development of the Special Effects Spark Generator.
JAMES M. REILLY, DOUGLAS W. NISHIMURA and MONIQUE C. FISCHER of the Rochester Institute of Technology for the creation of A-D Strips, a diagnostic tool for the detection of the presence of vinegar syndrome in processed acetate-based motion picture film.
JIM FRAZIER, for the design concept, and IAIN NEIL and RICK GELBARD for the further design and development of the Panavision/Frazier Lens System for motion picture photography.
JAMES F. FOLEY, CHARLES E. CONVERSE and F. EDWARD GARDNER of UCISCO; and to ROBERT W. STOKER, JR. and MATT SWEENEY for the development and realization of Liquid Synthetic Air.
JACK CASHIN, ROGER HIBBARD and LARRY JACOBSON for the design, development and implementation of a projection system analyzer.
RICHARD CHUANG, GLENN ENTIS and CARL ROSENDAHL for the concept and architecture of the Pacific Data Images (PDI) Animation System.
GREG HERMANOVIC, KIM DAVIDSON, MARK ELENDT and PAUL H. BRESLIN for the development of the procedural modeling and animation components of the Prisms software package.
JAMES J. KEATING, MICHAEL WAHRMAN and RICHARD HOLLANDER for their contributions that led to the Wavefront Advanced Visualizer computer graphics system.

1998

"If Shakespeare were alive today, he'd be driving a Porsche, living in Bel-Air, and he'd have a deal with Paramount."

—Marc Norman, co-screenwriter, *Shakespeare in Love*

It was almost preordained that Steven Spielberg's raw D-day epic *Saving Private Ryan* would sweep the Awards. And the general consensus promised that Oscar honoree director Elia Kazan (*On the Waterfront*, *A Streetcar Named Desire*), who surrendered eight of his peers to the House Un-American Activities Committee back in the McCarthy era, would be booed off the stage.

WHERE THERE'S A WILL

CEREMONY: March 21, 1999
Dorothy Chandler Pavilion, Los
Angeles Music Center, Los Angeles
HOST: Whoopi Goldberg

This first Sunday telecast in Oscar history was full of surprises. Goldberg opened the show in white face and tossed her first volley of Bill Clinton/Monica Lewinsky jokes, most of which landed with a thud. Elegance was briefly restored by Hollywood's newest golden girl, Gwyneth Paltrow, in prom-queen pink, who brought the audience to tears with her acceptance speech. Her Oscar made it clear that the reportedly $14 million publicity campaign launched by Miramax for *Shake-*

speare in Love had succeeded in leaving Spielberg beached on Normandy

After five uninspired dance numbers representing each Best Picture nominee and a lengthy film tribute to real-life heroes portrayed on film the longest telecast yet was finally alleviated by the explosive antics of Roberto Benigni. As his name was called, first for Best Foreign Film, then for Best Actor, Benigni leaped over chairs, kissed everyone but the conductor; and slaughtered the English language in a breathless tumult of nonsequiturs: "This is a terrible mistake because I used up all my English! I would like to be Jupiter and kidnap everybody and lie down in the firmament making love to everybody!"

Finally, the much anticipated moment of reckoning as Kazan appeared, protectively flanked by Robert De Niro and Martin Scorsese. Except for a few notables led by Ed Harris and Nick Nolte, who boycotted by sitting on their hands, Kazan was treated with tepid respect. Offering no hint of apology, he groped for words and finally eulogized himself: "I think I can just slip away." He did just that as the orchestra cut him off.

BEST PICTURE
SHAKESPEARE IN LOVE

Director John Madden thought "it would be great to have a movie about Shakespeare that could be sexy." After reading the screenplay by Marc Norman and Tom Stoppard (*Rosencrantz and Guildenstern Are Dead*, 1990), which had languished for years on the studio woodpile, he felt instantly passionate about it. "The story is ingeniously Shakespearean in its dimensions, including high and low comedy, coincidences, masquerades, jokes about itself, topical references and entrances with screwball timing," said the *Washington Post*.

The idea had come to Norman while talking to his son about *Romeo and Juliet*. What if the young, broke and burned-out Shakespeare was inspired to write the play after falling hopelessly in love? The idea would result in "a literate, wicked and funny screenplay," wrote Roger Ebert. With a cast "full of performances to savor," said Owen Glieberman in *Entertainment Weekly*. "Let the kids toy with their Rugrats and hold their Sandler high," pronounced the *Washington Post*. "*Shakespeare in Love* is a movie to please the rest of us, parched for a game of dueling, reeling romance." And *Newsweek*'s David Ansen exclaimed, "A glorious film that makes moviegoing fun again."

Gwyneth Paltrow, Joseph Fiennes

The envelope, please…

Steven Spielberg with Tom Hanks

BEST DIRECTOR
STEVEN SPIELBERG (B. 1947)
SAVING PRIVATE RYAN

A rarity in the Spielberg canon, *Ryan* was conceived without the technical wizardry usually associated with his films. "I wanted to achieve reality," he said. "Assuming the role of a combat cameraman, not assuming the role of an artist." The first twenty-four minutes, the landing of Allied troops on Normandy, are nightmarishly brutal. "I tried to put everybody in the situation of being under fire in extreme combat, where the details were the most important thing in each shot," Spielberg said. He insisted that his actors, including Tom Hanks, head off to boot camp for weeks before production. The effort paid off. "*Saving Private Ryan* is the best movie Spielberg ever made, but it is a terrific movie by any standard. Prepare to weep," wrote Bob Graham in the *San Francisco Chronicle*.

Roberto Benigni with Giorgio Cantarini

BEST ACTOR
ROBERTO BENIGNI (B. 1952)
LIFE IS BEAUTIFUL

"I'm so happy that every organ in my body is moving in a very bad way." Inspired by Buster Keaton and Charlie Chaplin, Benigni's frenetic slapstick comedy has made him the clown prince of his native Italy. Not only is he the star of *Life Is Beautiful*, but he also wrote and directed the fable of a loving father who uses his humor to help his young son survive the horrors of the concentration camps.

He appeared in American films, including Jim Jarmusch's *Down by Law* (1986), *Night on Earth* (1991), and *Son of the Pink Panther* (1993). There was little inkling, however, of the Benigni box-office earthquake to come ($130 million gross) with *Life Is Beautiful*.

BEST OF 1998
Best Picture: *Shakespeare in Love*
Best Director: Steven Spielberg, *Saving Private Ryan*
Best Actor: Roberto Benigni, *Life Is Beautiful*
Best Actress: Gwyneth Paltrow, *Shakespeare in Love*
Best Supporting Actor: James Coburn, *Affliction*
Best Supporting Actress: Judi Dench, *Shakespeare in Love*
Honorary Award: Elia Kazan

FIRSTS
- The Awards ceremony was moved to Sunday for the first time in its televised history.
- *Shakespeare in Love* was the first romantic comedy to win Best Picture since *Annie Hall* (1977).
- Roberto Benigni was the first foreign actor in a foreign-language film to win the gold since Sophia Loren in *Two Women* (1961).
- Roberto Benigni, up for Best Actor, Best Director, and Best Picture, joined the ranks of Orson Welles, Warren Beatty, and Woody Allen as the Academy's only trifecta nominees.

ROLE REVERSALS
- *Shakespeare in Love* was planned as a vehicle for Julia Roberts and Daniel Day-Lewis.
- A tale of twin Lizzies: Judi Dench and Cate Blanchett played the same queen, Elizabeth I, at different stages of her life in two nominated films, *Elizabeth* and *Shakespeare in Love*. The first-time-ever coincidence was heightened by the appearance of Joseph Fiennes and Geoffrey Rush in both films.

SINS OF OMISSION
Best Supporting Actor: Bill Murray, *Rushmore*.
Best Picture: *Sight Unseen*.
Best Supporting Actress: Lisa Kudrow, *The Opposite of Sex*.

UNMENTIONABLES
- Presenter Chris Rock set off a chorus of boos when he referred to Elia Kazan as "a rat."
- How much does it cost to look like a million? Gwyneth Paltrow's hair and makeup alone came to $10,000.
- This gets complicated: Best Supporting Actress nominee Lynn Redgrave split with her husband/manager just weeks before the Awards. She'd learned that he had a love child with his former assistant, who went on to marry her son. Completely in the dark, Redgrave helped raise the boy as her adopted grandson.
- Sharon Stone expressed her concern for Ms. Paltrow in the *Observer*: "She's very young and lives in a rarified air that's very thin. It's like she's not getting enough oxygen."
- "No, I didn't win, but I did get to meet Monica Lewinsky—that's not bad," said Sir Ian McKellen.
- Roberto Benigni's (*Life Is Beautiful*) father was a prisoner in a Nazi labor camp for two years.

BEST ACTRESS
GWYNETH PALTROW (B. 1973)
SHAKESPEARE IN LOVE

"There was not a dry eye in the house," observed the *Los Angeles Times* when Paltrow made her deeply felt thank-yous to Mom, actress Blythe Danner, her "soul mate," Joseph Fiennes, and dedicated her Oscar to Harrison Kravis, a teenage boyfriend who'd been killed in a car crash.

Playing Viola in *Shakespeare*, this was the third time Paltrow had played a Brit after *Emma* and *Sliding Doors* for British television. Paltrow is also blessed with glistening good looks and a penchant for high-profile offscreen romances. She's a darling of the tabloids—with a much-publicized engagement and breakup with Brad Pitt—and glamour magazines. She also won over the critics for her Oscar-winning role. The *New York Times*'s Janet Maslin found this to be her "first great, fully realized performance…she makes a heroine so breathtaking that she seems utterly plausible as Shakespeare's guiding light."

BEST SUPPORTING ACTOR
JAMES COBURN (1928–2002)
AFFLICTION

"I've been doing this work for over half my life. I finally got one right, I guess," said the actor with the lean, villainous good looks. Best known for his macho action role in *The Magnificent Seven* (1960) and *The Great Escape* (1963), and often stranded in far less worthy scripts, Coburn brought the full force of his dynamism to *Affliction*—a poignant film about the scarred psyches of American men based on the novel by Russell Banks. Suffering crippling arthritis, Coburn finally found treatment that allowed him to work again after a fifteen-year hiatus. Not one for self-pity, he maintained his growly smirk when he was asked how it felt to finally be an Academy Award nominee rather than a presenter: "You get a better seat!"

BEST SUPPORTING ACTRESS
JUDI DENCH (B. 1934)
SHAKESPEARE IN LOVE

"I feel, for eight minutes on the screen, I should only get a little bit of him," Dame Judi said as she held her first Oscar for a role that lasted all of eight minutes. Quality had clearly dominated quantity, according to the critics. "Judi Dench shines as a stern but fair Queen Elizabeth," said the *Washington Post*. Roger Ebert enjoyed "her wicked scene as Elizabeth, informing Wessex of his bride-to-be, 'You're a lordly fool; she's been plucked since I saw her last, and not by you. It takes a woman to know it.'"

The *San Francisco Examiner* proclaimed, "Dench is superb, dominating her scenes with splendid hauteur but not too regal to indulge in a few surprises." She was also nominated last year for playing another queen, Victoria, in *Mrs. Brown*—also directed by *Shakespeare* director Madden. While she is no stranger to monarchic roles, Dench got the biggest kick out of playing 007's boss lady in the Bond films: "Thrilling!" Though equally famous on the stage, Dench won her greatest popularity in a benign British sitcom, *A Fine Romance* (1991), playing opposite her actor/husband, Michael Williams.

PICTURE

ELIZABETH, Alison Owen, Eric Fellner and Tim Bevan, Gramercy Pictures

LIFE IS BEAUTIFUL, Elda Ferri and Gianluigi Braschi, Miramax Films

SAVING PRIVATE RYAN, Steven Spielberg, Ian Bryce, Mark Gordon and Gary Levinsohn, DreamWorks Pictures and Paramount Pictures

SHAKESPEARE IN LOVE, David Parfitt, Donna Gigliotti, Harvey Weinstein, Edward Zwick and Marc Norman, Miramax Films

THE THIN RED LINE, Robert Michael Geisler, John Roberdeau and Grant Hill, 20th Century-Fox

ACTOR

ROBERTO BENIGNI, *Life is Beautiful*, Miramax Films

TOM HANKS, *Saving Private Ryan*, DreamWorks Pictures and Paramount Pictures

IAN MCKELLEN, *Gods and Monsters*, Lions Gate Films

NICK NOLTE, *Affliction*, Lions Gate Films

EDWARD NORTON, *American History X*, New Line

ACTRESS

CATE BLANCHETT, *Elizabeth*, Gramercy Pictures

FERNANDA MONTENEGRO, *Central Station*, Sony Pictures Classics

GWYNETH PALTROW, *Shakespeare in Love*, Miramax Films

MERYL STREEP, *One True Thing*, Universal

EMILY WATSON, *Hilary and Jackie*, October Films

SUPPORTING ACTOR

JAMES COBURN, *Affliction*, Lions Gate Films

ROBERT DUVALL, *A Civil Action*, Buena Vista

ED HARRIS, *The Truman Show*, Paramount

Geoffrey Rush, *Shakespeare in Love*, Miramax Films

Billy Bob Thornton, *A Simple Plan*, Paramount and Mutual Film Company in association with Savoy Pictures

SUPPORTING ACTRESS

KATHY BATES, *Primary Colors*, Universal and Mutual Film Company

BRENDA BLETHYN, *Little Voice*, Miramax Films

JUDI DENCH, *Shakespeare in Love*, Miramax Films

RACHEL GRIFFITHS, *Hilary and Jackie*, October Films

LYNN REDGRAVE, *Gods and Monsters*, Lions Gate Films

DIRECTION

LIFE IS BEAUTIFUL, Roberto Benigni, Miramax Films

SAVING PRIVATE RYAN, Steven Spielberg, DreamWorks Pictures and Paramount Pictures

SHAKESPEARE IN LOVE, John Madden, Miramax Films

THE THIN RED LINE, Terrence Malick, 20th Century-Fox

THE TRUMAN SHOW, Peter Weir, Paramount

WRITING: BASED ON MATERIAL PREVIOUSLY PRODUCED OR PUBLISHED

GODS AND MONSTERS, Bill Condon, Lions Gate Films

OUT OF SIGHT, Scott Frank, Universal

PRIMARY COLORS, Elaine May, Universal and Mutual Film Company

A SIMPLE PLAN, Scott B. Smith, Paramount and Mutual Film Company in association with Savoy Pictures

THE THIN RED LINE, Terrence Malick, 20th Century-Fox

WRITING: DIRECTLY FOR THE SCREEN

BULWORTH, Warren Beatty and Jeremy Pikser, 20th Century-Fox

LIFE IS BEAUTIFUL, Vincenzo Cerami, Roberto Benigni, Miramax Films

SAVING PRIVATE RYAN, Robert Rodat, DreamWorks Pictures and Paramount Pictures

SHAKESPEARE IN LOVE, Marc Norman, Tom Stoppard, Miramax Films

THE TRUMAN SHOW, Andew Niccol, Paramount

CINEMATOGRAPHY

A CIVIL ACTION, Conrad L. Hall, Buena Vista

ELIZABETH, Remi Adefarasin, Gramercy Pictures

SAVING PRIVATE RYAN, Janusz Kaminski, DreamWorks Pictures and Paramount Pictures

SHAKESPEARE IN LOVE, Richard Greatrex, Miramax Films

THE THIN RED LINE, John Toll, 20th Century-Fox

ART DIRECTION—SET DECORATION

ELIZABETH, John Myhre, Gramercy Pictures

PLEASANTVILLE, Jeannine Oppewall, New Line

SAVING PRIVATE RYAN, Tom Sanders, DreamWorks Pictures and Paramount Pictures

SHAKESPEARE IN LOVE, Martin Childs, Miramax Films

WHAT DREAMS MAY COME, Eugenio Zanetti, PolyGram

COSTUME DESIGN

BELOVED, Colleen Atwood, Buena Vista

ELIZABETH, Alexandra Byrne, Gramercy Pictures

PLEASANTVILLE, Judianna Makovsky, New Line

SHAKESPEARE IN LOVE, Sandy Powell, Miramax Films

VELVET GOLDMINE, Sandy Powell, Miramax Films

SOUND

ARMAGEDDON, Kevin O'Connel, Greg P. Russell, Keith A. Wester, Buena Vista

THE MASK OF ZORRO, Kevin O'Connell, Greg P. Russell, Pud Cusack, TriStar

SAVING PRIVATE RYAN, Gary Rydstrom, Gary Summers, Andy Nelson, Ronald Judkins, DreamWorks Pictures and Paramount Pictures

SHAKESPEARE IN LOVE, Robin O'Donoghue, Dominic Lester, Peter Glossop, Miramax Films

THE THIN RED LINE, Andy Nelson, Anna Behlmer, Paul Brincat, 20th Century-Fox

FILM EDITING

LIFE IS BEAUTIFUL, Simona Paggi, Miramax Films

OUT OF SIGHT, Anne V. Coates, Universal

SAVING PRIVATE RYAN, Michael Kahn, DreamWorks Pictures and Paramount Pictures

SHAKESPEARE IN LOVE, David Gamble, Miramax Films

THE THIN RED LINE, Billy Weber, Leslie Jones, Saar Klein, 20th Century-Fox

SOUND EDITING

ARMAGEDDON, George Watters II, Buena Vista

THE MASK OF ZORRO, David McMoyler, TriStar

SAVING PRIVATE RYAN, Gary Rydstrom, Richard Hymns, DreamWorks Pictures and Paramount Pictures

SOUND EFFECTS EDITING

ARMAGEDDON, George Watters II, Buena Vista

THE MASK OF ZORRO, David McMoyler, TriStar

SAVING PRIVATE RYAN, Gary Rydstrom, Richard Hymns, DreamWorks Pictures and Paramount Pictures

VISUAL EFFECTS

ARMAGEDDON, Richard R. Hoover, Pat McClung, John Frazier, Buena Vista

MIGHTY JOE YOUNG, Rick Baker, Hoyt Yeatman, Allen Hall, Jim Mitchell, Buena Vista

WHAT DREAMS MAY COME, Joel Hynek, Nicholas Brooks, Stuart Robertson, Kevin Mack, PolyGram

SONG

ARMAGEDDON, Diane Warren (Song: "I Don't Want to Miss a Thing") Buena Vista

QUEST FOR CAMELOT, Carole Bayer Sager, David Foster, Tony Renis, Alberto Testa (Song: "The Prayer") Warner Bros.

THE HORSE WHISPERER, Allison Moorer, Gwil Owen (Song: "A Soft Place to Fall") Buena Vista

BABE: PIG IN THE CITY, Randy Newman (Song: "That'll Do") Universal

THE PRINCE OF EGYPT, Stephen Schwartz (Song: "When You Believe") DreamWorks SKG

SCORING: ORIGINAL MUSIC

ELIZABETH, David Hirschfelder, Gramercy Pictures

LIFE IS BEAUTIFUL, Nicola Piovani, Miramax Films

PLEASANTVILLE, Randy Newman, New Line

SAVING PRIVATE RYAN, John Williams, DreamWorks Pictures and Paramount Pictures

THE THIN RED LINE, Hans Zimmer, 20th Century-Fox

SCORING: MUSICAL OR COMEDY

A BUG'S LIFE, Randy Newman, Buena Vista

MULAN, Music by Matthew Wilder, Lyrics by David Zippel, Buena Vista

PATCH ADAMS, Marc Shaiman, Universal

THE PRINCE OF EGYPT, Music and Lyrics by Stephen Schwartz, Orchestral Score by Hans Zimmer, DreamWorks SKG

SHAKESPEARE IN LOVE, Stephen Warbeck, Miramax Films

MAKEUP

ELIZABETH, Jenny Shircore, Gramercy Pictures

SAVING PRIVATE RYAN, Lois Burwell, Conor O'Sullivan, Daniel C. Striepeke, DreamWorks Pictures and Paramount Pictures

SHAKESPEARE IN LOVE, Lisa Westcott, Veronica Brebner, Miramax Films

SHORT FILMS: ANIMATED

BUNNY, Chris Wedge, Blue Sky Studios, Inc.

THE CANTERBURY TALES, Christopher Grace, Jonathan Myerson, S4C/BBC Wales/HBO

JOLLY ROGER, Mark Baker, Astley Baker/Silver Bird for Channel Four

MORE, Mark Osborne, Steve Kalafer, Bad Clams Productions/Swell Productions/Flemington Pictures

WHEN LIFE DEPARTS, Karsten Kiilerich, Stefan Fjeldmark, A. Film

SHORT FILMS: LIVE ACTION

CULTURE, Will Speck, Josh Gordon, False Alarm Pictures

ELECTION NIGHT, Kim Magnusson, Anders Thomas Jensen, M&M

HOLIDAY ROMANCE, Alexander Jovy, JJ Keith, Jovy Junior Enterprises Ltd.

LA CARTE POSTALE (THE POSTCARD), Vivian Goffette, K2 S.A.

VICTOR, Simon Sandquist, Joel Bergvall, Bergvall Bilder/Hemikrania

DOCUMENTARY: SHORT SUBJECTS

THE PERSONALS: IMPROVISATIONS ON ROMANCE IN THE GOLDEN YEARS, Keiko Ibi Film

A PLACE IN THE LAND, Guggenheim

SUNRISE OVER TIANANMEN SQUARE,

National Film Board of Canada

DOCUMENTARY: FEATURE

DANCEMAKER, Four Oaks Foundation

THE FARM: ANGOLA, U.S.A., *Gabriel Films*

THE LAST DAYS, Survivors of the Shoah Visual History Foundation

LENNY BRUCE: SWEAR TO TELL THE TRUTH, Whyaduck

REGRET TO INFORM, Sun Fountain

FOREIGN LANGUAGE FILM

CENTRAL STATION, Sony Pictures Classics

CHILDREN OF HEAVEN, Miramax Films

THE GRANDFATHER, Miramax Films

LIFE IS BEAUTIFUL, Miramax Films

TANGO, Sony Pictures Classics

HONORARY AWARDS

To ELIA KAZAN in recognition of his indelible contributions to the art of motion picture direction.

To DAVID W. GRAY in appreciation for outstanding service and dedication in upholding the high standards of the Academy of Motion Pictures Arts and Sciences.

SCIENTIFIC OR TECHNICAL: ACADEMY AWARD OF MERIT

Editorial and Pre-production, AVID TECHNOLOGY

SCIENTIFIC OR TECHNICAL: SCIENTIFIC AND ENGINEERING AWARD

Sound, DR. THOMAS G. STOCKHAM, JR. and ROBERT B. INGEBRETSEN; JAMES A. MOORER; ROBERT PREDOVICH, JOHN SCOTT, MOHAMED KEN T. HUSAIN and CAMERON SHEARER

Lighting, STEPHEN J. KAY; and DEREK C. LIGHTBODY

Special Photographic, GARY TREGASKIS, DOMINIQUE BOISVERT, PHILIPPE PANZINI and ANDRÉ LEBLANC; ROY B. FERENCE, STEVEN R. SCHMIDT, RICHARD J. FEDERICO, ROCKWELL YARID and MICHAEL E. MCCRACKAN

Laboratory, COLIN MOSSMAN, HANS LEISINGER and GEORGE JOHN ROWLAND; RONALD E. UHLIG, THOMAS F. POWERS and FRED M. FUSS

Camera, ARNOLD & RICHTER CINE TECHNIK and ARRI USA, INC.

Lenses and Filters, ARNOLD & RICHTER CINE TECHNIK and the CARL ZEISS COMPANY; IAIN NEIL, TAKUO MIYAGISHIMA and PANAVISION, INCORPORATED

Camera Cranes, MARK ROBERTS, RONAN CARROLL, ASSAFF RAWNER, PAUL BARTLETT and SIMON WAKLEY; MICHAEL SORENSEN, RICHARD ALEXANDER and DONALD TRUMBULL

SCIENTIFIC OR TECHNICAL: TECHNICAL ACHIEVEMENT AWARD

Camera cranes, GARRETT BROWN and JERRY HOLWAY; JAMES RODNUNSKY, JAMES WEBBER, BOB WEBBER and TROU BAYLISS; MICHAEL MACKENZIE, MIKE BOLLES, UDO PAMPEL and JOSEPH FULMER; BARRY WALTON, BILL SCHULTZ, CHRIS BARKER and DAVID CORNELIUS; BURCE WILTON and CARLOS ICINKOFF

Photography, REMY SMITH, JAMES K. BRANCH and NASIR J. ZAIDI

Camera, IVAN KRUGLAK; TAKUO MIYAGISHIMA and ALBERT K. SAIKI

Special Photographic, DR. DOUGLAS R. ROBLE; THADDEUS BEIER; NICK FOSTER; and CARY PHILLIPS

Sound, MANFRED N. KLEMME and DONALD E. WETZEL

Lenses and Filters, DR. MITCHELL J. BOGDANOWICZ, JIM MEYER and STAN MILLER

Laboratory, DR. A. TULSI RAM, RICHARD C. SEHLIN, DR. CARL F. HOLTZ and DAVID F. KOPPERL; EDMUND M. DIGIULIO and JAMES BARTELL; ED ZWANEVELD and FREDERICK GASOI, MIKE LAZARIDIS and DALE BRUBACHER-CRESSMAN

Editorial and Pre-production, IVAN KRUGLAK and MIKE DENECKE

IRVING G. THALBERG MEMORIAL AWARD

NORMAN JEWISON

1999

The mild mystery of who would win this year's Oscars was surpassed by the stranger mystery of who had stolen them. Fifty-five gold statuettes went missing from a warehouse, and all but three were later discovered in a dumpster in L.A.'s Koreatown. That, and the scandal of several hundred Academy ballots misplaced by the U. S. Postal Service, provided returning host Billy Crystal with enough comic fodder to last the record four-hour-and-three minute ceremony. Crystal had plenty of time to stall, with the top prize winners almost a foregone conclusion. Even before its release, word was out: *American Beauty* and its star Kevin Spacey had it clinched. The same early projections held true for Hilary Swank and Angelina Jolie.

The show limped along despite the canceled "too dull to be campy" dance numbers. Gwyneth Paltrow wasn't the only star the cameras caught stifling a yawn. Crystal turned to a very pregnant Annette Bening for several punch lines: "If Warren [Beatty] is onstage for the Thalberg Award when Bening goes into labor, I'll have to be her Lamaze coach. But she's a pro, and I know she'll do it in one take." There was a bit of buzz when *The Matrix* managed to snag four technical-achievement Oscars from the supposed overdog, *Star Wars: The Phantom Menace*. What's usually a bathroom cue, the honorary Oscar presentation, was an exception this year, as Jane Fonda introduced American audiences to the stunning body of work by Polish auteur Andrzej Wajda.

A big laugh came at the expense of Spanish director Pedro Almodóvar, whose mangled acceptance speech was the perfect cue for Crystal: "He makes Roberto Benigni look like an English teacher." After that, it all came down to who was wearing what (backless and off-the-shoulder appeared to be the dress of the moment) and the reason for Whitney Houston's last-minute no-show. Her aunt, Dionne Warwick, stepped in as her replacement for a nostalgic Best Songs medley and brought down the house.

A "BEAUTY"-FUL NIGHT

**CEREMONY: March 26, 2000
Shrine Auditorium, Los Angeles
HOST: Billy Crystal**

**BEST PICTURE/
BEST DIRECTOR
SAM MENDES (B. 1965)
*AMERICAN BEAUTY***

First time director Sam Mendes made no bones about his adulation of Billy Wilder, to whom he dedicated his Oscar: "If my career amounts to one-tenth of what yours has been, I'll be a very, very happy man."

Beauty's tone was admittedly inspired by Wilder's *The Apartment* (1960), with its black humor laced with foreboding and mounting tension. Critics were nearly unanimous in their praise of this "unusually off-center studio venture." *Variety* went on to say that this dark tale of a suburban couple's emotional meltdown is "a real American original." Michael Wilmington in the *Chicago Tribune* wrote, "*American Beauty* has an intoxicating confidence and flow, gorgeous images and bracing irreverence." The *New York Post* proclaimed it "a flat-out masterpiece; indeed, an all-time classic."

Kevin Spacey, Mena Suvari

Mendes, a British stage director tapped by DreamWorks' Steven Spielberg for the assignment, was remarkably cool under fire. He had a vision of "creating a world that was banal but beautiful, sterile and empty but filled with poetry." Given such an arty overview, even he was surprised that audiences flocked to it. "I would have done this movie for free," Mendes quipped. "And I almost did. I think Steven Spielberg owes me a couple of quid."

The envelope, please...

Kevin Spacey with Annette Bening

BEST ACTOR
KEVIN SPACEY (B. 1959)
AMERICAN BEAUTY

"I'll be dead in a year," says Lester (Spacey) in almost the first words of the movie. "In a way, I'm dead already." The *Washington Post* said, "[Spacey's] portrayal of the beleaguered suburban male of the species is so achingly tender, our connection with him extends achingly beyond the grave." Mike Clark of *USA Today* effused, "*American Beauty* is a singular accomplishment so specifically keyed to Spacey's talents that it mandates going out on a limb to say it contains the performance that will ultimately be regarded as 'the one.'" Sam Mendes cast him "because he is capable of making the hair stand up on the back of your neck."

Spacey had come a long way from a routed military career, a battle with the bottle, and a reputation for nasty behavior. His film career began with a small part in *Heartburn* (1986). He was immediately noticed and cast for the TV series *Wiseguy*. He soon appeared in *Glengarry Glen Ross* (1992), *Swimming with Sharks* (1994), and his Oscar-winning performance in *The Usual Suspects* (1995). After appearing in Al Pacino's *Looking for Richard* (1996), Spacey made his own directorial debut with *Albino Alligator* (1997). He returned to the screen in *L.A. Confidential* and *Midnight in the Garden of Good and Evil* (both 1997). (For more on Spacey, see 1995.)

BEST ACTRESS
HILARY SWANK (B. 1974)
BOYS DON'T CRY

"We've come a long way...Mom, I guess it was worth living out of the car." Just nine years before her Oscar win, Hilary and Mrs. Swank had driven down from Seattle with just $75 dollars and a dream. The toothsome teen hit her first break on TV (*Growing Pains*, *Beverly Hills 90210*) before winning the role of Brandon Teena, the real-life young Nebraska woman who was raped and murdered for posing as a man.

Swank lived as a man for a month to prepare for the torturous role, and the effort paid off with uniformly rave reviews. "Extraordinary performance," wrote the *Chicago Tribune*'s Marc Caro. the *New York Times*'s Janet Maslin added, "Ms. Swank, who deserves to be remembered at the end of the year for a devastating portrayal, does account for much of the film's credibility." *Newsweek*'s Peter Ansen said, "Spectacularly accomplished." Swank also appeared in *The Affair of the Necklace* (2001).

BEST OF 1999
Best Picture: *American Beauty*
Best Director: Sam Mendes, *American Beauty*
Best Actor: Kevin Spacey, *American Beauty*
Best Actress: Hilary Swank, *Boys Don't Cry*
Best Supporting Actor: Michael Caine, *The Cider House Rules*
Best Supporting Actress: Angelina Jolie, *Girl, Interrupted*
Honorary Award: Warren Beatty

FIRSTS
- Angelina Jolie and Jon Voight joined Henry and Jane Fonda as the only father-daughter Oscar winners.
- The Academy was outraged by the *Wall Street Journal*, the first outside source to poll members before the Awards. (For the record: the *Journal* guessed every winner except Best Actor; it predicted Denzel Washington would nab the gold in a squeaker.)
- *American Beauty* was the first non-period, non-historical epic to win Best Picture since *Silence of the Lambs* (1991).
- Honoree Andrzej Wajda's acceptance speech was the first to be subtitled.

ROLE REVERSALS
Perhaps in tribute to cross-dressed Hilary Swank's Oscar, *South Park* creators Trey Parker and Matt Stone showed up in drag as Jennifer Lopez and Gwyneth Paltrow.

SINS OF OMISSION
Best Actor: Jim Carrey, *Man on the Moon*
Best Supporting Actor: Philip Seymour Hoffman, *The Talented Mr. Ripley*, John Malkovich, *Being John Malkovich*
Best Supporting Actress: Reese Witherspoon, *Election*

ALWAYS A BRIDESMAID, NEVER A BRIDE
Despite his more than twenty-five leading roles, including his performances in *Alfie* (1966) and *Sleuth* (1972), Michael Caine has never won a Best Actor Oscar.

UNMENTIONABLES
- The seductive little gift baskets given to this year's Oscar presenters included a baseball autographed by Joe DiMaggio, a limited-edition Tag Heuer watch, an 18-carat gold bracelet, a Kodak digital camera, and a Harry Winston sterling-silver travel frame in a leather case.
- Angelina Jolie's stomach tattoo in Latin reads: "That which feeds me, destroys me."
- The *F* word in the lyrics to "Blame Canada," from *South Park*, was covered by gasps from the choir.
- Michael Jackson paid $1.5 million for David O. Selznick's Best Picture Oscar for *Gone with the Wind*.

BEST SUPPORTING ACTOR
MICHAEL CAINE (B. 1933)
THE CIDER HOUSE RULES

In a playful nod to fellow nominee Tom Cruise (*Magnolia*), Caine said, "Your price would have gone down so fast if you had won this. Tom, do you have any idea what a supporting actor makes?" He was especially kind to 11-year-old nominee Haley Joel Osment (*The Sixth Sense*), his hottest competition in the polls.

With his two Supporting Actor wins under his belt (first for *Hannah and Her Sisters*, 1986), "Caine's riveting performance as an ether-addicted abortionist is one of his best," wrote Roger Ebert in the *Chicago Tribune*. *Zulu* (1964) was the first film to bring Caine international attention, and he had other Oscar-nominated roles in *Alfie* (1966), *Sleuth* (1972), and *Educating Rita* (1983). Caine also appeared in such lesser films as *Beyond the Poseidon Adventure* (1979), *Blame It on Rio* (1984), and *Sweet Liberty* (1986). (For more on Caine, see 1966.)

BEST SUPPORTING ACTRESS
ANGELINA JOLIE (B. 1976)
GIRL, INTERRUPTED

"I am in shock. I am just so in love with my brother." Jolie's look-alike sibling, James, had been her date for the Oscars two years in a row. The gossip was flying.

"Jolie is emerging as one of the great wild spirits of current movies, a loose cannon who somehow has deadly aim," wrote the *Chicago Sun-Times*'s Roger Ebert. Jolie began her professional career as a model and quickly established herself as a gifted actress in two TV movies (*George Wallace* and *GIA*). The daughter of Oscar-winner Jon Voight, she once admitted, "I love my father, but I'm not him."

IRVING G. THALBERG MEMORIAL AWARD
WARREN BEATTY (B. 1937)

Best friend Jack Nicholson introduced Beatty with a promise: "There will be no sex jokes."

Despite fourteen Oscar nominations and a Best Director win for *Reds* in 1982, Beatty's reputation as a lady-killer often superseded his enormous talent. Following tributes from Beatty's former co-stars, Nicholson went on to say, "Because of all these things, and because he's been such a good friend, and because we almost lost him to politics [Beatty had considered a run for the presidency], I present this award." "If I had to choose between this and the White House," said Beatty, "I think I'd stick to this."

Shirley MacLaine's younger, charismatic brother got his big break opposite Natalie Wood in Elia Kazan's *Splendor in the Grass* (1961). He broke out with his famous performance in *Bonnie and Clyde* (1967), after which he took a hiatus from films and returned to star in *The Only Game in Town* (1970), Robert Altman's *McCabe and Mrs. Miller* (1971), *The Parallax View* (1974), *The Fortune* (1975), *Shampoo* (1975, which he produced), *Heaven Can Wait* (1978), and *Reds* (1981, Oscar). (For more on Beatty, see 1961.)

Michael J. Pollard, Faye Dunaway, Warren Beatty, Estelle Parsons, Gene Hackman in Bonnie and Clyde

PICTURE
AMERICAN BEAUTY, Bruce Cohen and Dan Jinks, DreamWorks
THE CIDER HOUSE RULES, Richard N. Gladstein, Miramax Films
THE GREEN MILE, David Valdes and Frank Darabont, Warner Bros.
THE INSIDER, Michael Mann and Pieter Jan Brugge, Buena Vista
THE SIXTH SENSE, Frank Marshall, Kathleen Kennedy and Barry Mendel, Buena Vista

ACTOR
RUSSELL CROWE, *The Insider*, Buena Vista
RICHARD FARNSWORTH, *The Straight Story*, Buena Vista
SEAN PENN, *Sweet and Lowdown*, Sony Pictures Classics
KEVIN SPACEY, *American Beauty*, DreamWorks
DENZEL WASHINGTON, *The Hurricane*, Universal and Beacon

ACTRESS
ANNETTE BENING, *American Beauty*, DreamWorks
JANET MCTEER, *Tumbleweeds*, Fine Line Features
JULIANNE MOORE, *The End of the Affair*, Columbia
MERYL STREEP, *Music of the Heart*, Miramax Films
HILARY SWANK, *Boys Don't Cry*, Fox Searchlight

SUPPORTING ACTOR
MICHAEL CAINE, *The Cider House Rules*, Miramax Films
TOM CRUISE, *Magnolia*, New Line
MICHAEL CLARKE DUNCAN, *The Green Mile*, Warner Bros.
JUDE LAW, *The Talented Mr. Ripley*, Paramount and Miramax
HALEY JOEL OSMENT, *The Sixth Sense*, Buena Vista

SUPPORTING ACTRESS
TONI COLLETTE, *The Sixth Sense*, Buena Vista
ANGELINA JOLIE, *Girl Interrupted*, Columbia
CATHERINE KEENER, *Being John Malkovich*, USA Films
SAMANTHA MORTON, *Sweet and Lowdown*, Sony Pictures Classics
CHLOË SEVIGNY, *Boys Don't Cry*, Fox Searchlight

DIRECTION
AMERICAN BEAUTY, Sam Mendes, DreamWorks
BEING JOHN MALKOVICH, Spike Jonze, USA Films
THE CIDER HOUSE RULES, Lasse Hallström, Miramax Films
THE INSIDER, Michael Mann, Buena Vista
THE SIXTH SENSE, M. Night Shyamalan, Buena Vista

WRITING: BASED ON MATERIAL PREVIOUSLY PRODUCED OR PUBLISHED
THE CIDER HOUSE RULES, John Irving, Miramax Films
ELECTION, Alexander Payne, Jim Taylor, Paramount
THE GREEN MILE, Frank Darabont, Warner Bros.
THE INSIDER, Eric Roth, Michael Mann, Buena Vista

THE TALENTED MR. RIPLEY, Anthony Minghella, Paramount and Miramax

WRITING: DIRECTLY FOR THE SCREEN
AMERICAN BEAUTY, Alan Ball, DreamWorks
BEING JOHN MALKOVICH, Charlie Kaufman, USA Films
MAGNOLIA, Paul Thomas Anderson, New Line
THE SIXTH SENSE, M. Night Shyamalan, Buena Vista
TOPSY-TURVY, Mike Leigh, USA Films

CINEMATOGRAPHY
AMERICAN BEAUTY, Conrad L. Hall, DreamWorks
THE END OF THE AFFAIR, Roger Pratt, Columbia
THE INSIDER, Dante Spinotti, Buena Vista
SLEEPY HOLLOW, Emmanuel Lubezki, Paramount and Mandalay
SNOW FALLING ON CEDARS, Robert Richardson, Universal

ART DIRECTION—SET DECORATION
ANNA AND THE KING, Luciana Arrighi, Fox 2000
THE CIDER HOUSE RULES, David Gropman, Miramax Films
SLEEPY HOLLOW, Rick Heinrichs, Paramount and Mandalay
THE TALENTED MR. RIPLEY, Roy Walker, Paramount and Miramax
TOPSY-TURVY, Eve Stewart, USA Films

COSTUME DESIGN
ANNA AND THE KING, Jenny Beavan, Fox 2000
SLEEPY HOLLOW, Colleen Atwood, Paramount and Mandalay
THE TALENTED MR. RIPLEY, Ann Roth, Gary Jones, Paramount and Miramax
TITUS, Milena Canonero, Fox Searchlight
TOPSY-TURVY, Lindy Hemming, USA Films

SOUND
THE GREEN MILE, Michael Herbick, Willie D. Burton, Warner Bros.
THE INSIDER, Andy Nelson, Doug Hemphill, Lee Orloff, Buena Vista
THE MATRIX, John Reitz, Gregg Rudloff, David Campbell, David Lee, Warner Bros.
THE MUMMY, Leslie Shatz, Chris Carpenter, Rick Kline, Chris Munro, Universal
STAR WARS EPISODE I: THE PHANTOM MENACE, Gary Rydstrom, Tom Johnson, Shawn Murphy, John Midgley, Fox 2000

SOUND EDITING
FIGHT CLUB, Ren Klyce, Richard Hymns, Fox 2000
THE MATRIX, Dane A. Davis, Warner Bros.
STAR WARS EPISODE I: THE PHANTOM MENACE, Ben Burtt, Tom Bellfort, Fox 2000

SOUND EFFECTS EDITING
FIGHT CLUB, Ren Klyce, Richard Hymns, Fox 2000
THE MATRIX, Dane A. Davis, Warner Bros.
STAR WARS EPISODE I: THE PHANTOM MENACE, Ben Burtt, Tom Bellfort, Fox 2000

FILM EDITING
AMERICAN BEAUTY, Tariq Anwar, Christopher Greenbury, DreamWorks
THE CIDER HOUSE RULES, Lisa Zeno Churgin, Miramax Films
THE INSIDER, William Goldenberg, Paul Rubell, David Rosenbloom, Buena Vista
THE MATRIX, Zach Staenberg, Warner Bros.
THE SIXTH SENSE, Andrew Mondshein, Buena Vista

SONG
SOUTH PARK: BIGGER, LONGER & UNCUT, Trey Parker, Marc Shaiman [Song: "Blame Canada"] Paramount and Warner Bros.
MUSIC OF THE HEART, Diane Warren [Song: "Music of My Heart"] Miramax Films

MAGNOLIA, Aimee Mann [Song: "Save Me"] New Line
TOY STORY 2, Randy Newman [Song: "When She Loved Me"] Buena Vista
TARZAN, Phil Collins [Song: "You'll Be in My Heart"] Buena Vista

SCORING: ORIGINAL MUSIC
AMERICAN BEAUTY, Thomas Newman, DreamWorks
ANGELA'S ASHES, John Williams, Paramount-Universal Pictures International
THE CIDER HOUSE RULES, Rachel Portman, Miramax Films
THE RED VIOLIN, John Corigliano, Lions Gate Films
THE TALENTED MR. RIPLEY, Gabriel Yared, Paramount and Miramax

MAKEUP
AUSTIN POWERS: THE SPY WHO SHAGGED ME, Michèle Burke, Mike Smithson, New Line
BICENTENNIAL MAN, Greg Cannom, Buena Vista
LIFE, Rick Baker, Universal
TOPSY-TURVY, Christine Blundell, Trefor Proud, USA Films

SHORT FILMS: ANIMATED
HUMDRUM, Peter Peake, Aardman Animations Limited
MY GRANDMOTHER IRONED THE KING'S SHIRTS, Torill Kove, National Film Board of Canada & Studio Magica a.s.
THE OLD MAN AND THE SEA, Alexander Petrov, Productions Pascal Blais/Imagica Corp./Dentsu Tech./NHK Enterprise 21/ Panorama Studio of Yaroslavl
3 MISSES, Paul Driessen, CinéTé Film
WHEN THE DAY BREAKS, Wendy Tilby, Amanda Forbis, National Film Board of Canada

SHORT FILMS: LIVE ACTION
BROR, MIN BROR *(Teis and Nico)*, Henrik Ruben Genz, Michael W. Horsten, Nimbus Film and Dansk Novellefilm
KILLING JOE, Mehdi Norowzian, Steve Wax, Joy Films and Chelsea Pictures
KLEINGELD (SMALL CHANGE), Marc-Andreas Bochert, Gabriele Lins, Die Hochschule für Film und Fernsehen "Konrad Wolf" Potsdam-Babelsberg
MAJOR AND MINOR MIRACLES, Marcus Olsson, Dramatiska Institutet
MY MOTHER DREAMS THE SATAN'S DISCIPLES IN NEW YORK, Barbara Schock, Tammy Tiehel, Kickstart

DOCUMENTARY: FEATURE
BUENA VISTA SOCIAL CLUB, Road Movies
GENGHIS BLUES, Wadi Rum
ON THE ROPES, Highway Films
ONE DAY IN SEPTEMBER, Arthur Cohn
SPEAKING IN STRINGS, Counter Point Films

DOCUMENTARY: SHORT SUBJECTS
EYEWITNESS, Marbert Art Foundation
KING GIMP, Whiteford-Hadary/University of Maryland/Tapestry International
THE WILDEST SHOW IN THE SOUTH: THE ANGOLA PRISON RODEO, Gabriel Films

FOREIGN LANGUAGE FILM
ALL ABOUT MY MOTHER, Sony Pictures Classics
CARAVAN, Les Productions de la Guéville/ Les Productions JMH/Antelope (UK) Limited/National Studio Limted/Bac Films Production
EAST-WEST, Sony Pictures Classics
SOLOMON AND GAENOR, Sony Pictures Classics
UNDER THE SUN, Sweetwater AB Production

HONORARY AWARDS
To ANDRZEJ WAJDA in recognition of five decades of extraordinary film direction.
To FPC, INCORPORATED, under the leadership of BARRY M. STULTZ and MILTON JAN FRIEDMAN, for the development and implementation of an environmentally responsible program to recycle or destroy discarded motion picture prints.

To EDMUND M. DI GIULIO and TAKUO MIYAGISHIMA in appreciation for outstanding service and dedication in upholding the high standards of the Academy of Motion Picture Arts and Sciences.

IRVING G. THALBERG MEMORIAL AWARD
WARREN BEATTY

GORDON E. SAWYER AWARD
RODERICK T. RYAN

SCIENTIFIC OR TECHNICAL: SCIENTIFIC AND ENGINEERING AWARD
Stage Operations, NICK PHILLIPS
Camera, FRITZ GABRIEL BAUER; IAIN NEIL, RICK GELBARD and PANAVISION, INC.
Sound, HUW GWILYM, KARL LYNCH and MARK V. CRABTREE
Lenses and Filters, JAMES MOULTRIE, MIKE SALTER and MARK CRAIG GERCHMAN; and NAT TIFFEN
Projection, MARLOWE A. PICHEL; and L. RON SCHMIDT

SCIENTIFIC OR TECHNICAL: TECHNICAL ACHIEVEMENT AWARD
Sound, VIVIENNE DYER and CHRIS WOOLF; and LESLIE DREVER
Lenses and Filters, RICHARD C. SEHLIN and DR. MITCHELL J. BOGDANOWICZ and MARY L. SCHMOEGER
Laboratory, HOYT H. YEATMAN, JR.

VISUAL EFFECTS
THE MATRIX, John Gaeta, Janek Sirrs, Steve Courtley, Jon Thum, Warner Bros.
STAR WARS EPISODE I: THE PHANTOM MENACE, John Knoll, Dennis Muren, Scott Squires, Rob Coleman, 20th (*)
STUART LITTLE, John Dykstra, Jerome Chen, Henry F. Anderson III, Eric Allard, Columbia

ABOVE: Renee Zellweger shines in a lemon-yellow vintage gown by Jean Desses. (2001)

BELOW: Swathed in a column of pale pink ruffles, Nicole Kidman is luminous in this glamorous and thoroughly romantic dress. (2002)

ABOVE: Halle Berry is utterly beguiling in this embroidered, sleeveless gown that shows off her perfect figure. (2002)

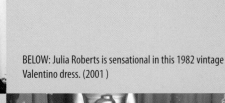

BELOW: Julia Roberts is sensational in this 1982 vintage Valentino dress. (2001)

THE LOOK OF THE DECADE

THE ONSET OF THE NEW MILLENNIUM was ushered in with much ceremony, but there was no sea change in the world of fashion. People did not start wearing silver spacesuits or begin donning futuristic outfits worthy of an episode of "The Jetsons," as many might have predicted. Instead, fashion began drawing on all the looks of the previous century, initiating an "anything goes" ethos in the world of style. Wearing vintage clothing, a trend that hadn't yet gone mainstream, was thrust into the spotlight as celebrities began showing up at the Oscars ceremonies in rare vintage finds. While anything was acceptable during the day, femininity and romance were hallmarks of the new style of dress for evening. Actresses evoked glamour in delicately pretty and romantic gowns, both new and old, that recalled the fashions of almost a century ago.

OPPOSITE: Like the woman herself, Björk's dress is thoroughly irreverent and flies in the face of convention. (2001)

2000

"I love it up here!"

—Julia Roberts

CROWE'S FEAT

CEREMONY: March 25, 2001
Shrine Auditorium, Los Angeles
HOST: Steve Martin

ith three Best Picture nominees bunched together at the starting gate, this was a "coin toss" year—no guaranteed sweep for *Gladiator*, *Traffic*, or *Crouching Tiger, Hidden Dragon*, the surprise martial-arts hit, up for both Best Picture and Best Foreign Film. Despite the tight contest, there was minimal excitement for all the nominees. Wisely, the show's producers focused on the evening's entertainment quotient and chose perhaps the funniest man in Hollywood to host, Steve Martin. "Over 800 million people are watching the telecast over the world, and right now every one of them is thinking the exact same thing: that we're all gay," Martin said. And with that opening crack he was off and running: "Hollywood is about all of us working together for one common love…publicity." The audience was forced to laugh loudly at itself. He even joked about the headline-making kidnapping attempt on *Gladiator*'s Russell Crowe: "The FBI has announced a suspect…and all I can say is, Tom Hanks, you should be ashamed of yourself." Hanks played along, making a contrite face for the camera. There was one big upset, and it came early. Kate Hudson had a lock on following in the footsteps of her mom, Goldie Hawn, by picking up Best Supporting Actress for her debut splash in *Almost Famous*. Hudson was all set to pop out of her seat as the envelope was opened. Then, a collective gasp; the winner was the relatively unknown Marcia Gay Harden for *Pollock*. Afterward, the ceremony coasted along on Martin's ripostes, reaching a fever pitch when Icelandic rock star/actress Bjork came out to perform the nominated dirge "I've Seen It All" from her film *Dancer in the Dark*. She was costumed in a bizarre papier-mâché swan with a wraparound neck. "I was going to wear my swan, too," Martin deadpanned, "But it was so…last year." John read the annual roll call of recently departed, which included Loretta Young, Alec Guinness, and the beloved Walter Matthau. A moment of silence was followed by a tribute to special Honoree, 84-year-old screenwriter Ernest Lehman (*The Sweet Smell of Success*, 1957; *North by Northwest*, 1959; *The Sound of Music*, 1965). Martin reminded the audience that at the beginning of the long evening, Lehman had been 24. Another honorary award went to cinematographer Jack Cardiff (*The African Queen*, 1951; *War and Peace*, 1956). Then, the Thalberg Memorial to Dino De Laurentiis, the last of the old-school showmen producers, with more than 600 films to his credit. Finally the ceremony sped to a climax, with the big prizes going to Julia Roberts; Russell Crowe, whose compelling performance was credited with putting *Gladiator* on the Oscar map; Steven Soderbergh for his direction of *Traffic*, and *Gladiator* for Best Picture. The face of its Oscar-snubbed director, Ridley Scott, was set in the imperious scowl of a fallen Caesar.

BEST PICTURE
GLADIATOR

"The story line is *Rocky* on downers," quipped Roger Ebert, who was no great fan of the Oscar winner. In his tale of betrayal and revenge in ancient Rome, director Ridley Scott's intention was to match the intensity of *Saving Private Ryan*: "Steven Spielberg set the new standard for battle scenes. They used to be just wide shots, like a ballet or a dance. Now you can take the audience inside the battle, like *Ryan* did. It's right in your lap in the theater." But for all that, this $100 million return to the "toga and sandals" spectacular of the 1950s couldn't have clicked without Crowe. Many critics concurred that Crowe *was* the movie. "Crowe has a patent on heroic plausibility… with him in the leading role, *Gladiator* doesn't have much to worry about," said Kenneth Turan of the *Los Angeles Times*. He also had high praise for Scott, who "has demonstrated a wonderful gift for ambiance, for making out-of-the-ordinary worlds come alive on the screen." While

Russell Crowe (right)

Ebert continued his criticism—"This is more like 'Spartacus Lite.' Or dark"—others, particularly the Academy, disagreed. The *San Francisco Chronicle* pronounced, "This Ridley Scott film, his best in years, re-envisions ancient Rome for the aughts and makes it safe to go back in the Colosseum."

The envelope, please...

Director Steven Soderbergh (center) with Michael Douglas (right)

BEST DIRECTOR
STEVEN SODERBERGH
(B. 1963)
TRAFFIC

"For someone my age, it's a lot easier to get drugs than it is to get alcohol," says a high-school student in *Traffic*.

Traffic, the film, was inspired by a five-part *Masterpiece Theater* series entitled *Traffik*, which ran ten years ago and traced the movement of heroin from the poppy fields of Turkey to the streets of Europe. In the film, all that had to be changed was the setting—North America. "Like Martin Scorsese's *GoodFellas*, *Traffic* is fascinating at one level simply because it shows how things work—how the

drugs are marketed, how the laws are sidestepped," wrote Roger Ebert in the *Chicago Sun-Times*. Soderbergh, whose *Erin Brockovich* was also released this year, has not only become a very accomplished director but has done some of his own camerawork as well. Under the pseudonym Peter Andrews, Soderbergh has done some very unusual, Costa-Gavras *Z*-style, hand-held, documentary-style filming. Soderbergh's first major break came in 1986, when he shot a full-length concert film for the rock group, Yes, which eventually earned him a Grammy nomination for the video. Recognition as an interesting young filmmaker came with the release of *sex, lies, and videotape* (1989), a film that earned him the Cannes Film Festival's Palme d'Or Award, the Independent Spirit Award for Best Director, and an Oscar nomination for Best Original Screenplay. Over the next six years he made such films as *Kafka* (1991), *King of the Hill* (1993), *Underneath* (1994) and *Gray's Anatomy* (1996). In 1998 Soderbergh made *Out of Sight*, his most critically and commercially successful film since *sex, lies, and videotape*.

BEST ACTOR
RUSSELL CROWE (B. 1964)
GLADIATOR

"If you grow up in the suburbs of anywhere, a dream like this seems kind of vaguely ludicrous and completely unattainable...but for anybody who's on the downside of advantage, and relying purely on courage, it's possible."

When Scott first discovered Crowe in 1992's *Romper Stomper*, he thought, This guy is an animal. "Only later when I met him did I realize how smart and articulate he was," Scott said.

In *Gladiator*, Crowe plays the hero, Maximus, a general from Spain. He is a favorite of the dying emperor Marcus

Aurelius (Richard Harris), who wants to pass the crown to Crowe, rather than to his own sons. "Watching him here," wrote Mick LaSalle of the *San Francisco Chronicle*, "it's clear that Crowe has that thing Gable had and Sean Connery has." Rumor had it that Crowe was a bad boy on the set and turned the shooting of *Gladiator* into "his own version of the Fall of the Roman Empire," recalled LaSalle. "But his temperament gives the picture a center: Maximus looks as if he has a thousand things on his mind, most of them unpleasant." The son of New Zealand film caterers, Crowe spent his early years dreaming of becoming another Elvis. But singing gave way to acting, and Hollywood couldn't get enough of him. In *L.A. Confidential* (1997) he appeared as a brutish but gold-hearted cop; he aged thirty years for his role in *The Insider* (2000), and finally created a fully dimensional, sensual alpha male for *Gladiator*. His charm could turn taciturn in a flash, as when he was asked by the press corps how he got to the heart of his character. "I'm an actor," he bristled. "I read the script, I learn the lines, I put the costume on, and Bob's your uncle."

BEST OF 2000
Best Picture: *Gladiator*
Best Director: Steven Soderbergh, *Traffic*
Best Actor: Russell Crowe, *Gladiator*
Best Actress: Julia Roberts, *Erin Brockovich*
Best Supporting Actor: Benicio Del Toro, *Traffic*
Best Supporting Actress: Marcia Gay Harden, *Pollock*

FIRSTS
- Steven Soderbergh's double Best Director nomination (*Traffic*, *Erin Brockovich*) was the first since 1938 when Michael Curtiz pulled it off for *Angels with Dirty Faces* and *Four Daughters*. (Curtiz didn't manage to win for either.)
- For the first time in fifty-one years, the Best Picture winner didn't pick up an additional Oscar for director or screenplay.

ROLE REVERSAL
Braveheart on the Tiber? The role of *Gladiator*'s Maximus was originally offered to Mel Gibson.

SIN OF OMISSION
Julia Roberts thanked everyone in her acceptance speech except the real Erin Brockovich. When she was later reminded of her gaffe, Roberts promised to "send her something special."

UNMENTIONABLES
- Oliver Reed died before his scenes in *Gladiator* were completed. His head was superimposed on a stand-in's body.
- Aside from his Oscar, Russell Crowe was rewarded for his work on *Gladiator* with a broken foot bone, a fractured hip, and a punctured cheek.
- "There have been reports that the badly behaved Mr. Crowe turned the shooting of *Gladiator* into his own version of the Fall of the Roman Empire," wrote Elvis Mitchell in the *New York Times*.
- A chorus of "foul play" went up when deep-pocketed Miramax was accused of "buying" the nomination for *Chocolat*.
- Steve Martin singled out Mike Myers with mock astonishment for "refusing to do a movie because the script wasn't good enough. What Hollywood is he in?" asked Martin.

BEST ACTRESS
JULIA ROBERTS (B. 1967)
ERIN BROCKOVICH

"Turn that clock off, it's making me nervous!" chided Roberts (giggling) to the man with the stopwatch. "I have some things to say." And with that she rambled prettily, admitting that she'd probably "never have the chance to be up here again." Since inhabiting the role of Erin Brockovich ("She even got the cleavage right!" said the real-life Erin), Roberts had the Oscar wrap as far as the reviews were concerned. "Roberts, in her most forceful, dramatic performance, allows us to take in every moment with fresh, impassioned eyes," wrote Owen Gleiberman in *Entertainment Weekly*. After two previous nominations for *Steel Magnolias* (1989) and *Pretty Woman* (1990), the reigning box-office queen was ready for her coronation. With her massive hair bun and vintage Oscar de la Renta, she looked every inch the part.

BEST SUPPORTING ACTOR
BENICIO DEL TORO (B. 1966)
TRAFFIC

After a very brief "Thank you," New Jersey-born Del Toro strode off briskly with his gold statuette. Inspired by Brando at an early age, Del Toro had the mark of a screen icon in the making in his performances in *The Usual Suspects* (1995) and *Fear and Loathing in Las Vegas* (1998). Almost unheard of for an actor, he asked *Traffic* director Soderbergh to cut much of his dialogue so that his face and his body could better reveal the heart of his character. The *Washington Post* declared, "As Javier Rodriguez, a Mexican policeman caught between overwhelming corruption and his granite-encased integrity, Del Toro's the best reason to watch this movie."

Marcia Gay Harden (center)

BEST SUPPORTING ACTRESS
MARCIA GAY HARDEN (B. 1959)
POLLOCK

The surprise winner weaved her way to the stage, looking as dumbfounded as the audience. "If I ever won an Oscar, I always said I'd thank all the waitresses who covered for me when I went to auditions—but I only had forty-five seconds." A Navy brat born in Japan, Harden was best known for her stage work until her appearance in *Miller's Crossing* (1990). She and Ed Harris met while doing a play, and the instant chemistry made her a natural choice for the role of Lee Krasner, the long-suffering wife of alcoholic artist Jackson Pollock. "The pleasure of watching Harris and Harden play figures of such stature without a trace of sentimentality is enormous," wrote Stephen Holden in the *New York Times*.

PICTURE
CHOCOLAT, David Brown, Kit Golden and Leslie Holleran, Miramax Films
CROUCHING TIGER, HIDDEN DRAGON, Bill Kong, Hsu Li Kong and Ang Lee, Sony Pictures Classics
ERIN BROCKOVICH, Danny DeVito, Michael Shamberg and Stacey Sher, Universal and Columbia
GLADIATOR, Douglas Wick, David Franzoni and Branko Lustig, DreamWorks and Universal
TRAFFIC, Edward Zwick, Marshall Herskovitz and Laura Bickford, USA Films

ACTOR
JAVIER BARDEM, *Before Night Falls*, Fine Line Features
RUSSELL CROWE, *Gladiator*, DreamWorks and Universal
TOM HANKS, *Castaway*, Fox 2000 and DreamWorks
ED HARRIS, *Pollock*, Sony Pictures Classics
GEOFFREY RUSH, *Quills*, Fox Searchlight

SUPPORTING ACTOR
JEFF BRIDGES, *The Contender*, DreamWorks and Cinerenta/Cinecontender
WILLEM DAFOE, *Shadow of the Vampire*, Lions Gate Films
BENICIO DEL TORO, *Traffic*, USA Films
ALBERT FINNEY, *Erin Brockovich*, Universal and Columbia
JOAQUIN PHOENIX, *Gladiator*, DreamWorks and Universal

ACTRESS
JOAN ALLEN, *The Contender*, DreamWorks and Cinerenta/Cinecontender
JULIETTE BINOCHE, *Chocolat*, Miramax Films
ELLEN BURSTYN, *Requiem for a Dream*, Artisan
LAURA LINNEY, *You Can Count on Me*, Paramount Classics/Shooting Gallery/Hart Sharp Entertainment in association with Cappa Productions
JULIA ROBERTS, *Erin Brockovich*, Universal and Columbia

SUPPORTING ACTRESS
JUDI DENCH, *Chocolat*, Miramax Films
MARCIA GAY HARDEN, *Pollock*, Sony Pictures Classics
KATE HUDSON, *Almost Famous*, DreamWorks and Columbia
FRANCES McDORMAND, *Almost Famous*, DreamWorks and Columbia
JULIE WATERS, *Billy Elliot*, Universal Focus

DIRECTION
BILLY ELLIOT, Stephen Daldry, Universal Focus
CROUCHING TIGER, HIDDEN DRAGON, Ang Lee, Sony Pictures Classics
ERIN BROCKOVICH, Steven Soderbergh, Universal and Columbia
GLADIATOR, Ridley Scott, DreamWorks and Universal
TRAFFIC, Steven Soderbergh, USA Films

WRITING: BASED ON MATERIAL PREVIOUSLY PRODUCED OR PUBLISHED
CHOCOLAT, Robert Nelson Jacobs, Miramax Films
CROUCHING TIGER, HIDDEN DRAGON, Wang Hui Ling, James Schamus, Tsai Kuo Jung, Sony Pictures Classics
O BROTHER, WHERE ART THOU?, Ethan Coen, Joel Coen, Buena Vista

TRAFFIC, Stephen Gaghan, USA Films
WONDER BOYS, Steve Kloves, Paramount and Mutual Film Company

WRITING: DIRECTLY FOR THE SCREEN
ALMOST FAMOUS, Cameron Crowe, DreamWorks and Columbia
BILLY ELLIOT, Lee Hall, Universal Focus
ERIN BROCKOVICH, Susannah Grant, Universal and Columbia
GLADIATOR, David Franzoni, John Logan, William Nicholson, DreamWorks and Universal
YOU CAN COUNT ON ME, Kenneth Lonergan, Paramount Classics/Shooting Gallery/Hart Sharp Entertainment in association with Cappa Productions

CINEMATOGRAPHY
CROUCHING TIGER, HIDDEN DRAGON, Peter Pau, Sony Pictures Classics
GLADIATOR, John Mathieson, DreamWorks and Universal
MALÈNA, Lajos Kotai, Miramax Films
O BROTHER, WHERE ART THOU?, Roger Deakins, Buena Vista
THE PATRIOT, Caleb Deschanel, Sony Pictures Releasing

ART DIRECTION—SET DECORATION
CROUCHING TIGER, HIDDEN DRAGON, Tim Yip, Sony Pictures Classics
DR. SEUSS' HOW THE GRINCH STOLE CHRISTMAS, Michael Corenblith, Universal
GLADIATOR, Arthur Max; DreamWorks and Universal
QUILLS, Martin Childs, Fox Searchlight
VATEL, Jean Rabasse, Miramax Films

COSTUME DESIGN
CROUCHING TIGER, HIDDEN DRAGON, Tim Yip, Sony Pictures Classics
DR. SEUSS' HOW THE GRINCH STOLE CHRISTMAS, Rita Ryack, Universal
GLADIATOR, Janty Yates, DreamWorks and Universal
102 DALMATIANS, Anthony Powell, Buena Vista
QUILLS, Jacqueline West, Fox Searchlight

SOUND
CAST AWAY, Randy Thom, Tom Johnson, Dennis Sands, William B. Kaplan, Fox 2000 and DreamWorks
GLADIATOR, Scott Millan Bob Beemer, Ken Weston, DreamWorks and Universal
THE PATRIOT, Kevin O'Connell, Greg P. Russell, Lee Orloff, Sony Pictures Releasing
THE PERFECT STORM, John Reitz, Gregg Rudloff, David Campbell, Keith A. Wester, Warner Bros.
U-571, Steve Maslow, Gregg Landaker, Rick Kline, Ivan Sharrock, Universal and Studio Canal

FILM EDITING
ALMOST FAMOUS, Joe Hutshing, Saar Klein, DreamWorks and Columbia
CROUCHING TIGER, HIDDEN DRAGON, Tim Squyres, Sony Pictures Classics
GLADIATOR, Pietro Scalia, DreamWorks and Universal
TRAFFIC, Stephen Mirrione, USA Films
WONDER BOYS, Dede Allen, Paramount and Mutual Film Company

SOUND EFFECTS EDITING
SPACE COWBOYS, Alan Robert Murray, Bub Asman, Warner Bros.
U-571, Jon Johnson, Universal and Studio Canal

VISUAL EFFECTS
GLADIATOR, John Nelson, Neil Corbould, Tim Burke, Rob Harvey, DreamWorks and Universal
HOLLOW MAN, Scott E. Anderson, Craig Hayes, Scott Stokdyk, Stan Parks, Sony Pictures Releasing
THE PERFECT STORM, Stefen Fangmeier, Habib Zargarpour, John Frazier, Walt Conti, Warner Bros.

SONG
MEET THE PARENTS, Randy Newman [Song: "A Fool in Love"] Universal and DreamWorks
DANCER IN THE DARK, Björk, Lars von Trier, Sjon Sigurdsson [Song: "I've Seen It All"] Fine Line Features

CROUCHING TIGER, HIDDEN DRAGON, Jorge Calandrelli, Tan Dun, James Schamus [Song: "A Love Before Time"] Sony Pictures Classics
THE EMPEROR'S NEW GROOVE, Sting, David Hartley [Song: "My Funny Friend and Me"] Buena Vista
WONDER BOYS, Bob Dylan [Song: "Things Have Changed"] Paramount and Mutual Film Company

SCORING: ORIGINAL MUSIC
CHOCOLAT, Rachel Portman, Miramax Films
CROUCHING TIGER, HIDDEN DRAGON, Tan Dun, Sony Pictures Classics
GLADIATOR, Hans Zimmer, DreamWorks and Universal
MALÈNA, Ennio Morricone, Miramax Films
THE PATRIOT, John Williams, Sony Pictures Releasing

MAKEUP
THE CELL, Michèle Burke, Edouard Henriques, New Line
DR. SEUSS' HOW THE GRINCH STOLE CHRISTMAS, Rick Baker, Gail Ryan, Universal
SHADOW OF THE VAMPIRE, Ann Buchanan, Amber Sibley, Lions Gate Films

SHORT FILMS: ANIMATED
FATHER AND DAUGHTER, Michael Dudok de Wit, CinéTé Filmproductie bv/ Cloudrunner Ltd.
THE PERIWIG-MAKER, Steffen Schäffler, Annete Schäffler, Ideal Standard Film
REJECTED, Don Hertzfeldt, Bitter Films

SHORT FILMS: LIVE ACTION
BY COURIER, Peter Riegert, Ericka Frederick, Two Tequila
ONE DAY CROSSING, Joan Stein, Christina Lazaridi, Open Eyes
QUIERO SER (I WANT TO BE...), Florian Gallenberger, Mondragon Films
SERAGLIO, Gail Lerner, Colin Campbell, Seraglio
A SOCCER STORY (UMA HISTORIA DE FUTEBOL), Paulo Machline, UM Filmes

DOCUMENTARY: SHORT SUBJECTS
BIG MAMA, Birthmark
CURTAIN CALL, NJN/White Whale
DOLPHINS, MacGillivray Freeman Films
THE MAN ON LINCOLN'S NOSE, Adama Films
ON TIPTOE: GENTLE STEPS TO FREEDOM, On Tip Toe

DOCUMENTARY: FEATURE
INTO THE ARMS OF STRANGERS STORIES OF THE KINDER-TRANSPORT, Warner Bros. Legacy, Nomadic Pictures
LONG NIGHT'S JOURNEY INTO DAY, Iris Films
SCOTTSBORO: AN AMERICAN TRAGEDY, Social Media
SOUND AND FURY, Aronson Film Associates and Public Policy

FOREIGN LANGUAGE FILM
AMORES PERROS, Lions Gate Films
CROUCHING TIGER, HIDDEN DRAGON, Sony Pictures Classics
DIVIDED WE FALL, Sony Pictures Classics
EVERYBODY FAMOUS!, Miramax Films
THE TASTE OF OTHERS, Offline Entertainment and Miramax Zoë

HONORARY AWARDS
To JACK CARDIFF, master of light and color.
To ERNEST LEHMAN, in appreciation of a body of varied and enduring work.
To IOAN ALLEN for the concept, ROBIN BRANSBURY for the design and MARK HARRAH for the implementation of the Trailer Audio Standards Association (TASA) Loudness Standard.
To N. PAUL KENWORTHY, JR. in appreciation for outstanding service and dedication in upholding the high standards of the Academy of Motion Picture Arts and Sciences.

IRVING G. THALBERG MEMORIAL AWARD
DINO DE LAURENTIIS

GORDON E. SAWYER AWARD
IRWIN W. YOUNG

SCIENTIFIC OR TECHNICAL: ACADEMY AWARD OF MERIT
Special Photographic, ROB COOK, LOREN CARPENTER and ED CATMULL

SCIENTIFIC OR TECHNICAL: SCIENTIFIC AND ENGINEERING AWARD
Camera, AL MAYER, SR. and AL MAYER, JR., IAIN NEIL and BRIAN DANG; ALVAH J. MILLER and PAUL JOHNSON
Laboratory, JOE WARY, GERALD PAINTER and COLIN F. MOSSMAN
Sound, AKAI DIGITAL; FAIRLIGHT; ADSG and TIMLINE, INCORPORATED

SCIENTIFIC OR TECHNICAL: TECHNICAL ACHIEVEMENT AWARD
Lighting, LEONARD PINCUS, ASHOT NALBANDYAN, GEORGE JOHNSON, THOMAS KONG and DAVID PRINGLE
Stage Operations, VIC ARMSTRONG; PHILIP GREENSTREET
Lenses and Filters, UDO SCHAUSS, HILDEGARD EBBESMEIER and KARL LENHARDT, RALF LINN and NORBERT BRINKER; GLENN M. BERGGREN, HORST LINGE and WOLFGANG REINECKE
Systems, BILL TONDREAU, ALVAH J. MILLER and PAUL JOHNSON and DAVID STUMP
Special Photographic, VENKAT KRISHNAMURTHY; and GEORGE BORSHUKOV, KIM LIBRERI and DAN PIPONI
Laboratory, JOHN P. PYTLAK

2001

*I*n a year of few monumental films or performances, the Academy Awards compensated by making history. The evening began with Whoopi Goldberg's dazzling descent from the flies in a *Moulin Rouge*-inspired concoction of eye-poking gold feathers. "Come and get me, boys!" she exclaimed. The first upset, Best Supporting Actor Jim Broadbent over heavy favorite Ian McKellen, signaled a sea change. Then it was two loners who rocked the Kodak. The first was Woody Allen, in a once-in-a-lifetime surprise appearance at the Awards. He responded to the ovation in typical Allen fashion: "That makes up for the strip search."

Next up was Oscar honoree Sidney Poitier, the pioneering black actor who single-handedly broke the stereotypic mold. His eloquent gratitude to all who helped make him a unique star was a harbinger of the historic turn the evening would take. Any pretense of composure evaporated when Halle Berry was announced as Best Actress. The beautiful 35-year-old, overcome with emotion, understood the full import of her selection. As she wept, even the most hardened industry veterans in the audience melted. It was the night's indelible moment. But there was more magic to come. The Best Actor Oscar was Russell Crowe's to lose. He had it wrapped with a bow—or so random polls had it—until his highly publicized bad boy antics caused Academy voters to change their minds and vote their hearts. The gold went to Denzel Washington. His emotional fervor couldn't match Berry's but his acceptance was an exercise in pure class, culminating in an Oscar salute to Poitier.

Dogged veteran director Ron Howard finally received his due along with his finely crafted *A Beautiful Mind*. Whatever else might be forgotten in fifty years or even five, the image of a near-catatonic Halle Berry clutching her Academy Award would be forever imprinted on Oscar's memory. Hollywood may have been grossly late in coming to it, but the last barrier had finally been broken.

A BEAUTIFUL CHANGE OF MIND

CEREMONY: March 24, 2002
Kodak Theatre, Hollywood
HOST: Whoopi Goldberg

BEST PICTURE/BEST DIRECTOR
RON HOWARD (B. 1954)
A BEAUTIFUL MIND

"Well, I am not a good enough actor anymore to be able to stand up here and make you believe that I haven't imagined this moment in my mind over the years and played it out about a thousand times," Howard said in his acceptance speech.

The biopic seemed to be in the bag if for no other reason than this was the Academy's most frequently awarded genre. The critics hated to love it, but, for the most part, they did. Kenneth Turan of the *Los Angeles Times* wrote, "There is more to admire in *A Beautiful Mind* than you might suspect, but less than its creators believe. When the film does succeed, it almost seems to do so despite itself, at those moments when the power of the underlying story structure and the strength of the actors overcome the film's inevitable weakness for hitting things too much on the nose." The *Rashomon* effect was clearly at work with Edward Guthmann of the *San Francisco Chronicle*, who saw quite a different film. "An unusually thoughtful look at mental illness and its disabling power," Guthmann wrote. "Inspiring and largely unsentimental, this is as much a love story as a tale of courage."

Russell Crowe

Ron Howard began his life in film as a child star, winning the heart of America as Opie on *The Andy Griffith Show* (1960–1968) and as the little boy with a lisp in *The Music Man* (1962). From the child in Mayberry, Howard grew into America's favorite teenager, Richie Cunningham, in *Happy Days* (1974–1980), and also appeared in films—among them *The Courtship of Eddie's Father* (1963), *American Graffiti* (1973), *Eat My Dust!*, and *The Shootist* (both 1976). Moving on fast forward, Howard outgrew his juvenile acting roles to become one of America's most successful mainstream directors and never looked back. His first film, *Grand Theft Auto* (1977), was made for low-budget icon Roger Corman. It didn't take long for him to break out on his own with such popular films as *Night Shift* (1982), *Splash* (1984), *Cocoon* (1985), and *Parenthood* (1989). His most recent films include *The Paper* (1994) and *Apollo 13* (1995). His brother Clint is an actor and appears in everything Ron directs.

The envelope, please…

BEST ACTOR
DENZEL WASHINGTON (B. 1954)
TRAINING DAY

"From the bottom of my heart, I thank you all. Forty years I've been chasing Sidney [Poitier]—they finally give it to me. What'd they do? They give it to him the same night. I'll always be chasing you, Sidney."

Reviewers lauded Washington's performance—though some believed he had performed more Oscar-worthy roles in earlier films without a nod. Roger Ebert, writing for the *Chicago Sun-Times* said, "Washington seems to enjoy a performance that's over the top and down the other side. For Denzel Washington, *Training Day* is a rare villainous role; he doesn't look, sound or move like his usual likable characters, and certainly there's no trace of the football coach from *Remember the Titans*."

He earned his first Academy Award nomination for his portrayal of Steven Biko in *Cry Freedom* (1987), and in 1989 he won the Oscar for Best Supporting Actor in the powerful historical film *Glory* (1989). Though he continued to co-star in features—among them *Courage Under Fire* (1996), a role for which he was paid $10 million—his range and versatility soon won him leading-man roles in *The Mighty Quinn* (1989), *Mo' Better Blues* (1990), *Ricochet* (1991), *Mississippi Masala* (1992), *Malcolm X* (1992, nom.), *The Pelican Brief* (1993), *Crimson Tide* and *Devil in a Blue Dress* (both 1995). *Finding Fish* (1999) put Washington on the other side of the camera in his directorial debut. (For more on Washington, see 1989.)

Halle Berry with Billy Bob Thornton

BEST ACTRESS
HALLE BERRY (B. 1968)
MONSTER'S BALL

"Oh, my God. Oh, my God. I'm sorry. This moment is so much bigger than me. This moment is for…every nameless, faceless woman of color that now has a chance because this door tonight has been opened. And I thank the Academy for choosing me to be the vessel for which His blessing might flow." The breathless intensity of Berry's acceptance speech was just another example of her tough and unstinting determination. It was that very same never-say-die drive that had won Berry this role, which was reported to have been intended for a white actress. Kevin Thomas of the *Los Angeles Times* saw it coming: "Berry combines a dazzling beauty and a soaring talent."

Born to a white mother and abandoned by her black father, Berry used her pageants and her modeling work to parlay a weekly TV series, *Living Dolls* (1989), where it became clear to everyone that Berry was "the genuine article." She lived her characters, even when the shooting stopped. For her role in Spike Lee's *Jungle Fever* (1991), Berry reportedly refused to bathe for days before performing as a crack addict. The film proved a breakthrough, and led to roles in *Boomerang* (1992), *The Flintstones* (1994), a highly publicized co-starring role with Jessica Lange in *Losing Isaiah* (1995), *Bulworth* (1998), and the box-office success *X-Men* (2000). But she won the greatest acclaim for her role as actress Dorothy Dandridge in the television drama *Introducing Dorothy Dandridge* (1999), for which she won a Golden Globe for Best Actress.

BEST OF 2001
Best Picture: *A Beautiful Mind*
Best Director: Ron Howard, *A Beautiful Mind*
Best Actor: Denzel Washington, *Training Day*
Best Actress: Halle Berry, *Monster's Ball*
Best Supporting Actor: Jim Broadbent, *Iris*
Best Supporting Actress: Jennifer Connelly, *A Beautiful Mind*
Honorary Awards: Sidney Poitier, Robert Redford

FIRSTS
• The Kodak Theatre debuted as the Oscars' new home. This was the Academy Awards' first Hollywood locale since 1959's presentation at the Pantages Theatre.

• Halle Berry was honored as the first African-American woman to win Best Actress.

• Denzel Washington was, in fact, the first African-American man to win Best Actor. His predecessor, Sidney Poitier, was of Jamaican heritage.

SINS OF OMISSION
Best Picture: *Mulholland Drive*, *Ghost World*
Best Actress: Naomi Watts, *Mulholland Drive*, Tilda Swinton, *The Deep End*
Best Supporting Actor: Steve Buscemi, *Ghost World*, Jude Law, *A.I.*

ALWAYS A BRIDESMAID, NEVER A BRIDE
Fifteen music nominations later, Randy Newman finally won Best Song for "If I Didn't Have You" (*Monsters, Inc.*)

UNMENTIONABLES
• In the final days of the campaign for Academy votes, a well-orchestrated smear campaign was launched against Best Picture front-runner *A Beautiful Mind*. It was asserted that its creators deleted certain facts from the biopic of Nobel laureate John Nash. Anonymous leaks to the media claimed he was an adulterous bisexual and a rabid anti-Semite.

• Russell Crowe verbally and physically assaulted the producer of the British Motion Picture Awards show. Crowe went ballistic when the last few lines of his acceptance speech for Best Actor were cut from the televised event.

• Halle Berry was named after a Cleveland department store. A severe beating at the hands of an ex-lover left Berry with a partial hearing loss. In 2000, Berry left the scene of a serious auto accident, claiming temporary amnesia.

• As a floundering 20-year-old, Denzel Washington was inspired by a spiritual prophet who foretold his stardom. According to a 1995 *Premiere* magazine article, Washington confronted Quentin Tarantino on the set of *Crimson Tide* and lambasted the director for his use of racial slurs in his films. The embarrassed Tarantino tried to move the argument to a quieter place. "No," said Washington, "if we're going to discuss it, let's discuss it now." Washington later assured reporters that he believed Tarantino was "a fine artist."

• Jennifer Connelly, on how it felt to win her first Oscar: "Well, it doesn't suck." Her de-energized state as she climbed the stairs to accept the award was perhaps due to the fact that she'd broken up with her boyfriend, Josh Charles, just hours earlier.

• Ryan O'Neal was outraged by unfounded rumors that he was at death's door. He admitted that the upside was being hit on by so many women who thought they'd have one last shot at him.

Jim Broadbent with Judy Dench

BEST SUPPORTING ACTOR
JIM BROADBENT (B. 1949)
IRIS

"Stone the crows. I'd like to thank the Academy for this wonderful honor. Making *Iris* was the most joyful, wonderful experience… And good luck, *Moulin Rouge* [another film in which he'd appeared that year]." Kenneth Turan of the *Los Angeles Times* wrote, praising Broadbent's performance, "Bolstered by an excellent performance by Broadbent, *Iris* does not shortchange the exasperation, even the fury felt by a man overmatched by a twist of fate." The *San Francisco Chronicle*'s Edward Guthmann wrote, "Jim Broadbent, as fine an actor as Dench, plays John Bayley, a physically clumsy but devoted and deeply affectionate man." Broadbent, one of today's most versatile British actors, trained at the London Academy of Music and Dramatic Arts and later performed at the Royal National Theatre and the Royal Shakespeare Company. Broadbent has also done a wide-ranging series of British TV work, including *Long Distance Information* and *The Last Company Car*. In addition, he wrote and starred in the award-winning short film *A Sense of History*, directed by Mike Leigh. Broadbent's feature film credits include *The Good Father* (1987), *Life Is Sweet* and *Enchanted April* (both 1991), *The Crying Game* (1992), the Woody Allen comedy *Bullets Over Broadway* (1994), *Rough Magic* (1995), *The Avengers* (1998), and *Bridget Jones's Diary* (2001). But it was his role as Gilbert, as part of the composing team of Gilbert and Sullivan in *Topsy-Turvy* (1999), that won him his greatest acclaim.

BEST SUPPORTING ACTRESS
JENNIFER CONNELLY (B. 1970)
A BEAUTIFUL MIND

"Hello. Okay. By some beautiful twist of fate I've landed in this vocation that demands that I feel and helps me to learn. I believe in love, that there is nothing more important. Alicia Nash [the character she plays in the film] is a true champion of love. And so thank you to her for her example."

Kenneth Turan of the *Los Angeles Times* wrote, "Jennifer Connelly in a career-best performance as [the genius's] beleaguered wife…is completely [Crowe's] match here, just as Alicia is John's in life. There's an intelligence and a tartness to her performance, an ability to be energized rather than fazed or intimidated by her co-star's powers, that leads to a noticeable on-screen sizzle between them."

The New York–born Connelly has been beautiful since birth. She became a model at the age of 10 and landed a role dancing in Sergio Leone's *Once Upon a Time in America* (1984). She danced her way through various rock videos, TV commercials, and even appeared in a British TV series and some B-level films, including *Creepers* and *Seven Minutes in Heaven* (both 1985), and *Labyrinth* (1986). After taking some time off from the screen, Connelly reemerged as a gorgeous teenager in *Some Girls* (1988), as a seductive "good girl" in *The Hot Spot* (1990), and as a spoiled heiress in *Career Opportunities* (1991). She continued making films as a grown-up actress, among them *The Rocketeer* (1991), *The Heart of Justice* (1993, TV), *Mulholland Falls* (1996), *Inventing the Abbots* (1997), John Singleton's *Higher Learning* (1995), and the independent film *Requiem for a Dream* (2000), which earned her a Spirit Award nomination. She followed this role with *Pollock* (2000), in which she played Pollock's mistress.

Sidney Poitier after winning Best Actor in 1963.

HONORARY AWARD
SIDNEY POITIER (B. 1924)

"I accept this award in memory of all the African-American actors and actresses who went before me in the difficult years, on whose shoulders I was privileged to stand to see where I might go."

Sidney Poitier was the first man of color to win a Best Actor Oscar, which he received for *Lilies of the Field* in 1963. In a career that has spanned more than fifty years, he never won again, not even for his more powerful performance for *In the Heat of the Night*. Prior to his Oscar win, Poitier was nominated for his 1958 star turn in *The Defiant Ones*.

Poitier, a passionate actor, began appearing in films in the 1950s and went on to star in *The Blackboard Jungle* (1955), *A Raisin in the Sun* (1961), *To Sir, With Love, Guess Who's Coming to Dinner*, and *In the Heat of the Night* (all 1967). Throughout the 1960s, he paved the way for black performers. After joining the American Negro Theater, he made his way to New York and appeared on Broadway in *Anna Lucasta* (1948). His film debut in *No Way Out* (1950) was a terrific role that led him to co-star with veteran black actor Canada Lee in *Cry, Beloved Country* (1951).

Poitier, who has long served as a symbol for the black struggle, was also a box-office draw. He made his writing debut with *For Love of Ivy* (1968), which was followed by his directing debut with *Buck and the Preacher* (1972). He then starred in and directed a trio of extremely popular all-black comedies: *Uptown Saturday Night* (1974), *Let's Do It Again* (1975), and *A Piece of the Action* (1977). The 1980s saw Poitier almost exclusively as a director, making such films as *Stir Crazy* (1980), *Hanky Panky* (1982), and *Fast Forward* (1985). He took more turns in front of the camera in *Shoot to Kill* (1988) and *Little Nikita* (1988). In one of his best roles, he played future Supreme Court justice Thurgood Marshall in the made-for-TV movie *Separate but Equal* (1991). (For more on Poitier, see 1963.)

Paul Newman with Robert Redford

HONORARY AWARD
ROBERT REDFORD (B. 1937)

"We have a great industry, and we all know that. I really believe it's going to be important in the years to come to make sure that we embrace the risks as well as the sure things…The world around us is in a sea change. And I think the glory of art is that it cannot only survive change, it can lead it."

The Hollywood pinup boy of the '70s scored his first Academy Award for the direction of *Ordinary People*. As an actor, Redford had been a big box-office draw for three decades, during which he appeared in *Inside Daisy Clover* (1966), *Butch Cassidy and the Sundance Kid* (1969), *The Candidate* (1972), *All the President's Men* (1977) and post-Oscar films *Out of Africa* (1985), *Indecent Proposal* (1993), and *The Legend of Bagger Vance* (2000). Redford's only close encounter for an acting Oscar was in 1973, for his performance in *The Sting*.

Directing allowed Redford to develop his own artistic vision. "The chance to be totally responsible for my own vision was exciting," he said. "I have a lot of fool's courage. Despite people telling me to stop, it wouldn't work, I just plunged right in and kept going." Following his directorial debut, he continued successfully working both sides of the camera in *The Milagro Beanfield War* (1988), *A River Runs Through It* (1992), *Quiz Show* (1994), and *The Legend of Bagger Vance* (2000). He received two nominations in 1994 for directing and producing Best Picture nominee *Quiz Show*. His ground-breaking Sundance Institute, which supports and showcases independent cinema, was founded when his film *Downhill Racer* proved a box-office failure. Sundance went on to become one of Redford's greatest accomplishments in film.

(For more on Redford, see 1980.)

AWARD NOMINATIONS 2001

PICTURE
A BEAUTIFUL MIND, Brian Grazer and Ron Howard, Universal and DreamWorks
GOSFORD PARK, Robert Altman, Bob Balaban and David Levy, USA Films
IN THE BEDROOM, Graham Leader, Ross Katz and Todd Field, Miramax Films
THE LORD OF THE RINGS: THE FELLOWSHIP OF THE RING, Peter Jackson, Fran Walsh and Barrie M. Osborne, New Line
MOULIN ROUGE, Martin Brown, Baz Luhrmann and Fred Baron, Fox 2000

ACTOR
RUSSELL CROWE, *A Beautiful Mind*, Universal and DreamWorks
SEAN PENN, *I Am Sam*, New Line
WILL SMITH, *Ali*, Sony Pictures Releasing
DENZEL WASHINGTON, *Training Day*, Warner Bros.
TOM WILKINSON, *In the Bedroom*, Miramax Films

SUPPORTING ACTOR
JIM BROADBENT, *Iris*, Miramax Films
ETHAN HAWKE, *Training Day*, Warner Bros.
BEN KINGSLEY, *Sexy Beast*, Fox Searchlight
IAN MCKELLEN, *The Lord of the Rings: The Fellowship of the Ring*, New Line
JON VOIGHT, *Ali*, Sony Pictures Releasing

ACTRESS
HALLE BERRY, *Monster's Ball*, Lions Gate Films
JUDI DENCH, *Iris*, Miramax Films
NICOLE KIDMAN, *Moulin Rouge*, Fox 2000
SISSY SPACEK, *In the Bedroom*, Miramax Films
RENÉE ZELLWEGER, *Bridget Jones's Diary*, Miramax/Universal/StudioCanal

SUPPORTING ACTRESS
JENNIFER CONNELLY, *A Beautiful Mind*, Universal and DreamWorks
HELEN MIRREN, *Gosford Park*, USA Films
MAGGIE SMITH, *Gosford Park*, USA Films
MARISA TOMEI, *In the Bedroom*, Miramax Films
KATE WINSLET, *Iris*, Miramax Films

ANIMATED FEATURE FILM
JIMMY NEUTRON: BOY GENIUS, Steve Oedekerk, John A. Davis, Paramount and Nickelodeon Movies
MONSTERS, INC., Pete Docter, John Lasseter, Buena Vista
SHREK, Aron Warner, DreamWorks

DIRECTION
A BEAUTIFUL MIND, Ron Howard, Universal and DreamWorks
BLACK HAWK DOWN, Ridley Scott, Sony Pictures Releasing
GOSFORD PARK, Robert Altman, USA Films
THE LORD OF THE RINGS: THE FELLOWSHIP OF THE RING, Peter Jackson, New Line
MULHOLLAND DRIVE, David Lynch, Universal and Studio Canal

WRITING: BASED ON MATERIAL PREVIOUSLY PRODUCED OR PUBLISHED
A BEAUTIFUL MIND, Akiva Goldsman, Universal and DreamWorks
GHOST WORLD, Daniel Clowes, Terry Zwigoff, United Artists through MGM
IN THE BEDROOM, Rob Festinger and Todd Field, Miramax Films

THE LORD OF THE RINGS: THE FELLOWSHIP OF THE RING, Fran Walsh, Philippa Boyens, Peter Jackson, New Line
SHREK, Ted Elliott, Terry Rossio, Joe Sillman and Roger S.H. Schulman, DreamWorks

WRITING: DIRECTLY FOR THE SCREEN
AMÉLIE, Guillaume Laurant and Jean-Pierre Jeunet, Miramax Zoë
GOSFORD PARK, Julian Fellowes, USA Films
MEMENTO, Christopher Nolan, Jonathan Nolan, Newmarket Films
MONSTER'S BALL, Milo Addica & Will Rokos, Lions Gate Films
THE ROYAL TENENBAUMS, Wes Andersen and Owen Wilson, Buena Vista

CINEMATOGRAPHY
AMÉLIE, Bruno Delbonnel, Miramax Zoë
BLACK HAWK DOWN, Slawomir Idziak, Sony Pictures Releasing
THE LORD OF THE RINGS: THE FELLOWSHIP OF THE RING, Andrew Lesnie, New Line
THE MAN WHO WASN'T THERE, Roger Deakins, USA Films
MOULIN ROUGE, Donald M. McAlpine, Fox 2000

ART DIRECTION—SET DECORATION
AMÉLIE, Aline Bonetto, Miramax Zoë
GOSFORD PARK, Stephen Altman, USA Films
HARRY POTTER AND THE SORCERER'S STONE, Stuart Craig, Warner Bros.
THE LORD OF THE RINGS: THE FELLOWSHIP OF THE RING, Grant Major, New Line
MOULIN ROUGE, Catherine Martin, Fox 2000

COSTUME DESIGN
THE AFFAIR OF THE NECKLACE, Milena Canonero, Warner Bros.
GOSFORD PARK, Jenny Beavan, USA Films
HARRY POTTER AND THE SORCERER'S STONE, Judianna Makovsky, Warner Bros.
THE LORD OF THE RINGS: THE FELLOWSHIP OF THE RING, Nglia Dickson, Richard Taylor, New Line
MOULIN ROUGE, Catherine Martin, Angus Strathie, Fox 2000

SOUND
AMÉLIE, Vincent Arnardi, Guillaum Leriche, Jean Umansky, Miramax Zoë
BLACK HAWK DOWN, Michael Minkler, Myron Nettinga, Chris Munro, Sony Pictures Releasing
THE LORD OF THE RINGS: THE FELLOWSHIP OF THE RING, Christopher Boyes, Michael Semanick, Gethin Creagh, Hammond Peek, New Line
MOULIN ROUGE, Andy Nelson, Anna Behlmer, Roger Savage, Guntis Sics, Fox 2000
PEARL HARBOR, Kevin O'Connell, Greg P. Russell, Peter J. Devlin, Buena Vista

FILM EDITING
A BEAUTIFUL MIND, Mike Hill, Dan Hanley, Universal and DreamWorks
BLACK HAWK DOWN, Pietro Scalia, Sony Pictures Releasing
THE LORD OF THE RINGS: THE FELLOWSHIP OF THE RING, John Gilbert, New Line
MEMENTO, Dody Dorn, Newmarket Films
MOULIN ROUGE, Jill Bilcock, Fox 2000

SOUND EFFECTS EDITING
MONSTERS, INC., Gary Rydstrom, Michael Silvers, Buena Vista
PEARL HARBOR, George Watters II, Christopher Boyes, Buena Vista

VISUAL EFFECTS
A.I. ARTIFICIAL INTELLIGENCE, Dennis Muren, Scott Farrar, Stan Winston, Michael Lantieri, Warner Bros.
THE LORD OF THE RINGS: THE FELLOWSHIP OF THE RING, Jim Rygiel, Randall William Cook, Richard Taylor, Mark Stetson, New Line
PEARL HARBOR, Eric Brevig, John Frazier, Ed Hirsh, Ben Snow, Buena Vista

SONG
MONSTERS, INC., Randy Newman [Song: "If I Didn't Have You"] Buena Vista

THE LORD OF THE RINGS: THE FELLOWSHIP OF THE RING, Enya, Nicky Ryan, Roma Ryan [Song: "May It Be"] New Line
PEARL HARBOR, Diane Warren [Song: "There You'll Be"] Buena Vista
KATE & LEOPOLD, Sting [Song: "Until"] Miramax Films
VANILLA SKY, Paul McCartney [Song: "Vanilla Sky"] Paramount

SCORING: ORIGINAL MUSIC
A.I. ARTIFICIAL INTELLIGENCE, John Williams, Warner Bros.
A BEAUTIFUL MIND, James Horner, Universal and DreamWorks
HARRY POTTER AND THE SORCERER'S STONE, John Williams Warner Bros.
THE LORD OF THE RINGS: THE FELLOWSHIP OF THE RING, Howard Shore, New Line
MONSTERS, INC., Randy Newman, Buena Vista

MAKEUP
A BEAUTIFUL MIND, Greg Cannom, Colleen Callaghan, Universal and DreamWorks
THE LORD OF THE RINGS: THE FELLOWSHIP OF THE RING, Peter Owen, Richard Taylor
MOULIN ROUGE, Maurizio Silvi, Aldo Signoretti, Fox 2000

SHORT FILMS: ANIMATED
FIFTY PERCENT GREY, Seamus Bryne, Zanita Films
FOR THE BIRDS, Ralph Eggleston, Pixar Animation Studios
GIVE UP YER AUL SINS, Cathal Gaffney, Darragh O'Connell, Irish Film Board/Radio Telefís Eireann/Arts Council/Brown Bag Films
STRANGE INVADERS, Cordell Barker, National Film Board of Canada
STUBBLE TROUBLE, Joseph E. Merideth, Calabash Animation

SHORT FILMS: LIVE ACTION
THE ACCOUNTANT, Ray McKinnon, Lisa Blount, Ginny Mule
COPY SHOP, Virgil Widrich, Virgil Widrich/ Multimediaproduktions G.m.b.H
GREGOR'S GREATEST INVENTION, Johannes Kiefer, Südwest Film
A MAN THING, Slawomir Fabicki, Bogumil Gofrejow, Polish National Film School
SPEED FOR THESPIANS, Kalman Apple, Shameela Bakhsh, Lester Films Ltd.

DOCUMENTARY: SHORT SUBJECTS
ARTISTS AND ORPHANS: A TRUE DRAMA, Not by Chance Production.
SING!, KCET/Hollywood and American Film Foundation
THOTH, Amateur Rabbit

DOCUMENTARY: FEATURE
CHILDREN UNDERGROUND, Belzberg Films
LALEE'S KIN: THE LEGACY OF COTTON, Maysles Films
MURDER ON A SUNDAY MORNING, Maha Productions/Pathé Doc/France 2/HBO
PROMISES, PROMISES, Film Project
WAR PHOTOGRAPHER, Christian Frei Filmproductions

FOREIGN LANGUAGE FILM
AMÉLIE, Miramax Zoë
ELLING, First Look Pictures
LAGAAN, SET Pictures
NO MAN'S LAND, United Artists through MGM
SON OF THE BRIDE, Sony Pictures Classics

HONORARY AWARDS
To SIDNEY POITIER, in recognition of his remarkable accomplishments as an artist and as a human being.
To ROBERT REDFORD—Actor, Director, Producer, Creator of Sundance, inspiration to independent and innovative filmmakers everywhere.
To RUNE ERICKSON for his pioneering development and 30 years of dedication to the Super 16mm format for motion pictures.

To the AMERICAN SOCIETY OF CINEMATOGRAPHERS (ASC) for the continued publication of "The American Cinematographer Manual."
To RAY FEENEY in appreciation for outstanding service and dedication in upholding the high standards of the Academy of Motion Picture Arts and Sciences.

JEAN HERSHOLT HUMANITARIAN AWARD
ARTHUR HILLER

GORDON E. SAWYER AWARD
EDMUND M. DI GIULIO

SCIENTIFIC OR TECHNICAL: SCIENTIFIC AND ENGINEERING AWARD
Sound, JOHN M. EARGLE, D.B. "DON" KEELE and MARK E. ENGEBRETSON; STEVEN GERLACH, GREGORY FARRELL and CHRISTIAN LURIN
Lenses and Filters, IAIN NEIL and AL SAIKI
Special Photographic, FRANZ KRAUS, JOHANNES STEURER and WOLFGANG RIEDEL; MAKOTO TSUKADA, SHOJI KANEKO and the TECHNICAL STAFF OF IMAGICA CORPORATION and DAIJIRO FUJIE; PAUL J. CONSTANTINE and PETER M. CONSTANTINE
Laboratory, PETER KURAN and SEAN COUGHLIN, JOSEPH A. OLIVIER and WILLIAM CONNER

SCIENTIFIC OR TECHNICAL: TECHNICAL ACHIEVEMENT AWARD
Photography, PETE ROMANO; and JORDAN KLEIN
Sound, BERNARD M. WERNER and WILLIAM GELOW; TOMLINSON HOLMAN
Camera, GEOFF JACKSON and ROGER WOODBURN
Camera Cranes, THOMAS MAJOR BARRON, CHAS SMITH, and GORDON SEITZ
Digital Imaging Technology, JOHN R. ANDERSON, JIM HOURIHAN, CARY PHILLIPS and SEBASTIAN MARINO; STEVE SULLIVAN and ERIC R. L. SCHAFER; BILL SPITZAK, PAUL VAN CAMP, JONATHAN EGSTAD and PRICE PETHEL; DR. LANCE J. WILLIAMS; DR. UWE SASSENBERG and ROLF SCHNEIDER; DR. GARLAND STERN
Special Photographic, CARL LUDWIG and JOHN M. CONSTANTINE, JR.
Stage Operations, MIC RODGERS and MATT SWEENEY

2002

> "You [Americans] are so. . .good."
> —Peter O'Toole, Honoree

> "Meryl Streep's performance really made me think——and for that, I will never forgive her."
> —Steve Martin

THE PRIME OF BRODY

CEREMONY: March 23, 2003
Kodak Theatre, Hollywood
HOST: Steve Martin

War toned down the paparazzi-splashed Red Carpet but not the fiery rhetoric inside the Kodak Theatre. *Bowling for Columbine* documentary winner Michael Moore's cry, "Shame on you, George Bush!" nearly sparked a tuxedoed riot of boos and huzzahs. "Right now, the Teamsters are helping Michael Moore into the trunk of his limo," quipped Steve Martin. Barbra Streisand was unruffled until she opened the envelope for Best Song and gasped at the name of Eminem! Wasn't U-2's Bono supposed to have a lock on this one? Suddenly, the stars weren't so implacably set in the firmament and sure-bet nominees shifted anxiously in their seats. Something was happening here.

Certainly the *Chicago* express chugged along smoothly toward a respectable six-statuette rack-up, including the evening's most pregnant pause as Catherine Zeta-Jones beat out favorite Meryl Streep for Best Supporting. Teary-eyed tough guy Chris Cooper was no surprise in the same category, and though we might not expect Jack Nicholson to have us reaching for the Kleenex, his neck-and-neck rival for Best Actor, Daniel Day-Lewis, just might. Either way it would be a highly entertaining acceptance. But nothing could have prepared the house for the sheer blast of joy as Halle Berry called out Adrien Brody's name. He stood transfixed as the audience spontaneously leapt to its feet. To deafening cheers, the loudest from his fellow nominees, the youngest Best Actor winner since Richard Dreyfuss leapt to the stage and swooped down on the unsuspecting Berry for a cinematic kiss. Brody then spoke eloquently off the cuff, shushing the orchestra so that he could express his mixed feelings at this time of uncertainty in the world, and his concern for a friend fighting on the Iraqi front. This, one of the biggest upsets in Oscar history, was nearly one-upped moments later by "the man who wasn't there," Roman Polanski, still a fugitive from the U.S. on a statutory rape charge. His directorial win for *The Pianist* left Martin Scorsese speechless and empty-handed yet again at the Oscars.

BEST PICTURE
CHICAGO

Producer Marty Richards spoke, and, on a night wet with tears of gratitude, he shed a few genuine tears himself. And it was no wonder: Seeing *Chicago* win the Oscar after he had labored to have the picture made for over three decades—ever since the Bob Fosse Broadway musical opened in 1975—was an unmitigated triumph. Though the majority of critics loved the film—"Big, brassy fun," wrote Roger Ebert of the *Chicago Sun-Times*—it also had a detractor or two: "It's rare to find a picture as exuberant, as shallow—and as exuberant about its shallowness," wrote Elvis Mitchell of the *New York Times*. Barreling through the door opened by *Moulin Rouge* the previous year, *Chicago* is a dazzling reimagination of the movie musical, in which songs and dances are interrupted by stories, instead of the other way around. *Chicago* grabbed six golden boys out of its thirteen nominations.

Renée Zellweger

The envelope, please...

BEST DIRECTOR
ROMAN POLANSKI (B. 1933)
THE PIANIST

Many thought it the best film, yet still more were startled by the win for a man who has for years been in exile as a fugitive from American justice for the rape of an underage girl. Martin Scorsese was the first to rise in applause for the brilliant filmmaker and for his work, about which Michael Wilmington of the *Chicago Tribune* wrote, "*The Pianist* is the film Roman Polanski may have been born to make." And he was not alone. "One of the very few non-documentary movies about Jewish life and death under the Nazis that can be called definitive," wrote A.O. Scott in the *New York Times*. *Time* magazine's Richard Schickel praised it, writing, "We admire this film for its harsh objectivity and refusal to seek our tears, our sympathies." Best known for his first Hollywood film, the chilling *Rosemary's Baby* (1968), Polanski immediately became a director to watch. His ironic, eccentric films explore personal themes of alienation and victimization. Polanski himself was a victim of the Holocaust: After his mother was killed in Auschwitz he was forced to wander and survive on his own. His outstanding directorial efforts include *Knife in the Water* (1962, Academy Award nomination), *Repulsion* (1965), *Rosemary's Baby* (1968), *The Fearless Vampire Killers*, featuring Sharon Tate (1969), *What?* (1973), *Chinatown* (1974), *The Tenant* (1976), *Tess*, his first film made in exile (1979, Academy Award nomination), *Frantic* (1987), *Death and the Maiden* (1994), and *The Ninth Gate* (2000).

BEST ACTOR,
ADRIEN BRODY (B. 1973)
THE PIANIST

No one was more surprised about Adrien Brody's win than Brody himself, perhaps with the exception of presenter Halle Berry, who received a giant, on-the-lips kiss from the winner, who said, "There comes a time in life when everything seems to make sense, and this is not one of those times." In another of the evening's tearful speeches (and lengthy, too; the winner indicated to the ever-time-conscious producers that he had no intention of stopping at their time limit), Brody ended his speech by saluting those who pray for a peaceful resolution to the war in Iraq and wishing for the quick return of a friend serving in Kuwait. About his role—based on real life—as a great pianist who survives the Holocaust on the run, J. Hoberman of the *Village Voice* wrote, "This passive hero is as much witness as protagonist ... who survived not because he was talented, but through an inexplicable combination of good luck and guardian angels." "Play[ed] ... with soulful elegance," wrote A.O. Scott in the *New York Times*. Brody has also appeared in *New York Stories* (1989), *The Thin Red Line* (1998), *Liberty Heights* (1999), *The Affair of the Necklace* (2001), and *The Singing Detective* (2003).

BEST OF 2002
Best Picture: *Chicago*
Best Director: Roman Polanksi, *The Pianist*
Best Actor: Adrien Brody, *The Pianist*
Best Actress: Nicole Kidman, *The Hours*
Best Supporting Actor: Chris Cooper, *Adaptation*
Best Supporting Actress: Catherine Zeta-Jones, *Chicago*
Honorary Awards: Peter O'Toole

FIRSTS

Thirty-year-old Adrien Brody becomes the youngest actor to win Best Actor since Richard Dreyfuss won, also at age 30, for *The Goodbye Girl* (1977).

ROLE REVERSALS

• John Travolta, Kevin Spacey, and Hugh Jackman were all considered for the role of Billy Flynn in *Chicago*.

• The role of Laura Brown in *The Hours* was originally intended for Emily Watson.

• In *The Hours*, Allison Janney was originally slated to play the woman in the flower shop, but successfully lobbied for the role of Meryl Streep's lover, instead.

• Madonna, Goldie Hawn, Kathy Bates, Rosie O'Donnell, Nicole Kidman, Gwyneth Paltrow, Cameron Diaz, and Britney Spears were all considered for roles in *Chicago*.

• In *Chicago*, the song "Class" was apparently filmed but not used because it didn't fit into the "show-within-Roxie's-mind" concept. Evidently it will be included as an appendix on the DVD release.

UNMENTIONABLES

• The director wanted Catherine Zeta-Jones to wear her natural long hair in the movie, but the actress insisted on the short bob. She explained to *People* magazine that she didn't want her hair to fall over her face and give people a reason to doubt that she did all the dancing herself.

• Kidman's false nose in *The Hours*, worn to make her look more like Virginia Woolf, has been discussed in print seemingly as much as any other element in the film.

• To look starved and near death, Adrien Brody lost 30 pounds by eating a daily diet of two boiled eggs and green tea for breakfast, a little chicken for lunch, and a small piece of fish or chicken with steamed vegetables for dinner, over a six-week period. Initially his weight was 160 pounds.

• In *The Pianist*, the character of the dancing old man leading a group of children in the Warsaw ghetto was based on Janusz Korczak, pedagogue and writer of books for children. He became a legend when he refused to leave the children of the ghetto, even though he had the chance, and died with them at the Treblinka concentration camp.

• Host Steve Martin was prepared to tell Saddam Hussein, "I hope your connection goes out just before we announce Best Picture," but decided to nix the joke just before the show.

• Producers tried to cut off Michael Moore's anti-war, anti-Bush speech by turning up the music. He continued—albeit in a rush—to say what he had to say. Among those booing Moore's speech were stagehands who confronted the director backstage. Rumor had it that there was a threat to withdraw Moore's Oscar. Insiders warned a U.K. daily that failure to award Moore's *Bowling for Columbine* the Oscar for Best Documentary Feature would be proof that Hollywood had reverted to "the witch-hunting 1950s."

• Many in the audience sported a squiggle-shaped pin representing a dove for Peace. When Joan Rivers asked her daughter what they meant, she replied, "Peace." "Every idiot in the world wants peace," Joan complained, adding that, the morning after, the pins will wind up for sale on eBay.

BEST ACTRESS
NICOLE KIDMAN, (B. 1967)
THE HOURS

Following in Adrien Brody's footsteps, Best Actress-winner **Nicole Kidman** was so overcome with tears that she had to stop her speech to pull herself together. "Russell Crowe said don't cry if you get up there, and now I'm crying." Like many before and after her, she expressed anxiety about the validity of the Oscars "when the world is in such turmoil," but added that art was its own justification. She then expressed her gratitude for the opportunity "to make my mother proud." Kidman's performance was roundly praised for its authentic portrait of the writer Virginia Woolf's battle with depression. "Kidman is galvanizing … full credit go[es] to Kidman's piercing performance, a powerful piece of acting that is unsettling in the best sense," wrote Kenneth Turan in the *Los Angeles Times*. Mike La Salle of the *San Francisco Chronicle* wrote, "Everyone who experiences *The Hours* will comment first on the acting, but it's Kidman, barely recognizable with her nose extended, who's the most impressive." Imaginatively based on Woolf's *Mrs. Dalloway*, the film follows three women, in three times and three places, all of whom battle depression and suicide. Kidman worked in Australia before coming to the U.S. *The Hours* was perhaps Kidman's most demanding role in a career that includes *Flirting* (1990), *Days of Thunder*, which was her first American film (1990), *Billy Bathgate* (1991), *Far and Away* (1992), *My Life* (1993), *Batman Forever* and *To Die For* (both 1995), *Eyes Wide Shut* (1999), *Moulin Rouge* (2001), and *Birthday Girl* (2002).

BEST SUPPORTING ACTOR
CHRIS COOPER (B. 1951)
ADAPTATION

Cooper seemed surprised, but all were elated upon hearing him win the Oscar for the role of the titular plant-robber in Susan Orlean's nonfiction bestseller *The Orchid Thief*, the book that is being adapted by the central character in the film. If the critics had been voting they would have seconded the decision. Kenneth Turan of the *Los Angeles Times*, among others, called it a "career-changing" performance. "Charismatically deprived of his front teeth, Cooper gives a career performance as a garrulous redneck genius; sensitively self-absorbed," wrote J. Hoberman in the *Village Voice*. Roger Ebert of the *Chicago Sun-Times* lauded his work, saying, "Chris Cooper plays a con man of extraordinary intelligence, who is attractive to a sophisticated New Yorker because he is so intensely *himself* in a world where few people are anybody." After his debut to great reviews in *Matewan* (1987), Cooper appeared in *Guilty by Suspicion* (1991), *A Time to Kill* (1996), *The Horse Whisperer* (1998), *American Beauty* (1999), *The Bourne Identity* (2002), and *Seabiscuit* (2003). Cooper has been featured in the TV miniseries *Lonesome Dove* (1989) and *Return to Lonesome Dove* (1993).

BEST SUPPORTING ACTRESS
CATHERINE ZETA-JONES (B. 1969)
CHICAGO

Looking like a great diva, the very pregnant Jones accepted her award for her breathtakingly high-stepping, belt-it-out performance in *Chicago*. Elvis Mitchell wrote in the *Village Voice*, "She pumps her majestic, long legs like the cylinders of a Corvette about to redline, but always knowing exactly when to stop short of throwing a piston." Zeta-Jones knew her way around a stage, having joined a song-and-dance troupe at the age of ten. As an adult, she played supporting roles in several films, including *Christopher Columbus: The Discovery* (1992), and a larger part in *The Phantom* (1996), before landing her break-through role in *The Mask of Zorro* (1998). She next starred in *Entrapment* (1999), *The Haunting* (1999), and *Traffic* (2000), for which many believed she deserved an Oscar.

HONORARY AWARD
PETER O'TOOLE (B. 1932)

"I signed up for five months. I wound up staying for over two years," said the witty and gracious actor about his *Lawrence of Arabia* experience, upon receiving his award so many years later. Rumor had it that O'Toole was ambivalent about showing up to receive an Honorary Oscar. Some of it showed when he announced, "Always a bridesmaid, never a bride, my foot!" The 70-year-old star had been nominated for seven Oscars over the years but had never won. During the making of *Lawrence*, O'Toole lost twenty pounds and his good health. "I find acting difficult. One hundred-thirty degrees in shade, sitting on a camel, and covered in vermin doesn't make it easier." His was an extraordinary film debut, coming from out of nowhere (the Shakespearean stage, to be precise), in a role that was neither romantic nor fully heroic. Nonetheless, his deeply felt intensity and startling good looks generated full-blast star power. Noel Coward famously cracked, "If he had been any prettier it would have been *Florence of Arabia*." O'Toole has been drawn to extreme character roles in a succession of landmark films, including *Becket* (1964), *Lion In Winter* (1968), *Goodbye, Mr. Chips* (1969), *The Ruling Class* (1971), *Man of La Mancha* (1972), *The Stunt Man* (1978), *Caligula* (1980), *My Favorite Year* (1982), and *The Last Emperor* (1987).

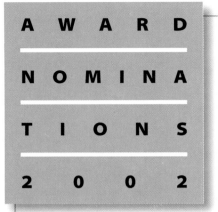

PICTURE

CHICAGO, Martin Richards, Miramax
GANGS OF NEW YORK, Alberto Grimaldi and Harvey Weinstein, Miramax
THE HOURS, Scott Rudin and Robert Fox, Paramount and Miramax
THE LORD OF THE RINGS: THE TWO TOWERS, Barrie M. Osborne, Fran Walsh and Peter Jackson, New Line
THE PIANIST, Roman Polanski, Robert Benmussa and Alain Sarde, Focus Features

ACTOR

ADRIEN BRODY, *The Pianist*, Focus Features
NICOLAS CAGE, *Adaptation*, Sony Pictures Releasing
MICHAEL CAINE, *The Quiet American*, Miramax and Intermedia
DANIEL DAY-LEWIS, *Gangs of New York*, Miramax
JACK NICHOLSON, *About Schmidt*, New Line

SUPPORTING ACTOR

CHRIS COOPER, *Adaptation*, Sony Pictures Releasing
ED HARRIS, *The Hours*, Paramount and Miramax
PAUL NEWMAN, *Road to Perdition*, DreamWorks and 20th Century Fox
JOHN C. REILLY, *Chicago*, Miramax
CHRISTOPHER WALKEN, *Catch Me If You Can*, DreamWorks

ACTRESS

SALMA HAYEK, *Frida*, Miramax
NICOLE KIDMAN, *The Hours*, Paramount and Miramax
DIANE LANE, *Unfaithful*, 20th Century Fox
JULIANNE MOORE, *Far from Heaven*, Focus Features
RENÉE ZELLWEGER, *Chicago*, Miramax

SUPPORTING ACTRESS

KATHY BATES, *About Schmidt*, New Line
JULIANNE MOORE, *The Hours*, Paramount and Miramax
QUEEN LATIFAH, *Chicago*, Miramax
MERYL STREEP, *Adaptation*, Sony Pictures Releasing
CATHERINE ZETA-JONES, *Chicago*, Miramax

ANIMATED FEATURE FILM

ICE AGE, Chris Wedge, 20th Century Fox
LILO & STITCH, Chris Sanders, Buena Vista
SPIRIT: STALLION OF THE CIMARRON, Jeffrey Katzenberg, DreamWorks
SPIRITED AWAY, Hayao Miyazaki, Buena Vista
TREASURE PLANET, Ron Clements, Buena Vista

DIRECTION

CHICAGO, Rob Marshall, Miramax
GANGS OF NEW YORK, Martin Scorsese, Miramax
THE HOURS, Stephen Daldry, Paramount and Miramax
THE PIANIST, Roman Polanski, Focus Features
TALK TO HER, Pedro Almodóvar, Sony Pictures Classics

WRITING: BASED ON MATERIAL PREVIOUSLY PRODUCED OR PUBLISHED

ABOUT A BOY, Peter Hedges, Chris Weitz and Paul Weitz, Universal
ADAPTATION, Charlie Kaufman and Donald Kaufman, Sony Pictures Releasing
CHICAGO, Bill Condon, Miramax
THE HOURS, David Hare, Paramount and Miramax
THE PIANIST, Ronald Harwood, Focus Features

WRITING: DIRECTLY FOR THE SCREEN

FAR FROM HEAVEN, Todd Haynes, Focus Features
GANGS OF NEW YORK, Jay Cocks, Steve Zaillian and Kenneth Lonergan, Miramax
MY BIG FAT GREEK WEDDING, Nia Vardalos, IFC/Gold Circle Films
TALK TO HER, Pedro Almodóvar, Sony Pictures Classic
Y TU MAMÁ TAMBIÉN, Carlos Cuarón and Alfonso Cuarón, IFC Films

CINEMATOGRAPHY

CHICAGO, Dion Beebe, Miramax
FAR FROM HEAVEN, Edward Lachman, Focus Features,
GANGS OF NEW YORK, Michael Ballhaus, Miramax
THE PIANIST, Pawel Edelman, Focus Features
ROAD TO PERDITION, Conrad L. Hall, DreamWorks and 20th Century Fox

ART DIRECTION – SET DECORATION

CHICAGO Miramax Art Direction: John Myhre; Set Decoration: Gordon Sim
FRIDA, Art Direction: Felipe Fernandez del Paso; Set Decoration: Hania Robledo, Miramax
GANGS OF NEW YORK, Art Direction: Dante Ferretti; Set Decoration: Francesca Lo Schiavo, Miramax
THE LORD OF THE RINGS: THE TWO TOWERS, Art Direction: Grant Major; Set Decoration: Dan Hennah and Alan Lee, New Line
ROAD TO PERDITION, Dennis Gassner, DreamWorks and 20th Century Fox

COSTUME DESIGN

CHICAGO, Colleen Atwood, Miramax
FRIDA, Julie Weiss, Miramax
GANGS OF NEW YORK, Sandy Powell, Miramax
THE HOURS, Ann Roth, Paramount and Miramax
THE PIANIST, Anna Sheppard, Focus Features

SOUND

CHICAGO, Michael Minkler, Dominick Tavella and David Lee, Miramax
GANGS OF NEW YORK, Tom Fleischman, Eugene Gearty and Ivan Sharrock, Miramax
THE LORD OF THE RINGS: THE TWO TOWERS, Christopher Boyes, Michael Semanick, Michael Hedges and Hammond Peek, New Line
ROAD TO PERDITION, Scott Millan, Bob Beemer and John Patrick Pritchett, DreamWorks and 20th Century Fox
SPIDER-MAN, Kevin O'Connell, Greg P. Russell and Ed Novick, Sony Pictures Releasing

FILM EDITING

CHICAGO, Martin Walsh, Miramax
GANGS OF NEW YORK, Thelma Schoonmaker, Miramax,
THE HOURS, Peter Boyle, Paramount and Miramax
THE LORD OF THE RINGS: THE TWO TOWERS, Michael Horton, New Line
THE PIANIST, Hervé de Luze, Focus Features

SOUND EFFECTS EDITING

THE LORD OF THE RINGS: THE TWO TOWERS, Ethan Van der Ryn and Michael Hopkins, New Line
MINORITY REPORT, Richard Hymns and Gary Rydstrom, 20th Century Fox and DreamWorks
ROAD TO PERDITION, Scott A. Hecker, DreamWorks and 20th Century Fox

VISUAL EFFECTS

THE LORD OF THE RINGS: THE TWO TOWERS, Jim Rygiel, Joe Letteri, Randall William Cook and Alex Funke, New Line
SPIDER-MAN, John Dykstra, Scott Stokdyk, Anthony LaMolinara and John Frazier, Sony Pictures Releasing
STAR WARS EPISODE II: ATTACK OF THE CLONES, Rob Coleman, Pablo Helman, John Knoll and Ben Snow, 20th Century Fox

SONG

FRIDA, Elliot Goldenthal and Julie Taymor [Song: "Burn It Blue"] Miramax
THE WILD THORNBERRYS MOVIE, Paul Simon [Song: "Father and Daughter"]
GANGS OF NEW YORK, Bono, The Edge, Adam Clayton and Larry Mullen [Song: "The Hands That Built America"] Miramax
CHICAGO, John Kander and Fred Ebb [Song: "I Move On"] Miramax
8 MILE, Eminem, Jeff Bass and Luis Resto [Song: "Lose Yourself"] Universal

SCORING: ORIGINAL MUSIC

CATCH ME IF YOU CAN, John Williams, DreamWorks
FAR FROM HEAVEN, Elmer Bernstein, Focus Features
FRIDA, Elliot Goldenthal, Miramax
THE HOURS, Philip Glass, Paramount and Miramax
ROAD TO PERDITION, Thomas Newman, DreamWorks and 20th Century Fox

MAKEUP

FRIDA, John Jackson and Beatrice De Alba, Miramax
THE TIME MACHINE, John M. Elliott, Jr. and Barbara Lorenz, DreamWorks and Warner Bros.

SHORT FILMS: ANIMATED

THE CATHEDRAL, Tomek Baginski, Platige Image
THE CHUBBCHUBBS! Eric Armstrong, Sony Pictures Imageworks, Columbia
DAS RAD, Chris Stenner and Heidi Wittlinger, Filmakademie Baden-Württemberg GmbH
MIKE'S NEW CAR, Pete Docter and Roger Gould, Buena Vista
MT. HEAD, Koji Yamamura, Yamamura Animation

SHORT FILMS: LIVE ACTION

FAIT D'HIVER, Dirk Beliën and Anja Daelemans, Another Dimension of an Idea
I'LL WAIT FOR THE NEXT ONE … (J'ATTENDRAI LE SUIVANT …), Philippe Orreindy and Thomas Gaudin, La Boite
INJA (DOG), Steven Pasvolsky and Joe Weatherstone, Australian Film TV & Radio School (AFTRS)
JOHNNY FLYNTON, Lexi Alexander and Alexander Buono, Red Corner
THIS CHARMING MAN (DER ER EN YNDIG MAND), Martin Strange-Hansen and Mie Andreasen, M&M Productions for Novellefilm

DOCUMENTARY: SHORT SUBJECTS

THE COLLECTOR OF BEDFORD STREET, Alice Elliott, Alice Elliott Productions
MIGHTY TIMES: THE LEGACY OF ROSA PARKS, Robert Hudson and Bobby Houston, Tell the Truth Pictures
TWIN TOWERS, Bill Guttentag and Robert David Port, Wolf Films/Shape Pictures/Universal/Mopo Entertainment
WHY CAN'T WE BE A FAMILY AGAIN? Roger Weisberg and Murray Nossel, Public Policy

DOCUMENTARY: FEATURE

BOWLING FOR COLUMBINE, Michael Moore and Michael Donovan, Salter Street Films/VIF 2/Dog Eat Dog Films, United Artists and Alliance Atlantis
DAUGHTER FROM DANANG, Gail Dolgin and Vincente Franco, Balcony Releasing in association with Cowboy Pictures
PRISONER OF PARADISE, Malcolm Clarke and Stuart Sender, Média Vérité/Café Productions, Alliance Atlantis
SPELLBOUND, Jeffrey Blitz and Sean Welch, Blitz/Welch, THINK Films
WINGED MIGRATION, Jacques Perrin, Sony Pictures Classics)
A Galatée Films/France 2 Cinéma/France 3 Cinéma/Les Productions de la Guéville/Bac Films/Pandora Film/Les Productions JMH/Wanda Vision/Eyescreen Production

FOREIGN LANGUAGE FILM

EL CRIMEN DEL PADRE AMARO, Alameda Films/BluFilms/Foprocine/Gob. del Estado de Veracruz-Llave
HERO, Beijing New Picture Film Company/Elite Group Enterprises
THE MAN WITHOUT A PAST, Sputnik Oy/Pandora Film/Pyramide Prods.
NOWHERE IN AFRICA, An MTM Medien & Television ZUS & ZO, Filmprodukties de Luwte

SCIENTIFIC OR TECHNICAL: ACADEMY AWARD OF MERIT

To Alias/Wavefront for the development of a 3D animation, dynamics, modeling and rendering production tool known as Maya.
To Arnold & Richter Cine Technik and to Panavision, Inc., for their continuing development and innovation in the design and manufacturing of advanced camera systems specifically designed for the motion picture entertainment industry.

SCIENTIFIC OR TECHNICAL: SCIENTIFIC AND ENGINEERING AWARD

To Glenn Sanders and Howard Stark of Zaxcom for the concept, design and engineering of the portable Deva Digital Audio Disk Recorder.
To Mark Elendt, Paul H. Breslin, Greg Hermanovic and Kim Davidson for their continued development of the procedural modeling and animation components of their Prisms program, as exemplified in the Houdini software package.
To Dr. Leslie Gutierrez, Diane E. Kestner, James Merrill and David Niklewicz for the design and development of the Kodak Vision Premier Color Print Film, 2393.
To Dedo Weigert for the concept, Dr. Depu Jin for the optical calculations, and Franz Petters for the mechanical construction of the Dedolight 400D.

SCIENTIFIC OR TECHNICAL: TECHNICAL ACHIEVEMENT AWARD

To Dick Walsh for the development of the PDI/ Dreamworks Facial Animation System.
To Thomas Driemeyer and to the Team of Mathematicians, Physicists and Software Engineers of Mental Images for their contributions to the Mental Ray rendering software for motion pictures.
To Eric Daniels, George Katanics, Tasso Lappas and Chris Springfield for the development of the Deep Canvas rendering software
To Jim Songer for his contributions to the technical development of video-assist in the motion picture industry.
To Pierre Chabert of Airstar for the introduction of balloons with internal light sources to provide set lighting for the motion picture industry.
To Rawdon Hayne and Robert W. Jeffs of Leelium Tubelite for their contributions to the development of internally lit balloons for motion picture lighting.

Best Picture, Best Actor, Best Actress, Best Supporting Actor, Best Supporting Actress By Year

Best Picture

1927–1928
WINGS, Paramount Famous Lasky. Produced by Lucien Hubbard.

1928–29
THE BROADWAY MELODY, MGM. Produced by Harry Rapf.

1929–30
ALL QUIET ON THE WESTERN FRONT, Universal. Produced by Carl Laemmle, Jr.

1930–31
CIMARRON, RKO Radio. Produced by William LaBaron.

1931–32
GRAND HOTEL, MGM. Produced by Irving Thalberg.

1932–33
CAVALCADE, Fox. Winfield Sheehan, studio head.

1934
IT HAPPENED ONE NIGHT, Columbia. Produced by Harry Cohn.

1935
MUTINY ON THE BOUNTY, MGM. Produced by Irving Thalberg, with Albert Lewin.

1936
THE GREAT ZIEGFELD, MGM. Produced by Hunt Stromberg.

1937
THE LIFE OF EMILE ZOLA, Warner Bros. Produced by Henry Blanke.

1938
YOU CAN'T TAKE IT WITH YOU, Columbia. Produced by Frank Capra.

1939
GONE WITH THE WIND, Selznick, MGM. Produced by David O. Selznick.

1940
REBECCA, Selznick, UA. Produced by David O. Selznick

1941
HOW GREEN WAS MY VALLEY, 20th Century-Fox. Produced by Darryl F. Zanuck.

1942
MRS. MINIVER, MGM. Produced by Sidney Franklin.

1943
CASABLANCA, Warner Bros. Produced by Hal B. Wallis.

1944
GOING MY WAY, Paramount. Produced by Leo McCarey.

1945
THE LOST WEEKEND, Paramount. Produced by Charles Brackett.

1946
THE BEST YEARS OF OUR LIVES, Goldwyn, RKO Radio. Produced by Samuel Goldwyn.

1947
GENTLEMAN'S AGREEMENT, 20th Century-Fox. Produced by Darryl F. Zanuck.

1948
HAMLET, Rank-Two Cities, U-I (British). Produced by Laurence Olivier.

1949
ALL THE KING'S MEN, Rossen, Columbia. Produced by Robert Rossen.

1950
ALL ABOUT EVE, 20th Century-Fox. Produced by Darryl F. Zanuck.

1951
AN AMERICAN IN PARIS, MGM. Produced by Arthur Freed.

1952
THE GREATEST SHOW ON EARTH, DeMille, Paramount. Produced by Cecil B. DeMille.

1953
FROM HERE TO ETERNITY, Columbia. Produced by Buddy Adler.

1954
ON THE WATERFRONT, Horizon-American, Columbia. Produced by Sam Spiegel.

1955
MARTY, Hecht-Lancaster, UA. Produced by Harold Hecht.

1956
AROUND THE WORLD IN 80 DAYS, Todd, UA. Produced by Michael Todd.

1957
THE BRIDGE ON THE RIVER KWAI, Horizon, Columbia. Produced by Sam Spiegel.

1958
GIGI, Freed, MGM. Produced by Arthur Freed.

1959
BEN-HUR, MGM. Produced by Sam Zimbalist.

1960
THE APARTMENT, Mirisch, UA. Produced by Billy Wilder.

1961
WEST SIDE STORY, Mirisch-B&P Enterprises, UA. Produced by Robert Wise.

1962
LAWRENCE OF ARABIA, Horizon-Spiegel-Lean, Columbia. Produced by Sam Spiegel.

1963
TOM JONES, Woodfall, UA-Lopert (British). Produced by Tony Richardson.

1964
MY FAIR LADY, Warner Bros. Produced by Jack L. Warner.

1965
THE SOUND OF MUSIC, Argyle, 20th Century-Fox. Produced by Robert Wise.

1966
A MAN FOR ALL SEASONS, Highland Films, Columbia. Produced by Fred Zinnemann.

1967
IN THE HEAT OF THE NIGHT, Mirisch, UA. Produced by Walter Mirisch.

1968
OLIVER!, Romulus, Columbia. Produced by John Woolf.

1969
MIDNIGHT COWBOY, Hellman-Schlesinger, UA. Produced by Jerome Hellman.

1970
PATTON, 20th Century-Fox. Produced by Frank McCarthy.

1971
THE FRENCH CONNECTION, D'Antoni-Schine-Moore, 20th Century-Fox. Produced by Philip D'Antoni.

1972
THE GODFATHER, Ruddy, Paramount. Produced by Albert S. Ruddy.

1973
THE STING, Universal-Bill/Phillips-George Roy Hill Film Prod., Zanuck/Brown Presentation, Universal. Tony Bill, Michael and Julia Phillips, producers.

1974
THE GODFATHER PART II, Coppola Company, Paramount. Produced by Francis Ford Coppola; Co-produced by Gray Frederickson and Fred Roos.

1975
ONE FLEW OVER THE CUCKOO'S NEST, Fantasy Films, UA. Produced by Saul Zaentz and Michael Douglas.

1976
ROCKY, Chartoff-Winkler, UA. Produced by Irwin Winkler and Robert Chartoff.

1977
ANNIE HALL, Rollins-Joffe, UA. Produced by Charles H. Joffe.

1978
THE DEER HUNTER, EMI/Cimino, Universal. Produced by Barry Spikings, Michael Deeley, Michael Cimino and John Peverall.

1979
KRAMER VS. KRAMER, Jaffe, Columbia. Produced by Stanley R. Jaffe.

1980
ORDINARY PEOPLE, Wildwood, Paramount. Produced by Ronald L. Schwary.

1981
CHARIOTS OF FIRE, Enigma, The Ladd Company/Warner Bros. Produced by David Puttnam.

1982
GANDHI, Columbia. Produced by Richard Attenborough.

1983
TERMS OF ENDEARMENT, Brooks, Paramount. Produced by James L. Brooks.

1984
AMADEUS, Zaentz, Orion. Produced by Saul Zaentz.

1985
OUT OF AFRICA, Universal. Produced by Sydney Pollack.

1986
PLATOON, Hemdale, Orion. Produced by Arnold Kopelson.

1987
THE LAST EMPEROR, Hemdale, Columbia. Produced by Jeremy Thomas.

1988
RAIN MAN, Guber-Peters, United Artists. Produced by Mark Johnson.

1989
DRIVING MISS DAISY, Zanuck Company, Warner Bros. Produced by Richard D. Zanuck and Lili Fini Zanuck.

1990
DANCES WITH WOLVES, Tig, Orion. Produced by Jim Wilson and Kevin Costner.

1991
THE SILENCE OF THE LAMBS, Strong Heart/Demme, Orion. Produced by Edward Saxon, Kenneth Utt and Ron Bozman.

1992
UNFORGIVEN, Warner Bros. Produced by Clint Eastwood.

1993
SCHINDLER'S LIST, Universal/Amblin, Universal. Steven Spielberg, Gerald R. Molen and Branko Lustig, Producers.

1994
FORREST GUMP, Steve Tisch/Wendy Finerman, Paramount. Wendy Finerman, Steve Tisch and Steve Starkey, Producers.

1995
BRAVEHEART, Icon/Ladd Company, Paramount. Mel Gibson, Alan Ladd, Jr. and Bruce Davey, Producers.

1996
THE ENGLISH PATIENT, Tiger Moth, Miramax. Saul Zaentz, Producer.

1997
TITANIC, Lightstorm Entertainment, 20th Century-Fox and Paramount. James Cameron and Jon Landau, Producers.

1998
SHAKESPEARE IN LOVE, Miramax Films, Universal Pictures, Bedford Falls Company Production; Miramax Films. (United Kingdom/U.S.) David Parfitt, Donna Gigliotti, Harvey Weinstein, Edward Zwick and Marc Norman, Producers.

1999
AMERICAN BEAUTY, Jinks/Cohen Company Production; DreamWorks. Bruce Cohen and Dan Jinks, Producers.

2000
GLADIATOR, Douglas Wick in association with Scott Free Production; DreamWorks and Universal. Douglas Wick, David Franzoni and Branko Lustig, Producers.

2001
A BEAUTIFUL MIND, Universal Pictures and Imagine Entertainment

Production; Universal and Dream-Works. Brian Grazer and Ron Howard, Producers.

2002
CHICAGO, Miramax, Zadan/Meron Productions. Produced by Martin Richards.

Best Actor

1927–1928
EMIL JANNINGS in *The Last Command*, Paramount Famous Lanky, and *The Way of All Flesh*, Paramount Famous Lanky.

1928–29
WARNER BAXTER in *In Old Arizona*, Fox.

1929–30
GEORGE ARLISS in *Disraeli*, Warner Bros., and *The Green Goddess*, Warner Bros.

1930–31
LIONEL BARRYMORE in *A Free Soul*, MGM.

1931–32
WALLACE BEERY in *The Champ*, MGM.

1932–33
CHARLES LAUGHTON in *The Private Life of Henry VIII*, London Films, UA (British).

1934
CLARK GABLE in *It Happened One Night*, Columbia.

1935
VICTOR McLAGLEN in *The Informer*, RKO Radio.

1936
PAUL MUNI in *The Story of Louis Pasteur*, Warner Bros.

1937
SPENCER TRACY in *Captains Courageous*, MGM.

1938
SPENCER TRACY in *Boys Town*, MGM.

1939
ROBERT DONAT in *Goodbye, Mr. Chips*, MGM (British).

1940
JAMES STEWART in *The Philadelphia Story*, MGM.

1941
GARY COOPER in *Sergeant York*, Warner Bros.

1942
JAMES CAGNEY in *Yankee Doodle Dandy*, Warner Bros.

1943
PAUL LUKAS in *Watch on the Rhine*, Warner Bros.

1944
BING CROSBY in *Going My Way*, Paramount.

1945
RAY MILLAND in *The Lost Weekend*, Paramount.

1946
FREDRIC MARCH in *The Best Years of Our Lives*, Goldwyn, RKO Radio.

1947
RONALD COLMAN in *A Double Life*, Kanin, U-I.

1948
LAURENCE OLIVIER in *Hamlet*, Rank-Two Cities, U-I (British).

1949
BRODERICK CRAWFORD in *All the King's Men*, Rossen, Columbia.

1950
JOSE FERRER in *Cyrano de Bergerac*, Kramer, UA.

1951
HUMPHREY BOGART in *The African Queen*, Horizon, UA.

1952
GARY COOPER in *High Noon*, Kramer, UA.

1953
WILLIAM HOLDEN in *Stalag 17*, Paramount.

1954
MARLON BRANDO in *On the Waterfront*, Horizon-American, Columbia.

1955
ERNEST BORGNINE in *Marty*, Hecht-Lancaster, UA.

1956
YUL BRYNNER in *The King and I*, 20th Century-Fox.

1957
ALEC GUINNESS in *The Bridge on the River Kwai*, Horizon, Columbia.

1958
DAVID NIVEN, in *Separate Tables*, Hecht-Hill-Lancaster, UA.

1959
CHARLTON HESTON in *Ben-Hur*, MGM.

1960
BURT LANCASTER in *Elmer Gantry*, Lancaster-Brooks, UA.

1961
MAXIMILIAN SCHELL in *Judgment at Nuremberg*, Kramer, UA.

1962
GREGORY PECK in *To Kill a Mockingbird*, Pakula-Mulligan-Brentwood, U-I.

1963
SIDNEY POITIER in *Lilies of the Field*, Rainbow, UA.

1964
REX HARRISON in *My Fair Lady*, Warner Bros.

1965
LEE MARVIN in *Cat Ballou*, Hecht, Columbia.

1966
PAUL SCOFIELD in *A Man for All Seasons*, Highland Films, Columbia.

1967
ROD STEIGER in *In the Heat of the Night*, Mirisch, UA.

1968
CLIFF ROBERTSON in *Charly*, ABC-Selmur, Cinerama.

1969
JOHN WAYNE in *True Grit*, Wallis, Paramount.

1970
GEORGE C. SCOTT in *Patton*, 20th Century-Fox.

1971
GENE HACKMAN in *The French Connection*, D'Antoni-Schine-Moore, 20th Century-Fox.

1972
MARLON BRANDO in *The Godfather*, Ruddy, Paramount.

1973
JACK LEMMON in *Save the Tiger*, Filmways-Jalem Cirandinha, Paramount.

1974
ART CARNEY in *Harry and Tonto*, 20th Century-Fox.

1975
JACK NICHOLSON in *One Flew Over the Cuckoo's Nest*, Fantasy Films, UA.

1976
PETER FINCH in *Network*, Gottfried/Chayefsky, MGM/UA.

1977
RICHARD DREYFUSS in *The Goodbye Girl*, Stark, MGM/Warner Bros.

1978
JON VOIGHT in *Coming Home*, Hellman, UA.

1979
DUSTIN HOFFMAN in *Kramer vs. Kramer*, Jaffe, Columbia.

1980
ROBERT DE NIRO in *Raging Bull*, Chartoff-Winkler, UA.

1981
HENRY FONDA in *On Golden Pond*, ITC/IPC, Universal.

1982
BEN KINGSLEY in *Gandhi*, Columbia.

1983
ROBERT DUVALL in *Tender Mercies*, EMI, Universal/AFD.

1984
F. MURRAY ABRAHAM in *Amadeus*, Zaentz, Orion.

1985
WILLIAM HURT in *Kiss of the Spider Woman*, Island Alive.

1986
PAUL NEWMAN in *The Color of Money*, Touchstone with Silver Screen Partners II, Buena Vista.

1987
MICHAEL DOUGLAS in *Wall Street*, Oaxatal, 20th Century-Fox.

1988
DUSTIN HOFFMAN in *Rain Man*, Guber-Peters, UA.

1989
DANIEL DAY LEWIS in *My Left Foot*, Ferndale/Granada, Miramax.

1990
JEREMY IRONS in *Reversal of Fortune*, Reversal Films, Warner Bros.

1991
ANTHONY HOPKINS in *The Silence of the Lambs*, Strong Heart/Demme, Orion.

1992
AL PACINO in *Scent of a Woman*, Universal Release/City Lights Films, Universal.

1993
TOM HANKS in *Philadelphia*, TriStar.

1994
TOM HANKS in *Forrest Gump*, Steve Tisch/Wendy Finerman, Paramount.

1995
NICOLAS CAGE in *Leaving Las Vegas*, Initial Productions, MGM/UA.

1996
GEOFFREY RUSH in *Shine*, Momentum Films, Fine Line Features.

1997
JACK NICHOLSON in *As Good As It Gets*, Gracie Films, TriStar.

1998
ROBERTO BENIGNI in *Life is Beautiful*, Miramax Films.

1999
KEVIN SPACEY in *American Beauty*, DreamWorks.

2000
RUSSELL CROWE in *Gladiator*, DreamWorks and Universal.

2001
DENZEL WASHINGTON in *Training Day*, Warner Bros.

2002
ADRIEN BRODY in *The Pianist*, Focus Features.

Best Actress

1927–1928
JANET GAYNOR in *7th Heaven*, Fox, *Street Angel*, Fox, and *Sunrise*, Fox.

1928–29
MARY PICKFORD in *Coquette*, Pickford, UA.

1929–30
NORMA SHEARER in *The Divorcee*, MGM.

1930–31
MARIE DRESSLER in *Min and Bill*, MGM.

1931–32
HELEN HAYES in *The Sin of Madelon Claudet*, MGM.

1932–33
KATHARINE HEPBURN in *Morning Glory*, RKO Radio.

1934
CLAUDETTE COLBERT in *It Happened One Night*, Columbia.

1935
BETTE DAVIS in *Dangerous*, Warner Bros.

1936
LUISE RAINER in *The Great Ziegfeld*, MGM1937
LUISE RAINER in *The Good Earth*, MGM.

1938
BETTE DAVIS in *Jezebel*, Warner Bros.

1939
VIVIEN LEIGH in *Gone With the Wind*, Selznick, MGM.

1940
GINGER ROGERS in *Kitty Foyle*, RKO Radio.

1941
JOAN FONTAINE in *Suspicion*, RKO Radio.

1942
GREER GARSON in *Mrs. Miniver*, MGM.

1943
JENNIFER JONES in *The Song of Bernadette*, 20th Century-Fox.

1944
INGRID BERGMAN in *Gaslight*, MGM.

1945
JOAN CRAWFORD in *Mildred Pierce*, Warner Bros.

1946
OLIVIA DE HAVILLAND in *To Each His Own*, Paramount.

1947
LORETTA YOUNG in *The Farmer's Daughter*, RKO Radio.

1948
JANE WYMAN in *Johnny Belinda*, Warner Bros.

1949
OLIVIA DE HAVILLAND in *The Heiress*, Paramount.

1950
JUDY HOLLIDAY in *Born Yesterday*, Columbia.

1951
VIVIEN LEIGH in *A Streetcar Named Desire*, Charles K. Feldman, Warner Bros.

1952
SHIRLEY BOOTH in *Come Back, Little Sheba*, Wallis, Paramount.

1953
AUDREY HEPBURN in *Roman Holiday*, Paramount.

1954
GRACE KELLY in *The Country Girl*, Perlberg-Seaton, Paramount.

1955
ANNA MAGNANI in *The Rose Tattoo*, Wallis, Paramount.

1956
INGRID BERGMAN in *Anastasia*, 20th Century-Fox.

1957
JOANNE WOOWARD in *The Three Faces of Eve*, 20th Century-Fox.

1958
SUSAN HAYWARD in *I Want to Live!*, Figaro, UA.

1959
SIMONE SIGNORET in *Room at the Top*, Romulus, Continental (British).

1960
ELIZABETH TAYLOR in *Butterfield 8*, Afton-Linebrook, MGM.

1961
SOPHIA LOREN in *Two Women*, Ponti, Embassy (Italian).

1962
ANNE BANCROFT in *The Miracle Worker*, Playfilms, UA.

1963
PATRICIA NEAL in *Hud*, Salem-Dover, Paramount.

1964
JULIE ANDREWS in *Mary Poppins*, Disney, Buena Vista.

1965
JULIE CHRISTIE in *Darling*, Anglo-Amalgamated, Embassy (British).

1966
ELIZABETH TAYLOR in *Who's Afraid of Virginia Woolf?*, Chenault, Warner Bros.

1967
KATHARINE HEPBURN in *Guess Who's Coming to Dinner*, Kramer, Columbia.

1968
KATHARINE HEPBURN in *The Lion in Winter*, Haworth, Avco Embassy.

1969
MAGGIE SMITH in *The Prime of Miss Jean Brodie*, 20th Century-Fox.

1970
GLENDA JACKSON in *Women in Love*, Kramer-Rosen, UA.

1971
JANE FONDA in *Klute*, Gus, Warner Bros.

1972
LIZA MINNELLI in *Cabaret*, ABC Pictures, Allied Artists.

1973
GLENDA JACKSON in *A Touch of Class*, Brut, Avco Embassy.

1974
ELLEN BURSTYN in *Alice Doesn't Live Here Anymore*, Warner Bros.

1975
LOUISE FLETCHER in *One Flew Over the Cuckoo's Nest*, Fantasy Films, UA.

1976
FAYE DUNAWAY in *Network*, Gottfried/Chayefsky, MGM/UA.

1977
DIANE KEATON in *Annie Hall*, Rollins-Joffe, UA.

1978
JANE FONDA in *Coming Home*, Hellman, UA.

1979
SALLY FIELD in *Norma Rae*, 20th Century-Fox.

1980
SISSY SPACEK in *Coal Miner's Daughter*, Schwartz, Universal.

1981
KATHARINE HEPBURN in *On Golden Pond*, ITC/IPC, Universal.

1982
MERYL STREEP in *Sophie's Choice*, ITC/Pakula-Barish, Universal/A.FD.

1983
SHIRLEY MacLAINE in *Terms of Endearment*, Brooks, Paramount.

1984
SALLY FIELD in *Places in the Heart*, Tri-Star.

1985
GERALDINE PAGE in *The Trip to Bountiful*, Island.

1986
MARLEE MATLIN in *Children of a Lesser God*, Sugarman, Paramount.

1987
CHER in *Moonstruck*, Palmer/Jewison, MGM.

1988
JODIE FOSTER in *The Accused*, Jaffe-Lansing, Paramount.

1989
JESSICA TANDY in *Driving Miss Daisy*, Zanuck Company, Warner Bros.

1990
KATHY BATES in *Misery*, Castle Rock Entertainment, Columbia.

1991
JODIE FOSTER in *The Silence of the Lambs*, Strong Heart/Demme, Orion.

1992
EMMA THOMPSON in *Howards End*, Merchant Ivory, Sony Pictures Classics.

1993
HOLLY HUNTER in *The Piano*, Jan Chapman & CIBY 2000, Miramax.

1994
JESSICA LANGE in *Blue Sky*, Robert H. Solo, Orion.

1995
SUSAN SARANDON in *Dead Man Walking*, Working Title/Havoc, Gramercy.

1996
FRANCES McDORMAND in *Fargo*, Working Title, Gramercy.

1997
HELEN HUNT in *As Good As It Gets*, Gracie Films, TriStar.

1998
GWYNETH PALTROW in *Shakespeare in Love*, Miramax Films.

1999
HILARY SWANK in *Boys Don't Cry*, Fox Searchlight.

2000
JULIA ROBERTS in *Erin Brockovich*, Universal and Columbia.

2001
HALLE BERRY in *Monster's Ball*, Lions Gate Films.

2002
NICOLE KIDMAN in *The Hours*, Paramount and Miramax.

Best Supporting Actor

1936
WALTER BRENNAN in *Come and Get It*, Goldwyn, UA.

1937
JOSEPH SCHILDKRAUT in *The Life of Emile Zola*, Warner Bros.

1938
WALTER BRENNAN in *Kentucky*, 20th Century-Fox.

1939
THOMAS MITCHELL in *Stagecoach*, Wanger, UA.

1940
WALTER BRENNAN in *The Westerner*, Goldwyn, UA.

1941
DONALD CRISP in *How Green Was My Valley*, 20th Century-Fox.

1942
VAN HEFLIN in *Johnny Eager*, MGM.

1943
CHARLES COBURN in *The More the Merrier*, Columbia.

1944
BARRY FITZGERALD in *Going My Way*, Paramount.

1945
JAMES DUNN in *A Tree Grows in Brooklyn*, 20th Century-Fox.

1946
HAROLD RUSSELL in *The Best Years of Our Lives*, Goldwyn, RKO Radio.

1947
EDMUND GWENN in *Miracle on 34th Street*, 20th Century-Fox.

1948
WALTER HUSTON in *The Treasure of the Sierra Madre*, Warner Bros.

1949
DEAN JAGGER in *12 O'Clock High*, 20th Century-Fox.

1950
GEORGE SANDERS in *All About Eve*, 20th Century-Fox.

1951
KARL MALDEN in *A Streetcar Named Desire*, Charles K. Feldman, Warner Bros.

1952
ANTHONY QUINN in *Viva Zapata!*, 20th Century-Fox.

1953
FRANK SINATRA in *From Here to Eternity*, Columbia.

1954
EDMOND O'BRIEN in *The Barefoot Contessa*, Figaro, UA.

1955
JACK LEMMON in *Mister Roberts*, Orange, Warner Bros.

1956
ANTHONY QUINN in *Lust for Life*, MGM.

1957
RED BUTTONS in *Sayonara*, Goetz, Warner Bros.

1958
BURL IVES in *The Big Country*, Anthony-Worldwide, UA.

1959
HUGH GRIFFITH in *Ben-Hur*, MGM.

1960
PETER USTINOV in *Spartacus*, Bryna, U-I.

1961
GEORGE CHAKIRIS in *West Side Story*, Mirisch-B&P Enterprises, UA.

1962
ED BEGLEY in *Sweet Bird of Youth*, Roxbury, MGM.

1963
MELVYN DOUGLAS in *Hud*, Salem-Dover, Paramount.

1964
PETER USTINOV in *Topkapi*, Filmways, UA.

1965
MARTIN BALSAM in *A Thousand Clowns*, Harrell, UA.

1966
WALTER MATTHAU in *The Fortune Cookie*, Phalanx Jalem-Mirisch, UA.

1967
GEORGE KENNEDY in *Cool Hand Luke*, Jalem, Warner Bros.-Seven Arts.

1968
JACK ALBERTSON in *The Subject Was Roses*, MGM.

1969
GIG YOUNG in *They Shoot Horses, Don't They?*, Chartoff-Winkler-Pollack, ABC Pictures, Cinerama.

1970
JOHN MILLS in *Ryan's Daughter*, Faraway, MGM.

1971
BEN JOHNSON in *The Last Picture Show*, BBS Productions, Columbia.

1972
JOEL GREY in *Cabaret*, ABC Pictures, Allied Artists.

1973
JOHN HOUSEMAN in *The Paper Chase*, Thompson-Paul, 20th Century-Fox.

1974
ROBERT DE NIRO in *The Godfather Part II*, Coppola Company, Paramount.

1975
GEORGE BURNS in *The Sunshine Boys*, MGM.

1976
JASON ROBARDS in *All the President's Men*, Wildwood, Warner Bros.

1977
JASON ROBARDS in *Julia*, 20th Century-Fox.

1978
CHRISTOPHER WALKEN in *The Deer Hunter*, EMI/Cimino, Universal.

1979
MELVYN DOUGLAS in *Being There*, Lorimar-Fernsehproduktion GmbH, UA.

1980
TIMOTHY HUTTON in *Ordinary People*, Wildwood, Paramount.

1981
JOHN GIELGUD in *Arthur*, Rollins, Joffe, Morra and Brezner, Orion.

1982
LOUIS GOSSETT JR. in *An Officer and a Gentleman*, Lorimar/Elfand, Paramount.

1983
JACK NICHOLSON in *Terms of Endearment*, Brooks, Paramount.

1984
HAING S. NGOR in *The Killing Fields*, Enigma, Warner Bros.

1985
DON AMECHE in *Cocoon*, Zanuck-Brown, 20th Century-Fox.

1986
MICHAEL CAINE in *Hannah and Her Sisters*, Rollins and Joffe, Orion.

1987
SEAN CONNERY in *The Untouchables*, Linson, Paramount.

1988
KEVIN KLINE in *A Fish Called Wanda*, Michael Shamberg-Prominent Features, MGM.

1989
DENZEL WASHINGTON in *Glory*, Tri-Star.

1990
JOE PESCI in *GoodFellas*, Warner Bros.

1991
JACK PALANCE in *City Slickers*, Castle Rock Entertainment, Columbia.

1992
GENE HACKMAN in *Unforgiven*, Warner Bros.

1993
TOMMY LEE JONES in *The Fugitive*, Warner Bros.

1994
MARTIN LANDAU in *Ed Wood*, Touchstone, Buena Vista.

1995
KEVIN SPACEY in *The Usual Suspects*, Blue Parrot, Gramercy.

1996
CUBA GOODING JR. in *Jerry Maguire*, TriStar.

1997
ROBIN WILLIAMS in *Good Will Hunting*, Be Gentlemen, Miramax.

1998
JAMES COBURN in *Affliction*, Lions Gate Films.

1999
MICHAEL CAINE in *The Cider House Rules*, Miramax Films.

2000
BENICIO DEL TORO in *Traffic*, USA Films.

2001
JIM BROADBENT in *Iris*, Miramax Films.

2002
CHRIS COOPER in *Adaptation*, Sony Pictures Releasing.

Best Supporting Actress

1936
GALE SONDERGAARD in *Anthony Adverse*, Warner Bros.

1937
ALICE BRADY in *In Old Chicago*, 20th Century-Fox.

1938
FAY BAINTER in *Jezebel*, Warner Bros.

1939
HATTIE McDANIEL in *Gone With the Wind*, Selznick, MGM.

1940
JANE DARWELL in *The Grapes of Wrath*, 20th Century-Fox.

1941
MARY ASTOR in *The Great Lie*, Warner Bros.

1942
TERESA WRIGHT in *Mrs. Miniver*, MGM.

1943
KATINA PAXINOU in *For Whom the Bell Tolls*, Paramount.

1944
ETHEL BARRYMORE in *None But the Lonely Heart*, RKO Radio.

1945
ANNE REVERE in *National Velvet*, MGM.

1946
ANNE BAXTER in *The Razor's Edge*, 20th Century-Fox.

1947
CELESTE HOLM in *Gentleman's Agreement*, 20th Century-Fox.

1948
CLAIRE TREVOR in *Key Largo*, Warner Bros.

1949
MERCEDES McCAMBRIDGE in *All the King's Men*, Rosen, Columbia.

1950
JOSEPHINE HULL in *Harvey*, U-I.

1951
KIM HUNTER in *A Streetcar Named Desire*, Charles K. Feldman, Warner Bros.

1952
GLORIA GRAHAME in *The Bad and the Beautiful*, MGM.

1953
DONNA REED in *From Here to Eternity*, Columbia.

1954
EVA MARIE SAINT in *On the Waterfront*, Horizon-American, Columbia.

1955
JO VAN FLEET in *East of Eden*, Warner Bros.

1956
DOROTHY MALONE in *Written on the Wind*, U-I.

1957
MIYOSHI UMEKI in *Sayonara*, Goetz, Warner Bros.

1958
WENDY HILLER in *Separate Tables*, Hecht-Hill-Lancaster, UA.

1959
SHELLEY WINTERS in *The Diary of Anne Frank*, 20th Century-Fox.

1960
SHIRLEY JONES in *Elmer Gantry*, Lancaster-Brooks, UA.

1961
RITA MORENO in *West Side Story*, Mirisch-B&P Enterprises, UA.

1962
PATTY DUKE in *The Miracle Worker*, Playfilms, UA.

1963
MARGARET RUTHERFORD in *The V.I.P.s*, MGM.

1964
LILA KEDROVA in *Zorba the Greek*, Rochley, 20th Century-Fox/International Classics.

1965
SHELLEY WINTERS in *A Patch of Blue*, Berman-Green, MGM.

1966
SANDY DENNIS in *Who's Afraid of Virginia Woolf?*, Chenault, Warner Bros.

1967
ESTELLE PARSONS in *Bonnie and Clyde*, Tatira Huller, Warner Bros.-Seven Arts.

1968
RUTH GORDON in *Rosemary's Baby*, Castle, Paramount.

1969
GOLDIE HAWN in *Cactus Flower*, Frankovich, Columbia.

1970
HELEN HAYES in *Airport*, Hunter, Universal.

1971
CLORIS LEACHMAN in *The Last Picture Show*, BBS Productions, Columbia.

1972
EILEEN HECKART in *Butterflies Are Free*, Frankovich, Columbia.

1973
TATUM O'NEAL in *Paper Moon*, Directors Company, Paramount.

1974
INGRID BERGMAN in *Murder on the Orient Express*, G.W. Films, Paramount.

1975
LEE GRANT in *Shampoo*, Rubeeker, Columbia.

1976
BEATRICE STRAIGHT in *Network*, Gottfried/Chayefsky, MGM/UA.

1977
VANESSA REDGRAVE in *Julia*, 20th Century-Fox.

1978
MAGGIE SMITH in *California Suite*, Stark, Columbia.

1979
MERYL STREEP in *Kramer vs. Kramer*, Jaffe, Columbia.

1980
MARY STEENBURGEN in *Melvin and Howard*, Linson/Phillips/Demme, Universal.

1981
MAUREEN STAPLETON in *Reds*, J.R.S., Paramount.

1982
JESSICA LANGE in *Tootsie*, Mirage/Punch, Columbia.

1983
LINDA HUNT in *The Year of Living Dangerously*, Fields, MGM/UA.

1984
PEGGY ASHCROFT in *A Passage to India*, G.W. Films, Columbia.

1985
ANJELICA HUSTON in *Prizzi's Honor*, ABC, 20th Century-Fox.

1986
DIANNE WIEST in *Hannah and Her Sisters*, Rollins and Joffe, Orion.

1987
OLYMPIA DUKAKIS in *Moonstruck*, Palmer/Jewison, MGM.

1988
GEENA DAVIS in *The Accidental Tourist*, Warner Bros.

1989
BRENDA FRICKER in *My Left Foot*, Ferndale/Granada, Miramax.

1990
WHOOPI GOLDBERG in *Ghost*, Howard W. Koch, Paramount.

1991
MERCEDES RUEHL in *The Fisher King*, TriStar.

1992
MARISA TOMEI in *My Cousin Vinny*, 20th Century-Fox.

1993
ANNA PAQUIN in *The Piano*, Jan Chapman & CIBY 2000, Miramax.

1994
DIANNE WIEST in *Bullets Over Broadway*, Jean Doumanian, Miramax.

1995
MIRA SORVINO in *Mighty Aphrodite*, Sweetheart, Miramax.

1996
JULIETTE BINOCHE in *The English Patient*, Tiger Moth, Miramax.

1997
KIM BASINGER in *L.A. Confidential*, Arnon Milchan/David L. Wolper, Warner Bros.

1998
JUDI DENCH in *Shakespeare in Love*, Miramax Films.

1999
ANGELINA JOLIE in *Girl, Interrupted*, Columbia.

2000
MARCIA GAY HARDEN in *Pollock*, Sony Pictures Classics.

2001
JENNIFER CONNELLY in *A Beautiful Mind*, Universal and DreamWorks.

2002
CATHERINE ZETA-JONES in *Chicago*, Miramax.

Index

333

334

Bibliography

Barraclough, David. *Movie Record Breakers*. London, England: Chartwell Books, A Quintet Book, 1992.

Bona, Damien and Mason Wiley. *Inside Oscar*. New York: Ballantine Books, 1987.

Canby, Vincent; Janet Maslin; and the Film Critics of *The New York Times*, Edited by Peter M. Nichols. The New York Times *Guide to the Best 1000 Movies Ever Made*. New York: Times Books, Random House, 1999.

Donnelly, Paul. *Fade to Black: A Book of Movie Obituaries*. London, England: Omnibus Press, 2000.

Ebert, Roger. *Movie Home Companion*. Kansas City, Missouri: Andrews and McMeel, 1990.

Halliwell, Leslie. *The Filmgoer's Companion*. 4th ed. New York: Farrar, Straus and Giroux, 1974.

Harkness, John. *The Academy Awards Handbook*. 8th ed. New York: Pinnacle Books, 2001.

Haun, Harry. *The Cinematic Century*. New York: Applause Books, 2000.

Holden, Anthony. *Behind the Oscar: The Secret History of the Academy Awards*. New York: Plume Books, 1993.

Katz, Ephraim. *The Film Encyclopedia*. New York: Thomas Y. Crowell, 1979.

Levy, Emanuel. *Oscar Fever*. New York: Continuum International Publishing Group, Inc., 2001.

Milne, Tom. *The Time Out Film Guide*. 3rd ed. New York: Penguin Books, 1993.

Mordden, Ethan. *Movie Star, A Look At The Women Who Made Hollywood*. New York: St. Martin's Press, 1983.

O'Neil, Tom. *Movie Awards: The Ultimate, Unofficial Guide to the Oscars, Golden Globes, Critics, Guild and Indie Honors*. New York: Perigee Books, 2001.

Osborne, Robert. *70 Years of the Oscar*. New York: Abbeville Press, 1989.

Peary, Danny. *Alternate Oscars*. New York: Bantam Doubleday Dell Publishing Group, Inc., 1993.

Peary, Danny, ed. *Close-Ups, The Movie Star Book*. New York: Workman Publishing Company, 1978.

Quinlan, David. *Quinlan's Film Stars*. 5th ed. hington, D.C.: Brassey's, Inc., 2000.

Rees, Nigel. *Cassell's Movie Quotations*. London, England: Wellington House, 2000.

Russo, Vito. *The Celluloid Closet, Revised Edition*. New York: Harper & Row, 1987.

Speck, Gregory. *Hollywood Royalty*. London, England: Robson Books, 1992.

Thompson, David. *A Biographical Dictionary of Film*. 3rd ed. New York: Knopf, 1996.

Walker, John, ed. *Halliwell's Film Guide*. 8th ed. New York: HarperCollins, 1991.

Internet Resource

International Movie Data Base: www.imdb.com.

Photography Credits

All photographs licensed from gettyimages except the following images licensed from Photofest on pages: 11, 15 (bottom), 16, 19, 20, 21 (all), 23, 24 (top), 25, 27 (top), 28 (bottom), 31, 39 (bottom), 43 (top), 48 (bottom), 52 (top), 55 (top right and bottom right), 73 (top), 89 (top), 97 (top right and bottom right), 120 (top), 127 (top), 142 (middle), 150 (top), 154 (middle), 157 (bottom), 158 (bottom), 170 (bottom), 195 (bottom), 212 (bottom), 230 (top), 241 (top), 258 (top and bottom), 256, 264, 268 (top), 272 (bottom), 280 (bottom), 296 (top), 310 (bottom), 312, 313 (top), 314 (top and bottom).

Robert Gedaliah

Gail Kinn has conceived and edited a wide range of film books, among them: *Screwball: The Great Romantic Comedies, Hollywood at Home: The Photographs of Sid Avery, The Zanucks of Hollywood, The Scorsese Picture* by David Ehrenstein, *The James Dean Scene,* and *Those Lips, Those Eyes.* She lives in New York City.

Jim Piazza is a screenwriter and playwright whose personal essays and writings about the media have appeared in *The Village Voice* and *Out* magazine. He has also been a script analyst for Columbia, Fox and Paramount Pictures. He lives in New York City.

They are the co-authors of *Four Stars: The 101 Greatest Movies of All Time.*